PEARSON

ALWAYS LEARNING

GO! with Microsoft® Office 2010 Introductory

Gaskin, Lawson, Ferrett, Giol, Vargas and McLellan

Fourth Custom Edition for
Miami Dade College
North Campus
Hialeah Campus
West Campus

Taken from:

Go! With Microsoft® Office 2010, Volume 1
by Shelley Gaskin, Robert L. Ferrett, Alicia Vargas, and Carolyn McLellan

Go! With Basic Computer Concepts, Getting Started
by Shelley Gaskin, Victor Giol

Go! With Microsoft® Windows 7, Getting Started
by Shelley Gaskin, Robert L. Ferrett

Go! With Microsoft® Internet Explorer 8, Getting Started
by Shelley Gaskin, Rebecca Lawson

Cover Art: Courtesy of PhotoDisc/Getty Images

Taken from:

Go! With Microsoft® Office 2010, Volume 1
by Shelley Gaskin, Robert L. Ferrett, Alicia Vargas, and Carolyn McLellan
Copyright © 2011 by Pearson Education, Inc.
Published by Prentice Hall
Upper Saddle River, New Jersey 07458

Go! With Basic Computer Concepts, Getting Started
by Shelley Gaskin, Victor Giol
Copyright © 2011 by Pearson Education, Inc.
Published by Prentice Hall

Go! With Microsoft® Windows 7, Getting Started
by Shelley Gaskin, Robert L. Ferrett
Copyright © 2011 by Pearson Education, Inc.
Published by Prentice Hall

Go! With Microsoft® Internet Explorer 8, Getting Started
by Shelley Gaskin, Rebecca Lawson
Copyright © 2011 by Pearson Education, Inc.
Published by Prentice Hall

All rights reserved. No part of this book may be reproduced, in any form or by any means, without permission in writing from the publisher.

This special edition published in cooperation with Pearson Learning Solutions.

All trademarks, service marks, registered trademarks, and registered service marks are the property of their respective owners and are used herein for identification purposes only.

Pearson Learning Solutions, 501 Boylston Street, Suite 900, Boston, MA 02116
A Pearson Education Company
www.pearsoned.com

Printed in the United States of America

1 2 3 4 5 6 7 8 9 10 V064 16 15 14 13 12 11

000200010270770596

MT

ISBN 10: 1-256-15918-2
ISBN 13: 978-1-256-15918-6

Contents

Basic Computer Concepts

Chapter 1 Basic Computer Concepts 1

Objective 1 Define Computer and Identify the Four Basic Computing Functions **2**

Objective 2 Identify the Different Types of Computers **5**
- Microcomputers 5
- Servers 7
- Supercomputers 8
- Embedded Computers 9

Objective 3 Describe Hardware Devices and Their Uses **9**
- System Unit 10
- Input Devices 11
- Keyboards 11
- The Mouse 12
- The Processor 14
- Different CPUs 14
- Output Devices 16
- Monitors 16
- Printers 18
- Speakers and Multimedia Projectors 19
- Storage Devices 20
- Ports 24
- Evaluating Your System 26

Objective 4 Identify Types of Software and Their Uses **29**
- System Software 30
- Operating Systems 30
- Utility Programs 34
- Application Software 35

Objective 5 Describe Networks and Define Network Terms **40**

Objective 6 Identify Safe Computing Practices **44**
- Computer Maintenance 44
- Viruses 51
- Spyware 52
- Protecting Yourself and Your Computer 53

Summary 56
Key Terms 56
Matching 58
Multiple Choice 59

Windows 7

Chapter 2 Getting Started with Windows 61

PROJECT 2A Familiarize Yourself with Windows 7 62

Objective 1 Get Started with Windows 7 63
Activity 2.1 Exploring the Windows 7 Desktop 63
Activity 2.2 Personalizing the Desktop 68
Activity 2.3 Adding and Removing Gadgets 71

Objective 2 Use the Start Menu and Manage Windows 73
Activity 2.4 Using the Start Menu 74
Activity 2.5 Adding Shortcuts to the Start Menu, Desktop, and Taskbar 76
Activity 2.6 Minimizing, Maximizing, and Restoring a Window 79
Activity 2.7 Hiding and Displaying Windows 80

Objective 3 Resize, Move, and Scroll Windows 81
Activity 2.8 Customizing and Using the Taskbar 82
Activity 2.9 Resizing, Moving, Scrolling, and Closing Windows 84

PROJECT 2B Manage Files and Folders 88

Objective 4 Create, Move, and Rename Folders 89
Activity 2.10 Opening and Navigating Windows Explorer 89
Activity 2.11 Creating a New Folder 91
Activity 2.12 Moving and Renaming Folders 93

Objective 5 Copy, Move, Rename, and Delete Files 95
Activity 2.13 Copying Files 95
Activity 2.14 Moving, Renaming, and Deleting Files 97
Activity 2.15 Compressing Files 100
Activity 2.16 Using the Address Bar to Navigate Drives and Folders 102

Objective 6 Find Files and Folders 103
Activity 2.17 Adding Descriptions and Tags to Files 103
Activity 2.18 Finding Files and Folders and Creating a Search Folder 105

Summary 108
Key Terms 108
Screen ID 109
Matching 110
Multiple Choice 111
Skills Review 112

Internet Explorer 8

Chapter 3 Getting Started with Internet Explorer 8 115

PROJECT 3A College and Career Information 116

Objective 1 Start Internet Explorer 8 and Identify Screen Elements **117**
Activity 3.1 Starting Internet Explorer 8 117

Objective 2 Navigate the Internet **120**
Activity 3.2 Navigating the Internet 120
Activity 3.3 Accessing Web Sites from the Address Bar 121
Activity 3.4 Opening a Second Web Site 125
Activity 3.5 Displaying Web Pages with Hyperlinks 126
Activity 3.6 Using Internet Explorer 8 History 129

Objective 3 Create and Manage Favorites **130**
Activity 3.7 Adding an Address to the Favorites List 130
Activity 3.8 Displaying a Favorite Web Site 131
Activity 3.9 Deleting a Web Address from Favorites 132

Objective 4 Search the Internet **133**
Activity 3.10 Adding a Search Engine and Searching the Internet 133

Objective 5 Save and Print Web Pages **135**
Activity 3.11 Downloading and Saving a Web Page 136
Activity 3.12 Downloading and Saving Graphics from a Web Page 137
Activity 3.13 Printing Web Pages 138
Activity 3.14 Printing Web Graphics 140
Activity 3.15 Printing Selected Text from Web Pages 141

Summary 144
Key Terms 144
Matching 144
Multiple Choice 145
Skills Review 146
Mastering Explorer 8 150
Rubric 156
Go! Think 157

Word

Chapter 4 Creating Documents with Microsoft Word 2010 159

PROJECT 4A Flyer 160

Objective 1 Create a New Document and Insert Text **161**
Activity 4.01 Starting a New Word Document and Inserting Text 161

Objective 2 Insert and Format Graphics **163**
Activity 4.02 Formatting Text Using Text Effects 163
Activity 4.03 Inserting and Resizing Pictures 164
Activity 4.04 Wrapping Text Around a Picture 165
Activity 4.05 Moving a Picture 166
Activity 4.06 Applying Picture Styles and Artistic Effects 167
Activity 4.07 Adding a Page Border 167

Objective 3 Insert and Modify Text Boxes and Shapes **168**
Activity 4.08 Inserting a Shape 168
Activity 4.09 Inserting a Text Box 170
Activity 4.10 Moving, Resizing, and Formatting Shapes and Text Boxes 170

Objective 4 Preview and Print a Document **172**
Activity 4.11 Adding a File Name to the Footer 172
Activity 4.12 Previewing and Printing a Document 174

PROJECT 4B Information Handout 176

Objective 5 Change Document and Paragraph Layout **177**
Activity 4.13 Setting Margins 177
Activity 4.14 Aligning Text 178
Activity 4.15 Changing Line Spacing 180
Activity 4.16 Indenting Text and Adding Space After Paragraphs 181

Objective 6 Create and Modify Lists **183**
Activity 4.17 Creating a Bulleted List 183
Activity 4.18 Creating a Numbered List 184
Activity 4.19 Customizing Bullets 187

Objective 7 Set and Modify Tab Stops **188**
Activity 4.20 Setting Tab Stops 188
Activity 4.21 Modifying Tab Stops 189

Objective 8 Insert a SmartArt Graphic **190**
Activity 4.22 Inserting a SmartArt Graphic 190
Activity 4.23 Modifying a SmartArt Graphic 191

Summary, Key Terms, Matching, and Multiple Choice 194-195
Skills Review 196
Mastering Word 202
GO! Fix It 208
GO! Make It 209
GO! Solve It 210
Rubric 212
GO! Think 213
You and GO! 214
GO! Collaborate 214

Chapter 5 Using Tables and Templates to Create Resumes and Cover Letters 215

PROJECT 5A Resume 216

Objective 1 Create a Table 217
Activity 5.01 Creating a Table 217

Objective 2 Add Text to a Table 218
Activity 5.02 Adding Text to a Table 218
Activity 5.03 Inserting Existing Text into a Table Cell 219
Activity 5.04 Creating Bulleted Lists in a Table 220

Objective 3 Format a Table 221
Activity 5.05 Changing the Width of Table Columns 221
Activity 5.06 Adding Rows to a Table 222
Activity 5.07 Merging Cells 223
Activity 5.08 Formatting Text in Cells 224
Activity 5.09 Changing the Table Borders 226

PROJECT 5B Cover Letter and Resume 229

Objective 4 Create a New Document from an Existing Document 230
Activity 5.10 Creating a Letterhead 230
Activity 5.11 Creating a Document from an Existing Document 231

Objective 5 Change and Reorganize Text 233
Activity 5.12 Recording AutoCorrect Entries 233
Activity 5.13 Creating a Cover Letter 234
Activity 5.14 Finding and Replacing Text 236
Activity 5.15 Selecting and Moving Text to a New Location 238
Activity 5.16 Inserting and Formatting a Table in a Document 240

Objective 6 Use the Proofing Options 240
Activity 5.17 Checking Spelling and Grammar Errors 241
Activity 5.18 Using the Thesaurus 243

Objective 7 Create a Document Using a Template 244
Activity 5.19 Locating and Opening a Template 244
Activity 5.20 Replacing Template Placeholder Text 245
Activity 5.21 Removing Template Controls and Formatting the Resume 248
Activity 5.22 Saving a Resume as a Web Page 249

Summary, Key Terms, Matching, and Multiple Choice 250-251
Skills Review 252
Mastering Word 259
GO! Fix It 266
GO! Make It 267
GO! Solve It 268
Rubric 270
GO! Think 271
You and GO! 272
GO! Collaborate 272

Chapter 6 Creating Research Papers, Newsletters, and Merged Mailing Labels **273**

PROJECT 6A Research Paper 274

Objective 1 Create a Research Paper **275**
Activity 6.01 Formatting Text and Page Numbers in a Research Paper 275

Objective 2 Insert Footnotes in a Research Paper **277**
Activity 6.02 Inserting Footnotes 278
Activity 6.03 Modifying a Footnote Style 279

Objective 3 Create Citations and a Bibliography in a Research Paper **282**
Activity 6.04 Adding Citations 282
Activity 6.05 Inserting Page Breaks 285
Activity 6.06 Creating a Reference Page 286
Activity 6.07 Managing Document Properties 287

PROJECT 6B Newsletter with Mailing Labels 290

Objective 4 Format a Multiple-Column Newsletter **291**
Activity 6.08 Changing One Column of Text to Two Columns 291
Activity 6.09 Formatting Multiple Columns 292
Activity 6.10 Inserting a Column Break 293
Activity 6.11 Inserting a ClipArt Image 294
Activity 6.12 Inserting a Screenshot 296

Objective 5 Use Special Character and Paragraph Formatting **296**
Activity 6.13 Applying the Small Caps Font Effect 296
Activity 6.14 Adding a Border and Shading to a Paragraph 298

Objective 6 Create Mailing Labels Using Mail Merge **299**
Activity 6.15 Opening the Mail Merge Wizard Template 299
Activity 6.16 Completing the Mail Merge Wizard 302
Activity 6.17 Previewing and Printing the Mail Merge Document 304

Summary, Key Terms, Matching, and Multiple Choice 306-307
Skills Review 308
Mastering Word 315
GO! Fix It 322
GO! Make It 323
GO! Solve It 324
Rubric 326
GO! Think 327
You and GO! 328
GO! Collaborate 328

Business Running Case 1: Word Chapters 4–6 ..... **329**

Excel

Chapter 7 Creating a Worksheet and Charting Data **335**

PROJECT 7A Sales Report with Embedded Column Chart and Sparklines 336

Objective 1 Create, Save, and Navigate an Excel Workbook **337**
Activity 7.01 Starting Excel and Naming and Saving a Workbook 337
Activity 7.02 Navigating a Worksheet and a Workbook 339

Objective 2 **Enter Data in a Worksheet** **340**
Activity 7.03 Entering Text and Using AutoComplete 340
Activity 7.04 Using Auto Fill and Keyboard Shortcuts 342
Activity 7.05 Aligning Text and Adjusting the Size of Columns 343
Activity 7.06 Entering Numbers 344
Objective 3 **Construct and Copy Formulas and Use the SUM Function** **346**
Activity 7.07 Constructing a Formula and Using the SUM Function 346
Activity 7.08 Copying a Formula by Using the Fill Handle 348
Objective 4 **Format Cells with Merge & Center and Cell Styles** **350**
Activity 7.09 Using Merge & Center and Applying Cell Styles 350
Activity 7.10 Formatting Financial Numbers 351
Objective 5 **Chart Data to Create a Column Chart and Insert Sparklines** **352**
Activity 7.11 Charting Data in a Column Chart 352
Activity 7.12 Creating and Formatting Sparklines 356
Objective 6 **Print, Display Formulas, and Close Excel** **357**
Activity 7.13 Changing Views, Creating a Footer, and Using Print Preview 357
Activity 7.14 Deleting Unused Sheets in a Workbook 359
Activity 7.15 Printing a Worksheet 360
Activity 7.16 Displaying, Printing, and Hiding Formulas 360
PROJECT 7B **Inventory Valuation** **362**
Objective 7 **Check Spelling in a Worksheet** **363**
Activity 7.17 Checking Spelling in a Worksheet 363
Objective 8 **Enter Data by Range** **365**
Activity 7.18 Entering Data by Range 365
Objective 9 **Construct Formulas for Mathematical Operations** **366**
Activity 7.19 Using Arithmetic Operators 366
Activity 7.20 Copying Formulas Containing Absolute Cell References 368
Objective 10 **Edit Values in a Worksheet** **371**
Activity 7.21 Editing Values in a Worksheet 371
Activity 7.22 Formatting Cells with the Percent Style 372
Objective 11 **Format a Worksheet** **372**
Activity 7.23 Inserting and Deleting Rows and Columns 372
Activity 7.24 Adjusting Column Widths and Wrapping Text 374
Summary, Key Terms, Matching, and Multiple Choice 378-379
Skills Review 380
Mastering Excel 386
GO! Fix It 392
GO! Make It 393
GO! Solve It 394
Rubric 396
GO! Think 397
You and GO! 399
GO! Collaborate 399

Chapter 8 **Using Functions, Creating Tables, and Managing Large Workbooks** **401**
PROJECT 8A **Inventory Status Report** **402**
Objective 1 **Use the SUM, AVERAGE, MEDIAN, MIN, and MAX Functions** **403**
Activity 8.01 Using the SUM and AVERAGE Functions 403

Activity 8.02 Using the MEDIAN Function 405
Activity 8.03 Using the MIN and MAX Functions 406

Objective 2 Move Data, Resolve Error Messages, and Rotate Text 407
Activity 8.04 Moving Data and Resolving a # # # # # Error Message 407
Activity 8.05 Rotating Text 408

Objective 3 Use COUNTIF and IF Functions and Apply Conditional Formatting 409
Activity 8.06 Using the COUNTIF Function 409
Activity 8.07 Using the IF Function 410
Activity 8.08 Applying Conditional Formatting by Using Highlight Cells Rules and Data Bars 412
Activity 8.09 Using Find and Replace 413

Objective 4 Use Date & Time Functions and Freeze Panes 414
Activity 8.10 Using the NOW Function to Display a System Date 414
Activity 8.11 Freezing and Unfreezing Panes 415

Objective 5 Create, Sort, and Filter an Excel Table 416
Activity 8.12 Creating an Excel Table 416
Activity 8.13 Sorting and Filtering an Excel Table 417
Activity 8.14 Converting a Table to a Range of Data 419

Objective 6 Format and Print a Large Worksheet 419
Activity 8.15 Printing Titles and Scaling to Fit 419

PROJECT 8B Weekly Sales Summary 423

Objective 7 Navigate a Workbook and Rename Worksheets 424
Activity 8.16 Navigating Among Worksheets, Renaming Worksheets, and Changing the Tab Color of Worksheets 424

Objective 8 Enter Dates, Clear Contents, and Clear Formats 425
Activity 8.17 Entering and Formatting Dates 425
Activity 8.18 Clearing Cell Contents and Formats 427

Objective 9 Copy and Paste by Using the Paste Options Gallery 429
Activity 8.19 Copying and Pasting by Using the Paste Options Gallery 429

Objective 10 Edit and Format Multiple Worksheets at the Same Time 430
Activity 8.20 Grouping Worksheets for Editing 430
Activity 8.21 Formatting and Constructing Formulas on Grouped Worksheets 432

Objective 11 Create a Summary Sheet with Column Sparklines 436
Activity 8.22 Constructing Formulas that Refer to Cells in Another Worksheet 436
Activity 8.23 Changing Values in a Detail Worksheet to Update a Summary Worksheet 438
Activity 8.24 Inserting Sparklines 439

Objective 12 Format and Print Multiple Worksheets in a Workbook 440
Activity 8.25 Moving and Formatting Worksheets in a Workbook 440
Activity 8.26 Printing All the Worksheets in a Workbook 441

Summary, Key Terms, Matching, and Multiple Choice 442-443
Skills Review 444
Mastering Excel 450
GO! Fix It 456
GO! Make It 457
GO! Solve It 458
Rubric 460
GO! Think 461
You and GO! 462
GO! Collaborate 462

Chapter 9 Analyzing Data with Pie Charts, Line Charts, and What-If Analysis Tools 463

PROJECT 9A Budget Pie Chart 464

Objective 1 **Chart Data with a Pie Chart** 465
Activity 9.01 Creating a Pie Chart and a Chart Sheet 465

Objective 2 **Format a Pie Chart** 468
Activity 9.02 Applying Percentages to Labels in a Pie Chart 468
Activity 9.03 Formatting a Pie Chart with 3-D 469
Activity 9.04 Rotating a Pie Chart 470
Activity 9.05 Exploding and Coloring a Pie Slice 471
Activity 9.06 Formatting the Chart Area 472
Activity 9.07 Inserting a Text Box in a Chart 473

Objective 3 **Edit a Workbook and Update a Chart** 474
Activity 9.08 Editing a Workbook and Updating a Chart 474
Activity 9.09 Inserting WordArt in a Worksheet 475

Objective 4 **Use Goal Seek to Perform What-If Analysis** 475
Activity 9.10 Using Goal Seek to Perform What-If Analysis 475
Activity 9.11 Preparing and Printing a Workbook with a Chart Sheet 477

PROJECT 9B Growth Projection with Line Chart 480

Objective 5 **Design a Worksheet for What-If Analysis** 481
Activity 9.12 Using Parentheses in a Formula to Calculate a Percentage Rate of Increase 481
Activity 9.13 Using Format Painter and Formatting as You Type 484
Activity 9.14 Calculating a Value After an Increase 486

Objective 6 **Answer What-If Questions by Changing Values in a Worksheet** 488
Activity 9.15 Answering What-If Questions and Using Paste Special 488

Objective 7 **Chart Data with a Line Chart** 491
Activity 9.16 Inserting Multiple Rows and Creating a Line Chart 491
Activity 9.17 Formatting Axes in a Line Chart 493
Activity 9.18 Formatting the Chart and Plot Areas 495
Activity 9.19 Preparing and Printing Your Worksheet 498

Summary, Key Terms, Matching, and Multiple Choice 500-501
Skills Review 502
Mastering Excel 508
GO! Fix It 514
GO! Make It 515
GO! Solve It 516
Rubric 518
GO! Think 519
You and GO! 521
GO! Collaborate 521

Business Running Case 1: Excel Chapters 7–9 523

Access

Chapter 10 Getting Started with Access Databases

Chapter 10 Getting Started with Access Databases 527

PROJECT 10A Contact Information Database with Two Tables 528

Objective 1 Identify Good Database Design **529**
Activity 10.01 Using Good Design Techniques to Plan a Database 529

Objective 2 Create a Table and Define Fields in a New Database **530**
Activity 10.02 Starting with a New Blank Database 531
Activity 10.03 Assigning the Data Type and Name to Fields 533
Activity 10.04 Renaming Fields and Changing Data Types in a Table 536
Activity 10.05 Adding a Record to a Table 537
Activity 10.06 Adding Additional Records to a Table 538
Activity 10.07 Importing Data from an Excel Workbook into an Existing Access Table 539

Objective 3 Change the Structure of Tables and Add a Second Table **542**
Activity 10.08 Deleting a Table Field in Design View 542
Activity 10.09 Modifying a Field Size and Adding a Description 543
Activity 10.10 Viewing a Primary Key in Design View 544
Activity 10.11 Adding a Second Table to a Database by Importing an Excel Spreadsheet 445
Activity 10.12 Adjusting Column Widths 547
Activity 10.13 Printing a Table 549

Objective 4 Create and Use a Query, Form, and Report **552**
Activity 10.14 Using the Simple Query Wizard to Create a Query 552
Activity 10.15 Creating and Printing a Form 554
Activity 10.16 Creating, Modifying, and Printing a Report 556

Objective 5 Save and Close a Database **558**
Activity 10.17 Closing and Saving a Database 558

PROJECT 10B Student Workshops Database 559

Objective 6 Create a Database Using a Template **560**
Activity 10.18 Creating a New Database Using a Template 560
Activity 10.19 Building a Table by Entering Records in a Multiple Items Form 561

Objective 7 Organize Objects in the Navigation Pane **564**
Activity 10.20 Organizing Database Objects in the Navigation Pane 564

Objective 8 Create a New Table in a Database Created with a Template **566**
Activity 10.21 Creating a New Table and Changing Its Design 566

Objective 9 Print a Report and a Table in a Database Created with a Template **568**
Activity 10.22 Viewing and Printing a Report 568
Activity 10.23 Printing a Table 568

Summary, Key Terms, Matching, and Multiple Choice 570-571
Skills Review 572
Mastering Access 579
GO! Fix It 586
GO! Make It 587
GO! Solve It 588
Rubric 590
GO! Think 591
You and GO! 592
GO! Collaborate 592

Chapter 11 Sort and Query a Database 593

PROJECT 11A Instructors and Courses Database 594

Objective 1 **Open an Existing Database** **595**
Activity 11.01 Opening and Renaming an Existing Database 595
Activity 11.02 Resolving Security Alerts and Renaming Tables 595

Objective 2 **Create Table Relationships** **596**
Activity 11.03 Creating Table Relationships and Enforcing Referential Integrity 596
Activity 11.04 Printing a Relationship Report and Displaying Subdatasheet Records 600

Objective 3 **Sort Records in a Table** **601**
Activity 11.05 Sorting Records in a Table in Ascending or Descending Order 601
Activity 11.06 Sorting Records in a Table on Multiple Fields 603

Objective 4 **Create a Query in Design View** **604**
Activity 11.07 Creating a New Select Query in Design View 604
Activity 11.08 Running, Saving, Printing, and Closing a Query 606

Objective 5 **Create a New Query from an Existing Query** **607**
Activity 11.09 Creating a New Query from an Existing Query 607

Objective 6 **Sort Query Results** **608**
Activity 11.10 Sorting Query Results 608

Objective 7 **Specify Criteria in a Query** **610**
Activity 11.11 Specifying Text Criteria in a Query 610
Activity 11.12 Specifying Criteria Using a Field Not Displayed in the Query Results 612
Activity 11.13 Using *Is Null* Criteria to Find Empty Fields 613

PROJECT 11B Athletic Scholarships Database 615

Objective 8 **Specify Numeric Criteria in a Query** **616**
Activity 11.14 Opening an Existing Database and Importing a Spreadsheet 616
Activity 11.15 Creating Table Relationships 617
Activity 11.16 Specifying Numeric Criteria in a Query 618
Activity 11.17 Using Comparison Operators 619
Activity 11.18 Using the Between... And Comparison Operator 620

Objective 9 **Use Compound Criteria** **621**
Activity 11.19 Using AND Criteria in a Query 621
Activity 11.20 Using OR Criteria in a Query 622

Objective 10 **Create a Query Based on More Than One Table** **623**
Activity 11.21 Creating a Query Based on More Than One Table 623

Objective 11 **Use Wildcards in a Query** **625**
Activity 11.22 Using a Wildcard in a Query 625

Objective 12 **Use Calculated Fields in a Query** **627**
Activity 11.23 Using Calculated Fields in a Query 627

Objective 13 **Calculate Statistics and Group Data in a Query** **630**
Activity 11.24 Using the MIN, MAX, AVG, and SUM Functions in a Query 630
Activity 11.25 Grouping Data in a Query 631

Objective 14 **Create a Crosstab Query** **633**
Activity 11.26 Creating a Crosstab Query Using One Table 633

Summary, Key Terms, Matching, and Multiple Choice 636-637
Skills Review 638
Mastering Access 645
GO! Fix It 653
GO! Make It 654
GO! Solve It 655

Rubric 657
GO! Think 658
You and GO! 659
GO! Collaborate 659

Chapter 12 Forms, Filters, and Reports 661

PROJECT 12A Students and Majors 662

Objective 1 Create and Use a Form to Add and Delete Records 663
Activity 12.01 Creating a Form 663
Activity 12.02 Adding Records to a Table by Using a Form 665
Activity 12.03 Deleting Records from a Table by Using a Form 667
Activity 12.04 Printing a Form 668

Objective 2 Create a Form by Using the Form Wizard 669
Activity 12.05 Creating a Form by Using the Form Wizard 669

Objective 3 Modify a Form in Layout View and in Design View 671
Activity 12.06 Grouping Controls and Applying a Theme to a Form in Layout View 671
Activity 12.07 Modifying a Form in Design View 673
Activity 12.08 Adding, Resizing, and Moving Controls in Layout View 675
Activity 12.09 Formatting and Aligning Controls in Layout View 676

Objective 4 Filter Records 679
Activity 12.10 Filtering Data by Selection of One Field 679
Activity 12.11 Using Filter By Form and Advanced Filter/Sort 681

PROJECT 12B Job Openings 684

Objective 5 Create a Report by Using the Report Tool 685
Activity 12.12 Creating a Report Using the Report Tool 685
Activity 12.13 Modifying a Report in Layout View and Printing a Report 686

Objective 6 Create Reports by Using the Blank Report Tool and the Report Wizard 688
Activity 12.14 Creating a Report Using the Blank Report Tool 688
Activity 12.15 Creating a Report by Using the Report Wizard 691

Objective 7 Modify the Design of a Report 695
Activity 12.16 Formatting and Deleting Controls in Layout View 695
Activity 12.17 Modifying Controls in Layout View 696
Activity 12.18 Aligning Controls in Design View 697

Objective 8 Print a Report and Keep Data Together 699
Activity 12.19 Keeping Data Together and Printing a Report 699
Summary, Key Terms, Matching, and Multiple Choice 702-703
Skills Review 704
Mastering Access 712
GO! Fix It 720
GO! Make It 721
GO! Solve It 722
Rubric 724
GO! Think 725
You and GO! 726
GO! Collaborate 726

Business Running Case 1: Access Chapters 10–12 727

PowerPoint

Chapter 13 Getting Started with Microsoft Office PowerPoint 731

PROJECT 13A Company Overview 732

Objective 1 Create a New Presentation **733**
Activity 13.01 Identifying Parts of the PowerPoint Window 733
Activity 13.02 Entering Presentation Text and Saving a Presentation 734
Activity 13.03 Applying a Presentation Theme 735

Objective 2 Edit a Presentation in Normal View **737**
Activity 13.04 Inserting a New Slide 737
Activity 13.05 Increasing and Decreasing List Levels 739
Activity 13.06 Adding Speaker's Notes to a Presentation 741
Activity 13.07 Displaying and Editing Slides in the Slide Pane 742

Objective 3 Add Pictures to a Presentation **744**
Activity 13.08 Inserting a Picture from a File 744
Activity 13.09 Applying a Style to a Picture 746
Activity 13.10 Applying and Removing Picture Artistic Effects 747

Objective 4 Print and View a Presentation **747**
Activity 13.11 Viewing a Slide Show 747
Activity 13.12 Inserting Headers and Footers 748
Activity 13.13 Printing a Presentation 749

PROJECT 13B New Product Announcement 752

Objective 5 Edit an Existing Presentation **753**
Activity 13.14 Displaying and Editing the Presentation Outline 753
Activity 13.15 Inserting Slides from an Existing Presentation 754
Activity 13.16 Finding and Replacing Text 757

Objective 6 Format a Presentation **757**
Activity 13.17 Changing Fonts, Font Sizes, Font Styles, and Font Colors 757
Activity 13.18 Aligning Text and Changing Line Spacing 759
Activity 13.19 Modifying Slide Layout 760

Objective 7 Use Slide Sorter View **760**
Activity 13.20 Deleting Slides in Slide Sorter View 761
Activity 13.21 Moving Slides in Slide Sorter View 761

Objective 8 Apply Slide Transitions **763**
Activity 13.22 Applying Slide Transitions to a Presentation 763
Activity 13.23 Displaying a Presentation in Reading View 764

Summary, Key Terms, Matching, and Multiple Choice 766-767
Skills Review 768
Mastering PowerPoint 774
GO! Fix It 780
GO! Make It 781
GO! Solve It 782
Rubric 784
GO! Think 785
You and GO! 787
GO! Collaborate 787

Chapter 14 Formatting PowerPoint Presentations 789

PROJECT 14A Employee Training Presentation **790**

Objective 1 Format Numbered and Bulleted Lists **791**
Activity 14.01 Selecting Placeholder Text 791
Activity 14.02 Changing a Bulleted List to a Numbered List 792
Activity 14.03 Modifying a Bulleted List Style 793
Activity 14.04 Removing a Bullet Symbol from a Bullet Point 794

Objective 2 Insert Clip Art **795**
Activity 14.05 Inserting Clip Art 795
Activity 14.06 Moving and Sizing Images 797
Activity 14.07 Changing the Shape of a Picture 799

Objective 3 Insert Text Boxes and Shapes **800**
Activity 14.08 Inserting a Text Box 800
Activity 14.09 Inserting, Sizing, and Positioning Shapes 802
Activity 14.10 Adding Text to Shapes 803

Objective 4 Format Objects **804**
Activity 14.11 Applying Shape Fills, Outlines, and Styles 804
Activity 14.12 Applying Shape and Picture Effects 806
Activity 14.13 Duplicating Objects 807
Activity 14.14 Aligning and Distributing Objects 808

PROJECT 14B Event Announcement **812**

Objective 5 Remove Picture Backgrounds and Insert WordArt **813**
Activity 14.15 Removing the Background from a Picture and Applying Soft Edge Options 813
Activity 14.16 Applying WordArt Styles to Existing Text 816
Activity 14.17 Inserting a WordArt Object 817

Objective 6 Create and Format a SmartArt Graphic **818**
Activity 14.18 Creating a SmartArt Graphic from Bulleted Points 819
Activity 14.19 Adding Shapes in a SmartArt Graphic 820
Activity 14.20 Creating a SmartArt Graphic Using a Content Layout 821
Activity 14.21 Changing the SmartArt Layout 823
Activity 14.22 Changing the Color and Style of a SmartArt Graphic 823
Activity 14.23 Customize the Size and Shape of a SmartArt Graphic 824
Activity 14.24 Converting a SmartArt to Text 825

Summary, Key Terms, Matching, and Multiple Choice 826-827
Skills Review 828
Mastering PowerPoint 834
GO! Fix It 840
GO! Make It 841
GO! Solve It 842
Rubric 844
GO! Think 845
You and GO! 847
GO! Collaborate 847

Chapter 15 Enhancing a Presentation with Animation, Video, Tables, and Charts 849

PROJECT 15A Informational Presentation 850

Objective 1 Customize Slide Backgrounds and Themes **851**
Activity 15.01 Changing the Theme Colors and Theme Fonts 851
Activity 15.02 Applying a Background Style 852
Activity 15.03 Hiding Background Graphics 853
Activity 15.04 Formatting a Slide Background with a Picture 854
Activity 15.05 Applying a Background Fill Color and Resetting a Slide Background 857

Objective 2 Animate a Slide Show **858**
Activity 15.06 Applying Animation Entrance Effects and Effect Options 858
Activity 15.07 Setting Animation Timing Options 861
Activity 15.08 Using Animation Painter and Removing Animation 864

Objective 3 Insert a Video **865**
Activity 15.09 Inserting a Video 866
Activity 15.10 Formatting a Video 868
Activity 15.11 Editing and Compressing a Video 870

PROJECT 15B Summary and Analysis Presentation 874

Objective 4 Create and Modify Tables **875**
Activity 15.12 Creating a Table 875
Activity 15.13 Modifying the Layout of a Table 877
Activity 15.14 Modifying a Table Design 879

Objective 5 Create and Modify Charts **880**
Activity 15.15 Creating a Column Chart and Applying a Chart Style 880
Activity 15.16 Creating a Line Chart and Deleting Chart Data 883
Activity 15.17 Animating a Chart 885

Summary, Key Terms, Matching, and Multiple Choice 886-887
Skills Review 888
Mastering PowerPoint 894
GO! Fix It 900
GO! Make It 901
GO! Solve It 902
Rubric 904
GO! Think 905
You and GO! 907
GO! Collaborate 907

Business Running Case 1: PowerPoint Chapters 13–15 .... **909**

Glossary G-1

Index I-1

Chapter 1 taken from *Go! With Basic Computer Concepts, Getting Started* by Shelley Gaskin, Victor Giol.

Chapter 2 taken from *Go! With Microsoft® Windows 7, Getting Started* by Shelley Gaskin, Robert L. Ferrett.

Chapter 3 taken from *Go! With Microsoft® Internet Explorer 8, Getting Started* by Shelley Gaskin, Rebecca Lawson.

Chapter 4–15 taken from *Go! With Microsoft® Windows 7, Getting Started* by Shelley Gaskin, Robert L. Ferrett, Alicia Vargas, and Carolyn McLellan.

Basic Computer Concepts

OBJECTIVES

Mastering these objectives will enable you to:

1. Define Computer and Identify the Four Basic Computing Functions (p. 2)
2. Identify the Different Types of Computers (p. 5)
3. Describe Hardware Devices and Their Uses (p. 9)
4. Identify Types of Software and Their Uses (p. 29)
5. Describe Networks and Define Network Terms (p. 40)
6. Identify Safe Computing Practices (p. 44)

In This Chapter

Computers are an integral part of our lives. They are found in homes, offices, stores, hospitals, libraries, and many other places. Computers are part of cars and phones, and they enable you to access bank accounts from home, shop online, and quickly communicate with people around the world by means of e-mail and the Internet. It is difficult to find a business or occupation that doesn't rely on computers. Whether it's a truck driver who keeps an electronic travel log or a high-powered stockbroker who needs up-to-the-second market information, computers can make these tasks faster, easier, more efficient, and more accurate.

Computers are all around us, which makes it important to learn basic computing skills and gain the knowledge to be a responsible computer user. Knowing how to use a computer makes you ***computer fluent***.

This chapter looks at different types of computers and their functions. It discusses computer hardware and software and the benefits of networking. In addition, this chapter also discusses the importance of safe computing practices and the ways that you can protect your computer from various threats.

Objective 1 | Define Computer and Identify the Four Basic Computing Functions

What are the benefits of becoming computer fluent? Becoming computer fluent can benefit you in several ways. The advantage of being computer fluent is that it makes employees more attractive to potential employers. Many employers expect employees to have basic computer skills when they are hired. Computers have certainly changed the way we work. The traditional memo has given way to e-mail messages. Business reports can now be shared on a network, enabling a group of individuals to collaborate by adding their own notes and comments before the final report is finalized. Presentations are seldom delivered via overhead transparencies; presentation graphic software is widely used to share information with an audience in a conference room or via the company's intranet. Spreadsheet software is a key tool in presenting financial information and developing sound business plans.

On the other hand, if you are knowledgeable about computers and their uses, it also makes you a better consumer. You feel more comfortable when it comes to purchasing the right computer hardware and software for your needs, adding a peripheral for a specific use, or detecting basic problems when a system does not work properly. Also, if you have a basic understanding of today's technology, you can better understand and use *new* technologies.

What are the basic functions of a computer? A ***computer*** is a programmable electronic device that can input, process, output, and store data. The term ***programmable*** signifies that a device can be instructed to perform a task or a function when fed with a program or software. A computer takes data and converts it into information. ***Data*** represents text, numbers, graphics, sounds, and videos entered into the computer's memory during input operations.

Information is data that has been processed so that it can be presented in an organized and meaningful way. Think of data as the pieces of a jigsaw puzzle and information as the finished puzzle. Putting the pieces of the puzzle together gives you the overall picture. For example, CIS1100, the letter B, and the name Amy Stevens are pieces of data. Individually, these pieces of data seem meaningless. However, when processed, this data becomes the information on a grade report that indicates Amy Stevens received a grade of B in her CIS 1100 class.

These four basic computer functions work in a cycle known as the ***information processing cycle***. See Figure 1.1.

The functions of this cycle are:

- ***Input***—The computer gathers data or enables a user to enter data.
- ***Process***—Data is manipulated and converted into information.
- ***Output***—Information is displayed or shown to the user in a way that is understandable.
- ***Storage***—Data and/or information is stored for future use.

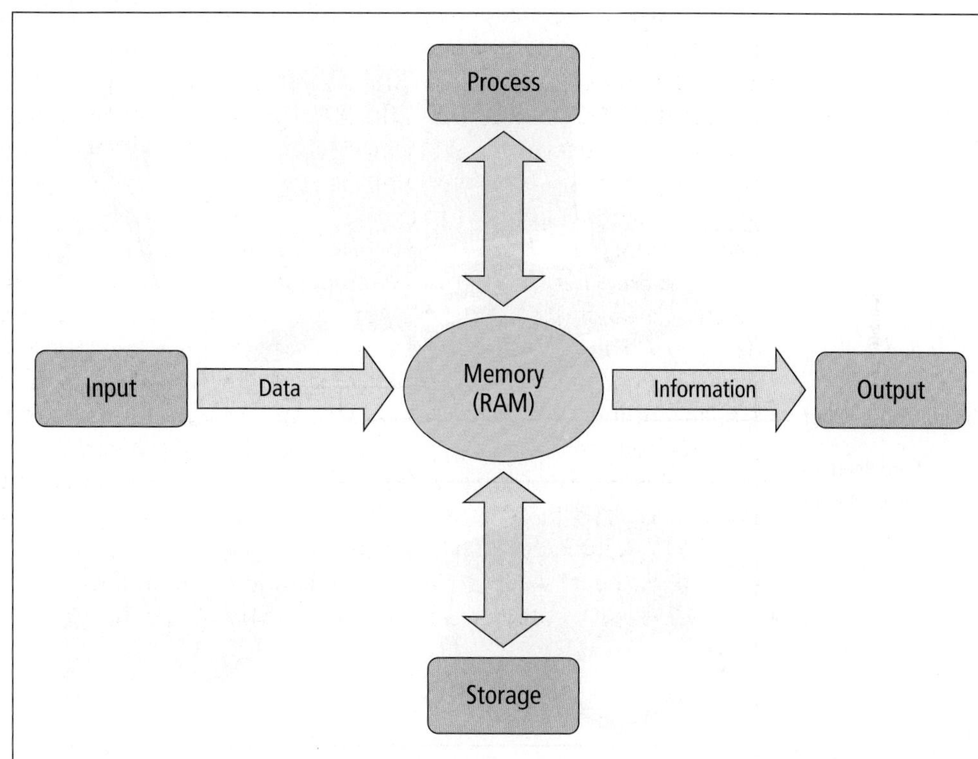

Figure 1.1

These are the four computer functions within the information processing cycle. Memory is not considered a function, but it is the center of flow of data and information within this cycle.

In the grade report, the instructor used a computer to enter, or input, the students' grades into the school's computerized grading system. A computer then processed this data along with data for other classes the students might have taken. In the example, the student Amy then received a written record of her grade or she accessed her grades online. The grade report was output by the computer. In addition, her grades remain stored in the system so they can be used to generate her transcript or to determine her future grade point average as she continues to take classes. See Figure 1.2.

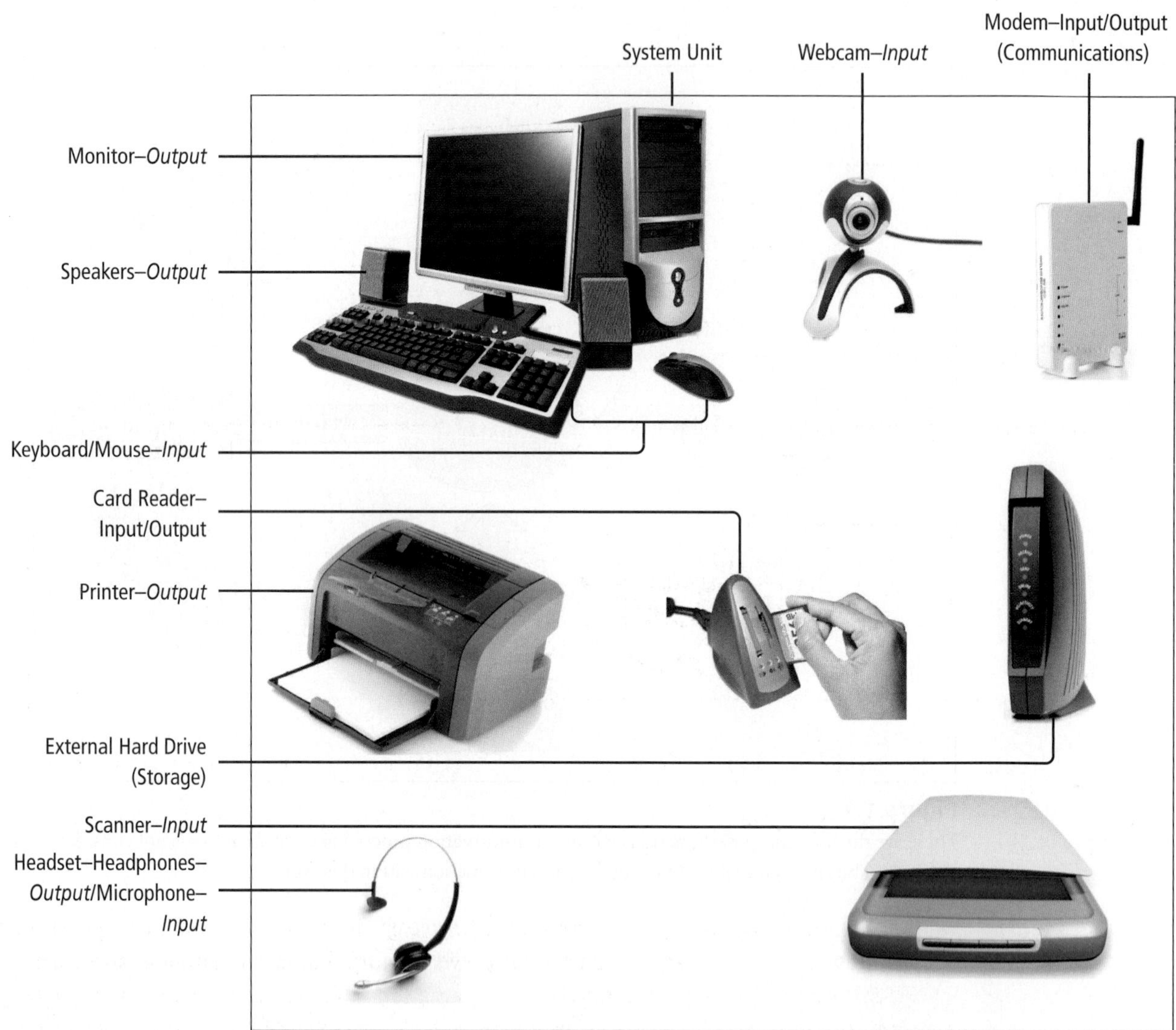

Figure 1.2
The components of a typical computer system and the appropriate step in the information processing cycle.

Objective 2 | Identify the Different Types of Computers

What are the different types of computers and what are their uses? Although computers come in a variety of sizes and shapes, the basic components required to complete the information processing cycle must be present in them. In addition to ***microcomputers***, the desktop and notebook computers and mobile devices that many of us are familiar with, there are also specialty computers, including servers, mainframes, supercomputers, and embedded computers. See Figure 1.3.

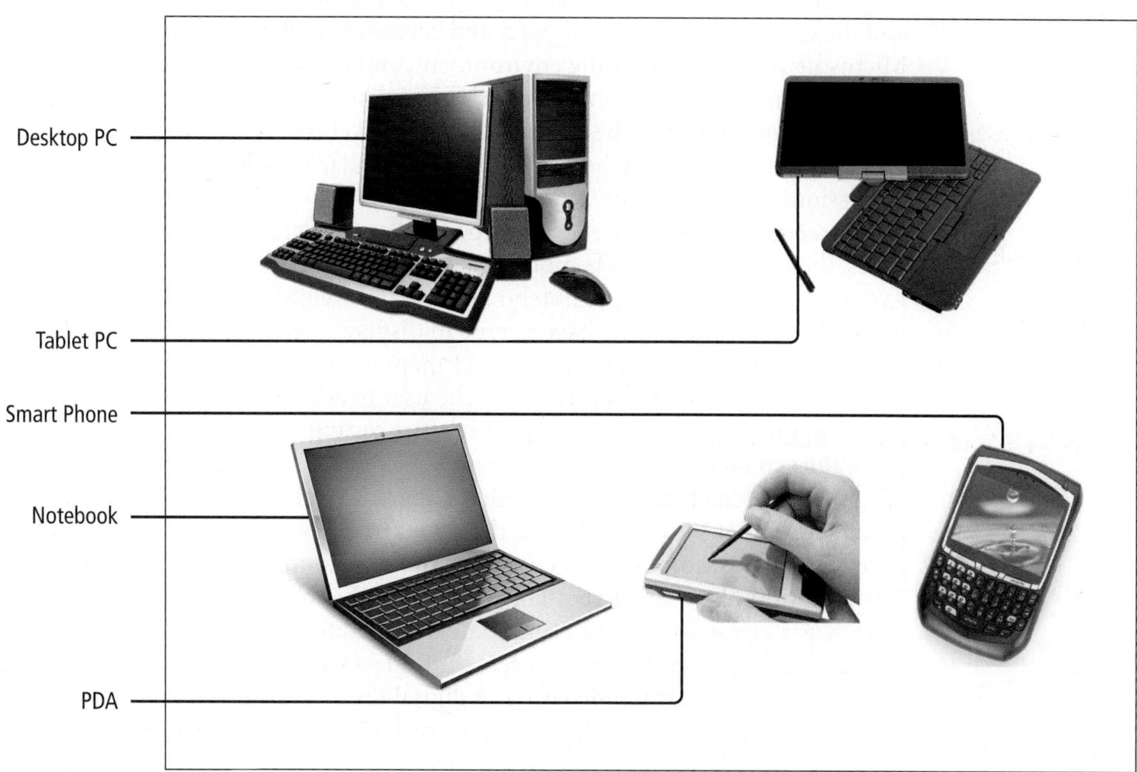

Figure 1.3
Types of microcomputers

Microcomputers

What are microcomputers? The term microcomputer means that the main component of a computer is a microprocessor, a tiny but powerful chip that is very small in size compared to a mainframe or a supercomputer. Microcomputers are classified as small, inexpensive, and designed for personal use or as part of a network of computers in a business environment. Computers in this category range in size from a desktop size system that is ideal when portability is not required to handheld devices that fit in your pocket. Some of the most common types of microcomputers include the following:

- ***Desktop computers*** are computers that sit on the desk, floor, or table, and typically have a detachable keyboard, mouse, monitor, and possibly other peripheral devices, such as digital cameras, scanners, and music players. Desktop computers are used in most homes and in business applications where portability is not needed. They can be configured in a multitude of arrangements depending on the specific needs and budget constraints. To ***configure*** means to put together by selecting a specific combination of components, features, and options.
- ***Gaming computers*** are mostly used by video game enthusiasts. They are usually configured with a fast CPU, large amount of memory, a special video card, joystick or game pad, and sound card with surround sound speaker system.

Desktop computers generally fall into two main categories: PCs or Macs. The PC, or personal computer, originally referred to as the IBM personal computer when it was released in the early 1980s, is now manufactured by a variety of companies including Hewlett-Packard, Dell, and Gateway. Today the term *PC* applies to any personal computer based on an Intel microprocessor, or on an Intel-compatible microprocessor. The Apple Macintosh computer, now known as Mac, is manufactured exclusively by Apple Inc. with an Intel microprocessor and can perform the same functions as the PC.

There are pros and cons to both types of computers, but in reality, both are good systems and the choice usually comes down to personal preference. The primary differences between the PC and the Mac relate to the different user interface, the application software, and the cost and availability of parts and accessories. The PC is typically used in a Microsoft Windows operating environment, and the Mac uses the Mac operating system. Although and the PC and the Mac each process information differently, both can perform the same types of tasks. The PC has a larger market share among general computer users and in business settings, whereas the Mac is popular with graphic design, advertising, and professional audio and film industries.

Notebook computers are ideal for people "on-the-go." Equipped with rechargeable batteries, they are designed to be portable, permitting them to be used in a variety of places. Averaging about 6 pounds, a notebook's size and weight can also limit its computing power. Notebooks typically have a built-in display screen, a keyboard, and a pointing device, although it is possible to connect them to detachable devices for more comfortable desktop use. A ***docking station*** enables the user to connect a notebook to a full-size keyboard, monitor, and other devices in an office setting.

Tablet computers are similar to notebooks because they are portable; however, they have some special features that set them apart. Tablet computers have a convertible ***touch screen*** that swivels, enabling the tablet to be used like a standard notebook computer in one position or like a clipboard in the second position. When used in the tablet configuration, the user can actually write directly on the screen using a special pen known as a ***stylus***, which is a pointed device used to input information and access various features right on the device's screen. Tablets use advanced handwriting-recognition technology to convert handwriting to digital text. Many also use ***speech-recognition*** technology, which enables the user to record discussions or lectures, or to control the computer functions using voice commands.

Mobile devices include items such as ***personal digital assistants (PDAs)***, ***handheld computers*** (Pocket PCs), and ***smartphones***. These devices vary in size and purpose, but they are all ultra-lightweight and portable. PDAs were initially designed to provide a convenient resource for maintaining an organized calendar and list of business and personal associates. Handheld computers enable users to access personal productivity software and send e-mail over the Internet, while smartphones add Internet capability to the wireless communication aspects of cell phones.

The newest mobile devices are often referred to simply as "handhelds." Many handheld devices now include personal productivity software and enable the user to play music, take photos and video, make phone calls, and access the Internet. PDAs and Pocket PCs often use a stylus. It is not uncommon for these devices to use a small detachable keyboard for text and data entry. As the features of mobile devices continue to converge, permitting them to perform similar tasks, it becomes more difficult to differentiate between them. If you are in the process of buying one of these handhelds, you need to do some research and make sure that you get the features and functions you want.

Servers

What are servers? When computers are connected together in a ***network*** environment, ***servers*** are specialized computers that manage network resources through the use of administrative software (see Figure 1.4). They provide other computers with access to the network and can handle a variety of functions or may be assigned to just one particular type of task. Thus, within the same company, you might find a Web server that holds and delivers the organization's Web pages, a file server that handles the storage and retrieval tasks for all of the company's files, and a printer server that handles all print requests. Also, virtual servers (not real, but an abstraction) can manage other specialized servers without the added cost of additional hardware.

Figure 1.4
Network server

What are mainframe computers? ***Mainframe computers*** are large computers often found in large businesses, organizations, and government agencies where thousands of users need to simultaneously use the data and resources of their institution (see Figure 1.5). Mainframe computers ***multitask***; that is, they can perform more than one task at a time. Mainframes can store vast amounts of data using a variety of storage. Mainframes are often used for high-security applications, bulk data processing such as data surveys and census, and statistics. Early mainframe computers were very large and required separate rooms to house them, while today's mainframes are significantly smaller, faster, and more powerful than their predecessors.

Figure 1.5
Mainframe computer

Supercomputers

What are supercomputers? ***Supercomputers*** are large, powerful, and ultrafast computers that perform specialized tasks. Some of these are used for research, processing intensive scientific calculations, and multi-scale simulations. Since June 2008, the IBM nicknamed "Roadrunner," at the Department of Energy's Los Alamos National Laboratory in New Mexico, holds top spot as the world's fastest supercomputer. (See http://www.top500.org/ for more information about Roadrunner.)

Supercomputers (see Figure 1.6) are the fastest and most expensive computers. Unlike a mainframe computer that can handle a number of programs simultaneously, the supercomputer is designed to run fewer programs at one time, but to do so as quickly as possible. They perform sophisticated mathematical calculations, track weather patterns, monitor satellites, and perform other complex, dedicated tasks.

Figure 1.6
Supercomputer

Embedded Computers

What are embedded computers? ***Embedded computers*** are small specialized computers built into larger components such as automobiles and appliances. Functions such as emission control systems, antilock braking systems (ABS), airbags, and stability control systems are common in today's vehicles. These computers use a specially programmed microprocessor to perform a set of predefined tasks, and may require little or no input from the user. Other examples include electronic appliances, microwave ovens, digital cameras, programmable thermostats, medical devices, and diagnostic equipment.

Objective 3 | Describe Hardware Devices and Their Uses

What is computer hardware? ***Hardware*** is the computer and any equipment connected to it. Hardware devices are the physical components of the computer. Items such as the monitor, keyboard, mouse, and printer are also known as ***peripherals*** because they attach to the computer. In Figure 1.3, the computer and different peripherals are matched with the individual steps of the information processing cycle.

The computer itself is known as the ***system unit***, and it contains many of the critical hardware and electrical components. The system unit is sometimes referred to as the tower, box, or console. When the system unit is combined with the appropriate peripheral devices, the system can perform the four basic computer functions: input, process, output, and storage. Peripheral devices are used to input and output data and information, and the system unit processes and stores the data.

System Unit

What is inside the system unit? If you remove the cover from the system unit, you will find several key components inside. One of the most essential components is the ***motherboard***, a large printed circuit board to which all the other components are connected (see Figure 1.7). The ***microprocessor chip***, also known as the ***central processing unit (CPU)*** and RAM, the computer's main memory, are connected to the motherboard (see the table in Figure 1.8). The motherboard also provides some of the ports used to connect peripheral devices to the system. Ports are explained and illustrated later in this chapter.

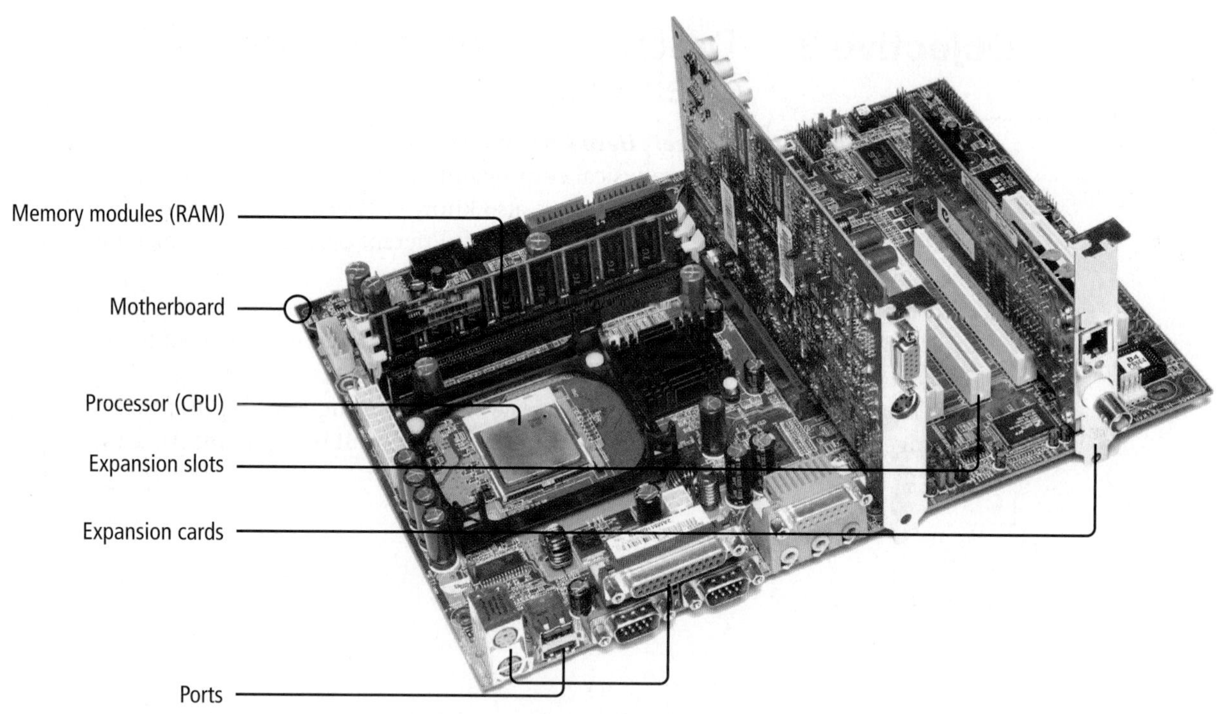

Figure 1.7
The motherboard and some of its components

Motherboard Features

Component	Description
Motherboard / System board	The main computer circuit board into which all components are plugged. It is installed safely inside the box or case called the system unit.
CPU	The central processing unit is responsible for getting data from memory, performing arithmetic and logical operations, and converting data to information.
Memory modules (RAM)	Temporary storage area where data is stored before processing, output, or storage. RAM is the center of flow of data and information within the information processing cycle.
Expansion slots	Slots or connectors on the motherboard that allow you to connect expansion cards.
Expansion cards	Removable circuit boards used to add new peripherals or increase the computer's capabilities. If the motherboard does not have a specific port to connect a peripheral device, the appropriate expansion card will allow you to do so.
Ports	Connecting points used as an interface between peripherals and the motherboard.

Figure 1.8
Motherboard features

Input Devices

Input devices are used to enter data into memory (RAM). The two most familiar input devices are the keyboard and the mouse, but they are not the only ones. See Figure 1.9.

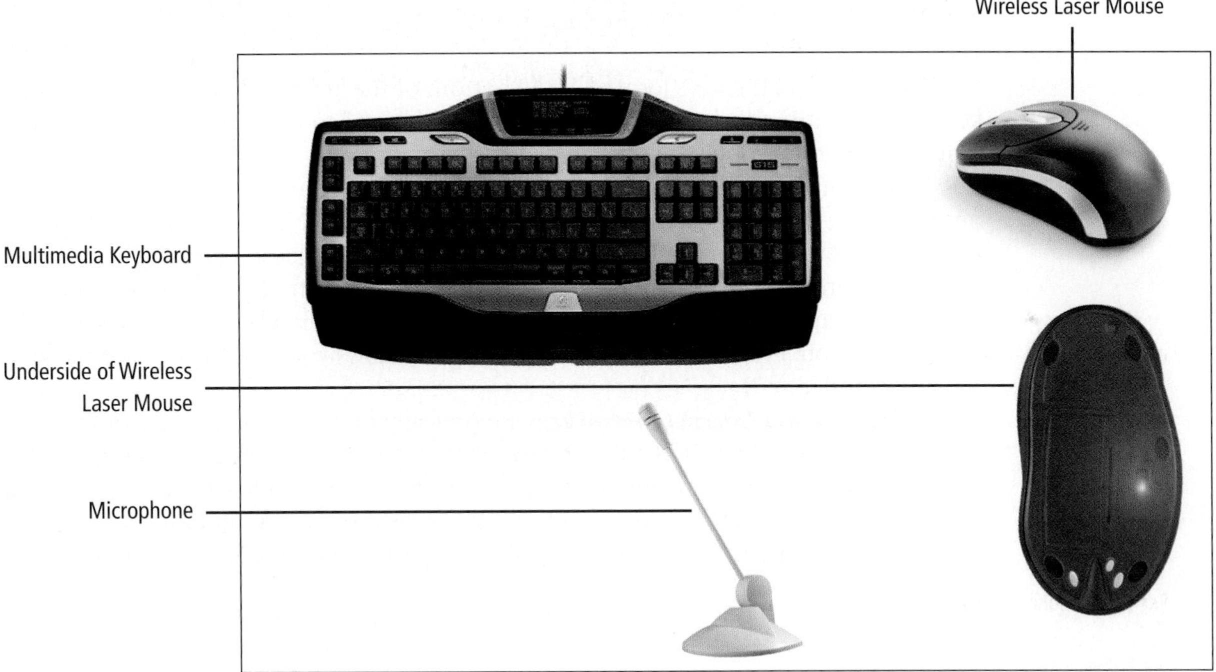

Figure 1.9
Input devices

Keyboards

Are there different types of keyboards? The ***keyboard*** is the primary input device for computers. There are actually several different kinds of keyboards. The QWERTY keyboard is the one most common. It is based on the original typewriter keyboard and is named for the arrangement of the letters on the upper left alphabetic row of keys. Another style is the Dvorak keyboard, which arranges the letters and numbers in a different pattern for increased typing speed. Some ergonomic keyboards use a split keyboard arrangement, offsetting each half at an angle to reduce the incidence of repetitive stress injuries such as carpal tunnel syndrome.

Keyboard size and layout on notebook and tablet computers can differ slightly from a standard keyboard due to space constraints. Keyboards usually send information to the computer through a cable connected to a USB port; however, ***wireless*** or remote keyboards are gaining in popularity. A wireless keyboard communicates with the computer by infrared or radio frequency technology. These wireless devices require batteries.

What are all these other keys used for? In addition to the standard alphanumeric keys originally found on typewriters, computer keyboards have a variety of keys that provide additional functionality.

Control keys, such as the Ctrl, Alt, and Windows keys, often provide shortcuts or increased functionality to the keyboard when used in combination with another key. If you press the Shift key and a letter, the result is an uppercase, rather than a lowercase, letter. In the same way, using one of the control keys enables the standard keys to be used for additional purposes. For example, pressing Ctrl and the letter P opens the Print dialog box. Another example of a control key is the Esc key, which can often be used to stop, or *escape*, from a currently running task. A unique control key that is found only on Windows-based keyboards is the Windows key.

The ***numeric keypad***, located at the right of the keyboard, provides an alternative method of quickly entering numbers. This is useful for individuals who are accustomed to using an adding machine or calculator.

Function keys are located above the standard row of number keys. Numbered F1 through F12, these keys are generally associated with certain software-specific commands. Pressing the F1 key will usually open the Help menu for a program; however, pressing one of the other function keys can produce different results, depending on the software program running.

Arrow keys are the keys located at the bottom of the keyboard between the standard keys and the numeric keypad. These keys enable the user to move the insertion point around the window one space at a time.

Toggle and other keys, which are located just above the arrow keys, are used for various purposes, including navigation and editing. The Insert, Num Lock, and Caps Lock keys are all examples of toggle keys. A ***toggle key*** works just like a light switch; press it once and the feature is turned on, press it again and it is turned off. If you've ever accidentally pressed the Caps Lock key and typed a long string of all capital letters, you've seen this feature in action. Pressing the Caps Lock key again allows you to return to normal keyboarding mode.

Multimedia and Internet control keys are typically found at the top edge of the keyboard. The precise placement and function of these keys usually depends on the keyboard manufacturer. However, most modern keyboards have at least a few keys or buttons that can be used for such tasks as muting or adjusting speaker volume, opening a ***Web browser***, and sending an e-mail. Generally, each button has an icon that indicates its function.

The Mouse

Is there an easier way to control the action on the computer screen? Yes, the ***mouse*** is an input device (also called a pointing device) that, together with the keyboard, enables the user to control the operations of the computer. The mouse became popular with the introduction of graphical user interfaces, such as Microsoft Windows. This point-and-click device is useful for positioning the ***insertion point*** by translating hand movements into corresponding actions on the screen. The mouse is represented on the screen by a symbol called the ***mouse pointer***. The user can move the mouse and position this pointer anywhere on the screen to move objects or make selections from available program icons or menus.

Some mice have a roller ball on the bottom that, as you move it, translates your movement into electrical impulses. Others use laser technology (optical) to control the pointer movement. Because the bottom of an optical mouse is sealed, dirt and debris are less likely to get inside and interfere with the mouse's internal mechanisms. This laser beam can be harmful if pointed to your eyes; do not look at it directly or point it at anybody else's eyes. See Figure 1.4. Just like a keyboard, the mouse can be wired or wireless. Notebook and tablet computers can use a mouse, but most of them have a built-in touchpad, a trackball, or track point to move the insertion point and mouse pointer. Most mice today are equipped with two buttons and a wheel button in the center that provides easy zoom and scroll functions.

How can the mouse be used more efficiently? Although there are different kinds of mice, the traditional mouse has two buttons and a scroll wheel. The palm of your hand should rest comfortably over the mouse in such a way that your index finger rests on the left mouse button and the middle finger on the right mouse button. The following provides a brief description of some of the ways the mouse can be used:

- ***Click***—By default, the left mouse button is considered the primary button. When instructed to click, it is understood that the mouse pointer is moved to a certain location on the screen and the left mouse button is be pressed and released one time.

- ***Double-click***—When instructed to double-click, it is understood that the mouse pointer is moved to a certain location on the screen and the left mouse button is pressed and released twice in rapid succession. It is important that the mouse does not move while double-clicking or the command will not produce the expected results.
- ***Drag***—This means to press the left mouse button and continue to hold it while dragging, or moving, the mouse then releasing it. This action can be used to select large blocks of text, to move objects, or to resize other objects.
- ***Right-click***—Pressing and releasing the right mouse button one time will open a ***shortcut menu***. Shortcut menus are usually context-sensitive, which means they will vary depending on what or where you have clicked and what program you are using. The right mouse button is also known as the secondary button and is not typically pressed more than one time; no double-clicking for the right button. After the shortcut menu has been opened, you select the appropriate choice by clicking it with the left mouse button.
- ***Right-drag***—This is done by pressing the right mouse button and continuing to hold it while dragging, or moving, the mouse. This action is used when copying or moving files or folders within different storage devices.
- ***Scroll wheel***—If your mouse is equipped with a scroll wheel, it can be used to quickly move a page up or down in a window, thus the name of the action to ***scroll***. It is an easy way to navigate through lengthy documents or websites.

Are there other input devices? Although the keyboard and mouse are the two most common input devices, there are many other input devices. ***Scanners*** are similar to copy machines, but instead of producing a paper copy, they convert documents or photos to digital files that can then be saved on your computer. ***Microphones*** are used to digitally capture and record sounds. Game controls such as ***joysticks*** are used to control movement within video games. ***Digital cameras*** and ***digital video recorders*** enable you to capture digital images and movies and transfer them directly to your computer.

The Processor

What does the CPU do? The CPU (see Figure 1.10) is the brain of the computer and is responsible for executing program instructions and manipulating data to convert to information. It has two main parts—the ***control unit*** and the ***arithmetic logic unit (ALU)***. The control unit is responsible for obtaining and executing instructions from the computer's memory. Example: The user wants to print a document and selects the "Print" command from an icon on the screen. The CPU gets the command from memory (RAM), interprets the command, and sends the document as output to a selected printer. In other words, the CPU coordinates the internal activities and the activities of all the other computer components. The arithmetic logic unit (ALU) performs the arithmetic and logic functions for the computer. The ALU handles addition, subtraction, multiplication, and division, and also makes logical and comparison decisions. This enables the CPU to perform tasks such as sorting data alphabetically or numerically and filtering data to locate specific criteria.

Figure 1.10
Two sides of a CPU

Different CPUs

As important as the CPU is to your computer, you might expect it to take up a large amount of space in the console. However, the CPU is actually rather small, thus the term *microchip*. Over the years, manufacturers have successfully reduced the size of microprocessor chips while continuing to increase their computing power. In fact, Moore's law (formulated in 1965 by Gordon Moore, cofounder of Intel) addresses this increase in computing power, observing that current production methods enable CPU capacity to double about every 24 months or so!

Are there different brands of CPUs? Yes, the most well-known chip manufacturers include Intel and Advanced Micro Devices (AMD). Chip manufacturers often produce several different models of chips. Some of the chips that Intel makes include the *Intel® Core™ i7 processor Extreme Edition*, the *Intel® Core™2 Quad Processor* for desktops, and the *Intel® Centrino® 2 Processor Technology* for portable computers. AMD manufactures chips such as the *AMD Phenom™ II X4* for desktops, and the *AMD Turion™ X2 Ultra Dual-Core Mobile Processor* for portable computers. Intel and AMD chips are the mainstays for PCs. Using multiple processors (dual core or quad core) has several advantages over a single-processor CPU, including improved multitasking capabilities and system performance, lower power consumption, reduced usage of system resources, and lower heat emissions.

How is a CPU's processing power measured? One indicator of a CPU's processing power is its ***clock speed***. Clock speed measures the speed at which a CPU processes data (number of instructions per second) and is measured in ***megahertz (MHz)*** or ***gigahertz***

(GHz), depending on the age of the CPU. Early computers had CPUs that processed at speeds of less than 5 MHz, whereas modern processors can operate at over 3 GHz (the equivalent of 3,000 MHz) and newer processors continue to surpass these numbers.

What types of memory does a computer have? Memory is another critical computer component of a computer system. The term *memory* signifies storage. There are two basic types of memory: temporary or ***volatile*** and permanent or ***nonvolatile***.

Permanent memory includes ***Read-Only Memory (ROM),*** which is prerecorded on a chip. The information on a ROM chip cannot be changed, removed, or rewritten, and is generally inaccessible to the computer user. ROM is nonvolatile memory because it retains its contents even if the computer is turned off. ROM contains critical information, such as the program used to start up or boot—start— the computer.

Storage devices such as hard disks and flash drives and storage media such as CDs and DVDs are considered permanent or nonvolatile memory. These are presented later in this chapter.

Temporary memory, the computer's temporary or volatile memory, is ***Random Access Memory (RAM)***. RAM (see Figure 1.11) acts as the computer's short-term memory and stores data and program instructions waiting to be processed. RAM is considered volatile because its contents are erased when the computer is turned off.

Figure 1.11
Random Access Memory (RAM) / RAM chips

Why is it important to have enough RAM? The more tasks your computer performs at the same time, or the more programs you have open, the more RAM it uses. We described RAM earlier as the center of the flow of data and information in the information processing cycle (see Figure 1.1). That flow slows down when there is not enough RAM. Your computer's RAM is like the top of your desk. The size of the desk that you need is determined by the work you do at a given moment. You may need to use a notebook computer, several books, a clipboard with notes, a holder for pens and pencils, and a telephone. If your desk is not big enough to fit these items, you cannot work with all of them at the same time. If you do not have a sufficient amount of RAM in your system, you might notice your computer slows down or even stops responding when you try to perform tasks.

Computer users often think this means they have too much information saved on their computers' hard drives. What it actually means is that they are running out of memory, not permanent storage space. To fix this problem, you can reduce the number of programs running at the same time, disable some features of the Operating System, or simply add more RAM to your system. Installing additional memory is one of the most inexpensive and easiest upgrades for your computer and often results in noticeable performance improvements.

Memory is measured in several units such as ***megabytes (MB)***, which is approximately one million bytes, ***gigabytes (GB)***, which is approximately one billion bytes, or ***terabytes (TR)***, which is one trillion bytes. Study the table in Figure 1.12.

Units to Measure Memory

Name	Abbreviation	Number of Bytes	Relative Size
Byte	B	1 byte	Holds one character of data
Kilobyte	KB	1,024 bytes	Holds about a half page of double-spaced text
Megabyte	MB	1,048,576 bytes	Holds about 768 pages of typed text
Gigabyte	GB	1,073,741,824 bytes	Holds approximately 786,432 pages of text
Terabyte	TB	1,099,511,627,776 bytes	This represents a stack of typewritten pages almost 51 miles high
Petabyte	PB	1,125,899,906,842,624 bytes	This represents a stack of typewritten pages almost 52,000 miles high

Figure 1.12
Measuring memory—these units are used to measure the size and capacity of RAM and also of storage devices/media

RAM size requirements vary depending on the operating system in use. Older computers that run Windows XP should have between 512 MB to 1 GB of RAM. For newer computers, a minimum of 2GB possibly more is recommended.

Output Devices

Output devices display information after data has been processed in a useful format. This format can be text, graphics, audio, or video. Monitors and printers are the two most common output devices.

Monitors

What are monitors? Monitors are display devices that show images of text, graphics, and video once data has been processed. The image on a monitor is called ***soft copy***; you can view it, but you cannot touch it. See Figure 1.13.

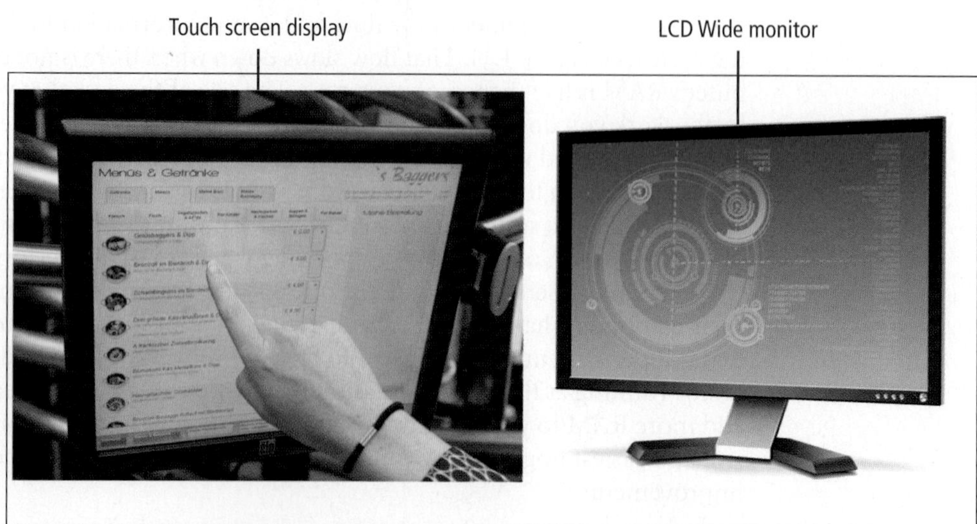

Figure 1.13
Output devices—monitors

What is an LCD monitor? Monitors come in a variety of sizes and styles, but the standard today is the ***LCD (liquid crystal display)***. ***Flat-panel*** LCD monitors use a liquid crystal display and are thin and energy efficient.

What factors determine a monitor's display quality? The number of ***pixels***, a monitor's display, is made up of millions of tiny dots known as pixels or picture element. Each pixel represents a single point on a display screen or in a graphic image. The number of pixels on the screen determines a monitor's sharpness and clarity, also known as its ***resolution***. A higher number of pixels results in a clearer and sharper monitor resolution. A standard screen resolution might be expressed as 1024 x 768, which means there are 1,024 columns, each containing 768 pixels, for a total of more than 786,000 pixels on the screen. Monitor sizes are determined by measuring their screens diagonally.

Dot pitch is another display characteristic and refers to the diagonal distance between two pixels of the same color. Dot pitch is measured in millimeters with smaller measurements resulting in a crisper viewing image because there is less blank space between the pixels. For best viewing, monitors should have a dot pitch measurement of .28 mm or less. LCD monitors use an electric current to illuminate the pixels.

Refresh rate is the speed at which the pixels are reilluminated and it's measured in cycles per second, expressed as hertz (Hz). Refresh rates generally average between 75 and 85 Hz, which means the screen image is redrawn 75 to 85 times per second. Higher refresh rates result in less screen flicker and less eye strain.

What are touch screen monitors? Touch screen monitors are both input and output devices. They display images just like regular monitors but also enable users to touch their surfaces and make selections directly from the screen. These monitors are widely used in retail stores at checkout counters, in airports for passengers' fast check-ins, and HP has released a personal computer in which the monitor is also the system unit and uses touch screen technology.

Which monitor is best? Choosing the right monitor is always a combination of what you like, want, and can afford. A higher resolution, small dot pitch, fast refresh rate, and large monitor size are desirable, but all come with a higher price tag.

Printers

Using a monitor is a good way to view the information on your computer, but sometimes a soft copy isn't sufficient for your needs. ***Printers*** generate a ***hard copies*** or ***printouts***, which are a permanent record of your work on paper. See Figure 1.14.

Figure 1.14
Output devices—printers

What types of printers are available? There are two categories of printers: impact and nonimpact. ***Impact*** printers have small hammers, similar to a typewriter's, that strike an ink ribbon against paper, leaving behind the image of the character or symbol. The ***dot matrix*** printer is an impact printer. Once very popular because of their low cost, dot matrix printers are still in use today, limited only to certain applications that require continuous forms or multipart forms (an original and several copies), such as invoices or purchase orders.

How does a nonimpact printer work? Nonimpact printers do not actually touch the paper when printing. There are a variety of nonimpact printers, but the two most commonly used with home computers are the ink-jet printer and the laser printer. The ***ink-jet*** printer uses a special nozzle and ink cartridges to spray ink in small droplets onto the surface of the paper. Ink-jet printers easily print in color, in black, and in grayscale to produce good quality printouts. They are relatively inexpensive to buy and maintain. ***Laser printers*** use the same process as photocopiers to produce their output. They use a special cylinder known as a drum, dry ink or toner, and a laser. Static electricity attracts toner to the surface of the drum, and the laser distributes the toner in the correct pattern. The drum transfers the toner to the paper and heat is used to permanently fuse the toner to the paper. Laser printers are generally more expensive to purchase than ink-jet printers, although they often print more quickly and are more cost effective. Lower-end laser printers print only in black and white; however, more expensive printers can produce color copies.

How do you assess a printer's capabilities? When you select a printer, there are some key characteristics to consider.

Print speed is often expressed as ***pages per minute (ppm)***. Print speed can vary depending on the manufacturer and model, and is also affected by whether the page is text-only, if it includes graphics, and if the printout is in color or in black and grayscale.

Just as with monitors, resolution is also important to print quality. For printing purposes, resolution is expressed as ***dots per inch*** or ***dpi***. The higher the dpi, the better the print quality. Print qualities of 300 to 600 dpi are typical of most printers, although special photo printers can offer resolutions up to 1,200 dpi. Professional printers can reach even higher values.

Color output and its related cost is another important consideration. Ink-jet printers offer four- or six-color options. Many ink-jet printers use one cartridge for black ink and one or more cartridges for color. When available, printers that offer a separate cartridge for each color are a practical choice because you need to replace only one color at a time as the cartridges run out. Laser printers use separate toner cartridges for each color.

What are all-in-one printers? All-in-one printers bundle multiple capabilities in one device. All-in-one devices usually include:

- A printer, either ink-jet (color or black and grayscale) or laser (output)
- A scanner to convert text or images into files that can be stored and further manipulated by the computer (input)
- A facsimile (fax) function to send and receive documents via the telephone (communications)
- A copier function to duplicate documents (output)
- Network capabilities to enable this ***multifunction device (MFD)*** to work as part of a network environment both wired or wireless (communications)

Speakers and Multimedia Projectors

Are there other output devices? Speakers and ***multimedia projectors*** are also examples of output devices. Many computers include small speakers to enable the user to listen to CDs or DVDs and hear any auditory signals the computer sends. However, if you're serious about multimedia, you will probably want to invest in a better set of speakers for improved performance. Multimedia projectors are used to conduct presentations and training sessions. These projectors enable information to be displayed on a big screen so it can be easily viewed by a large group of attendees.

Under what category do digital cameras fall? A digital camera is a device that stores pictures digitally rather than using conventional film. After images are captured, they are stored in the camera's internal memory. Some cameras use removable flash memory cards as storage media. These cards can be read by a computer, which can then edit them and save them as files. So, the camera itself is a form of "hand-held" computer, which, if connected to a computer, serves as an input/output device. The same thing can be said to describe camcorders.

Storage Devices

What are storage devices? ***Storage devices*** are used to store the data, information, and programs for future use. This storage is often referred to as permanent memory because, unlike data that is in RAM, data saved to a storage device remains there until the user deletes or overwrites it. Data can be stored using internal hardware devices located in the system unit or in removable units that enable portability. See Figure 1.15.

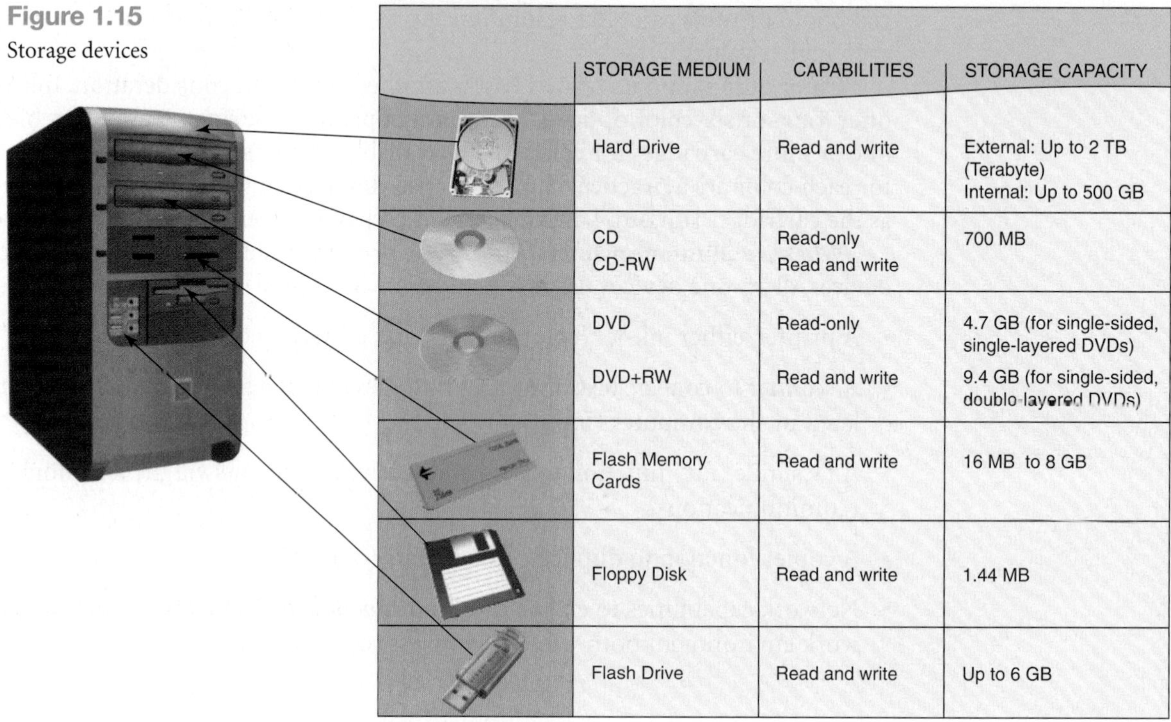

STORAGE MEDIUM	CAPABILITIES	STORAGE CAPACITY
Hard Drive	Read and write	External: Up to 2 TB (Terabyte) Internal: Up to 500 GB
CD CD-RW	Read-only Read and write	700 MB
DVD DVD+RW	Read-only Read and write	4.7 GB (for single-sided, single-layered DVDs) 9.4 GB (for single-sided, doublo-layered DVDs)
Flash Memory Cards	Read and write	16 MB to 8 GB
Floppy Disk	Read and write	1.44 MB
Flash Drive	Read and write	Up to 6 GB

Figure 1.15
Storage devices

How is a storage device different than storage media? A ***device*** is a piece of hardware such as a hard drive or a DVD drive. Media is the removable part that actually contains the stored data. Media requires a device to ***read*** and ***write*** on it. Read is the action of retrieving or opening existing data and write is the action of saving or storing data. Following is a list of devices and their media:

- CD and DVD optical drives read and write on CDs and DVDs, which are the media.
- Card readers read and write on flash memory cards, which are the media.
- Flash drives or thumb drives are media that require a connection to a USB port for read/write operations.
- Tape backup drives read and write onto tape cartridges, which are the media.
- The exception to this is the hard drive, in which the hardware and the media are all contained in a sealed unit that cannot be taken apart.

How is data stored? Data is generally stored using one of three forms of storage: magnetic, optical, or flash memory:

- ***Magnetic*** storage uses tape or film covered in a thin, magnetic coating that enables data to be saved as magnetic impulses. It works in much the same fashion as an audiocassette or videotape works. Hard drives and backup tape drives are both forms of magnetic storage. Before magnetic storage can occur, media has to be formatted. This is the process in which media is divided into ***tracks*** and ***sectors***. Tracks are magnetic concentric circles and sectors are segments within those circles Data is stored magnetically within the spaces created by these tracks sectors. Magnetic media has read/write capability, which means it is possible to use it over and over again, enabling you to delete or revise existing data and save new data.

- ***Optical*** storage uses flat plastic discs coated in a special reflective material. Data is saved by using a laser beam to burn tiny pits into the storage medium. A less intensive laser is used to read the saved data. The saved data is organized using tracks and sectors, similar to those used in magnetic media. ***Compact discs (CDs)*** and ***digital video discs (DVDs)*** are examples of optical media. Unlike magnetic media, not all optical storage is read/write capable. ***CD-ROMs***—CD media that was burned once and from that moment on can only be read—and ***DVD-ROMs***—DVD media that is burned once and from that moment on can only be read—are considered read-only media (ROM). The information contained on them can be read, but not changed or deleted, and it is not possible to save new data to them. If you purchase new software, music, or a movie, it is most likely on a CD-ROM or DVD-ROM. A record-only disc (CD-R) enables you to record, or ***burn***, information to the disc one time only; information saved this way cannot be deleted or rewritten. A rewritable disc (CD-RW) enables information to be recorded, revised, or deleted, and new data can also be written to the disc, similar to magnetic media. The same possibilities are available in DVDs. However, there are currently two competing formats DVD-R/RW, known as "DVD dash," and DVD+R/RW, known as "DVD plus." The R/RW suffix indicates the DVD can be used to record and can also be rewritten. Although most DVD players can play either format, if you want to record to a DVD, you need to know which format the DVD recorder requires.

What is LightScribe? LightScribe is a disc-labeling technology that burns text and graphics onto the surface of a specially coated LightScribe CD or DVD. This is an alternative to printing a conventional sticker label and attaching it to a regular CD or DVD but it does require that you purchase LightScribe media. See Figure 1.16.

Figure 1.16
LightScribe direct disc labeling

- ***Flash memory*** uses solid-state technology. It is completely electronic and has no moving mechanical parts. Flash memory is a quick and easy form of rewritable storage and is often used in mobile devices such as PDAs, digital cameras, and MP3 players. Depending on the manufacturer, flash memory cards may be called Memory Stick, CompactFlash, Secure Digital, or MultiMediaCard. Typically, a device can use only one style of memory card; however, a computer equipped with the appropriate card reader can read any of them. Small, removable storage devices known as flash drives or thumb drives also use flash technology, require a USB port to connect to the system unit, and are very popular to transport data.

What are the main types of storage devices? Depending on the age and type of computer you have, you might find some or all of the following internal storage options:

- ***Hard disk drive***—A hard disk drive is the computer's main internal storage device. Also referred to as a hard drive, its storage space is usually measured in gigabytes (GB), with newer computers ranging in size from 80 GB to 750 GB, although it is possible to find some specialized, high-end computers with storage space measuring up to 2 terabytes (TB). As with everything else in computing, these numbers tend to increase with each new model. Hard drives are traditionally permanent storage devices fixed inside the system unit.
- ***Floppy disk drive***—This is a device that reads/writes floppy diskettes that have a maximum storage capacity of 1,450 MB. Because of this limited storage capacity compared to other media, you will seldom see floppy disks used by computer users today.

- ***CD and/or DVD drives***—Your computer may have one or two of these optical drives in the system unit. It's important to know whether these drives are simple CD-ROM drives, which can only read CDs, or if it is a ***CD-RW*** drive, also known as a CD burner. A ***CD burner*** gives you the ability to save, or burn, files to a CD-R (compact disk recordable). You might also have a separate drive that can read and/or write DVDs.

Although CDs and DVDs look alike, DVDs are capable of holding much more information than CDs. A CD can hold up to 700 MB of data, but a DVD can store almost 10 GB! Because of their differences, a CD drive is unable to read DVDs, although a DVD drive can read CDs.

Is it possible to add a storage device to a system? If you are running out of hard disk space or your system doesn't have a particular storage device, it may be possible to add a storage device, provided your system has enough room for it. You would need an available drive bay, which is the physical location within the system unit, or you might consider removing an existing device and replacing it with another. For instance, if you only have a CD-ROM drive, you could remove that and replace it with a CD-RW/DVD drive, thereby giving you the ability to read and burn CDs and play DVDs too. It is also possible to purchase many of these units as external storage devices. An external storage device is a peripheral that attaches to the computer via a port and performs the same tasks as its corresponding internal device. One of the most popular of these today is the external hard drive, which can greatly increase a computer's storage capacity and make your data fully portable.

Are there other types of storage devices? Other storage devices you might be familiar with include flash drives, a currently popular form of data storage, and older but still reliable backup tape drives.

Flash drives are removable storage devices that use flash memory and connect to the computer by a USB port. Flash drives are also known as thumb drives, universal serial bus (USB) drives, and jump drives. The flash drive is typically a device small enough to fit on a keychain or in a pocket and, because of its solid-state circuitry and lack of moving parts, it is extremely durable. Available in several storage sizes ranging from 16 MB to 64 GB, a flash drive is a quick and easy way to save and transport files. As an example, a 64-MB flash drive, which is relatively small, holds the equivalent of almost 45 floppy disks! To use one of these devices, you simply plug it into a computer's USB port. The computer recognizes the new device and enables the user to save or retrieve files from the flash drive.

Backup tape drives are storage devices that resemble audiocassette tape recorders and save data to magnetic tape media. Although they are rarely used for home computers anymore, many businesses and organizations still rely on tape backup systems to safeguard their data on a daily basis. See Figure 1.17.

The capacity of the components found in your system unit is measured in terms of storage size or speed. Computer systems continue to increase in storage capacity and

Figure 1.17
Tape backup drive and media

computing speed, while decreasing in size. Generally, higher measurements indicate a system that is quicker and more powerful than a system with lower measurements. However, it is important to balance size and speed with financial considerations too. Although it is tempting to consider buying a computer with the most power possible, a lesser computer may be more reasonably priced and still be sufficient for the typical user's needs. Recall that CPU speed is measured in megahertz (MHz) or gigahertz (GHz). The amount of RAM in a computer is generally measured in megabytes (MB), while storage space is usually measured in megabytes or gigabytes (GB), depending on the device.

Ports

What are ports? A ***port*** acts as an interface or connector between a system's peripheral devices and the computer, enabling data to be exchanged easily. Ports (see Figure 1.18) have different shapes and sizes. The same ports are typically found on a desktop too, although they might be arranged in a different order. Various input and output devices use different data exchange methods, requiring different types of ports and connectors (or plugs). If your computer does not have a particular port, you can buy an expansion card that connects to the motherboard and provides the needed connection.

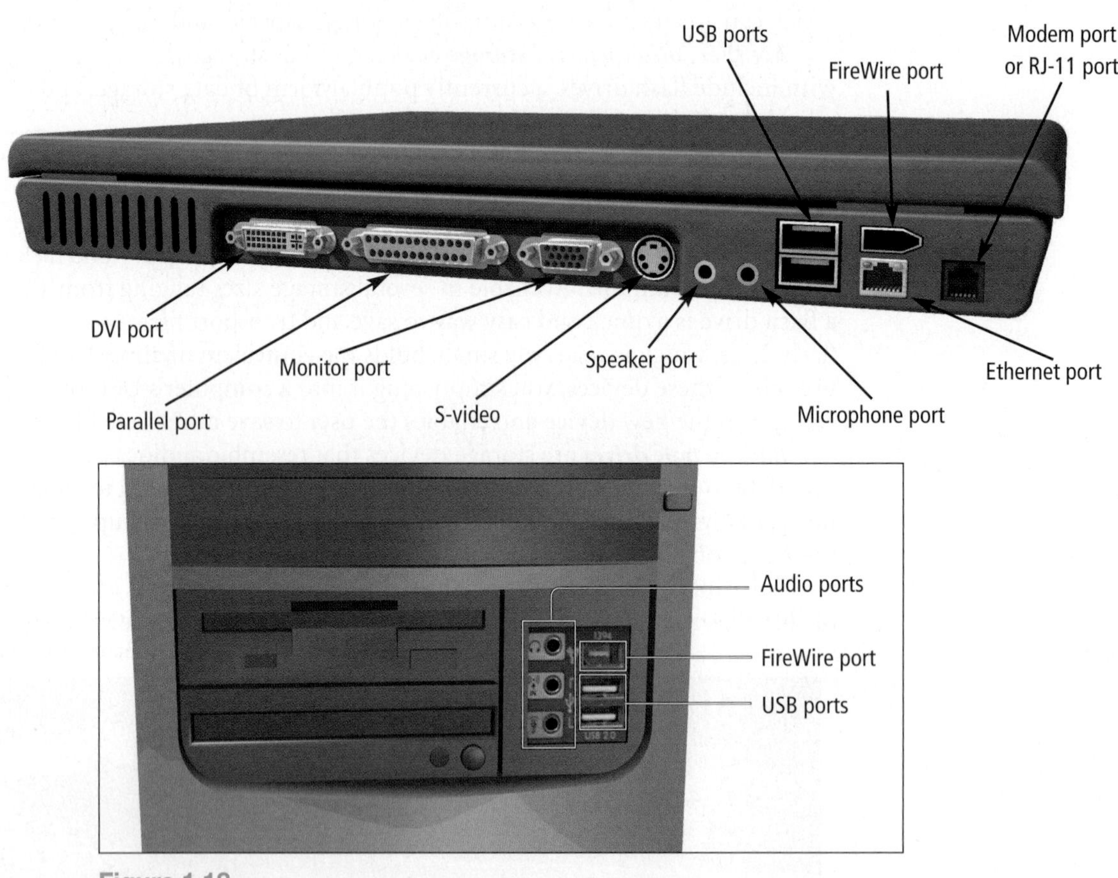

Figure 1.18
Ports

How do you determine which port a peripheral device needs? Manufacturers have attempted to make the process of connecting peripheral devices less complicated on newer computers. Rather than trying to match the size and shape of a connector to its port, many manufacturers now use a color-coding system that coordinates the colors of the connectors with their corresponding ports. Additionally, many newer desktop computers include ports, such as USB and audio ports, on the front panel of the system unit to provide easier access to them. Locating these ports on the front or back panels makes it a simple process to connect and disconnect devices that are used only occasionally, such as digital cameras, external hard drives, or MP3 players. Peripherals that are rarely disconnected, such as a keyboard or printer, are generally plugged into the ports on the back of the computer.

What are the different ports used for? Serial and parallel ports are two of the oldest types of ports found on a computer. ***Serial ports*** are ports that can send data only one bit at a time, so the data exchange rate is slow compared to newer technology. The maximum rate at which a standard serial port can transfer data is 115 ***kilobits*** or one thousand bits per second (Kbps). The mouse and modem are examples of devices that might use a serial port. A ***parallel port*** is a port that sends data in groups of bits, at transfer rates of up to 500 Kbps, so it is a considerably faster method of transferring data than the serial port. Older printers were often connected to a computer through a parallel port.

Are there faster ports? Over the years, newer ports have come into existence. One of these is the ***universal serial bus (USB) port***. This type of port is able to interface with several different peripheral devices, which reduces the need for individual, dedicated ports. USB ports are also able to transfer data at extremely high rates of speed. Original USB ports, known as USB 1.1, are capable of speeds of 12 ***megabits*** or one million bits per second (Mbps). The newest version, USB 2.0, can attain a rate of 480 Mbps, 40 times faster than USB 1.1 technology and over 400 times faster than a serial port! USB 2.0 ports are backwards compatible, which means that older USB devices work with them; however, data will transfer only at the slower USB 1.1 speed. The higher data transfer capabilities of USB ports, coupled with their capability to work with multiple devices, have made the older serial and parallel ports obsolete. Because of the USB port's speedy data transfer rate and its capability to be used with numerous devices, new computers often include six or more USB ports. Devices using USB ports include keyboards, mice, printers, scanners, digital cameras, MP3 players, and PDAs. In general, it's a good idea to get a computer with as many USB ports as possible. See the table in Figure 1.19.

Ports and Their Uses

Port Name	Data Transfer Speed	Typical Use
Serial	115 Kbps	Mice / External modems
Parallel	500 Kbps	Printers / External Zip drives
USB 1.1	12 Mbps	Mice / Keyboards / Printers / Scanners / Game controllers
USB 2.0	400 Mbps	Same as USB 1.1 but at faster transfer rates. Also, camcorders, digital cameras, and MP3 players. It maintains compatibility with USB 1.1.
FireWire / FireWire 800	400 Mbps / 800 Mbps	Digital video camcorders / Digital cameras
Ethernet / Gigabit Ethernet	Up to 100 Mbps / Up to 1,000 Mbps	Network connections / Cable modems

Figure 1.19
Port speeds and uses

The ***FireWire port***, developed by Apple and also known as IEEE 1394, is another means of transferring data quickly. The FireWire 400 has a data transfer rate of 400 Mbps, while the newer FireWire 800 transfers data at a blazing 800 Mbps! This port is typically used to connect devices that need to transfer huge amounts of data to a computer quickly, such as digital cameras or digital video recorders, or external hard drives. FireWire ports are standard on many Apple products, but are usually found only on higher-end Windows PCs and peripheral devices. Some peripheral devices offer users a choice of connecting using a USB port or a FireWire port.

What kind of port is used to connect to another computer? Connectivity ports, such as Ethernet and modem ports, are used to connect a computer to a local network or to the Internet. An ***Ethernet port***, also known as an RJ-45 jack, resembles a standard phone jack, but is slightly larger. The Ethernet port is used for network access and can also be used to connect a cable modem or router for Internet access. A ***modem port*** is the same size and shape as a phone jack and is used to connect the modem to a phone system, enabling ***digital subscriber line (DSL)*** or dial-up Internet access. DSL is a type of communications line in which signals travel through copper wires between a telephone switching station and a home or business. The maximum data transfer rate for a modem is 56 Kbps, whereas the most common Ethernet standard, Fast Ethernet, transfers data at the rate of 100 Mbps. However, Gigabit Ethernet, with a potential transfer rate of 1,000 Mbps, is becoming an option on higher-end systems and is standard on many Mac systems.

Even faster Ethernet technologies, such as 10 Gigabit Ethernet or 10 GbE exist, but they are currently used for network backbones and enterprise network infrastructures rather than home users.

Are there special purpose ports? Despite the prevalence of USB ports, which can be used for a variety of peripherals, there are still some devices that require special ports. These ports include Musical Instrument Digital Interface (MIDI), IrDA, Bluetooth, video, and audio ports.

MIDI ports are used to connect electronic musical devices, such as keyboards and synthesizers, to a computer, enabling musicians to create digital music files.

The ***IrDA port*** is used to enable devices such as PDAs, keyboards, mice, and printers to transmit data wirelessly to another device by using infrared light waves. In order to transmit information, each of the devices must have an IrDA port, and a clear line of sight, with no other objects blocking the transmission.

Bluetooth is another type of wireless technology that relies on radio wave transmission and doesn't require a clear line of sight. Bluetooth-enabled devices such as PDAs or other mobile devices can communicate only with each other over short distances, typically less than 30 feet.

Video ports include standard monitor ports, DVI ports, and S-video ports. A ***monitor port*** is used to connect the monitor to the graphics processing unit, which is usually located on the motherboard or on a video card. However, to get the best results from a flat-panel (LCD) monitor, the ***Digital Video Interface (DVI) port*** should be used instead. The DVI port transmits a pure digital signal, eliminating the need for digital-to-analog conversion and resulting in a higher quality transmission and a clearer picture on the monitor. The ***S-video port*** is typically used to connect other video sources, such as a television, projector, or digital recorder, to the computer.

Similar to video ports, ***audio ports*** connect audio devices, such as speakers, headphones, and microphones, to the computer's sound card. These jacks will be familiar to anyone who is used to using standard stereo components.

Evaluating Your System

Each computer might have a different configuration. The way a computer system is set up or the combination of components that make up the system is called its ***configuration***. This is important when buying a computer, expanding an existing system, or when connecting computers together in a network environment.

Now that you have learned most of the hardware components of a typical personal computer, you are ready to explore the computer's configuration, specifications, and features. If you didn't buy your computer brand new, you might not know all the details about your computer. If you did buy a new computer, the easiest way is to check your paperwork; all the basic information should be there. However, if your computer isn't new or you didn't keep the paperwork, there are some ways to determine exactly what is in your system. Also if you start a new job or a new position and are given a computer system, you can do a number of things again to determine exactly what is in your system.

What kind of computer do you have? This is one of the easiest questions to answer. Like almost every other appliance you've used, you can probably find the manufacturer's name and a brand name or model number on the case of the computer. If not, check the back of the unit; there should be a metal tag that includes the manufacturer's name, model number, and serial number. This information might be necessary if you have to have service performed under warranty. Use the following steps to see your system properties, which will answer some questions.

If you are a Windows XP user and you have the My Computer icon on the desktop:

1. Right-click My Computer.
2. Select Properties and read the contents of the General tab.

If you do not have the My Computer icon on the desktop, follow these steps:

1. Click the **Start** menu, select **Settings**, and then click **Control Panel**.
2. From the next window, click **Performance** and **Maintenance**.
3. Then click **System** and read the contents of the **General** tab.

Windows Vista users can follow these steps:

1. Right-click the **My Computer** icon on the desktop and select **Properties**.
2. If the icon is not on the desktop, open the **Start** menu and then right-click the **Computer** button and select **Properties**. See Figure 1.20.

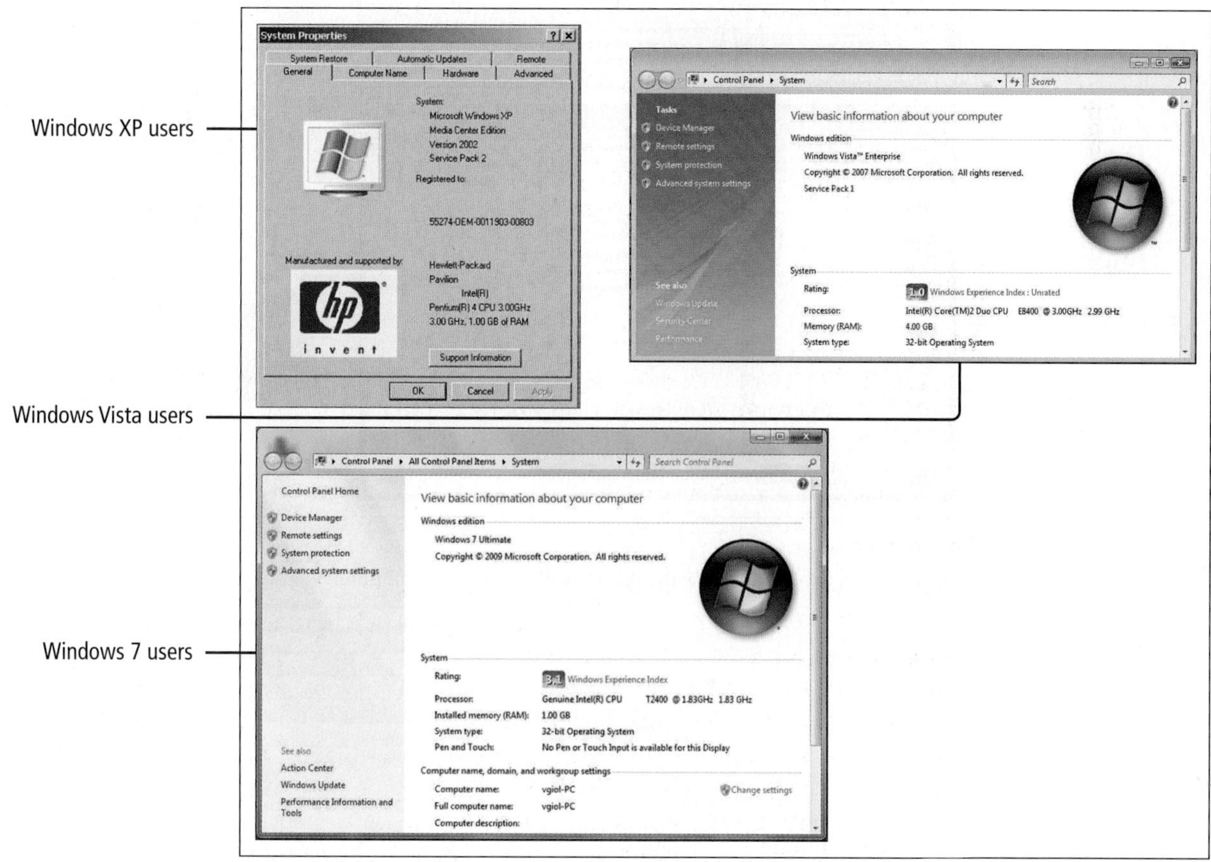

Figure 1.20
Evaluating your system—General Properties

What operating system does the computer use? If you watch carefully as a computer boots up, you can often determine the operating system. You will usually see a ***splash screen*** showing the version of Windows that runs—for example, Windows ME, Windows XP, Windows Vista, or Windows 7, which is the working name for a new version of Windows to be released sometime in 2010.

How much memory is in the computer? What is the type and speed of the CPU? Figure 1.21 displays (for several versions of Windows) a window with information on the computer's operating system, the type and speed of the CPU, and the storage capacity of RAM.

How do you determine what drives are on the system and how much storage space is available? It's important to know how much information you can store on your computer, what disk drives are available, and how much room you have left on each drive. Is there enough storage space or are the storage devices getting full? Use My Computer (or Computer) to find the answers. If the desktop does not have a My Computer (or Computer) icon, you can access it through the Start menu.

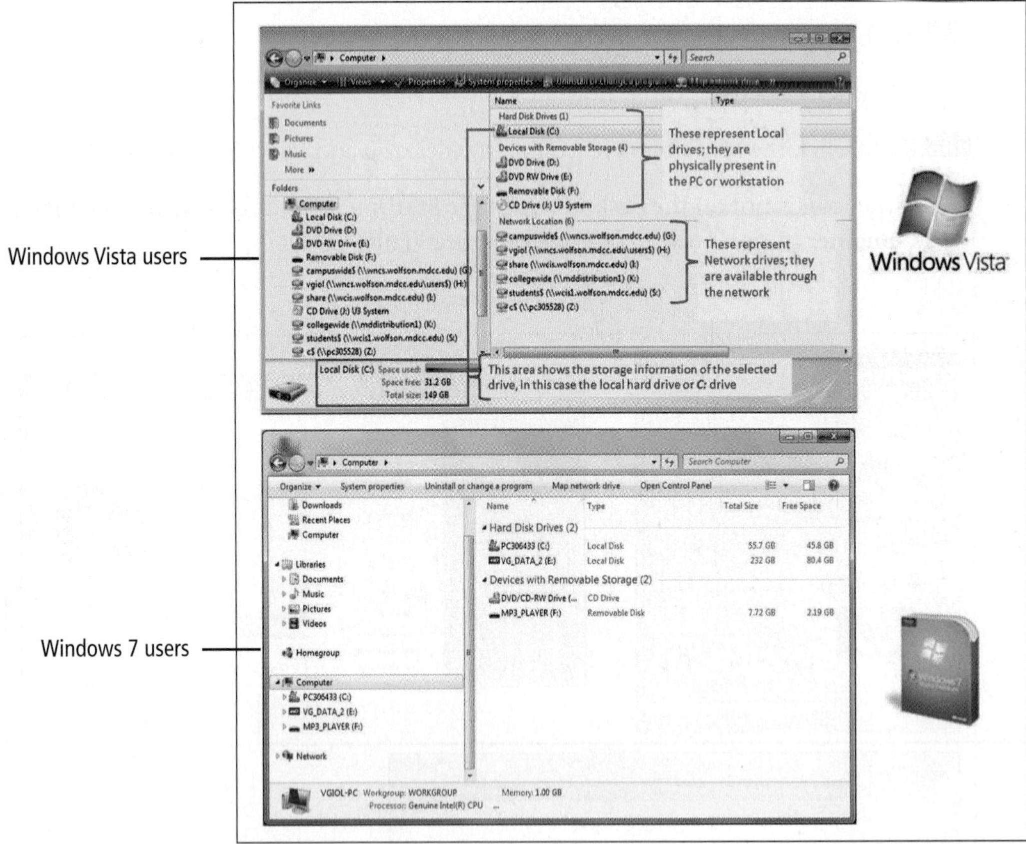

Figure 1.21

Using Windows Explorer to view the drives available to your computer

Figure 1.22 shows the Computer (or Windows Explorer) window in which the user can see all available local drives (devices within the system unit or peripherals to that unit) and network drives (devices available through a network). Also, right-click on any drive symbol, and select Properties from the shortcut menu. A new dialog box displays the drive's information similar to the one shown in Figure 1.22. The pie chart displayed on the General tab is a good visual tool that shows the size of your storage device and how much space is free.

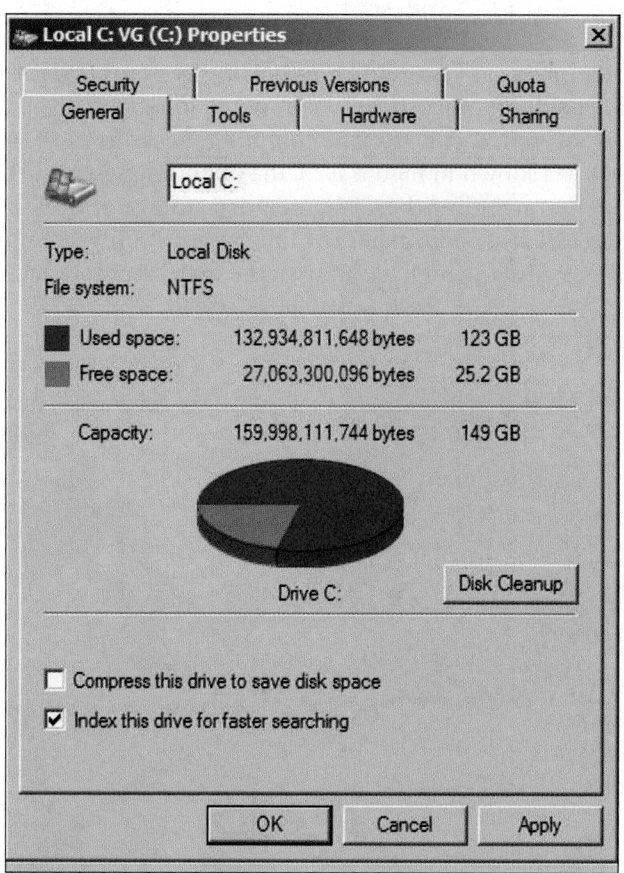

Figure 1.22
The properties of one of the storage drives (the hard drive)

Objective 4 | Identify Types of Software and Their Uses

So far we have described computer hardware, the physical components of the system. However, without software, the computer would just be a collection of useless electronic and mechanical parts. Software provides the instructions or commands that tell the computer what to do. To perform various tasks, the computer requires a set of instructions called ***programs***. These programs enable individuals to use the computer without the need for special programming skills. There are two categories of computer software—***system software*** and ***application software***. Both types of software are required to work effectively with your computer.

System Software

System software provides the instructions that the computer needs to run. It contains the directions needed to start up the computer (known as the ***boot process***), checks to ensure everything is in good working order, and enables you to interface or interact with the computer and its peripheral devices so that you can use them. System software consists of two main programs: the ***operating system*** and ***utility programs***.

Operating Systems

What is the operating system? The **operating system (*OS*)** is a special computer program that is present on every desktop computer, notebook, PDAs, or mainframes. The operating system controls the way the computer works from the time it is turned on until it is shut down. As shown in Figure 1.23, the operating system manages the various hardware components, including the CPU, memory, storage devices, peripheral devices, and network devices. It also coordinates with the various software applications presently running and provides the interaction with the user (user interface).

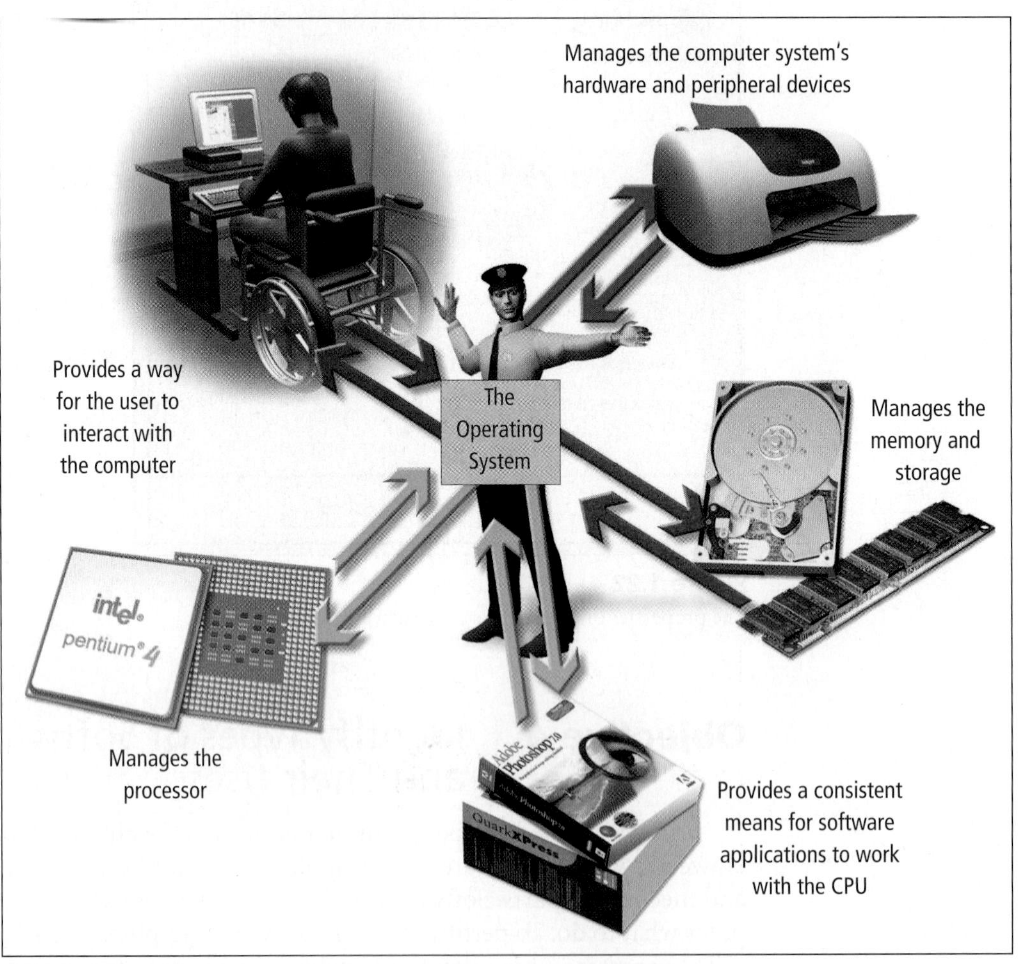

Figure 1.23
The operating system

Is it possible to communicate with the operating system? Although the operating system communicates with the computer and its peripherals, it also includes a ***user interface*** that you can use to interact and communicate with the computer. Early operating systems used a text-based or keyboard-driven interface. The early ***Disk Operating System (DOS)*** required knowledge of special commands that had to be typed accurately to achieve the desired results. This type of system was not very "***user friendly.***" Most current operating systems use a point-and-click format known as a ***graphical user interface (GUI)***. GUIs are more user friendly and intuitive than DOS systems. Rather than typing specific commands, you can use a mouse to select from on screen objects such as ***icons*** (a graphical depiction of an object such as a file or program), ***menus*** (lists of available commands), or ***dialog boxes*** (windows used to make choices or give the system specific instructions as to the action you want to take or task to perform). GUI operating systems display information on the monitor in the form of rectangular boxes called ***windows***. Although you interact with system software every time you use the computer, in some ways you don't notice it.

Do all computers need an operating system? Yes, the operating system is a critical part of a computer system. Without an OS to provide specific instructions, the computer would be unable to fulfill its four main functions. However, different computers require different types of operating systems. There are several popular operating systems available for home computers. They include Microsoft Windows, Mac OS, and Linux.

Microsoft Windows has the largest market share of the three main operating systems and is found on most of today's desktop and notebook computers. There have been many versions of Microsoft Windows, including Windows 3.0, Windows 95, Windows 98, Windows Me, Windows Vista, and Windows 7 to be released in 2010. Although a previous version of Windows might be found on an older computer, Windows Vista is the current version installed on most computers. A sample Windows Vista desktop is displayed in Figure 1.24.

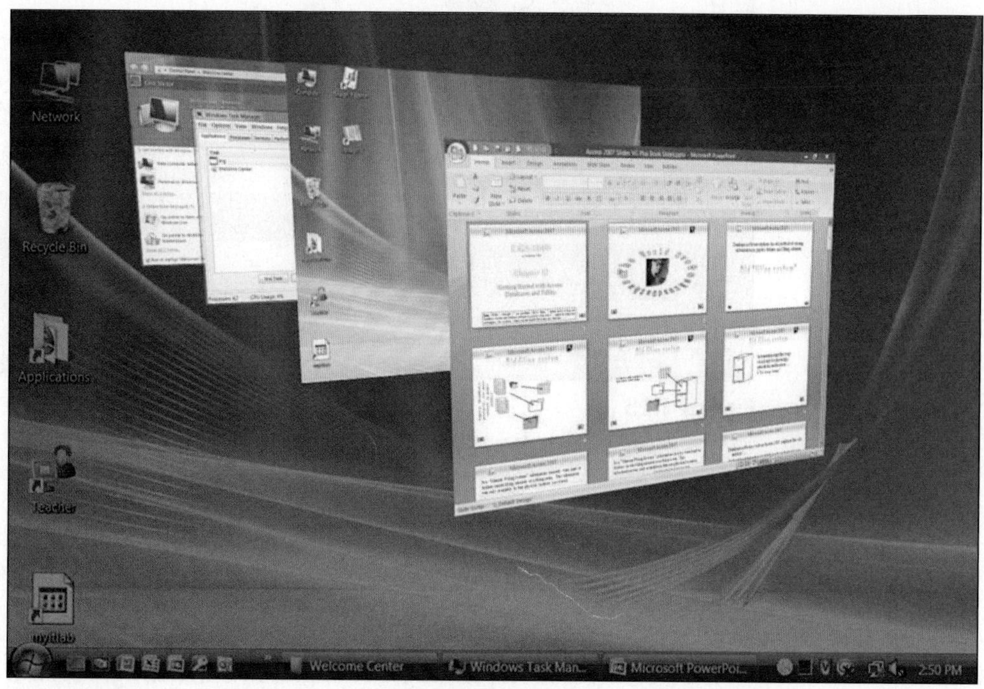

Figure 1.24
A sample of the Windows VISTA desktop

Why are there so many versions of Windows? Software developers are always updating and refining their software to adapt to new technology, respond to vulnerabilities, and improve their product. Because Microsoft also manufactures application software, some of its products have similar names and users can become confused. It's important to note that even though your computer might use Microsoft Windows for its operating system, it might not have Microsoft Office (an application software suite) installed.

Mac OS is an operating system designed specifically for Apple's Macintosh computers. Figure 1.25 shows the Mac OS desktop that is similar to Windows because it also uses a GUI. In fact, Apple was the first company to introduce a commercially successful GUI operating system for the consumer market. But, because of the popularity of the Windows-based PCs, Mac OS has a much smaller market share. If you are looking to purchase a PC or a peripheral for a PC, you have a variety of choices among different manufacturers. Only Apple manufactures Apple products and peripherals for its computers and they tend to be a bit pricier.

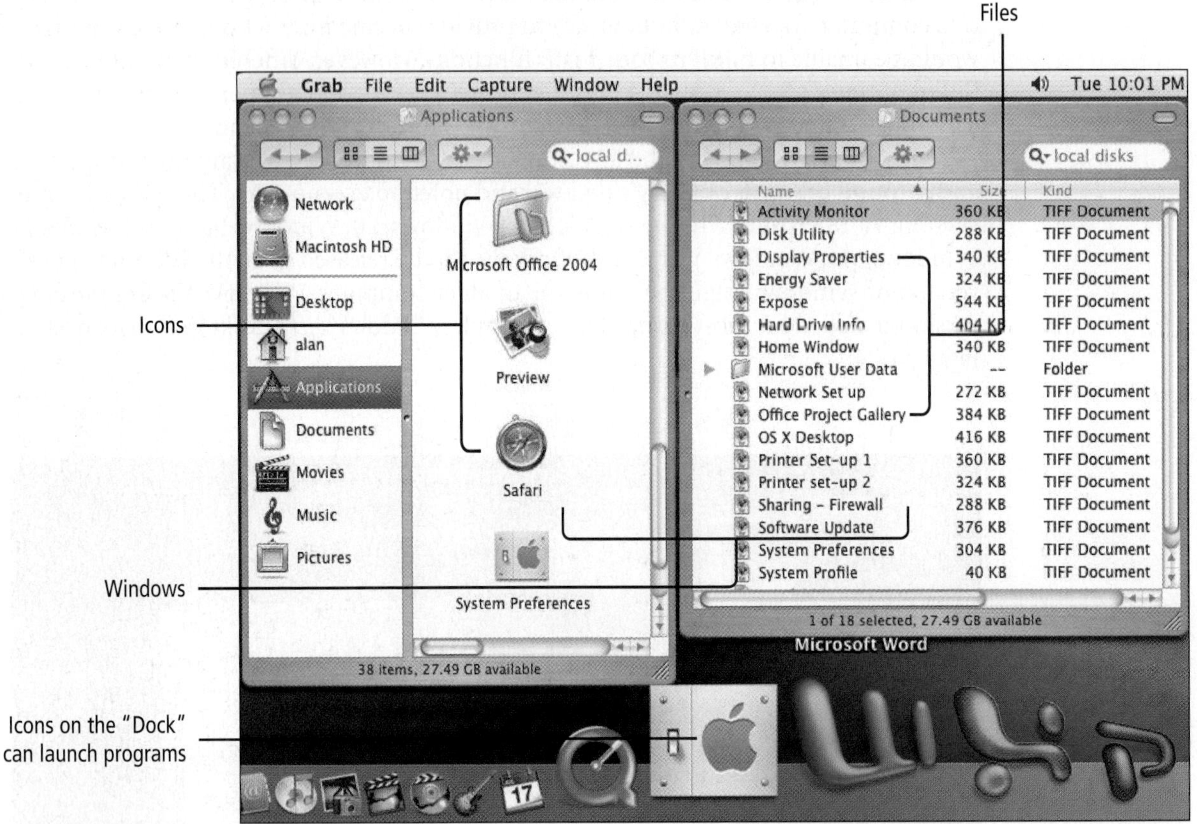

Figure 1.25
Mac OS desktop

Can Windows run on an Apple computer? Until recently, the Mac OS could not run on a PC, and the Windows OS could not run on a Mac. Software is available to start a Mac that will run Windows applications. Microsoft's Virtual PC for Mac features specifications such as:

- Access PC-only software, files, networks, and devices with your Mac
- Zero-configuration printing; better graphics handling; expanded preferences
- Cut and paste between platforms; share folders and other media between platforms
- Easily shut down virtual PC and relaunch right where it left off
- Use PC and Mac peripherals

Linux is an alternative operating system. Based on the UNIX operating system developed for mainframe computers, it also has a dedicated group of users. Linux is an ***open-source*** operating system, which means it is not owned by a single company and some versions are available at no cost.

How is open-source software different from other types of software? Open-source software makes its source code, essentially the program instructions, available to anyone who would like to see it. Programmers are encouraged to work with and change the code as they see fit, in the hope that having many "eyes" looking at the code will streamline and improve it. Proprietary software, such as Microsoft Windows, keeps this code secret and inaccessible to programmers who are not authorized by the software development company.

Why is Linux used? Linux is rarely used by novice computer users, although it is popular among developers and other technologically advanced individuals who prefer to use an alternative operating system. Some people appreciate the opportunity to work in this more "open" programming environment. However, one of the disadvantages of Linux is that, because no single company is responsible for it, technical support is not easily found. Users might find help from various resources such as user groups and Internet communities. Alternatively, some software companies have chosen to develop and sell a version of Linux that includes a warranty and technical support as a way of alleviating user concerns. Figure 1.26 shows an example of one version of the Linux operating system.

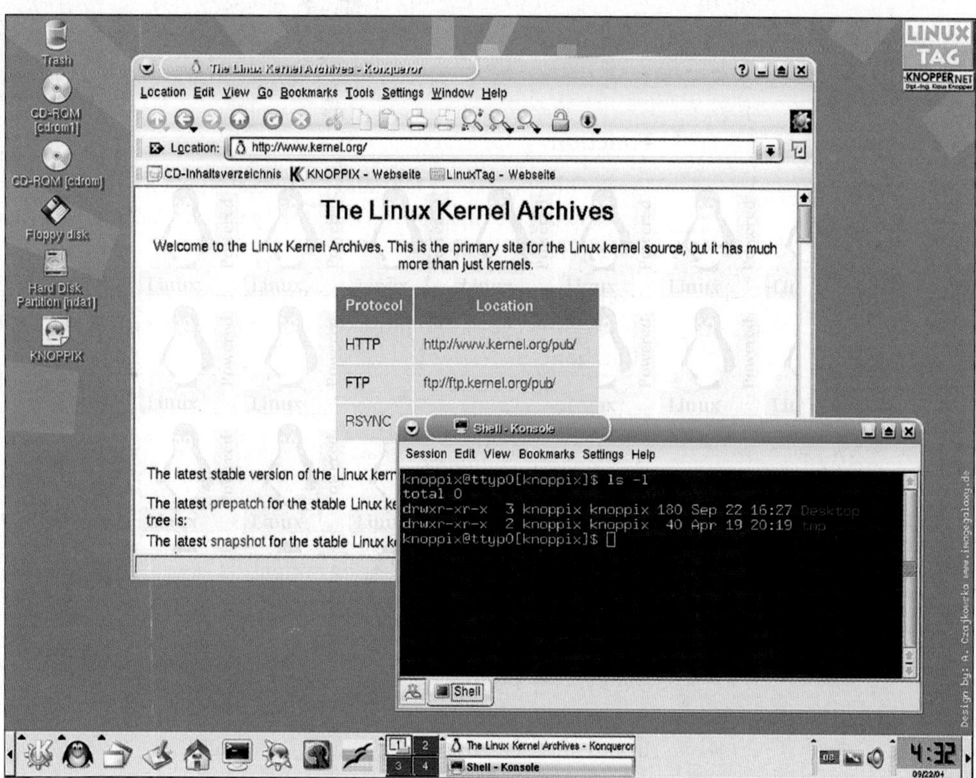

Figure 1.26

Example of one of the versions of the Linux operating system

Utility Programs

What are utility programs? Operating system software is the most critical software on the computer, because nothing can run without it. However, utility programs are another important component of system software. These small applications handle many important tasks involved with the management and maintenance of your system. Utility programs can be used to help back up important files, remove unwanted files or programs from your system, and schedule various tasks to keep your system running smoothly. Some of these utilities are included with the operating system, whereas others are stand-alone versions that you can purchase or download for free. The table in Figure 1.27 displays a variety of utility programs that ship with the Windows operating system and compares them with similar stand-alone products, describing the function of each utility.

Windows Utility Programs

Program	Function
Windows Explorer	Create folders, manage files, and compress/extract files. Read disk drive's properties including view storage capacity and free disk space, check drive for errors, defragment utility, and back up/restore utility
Windows Task Manager (Ctrl + Alt+ Delete)	Lets the user view the list of active applications, and switch or end any of them. Also, check the performance of the computer including CPU usage, RAM availability, and network utilization
Control Panel	
• System and Security	Review your computer's status Back up your computer Find and fix problems
• Network and Internet	View network status and tasks Choose home group and sharing options
• Hardware and sound	View devices and printers Add a device Connect to a projector Adjust commonly used mobility settings
• Programs	Install/uninstall programs Add desktop gadgets
• User Accounts and Family Safety	Add or remove user accounts Set up parental controls for any user
• Appearance and Personalization	Change the theme Change desktop background Adjust screen resolution
• Clock, Language, and Region	Change keyboards or other input methods Change display language Let Windows suggest settings
• Ease of Access	Optimize visual display
Administrative Tools	Schedule tasks
Security	
• Security Configuration Manager	Set account policies, local policies, network list manager policies, software restriction policies, and application control policies
• Firewall and Advanced Security	Set firewall and advanced security on local computer

Figure 1.27
Windows utility programs

Application Software

Application software or applications are comprised of programs that enable you to accomplish tasks and use the computer in a productive manner. Applications are programs created to perform a specific task, solve a specific problem, or address a specific need.

How do system software and application software work together? System software is like the breathing you need to do to live; however, you don't usually think much about it unless something goes wrong. Application software might be compared to a musical instrument like a flute. When a musician combines each of these breaths and her flute, the result may be a beautiful melody (if she has practiced, of course!). Computer software works together similarly; the system software acts as the "breath," while the application software provides the "instrument," enabling you to create something.

There are many different kinds of application software, although they often fall into one of several general categories, each of which has a different purpose. These categories include financial and business-related software, graphics and multimedia software, educational and reference software, entertainment software, and communication software. You might be most familiar with productivity software, which includes the following applications.

- ***Word processing software*** is used to create, edit, format, print, and save documents and other text-based files. Word processing software enables you to create or edit letters, reports, memos, and many other types of written documents that you can print or attach to an e-mail message. Revisions to existing documents can be made quickly and easily, without having to re-create the entire document. Documents created with this type of software can also include pictures, charts, ***hyperlinks,*** and other graphic elements. A hyperlink is a connection to another area of a document or a connection to an Internet URL. Microsoft Word, Lotus Word Pro, and Corel WordPerfect are all examples of word processing programs. A document created using Microsoft Word 2007 is shown in Figure 1.28. Notice that the document

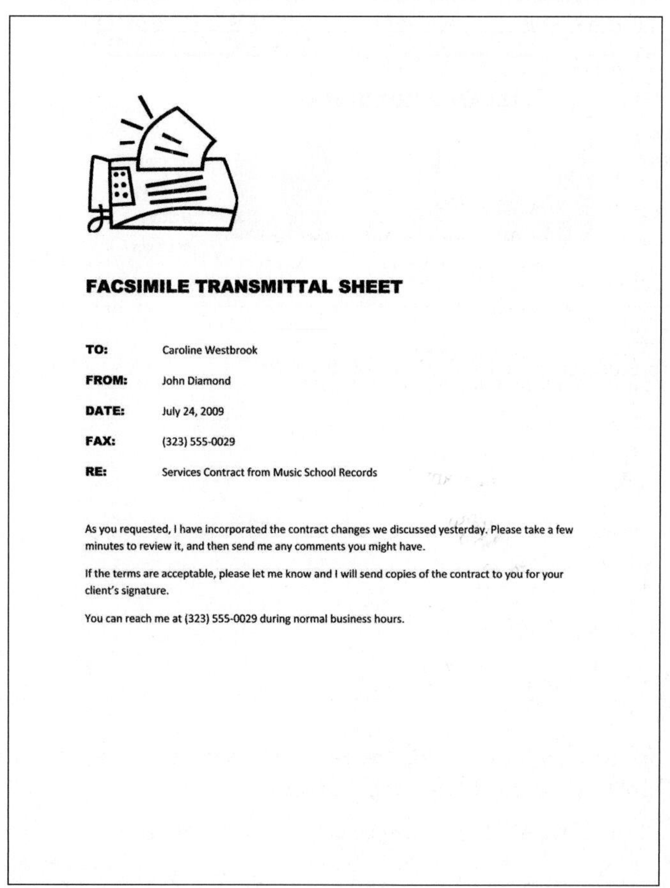

FACSIMILE TRANSMITTAL SHEET

TO: Caroline Westbrook

FROM: John Diamond

DATE: July 24, 2009

FAX: (323) 555-0029

RE: Services Contract from Music School Records

As you requested, I have incorporated the contract changes we discussed yesterday. Please take a few minutes to review it, and then send me any comments you might have.

If the terms are acceptable, please let me know and I will send copies of the contract to you for your client's signature.

You can reach me at (323) 555-0029 during normal business hours.

Figure 1.28
Sample document created with Microsoft Word 2007

contains a graphic element as well as text. Using word processing software replaces the use of conventional typewriters, on which editing was virtually impossible once the document was finished.

- ***Spreadsheet software*** enables the user to enter data in rows and columns format and:
  - Perform calculations on numeric data with user-defined formulas.
  - Convert part of the data into one or more charts, such as a column chart, a pie chart, or a line chart.
  - Work with lists to organize data and sort it in alphabetic or numeric order.
  - Create different scenarios and perform "what-if" analyses, the basis for sound decision making.

A key advantage of spreadsheet software is its capability to recalculate spreadsheets without user intervention. When data used in a calculation or a formula is changed, the spreadsheet software automatically updates the worksheet with the correct result. Microsoft Excel, Lotus 1-2-3, and Corel Quattro Pro are examples of spreadsheet programs. Figure 1.29 shows a worksheet and a chart created with Microsoft Excel 2007. The use of spreadsheet software replaces the old manual method of entering data in ledgers or journals and using a desktop calculator to do the math computations.

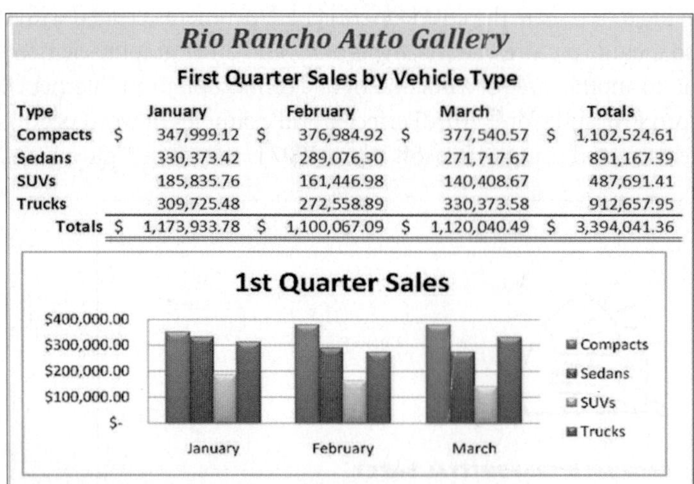

Rio Rancho Auto Gallery

First Quarter Sales by Vehicle Type

Type	January	February	March	Totals
Compacts	$ 347,999.12	$ 376,984.92	$ 377,540.57	$ 1,102,524.61
Sedans	330,373.42	289,076.30	271,717.67	891,167.39
SUVs	185,835.76	161,446.98	140,408.67	487,691.41
Trucks	309,725.48	272,558.89	330,373.58	912,657.95
Totals	$ 1,173,933.78	$ 1,100,067.09	$ 1,120,040.49	$ 3,394,041.36

Figure 1.29

Example spreadsheet created with Microsoft Excel 2007

A database is a collection of data or unorganized facts. ***Database software*** is used to store, organize, update, and retrieve large amounts of data. ***Relational database software (RDBMS)*** stores information in tables, which enable users quick access to the data by connecting tables with common fields. ***Data mining*** is a function in some databases that looks for hidden patterns in the data to anticipate future patterns. This is commonly used in scientific applications and as a marketing tool to predict future consumer trends. Typically, database software can be used to manage various types of information, such as that found in large mailing lists, inventories, students' records, order histories, and invoicing. Databases help you to enter, store, sort, filter, retrieve, and summarize the information they contain and then generate meaningful reports. Common database programs include Microsoft Access, Lotus Approach, and Corel Paradox. Figure 1.30 shows a database object created in Microsoft Access 2007. Database software replaces an old manual filing system where information is stored in filing cabinets in a single location.

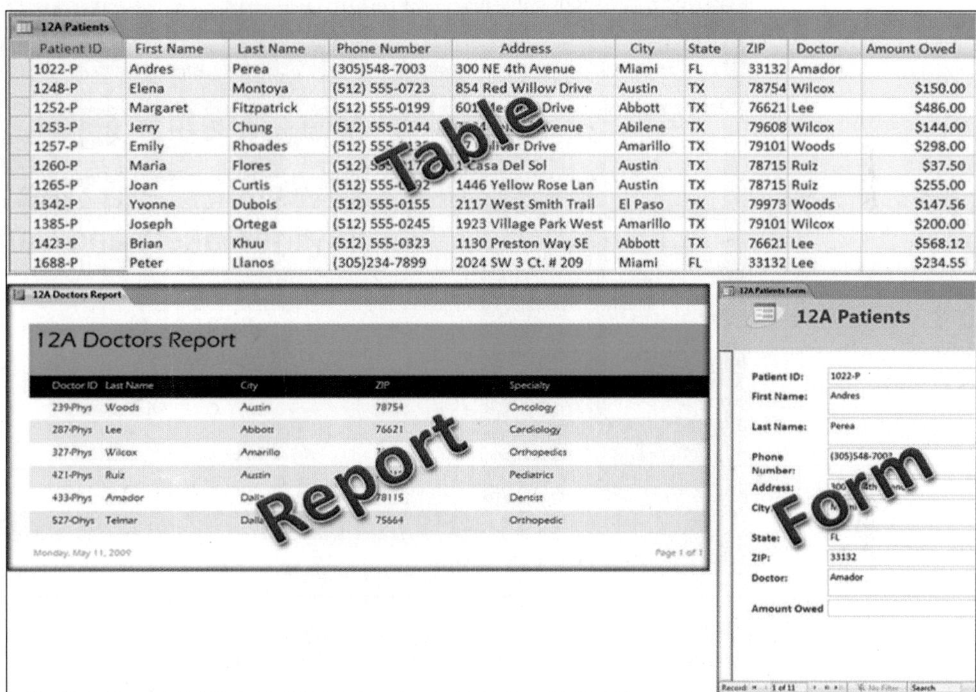

Figure 1.30
Examples of database software objects

Presentation software has become a standard in replacing flip charts, slide projectors, or overhead transparencies used by speakers and lecturers. This software is used to create electronic slides and project slide shows to visually present materials and ideas to large groups in a conference room or on the Web. Presentation software is also used to create audience handouts, speaker notes, and other materials that can be used during an oral presentation or for distribution to a group of participants. Microsoft PowerPoint, Lotus Freelance Graphics, and Corel Presentations are examples of presentation software programs. Figure 1.31 shows a presentation created with Microsoft PowerPoint 2007.

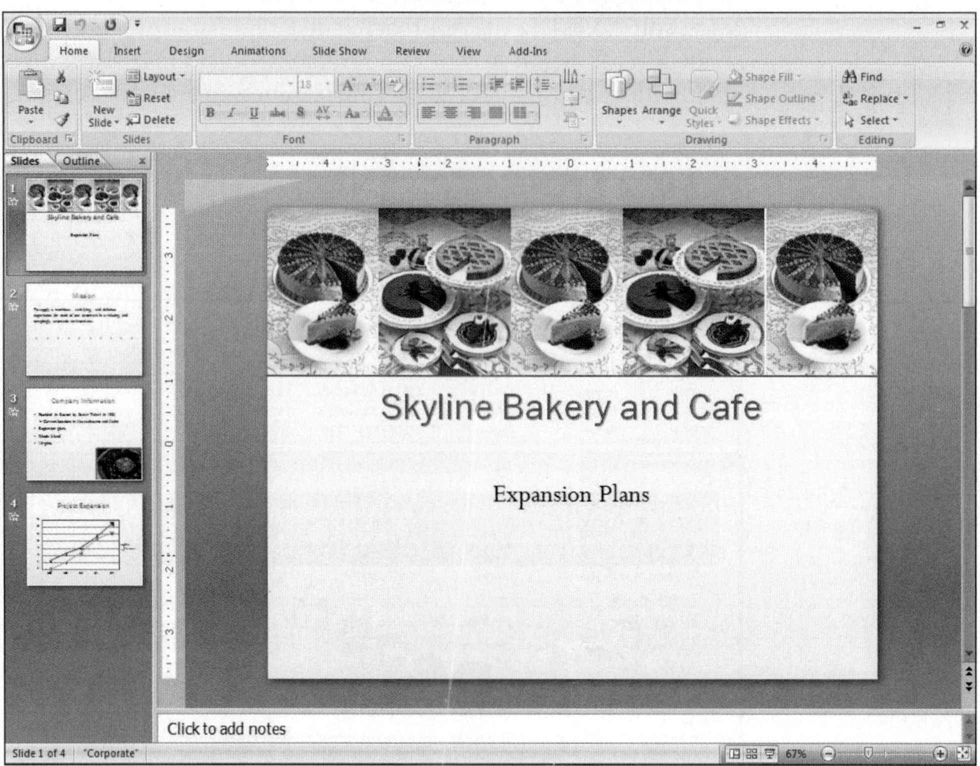

Figure 1.31
Example presentation created with Microsoft PowerPoint 2007

Communication and organizational software—Communication software can cover a broad range of tasks including videoconferencing and telephony. However, applications in the productivity category are most often used to send and receive e-mail. These applications typically include an address book (contacts list), a scheduler, a calendar, and task functions, which help users organize their personal and professional responsibilities. Microsoft Outlook, Lotus Notes, and Corel WordPerfect Mail are examples of communication and organizational software. Figure 1.32 shows an example of a calendar in Microsoft Outlook 2007.

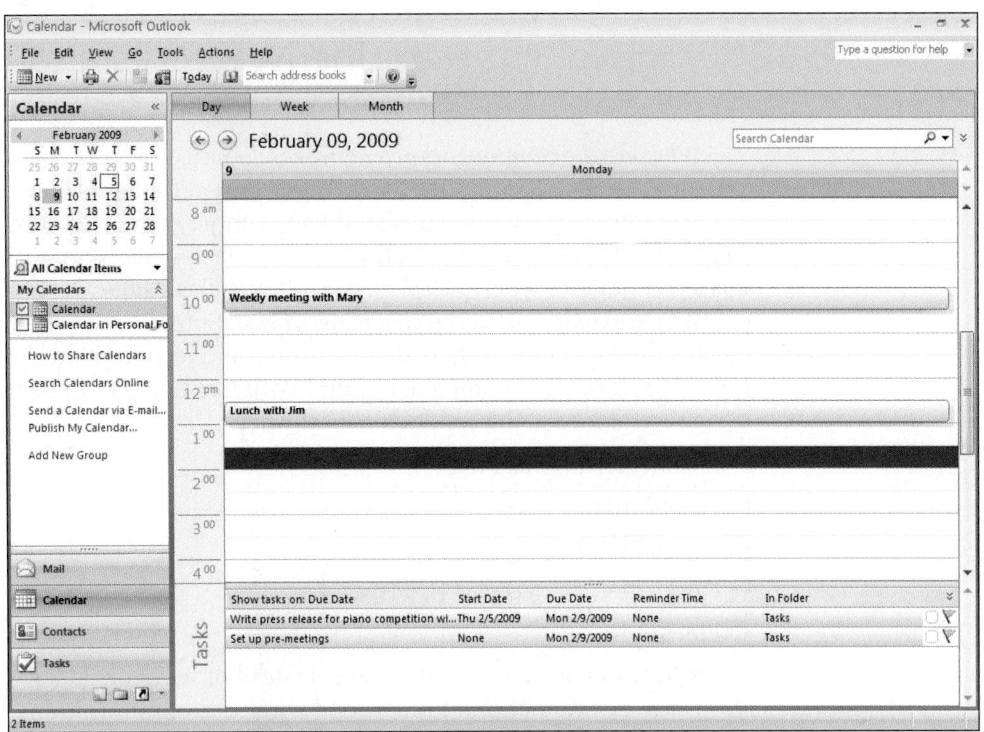

Figure 1.32

Example of a calendar in Microsoft Outlook 2007

What is a software suite? Although it is possible to buy any of the previous applications separately, most software manufacturers, including Microsoft, Corel, and Lotus, also group applications together into a package called a ***suite***. There is an alternative suite called OpenOffice and it's free. It is designed as an open source software in such a way that users can report bugs, request new features, or change and improve the software.

Another advantage of using a suite is that because products from the same company have many common elements, such as basic window design and layout, toolbars containing similar tools, dictionaries, and media galleries, many users find this familiarity makes it easier to switch between the programs in a suite. Examples of suites include Microsoft Office, Corel WordPerfect Office, and Lotus SmartSuite.

What are some other common software applications? As mentioned earlier, there are many different types of application software besides productivity software, each one with a specific function. Some of these are the following:

- You might use Microsoft Publisher or QuarkXPress to create newsletters or brochures.
- Bookkeepers rely on special accounting packages such as Peachtree Accounting or QuickBooks to balance the books and handle other accounting functions.
- Graphic designers turn to packages such as Adobe Photoshop or Adobe Illustrator to develop creative artwork.
- You might use Microsoft Expression Web or Macromedia Dreamweaver to create your own Web site.

- ***IM*** (instant messaging) software enables users to communicate in real time like a phone conversation but using text only. The software can alert you if a member of your group is online at that moment.
- Web browsers are software used to locate and display Web pages and navigate through them. They also enable users to store their frequently used sites for quick access.

If you have a specific need, chances are there is software that will address those needs. Today the best way to find software is to do a Web search using a search engine.

Objective 5 | Describe Networks and Define Network Terms

What are the components of a network? Connecting one computer to another creates a network. Recall that computers and the various peripherals that are connected to them are called hardware. Networks consist of two or more connected computers plus the various peripheral devices that are attached to them. Each object connected to a network, whether it is a computer or a peripheral device, is known as a ***node***.

Why are computers connected to networks? Some of the benefits of computer networks include the capability to share data, software, and resources such as printers, scanners, Internet access, video conferencing, and VoIP. Computers can be connected to a network using several media, the conductors of the network signals:

- Existing telephone wires
- Power lines
- Coaxial cables
- Unshielded twisted pair (UTP) cables
- Fiber optic

Wireless networks use radio waves instead of wires or cables to connect. Most networks use a combination of media and wireless communications (see Figure 1.33).

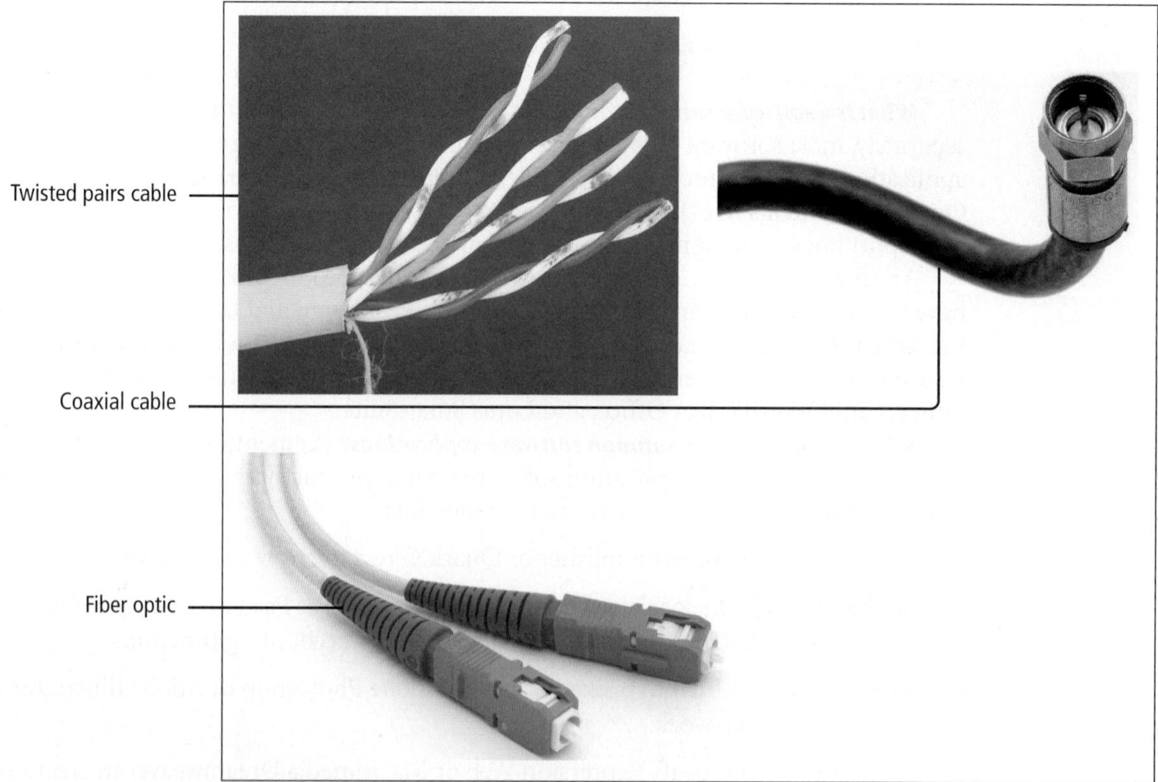

Figure 1.33
Network media, the conductor of network signals

Today, using computer networks, institutions are able to ***video conference***, that is, communicate audio and/or video between two or more individuals in different locations, optimizing communications, information sharing, and decision making.

Voice over Internet Protocol (***VoIP***) enables voice, facsimile, and voice-messaging communications over networks and the Internet.

Can networks be different sizes? A network that connects computers reasonably close together, say within a few city blocks in adjacent buildings, is called a ***local area network (LAN)***. See Figure 1.34.

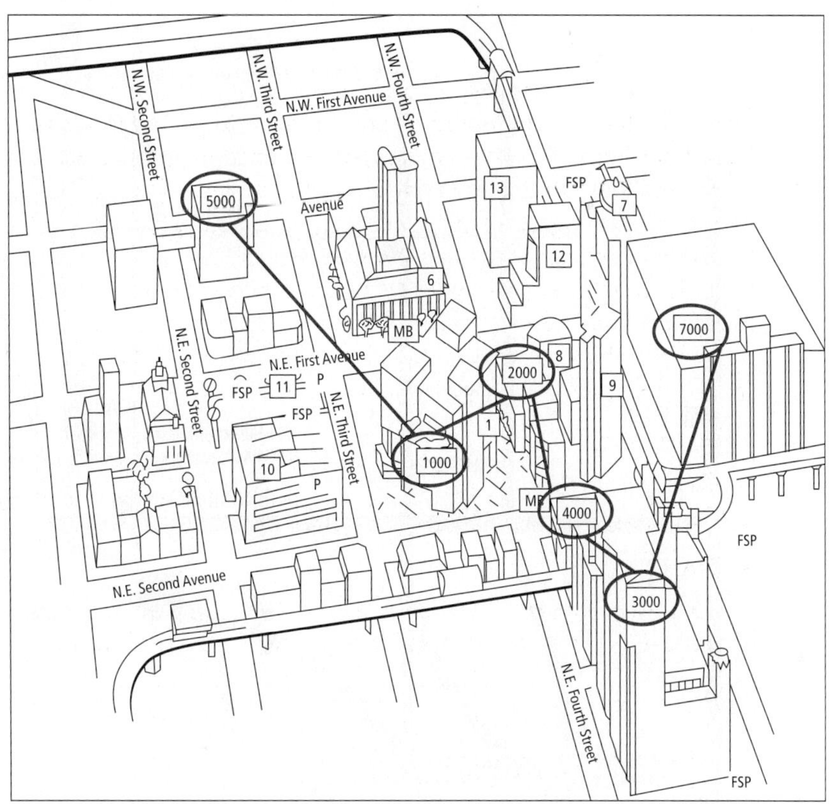

Figure 1.34

Example of a local area network, a college campus network that covers several buildings within a few city blocks

If the network grows to cover a larger geographic area or begins to include other networks, it becomes a ***wide area network (WAN)***. An example is a state college campus that connects its computers with a LAN while all of its campuses connected together form a WAN. Because the different campuses are connected through WANs, students, faculty, staff, and administrators can easily and seamlessly use the resources of the entire network. Both LANs and WANs can be wired, wireless, or a combination of both. See Figure 1.35. The Internet is actually the largest WAN because it connects computer networks all around the world.

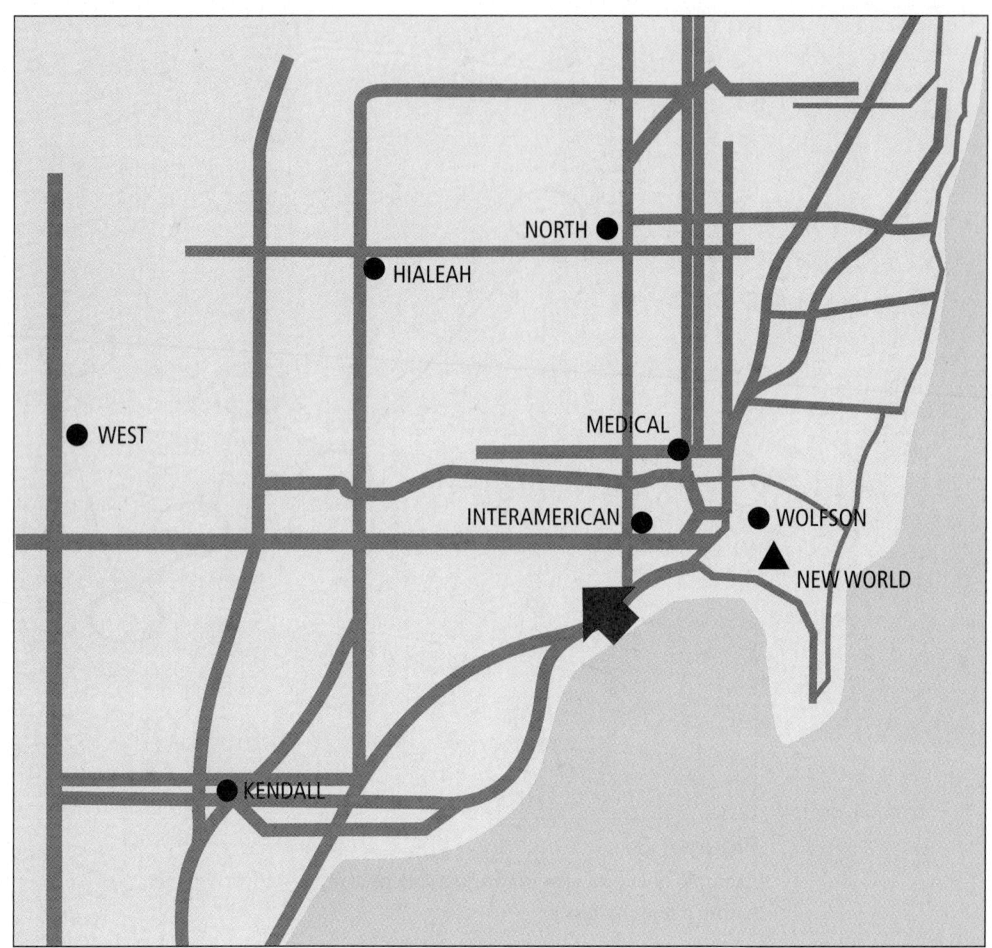

Figure 1.35
Example of a wide area network, which is a college network that links campus LANs in several cities within a county

Are networks public or private? They can be either. If you want to post information and make it available to any user, you post it on a website with no restrictions. If you want to protect certain information, you create an ***intranet*** in which access is restricted to authorized users only. Within an intranet, network administrators can limit the specific rights and privileges of different users.

How are networks configured? Networks can be configured in several ways. There are two main categories: peer-to-peer and client/server. ***Peer-to-peer*** or ***P2P networks*** are most commonly found in homes and small businesses. In a peer-to-peer network, each node can communicate with every other node without a dedicated server or hierarchy among computers. Peer-to-peer networks are relatively easy to set up, but tend to be rather small. This makes them ideal for home use, although not as desirable in the workplace. If a network grows to more than, say, ten to fifteen nodes, it is generally best to use the ***client/server network***. In a client/server network, the server manages and controls all network resources. A node can be a computer, printer, scanner, modem, an external hard disk, or any other peripheral device connected to a computer. Therefore, it isn't difficult to find more than ten nodes in an office or business setting.

How is a client/server network different from a P2P network? Client/server networks typically have two different types of computers. The ***client*** is the computer used at your desk or workstation to write letters, send e-mail, produce invoices, or perform any of the many tasks that can be accomplished with a computer. The client computer is the one most people directly interact with. In contrast, the server computer is typically kept in a secure location and is used by network technicians and administrators to manage network resources. If a server is assigned to handle only specific tasks, it is known as a ***dedicated server.*** For instance, a Web server is used to store and deliver Web pages, a file server is used to store and archive files, and a print server manages the printing resources for the network. Each of these is a dedicated server.

As a client/server network grows in number of nodes and geographical distance covered, servers are assisted by distance-spanning devices such as switches and routers to optimize data traffic.

Network topology describes the different types of network architecture used for client/server networks (see Figure 1.36). Just as there are different sizes and styles of buildings that are designed for different purposes, networks are designed to be physically configured and connected in different ways.

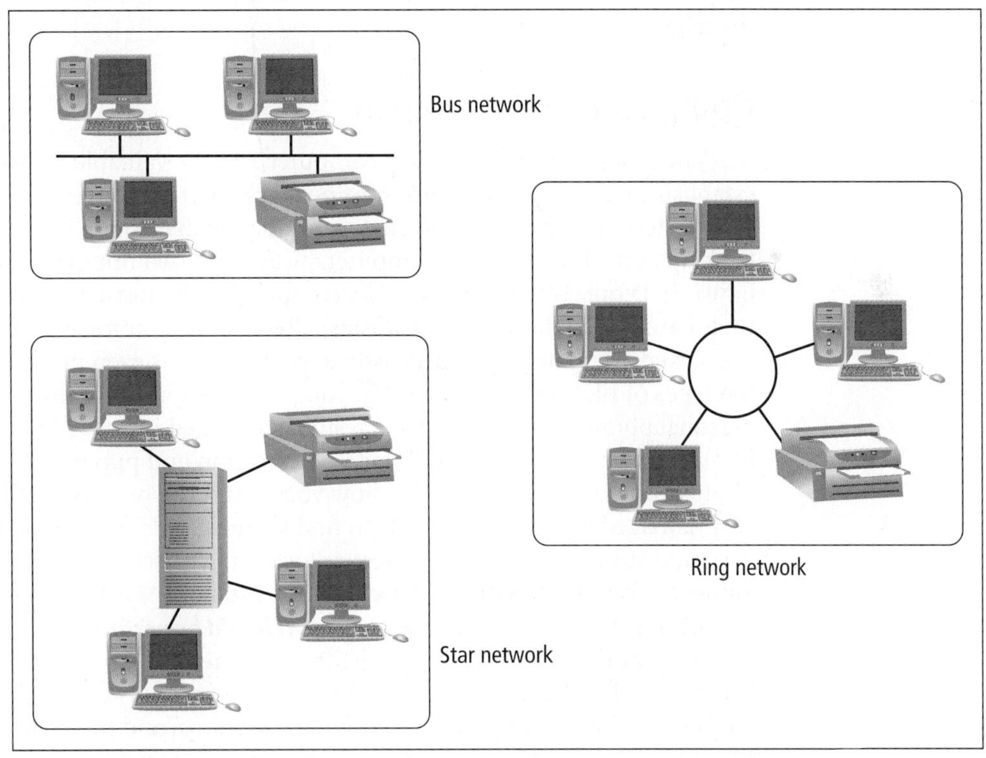

Figure 1.36
Common network topologies

Which topologies are used most often? The three most common layouts are explained in the following list:

- ***Bus topology*** connects each node to a single, central high-speed line known as a bus. No server is used, and although it is possible for each node to communicate with all the others, they can only do so one at a time. If one computer or device is sending over the network, all the others must wait until the transmission is complete before they can begin. Because this is an inexpensive and easy way to connect, this topology is often found in peer-to-peer networks.

- ***Ring topology***, sometimes known as ***token-ring topology***, connects each node to the next, forming a loop or a circle. The data that's sent is passed from node to node, traveling around the circle in only one direction. A token travels around the ring until one of the nodes is ready to send a transmission. The node then holds the token until the transmission is finished, preventing any of the other devices from sending until the token is released to make its way around the circle again. This type of topology gives each device an equal chance of being able to send data and prevents one node from doing all the communicating. This topology is being retired in favor of star topology.
- ***Star topology*** is the most frequent networking style used for businesses and homes. It offers a high degree of flexibility. Each node is connected to a special device known as a switch, which is centrally located. Each node must go through the switch to communicate with the others. If something happens to one node, the others are still able to communicate.

Objective 6 | Identify Safe Computing Practices

Being computer fluent implies you are a responsible computer user. This means more than just understanding the key components of a computer or the differences between hardware and software. Responsible computer users also know how to properly maintain their computers, back up necessary data, and protect themselves and others from security breaches and attacks.

Computer Maintenance

The first step to protect your computer and the valuable information it contains is to establish a regular maintenance routine. Backup utility programs, which may be part of your system software or purchased separately, enable you to back up your files. You can back up everything on your computer, just one or two important files, or anything in between. People often think that the computer is the most expensive item to replace if their hard drive fails. In reality, it is usually all the lost information that was contained on the hard drive that is the most costly to replace, if it is even possible to do so. Think about the types of files you might have on your own computer like financial records, your personal phone/address directory, resumes, scanned images of important documents, homework or school projects, your CD collection and purchased music files, and family photos and videos. Now imagine how you would re-create these files if they were irretrievably damaged. Would you be able to find them again? If you back up files on a regular basis and store the backups in a secure location, you lessen the impact that a mechanical failure or security breach will have on your data.

What other types of maintenance tasks should be performed? In addition to backing up files, regular file maintenance also helps to maintain order in your system. Several useful Windows utilities can be accessed from the System Tools folder. You can access the System Tools folder by clicking Start, clicking All Programs, and then clicking Accessories. Disk Cleanup scans the hard drive and removes unnecessary files such as those found in the Recycle Bin, in addition to temporary Internet files and other temporary files created by various programs. It is possible to adjust the settings and select which files to delete and which files to retain.

Similarly, the Disk Defragmenter scans the hard drive. However, rather than removing files, it attempts to reallocate files so they use the available hard drive space more efficiently. Recall that data is stored on hard drives in sectors and tracks. As file sizes change, they can outgrow their original location. When that happens, the remaining portion of the file may be stored elsewhere. If a file size decreases, or a file is deleted, this can create a blank area on the hard drive. Defragmenting a hard drive enables scattered portions of files to be regrouped and open spaces to be rearranged. This results in faster and more efficient file access, which improves the response time of the hard drive.

Is there a way to automate these maintenance tasks? Running these programs can be time-consuming, especially when you want to use your computer for other tasks. It is also easy to forget to do these things on a regular basis. That is why newer versions of Windows include a Task Scheduler. This utility enables you to create a task and select the best time for each task to run, in addition to how often, which makes the whole process automatic. Figures 1.37 and 1.38 show the steps to follow to reach the Task Scheduler dialog box for Windows Vista users and Windows 7 users, respectively.

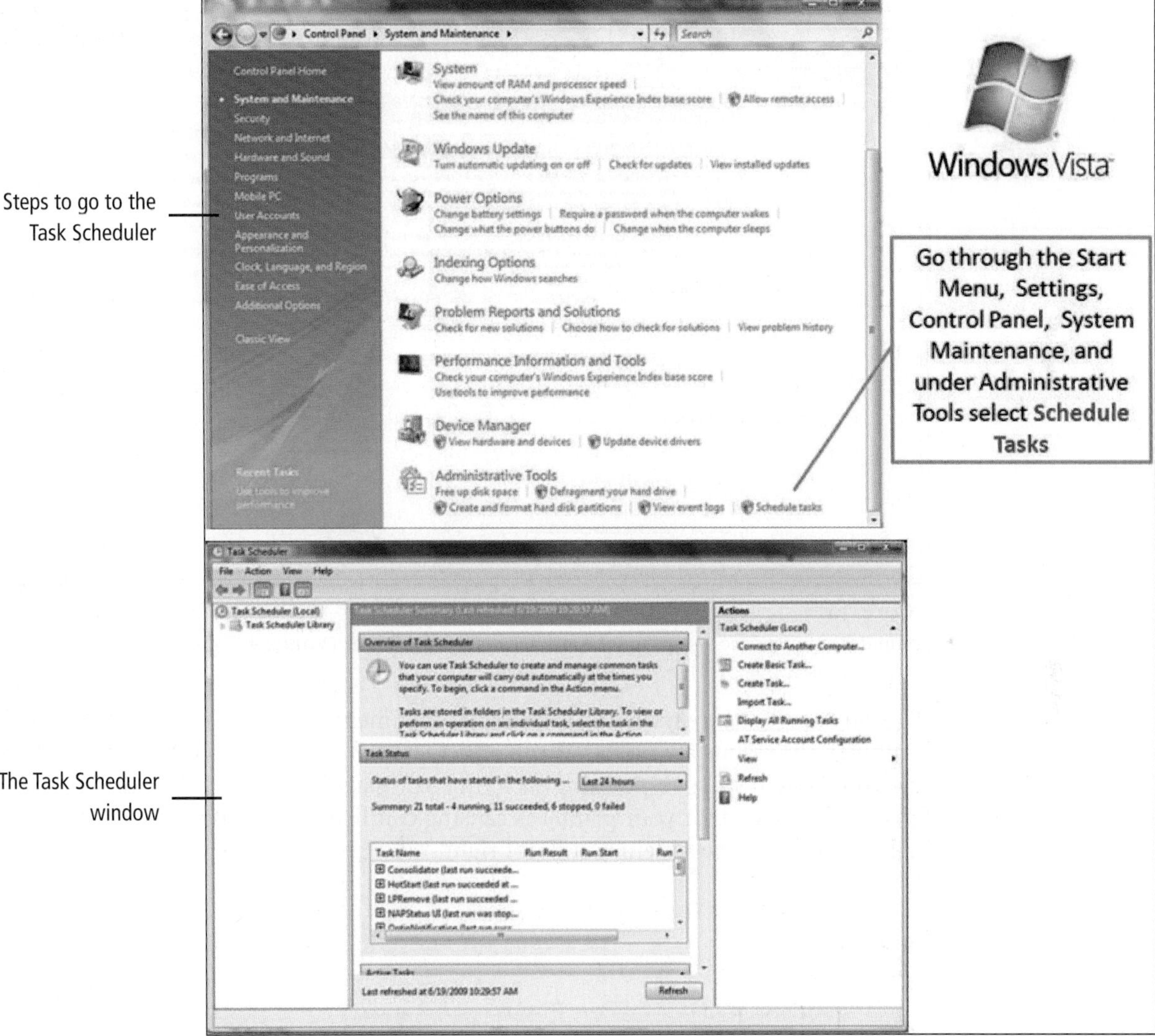

Figure 1.37
Computer maintenance—Task Scheduler (Windows Vista users)

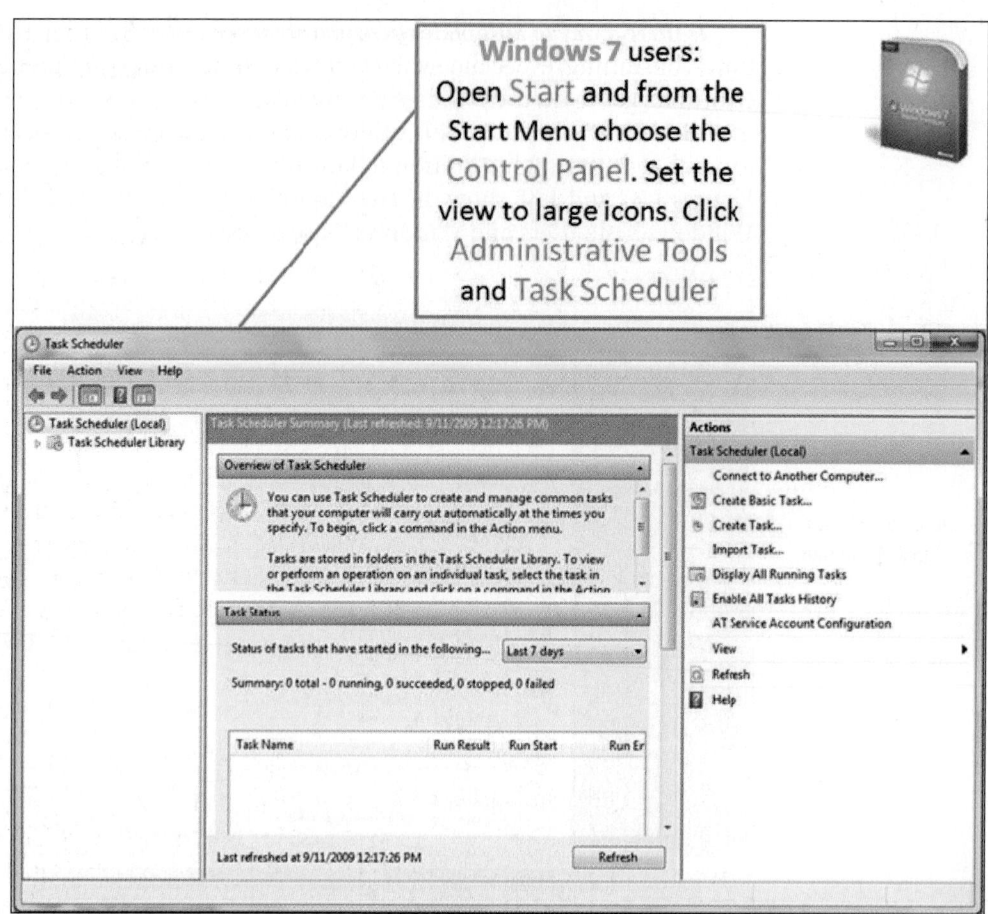

Figure 1.38
Computer maintenance—steps to set a task in the Task Scheduler (Windows 7 users)

Can changes to my system be undone? Sometimes when new software is installed on a computer, the results are not what you anticipated. Instead of playing a new game, you find your system stops responding each time you start it. Or, you might find the new driver you installed for your printer is causing conflicts. Even though you've tried to uninstall the software, the system is still not right.

Fortunately, if you are running a newer version of Windows, the System Restore utility come to the rescue. Periodically, Windows creates a ***restore point***, which records all the settings for your system. It's similar to taking a picture of how everything is currently set up. Figures 1.39 and 1.40 show steps to create a restore point for Windows Vista and Windows 7 users, respectively.

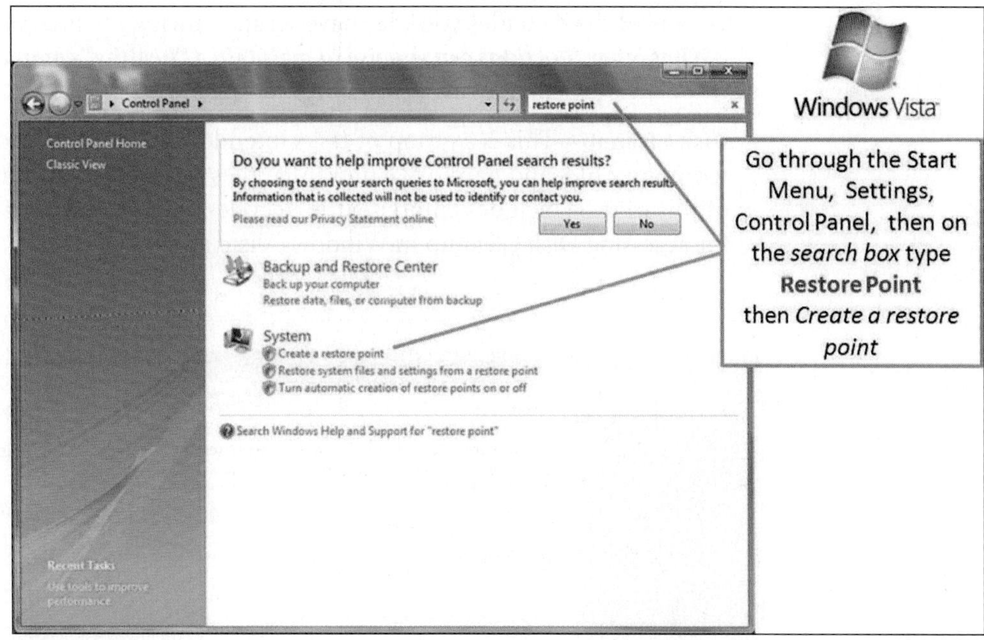

Figure 1.39
Computer maintenance—steps to create a Restore Point (Windows Vista users)

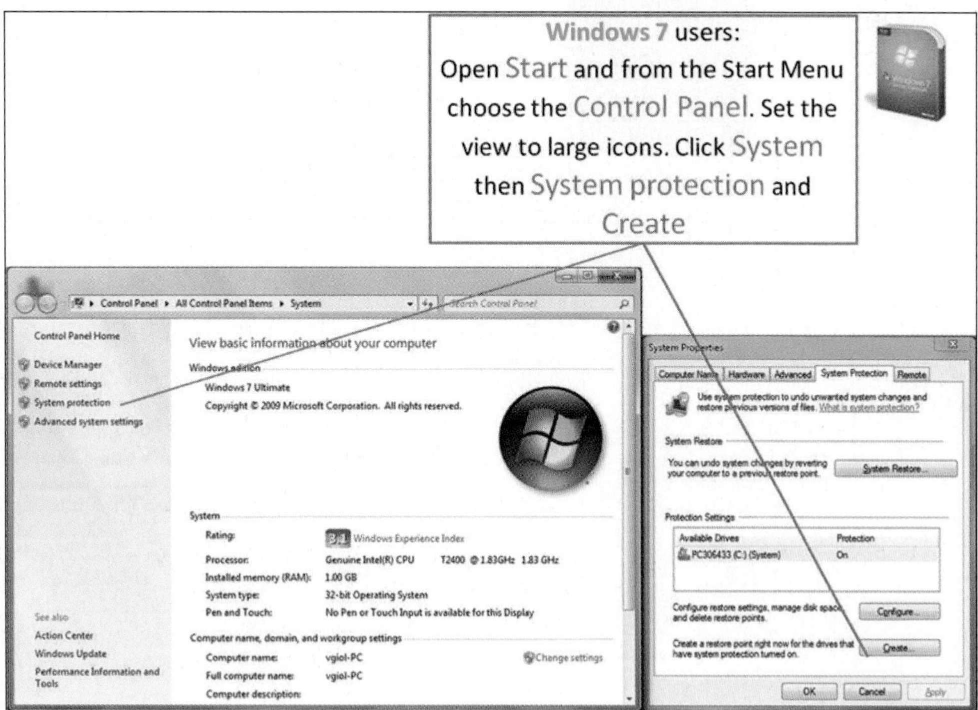

Figure 1.40
Computer maintenance—steps to create a Restore Point (Windows 7 users)

It is also possible to set manual restore points, and it is highly recommended that you set one before installing new software or hardware, or when making any major changes to your system. If you experience a problem with your system after the new software is installed, you can roll your system back to an earlier restore point when the system was working correctly. Think of it as an Undo button for your operating system. The good news is, returning to an earlier restore point affects only your system settings. It does not delete any of the data files you may have created during the interval.

What other functions can you use to maintain a "healthy" computer? Following are some of the other things that keep computers healthy:

- **Disk Cleanup**—This is a group of tasks intended to free disk space cause by Internet temporary files and hard drive unwanted files that accumulate from time to time. Part of this routine includes emptying the Recycle Bin. Figures 1.41 and 1.42 show the steps for accessing Disk Cleanup in Windows Vista and Windows 7.

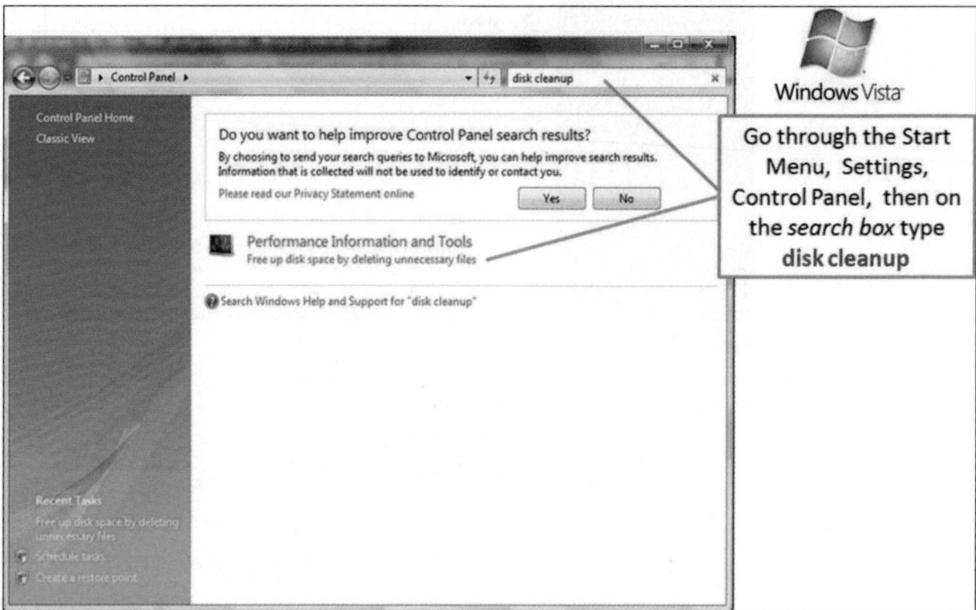

Figure 1.41
Computer maintenance—steps to access Disk Cleanup (Windows Vista users)

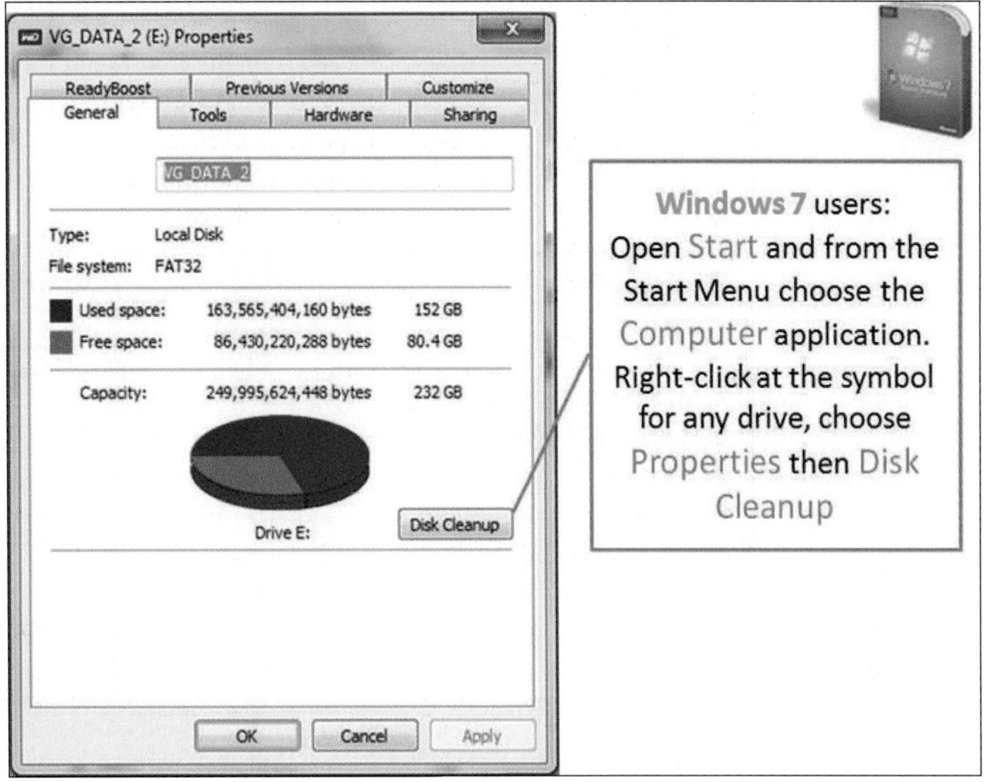

Figure 1.42

Computer maintenance—steps to access Disk Cleanup (Windows 7 users)

- **Activate and set up the Internet Pop-up Blocker**—This lets the user the select options to allow or to block advertising and other pop-up windows while surfing the Net. Figures 1.43 and 1.44 show the steps for accessing Pop-up Blocker in Windows Vista and Windows 7.

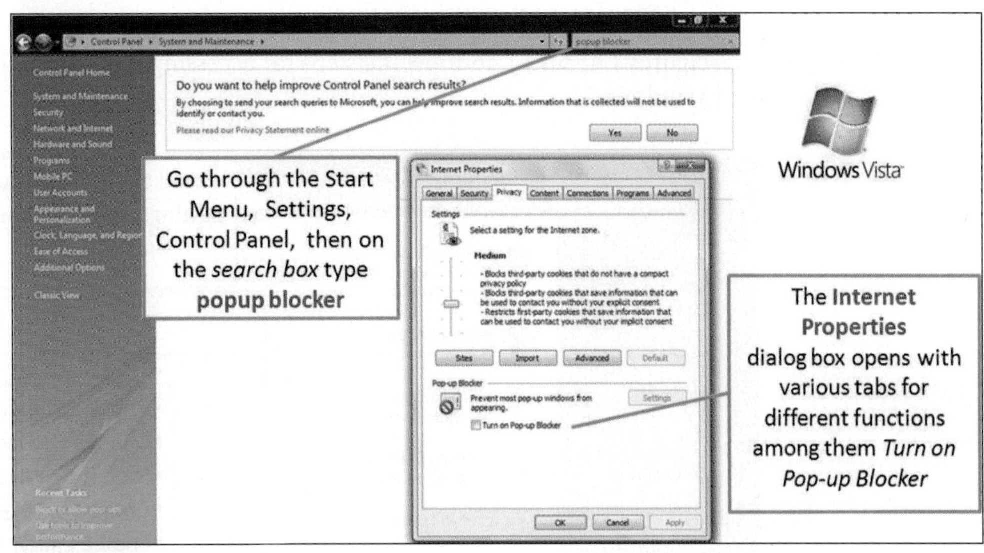

Figure 1.43

Computer maintenance—steps to access the Pop-up Blocker (Windows Vista users)

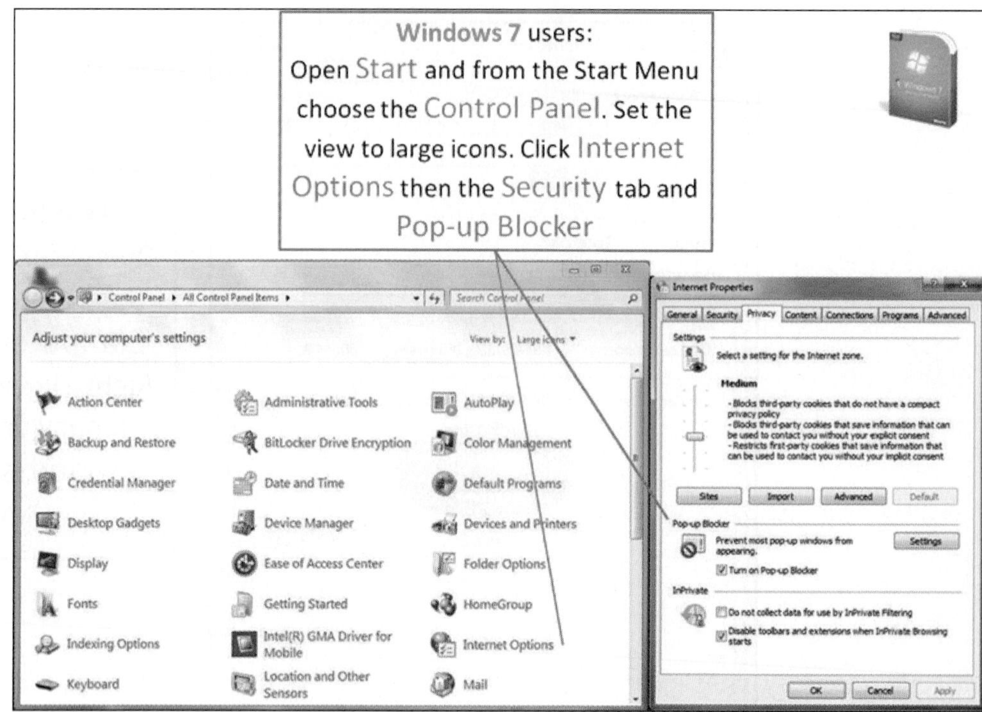

Figure 1.44

Computer maintenance—steps to access the Pop-up Blocker (Windows 7 users)

- **Access and set up Security settings**—You can set security settings, such as:
  - Check for security updates
  - Select the settings for the Windows Firewall
  - Check for Windows software updates
  - Scan for spyware and other potentially unwanted software
  - Change Internet security options

Figures 1.45 and 1.46 show the steps for accessing security settings in Windows Vista and Windows 7.

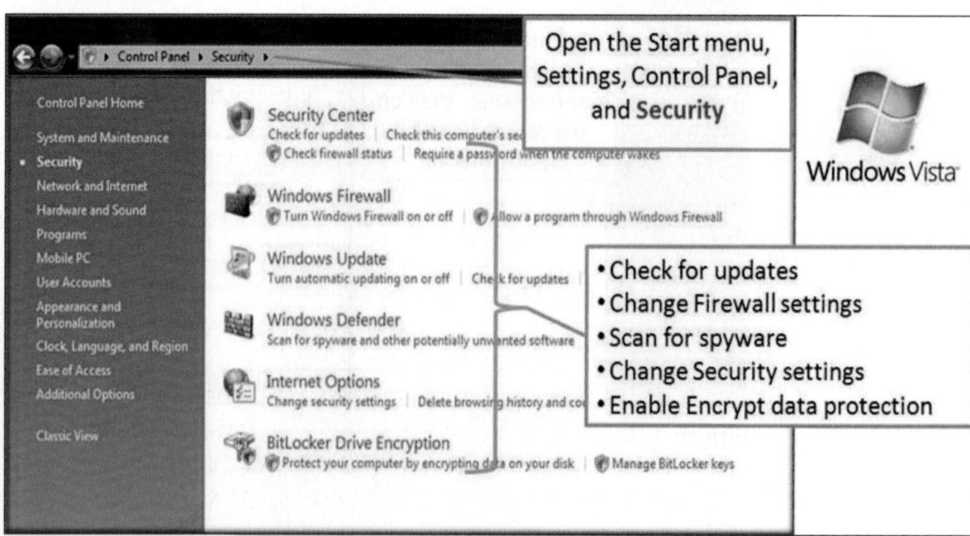

Figure 1.45

Computer maintenance—steps to access the Security settings (Windows Vista users)

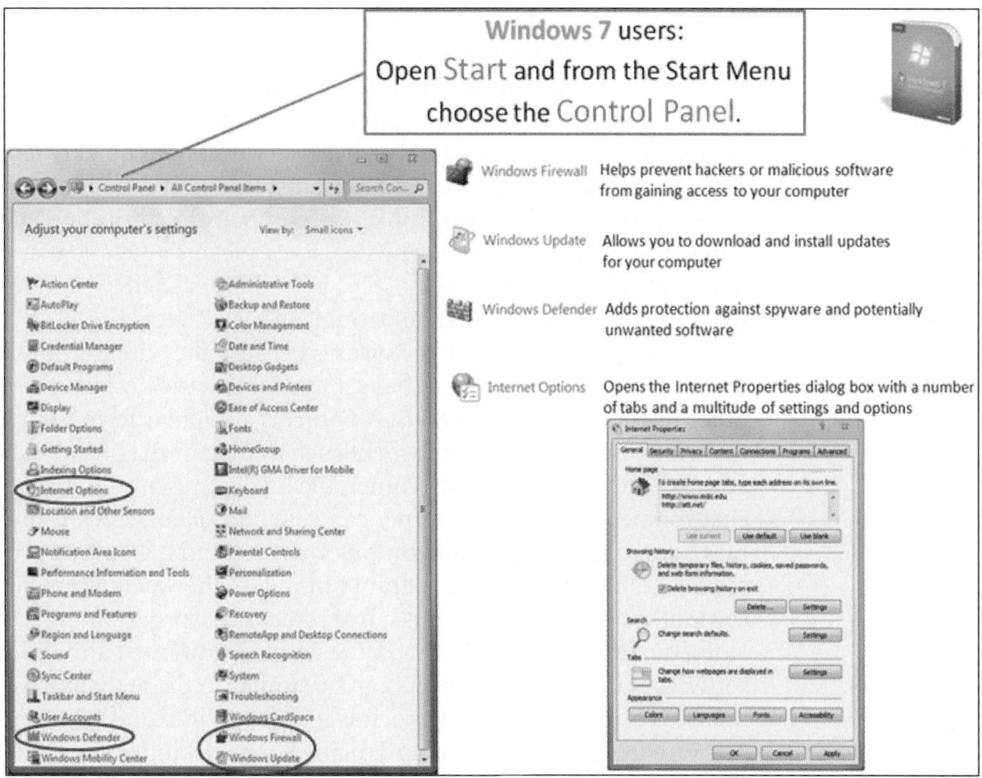

Figure 1.46

Computer maintenance—steps to access the Security settings and other functions (Windows 7 users)

Viruses

Establishing the habit of performing regular maintenance on your computer is one way to protect it, and yourself, from data loss. But there are many other dangers you need to be aware of too. Viruses, spyware, and ***hackers*** are all out there waiting to pounce on the unwary computer user. The term *hacker*, as used here, signifies an expert in computers and programming languages who uses his/her expertise to obtain unauthorized access to computer systems with the purpose corrupting data and/or stealing information.

What are viruses and how do they get on the computer? Computer ***viruses*** are malicious codes or software designed to invade your computer system and alter or destroy data without your knowledge and against your wishes. The severity of a virus can vary. Some viruses merely seem to be nuisances or might not even be obvious to the user; some cause files to be corrupted or erased; and others are capable of shutting down a computer and erasing the entire hard drive. Viruses infect a system and then attach themselves to a program or file to spread to other users.

Viruses can be distributed in several ways. In the early days of computers, viruses were spread by sharing infected floppy disks. Now, due to the ease in which files can be shared over the Internet, viruses are able to spread much more quickly. One of the most common ways to send a virus is through e-mail attachments. Security experts recommend that you never open an e-mail attachment unless you have first scanned it with antivirus software to determine that it is virus-free. Experts also recommend that unless you know the sender and have been expecting the e-mail attachment, it is best to delete the attachment without ever opening it. File-sharing services are another source for these types of problems.

Are viruses and worms the same thing? Worms are similar to viruses because they are also malicious programs that spread from computer to computer; however, unlike viruses, worms are able to do this without any human interaction and are able to replicate themselves so numerous copies can be sent. Worms can burrow into your e-mail address book, or locate e-mail addresses on files saved on your hard drive, then send themselves out without any help from you. When it reaches the e-mail recipient, it does the same thing to the recipient's address book. Also, because worms can quickly replicate themselves, they can repeat this scenario over and over. Just the sheer amount of traffic they cause on a network can be enough to bring an entire company to a grinding halt. Worms can also open a "back door" to your system, which enables hackers access to it and gives them the ability to control your computer remotely. Sasser, Blaster, NetSky, and MyDoom are all worms that have created a great deal of trouble in recent years.

Trojan horses are not truly viruses because they do not duplicate themselves or infect other files; however, they can be just as problematic because they open your system for other intruders such as ***botnets***. A ***botnet*** is a popular term for a group of software robots that run automatically in networks such as instant massagers, chat rooms, and discussion groups that have been made vulnerable by the presence of Trojan horses. Once inside a chat room, for instance, a botnet can generate ***spam,*** which is bulk unsolicited e-mail messages to random lists of computer users. At first glance, a Trojan horse often appears to be a desirable software program but in fact they facilitate unauthorized access to a computer system. Perhaps it is a free screensaver program or a set of animated cursors. Unfortunately, these programs come with an unwanted and hidden agenda. After the software is installed, the effects can be similar to those that viruses or worms cause. Before you install new software, it is important to scan the program files with antivirus software to ensure there are no Trojan horses lurking there. And, as with unknown e-mail attachments, it is important to be skeptical about free software; it's not often that you really get something for nothing!

Spyware

How is spyware different from viruses? ***Spyware*** is software designed to capture personal and confidential information that resides on your system and send it elsewhere. It has quickly become as large a problem as viruses. Spyware's primary threat is to your privacy and confidentiality. Although spyware is not usually intended to harm your system, it can sometimes have that effect on it. ***Adware*** is spyware that tracks your Internet browsing and can install malicious cookies on your computer. A ***cookie*** is a small text file that contains information that can identify you to a website. Cookies are not necessarily bad. They are useful when they are used to help personalize your Web browsing experience, but cookies can threaten your privacy if they are used to reveal too much information.

How can you tell if spyware is on a computer? One symptom that indicates adware is on a computer is an increase in the number of pop-up ads the user receives, some of which might even address the user by name! Adware can generate pop-up ads even when you're not online. Some types of adware can also reset a Web browser's home page to a page of its choosing and take control of the search engine, directing you to websites that have been predetermined by the adware.

Are there other privacy threats? ***Key loggers*** are another type of spyware. In this case, a software program records every keystroke made on the computer. Key loggers can capture all sorts of confidential information this way—passwords, credit card numbers, bank account numbers, and so on—and then relay this information elsewhere. Entire e-mail messages and instant messaging conversations can be recorded this way too. Some key loggers are hardware, rather than software, although they perform the same devious function. Such hardware devices can be attached between the keyboard and the computer. The information stolen through the use of key loggers can easily make you a victim of identity theft. Trojan horses can be used to distribute key loggers and other types of spyware just as easily as they deliver viruses.

How can you avoid being a victim? To minimize the risk of having spyware installed on your computer, there are some practical precautions you can take. One of the most prevalent methods of spreading spyware is through file-sharing services, such as Morpheus or Kazaa. Not only can the file-sharing software include spyware, but often the files you think you are downloading for free are infected too. Although it's tempting to get the newest song or video for free from such a site, don't risk it!

This problem can be avoided if you use one of the legitimate, pay-as-you-go file-sharing services such as iTunes or the reincarnated Napster. Do not trust files or software sent by friends or acquaintances. Additionally, be cautious when you download and install freeware or shareware software. Make sure you deal with a reputable software publisher, scan the downloaded software for viruses and spyware, and read the licensing agreement. Some licensing agreements actually include information about additional software that will be automatically installed if you accept it.

Another way to prevent spyware is to avoid pop-up and banner ads whenever possible. You should never click on them. Often the "No Thanks" button is just a ruse to get you to click it and enable the spyware installation. Close pop-up ads by clicking the Close button in the top right corner. Installing pop-up blocking software can help to eliminate this risk almost entirely.

If you are running the most recent version of Windows, you already have a pop-up blocker available to you. You can view the pop-up blocker settings for Windows Vista in Figure 1.43 and access this dialog box through Internet Explorer's Tools menu. Many popular search engines, such as Google and Yahoo!, also include pop-up blocking features in their toolbars, which you can download at no charge. It is also wise to avoid questionable websites, because some of them can install spyware on your system just by visiting the site.

Protecting Yourself and Your Computer

In addition to being cautious in your Internet travels, there are some proactive measures you can take to protect yourself and your computer from viruses and spyware. These include:

- ***Software updates* and *patches***—Keeping your operating system and software up to date is critical. Software manufacturers are constantly on the lookout for security threats, and they issue updates and patches to help protect your system. Check for these and install them regularly. Software manufacturers have begun to implement automated procedures to check and install such updates. If your computer has this capability, it's a good idea to use this feature.

- ***Antivirus and antispyware software***—***Antivirus software*** is a utility program used to search your hard drive and files for viruses, and remove those that are found. ***Antispyware software*** works in a similar fashion, but searches for spyware rather than viruses. No computer should be without this protection. Many users erroneously think that because they aren't regularly online or use only a slow dial-up connection, they aren't a target. Nothing could be further from the truth! Recent studies show more than two-thirds of all computer users have some form of virus or spyware on their system.

There are a variety of antivirus and antispyware products available. Unfortunately, there are also a lot of dishonest companies purporting to offer these products. Too often, these are really scams that will actually install spyware or viruses on your system! To avoid being scammed or downloading something malicious, you should never respond to offers that are received in a pop-up ad or unsolicited e-mail. To obtain legitimate products, it is best to purchase them from the manufacturer's website or from a local retailer. Additionally, some internet service providers are beginning to provide some of these products as part of their services.

Some well-known antivirus products include Norton AntiVirus (*www.symantec.com*), McAfee VirusScan (*www.mcafee.com*), and AVG Anti-Virus (*www.grisoft.com*).

Antispyware products include eTrust PestPatrol (*www.pestpatrol.com*), Ad-Aware (*www.lavasoft.com*), and Spybot Search & Destroy (*www.safer-networking.org*). You can search for other products at popular download sites such as Download.com (*www.download.com*) or Tucows (*www.tucows.com*) but you should be sure to read the software reviews and evaluate their usefulness before downloading or installing them.

It is best to use only one antivirus product, because running more than one can cause conflicts between the programs. However, because there are so many different types of spyware, antispyware products may address these problems in different ways. Experts recommend running at least two different antispyware applications in order to catch as many spyware programs as possible. It's not enough to install antivirus and antispyware software on your system; you need to update it frequently, at least once a week. Doing so will protect you against any new viruses or spyware created since the last time you checked. Software should be set to scan incoming data files, e-mail, and so on but regular full-system scans should be conducted on a weekly basis as well.

Personal firewalls—Firewalls may be software programs or hardware devices, although their purpose is the same to prevent unauthorized access to your computer. When a firewall is installed properly, it can make your computer invisible to hackers and other invaders. Not only can a good firewall help prevent infections and identity theft; it can also prevent hackers from accessing your computer and turning it into a ***zombie***. A zombie computer is one that can be controlled remotely and can be used to help spread viruses, spyware, or junk e-mail known as spam. Zombie computers can also be used in ***denial of service (DoS)*** attacks. DoS attacks occur when a large number of computers try to access a website at the same time, effectively overloading it and causing it to shut down. If you are using Windows XP or Windows Vista, you already have a firewall available to you.

You can access the firewall settings by clicking the Start button, settings, Control Panel, Security, and Windows Firewall.

What else should I look for? It might sound simple, but when online, do not give out personal information unless it is for legitimate purposes. It is important to avoid spam e-mail and ***phishing*** attacks e-mails that masquerade as authentic entities, such as banks and credit card companies, and ask for confidential information. Legitimate organizations will not ask for passwords, bank account numbers, or credit card details through e-mail. It is also possible to check for hoaxes and scams at a variety of websites, including many of the antivirus and antispyware sites. When in doubt, do some research to see if the request you've received is legitimate. If necessary, make a telephone call to the agency in question. Viewing such requests with a critical eye can help you avoid online scams and hoaxes.

Content-Based Assessments

Summary

In this chapter, you examined the benefits of computer fluency and identified the four basic functions of computing. You explored the various types of computers and their components, including CPUs, RAM, and storage devices. This chapter also discussed how to evaluate a computer system and understand the terminology used to measure storage capacity, memory, and microprocessor speed. Various hardware and peripheral devices were reviewed, including input and output devices, and different types of storage devices and media. You explored the basic types of computer software system software and application software and the different uses for each type. You identified various types of networks and the different ways networks can be configured. You also reviewed ways to maintain your computer and keep it safe from various threats, including viruses and spyware.

Key Terms

Adware 52
Antispyware software 53
Antivirus software 53
Application software 29
Arithmetic logic unit (ALU) 14
Arrow keys 12
Audio port 26
Backup tape drive 23
Bluetooth 26
Boot 52
Botnet 52
Boot process 30
Browser 26
Burn 21
Bus topology 43
CD 21
CD burner 23
CD drive 23
CD-ROM 21
CD-R 23
CD-RW 23
Central processing unit (CPU) 10
Click 12
Client 43
Client/server network 42
Clock speed 14
Communication and organizational software 39
Compact disk 21
Computer 2
Computer fluent 1
Configuration 26
Connectivity port 26
Control keys 1
Control unit 14
Cookie 52
CPU 10
Data 2
Database software 37
Data mining 37
Dedicated server 43
Denial of service (DoS) 54
Desktop computer 5
Device 20
Dialog box 31
Digital camera 13
Digital video recorder 13
Digital Video Interface (DVI) port 26
Docking station 6
DOS 30
Dot matrix 18
Dot pitch 17
Dots per inch (dpi) 19
Double-click 13
Drag 13
DSL 26
DVD 21
DVD drive 23
DVD-ROM 21
DVI port 26
Embedded computers 9
Ethernet port 26
Firewall 54
FireWire port 25
Flash drive 23
Flash memory 22
Flat-panel displays 17
Floppy diskette 22
Floppy disk drive 22
Function keys 12
Gaming computers 5
Gigabyte (GB) 16
Gigahertz (GHz) 14
Graphical user interface (GUI) 31
GUI 31
Hackers 51
Handheld computers 6
Hard copy 18
Hard disk drive 22
Hardware 9
Hyperlinks 35
Icon 31
IM 40
Impact 18
Information 2
Information processing cycle 3

Ink-jet 18
Input 3
Input devices 11
Insertion point 12
Internet control key 12
Intranet 42
IrDA port 26
Joysticks 13
Key logger 52
Keyboard 11
Kilobit 25
Kilobyte 16
LAN 41
Laser printer 18
LCD 17
LightScribe 22
Linux 32
Liquid crystal display (LCD) 17
Local area network (LAN) 41
Mac OS 32
Magnetic 20
Mainframe computers 8
Megabit (Mb) 25
Megabyte (MB) 16
Megahertz (MHz) 14
Memory 15
Menu 31
MFD 19
Microcomputer 5
Microphones 13
Microprocessor chip 10
Microsoft Windows 31
MIDI port 26
Mobile devices 6
Modem port 26
Monitor (or display screen) 16
Monitor port 26
Motherboard 10
Mouse 12
Mouse pointer 12
Multifunction device (MFD) 19
Multimedia control key 12
Multimedia projectors 19
Multitask 8
Network 7
Network topology 43
Node 40
Nonimpact 18
Nonvolatile 15
Notebook computer 6
Numeric keypad 12
Open-source 32
Operating system (OS) 30
Optical 21
OS 30
Output 3
Output device 16
P2P network (Peer-to-peer) 42
Parallel port 25
PDA 6
Peripheral 9
Permanent memory 15
Personal digital assistant (PDA) 6
Personal firewall 54
Phishing 54
Pixel 17
Port 24
Ppm (pages per minute) 19
Presentation software 38
Printer 18
Printout 18
Process 3
Program 29
Programmable 2
RAM 15
Random Access Memory (RAM) 15
RDBMS 37
Read-Only Memory (ROM) 15
Read/write 20
Refresh rate 17
Resolution 17
Restore point 47
Right-click 13
Right-drag 13
Ring (or token-ring) topology 46
ROM 15
S-video port 26
Scanners 13
Scroll 13
Scroll wheel 13
Sectors 20
Serial port 25
Server 7
Shortcut menu 13
Smartphones 6
Soft copy 16
Software patches or Software updates 53
Spam 54
Speech recognition 6
Speakers 19
Splash screen 28
Spreadsheet software 36
Spyware 52
Star topology 44
Storage 3
Storage devices 20
Stylus 6
Suite 39
Supercomputer 8
System software 29
System unit 9
Tablet computer 6
Toggle key 12
Temporary memory 15
Terabyte 16
Token-ring topology 44
Touch screen 6
Tracks 20
Trojan horse 52
Universal serial bus (USB) port 25
User friendly 30

User interface 30
Utility program 30
Video conferencing 41
Virus.................................51
VoIP 41
Volatile.............................15
WAN.................................42
Web browser....................12
Wide area network (WAN)...........................42
Windows 31
Wireless..........................11
Wireless network 40
Word processing software 35
Worm 51
Zombie 54

Matching

A Application software
B Computer
C Computer network
D Console/system unit
E CPU
F Hardware
G DVDs or CDs
H Memory (RAM)
I Motherboard/ system board
J Peripherals
K Port
L Server
M Software
N Spyware
O Topology

Match each term in the second column with its correct definition in the first column. Write the letter of the term on the blank line in front of the correct definition.

_____ 1. Computer programs.

_____ 2. Programs that enable you to accomplish a specific tasks or solve a specific need.

_____ 3. Two or more computers connected together to enable resource sharing.

_____ 4. Used to manage network resources, this type of computer can be dedicated to a specific task.

_____ 5. Optical disk drives use this type of storage media.

_____ 6. The layout or design/arrangement of computers connected to a network.

_____ 7. A peripheral device uses this to attach to the computer.

_____ 8. A programmable electronic device that can input, process, output, and store data.

_____ 9. The physical components of a computer system.

_____ 10. Hardware connected outside the computer's system unit.

_____ 11. The hardware unit that typically contains the CPU, RAM, a hard disk, and a power supply.

_____ 12. A large printed circuit board to which all the other components are connected.

_____ 13. The temporary storage that holds data and instructions waiting to be processed.

_____ 14. The processing unit.

_____ 15. This type of program threatens a user's privacy.

Multiple Choice

Circle the correct response.

1. Which of the following requires one byte of storage?
   a. Page **b.** Paragraph **c.** Sentence **d.** Character
2. Which of the following units represents the fastest CPU clock speed?
   a. 733 MHz **b.** 286 MHz **c.** 2 GHz **d.** 2 GB
3. Which of the following is not an input device?
   a. Keyboard **b.** Speaker **c.** Mouse **d.** Stylus
4. Which of the following is an example of optical storage media?
   a. Disk drive **b.** Flash card **c.** RAM **d.** Compact disc
5. Which of the following is not a type of computer?
   a. Mainframe **b.** Multitask **c.** Server **d.** Supercomputer
6. Before a computer can process data, where must data be stored?
   a. In RAM **b.** On a disk **c.** In the control unit **d.** On the monitor
7. What term, related to computers, means billions?
   a. Byte **b.** Mega **c.** Giga **d.** Hertz
8. Which of the following is not a type of microcomputer?
   a. Desktop **b.** Notebook **c.** Personal digital assistant **d.** Microprocessor
9. Which of the following can prevent the easy and casual connection to your computer by a nonauthorized user?
   a. Disk defragmenter **b.** Antivirus software **c.** Firewall **d.** Key logger
10. Which of the following is capable of opening a "back door" on a computer and is able to spread without human interaction?
    a. Trojan horse **B.** Worm **c.** Adware **d.** Zombie

Getting Started with Windows 7

OUTCOMES At the end of this chapter, you will be able to:	**OBJECTIVES** Mastering these objectives will enable you to:
PROJECT 2A Familiarize Yourself with Windows 7.	**1.** Get Started with Windows 7 (p. 63) **2.** Use the Start Menu and Manage Windows (p. 73) **3.** Resize, Move, and Scroll Windows (p. 81)
PROJECT 2B Manage Files and Folders.	**4.** Create, Move, and Rename Folders (p. 89) **5.** Copy, Move, Rename, and Delete Files (p. 95) **6.** Find Files and Folders (p. 103)

Dmitriy Shironosov/Shutterstock

In This Chapter

Windows 7 is the software that coordinates the activities of your computer's hardware. Windows 7 controls how your screen is displayed, how you open and close programs, and the start-up, shut-down, and navigation procedures for your computer. It is useful to become familiar with the basic features of the Microsoft Windows operating system, especially working with the Start button and the taskbar; opening, closing, moving, and resizing windows; and finding, saving, and managing files and folders.

Project 2A Familiarize Yourself with Windows 7

Project Activities

In Activities 2.01 through 2.09, you will explore the Windows 7 screen and practice navigating Windows 7. You will open, close, resize, and move windows, and you will open several windows at one time. The screens that you will be working with will look similar to those in Figure 2.1.

Project Files

For Project 2A, you will need the following files:

No files are needed for this project

You will save your documents as

Lastname_Firstname_1A_Taskbar (not submitted)
Lastname_Firstname_1A_Windows (not submitted)
Lastname_Firstname_1A_WordPad

Project Results

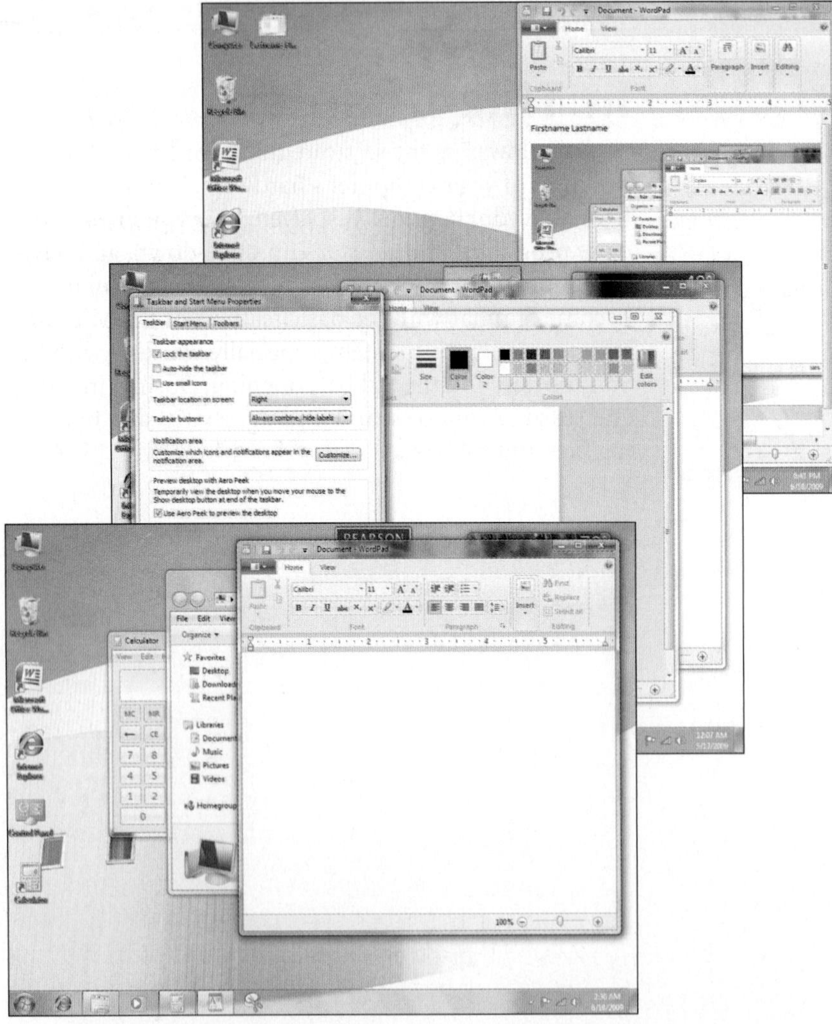

Figure 2.1

Objective 1 | Get Started with Windows 7

Windows 7 is an ***operating system***—software that controls the ***hardware*** attached to your computer, including its memory, disk drive space, attached devices such as printers and scanners, and the central processing unit. Windows 7 and earlier versions of Windows are similar; they use a ***graphical user interface (GUI)***. A GUI uses graphics or pictures to represent commands and actions and lets you see document formatting on the screen as it will look when printed on paper. ***Windows***, when spelled with a capital *W*, refers to the operating system that runs your computer.

Starting Windows is an automatic procedure; you turn on your computer, and after a few moments, the version of Windows installed on your computer displays. Some computers require that you log in, and some do not. Windows 7 is available in several versions: Starter, Home Premium, Professional, and Ultimate. For large institutions, there is also an Enterprise edition. For most tasks, the Home Premium, Professional, and Ultimate editions work the same. The Starter edition is typically used only on small notebook computers.

Alert! | Does your screen differ?

This chapter uses Windows 7 Ultimate edition, and there may be some differences in the look of this edition and the other editions. More importantly, the look of the screen will depend largely on the setting options that have been selected for your computer, the shape of your monitor, and on the type of hardware installed in your computer—especially the video card and memory.

Activity 2.01 | Exploring the Windows 7 Desktop

In this activity, you will examine the different components of the Windows 7 desktop.

1. Turn on your computer and wait for the Windows program to display, or follow the log-on instructions required for the computer you are using. For example, you might have to click a name on a Welcome screen, or enter a user ID or password. If this is your home computer and you are the only user, it is likely that you need do nothing except wait for a few moments.

   The Windows ***desktop***, which is the working area of the Windows 7 screen, displays. The screen look will vary, depending on which version of Windows you are using and what you have on your own desktop.

2 Compare your Windows desktop with Figure 2.2 and then take a moment to study the Windows elements identified in the table in Figure 2.3. Your icons may vary.

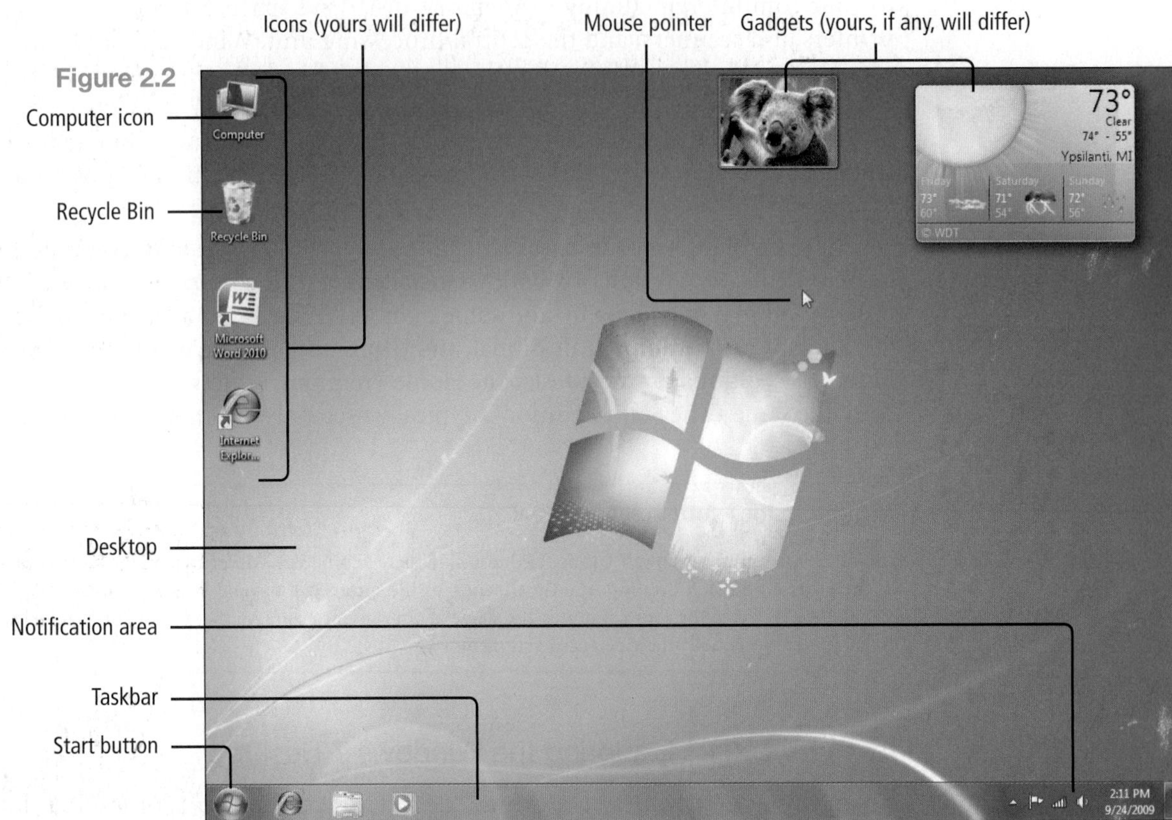

Figure 2.2

Windows Screen Elements

Screen Element	Description
Command bar	A toolbar that offers easy access to settings or features.
Computer icon	An icon that represents the computer on which you are working, and that provides access to the drives, folders, and files on your computer.
Desktop	The working area of the Windows 7 screen, consisting of program icons, a taskbar, gadgets (optional), and a Start button.
Gadgets	Small dynamic programs that run on the desktop, such as a clock, a stock market ticker, or a weather forecast.
Icon	A graphic representation of an object that you can select and open, such as a drive, a disk, a folder, a document, or a program.
Mouse pointer	The arrow, I-beam, or other symbol that moves when you move the mouse or other pointing device, and that indicates a location or position on your screen—also called the ***pointer***.
Notification area	The area on the right side of the taskbar, formerly called the ***system tray*** or ***status area***, where the clock and system notifications display. These notifications keep you informed about active processes.
Recycle Bin	A temporary storage area for files that you have deleted from hard drives. Files can be either recovered or permanently removed from the Recycle Bin.
Start button	The button on the left side of the taskbar that is used to start programs, change system settings, find Windows help, search for programs or documents, or shut down the computer.
Taskbar	Displays the Start button and icons for any open programs. The taskbar also displays shortcut buttons for other programs.

Figure 2.3

3 On the left side of the taskbar, ***click***—press the left mouse button one time—the **Windows Explorer** button . Compare your screen with Figure 2.4, and then take a moment to study the *Windows Explorer* window elements in the table in Figure 2.5. ***Windows Explorer*** is a program used to create and manage folders, and to copy, move, sort, and delete files. If the Windows Explorer button does not display on your taskbar, click the Start button, click All Programs, click Accessories, and then click Windows Explorer. If the Menu bar does not display, on the Toolbar, click the Organize button, point to Layout, and then click Menu bar.

The Windows Explorer window displays. When you click the Windows Explorer button, the window opens with *Libraries* selected in the Navigation pane and displayed in the file list. A ***window***—spelled with a lowercase *w*—is a rectangular box that displays information or a program. When a window is open, the name of the window is sometimes displayed in the title bar.

> **Alert! | Does your screen differ?**
>
> Because the configuration of your Windows Explorer window depends on how it was last used, your window may not display all of the elements shown in Figure 2.4, in particular the Menu bar, Details pane, Navigation pane, and Search pane. A Preview pane may display on the right side of the window, and the window may cover the entire screen.

Figure 2.4

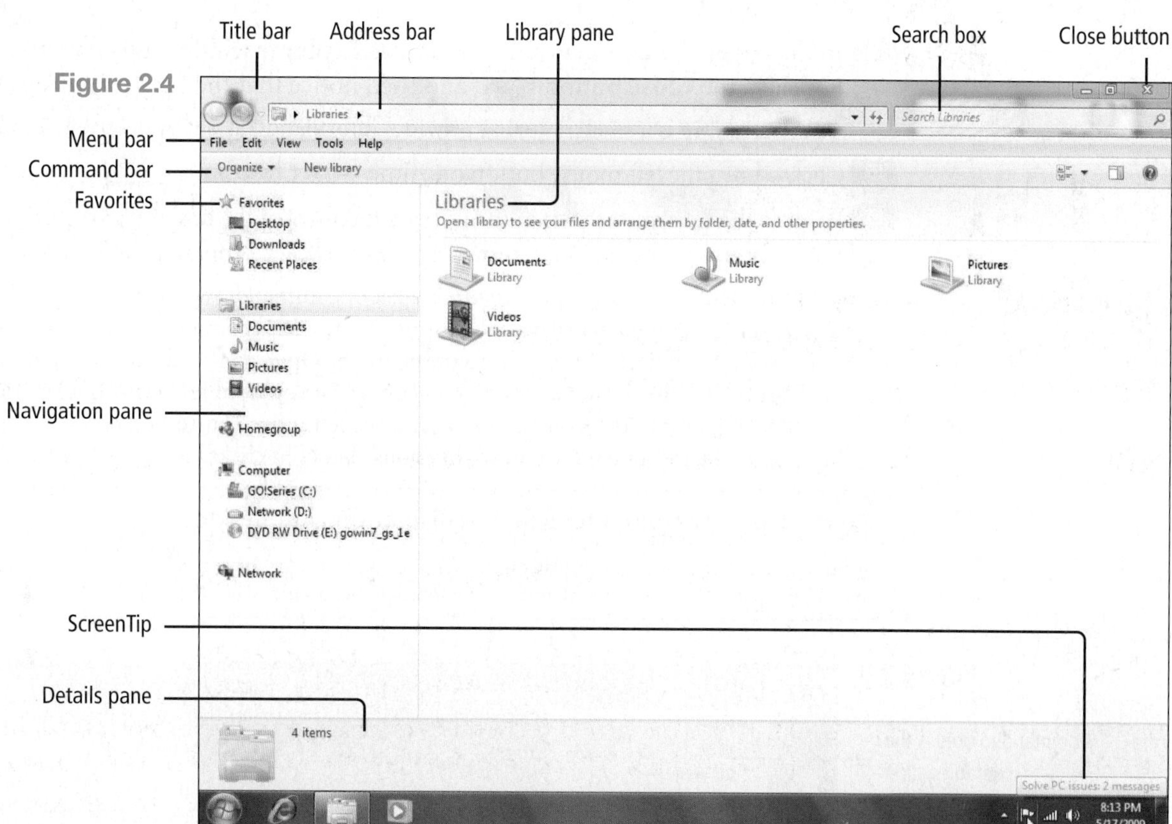

Parts of a Window

Screen Element	Description
Address bar	A toolbar that displays the organizational path to the active file, folder, or window.
Close button	A button in a title bar that closes a window or a Program
Details pane	Displays details about the drive, folder, or file selected in the file list.
Favorites	The upper part of the Navigation pane that displays favorite destinations associated with the current user.
File list	Displays the contents of the current folder or library.
Library pane	Displays above the file list when a Library is selected in the Navigation pane.
Menu bar	The bar near the top of a window that lists the names of menu categories.
Navigation pane	The pane on the left side of the Windows Explorer window that contains personal Favorites, Libraries, access to personal files and folders, and other items.
ScreenTip	A small box, activated by pointing to a button or other screen object, that displays the name of or further information about the screen element.
Search box	A box in which you type a search word or phrase.
Title bar	The area at the top of a window that includes the Minimize, Maximize, and Close buttons. The title bar also often contains the name of the program and the name of the open document.
Toolbar	A row of buttons that activates commands with a single click of the left mouse button.

Figure 2.5

4 In the upper right corner of the **Windows Explorer** window title bar, point to, but do not click, the **Close** button, and then notice that the ScreenTip *Close* displays.

A ***ScreenTip*** is a small note that provides information about or describes a screen element.

5 Click—press the left mouse button one time—the **Close** button to close the window.

6 Point to the **Computer** icon in the upper left corner of the desktop and click the right mouse button—this action is known as a ***right-click***. Compare your screen with Figure 2.6.

A shortcut menu displays. A ***menu*** is a list of commands within a category. ***Shortcut menus*** list ***context-sensitive commands***—commands commonly used when working with the selected object. On this shortcut menu, the Open command is displayed in bold because it is the default action that occurs when you double-click this icon. To ***double-click*** an icon, point to the icon and then press the left mouse button quickly two times in succession, taking care not to move the mouse between clicks.

Alert! | Does the Computer icon not display on your desktop?

If the Computer icon does not display on the desktop, click the Start button. On the right side of the Start menu, right-click Computer, and then from the shortcut menu, click *Show on Desktop*.

Figure 2.6

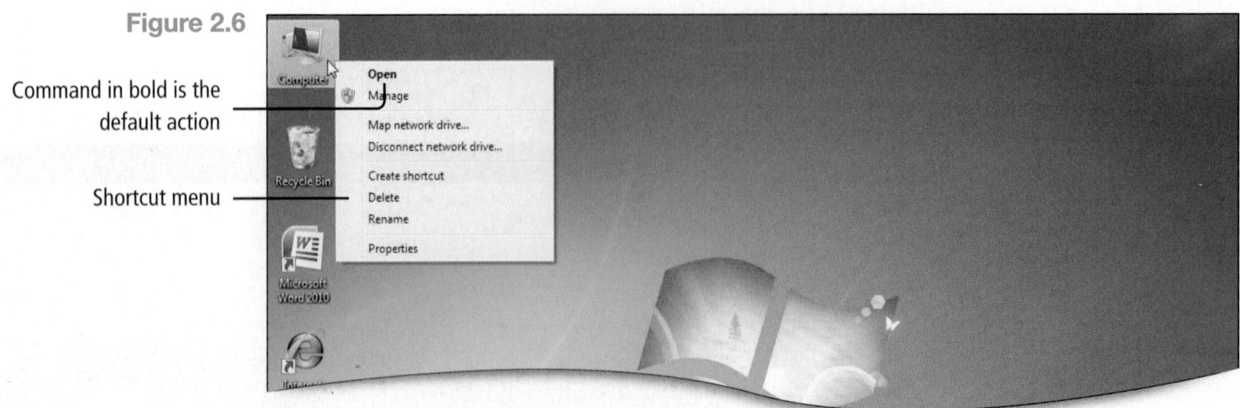

7 From the displayed shortcut menu, point to **Open** to select the command, and then click one time. Compare your screen with Figure 2.7.

The Windows Explorer window displays, but this time the pane on the right is a file list, not a Libraries pane. The ***file list*** displays the contents of the item selected in the Navigation pane; in this case, the fixed and removable drives attached to the computer. A ***drive*** is an area of storage that is formatted with the Windows file system, and that has a drive letter such as C, D, E, and so on. The main drive inside your computer is referred to as the ***hard drive***—there may be more than one hard drive in a computer. Also, network drives may display here.

Figure 2.7

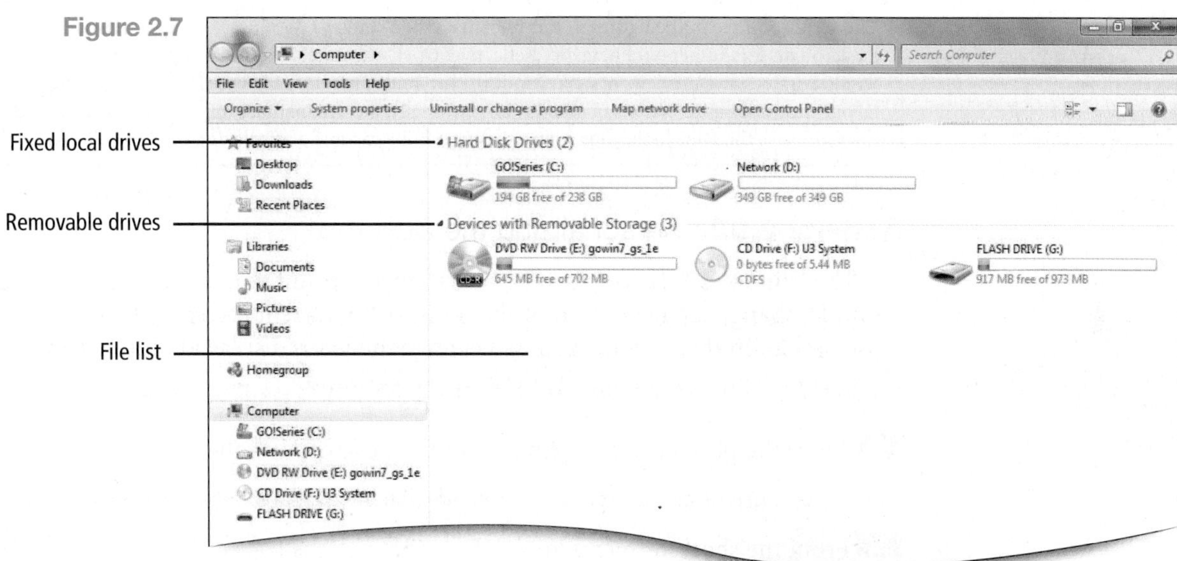

8 Near the top of the **file list**, point to and then click the disk drive labeled **(C:)**, and then notice the **Details** pane. Compare your screen with Figure 2.8.

Figure 2.8

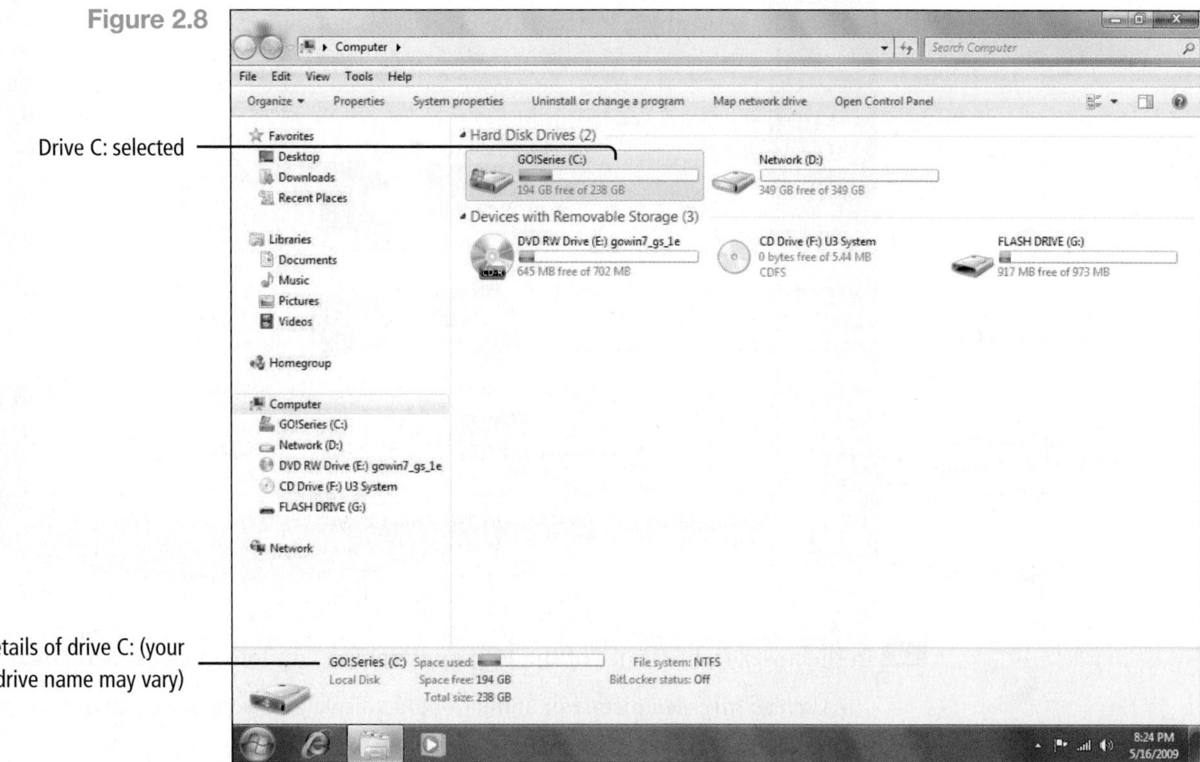

> **Alert! | Is your Details pane missing?**
>
> Recall that the configuration of your Windows Explorer window may vary, depending on how it was last configured. If your Details pane does not display, in the Command bar, click Organize, point to Layout, and then click *Details pane*.

9 In the **Windows Explorer** window title bar, click the **Close** button.

> **More Knowledge | The Windows Aero User Interface**
>
> The screen you see in the figures in this book uses the Windows Aero user interface. ***Windows Aero***—which is an acronym for ***A***uthentic, ***E***nergetic, ***R***eflective, ***O***pen—features a three-dimensional look, with transparent window frames, live previews of open windows, and multiple color schemes. This user interface is available with all but the most basic versions of Windows 7, but requires extra memory and a good video card. If your screen does not have the same look, your computer may not be capable of displaying the Aero interface.

Activity 2.02 | Personalizing the Desktop

The Windows 7 desktop can be personalized to suit your needs and tastes. You can, for example, change the resolution of the monitor to make it easier to read or display more information. In this activity, you will change the icons displayed on the desktop, change the screen saver, and change the desktop background.

1 Move the pointer to an open area of the desktop, and then right-click.

A shortcut menu displays commands that are available for your desktop.

2 From the shortcut menu, move the pointer to the bottom of the list, and then click **Personalize**. Notice that the Personalization window displays, as shown in Figure 2.9.

Figure 2.9

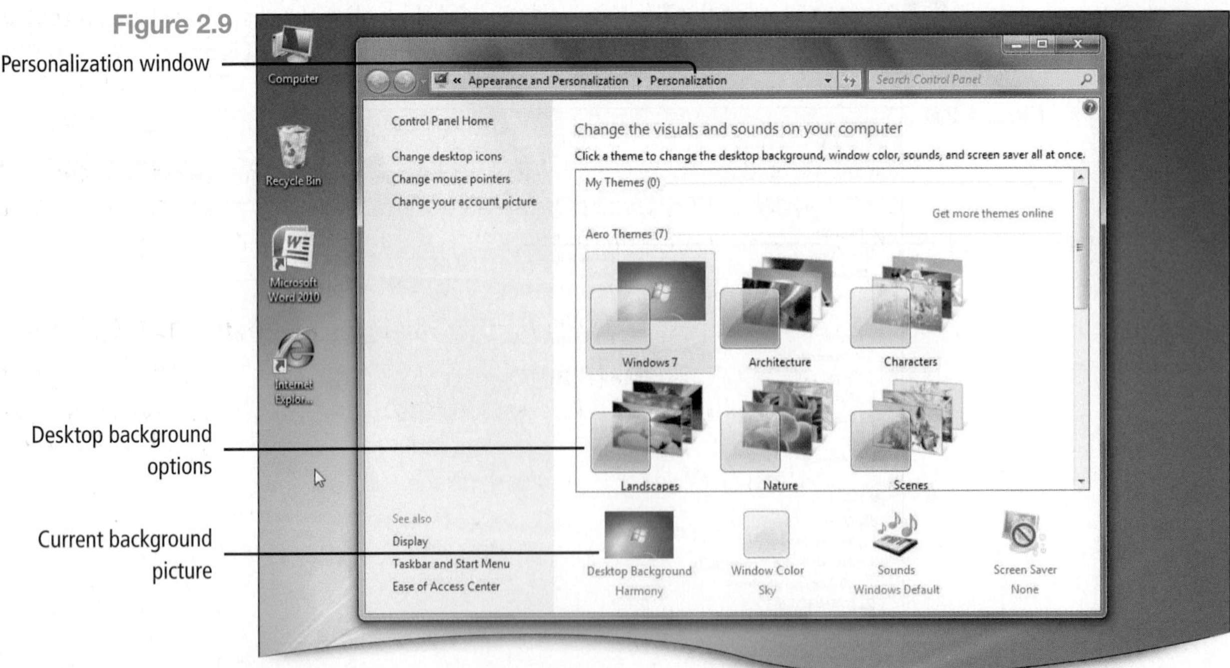

3 In the lower right corner of the **Personalization** window, click **Screen Saver**.

A ***screen saver*** is a picture or animation that displays on your screen after a preset period of computer inactivity.

4 In the **Screen Saver Settings** dialog box, click the **Screen saver box arrow**. From the displayed list, click **Ribbons**, and then compare your screen with Figure 2.10.

A ***dialog box*** is a box that asks you to make a decision about an individual object or topic. The Ribbons screen saver is selected, and a preview displays near the top of the dialog box. The default length of inactivity to trigger the screen saver is 1 minute.

Figure 2.10

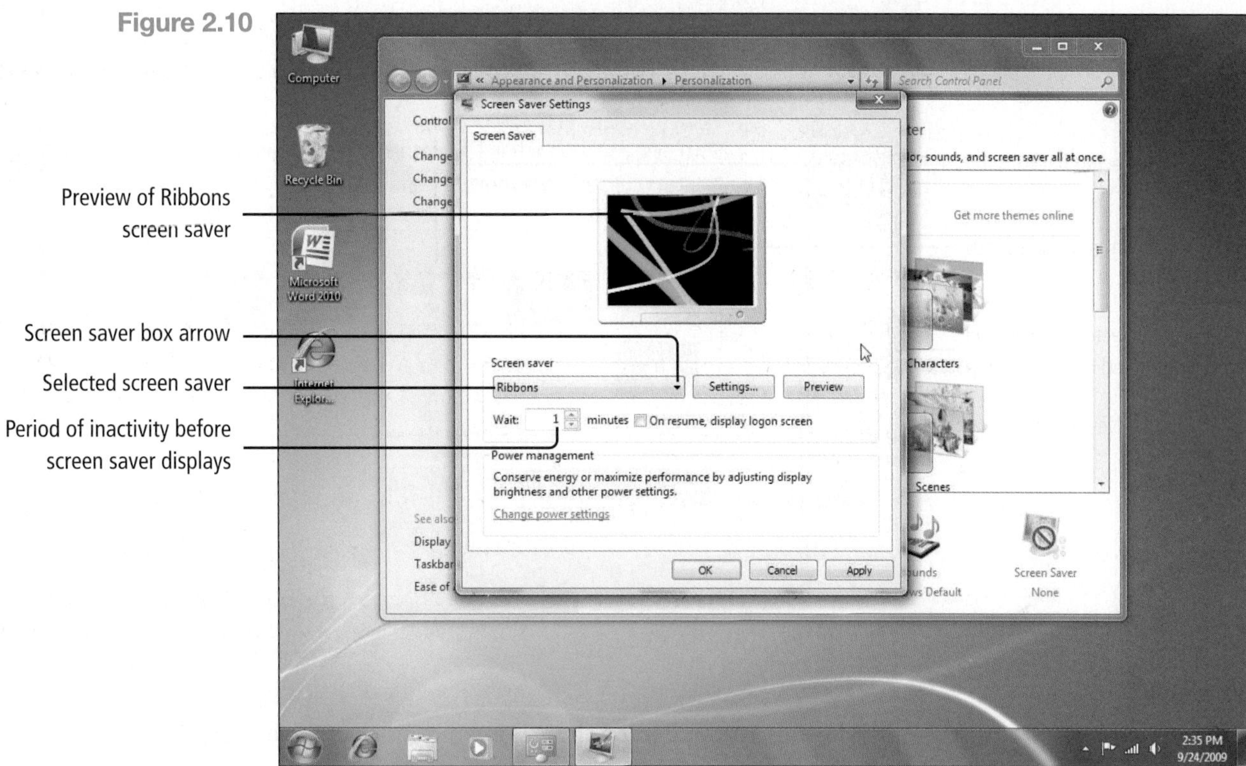

5 In the **Screen Saver Settings** dialog box, click the **Preview** button to preview a full-screen version of the screen saver. When you are through, move the mouse to turn off the full-screen screen saver preview. If you want to turn on the screen saver, click **OK**; otherwise, click **Cancel**.

6 In the left panel of the **Personalization** window, click **Change desktop icons**.

7 At the top of the **Desktop Icon Settings** dialog box, select—click to add a check mark to—the **Control Panel** check box. Click **OK** to save your changes and close the Desktop Icon Settings dialog box. Notice that a Control Panel icon is added to the left side of the desktop.

8 At the bottom of the **Personalization** window, click **Desktop Background**. Click the **up arrow** [▲] at the top of the scroll bar several times to move to the top of the backgrounds list. Under **Architecture**, click the third picture—the picture of the white building. The new background previews on the screen, as shown in Figure 2.11.

The ***desktop background*** is the picture, pattern, or color that displays on the desktop.

Figure 2.11

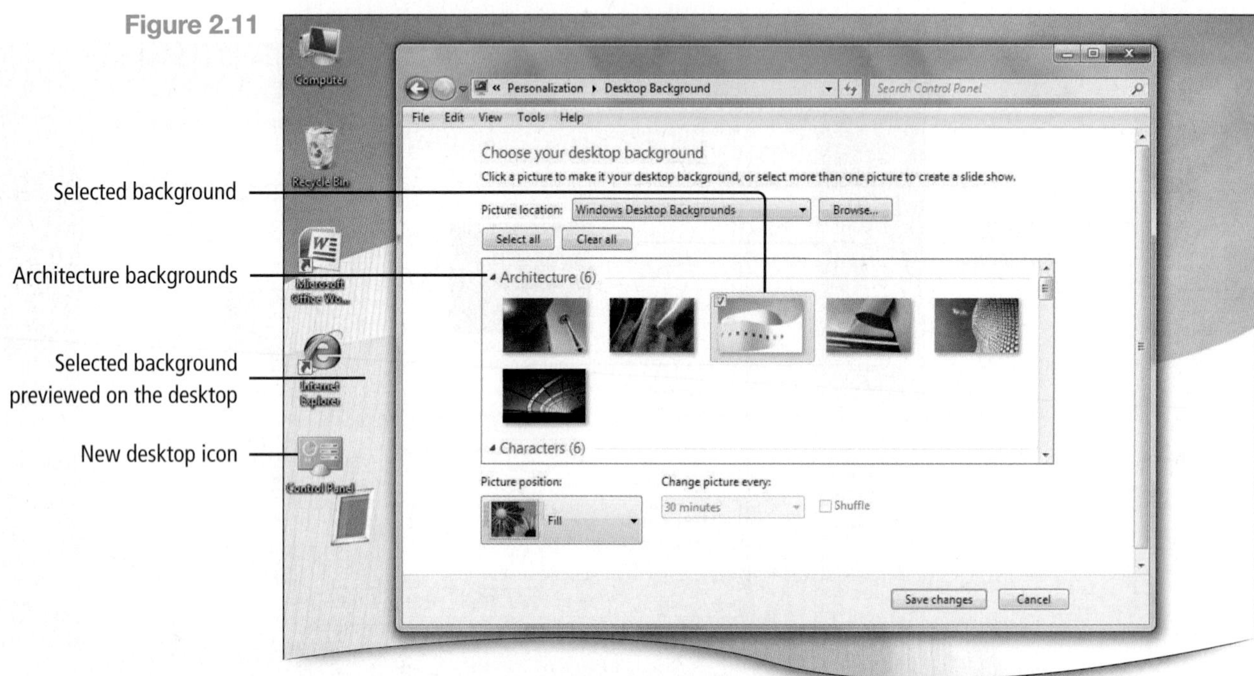

9 At the bottom of the **Personalization** window, click **Save changes**.

10 In the upper right corner of the **Personalization** window, click the **Close** button [X], and then compare your screen with Figure 2.12.

Figure 2.12

Activity 2.03 | Adding and Removing Gadgets

Gadgets are used to display dynamic programs such as a currency converter, a calendar, a stock market ticker, or a clock. You can move the gadgets anywhere on the screen, and you can modify or resize most of them.

1 In an open area of the desktop, right-click to display a shortcut menu. On the shortcut menu, click **Gadgets**. Compare your screen with Figure 2.13.

Figure 2.13

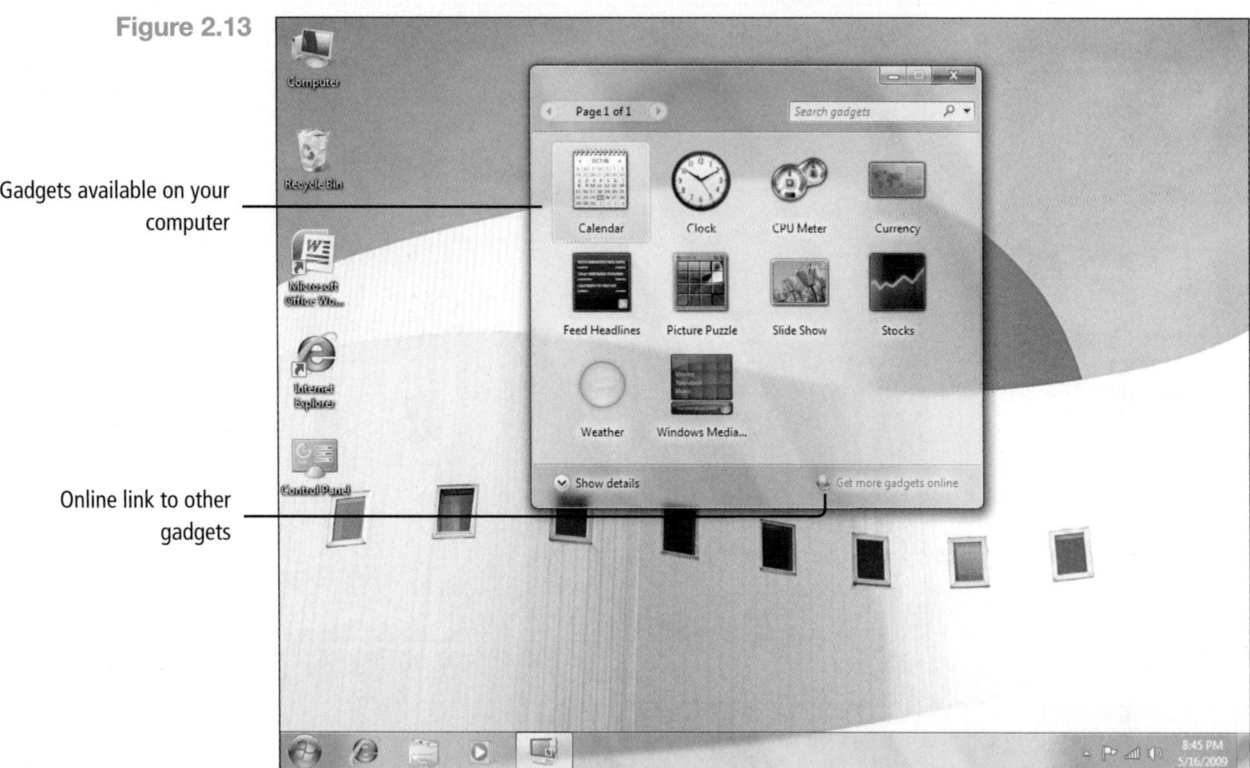

2 In the **Gadgets** window, double-click the **Weather** gadget. In the upper right corner of the **Gadgets** dialog box, click the **Close** button.

Alert! | Are there already gadgets on your desktop?

Your desktop may contain one or more gadgets, including a Weather gadget. In fact, you can have more than one of the same gadgets on the desktop at a time. For example, if you are interested in the weather in two different locations, you can add two weather gadgets to the desktop and keep an eye on two locations at one time.

3 Point to the **Weather** gadget. Notice that a four-button tool set, called the ***gadget controls***, displays on the right, as shown in Figure 2.14. Take a moment to study the functions of the buttons, as shown in the table in Figure 2.15.

Figure 2.14

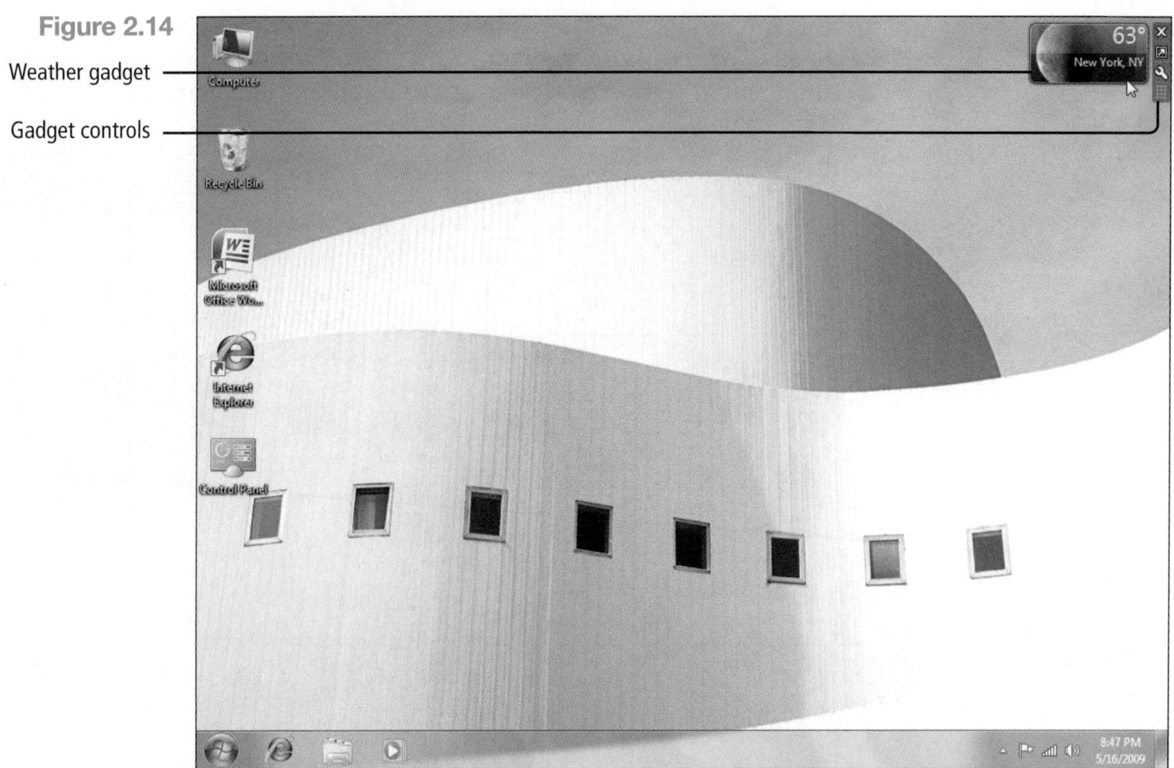

Gadget Controls

Button Name	Button	Description
Close	✕	Closes the gadget.
Larger size	⧉	Increases the size of the gadget; occupies the same position as the Smaller size button.
Smaller size	⧉	Decreases the size of the gadget; occupies the same position as the Larger size button.
Options	🔧	Displays different settings for each gadget.
Drag gadget	⋮⋮	Used to move the gadget anywhere on the desktop.

Figure 2.15

4 Point to the **Weather** gadget, click the **Larger size** button, and then click the **Options** button. In the **Select current location** box, type **Madison, Wisconsin** and then press Enter. Click **OK**, and then compare your screen with Figure 2.16.

Figure 2.16

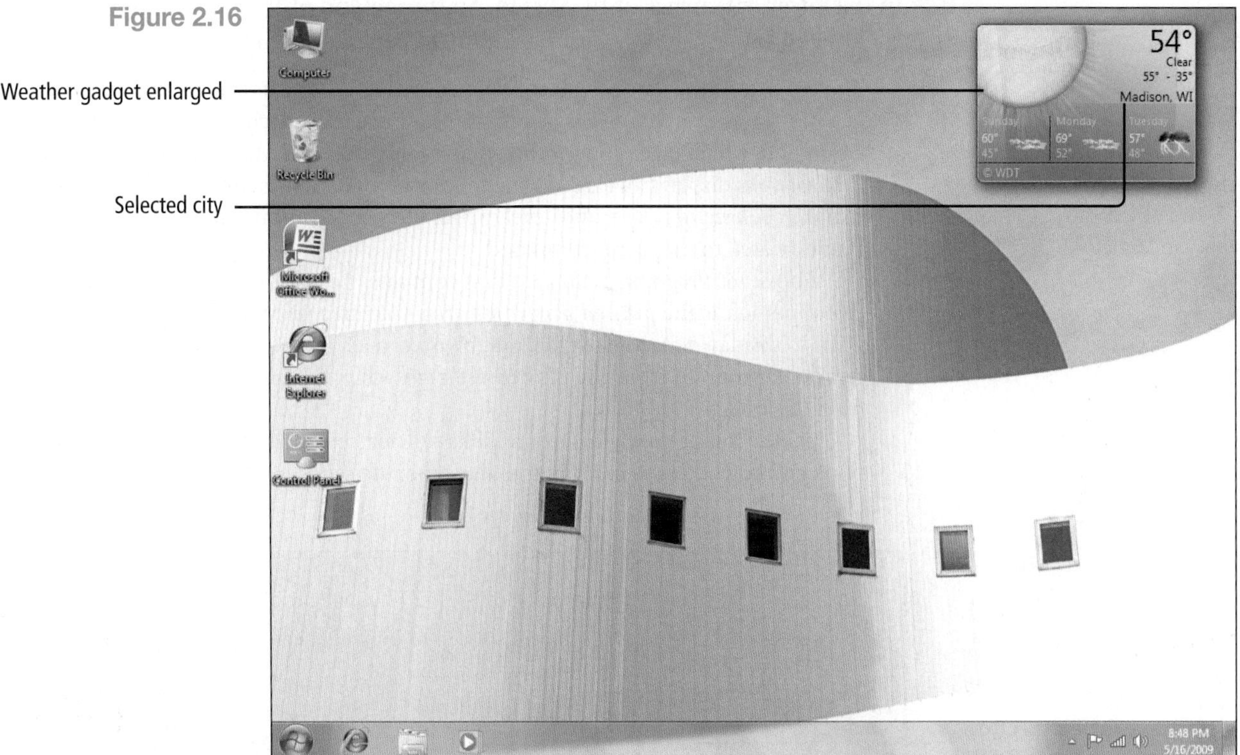

5 In an open area of the desktop, right-click to display a shortcut menu. On the shortcut menu, click **Gadgets**. In the **Gadgets** window, double-click the **Slide Show** gadget, and then double-click the **Slide Show** gadget again. In the upper right corner of the **Gadgets** dialog box, click the **Close** button.

Two additional gadgets are added to the desktop.

6 Point to either of the **Slide Show** gadgets, and then in the gadget controls, click the **Close** button to remove the gadget from the desktop.

7 Point to the remaining **Slide Show** gadget, point to the **Drag gadget** button, and then drag the gadget near the upper edge of the desktop. Notice that as you move near the top of the desktop, the gadget snaps into position, slightly below the top of the desktop.

Objective 2 | Use the Start Menu and Manage Windows

Some programs and documents are available from the desktop. For most things, however, you will turn to the Start menu. The ***Start menu*** gives you access to all of the programs on your computer, and also enables you to change the way Windows operates, to access and configure your network, and to get help and support when it is needed. After you have opened several programs, you can rearrange and resize the program windows to fit your needs.

Activity 2.04 | Using the Start Menu

In this activity, you will use the Start menu to open a program, and also to open the Windows Explorer window.

> **Another Way**
>
> Press the Start button on your keyboard—a key with the Windows logo, often found to the left of the spacebar.

1 In the lower left corner of the screen, on the left end of the taskbar, point to and then click the **Start** button. Compare your screen with Figure 2.17.

The left side of the Start menu contains four areas. At the bottom is the Search box, which enables you to search for files or programs. Above the Search box is the ***All Programs*** command, which takes you to a list of all of the programs you can access on the computer. *All Programs* displays an arrow, which indicates that a submenu is available for a command. A ***submenu*** is a second-level menu; the arrow indicates that more items can be found related to the menu command.

Above *All Programs* is an area that contains the most recently opened programs. On the upper left is the ***pinned programs area***—an area reserved for programs that you want to display permanently, although you can also remove programs from this area. To remove a program from the pinned list, right-click the program, and then click *Remove from this list*.

On the top of the right side are links to your personal folders, while the bottom sections give you access to computer management features.

Figure 2.17

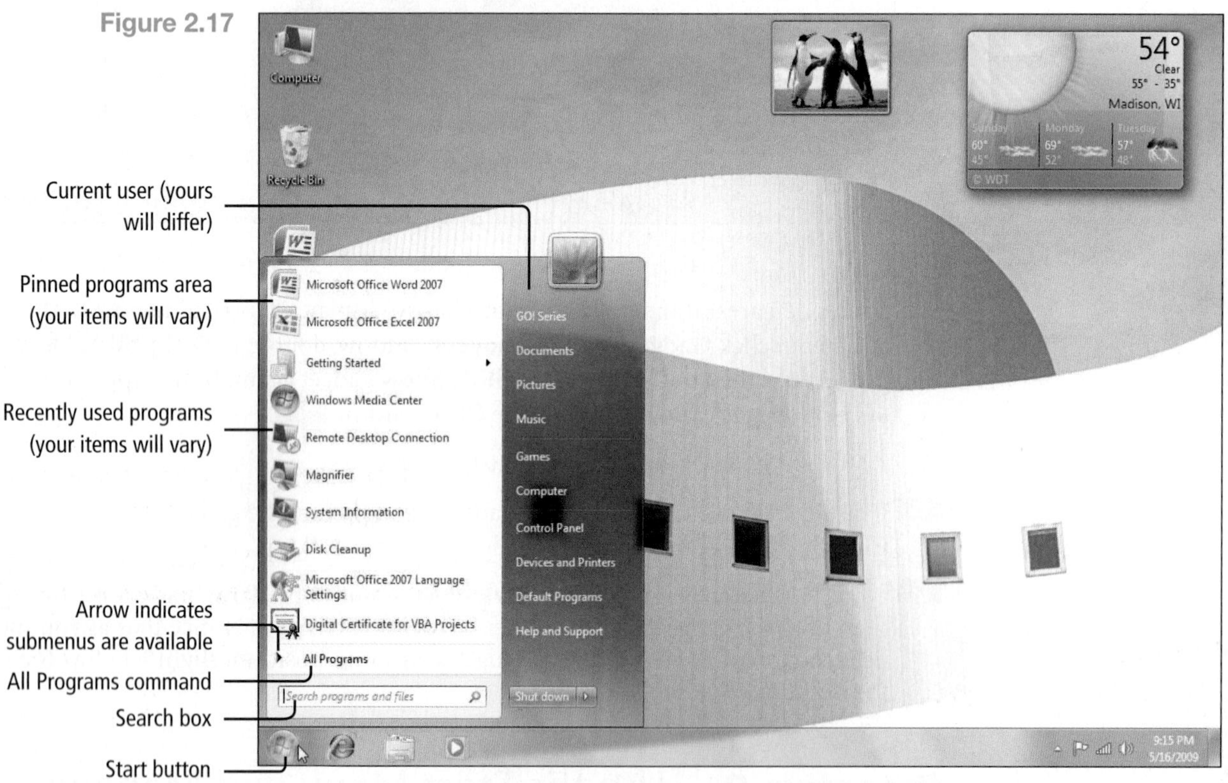

> **Alert! | Is your taskbar hidden?**
>
> Some computers are set up to hide the taskbar when it is not in use. This adds more workspace to the desktop, and is particularly useful on portable computers with small screens. When the taskbar is hidden, move the pointer to the bottom of the screen, and it will display. However, in this chapter, it is assumed that the taskbar is displayed at all times.
>
> To keep the taskbar displayed on your screen, find an open area on the taskbar, right-click, and then from the shortcut menu, click Properties. In the Taskbar and Start Menu Properties dialog box, on the Taskbar tab, locate the *Auto-hide the taskbar* check box. If the taskbar is hidden, there will be a check mark in the check box. To remove the Auto-hide feature, click the check box one time to clear—remove—the check mark.

2 From the **Start** menu, point to, but do not click, the **All Programs** command. Compare your screen with Figure 2.18.

The All Programs submenu displays—displaying a portion of the contents found within All Programs—and the *All Programs* command changes to a *Back* command. Your menu will differ from the one shown in Figure 2.18 because your computer will have different programs installed. Folders in the menu contain more programs or more folders or some of each.

Figure 2.18

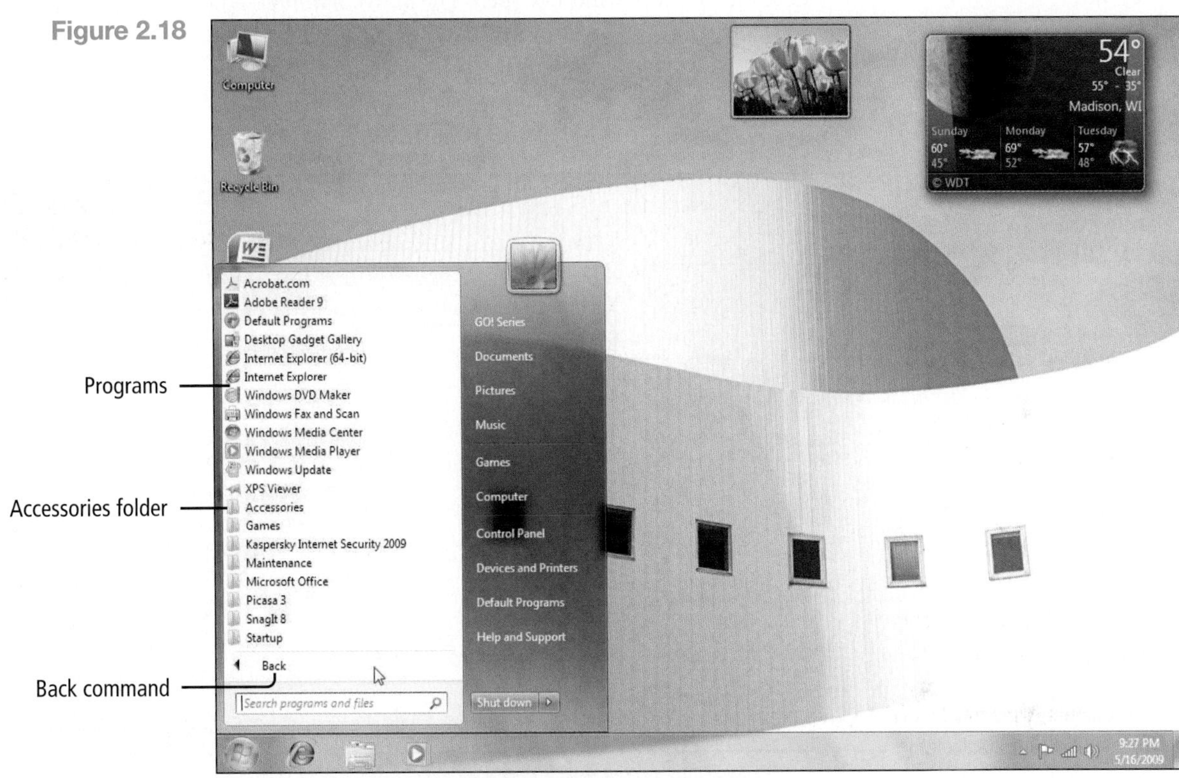

3 Click the **Accessories** folder, and then from the displayed list, click **Calculator**. Notice that the ***window name***—*Calculator*—displays in the title bar.

The Calculator window opens, and the Start menu closes. You can access the Accessories programs from the Start menu and use them while you are using other programs. For example, you might want to make a quick calculation while you are typing a document in Microsoft Word. You can open the calculator, make the calculation, and then place the result in your Word document without closing Word.

4 Click the **Start** button again, and near the middle of the right side of the **Start menu**, click **Computer**. If the Windows Explorer window fills the entire screen, near the right side of the title bar, click the Restore Down button . Compare your screen with Figure 2.19.

The Windows Explorer window opens, but the Calculator window is either partially or completely hidden, as shown in Figure 2.19. The buttons in the taskbar, however, indicate that two programs are open. The buttons that are outlined indicate the programs that have one or more windows open. The ***active window***—the window in which the pointer movements, commands, or text entry occur when two or more windows are open—displays a darker title bar.

Figure 2.19

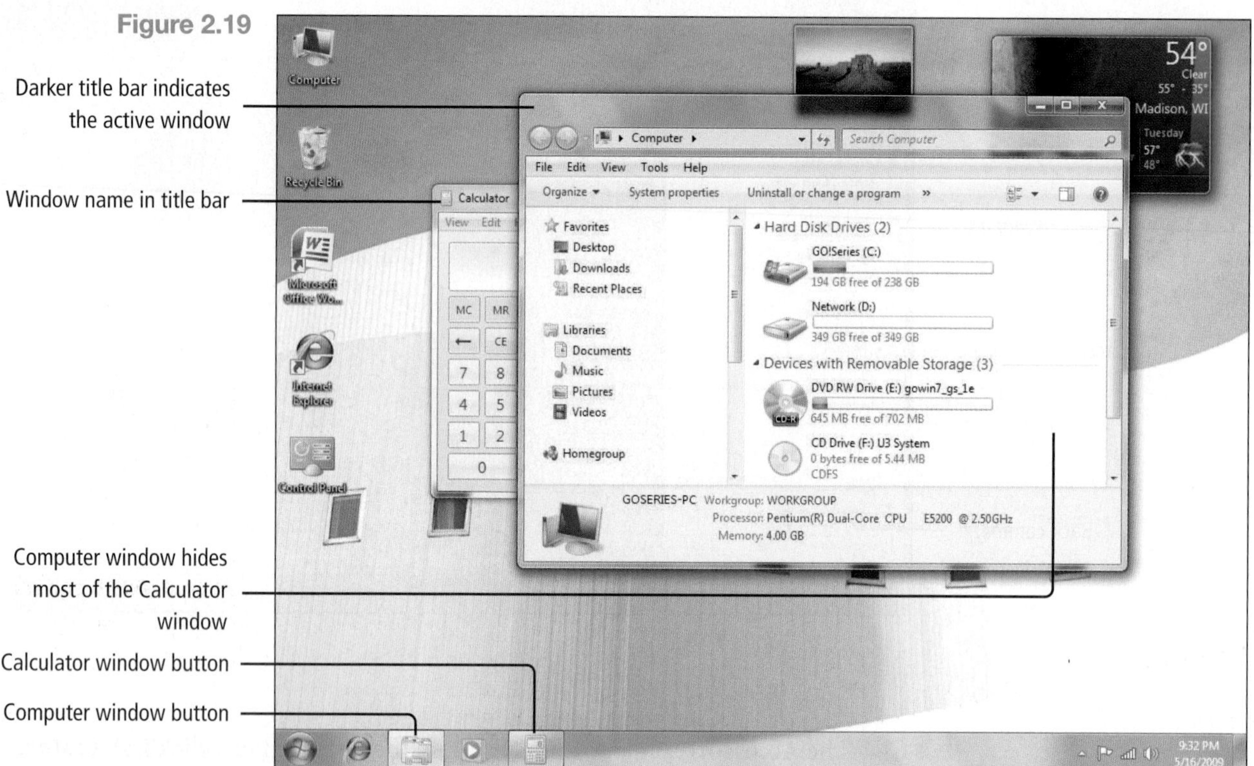

5 Click the **Start** button , and then click in the **Search programs and files** box. Type **wordpad** and press Enter. If the WordPad window fills the entire screen, near the right side of the title bar, click the Restore Down button .

If you type a program name into the Start menu Search box, the program will open, which enables you to quickly open programs rather than try to find them. ***WordPad*** is a simple word processing program that comes with Windows 7.

Activity 2.05 | Adding Shortcuts to the Start Menu, Desktop, and Taskbar

There are programs that you will seldom use, and there are programs that you will use all the time. To make frequently used programs easily and quickly available, you can pin a shortcut to the program in the Start menu *pinned programs area*, or you can add a shortcut icon to the desktop or pin the program to the taskbar.

1 Click the **Start** button , point to **All Programs**, click **Accessories**, and then right-click **Calculator**.

2 From the displayed shortcut menu, click **Pin to Start Menu**. At the bottom of the **Start menu**, click the **Back** button, and notice that *Calculator* has been added to the pinned programs area, as shown in Figure 2.20.

Figure 2.20

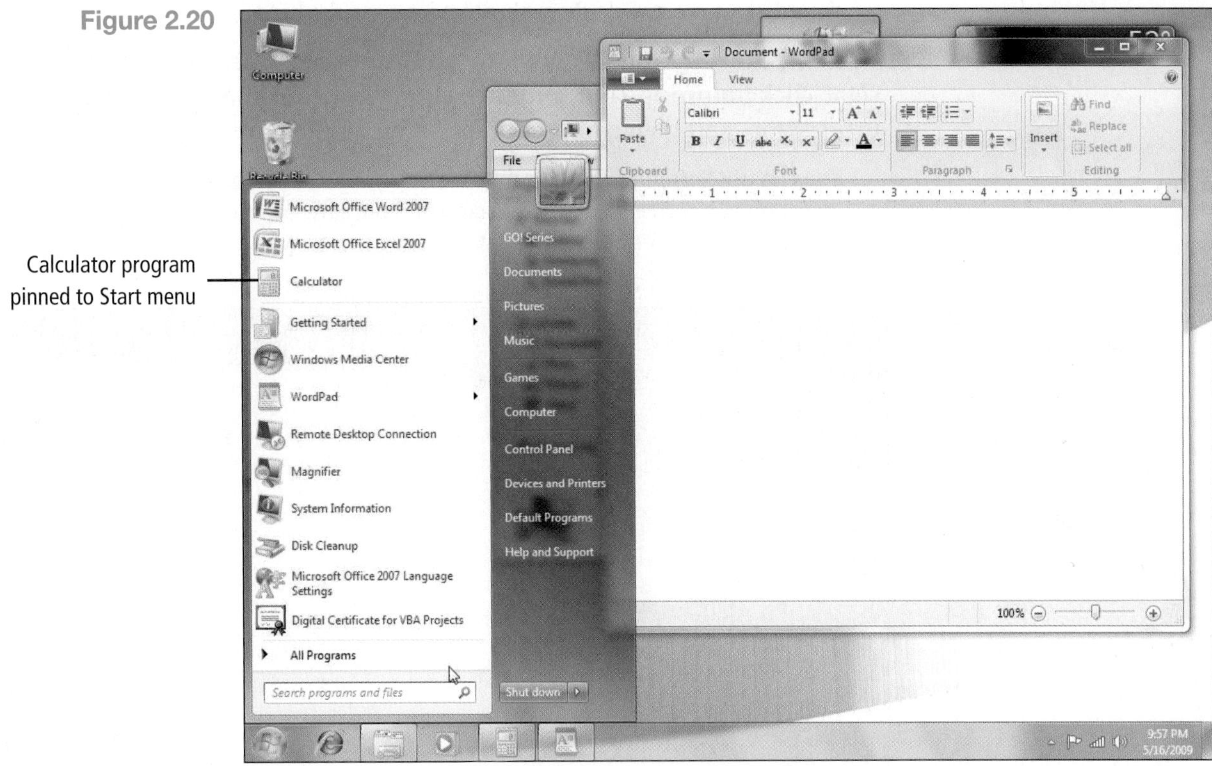

3 Click the **Start** button, point to **All Programs**, if necessary click **Accessories**, right-click **Calculator**, and then point to—but do not click—**Send to**. Notice the available commands on the *Send to* list, as shown in Figure 2.21.

Figure 2.21

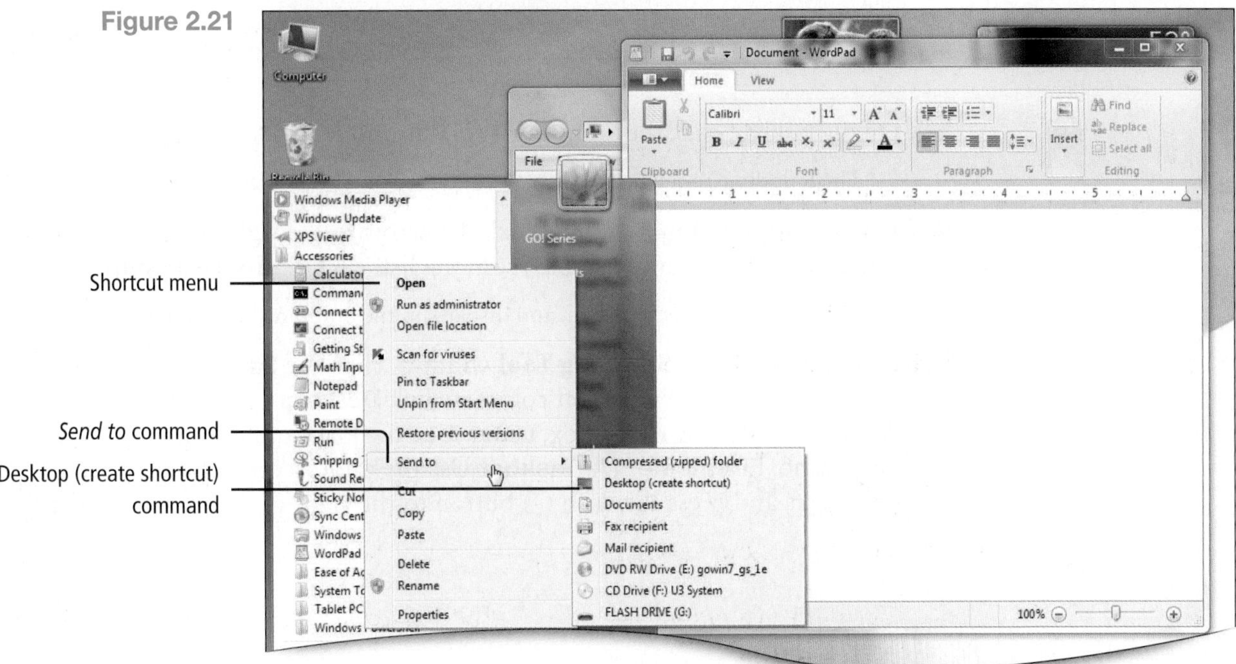

4. From the displayed shortcut menu, click **Desktop (create shortcut)**, and then click in any open area of the desktop.

   A Calculator icon is placed on the desktop. The shortcut icon has a small blue arrow in the lower left corner. Depending on the windows you have open, and the number of icons on your desktop, your Calculator shortcut icon may be hidden.

5. Click the **Start** button, point to **All Programs**, if necessary click **Accessories**, right-click **Snipping Tool**, and then click **Pin to Taskbar**. Click in an open area on the desktop, and then compare your screen with Figure 2.22.

   You can use ***Snipping Tool*** to capture a screen shot, or ***snip***, of the entire screen or of any object on your screen, and then make notes on, save, or share the image. You will use this tool throughout this chapter.

Figure 2.22

6. On the taskbar, click the **Snipping Tool** button.

   The Snipping Tool window displays, and the rest of the screen appears faded.

7. In the **Snipping Tool** window, click the arrow to the right of the **New** button to display a list of potential snips. From the list, click **Full-screen Snip**.

   The entire screen is captured, and displays in the Snipping Tool window.

8. Near the top of the **Snipping Tool** window, click the **Save Snip** button. In the **Save As** dialog box, in the left column, click **Desktop** to save the snip to the desktop. In the **File name** box, using your own last and first names, type **Lastname_Firstname_1A_Taskbar** Use the underscore between words—hold down Shift and press the dash (-) button to the right of the numbers near the top

of the keyboard. Click in the **Save as type** box, and then from the menu, click **JPEG file**. Compare your screen with Figure 2.23.

Figure 2.23

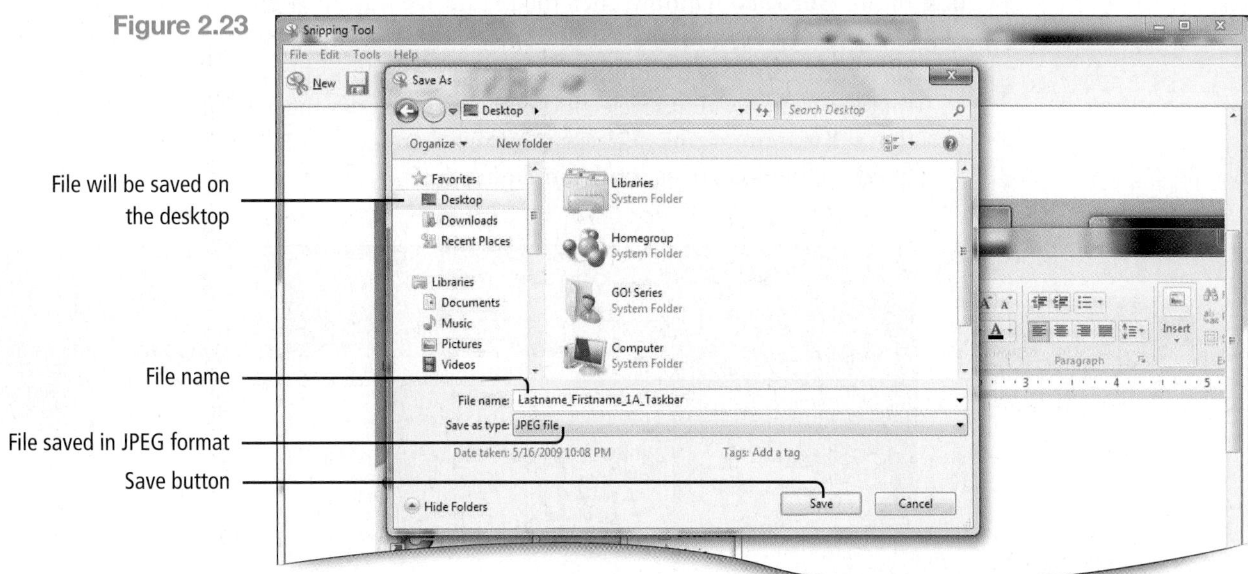

9 At the bottom of the **Save As** dialog box, click **Save** to save the snip on the desktop.

10 In the upper right corner of the **Snipping Tool** window, click the **Close** button. Notice that your file displays as an icon on the desktop.

Activity 2.06 | Minimizing, Maximizing, and Restoring a Window

You can ***maximize*** a window, which enlarges the window to occupy the entire screen, and you can ***restore*** a window, which reduces the window to the size it was before being maximized. You can also ***minimize*** a window, which reduces the window to a button on the taskbar, removing it from the screen entirely without actually closing it. When you need to view the window again, you can click the taskbar button to bring it back into view.

1 Click anywhere in the **WordPad** window to make it the active window, and then examine the three buttons in the upper right corner of the window. The left button is the **Minimize** button, the middle button is the **Maximize** button, and the right button is the **Close** button.

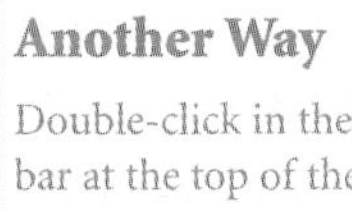

Another Way

Double-click in the bar at the top of the window.

2 In the **WordPad** window, click the **Maximize** button. Notice that the window expands to cover the entire screen, and the Maximize button changes to a Restore Down button, as shown in Figure 2.24.

Figure 2.24

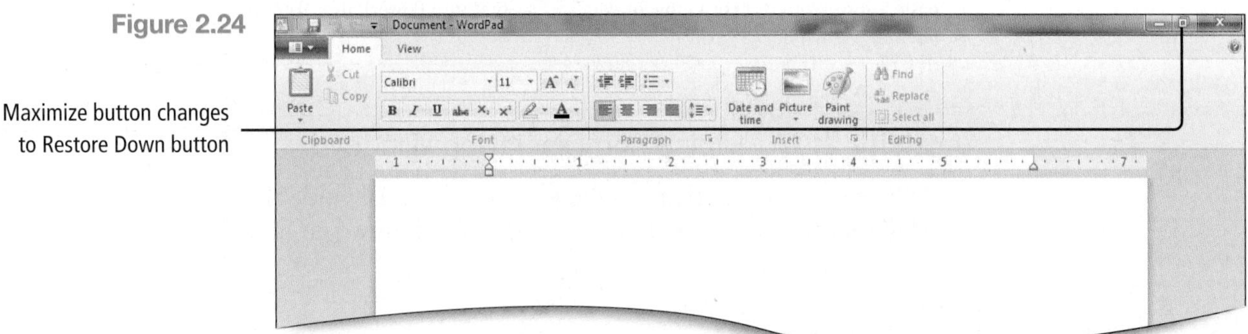

> **Another Way**
>
> Double-click in the title bar at the top of the window.

3. In the **WordPad** window, click the **Restore Down** button. Notice that the window resumes its former shape, size, and location.

4. In the **WordPad** window, click the **Minimize** button. In the taskbar, click the **Calculator** button to make it the active window, and then in the **Calculator** window, click the **Minimize** button to display the Windows Explorer window. Notice that the Windows Explorer window now displays as the active window. Notice also that the two programs that you minimized are not closed—their buttons are still outlined on the taskbar, as shown in Figure 2.25.

Figure 2.25

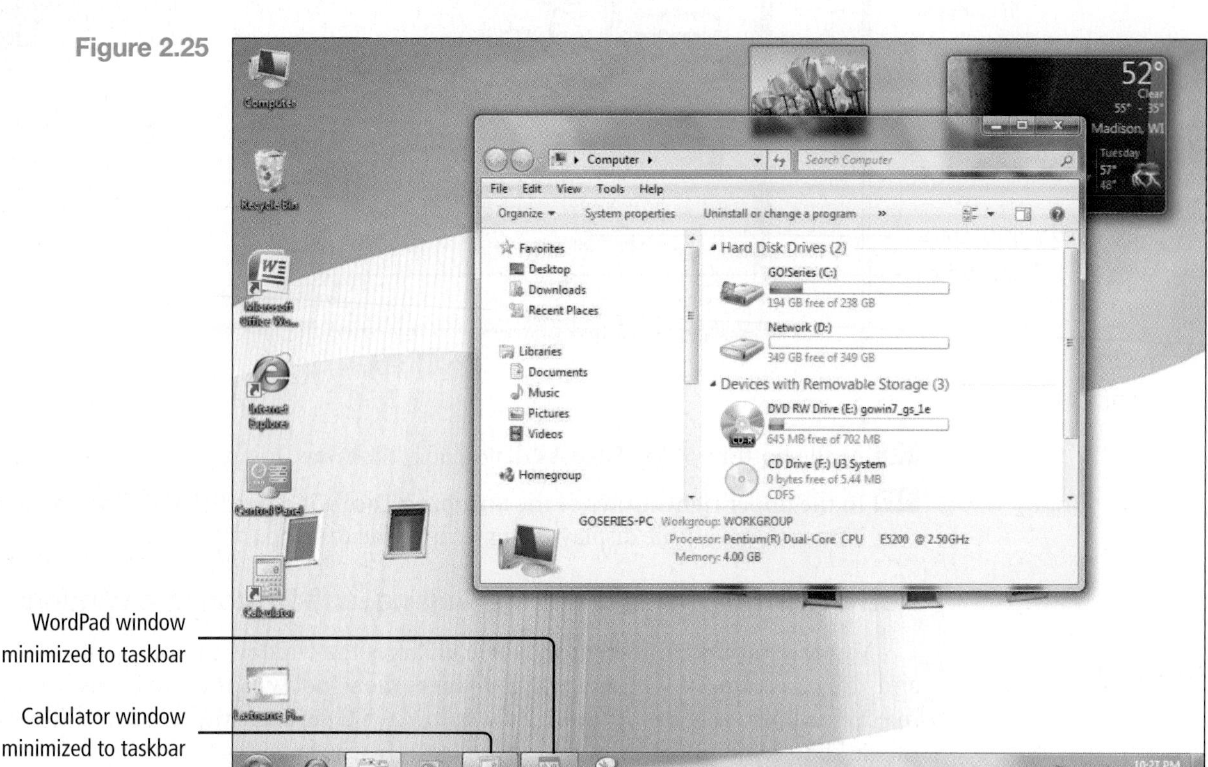

5. In the taskbar, click the **Calculator** button to restore the Calculator window. Then, click the **WordPad** button to restore the WordPad window.

> **More Knowledge | Keeping More Than One Program Window Open at a Time**
>
> The ability to keep more than one window open at a time will become more useful as you become more familiar with Microsoft Office. For example, if you want to take information from two word processing documents to create a third document, you can open all three documents and use the taskbar to move among them, copying and pasting text from one document to another. Or, you could copy a chart from Excel and paste it into Word or take a table of data and paste it into PowerPoint. You can even have the same document open in two windows.

Activity 2.07 | Hiding and Displaying Windows

There is a shortcut that enables you to temporarily hide all open windows and view the desktop, and also a way to display just one window and hide the rest.

1 Move the pointer to the lower-right corner of the desktop to point to the **Show desktop** button. Notice that all open windows become transparent to give you a ***peek*** at the desktop—all desktop items display, as shown in Figure 2.26.

This only works if the Aero interface is turned on.

Figure 2.26

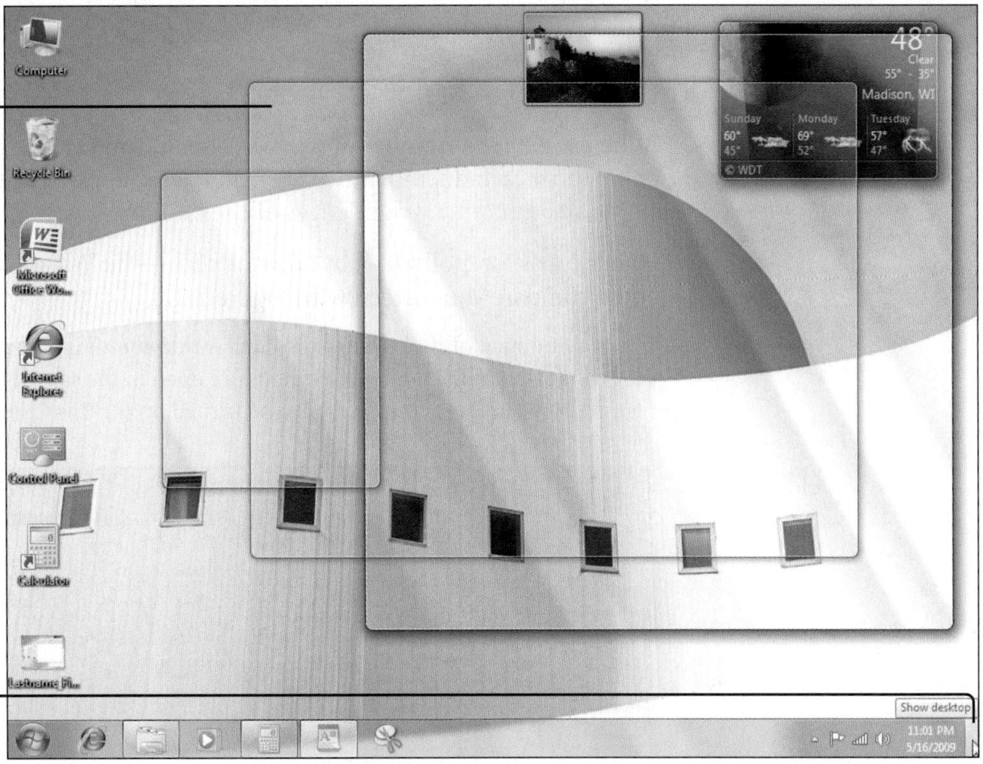

Outlines of transparent windows

Show desktop button

2 Move the pointer away from the **Show desktop** button and notice that the windows display again.

3 Point to the **Show desktop** button, but this time click the button. Notice that all open windows are hidden, and no outlines display.

4 Click the **Show desktop** button again to display all open windows.

5 In the taskbar, locate and click the **Calculator** button to make the Calculator the active window. Notice that the background of the Calculator icon on the taskbar is brighter than the icons for the other open windows.

6 Point to the **Calculator** title bar, hold down the left mouse button, and then ***shake***—move the window back and forth quickly—the window.

All windows except the shaken window are hidden.

7 Shake the **Calculator** window again to display all of the open windows.

Objective 3 | Resize, Move, and Scroll Windows

When a window opens on your screen, it generally opens in the same size and shape as it was when last used. If you are using more than one window at a time, you can increase or decrease the size of a window, or move a window so that you can see the information you need.

As you work within a program, the information you create will likely grow larger than the screen can display. When the information in a window extends beyond the right or lower edges of the window, scroll bars display at the bottom and right. Using the ***horizontal scroll bar***, you can move left and right to view information that extends beyond the left or right edge of the screen. Using the ***vertical scroll bar***, you can move up and down to view information that extends beyond the top or bottom of the screen.

Activity 2.08 | Customizing and Using the Taskbar

When you have a number of windows open, you can use the taskbar to quickly review the contents of each document to determine which one to use. You can also move the taskbar to the top, left, or right edges of the desktop.

1 On the taskbar, point to—but do not click—the **Windows Explorer** button, and then compare your screen with Figure 2.27.

A thumbnail of the window displays. A ***thumbnail*** is a miniature representation of a window or a file. If two documents are open in the same program, two thumbnails will display. The Aero interface must be turned on for this feature to work.

Figure 2.27

2 On the taskbar, point to—but do not click—the **Calculator** button. Move the pointer and point to the **WordPad** button.

3 Click the **Start** button, point to **All Programs**, click **Accessories**, and then click **Paint**.

If the Paint window is maximized, click the Restore Down button.

Paint is a simple drawing program that comes with Windows 7. Four programs are now open, and there are icons on the taskbar for other unopened programs, such as Snipping Tool.

4 Hold down the Alt key, and then press the Tab key. Compare your screen with Figure 2.28.

The screen displays thumbnails of the windows that are open, including the desktop; if the Aero interface is not turned on, only the program icons display.

Figure 2.28

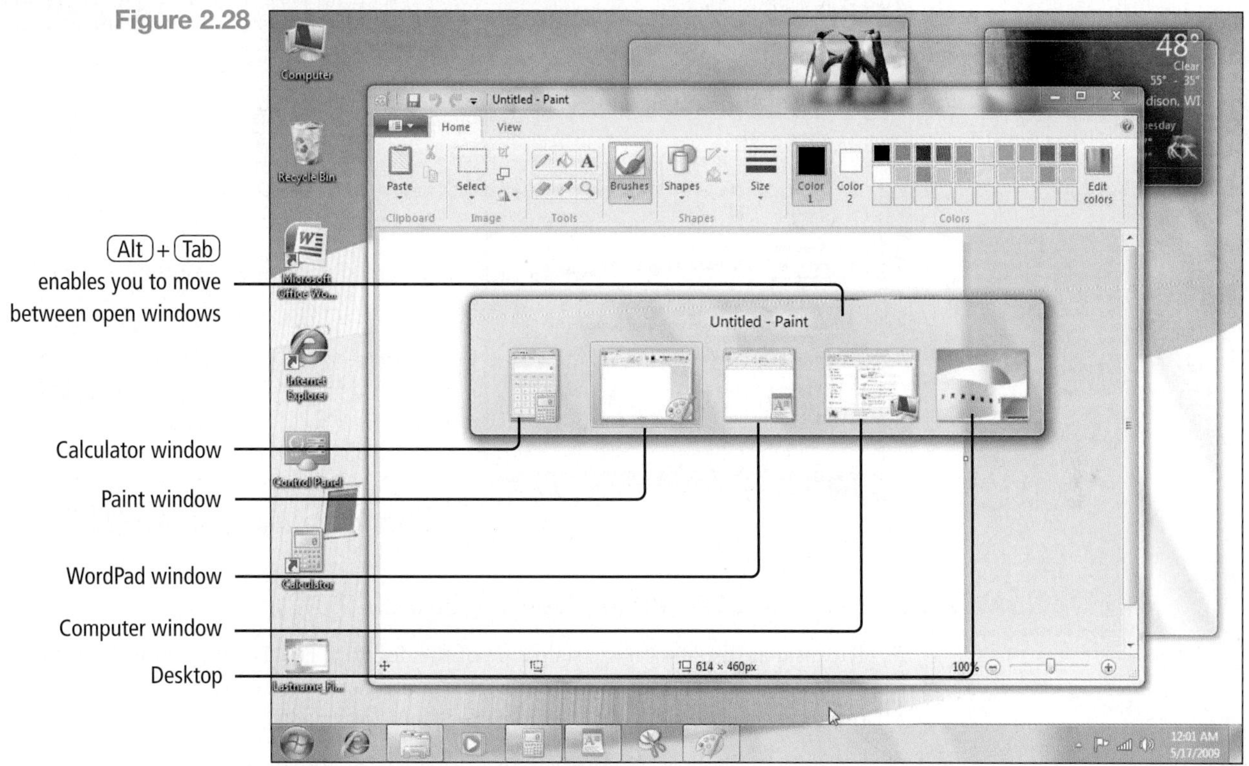

5 Continue to hold down Alt, but press Tab several times. Notice that the selected window moves from left to right in the list of thumbnails.

When you release the Alt key, the window in the active thumbnail becomes the active window on the desktop.

6 Move to the **Calculator** window, and then release the Alt button.

7 On the taskbar, point to the **Windows Explorer** window, and then right-click.

A ***jump list*** displays frequent destinations you might want to jump to from the Windows Explorer window. If you display a jump list for a program such as a word processor or a spreadsheet, a list of recently edited files also displays, enabling you to quickly open any desired files.

8 Right-click an open area of the taskbar, and then from the shortcut menu, click **Properties**.

9 In the **Properties** dialog box, be sure the Taskbar tab is selected. Under **Taskbar appearance**, click the **Taskbar location on screen arrow**, and then click **Right**. Compare your screen with Figure 2.29.

Figure 2.29

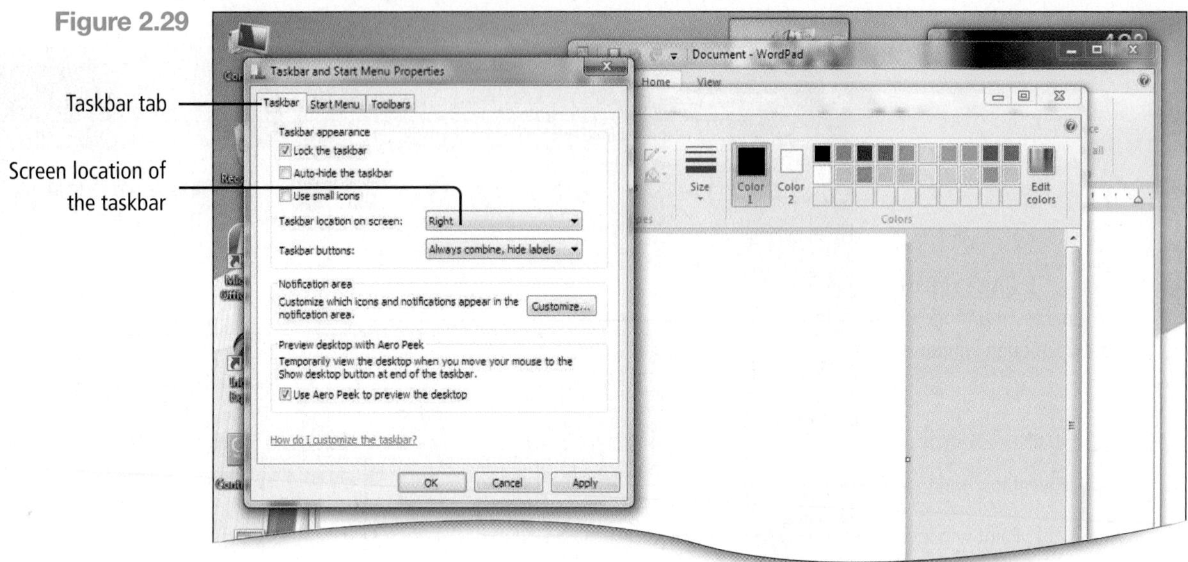

10 At the bottom of the **Properties** dialog box, click **OK**.

The taskbar displays on the right side of the desktop. This is an ideal location if you are using a widescreen monitor or a portable computer with a wide monitor because it gives you more vertical space on the screen for your documents.

11 In the taskbar, click the **Snipping Tool** button. In the **Snipping Tool** window, click the arrow to the right of the **New** button to display a list of potential snips. From the list, click **Full-screen Snip**.

12 Near the top of the **Snipping Tool** window, click the **Save Snip** button. In the **Save As** dialog box, in the left column, click **Desktop**. In the **File name** box, using your own last and first names, type **Lastname_Firstname_1A_Windows** Click in the **Save as type** box and be sure **JPEG file** is selected.

13 At the bottom of the **Save As** dialog box, click **Save** to save the snip on the desktop.

14 In the upper right corner of the **Snipping Tool** window, click the **Close** button. Notice that your file displays as an icon on the desktop.

15 Use the procedure you practiced in Steps 8 through 10 to return the taskbar to the bottom of the desktop.

Activity 2.09 | Resizing, Moving, Scrolling, and Closing Windows

In the following activity, you will resize and move the Windows Explorer window. You will also use the vertical scroll bar in the window to view information that does not fit in the window.

1 On the right end of the taskbar, click the **Show desktop** button to hide all of the windows.

2 On the taskbar, click the **Windows Explorer** button to display the Windows Explorer window.

3 Move the pointer to the lower right corner of the window to display the diagonal resize pointer, and then compare your screen with Figure 2.30.

When the mouse pointer is in this shape, you can use it to change the size and shape of a window.

Figure 2.30

4 Hold down the left mouse button, ***drag***—move the mouse while holding down the left mouse button and then release at the appropriate time—diagonally up and to the left until you see a scroll bar at the right side of the window, and then release the mouse button. Adjust as necessary so that the Windows Explorer window is the approximate size of the one shown in Figure 2.31.

Notice that a vertical scroll bar displays on the right side of the window, and another one displays on the right side of the Navigation pane. A scroll bar is added to the window whenever the window contains more than it can display.

Figure 2.31

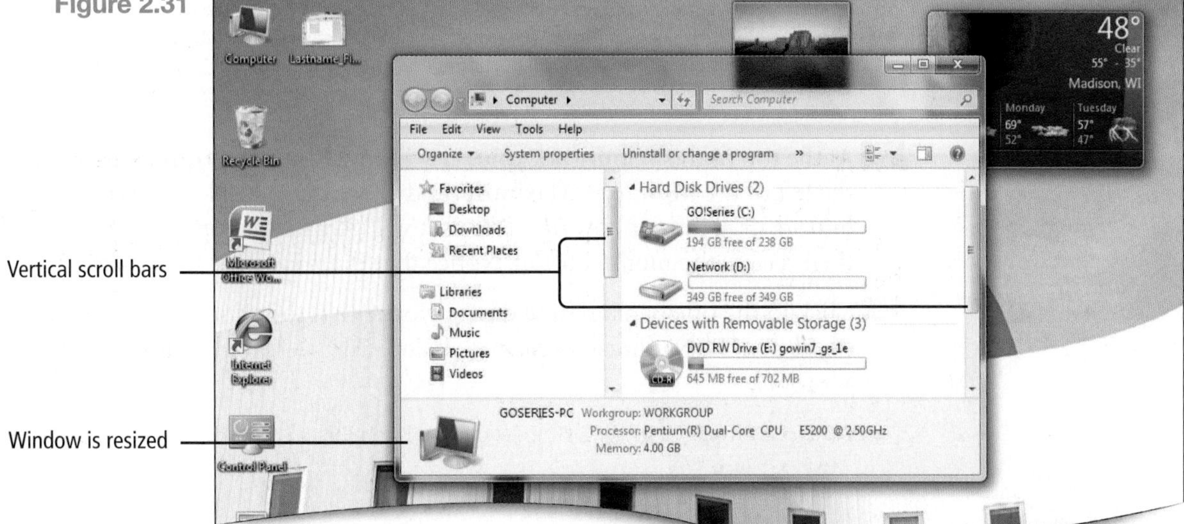

5 In the **Windows Explorer** window **file list**, at the bottom of the vertical scroll bar, point to the **down arrow** [▼] and click two times. Notice that information at the bottom of the window scrolls up so that you can see the information that was not visible before, as shown in Figure 2.32.

Figure 2.32

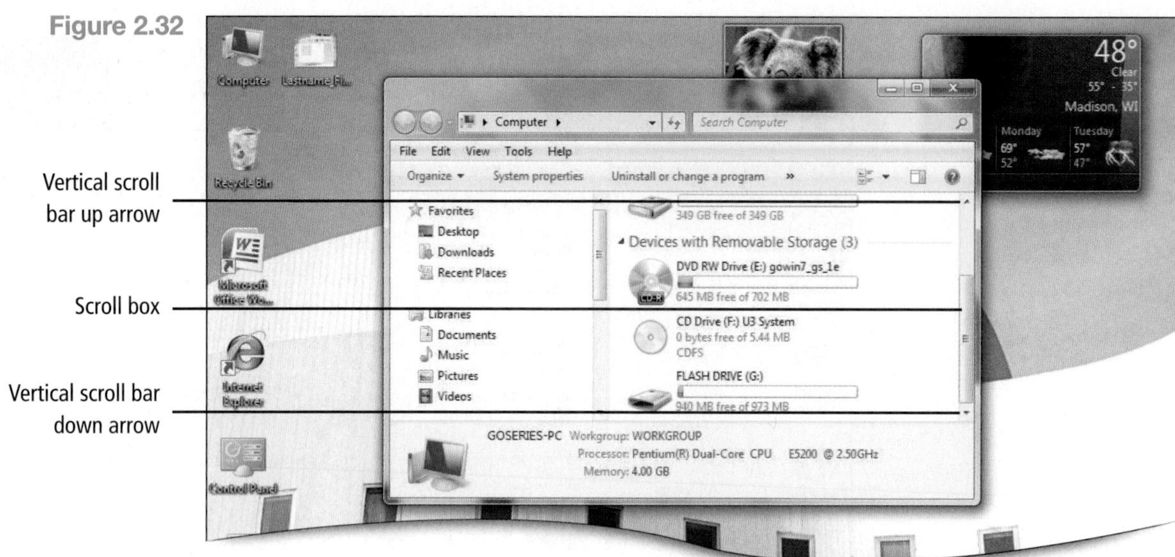

6 On the same scroll bar, point to the **up arrow** [▲], and then click and hold down the left mouse button.

The window scrolls to the top of the file list. You can click and hold down the left mouse button on the up or down scroll arrows to scroll rapidly through a long list of information.

7 Point to the scroll box, and then drag it downward.

The ***scroll box*** displays within the vertical and horizontal scroll bars and provides a visual indication of your location within the information displayed. It can also be used with the mouse to reposition the information on the screen. Moving the scroll box gives you more control as you scroll because you can see the information as it moves up or down in the window.

Note | Moving a Screen at a Time

You can move up or down a screen at a time by clicking in the gray area above or below the vertical scroll box. You can also move left or right a screen at a time by clicking in the area to the left or right of a horizontal scroll box. The size of the scroll box indicates the relative size of the display to the whole document. If the scroll box is small, it means that the display is a small portion of the entire document.

8 At the top of the **Windows Explorer** window, point to a blank area in the title bar to the left of the Minimize, Maximize, and Close buttons. Hold down the left mouse button, drag the window up as far as it will go past the top edge of the window, and then release the mouse button. Notice that the window is maximized.

9 Click in the title bar and drag down. Notice that the window is restored to its original size, but not its original location.

10 In the **Windows Explorer** window title bar, click the **Close** button. In the taskbar, right-click the **Paint** button, and then click **Close window**. Use the same technique to close the **Calculator** window.

11 In the taskbar, click the **WordPad** button to display the WordPad window. Using the title bar, drag the WordPad window to the right edge of the desktop until it changes shape to occupy the right half of the desktop, and then release the mouse button.

You can use this method to open two windows side by side if you drag a second window to the left border.

12 Click in the WordPad window, type your first and last names, and then press Enter. Locate the **Lastname_Firstname_1A_Taskbar** icon on the desktop—you may have to click the two snip files to find the correct file.

13 Drag the **Lastname_Firstname_1A_Taskbar** file to the line below your name in the WordPad document, and then release the mouse button. Compare your screen with Figure 2.33.

The contents of the file you dragged are pasted into the WordPad document.

Figure 2.33

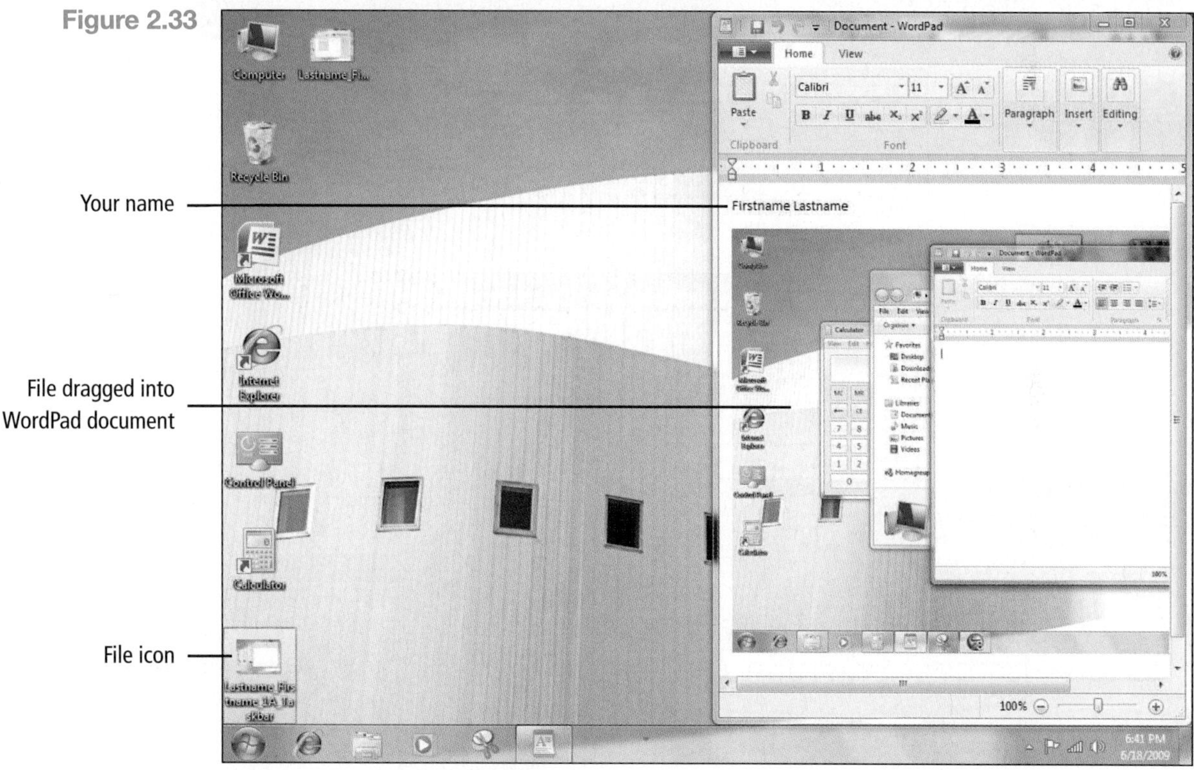

14 Drag the **Lastname_Firstname_1A_Windows** file to the line below the figure you just inserted into the WordPad document. In the WordPad title bar, click the **Save** button.

15 In the **Save As** dialog box, in the **Navigation** pane, click **Desktop**. In the **File name** box, type **Lastname_Firstname_1A_WordPad** and then click **Save**.

16 If you are to print your document, hold down Ctrl and then press P to display the Print dialog box. Be sure the correct printer is selected, and then click **Print**. If you are to submit this document electronically, follow your instructor's directions.

17 **Close** the WordPad window.

End **You have completed Project 2A**

Project 2B Manage Files and Folders

Project Activities

In Activities 2.10 through 2.18 you will create folders, and then copy, move, rename, and delete files and folders. You will add tags to files and use the Windows 7 search features to search for files. Your screens will look similar to those in Figure 2.34.

Project Files

For Project 2B, you will need the following files:

36 sample files, and two folders containing 14 additional files

You will save your documents as:

Lastname_Firstname_1B_Renamed_Folder
Lastname_Firstname_1B_Compressed_Folder
Lastname_Firstname_1B_Search_Folder

Project Results

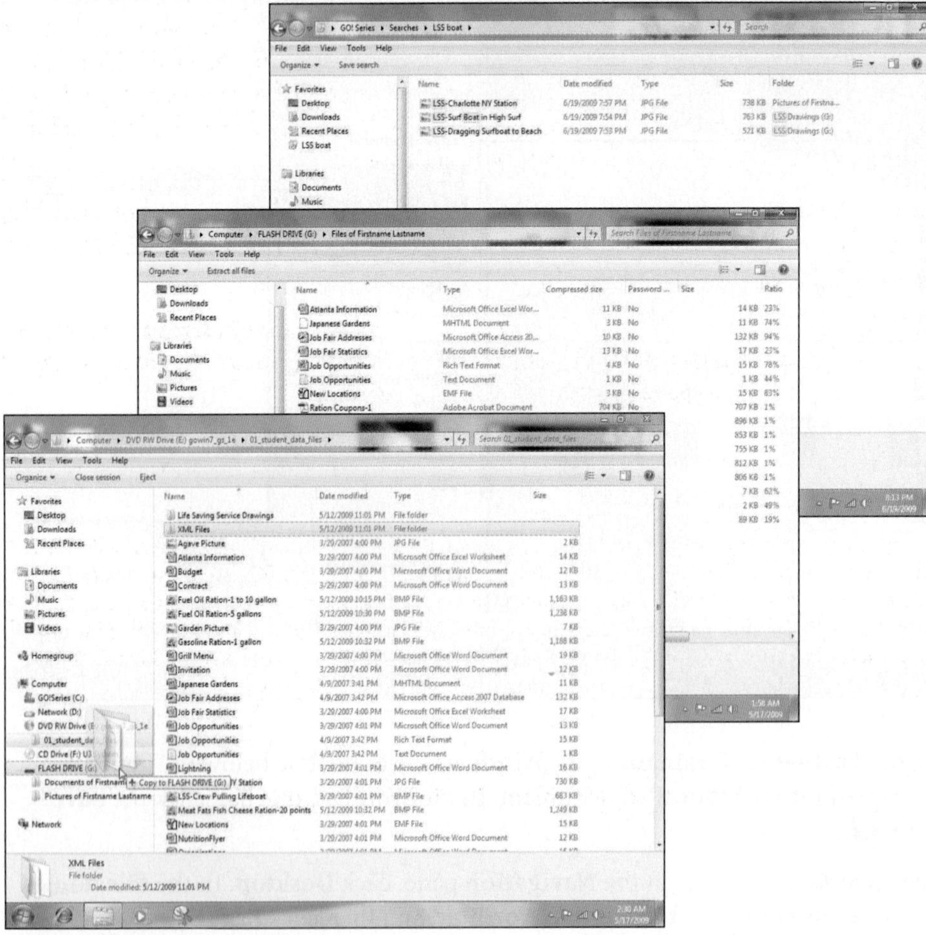

Figure 2.34

Objective 4 | Create, Move, and Rename Folders

Information that you create in a computer program is stored in the computer's memory, which is a temporary storage location. This data will be lost if the computer is turned off. To keep the information you create, you must save it as a file on one of the drives available to you. For example, a five-page term paper that you create in a word processing program such as Microsoft Word, when saved, is a ***file***. Files can be stored directly on a drive, but more commonly are stored in a folder on the drive. A ***folder*** is a container for programs and files, represented on the screen by a picture of a common paper file folder.

Use folders to organize your files so that you can easily locate them for later use. Folders and files must be created and stored on one of the drives attached to your computer. Your available drives fall into three categories: 1) the nonremovable hard drive, also called the ***local disk***, inside the computer; 2) removable drives that you insert into the computer, such as a flash drive, an external hard drive, or a writable CD or DVD; or 3) a shared network drive connected to your computer through a computer network, such as the network at your college.

Activity 2.10 | Opening and Navigating Windows Explorer

Windows Explorer is a program that enables you to create and manage folders, and copy, move, sort, and delete files. In the following activity, you will create a folder on one of the three types of drives available to you—the local disk (hard drive), a removable drive (USB flash drive, an external hard drive, or some other type of removable drive), or a network drive. If you are using a computer in a college lab, you may have space assigned to you on a shared network drive. You can create these folders on any drive that is available to you. For the rest of this chapter, a flash drive will be used.

1 On the taskbar, click the **Windows Explorer** button. If this button is not available, click the **Start** button, point to All Programs, click Accessories, and then click Windows Explorer.

The Windows Explorer window opens, with the Navigation pane displayed on the left, and the Libraries pane displayed on the right. You may also see a Details pane just above the taskbar and a Preview pane on the right side of the window.

More Knowledge | Using Libraries

Libraries are folders used to sort files with similar content. By default, Windows 7 sets up four libraries: Documents, Music, Pictures, and Videos. Each of these libraries is assigned two folders—a user folder and a public folder. For example, the Documents library contains the My Documents subfolder for the current user, along with the Public Documents subfolder on the hard disk, which contains files that can be shared with all users. If you have other fixed drives on your computer, or permanent network drives, you can add other folders to a library so that all files of a similar type can be accessed quickly using the library.

Another Way

On the right side of the title bar, click the Maximize button.

2 If the window is not maximized, drag the title bar to the top of the screen.

3. On the Command bar, click the **Organize** button, and then point to **Layout**. If the Details pane does not display at the bottom of your window, click Details Pane. If the Navigation pane does not display on the left side of your window, repeat the procedure and click Navigation Pane. Compare your screen with Figure 2.35.

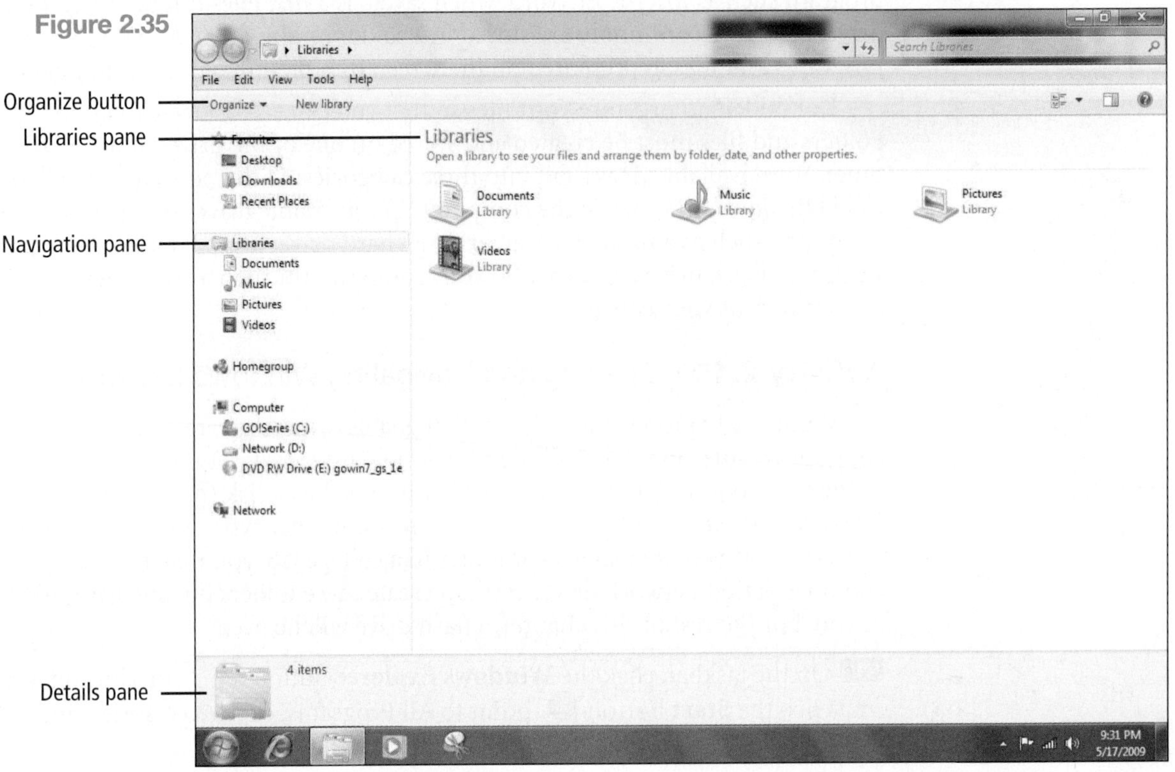

4. In the **Navigation** pane, if necessary scroll down, and then click **Computer**.

   The file list displays a list of hard drives, removable storage devices, network drives, and other devices connected to the computer.

5. In the **Navigation** pane, if necessary, to the left of **Computer**, click the open arrow. Notice that the arrow changes to a filled arrow pointing downward at an angle.

   The open arrow indicates that there are other folders and drives to be displayed. When you click the open arrow, the next level of folders and drives displays. The list of drives in the Navigation pane matches the list of drives in the file list.

6. Insert your USB flash drive or other removable drive. If an AutoPlay dialog box displays asking what you want Windows to do, click the Close button. In the **Navigation** pane, under **Computer**, click your removable drive—for this chapter, the removable drive name will be FLASH DRIVE (G:); yours will be different.

7 Compare your screen with Figure 2.36. Notice that the file list in the figure is empty; your storage device or drive may already contain files and folders.

Figure 2.36

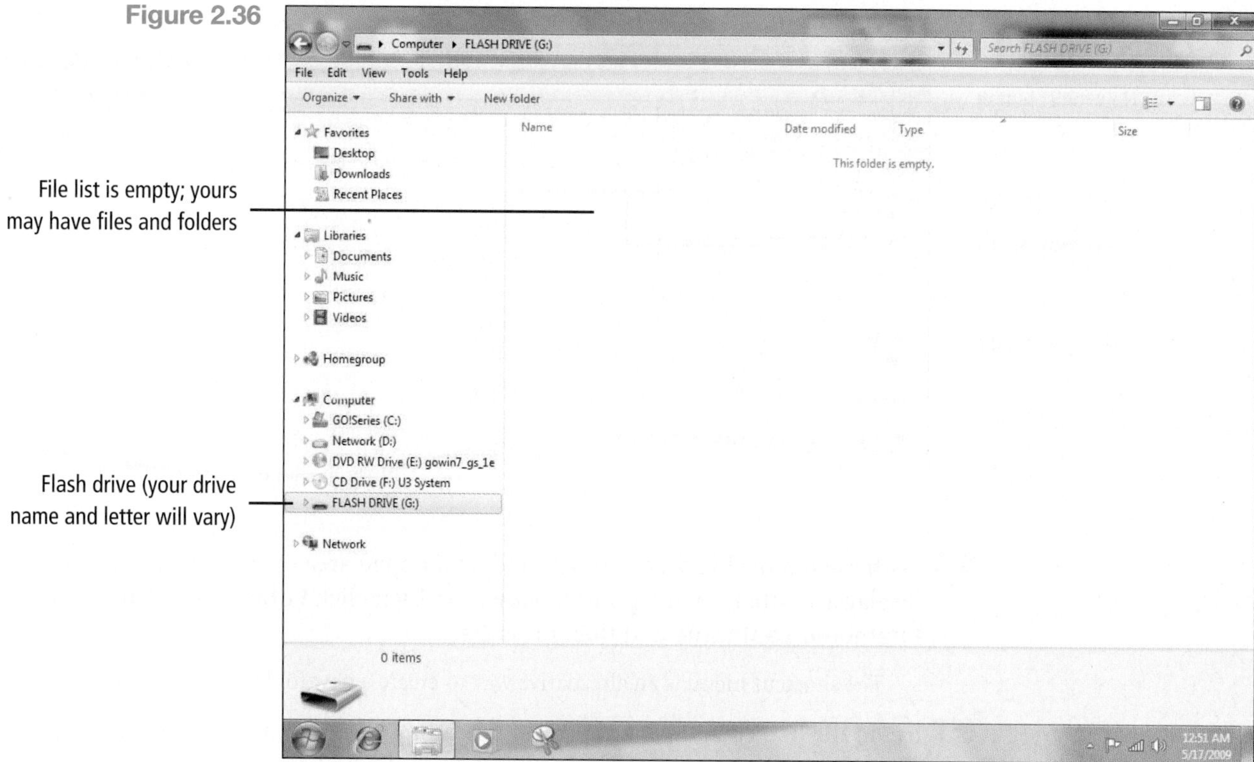

> **More Knowledge | Computer Storage Devices**
>
> The hard drive (local disk) is usually identified on your computer by the notation C: (and sometimes D:, E:, and so on for additional drives). ***Flash drives***—also known as ***USB drives*** or ***thumb drives***—are small storage devices that plug into a computer's Universal Serial Bus (USB) port, which provides a connection between a computer and a peripheral device such as a printer, a mouse, a keyboard, or a USB drive.
>
> You may also have access to files on another type of storage device, a ***CD***—Compact Disc, or a ***DVD***—Digital Video (or Versatile) Disc. CD and DVD drives are optical storage devices that come in two formats—read-only and read-write. If you are using files stored on a read-only CD or a DVD disc, you will need to open a file from the disc, and then save it to a writable drive, or copy a file to another disk and then open it.

Activity 2.11 | Creating a New Folder

It is always a good idea to create a new folder when you have a new category of files to store. You do not need to create a new folder for each type of file, however. You can store many different kinds of files in the same folder.

> **Another Way**
>
> If you accidentally press Enter before you have a chance to name the folder, you can still rename it. Right-click the folder, click Rename from the shortcut menu, type a new name, and then press Enter.

1 With the flash drive selected, in the Command bar, click the **New folder** button.

A new folder—named *New folder*—is created with the name of the folder displayed in the ***edit mode***. Edit mode enables you to change the name of a file or folder, and works the same in all Windows programs.

2 With *New Folder* selected, substitute your name where indicated, and type **Pictures of Firstname Lastname** and then press Enter. Click anywhere in the blank area of the file list to deselect the new folder and compare your screen with Figure 2.37.

Figure 2.37

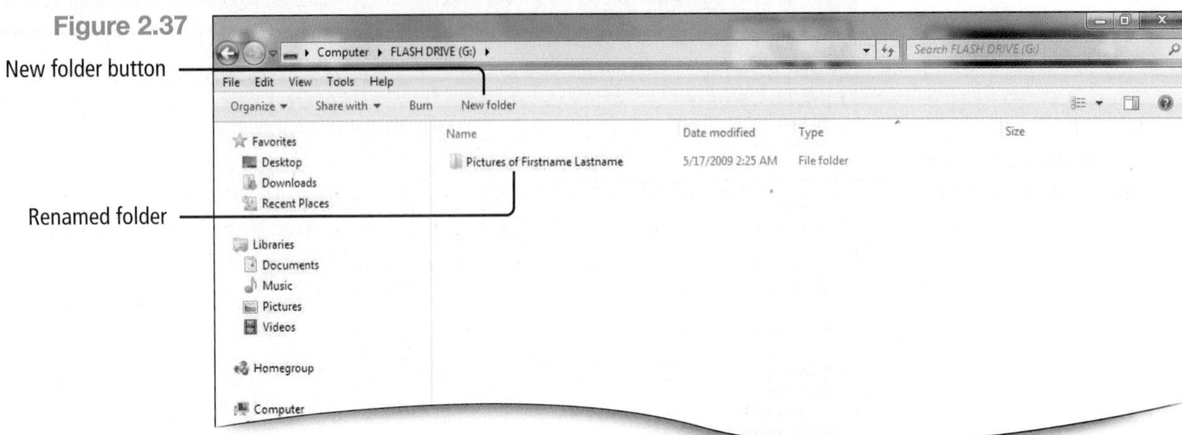

3 With the removable drive still selected, in an open area of the **file list**, right-click to display a shortcut menu, point to **New**, and then click **Folder**. Type **Documents of Firstname Lastname** and then press Enter.

The shortcut menu is an alternative way to create a new folder.

4 In the **file list**, click the **Name** column heading several times to sort the folders and file names from *a* to *z* and from *z* to *a*. Notice that the arrow in the Name column heading points up when the folders are displayed in ***ascending order*** (*a* to *z*), and points down when the folders are displayed in ***descending order*** (*z* to *a*). Stop when the folders are sorted in descending alphabetical order—from *z* to *a*.

5 In the **file list**, move the pointer to the line at the right of the **Name** column heading to display the resize pointer ↔, as shown in Figure 2.38. Drag the resize pointer ↔ to the right or left to make the column slightly wider than the longest folder name.

Figure 2.38

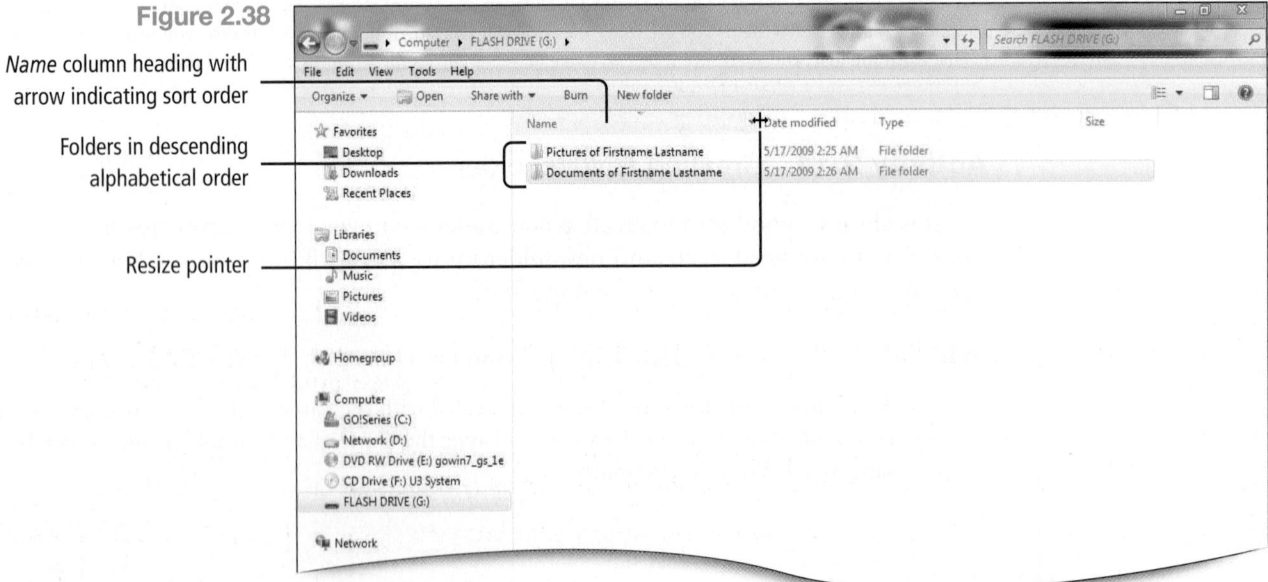

Activity 2.12 | Moving and Renaming Folders

Your student files and folders for this book are stored on a CD or another location chosen by your instructor. You can move the folders, including the files in the folders, from another location to your flash drive or other storage device.

1 Navigate to the location where your student files for this book are stored. They may be stored on a CD, in a course management system, on a hard drive, or on a shared network drive. In this chapter, the data CD is used.

2 In the **Navigation** pane, on the data CD, click the open arrow ▷ to display the folder on the disc. Click the **01_student_data_files** folder, and then compare your screen with Figure 2.39. If your files and folders do not display the way they display in the figure, on the Command bar, to the right of the *Change your view* button, click the *More options* arrow, and then click Details.

There are two folders and a number of files in this folder. The total number of files and folders is displayed in the Details pane at the bottom of the screen. There are more files in the two folders, but they are not included in the totals in the Details pane—only the files and the folders currently displayed in the file list are counted.

Figure 2.39

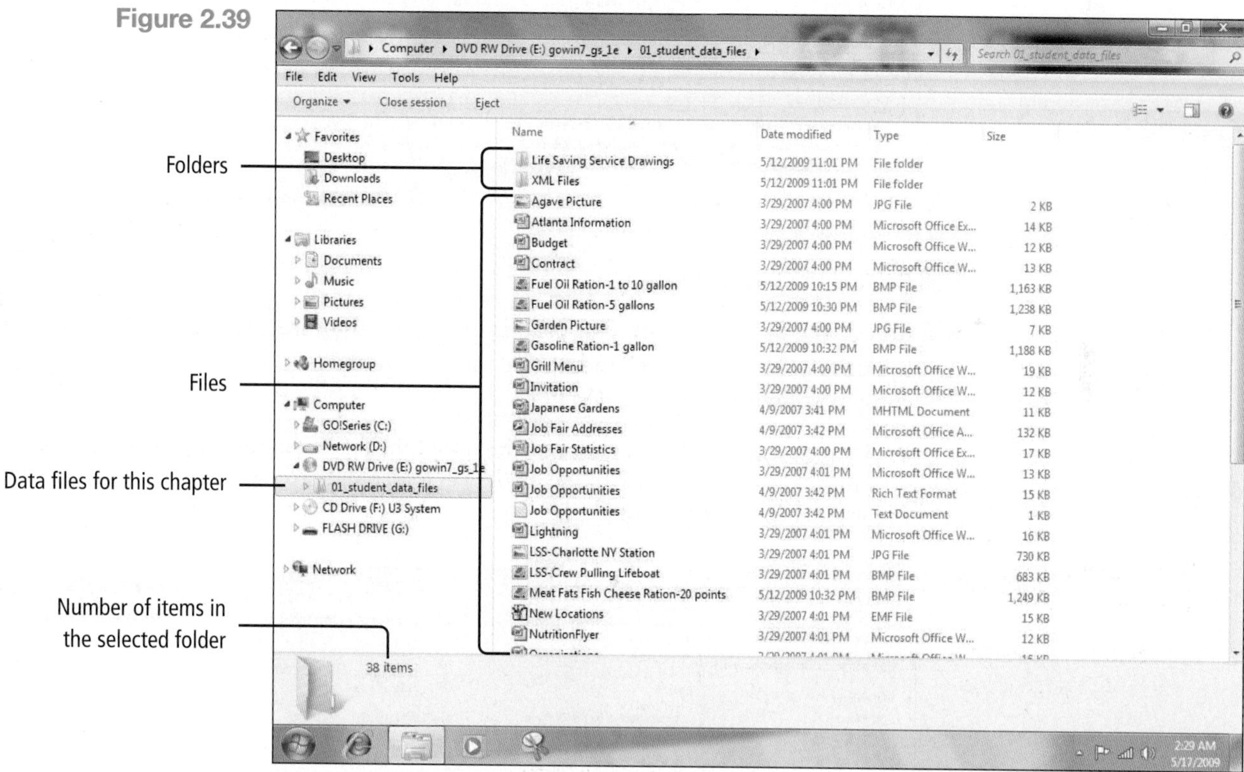

3 In the **file list**, move the pointer to the right border of the **Name** column heading to display the ↔ pointer. Double-click to resize the border to the widest folder or file name. Repeat this procedure to display the full **Date modified** and **Type** column contents.

> **Note | Changing the Columns that Display in the File List**
>
> If one or more of the columns displayed in Figure 2.39 do not display, right-click anywhere in the file list column titles, and then click the desired column.

4 In the **Navigation** pane, if necessary, click the open arrow ▷ to the left of your flash drive. Be sure your student files and folders from the data CD still display in the file list.

5 Near the top of the **file list**, locate the **XML Files** folder. Click on the folder, hold the mouse button down, and drag the folder to the **Navigation** pane directly on top of your storage drive, as shown in Figure 2.40. Notice that a folder displays attached to the pointer, and a ScreenTip says *Copy to FLASH DRIVE (G:)*—your folder or drive name will vary.

Figure 2.40

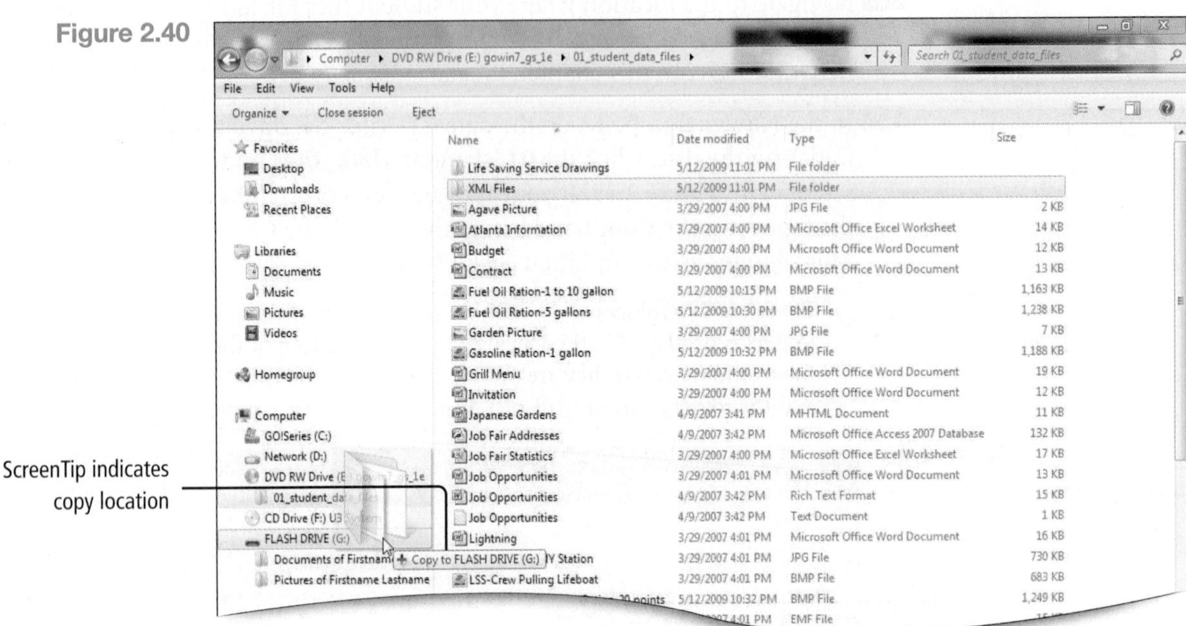

6 Release the mouse button.

7 Repeat the procedure you just practiced to copy the **Life Saving Service Drawings** folder to your flash drive, and notice that a message box indicates the progress of the copy, as shown in Figure 2.41.

The message box displays because the size of the *Life Saving Service Drawings* folder is much larger than the size of the *XML Files* folder and takes a few seconds to copy. The original files remain on the CD.

Figure 2.41

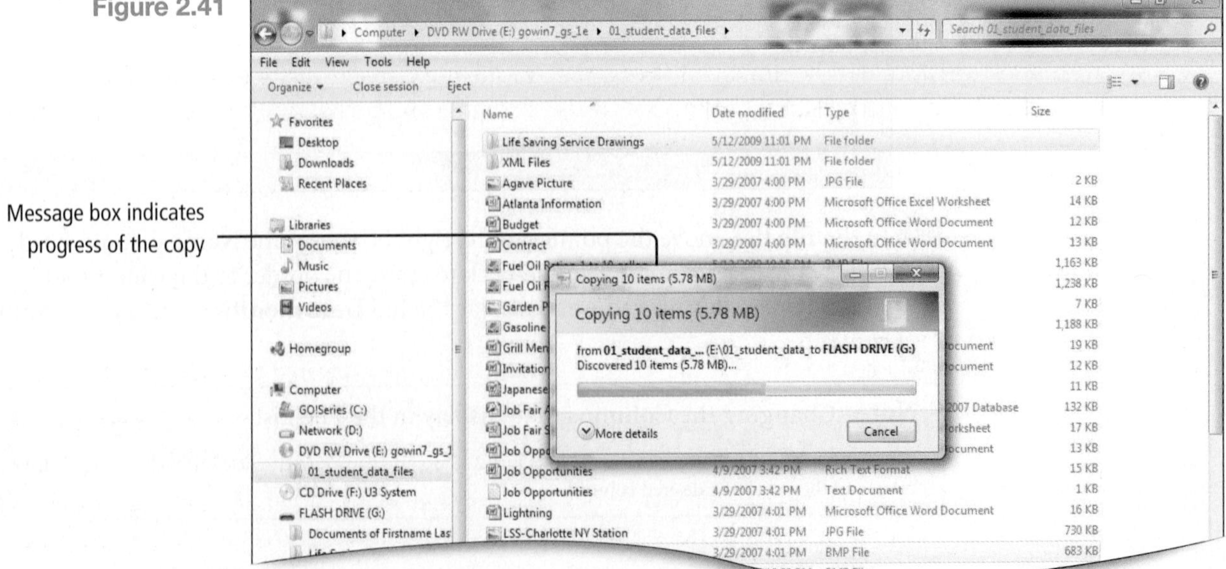

8 In the **Navigation** pane, click the flash drive or other device where you are storing your files and folders. In the **file list**, right-click the **Life Saving Service Drawings** folder, and then from the displayed shortcut menu, click **Rename**.

9 With the folder name in edit mode, type **LSS Drawings** and then press Enter.

The folder name is changed. When text is selected, typing replaces all of the selected text.

10 Use the skills you practiced earlier to create a **Full-screen Snip**. Click the **Save Snip** button. In the **Save As** dialog box, in the left pane, scroll down to display the **Computer** drives. Click your flash drive, and then in the Command bar, click the **New folder** button. Name the new folder **Windows Chapter 2** Press Enter, and then press Enter again to open the new folder. In the **File name** box, type **Lastname_Firstname_1B_Renamed_Folder** Click **Save**, and then **Close** the Snipping Tool window.

Objective 5 | Copy, Move, Rename, and Delete Files

Copying files from one folder to another is a frequent data management task. For example, you might want to make a backup copy of important information, copy a file from a CD to a local disk, or copy information from your local disk drive to a removable drive. Copying files works the same regardless of the type of drive.

Performing other operations on files, such as deleting them or moving them, also works the same regardless of the type of drive. As you accumulate files, you will likely need to delete some to reduce clutter on your hard drive. You might also want to move documents into other folders on another drive to ***archive*** them—place them somewhere for long-term storage. Finally, you may want to change the names of file to make the names more descriptive. All of these tasks are functions of your Windows 7 operating system.

Activity 2.13 | Copying Files

1 In the **Navigation** pane, under **Computer**, scroll to the location where your student data files for this book are stored. Locate and click the folder named **01_student_data_files** to display the files and folders in the folder.

2 In the **Navigation** pane, scroll as necessary to display your flash drive or other storage device. Be sure your student data files and folders still display in the file list.

3 Near the middle of the **file list**, locate the **Garden Picture** file, and then drag it to your storage device. Recall that dragging also includes releasing the mouse button at the destination location.

When you drag a file or folder from one device to another, it is copied, which means that the original file remains on the original drive and a copy of the file is placed on the new drive. If you drag a file or folder to another place (such as a folder) on the same drive—for example, from one folder to another—the file or folder is moved and no longer resides in the original location.

4 Locate the **Grill Menu** file, right-click the file, and then click **Copy**.

This creates a copy of the Grill Menu file and places it in a temporary storage area called the ***Clipboard***. Files in the Clipboard can be placed in other folders using the Paste command.

5 In the **Navigation** pane, click your storage device. In the **file list**, right-click in an open area, and then from the shortcut menu, click **Paste**. Notice that the file is copied to the open folder.

6 Click the **Name** column heading as necessary to sort the folders in ascending order—the arrow in the column heading should be pointing up. Compare your screen with Figure 2.42.

The file list should display five folders—the three that you created and the two that you copied. In addition, the two files that you copied should display below the folders. When you sort a folder in ascending order, the folders always display first.

Figure 2.42

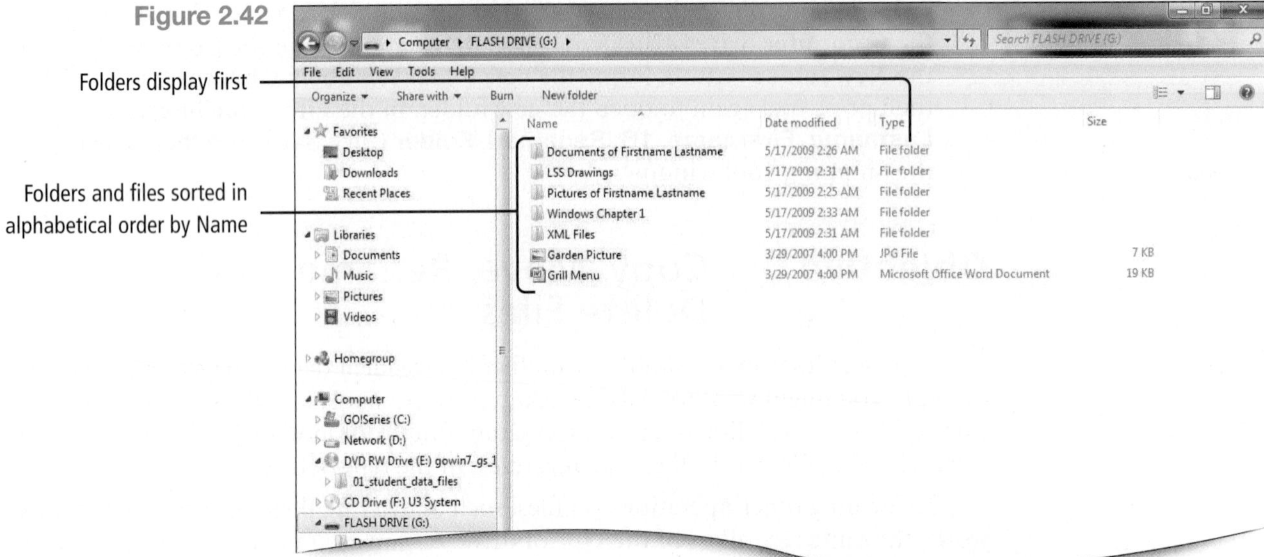

7 Display the files and folders in the **01_student_data_files** folder again. Click the **Atlanta Information** file, hold down Shift, and then click the **Fuel Oil Ration-1 to 10 gallon** file.

By holding down the Shift key, you select the two files you click and all of the files in between.

8 In the **Navigation** pane, scroll as necessary to display your storage area. Drag the selected files to your storage area.

9 Click the **Agave Picture** file, hold down Ctrl, and then click the **Fuel Oil Ration-5 gallons** file, and then the **Gasoline Ration-1 gallon** file. Notice that by using the Control key, you can select several files that are not next to each other, as shown in Figure 2.43.

Figure 2.43

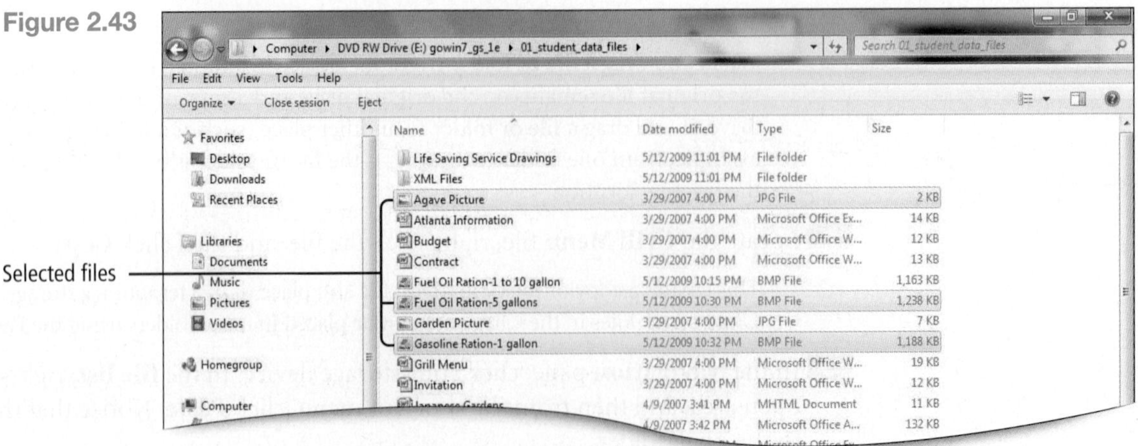

10 Drag the selected files to your storage area.

11 In the **file list**, click the **Invitation** file, and then use the vertical scroll bar to scroll to the bottom of the file list. Hold down Shift, and then click the **Volunteers** file. In the Detail area, notice that the number of files displays, as shown in Figure 2.44. If the total size of the files does not display, in the Details pane, click Show more details.

Figure 2.44

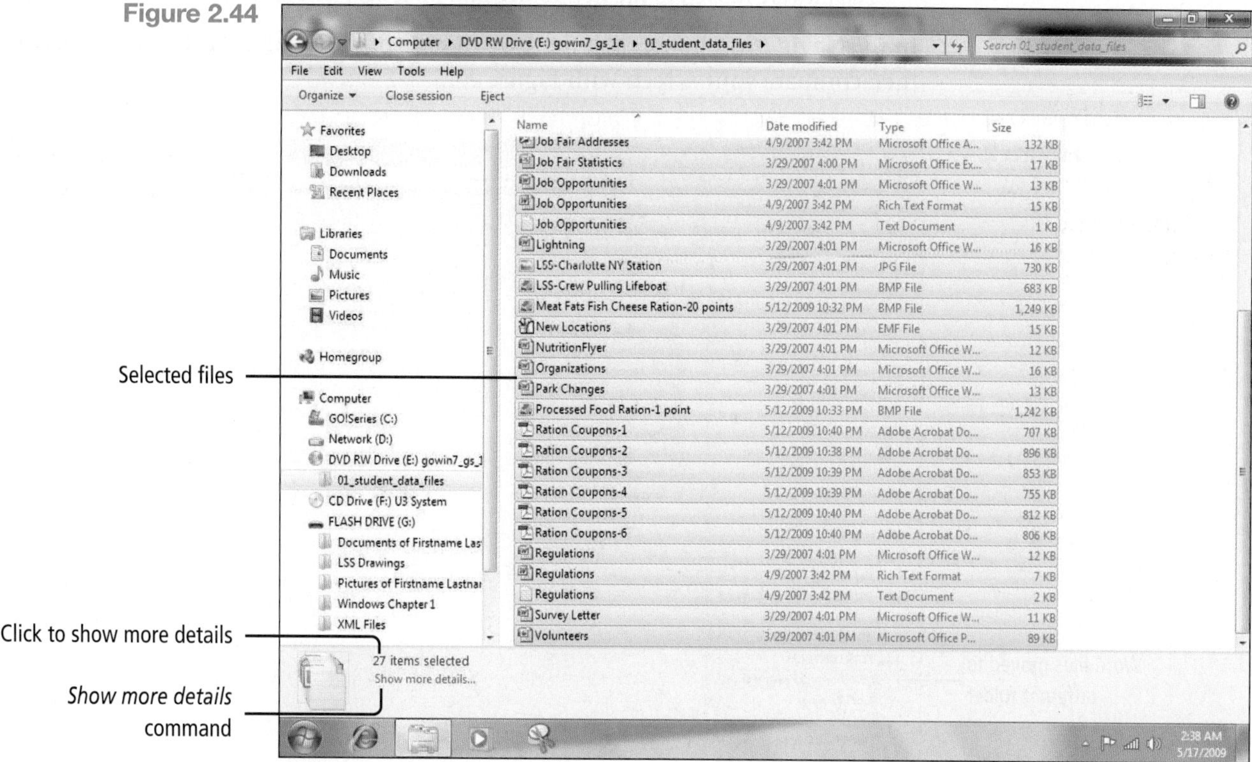

12 Drag the selected files to your storage area.

> **More Knowledge** | **File Extensions**
>
> The files you see may display three or four letters following the file name, such as *.docx*. These are ***file extensions***, and most files have these extensions—although they may or may not display on your system. Files created by Microsoft Office programs have a standard set of extensions that identify the type of program used to create the file. For example, Microsoft Word documents end in *.doc* or *.docx*, Excel worksheets end in *.xls* or *.xlsx*, PowerPoint presentations end with *.ppt* or *pptx*, and so on. The default setting in Windows 7 is to hide the file extensions.

Activity 2.14 | Moving, Renaming, and Deleting Files

In the following activity, you will move files from one location on your removable drive to another location on the same drive. You will also rename and delete files.

1 In the **Navigation** pane, scroll as necessary and then click on your flash drive or other storage device.

Your storage device should display five folders at the top, and a total of 36 files in the drive—41 objects, as displayed in the Details pane.

2 In the **file list**, click the **Type** column header to sort the files by file type. Move the pointer to the right border of the **Type** column heading to display the ✛ pointer. Double-click to resize the border to the widest file type.

3 In the **file list**, use the wheel in the middle of your mouse, or the vertical scroll bar, to scroll down until you can see all of the **Microsoft Office Word Document** files.

4 Click the **Budget** file, hold down Shift, and then click the **Survey Letter** file to select all of the Word documents. Drag the selected files to the **Documents of Firstname Lastname** folder.

The files are moved to the new folder, and no longer display in their original location.

5 In the **Navigation** pane, click the **Documents of Firstname Lastname** folder, and then compare your screen with Figure 2.45.

Figure 2.45

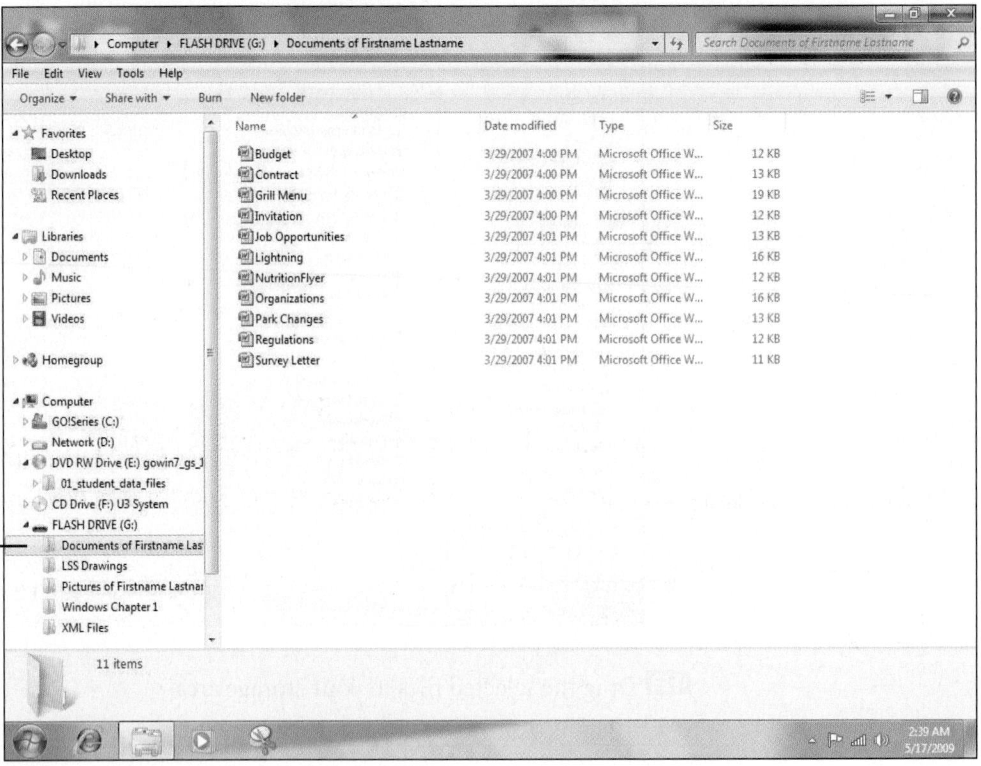

Word files moved to different folder

6 In the **Navigation** pane, click on your flash drive or other storage device. Using the technique you just practiced, select the three **JPG Images**, and then drag them to the **Pictures of Firstname Lastname** folder.

> **Alert! | What if your file types differ?**
>
> Files can be associated with several different programs, and will display a different file type in the Type column. For example, the three files labeled JPG in Figure 2.46 could be called JPEG files on your computer.

7 Select the six **BMP Files** and drag them to the **Pictures of Firstname Lastname** folder. If you do not see files labeled *BMP File*, select the six files beginning with *Fuel Oil Ration-1 to 10 gallon* and ending with *Processed Food Ration-1 point.*

8 In the **Navigation** pane, click the **Pictures of Firstname Lastname** folder, and then compare your screen with Figure 2.46.

Figure 2.46

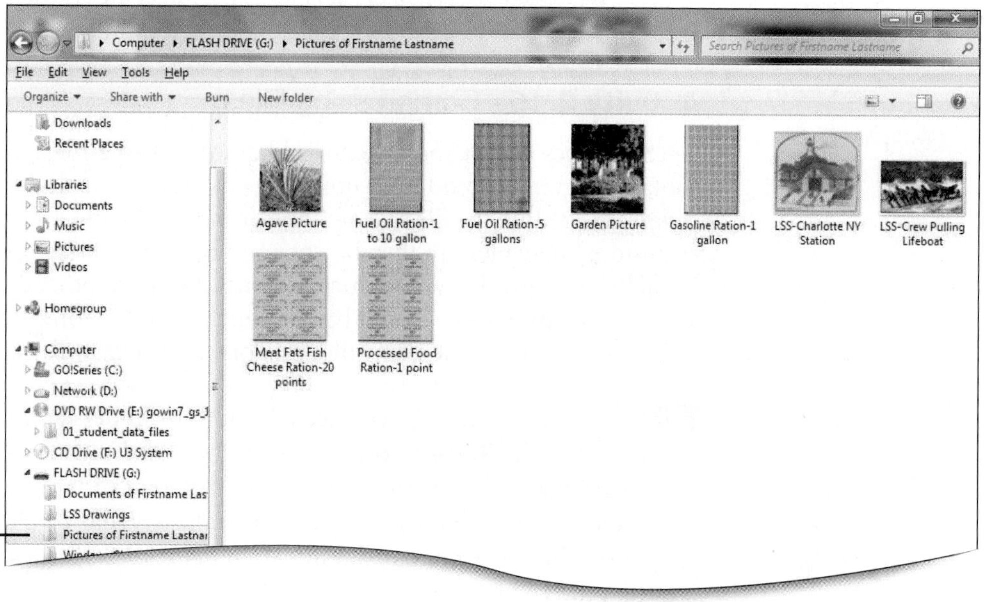

Picture files moved to new folder

9 If thumbnails do not display for the files, on the Command bar, to the right of the **Change your view** button, click the **More options arrow**, and then click **Large Icons**.

10 In the **file list**, right-click the **Agave Picture** file, and then click **Rename**. Type **Agave Cactus** and then press Enter.

11 In the **file list**, right-click the **Garden Picture** file, and then click **Delete**. The **Delete File** message box displays, as shown in Figure 2.47.

Figure 2.47

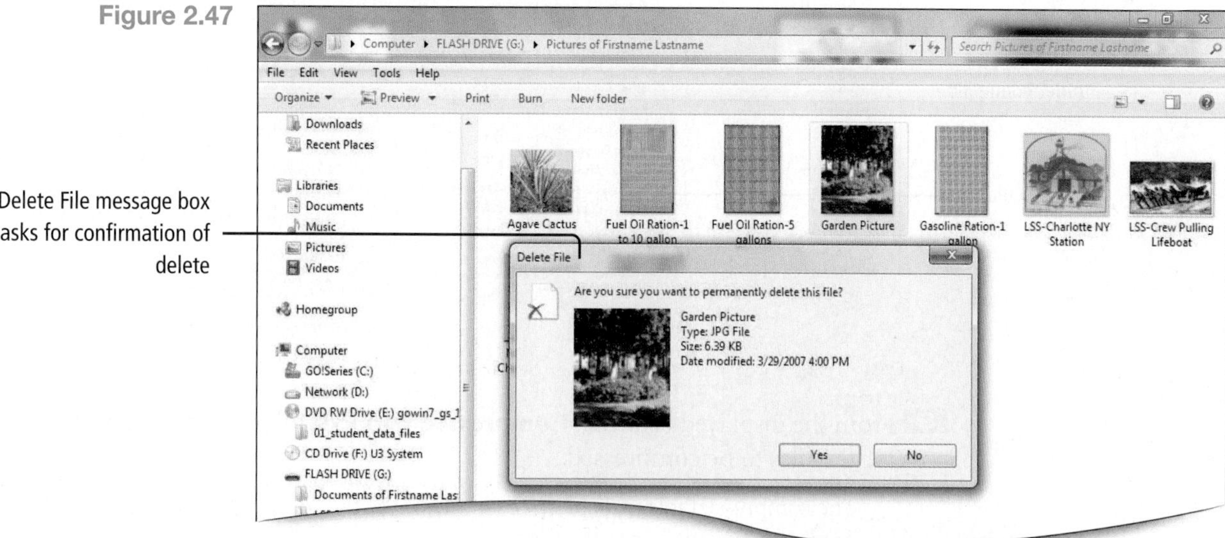

Delete File message box asks for confirmation of delete

12 In the **Delete File** message box, click **Yes** to send the file to the Recycle Bin.

13 In the upper left corner of the window, click the **Back** button to move back to your main storage area.

Another Way

In the Navigation pane, click your flash drive or other storage location name.

14 In the **file list**, right-click the **XML Files** folder, and then click **Delete**. In the displayed **Delete Folder** message box, click **Yes**.

When you delete a folder, all files in the folder are also deleted.

Activity 2.15 | Compressing Files

Some files may be too large to send quickly as an e-mail attachment. For example, files containing graphics tend to be quite large. Windows 7 includes a feature with which you can ***compress***—reduce the file size of—one or more files into a single file that uses a *.zip* file extension. These files can then be uncompressed for editing on any other computer running Windows 7. Many file types—such as most Microsoft Office 2007 files, Adobe Acrobat files, and JPEG picture files—do not benefit much from file compression. However, compression is often used to combine many files into one file for easy distribution.

1 With your storage device selected, and four folders and 16 files displayed in the **file list**, click the **Ration Coupons-1** file, hold down Shift, and then click the second **Regulations** file. If your files are in a different order, select all 16 files, but not the folders. Notice that the Details pane indicates that 16 files are selected. If the total size of the files does not display, under *16 items selected*, click *Show more details*. Notice that the 16 files have a total size of 5.00 MB.

2 In the **file list**, right-click any of the selected files, and then from the displayed shortcut menu, point to **Send to**. Compare your screen with Figure 2.48.

Figure 2.48

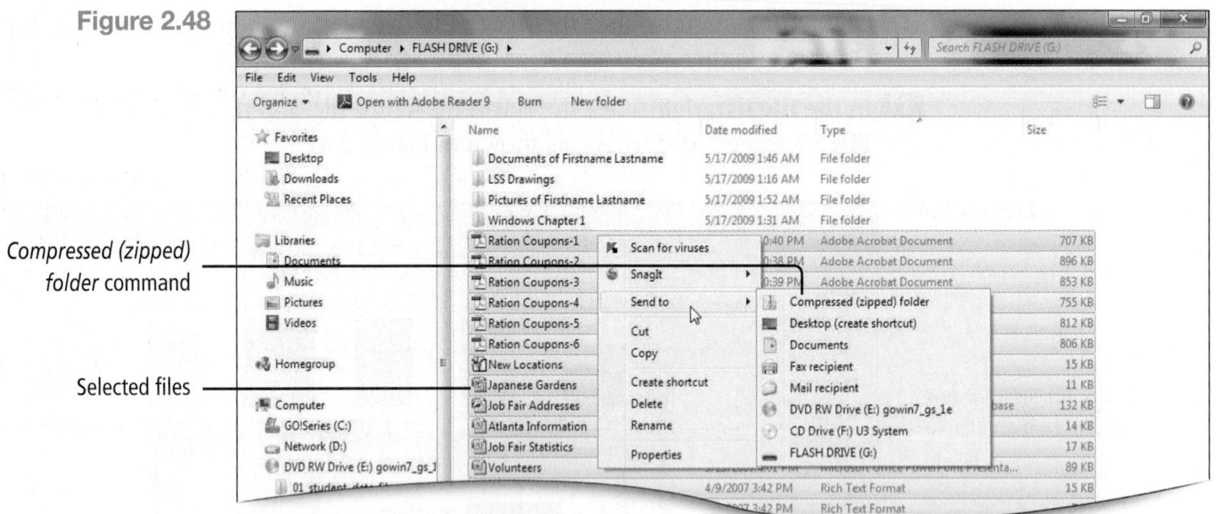

3 From the displayed list, click **Compressed (zipped)** folder, and then wait a moment for the files to be compressed.

The compressed folder displays the name of the file you right-clicked, but displays in edit mode so you can change the file name.

> **Note | To Work with Third-Party Zip Programs**
>
> If you are using a third-party zip program, such as WinZip™ or PKZIP™, you will need to use that program to complete this task—the procedure listed below will not work.

4 With the compressed folder name still in edit mode, type **Files of Firstname Lastname** and then press Enter. Notice that the compressed folder size is approximately 4.9 MB, which is not a great space savings. Compare your screen with Figure 2.49.

Figure 2.49

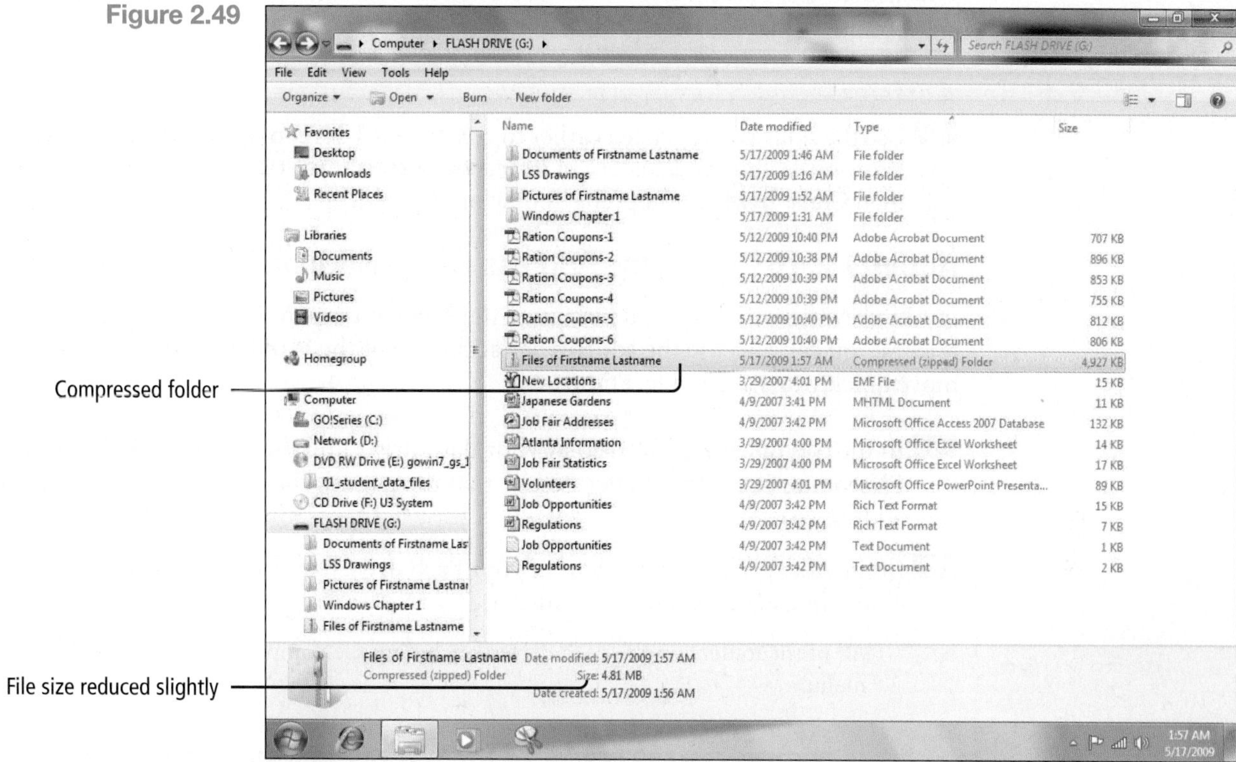

5 In the **file list**, double-click the **Files of Firstname Lastname** compressed folder. Compare your screen with Figure 2.50.

The files in the compressed folder are listed, along with their original sizes and their compressed sizes. The percent of space saved is indicated for each file. Some of the files show very little space savings, while in others the space saved is considerable. To extract the files from the compressed folder, you would click the *Extract all files* button on the Command bar. You can also open the files directly from the compressed folder.

Figure 2.50

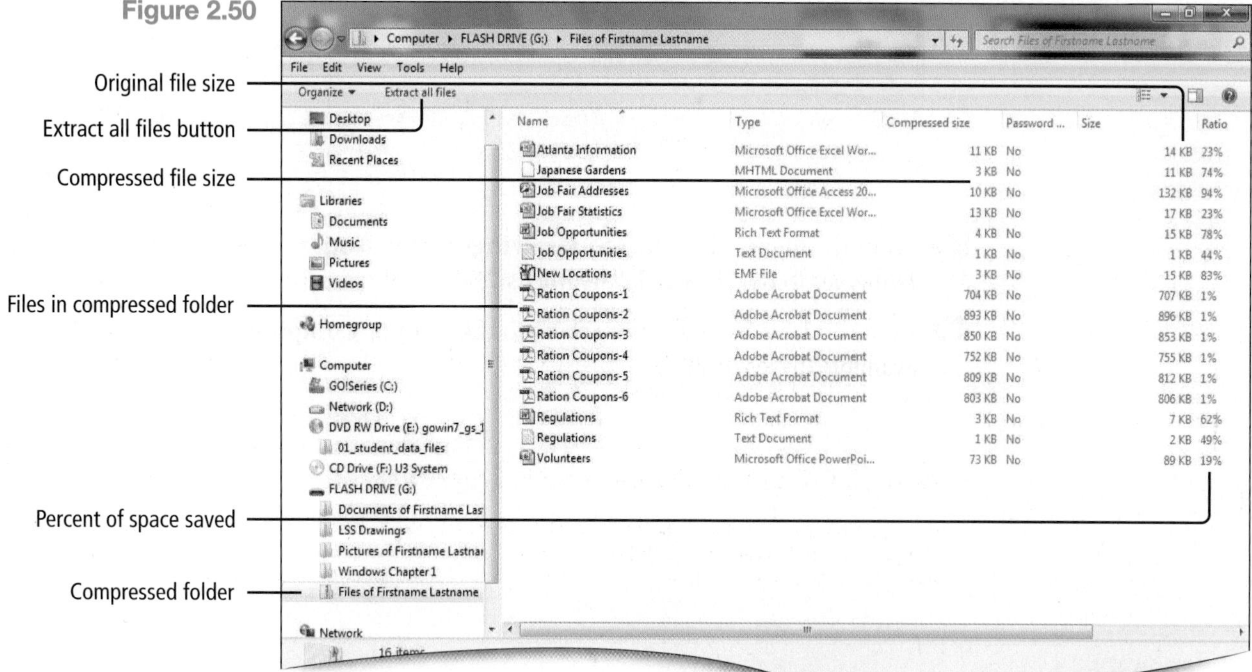

More Knowledge | Adding More Items to a Compressed Folder

You can add more files to an existing compressed folder by dragging files and dropping them on the compressed folder. You can drag the files to the folder from anywhere, and you can also drag folders into a compressed folder.

6 Use the skills you practiced earlier to create a **Full-screen Snip**. **Save Snip** to your **Windows Chapter 2** folder as **Lastname_Firstname_1B_Compressed_Folder** and then **Close** the Snipping Tool window.

Activity 2.16 | Using the Address Bar to Navigate Drives and Folders

In previous activities, you have used the Navigation pane to move between drives and folders. You can also use the address bar at the top of the Windows Explorer window to move quickly to a desired location.

1 In the **Navigation** pane, display your flash drive, and then click the **Pictures of Firstname Lastname** folder. Notice that the path to the current folder displays in the address bar.

2 In the Address bar, to the right of your flash drive name, click the **arrow**, and then compare your screen with Figure 2.51.

All of the folders on the flash drive—including the compressed folder—display in a menu.

Figure 2.51

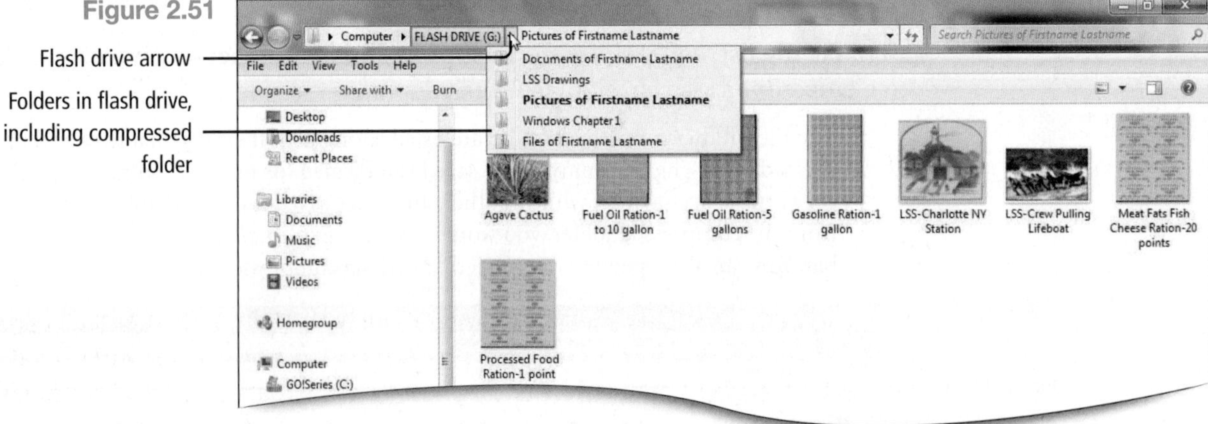

3 From the menu, click the **LSS Drawings** folder. Notice that the contents of the *LSS Drawings* folder display in the file list.

4 In the address bar, click the **arrow** to the right of **Computer**. Notice that all of the available drives display.

5 To the left of **Computer**, click the **arrow**, and then compare your screen with Figure 2.52.

The top-level items in the Navigation pane display in a menu, along with commands for the Control Panel and the Recycle Bin.

Figure 2.52

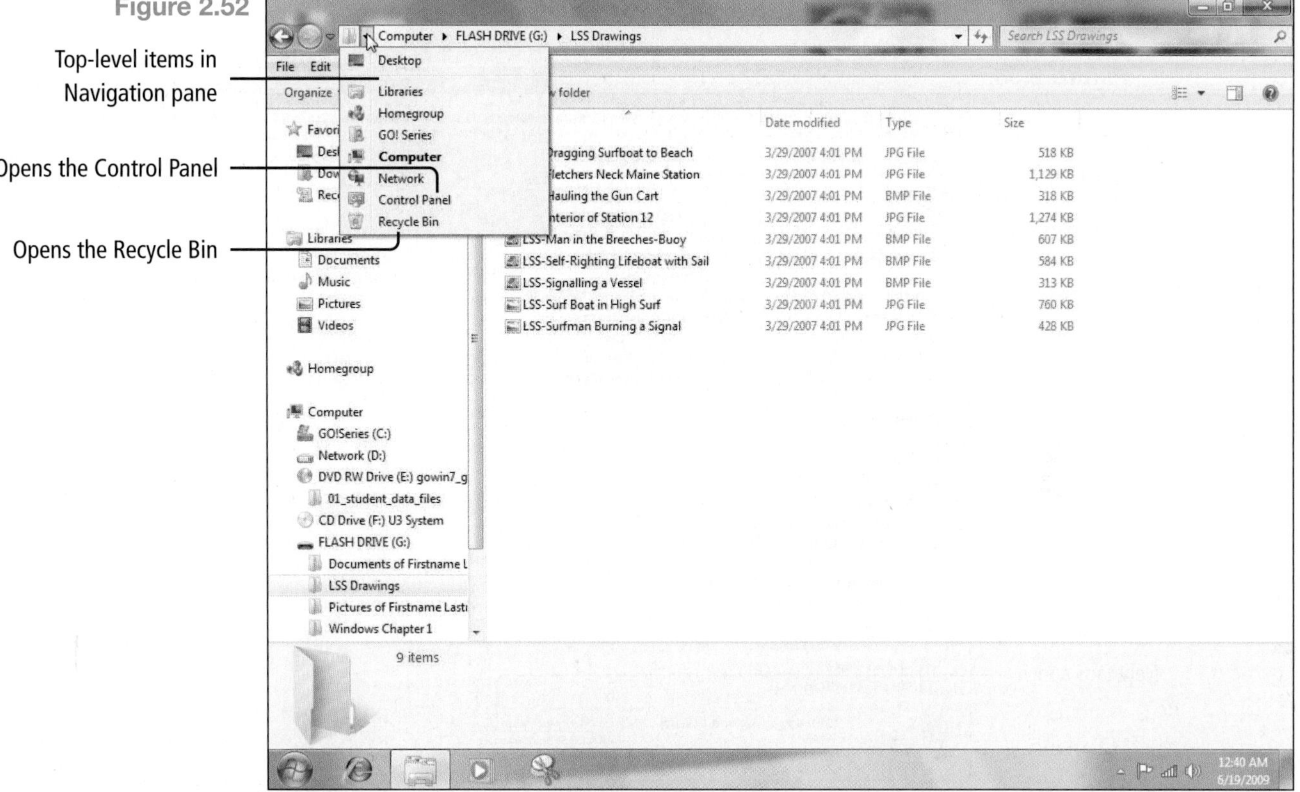

6 Click anywhere in the **file list** to close the menu.

Objective 6 | Find Files and Folders

As you use a computer, you will likely accumulate a large number of files and folders. It's easy to forget where you stored a file, or what you named it. Windows 7 provides several search functions with which you can find files and folders. You can also add tags to files. ***Tags*** are custom file properties that help you find and organize your files. Tags are part of a file's ***metadata***—items that record and display information about a file, such as a title, a rating, the file name, and the file size.

Activity 2.17 | Adding Descriptions and Tags to Files

1 Be sure your storage device is selected, with the contents of the **LSS Drawings** folder displayed in the file list. Also be sure the **Details** pane is open at the bottom of the window.

2 Click the first file in the **file list—LSS-Dragging Surfboat to Beach**. Move the pointer to the line at the top of the **Details** pane to display the [↕] pointer, and then drag the top of the Details pane to display three lines of details.

3 In the **Details** pane, click in the **Tags** box—to the right of the word *Tags*. Type **LSS** and then press →. Type **LSS Boat** and then press →. Type **Surfboat** and then compare your screen with Figure 2.53. Notice on the left side of the Details pane that the file type for this file is JPG—one of a number of image file types.

When you add a tag, a semicolon immediately displays to the right of the insertion point. Semicolons separate multiple tags.

Figure 2.53

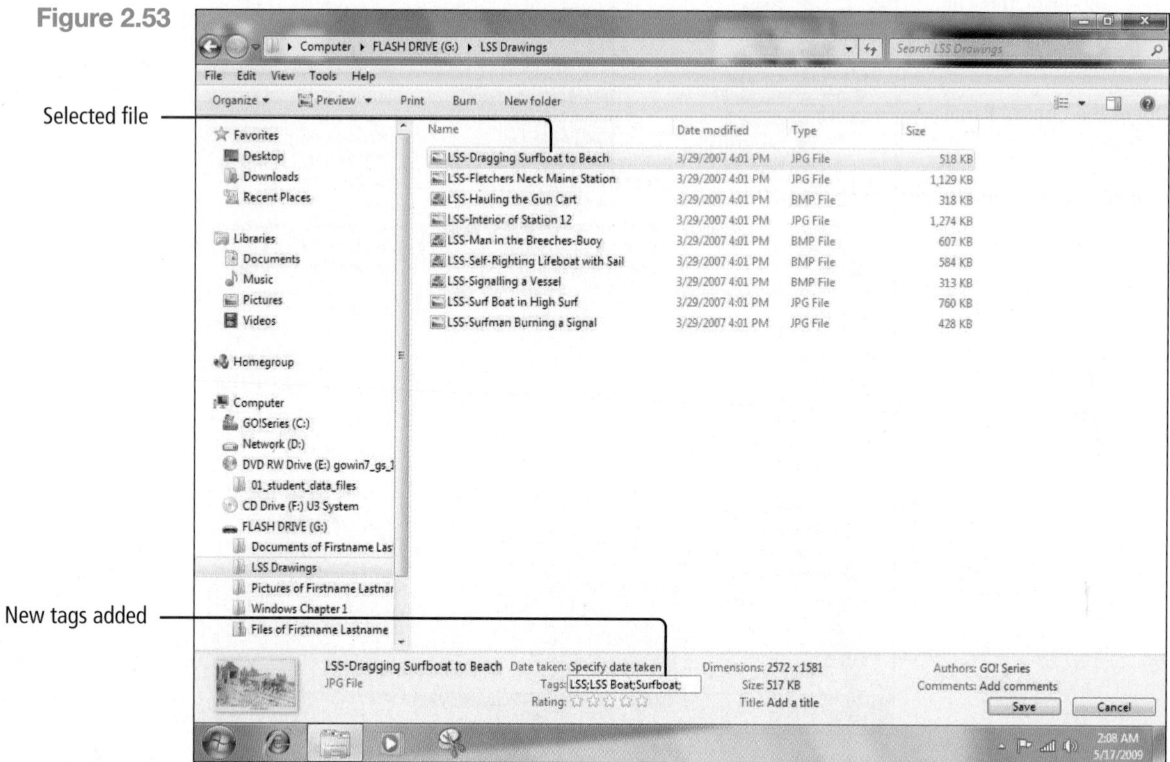

4 Press Enter to confirm the tags. Using the procedure you just practiced, add the same three tags to the **LSS-Surf Boat in High Surf** file. Notice on the left side of the Details pane that the file type for this file is JPG or JPEG.

5 Click the **LSS-Self-Righting Lifeboat with Sail** file. Notice that there is no place to add a tag.

This image is a bitmap image, which does not support tags. Most Microsoft Office 2007 and 2010 default file formats support tags, as do many other file formats.

6 In the **Navigation** pane, click the **Pictures of Firstname Lastname** folder, and then click the file **LSS-Charlotte NY Station**. Add the following tags: **LSS** and **LSS Boat** and **LSS Boat Ramp** and then press Enter.

7 In the **Details** pane, click the **Title** box, type **Life Saving Station at Charlotte, NY** and then press Enter.

8 In the **file list**, right-click the **LSS-Charlotte NY Station** file, and then from the shortcut menu, click **Properties**. In the **Properties** dialog box, click the **Details tab**.

The items you entered in the Details pane display, and there are several other categories of tags that you can add, including a rating of the picture or document.

9 In the **Properties** dialog box, under **Description**, click the fourth **Rating** star from the left. Under **Origin**, click the **Copyright** box, type **Public Domain** and then compare your screen with Figure 2.54.

Figure 2.54

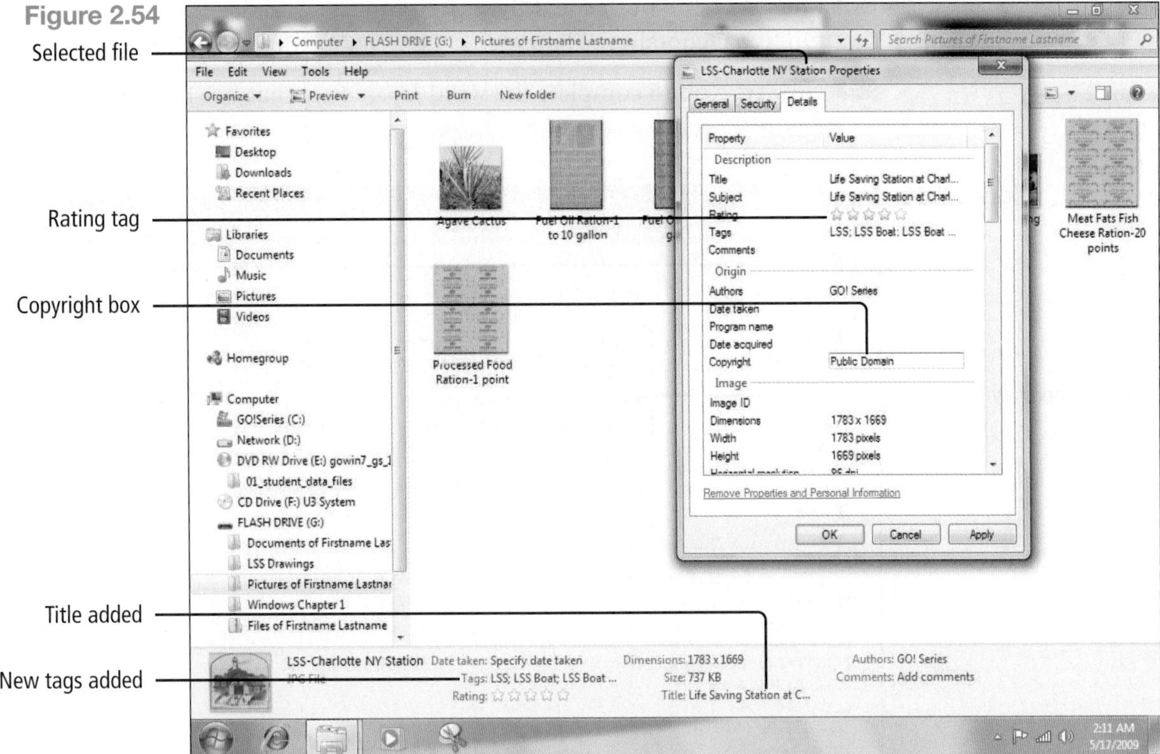

10 At the bottom of the **Properties** dialog box, click **OK**.

Activity 2.18 | Finding Files and Folders and Creating a Search Folder

1 In the **Navigation** pane, click your storage location name. Be sure your storage device is selected, and four folders, one compressed folder, and 16 files display in the file list.

2 Near the upper right corner of the window, click in the **Search** box, type **J** and then in the **file list**, examine the results of your search, as shown in Figure 2.55. If your search results do not display in the list format, to the right of the *Change your view* button, click the *More options* arrow, and then click Details.

The program found all files and folders with words that begin with the letter *J*, along with all file types (file extensions) with words that begin with the letter *J*—in this case, all JPEG image files. Your files may display in a different order.

Figure 2.55

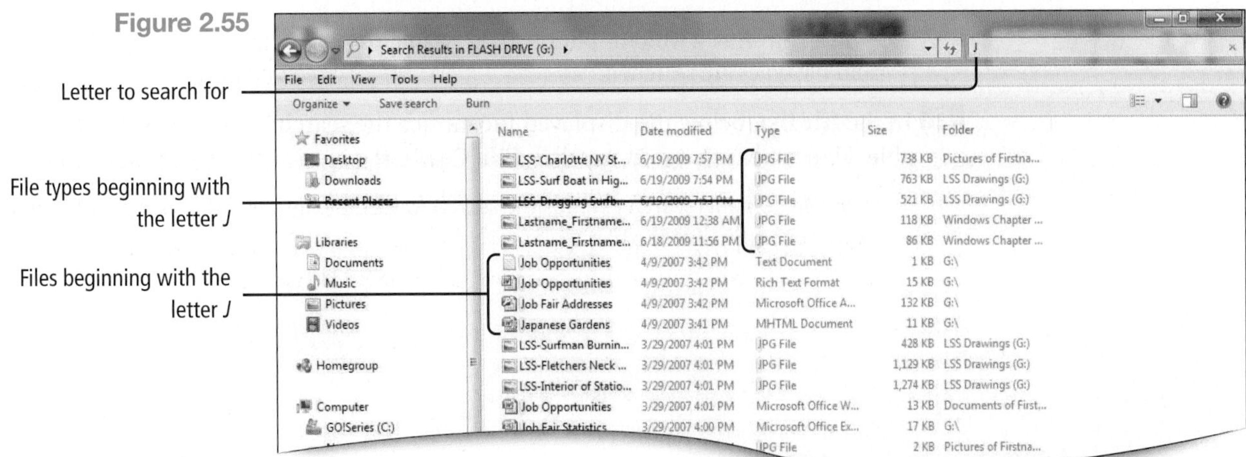

3 With the letter *J* already in the **Search** box, type the letter **P** and examine the search results. Notice that the only files, folders, or file types in your storage device that begin with the letters *JP* are the JPEG image files.

4 Press Bksp, and notice that the search results again display all files, folders, and file types that contain the letter *J*.

5 Now type **ob** to complete the word *Job*. Notice that five files display, as shown in Figure 2.56.

Figure 2.56

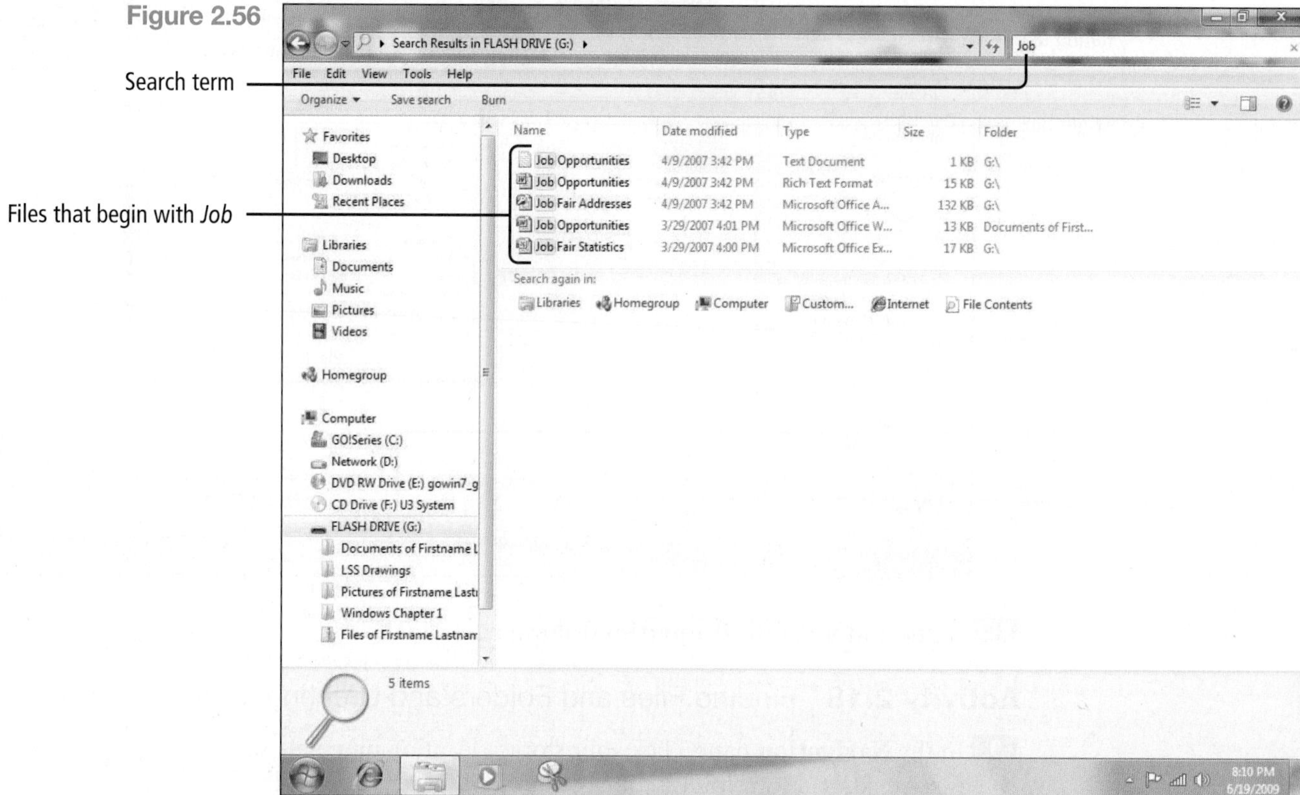

6 Press Bksp three times, type **LSS** and then notice that files and folders from various locations display in the file list.

7 Press Spacebar, type **boat** and then notice that only one file or folder meets this search condition, even though you added *LSS Boat* as a tag to several files. Also notice that the file that was found had both search words, but they do not have to be next to each other.

When you enter a word or phrase in the Search pane, only the file names, folder names, and file types are searched.

8 In the **file list**, below the displayed file, notice the search alternatives that are available. Under **Search again in**, click **File Contents**. Notice that three files display.

The *File Contents* search extends the search to include tags, text that is a portion of a file name, or text inside the file.

9 On the Command bar, click the **Save search** button. In the displayed **Save As** dialog box, click **Save**. Compare your screen with Figure 2.57.

A ***search folder*** is saved on your computer under **Favorites**—not on your removable storage device. A search folder retains all of the search conditions you specified during your search, and recreates the search every time you click the search folder. As you add more pictures with the *LSS Boat* tag to your removable storage device, the search folder will find them. It is important to remember that the search folder will only search the location you specified—it will not search the rest of the computer.

Figure 2.57

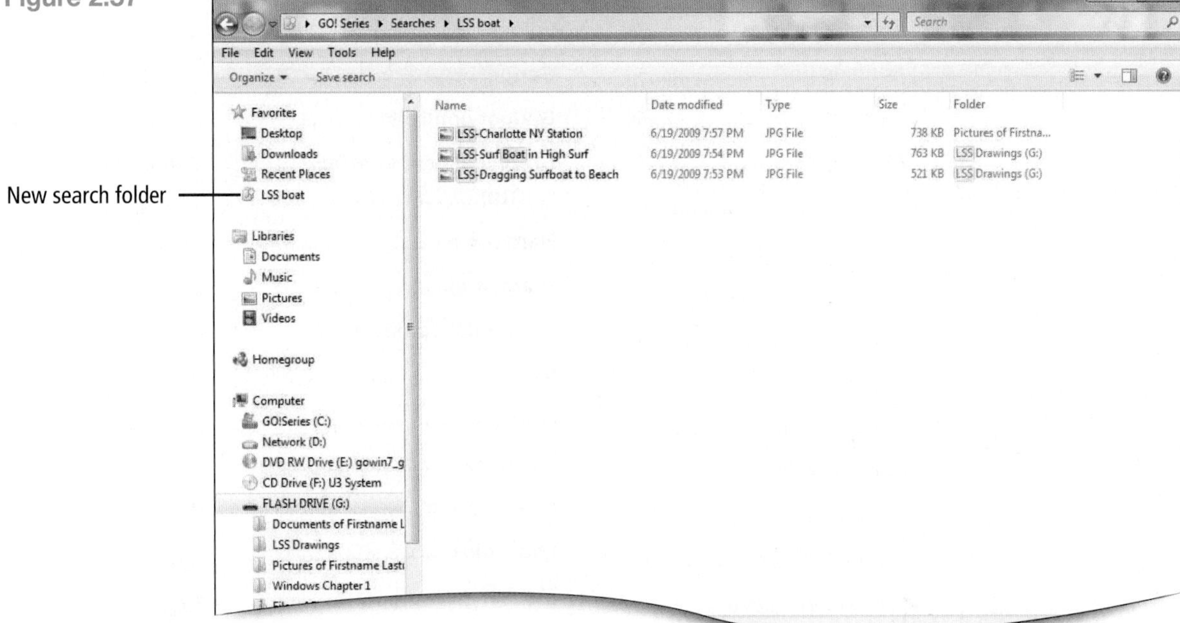

10 Use the skills you practiced earlier to create a **Full-screen Snip**. **Save** the snip to your **Windows Chapter 2** folder as **Lastname_Firstname_1B_Search_Folder** and submit all three file snips from Project 2B as directed. If you are directed to print the files, use the skills practiced in Activity 2.9 to create a WordPad document, add your name, drag the three snip files from this project, and then print the document. It is not necessary to save the WordPad file once you have printed it.

11 In the title bar, click the **Close**  button to close the Windows Explorer window. Select and **Delete** the files and shortcuts you saved on the desktop, and then **Close** the gadgets that you added to the desktop.

More Knowledge | Using Wildcards in Searches

When you are searching for a particular type of file, you can specify the extension by using a wildcard, followed by the extension. A ***wildcard*** takes the place of one or more characters in a search. For example, if you wanted to search for all of your Excel 2007 files in the My Documents folder, select the folder, and then type **.xlsx* in the Search box. All files with the *.xlsx* extension will display. If you want to display all of your Excel files, including older versions (with the *.xls* extension), type **.xls*. This search will locate all *.xls* and *.xlsx* files. Similarly, you can search for all files beginning with *Fun* by typing *Fun**, which will return all files with those first three letters, including *Fundamentals of Business* and *Fun with Trombones*.

End **You have completed Project 2B**

Summary

Windows 7 is a robust operating system that enables you to easily locate information and programs. It enables you to create, rename, move, copy, and delete files and folders. You can add key words and other information to the files to make searching easier and more accurate.

Key Terms

Active window 76
Address bar 66
Aero 68
All Programs 74
Archive 95
Ascending order 92
CD 91
Click 65
Clipboard 95
Close button 66
Command bar 64
Compress 100
Computer icon 64
Context-sensitive command 66
Descending order 92
Desktop 63
Desktop background 70
Details pane 66
Dialog box 69
Double-click 66
Drag 85
Drive 67
DVD 91
Edit mode 91
Favorites 66
File 89
File extension 97
File list 67
Flash drive 91
Folder 89
Gadget 71
Gadget controls 72
Graphical user interface (GUI) 67
Hard drive 67
Hardware 63
Horizontal scroll bar 82
Icon 64
Jump list 83
Libraries 65
Library pane 66
Local disk 89
Maximize 79
Menu 66
Menu bar 66
Metadata 103
Minimize 79
Mouse pointer 64
Navigation pane 66
Notification area 64
Operating system 63
Paint 82
Peek 81
Pinned programs area 74
Pointer 64
Recycle Bin 64
Restore 79
Right-click 66
Screen saver 68
ScreenTip 66
Scroll box 86
Search box 66
Search folder 107
Shake 81
Shortcut menu 66
Snip 78
Snipping Tool 78
Start button 64
Start menu 73
Status area 64
Submenu 74
System tray 64
Tags 103
Taskbar 64
Thumb drive 91
Thumbnail 82
Title bar 66
Toolbar 66
USB drive 91
Vertical scroll bar 82
Wildcard 107
Window 65
Window name 75
Windows 63
Windows Aero 68
Windows Explorer 65
WordPad 76

Screen ID

Identify each element of the screen by matching callout numbers shown in Figure 2.58 to a corresponding description.

Figure 2.58

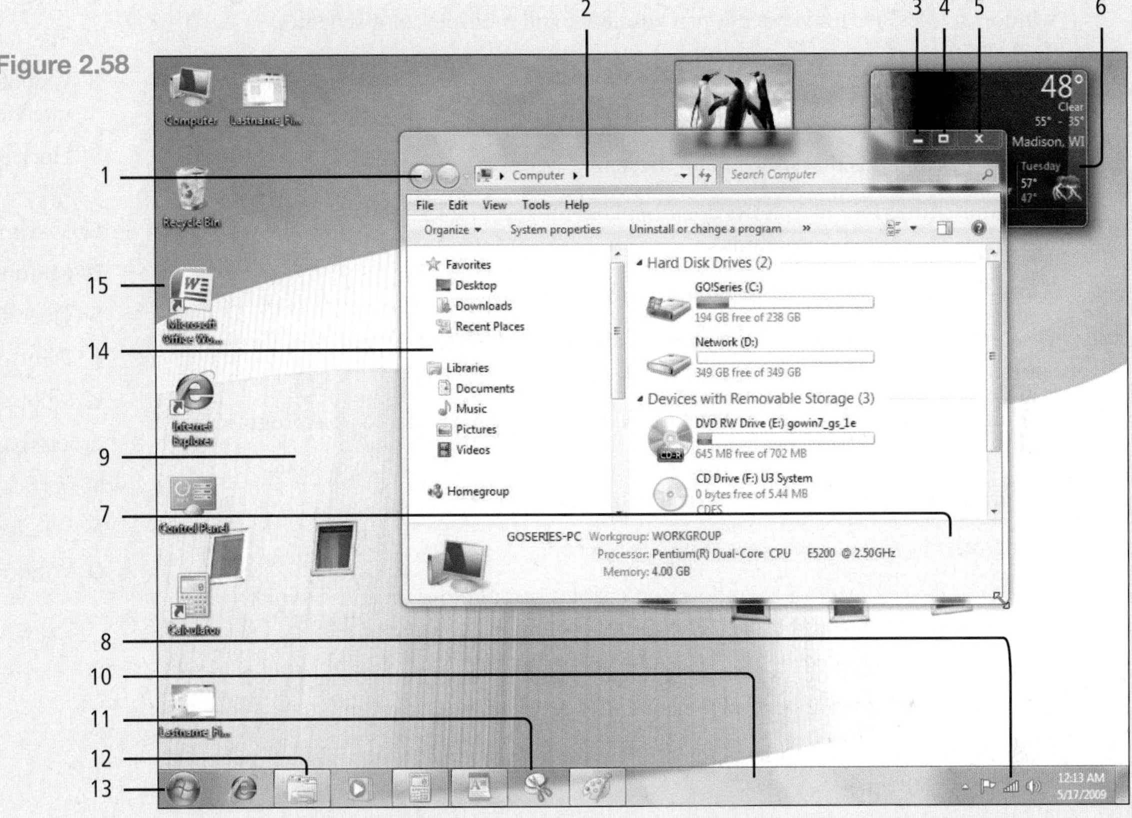

_____ A. Address bar

_____ B. Back button

_____ C. Close button

_____ D. Desktop

_____ E. Details pane

_____ F. Gadget

_____ G. Icon

_____ H. Maximize button

_____ I. Minimize button

_____ J. Navigation pane

_____ K. Notification area

_____ L. Snipping Tool button

_____ M. Start button

_____ N. Taskbar

_____ O. Windows Explorer button

Content-Based Assessments

Matching

Match each term in the second column with its correct definition in the first column. Write the letter of the term on the blank line in front of the correct definition.

____ 1. The Windows 7 user interface that features a three-dimensional look, with transparent window frames, live previews of open windows, and multiple color schemes.

____ 2. A program that captures a screen or part of a screen.

____ 3. Displays information about the drive, folder, or file selected in the file list.

____ 4. A set of instructions that coordinates the activities of your computer.

____ 5. A computer interface that shows documents as they will look in their final form and uses icons to represent programs.

____ 6. A simple drawing program included with Windows 7.

____ 7. Displays the Start button and the name of any open documents; it may also display shortcut buttons for other programs.

____ 8. Command at the bottom of the Start menu that takes you to all available programs on your computer.

____ 9. To remove the window from the screen without closing it.

____ 10. To increase the size of a window to fill the screen.

____ 11. The bar at the right side of a window that enables you to move up and down to view information that extends beyond the top and bottom of the screen.

____ 12. The bar at the bottom of a window that enables you to move left and right to view information that extends beyond the left and right edges of the screen.

____ 13. Move the mouse pointer while holding down the left mouse button, and then release at the appropriate time.

____ 14. Work that you save and store on a drive, such as a Word document or a PowerPoint presentation.

____ 15. A program that enables you to create and manage folders, and copy, move, sort, and delete files.

A All Programs
B Details pane
C Drag
D File
E Graphical user interface
F Horizontal scroll bar
G Maximize
H Minimize
I Operating system
J Paint
K Snipping Tool
L Taskbar
M Vertical scroll bar
N Windows Aero
O Windows Explorer

Content-Based Assessments

Multiple Choice

Circle the correct answer.

1. In the Windows Explorer window, this pane displays Favorites, Libraries, Computer, and Network information.
   a. Preview **b.** Navigation **c.** Details
2. The working area of the Windows 7 screen—consisting of program icons, a taskbar, a Start button, and gadgets—is the:
   a. desktop **b.** window **c.** Notification area
3. The arrow, I-beam, or other symbol that shows the location or position of the mouse on your screen is the mouse:
   a. button **b.** cursor **c.** pointer
4. The area on the right side of the taskbar that keeps you informed about processes that are occurring in the background, such as antivirus software, network connections, and other utility programs, is the:
   a. Quick Launch toolbar **b.** Notification area **c.** program icon
5. Custom file properties such as names, places, and descriptions that are added to files are called:
   a. jump lists **b.** details **c.** metadata
6. You can activate this by pointing to an object and clicking the right mouse button.
   a. active window **b.** shortcut menu **c.** gadget
7. When you create a new folder, the folder name displays:
   a. in edit mode **b.** in the Details pane **c.** on the desktop
8. When you create a search folder, it displays in the Navigation pane under this category:
   a. Favorites **b.** Computer **c.** Libraries
9. A dynamic program—such as a clock, a stock market ticker, or a weather window—that displays on the desktop is a:
   a. gadget **b.** tag **c.** snip
10. The three or four characters to the right of the period in a file name is called:
    a. metadata **b.** a wildcard **c.** a file extension

Skills Review | Project 2C Using Windows 7

Apply a combination of the 2A and 2B skills.

In the following Skills Review, you will copy files from your student data disk to a flash drive, create and rename folders, and move files. You will also add tags to files and search for files using the Search box. Your completed documents will look similar to the ones shown in Figure 2.59.

Project Files

For Project 2C, you will need the following files:

36 sample files, and two folders containing 14 additional files

You will save your documents as:

Lastname_Firstname_1C_Screen_Saver
Lastname_Firstname_1C_Desktop
Lastname_Firstname_1C_Folders
Lastname_Firstname_1C_Tags

Project Results

Figure 2.59

(Project 2C Using Windows 7 continues on the next page)

Skills Review | Project 2C Using Windows 7 (continued)

1 Turn on your computer and if necessary follow the log-on instructions required for the computer you are using.

2 Move the pointer to an open area of the desktop, and then right-click. From the shortcut menu, move the pointer to the bottom of the list, and then click **Personalize**. At the bottom of the **Personalization** window, click the **Screen Saver** button. Click the **Screen saver box arrow**, and then from the displayed list, click **Bubbles**.

3 If the **Snipping Tool** does not display on your taskbar, click the **Start** button, point to **All Programs**, click **Accessories**, right-click **Snipping Tool**, and then click **Pin to Taskbar**. On the taskbar, click the **Snipping Tool** button. In the **Snipping Tool** window, click the arrow to the right of the **New** button, and then click **Full-screen Snip**.

4 In the **Snipping Tool** window, click the **Save Snip** button. In the **Save As** dialog box, in the left pane, scroll down to display the **Computer** drives. Click your flash drive, and then in the Command bar, click the **New folder** button. Name the new folder **Windows Project C** Press Enter, and then press Enter again to open the new folder. In the **File name** box, type **Lastname_Firstname_1C_Screen_Saver** Be sure the **Save as type** box displays *JPEG file*. Click **Save**, and then **Close** the Snipping Tool window.

5 If you want to use the Bubbles screen saver, at the bottom of the Screen Saver Settings dialog box, click OK; otherwise, click Cancel.

6 At the bottom of the **Personalization** window, click **Desktop Background**. Use the vertical scroll bar to display the **United States** desktop backgrounds, and then click the picture of the **stone arch**. Click **Save changes** to apply the new background, and then **Close** the Personalization window.

7 Click the **Start** button, point to **All Programs**, and then click **Accessories**. Right-click **WordPad**, point to **Send to**, click **Desktop (create shortcut)**, and then click in any open area of the desktop.

8 In an open area of the desktop, right-click to display a shortcut menu, and then click **Gadgets**. Double-click the **Clock** gadget, double-click the **Stocks** gadget, and then double-click the **CPU Meter** gadget. **Close** the Gadgets window. Point to the **CPU Usage** gadget, and then click the **Larger size** button. Drag the **CPU Usage** gadget to the top of the desktop.

9 Use the skills you practiced to create a **Full-screen Snip** of the desktop, **Save** it in the **Windows Project C** folder as **Lastname_Firstname_1C_Desktop** and then **Close** the Snipping Tool window.

10 On the taskbar, click the **Windows Explorer** button. If this button is not available, click the Start button, point to All Programs, click Accessories, and then click Windows Explorer. Insert your student data CD. In the **Windows Explorer** window, in the **Navigation** pane, click the drive that contains your student data files. To the left of the drive name, click the open arrow to display the **01_student_data_files** folder, and then click that folder to display the folders and files in the file list.

11 In the **Navigation** pane, in the drive that contains your student files, be sure the folders display. In the **file list**, drag the **XML Files** folder to the **Windows Project C** folder on your flash drive.

12 At the top of the **file list**, click the **Type** column heading. Widen the **Type** column so you can see all of the file types. Click the first **Adobe Acrobat** document—*Ration Coupons-1*—, hold down Shift, and then click the last **Adobe Acrobat** document—*Ration Coupons-6*. Drag the selected files to the **Windows Project C** folder on your flash drive. Then, select all of the files with a **Type** that begins *Microsoft Office*. Drag these 15 files to the **Windows Project C** folder on your flash drive.

13 In the **Navigation** pane, locate your flash drive, and then click the **Windows Project C** folder. On the Command bar click the **New Folder** button, and then name the folder **Adobe Acrobat Files** Select the six **Adobe Acrobat Files** and drag them to the folder you just created. In the **Navigation** pane, expand the **Windows Project C** folder, and then click the **Windows Project C** folder to display the folder contents.

14 In the **file list**, right-click the file **Volunteers**, and then click **Rename**. Rename the file **Job Fair Volunteers** In the same list of files, right-click the **Lightning** file, and then from the shortcut menu, click **Delete**. In the message box, click **Yes**.

15 At the top of the **file list**, click the **Name** column heading as necessary to display the folders and files in ascending (*a* to *z*) order. Use the skills you practiced to create a **Full-screen Snip** of the Windows Explorer window, **Save** it in the **Windows Project C** folder as

(Project 2C Using Windows 7 continues on the next page)

Skills Review | Project 2C Using Windows 7 (continued)

Lastname_Firstname_1C_Folders and then **Close** the Snipping Tool window.

16 In the **file list**, click the **Job Fair Statistics** file. In the **Details** pane, click to the right of **Tags**. In the **Tags** box, type **Atlanta** press →, and then type **Job Fair** Add the same tags to the **Atlanta Information** file.

17 In the **Search** box, type **Atlanta** and then press Enter. In the **file list**, click **File Contents** to include files with the word *Atlanta* in the files or in the file tags. If necessary, change the display to Details. Use the skills you practiced to create a **Full-screen Snip** of the Windows Explorer window, **Save** it in the **Windows Project C** folder as **Lastname_Firstname_1C_Tags** and then **Close** the Snipping Tool window.

18 Submit all four snips as directed. If you are directed to print the files, use the skills practiced in Activity 2.9 to create a WordPad document, add your name, drag the four snip files from this project, and then print the document. It is not necessary to save the WordPad file once you have printed it.

19 Remove all desktop and taskbar shortcuts that you created in this project, and then **Close** all three gadgets that you added.

End **You have completed Project 2C**

Getting Started with Internet Explorer 8

OBJECTIVES

At the end of this chapter you will be able to:

PROJECT 3A

Use Internet Explorer 8 to Navigate and Search the Internet, Create and Manage Favorite Internet Sites, and Save and Print Web Pages.

OUTCOMES

Mastering these objectives will enable you to:

1. Start Internet Explorer 8 and Identify Screen Elements (p. 117)
2. Navigate the Internet (p. 120)
3. Create and Manage Favorites (p. 130)
4. Search the Internet (p. 133)
5. Save and Print Web Pages (p. 135)

Monkey Business Images/Shutterstock

In This Chapter

Lake Michigan City College is located along the lakefront of Chicago—one of the nation's most exciting cities. The college serves its large and diverse student body and makes positive contributions to the community through relevant curricula, partnerships with businesses and nonprofit organizations, and learning experiences that enable students to be full participants in the global community. The college offers three associate degrees in 20 academic areas, adult education programs, and continuing education classes on campus, at satellite locations, and online.

The Internet got its start in the 1960s as an experiment by the Department of Defense as a way for large computers to communicate with other large computers. The Internet has evolved into the largest online computer network in the world—one accessed by hundreds of millions of people every day.

Today, using the Internet, you are able to locate old classmates, communicate with friends by using email or chat, or find phone numbers, directions, and maps so you can arrange visits. The Internet enables you to explore the museums of the world or shop for items that are unavailable at your local mall, all with the click of a button. You can control your finances or improve your mind with educational opportunities any time of day and from any location. The Internet gives you a greater connection to the world.

This introduction to Internet Explorer 8 provides a basic overview of Internet Explorer 8 features and how to use them to explore the Internet. You will practice accessing Web sites, navigating the Internet, saving your favorite Web sites, searching for information, and saving and printing Web pages.

Project 3A College and Career Information

Project Activities

In Activities 3.1 through 3.15, you and the students in Mr. Tony Adair's CIS 101 course will use Internet Explorer 8 to find information about opportunities after graduating from Lake Michigan City College. Some students are interested in transferring to a four-year college and others want to begin a job and work before thinking about more college. Your completed projects will look similar to those shown in Figure 3.1.

Project Files

For Project 3A, you will need the following file:

New blank Word document

You will save your documents as

Lastname_Firstname_1A_College_Money
Lastname_Firstname_1A_Career_Info

Project Results

Figure 3.1
Project 3A College and Career Information

Objective 1 | Start Internet Explorer 8 and Identify Screen Elements

Internet Explorer 8 is a software program that enables you to view the contents of the World Wide Web. Software of this type is called a ***Web browser***. By using Internet Explorer as your Web browser, you can connect to the Internet to search for information, display Web pages, and receive email. Internet Explorer also assists with downloading and transferring files from the Internet, displaying the graphics on a Web site, playing audio and video files associated with a Web site, and executing small programs found in Web sites.

Activity 3.1 | Starting Internet Explorer 8

In the following activity, you will start Internet Explorer 8 and identify features of the Internet Explorer program window. The way you start Internet Explorer 8 will vary depending on the version of Windows you are using and the way your system has been set up by you, your college, or your organization. The standard installation of Windows places Internet Explorer at the top of the Start menu.

1 On the Windows taskbar, click the **Start** button, and then using Figure 3.2 as a guide, locate Internet Explorer on your system.

Organizations can customize the arrangement of programs on the Start menu. If Internet Explorer is used as the standard browser program on your computer, it displays at the top of the Start menu. In other cases, Internet Explorer will display in the All Programs list. If the Internet Explorer logo displays as an icon on your desktop, you can double-click the desktop icon to start the program. The Internet Explorer logo might also display on the Quick Launch toolbar.

Figure 3.2

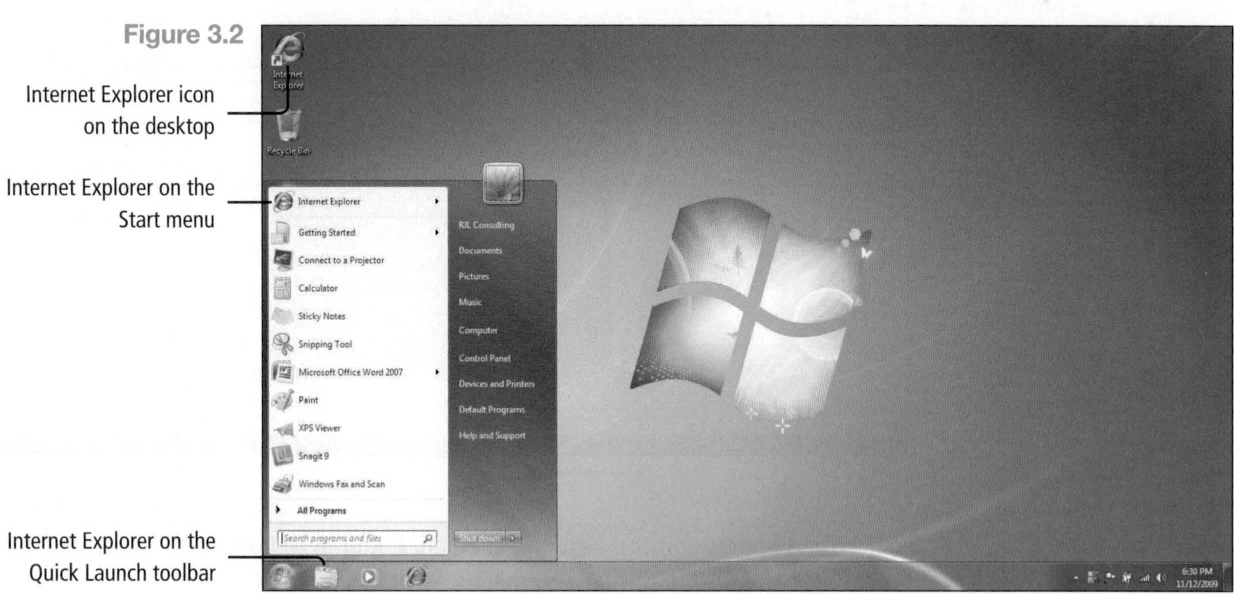

> **Alert! | Are you sure that you have an Internet connection?**
>
> To complete the activities in this chapter, your system must be connected to the Internet. This connection might be through your college or organization's network or your personal ***Internet Service Provider (ISP)***. An Internet Service Provider is a company that provides an Internet connection through a regular telephone line, a special high-speed telephone line, or a cable. These services are provided by companies such as AT&T, Yahoo!, Verizon, or Comcast, or by local cable and telephone companies.

2 On your system, click **Internet Explorer**. In the upper right corner, **Maximize** the window if it is not already maximized.

Each time you start Internet Explorer 8 when your system is connected to the Internet, the home page that has been set on your system displays. Your ***home page*** is the Web page that displays every time you start Internet Explorer 8 and can be any Web page. In a college environment, the home page is usually set to the college's Web page. On your own system, you can choose any Web page.

A ***Web page*** is a document on the World Wide Web that displays as a screen with associated links, frames, pictures, and other features of interest. A ***Web site*** is a group of related Web pages published to a specific location on the World Wide Web; for example, all the various screens—pages—that comprise your college's Web site. Each Web site has its own unique address, called a ***Uniform Resource Locator*** or ***URL***.

3 In the **Address bar**, type **microsoft.com**, and then press Enter. As you type the first few characters in the Address bar, Internet Explorer 8 recalls sites that you have visited in past browsing sessions. These sites are displayed as a drop-down list directly beneath the Address bar. Matching characters are highlighted in blue. Compare your screen with Figure 3.3.

Because Web sites are regularly updated, your screen might look slightly different than Figure 3.3. The Windows Live toolbar is an optional toolbar to make searching easier. It is not a default feature of Internet Explorer 8.

Figure 3.3

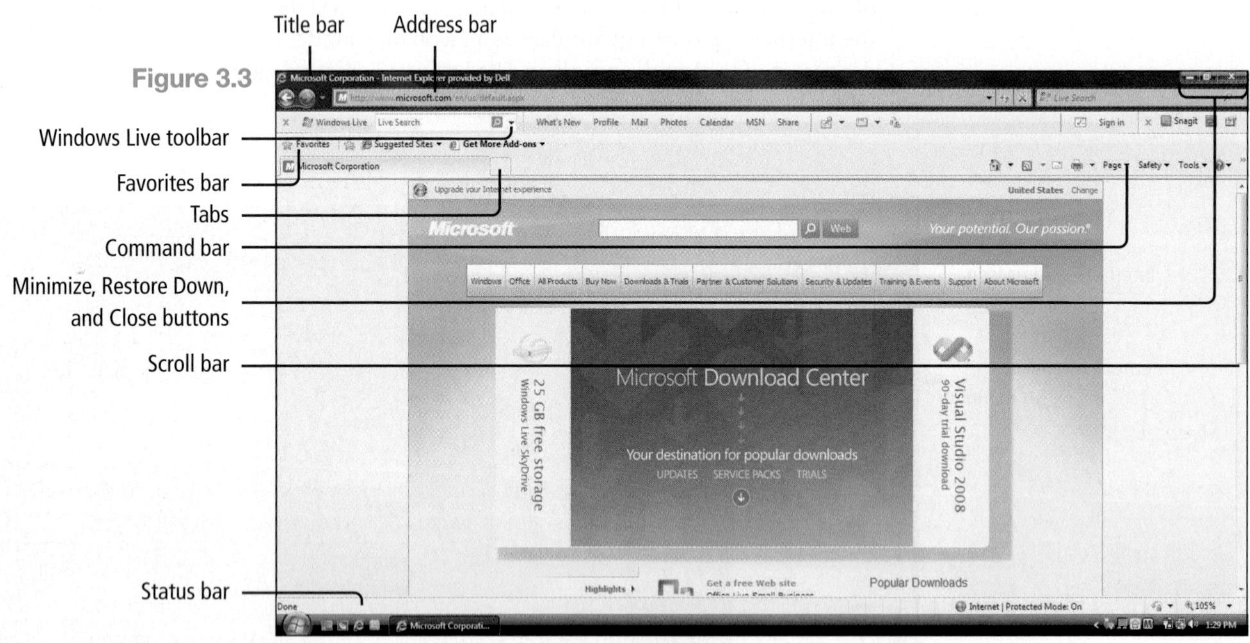

4 Click the **Favorites** button, and then click **Add to Favorites** to display the **Add a Favorite** dialog box. Compare your screen with Figure 3.4.

Figure 3.4

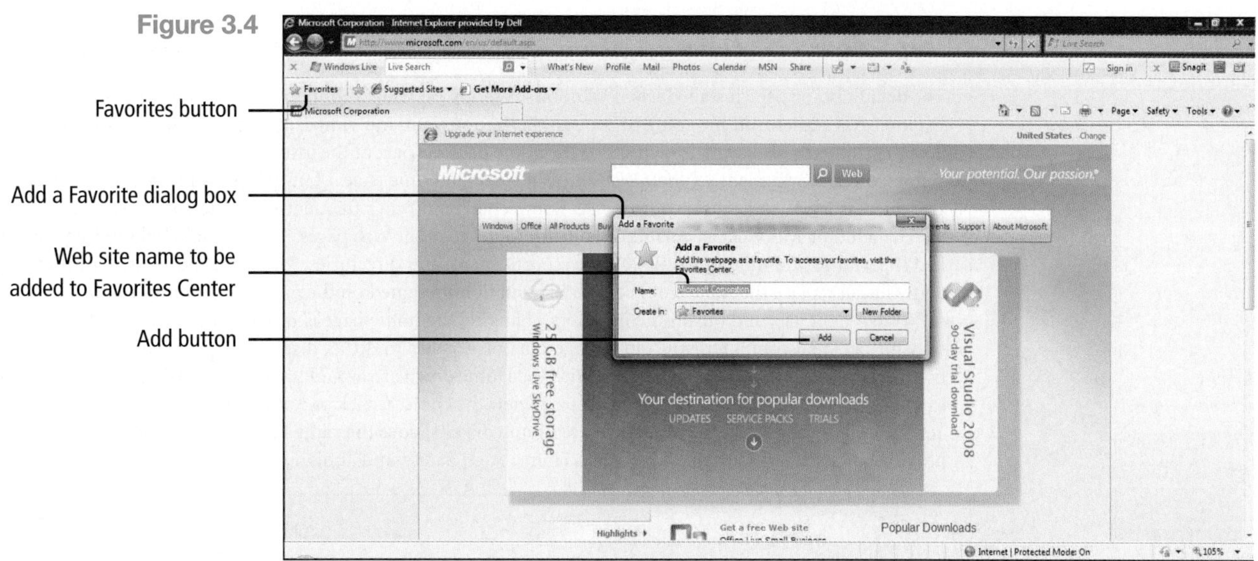

5 In the **Add a Favorite** dialog box, click the **Add** button. Take a moment to review the Microsoft Internet Explorer 8 screen elements shown in the table in Figure 3.5.

The Web page has been added to your Favorites Center.

Internet Explorer 8 Screen Elements

Screen Element	Description
Title bar	Identifies the program as Windows Internet Explorer and also displays the name of the active Web page.
Minimize, Restore Down, and Close buttons	Provide a way to vary the size of the window you are viewing.
Command bar	The toolbar located immediately above the right side of the browser window that can provide quick access to commands such as Home, Page, Safety, and Tools.
Address bar	Displays the address of the active Web page.
Favorites bar	The toolbar located immediately above the left side of the browser window that can provide quick access to a favorite Web site.
Mouse pointer	Displays as a pointing hand when you point to a link (Link Select pointer).
Hyperlinks	When clicked, display other Web pages in this site, or other Web sites. Links can also take you to a document, email address, picture, or sound clip.
Scroll bar	Allows vertical or horizontal navigation of a Web page.
Status bar	Provides information about the security of a site and information about a link's destination as you point to a link.
Tabs	Allow multiple Web sites to be open at the same time.

Figure 3.5

> **More Knowledge | Home Pages and Portals**
>
> The default home page installed when Windows is set up on your computer is a Microsoft site because Internet Explorer 8 is a Microsoft program. Schools, organizations, and individuals that have Web sites often change the default settings to display their own site as the home page. As part of the installation process, ISPs such as AT&T, Yahoo!, or Comcast might set their Web site as the default home page. Many people want their home page set to sites such as MSN and Yahoo! to make accessing email and other frequently used features easier. These home pages, including MSN, act as ***portals*** or launching sites to other Web pages. They contain links to frequently visited sites, up-to-the-minute news, weather reports, maps, and directories. The portal pages are customizable so that you can replace the standard links and information presented on the page with features you use.
>
> On school, lab, and business computers, changing the home page is usually not recommended. However, on your personal computer, you can change the home page. To do so, display the page you want to set as the home page. Then, on the Command bar, click the Home down arrow and then click Add or Change Home Page. In the Add or Change Home Page dialog box, review the choices, click one of the option buttons, and then click Yes. The ***Command bar*** is the toolbar located immediately above the right side of the browser window that can provide quick access to commands such as Home, Page, Safety, and Tools.

Objective 2 | Navigate the Internet

Most Web pages contain links that you can use to navigate to other sites on the Internet. Internet Explorer 8 also provides commands that are accessible on the toolbars, a History list, and the Address bar, all of which you can use to navigate the Web. Internet Explorer 8 has tabs that enable you to have multiple Web sites open at the same time. In Activities 3.2 through 3.6, you will use each of these tools to access different Web sites.

Activity 3.2 | Navigating the Internet

1. Click the **Back** button to return to your home page, and then notice that the **Forward** button becomes available.
2. On the **Address bar**, point to, but do not click, the **Forward** button, and then compare your screen with Figure 3.6.

   A ScreenTip identifies the Web page that will display when you click the button. A ***ScreenTip*** is a small note that displays information about a screen element and is activated by pointing to a button or other screen object.

Figure 3.6

3 On the **Address bar**, click the **Forward** button [icon] to redisplay the **Microsoft.com** home page.

4 On the Command bar, click the **Home** button [icon].

Regardless of how many Web pages you view or Web sites you visit, clicking the Home button returns you to the site that is set as the home page on the system at which you are working.

Activity 3.3 | Accessing Web Sites from the Address Bar

1 Near the top of the **Internet Explorer** window, click anywhere in the **Address bar**.

The existing Web address is highlighted indicating that it is selected.

2 With the current Web address selected, type **www.usa.gov** Press Enter, and then compare your screen with Figure 3.7.

The USA.gov site's home page displays. When an existing Web address is selected, typing a new address replaces the selected text. As you type, a history list might display. Internet Explorer displays a list of all the sites you have accessed recently that begin with the characters you type. If you see the site you are typing in the history list, you can click the site name in the list rather than type the complete address.

Figure 3.7

Web site address in Address bar

Home page of USA.gov Web site (your screen will likely differ)

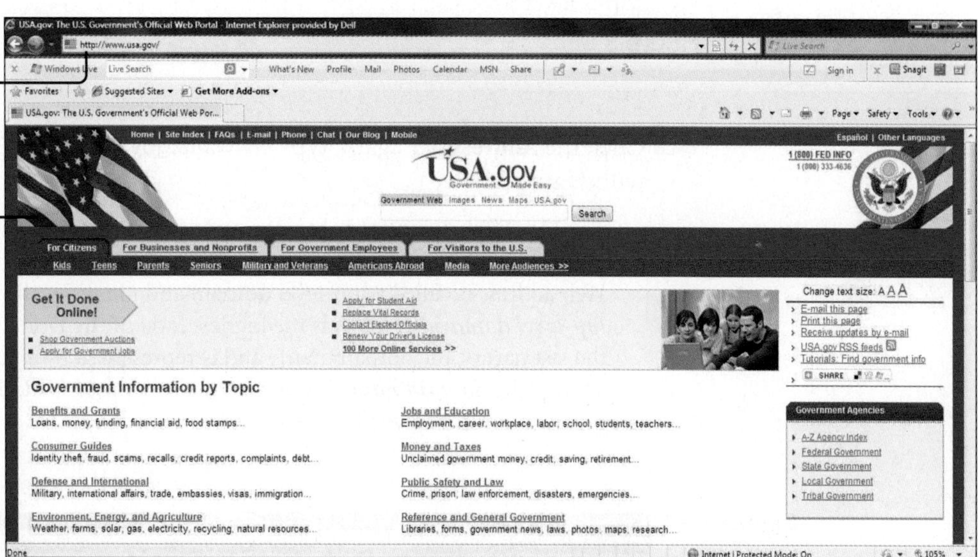

3 Take a moment to study the table in Figure 3.8 that describes how Web addresses are formed.

Parts of the Web Address

Parts of the Web Address	Description
http	The abbreviation of Hypertext Transfer Protocol—the standard ***protocol*** for retrieving Web sites. A protocol is a set of rules for transferring data over the Internet. Another protocol is ***ftp***, or ***File Transfer Protocol***. FTP is a protocol that enables individuals to copy files from one computer to another on a network.
://	Three characters identified by Internet creators for separating the protocol from the rest of the Web address. These three characters were identified because they had never appeared together in computer programs and other computer-related contexts.
www.USA.gov	The domain name. In this case, the domain name includes the abbreviation for World Wide Web *(www)*, the name of the organization, and top-level domain—*.gov* stands for government. Not all domain names start with www, but many do. Other domain types include *.com* (commercial), *.edu* (education), *.org* (organization), *.net* (network), and *.mil* (military). Most countries have their own domain types such as *.ca* for Canada and *.fr* for France.

Figure 3.8

4 Click the **Address bar** again, type **www.bls.gov** and press Enter. Compare your screen with Figure 3.9.

The U.S. Department of Labor, Bureau of Labor Statistics Web site displays. Because sites are regularly updated, your screen will likely not match Figure 3.9 exactly. The *.gov* in the Web address is called a top-level domain and identifies the site as a government site. A ***top-level domain***, or ***TLD***, is the highest level of the Domain Name System expressed as the last part of the domain name and is represented by a period followed by three or four letters. The ***domain name*** is the part of a text-based URL that identifies the company or organization that owns the Web site.

Figure 3.9

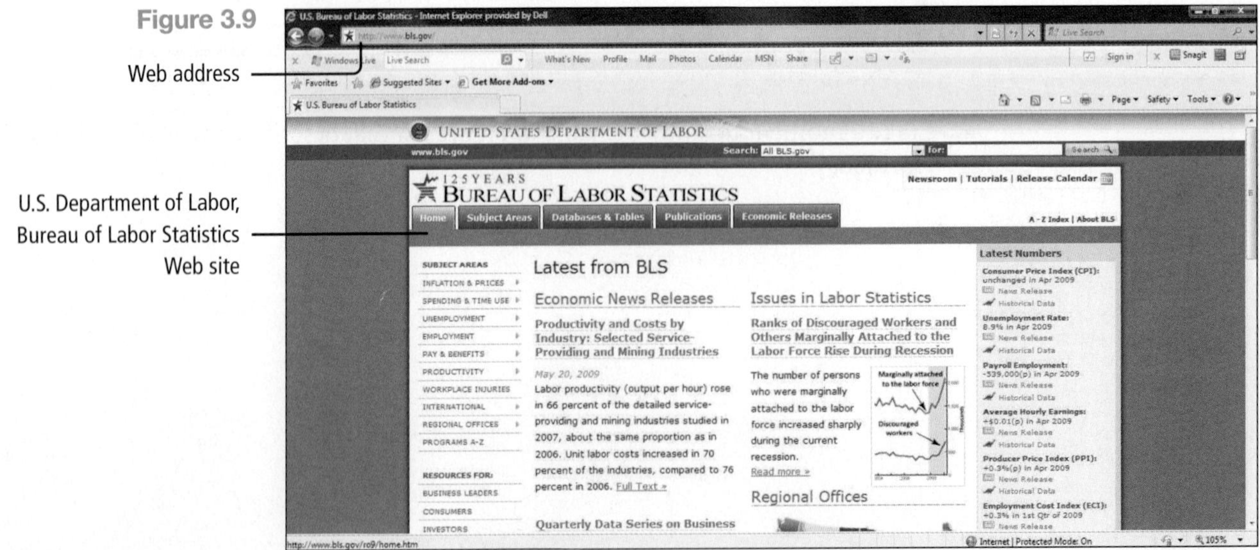

5 At the right end of the **Address bar**, click the **Address bar down arrow** and point to but do not click the **http://www.usa.gov** Web address. Compare your screen with Figure 3.10.

The list of recently accessed Web sites on your computer will differ from those shown in Figure 3.10. The sites listed represent those most frequently visited on your system.

Figure 3.10

Site to select

Address Bar down arrow

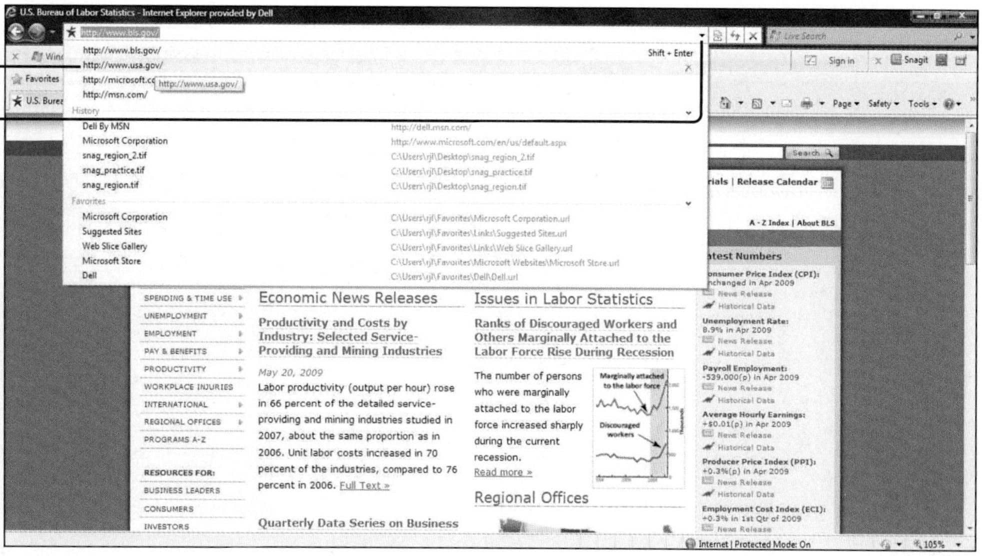

6 In the displayed list, click the **http://www.usa.gov** Web address to display that Web site. Then, in the **Address bar**, type **www.ed.gov** and press Enter.

The U.S. Department of Education Web site displays.

7 On the **Address bar**, locate the **Recent Pages button down arrow** to the right of the Forward button, and then click the arrow to display the most recently visited Web sites. Click the listing for the **USA.gov** Web site. Then, click the **Forward** button to return to the **U.S. Department of Education** Web site. Compare your screen with Figure 3.11.

The U.S. Department of Education Web site displays, and the Forward button is unavailable because you have used it to return to this Web site.

Figure 3.11

Forward button (which is unavailable because you used it to get to this site)

Recent Pages button down arrow

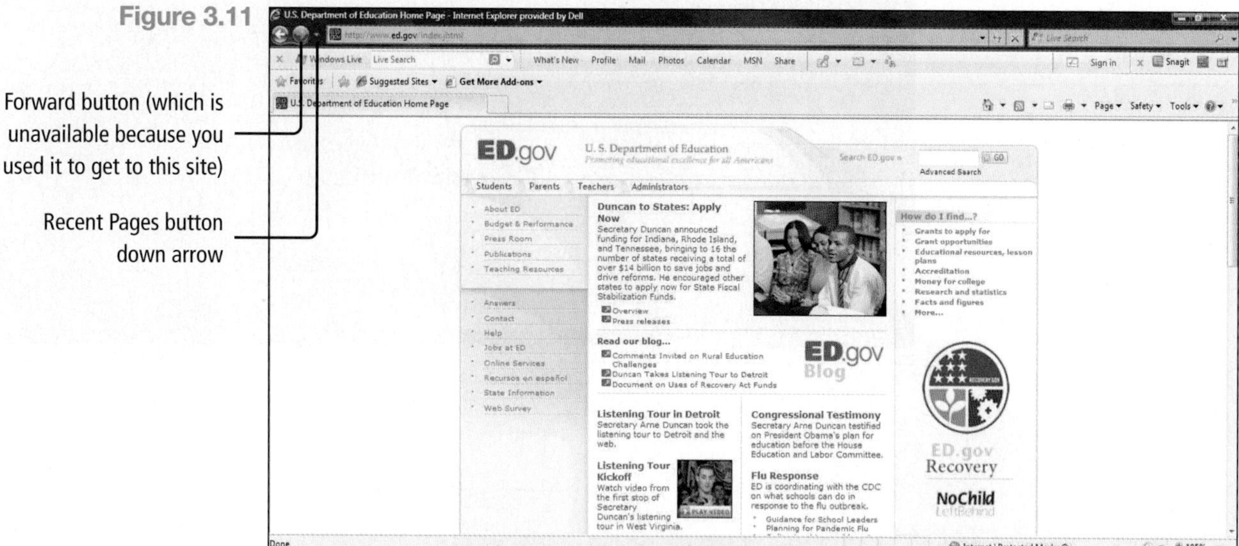

8 On the Favorites bar, if necessary, click the **Favorites Center** button to display the task pane. Click **Microsoft Corporation**. Compare your screen with Figure 3.12.

The ***Favorites Center*** enables you to view the Favorites, Feeds, and History lists. With Internet Explorer 8, you can add Web pages directly to the Favorites bar for easy access. The ***Favorites bar*** is the toolbar located immediately above the left side of the browser window that can provide quick access to a favorite Web site.

Figure 3.12

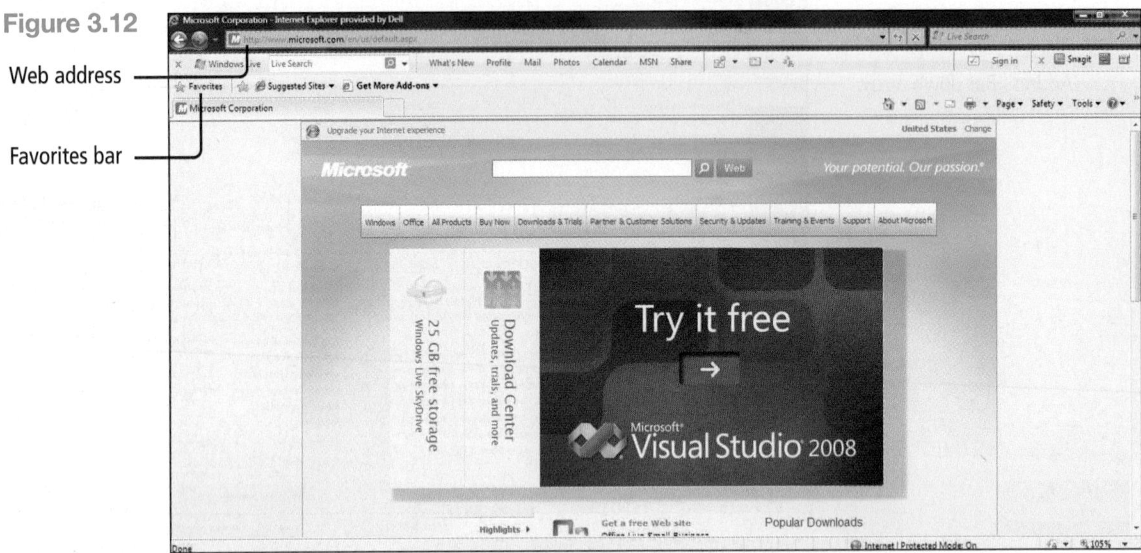

9 In the **Address bar**, click and type **www.psu.edu** and press Enter. Compare your screen with Figure 3.13.

Internet Explorer displays the Penn State Web site. The top-level domain *.edu,* is the domain type reserved for colleges and universities.

Figure 3.13

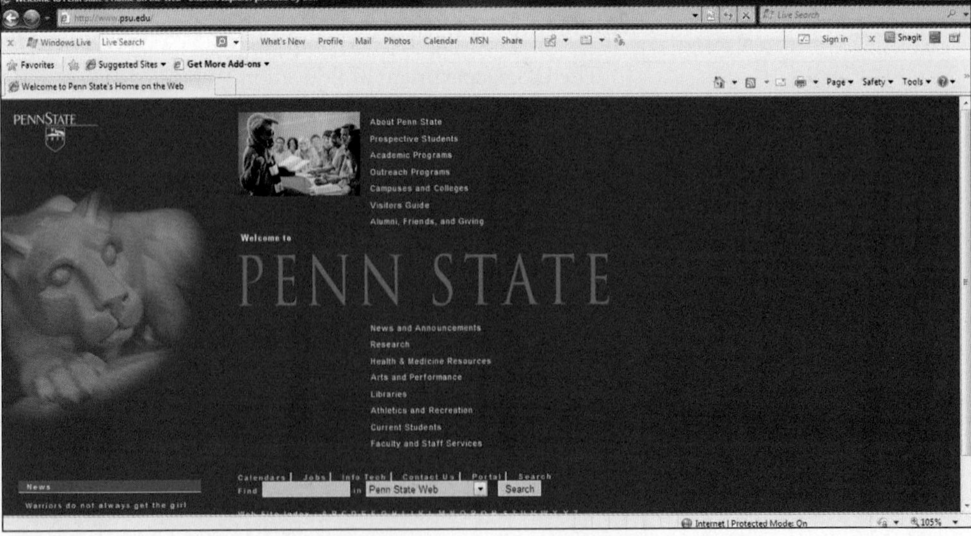

Activity 3.4 | Opening a Second Web Site

1 Near the right of the **Welcome to Penn State's Home on the Web tab**, position your mouse pointer over the **New Tab** button, but do not click. Compare your screen with Figure 3.14.

A ScreenTip displays, indicating a new tab will be opened.

Tabs in Internet Explorer 8 enable you to have multiple Web pages open at the same time without having to open multiple instances of the browser.

Figure 3.14

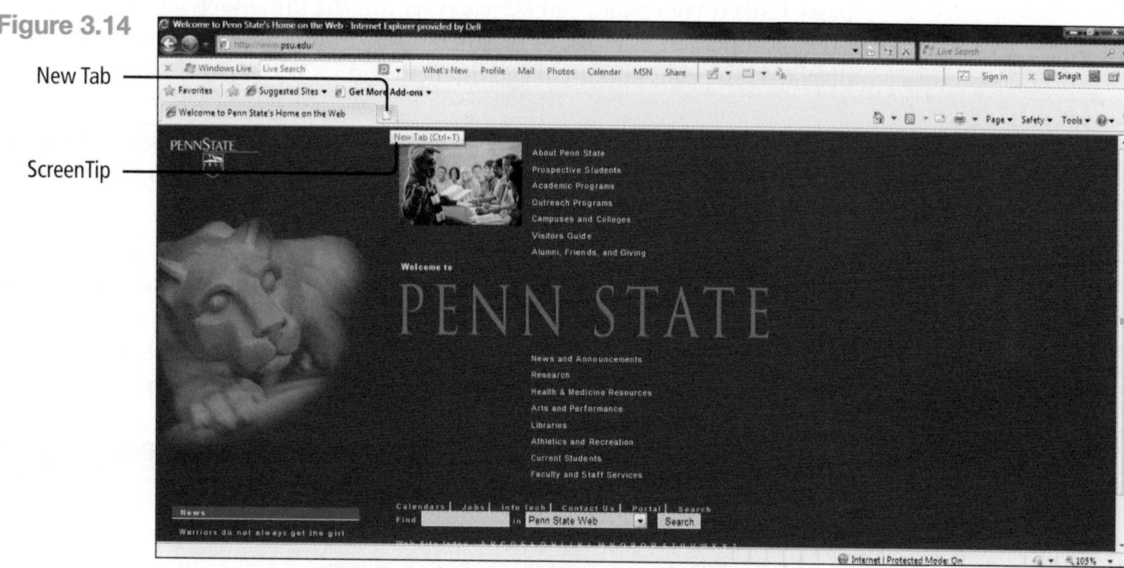

2 Click **New Tab**.

A new tab displays that enables you to view another Web site while keeping the Penn State Web site open.

3 In the **Address bar**, type the URL for the Web site of your school, and then press Enter. Compare your screen with Figure 3.15.

Your school's Web site displays and the name of the Web page displays on the New Tab along with a Close Tab button.

Figure 3.15

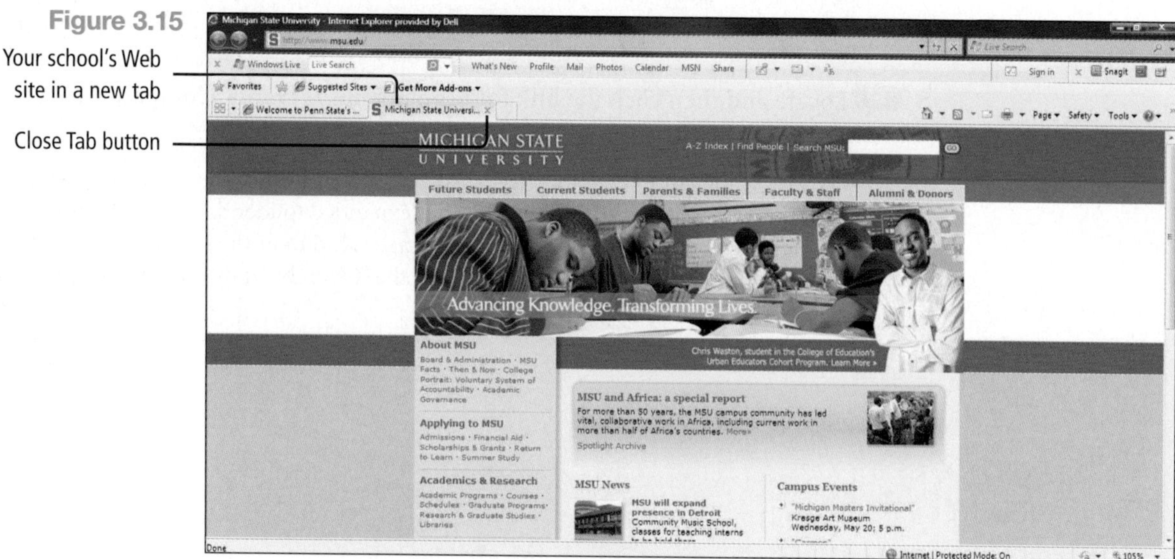

4 Use the **Close Tab** button [×] to close the tab displaying your school's Web page.

5 On the Command bar, click the **Home** button [Home] to return to the home page that is set on your computer.

Activity 3.5 | Displaying Web Pages with Hyperlinks

Most Web sites contain ***hyperlinks,*** which provide another navigation tool for browsing Web pages. Hyperlinks are text, buttons, pictures, or other objects displayed on Web pages that, when clicked, access other Web pages or display other sections of the active page. Linked Web pages can be pages within the same Web site or Web pages on sites of other companies, schools, or organizations. In this activity, you will use hyperlinks to display Web pages about college financial aid.

1 In the **Address bar**, type **www.students.gov** and then press Enter. Move the mouse pointer to various parts of the screen to locate areas where the **Link Select pointer** [pointer] displays, as shown in Figure 3.16.

Internet Explorer displays the students.gov home page. As you review Figure 3.16, notice that the mouse pointer displays as a pointing hand—the ***Link Select pointer***—when you point to an item that links to another Web page. Web sites contain Web pages with links that connect to other pages on the site. These other pages contain links that lead to still other pages and also link back to the home page of the Web site.

Figure 3.16

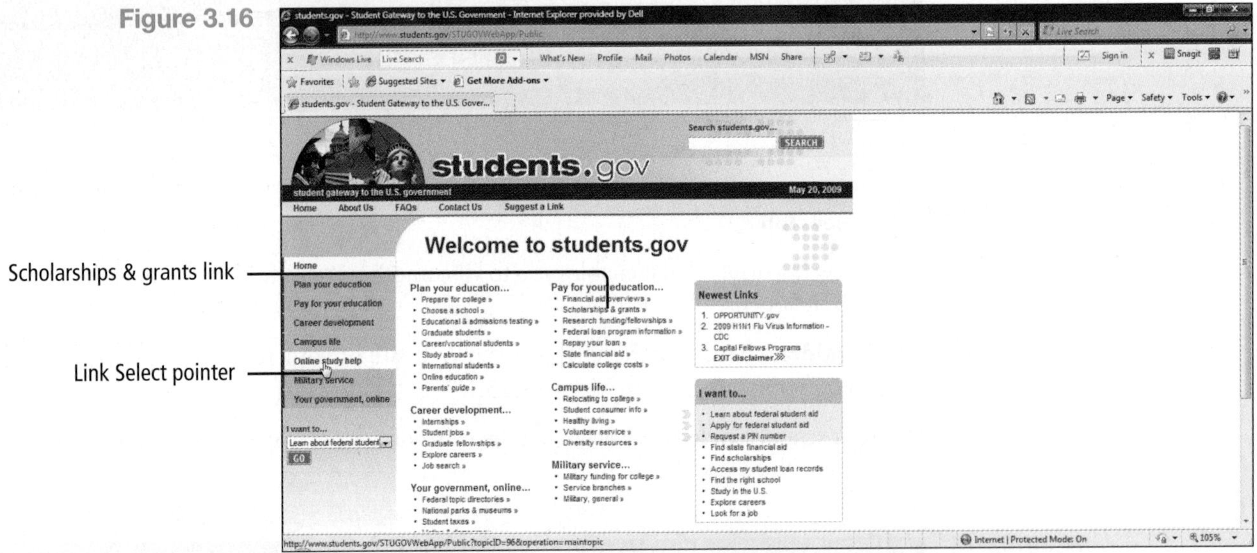

2 Locate and then click the link for **Scholarships & grants.** Compare your screen with Figure 3.17.

The Scholarships & grants page displays. The address in the Address bar still shows the *students.gov* Web site, but the URL has expanded to identify the ***path*** for this page. A path is the sequential description of the storage location of the HTML documents and files making up the Web page and stored in the hierarchy of directories and folders on the Web server.

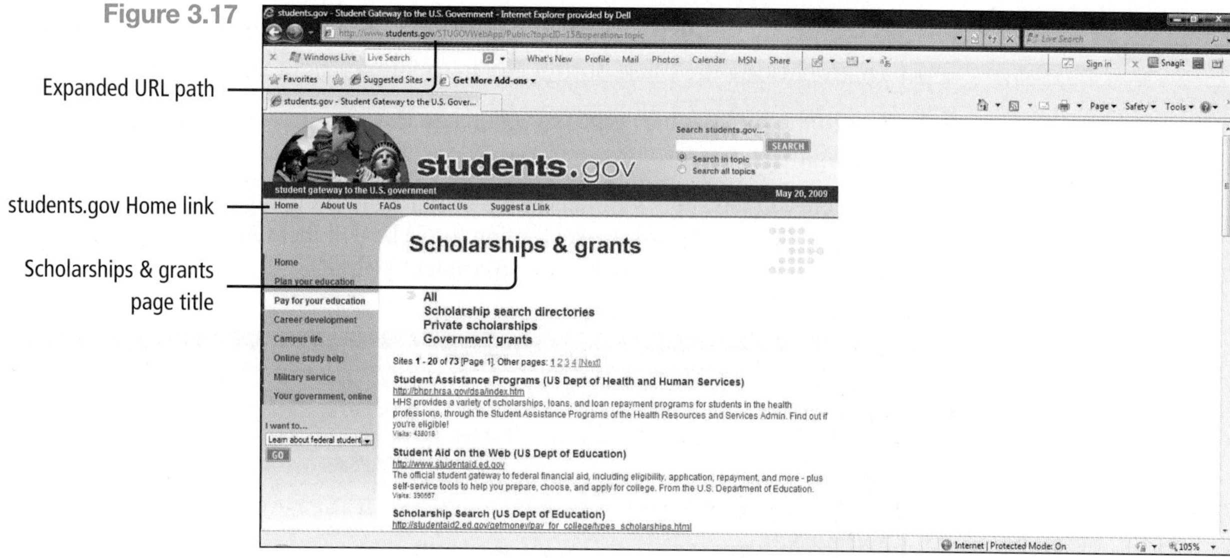

Figure 3.17

Alert! | Is the Web page available?

Because Web sites are updated frequently, the links on the Web sites also change. If the Scholarships & grants link on the *students.gov* Web site does not display, choose another link to follow.

3. On the **Address bar**, click the **Back** button.

   The *students.gov* home page displays.

4. Scroll down as necessary to locate the link for **State financial aid** and click it. Compare your screen with Figure 3.18. Click on your state to try to find information about your state's financial aid. One or more links to information about financial aid in your state will display below the list of states. Click any one of these links.

   Internet Explorer opens the individual state's financial aid links in a new window. Each Web page contains settings that control whether linked pages open in a separate window or in the same window. In addition, settings that are active on your computer control the linked page's display.

   The new Web page opens in a separate window on top of the State financial aid window.

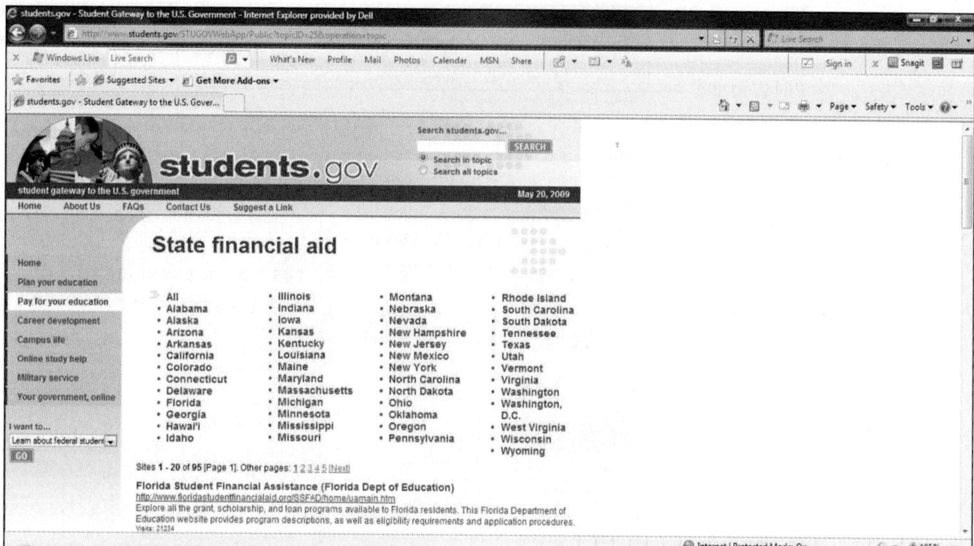

Figure 3.18

5 When you are finished viewing the information, return to the State financial aid Web page by clicking the **Close** button in the upper right corner of the new window.

6 Click in the **Address bar**, type **www.fafsa.ed.gov** and press Enter. Compare your screen with Figure 3.19.

Before you can apply for financial aid such as scholarships, grants, or loans, you will need to fill out a FAFSA or Free Application for Federal Student Aid. The TLD, *.gov*, shows that the application is completed at a government Web site.

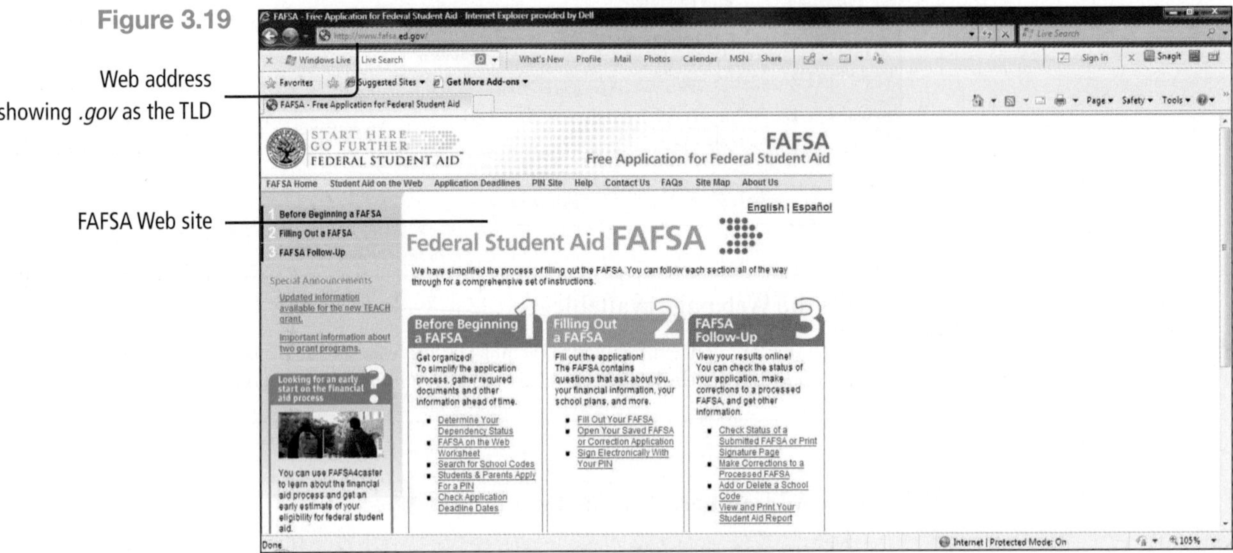

Figure 3.19

7 At the top of the FAFSA Web page, locate and then click the link for **PIN Site**. Compare your screen with Figure 3.20. The PIN Federal Student Aid Web site displays in a new window. You can see that the new Web page opens in a separate window on top of the FAFSA window.

Notice that the top-level domain name (*.gov*) in the Address bar shows that this is a government Web site. Both you and your parents can apply for a Federal Student Aid PIN at this site. Your PIN, or Personal Identification Number, serves as an electronic signature for your FAFSA.

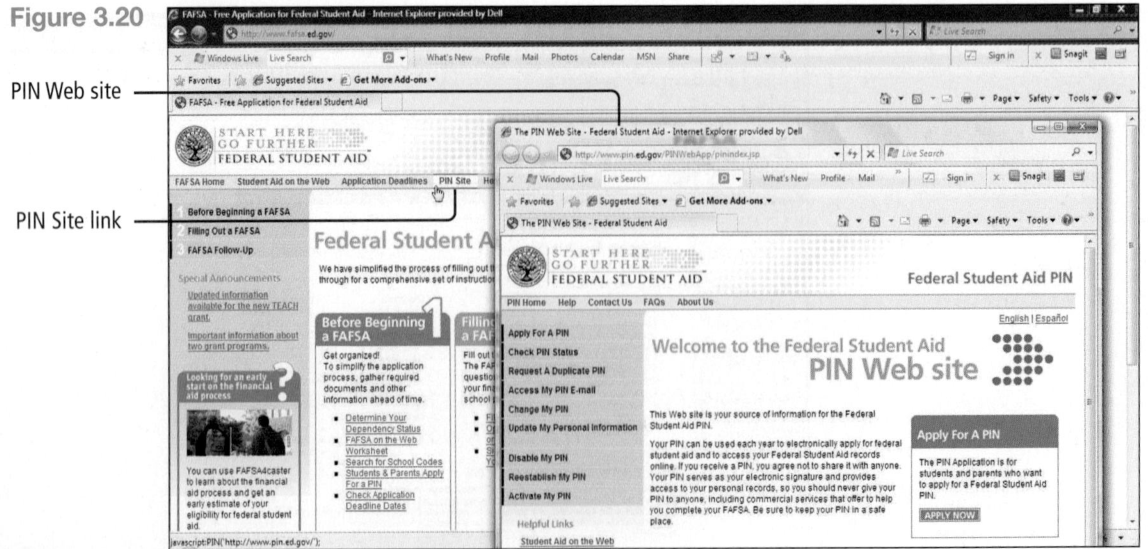

Figure 3.20

8 On the displayed Web site's title bar, click the **Close** button to close the new window. Then click the **Home** button to return to your home page.

Activity 3.6 | Using Internet Explorer 8 History

The Internet Explorer 8 ***History*** feature tracks recently visited Web sites. You can display the History list by using the Favorites Center button, and then clicking the History tab to view a site that you recently visited. You can view the History list by Date, Site, Most Visited, and by Order Visited Today. You can also use the Search History option to locate sites. In this activity, you will use the History list to display recently visited sites.

1 On the Favorites bar, click the **Favorites** button, and then if necessary, click the **History** tab. The History list displays on the left side of the Internet Explorer window. If necessary, click the down arrow to locate and click **View By Date**, and then click **Today**. Compare your screen with Figure 3.21.

The listings of items on your computer may differ from those shown in the figure. However, many of the listings shown for Today should be the same. Notice that the sites accessed today display in alphabetical order.

Figure 3.21

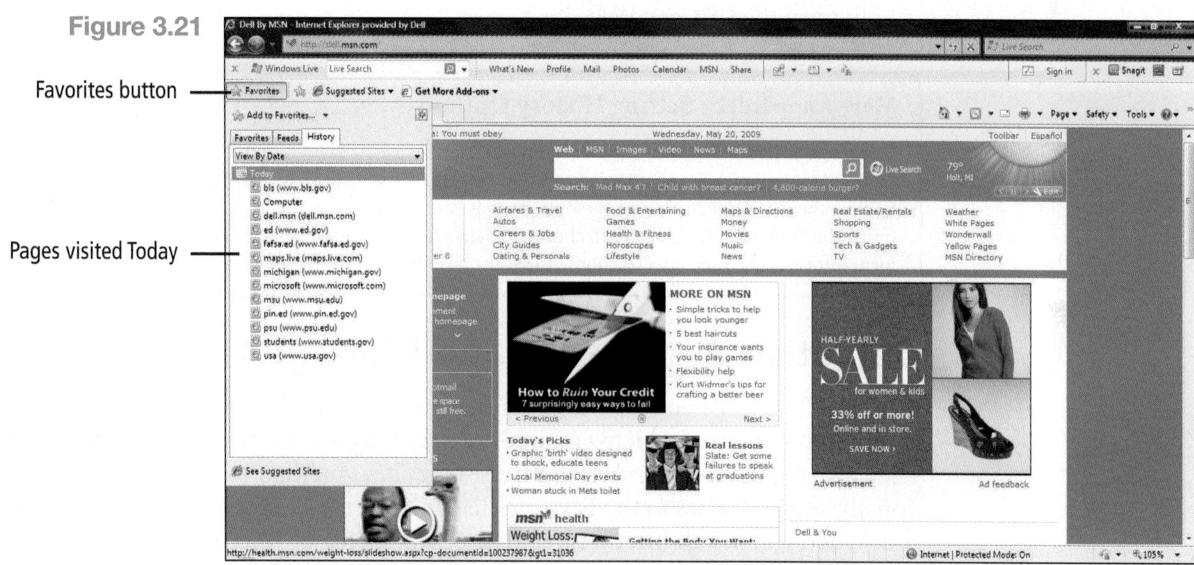

2 In the **History** list, click **bls** (**www.bls.gov**), and then compare your screen with Figure 3.22.

The Web site name associated with the URL displays as a link below the URL. If you click the link, the Web site will open. This is another way to open a Web site. You can also locate and open a Web site by clicking the **View By Date down arrow** and choosing the Search History option. Then type keywords into the Search for box.

Figure 3.22

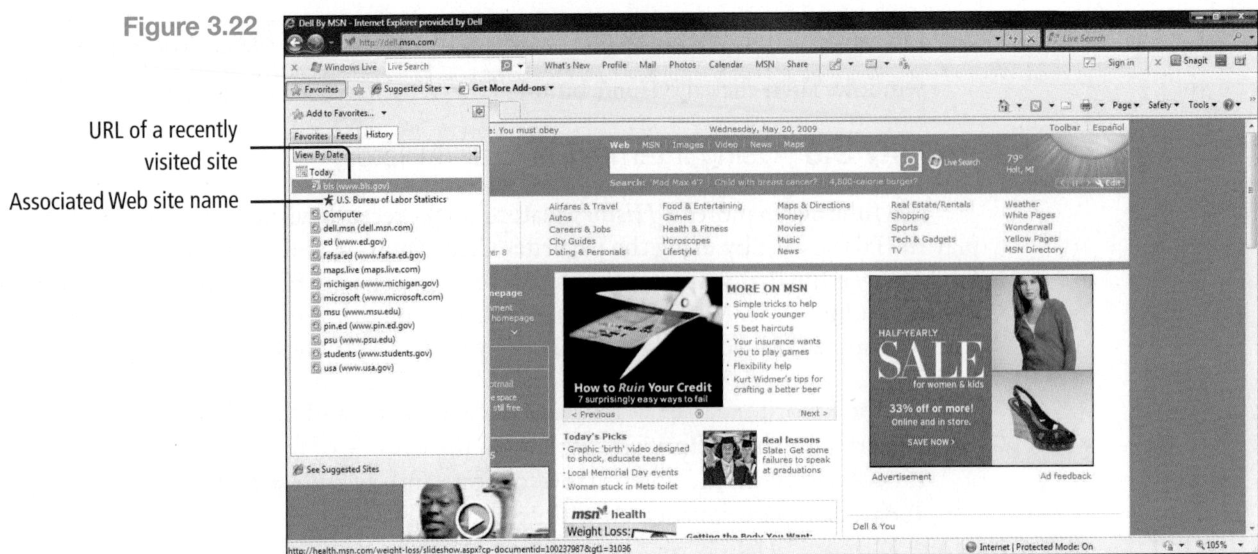

3. Scroll down the **History** list as necessary, and then click **usa (www.usa.gov)** to display the associated Web site name for the USA.gov Web site. Click on the Web site name link to open the **USA.gov** Web site.

> **More Knowledge | Setting History Options**
>
> By default, Internet Explorer 8 tracks sites visited in the last 20 days. To reduce the amount of disk storage space required to maintain the History list, you can customize the settings to change the number of days tracked and to clear the list. You can change the options that control and clear the History list by setting Internet Options under the Tools command. You can choose to delete temporary files, history, cookies, saved passwords, and Web form information. You can also choose to set the amount of disk space to use.

Objective 3 | Create and Manage Favorites

The History list automatically tracks sites that you visit each time you start Internet Explorer 8—many of which you may never visit again. The Favorites list works differently. The Favorites list contains Web addresses for sites you plan to visit frequently. You intentionally add addresses to the Favorites list and Internet Explorer 8 keeps the list for you. When you install Internet Explorer 8, a short list of Microsoft sites is added to the Favorites list. You can delete these addresses, add new addresses, and organize favorite site addresses into folders. For example, you may have a folder for Travel Sites, for College Sites, and so on. In Activities 3.7 through 3.9, you will add a new favorite, create a new folder, navigate to a site listed in the favorites, and delete a favorite.

Activity 3.7 | Adding an Address to the Favorites List

In this activity, you will display a Web page and add it to the Favorites list, using the Add to Favorites button.

1. In the **Address bar**, type **www.prenhall.com/go** and then press Enter.
2. On the Favorites bar, click the **Favorites** button, and the Favorites tab, if necessary. Then click **Add to Favorites** to display the **Add a Favorite** dialog box. Compare your screen with Figure 3.23.

   The Add a Favorite dialog box displays with the title of the Web site indicated in the Name box.

Figure 3.23

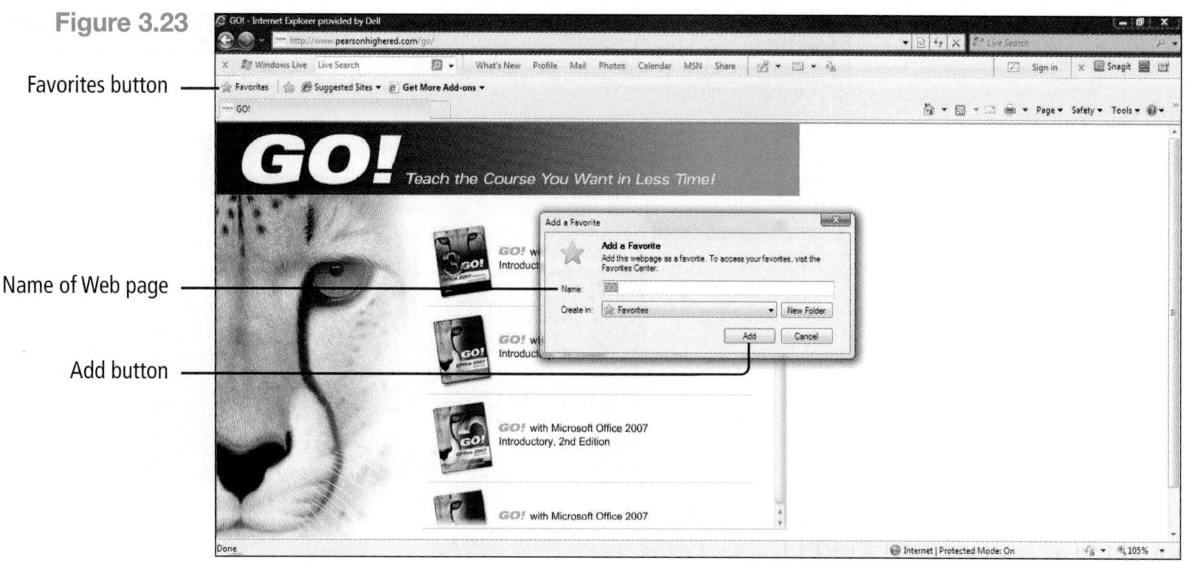

3 In the **Add a Favorite** dialog box, click **Add.**

You can also add a shortcut to a favorite directly to the Favorites bar by clicking the Add to Favorites Bar button.

4 On the Favorites bar, click the **Favorites** button. Click the **Favorites** tab, if necessary, to display the Favorites. Click the **Add to Favorites down arrow**, and then click **Organize Favorites**. Near the bottom of the **Organize Favorites** dialog box, click the **New Folder** button. In the new folder that was added to the list, type **Textbook Sites** and then press Enter.

The folder is created and displays in the listing of all folders and Web site favorites that is already established. When you have a number of sites that are related to a specific topic, you can create a new folder and use it to store related site addresses. The Organize Favorites dialog box displays a list of folders and links contained in the Favorites list and command buttons for creating folders, renaming folders and links, moving links to folders, and deleting folders and links from Favorites.

5 In the **Organize Favorites** dialog box, click the **GO! Web page**, and then click the **Move** button. In the **Browse For Folder** dialog box, click the **Textbook Sites** folder, and then click **OK**. In the **Organize Favorites** dialog box, click the **Close** button.

Another Way

To move a Web site after the folder is created, in the Organize Favorites dialog box, drag the Web site to the desired folder.

Internet Explorer 8 adds the GO! Web page address to the Textbook Sites folder in the Favorites list.

6 Click the **Home** button to display your home page.

Activity 3.8 | Displaying a Favorite Web Site

In this activity, you will use the Favorites list to display a Web site.

1 If necessary, on the Favorites bar, click the **Favorites** button. Click the **Favorites tab**, click the **Textbook Sites** folder, and then notice that the link to the GO! Web site displays, as shown in Figure 3.24.

Figure 3.24

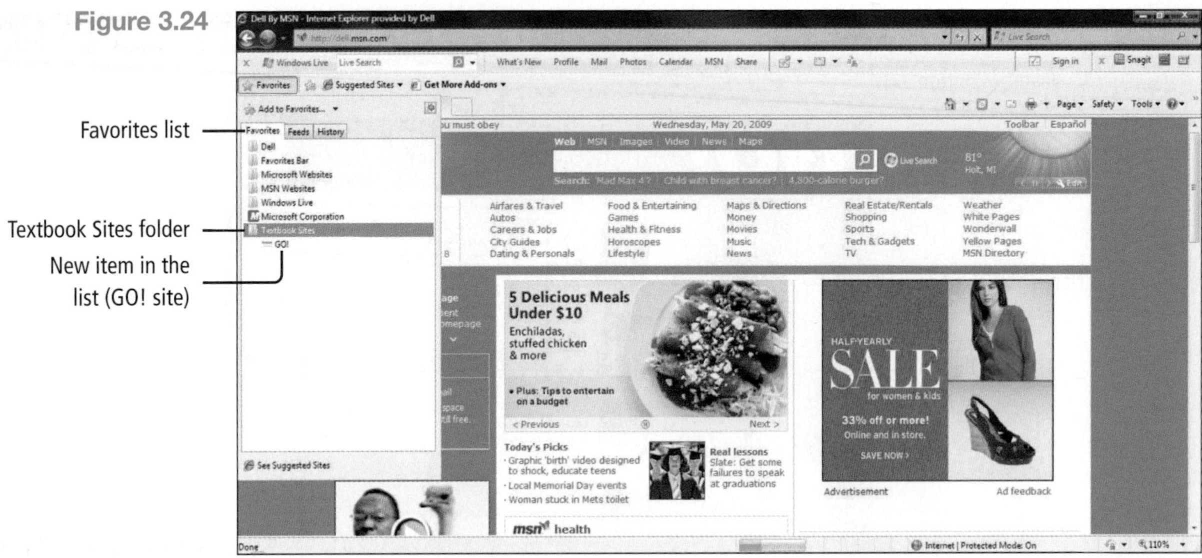

2 Click the link to the **GO! Web site.**

The GO! Web site displays.

Activity 3.9 | Deleting a Web Address from Favorites

In this activity, you will remove an address from the Favorites list.

1 On the Favorites bar, click the **Favorites** button, click the **Add to Favorites down arrow**, and then click **Organize Favorites**. Compare your screen with Figure 3.25.

Figure 3.25

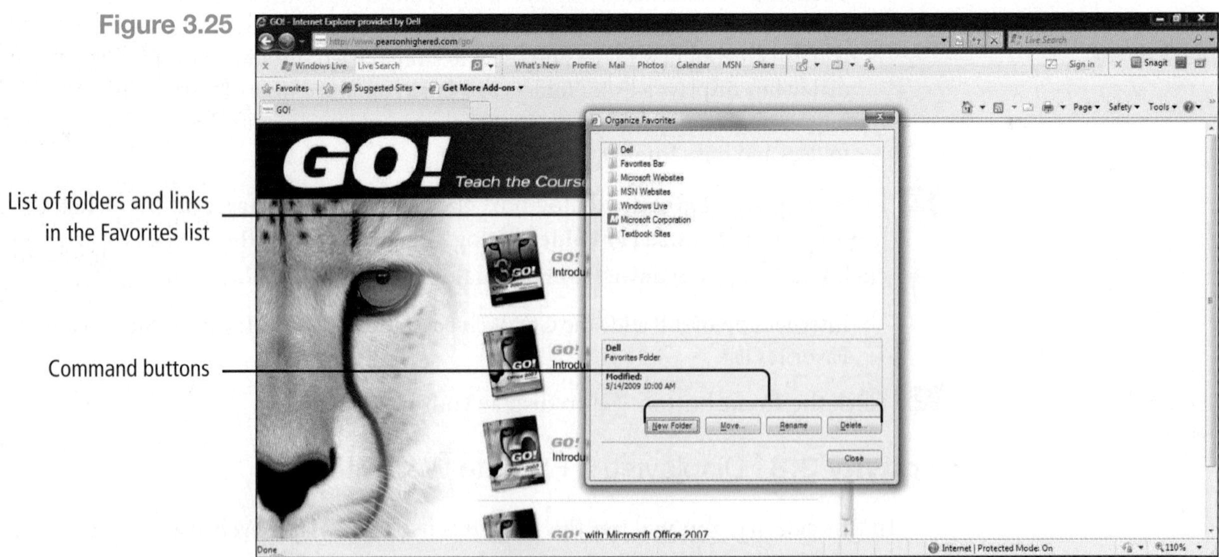

2 In the **Organize Favorites** dialog box, scroll down if necessary and click the **Textbook Sites** folder to list its contents. Click the **GO! Web page** link one time to select it.

3 In the **Organize Favorites** dialog box, click the **Delete** button, and then compare your screen with Figure 3.26.

Figure 3.26

Delete File dialog box

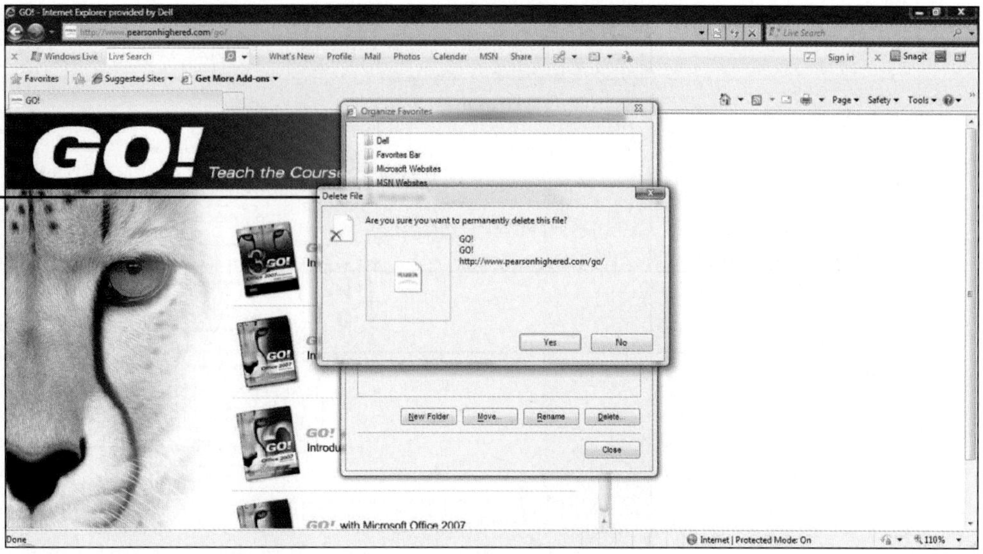

4 In the **Delete File** dialog box, click **Yes**, and then in the **Organize Favorites** dialog box, click the **Close** button.

Internet Explorer 8 removes the GO! Web site from the Favorites list and closes the Organize Favorites dialog box.

5 On the Command bar, click the **Home** button to display your home page.

Objective 4 | Search the Internet

When you know the name of an organization or the Web address you want to locate, accessing the site is easy and straightforward. When you want to locate information about topics from a variety of sources or find sites for businesses, journals, and other sources, it presents a greater challenge because of the large number of sites available on the Internet. There are several Web sites with search capabilities called ***search engines***, programs that search for keywords in files and documents or other Web sites found on the Internet.

Internet Explorer 8 includes an Instant Search box that connects to a default search engine (such as Live Search or Bing) and easily allows you to add additional search engines. With Internet Explorer 8, Instant Search makes it easier to search for keywords within the text of the current Web page. In this activity, you will search the Internet for topics related to student financial aid.

Activity 3.10 | Adding a Search Engine and Searching the Internet

1 On right side of the **Address bar**, click the **Search down arrow**, and then click **Find More Providers.**

The Add-ons Gallery: Search Providers Web page opens. It enables you to add additional search providers to Internet Explorer.

2 In the **Add-ons Gallery: Search Providers** list, scroll down or go to page 2 to locate **Google Search Suggestions**. Then click the **Add to Internet Explorer button.** In the **Add Search Provider** dialog box, click the **Make this my default search provider** check box. Compare your screen with Figure 3.27.

Figure 3.27

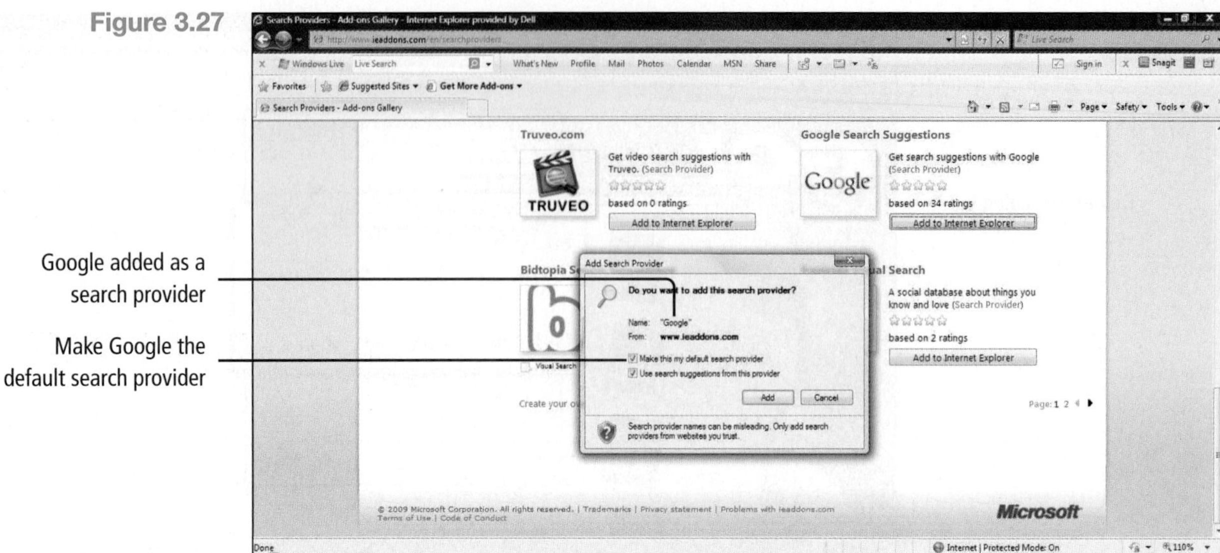

3 Click the **Add** button.

Google now displays as the default search provider in the Instant Search box.

4 On the **Address bar** in the **Instant Search** box, type **"student financial aid"** including the quotation marks, and then press Enter. Compare your screen with Figure 3.28.

You can begin a search by typing a single word, a phrase, a question, or a statement. You can easily change the size of the Instant Search textbox by dragging the edge. This makes it easier to see all of the characters in a long search string. Typing *student financial aid* without the quotation marks directs the search engine to look for three different terms. Placing the text in quotation marks ensures that the search engine looks for sites that contain the entire phrase. You can see that the number of sites found during this particular search that contain the phrase *"student financial aid"* is quite large. Internet Explorer 8 displays links to the Web sites in a ranked order based on the quality and quantity of the content at the Web sites it returns. Several factors are considered, such as how closely the site matches the search phrase, the number of references to the search text contained in the site, the number of other links to that site, and how recently the site has been updated.

Figure 3.28

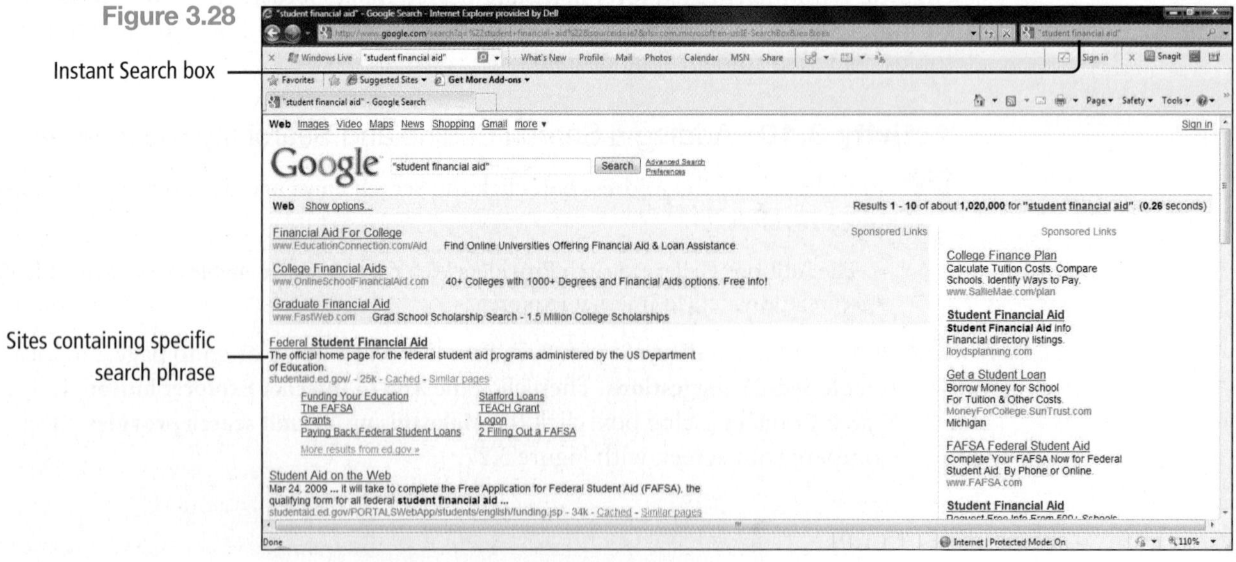

5. On the right side of the screen, under **Sponsored Links**, click the first link. Compare your screen with Figure 3.29.

   Sponsored links are sites that pay to be displayed with results on a search engine site. Sponsored links are frequently placed near the top or on the right side of the search engine results page so they are easily seen and clicked. Sponsored links generally are commercial sites, so they stand to gain from increasing traffic to their Web site. The top-level domain is *.com* for commercial sites.

Figure 3.29

Web address of first sponsored site (yours will vary)

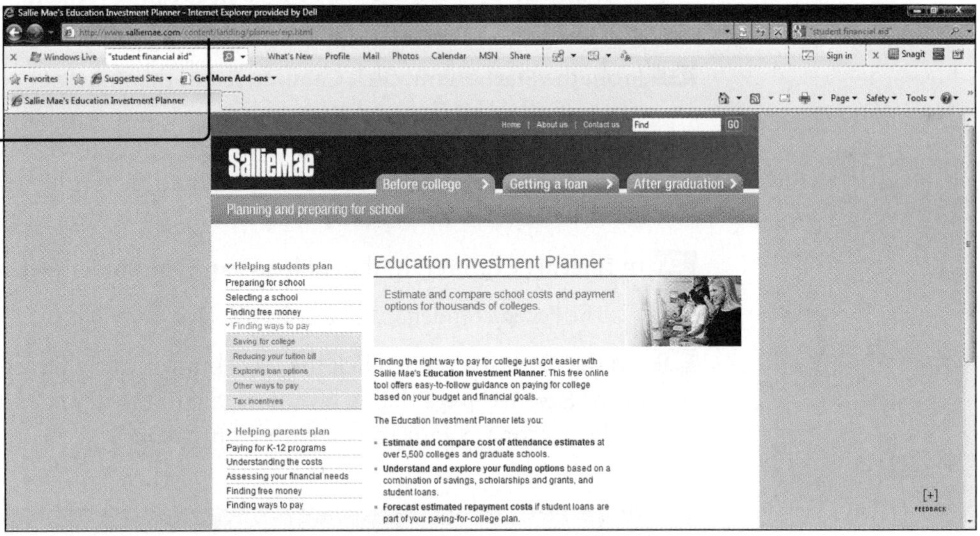

6. Click the **Back** button to return to your search results. Scroll as necessary, and then locate and click the link for **Federal Student Financial Aid**.

   The home page for student aid programs administered by the U.S. Department of Education displays. If you are interested in this information, you can print it or put it on your Favorites list to examine at a later time. Financial aid information found at a sponsored Web site (*.com*) is likely to be a loan opportunity, whereas a government financial aid Web site (*.gov*) is more likely to offer information on grant and scholarship opportunities.

7. On the Command bar, click the **Home** button to display your home page.

Objective 5 | Save and Print Web Pages

Saving a copy of a Web page on your system or storage device is referred to as ***downloading***. Downloading means that you request a copy of a file or program from a remote server, such as a Web server, and save it on your local system or storage device. You can also download other types of Web files, such as graphics, and save them on your computer or disk so that you can review them later. When you download a Web page displayed in Internet Explorer 8, Internet Explorer 8 creates a new folder at the location you indicate to save all associated graphics, pictures, and other features of the Web page so that when you view the file offline, it resembles the entire page as it was displayed on the Web. Other techniques for accessing Web pages include setting a desktop shortcut to the Web page and sending a link to a Web page to someone through email. Setting a desktop shortcut creates an icon on your desktop for the Web page so that it opens very quickly. Both techniques are accomplished from the Page button on the Command bar.

Because of the widespread threat of system viruses, as a general precaution, avoid downloading or saving files from unknown Web sites, and be sure your virus protection program is up-to-date before downloading Web files on your system. You must also be careful not to violate copyright-protected Web materials.

Activity 3.11 | Downloading and Saving a Web Page

In this activity, you will download and save a Web page.

1. Determine where you will be storing your files for this chapter, for example, on your own disk or USB flash drive or on a network drive, and be sure that storage location is available. If necessary, check with your instructor or lab coordinator.

2. From the **Start** menu, click **Computer**, and then navigate to the drive—USB flash drive, computer hard drive, or network drive—where you will be storing your files. In the right pane of the **Computer** window, right-click an empty space. In the context-sensitive menu that displays, click **New**, and then roll over and click **Folder.** With **New Folder** selected, type **IE8 Chapter** and then press Enter. **Close** the window.

3. In **Internet Explorer**, in the **Address bar**, type **studentaid.ed.gov** and then press Enter.

   The Federal Student Aid Web site displays.

4. On the Command bar, click the **Page** button, and then click **Save As**. In the left pane of the **Save Webpage** dialog box, navigate to the drive, and then to your **IE8 Chapter** folder. Compare your screen with Figure 3.30.

Figure 3.30

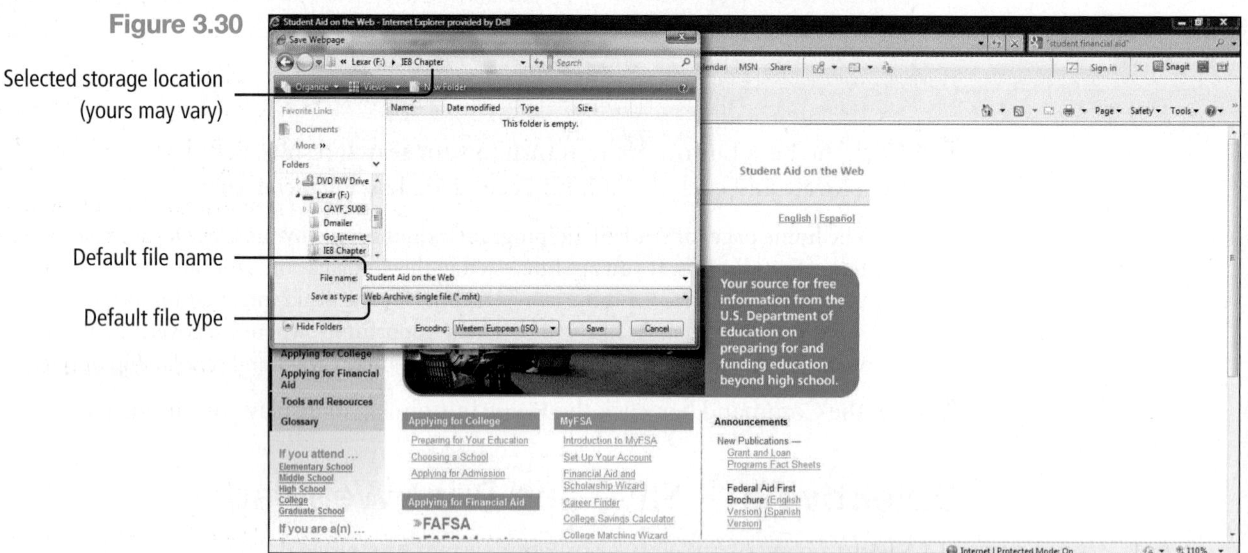

5. At the bottom of the **Save Webpage** dialog box, click the **Save as type arrow** and if necessary, click **Web Archive, single file (*.mht)**. Click in the **File name** box to select the existing text, and then replace the selected text by typing **Lastname_Firstname_1A_College_Money** substituting your own names for Lastname and Firstname, and instead of spaces between words, use the underscore key, which is Shift + -. Then, in the lower right corner, click the **Save** button.

   An ***MHTML*** file— which has a file extension of ***.mht***—is a format used to save Web pages into a single archive, including all the page elements such as text and graphics.

6. Click the **Home** button. In the **Address bar**, type the drive, such as **f:** or the location where you saved the file, and the most recent files in that location will display. Compare your screen with Figure 3.31.

Figure 3.31

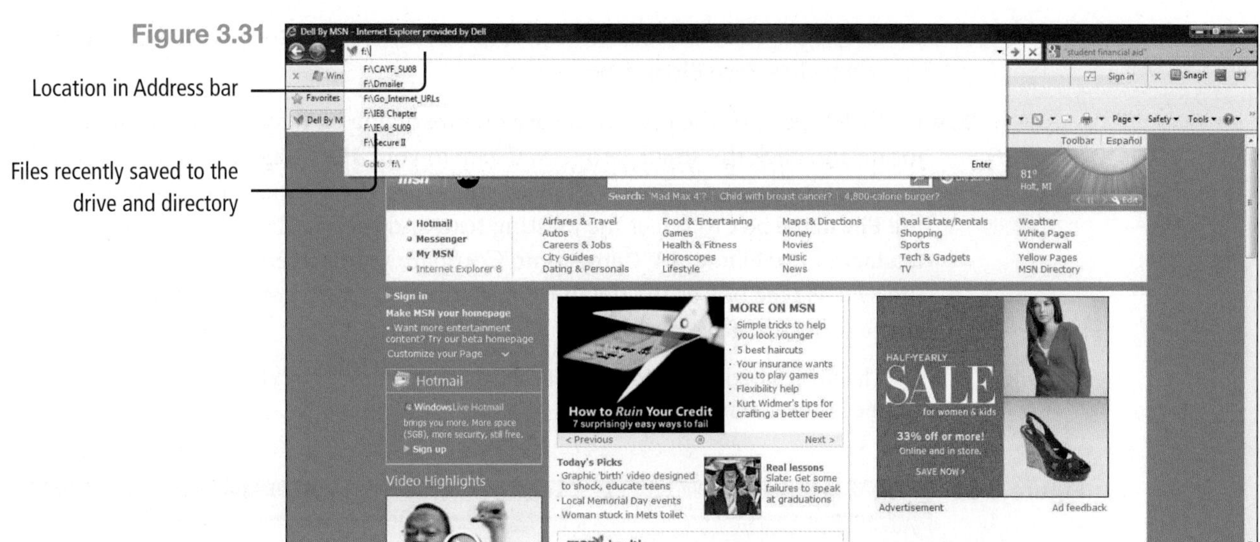

7 Scroll down as necessary, and click the **IE8 Chapter folder**. In the **Computer** window, if necessary, double-click the IE8 Chapter folder. Then double-click the **Lastname_Firstname_1A_College_Money** MHTML document.

The Web page opens in a new tab. Notice the Address bar shows the Web page address as the location where you saved the Web page as a MHTML file. If you were looking at the actual Web page, the Address bar would display the URL as *http://studentaid.ed.gov/PORTALSWebApp/students/english/index.jsp*.

Even though a Web page may look as if it is one single file, it is actually made up of several objects and files. Each graphic is its own file and the text content is another file. In addition, the Web page may be divided into ***frames***. Frames are used to divide a Web page into separate panes that still display as one complete Web page. Navigation is controlled by one of the panes while viewing several different pages of content displayed within a single browser window. The MHTML format saves all of the objects, files, and frames together as one Web archive for viewing offline.

8 **Close** [x] the new tab displaying the Federal Student Aid MHTML file.

9 If necessary, on the Command bar, click the **Home** button to display your home page.

> **More Knowledge | Downloading New Programs**
>
> Downloading, as you used it in Activity 3.11, saves a Web page and associated files in the folder you specify. You can also download entire software programs and other items from the Internet. For example, if you display the Microsoft.com Web site, you can download free trial programs, install them on your system, and try them before you purchase them. When sites offer free downloads, a **Download** link usually displays on the page. When you click the link, Internet Explorer 8 prompts you to save the file on your system. The prompt message also provides an option to open or run the program from the server.
>
> It is generally recommended that you download and save the file on your system before trying to install it. After it is saved to your system, run the program file through your virus protection software before installing the new program. A good rule to follow is to be careful what you download, and download only from well-known and trusted sites.

Activity 3.12 | Downloading and Saving Graphics from a Web Page

1 In the **Address bar**, type **www.bls.gov** and then press Enter. On the **Bureau of Labor Statistics Web site home page**, scroll toward the bottom of the page, and then locate and click the **Career Information for Kids** link. Point anywhere in the displayed picture, right-click the mouse button to display a context-sensitive shortcut menu, and then click **Save Picture As**.

2. In the left pane of the displayed **Save Picture** dialog box, to the left of **Computer**, locate and click the small arrow. Navigate to your **IE8 Chapter** folder and double-click it so that its name displays in the **Save in** box. At the bottom of the dialog box, click in the **File name** box to select the existing text, and then replace it by typing **Lastname_Firstname_1A_Career_Info** Compare your screen with Figure 3.32. Leave the **Save as type** box as the default type—JPEG (*.jpg)—and then in the lower right corner, click the **Save** button.

   The file is saved as a JPEG file. The Save Picture dialog box closes and you are returned to the browser window.

Figure 3.32

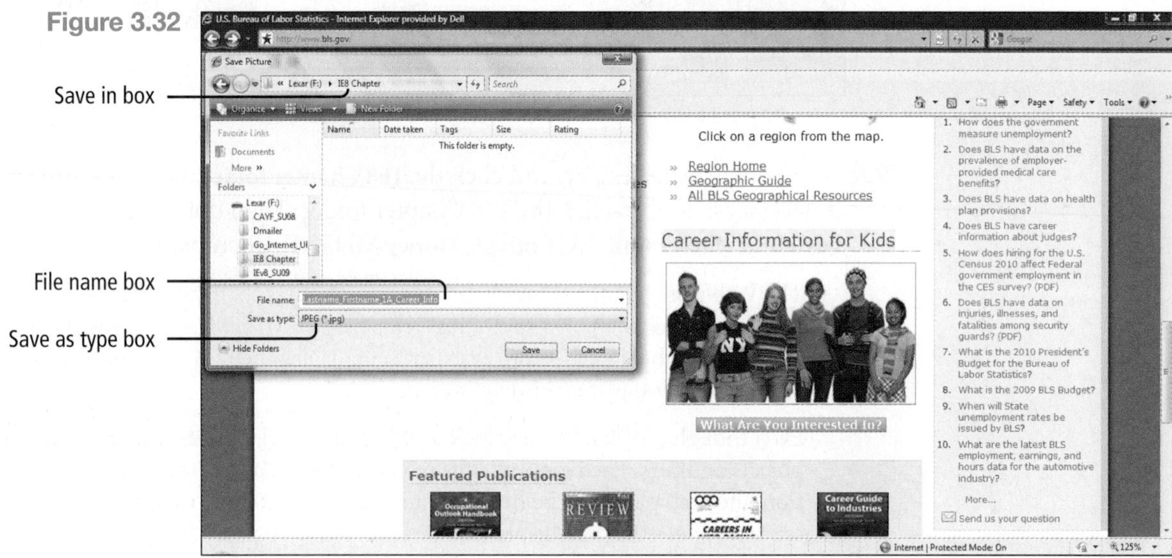

3. On the Command bar, click the **Home** button to display your home page.

Activity 3.13 | Printing Web Pages

Web pages are constructed to contain a variety of different elements—pictures, navigation panes, links, text, and so on. When you print Web pages, all the elements displayed on the Web page print unless you select the specific text, picture, or frame you want to print. Most of the options contained in the Print dialog box in Internet Explorer 8 are the same as those seen in the Print dialog box for other programs. However, the Print dialog box in Internet Explorer 8 contains options that enable you to print pages, frames within a Web page, or a table of pages that are linked to the active Web page.

Because frames and objects are placed so closely together on the Web page, selecting just the information you want to print can be a challenge without activating a hyperlink or selecting additional information as well. In this activity, you will review options in the Print dialog box and print a Web page.

1. From the **Start** menu, click **Computer**, and then navigate to the drive—USB flash drive, computer hard drive, or network drive—where you stored your files for this chapter. Locate and then double-click your MHTML file **Lastname_Firstname_1A_College_Money**. Compare your screen with Figure 3.33.

Figure 3.33

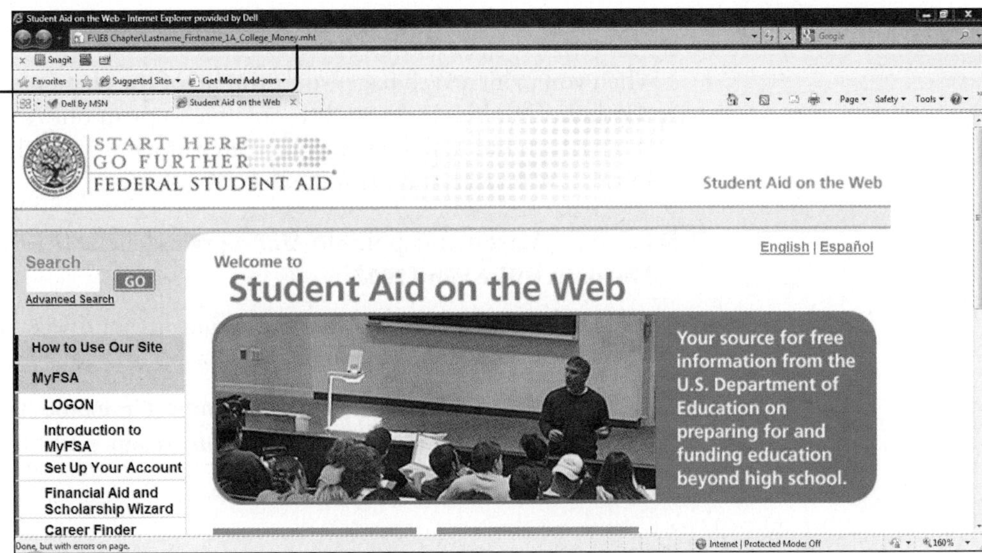

2 On the Command bar, click the **Print button down arrow**, and then click **Page Setup** to display the Page Setup dialog box. Locate the three **Header**: **down arrows** and click **Empty** for each. Locate the section labeled **Footer**: Using the first down arrow, click **URL**. Using the second down arrow, click **Title.** In the third down arrow, click **Date in Short Format.** Compare your screen with Figure 3.34.

Figure 3.34

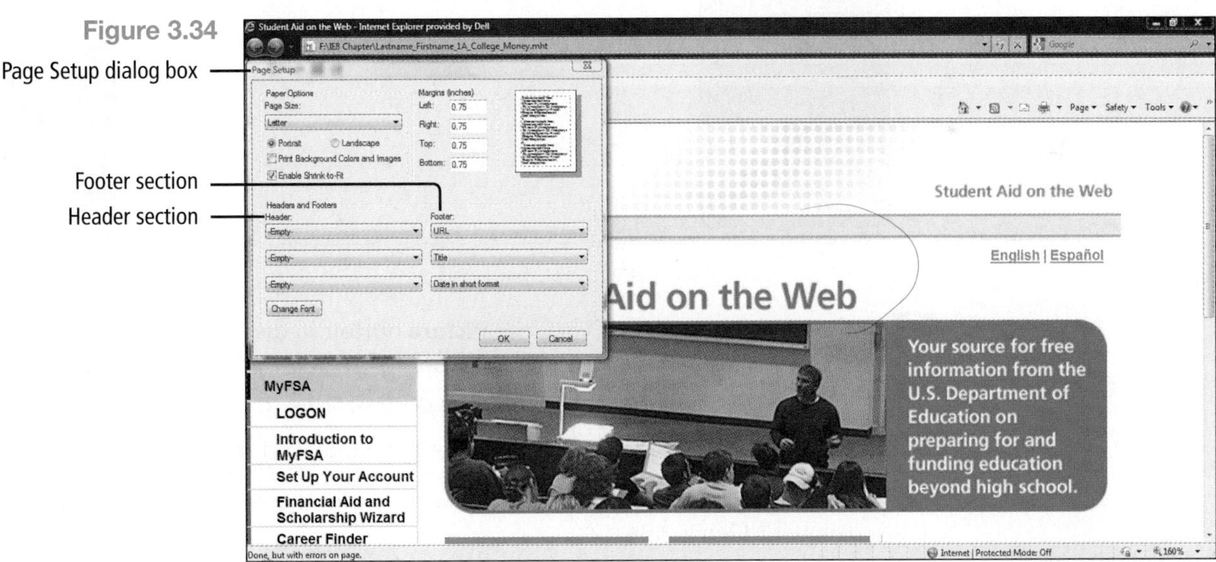

3 In the **Page Setup** dialog box, click **OK**. On the Command bar, click the **Print button down arrow**, click **Print**, and then at the bottom of the displayed **Print** dialog box, click the **Print** button.

The saved Web page print. It is likely that two or more pages will print. At the bottom of each page, the footer you created displays.

4 On the Command bar, click the **Home** button to display your home page. Submit it as directed by your instructor.

Activity 3.14 | Printing Web Graphics

When you print a Web page, you print all of the elements that make up that Web page, both the graphics and text. It is possible to print only the graphics that are part of the Web page. In this activity you will create a document with a graphic that you have saved from a Web page and print the document.

1 From the **Start** menu, point to **All Programs**, click **Microsoft Office**, and then click **Microsoft Office Word 2007**.

Microsoft Office Word, a word processing program, will open a new document. You will add text and graphics to this new document.

2 In the new **Word** document, type **Lastname_Firstname_1A_Career_Info** and then press Enter. On the **Insert tab**, in the **Illustrations group**, point to **Picture** (but do not click). Compare your screen with Figure 3.35.

Figure 3.35

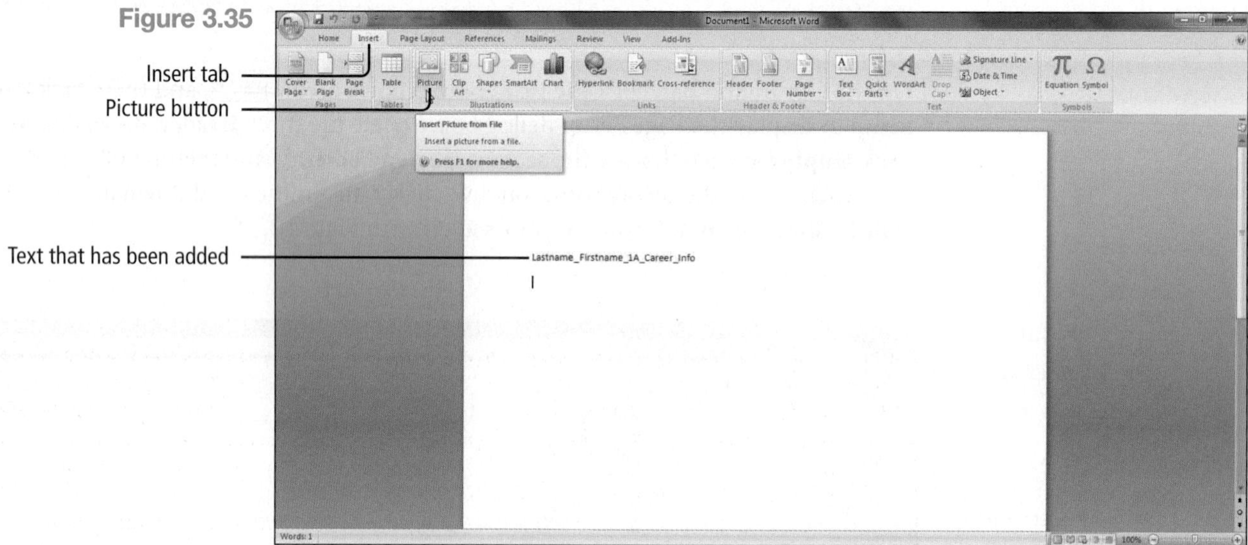

3 In the **Illustrations group**, click the **Picture** button to display the **Insert Picture** dialog box. Navigate to the file **Lastname_Firstname_1A_Career_Info** in your **IE8 Chapter** folder. This graphic was downloaded in Activity 3.12.

4 In the **Insert Picture** dialog box, click the file name, and then click **Insert**.

5 The Web graphic displays underneath your text in the new document. Compare your screen with Figure 3.36.

Figure 3.36

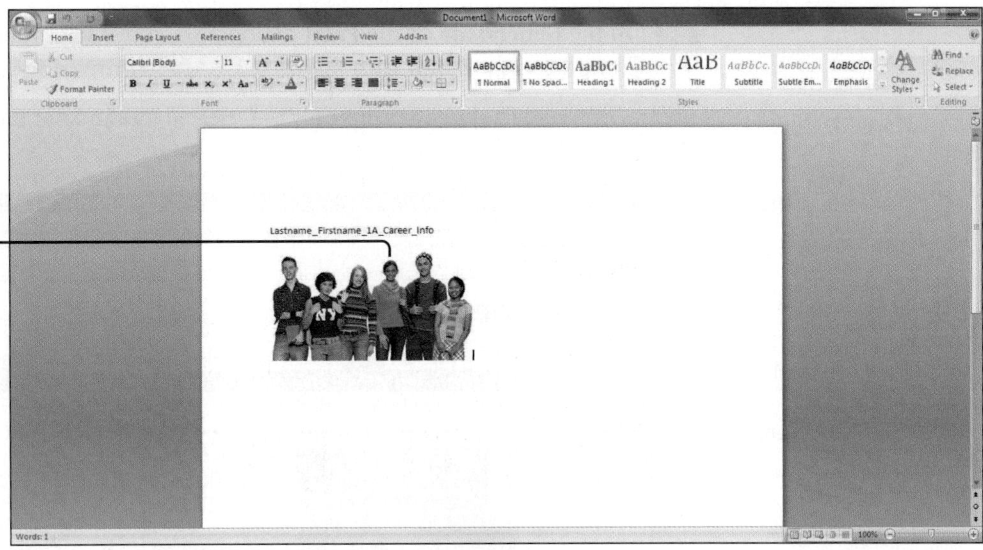

6 From the **Office** button, click **Save As** and then navigate to your **IE8 Chapter** folder so that its name displays in the **Save in** box. At the bottom of the dialog box, click in the **File name** box to select the existing text, and then replace it by typing **Lastname_Firstname_1A_Career_Info** Leave the **Save as type** box as the default type, and then in the lower right corner, click the **Save** button.

> **More Knowledge | Be Aware of Copyright Issues**
>
> Almost everything you find on the Web is protected by copyright law, which protects authors of original works, including text, art, photographs, and music. If you want to use text or graphics that you find online, you will need to get permission. One of the exceptions to this law is the use of small amounts of information for educational purposes, which falls under Fair Use Guidelines. Another exception is to use work that is considered in the ***public domain***. These works are created with the intention of letting anyone use them for any reason; also a work becomes public domain when the copyright has expired.
>
> Copyright laws in the United States are open to different interpretations, and copyright laws can be very different in other countries. As a general rule, if you want to use someone else's material, get permission first.

7 From the **Office** button, click **Print**, and then at the bottom of the displayed **Print** dialog box, click the **OK** button. Submit as directed by your instructor.

The document containing the saved Web graphic prints.

8 **Close** Word to return to the **Internet Explorer** window.

Activity 3.15 | Printing Selected Text from Web Pages

1 In the **Address bar**, type **www.denverpost.com** and press Enter.

The Denver Post Web site displays current information and news items.

2 On the Web page, drag your mouse over the first paragraph under the article heading in the left column to select it.

The paragraph will display as light text on a dark background.

3 On the Command bar, click the **Print button down arrow**, and then click **Print** to display the **Print** dialog box.

4 On the **General tab** of the **Print** dialog box, under **Page Range,** click the **Selection** option. Compare your screen with Figure 3.37. After comparing your screen, click **Print**.

Internet Explorer 8 prints only the selected text and not the entire Web page.

Figure 3.37

5 On the Internet Explorer title bar, click the program's **Close** button.

End **You have completed Project 3A**

Content-Based Assessments

Summary

In this project, you explored basic Internet Explorer 8 features such as starting the browser, navigating among Web pages, and working with Favorites. You learned how to search for Web sites containing information about topics you specify and how to download and save Web pages and graphics. You learned how to print a Web page, a graphic saved from a Web page, and selected text on a Web page.

Key Terms

Command bar 120
Domain name 122
Downloading 135
Favorites bar 124
Favorites Center 124
File Transfer Protocol (FTP) 122
Frames 137
History 129
Home page 118
Hyperlinks 126
Internet Explorer 8 117
Internet Service Provider (ISP) 117
Link Select pointer 126
MHTML 136
Path 126
Portal 120
Protocol 122
Public domain 141
ScreenTip 120
Search engine 133
Sponsored link 135
Tabs 125
Top-level domain (TLD) 122
Uniform Resource Locator (URL) 118
Web browser 117
Web page 118
Web site 118

Matching

Match each term in the second column with its correct definition in the first column. Write the letter of the term on the blank line in front of the correct definition.

____ 1. A protocol that enables individuals to copy files from one computer to another on a network.

____ 2. A Microsoft software program that enables you to view the contents of the World Wide Web.

____ 3. A company that provides an Internet connection through a regular telephone line, a special high-speed telephone line, or a cable.

____ 4. Software that enables you to use the World Wide Web and navigate from page to page and site to site.

____ 5. The unique address used to locate a Web page or Web site.

____ 6. A small note that displays information about a screen element and is activated by pointing to a button or other screen object.

____ 7. An Internet Explorer 8 feature that enables you to view the Favorites, Feeds, and History lists.

____ 8. The toolbar located immediately above the right side of the browser window that can provide quick access to commands such as Home, Page, Safety, and Tools.

____ 9. A browser feature that enables you to have multiple Web pages open at the same time without having to open multiple browsers.

____ 10. The sequential description of the storage location of the HTML documents and files making up the Web page and stored in the hierarchy of directories and folders on the Web server.

A Command bar
B Downloading
C Favorites Center
D File Transfer Protocol (FTP)
E History
F Internet Explorer 8
G Internet Service Provider (ISP)
H MHTML
I Path
J ScreenTip
K Sponsored link
L Tabs
M Uniform Resource Locator (URL)
N Web browser
O Web page

_____ 11. An Internet Explorer 8 feature that tracks recently visited Web pages and sites.

_____ 12. A site that pays to be displayed with results at a search engine site.

_____ 13. To request a copy of a file or program from a remote server, such as a Web server, and then to save it on your local system or storage device.

_____ 14. A format used to save Web pages into a single archive, including all the page elements such as text and graphics.

_____ 15. A document on the World Wide Web that displays as a screen with associated links, frames, pictures, and other features of interest.

Multiple Choice

Circle the correct response.

1. The part of a text-based URL that identifies the company or organization that owns the Web site is called a:
   a. Top-level domain **b.** Public domain **c.** Domain name

2. The Web page that displays when you start Internet Explorer 8 is called a:
   a. Portal **b.** Home page **c.** Sponsored link

3. A group of related Web pages published to a specific location on the World Wide Web is called a:
   a. Favorites bar **b.** Home page **c.** Web site

4. A home page that contain links to frequently visited sites, up-to-the-minute news, weather reports, maps, and directories is called a:
   a. Portal **b.** Favorites Center **c.** Public domain

5. The highest level of the Domain Name System expressed as the last part of the domain name and represented by a period followed by three or four letters is called the:
   a. FTP **b.** TLD **c.** ISP

6. The toolbar located above the left side of the browser window that provides immediate access to a favorite Web site is called the:
   a. History **b.** Command bar **c.** Favorites bar

7. Text, buttons, pictures, or other objects displayed on Web pages that, when clicked, access other Web pages or display other sections of the active page are called:
   a. Hyperlinks **b.** Link Select pointers **c.** ScreenTips

8. The method used to divide a Web page into separate panes that appear to be one complete Web page is called:
   a. Tabs **b.** Portals **c.** Frames

9. A program that searches for keywords in files and documents or other Web sites found on the Internet is called a:
   a. Search engine **b.** Portal **c.** File Transfer Protocol

10. The set of rules for transferring data over the Internet is called a:
    a. Path **b.** Protocol **c.** Public domain

Apply 3A skills from these Objectives:

1. Start Internet Explorer 8 and Identify Screen Elements
2. Navigate the Internet
3. Create and Manage Favorites
4. Search the Internet
5. Save and Print Web Pages

Skills Review | Project 3B Playing Music from a Favorite Link

In the following Skills Review project, you will open a Web site, save it in Favorites, and locate and listen to a radio station that is near Lake Michigan City College. You can use the radio tuner to locate radio stations in your area and, if you have a sound card, you can listen to the radio as you work. Your screen will look similar to Figure 3.38.

Project Files

For Project 3B, you will save your file as:

Lastname_Firstname_1B_Radio

Project Results

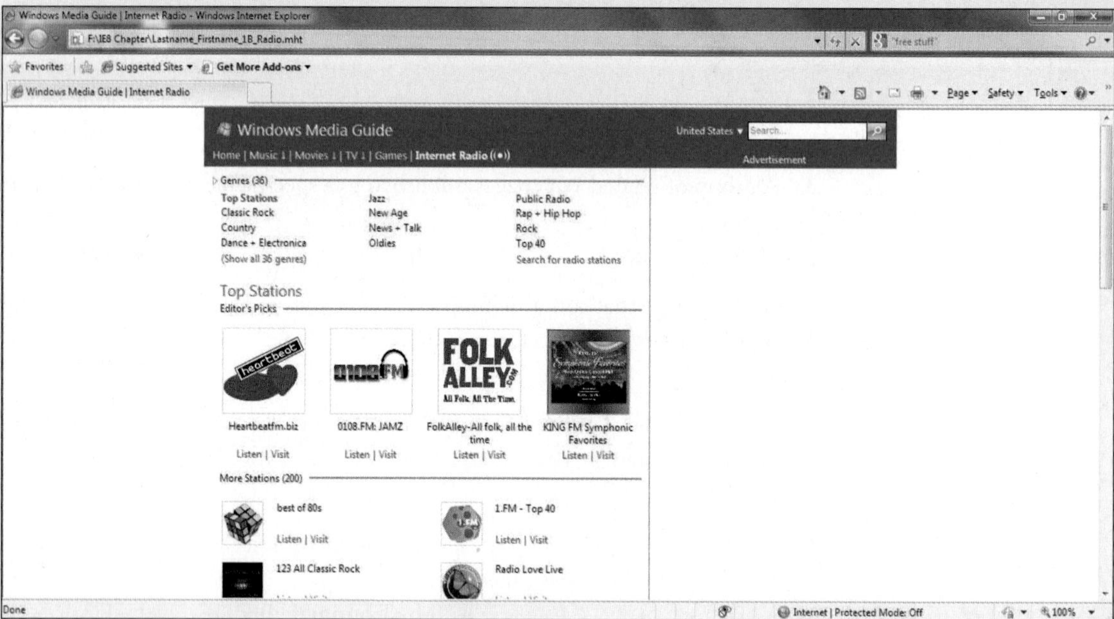

Figure 3.38

(Project 3B Playing Music from a Favorite Link continues on the next page)

Skills Review | Project 3B Playing Music from a Favorite Link (continued)

1. On the Windows taskbar, click the **Start** button, and then locate **Internet Explorer 8** on your system. On your system, click **Internet Explorer**. In the **Address bar**, type **http://windowsmedia.com/radiotuner** Press Enter.
2. On the Favorites bar, click the **Favorites** button, and if necessary, click the Favorites tab. Then click **Add to Favorites** to display the **Add a Favorite** dialog box.
3. In the **Add a Favorite** dialog box, change the name to **Radio Station Guide** and then click the **Add** button.

   Each category under Genres can be clicked to display additional stations. You can use links to visit a radio station or listen to the station. You can locate more stations by looking in the More Stations section or by using the Search box.
4. In the **Top Stations** list, click the first station to open the Windows Media Player.
5. In the Windows Media Player that displays, notice the buttons to pause the music and to close the Windows Media Player when you are finished listening.

   The Windows Media Player opens and the station plays. This may take a few seconds as the streaming process occurs. Depending on the active settings on your system, Internet Explorer 8 may present a message box asking if you want to play the station in Internet Explorer. If you are prompted, click Yes to play the station.
6. On the Command bar, click **Page** and then click **Save As** to display the **Save Webpage** dialog box. In the **File name** box, type **Lastname_Firstname_1B_Radio** Change the **Save as type** to **Web Archive, single file (*.mht)**. In the **Save in** box, navigate to the **IE8 Chapter** folder that you created earlier in this chapter.
7. In the **Save Webpage** dialog box, click **Save**.
8. In the **Address bar**, type the drive—for example **f:**—and the location where you saved the file, and the most recent files in that location will display. Scroll down as necessary, and click the file name that you saved in Step 6.
9. On the Command bar, click the **Print down arrow** to open the **Print** dialog box. Click the **Print** button to print the saved Web page. Submit it as directed by your instructor.
10. In the **Windows Media Player** window, click the **Stop** button to stop the live broadcast, and then click the Media Player's **Close** button to close the pane.
11. Click the **Close** button to close Internet Explorer.

End You have completed Project 3B

Apply **2A** skills from these Objectives:

1. Start Internet Explorer 8 and Identify Screen Elements
2. Navigate the Internet
5. Save and Print Web Pages

Skills Review | Project 3C Searching for Multimedia

In the following Skills Review, you will search for free downloads of multimedia for your music appreciation class at Lake Michigan City College.

The Internet provides opportunities to locate and download several types of multimedia, such as animated graphics and sound or video files. However, the ease with which it is possible to copy these files does not always make it legally acceptable. The Fair Use Guidelines for Educational Multimedia allow for the use of copyrighted materials for educational purposes under certain circumstances. These circumstances address the purpose of use and the quantity of materials to be used. In addition, consideration must be given to whether the work has been put into the public domain, and there must be no effect on any potential market. Follow these instructions to perform a search for copyright-free sound files. Your screen will look similar to Figure 3.39.

Project Files

For Project 3C, you will save your file as:

Lastname_Firstname_1C_Multimedia

Project Results

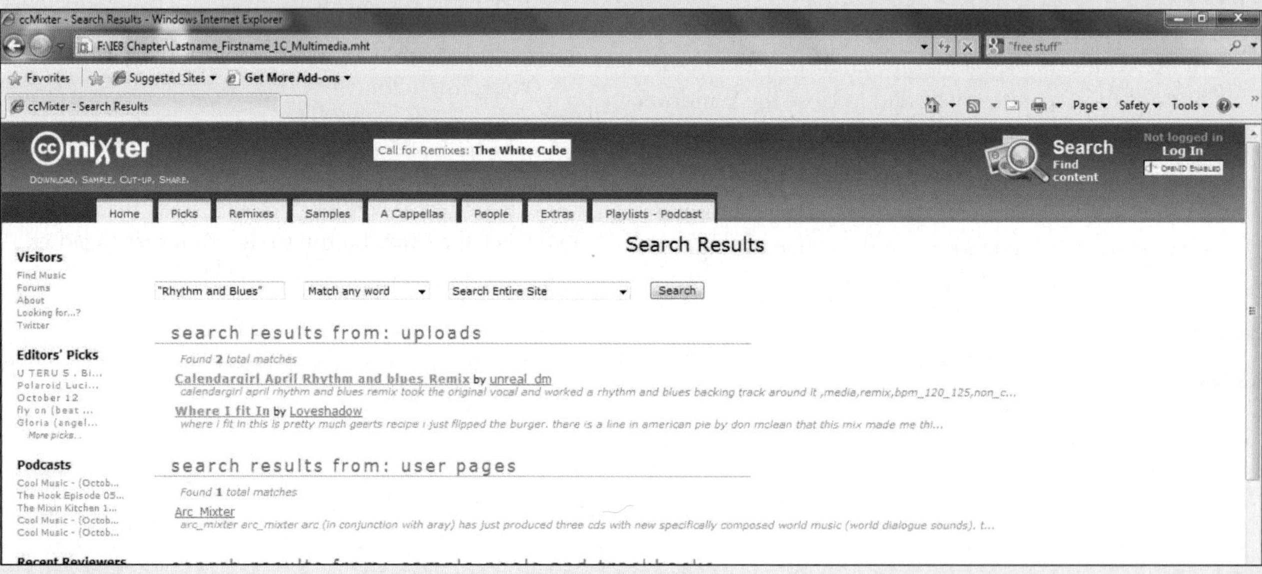

Figure 3.39

(Project 3C Searching for Multimedia continues on the next page)

Skills Review | Project 3C Searching for Multimedia (continued)

1. On the Windows taskbar, click the **Start** button, and then locate **Internet Explorer 8** on your Start menu. On your system, click **Internet Explorer**.
2. In the **Address bar**, type **ccmixter.org** and then press Enter.

   The ccMixter Web site displays. This site offers copyright-free and royalty-free sound files that are available for listening, downloading, remixing, and sharing through a Creative Commons license.
3. In the upper right corner, click the **Search Find Content** link.
4. In the **SearchFind content** pop-up that displays, in the **Search Text** box, type **"Rhythm and Blues"** including the quotation marks. Leave the default Match and What choices selected. Click the **Search** button.
5. On the Command bar, click **Page** and then click **Save As** to display the **Save Webpage** dialog box. In the **File name** box, type **Lastname_Firstname_1C_Multimedia** Change the **Save as type** to **Web Archive, single file (*.mht)**. In the **Save in** box, navigate to the **IE8 Chapter** folder that you created earlier in this chapter.
6. In the **Save Webpage** dialog box, click **Save**.
7. In the **Address bar**, type the drive—for example **f:**—and the location where you saved the file, and the most recent files in that location will display. Scroll down as necessary, and click the file name that you saved in Step 5.
8. On the Command bar, click **Print down arrow** to open the **Print** dialog box. Click the **Print** button to print the saved Web page. Submit it as directed by your instructor. **Close** Internet Explorer.

End **You have completed Project 3C**

Apply 3A skills from these Objectives:

1. Start Internet Explorer 8 and Identify Screen Elements
4. Search the Internet
5. Save and Print Web Pages

Mastering | Project 3D Searching for Picture Space

In this project, you will search for free photographic services for the Alumni Club at Lake Michigan City College. The festivities on Homecoming Weekend were a great success and brought in alumni from around the state. Many sites on the Internet offer free space for storing and sharing pictures. From these sites, friends and family can view pictures and order copies of those pictures they want to keep. You can locate these services by searching the Internet. Follow these steps to locate and explore sites to determine which one best meets your needs. Your screens will look similar to Figure 3.40.

Project Files

For Project 3D, you will save your files as:

Lastname_Firstname_1D_Photo_1
Lastname_Firstname_1D_Photo_2

Project Results

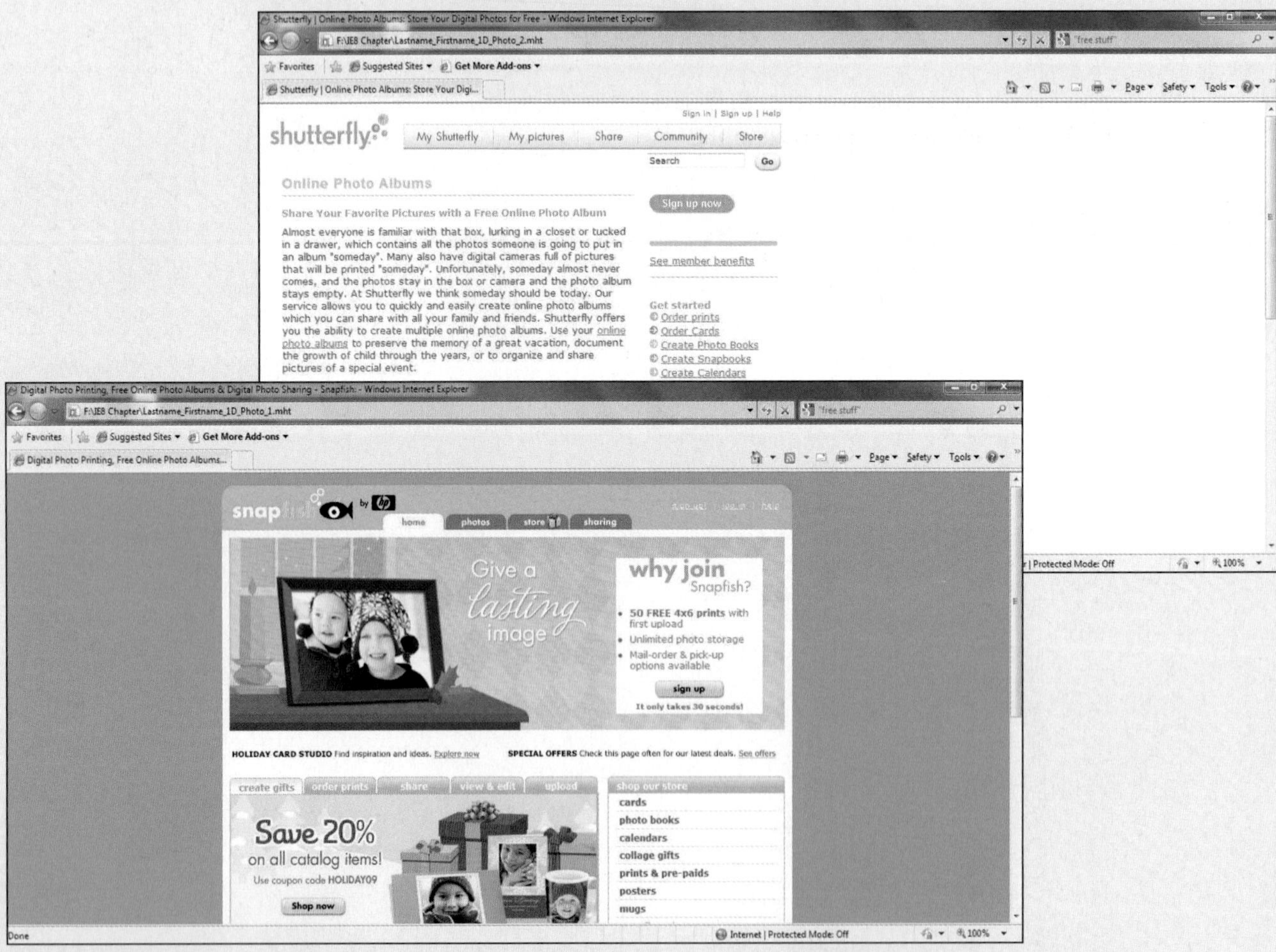

Figure 3.40

(Project 3D Searching for Picture Space continues on the next page)

Mastering | Project 3D Searching for Picture Space (continued)

1. Open **Internet Explorer 8**.
2. On the **Address bar**, in the **Search** box, type **"free online photo albums"** and then press Enter. Several Web sites that offer free photographic services, such as storage and online photo albums, display.
3. In the list of **Web Results**, click the first link to display a Web site providing a free online photo album that is not a sponsored site. Scroll down the Web page until you locate information about how that online photo album works.
4. On the Command bar, click the **Page** button, and then click **Save As** to display the **Save Webpage** dialog box. In the **File name** box, type **Lastname_Firstname_1D_Photo_1** Change the **Save as type** to **Web Archive, single file (*.mht)**, and then in the **Save in** box, navigate to the **IE8 Chapter** folder that you created earlier in the chapter.
5. In the **Save Webpage** dialog box, click **Save**. Click the **Back** button to return to the search results.
6. Click another link in the list of Web Results to display another Web site providing a free online photo album. Scroll down that Web page until you locate information about how that online photo album works.
7. On the Command bar, click the **Page** button, and then click **Save As** to display the **Save Webpage** dialog box. In the **File name** box, type **Lastname_Firstname_1D_Photo_2** Change the **Save as type** to **Web Archive, single file (*.mht)**, and then in the **Save in** box, navigate to the **IE8 Chapter** folder that you created earlier in the chapter.
8. In the **Save Webpage** dialog box, click **Save**.
9. Use the **Address bar** to open each of the two saved files and then on the Command bar, click the **Print** button to print each of the saved files. Submit them as directed by your instructor.
10. **Close** Internet Explorer.

End **You have completed Project 3D**

Apply 3A skills from these Objectives:

1 Start Internet Explorer 8 and Identify Screen Elements
3 Create and Manage Favorites
4 Search the Internet
5 Save and Print Web Pages

Mastering | Project 3E Locating Free Items

In the following project, you will search for free coupons, offers, and programs available on the Internet as marketing giveaway items for a club at Lake Michigan City College. As you become more familiar with the Internet, you will find free items such as software programs, computer equipment, computer services, and so on—available from Web sites. Not all of these offers are legitimate. Search the Internet for free items and review some of the offers. As you explore and evaluate the sites, remember that you should download programs and information only from sites you know and trust. Determine which sites make legitimate offers and which do not. Several criteria will help you with this determination. The following set of questions will be helpful as you perform an evaluation of a Web site:

- Is the site attractive and professional looking?
- When was the last time that the Web site was updated? Are there broken links or misspelled words?
- Who owns or sponsors the site? Do they seem qualified to make this type of offer?
- Are you required to provide personal data such as name, location, age, or credit or financial information in order to receive "free" items?

Your screens will look similar to Figure 3.41.

Project Files

For Project 2E, you will save your files as:

Lastname_Firstname_1E_Free_1
Lastname_Firstname_1E_Free_2

Project Results

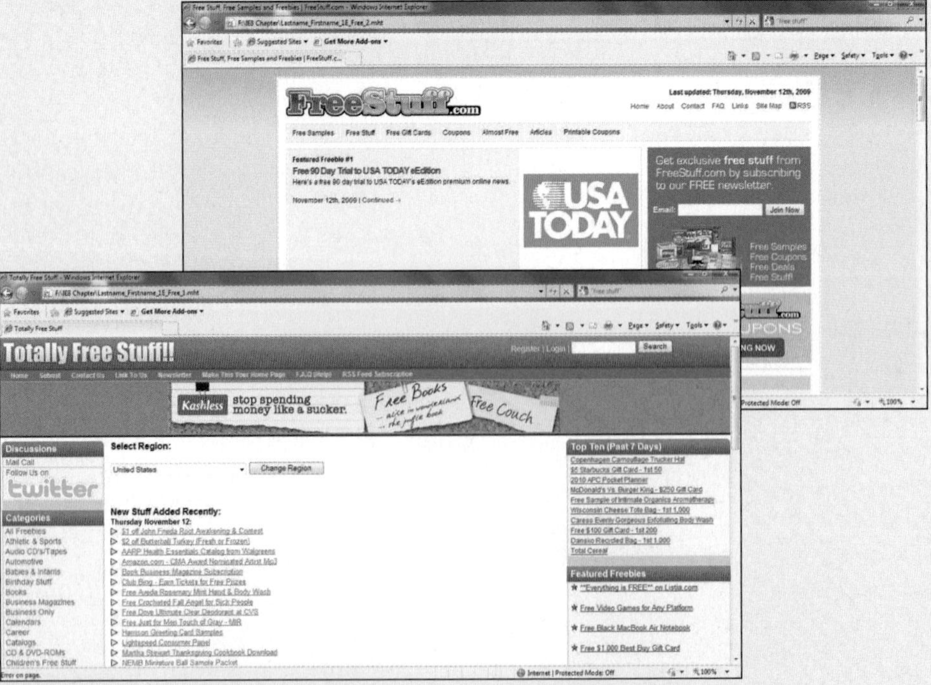

Figure 3.41

(Project 3E Locating Free Items continues on the next page)

Mastering | Project 3E Locating Free Items (continued)

1. Open **Internet Explorer 8**.
2. On the Address bar, in the **Search** box, type **"free stuff"** and then press Enter.
3. In the list of **Web Results**, click on the first link to display a Web site providing free stuff that is not a sponsored site. Scroll down the Web page until you locate the answers to the set of questions in the previous list to help you determine the legitimacy of the free offers.
4. On the Favorites bar, click the **Favorites** button, and then click **Add to Favorites** to open the **Add a Favorite** dialog box.
5. In the **Add a Favorite** dialog box, click the **New Folder** button. In the **Folder Name** box, type **Free Stuff** Click **Create**, and then click **Add** to add the Web site to the folder. A new folder named Free Stuff displays in the list of Favorites and the current Web site has been added to it.
6. On the Command bar, click the **Page** button, and then click **Save As** to display the **Save Webpage** dialog box. In the **File name** box, type **Lastname_Firstname_1E_Free_1** If necessary, change the Save as type to Web Archive, single file (*.mht), and then navigate to the **IE8 Chapter** folder that you created earlier in the chapter. Click **Save**.
7. Use the **Address bar** to open the saved file and then on the Command bar, use the **Print** button to print the saved file. Submit it as directed by your instructor.
8. On the **Address bar**, click **Back** to return to the Web Results. Scroll down the list to choose another Web site offering free stuff. Click the link to that Web site and answer the same set of questions to determine the legitimacy of the free offers.
9. On the Favorites bar, click the **Favorites** button, and then if necessary, click Add to Favorites to display the Add a Favorite dialog box. Be sure the **Free Stuff** folder is displayed in the **Create in** box, and then click the **Add** button.
10. On the Command bar, click the **Page** button, and then click **Save As** to display the **Save Webpage** dialog box. In the **File name** box, type **Lastname_Firstname_1E_Free_2** If necessary, change the Save as type to Web Archive, single file (*.mht), and then navigate to the **IE8 Chapter** folder that you created earlier in the chapter. Click **Save**.
11. Use the **Address bar** to open the saved file and then on the Command bar, use the **Print** button to print the saved file. Submit it as directed by your instructor.
12. On the Favorites bar, click the **Favorites** button if necessary, scroll down, and then click on the **Free Stuff** folder to display the two Web sites that you added to the folder.
13. Click anywhere outside the **Favorites** list to close it. **Close** Internet Explorer.

End **You have completed Project 3E**

Apply 3A skills from these Objectives:

1. Start Internet Explorer 8 and Identify Screen Elements
4. Search the Internet
5. Save and Print Web Pages

Mastering | Project 3F Protecting Your Privacy

In this project, you will search the Internet for information about yourself or other members of your family as part of your sociology project at Lake Michigan City College. The World Wide Web stores information about individuals in addition to companies. Many businesses store data about their clients and customers in databases on the Web so that they can place orders online. Families often store family trees on Web sites so that others can track their family history. Search the Internet for information about yourself to see what information is stored about you and others with your name. You might prefer to search for information about your family name to see if family tree data is available. The World Wide Web provides a means to easily gather personal information about you and your family. One of the best ways to learn about protecting your family and yourself is to look at the privacy policies of Web sites that you visit. Locate and review the privacy policy at any Web site you find that contains information about you or your family. Answer these questions:

- How does the Web site collect information about you?
- How is the information used?
- Are there options for you to prevent the collection and sharing of your personal data?

Your screen will look similar to Figure 3.42.

Project Files

For Project 2F, you will save your file as:
Lastname_Firstname_1F_Privacy

Project Results

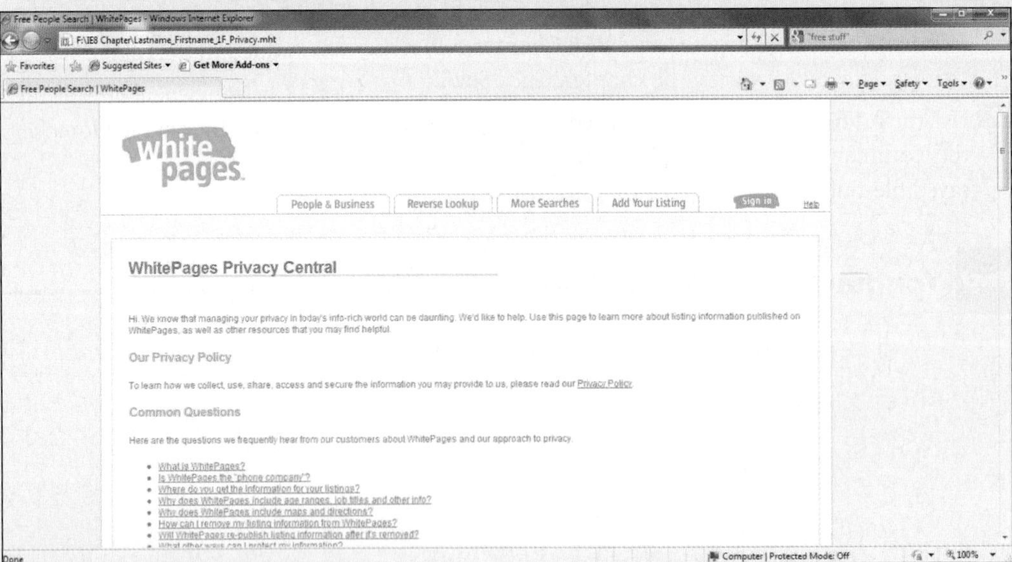

Figure 3.42

(Project 3F Protecting Your Privacy continues on the next page)

Mastering | Project 3F Protecting Your Privacy (continued)

1. Open **Internet Explorer 8**.
2. In the **Address bar**, type **www.whitepages.com** and then press Enter to display the **WhitePages** home page.
3. Under **Find People**, type your first name, last name, your city, and your state in the appropriate boxes. Click the **Find** button. A number of results are displayed. Take a moment to review them.
4. Scroll down to the bottom of the results page. Click the **Privacy** link. Read the privacy policy to determine the answers to the questions listed at the beginning of this project.
5. On the Command bar, click the **Page** button, and then click **Save As** to display the **Save Webpage** dialog box. In the **File name** box, type **Lastname_Firstname_1F_Privacy** If necessary, change the Save as type to Web Archive, single file (*.mht), and then navigate to the **IE8 Chapter** folder that you created earlier in the chapter. Click **Save**.
6. Use the **Address bar** to open the saved file and then on the Command bar, use the **Print** button to print the saved file. Submit it as directed by your instructor.
7. **Close** Internet Explorer.

End **You have completed Project 3F**

Outcomes-Based Assessments

Rubric

The following Outcomes-Based Assessment is an open-ended assessment. That is, there is no specific correct result; your result will depend on your approach to the information provided. Make Professional Quality your goal. Use the following scoring rubric to guide you in how to approach the problem and then to evaluate how well your approach solves the problem.

The *criteria*—Software Mastery, Content, Format and Layout, and Process—represent the knowledge and skills you have gained that you can apply to solving the problem. The *levels of performance*—Professional Quality, Approaching Professional Quality, or Needs Quality Improvements—help you and your instructor evaluate your result.

	Your completed project is of Professional Quality if you:	**Your completed project is Approaching Professional Quality if you:**	**Your completed project Needs Quality Improvements if you:**
1-Software Mastery	Choose and apply the most appropriate skills, tools, and features and identify efficient methods to solve the problem.	Choose and apply some appropriate skills, tools, and features, but not in the most efficient manner.	Choose inappropriate skills, tools, or features, or are inefficient in solving the problem.
2-Content	Construct a solution that is clear and well organized, contains content that is accurate, appropriate to the audience and purpose, and is complete. Provide a solution that contains no errors of spelling, grammar, or style.	Construct a solution in which some components are unclear, poorly organized, inconsistent, or incomplete. Misjudge the needs of the audience. Have some errors in spelling, grammar, or style, but the errors do not detract from comprehension.	Construct a solution that is unclear, incomplete, or poorly organized, contains some inaccurate or inappropriate content; and contains many errors of spelling, grammar, or style. Do not solve the problem.
3-Format and Layout	Format and arrange all elements to communicate information and ideas, clarify function, illustrate relationships, and indicate relative importance.	Apply appropriate format and layout features to some elements, but not others. Overuse features, causing minor distraction.	Apply format and layout that does not communicate information or ideas clearly. Do not use format and layout features to clarify function, illustrate relationships, or indicate relative importance. Use available features excessively, causing distraction.
4-Process	Use an organized approach that integrates planning, development, self-assessment, revision, and reflection.	Demonstrate an organized approach in some areas, but not others; or, use an insufficient process of organization throughout.	Do not use an organized approach to solve the problem.

Apply a combination of the 3A skills.

GO! Think | Project 3G Exploring Copyright Laws

Use the skills you practiced in this chapter to locate information on copyright laws and the appropriate use of copyrighted information for educational purposes. The major focus of legislation in this area includes findings on Fair Use.

Project Files

For Project 3G, you will save your files as:

Lastname_Firstname_1G_Copyright
Lastname_Firstname_1G_Fair_Use

Conduct a search to locate the Web site of the government organization that oversees copyright law and a Web site of an educational institution that pertains to Fair Use. Explore these Web sites to locate information on copyright and Fair Use. Save the government Web page as **Lastname_Firstname_1G_Copyright** Save the educational institution Web page as **Lastname_Firstname_1G_Fair_Use** Print each Web page and submit the documents as directed.

End **You have completed Project 3G**

Creating Documents with Microsoft Word 2010

OUTCOMES

At the end of this chapter you will be able to:

OBJECTIVES

Mastering these objectives will enable you to:

PROJECT 4A
Create a flyer with a picture.

1. Create a New Document and Insert Text (p. 161)
2. Insert and Format Graphics (p. 163)
3. Insert and Modify Text Boxes and Shapes (p. 168)
4. Preview and Print a Document (p. 172)

PROJECT 4B
Format text, paragraphs, and documents.

5. Change Document and Paragraph Layout (p. 177)
6. Create and Modify Lists (p. 183)
7. Set and Modify Tab Stops (p. 188)
8. Insert a SmartArt Graphic (p. 190)

Joy Brown/Shutterstock

In This Chapter

In this chapter, you will use Microsoft Word, which is one of the most common programs found on computers and one that almost everyone has a reason to use. You will use many of the new tools found in Word 2010. When you learn word processing, you are also learning skills and techniques that you need to work efficiently on a computer. You can use Microsoft Word to perform basic word processing tasks such as writing a memo, a report, or a letter. You can also use Word to complete complex word processing tasks, such as creating sophisticated tables, embedding graphics, writing blogs, creating publications, and inserting links into other documents and the Internet. Word is a program that you can learn gradually, and then add more advanced skills one at a time.

The projects in this chapter relate to **Laurel College**. The college offers this diverse geographic area a wide range of academic and career programs, including associate degrees, certificate programs, and non-credit continuing education and personal development courses. The college makes positive contributions to the community through cultural and athletic programs and partnerships with businesses and nonprofit organizations. The college also provides industry-specific training programs for local businesses through its growing Economic Development Center.

Project 4A Flyer

Project Activities

In Activities 4.01 through 4.12, you will create a flyer announcing a new rock climbing class offered by the Physical Education Department at Laurel College. Your completed document will look similar to Figure 4.1.

Project Files

For Project 4A, you will need the following files:

New blank Word document
w01A_Fitness_Flyer
w01A_Rock_Climber

You will save your document as:

Lastname_Firstname_1A_Fitness_Flyer

Project Results

Figure 4.1
Project 4A Fitness Flyer

Objective 1 | Create a New Document and Insert Text

When you create a new document, you can type all of the text, or you can type some of the text and then insert additional text from another source.

Activity 4.01 | Starting a New Word Document and Inserting Text

1. **Start** Word and display a new blank document. On the **Home tab**, in the **Paragraph group**, if necessary click the Show/Hide button ¶ so that it is active (glows orange) to display the formatting marks. If the rulers do not display, click the View tab, and then in the Show group, select the Ruler check box.

2. Type **Rock Climbing 101** and then press Enter two times. As you type the following text, press the Spacebar only one time at the end of a sentence: **Increase your fitness level by learning basic rock climbing using the new Laurel College Gymnasium rock climbing wall. The Physical Education Department is offering Rock Climbing 101 as part of its Recreational Fitness Program.**

   As you type, the insertion point moves to the right, and when it approaches the right margin, Word determines whether the next word in the line will fit within the established right margin. If the word does not fit, Word moves the entire word down to the next line. This feature is called ***wordwrap*** and means that you press Enter *only* when you reach the end of a paragraph—it is not necessary to press Enter at the end of each line of text.

> **Note** | Spacing Between Sentences
> Although you might have learned to add two spaces following end-of-sentence punctuation, the common practice now is to space only one time at the end of a sentence.

3. Press Enter one time. Take a moment to study the table in Figure 4.2 to become familiar with the default document settings in Microsoft Word, and then compare your screen with Figure 4.3.

   When you press Enter, Spacebar, or Tab on your keyboard, characters display in your document to represent these keystrokes. These characters do not print and are referred to as ***formatting marks*** or ***nonprinting characters***. These marks will display throughout this instruction.

Default Document Settings in a New Word Document

Setting	Default format
Font and font size	The default font is Calibri and the default font size is 11.
Margins	The default left, right, top, and bottom page margins are 1 inch.
Line spacing	The default line spacing is 1.15, which provides slightly more space between lines than single spacing does—an extra 1/6 of a line added between lines than single spacing.
Paragraph spacing	The default spacing after a paragraph is 10 points, which is slightly less than the height of one blank line of text.
View	The default view is Print Layout view, which displays the page borders and displays the document as it will appear when printed.

Figure 4.2

Figure 4.3

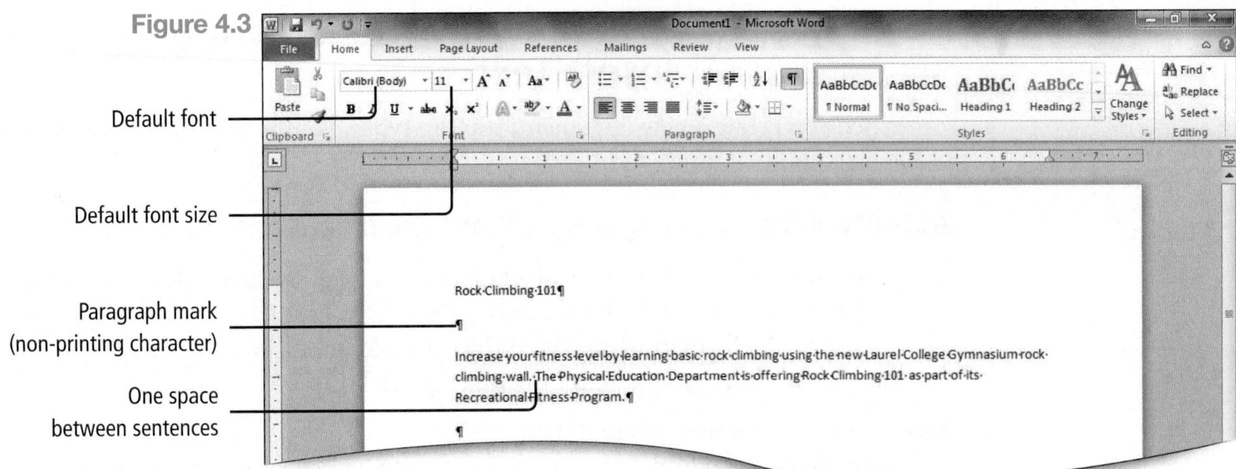

4 On the Ribbon, click the **Insert tab**. In the **Text group**, click the **Object button arrow**, and then click **Text from File**.

> **Alert! | Does the Object Dialog Box Display?**
>
> If the Object dialog box displays, you probably clicked the Object *button* instead of the Object *button arrow*. Close the Object dialog box, and then in the Text group, click the Object button arrow, as shown in Figure 4.4. Click *Text from File*, and then continue with Step 5.

> **Another Way**
>
> Open the file, copy the required text, close the file, and then paste the text into the current document.

5 In the **Insert File** dialog box, navigate to the student files that accompany this textbook, locate and select **w01A_Fitness_Flyer**, and then click **Insert**. Compare your screen with Figure 4.4.

A *copy* of the text from the w01A_Fitness_Flyer file displays at the insertion point location; the text is not removed from the original file.

Figure 4.4

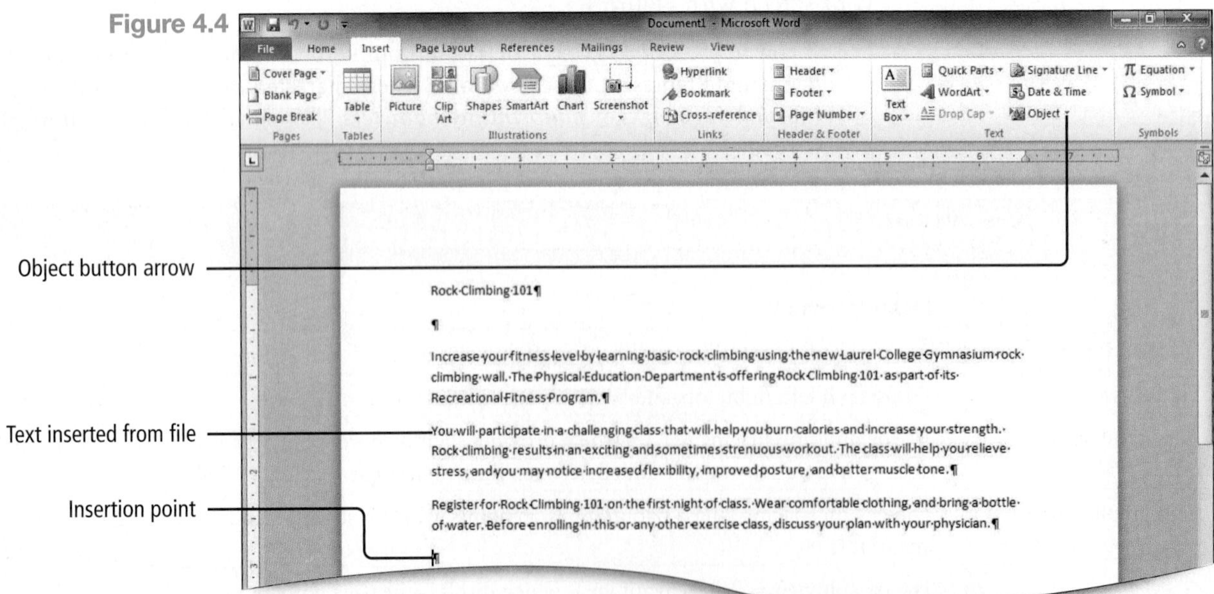

6 On the **Quick Access Toolbar**, click the **Save** button. In the **Save As** dialog box, navigate to the location where you are saving your files for this chapter, and then create and open a new folder named **Word Chapter 1** In the **File name** box, replace the existing text with **Lastname_Firstname_1A_Fitness_Flyer** and then click **Save**.

> **More Knowledge | Word's Default Settings Are Easier to Read Online**
>
> Until just a few years ago, word processing programs used single spacing, an extra blank paragraph to separate paragraphs, and 12 pt Times New Roman as the default formats. Now, studies show that individuals find the Word default formats described in Figure 4.2 to be easier to read online, where many documents are now viewed and read.

Objective 2 | Insert and Format Graphics

To add visual interest to a document, insert ***graphics***. Graphics include pictures, clip art, charts, and ***drawing objects***—shapes, diagrams, lines, and so on. For additional visual interest, you can convert text to an attractive graphic format; add, resize, move, and format pictures; and add an attractive page border.

Activity 4.02 | Formatting Text Using Text Effects

Text effects are decorative formats, such as shadowed or mirrored text, text glow, 3-D effects, and colors that make text stand out.

1. Including the paragraph mark, select the first paragraph of text—*Rock Climbing 101.* On the **Home tab**, in the **Font group**, click the **Text Effects** button.
2. In the displayed **Text Effects** gallery, in the first row, point to the second effect to display the ScreenTip *Fill - None, Outline - Accent 2* and then click this effect.
3. With the text still selected, in the **Font group**, click in the **Font Size** box to select the existing font size. Type **60** and then press Enter.

   When you want to change the font size of selected text to a size that does not display in the Font Size list, type the number in the Font Size button box and press Enter to confirm the new font size.
4. With the text still selected, in the **Paragraph group**, click the **Center** button to center the text. Compare your screen with Figure 4.5.

Figure 4.5

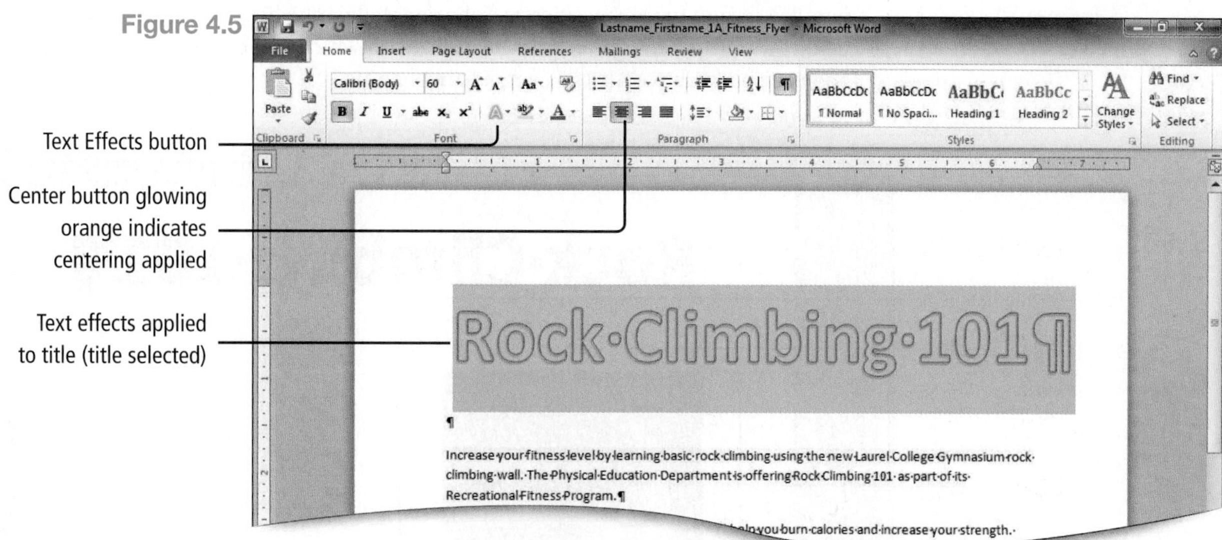

5. With the text still selected, in the **Font group**, click the **Text Effects** button. Point to **Shadow**, and then under **Outer**, in the second row, click the third style—**Offset Left**.
6. With the text still selected, in the **Font group**, click the **Font Color button arrow**. Under **Theme Colors**, in the fourth column, click the first color—**Dark Blue, Text 2**.

7. Click anywhere in the document to deselect the text, and then compare your screen with Figure 4.6.

Figure 4.6

8. **Save** your document.

Activity 4.03 | Inserting and Resizing Pictures

1. In the paragraph that begins *Increase your fitness*, click to position the insertion point at the beginning of the paragraph.

2. On the **Insert tab**, in the **Illustrations group**, click the **Picture** button. In the **Insert Picture** dialog box, navigate to your student data files, locate and click **w01A_Rock_Climber**, and then click **Insert**.

   Word inserts the picture as an ***inline object***; that is, the picture is positioned directly in the text at the insertion point, just like a character in a sentence. Sizing handles surround the picture indicating it is selected.

3. If necessary, scroll to view the entire picture. Notice the round and square sizing handles around the border of the selected picture, as shown in Figure 4.7.

   The round corner sizing handles resize the graphic proportionally. The square sizing handles resize a graphic vertically or horizontally only; however, sizing with these will distort the graphic. A green rotate handle, with which you can rotate the graphic to any angle, displays above the top center sizing handle.

Figure 4.7

4 At the lower right corner of the picture, point to the round sizing handle until the pointer displays. Drag upward and to the left until the bottom of the graphic is aligned at approximately **4 inches on the vertical ruler**. Compare your screen with Figure 4.8. Notice that the graphic is proportionally resized.

Figure 4.8

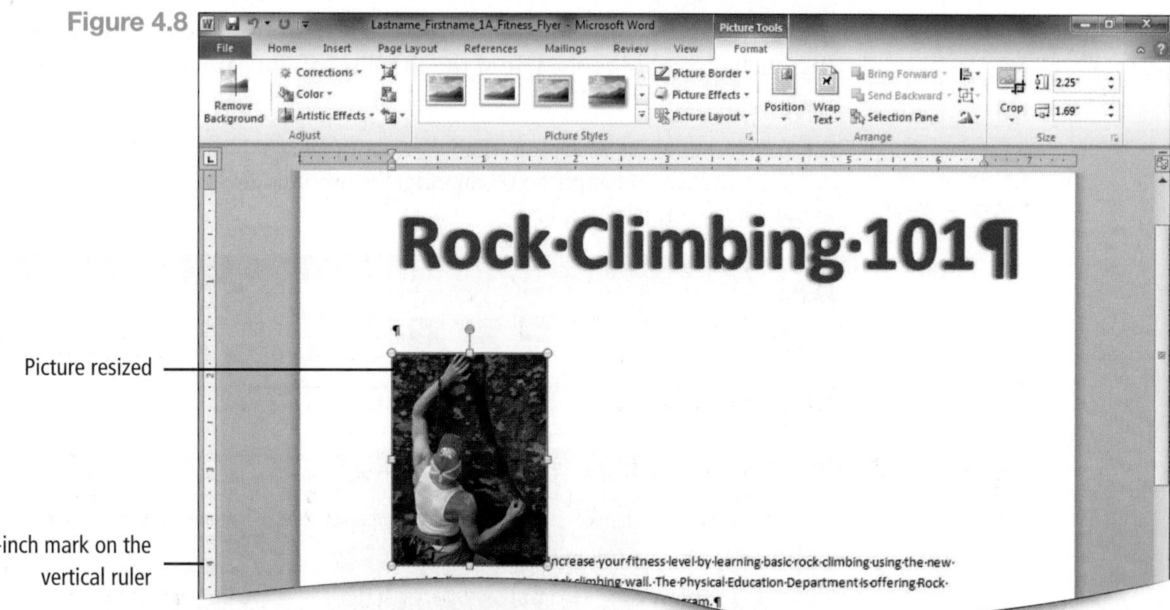

Another Way

Click the Undo button to undo the change.

5 On the **Format tab**, in the **Adjust group**, click the **Reset Picture button arrow**, and then click **Reset Picture & Size.**

6 In the **Size group**, click the **Shape Height spin box up arrow** as necessary to change the height of the picture to **4.5"**. Scroll down to view the entire picture on your screen, compare your screen with Figure 4.9, and then **Save** your document.

When you use the Height and Width ***spin boxes*** to change the size of a graphic, the graphic will always resize proportionally; that is, the width adjusts as you change the height and vice versa.

Figure 4.9

Activity 4.04 | Wrapping Text Around a Picture

Graphics inserted as inline objects are treated like characters in a sentence, which can result in unattractive spacing. You can change an inline object to a ***floating object***—a graphic that can be moved independently of the surrounding text characters.

1 Be sure the picture is selected—you know it is selected if the sizing handles display.

2 On the **Format tab**, in the **Arrange group**, click the **Wrap Text** button to display a gallery of text wrapping arrangements.

Text wrapping refers to the manner in which text displays around an object.

3 From the gallery, click **Square** to wrap the text around the graphic, and then notice the ***anchor*** symbol to the left of the first line of the paragraph. Compare your screen with Figure 4.10.

Select square text wrapping when you want to wrap the text to the left or right of the image. When you apply text wrapping, the object is always associated with—anchored to—a specific paragraph.

Figure 4.10

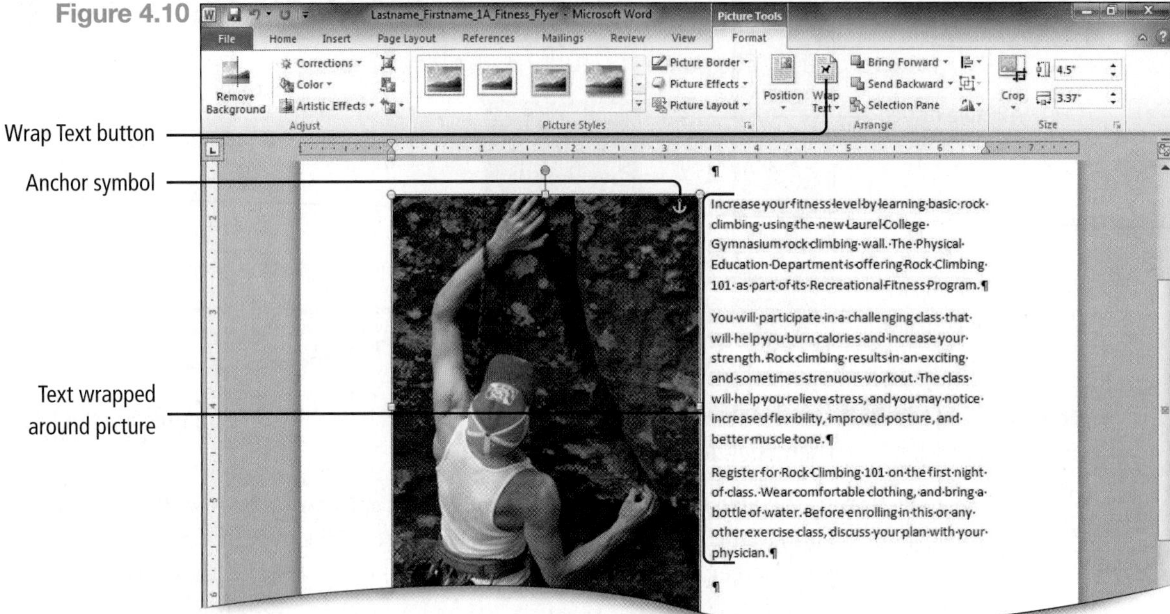

4 **Save** your document.

Activity 4.05 | Moving a Picture

1 Point to the rock climber picture to display the pointer.

2 Hold down Shift and drag the picture to the right until the right edge of the picture aligns at approximately **6.5 inches on the horizontal ruler**. Notice that the picture moves in a straight line when you hold down Shift. Compare your screen with Figure 4.11.

Figure 4.11

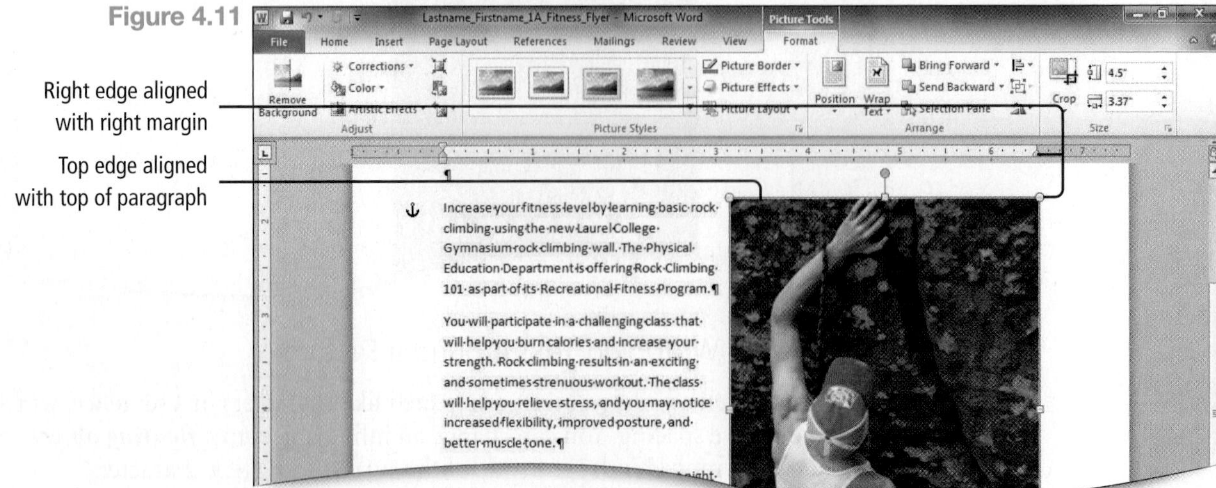

3. If necessary, press any of the arrow keys on your keyboard to ***nudge***—move in small increments—the picture in any direction so that the text wraps to match Figure 4.11. **Save** your document.

Activity 4.06 | Applying Picture Styles and Artistic Effects

Picture styles include shapes, shadows, frames, borders, and other special effects with which you can stylize an image. ***Artistic effects*** are formats that make pictures look more like sketches or paintings.

1. Be sure the rock climber picture is selected. On the **Format tab**, in the **Picture Styles group**, click the **Picture Effects** button. Point to **Soft Edges**, and then click **5 Point**.

   The Soft Edges feature fades the edges of the picture. The number of points you choose determines how far the fade goes inward from the edges of the picture.

2. On the **Format tab**, in the **Adjust group**, click the **Artistic Effects** button. In the first row of the gallery, point to, but do not click, the third effect—**Pencil Grayscale**.

   Live Preview displays the picture with the *Pencil Grayscale* effect added.

3. In the second row of the gallery, click the third effect—**Paint Brush**. Notice that the picture looks like a painting, rather than a photograph, as shown in Figure 4.12. **Save** your document.

Figure 4.12

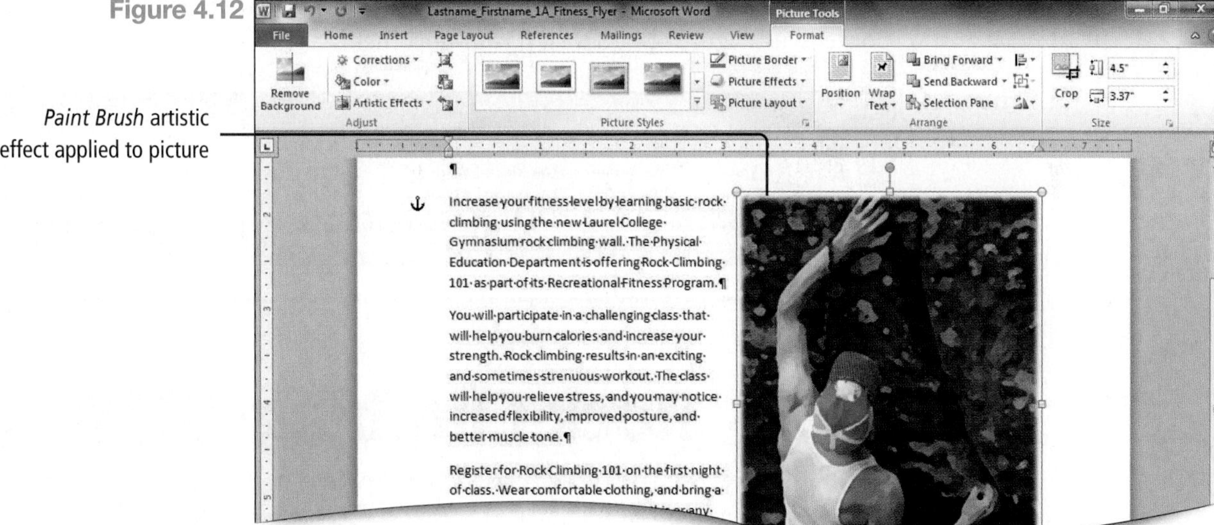

Paint Brush artistic effect applied to picture

Activity 4.07 | Adding a Page Border

Page borders frame a page and help to focus the information on the page.

1. Click anywhere outside the picture to deselect it. On the **Page Layout tab**, in the **Page Background group**, click the **Page Borders** button.

2. In the **Borders and Shading** dialog box, under **Setting**, click **Box**. Under **Style**, scroll down the list about a third of the way and click the heavy top line with the thin bottom line—check the **Preview** area to be sure the heavier line is the nearest to the edges of the page.

3. Click the **Color arrow**, and then in the fourth column, click the first color—**Dark Blue, Text 2**.

4 Under **Apply to**, be sure *Whole document* is selected, and then compare your screen with Figure 4.13.

Figure 4.13

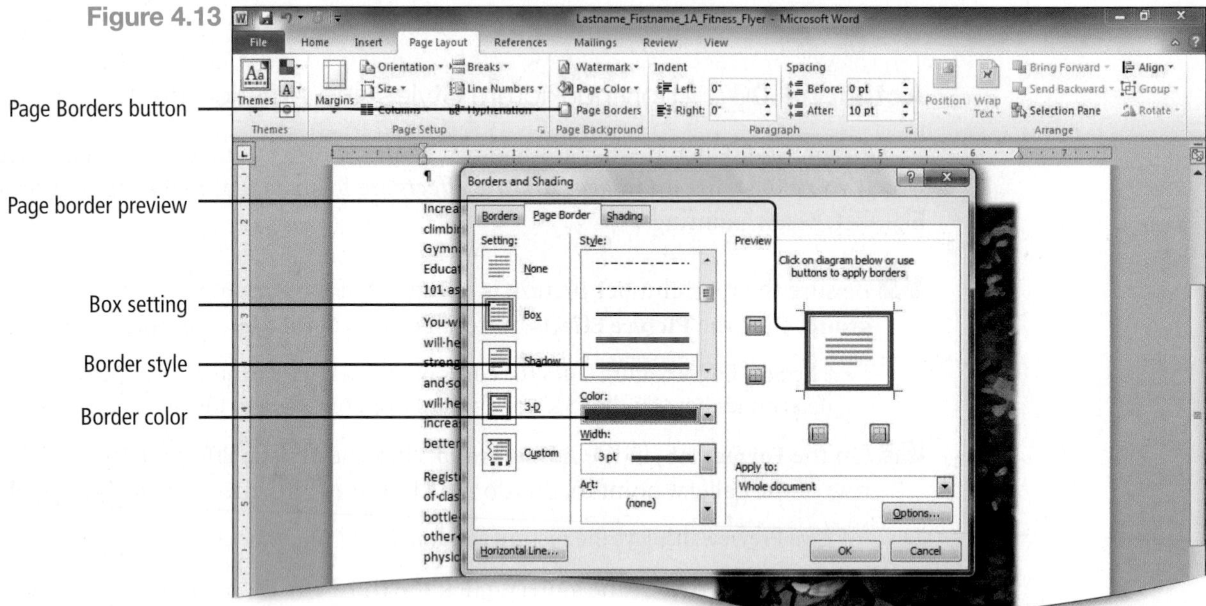

5 At the bottom of the **Borders and Shading** dialog box, click **OK**.

6 Press Ctrl + Home to move to the top of the document, and then compare your page border with Figure 4.14. **Save** your document.

Figure 4.14

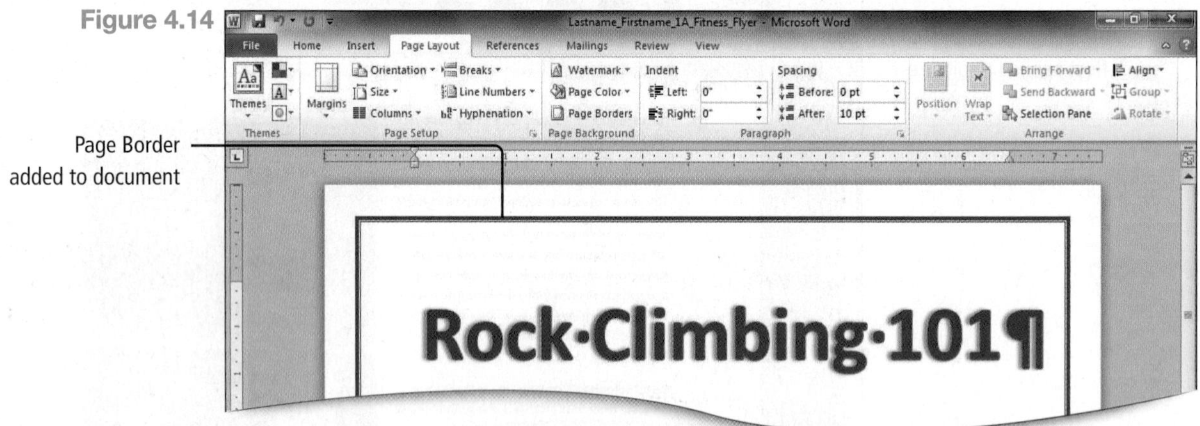

Objective 3 | Insert and Modify Text Boxes and Shapes

Word provides predefined ***shapes*** and ***text boxes*** that you can add to your documents. A shape is an object such as a line, arrow, box, callout, or banner. A text box is a movable, resizable container for text or graphics. Use these objects to add visual interest to your document.

Activity 4.08 | Inserting a Shape

1 Press ↓ one time to move to the blank paragraph below the title. Press Enter four times to make space for a text box, and notice that the picture anchored to the paragraph moves with the text.

2 Press Ctrl + End to move to the bottom of the document, and notice that your insertion point is positioned in the empty paragraph at the end of the document.

3 Click the **Insert tab**, and then in the **Illustrations group**, click the **Shapes** button to display the gallery. Compare your screen with Figure 4.15.

Figure 4.15

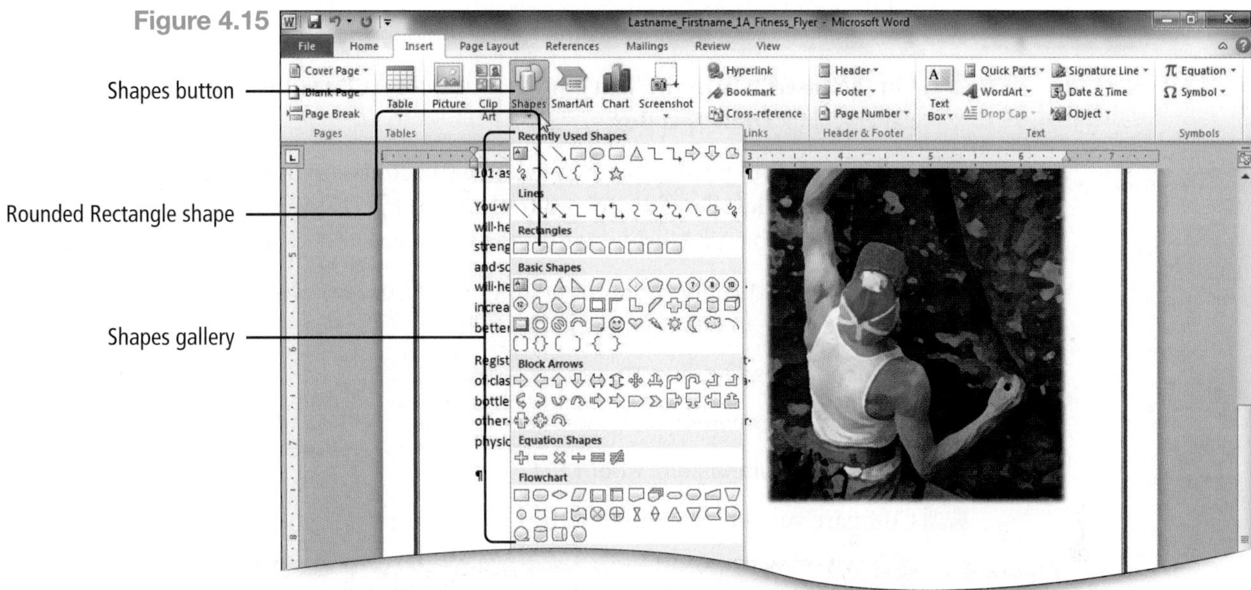

4 Under **Rectangles**, click the second shape—**Rounded Rectangle**, and then move your pointer. Notice that the [+] pointer displays.

5 Position the [+] pointer just under the lower left corner of the picture, and then drag down approximately **1 inch** and to the right edge of the picture.

6 Point to the shape and right-click, and then from the shortcut menu, click **Add Text**.

7 With the insertion point blinking inside the shape, point inside the shape and right-click, and then on the Mini toolbar, change the **Font Size** to **16**, and be sure **Center** alignment is selected.

8 Click inside the shape again, and then type **Improve your strength, balance, and coordination** If necessary, use the lower middle sizing handle to enlarge the shape to view your text. Compare your screen with Figure 4.16. **Save** your document.

Figure 4.16

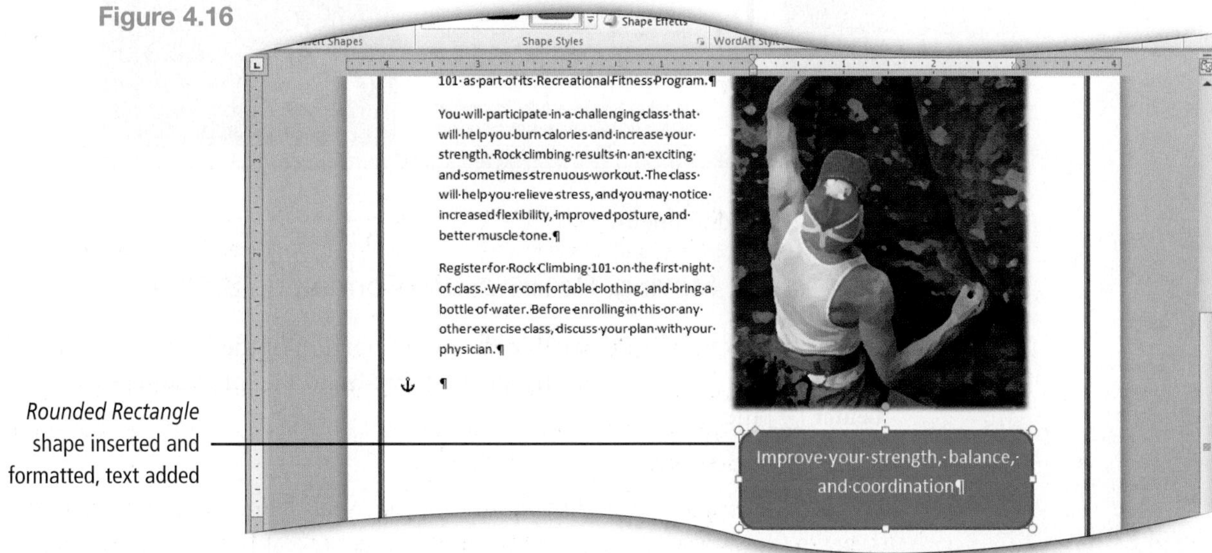

Activity 4.09 | Inserting a Text Box

A text box is useful to differentiate portions of text from other text on the page. You can move a text box anywhere on the page.

1 Press Ctrl + Home to move to the top of the document.

2 On the **Insert tab**, in the **Text group**, click the **Text Box** button. At the bottom of the gallery, click **Draw Text Box**.

3 Position the pointer below the letter *k* in *Rock*—at approximately **1.5 inches on the vertical ruler**. Drag down and to the right to create a text box approximately **1.5 inches** high and **3 inches** wide—the exact size and location need not be precise.

4 With the insertion point blinking in the text box, type the following, pressing Enter after each line to create a new paragraph:

Meets Tuesdays and Thursdays, 7-9 p.m.

Begins September 13, ends December 16

College Gymnasium, Room 104

5 Compare your screen with Figure 4.17.

Figure 4.17

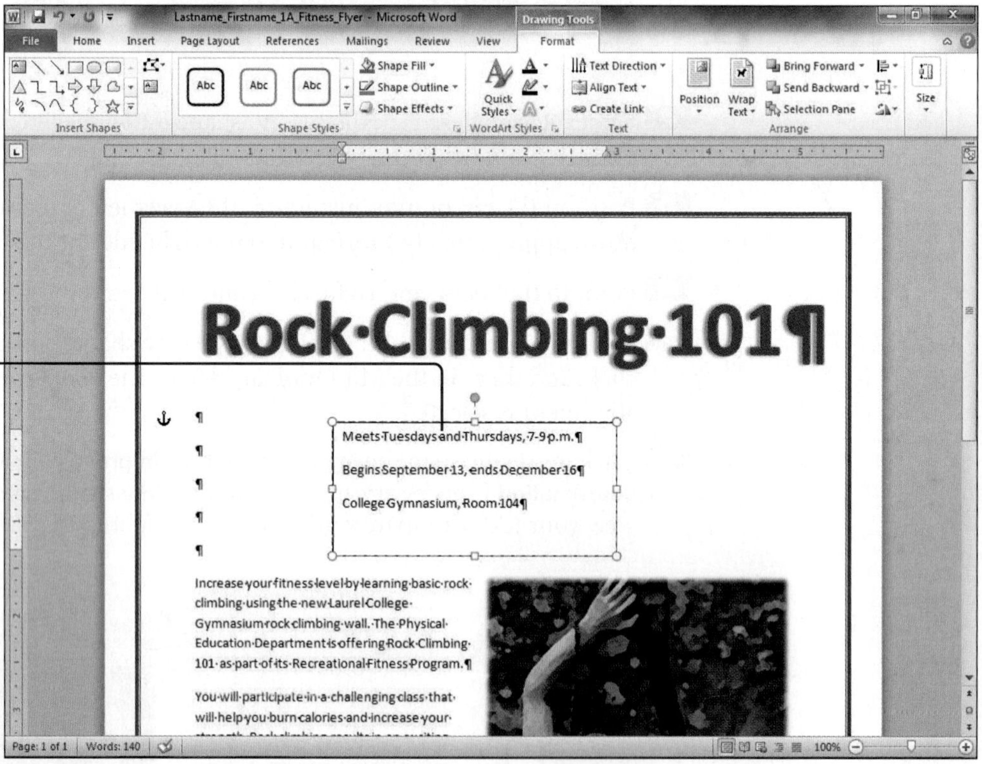

Text box with inserted text

6 **Save** your document.

Activity 4.10 | Moving, Resizing, and Formatting Shapes and Text Boxes

1 In the text box you just created in the upper portion of the flyer, select all of the text. From the Mini toolbar, change the **Font Size** to **14**, apply **Bold**, and then **Center** the text.

2 On the **Format tab**, in the **Size group**, if necessary, click the **Size** button. Click the **Shape Height spin arrows** [1.5"] as necessary to set the height of the text box to **1.2"**. Click the **Shape Width spin arrows** [1.37"] as necessary to set the width of the text box to **4"**.

3 In the **Shape Styles group**, click the **Shape Effects** button. Point to **Shadow**, and then under **Outer**, in the first row, click the first style—**Offset Diagonal Bottom Right**.

4 In the **Shape Styles group**, click the **Shape Outline button arrow**. In the fourth column, click the first color—**Dark Blue, Text 2** to change the color of the text box border.

5 Click the **Shape Outline button arrow** again, point to **Weight**, and then click **3 pt**.

6 Click anywhere in the document to deselect the text box. Notice that with the text box deselected, you can see all the measurements on the horizontal ruler.

7 Click anywhere in the text box and point to the text box border to display the pointer. By dragging, visually center the text box vertically and horizontally in the space below the *Rock Climbing 101* title. Then, if necessary, press any of the arrow keys on your keyboard to nudge the text box in precise increments to match Figure 4.18.

Figure 4.18

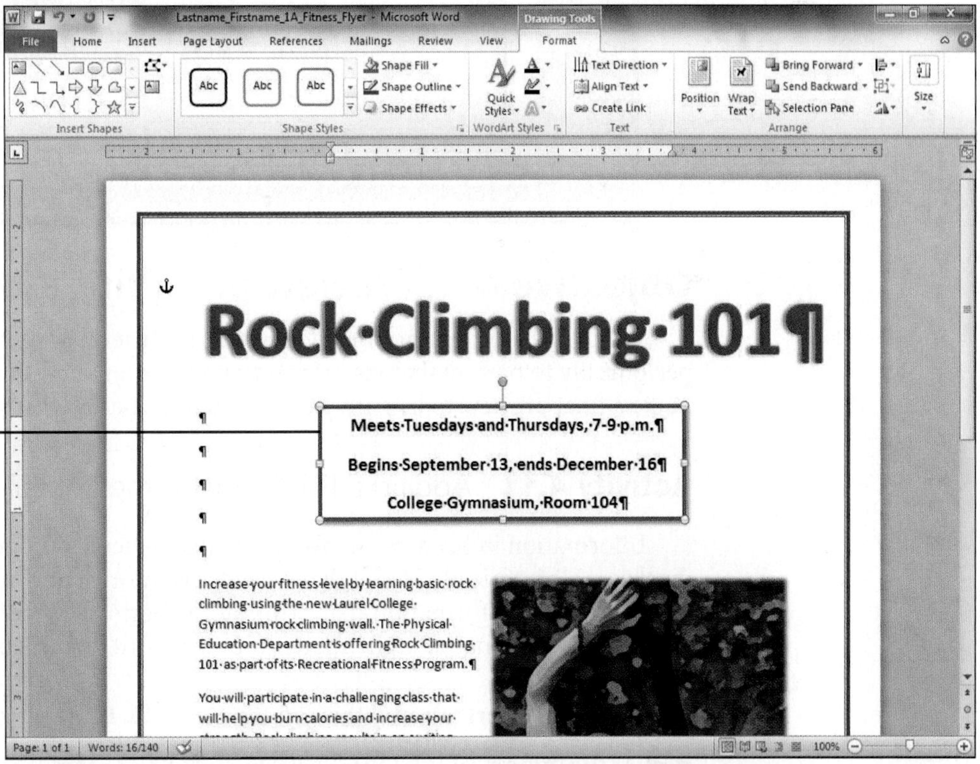

Text formatted and centered in text box, shadow added, border color and weight changed

8 Press Ctrl + End to move to the bottom of the document. Click on the border of the rounded rectangular shape to select it.

9 On the **Format tab**, in the **Size group**, if necessary, click the **Size** button. Click the **Shape Height spin arrows** [1.5"] as necessary to change the height of the shape to **0.8"**.

10 In the **Shape Styles group**, click the **Shape Fill button arrow**, and then at the bottom of the gallery, point to **Gradient**. Under **Dark Variations**, in the third row click the first gradient—**Linear Diagonal - Bottom Left to Top Right**.

11 In the **Shape Styles group**, click the **Shape Outline button arrow**. In the sixth column, click the first color—**Red, Accent 2**.

12 Click the **Shape Outline button arrow** again, point to **Weight**, and then click **1 1/2 pt**. Click anywhere in the document to deselect the shape. Compare your screen with Figure 4.19, and then **Save** your document.

Figure 4.19

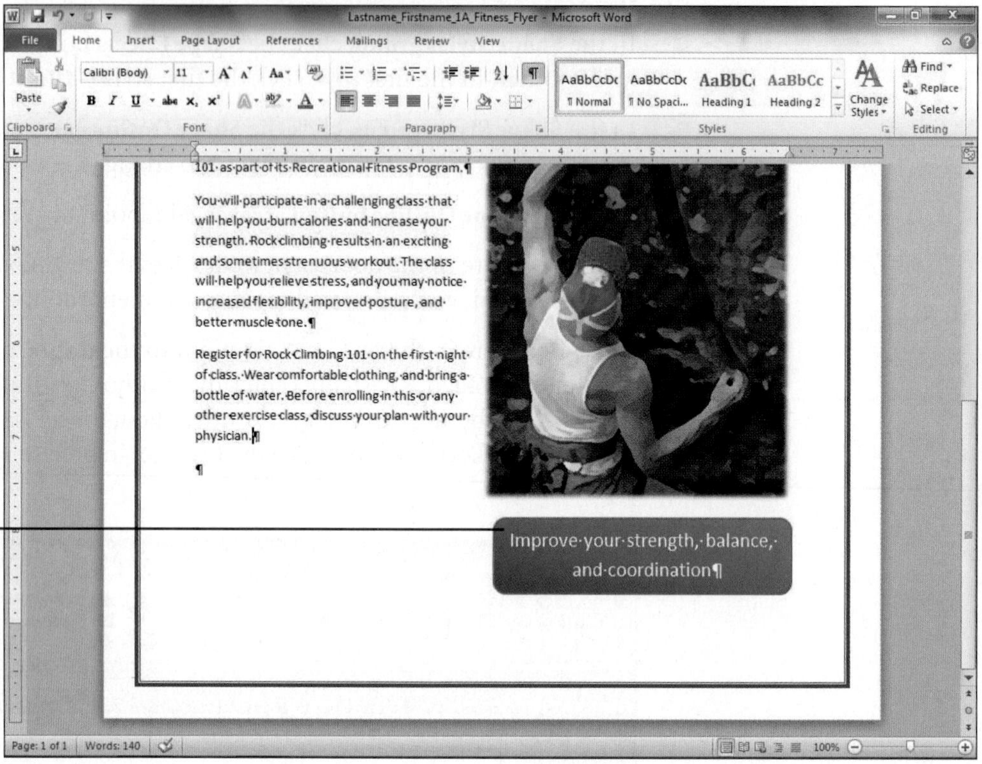

Gradient fill added, shape outline formatted

Objective 4 | Preview and Print a Document

While you are creating your document, it is useful to preview your document periodically to be sure that you are getting the result you want. Then, before printing, make a final preview to be sure the document layout is what you intended.

Activity 4.11 | Adding a File Name to the Footer

Information in headers and footers helps to identify a document when it is printed or displayed electronically. Recall that a header is information that prints at the top of every page; a footer is information that prints at the bottom of every page. In this textbook, you will insert the file name in the footer of every Word document.

Another Way
At the bottom edge of the page, right-click; from the shortcut menu, click Edit Footer.

1 Click the **Insert tab**, and then, in the **Header & Footer group**, click the **Footer** button.

2 At the bottom of the **Footer** gallery, click **Edit Footer**.

The footer area displays with the insertion point blinking at the left edge, and on the Ribbon, the Header & Footer Tools display and add the Design tab.

3 On the **Design tab**, in the **Insert group**, click the **Quick Parts** button, and then click **Field**. In the **Field** dialog box, under **Field names**, use the vertical scroll bar to examine the items that you can insert in a header or footer.

A ***field*** is a placeholder that displays preset content such as the current date, the file name, a page number, or other stored information.

4 In the **Field names** list, scroll as necessary to locate and then click **FileName**. Compare your screen with Figure 4.20.

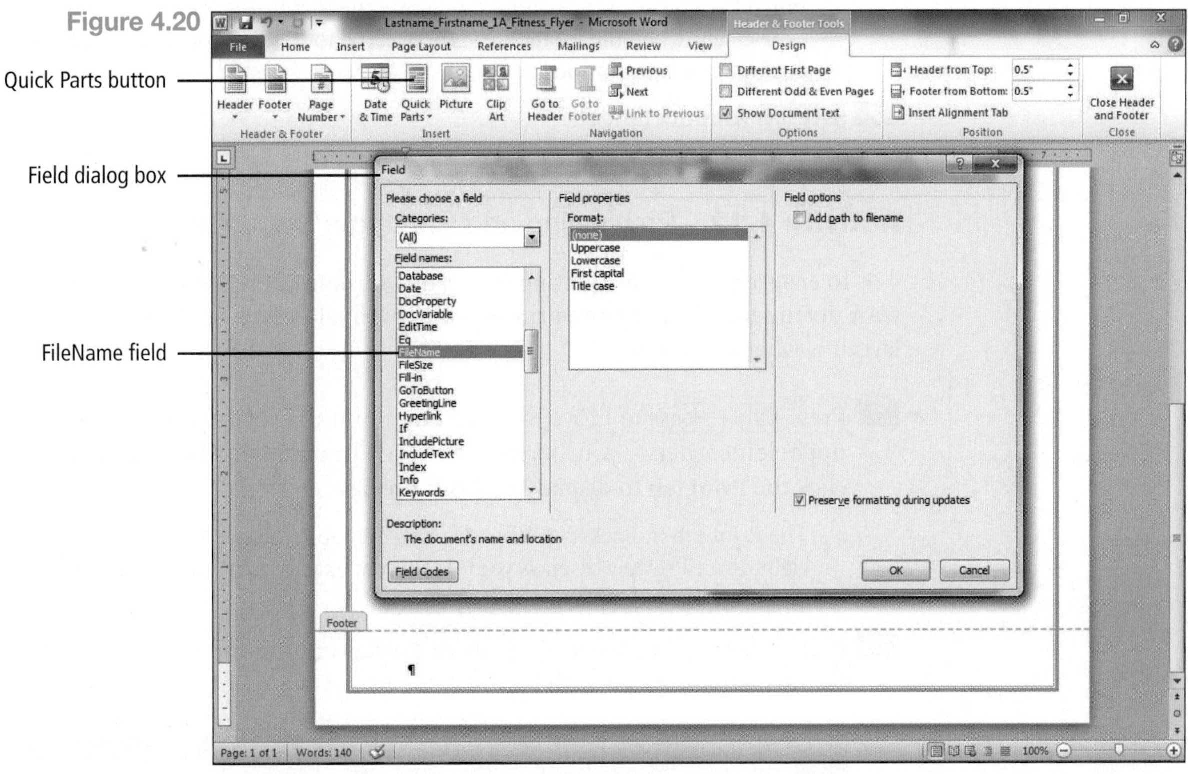

Figure 4.20

5 In the lower right corner of the **Field** dialog box, click **OK**, and then compare your screen with Figure 4.21.

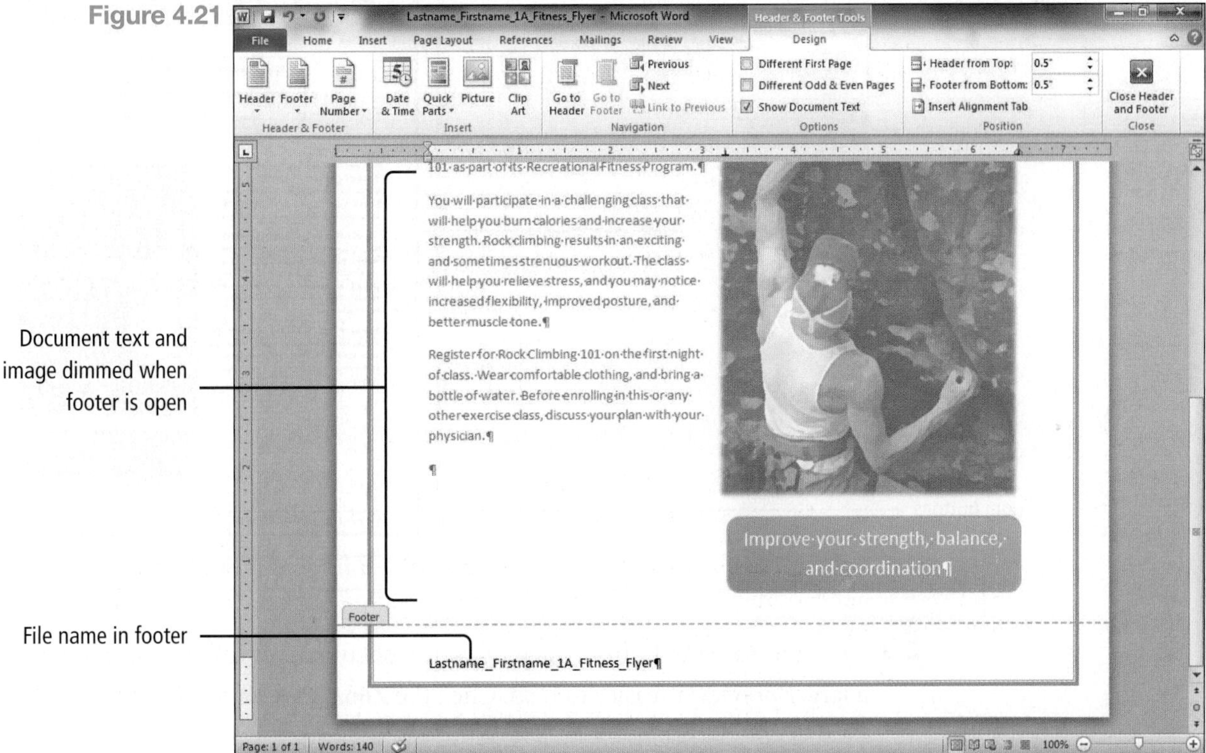

Figure 4.21

Another Way

Double-click anywhere in the document to close the footer area.

6 On the **Design tab**, at the far right in the **Close group**, click the **Close Header and Footer** button.

When the body of the document is active, the footer text is dimmed—displays in gray. Conversely, when the footer area is active, the footer text is not dimmed; instead, the document text is dimmed.

7 **Save** your document.

Activity 4.12 | Previewing and Printing a Document

To ensure that you are getting the result you want, it is useful to periodically preview your document. Then, before printing, make a final preview to be sure the document layout is what you intended.

Another Way

Press Ctrl + F2 to display Print Preview.

1 Press Ctrl + Home to move the insertion point to the top of the document. In the upper left corner of your screen, click the **File tab** to display **Backstage** view, and then click the **Print tab** to display the **Print Preview**.

The Print tab in Backstage view displays the tools you need to select your settings. On the right, Print Preview displays your document exactly as it will print; the formatting marks do not display.

2 In the lower right corner of the **Print Preview**, notice the zoom buttons that display. Compare your screen with Figure 4.22.

Figure 4.22

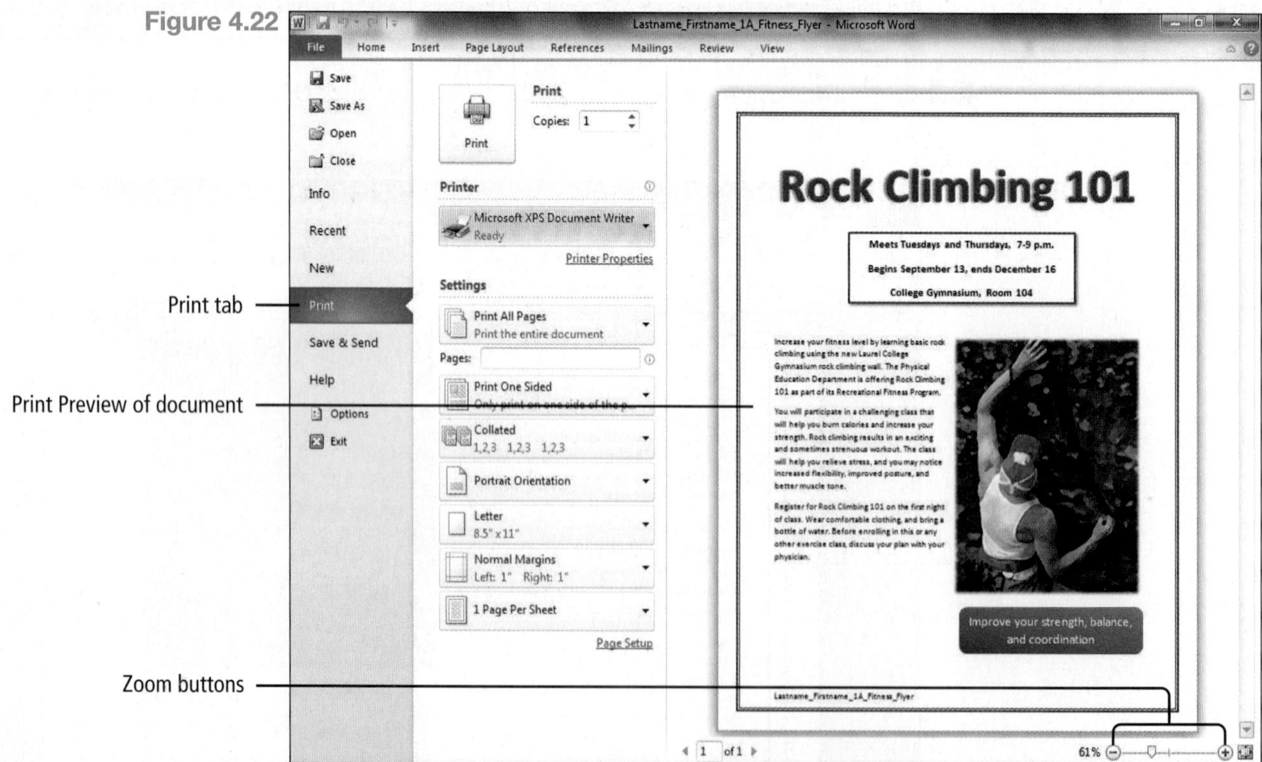

3 Click the **Zoom In** button to view the document at full size, and notice that a larger preview is easier to read. Click the **Zoom Out** button to view the entire page.

4. Click the **Info tab**. On the right, under the screen thumbnail, click **Properties**, and then click **Show Document Panel**.

   Here you can adjust the document properties.

5. In the **Author** box, delete any text and then type your firstname and lastname. In the **Subject** box type your course name and section number, and in the **Keywords** box type **fitness, rock climbing Close** the Document Panel.

6. **Save** your document. To print, display **Backstage** view, and then on the **navigation bar**, click **Print**. In the **Settings** group, be sure the correct printer is selected, and then in the **Print group**, click the **Print** button. Or, submit your document electronically as directed by your instructor.

7. In **Backstage** view, click **Exit** to close the document and exit Word.

End You have completed Project 4A

Project 4B Information Handout

Project Activities

In Activities 4.13 through 4.23, you will format and add lists to an information handout that describes student activities at Laurel College. Your completed document will look similar to Figure 4.23.

Project Files

For Project 4B, you will need the following file:

w01B_Student_Activities

You will save your document as:

Lastname_Firstname_1B_Student_Activities

Project Results

Every spring, students vote for the President, Vice President, Treasurer, Secretary, and Student Trustee for the following year. Executive Officers work with the college administration to manage campus activities and to make changes to policies and procedures. For example, the Student Trustee is a

Associated Students of Laurel College

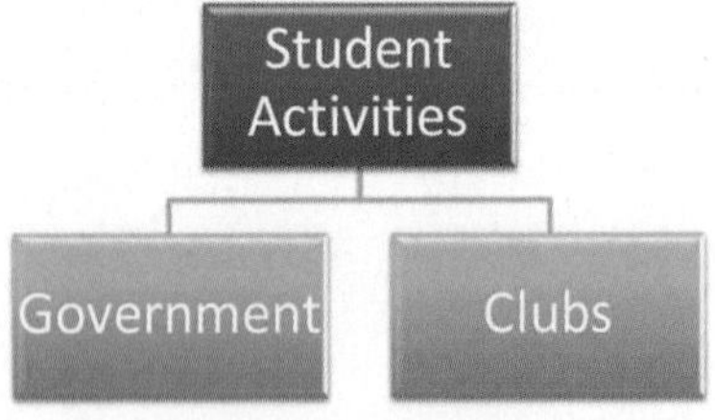

Get Involved in Student Activities

Your experience at Laurel College will be richer and more memorable if you get involved in activities that take you beyond the classroom. You will have the opportunity to meet other students, faculty, and staff members and will participate in organizations that make valuable contributions to your college and to the community.

Consider becoming involved in student government or joining a club. You might take part in activities such as these:

- ✓ Volunteering to help with a blood drive
- ✓ Traveling to a foreign country to learn about other cultures
- ✓ Volunteering to assist at graduation
- ✓ Helping to organize a community picnic
- ✓ Planning and implementing advertising for a student event
- ✓ Meeting with members of the state legislature to discuss issues that affect college students—for example, tuition costs and financial aid

Student Government

As a registered student, you are eligible to attend meetings of the Executive Officers of the Associated Students of Laurel College. At the meetings, you will have the opportunity to learn about college issues that affect students. At the conclusion of each meeting, the Officers invite students to voice their opinions. Eventually, you might decide to run for an office yourself. Running for office is a three-step process:

1. Pick up petitions at the Student Government office.
2. Obtain 100 signatures from current students.
3. Turn in petitions and start campaigning.

Lastname_Firstname_1B_Student_Activities

Figure 4.23
Project 4B Student Activities

Objective 5 | Change Document and Paragraph Layout

Document layout includes ***margins***—the space between the text and the top, bottom, left, and right edges of the paper. Paragraph layout includes line spacing, indents, and tabs. In Word, the information about paragraph formats is stored in the paragraph mark at the end of a paragraph. When you press the Enter, the new paragraph mark contains the formatting of the previous paragraph, unless you take steps to change it.

Activity 4.13 | Setting Margins

1 **Start** Word. From **Backstage** view, display the **Open** dialog box. From your student files, locate and open the document **w01B_Student_Activities.** On the **Home tab**, in the **Paragraph group**, be sure the **Show/Hide** button ¶ is active—glows orange—so that you can view the formatting marks.

2 From **Backstage** view, display the **Save As** dialog box. Navigate to your **Word Chapter 1** folder, and then **Save** the document as **Lastname_Firstname_1B_Student_Activities**

3 Click the **Page Layout tab.** In the **Page Setup group**, click the **Margins** button, and then take a moment to study the buttons in the Margins gallery.

The top button displays the most recent custom margin settings, while the other buttons display commonly used margin settings.

4 At the bottom of the **Margins** gallery, click **Custom Margins.**

5 In the **Page Setup** dialog box, press Tab as necessary to select the value in the **Left** box, and then, with *1.25"* selected, type **1**

This action will change the left margin to 1 inch on all pages of the document. You do not need to type the inch (") mark.

6 Press Tab to select the margin in the **Right** box, and then type **1** At the bottom of the dialog box, notice that the new margins will apply to the **Whole document.** Compare your screen with Figure 4.24.

Figure 4.24

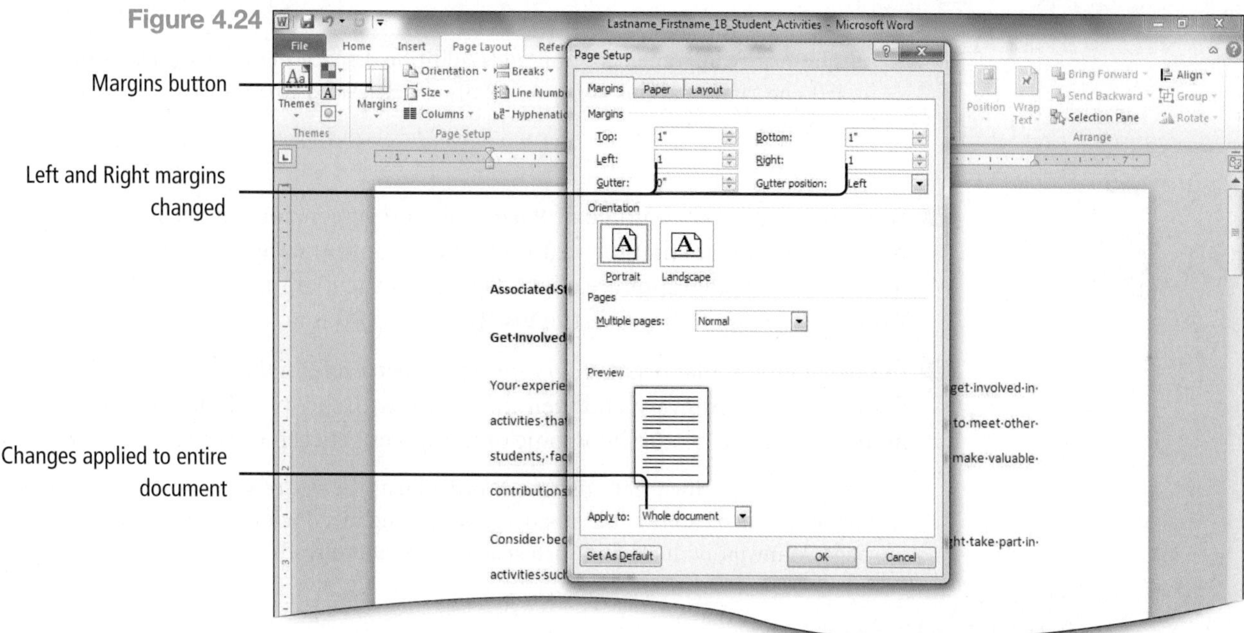

Another Way

Click the View tab, and then in the Show group, select the Ruler check box.

7 Click **OK** to apply the new margins and close the dialog box. If the ruler below the Ribbon is not displayed, at the top of the vertical scroll bar, click the View Ruler button.

8 Scroll to view the bottom of **Page 1** and the top of **Page 2**. Notice that the page edges display, and the page number and total number of pages display on the left side of the status bar.

9 Near the bottom edge of **Page 1**, point anywhere in the margin area, right-click, and then click **Edit Footer** to display the footer area.

10 On the **Design tab**, in the **Insert group**, click the **Quick Parts** button, and then click **Field**. In the **Field** dialog box, under **Field names**, locate and click **FileName**, and then click **OK**.

11 Double-click anywhere in the document to close the footer area, and then **Save** your document.

Activity 4.14 | Aligning Text

Alignment refers to the placement of paragraph text relative to the left and right margins. Most paragraph text uses ***left alignment***—aligned at the left margin, leaving the right margin uneven. Three other types of paragraph alignment are: ***center alignment***—centered between the left and right margins; ***right alignment***—aligned at the right margin with an uneven left margin; and ***justified alignment***—text aligned evenly at both the left and right margins. See the table in Figure 4.25.

Paragraph Alignment Options

Alignment	Button	Description and Example
Align Text Left		Align Text Left is the default paragraph alignment in Word. Text in the paragraph aligns at the left margin, and the right margin is uneven.
Center		Center alignment aligns text in the paragraph so that it is centered between the left and right margins.
Align Text Right		Align Text Right aligns text at the right margin. Using Align Text Right, the left margin, which is normally even, is uneven.
Justify		The Justify alignment option adds additional space between words so that both the left and right margins are even. Justify is often used when formatting newspaper-style columns.

Figure 4.25

1 Scroll to position the middle of **Page 2** on your screen, look at the left and right margins, and notice that the text is justified—both the right and left margins of multiple-line paragraphs are aligned evenly at the margins. On the **Home tab**, in the **Paragraph group**, notice that the **Justify** button is active.

2 In the paragraph that begins *Every spring, students vote*, in the first line, look at the space following the word *Every*, and then compare it with the space following the word *Trustee* in the second line. Notice how some of the spaces between words are larger than others.

To achieve a justified right margin, Word adjusts the size of spaces between words in this manner, which can result in unattractive spacing in a document that spans the width of a page. Many individuals find such spacing difficult to read.

Another Way

On the Home tab, in the Editing group, click the Select button, and then click Select All.

3. Press Ctrl + A to select all of the text in the document, and then on the **Home tab**, in the **Paragraph group**, click the **Align Text Left** button.

4. Press Ctrl + Home. At the top of the document, in the left margin area, point to the left of the first paragraph—*Associated Students of Laurel College*—until the pointer displays, and then click one time to select the paragraph. On the Mini toolbar, change the **Font Size** to **26**.

   Use this technique to select entire lines of text.

5. Point to the left of the first paragraph—*Associated Students of Laurel College*—to display the pointer again, and then drag down to select the first two paragraphs, which form the title and subtitle of the document.

6. On the Mini toolbar, click the **Center** button to center the title and subtitle between the left and right margins, and then compare your screen with Figure 4.26.

Figure 4.26

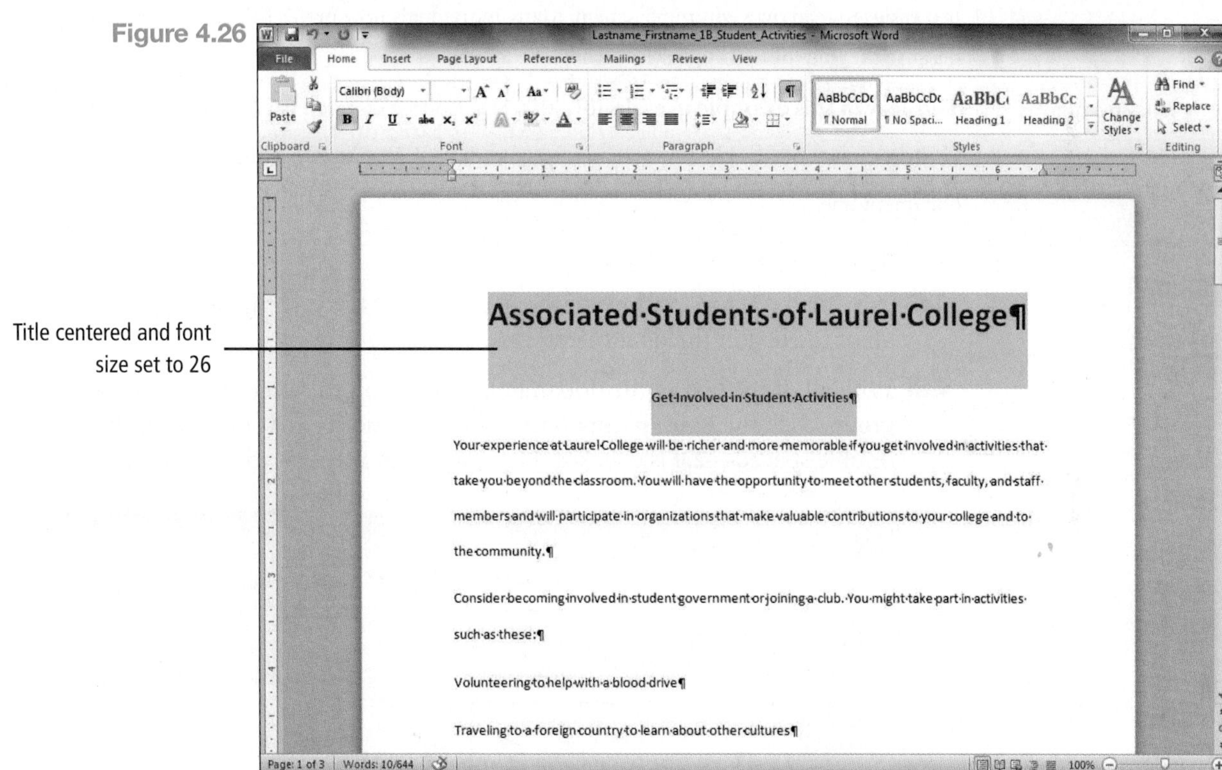

7. Scroll down to view the bottom of **Page 1**, and then locate the first bold subheading—*Student Government*. Point to the left of the paragraph to display the pointer, and then click one time.

8. With *Student Government* selected, use your mouse wheel or the vertical scroll bar to bring the lower portion of **Page 2** into view. Locate the subheading *Clubs*. Move the pointer to the left of the paragraph to display the pointer, hold down Ctrl, and then click one time.

   Two subheadings are selected; in Windows-based programs, you can hold down Ctrl to select multiple items.

9. On the Mini toolbar, click the **Center** button to center both subheadings, and then click **Save**.

Activity 4.15 | Changing Line Spacing

Line spacing is the distance between lines of text in a paragraph. Three of the most commonly used line spacing options are shown in the table in Figure 4.27.

Line Spacing Options

Alignment	Description, Example, and Information
Single spacing	**This text in this example uses single spacing**. Single spacing was once the most commonly used spacing in business documents. Now, because so many documents are read on a computer screen rather than on paper, single spacing is becoming less popular.
Multiple 1.15 spacing	**This text in this example uses multiple 1.15 spacing**. The default line spacing in Microsoft Word 2010 is 1.15, which is equivalent to single spacing with an extra 1/6 line added between lines to make the text easier to read on a computer screen. Many individuals now prefer this spacing, even on paper, because the lines of text appear less crowded.
Double spacing	**This text in this example uses double spacing**. College research papers and draft documents that need space for notes are commonly double-spaced; there is space for a full line of text between each document line.

Figure 4.27

1. Press Ctrl + Home to move to the beginning of the document. Press Ctrl + A to select all of the text in the document.

2. With all of the text in the document selected, on the **Home tab**, in the **Paragraph group**, click the **Line Spacing** button, and notice that the text in the document is double spaced—**2.0** is checked. Compare your screen with Figure 4.28.

Figure 4.28

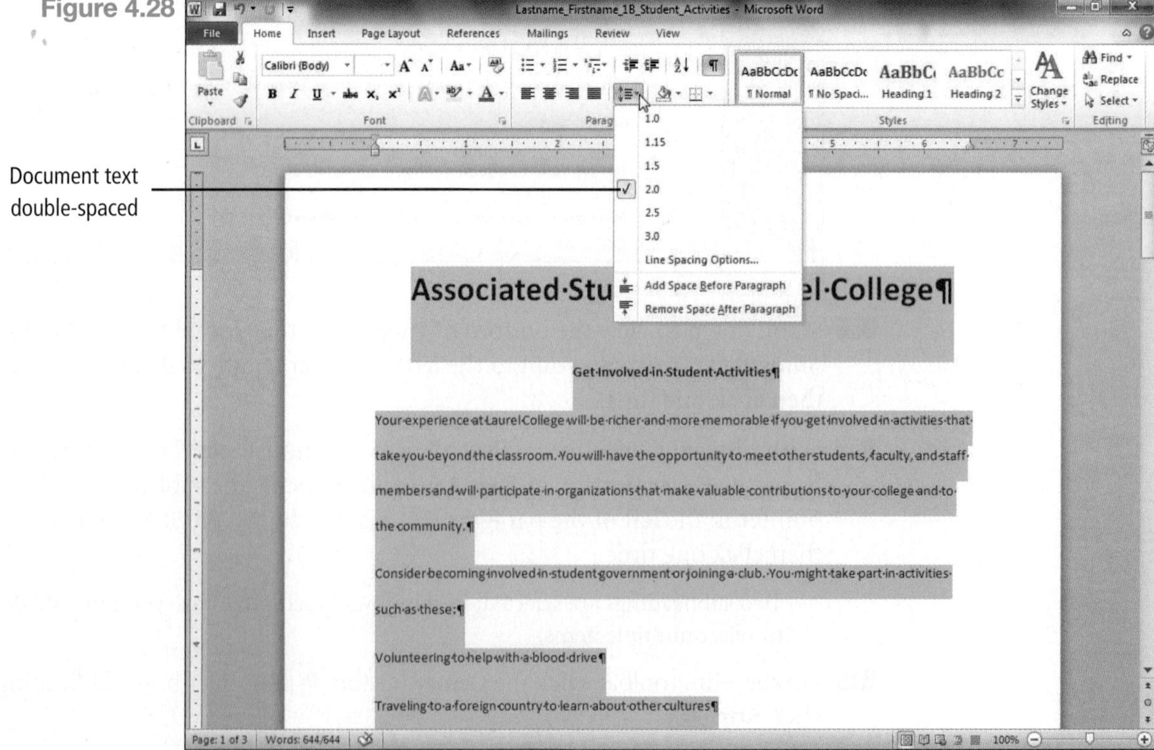

3 On the **Line Spacing** menu, click the *second* setting—**1.15**—and then click anywhere in the document. Compare your screen with Figure 4.29, and then **Save** your document.

Double spacing is most commonly used in research papers and rough draft documents. Recall that 1.15 is the default line spacing for new Word documents. Line spacing of 1.15 has slightly more space between the lines than single spacing. On a computer screen, spacing of 1.15 is easier to read than single spacing. Because a large percentage of Word documents are read on a computer screen, 1.15 is the default spacing for a new Word document.

Figure 4.29

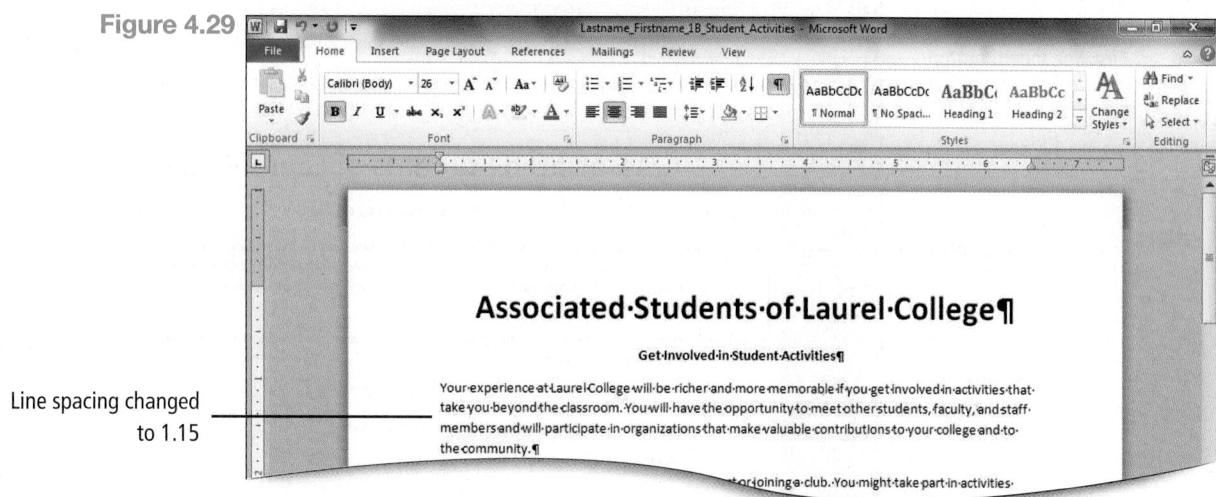

Activity 4.16 | Indenting Text and Adding Space After Paragraphs

Common techniques to distinguish paragraphs include adding space after each paragraph, indenting the first line of each paragraph, or both.

1 Below the title and subtitle of the document, click anywhere in the paragraph that begins *Your experience.*

2 On the **Home tab**, in the **Paragraph group**, click the **Dialog Box Launcher**.

3 In the **Paragraph** dialog box, on the **Indents and Spacing tab**, under **Indentation**, click the **Special arrow**, and then click **First line** to indent the first line by 0.5″, which is the default indent setting. Compare your screen with Figure 4.30.

Figure 4.30

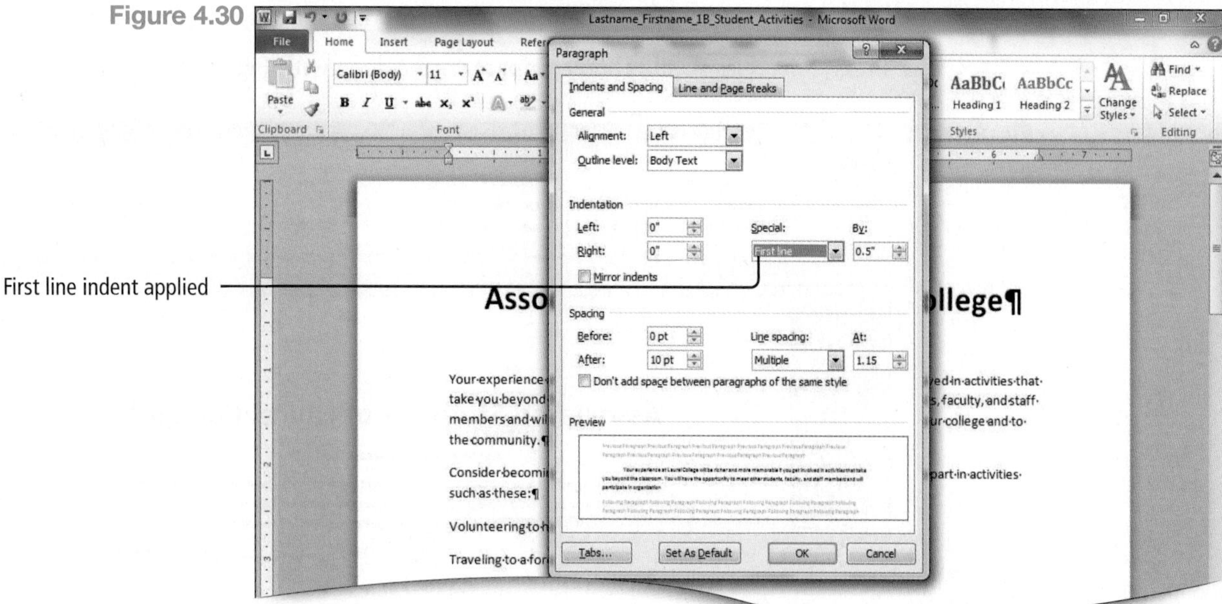

4 Click **OK**, and then click anywhere in the next paragraph, which begins *Consider becoming*. On the ruler under the Ribbon, drag the **First Line Indent** button to **0.5 inches on the horizontal ruler**, and then compare your screen with Figure 4.31.

Figure 4.31

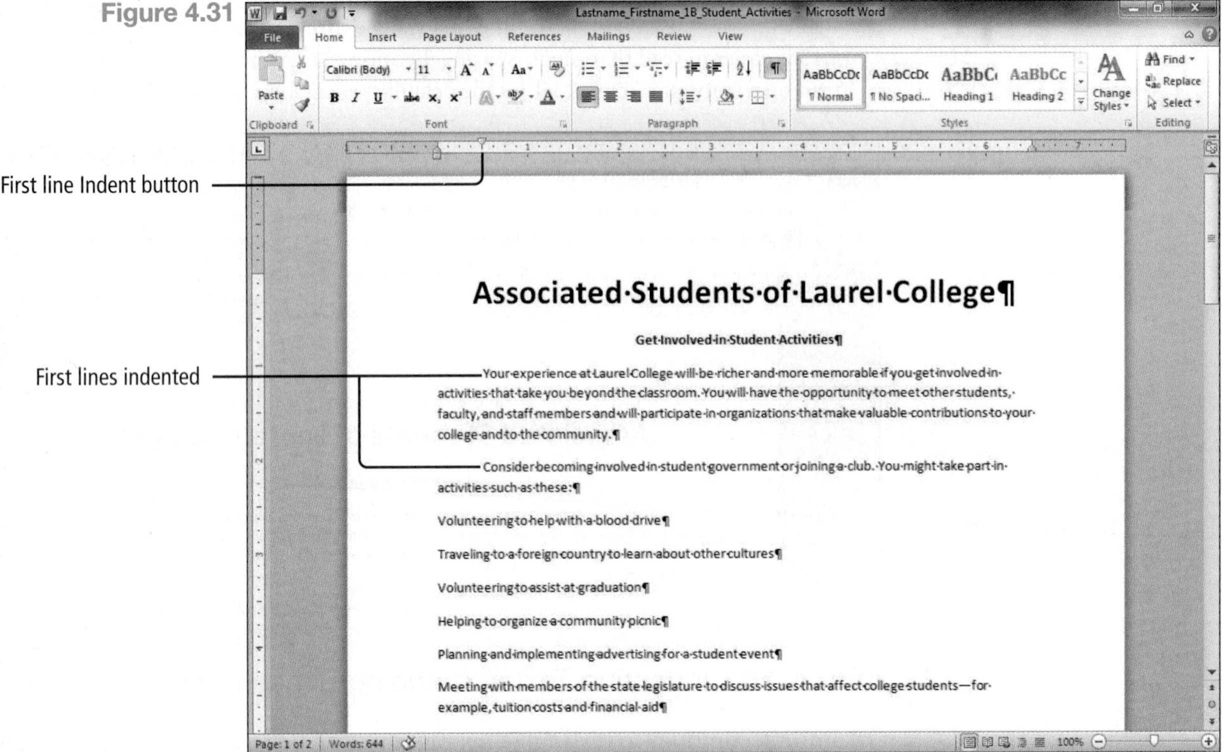

Another Way

On either the Home tab or the Page Layout tab, display the Paragraph dialog box from the Paragraph group, and then under Spacing, click the spin box arrows as necessary.

5 By using either of the techniques you just practiced, or by using the Format Painter, apply a first line indent of **0.5″** in the paragraph that begins *As a registered* to match the indent of the remaining paragraphs in the document.

6 Press Ctrl + A to select all of the text in the document. Click the **Page Layout tab**, and then in the **Paragraph group**, under **Spacing**, click the **After spin box down arrow** one time to change the value to **6 pt**.

To change the value in the box, you can also select the existing number, type a new number, and then press Enter. This document will use 6 pt spacing after paragraphs.

7 Press Ctrl + Home, and then compare your screen with Figure 4.32.

Figure 4.32

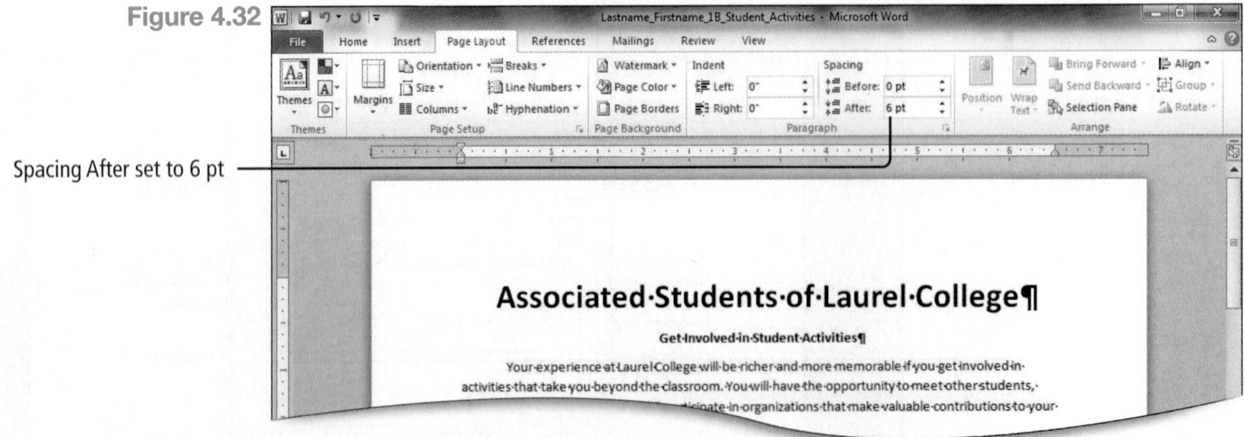

8 Scroll to view the lower portion of **Page 1**. Select the subheading *Student Government*, including the paragraph mark following it, hold down Ctrl, and then select the subheading *Clubs*.

9 With both subheadings selected, in the **Paragraph group**, under **Spacing**, click the **Before up spin box arrow** two times to set the **Spacing Before** to **12 pt**. Compare your screen with Figure 4.33, and then **Save** your document.

This action increases the amount of space above each of the two subheadings, which will make them easy to distinguish in the document. The formatting is applied only to the two selected paragraphs.

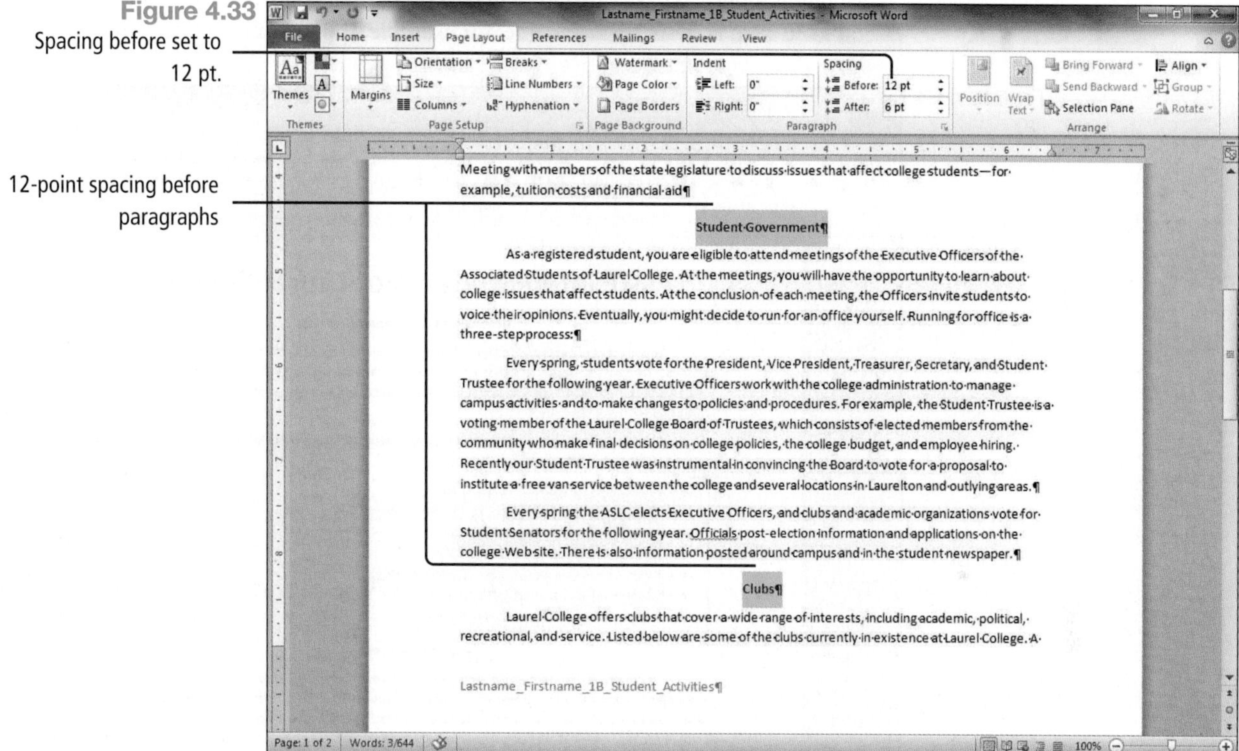

Figure 4.33

Objective 6 | Create and Modify Lists

To display a list of information, you can choose a ***bulleted list***, which uses ***bullets***—text symbols such as small circles or check marks—to introduce each item in a list. You can also choose a ***numbered list***, which uses consecutive numbers or letters to introduce each item in a list.

Use a bulleted list if the items in the list can be introduced in any order; use a numbered list for items that have definite steps, a sequence of actions, or are in chronological order.

Activity 4.17 | Creating a Bulleted List

1 In the upper portion of **Page 1**, locate the paragraph that begins *Volunteering to help*, and then point to this paragraph from the left margin area to display the pointer. Drag down to select this paragraph and the next five paragraphs.

2 On the **Home tab**, in the **Paragraph group**, click the **Bullets** button to change the selected text to a bulleted list.

The spacing between each of the bulleted points changes to the spacing between lines in a paragraph—in this instance, 1.15 line spacing. The spacing after the last item in the list is the same as the spacing after each paragraph—in this instance, 6 pt. Each bulleted item is automatically indented.

3 On the ruler, point to the **First Line Indent** button and read the ScreenTip, and then point to the **Hanging Indent** button. Compare your screen with Figure 4.34.

By default, Word formats bulleted items with a first line indent of 0.25″ and adds a Hanging Indent at 0.5″. The hanging indent maintains the alignment of text when a bulleted item is more than one line, for example, the last bulleted item in this list.

Figure 4.34

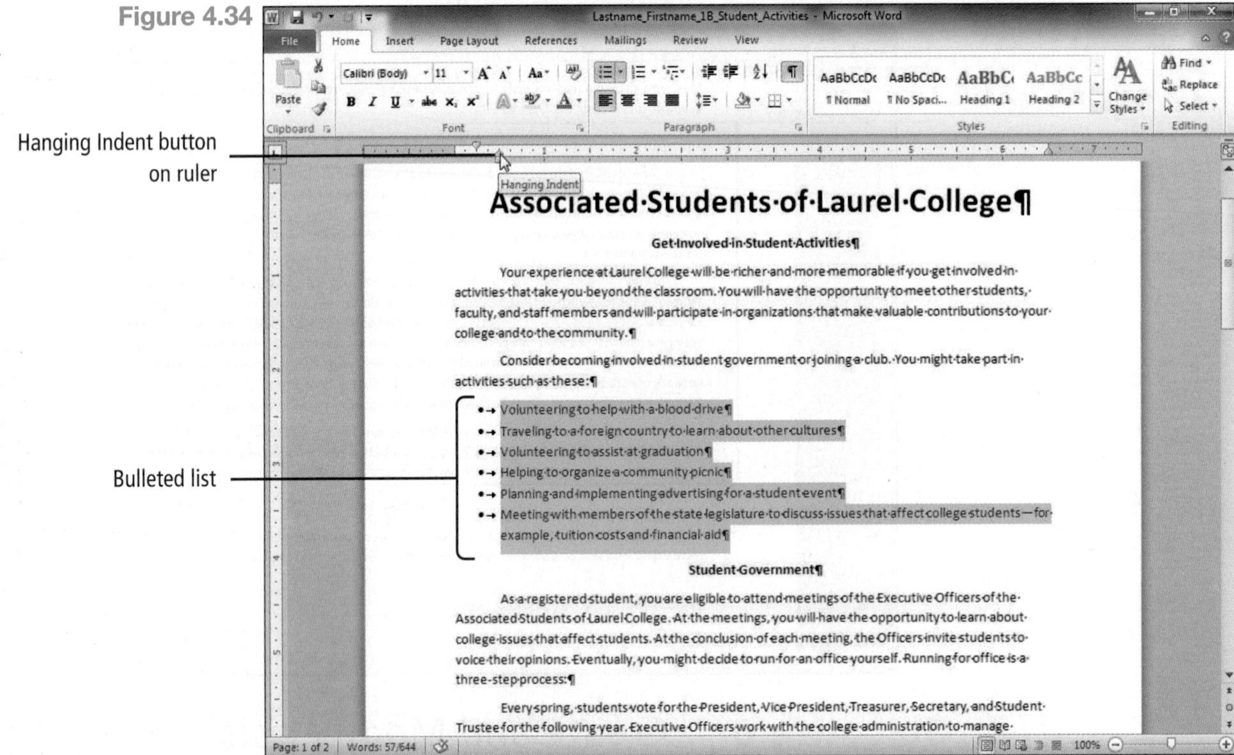

4 Scroll down to view **Page 2**. By using the pointer from the left margin area, select all of the paragraphs that indicate the club names and meeting dates, beginning with *Chess Club* and ending with *Theater Club.*

5 In the **Paragraph group**, click the **Bullets** button, and then **Save** your document.

Activity 4.18 | Creating a Numbered List

1 Scroll to view **Page 1**, and then under the subheading *Student Government*, in the paragraph that begins *As a registered student*, click to position the insertion point at the *end* of the paragraph following the colon. Press Enter to create a blank paragraph.

2 Notice that the paragraph is indented, because the First Line Indent from the previous paragraph carried over to the new paragraph.

3 To change the indent formatting for this paragraph, on the ruler, drag the **First Line Indent** button [▽] to the left so that it is positioned directly above the lower button. Compare your screen with Figure 4.35.

Figure 4.35

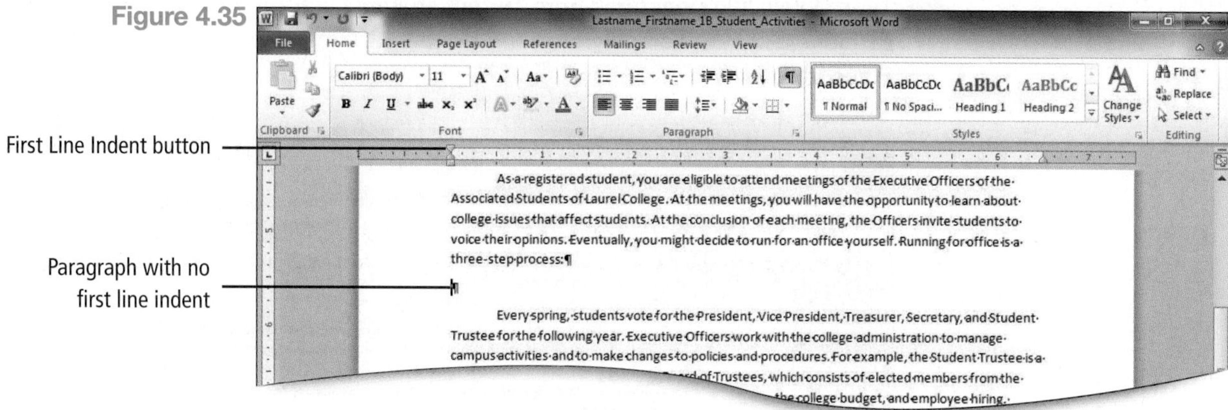

4 Being sure to include the period, type **1.** and press Spacebar.

Word determines that this paragraph is the first item in a numbered list and formats the new paragraph accordingly, indenting the list in the same manner as the bulleted list. The space after the number changes to a tab, and the AutoCorrect Options button displays to the left of the list item. The tab is indicated by a right arrow formatting mark.

> **Alert! | Activating Automatic Numbered Lists**
>
> If a numbered list does not begin automatically, display Backstage view, and then click the Options tab. On the left side of the Word Options dialog box, click Proofing. Under AutoCorrect options, click the AutoCorrect Options button. In the AutoCorrect dialog box, click the AutoFormat As You Type tab. Under *Apply as you type*, select the *Automatic numbered lists* check box, and then click OK two times to close both dialog boxes.

5 Click the **AutoCorrect Options** button [icon], and then compare your screen with Figure 4.36.

From the displayed list, you can remove the automatic formatting here, or stop using the automatic numbered lists option in this document. You also have the option to open the AutoCorrect dialog box to *Control AutoFormat Options.*

Figure 4.36

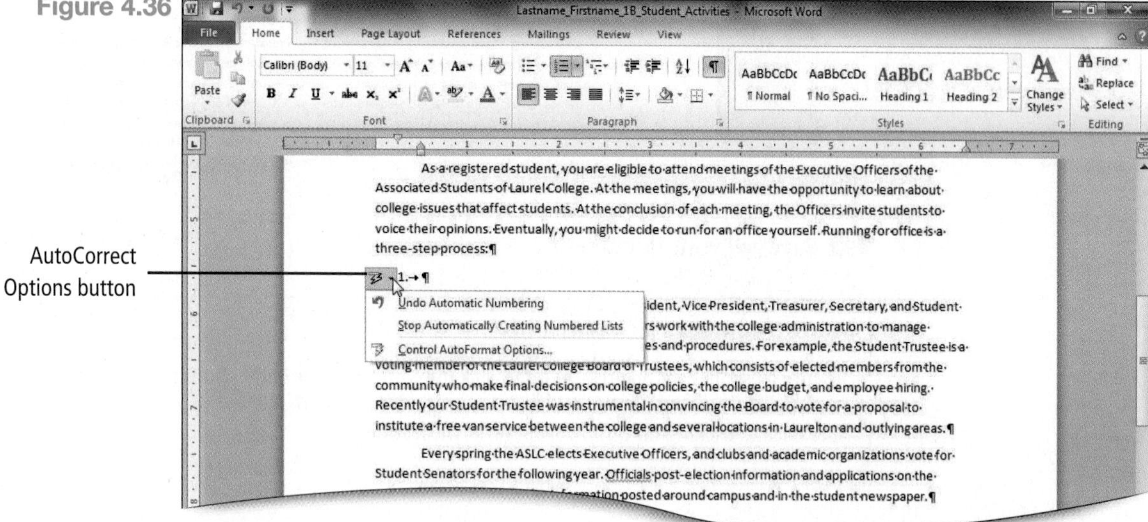

6 Click the **AutoCorrect Options** button again to close the menu without selecting any of the commands. Type **Pick up petitions at the Student Government office.** and press Enter. Notice that the second number and a tab are added to the next line.

7 Type **Obtain 100 signatures from current students.** and press Enter. Type **Turn in petitions and start campaigning.** and press Enter. Compare your screen with Figure 4.37.

Figure 4.37

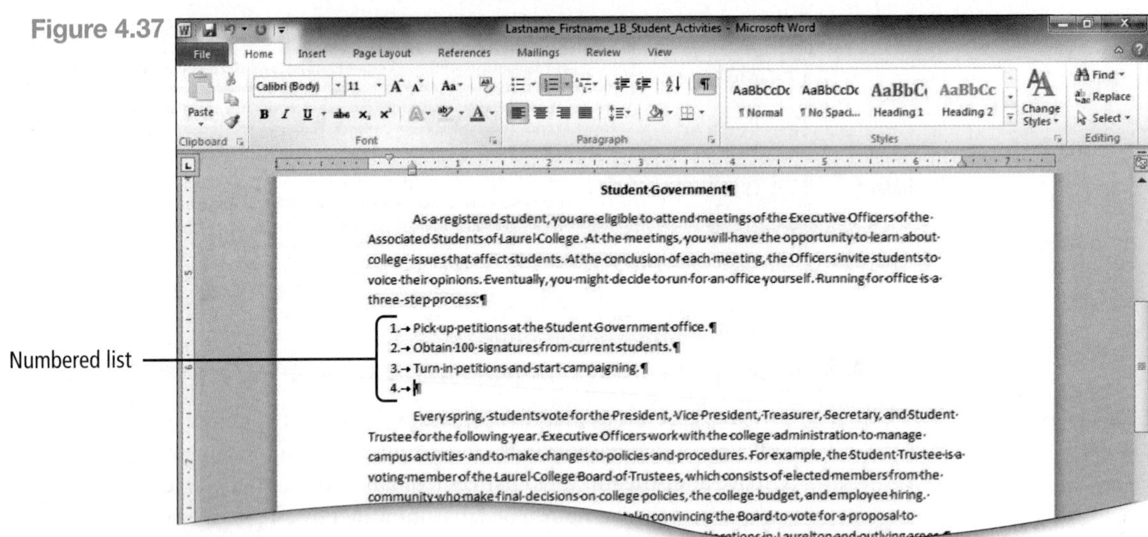

8 Press ←Bksp to turn off the list numbering. Then, press ←Bksp three more times to remove the blank paragraph. Compare your screen with Figure 4.38.

Figure 4.38

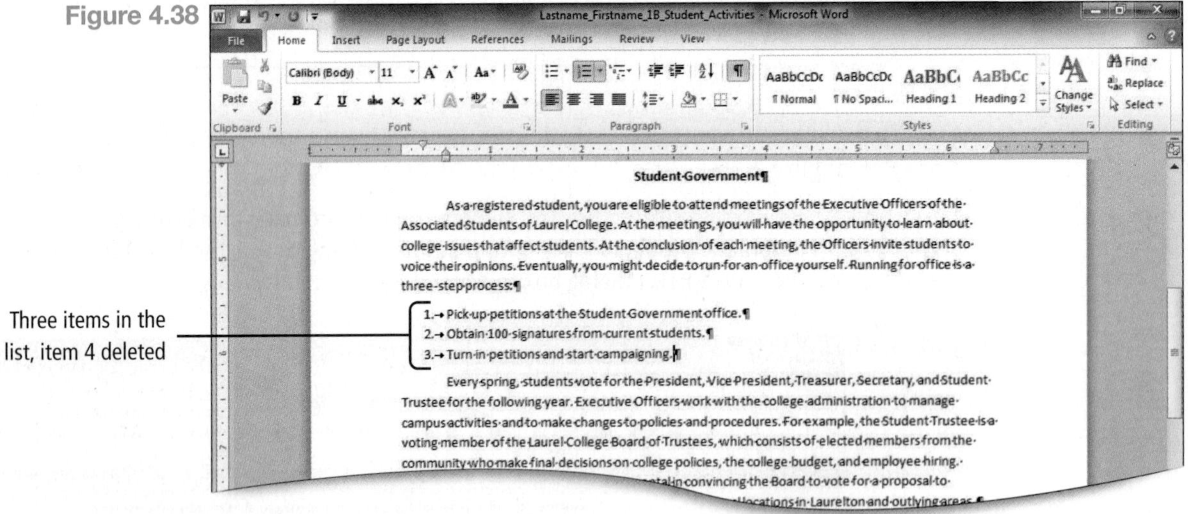

9 **Save** your document.

More Knowledge | To End a List

To turn a list off, you can press ←Bksp, click the Numbering or Bullets button, or press Enter a second time. Both list buttons—Numbering and Bullets—act as ***toggle buttons***; that is, clicking the button one time turns the feature on, and clicking the button again turns the feature off.

Activity 4.19 | Customizing Bullets

1 Press Ctrl + End to move to the end of the document, and then scroll up as necessary to display the bulleted list containing the list of clubs.

2 Point to the left of the first list item to display the pointer, and then drag down to select all the clubs in the list—the bullet symbols are not highlighted.

3 Point to the selected list and right-click. From the shortcut menu, point to **Bullets**, and then compare your screen with Figure 4.39.

Figure 4.39

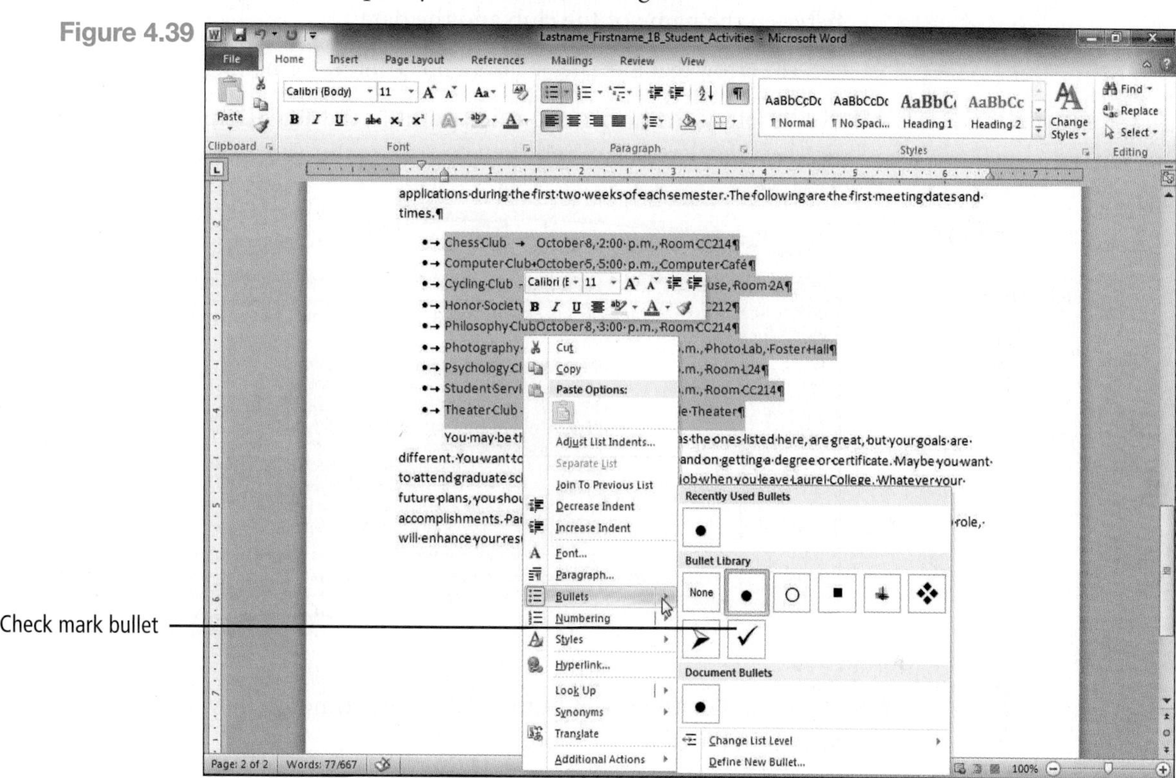

4 Under **Bullet Library**, click the **check mark** symbol. If the check mark is not available, choose another bullet symbol.

> **Another Way**
> On the Home tab, in the Clipboard group, click the Format Painter button.

5 With the bulleted list still selected, right-click over the list, and then on the Mini toolbar, click the **Format Painter** button.

6 Use the vertical scroll bar or your mouse wheel to scroll to view **Page 1**. Move the pointer to the left of the first item in the bulleted list to display the pointer, and then drag down to select all of the items in the list and to apply the format of the second bulleted list to this list. Compare your screen with Figure 4.40, and then **Save** your document.

Figure 4.40

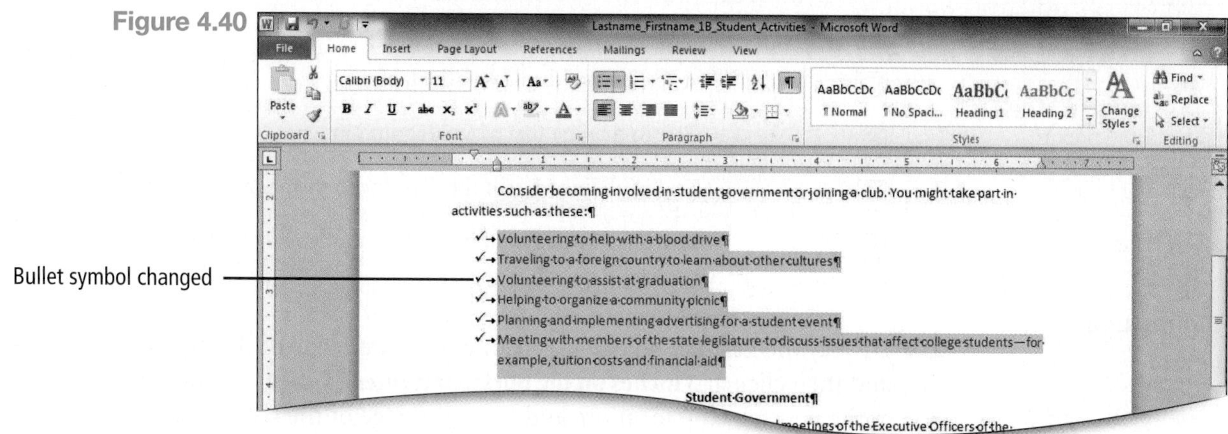

Objective 7 | Set and Modify Tab Stops

Tab stops mark specific locations on a line of text. Use tab stops to indent and align text, and use the Tab key to move to tab stops.

Activity 4.20 | Setting Tab Stops

1 Scroll to view the middle of **Page 2**, and then by using the pointer at the left of the first item, select all of the items in the bulleted list. Notice that there is a tab mark between the name of the club and the date.

The arrow that indicates a tab is a nonprinting formatting mark.

2 To the left of the horizontal ruler, point to the **Tab Alignment** button to display the *Left Tab* ScreenTip, and then compare your screen with Figure 4.41.

Figure 4.41

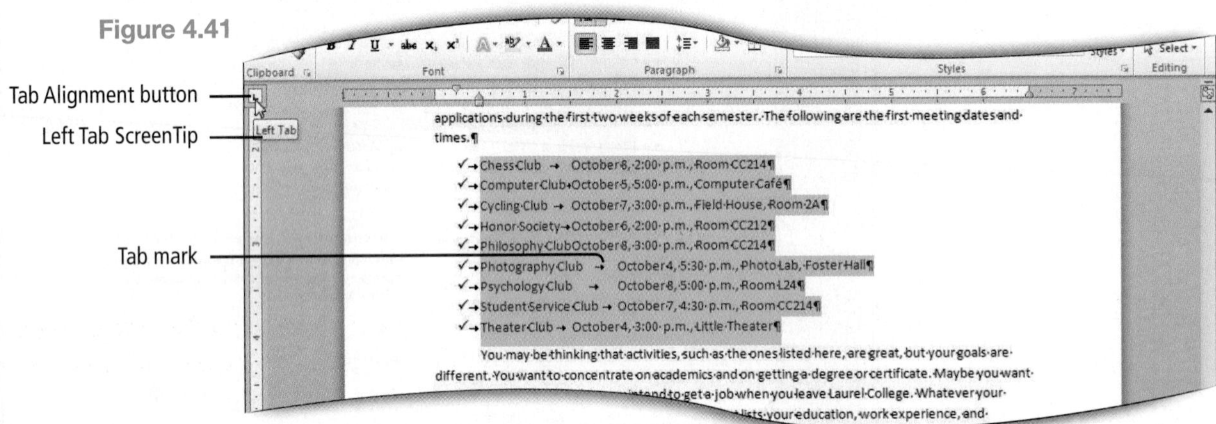

3 Click the **Tab Alignment** button several times to view the tab alignment options shown in the table in Figure 4.42.

Tab Alignment Options

Type	Tab Alignment Button Displays This Marker	Description
Left		Text is left aligned at the tab stop and extends to the right.
Center		Text is centered around the tab stop.
Right		Text is right aligned at the tab stop and extends to the left.
Decimal		The decimal point aligns at the tab stop.
Bar		A vertical bar displays at the tab stop.
First Line Indent		Text in the first line of a paragraph indents.
Hanging Indent		Text in all lines except the first line in the paragraph indents.
Left Indent		Moves both the First Line Indent and Hanging Indent buttons.

Figure 4.42

4 Display the **Left Tab** button. Along the lower edge of the horizontal ruler, point to and then click at **3 inches on the horizontal ruler**. Notice that all of the dates left align at the new tab stop location, and the right edge of the column is uneven.

5 Compare your screen with Figure 4.43, and then **Save** your document.

Figure 4.43

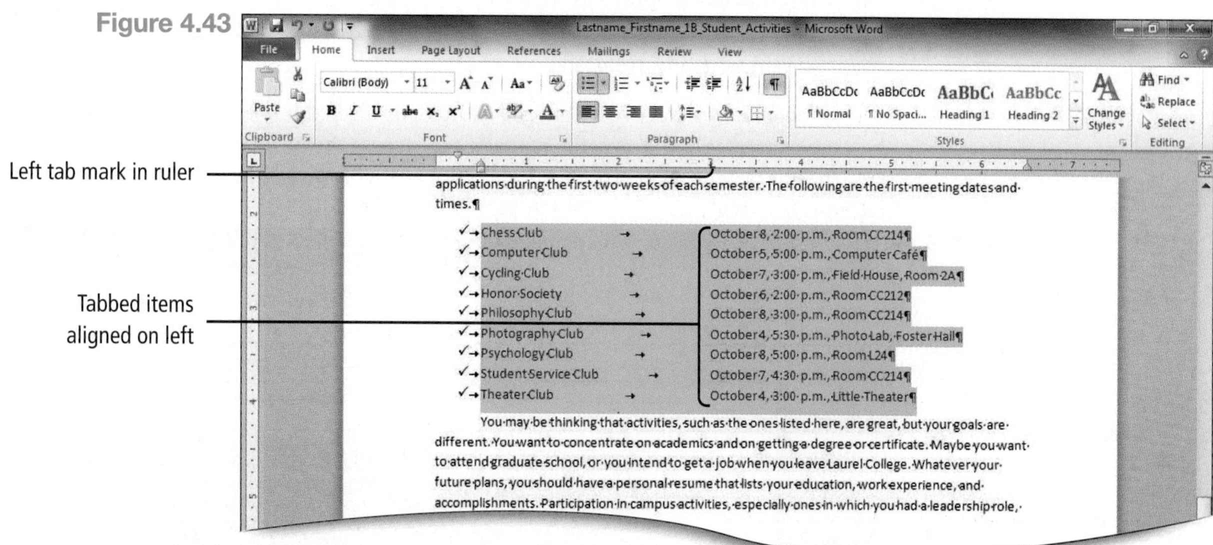

Activity 4.21 | Modifying Tab Stops

Tab stops are a form of paragraph formatting, and thus, the information about tab stops is stored in the paragraph mark in the paragraphs to which they were applied.

1 With the bulleted list still selected, on the ruler, point to the new tab marker, and then when the *Left Tab* ScreenTip displays, drag the tab marker to **3.5 inches on the horizontal ruler**.

In all of the selected lines, the text at the tab stop left aligns at 3.5 inches.

Another Way

On the Home tab, in the Paragraph group, click the Dialog Box Launcher. At the bottom of the Paragraph dialog box, click the Tabs button.

2 On the ruler, point to the tab marker to display the ScreenTip, and then double-click to display the **Tabs** dialog box.

3 In the **Tabs** dialog box, under **Tab stop position**, if necessary select *3.5″* and then type **6**

4 Under **Alignment**, click the **Right** option button. Under **Leader**, click the **2** option button. Near the bottom of the **Tabs** dialog box, click **Set**.

Because the Right tab will be used to align the items in the list, the tab stop at 3.5″ is no longer necessary.

5 In the **Tabs** dialog box, in the **Tab stop position** box, click **3.5″** to select this tab stop, and then in the lower portion of the **Tabs** dialog box, click the **Clear** button to delete this tab stop, which is no longer necessary. Compare your screen with Figure 4.44.

Figure 4.44

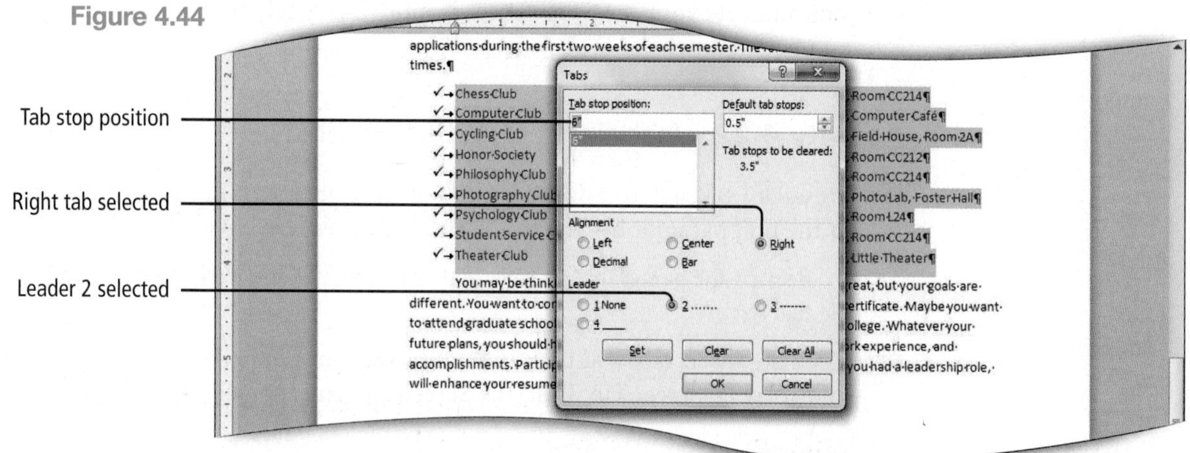

6 Click **OK**. On the ruler, notice that the left tab marker at *3.5"* no longer displays, a right tab marker displays at *6"*, and a series of dots—a ***dot leader***—displays between the columns of the list. Notice also that the right edge of the column is even. Compare your screen with Figure 4.45.

A ***leader character*** creates a solid, dotted, or dashed line that fills the space to the left of a tab character and draws the reader's eyes across the page from one item to the next. When the character used for the leader is a dot, it is commonly referred to as a dot leader.

Figure 4.45

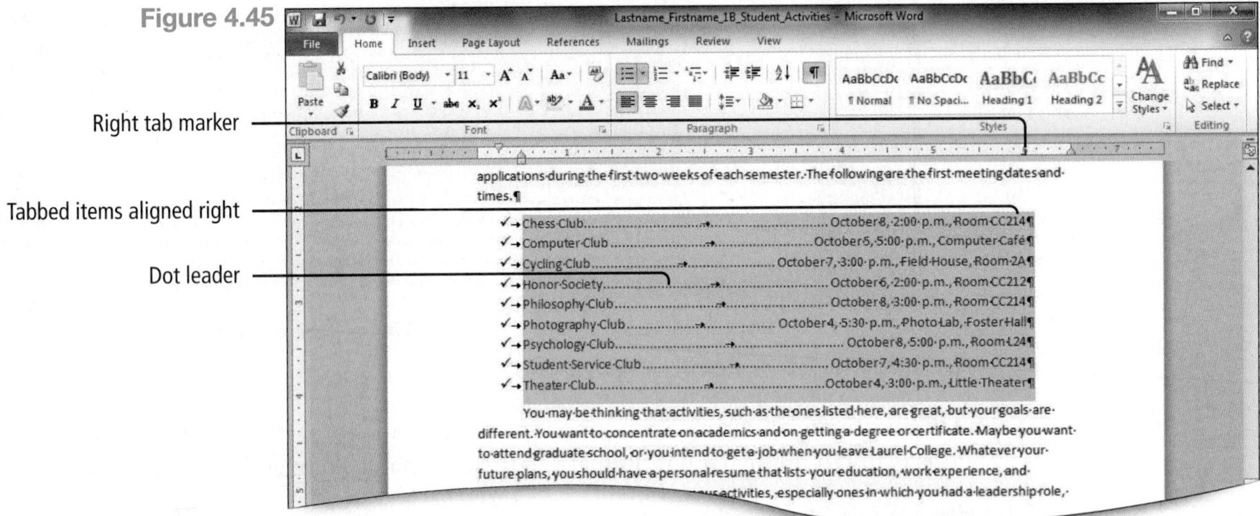

7 In the bulleted list that uses dot leaders, locate the *Honor Society* item, and then click to position the insertion point at the end of that line. Press Enter to create a new blank bullet item.

8 Type **Math Club** and press Tab. Notice that a dot leader fills the space to the tab marker location.

9 Type **October 6, 4:00 p.m., Math Tutoring Lab, L35** and notice that the text moves to the left to maintain the right alignment of the tab stop.

10 **Save** your document.

Objective 8 | Insert a SmartArt Graphic

SmartArt graphics are designer-quality visual representations of information, and Word provides many different layouts from which you can choose. A SmartArt graphic can communicate your messages or ideas more effectively than plain text and adds visual interest to a document or Web page.

Activity 4.22 | Inserting a SmartArt Graphic

1 Press Ctrl + Home to move to the top of the document. Press End to move to the end of the first paragraph—the title—and then press Enter to create a blank paragraph.

Because the paragraph above is 26 pt font size, the new paragraph mark displays in that size.

2 Click the **Insert tab**, and then in the **Illustrations group**, point to the **SmartArt** button to display its ScreenTip. Read the ScreenTip, and then click the button.

3 In the center portion of the **Choose a SmartArt Graphic** dialog box, scroll down and examine the numerous types of SmartArt graphics available.

4 On the left, click **Hierarchy**, and then in the first row, click the first graphic—**Organization Chart**.

At the right of the dialog box, a preview and description of the graphic displays.

5 Compare your screen with Figure 4.46.

Figure 4.46

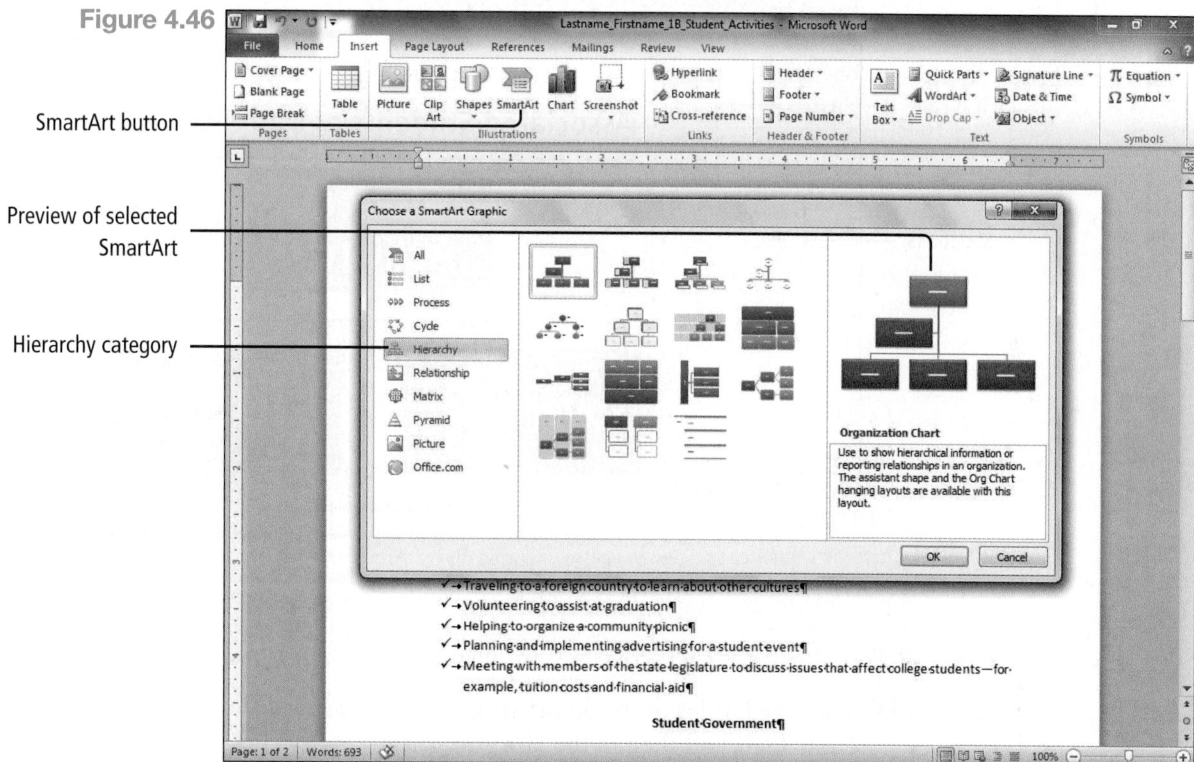

6 Click **OK**. If the pane indicating *Type your text here* does not display on the left side of the graphic, on the Design tab, in the Create Graphic group, click the Text Pane button. **Save** your document.

The SmartArt graphic displays at the insertion point location and consists of two parts—the graphic itself, and the Text Pane. On the Ribbon, the SmartArt Tools add the Design tab and the Format tab. You can type directly into the graphics, or type in the Text Pane. By typing in the Text Pane, you might find it easier to organize your layout.

Activity 4.23 | Modifying a SmartArt Graphic

1 In the SmartArt graphic, in the second row, click the border of the *[Text]* box to display a *solid* border and sizing handles, and then press Del. Repeat this procedure in the bottom row to delete the middle *[Text]* box.

Another Way

Close the Text Pane and type the text directly in the SmartArt boxes.

2 In the **Text Pane**, click in the top bulleted point, and then type **Student Activities** Notice that the first bulleted point aligns further to the left than the other points.

The ***top-level points*** are the main points in a SmartArt graphic. ***Subpoints*** are indented second-level bullet points.

3 Press [↓]. Type **Government** and then press [↓] again. Type **Clubs** and then compare your screen with Figure 4.47.

Figure 4.47

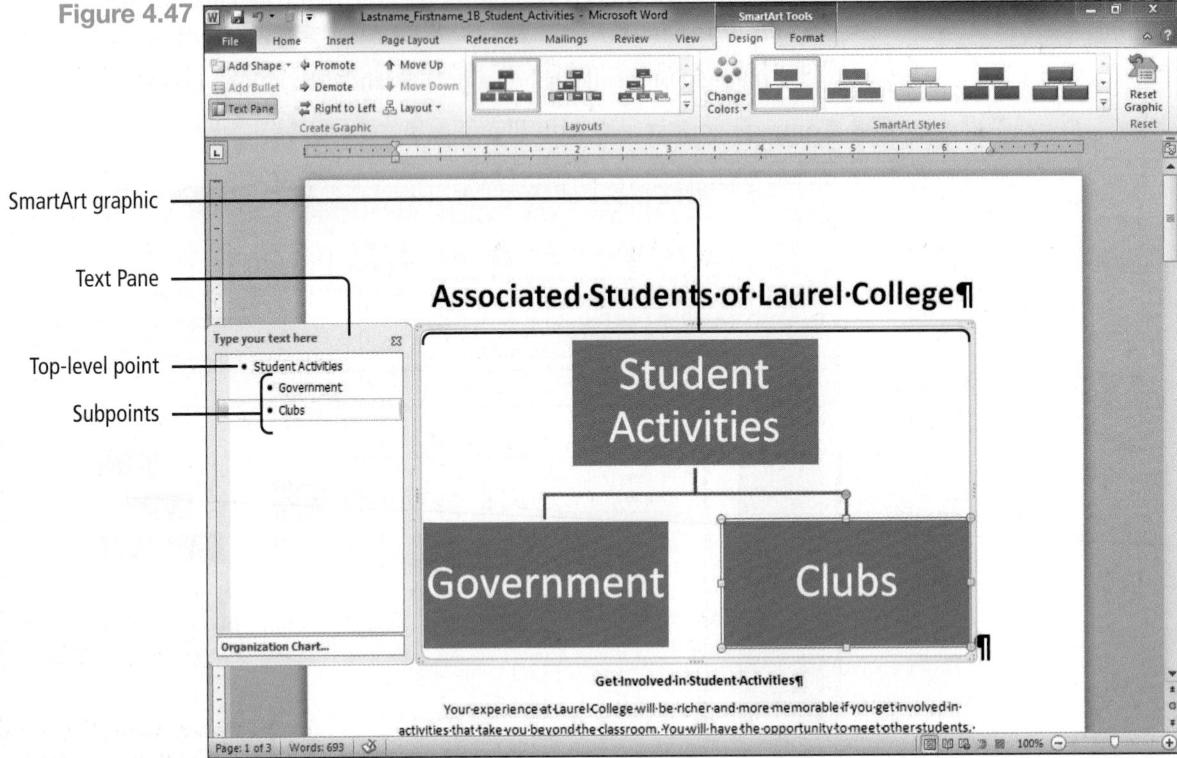

4 In the upper right corner of the **Text Pane**, click the **Close** button.

5 Click the border of the SmartArt graphic—a pale border surrounds it. Click the **Format tab**, and then in the **Size group**, if necessary click the **Size** button to display the **Shape Height** and **Shape Width** boxes.

6 Set the **Height** to **2.5″** and the **Width** to **4.2″**, and then compare your screen with Figure 4.48.

Figure 4.48

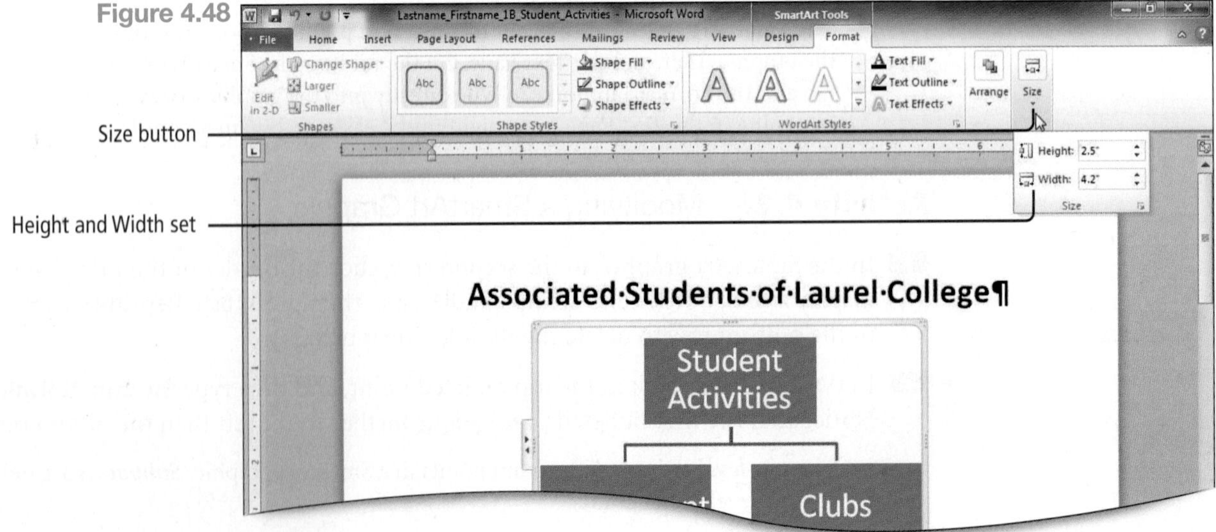

7 With the SmartArt graphic still selected, click the **Design tab**, and then in the **SmartArt Styles group**, click the **Change Colors** button. Under **Colorful**, click the second style—**Colorful Range - Accent Colors 2 to 3**.

8 On the **Design tab**, in the **SmartArt Styles group**, click the **More** button. Under **3-D**, click the first style—**Polished**. Compare your screen with Figure 4.49.

Figure 4.49

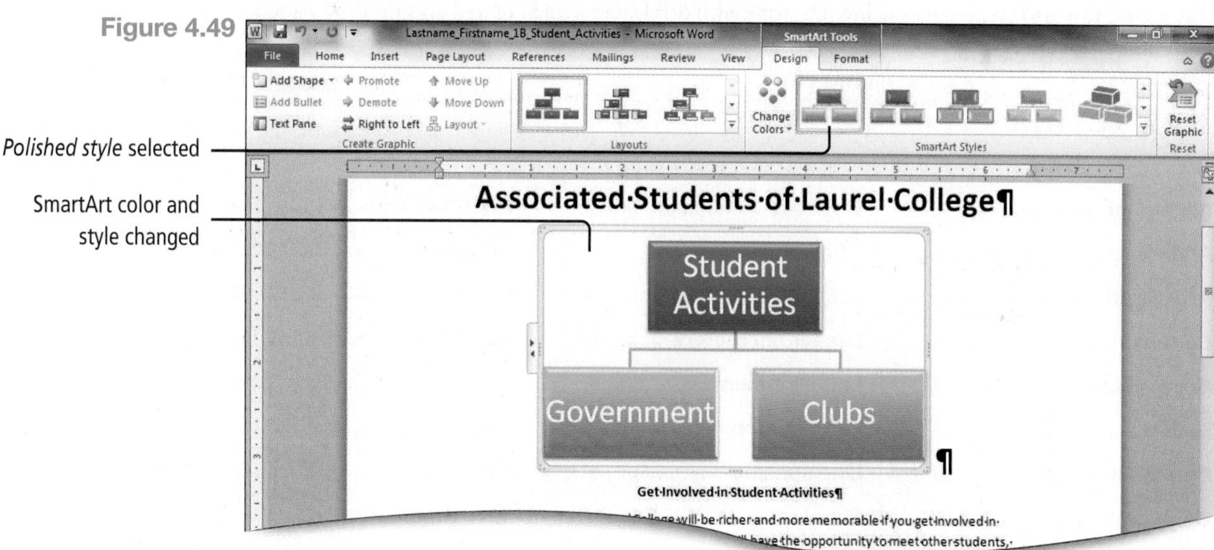

9 Click outside of the graphic to deselect it. Display **Backstage** view. On the right, under the screen thumbnail, click **Properties**, and then click **Show Document Panel**. In the **Author** box, delete any text and then type your firstname and lastname. In the **Subject** box, type your course name and section number, and in the **Keywords** box type **Student Activities, Associated Students Close** the Document Panel and **Save** your document.

10 Display **Backstage** view, and then click **Print** to display **Print Preview**. At the bottom of the preview, click the **Next Page** and **Previous Page** buttons to move between pages. If necessary, return to the document and make any necessary changes.

11 As directed by your instructor, print your document or submit it electronically. **Close** Word.

> **More Knowledge | Changing the Bullet Level in a SmartArt Graphic**
>
> To increase or decrease the level of an item, on the Design tab, in the Create Graphic group, click either the Promote or the Demote button.

End **You have completed Project 4B**

Content-Based Assessments

Summary

In this chapter, you created and formatted documents using Microsoft Word 2010. You inserted and formatted graphics, created and formatted bulleted and numbered lists, and created and formatted text boxes. You also created lists using tab stops with dot leaders, and created and modified a SmartArt graphic.

Key Terms

Alignment 178
Anchor 166
Artistic effects 167
Bar tab stop 188
Bulleted list 183
Bullets 183
Center alignment 178
Center tab stop 188
Decimal tab stop 188
Dot leader 190
Drawing objects 163
Field 172
Floating object 165
Formatting marks 161
Graphics 163
Inline object 164
Justified alignment 178
Leader characters 190
Left alignment 178
Left tab stop 188
Line spacing 180
Margins 177
Nonprinting characters 161
Nudge 167
Numbered list 183
Picture styles 167
Right alignment 178
Right tab stop 188
Shapes 168
SmartArt 190
Spin box 165
Subpoints 191
Tab stop 188
Text box 168
Text effects 163
Text wrapping 166
Toggle button 186
Top-level points 191
Wordwrap 161

Matching

Match each term in the second column with its correct definition in the first column by writing the letter of the term on the blank line in front of the correct definition.

____ 1. Formats that make pictures look more like sketches or paintings.

____ 2. A small box with an upward- and downward-pointing arrow that enables you to move rapidly through a set of values by clicking.

____ 3. Small circles in the corners of a selected graphic with which you can resize the graphic proportionally.

____ 4. The manner in which text displays around an object.

____ 5. An object or graphic that can be moved independently of the surrounding text.

____ 6. The process of using the arrow keys to move an object in small precise increments.

____ 7. An object or graphic inserted in a document that acts like a character in a sentence.

____ 8. Frames, shapes, shadows, borders, and other special effects that can be added to an image to create an overall visual style for the image.

____ 9. Predefined drawing objects, such as stars, banners, arrows, and callouts, included with Microsoft Office, and that can be inserted into documents.

A Artistic effects
B Bullets
C Floating object
D Inline object
E Justified alignment
F Left alignment
G Line spacing
H Nudge
I Picture styles
J Shapes
K Sizing handles
L SmartArt
M Spin box
N Tab stop
O Text wrapping

_____ 10. A commonly used alignment of text in which text is aligned at the left margin, leaving the right margin uneven.

_____ 11. An alignment of text in which the text is evenly aligned on both the left and right margins.

_____ 12. The distance between lines of text in a paragraph.

_____ 13. Text symbols such as small circles or check marks that introduce items in a list.

_____ 14. A mark on the ruler that indicates the location where the insertion point will be placed when you press the Tab key.

_____ 15. A designer-quality graphic used to create a visual representation of information.

Multiple Choice

Circle the correct answer.

1. Characters that display on the screen to show the location of paragraphs, tabs, and spaces, but that do not print, are called:
A. text effects **B.** bullets **C.** formatting marks

2. The placement of paragraph text relative to the left and right margins is referred to as:
A. alignment **B.** spacing **C.** indents

3. The symbol that indicates to which paragraph an image is attached is:
A. a small arrow **B.** an anchor **C.** a paragraph mark

4. A movable, resizable container for text or graphics is a:
A. text box **B.** dialog box **C.** SmartArt graphic

5. A banner is an example of a predefined:
A. paragraph **B.** format **C.** shape

6. A placeholder that displays preset content, such as the current date, the file name, a page number, or other stored information is:
A. a leader **B.** a field **C.** a tab

7. The space between the text and the top, bottom, left, and right edges of the paper are referred to as:
A. alignment **B.** margins **C.** spacing

8. A group of items in which items are displayed in order to indicate definite steps, a sequence of actions, or chronological order is a:
A. numbered list **B.** bulleted list **C.** outline list

9. A series of dots following a tab that serve to guide the reader's eye is a:
A. leader **B.** field **C.** shape

10. Tab stops are a form of:
A. line formatting **B.** document formatting **C.** paragraph formatting

Content-Based Assessments

Apply 4A skills from these Objectives:

1. Create a New Document and Insert Text
2. Insert and Format Graphics
3. Insert and Modify Text Boxes and Shapes
4. Preview and Print a Document

Skills Review | Project 4C Welcome Week

In the following Skills Review, you will create and edit a flyer for the Laurel College New Student Welcome Week. Your completed document will look similar to Figure 4.50.

Project Files

For Project 4C, you will need the following files:

New blank Word document
w01C_Welcome_Text
w01C_Welcome_Picture

You will save your document as:

Lastname_Firstname_1C_Welcome_Week

Project Results

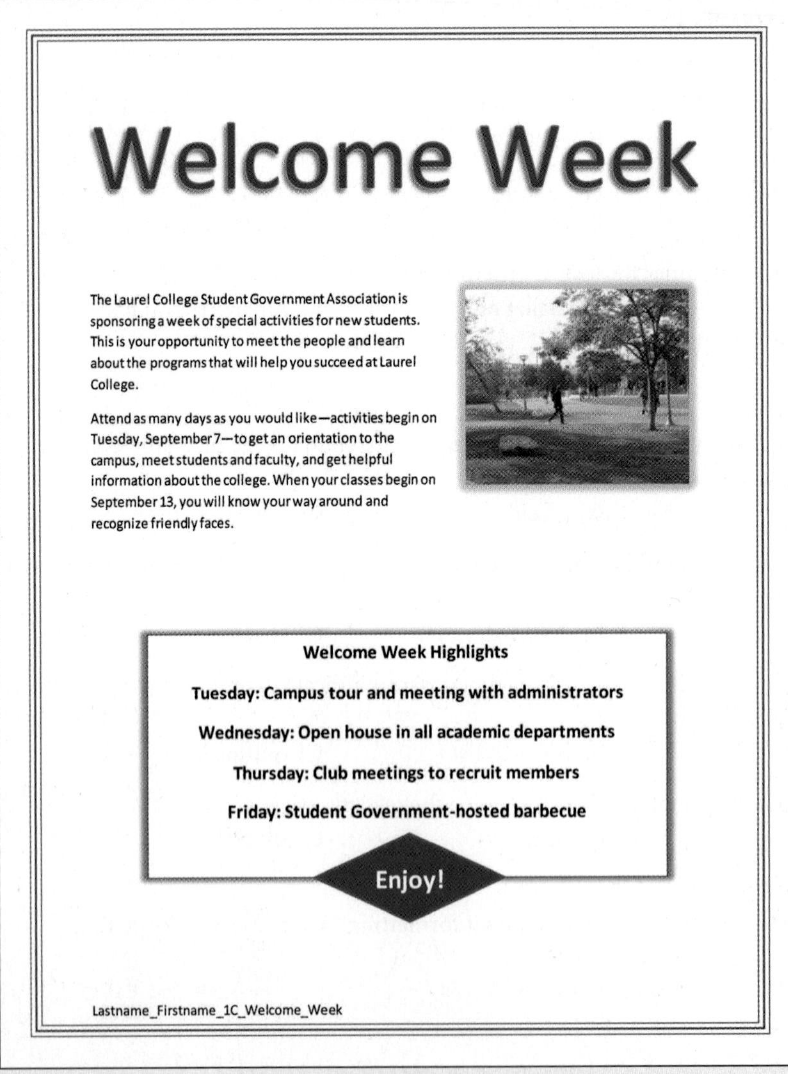

Figure 4.50

(Project 4C Welcome Week continues on the next page)

Skills Review | Project 4C Welcome Week (continued)

1 **Start** Word and display a new blank document. On the **Home tab**, in the **Paragraph group**, be sure the **Show/Hide ¶** button is active so that you can view formatting marks. In the **Quick Access Toolbar**, click the **Save** button, navigate to your **Word Chapter 1** folder, and then **Save** the document as **Lastname_Firstname_1C_Welcome_Week**

- **a.** Type **Welcome Week** and then press Enter two times.
- **b.** Type **The Laurel College Student Government Association is sponsoring a week of special activities for new students. This is your opportunity to meet the people and learn about the programs that will help you succeed at Laurel College.**
- **c.** Press Enter one time. Click the **Insert tab**. In the **Text group**, click the **Object button arrow**, and then click **Text from File**. Navigate to your student files, select the file **w01C_Welcome_Text**, and then at the bottom of the **Insert File** dialog box, click **Insert**. **Save** your document.

2 At the top of the document, in the left margin area, point to the left of the first paragraph—*Welcome Week*—until the pointer displays, and then click one time to select the paragraph. On the **Home tab**, in the **Font group**, click the **Text Effects** button. In the displayed **Text Effects** gallery, in the first row, click the fourth effect—**Fill - White, Outline - Accent 1**.

- **a.** With the text still selected, in the **Font group**, click the **Font Size button arrow**, and then click **72**. In the **Paragraph group**, click the **Center** button.
- **b.** With the text still selected, in the **Font group**, click the **Text Effects** button. Point to **Shadow**, and then under **Outer**, in the first row click the third style—**Offset Diagonal Bottom Left**. In the **Font group**, click the **Font Color button arrow**. Under **Theme Colors**, in the fourth column, click the first color—**Dark Blue, Text 2**.
- **c.** In the paragraph that begins *The Laurel College*, click to position the insertion point at the beginning of the paragraph. On the **Insert tab**, in the **Illustrations group**, click the **Picture** button. From your student data files, **Insert** the file **w01C_Welcome_Picture**. On the **Format tab**, in the **Size group**, click the **Shape Height down spin arrow** as necessary to change the height of the picture to **2″**.
- **d.** With the picture still selected, on the **Format tab**, in the **Arrange group**, click the **Wrap Text** button. From the **Wrap Text** gallery, click **Square**.
- **e.** Hold down Shift and point anywhere in the picture to display the pointer. Drag the picture to align the right edge of the picture just to the left of the right margin.
- **f.** On the **Format tab**, in the **Picture Styles group**, click the **Picture Effects** button. Point to **Glow**, and then under **Glow Variations**, in the third row, click the first style—**Blue, 11 pt glow, Accent color 1**. Nudge as necessary to match the picture position shown in Figure 4.50.
- **g.** Click anywhere to deselect the picture. Click the **Page Layout tab**, and then in the **Page Background group**, click the **Page Borders** button. In the **Borders and Shading** dialog box, under **Setting**, click **Box**. Under **Style**, scroll down the list. About two-thirds down the list, click the style with a thin top and bottom line and a slightly thicker middle line.
- **h.** Click the **Color arrow**, and then under **Theme Colors**, in the fourth column, click the first color—**Dark Blue, Text 2**. Click **OK**, and then **Save** your document.

3 Press Ctrl + End to move to the bottom of the document. On the **Insert tab**, in the **Text group**, click the **Text Box** button. At the bottom of the **Text Box** gallery, click **Draw Text Box**.

- **a.** At the bottom of the document, position the pointer in an open area near the left margin, and then drag down and to the right to create a text box approximately **2.5 inches** high and **5.5 inches** wide; you need not be precise.
- **b.** With the insertion point positioned in the text box, type the following:

  Welcome Week Highlights

  Tuesday: Campus tour and meeting with administrators

  Wednesday: Open house in all academic departments

  Thursday: Club meetings to recruit members

  Friday: Student Government-hosted barbecue

(Project 4C Welcome Week continues on the next page)

Skills Review | Project 4C Welcome Week (continued)

c. In the text box, select all of the text. On the Mini toolbar, click the **Font Size button arrow**, and then click **14**. Click the **Bold** button, and then click the **Center** button.

d. On the **Format tab**, in the **Size group**, if necessary click the **Size** button. Click the **Shape Height spin arrows** as necessary to change the height of the text box to **2.5″**. Click the **Shape Width button up spin arrow** as necessary to widen the text box to **5.5″**.

e. In the **Shape Styles group**, click the **Shape Effects** button. Point to **Shadow**, and then under **Outer**, in the second row, click the second style—**Offset Center**. In the **Shape Styles group**, click the **Shape Outline button arrow**. Under **Theme Colors**, in the fourth column, click the first color—**Dark Blue, Text 2**.

f. If necessary, click anywhere inside the text box. Point to the text box border to display the [move] pointer. Drag the text box to align the left edge at approximately **0.5 inches on the horizontal ruler** and to align the top edge at approximately **5.5 inches on the vertical ruler**. You may have to click outside the text box several times to see the exact location on the rulers.

g. On the **Insert tab**, in the **Illustrations group**, click the **Shapes** button. Under **Basic Shapes**, in the first row, click the seventh shape—**Diamond**.

h. Position the [+] pointer slightly under the text box and at approximately **2 inches on the horizontal ruler**. Drag down approximately **1 inch** and to the right approximately **2 inches**. On the **Format tab**, in the **Size group**, adjust the **Shape Height** to **0.9″** and the **Shape Width** to **2″**.

i. Right-click the new shape, and then click **Add Text**. Type **Enjoy!** and then select the text you typed. On the Mini toolbar, click the **Font Size button arrow**, and then click **20**. Click the **Bold** button, and then if necessary, click the **Center** button.

j. On the **Format tab**, in the **Shape Styles group**, click the **Shape Fill button arrow**, and then under **Theme Colors**, in the fourth column, click the first color—**Dark Blue, Text 2**.

k. Point to the shape border until the [move] pointer displays, and then position the shape with its widest points aligned with the lower edge of the text box and approximately centered. As necessary, move the shape in small increments by pressing the arrow keys on your keyboard. Refer to Figure 4.50 for approximate placement. **Save** your document.

4 Click the **Insert tab**, and then, in the **Header & Footer group**, click the **Footer** button. At the bottom of the **Footer** gallery, click **Edit Footer**.

a. On the **Design tab**, in the **Insert group**, click the **Quick Parts** button, and then click **Field**. In the **Field names** list, scroll as necessary to locate and click **FileName**. Click **OK**, and then double-click anywhere in the document.

b. Press Ctrl + Home to move the insertion point to the beginning of the document. Display **Backstage** view. On the right, under the screen thumbnail, click **Properties**, and then click **Show Document Panel**. In the **Author** box, delete any text and then type your firstname and lastname. In the **Subject** box, type your course name and section number, and in the **Keywords** box type **Welcome Week**

c. **Close** the Document Panel. In **Backstage** view, click the **Print tab** to display the **Print Preview**. If necessary, return to the document to make any corrections or adjustments.

d. **Save** your document, print or submit electronically as directed by your instructor, and then **Close** Word.

End **You have completed Project 4C**

Apply 4B skills from these Objectives:

5 Change Document and Paragraph Layout
6 Create and Modify Lists
7 Set and Modify Tab Stops
8 Insert a SmartArt Graphic

Skills Review | Project 4D Constitution

In the following Skills Review, you will edit the constitution of the Associated Students of Laurel College. Your completed document will look similar to Figure 4.51.

Project Files

For Project 4D, you will need the following file:

w01D_Constitution

You will save your document as:

Lastname_Firstname_1D_Constitution

Project Results

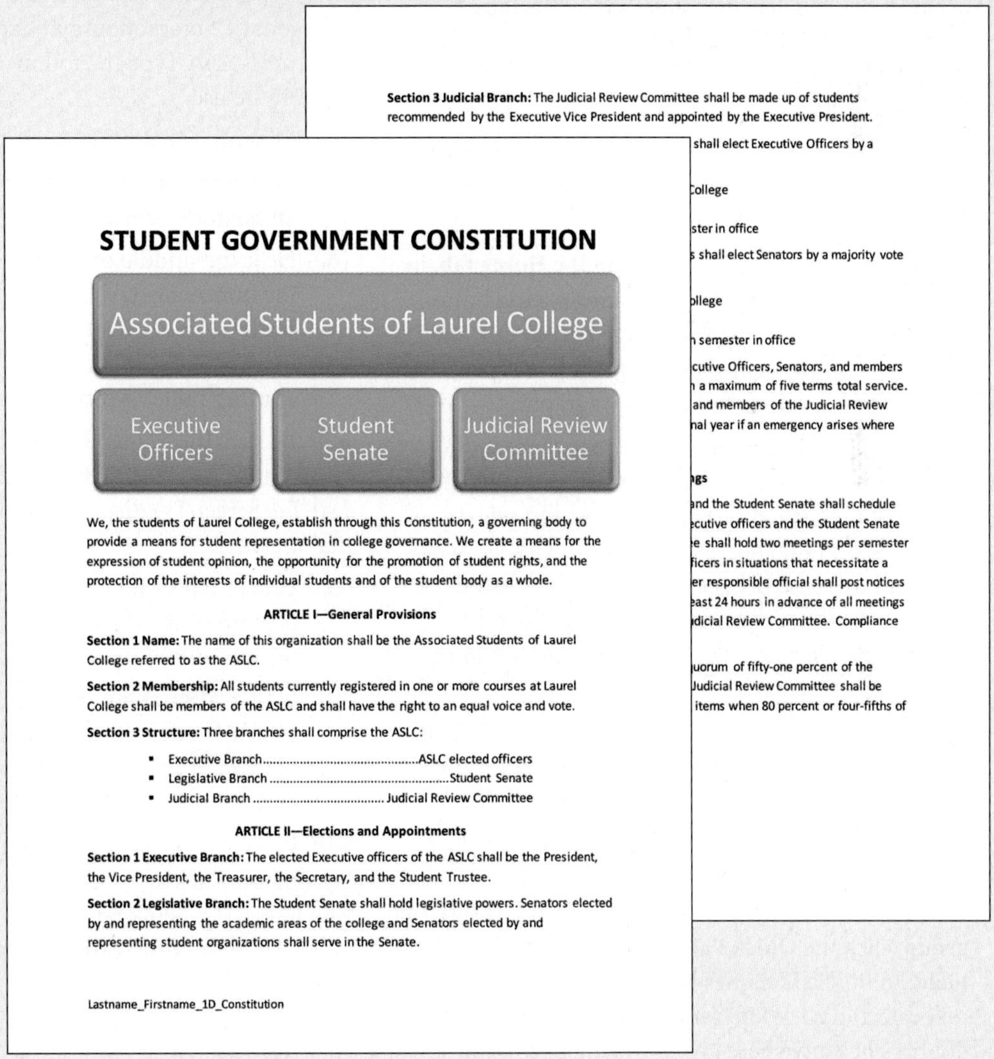

Section 3 Judicial Branch: The Judicial Review Committee shall be made up of students recommended by the Executive Vice President and appointed by the Executive President.

STUDENT GOVERNMENT CONSTITUTION

Associated Students of Laurel College

Executive Officers | Student Senate | Judicial Review Committee

We, the students of Laurel College, establish through this Constitution, a governing body to provide a means for student representation in college governance. We create a means for the expression of student opinion, the opportunity for the promotion of student rights, and the protection of the interests of individual students and of the student body as a whole.

ARTICLE I—General Provisions

Section 1 Name: The name of this organization shall be the Associated Students of Laurel College referred to as the ASLC.

Section 2 Membership: All students currently registered in one or more courses at Laurel College shall be members of the ASLC and shall have the right to an equal voice and vote.

Section 3 Structure: Three branches shall comprise the ASLC:

- Executive Branch..ASLC elected officers
- Legislative Branch...Student Senate
- Judicial Branch..................................... Judicial Review Committee

ARTICLE II—Elections and Appointments

Section 1 Executive Branch: The elected Executive officers of the ASLC shall be the President, the Vice President, the Treasurer, the Secretary, and the Student Trustee.

Section 2 Legislative Branch: The Student Senate shall hold legislative powers. Senators elected by and representing the academic areas of the college and Senators elected by and representing student organizations shall serve in the Senate.

Lastname_Firstname_1D_Constitution

Figure 4.51

(Project 4D Constitution continues on the next page)

Content-Based Assessments

Skills Review | Project 4D Constitution (continued)

1 **Start** Word. From your student files, locate and open the document **w01D_Constitution**. Display **Backstage** view, click **Save As**, and then navigate to your **Word Chapter 1** folder. **Save** the document as **Lastname_Firstname_1D_Constitution**

a. On the **Home tab**, in the **Paragraph group**, be sure the **Show/Hide** button is active so you can view formatting marks. Click the **Page Layout tab**. In the **Page Setup group**, click the **Margins** button, and then at the bottom of the **Margins** gallery, at the bottom of the list, click **Custom Margins**. In the **Page Setup** dialog box, in the **Top** box, type **1** Press Tab as necessary to select the values in the **Bottom**, **Left**, and **Right** boxes and change all margins to **1**. Click **OK**.

b. Press Ctrl + A to select all of the text in the document. On the **Home tab**, in the **Paragraph group**, click the **Align Text Left** button to change the alignment from justified to left aligned.

c. With all of the text still selected, on the **Home tab**, in the **Paragraph group**, click the **Line Spacing** button, and then click **1.15**. Click the **Page Layout tab**, and then in the **Paragraph group**, under **Spacing**, set **After** to **6 pt** spacing after each paragraph.

d. At the top of the document, click anywhere in the title, right-click, and then on the Mini toolbar, click **Center**. Near the top of **Page 1**, locate and select the paragraph that begins *ARTICLE 1*. Hold down Ctrl, and then use the vertical scroll bar to scroll through the document, and then select the other two paragraphs that begin *ARTICLE*. On the Mini toolbar, click **Center**.

e. With the three subheadings that begin *ARTICLE* still selected, on the **Page Layout tab**, in the **Paragraph group**, under **Spacing**, set **Before** to **12 pt**.

f. Scroll to view the bottom of **Page 1**, point anywhere in the bottom margin area, right-click, and then click **Edit Footer**. On the **Design tab**, in the **Insert group**, click the **Quick Parts** button, and then click **Field**. In the **Field names** list, scroll as necessary to locate and click **FileName**. Click **OK**, and then double-click anywhere in the document to exit the footer area.

2 Near the middle of **Page 1**, *above* the *ARTICLE II* subheading, locate the paragraph that begins *Executive Branch*, and then move the pointer into the left margin area to display the pointer. Drag down to select this paragraph and the next two paragraphs. On the **Home tab**, in the **Paragraph group**, click the **Bullets** button.

a. Scroll to view the bottom of **Page 1**, and then locate the paragraph that begins *Completion of at least*. Select that paragraph and the next two paragraphs. On the **Home tab**, in the **Paragraph group**, click the **Numbering** button.

b. Locate the paragraph that begins *Section 4 Elections*. Click to position the insertion point at the *end* of that paragraph after the colon, and then press Enter.

c. Type **1.** and press Spacebar. Type **Completion of at least 12 credit hours at Laurel College** and then press Enter. Type the following text for items 2 and 3 in the list:

Minimum GPA of 2.75

Enrollment in at least six credit hours each semester in office

d. Near the middle of **Page 1**, select the three items in the bulleted list, right-click the list, and then point to **Bullets**. Under **Bullet Library**, click the **black square** symbol. If the black square is not available, choose another bullet symbol. **Save** your document.

3 Be sure the bulleted list is still selected. Point to the left tab marker at **2″ on the horizontal ruler**. When the *Left Tab* ScreenTip displays, double-click to open the **Tabs** dialog box.

a. Under **Tab stop position**, with *2″* selected, at the bottom of the dialog box, click **Clear** to delete this tab stop. Then, type **5.5** in the **Tab stop position** box.

b. Under **Alignment**, click the **Right** option button. Under **Leader**, click the **2** option button. At the bottom of the **Tabs** dialog box, click the **Set** button, and then click **OK**.

4 Press Ctrl + Home to move to the top of the document. Click at the end of the title, and then press Enter to insert a blank paragraph. Click the **Insert tab**, and then in the **Illustrations group**, click the **SmartArt** button.

a. In the **Choose a SmartArt Graphic** dialog box, on the left, click **Hierarchy**, and in the second row, click the fourth style—**Table Hierarchy**. At the bottom of the **Choose a SmartArt Graphic** dialog box, click **OK**. If necessary, on the Design tab, in the Create Graphic group, activate the Text Pane button.

(Project 4D Constitution continues on the next page)

Skills Review | Project 4D Constitution (continued)

b. In the SmartArt graphic, in the second row, click the border of the first *[Text]* box, and then press Del. Press Del again to delete a second *[Text]* box. In the **Text Pane**, under **Type your text here** box, click in the last bulleted point. On the **Design tab**, in the **Create Graphic group**, click the **Promote** button to move the list item up one level.

c. In the **Text Pane**, click in the top bulleted point, type **Associated Students of Laurel College** and then press ↓. Type the following in the three remaining boxes:

Executive Officers

Student Senate

Judicial Review Committee

d. In the upper right corner of the **Text Pane**, click the **Close** button. Be sure the graphic is selected—a pale border surrounds the entire graphic, and then click the outside border one time. Click the **Format tab**, and then in the **Size group**, if necessary click the **Size** button. By clicking the spin box arrows, change the **Shape Height** to **2.6″** and the **Shape Width** to **6.5″**.

e. With the SmartArt graphic still selected, on the **Design tab**, in the **SmartArt Styles group**, click the **Change Colors** button. Scroll down, and then under **Accent 5**, click the second style—**Colored Fill - Accent 5**.

f. On the **Design tab**, in the **SmartArt Styles group**, click the **More** button. Under **3-D**, click the second style—**Inset**. Click anywhere in the document to deselect the graphic. Press Ctrl + Home to move the insertion point to the beginning of the document.

g. Display **Backstage** view, on the right, under the screen thumbnail, click **Properties**, and then click **Show Document Panel**. In the **Author** box, type your firstname and lastname. In the **Subject** box type your course name and section number, and in the **Keywords** box type **student constitution**

h. **Close** the Document Panel. Click **Save**. Display **Backstage** view and click the **Print tab**. Examine the **Print Preview**. Print or submit electronically as directed. **Close** Word.

End **You have completed Project 4D**

Content-Based Assessments

Apply 4A skills from these Objectives:

1. Create a New Document and Insert Text
2. Insert and Format Graphics
3. Insert and Modify Text Boxes and Shapes
4. Preview and Print a Document

Mastering Word | Project 4E Retreat

In the following Mastering Word project, you will create a flyer announcing a retreat for the Associated Students of Laurel College Board. Your completed document will look similar to Figure 4.52.

Project Files

For Project 4E, you will need the following files:

New blank Word document
w01E_Retreat_Text
w01E_Retreat_Picture

You will save your document as:

Lastname_Firstname_1E_Retreat

Project Results

ASLC Board Retreat

College President Diane Gilmore is pleased to announce a retreat for the Board of the Associated Students of Laurel College.

Invitees include the ASLC Board, consisting of the Executive Officers and their appointed directors, Student Senators, Club Presidents, and members of the Judicial Review Committee. The retreat will be held at the Fogelsville campus of Penn State University on Friday, November 12.

The morning session will begin with a continental breakfast at 8:30 a.m., and will include presentations on effective ways to set and achieve goals. Lunch will be served at noon. The afternoon session will begin at 1:30 p.m., and will include small breakout sessions for the sharing and development of goals and a series of exercises to facilitate group interaction.

In addition to goal setting, the retreat is organized to provide a means for Board members to get to know one another. Students are so busy with courses, student government duties, and personal responsibilities that they rarely get to interact with other Board members outside of their immediate circles. The afternoon will be devoted to a series of exercises specially designed for this retreat. It will enable all participants to meet every other person in attendance and to exchange ideas. We have hired the well-known group, Mountain Retreat Planners, to conduct this portion of the program. They have some entertaining activities planned that will help break down barriers to becoming acquainted with other participants.

Prize drawings at lunch include concert tickets, college football jerseys, coffee mugs, and restaurant gift cards.

Lastname_Firstname_1E_Retreat

Figure 4.52

(Project 4E Retreat continues on the next page)

Mastering Word | Project 4E Retreat (continued)

1 **Start** Word and display a new blank document. **Save** the document in your **Word Chapter 1** folder as **Lastname_Firstname_1E_Retreat** and then add the file name to the footer. Be sure the formatting marks and rulers display.

2 Type **ASLC Board Retreat** and press Enter two times. Type **College President Diane Gilmore is pleased to announce a retreat for the Board of the Associated Students of Laurel College.** Press Enter one time. **Insert** the file **w04E_Retreat_Text**.

3 Select the title *ASLC Board Retreat*. On the **Home tab**, in the **Font group**, display the **Text Effects** gallery, and then in the third row, apply the first effect—**Fill - White, Gradient Outline - Accent 1**. Change the **Font Size** to **56** pt. Apply a **Shadow** text effect using the first effect under **Outer—Offset Diagonal Bottom Right**. Change the **Font Color** to **Olive Green, Accent 3, Darker 25%**—in the seventh column, the fifth color.

4 Click to position the insertion point at the beginning of the paragraph that begins *College President*, and then from your student files, **Insert** the picture **w01E_Retreat_Picture**. Change the **Shape Height** of the picture to **2″**, and then set the **Wrap Text** to **Square**. Move the picture so that the right edge aligns with the right margin, and the top edge aligns with the top edge of the text that begins *College President*. Apply a **Film Grain Artistic Effect**—the third effect in the third row. From **Picture Effects**, add a **5 Point Soft Edge**.

5 Scroll to view the lower portion of the page. **Insert** a **Text Box** beginning at the left margin and at approximately **7 inches on the vertical ruler** that is approximately 1″ high and 4.5″ wide. Then, in the **Size group**, make the measurements exact by setting the **Height** to **1″** and the **Width** to **4.6″**. Type the following text in the text box:

> **Prize drawings at lunch include concert tickets, college football jerseys, coffee mugs, and restaurant gift cards.**

6 Select the text in the text box. Change the **Font Size** to **16** pt, apply **Bold**, and **Center** the text. Add a **Shape Fill** to the text box using the theme color **Olive Green, Accent 3, Lighter 40%**. Then apply a **Gradient** fill using the **Linear Right** gradient. Change the **Shape Outline** color to **White, Background 1**. Drag the text box as necessary to center it horizontally between the left and right margins, and vertically between the last line of text and the footer.

7 Display the **Document Panel**. Type your firstname and lastname in the **Author** box, your course name and section number in the **Subject** box, and then in the **Keywords** box type **retreat, ASLC**

8 **Close** the Document Panel. **Save** and preview your document, make any necessary adjustments, and then print your document or submit it electronically as directed. **Close** Word.

End **You have completed Project 4E**

Apply 4B skills from these Objectives:

5 Change Document and Paragraph Layout
6 Create and Modify Lists
7 Set and Modify Tab Stops
8 Insert a SmartArt Graphic

Mastering Word | Project 4F Cycling Trip

In the following Mastering Word project, you will create an informational handout about a planned trip by the Laurel College Cycling Club. Your completed document will look similar to Figure 4.53.

Project Files

For Project 4F, you will need the following file:

w01F_Cycling_Trip

You will save your document as:

Lastname_Firstname_1F_Cycling_Trip

Project Results

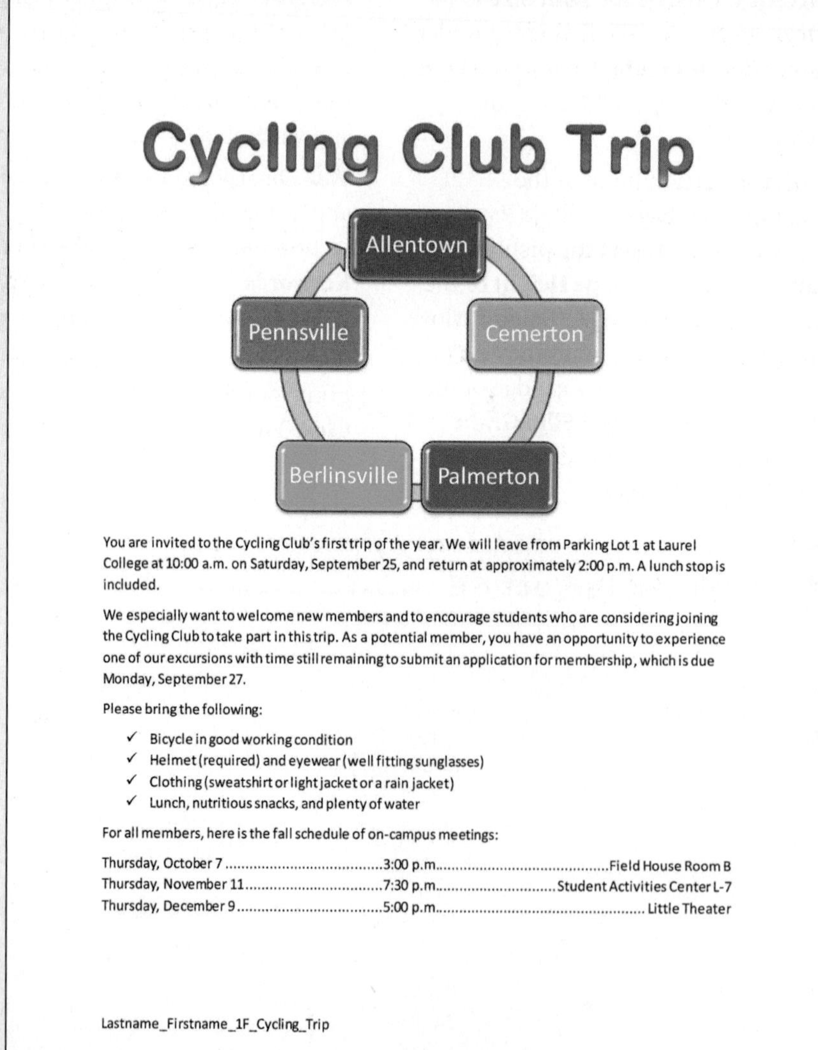

Cycling Club Trip

Allentown
Cemerton
Palmerton
Berlinsville
Pennsville

You are invited to the Cycling Club's first trip of the year. We will leave from Parking Lot 1 at Laurel College at 10:00 a.m. on Saturday, September 25, and return at approximately 2:00 p.m. A lunch stop is included.

We especially want to welcome new members and to encourage students who are considering joining the Cycling Club to take part in this trip. As a potential member, you have an opportunity to experience one of our excursions with time still remaining to submit an application for membership, which is due Monday, September 27.

Please bring the following:

- ✓ Bicycle in good working condition
- ✓ Helmet (required) and eyewear (well fitting sunglasses)
- ✓ Clothing (sweatshirt or light jacket or a rain jacket)
- ✓ Lunch, nutritious snacks, and plenty of water

For all members, here is the fall schedule of on-campus meetings:

Thursday, October 7 .... 3:00 p.m. .... Field House Room B
Thursday, November 11 .... 7:30 p.m. .... Student Activities Center L-7
Thursday, December 9 .... 5:00 p.m. .... Little Theater

Lastname_Firstname_1F_Cycling_Trip

Figure 4.53

(Project 4F Cycling Trip continues on the next page)

Mastering Word | Project 4F Cycling Trip (continued)

1 **Start** Word. From your student files open the document **w01F_Cycling_Trip**. **Save** the document in your **Word Chapter 1** folder as **Lastname_Firstname_1F_Cycling_Trip** Add the file name to the footer. Display formatting marks.

2 Display the **Page Setup** dialog box. Set the **Top** margin to **1.25″** and the other three margins to **1″**. Select all of the text in the document, including the title. Add **6 pt** spacing after all paragraphs. Change the **Line Spacing** to **1.15**. Change the alignment to **Align Text Left**. **Center** the document title—*Cycling Club Trip*.

3 Locate the paragraph that begins *Bicycle in good.* Select that paragraph and the three paragraphs that follow it. Create a bulleted list from the selected text. Use the shortcut menu to display bullet options, and change the bullet character to a **check mark** or another symbol if the check mark is unavailable.

4 Position the insertion point in the blank paragraph at the end of the document. Add a **Right** tab stop at **3.5″**. Display the **Tabs** dialog box and add a dot leader. **Set** the tab stop, and then add and **Set** another **Right** tab stop with a dot leader at **6.5″**.

5 Type the text shown in **Table 1**, pressing Tab between columns and Enter at the end of each line. Refer to Figure 4.53.

6 Select the first two lines in the tabbed list and change the **Space After** to **0 pt**. Near the top of the document, position the insertion point in the blank line below the title. Display the **Choose a SmartArt Graphic** dialog box, select the **Cycle** category, and then in the second row, select the first style—**Continuous Cycle**.

7 Display the **Text Pane**. Add the following cities in this order: **Allentown** and **Cemerton** and **Palmerton** and **Berlinsville** and **Pennsville**

8 **Close** the Text Pane. Click the SmartArt border. On the **Format tab**, set the **Shape Width** of the SmartArt graphic to **6.5″** and the **Shape Height** to **3″**. On the **Design tab**, from the **SmartArt Styles** gallery, apply the **Cartoon 3-D** style, and change the colors to the first color under **Colorful—Colorful – Accent Colors**.

9 Display the **Document Panel**, type your firstname and lastname in the **Author** box, your course name and section number in the **Subject** box, and then in the **Keywords** box type **cycling, cycling club**

10 **Close** the Document Panel. **Save** your document. Preview your document, check for and make any adjustments, and then print your document or submit it electronically as directed. **Close** Word.

Table 1

Thursday, October 7	**3:00 p.m.**	**Field House Room B**
Thursday, November 11	**7:30 p.m.**	**Student Activities Center L-7**
Thursday, December 9	**5:00 p.m.**	**Little Theater**

(Return to Step 6)

End **You have completed Project 4F**

Content-Based Assessments

Apply a combination of 4A and 4B skills:

1. Create a New Document and Insert Text
2. Insert and Format Graphics
3. Insert and Modify Text Boxes and Shapes
4. Preview and Print a Document
5. Change Document and Paragraph Layout
6. Create and Modify Lists
7. Set and Modify Tab Stops
8. Insert a SmartArt Graphic

Mastering Word | Project 4G Web Sites

In the following Mastering Word project, you will edit guidelines for club Web sites at Laurel College. Your completed document will look similar to Figure 4.54.

Project Files

For Project 4G, you will need the following files:

New blank Word document
w01G_Chess_Club_Picture
w01G_Web_Sites_Text

You will save your document as:

Lastname_Firstname_1G_Web_Sites

Project Results

Club Web Sites

Published by Student Computing Services

The Web site that your club develops will represent your club and its membership. The site can promote interest in your club and attract new members—think of it as advertising. The site is also a main source of information for current members. Always consider how others will view or interpret the content of your site. Use the guidelines listed below as you develop and update the information you publish.

The college Student Computing Services office is available to assist clubs with Web site development and maintenance. Consult the contact information, listed at the end of these guidelines, to set up a meeting with one of our staff members.

General Information Guidelines

Be sure that:

- All information on the Web site is club related.
- No personal information or links to personal information is on the Web site unless the content has a specific relationship to the club.
- Updates to the Web site are frequent enough to eliminate outdated content and to add new content.
- Instruction is available to club members regarding proper use of bulletin boards, including general etiquette rules.
- Protected information on the Web site is available only to club members who have been issued user names and passwords.
- The club's faculty advisor approves all Web site content and updates to the site.

General information about the club should include:

1. Purpose and goals of the club
2. Names of club officers and their campus email addresses
3. Dates and locations of club meetings
4. Dates and locations of special events
5. Applications for club membership
6. Information about election of officers and nomination forms

Lastname_Firstname_1G_Web_Sites

lines.
ng carefully.
d what they need quickly.
s and colors, background colors and
ult to read and navigate.
g of Web pages.
and unusual fonts to make your site
ther help with designing your club's Web
... 8 a.m. to 10 p.m.
..... 8 a.m. to 5 p.m.
... 8 a.m. to 12 noon
s office is located in
call (215) 555-0932.

Figure 4.54

(Project 4G Web Sites continues on the next page)

Mastering Word | Project 4G Web Sites (continued)

1 **Start** Word and display a new blank document. Display formatting marks and rulers. **Save** the document in your **Word Chapter 1** folder as **Lastname_Firstname_1G_Web_Sites** Add the file name to the footer.

Type **Club Web Sites** and then press Enter. Select the title you just typed. From the **Text Effects** gallery, in the fourth row, apply the second effect—**Gradient Fill - Orange, Accent 6, Inner Shadow**, change the **Font Size** to **72** pt, and **Center** the title.

2 Click in the blank line below the title. Locate and insert the file **w01G_Web_Sites_Text**. *Except* for the document title, select all of the document text. **Align Text Left**, change the **Line Spacing** to **1.15**, and change the **Spacing After** to **6 pt**. Locate and **Center** the document subtitle that begins *Published by.*

3 In the middle of **Page 1**, under the subheading *Be sure that,* select the six paragraphs down to, but not including, the *General information* subheading. Format the selected text as a bulleted list. Near the bottom of **Page 1** and the top of **Page 2**, under the *Web Site Design Guidelines* subheading, select all of the paragraphs to the end of the document—not including the blank paragraph mark—and create another bulleted list.

4 Under the subheading that begins *General information,* select the six paragraphs and apply **Numbering** to create a numbered list.

Near the top of the document, position the insertion point to the left of the paragraph that begins The Web site. **Insert** the picture **w01G_Chess_Club_Picture**. Set the **Wrap Text** to **Square**. Decrease the picture **Width** to **2.7″**. From the **Picture Effects** gallery, apply the **Soft Edges** effect using **5 Point**.

5 Press Ctrl + End to move to the blank line at the end of the document. Type **For assistance, Student Computing Services hours are:** and then press Enter. Set a **Left** tab stop at **1.5″**. Display the **Tabs** dialog box. At **5″** add a **Right** tab stop with a **dot leader** and click **Set**. Click **OK** to close the dialog box, press Tab to begin, and then type the following information; be sure to press Tab to begin each line and press Tab between the days and the times and press Enter at the end of each line:

Monday–Thursday	**8 a.m. to 10 p.m.**
Friday	**8 a.m. to 5 p.m.**
Saturday	**8 a.m. to 12 noon**

6 At the top of **Page 2**, position the insertion point to the left of the subheading *Web Site Design Guidelines.* Press Enter one time, and then click in the blank paragraph you just created. **Insert** a **SmartArt** graphic, and then from the **Process** group, select the **Basic Chevron Process**—in the fourth row, the third graphic. Click the border of the graphic, and then on the **Format tab**, set the **Shape Height** of the graphic to **1″** and the **Shape Width** of the graphic to **6.5″**. From the **Design tab**, display the **Text Pane**, and then type **Club** and **Web Site** and **New Members Close** the **Text Pane**. Change style to **3-D Inset** and the colors to **Colored Fill – Accent 6**, which is in the last set of colors.

7 At the bottom of **Page 2**, **Insert** a **Text Box** and set the height to **0.7″** and the width to **5″**. In the text box, type: **The Student Computing Services office is located in the Cedar Building, Room 114, call (215) 555-0932.**

Select the text in the text box. From the Mini toolbar, change the **Font Size** to **16** pt, apply **Bold**, and **Center** the text. Change the **Shape Fill** to **Orange, Accent 6, Darker 25%.** From the **Shape Effects** gallery, apply a **Circle Bevel.** By using the pointer, visually center the text box horizontally between the left and right margins and vertically between the tabbed list and the footer.

8 As the document properties, type your firstname and lastname in the **Author** box, your course name and section number in the **Subject** box, and then in the **Keywords** box type **Web sites, guidelines, Student Computing Services** **Save** your document, examine the Print Preview, check for and make any adjustments, and then print your document or submit it electronically as directed. **Close** Word.

End **You have completed Project 4G**

Content-Based Assessments

Apply a combination of the 4A and 4B skills.

GO! Fix It | Project 4H Guidelines

Project Files

For Project 4H, you will need the following file:

w01H_Guidelines

You will save your document as:

Lastname_Firstname_1H_Guidelines

From the student files that accompany this textbook, locate and open the file w01H_More_Guidelines, and then save the file in your Word Chapter 1 folder as **Lastname_Firstname_1H_Guidelines**

This document contains errors that you must find and correct. Read and examine the document, and then edit to correct any errors that you find and to improve the overall document format. Types of errors could include, but are not restricted to:

- Wasted space due to text not wrapping around pictures
- Inconsistent line spacing in paragraphs
- Inconsistent spacing between paragraphs
- Inconsistent paragraph indents
- Inconsistent indenting of lists
- Titles that do not extend across the page
- Text boxes that are too small
- Tabbed lists with wide spaces that do not contain leaders
- Spaces between paragraphs created using empty paragraphs rather than space after paragraphs

Things you should know to complete this project:

- Displaying formatting marks will assist in locating spacing errors.
- There are no errors in the fonts, although the title font size is too small.
- The final flyer should fit on one page.

Save your document and add the file name to the footer. In the Document Panel, type your firstname and lastname in the Author box and your course name and section number in the Subject box. In the Keywords box type **Web site guidelines** and then save your document and submit as directed.

End You have completed Project 4H

Apply a combination of the 4A and 4B skills.

GO! Make It | Project 4I Flyer

Project Files

For Project 4I, you will need the following files:

w01I_Team_Building   w01I_Park_Picture

You will save your document as:

Lastname_Firstname_1I_Team_Building

From the student files that accompany this textbook, locate and open the file w01I_Team_Building, and then save the file in your chapter folder as **Lastname_Firstname_1I_Team_Building**

Use the skills you have practiced, create the document shown in Figure 4.55. The title uses Gradient Fill – Blue, Accent 1, 48 pt. The SmartArt graphic uses the Radial Cycle with an Intense Effect style, is 3″ high and 6.5″ wide, has the Colorful Range – Accent Colors 2 to 3 applied. The w01I_Park_Picture picture has a 2.5 pt soft edge, and is 2.5″ wide. The page border uses Dark Blue, Text 2.

Add the file name to the footer; in the Document Panel, add your name and course information and the Keywords **team building**; save your document; and then submit as directed.

Project Results

Team Building Session

The administration at Laurel College is organizing a retreat for the ASLC Board, consisting of the Executive Officers and their appointed directors, Student Senators, Club Presidents, and members of the Judicial Review Committee. The retreat will be held at the Fogelsville campus of Penn State University on Friday, November 12.

The afternoon session will begin at 1:30 p.m. When the retreat was first organized, the afternoon session was to include small group work sessions for the sharing and development of goals and a series of exercises to facilitate group interaction. However, we have been fortunate to secure the services of F. B Lewis, the nationally-renowned team-building expert. Therefore, the afternoon session will consist of an outdoor team-building exercise.

The exercise will be held in Westfield Park, which is shown in the picture, and will enable each participant to:

- Decide when teams are appropriate, and when they are not
- Devise new conflict resolution strategies
- Strengthen leadership skills
- Strengthen interpersonal skills
- Value and understand diversity

Lastname_Firstname_1I_Team_Building

Figure 4.55

End You have completed Project 4I

Content-Based Assessments

Apply a combination of the 4A and 4B skills.

GO! Solve It | Project 4J Food Drive

Project Files

For Project 4J, you will need the following file:

New blank Word document
w01J_Food_Drive

You will save your document as:

Lastname_Firstname_1J_Food_Drive

Create a new document and save it in your Word Chapter 1 folder as **Lastname_Firstname_1J_Food_Drive** Use the following information to create a flyer that includes a title that uses Text Effects, introductory text, two lists of an appropriate type, one text box, and a picture with appropriate formatting and text wrapping. Use your own picture or w01J_Food_Drive.

This Thanksgiving, the Associated Students of Laurel College is sponsoring a food drive for the local community. All college clubs are invited to participate. Results will be adjusted for club membership by measuring the results in pounds of food per member. Three kinds of food are acceptable: canned goods, non-perishable dry goods, and boxed or canned dry drink mixes, such as coffee, tea, or lemonade.

To participate, a club must follow this procedure: fill out a competition form, collect the goods, and then turn the food in on November 13. The address and telephone number for the ASLC is the Cedar Building, Room 222, Laurelton, PA 19100, (215) 555-0902.

Add the file name to the footer. To the Properties area, add your name, your course name and section number, and the keywords **food drive, clubs**

Performance Criteria	Performance Level: Exemplary: You consistently applied the relevant skills	Proficient: You sometimes, but not always, applied the relevant skills	Developing: You rarely or never applied the relevant skills
Create and format lists	Both lists use the proper list type and are formatted correctly.	One of the lists is formatted correctly.	Neither of the lists are formatted correctly.
Insert and format a picture	The picture is inserted and positioned correctly, and text is wrapped around the picture.	The picture is inserted but not formatted properly.	No picture is inserted.
Insert a text box	A text box with appropriate information is inserted and formatted.	A text box is adequately formatted but is difficult to read or unattractive.	No text box is inserted.
Insert introductory text	Introductory text explains the reason for the flyer, with no spelling or grammar errors.	Some introductory text is included, but does not contain sufficient information and/or includes spelling or grammar errors.	No introductory text, or insufficient introductory text.
Insert title using Text Effects	Text Effects title inserted and centered on the page.	Text Effects title is inserted, but not centered or formatted attractively on the page.	No Text Effects title is included.

End You have completed Project 4J

Apply a combination of the 4A and 4B skills..

GO! Solve It | Project 4K Fitness Services

Project Files

For Project 4K, you will need the following files:

New blank Word document
w01K_Volleyball

You will save your document as:

Lastname_Firstname_1K_Fitness_Services

Create a new file and save it as **Lastname_Firstname_1K_Fitness Services** Use the following information to create a flyer that includes introductory text, a SmartArt graphic, a title that uses Text Effects, and a picture that has an artistic effect applied and uses text wrapping. Use your own picture or w01K_Volleyball.

The Associated Students of Laurel College sponsors fitness activities. These take place both on campus and off campus. The activities fall into two categories: Fitness Services and Intramural Sports. Fitness Services are noncompetitive activities, with the most popular being Kickboxing, Jogging, and Aerobics. The most popular Intramural Sports activities—which include competitive team and club sports—are Field Hockey, Volleyball, and Basketball.

Add the file name to the footer, and add your name, your course name and section number, and the keywords **fitness, sports** to the Properties area.

Performance Criteria	Performance Level		
	Exemplary: You consistently applied the relevant skills	Proficient: You sometimes, but not always, applied the relevant skills	Developing: You rarely or never applied the relevant skills
Insert title using Text Effects	Text Effects title inserted and centered on the page.	Text Effects title is inserted, but not centered on the page.	No Text Effects title is included.
Insert introductory text	Introductory text explains the reason for the flyer, with no spelling or grammar errors.	Some introductory text is included, but does not sufficiently explain the topic and/or includes spelling or grammar errors.	No or insufficient introductory text is included.
Insert and format a picture	The picture is inserted and positioned correctly, an artistic effect is applied, and text is wrapped around the picture.	The picture is inserted but not formatted properly.	No picture is inserted in the document.
Insert and format SmartArt	The SmartArt graphic displays both categories of fitness activities and examples of each type.	The SmartArt graphic does not display fitness activities by category.	No SmartArt graphic inserted.

End You have completed Project 4K

Outcomes-Based Assessments

Rubric

The following outcomes-based assessments are *open-ended assessments.* That is, there is no specific correct result; your result will depend on your approach to the information provided. Make *Professional Quality* your goal. Use the following scoring rubric to guide you in *how* to approach the problem and then to evaluate *how well* your approach solves the problem.

The *criteria*—Software Mastery, Content, Format and Layout, and Process—represent the knowledge and skills you have gained that you can apply to solving the problem. The *levels of performance*—Professional Quality, Approaching Professional Quality, or Needs Quality Improvements—help you and your instructor evaluate your result.

	Your completed project is of Professional Quality if you:	**Your completed project is Approaching Professional Quality if you:**	**Your completed project Needs Quality Improvements if you:**
1-Software Mastery	Choose and apply the most appropriate skills, tools, and features and identify efficient methods to solve the problem.	Choose and apply some appropriate skills, tools, and features, but not in the most efficient manner.	Choose inappropriate skills, tools, or features, or are inefficient in solving the problem.
2-Content	Construct a solution that is clear and well organized, contains content that is accurate, appropriate to the audience and purpose, and is complete. Provide a solution that contains no errors in spelling, grammar, or style.	Construct a solution in which some components are unclear, poorly organized, inconsistent, or incomplete. Misjudge the needs of the audience. Have some errors in spelling, grammar, or style, but the errors do not detract from comprehension.	Construct a solution that is unclear, incomplete, or poorly organized; contains some inaccurate or inappropriate content; and contains many errors in spelling, grammar, or style. Do not solve the problem.
3-Format and Layout	Format and arrange all elements to communicate information and ideas, clarify function, illustrate relationships, and indicate relative importance.	Apply appropriate format and layout features to some elements, but not others. Overuses features, causing minor distraction.	Apply format and layout that does not communicate information or ideas clearly. Do not use format and layout features to clarify function, illustrate relationships, or indicate relative importance. Use available features excessively, causing distraction.
4-Process	Use an organized approach that integrates planning, development, self-assessment, revision, and reflection.	Demonstrate an organized approach in some areas, but not others; or, uses an insufficient process of organization throughout.	Do not use an organized approach to solve the problem.

Outcomes-Based Assessments

Apply a combination of the 4A and 4B skills..

GO! Think | Project 4L Academic Services

Project Files

For Project 4L, you will need the following file:

New blank Word document

You will save your document as:

Lastname_Firstname_1L_Academic_Services

The Services Coordinator of the Associated Students of Laurel College needs to create a flyer to inform students of academic services available at the ASLC office. Referrals are available for medical, legal, and counseling services, as well as tutoring and volunteer organizations. Among the services offered at the ASLC office are free printing (up to 250 pages per semester), help with minor legal issues, housing information, bicycle repair, minor computer repair, and help placing students with volunteer organizations.

Create a flyer with basic information about the services provided. Be sure the flyer is easy to read and understand and has an attractive design. If you need more information about student services available at other colleges, search the Web for **student government** and add whatever services you think might be (or should be) available at your college. Add appropriate information to the Document Panel. Save the document as **Lastname_Firstname_1L_Academic_Services** and submit it as directed.

End You have completed Project 4L

Apply a combination of the 4A and 4B skills.

GO! Think | Project 4M Campus Bookstore

Project Files

For Project 4M, you will need the following files:

New blank Word document
w01L_Campus_Bookstore

You will save your document as:

Lastname_Firstname_1M_Campus_Bookstore

The manager of the Laurel College Bookstore needs to create a flyer that can be handed out by the ASLC to students during Welcome Week. The bookstore gives students attending Welcome Week a discount of 20% on special items such as sweatshirts and other college-related clothing, coffee mugs, calendars, and similar items. Door prizes will also be awarded. The bookstore is open Monday and Thursday from 8 a.m. to 10 p.m., Tuesday and Wednesday from 8 a.m. to 8 p.m., and Friday from 8 a.m. to 5 p.m.

Using your own campus bookstore as an example, create a flyer that gives general information about the bookstore, provides one or more lists of items that are on sale, displays the picture w01M_ Campus_Bookstore, and has a highlighted area that gives the store hours.

Add appropriate information to the Document Panel. Save the document as **Lastname_Firstname_1M_Campus_Bookstore** and submit it as directed.

End You have completed Project 4M

Apply a combination of the 4A and 4B skills.

You and GO! | Project 4N Family Flyer

Project Files

For Project 4N, you will need the following file:

New blank Word document

You will save your document as

Lastname_Firstname_1N_Family_Flyer

In this project, you will create a one-page flyer that you can send to your family. Include any information that may interest your family members, such as work-related news, school events, vacation plans, and the activities and accomplishments of you, your spouse, your friends, or other family members. Choose any writing style that suits you—chatty, newsy, entertaining, or humorous.

To complete the assignment, be sure to include a title, at least one list, a picture, and either a SmartArt graphic or a text box or shape. Before you submit the flyer, be sure to check it for grammar and spelling errors, and also be sure to format the document in an attractive manner, using the skills you practiced in this chapter.

Save the file as **Lastname_Firstname_1N_Family_Flyer** Add the file name to the footer, and add your name, your course name and section number, and the keywords **flyer** and **family** to the Properties area. Submit your file as directed.

You have completed Project 4N

Apply a combination of the 4A and 4B skills.

GO! Collaborate | Project 4O Bell Orchid Hotels Group Running Case

This project relates to the **Bell Orchid Hotels**. Your instructor may assign this group case project to your class. If your instructor assigns this project, he or she will provide you with information and instructions to work as part of a group. The group will apply the skills gained thus far to help the Bell Orchid Hotels achieve their business goals.

End **You have completed Project 4O**

Using Tables and Templates to Create Resumes and Cover Letters

OUTCOMES At the end of this chapter you will be able to:	**OBJECTIVES** Mastering these objectives will enable you to:
PROJECT 5A Create a resume by using a Word table.	1. Create a Table (p. 217) 2. Add Text to a Table (p. 218) 3. Format a Table (p. 221)
PROJECT 5B Create a cover letter and resume by using a template.	4. Create a New Document from an Existing Document (p. 230) 5. Change and Reorganize Text (p. 233) 6. Use the Proofing Options (p. 240) 7. Create a Document Using a Template (p. 244)

James Thew/Shutterstock

In This Chapter

Tables are useful for organizing and presenting data. Because a table is so easy to use, many individuals prefer to arrange tabular information in a Word table rather than setting a series of tabs. Use a table when you want to present rows and columns of information or to create a structure for a document such as a resume.

When using Word to write business or personal letters, use a commonly approved letter format. You will make a good impression on prospective employers if you use a standard business letter style when you are writing a cover letter for a resume. You can create a resume using one of the Microsoft resume templates included with Microsoft Office or available online.

The projects in this chapter relate to **Madison Staffing Services**. Many companies prefer to hire employees through a staffing service, so that both the employer and the employee can determine if the match is a good fit. Madison Staffing Services takes care of the details of recruiting, testing, hiring, and paying the employee. At the end of the employment assignment, neither the employer nor the employee is required to make a permanent commitment. Many individuals find full-time jobs with an employer for whom they initially worked through a staffing agency.

Project 5A Resume

Project Activities

In Activities 5.01 through 5.09, you will create a table to use as the structure for a resume for one of Madison Staffing Services' clients. Your completed document will look similar to Figure 5.1.

Project Files

For Project 5A, you will need the following file:

w02A_Experience

You will save your document as:

Lastname_Firstname_2A_Resume

Project Results

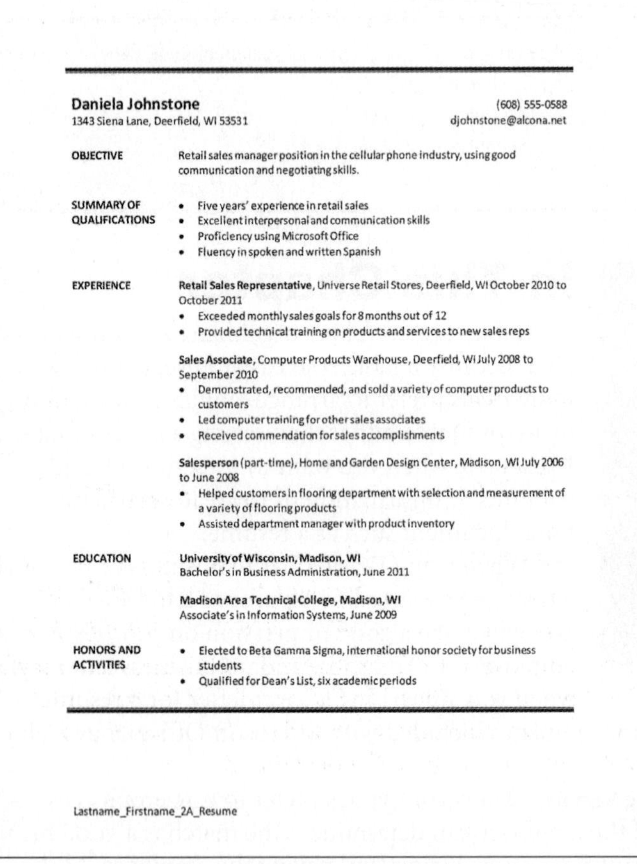

Daniela Johnstone (608) 555-0588
1343 Siena Lane, Deerfield, WI 53531 djohnstone@alcona.net

OBJECTIVE	Retail sales manager position in the cellular phone industry, using good communication and negotiating skills.
SUMMARY OF QUALIFICATIONS	• Five years' experience in retail sales • Excellent interpersonal and communication skills • Proficiency using Microsoft Office • Fluency in spoken and written Spanish
EXPERIENCE	**Retail Sales Representative**, Universe Retail Stores, Deerfield, WI October 2010 to October 2011 • Exceeded monthly sales goals for 8 months out of 12 • Provided technical training on products and services to new sales reps **Sales Associate**, Computer Products Warehouse, Deerfield, WI July 2008 to September 2010 • Demonstrated, recommended, and sold a variety of computer products to customers • Led computer training for other sales associates • Received commendation for sales accomplishments **Salesperson** (part-time), Home and Garden Design Center, Madison, WI July 2006 to June 2008 • Helped customers in flooring department with selection and measurement of a variety of flooring products • Assisted department manager with product inventory
EDUCATION	**University of Wisconsin, Madison, WI** Bachelor's in Business Administration, June 2011 **Madison Area Technical College, Madison, WI** Associate's in Information Systems, June 2009
HONORS AND ACTIVITIES	• Elected to Beta Gamma Sigma, international honor society for business students • Qualified for Dean's List, six academic periods

Lastname_Firstname_2A_Resume

Figure 5.1
Project 5A Resume

Objective 1 | Create a Table

A ***table*** is an arrangement of information organized into rows and columns. The intersection of a row and a column in a table creates a box called a ***cell*** into which you can type. Tables are useful to present information in a logical and orderly manner.

Activity 5.01 | Creating a Table

1. Start **Word**, and in the new blank document, display formatting marks and rulers.
2. Click the **File tab**, and then in **Backstage** view, click **Save As**. In the **Save As** dialog box, navigate to the location where you are storing your projects for this chapter. Create a new folder named **Word Chapter 5**
3. **Save** the file in the **Word Chapter 5** folder as **Lastname_Firstname_2A_Resume**
4. Scroll to the end of the document, right-click near the bottom of the page, and then click **Edit Footer**. On the **Design tab**, in the **Insert group**, click the **Quick Parts** button, and then click **Field**.
5. Under **Field names**, scroll down, click **FileName**, and then click **OK. Close** the footer area.
6. On the **Insert tab**, in the **Tables group**, click the **Table** button. In the **Table** grid, in the fourth row, point to the second square, and notice that the cells display in orange and *2 × 4 Table* displays at the top of the grid. Compare your screen with Figure 5.2.

Figure 5.2

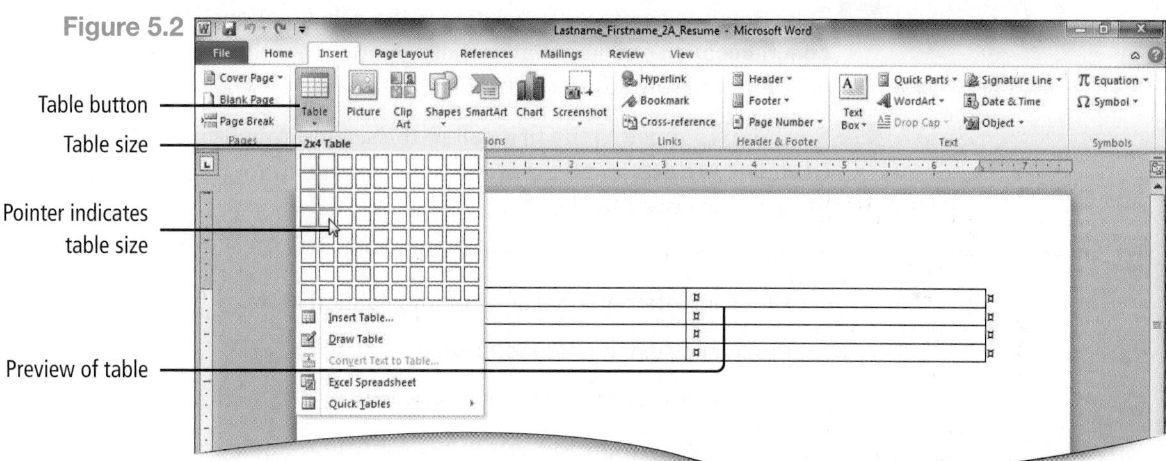

7. Click one time to create the table. Notice that formatting marks in each cell indicate the end of the contents of each cell and the mark to the right of each *row* indicates the row end. **Save** your document, and then compare your screen with Figure 5.3.

   A table with four rows and two columns displays at the insertion point location, and the insertion point displays in the upper left cell. The table fills the width of the page, from the left margin to the right margin. On the Ribbon, Table Tools display and add two tabs—*Design* and *Layout*. Borders display around each cell in the table.

Figure 5.3

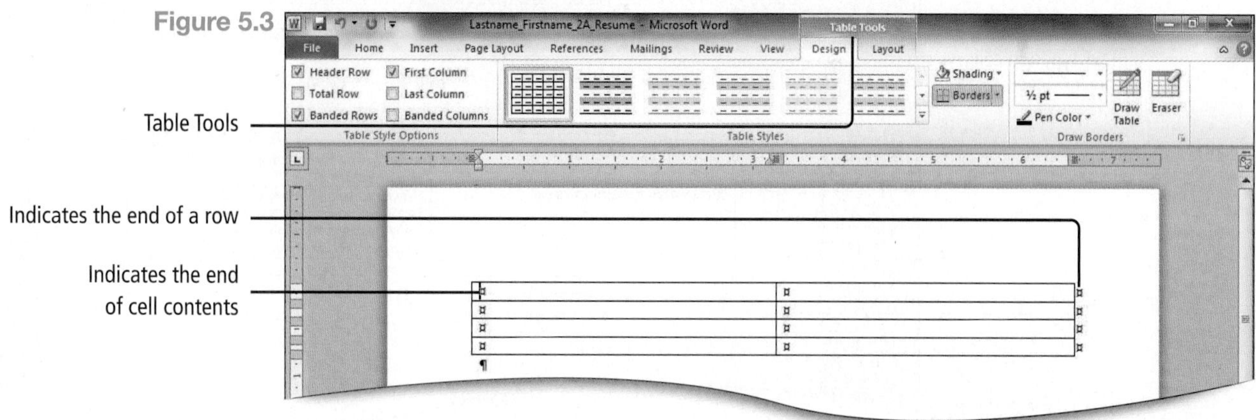

Objective 2 | Add Text to a Table

In a Word table, each cell behaves similarly to a document. For example, as you type in a cell, when you reach the right border of the cell, wordwrap moves the text to the next line. When you press Enter, the insertion point moves down to a new paragraph in the same cell. You can also insert text from another document into a table cell.

Activity 5.02 | Adding Text to a Table

There are numerous acceptable formats for resumes, many of which can be found in Business Communications textbooks. The layout used in this project is suitable for a recent college graduate and places topics in the left column and details in the right column.

1. Scroll up to view the top of the document. With the insertion point blinking in the first cell in the first row, type **OBJECTIVE** and then press Tab.

   Pressing Tab moves the insertion point to the next cell in the row, or, if the insertion point is already in the last cell in the row, pressing Tab moves the insertion point to the first cell in the following row.

2. Type **Retail sales manager position in the cellular phone industry, using good communication and negotiating skills.** Notice that the text wraps in the cell and the height of the row adjusts to fit the text.

3. Press Tab to move to the first cell in the second row. Type **SUMMARY OF QUALIFICATIONS** and then press Tab. Type the following, pressing Enter at the end of each line *except* the last line:

   Five years' experience in retail sales

   Excellent interpersonal and communication skills

   Proficiency using Microsoft Office

   Fluency in spoken and written Spanish

   The default font and font size in a table are the same as for a document—Calibri 11 pt. The default line spacing in a table is single spacing with no space before or after paragraphs, which differs from the defaults for a document.

4. **Save** your document, and then compare your screen with Figure 5.4.

Figure 5.4

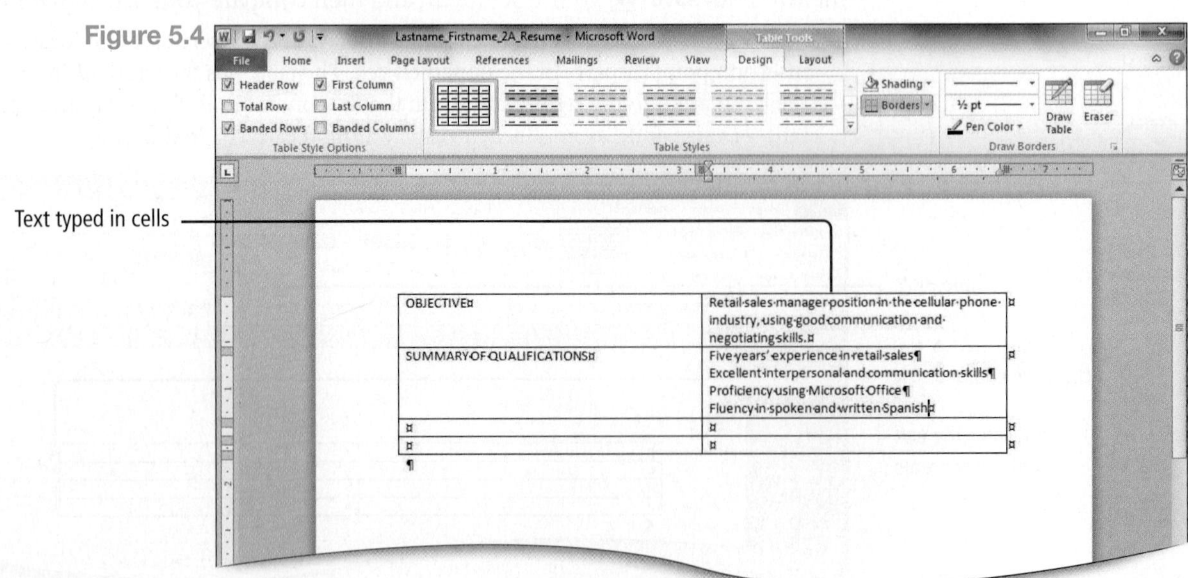

Activity 5.03 | Inserting Existing Text into a Table Cell

1 Press [Tab] to move to the first cell in the third row. Type **EXPERIENCE** and then press [Tab].

2 Type the following, pressing [Enter] after each line:

> **Retail Sales Representative, Universe Retail Stores, Deerfield, WI October 2010 to October 2011**
>
> **Exceeded monthly sales goals for 8 months out of 12**
>
> **Provided technical training on products and services to new sales reps**

3 Be sure your insertion point is positioned in the second column to the left of the cell marker below *sales reps*. Compare your screen with Figure 5.5.

Figure 5.5

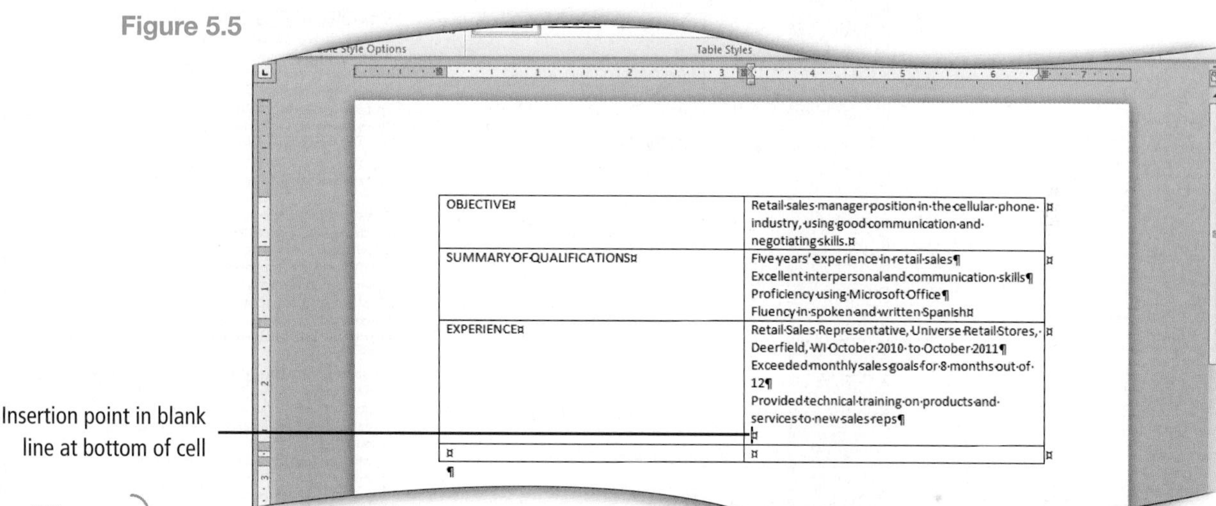

Another Way

Open the second document and select the text you want. Copy the text, and then paste at the desired location.

4 On the **Insert tab**, in the **Text group**, click the **Object button arrow**, and then click **Text from File**. Navigate to your student files, select **w02A_Experience**, and then click **Insert**.

5 Press [Backspace] one time to remove the blank line at the end of the inserted text, and then compare your screen with Figure 5.6.

Figure 5.6

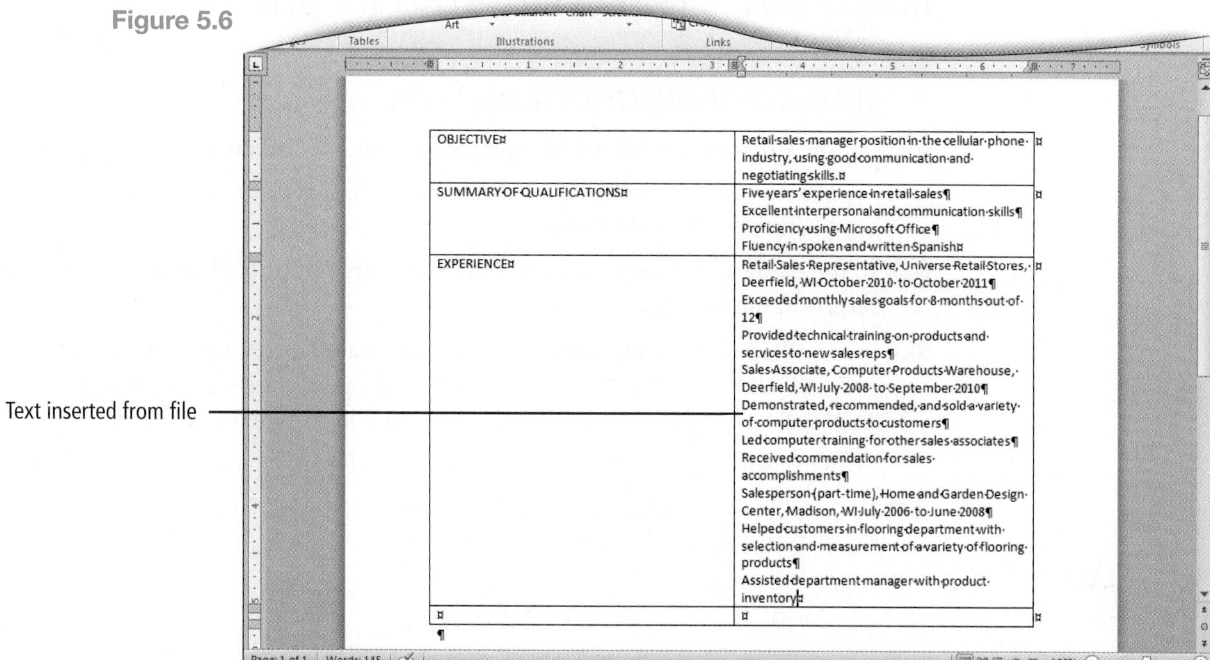

6 Press Tab to move to the first cell in the fourth row. Type **EDUCATION** and then press Tab.

7 Type the following, pressing Enter at the end of each item *except* the last one:

University of Wisconsin, Madison, WI

Bachelor's in Business Administration, June 2011

Madison Area Technical College, Madison, WI

Associate's in Information Systems, June 2009

8 Compare your screen with Figure 5.7.

Figure 5.7

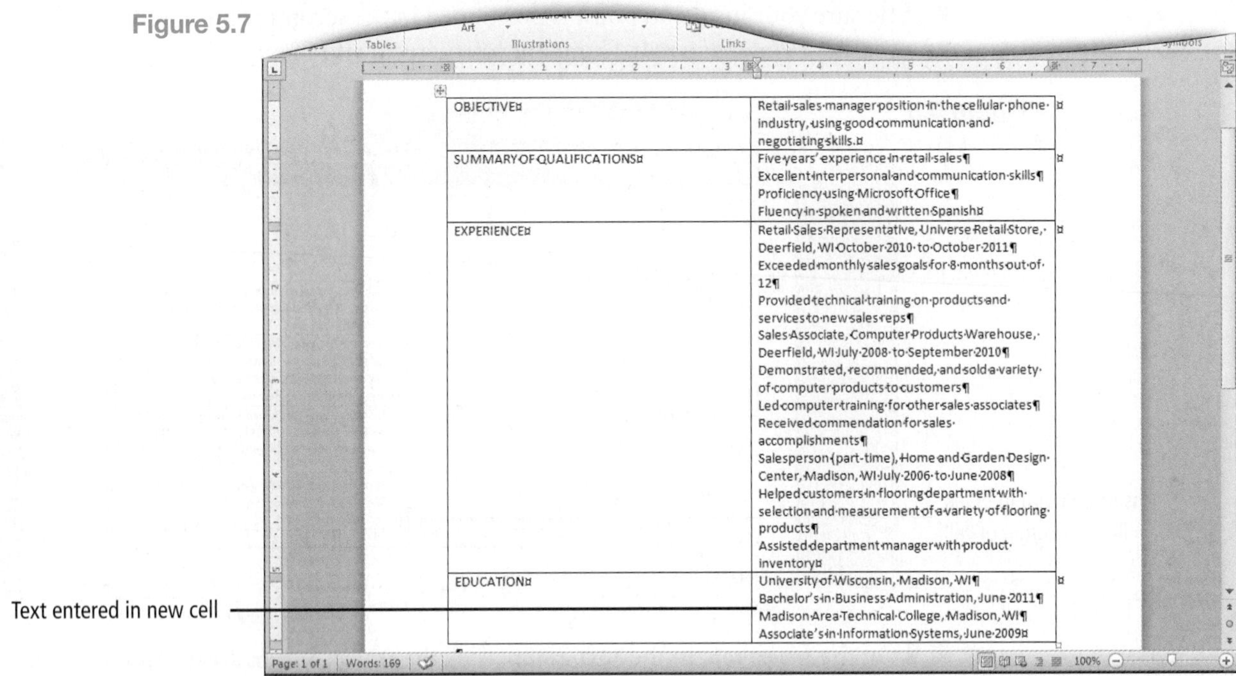

OBJECTIVE	Retail sales manager position in the cellular phone industry, using good communication and negotiating skills.
SUMMARY OF QUALIFICATIONS	Five years' experience in retail sales Excellent interpersonal and communication skills Proficiency using Microsoft Office Fluency in spoken and written Spanish
EXPERIENCE	Retail Sales Representative, Universe Retail Store, Deerfield, WI October 2010 to October 2011 Exceeded monthly sales goals for 8 months out of 12 Provided technical training on products and services to new sales reps Sales Associate, Computer Products Warehouse, Deerfield, WI July 2008 to September 2010 Demonstrated, recommended, and sold a variety of computer products to customers Led computer training for other sales associates Received commendation for sales accomplishments Salesperson (part-time), Home and Garden Design Center, Madison, WI July 2006 to June 2008 Helped customers in flooring department with selection and measurement of a variety of flooring products Assisted department manager with product inventory
EDUCATION	University of Wisconsin, Madison, WI Bachelor's in Business Administration, June 2011 Madison Area Technical College, Madison, WI Associate's in Information Systems, June 2009

9 **Save** your document.

Activity 5.04 | Creating Bulleted Lists in a Table

1 Scroll to view the top of your document, and then in the cell to the right of *SUMMARY OF QUALIFICATIONS*, select all of the text.

2 On the **Home tab**, in the **Paragraph group**, click the **Bullets** button.

The selected text displays as a bulleted list. Using a bulleted list in this manner makes each qualification more distinctive.

3 In the **Paragraph group**, click the **Decrease Indent** button one time to align the bullets at the left edge of the cell.

4 In the **Clipboard group**, double-click the **Format Painter** button. In the cell to the right of *EXPERIENCE*, select the second and third paragraphs—beginning *Exceeded* and *Provided*—to create the same style of bulleted list as you did in the previous step.

When you double-click the Format Painter button, it remains active until you turn it off.

5 In the same cell, under *Sales Associate*, select the three paragraphs that begin *Demonstrated* and *Led* and *Received* to create another bulleted list aligned at the left edge of the cell.

Another Way

Click the Format Painter again.

6 With the Format Painter pointer still active, in the same cell, select the paragraphs that begin *Helped* and *Assisted* to create the same type of bulleted list.

7 Press Esc to turn off the Format Painter. Click anywhere in the table to deselect the text, and then compare your screen with Figure 5.8.

Figure 5.8

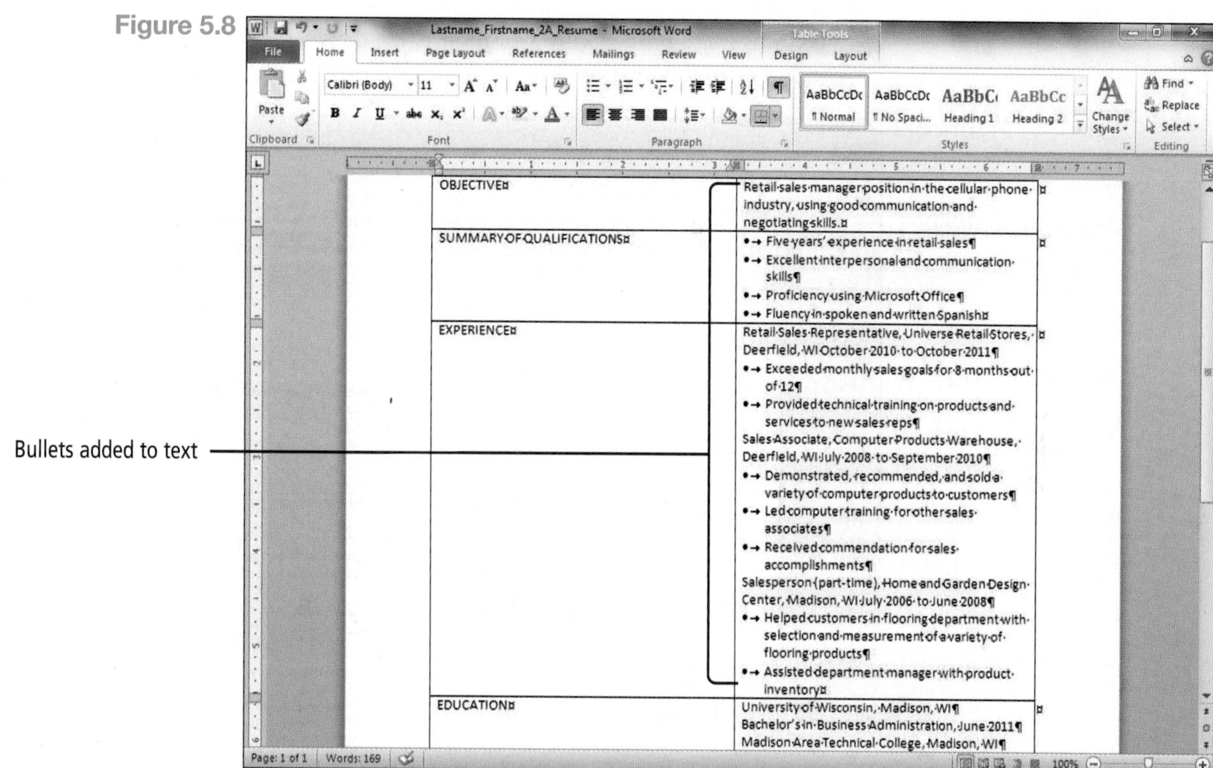

8 **Save** your document.

Objective 3 | Format a Table

Use Word's formatting tools to make your tables attractive and easy to read. Types of formatting you can add to a table include changing the row height and the column width, removing or adding borders, increasing or decreasing the paragraph or line spacing, or enhancing the text.

Activity 5.05 | Changing the Width of Table Columns

When you create a table, all of the columns are of equal width. In this activity, you will change the width of the columns.

1 In any row, point to the vertical border between the two columns to display the pointer.

2 Drag the column border to the left to approximately **1.25 inches on the horizontal ruler**.

3 Scroll to the top of the document. Notice that in the second row, the text *SUMMARY OF QUALIFICATIONS* wraps to two lines to accommodate the new column width.

4 If necessary, in the left column, click in any cell. On the Ribbon, under **Table Tools**, click the **Layout tab**.

5 In the **Cell Size group**, click the **Table Column Width button spin arrows** [1.37"] as necessary to change the width of the first column to **1.4"**. Compare your screen with Figure 5.9.

After dragging a border with your mouse, use the Width button to set a precise measurement if necessary.

Figure 5.9

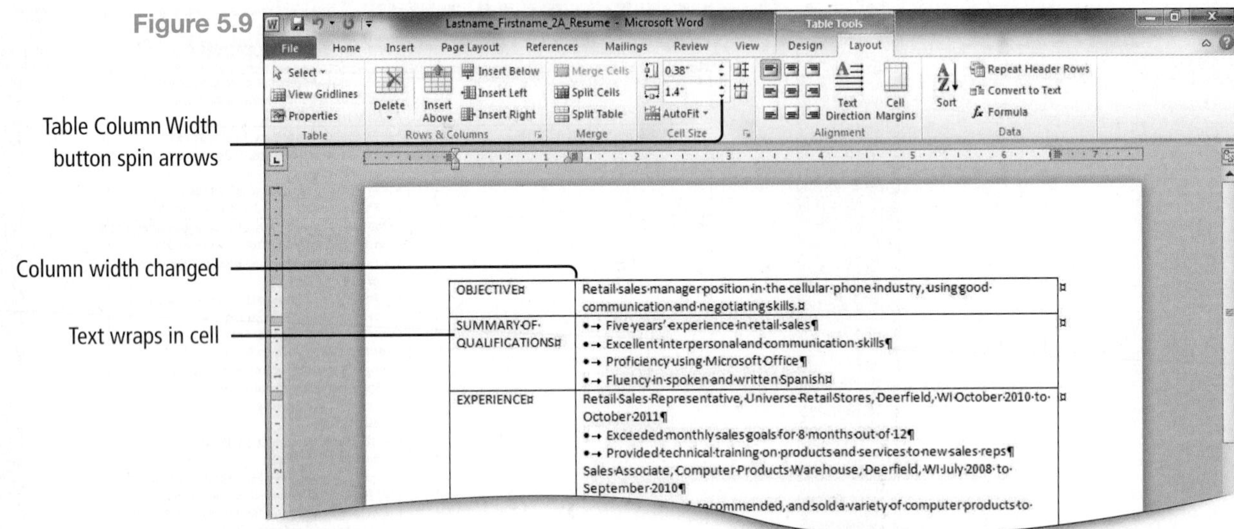

6 **Save** your document.

> **More Knowledge | Changing Column Widths**
>
> You will typically get the best results if you change the column widths starting at the left side of the table, especially in tables with three or more columns. Word can also calculate the best column widths for you. To do this, select the table. Then, on the Layout tab, in the Cell Size group, click the AutoFit button and click AutoFit Contents.

Activity 5.06 | Adding Rows to a Table

You can add rows or columns anywhere in a table.

1 Scroll to view the lower portion of the table. In the last row of the table, click anywhere in the *second* cell that contains the educational information, and then press Tab.

A new row displays at the bottom of the table. When the insertion point is in the last cell in the bottom row of a table, you can add a row by pressing the Tab key; the insertion point will display in the first cell of the new row.

2 Type **HONORS AND ACTIVITIES** and then press Tab.

3 Type the following, pressing Enter after the first item but not the second item:

Elected to Beta Gamma Sigma, international honor society for business students

Qualified for Dean's List, six academic periods

4 Select the text you typed in the last cell of the bottom row. On the **Home tab**, in the **Paragraph group**, click the **Bullets** button, and then click the **Decrease Indent** button one time to align the bullets at the left edge of the cell.

5 Scroll up to view the entire table, click anywhere in the table to deselect the text, and then compare your screen with Figure 5.10.

Figure 5.10

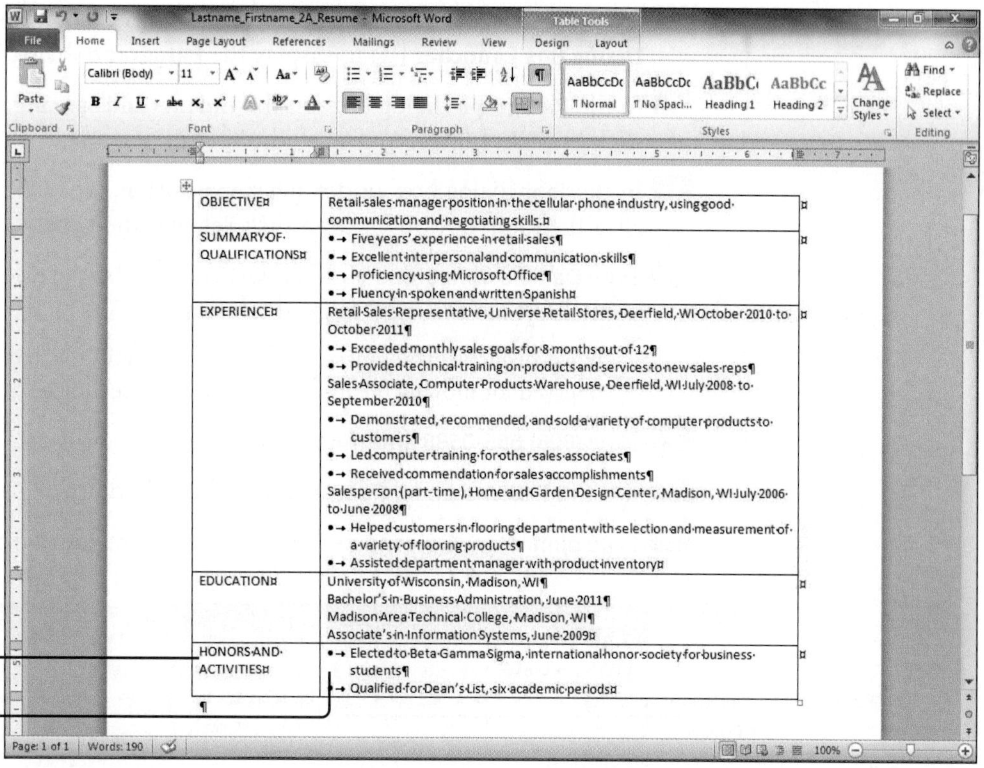

Row added to table

Bullets added to text

6 Click anywhere in the top row of the table.

Another Way

Right-click in the top row, point to Insert, and then click Insert Rows Above.

7 On the **Layout tab**, in the **Rows & Columns group**, click the **Insert Above** button. Compare your screen with Figure 5.11.

A new row displays above the row that contained the insertion point, and the new row is selected.

Figure 5.11

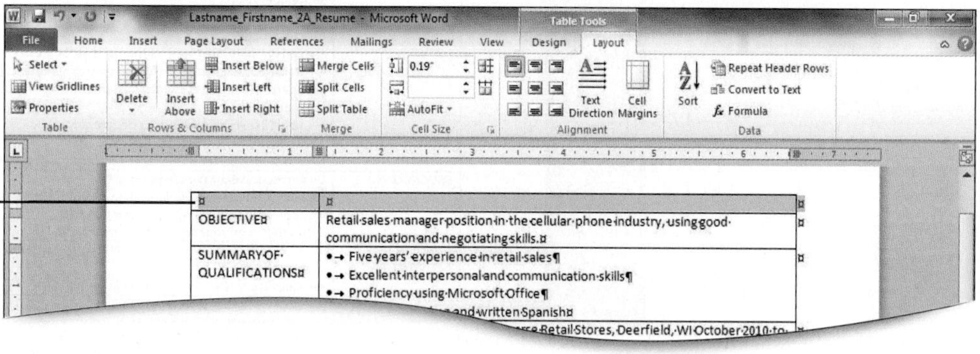

Row inserted at top of table

8 **Save** your document.

Activity 5.07 | Merging Cells

The title of a table typically spans all of the columns. In this activity, you will merge cells so that you can position the personal information across both columns.

1 Be sure the two cells in the top row are selected; if necessary, drag across both cells to select them.

> **Another Way**
> Right-click the selected row and click Merge Cells on the shortcut menu.

2 On the **Layout tab**, in the **Merge group**, click the **Merge Cells** button.

The cell border between the two cells no longer displays.

3 With the merged cell still selected, on the **Home tab**, in the **Paragraph group**, click the **Dialog Box Launcher** to display the **Paragraph** dialog box.

4 In the **Paragraph** dialog box, on the **Indents and Spacing tab**, in the lower left corner, click the **Tabs** button to display the **Tabs** dialog box.

5 In the **Tabs** dialog box, under **Tab stop position**, type **6.5** and then under **Alignment**, click the **Right** option button. Click **Set**, and then click **OK** to close the dialog box.

6 Type **Daniela Johnstone** Hold down Ctrl and then press Tab. Notice that the insertion point moves to the right-aligned tab stop at 6.5″.

In a Word table, you must use Ctrl + Tab to move to a tab stop, because pressing Tab is reserved for moving the insertion point from cell to cell.

7 Type **(608) 555-0588** and then press Enter.

8 Type **1343 Siena Lane, Deerfield, WI 53531** Hold down Ctrl and then press Tab.

9 Type **djohnstone@alcona.net** and then compare your screen with Figure 5.12.

Figure 5.12

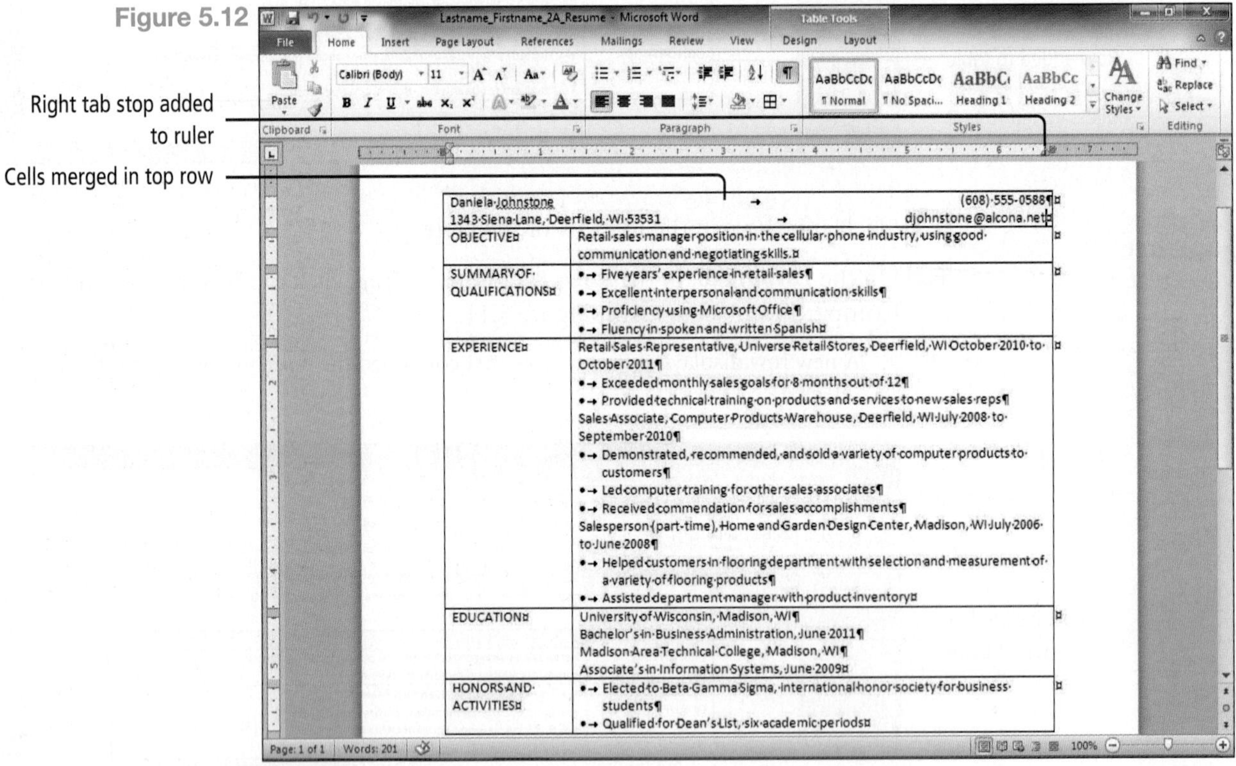

10 **Save** your document.

Activity 5.08 | Formatting Text in Cells

1 In the first row of the table, select the name *Daniela Johnstone*, and then on the Mini toolbar, apply **Bold** and change the **Font Size** to **16**.

2 Under *Daniela Johnstone*, click anywhere in the second line of text, which contains the address and e-mail address.

3 On the **Page Layout tab**, in the **Paragraph group**, click the **Spacing After up spin arrow** three times to add **18 pt** spacing between the first row of the table and the second row. Compare your screen with Figure 5.13.

These actions separate the personal information from the body of the resume and adds focus to the applicant's name.

Figure 5.13

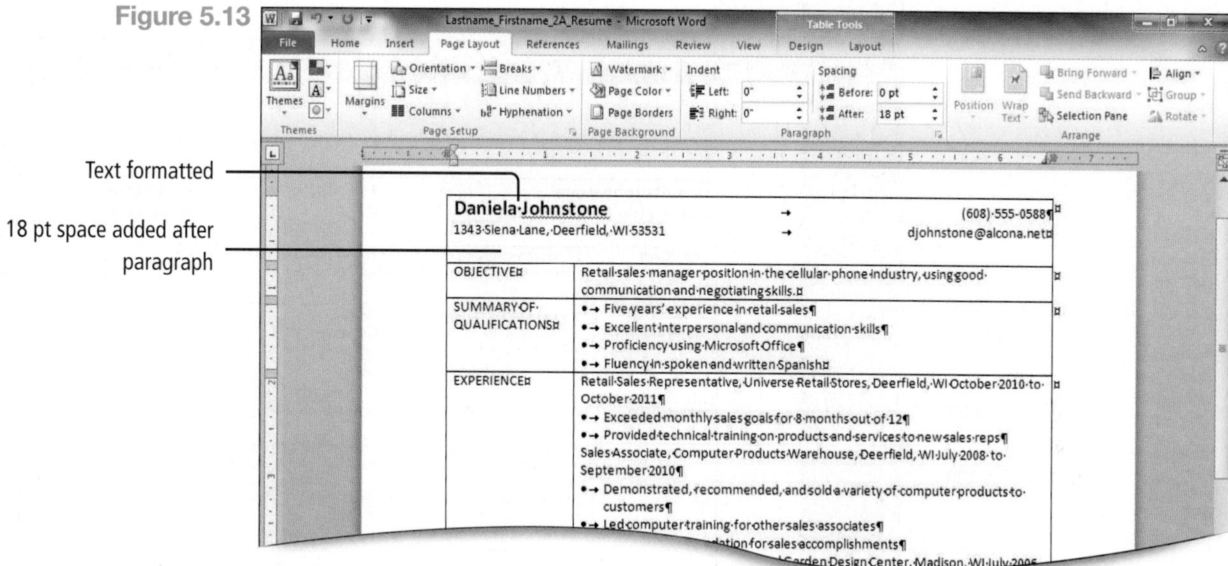

4 Using the technique you just practiced, in the second column, click in the last paragraph of every cell and add **18 pt Spacing After** the last paragraph of all rows including the last row; a border will be added to the bottom of the table, and spacing will be needed between the last row and the border.

5 In the second row, point to the word *OBJECTIVE*, hold down the left mouse button, and then drag downward in the first column only to select all the headings in uppercase letters. On the Mini toolbar, click the **Bold** button **B**.

Note | Selecting Only One Column

When you drag downward to select the first column, a fast mouse might also begin to select the second column when you reach the bottom. If this happens, drag upward slightly to deselect the second column and select only the first column.

6 In the cell to the right of *EXPERIENCE*, without selecting the following comma, select *Retail Sales Representative* and then on the Mini toolbar, click the **Bold** button **B**.

7 In the same cell, apply **Bold** **B** to the other job titles—*Sales Associate* and *Salesperson*—but do not bold *(part time)*.

8 In the cell to the right of *EDUCATION*, apply **Bold** **B** to *University of Wisconsin, Madison, WI* and *Madison Area Technical College, Madison, WI*.

9 In the same cell, click anywhere in the line beginning *Bachelor's*. On the **Page Layout tab**, in the **Paragraph group**, click the **Spacing After up spin arrow** two times to add **12 pt** spacing after the paragraph.

10 In the cell to the right of *EXPERIENCE*, under *Retail Sales Representative*, click anywhere in the second bulleted item, and then add **12 pt Spacing After** the item.

11 In the same cell, repeat this process for the last bulleted item under *Sales Associate*.

12 Scroll to the top of the screen, and then compare your screen with Figure 5.14.

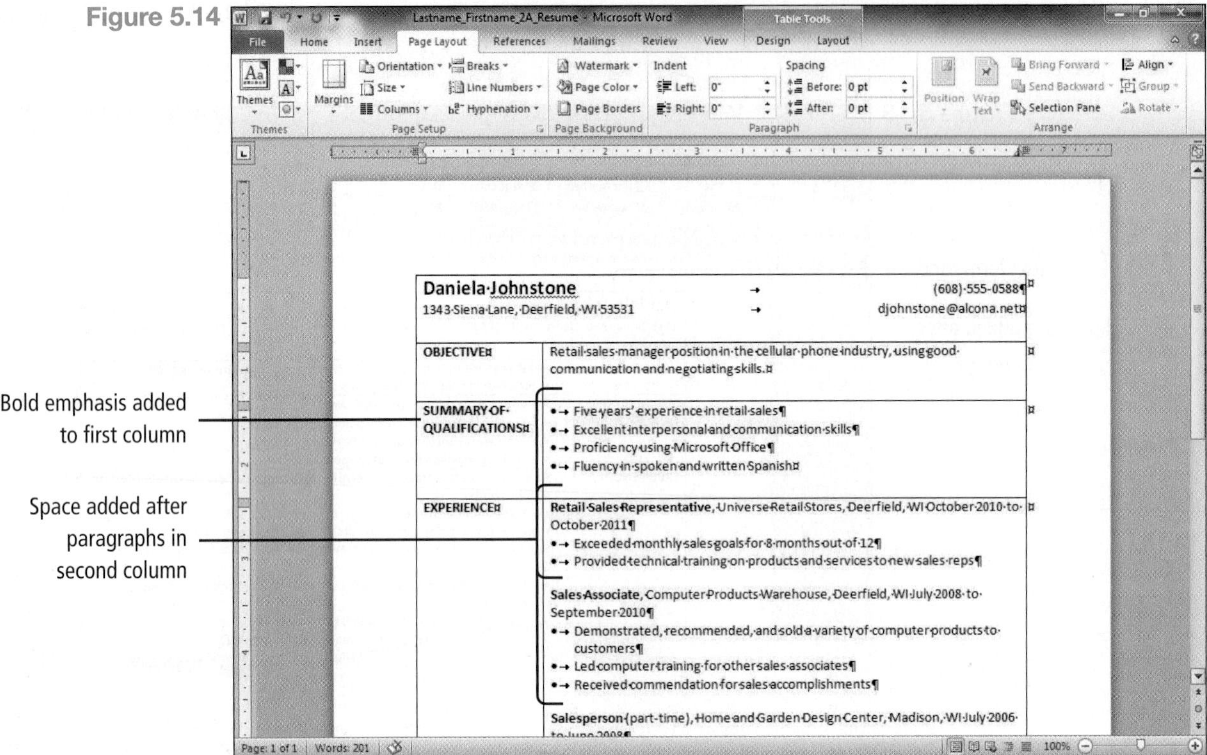

Figure 5.14

13 **Save** your document.

Activity 5.09 | Changing the Table Borders

When you create a table, all of the cells have black borders. Most resumes do not display any cell borders. A border at the top and bottom of the resume, however, is attractive and adds a professional look to the document.

1 If necessary, press Ctrl + Home to move the insertion point to the top of the table, and then point slightly outside of the upper left corner of the table to display the **table move handle**.

2 With the pointer, click one time to select the entire table, and notice that the row markers at the end of each row are also selected.

Shaded row markers indicate that the entire row is selected.

3 Click the **Design tab**. In the **Table Styles group**, click the **Borders button arrow**, and then click **No Border**.

The black borders no longer display; instead, depending on your setup, either no borders—the default setting—or nonprinting blue dashed borders display.

4 Click the **File tab** to display **Backstage** view, and then click the **Print tab** to preview the table. Notice that no borders display in the preview, as shown in Figure 5.15.

Figure 5.15

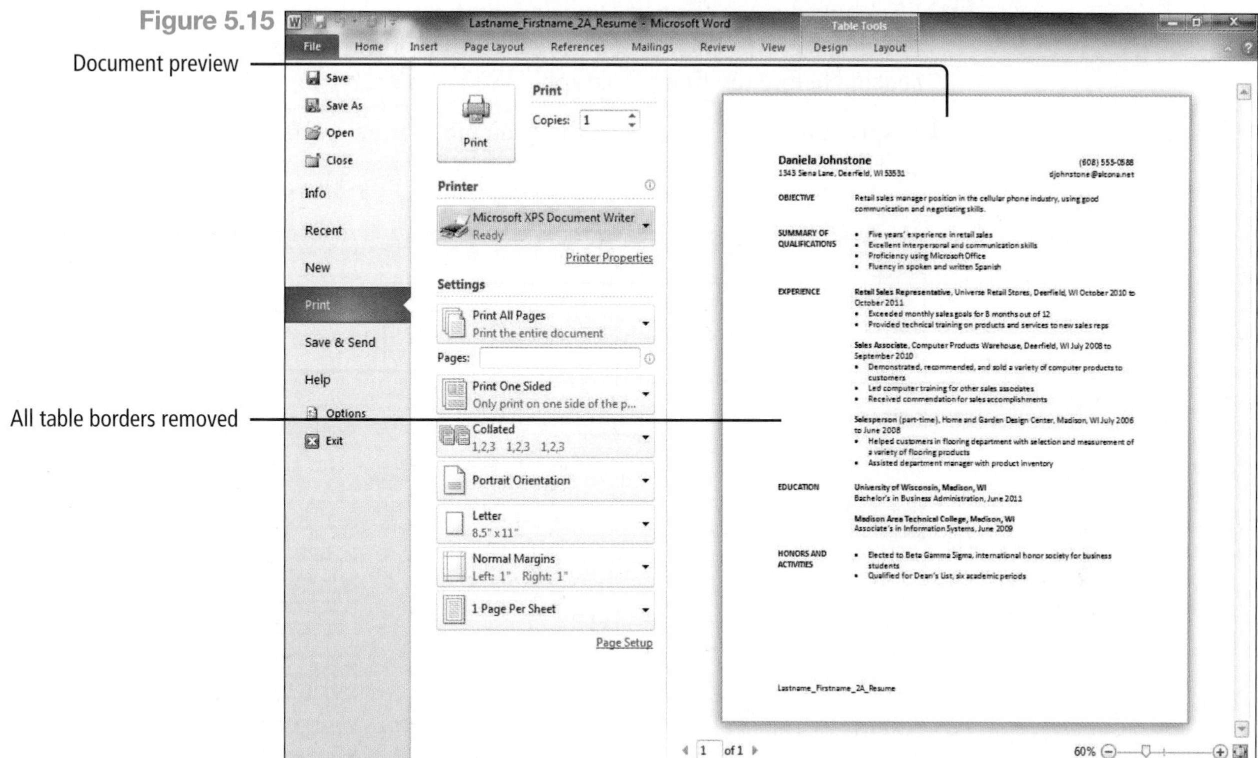

> **Another Way**
> Right-click the selected table, click Borders and Shading, and then click the Borders tab.

5 Click the **Design tab**; be sure the table is still selected. In the **Table Styles group**, click the **Borders button arrow**, and then at the bottom of the **Borders** gallery, click **Borders and Shading**.

6 Under **Setting**, click the **Custom** button. Under **Style**, scroll down about a third of the way and click the style with the thick upper line and the thin lower line.

> **Another Way**
> Click the top border button, which is one of the buttons that surround the Preview.

7 In the **Preview** box at the right, point to the *top* border of the small preview and click one time.

8 Under **Style**, click the style with the thin upper line and the thick lower line, and then in the **Preview** box, click the *bottom* border of the preview. Compare your screen with Figure 5.16.

Figure 5.16

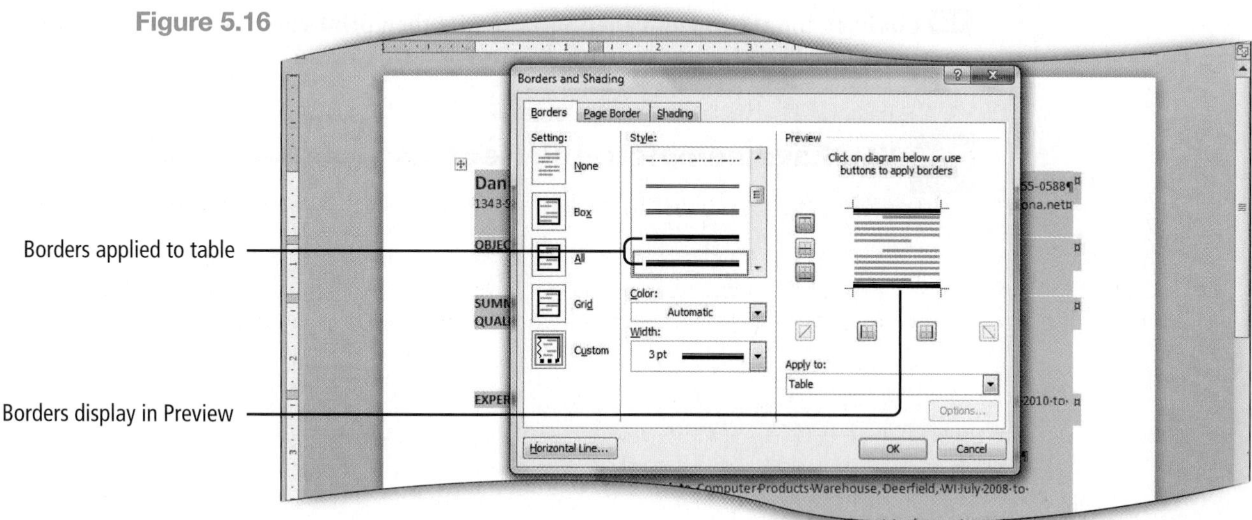

9 Click **OK**, click anywhere to cancel the selection, and then notice that there is only a small amount of space between the upper border and the first line of text.

10 Click anywhere in the text *Daniela Johnstone*, and then on the **Page Layout tab**, in the **Paragraph group**, click the **Spacing Before up spin arrow** as necessary to add **18 pt** spacing before the first paragraph.

11 Display **Backstage** view. Click the **Print tab** to preview the table. Compare your screen with Figure 5.17.

Figure 5.17

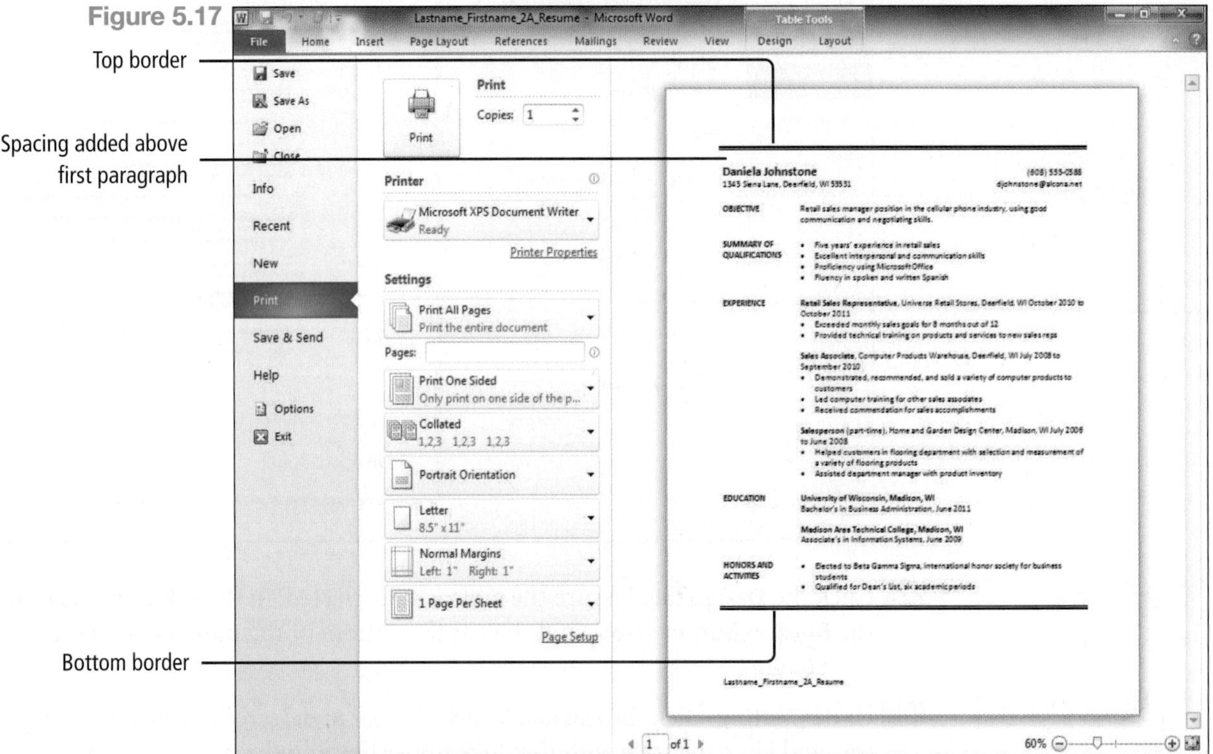

12 In **Backstage** view, click the **Info tab**. On the right, under the document thumbnail, click **Properties**, and then click **Show Document Panel**. In the **Author** box, delete any text and then type your firstname and lastname. In the **Subject** box, type your course name and section number, and in the **Keywords** box type **resume, Word table**

13 **Close** the **Document Panel**. **Save** and then print your document, or submit it electronically, as directed by your instructor. **Exit** Word.

End **You have completed Project 5A**

Project 5B Cover Letter and Resume

Project Activities

In Activities 5.10 through 5.22, you will create a letterhead, and then use the letterhead to create a cover letter. You will also create a short resume using a Microsoft template and save it as a Web page. Your completed documents will look similar to Figure 5.18.

Project Files

For Project 5B, you will need the following file:

w02B_Cover_Letter_Text

You will save your documents as:

Lastname_Firstname_2B_Letterhead
Lastname_Firstname_2B_Cover_Letter
Lastname_Firstname_2B_Brief_Resume
Lastname_Firstname_2B_HTML_Resume

Project Results

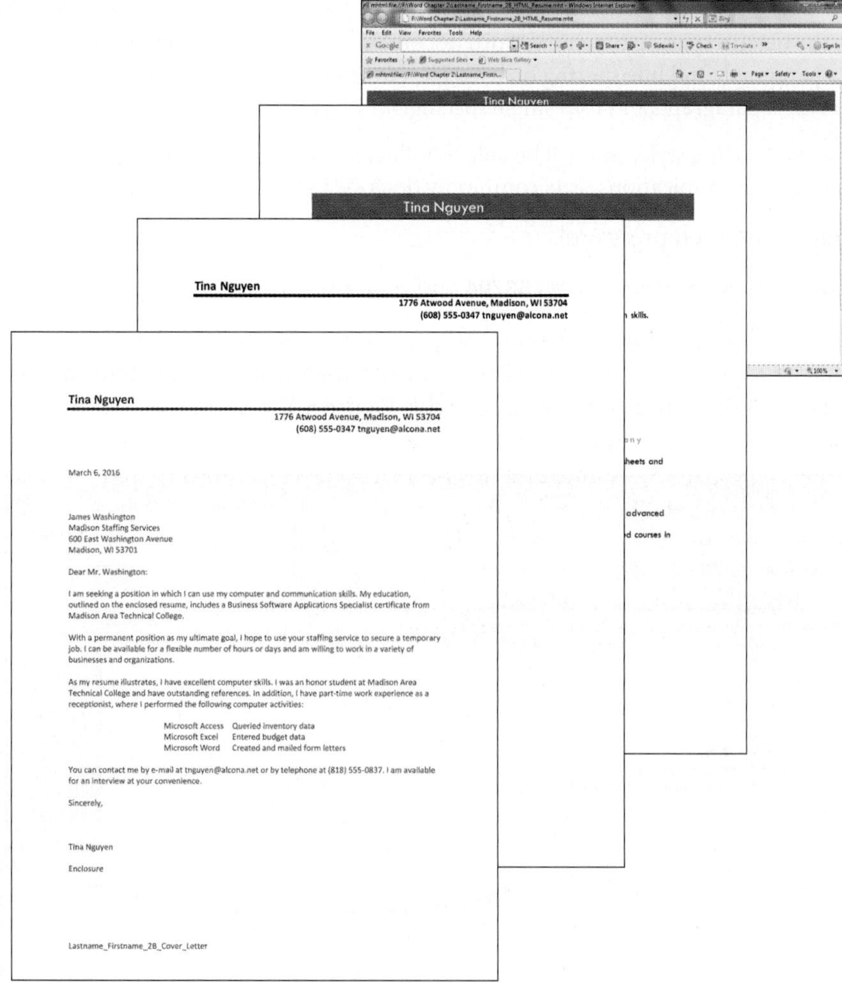

Tina Nguyen

1776 Atwood Avenue, Madison, WI 53704
(608) 555-0347 tnguyen@alcona.net

March 6, 2016

James Washington
Madison Staffing Services
600 East Washington Avenue
Madison, WI 53701

Dear Mr. Washington:

I am seeking a position in which I can use my computer and communication skills. My education, outlined on the enclosed resume, includes a Business Software Applications Specialist certificate from Madison Area Technical College.

With a permanent position as my ultimate goal, I hope to use your staffing service to secure a temporary job. I can be available for a flexible number of hours or days and am willing to work in a variety of businesses and organizations.

As my resume illustrates, I have excellent computer skills. I was an honor student at Madison Area Technical College and have outstanding references. In addition, I have part-time work experience as a receptionist, where I performed the following computer activities:

Microsoft Access	Queried inventory data
Microsoft Excel	Entered budget data
Microsoft Word	Created and mailed form letters

You can contact me by e-mail at tnguyen@alcona.net or by telephone at (818) 555-0837. I am available for an interview at your convenience.

Sincerely,

Tina Nguyen

Enclosure

Lastname_Firstname_2B_Cover_Letter

Figure 5.18
Project 5B Cover Letter and Resume

Objective 4 | Create a New Document from an Existing Document

A ***template*** is an *existing* document that you use as a starting point for a *new* document. The template document opens a copy of itself, unnamed, and then you use the structure—and possibly some content, such as headings—as the starting point for a new document.

All documents are based on a template. When you create a new blank document, it is based on Word's ***Normal template***, which serves as the starting point for all new Word documents.

Activity 5.10 | Creating a Letterhead

A ***letterhead*** is the personal or company information that displays at the top of a letter, and which commonly includes a name, address, and contact information. The term also refers to a piece of paper imprinted with such information at the top.

1 **Start** Word, and in the new blank document, be sure that formatting marks and rulers display.

2 On the **Home tab**, in the **Styles group**, click the **More** button. In the displayed gallery, click the **No Spacing** button.

Recall that the default spacing for a new Word document is 10 points of blank space following a paragraph and line spacing of 1.15. The ***No Spacing style*** inserts *no* extra space following a paragraph and uses single spacing.

By using the No Spacing style, you will be able to follow the prescribed format of a letter, which Business Communications texts commonly describe in terms of single spacing.

3 Type **Tina Nguyen** and then press Enter.

4 Type **1776 Atwood Avenue, Madison, WI 53704** and then press Enter.

5 Type **(608) 555-0347 tnguyen@alcona.net** and then press Enter. If the e-mail address changes to blue text, right-click the e-mail address, and then from the shortcut menu, click **Remove Hyperlink**. Compare your screen with Figure 5.19.

Figure 5.19

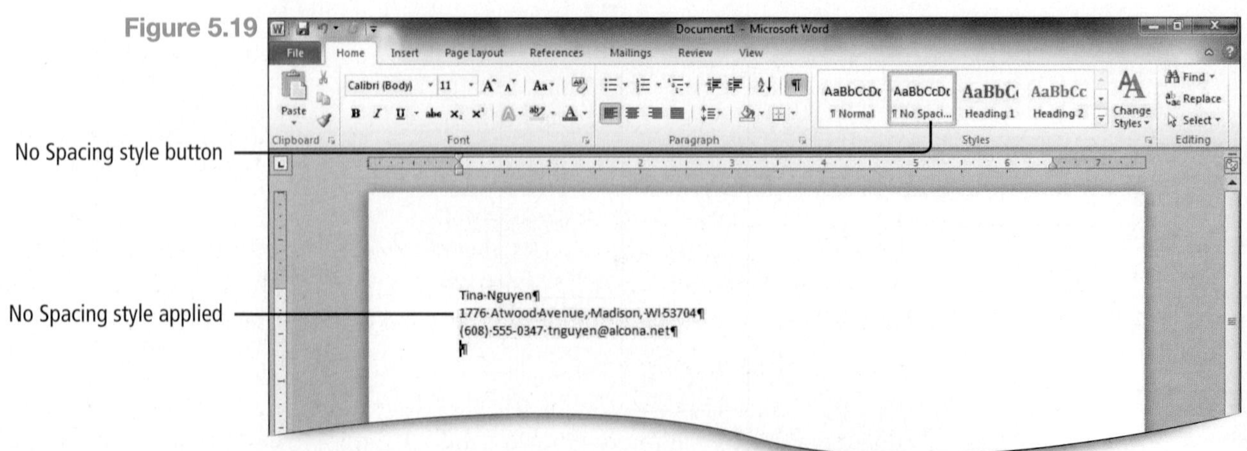

6 Select the first paragraph—*Tina Nguyen*—and then on the Mini toolbar, apply **Bold** and change the **Font Size** to **16**.

> **Another Way**
> Press Ctrl + R to align text to the right.

> **Another Way**
> Alternatively, click the bottom border button.

7. Select the second and third paragraphs. On the Mini toolbar, apply **Bold** and change the **Font Size** to **12**.
8. With the two paragraphs still selected, on the **Home tab**, in the **Paragraph group**, click the **Align Text Right** button.
9. Click anywhere in the first paragraph—*Tina Nguyen*. In the **Paragraph group**, click the **Borders button arrow**, and then at the bottom, click **Borders and Shading**.
10. In the **Borders and Shading** dialog box, under **Style**, be sure the first style—a single solid line—is selected.
11. Click the **Width arrow**, and then click **3 pt**. To the right, under **Preview**, click the bottom border of the diagram. Under **Apply to**, be sure *Paragraph* displays. Compare your screen with Figure 5.20.

Figure 5.20

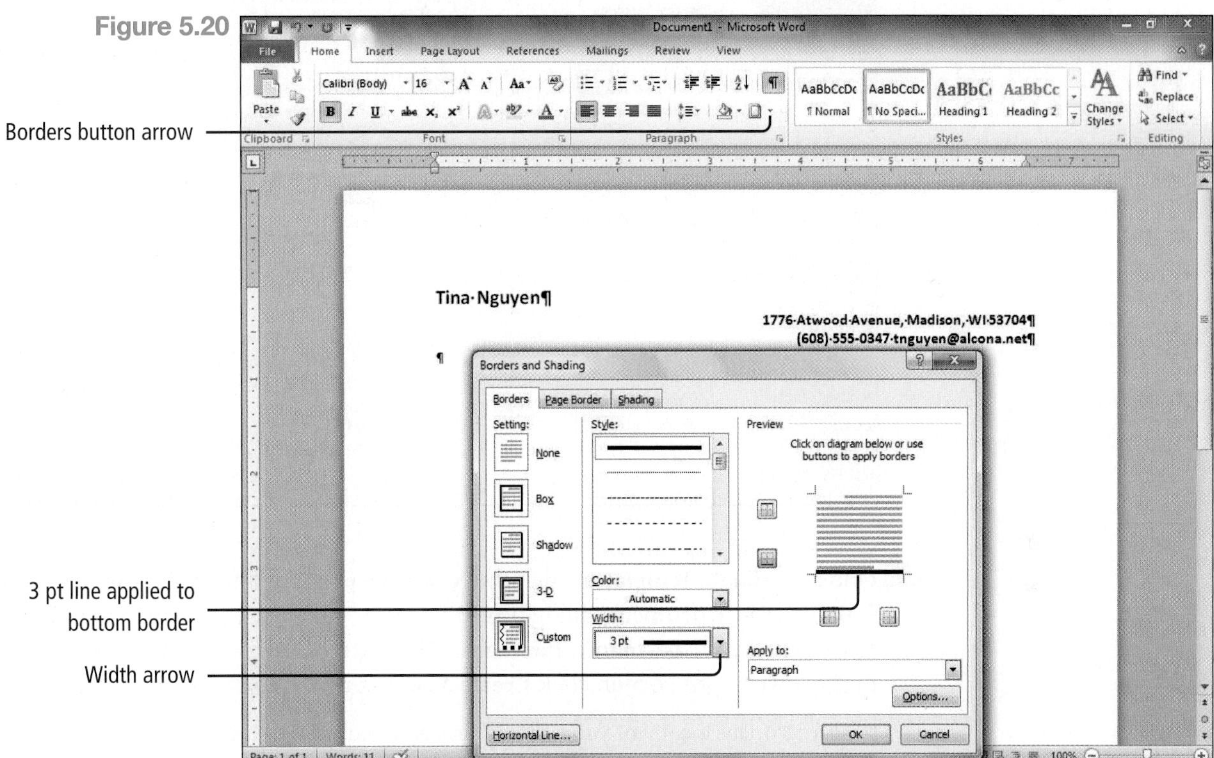

12. Click **OK** to display a 3 pt line below *Tina Nguyen*, which extends from the left margin to the right margin.
13. Display **Save As** dialog box, **Save** the document in your **Word Chapter 5** folder as **Lastname_Firstname_2B_Letterhead** and then add the file name to the footer.
14. Display **Backstage** view, click the **Info tab**, and then on the right, under the document thumbnail, click **Properties**. Click **Show Document Panel**. In the **Author** box, delete any text and then type your firstname and lastname. In the **Subject** box, type your course name and section number, and in the **Keywords** box type **personal letterhead**
15. **Close** the **Document Panel**.
16. **Save** your document. Display **Backstage** view, and then click **Close** to close the document but leave Word open. Hold this file until you complete this project.

Activity 5.11 | Creating a Document from an Existing Document

To use an existing document as the starting point for a new document, Word provides the *New from existing* command.

1 Click the **File tab** to display **Backstage** view, and then click **New** to display the new document options. Compare your screen with Figure 5.21.

Here you can create a new document in a variety of ways, including from an existing document.

Figure 5.21

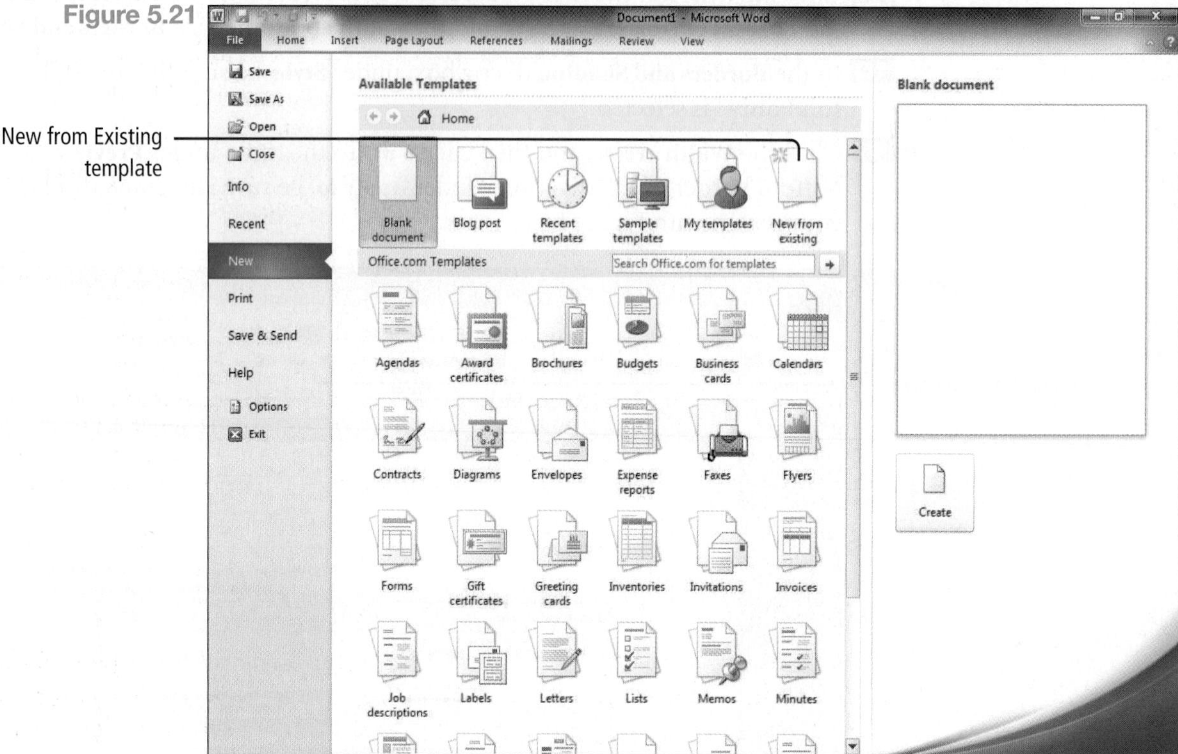

2 Under **Available Templates**, click the **New from existing** button. In the displayed **New from Existing Document** dialog box, if necessary, navigate to your **Word Chapter 5** folder, click your **Lastname_Firstname_2B_Letterhead** document to select it, and then in the lower right corner, click **Create New**. Compare your screen with Figure 5.22.

Word opens a copy of your 2B_Letterhead document in the form of a new Word document—the title bar indicates *Document* followed by a number. You are not opening the original document, and changes that you make to this new document will not affect the contents of your 2B_Letterhead document.

Figure 5.22

3 Display the **Save As** dialog box, and then navigate to your **Word Chapter 5** folder. **Save** the file as **Lastname_Firstname_2B_Cover_Letter**

The personal information that you typed in the 2B_Letterhead Document Panel remains in the new document.

4 Scroll down to view the footer area, and notice that a footer displays.

The footer displays because it was included in the document that you saved as a template. The *FileName* field does not automatically update to the new file name.

5 Point to the footer and right-click, and then click **Edit Footer**. Point to the highlighted footer text, right-click, and then from the shortcut menu, click **Update Field**. At the far right end of the Ribbon, click the **Close Header and Footer** button.

6 **Save** your document.

More Knowledge | Creating a Template File

You can also identify an original document so that your Windows operating system always knows that you want to create a new unnamed copy. To do so, save your document as a template file instead of a document. Word will then attach the dotx extension to the file, instead of the docx extension that is applied for a document, and will store the template file in a special location with other templates. Then, you can open the template from the New Document dialog box by clicking *My templates*.

Objective 5 | Change and Reorganize Text

Business letters follow a standard format and contain the following parts: the current date, referred to as the ***date line***; the name and address of the person receiving the letter, referred to as the ***inside address***; a greeting, referred to as the ***salutation***; the text of the letter, usually referred to as the ***body*** of the letter; a closing line, referred to as the ***complimentary closing***; and the ***writer's identification***, which includes the name or job title (or both) of the writer, and which is also referred to as the ***writer's signature block***.

Some letters also include the initials of the person who prepared the letter, an optional ***subject line*** that describes the purpose of the letter, or a list of ***enclosures***—documents included with the letter.

Activity 5.12 | Recording AutoCorrect Entries

You can correct commonly misspelled words automatically by using Word's ***AutoCorrect*** feature. Commonly misspelled words—such as *teh* instead of *the*—are corrected using a built-in list that is installed with Office. If you have words that you frequently misspell, you can add them to the list for automatic correction.

1 Click the **File tab** to display **Backstage** view. On the **Help tab**, click **Options** to display the **Word Options** dialog box.

2 On the left side of the **Word Options** dialog box, click **Proofing**, and then under **AutoCorrect options**, click the **AutoCorrect Options** button.

3. In the **AutoCorrect** dialog box, click the **AutoCorrect tab**. Under **Replace**, type **resumee** and under **With**, type **resume**

   If another student has already added this AutoCorrect entry, a Replace button will display.

4. Click **Add**. If the entry already exists, click Replace instead, and then click Yes.

5. In the **AutoCorrect** dialog box, under **Replace**, type **computr** and under **With**, type **computer** and then compare your screen with Figure 5.23.

Figure 5.23

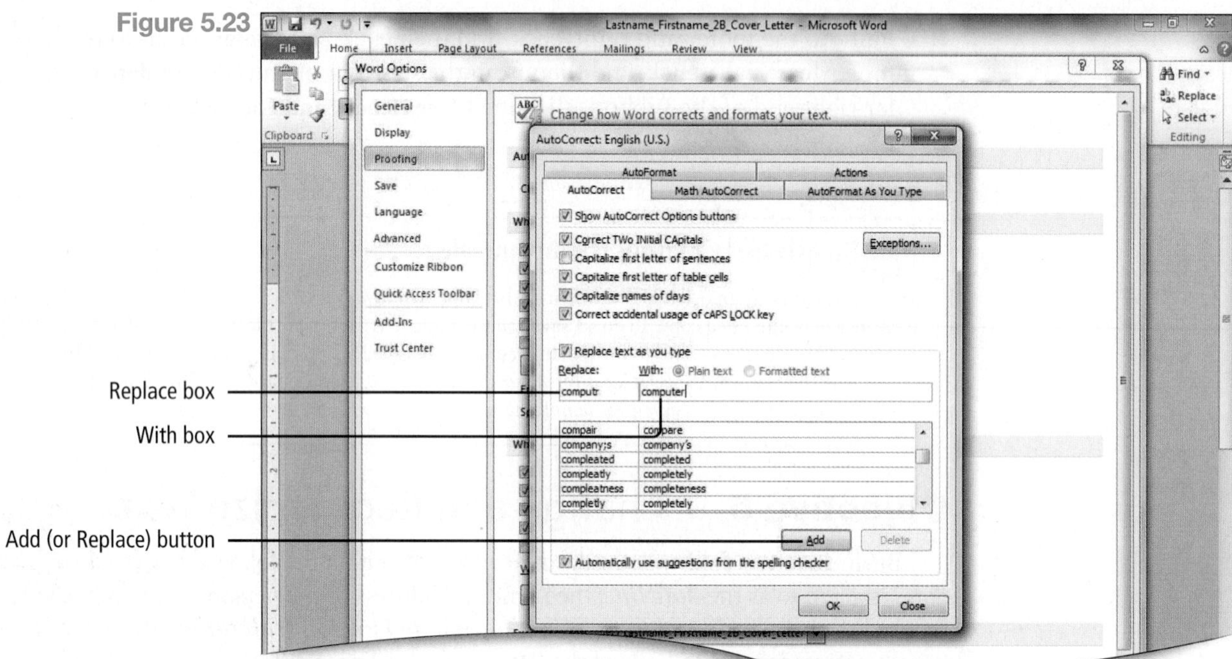

6. Click **Add** (or Replace) and then click **OK** two times to close the dialog boxes.

Activity 5.13 | Creating a Cover Letter

There are a variety of accepted letter formats that you will see in reference manuals and Business Communication texts. The one used in this chapter is a block style cover letter taken from *Business Communication Today*.

1. Press Ctrl + End to move the insertion point to the blank line below the letterhead. Press Enter three times, and then type **March 16, 2016** to create the dateline.

   Most Business Communication texts recommend that the dateline be positioned at least 0.5 inch (3 blank lines) below the letterhead; or, position the dateline approximately 2 inches from the top edge of the paper.

2. Press Enter four times, which leaves three blank lines. Type the following inside address on four lines, but do not press Enter following the last line:

   James Washington

   Madison Staffing Services

   600 East Washington Avenue

   Madison, WI 53701

   The recommended space between the dateline and inside address varies slightly among Business Communication texts and office reference manuals. However, all indicate that the space can be from one to 10 blank lines depending on the length of your letter.

3 Press Enter two times to leave one blank line. Compare your screen with Figure 5.24.

Figure 5.24

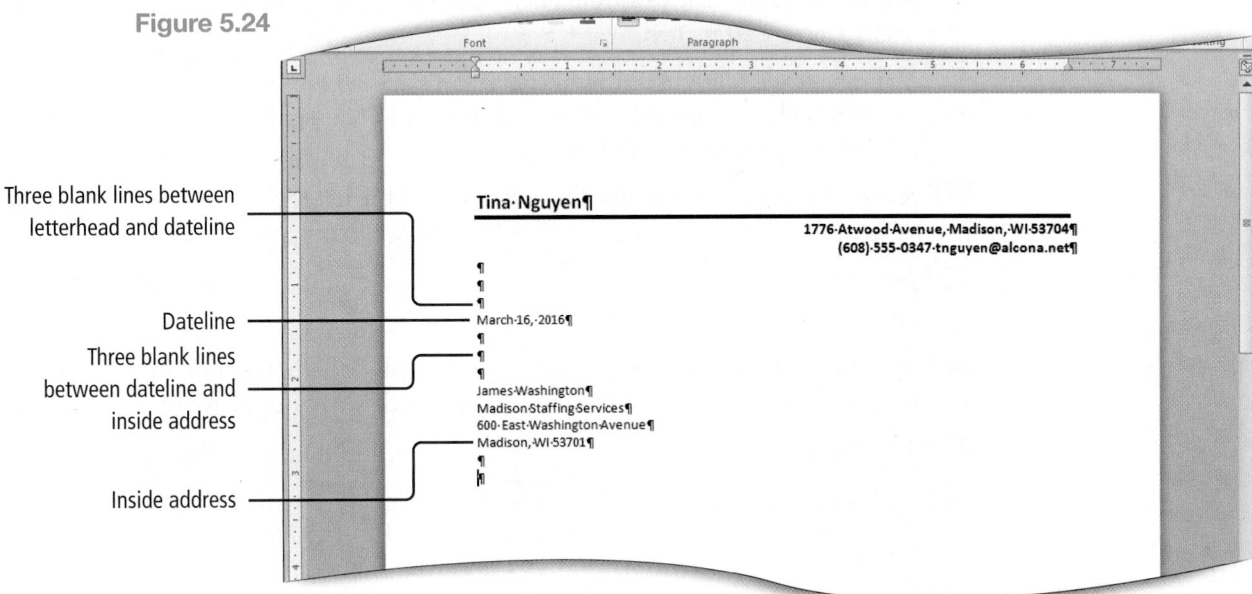

4 Type the salutation **Dear Mr. Washington:** and then press Enter two times.

Always leave one blank line above and below the salutation.

5 Type, exactly as shown, the following opening paragraph that includes an intentional word usage error: **I am seeking a position in witch I can use my** and press Spacebar. Type, exactly as shown, **computr** and then watch *computr* as you press Spacebar.

The AutoCorrect feature recognizes the misspelled word, and then changes *computr* to *computer* when you press Spacebar, Enter, or a punctuation mark.

6 Type the following, including the misspelled last word: **and communication skills. My education, outlined on the enclosed resumee** and then type **,** (a comma). Notice that when you type the comma, AutoCorrect replaces *resumee* with *resume*.

7 Press Spacebar. Complete the paragraph by typing **includes a Business Software Applications Specialist certificate from MATC.** Compare your screen with Figure 5.25.

Figure 5.25

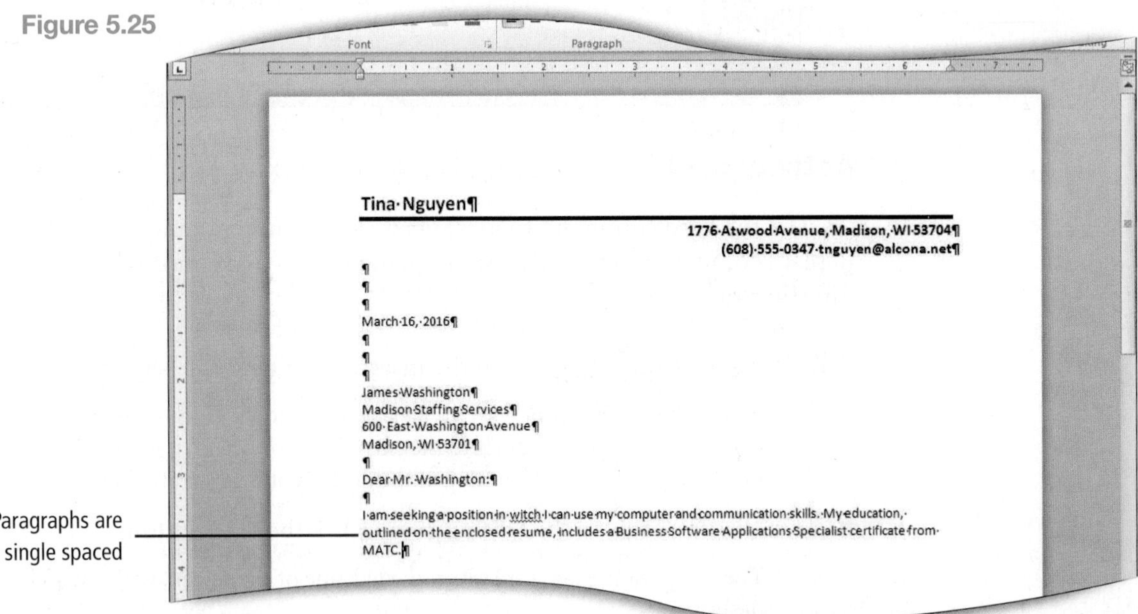

8 Press Enter two times. On the **Insert tab**, in the **Text group**, click the **Object button arrow**, and then click **Text from File**. From your student files, locate and **Insert** the file **w02B_Cover_Letter_Text**.

Some of the words in the cover letter text display red, green, or blue wavy underlines. These indicate potential spelling, grammar, or word usage errors, and you will correct them before the end of this project.

9 Scroll as necessary to display the lower half of the letter on your screen, and be sure your insertion point is positioned in the blank paragraph at the end of the document.

10 Press Enter one time to leave one blank line between the last paragraph of the letter and the complimentary closing.

11 Type **Sincerely,** as the complimentary closing, and then press Enter four times to leave three blank lines between the complimentary closing and the writer's identification.

12 Type **Tina Nguyen** as the writer's identification, and then press Enter two times.

13 Type **Enclosure** to indicate that a document is included with the letter. **Save** your document, and then compare your screen with Figure 5.26.

Figure 5.26

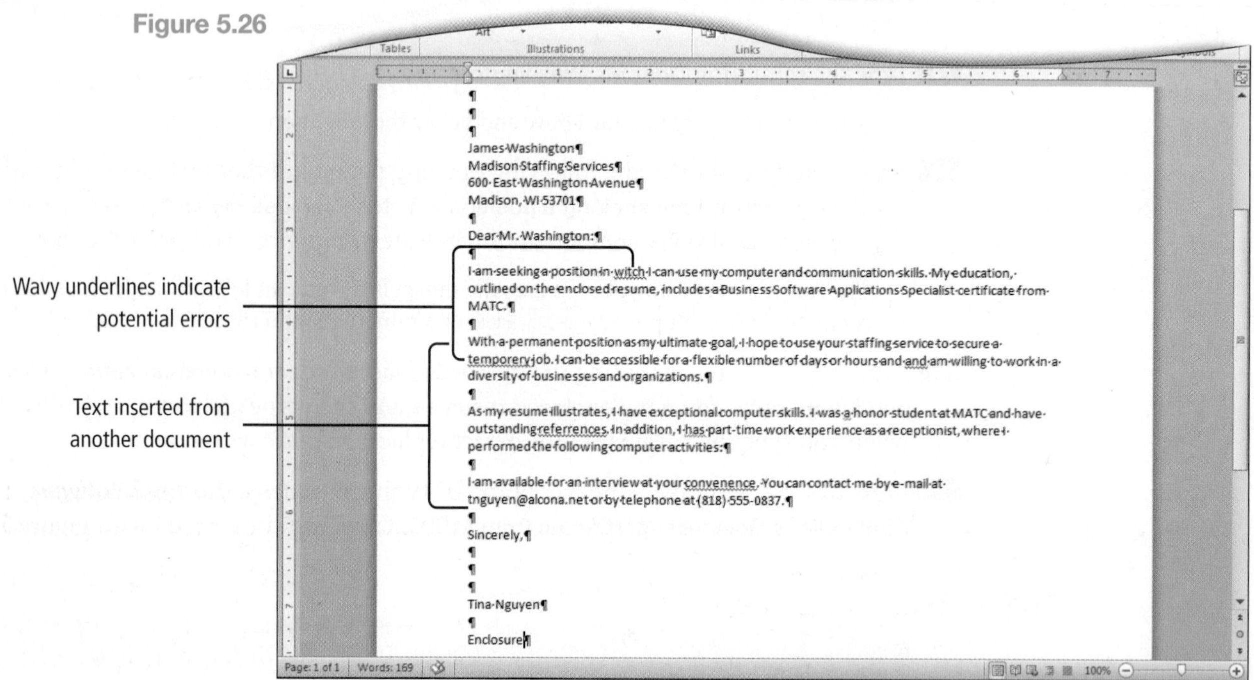

Activity 5.14 | Finding and Replacing Text

Use the Find command to locate text in a document quickly. Use the Find and Replace command to make the same change, or to make more than one change at a time, in a document.

1 Press Ctrl + Home to position the insertion point at the beginning of the document.

Because a find operation—or a find and replace operation—begins from the location of the insertion point and proceeds to the end of the document, it is good practice to position the insertion point at the beginning of the document before initiating the command.

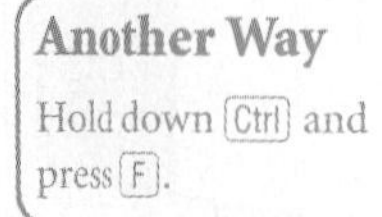
Another Way
Hold down Ctrl and press F.

2 On the **Home tab**, in the **Editing group**, click the **Find** button.

The Navigation Pane displays on the left side of the screen, with a search box at the top of the pane.

3 In the search box, type **ac** If necessary, scroll down slightly in your document to view the entire body text of the letter, and then compare your screen with Figure 5.27.

In the document, the search letters *ac* are selected and highlighted in yellow for all three words that contain the letters *ac* together. In the Navigation Pane, the three instances are shown in context—*ac* displays in bold.

Figure 5.27

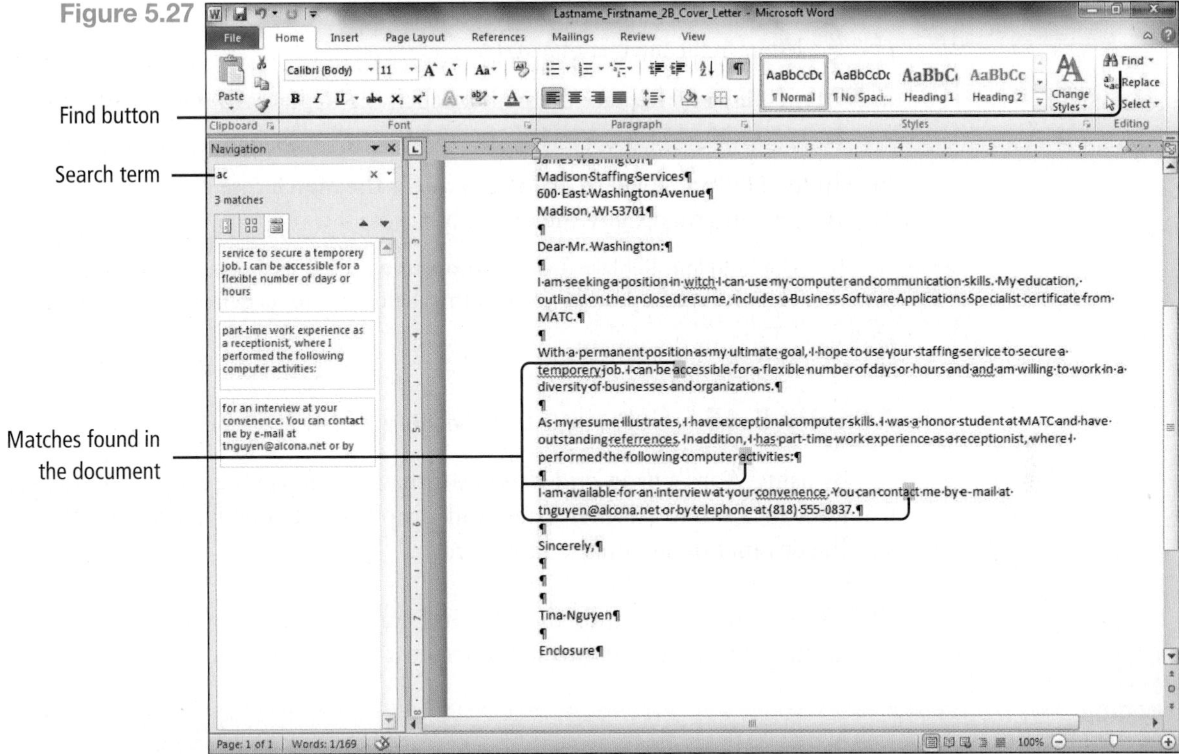

4 In the search box, complete the word **accessible.**

One match for the search term displays in context in the Navigation Pane and is highlighted in the document.

5 In the document, point to the yellow highlighted word *accessible*, double-click, and then type **available** to replace the word. Notice that the list of results is now empty.

6 **Close** the **Navigation Pane**, and then on the **Home tab**, in the **Editing group**, click the **Replace** button.

7 In the **Find and Replace** dialog box, in the **Find what** box, replace the existing text by typing **MATC** In the **Replace with** box, type **Madison Area Technical College** and then compare your screen with Figure 5.28

Figure 5.28

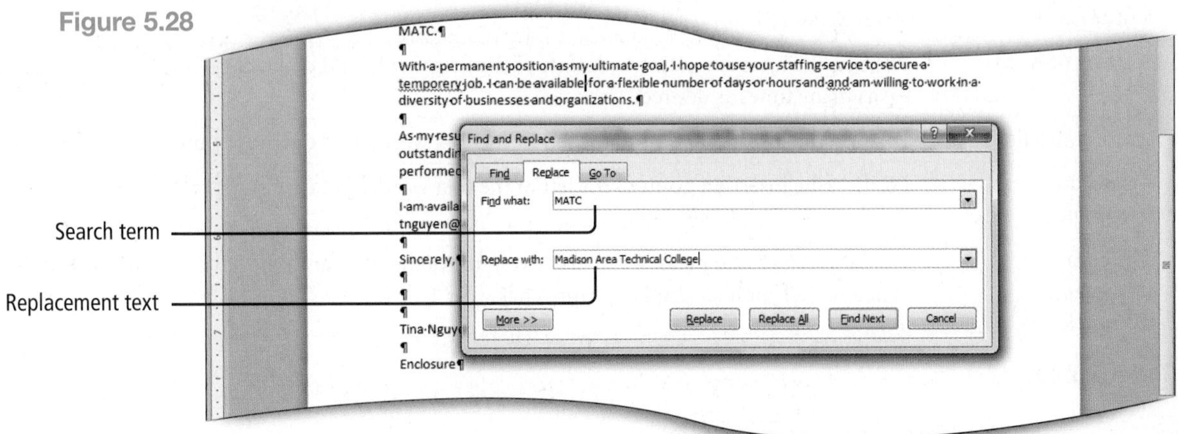

8 In the lower left corner of the dialog box, click the **More** button to expand the dialog box, and then under **Search Options**, select the **Match case** check box.

The acronym *MATC* appears in the document two times. In a formal letter, the reader may not know what the acronym means, so you should include the full text instead of an acronym. In this instance, you must select the *Match case* check box so that the replaced text will match the case you typed in the Replace with box, and *not* display in all uppercase letters in the manner of *MATC*.

9 In the **Find and Replace** dialog box, click the **Replace All** button to replace both instances of *MATC*. Click **OK** to close the message box.

10 In the **Find and Replace** dialog box, clear the **Match case** check box, click the **Less** button, and then **Close** the dialog box.

The Find and Replace dialog box opens with the settings used the last time it was open. Thus, it is good practice to reset this dialog box to its default settings each time you use it.

11 **Save** your document.

Activity 5.15 | Selecting and Moving Text to a New Location

By using Word's ***drag-and-drop*** feature, you can use the mouse to drag selected text from one location to another. Drag-and-drop is most effective when the text to be moved and the destination are on the same screen.

1 Take a moment to study the table in Figure 5.29 to become familiar with the techniques you can use to select text in a document quickly.

Selecting Text in a Document

To Select	Do This
A portion of text	Click to position the insertion point at the beginning of the text you want to select, hold down Shift, and then click at the end of the text you want to select. Alternatively, hold down the left mouse button and drag from the beginning to the end of the text you want to select.
A word	Double-click the word.
A sentence	Hold down Ctrl and click anywhere in the sentence.
A paragraph	Triple-click anywhere in the paragraph; or, move the pointer to the left of the line, into the margin area. When the pointer displays, double-click.
A line	Move the pointer to the left of the line. When the pointer displays, click one time.
One character at a time	Position the insertion point to the left of the first character, hold down Shift, and press ← or → as many times as desired.
A string of words	Position the insertion point to the left of the first word, hold down Shift and Ctrl, and then press ← or → as many times as desired.
Consecutive lines	Position the insertion point to the left of the first word, hold down Shift and press ↑ or ↓.
Consecutive paragraphs	Position the insertion point to the left of the first word, hold down Shift and Ctrl and press ↑ or ↓.
The entire document	Hold down Ctrl and press A. Alternatively, move the pointer to the left of any line in the document. When the pointer displays, triple-click.

Figure 5.29

2 Be sure you can view the entire body of the letter on your screen. In the paragraph that begins *With a permanent position*, in the second line, locate and double-click *days*.

3 Point to the selected word to display the [pointer icon] pointer.

4 Drag to the right until the dotted vertical line that floats next to the pointer is positioned to the right of the word *hours* in the same line, as shown in Figure 5.30.

Figure 5.30

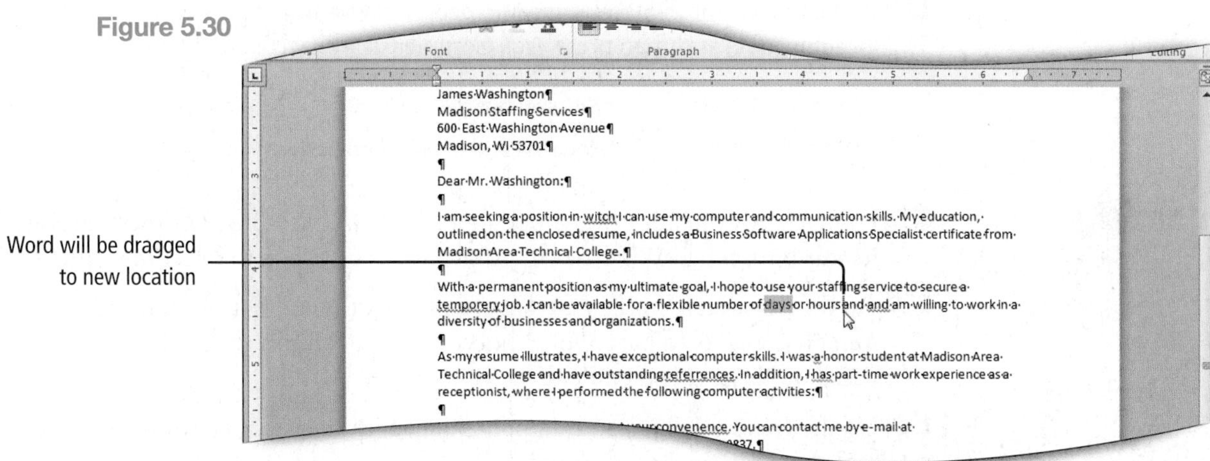

5 Release the mouse button to move the text. Select the word *hours* and drag it to the left of the word *or*—the previous location of the word *days*. Click anywhere in the document to deselect the text.

6 Examine the text that you moved, and add or remove spaces as necessary.

7 Hold down Ctrl, and then in the paragraph that begins *I am available*, click anywhere in the first sentence to select the entire sentence.

8 Drag the selected sentence to the end of the paragraph by positioning the small vertical line that floats with the pointer to the left of the paragraph mark. Compare your screen with Figure 5.31.

Figure 5.31

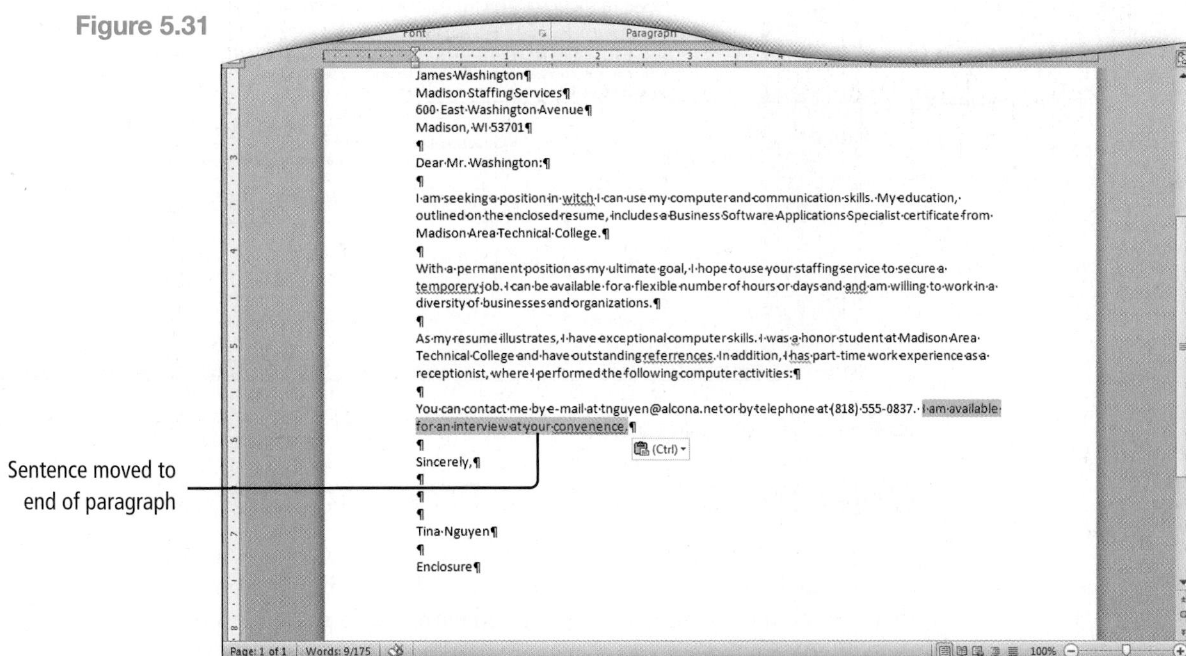

9 **Save** your document.

Activity 5.16 | Inserting and Formatting a Table in a Document

1 Locate the paragraph that begins *As my resume*, and then click to position the insertion point in the blank line below that paragraph. Press Enter one time.

2 On the **Insert tab**, in the **Tables group**, click the **Table** button. In the **Table** grid, in the third row, click the second square to insert a 2 × 3 table.

3 In the first cell of the table, type **Microsoft Access** and then press Tab. Type **Queried inventory data** and then press Tab. Complete the table using the following information:

Microsoft Excel	Entered budget data
Microsoft Word	Created and mailed form letters

4 Point slightly outside of the upper left corner of the table to display the **table move handle** button. With the pointer, click one time to select the entire table.

5 On the **Layout tab**, in the **Cell Size group**, click the **AutoFit** button, and then click **AutoFit Contents** to have Word choose the best column widths for the two columns based on the text you entered.

6 On the **Home tab**, in the **Paragraph group**, click the **Center** button to center the table between the left and right margins.

7 On the **Design tab**, in the **Table Styles group**, click the **Borders button arrow**, and then click **No Border**. Click anywhere to cancel the selection of the table, and then compare your screen with Figure 5.32.

A light dashed line may display in place of the original table borders if your default settings have been changed.

Figure 5.32

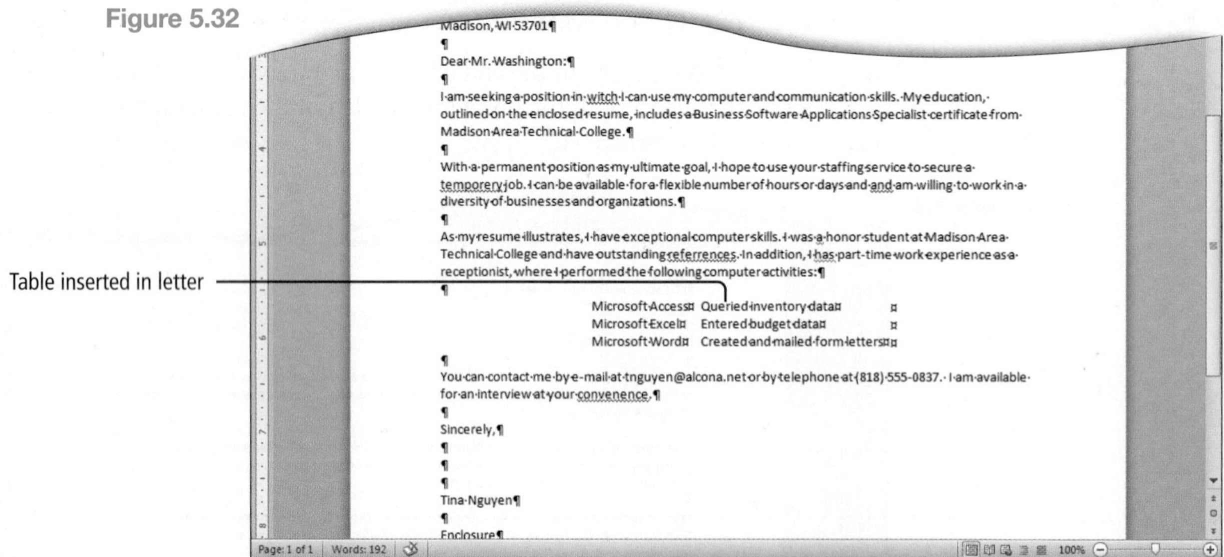

8 **Save** your document.

Objective 6 | Use the Proofing Options

Word compares your typing to words in the Office dictionary and compares your phrases and punctuation to a list of grammar rules. This automatic proofing is set by default. Words that are not in the dictionary are marked with a wavy red underline. Phrases and punctuation that differ from the grammar rules are marked with a wavy green underline.

Word also compares commonly misused words with a set of word usage rules, and marks misused words with a wavy blue underline; for example the misuse of *their*, *there*, and *they're*. However, Word will not flag the word *sign* as misspelled even though you intended to type *sing a song* rather than *sign a song*, because both are words contained within Word's dictionary. Your own knowledge and proofreading skills are still required, even when using a sophisticated Word processing program like Word.

Activity 5.17 | Checking Spelling and Grammar Errors

There are two ways to respond to spelling and grammar errors flagged by Word. You can right-click a flagged word or phrase, and then from the shortcut menu choose a correction or action. Or, you can initiate the Spelling and Grammar command to display the Spelling and Grammar dialog box, which provides more options than the shortcut menus.

Alert! | Spelling and Grammar Checking

If you do not see any wavy red, green, or blue lines under words, the automatic spelling and/or grammar checking has been turned off on your system. To activate the spelling and grammar checking, display Backstage view, on the Help tab, click Options, click Proofing, and then under *When correcting spelling in Microsoft Office programs*, select the first four check boxes. Under *When correcting spelling and grammar in Word*, select the first four check boxes, and then click the Writing Style arrow and click Grammar Only. Under *Exceptions for*, clear both check boxes. To display the flagged spelling and grammar errors, click the Recheck Document button, and then close the dialog box.

1 Position the body of the letter on your screen, and then examine the text to locate green, red, and blue wavy underlines. Compare your screen with Figure 5.33.

A list of grammar rules applied by a computer program like Word can never be exact, and a computer dictionary cannot contain all known words and proper names. Thus, you will need to check any words flagged by Word with wavy underlines, and you will also need to proofread for content errors.

Figure 5.33

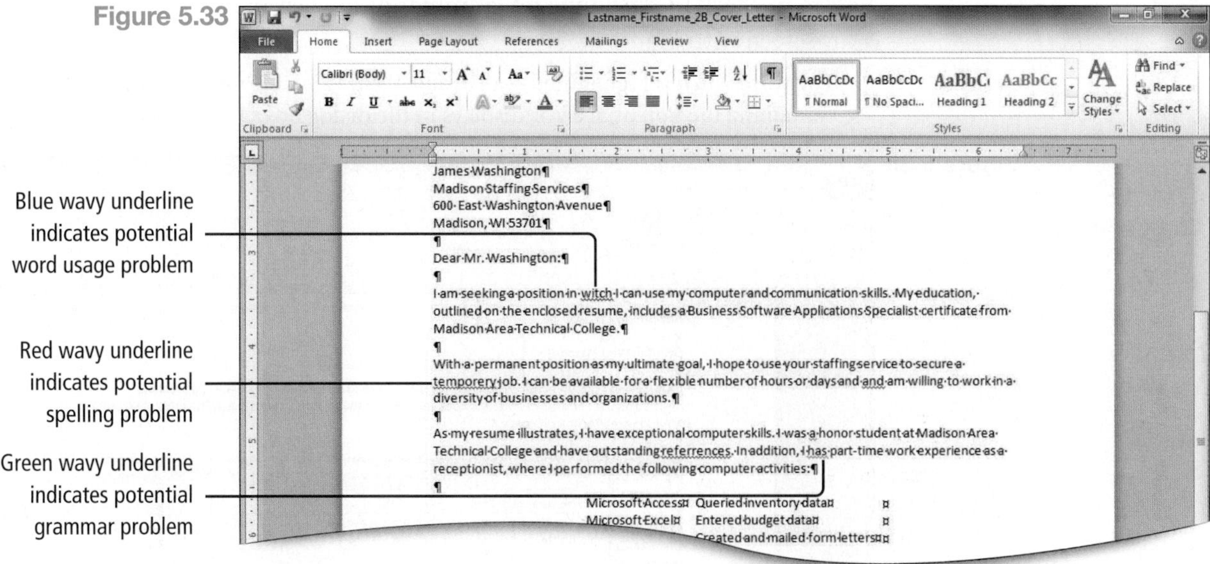

2 In the lower left corner of your screen, in the status bar, locate and point to the icon to display the ScreenTip *Proofing errors were found. Click to correct.*

If this button displays, you know there are potential errors identified in the document.

3 In the paragraph that begins *With a permanent*, locate the word *temporery* with the wavy red underline. Point to the word and right-click to display the shortcut menu, and then compare your screen with Figure 5.34.

Figure 5.34

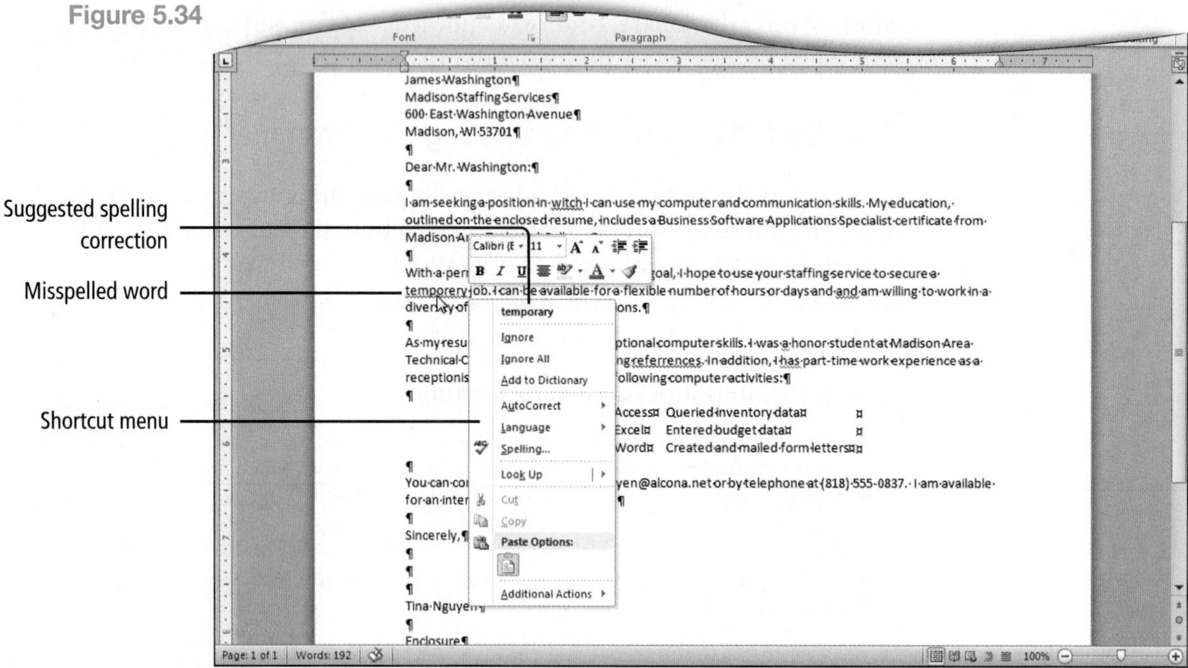

4 On the shortcut menu, click **temporary** to correct the spelling error.

5 In the next line, locate the word *and* that displays with a wavy red underline, point to word and right-click, and then from the shortcut menu, click **Delete Repeated Word** to delete the duplicate word.

Another Way

Press F7 to start the Spelling & Grammar command.

6 Press Ctrl + Home to move the insertion point to the beginning of the document. Click the **Review tab**, and then in the **Proofing group**, click the **Spelling & Grammar** button to check the spelling and grammar of the text in the document. Compare your screen with Figure 5.35.

The word *witch* is highlighted—a *Possible Word Choice Error*—and the sentence containing the potential error displays in the dialog box. A suggested change also displays.

Figure 5.35

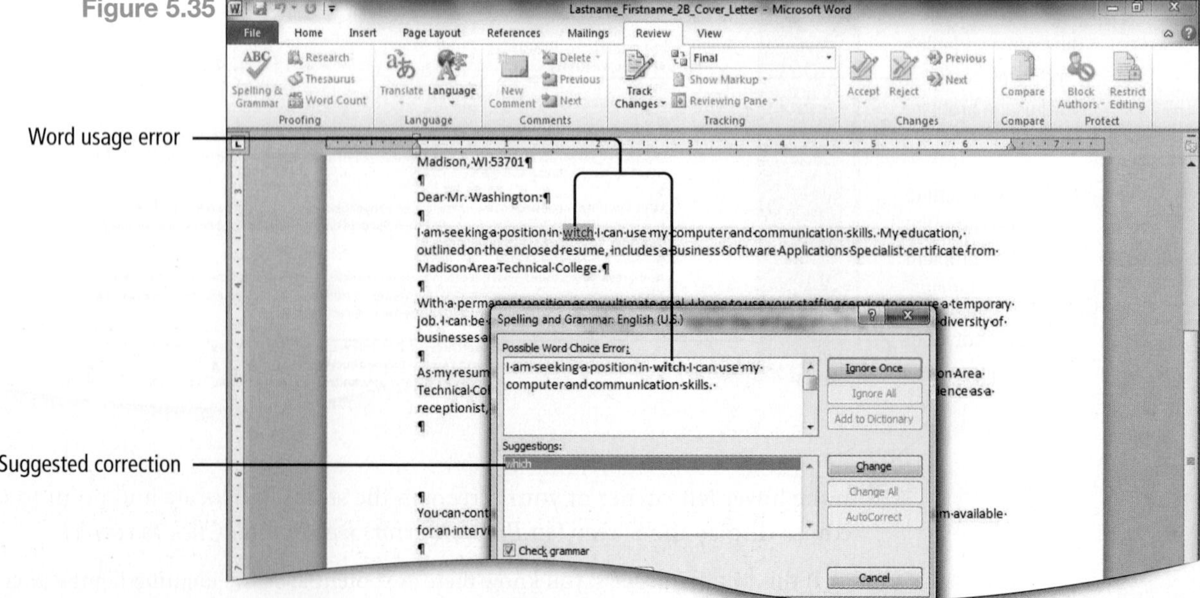

7 In the **Spelling and Grammar** dialog box, click the **Change** button to change to the correct usage *which*.

The next marked word—a possible spelling error—displays.

8 Click the **Change** button to change *referrences* to *references*. Notice that the next error is a possible grammar error.

9 Click the **Change** button to change *a* to *an*. Continue the spelling and grammar check and change *has* to *have* and correct the spelling of *convenence*.

10 When Word indicates *The spelling and grammar check is complete*, click **OK**.

11 **Save** your document.

Activity 5.18 | Using the Thesaurus

A ***thesaurus*** is a research tool that lists ***synonyms***—words that have the same or similar meaning to the word you selected.

1 Scroll so that you can view the body of the letter. In the paragraph that begins *With a permanent*, at the end of the second line, locate and right-click the word *diversity*.

2 On the shortcut menu, point to **Synonyms**, and then compare your screen with Figure 5.36.

A list of synonyms displays; the list will vary in length depending on the selected word.

Figure 5.36

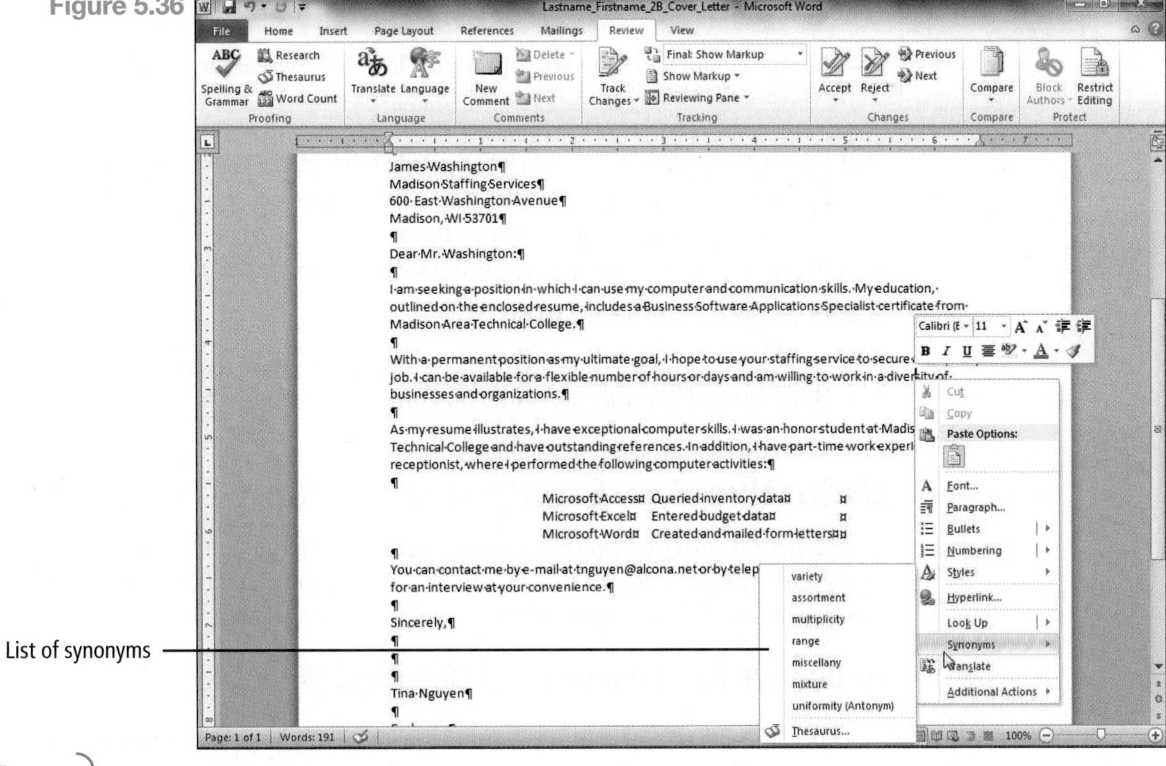

Another Way

Click the word, and then on the Review tab, in the Proofing group, click the Thesaurus button.

3 From the list of synonyms, click **variety** to replace *diversity* with *variety*.

4 In the paragraph that begins *As my resume*, point to the word *exceptional*, right-click, point to **Synonyms**, and then at the bottom of the shortcut menu, click **Thesaurus** to display the **Research** task pane.

5 In the **Research** task pane, under **Thesaurus**, point to the non-bold word *excellent*, and then click the **arrow**. Compare your screen with Figure 5.37.

Figure 5.37

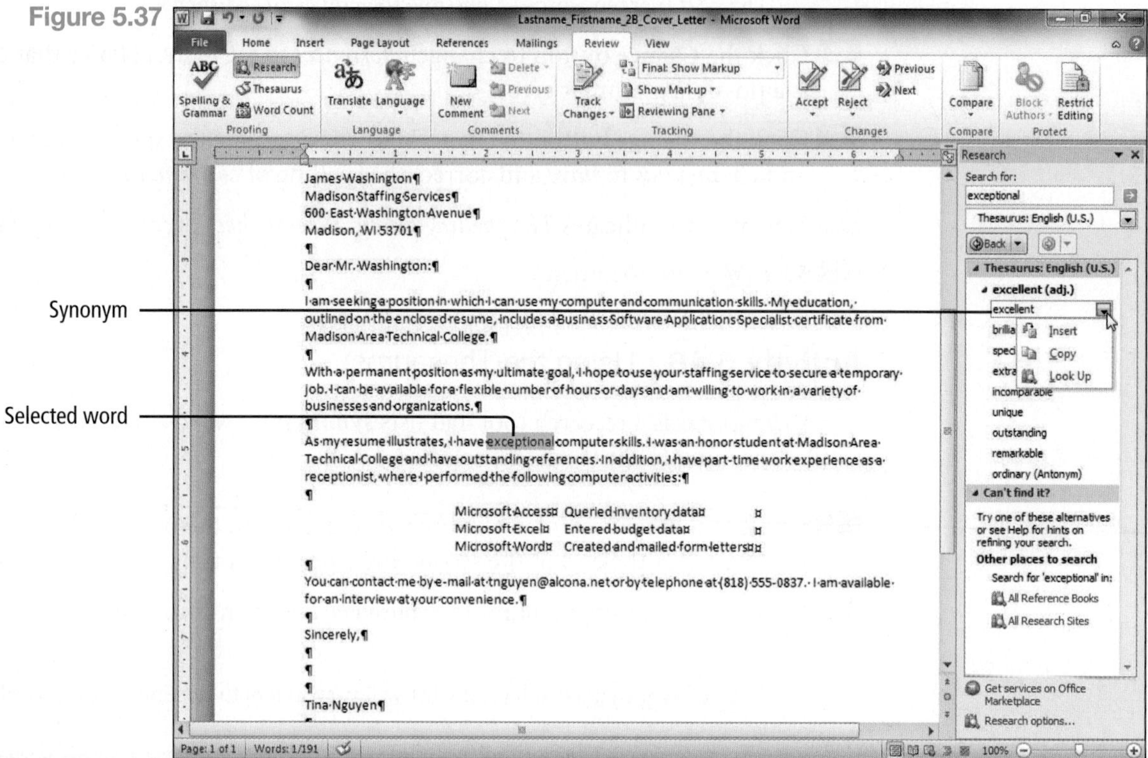

6 On the menu, click **Insert**, and then **Close** the **Research** task pane.

excellent replaces the word *exceptional.*

7 Display **Backstage** view and click the **Info tab**. On the right, under the document thumbnail, click **Properties**, and then click **Show Document Panel**. In the **Author** box, type your firstname and lastname. Be sure your course name and section number display in the **Subject** box, and as the **Keywords**, replace any existing text with **cover letter**

8 **Close** the **Document Panel**.

9 **Save**, and then display **Backstage** view. Click **Close** to close the document but leave Word open. Hold this file until you complete this project.

Objective 7 | Create a Document Using a Template

Microsoft provides pre-designed templates for letters, resumes, invoices, and other types of documents. Recall that when you open a template, it opens unnamed so that you can reuse it as often as you need to do so.

Activity 5.19 | Locating and Opening a Template

If you need to create a short resume quickly, or if you need ideas about how to format your resume, Microsoft Word provides pre-designed resume templates. Some templates are available on your computer; many more are available online. After opening a template, you can add text as indicated, modify the layout and design, and add or remove resume elements.

1 Close any open documents, and then from **Backstage** view, click **New**.

2 Under **Available Templates**, click **Sample templates**.

3 Under **Available Templates**, scroll toward the bottom of the window, and then click **Median Resume**. Notice that a preview of the *Median Resume* template displays on the right. Compare your screen with Figure 5.38.

Figure 5.38

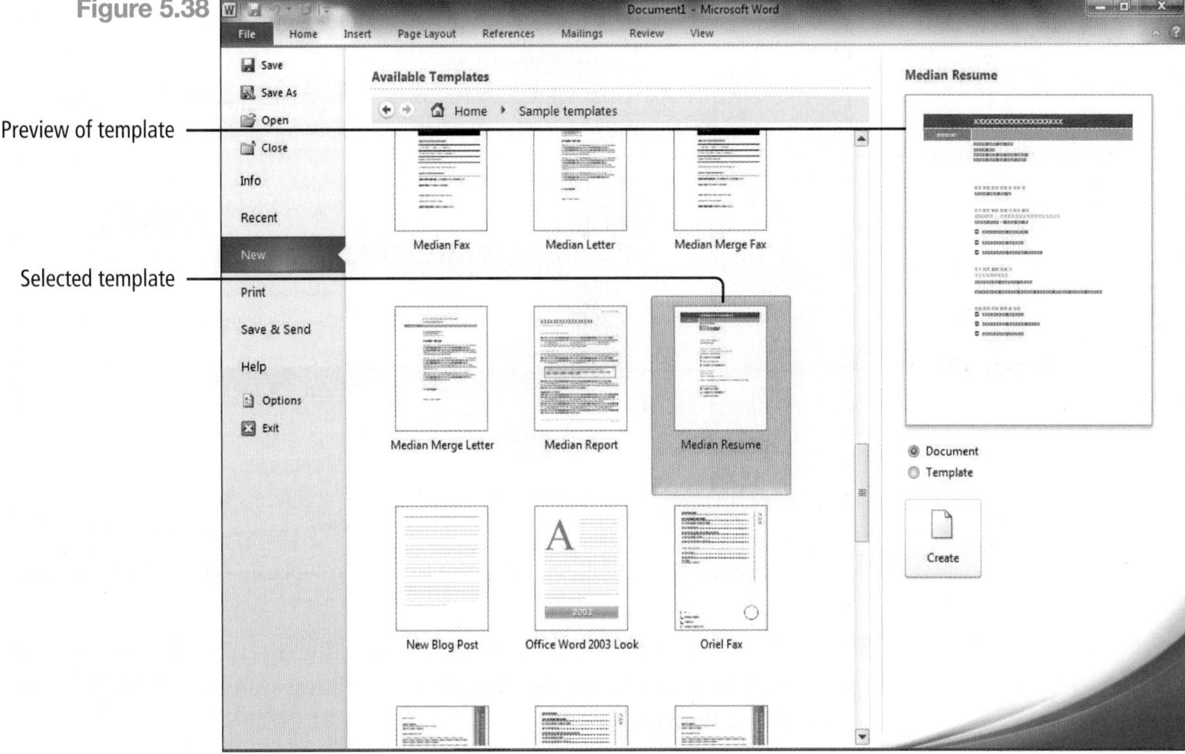

4 In the lower right corner, click the **Create** button.

The template opens a copy of itself in the form of a new Word document—the title bar indicates *Document* followed by a number. Recall that you are not opening the template itself, and that changes you make to this new document will not affect the contents of the template file.

5 Display the **Save As** dialog box. **Save** the document in your **Word Chapter 5** folder as **Lastname_Firstname_2B_Brief_Resume** and then add the file name to the footer—called the *First Page Footer* in this template.

6 **Save** your document.

Activity 5.20 | Replacing Template Placeholder Text

After you save the template file as a Word document, you can begin to substitute your own information in the indicated locations. You can also remove unneeded resume elements that are included with the template.

1 Click on the picture, and notice that a Picture Tool tab is added to the Ribbon.

2 Click the **Layout tab**, and then in the **Table group**, click the **View Gridlines** button to display non-printing table borders.

This template consists of two Word tables, and the name in the first row of the upper table displays either the user name or the text *[Type your name]* in square brackets.

3 At the top of the upper table, click the **Resume Name tab arrow**, and then compare your screen with Figure 5.39.

There are two styles available with the Median template—with or without a photo. You should not include a picture on a resume unless physical appearance is directly related to the job for which you are applying—for example, for a job as an actor or a model.

Figure 5.39

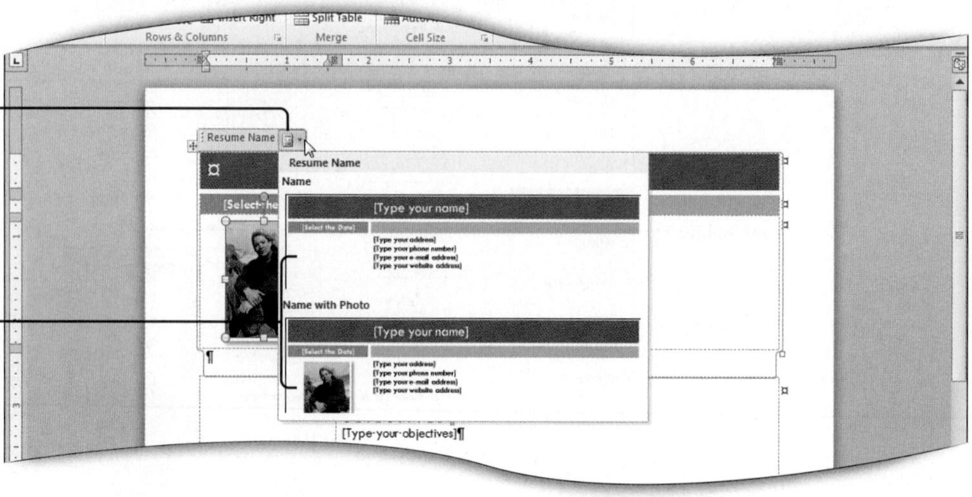

Resume Name tab arrow

Two styles available

4 In the **Resume Name** gallery, click the first style—**Name**—to switch to the style with no picture.

5 In the first row of the table, select the displayed text—typically the name of your computer as indicated in your Windows operating system—and replace the text by typing **Tina Nguyen**

Another Way

Select the entire row, right-click, and then from the shortcut menu, click Delete Rows.

6 In the second row, click anywhere in the date control *[Select the Date]*. On the Ribbon, click the **Layout tab**. In the **Rows & Columns group**, click the **Delete** button, and then click **Delete Rows**.

Text surrounded by brackets is called a ***content control***. There are several different types of content controls, including date, picture, and ***text controls***. Most of the controls in this template are text controls. Because resumes do not typically include a date, you can delete this row.

7 Click anywhere in the content control *[Type your address]*. Compare your screen with Figure 5.40.

For the name and address at the top of the document, all of the text controls are grouped together. Each control has ***placeholder text***, text that indicates the type of information to be entered. The name in the first row may also be a content control with placeholder text.

Figure 5.40

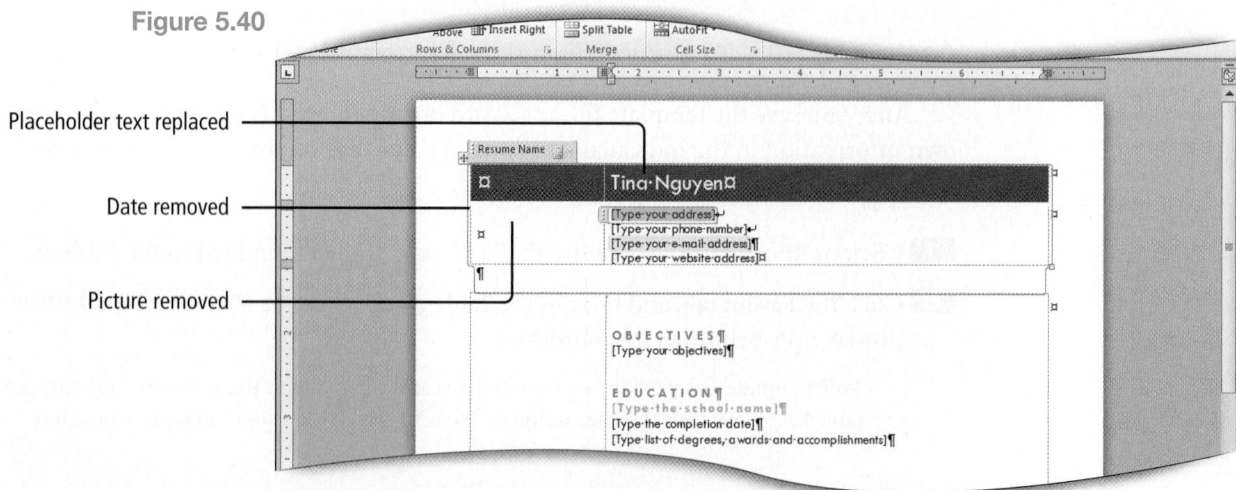

8 Complete the personal information by using the following information:

[Type your address]	**1776 Atwood Avenue, Madison, WI 53704**
[Type your phone number]	**(608) 555-0347**
[Type your e-mail address]	**tnguyen@alcona.net**
[Type your website address]	(leave this blank)

9 In the lower table, click in the *[Type your objectives]* control, and then type **To obtain a position using my computer and communications skills.**

10 Complete the **Education** section by using the following information:

[Type the school name]	**Madison Area Technical College**
[Type the completion date]	**June 2015**
[Type list of degrees, awards and accomplishments] *(type three separate lines)*	**Business Computing Specialist certificate** **Dean's List, four semesters** **President, Community Service Club**

11 Complete the **Experience** section by using the following information:

[Type the job title]	**Office Assistant (part-time)**
[Type the company name]	**The Robinson Company**
[Type the start date]	**September 2014**
[Type the end date]	**present**
[Type list of job responsibilities]	**Data entry and report generation using company spreadsheets and databases.**

12 Click in the *[Type list of skills]* control, type **Proficiency using Word, Excel, and Access (completed advanced courses in Microsoft Office programs)** and then press Enter.

13 As the second bulleted point, type **Excellent written and verbal communications (completed courses in Business Communications, PowerPoint, and Speech)** and then compare your screen with Figure 5.41. **Save** your document.

Figure 5.41

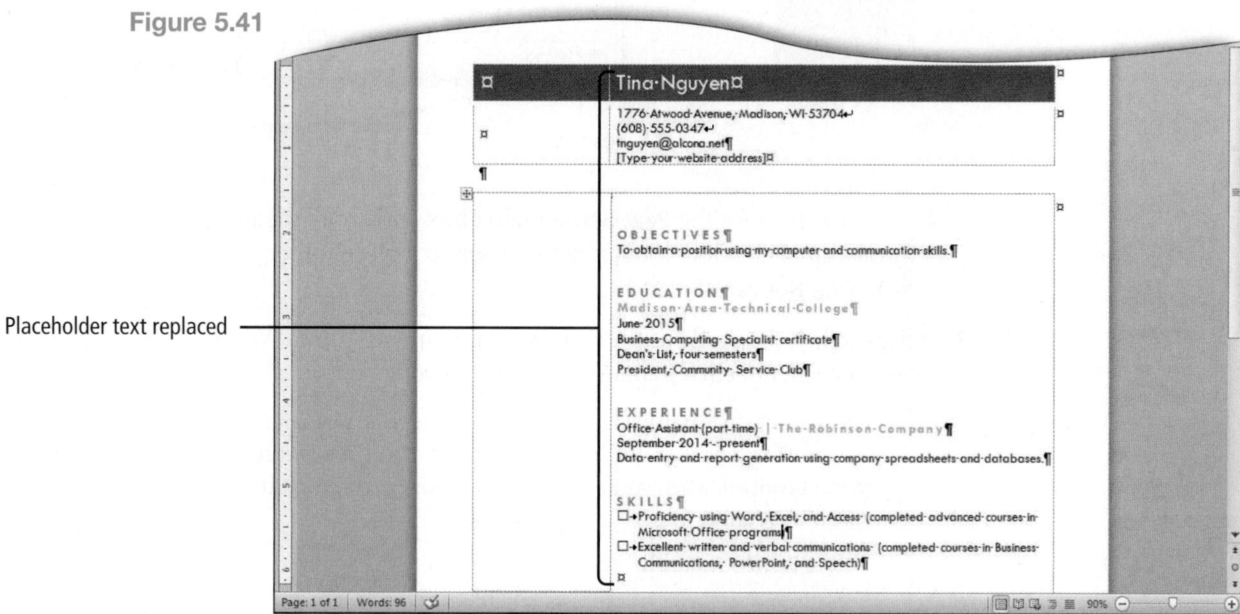

Activity 5.21 | Removing Template Controls and Formatting the Resume

1 Near the top of the document, point to the text control that you did not use—*[Type your website address]*. Right-click the control, and then from the shortcut menu, click **Remove Content Control**. Press Backspace as necessary to position the insertion point at the end of the e-mail address. Select the three lines with the address, phone, and e-mail information. On the Mini toolbar, notice that the text size is *11.5*. Click the **Font Size button arrow**, and then click **12**.

2 Click anywhere in lower table—the table with the *Objectives* row at the top—and then point to the upper left corner of the active table to display the **move table handle**. Click one time to select the lower table.

3 On the Mini toolbar, change the **Font Size** to **12** to match the table above.

4 Click anywhere to cancel the selection. On the **Page Layout tab**, in the **Page Setup group**, click the **Margins** button, and then click **Custom Margins**. Change the **Top** margin to **1.5** and the **Left** and **Right** margins to **1** to make this short resume better fill the page. Compare your screen with Figure 5.42.

Figure 5.42

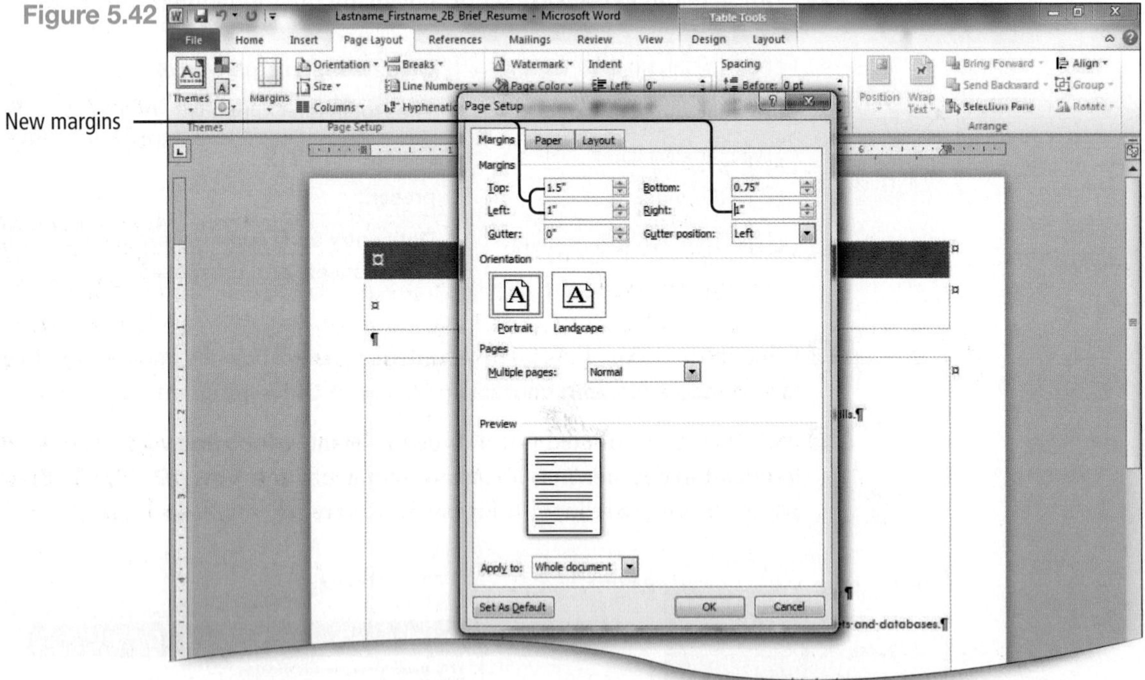

5 Click **OK** to close the **Page Setup** dialog box and apply the new margins. If the name at the top of the document changes back to a placeholder, click the control and type **Tina Nguyen**

6 Right-click the name at the top of the document—*Tina Nguyen*—and then from the shortcut menu, click **Remove Content Control**.

This action will leave the name but remove the control. Remove the control if the Document Properties will have an author other than the name in this control. If you do *not* remove the content control, when you add document properties, the name will change to the name you type in the Author box.

7 Press Ctrl + F2 to display the Print Preview in **Backstage** view. Click the **Info tab**. On the right, under the document thumbnail, click **Properties**, and then click **Show Document Panel**. In the **Author** box, delete any text and then type your firstname and lastname. In the **Subject** box, type your course name and section number, and in the **Keywords** box, type **short resume, template**

8 **Close** the **Document Panel**. **Save** your document, and then hold this file until you complete this project. Leave the resume displayed on your screen.

Activity 5.22 | Saving a Resume as a Web Page

You can save your resume as a Web page. This enables you to post the Web page on your own Web site or on Web space provided by your college. It also enables you to send the resume as an e-mail attachment that can be opened using any Web browser.

1 With your **2B_Brief_Resume** still open on your screen, click **Save** to be sure the current version of the document is saved.

2 Display the **Save As** dialog box. In the lower portion of the **Save As** dialog box, click the **Save as type arrow**, and then click **Single File Web Page**.

A ***Single File Web Page*** is a document saved using the ***Hypertext Markup Language (HTML)***. HTML is the language used to format documents that can be opened using a Web browser such as Internet Explorer.

3 In the **Save As** dialog box, in the **File name** box, type **Lastname_Firstname_2B_HTML_Resume** Click **Save**, and then click **Yes** if a message box displays. Notice that the Web page displays in Word.

4 Display **Backstage** view. On the right, click **Properties**, and then click **Advanced Properties**. In the **Properties** dialog box, on the **Summary tab**, in the **Subject** box, be sure your course name and section number display. In the **Author** box, be sure your first and last names display. In the **Keywords** box, replace the existing text with **HTML** Click **OK**, and then click the **Home tab**. **Save** the document; print or submit electronically as directed.

5 **Exit** Word. From the **Start** menu, click **Computer**. Navigate to your **Word Chapter 5** folder, and then double-click your **Lastname_Firstname_2B_HTML_Resume** file to open the resume in your Web browser. Compare your screen with Figure 5.43.

Figure 5.43

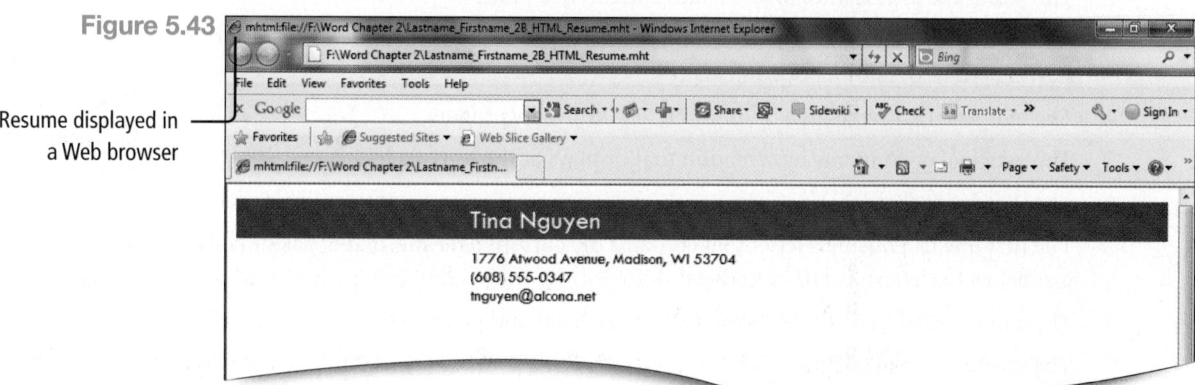

6 **Close** your Web browser. As directed by your instructor, print or submit electronically the four files from this project—2B_Letterhead, 2B_Cover_Letter, 2B_Brief_Resume, and 2B_HTML_Resume.

End You have completed Project 5B

Content-Based Assessments

Summary

In this chapter, you created a table, and then used the table to create a resume. You created a letterhead template, and then created a document using a copy of the letterhead template. You created a cover letter for the resume, moved text, corrected spelling and grammar, and used the built-in thesaurus. Finally, you created a short resume using a template, and also saved the resume as a Web page.

Key Terms

AutoCorrect 233
Body.................................233
Cell..................................217
Complimentary closing 233
Content control.............246
Date line 233
Drag and drop................238
Enclosures 233
HTML 249
Hypertext Markup Language (HTML) 249
Inside address 233
Letterhead......................230
New from existing 231
No Spacing style...........230
Normal template............230
Placeholder text 246
Salutation 233
Single File Web Page 249
Subject line 233
Synonyms 243
Table 217
Template 230
Text control 246
Thesaurus 243
Writer's identification 233
Writer's signature block 233

Matching

Match each term in the second column with its correct definition in the first column by writing the letter of the term on the blank line in front of the correct definition.

____ 1. An arrangement of information organized into rows and columns.
____ 2. The box at the intersection of a row and column in a table.
____ 3. A document structure that opens a copy of itself, opens unnamed, and is used as the starting point for another document.
____ 4. The template that serves as a basis for all new Word documents.
____ 5. The personal or company information that displays at the top of a letter.
____ 6. The Word style that inserts no extra space following a paragraph and uses single spacing.
____ 7. The first line in a business letter that contains the current date and that is positioned just below the letterhead if a letterhead is used.
____ 8. The name and address of the person receiving a letter and positioned below the date line.
____ 9. The greeting line of a letter.
____ 10. A parting farewell in a letter.
____ 11. The name and title of the author of a letter, placed near the bottom of the letter under the complimentary closing.
____ 12. The optional line following the inside address in a business letter that states the purpose of the letter.

A AutoCorrect
B Cell
C Complimentary closing
D Date line
E Drag and drop
F Enclosures
G Inside address
H Letterhead
I No Spacing
J Normal template
K Salutation
L Subject line
M Table
N Template
O Writer's identification

_____ 13. Additional documents included with a business letter.

_____ 14. A Word feature that corrects common spelling errors as you type, for example changing *teh* to *the*.

_____ 15. A technique by which you can move, by dragging, selected text from one location in a document to another.

Multiple Choice

Circle the correct answer.

1. When you create a table, the width of all of cells in the table is:
A. equal **B.** proportional **C.** 1 inch

2. To indicate words that might be misspelled because they are not in Word's dictionary, Word flags text with:
A. blue wavy underlines **B.** green wavy underlines **C.** red wavy underlines

3. To indicate possible grammar errors, Word flags text with:
A. blue wavy underlines **B.** green wavy underlines **C.** red wavy underlines

4. To indicate possible errors in word usage, Word flags text with:
A. blue wavy underlines **B.** green wavy underlines **C.** red wavy underlines

5. A research tool that provides a list of words with similar meanings is:
A. a thesaurus **B.** a dictionary **C.** an encyclopedia

6. A word with the same or similar meaning as another word is:
A. an acronym **B.** a search term **C.** a synonym

7. In a template, an area indicated by placeholder text into which you can add text, pictures, dates, or lists is a:
A. text control **B.** content control **C.** quick control

8. A document saved in HTML, which can be opened using a Web browser, is a:
A. Web page **B.** template **C.** resume

9. Using drag-and-drop to move text is most useful when both the text and the destination are on the same:
A. document **B.** section **C.** screen

10. To locate specific text in a document quickly, use the:
A. Find command **B.** Replace command **C.** Locate command

Apply 5A skills from these Objectives:

1. Create a Table
2. Add Text to a Table
3. Format a Table

Skills Review | Project 5C Student Resume

In the following Skills Review, you will use a table to create a resume for Joshua Green. Your completed resume will look similar to Figure 5.44.

Project Files

For Project 5C, you will need the following files:

New blank Word document
w02C_Skills
w02C_Experience

You will save your document as:

Lastname_Firstname_2C_Student_Resume

Project Results

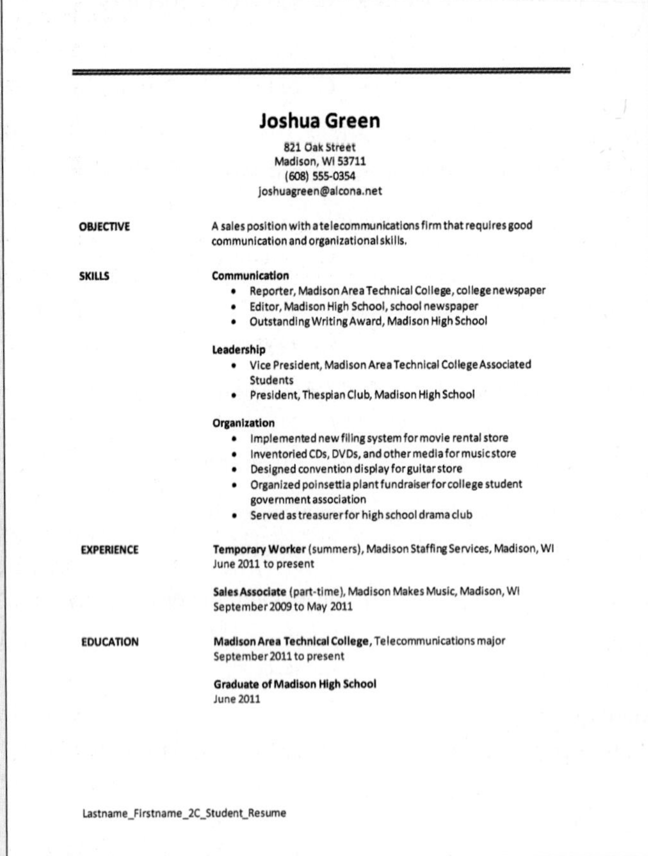

Joshua Green

821 Oak Street
Madison, WI 53711
(608) 555-0354
joshuagreen@alcona.net

OBJECTIVE	A sales position with a telecommunications firm that requires good communication and organizational skills.
SKILLS	**Communication** • Reporter, Madison Area Technical College, college newspaper • Editor, Madison High School, school newspaper • Outstanding Writing Award, Madison High School **Leadership** • Vice President, Madison Area Technical College Associated Students • President, Thespian Club, Madison High School **Organization** • Implemented new filing system for movie rental store • Inventoried CDs, DVDs, and other media for music store • Designed convention display for guitar store • Organized poinsettia plant fundraiser for college student government association • Served as treasurer for high school drama club
EXPERIENCE	**Temporary Worker** (summers), Madison Staffing Services, Madison, WI June 2011 to present **Sales Associate** (part-time), Madison Makes Music, Madison, WI September 2009 to May 2011
EDUCATION	**Madison Area Technical College**, Telecommunications major September 2011 to present **Graduate of Madison High School** June 2011

Lastname_Firstname_2C_Student_Resume

Figure 5.44

(Project 5C Student Resume continues on the next page)

Skills Review | Project 5C Student Resume (continued)

1 **Start** Word. In the new blank document, be sure that formatting marks and rulers display. **Save** the document in your **Word Chapter 5** folder as **Lastname_Firstname_2C_Student_Resume**

a. Add the file name to the footer, and then close the footer area. Click the **Insert tab**, and then in the **Tables group**, click the **Table** button. In the **Table** grid, in the fourth row, click the second square to insert a **2 × 4** table.

b. In the first cell of the table, type **Joshua Green** and then press Enter. Type the following text, pressing Enter after each line *except* the last line:

821 Oak Street

Madison, WI 53711

(608) 555-0354

joshuagreen@alcona.net

c. Press ↓ to move to the first cell in the second row. Type **SKILLS** and then press ↓ to move to the first cell in the third row.

d. Type **EXPERIENCE** and then press ↓. Type **EDUCATION**

e. In the first cell, if the e-mail address displays in blue, right-click the e-mail address, and then from the shortcut menu, click **Remove Hyperlink**. **Save** your document

2 Click in the cell to the right of *SKILLS*, and then type the following, pressing Enter after each item:

Communication
Reporter, Madison Area Technical College, college newspaper
Editor, Madison High School, school newspaper
Outstanding Writing Award, Madison High School

a. With the insertion point in the new line at the end of the cell, click the **Insert tab**. In the **Text group**, click the **Object button arrow**, and then click **Text from File**.

b. Navigate to your student files, select **w02C_Skills**, and then click **Insert**. Press Backspace one time to remove the blank line.

c. Click in the cell to the right of *EXPERIENCE*, and then insert the file **w02C_Experience**. Press Backspace one time to remove the blank line.

d. Click in the cell to the right of *EDUCATION*, and then type the following, pressing Enter after all *except* the last item:

Madison Area Technical College, Telecommunications major

September 2011 to present

Graduate of Madison High School

June 2011

3 Click anywhere in the top row of the table. Click the **Layout tab**, and then in the **Rows & Columns group**, click the **Insert Below** button. Type **OBJECTIVE** and then press Tab.

a. Type **A sales position with a telecommunications firm that requires good communication and organizational skills.**

b. In any row, point to the vertical border between the two columns to display the ⫲ pointer. Drag the column border to the left to approximately **1.75 inches on the horizontal ruler**.

c. Click anywhere in the left column. Click the **Layout tab**. In the **Cell Size group**, in the **Table Column Width** box, if necessary, type **1.75** and press Enter.

d. In the first row of the document, drag across both cells to select them. On the **Layout tab**, in the **Merge group**, click the **Merge Cells** button. Right-click the selected cell, and then from the Mini toolbar, click the **Center** button.

e. In the top row, select the first paragraph of text—*Joshua Green*. From the Mini toolbar, increase the **Font Size** to **20** and apply **Bold**.

f. In the second row, point to the word *OBJECTIVE*, hold down the left mouse button, and then drag down to select the row headings in uppercase letters. On the Mini toolbar, click the **Bold** button. **Save** your document.

4 Click in the cell to the right of *OBJECTIVE*. On the **Page Layout tab**, in the **Paragraph group**, click the **Spacing After up spin arrow** three times to change the spacing to **18 pt**.

a. In the cell to the right of *SKILLS*, apply **Bold** to the words *Communication*, *Leadership*, and *Organization*. Then, under each bold heading in the cell, select the lines of text, and create a bulleted list.

b. In the first two bulleted lists, click in the last bullet item, and then on the **Page Layout tab**, in the **Paragraph group**, set the **Spacing After** to **12 pt**.

(Project 5C Student Resume continues on the next page)

Skills Review | Project 5C Student Resume (continued)

c. In the last bulleted list, click in the last bullet item, and then set the **Spacing After** to **18 pt**.

d. In the cell to the right of *EXPERIENCE*, apply **Bold** to *Temporary Worker* and *Sales Associate*. Click in the line *June 2011 to present* and apply **Spacing After** of **12 pt**. Click in the line *September 2009 to May 2011* and apply **Spacing After** of **18 pt**.

e. In the cell to the right of *EDUCATION*, apply **Bold** to *Madison Area Technical College* and *Graduate of Madison High School*.

f. In the same cell, click in the line *September 2011 to present* and apply **Spacing After** of **12 pt**.

g. In the first row, click in the last line—*joshuagreen@alcona.net*—and then change the **Spacing After** to **18 pt**. Click in the first line—*Joshua Green*—and set the **Spacing Before** to **30 pt** and the **Spacing After** to **6 pt**.

5 Point to the upper left corner of the table, and then click the displayed **table move handle** button to select the entire table. On the **Design tab**, in the **Table Styles group**, click the **Borders button arrow**, and then click **No Border**.

a. On the **Design tab**, in the **Table Styles group**, click the **Borders button arrow** again, and then at the bottom of the gallery, click **Borders and Shading**. In the **Borders and Shading** dialog box, under **Setting**, click **Custom**. Under **Style**, scroll down slightly, and then click the style with two equal lines.

b. Click the **Width arrow**, and then click **1 1/2 pt**. Under **Preview**, click the top border of the preview box, and then click **OK**.

c. Click the **File tab** to display **Backstage** view, and then click the **Print tab** to display the Print Preview.

d. Click the **Info tab**. On the right side, under the document thumbnail, click **Properties**, and then click **Show Document Panel**.

e. In the **Author** box, delete any text and then type your firstname and lastname. In the **Subject** box, type your course name and section number, and in the **Keywords** box type **resume, table**

f. **Close** the **Document Panel**. **Save** and then, as directed by your instructor, print your document or submit it electronically. **Exit** Word.

End **You have completed Project 5C**

Content-Based Assessments

Apply **5B** skills from these Objectives:

- **4** Create a New Document from an Existing Document
- **5** Change and Reorganize Text
- **6** Use the Proofing Options
- **7** Create a Document Using a Template

Skills Review | Project **5D** Ross Letter

In the following Skills Review, you will create a letterhead, and then create a new document from the letterhead to create a resume cover letter. You will also create a short resume using a Microsoft template and save it as a Web page. Your completed documents will look similar to Figure 5.45.

Project Files

For Project 5D, you will need the following files:

New blank Word document
w02D_Letter_Text
Equity Resume Template from Word's installed templates

You will save your documents as:

Lastname_Firstname_2D_Ross_Letterhead
Lastname_Firstname_2D_Ross_Letter
Lastname_Firstname_2D_Resume
Lastname_Firstname_2D_Web_Resume

Project Results

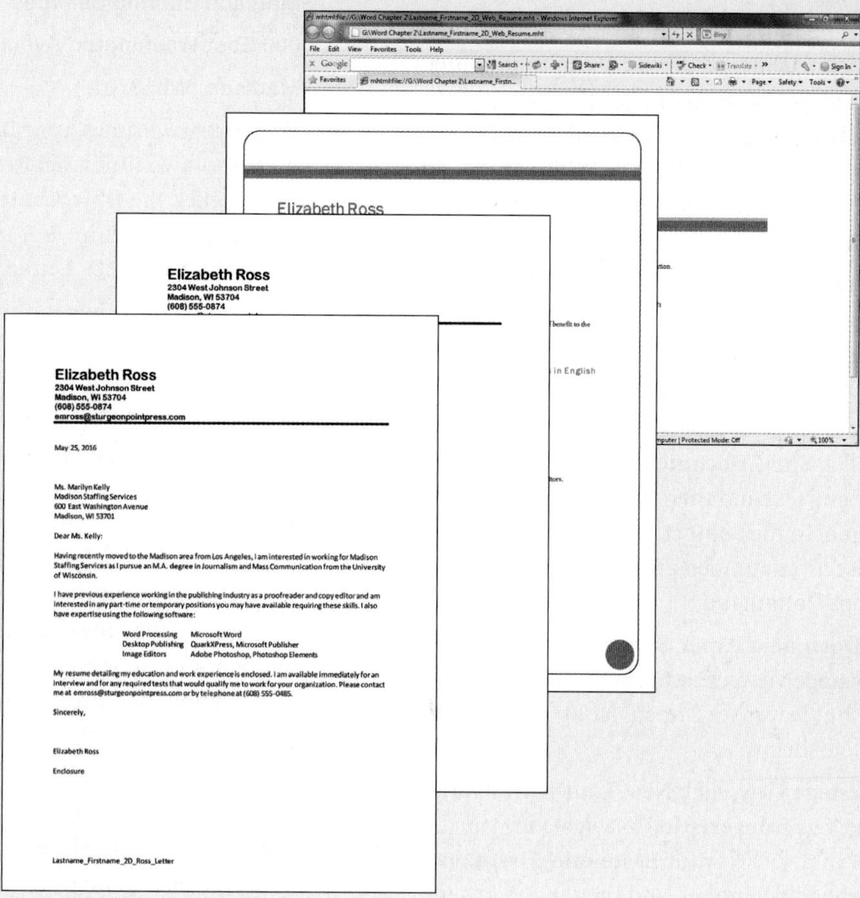

Elizabeth Ross
2304 West Johnson Street
Madison, WI 53704
(608) 555-0874
emross@sturgeonpointpress.com

May 25, 2016

Ms. Marilyn Kelly
Madison Staffing Services
600 East Washington Avenue
Madison, WI 53701

Dear Ms. Kelly:

Having recently moved to the Madison area from Los Angeles, I am interested in working for Madison Staffing Services as I pursue an M.A. degree in Journalism and Mass Communication from the University of Wisconsin.

I have previous experience working in the publishing industry as a proofreader and copy editor and am interested in any part-time or temporary positions you may have available requiring these skills. I also have expertise using the following software:

Word Processing	Microsoft Word
Desktop Publishing	QuarkXPress, Microsoft Publisher
Image Editors	Adobe Photoshop, Photoshop Elements

My resume detailing my education and work experience is enclosed. I am available immediately for an interview and for any required tests that would qualify me to work for your organization. Please contact me at emross@sturgeonpointpress.com or by telephone at (608) 555-0485.

Sincerely,

Elizabeth Ross

Enclosure

Lastname_Firstname_2D_Ross_Letter

Figure 5.45

(Project 5D Ross Letter continues on the next page)

Skills Review | Project 5D Ross Letter (continued)

1 **Start** Word. In the new blank document, be sure that formatting marks and rulers display. On the **Home tab**, in the **Styles group**, click the **No Spacing** button.

a. Type **Elizabeth Ross** and then press Enter. Type **2304 West Johnson Street** and press Enter. Type **Madison, WI 53704** and then press Enter.

b. Type **(608) 555-0874** and then press Enter. Type **emross@sturgeonpointpress.com** and then press Enter three times. If the e-mail address changes to blue text, right-click the e-mail address, and then click Remove Hyperlink.

c. Select all five lines of the personal information, but do not select the blank paragraphs. From the Mini toolbar, change the **Font** to **Arial Rounded MT Bold**. Select the first paragraph—*Elizabeth Ross*—and then on the Mini toolbar, apply **Bold** and change the **Font Size** to **20**.

d. Click anywhere in the fifth line of text—the e-mail address. On the **Home tab**, in the **Paragraph group**, click the **Borders button arrow**, and then click **Borders and Shading**. Under **Style**, click the first style—a single solid line. Click the **Width arrow**, and then click **3 pt**. In the **Preview** area, click the bottom border, and then click **OK**.

e. Display **Backstage** view, and then click **Save As**. Save the document in your **Word Chapter 5** folder as **Lastname_Firstname_2D_Ross_Letterhead**

f. Add the file name to the footer, and then close the footer area. Display **Backstage** view, click **Properties**, and then click **Show Document Panel**. In the **Author** box, delete any text and then type your firstname and lastname. In the **Subject** box, type your course name and section number, and in the **Keywords** box, type **personal letterhead**

g. **Close** the **Document Panel**. **Save** your document. From **Backstage** view, click **Close** to close the document but leave Word open. Hold this file until you complete the project.

2 From **Backstage** view, click **New**. Under **Available Templates**, click **New from existing**. Navigate to your **Word Chapter 5** folder, click your **Lastname_Firstname_2D_Ross_Letterhead** document, and then in the lower right corner, click **Create New**. From **Backstage** view, click **Save As**. Navigate to your **Word Chapter 5** folder, and **Save** the file as **Lastname_Firstname_2D_Ross_Letter** Double-click the footer, right-click the file name, and then click **Update Field**. Close the footer area.

a. From **Backstage** view, display the **Word Options** dialog box. In the **Word Options** list, click **Proofing**, and then under **AutoCorrect options**, click the **AutoCorrect Options** button.

b. In the **AutoCorrect** dialog box, click the **AutoCorrect tab**. Under **Replace**, type **expereince** and under **With**, type **experience** Click **Add**. If the entry already exists, click Replace instead, and then click Yes. Click **OK** two times to close the dialog boxes.

c. Press Ctrl + End, type **May 25, 2016** and then press Enter four times. Type the following inside address using four lines:

Ms. Marilyn Kelly

Madison Staffing Services

600 East Washington Avenue

Madison, WI 53701

d. Press Enter two times, type **Dear Ms. Kelly:** and then press Enter two times. On the **Insert tab**, in the **Text group**, click the **Object button arrow**, and then click **Text from File**. From your student files, locate and insert the file **w02D_Letter_Text**.

e. Scroll to view the lower portion of the page, and be sure your insertion point is in the empty paragraph mark at the end. Press Enter, type **Sincerely,** and then press Enter four times. Type **Elizabeth Ross** and press Enter two times. Type **Enclosure** and then **Save** your document.

f. Near the bottom of the document, locate the paragraph that begins *I am available* and click to position the insertion point at the beginning of the paragraph. Type **My resume detailing my education and work** Press Spacebar and then type the misspelled word **expereince** Press Spacebar and notice that AutoCorrect corrects the misspelling. Type **is enclosed.** and then press Spacebar.

g. Press Ctrl + Home. On the **Home tab**, in the **Editing group**, click the **Replace** button. In the **Find what** box, type **association** In the **Replace with** box, type **organization** and then click **Replace All**. Click **OK** to close the message box, and then **Close** the **Find and Replace** dialog box.

(Project 5D Ross Letter continues on the next page)

Skills Review | Project 5D Ross Letter (continued)

h. In the paragraph that begins *I have previous*, double-click *experience*. Point to the selected word to display the [pointer icon] pointer, and then drag the word to the left of *working*. Adjust spacing as necessary.

i. Below the paragraph that begins *I have previous*, position the insertion point in the second blank line. On the **Insert tab**, in the **Tables group**, click the **Table** button. In the **Table** grid, in the third row, click the second square to insert a 2 × 3 table. Type the following information in the table:

Word Processing	**Microsoft Word**
Desktop Publishing	**QuarkXPress, Microsoft Publisher**
Image Editors	**Adobe Photoshop, Photoshop Elements**

j. Point outside of the upper left corner and click the **table move handle** button to select the entire table. On the **Layout tab**, in the **Cell Size group**, click the **AutoFit** button, and then click **AutoFit Contents**. On the **Home tab**, in the **Paragraph group**, click the **Center** button. On the **Design tab**, in the **Table Styles group**, click the **Borders button arrow**, and then click **No Border**. **Save** your document.

3 If you do not see any wavy red and green lines under words, refer to the Alert in Activity 5.17 to enable the default settings for automatic proofing.

a. In the paragraph that begins *Having lately*, in the second line, locate and right-click the phrase *an M.A. degrees*, and then from the shortcut menu, click *an M.A. degree*. In the same paragraph, locate and right-click *Journlism*. From the shortcut menu, click *Journalism*.

b. Press Ctrl + Home. On the **Review tab**, in the **Proofing group**, click the **Spelling & Grammar** button. In the **Spelling and Grammar** dialog box, click the **Change** button to change *are* to *am*. For the misspelled word *expertis*, under **Suggestions**, be sure *expertise* is selected, and then click **Change**.

c. **Change** *qualifie* to *qualify*, and then click **OK** to close the message box.

d. Near the top of the document, in the paragraph that begins *Having lately*, right-click *lately*. In the shortcut menu, point to **Synonyms**, and then click *recently*. In the same line, right-click *region*, and replace it with the synonym *area*.

e. Display **Backstage** view, click **Properties**, and then click **Show Document Panel**. Type your firstname and lastname as the **Author** and your course number and section as the **Subject**. In the **Keywords** box, replace any existing text with **cover letter** **Close** the **Document Panel**. **Save** your document. From **Backstage** view, **Close** the document but leave Word open. Hold this file until you complete the project.

4 Display **Backstage** view, and then click **New**. Under **Available Templates**, click **Sample templates**. Locate and click **Equity Resume**. In the lower right corner, click **Create**.

a. **Save** the document in your **Word Chapter 5** folder as **Lastname_Firstname_2D_Resume** and then add the file name to the footer—called *First Page Footer* in this template. At the top of the resume, select the text in the first control, which displays the name of the computer at which you are working. Replace this text by typing **Elizabeth Ross** Right-click the name, and then from the shortcut menu, click **Remove Content Control**.

b. Click the *[Type your phone number]* control, and then type **(608) 555-0874** Click the *[Type your address]* control, type **2304 West Johnson Street** and press Enter. Type **Madison, WI 53703**

c. Click the *[Type your e-mail address]* control, and then type **emross@sturgeonpointpress.com** Right-click the *[Type your website]* control, and then from the shortcut menu, click **Remove Content Control**. Press Backspace to remove the *website* line.

d. Click the *[Type the objectives]* control, and then type **A copy editing or proofreading position where my editing and advanced computer skills will be of benefit to the organization.**

e. Under *Education*, click the *[Type the completion date]* control, and then type **University of Wisconsin-Milwaukee, May 2015** Click the *[Type the degree]* control, and then type **Bachelor of Arts in English** For the *[Type list of accomplishments]* bulleted list, type:

Dean's list, six terms

Harriet McArthur Creative Writing Award

(Project 5D Ross Letter continues on the next page)

Skills Review | Project 5D Ross Letter (continued)

Assistant Editor of college newspaper

3.8 GPA

f. Under *Experience*, enter the text shown in **Table 1** below.

g. Click the *[Type list of skills]* control and type **Word Press** Enter, and then type two additional bullet points with **QuarkXPress** and **Adobe Photoshop**

h. Display **Backstage** view, click **Properties**, and then click **Show Document Panel**. Type your firstname and lastname as the **Author**. In the **Subject** box, type your course and section number. In the **Keywords** box, **resume, template Close** the **Document Panel**.

i. **Save** your document.

j. Display **Backstage** view, click **Save As**, and then in the **Save as type** box, click **Single File Web Page**. Navigate to your **Word Chapter 5** folder. In the **File name** box, type **Lastname_Firstname_2D_Web_Resume** Click **Save**.

k. Display **Backstage** view, click **Properties**, and then click **Advanced Properties**. In the **Properties** dialog box, be sure your name displays in the *Author* box, and then in the **Keywords** box, add **HTML** to the list of keywords. Click **OK** and **Save** your document.

l. **Exit** Word. From the **Start** menu, click **Computer** (or My Computer). Navigate to your **Word Chapter 5** folder, and then double-click your **2D_Web_Resume** file to open the resume in your Web browser. **Close** the Web browser. As directed by your instructor, print or submit electronically the four files that are the results of this project—2D_Ross_Letterhead, 2D_Ross_Letter, 2D_Resume, and 2D_Web_Resume.

Table 1

[Type the start date]	**May 2012**
[Type the end date]	**Present-**
[Type the job title]	**Senior Copy Editor**
[Type the company name]	**Sturgeon Point Press**
[Type the company address]	**Milwaukee, WI**
[Type job responsibilities]	**Produced final edited copy of books, technical manuals, and pamphlets; supervised three copy editors.**

(Return to Step 4-g)

End You have completed Project 5D

Apply 5A skills from these Objectives:

1 Create a Table
2 Add Text to a Table
3 Format a Table

Mastering Word | Project 5E Job Listings

In the following Mastering Word project, you will create an announcement for new job postings at Madison Staffing Services. Your completed document will look similar to Figure 5.46.

Project Files

For Project 3E, you will need the following files:

New blank Word document
w02E_New_Jobs

You will save your document as:

Lastname_Firstname_2E_Job_Listings

Project Results

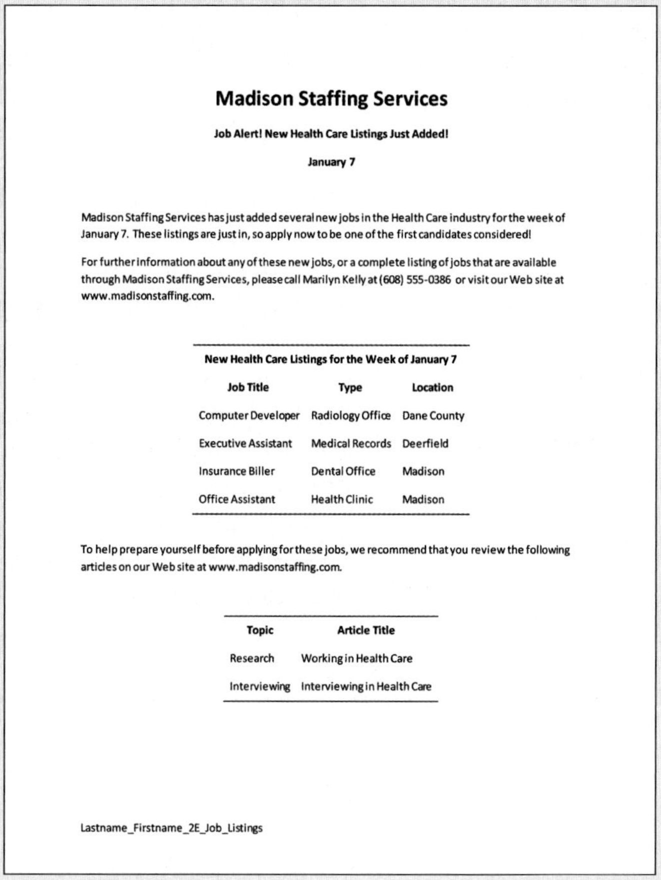

Madison Staffing Services

Job Alert! New Health Care Listings Just Added!

January 7

Madison Staffing Services has just added several new jobs in the Health Care industry for the week of January 7. These listings are just in, so apply now to be one of the first candidates considered!

For further information about any of these new jobs, or a complete listing of jobs that are available through Madison Staffing Services, please call Marilyn Kelly at (608) 555-0386 or visit our Web site at www.madisonstaffing.com.

New Health Care Listings for the Week of January 7

Job Title	Type	Location
Computer Developer	Radiology Office	Dane County
Executive Assistant	Medical Records	Deerfield
Insurance Biller	Dental Office	Madison
Office Assistant	Health Clinic	Madison

To help prepare yourself before applying for these jobs, we recommend that you review the following articles on our Web site at www.madisonstaffing.com.

Topic	Article Title
Research	Working in Health Care
Interviewing	Interviewing in Health Care

Lastname_Firstname_2E_Job_Listings

Figure 5.46

(Project 5E Job Listings continues on the next page)

Content-Based Assessments

Mastering Word | Project 5E Job Listings (continued)

1 **Start** Word and display a new blank document; display formatting marks and rulers. **Save** the document in your **Word Chapter 5** folder as **Lastname_Firstname_2E_Job_Listings** and then add the file name to the footer.

2 Type **Madison Staffing Services** and press Enter. Type **Job Alert! New Health Care Listings Just Added!** and press Enter. Type **January 7** and press Enter two times. **Insert** the file **w02E_New_Jobs**.

3 At the top of the document, select and **Center** the three title lines. Select the title *Madison Staffing Services* and change the **Font Size** to **20** pt and apply **Bold**. Apply **Bold** to the second and third title lines. Locate the paragraph that begins *For further information*, and then below that paragraph, click to position the insertion point in the second blank paragraph. **Insert** a **3** × **4** table. Enter the following:

Job Title	Type	Location
Executive Assistant	Medical Records	Deerfield
Insurance Biller	Dental Office	Madison
Office Assistant	Health Clinic	Madison

4 In the table, click anywhere in the second row, and then insert a row above. Add the following information so that the job titles remain in alphabetic order:

Computer Developer	Radiology Office	Dane County

5 Select the entire table. On the **Layout tab**, in the **Cell Size group**, use the **AutoFit** button to **AutoFit Contents**. With the table still selected, **Center** the table. With the table still selected, on the **Page Layout tab**, add **6 pt Spacing Before** and **6 pt Spacing After**.

6 With the table still selected, remove all table borders, and then add a **Custom 1 pt** solid line top border and bottom border. Select all three cells in the first row, apply **Bold**, and then **Center** the text. Click anywhere in the first row, and then insert a new row above. Merge the three cells in the new top row, and then type **New Health Care Listings for the Week of January 7** Notice that the new row keeps the formatting of the row from which it was created.

7 At the bottom of the document, **Insert** a **2** × **3** table. Enter the following:

Topic	Article Title
Research	Working in Health Care
Interviewing	Interviewing in Health Care

8 Select the entire table. On the **Layout tab**, in the **Cell Size group**, use the **AutoFit** button to **AutoFit Contents**. On the **Home tab**, **Center** the table. On the **Page Layout tab**, add **6 pt Spacing Before** and **6 pt Spacing After**.

9 With the table still selected, remove all table borders, and then add a **Custom 1 pt** solid line top border and bottom border. Select the cells in the first row, apply **Bold**, and then **Center** the text.

10 In the **Document Panel**, add your name and course information and the **Keywords new listings, health care** **Save** and then print or submit the document electronically as directed. **Exit** Word.

You have completed Project 5E

Apply **5B** skills from these Objectives:

- **4** Create a New Document from an Existing Document
- **5** Change and Reorganize Text
- **6** Use the Proofing Options
- **7** Create a Document Using a Template

Mastering Word | Project 5F Job Tips

In the following Mastering Word project, you will create a fax and a memo that includes job tips for Madison Staffing Services employees. Your completed documents will look similar to Figure 5.47.

Project Files

For Project 5F, you will need the following files:

w02F_Memo_Heading
w02F_Memo_Text
Origin Fax template from Word's installed templates

You will save your documents as:

Lastname_Firstname_2F_Job_Tips
Lastname_Firstname_2F_Fax

Project Results

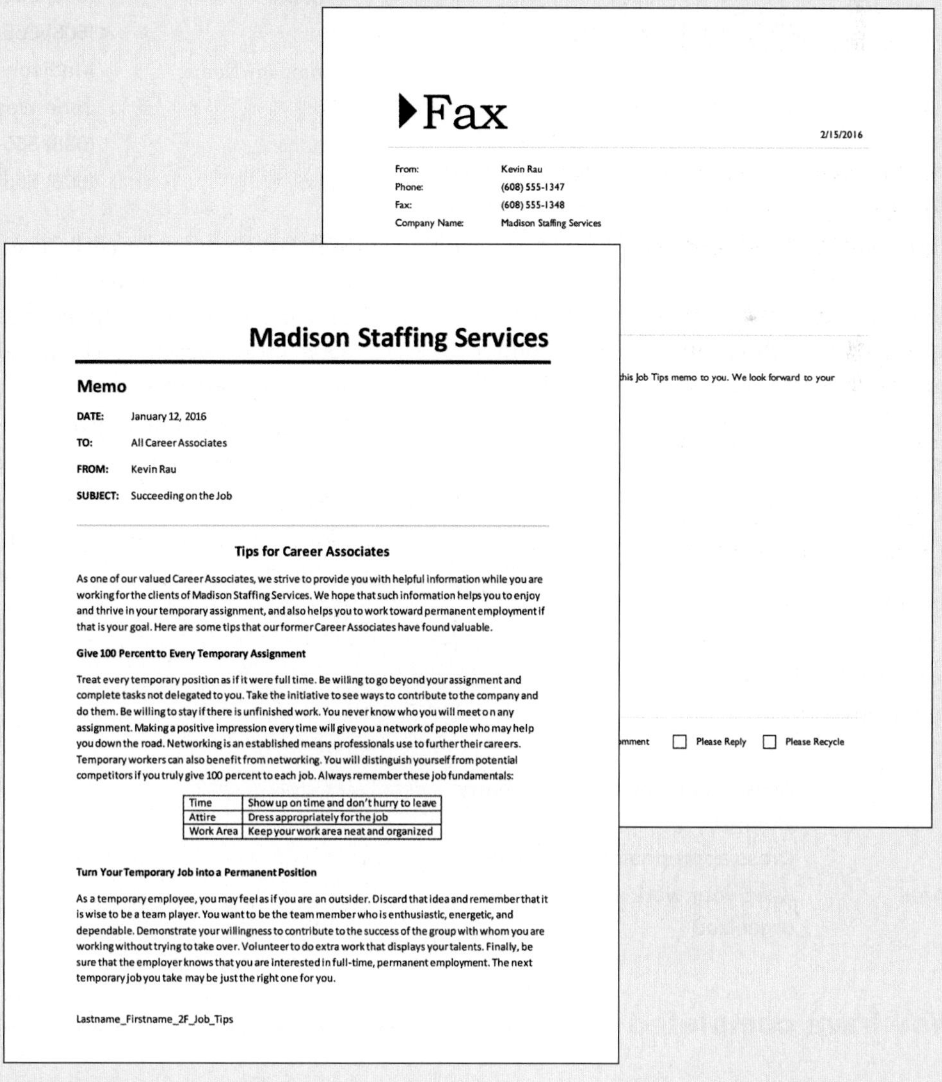

Fax

2/15/2016

From: Kevin Rau
Phone: (608) 555-1347
Fax: (608) 555-1348
Company Name: Madison Staffing Services

...his Job Tips memo to you. We look forward to your

...mment ☐ Please Reply ☐ Please Recycle

Madison Staffing Services

Memo

DATE: January 12, 2016
TO: All Career Associates
FROM: Kevin Rau
SUBJECT: Succeeding on the Job

Tips for Career Associates

As one of our valued Career Associates, we strive to provide you with helpful information while you are working for the clients of Madison Staffing Services. We hope that such information helps you to enjoy and thrive in your temporary assignment, and also helps you to work toward permanent employment if that is your goal. Here are some tips that our former Career Associates have found valuable.

Give 100 Percent to Every Temporary Assignment

Treat every temporary position as if it were full time. Be willing to go beyond your assignment and complete tasks not delegated to you. Take the initiative to see ways to contribute to the company and do them. Be willing to stay if there is unfinished work. You never know who you will meet on any assignment. Making a positive impression every time will give you a network of people who may help you down the road. Networking is an established means professionals use to further their careers. Temporary workers can also benefit from networking. You will distinguish yourself from potential competitors if you truly give 100 percent to each job. Always remember these job fundamentals:

Time	Show up on time and don't hurry to leave
Attire	Dress appropriately for the job
Work Area	Keep your work area neat and organized

Turn Your Temporary Job into a Permanent Position

As a temporary employee, you may feel as if you are an outsider. Discard that idea and remember that it is wise to be a team player. You want to be the team member who is enthusiastic, energetic, and dependable. Demonstrate your willingness to contribute to the success of the group with whom you are working without trying to take over. Volunteer to do extra work that displays your talents. Finally, be sure that the employer knows that you are interested in full-time, permanent employment. The next temporary job you take may be just the right one for you.

Lastname_Firstname_2F_Job_Tips

Figure 5.47

(Project 5F Job Tips continues on the next page)

Content-Based Assessments

Mastering Word | Project 5F Job Tips (continued)

1 **Start** Word; display rulers and formatting marks. In **Backstage** view, create a **New** document using the **New from existing** template. In the **New from Existing Document** dialog box, navigate to your student files, click **w02F_Memo_Heading**, and then click **Create New**.

2 Display the **Document Panel**, add your name and course information and the **Keywords memo, associates**

3 **Save** the document in your **Word Chapter 5** folder as **Lastname_Firstname_2F_Job_Tips** Add the file name to the footer.

4 At the top of your document, in the *DATE* paragraph, click to the right of the tab formatting mark, and then type **January 12, 2016** Use a similar technique to add the following information:

TO:	**All Career Associates**
FROM:	**Kevin Rau**
SUBJECT:	**Succeeding on the Job**

5 Position the insertion point in the blank paragraph below the memo heading. **Insert** the file **w02F_Memo_Text** and press Backspace to remove the blank line at the end of the selected text.

6 Select and **Center** the title *Tips for Career Associates.* By using either the **Spelling and Grammar** dialog box, or by right-clicking selected words, correct all spelling, grammar, and word usage errors.

7 In the first line of the paragraph that begins *Treat every*, locate and right-click *provisional*. Use the shortcut menu to change the word to the synonym *temporary*. In the second line of the same paragraph, change *donate* to the synonym *contribute*.

8 At the end of the paragraph that begins *Treat every temporary*, create a blank paragraph. **Insert** at **2** × **3** table, and then type the following information:

Time	**Show up on time and don't hurry to leave**
Attire	**Dress appropriately for the job**
Work Area	**Keep your work area neat and organized**

9 Select the entire table. **AutoFit Contents**, **Center** the table, and remove the table borders. Display **Backstage** view and preview the document. **Save** and **Close** the document but leave Word open. Hold this file until you complete this project.

10 From **Sample templates**, create a document based on the **Origin Fax** template. Save the document in your **Word Chapter 5** folder as **Lastname_Firstname_2F_Fax** and then add the file name to the footer—called the *First Page Footer* in this template.

11 Click the *Pick a date* placeholder, type **2/15/2016** and then type the following for the remaining controls:

From:	**Kevin Rau**
Phone:	**(608) 555-1347**
Fax:	**(608) 555-1348**
Company Name:	**Madison Staffing Services**
To:	**Jane Westerfield**
Phone:	**(608) 555-0034**
Fax:	**(608) 555-0035**

12 Locate and right-click *Kevin Rau*; remove the content control. Delete the lower *Company Name* text and remove the control to its right. In the *Type comments* control, type **Jane: I know you are on leave, so I thought I would fax this Job Tips memo to you. We look forward to your return.**

13 In the **Document Panel**, add your name and course information and the **Keywords job tips, fax Save** the document.

14 As directed by your instructor, print or submit electronically the two files that are the results of this project. **Exit** Word.

End **You have completed Project 5F**

Apply **5A** and **5B** skills from these Objectives:

1. Create a Table
2. Add Text to a Table
3. Format a Table
4. Create a New Document from an Existing Document
5. Change and Reorganize Text
6. Use the Proofing Options
7. Create a Document Using a Template

Mastering Word | Project 5G Job Letter

In the following Mastering Word project, you will create a new document from an existing document, format a table, and then create a fax cover using a template. Your completed documents will look similar to Figure 5.48.

Project Files

For Project 5G, you will need the following files:

w02G_Letter_Text
w02G_Letterhead
w02G_Resume
Equity Fax template from Word's installed templates

You will save your documents as:

Lastname_Firstname_2G_Job_Letter
Lastname_Firstname_2G_Resume
Lastname_Firstname_2G_Fax

Project Results

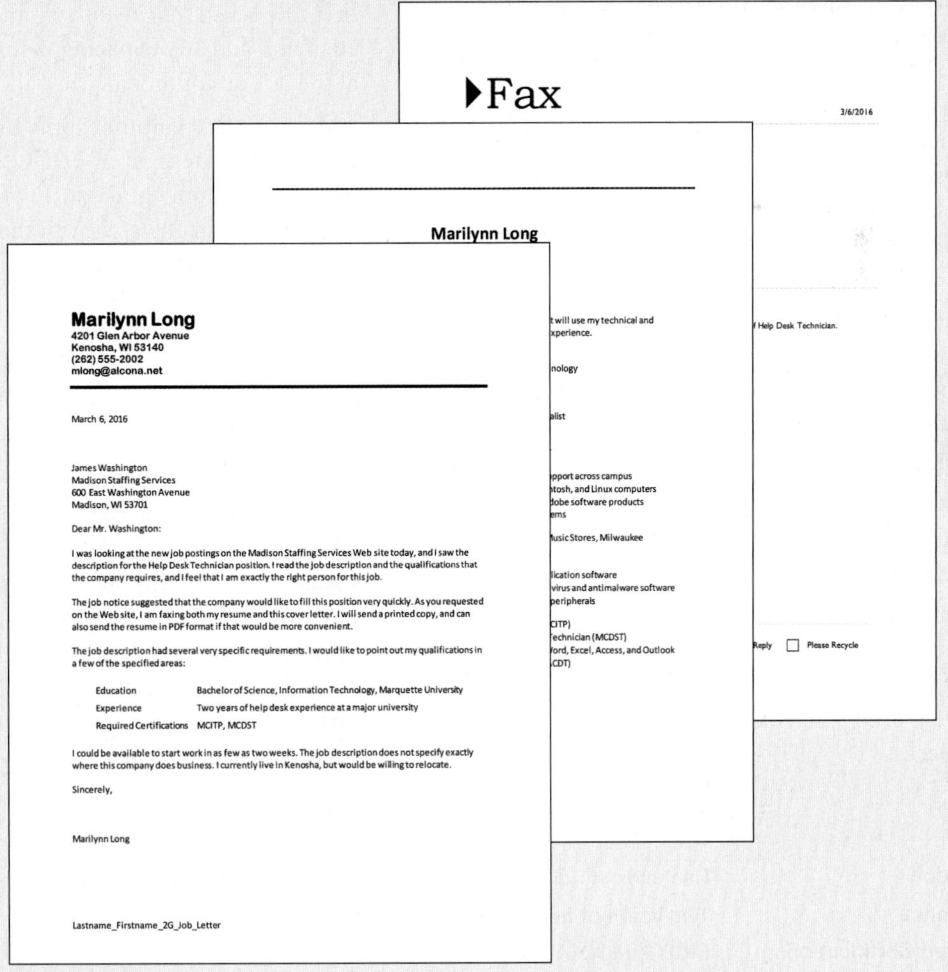
Fax

3/6/2016

Marilynn Long

Marilynn Long
4201 Glen Arbor Avenue
Kenosha, WI 53140
(262) 555-2002
mlong@alcona.net

March 6, 2016

James Washington
Madison Staffing Services
600 East Washington Avenue
Madison, WI 53701

Dear Mr. Washington:

I was looking at the new job postings on the Madison Staffing Services Web site today, and I saw the description for the Help Desk Technician position. I read the job description and the qualifications that the company requires, and I feel that I am exactly the right person for this job.

The job notice suggested that the company would like to fill this position very quickly. As you requested on the Web site, I am faxing both my resume and this cover letter. I will send a printed copy, and can also send the resume in PDF format if that would be more convenient.

The job description had several very specific requirements. I would like to point out my qualifications in a few of the specified areas:

Education	Bachelor of Science, Information Technology, Marquette University
Experience	Two years of help desk experience at a major university
Required Certifications	MCITP, MCDST

I could be available to start work in as few as two weeks. The job description does not specify exactly where this company does business. I currently live in Kenosha, but would be willing to relocate.

Sincerely,

Marilynn Long

Lastname_Firstname_2G_Job_Letter

Figure 5.48

(Project 5G Job Letter continues on the next page)

Content-Based Assessments

Mastering Word | Project 5G Job Letter (continued)

1 **Start** Word and display rulers and formatting marks. By using the **New from existing** template, create a document from the file **w02G_Letterhead**. **Save** the document in your **Word Chapter 5** folder as **Lastname_Firstname_2G_Job_Letter** Add the file name to the footer. Move to the end of the document, and then on the **Home tab**, apply the **No Spacing** style. Type **March 6, 2016** and then press Enter four times. Type the following:

James Washington
Madison Staffing Services
600 East Washington Avenue
Madison, WI 53701

2 Press Enter two times, type **Dear Mr. Washington:** and press Enter two times. **Insert** the text from the file **w02G_Letter_Text** and remove the blank line at the bottom of the selected text.

3 Move to the top of the document, and then by using either the **Spelling and Grammar** dialog box, or by right-clicking selected words, correct spelling, grammar, and word usage errors. In the paragraph that begins *I was looking*, in the third line, locate and right-click *corporation*. Use the shortcut menu to open the **Thesaurus** and change the word to the synonym *company*. In the same line, change *correct* to the synonym *right*.

4 In the paragraph that begins *I currently*, select the first sentence of the paragraph and drag it to the end of the same paragraph. In the second blank line below the paragraph that begins *The job description*, **Insert** a **2 × 3** table, and then type the text shown in **Table 1** below.

5 Select the entire table. **AutoFit Contents**, **Center** the table, remove the table borders, and then add **3 pt** spacing before and after by typing **3** in the **Spacing** boxes and pressing Enter.

6 In the **Document Panel**, add your name and course information and the **Keywords job letter** Preview the document. **Save** and **Close** the document but leave Word open. Hold the file until you complete this project.

7 From your student files, open **w02G_Resume**. **Save** the document in your **Word Chapter 5** folder as **Lastname_Firstname_2G_Resume** Add the file name to the footer.

8 **Insert** a new second row in the table. In the first cell of the new row, type **OBJECTIVE** and then press Tab. Type **To obtain a Help Desk Technician position that will use my technical and communication skills and computer support experience.** In the same cell, add **12 pt Spacing After**.

9 Select the entire table. On the **Layout tab**, **AutoFit Contents**. Remove the table borders, and then display the **Borders and Shading** dialog box. With the table selected, create a **Custom** single solid line **1 1/2 pt** top border.

10 In the first row of the table, select both cells and then **Merge Cells**. **Center** the five lines and apply **Bold**. In the first row, select *Marilynn Long* and change the **Font Size** to **20 pt** and add **36 pt Spacing Before**. In the e-mail address at the bottom of the first row, add **24 pt Spacing After**.

11 In the first column, apply **Bold** to the four headings. In the cell to the right of *EDUCATION*, **Bold** the names of the two schools, and add **12 pt Spacing After** the two lines that begin *September*. In the cell to the right of *RELEVANT EXPERIENCE*, bold the names of the two jobs—*IT Help Desk Specialist* and *Computer Technician*. In the same cell, below the line that begins *January 2014*, apply bullets to the four lines that comprise the job duties. Create a similar bulleted list for the duties as a Computer Technician. Add **12 pt Spacing After** to the last line of each of the bulleted lists.

12 In the cell to the right of *CERTIFICATIONS*, select all four lines and create a bulleted list. In the **Document Panel**, add your name and course information and the **Keywords help desk resume** and then submit your document as directed. **Save** and **Close** the document but leave Word open.

13 From **Sample templates**, create a document based on the **Origin Fax** template. **Save** the document in your **Word**

Table 1

Education	Bachelor of Science, Information Technology, Marquette University
Experience	Two years of help desk experience at a major university
Required Certifications	MCITP, MCDST

(Return to Step 5)

(Project 5G Job Letter continues on the next page)

Mastering Word | Project 5G Job Letter (continued)

Chapter 5 folder as **Lastname_Firstname_2G_Fax** and then add the file name to the footer—called a *First Page Footer* in this template.

14 Type the text shown in **Table 2** for the content controls.

15 Locate and right-click *Marilynn Long*; remove the content control. In the **Document Panel**, add your name and course information and the **Keywords fax cover page** As directed by your instructor, print or submit electronically the three files from this project. **Exit** Word.

Table 2

Pick a date	**3/6/2016**
From:	**Marilynn Long**
Phone:	**(608) 555-0967**
Fax:	**(608) 555-0966**
Company Name:	Remove this content control and row heading
To:	**James Washington, Recruiter**
Phone:	**(608) 555-0034**
Fax:	**(608) 555-0035**
Company Name	**Madison Staffing Services**
Comments:	**Two pages to follow that include my resume and a cover letter for the position of Help Desk Technician.**

(Return to Step 15)

End **You have completed Project 5G**

Apply a combination of the 5A and 5B skills.

GO! Fix It | Project 5H New Jobs

In this project, you will construct a solution by applying any combination of the skills you practiced from the Objectives in Projects 5A and 5B.

Project Files

For Project 5H, you will need the following file:

w02H_New_Jobs

You will save your document as:

Lastname_Firstname_2H_New_Jobs

From the student files that accompany this textbook, locate and open the file w02H_New_Jobs, and then save the file in your Word Chapter 5 folder as **Lastname_Firstname_2H_New_Jobs**

This document contains errors that you must find and correct. Read and examine the document, and then edit to correct the errors that you find and to improve the overall document format. Types of errors could include, but are not restricted to:

- Spelling errors
- Grammar errors
- Word choice errors
- Duplicate words
- Unattractive table column widths
- Title not merged across the top row of the table
- Inconsistent spacing before and after paragraphs in the table

Things you should know to complete this project:

- Viewing the document in Print Preview will help identify some of the problems
- The Spelling and Grammar checker will be useful
- Adjust the column widths *before* merging the title

Save your document and add the file name to the footer. In the Document Panel, type your firstname and lastname in the Author box and your course name and section number in the Subject box. In the Keywords box type **job listings** and then save your document and submit as directed.

End You have completed Project 5H

Apply a combination of the 5A and 5B skills.

GO! Make It | Project 5I Training

Project Files

For Project 5I, you will need the following file:

New blank Word document

You will save your document as:

Lastname_Firstname_2I_Training

Start Word, and then save the file in your Word Chapter 5 folder as **Lastname_Firstname_2I_Training**

Use the skills you practiced in this chapter to create the table shown in Figure 5.49. The first row font is Cambria 16 pt, the remainder is Cambria 14 pt. The spacing after the first row is 36 pt, the spacing at the bottom of the rows is 12 pt.

Add the file name to the footer; in the Document Panel, add your name and course information and the Keywords **online training** Save your document, and then submit as directed.

Project Results

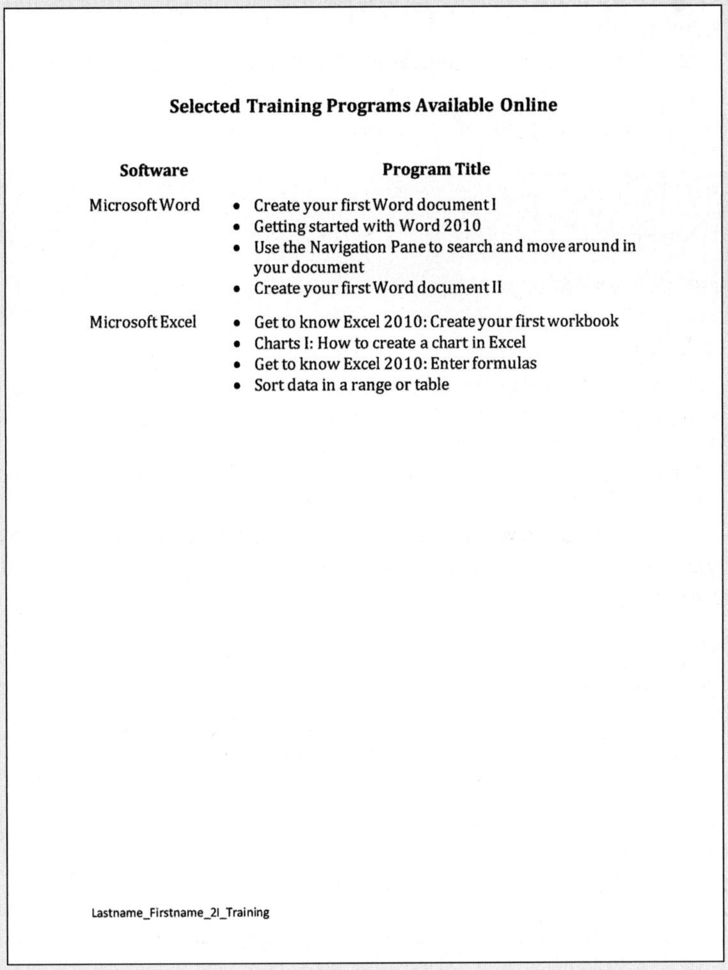

Selected Training Programs Available Online

Software	Program Title
Microsoft Word	• Create your first Word document I • Getting started with Word 2010 • Use the Navigation Pane to search and move around in your document • Create your first Word document II
Microsoft Excel	• Get to know Excel 2010: Create your first workbook • Charts I: How to create a chart in Excel • Get to know Excel 2010: Enter formulas • Sort data in a range or table

Lastname_Firstname_2I_Training

Figure 5.49

End You have completed Project 5I

Apply a combination of the 5A and 5B skills.

GO! Solve It | Project 5J Job Postings

Project Files

For Project 5J, you will need the following files:

New blank Word document
w02J_Job_Postings

You will save your documents as:

Lastname_Firstname_2J_Letterhead
Lastname_Firstname_2J_Job_Postings

Print the w02J_Job_Postings document, and use the information to complete this project. Create a new company letterhead and save it in your Word Chapter 5 folder as **Lastname_Firstname_2J_Letterhead** Add the file name to the footer. Add your name, your course name and section number, and the keyword **letterhead** to the Properties area.

Create a new document based on the existing document you just created. The new document will be a list of new jobs posted by Madison Staffing Services. The job posting should include the letterhead, introductory text, and a table that includes the information about the new jobs that are currently available. The job list should be in table format. Use either two or three columns, and label the columns appropriately. Format the table, the table borders, and the text in an attractive, readable manner.

Save the document as **Lastname_Firstname_2J_Job_Postings** Add the file name to the footer, and add your name, your course name and section number, and the keywords **new jobs** to the Properties area. Submit your two files as directed.

Performance Element	Performance Level: Exemplary: You consistently applied the relevant skills	Proficient: You sometimes, but not always, applied the relevant skills	Developing: You rarely or never applied the relevant skills
Create and format a letterhead template	The text in the letterhead is appropriately formatted, the company name stands out, and the spacing between paragraphs is attractive.	The letterhead is complete, but the line spacing or text formatting is not appropriate for a letterhead.	The spacing and formatting is not appropriate for a letterhead.
Insert a table	The inserted table has the appropriate number of columns and rows to display the information.	The table is not structured to effectively display the information.	No table is inserted in the document.
Format the table structure	Table column widths fit the information, extra space is added between the rows, and borders are attractively formatted.	The column widths do not reflect the amount of information in the column, and the spacing between the cells is insufficient.	Table displays only default column widths and spacing.
Format the text in the table	Important text is highlighted and formatted appropriately, making the text easy to read and interpret.	Some text formatting is added, but the formatting does not highlight the important information.	No text formatting is included.

End You have completed Project 5J

Apply a combination of the 5A and 5B skills.

GO! Solve It | Project 5K Agenda

Project Files

For Project 5K, you will need the following file:

Agenda template from Word's Online templates

You will save your document as:

Lastname_Firstname_2K_Agenda

Create a new document based on an agenda template—such as the *Formal meeting agenda* template—from the Agenda templates at Microsoft Office Online. Save the agenda as **Lastname_Firstname_2K_Agenda** Use the following information to prepare an agenda for a Madison Staffing Services meeting.

The meeting will be chaired by Marilyn Kelly and will be the monthly meeting of the company administrators—Kevin Rau, Marilyn Kelly, Andre Randolph, Susan Nguyen, and Charles James. The meeting will be held on March 15, 2016, at 3:00 p.m. The old business (open issues) include 1) expanding services into the printing and food service industries; 2) recruitment at the UW-Madison and MATC campuses; and 3) the addition of a part-time trainer. The new business will include 1) recruitment at the University of Wisconsin, Milwaukee; 2) rental of office space in or around Milwaukee; 3) purchase of new computers for the training room; and 4) renewal of snow removal service contract.

Add the file name to the footer, and add your name, your course name and section number, and the keywords **agenda, monthly administrative meeting** to the Properties area. Submit as directed.

Performance Element	Performance Level: Exemplary: You consistently applied the relevant skills	Proficient: You sometimes, but not always, applied the relevant skills	Developing: You rarely or never applied the relevant skills
Select an agenda template	Agenda template is appropriate for the information provided for the meeting.	Agenda template is used, but does not fit the information provided.	No template is used for the agenda.
Add appropriate information to the template	All information is inserted in the appropriate places. All unused controls are removed.	All information is included, but not in the appropriate places, and not all of the unused controls are removed.	Information is missing and unused placeholders are not removed.
Format template information	All text in the template is properly aligned and formatted.	All text is included, but alignment or formatting is inconsistent.	No additional formatting has been added.

End **You have completed Project 5K**

Outcomes-Based Assessments

Rubric

The following outcomes-based assessments are *open-ended assessments*. That is, there is no specific correct result; your result will depend on your approach to the information provided. Make *Professional Quality* your goal. Use the following scoring rubric to guide you in *how* to approach the problem and then to evaluate *how well* your approach solves the problem.

The *criteria*—Software Mastery, Content, Format and Layout, and Process—represent the knowledge and skills you have gained that you can apply to solving the problem. The *levels of performance*—Professional Quality, Approaching Professional Quality, or Needs Quality Improvements—help you and your instructor evaluate your result.

	Your completed project is of Professional Quality if you:	**Your completed project is Approaching Professional Quality if you:**	**Your completed project Needs Quality Improvements if you:**
1-Software Mastery	Choose and apply the most appropriate skills, tools, and features and identify efficient methods to solve the problem.	Choose and apply some appropriate skills, tools, and features, but not in the most efficient manner.	Choose inappropriate skills, tools, or features, or are inefficient in solving the problem.
2-Content	Construct a solution that is clear and well organized, contains content that is accurate, appropriate to the audience and purpose, and is complete. Provide a solution that contains no errors in spelling, grammar, or style.	Construct a solution in which some components are unclear, poorly organized, inconsistent, or incomplete. Misjudge the needs of the audience. Have some errors in spelling, grammar, or style, but the errors do not detract from comprehension.	Construct a solution that is unclear, incomplete, or poorly organized; contains some inaccurate or inappropriate content; and contains many errors in spelling, grammar, or style. Do not solve the problem.
3-Format and Layout	Format and arrange all elements to communicate information and ideas, clarify function, illustrate relationships, and indicate relative importance.	Apply appropriate format and layout features to some elements, but not others. Overuse features, causing minor distraction.	Apply format and layout that does not communicate information or ideas clearly. Do not use format and layout features to clarify function, illustrate relationships, or indicate relative importance. Use available features excessively, causing distraction.
4-Process	Use an organized approach that integrates planning, development, self-assessment, revision, and reflection.	Demonstrate an organized approach in some areas, but not others; or, use an insufficient process of organization throughout.	Do not use an organized approach to solve the problem.

Apply a combination of the 5A and 5B skills.

GO! Think | Project 5L Workshops

Project Files

For Project 5L, you will need the following files:

New blank Word document
w02L_Workshop_Information

You will save your document as:

Lastname_Firstname_2L_Workshops

Madison Staffing Services offers a series of workshops for its employee-clients. Any temporary employee who is available during the workshop hours can attend the workshops and there is no fee. Currently, the company offers three-session workshops covering Excel and Word, a two-session workshop covering Business Communication, and a one-session workshop covering *Creating a Resume*.

Print the w02L_Workshop_Information file and use the information to complete this project. Create an announcement with a title, an introductory paragraph, and a table listing the workshops and the topics covered in each workshop. Use the file w02L_Workshop_Information for help with the topics covered in each workshop. Format the table cells appropriately. Add an appropriate footer and information to the Document Panel. Save the document as **Lastname_Firstname_2L_Workshops** and submit it as directed.

End **You have completed Project 5L**

Apply a combination of the 5A and 5B skills.

GO! Think | Project 5M Planner

Project Files

For Project 5M, you will need the following files:

Weekly appointment sheet template from Word's Online templates
w02M_Workshop_Information

You will save your document as:

Lastname_Firstname_2M_Planner

To keep track of workshops provided to employees, the trainer fills out a weekly schedule. Each workshop lasts two hours. Print the w02M_Workshop_Information file and use part or all of the information to complete this project.

Create a new document using a template, for example the *Weekly appointment sheet* template found in the Planners category in the online template list. Create a template for a week, and include the first part of each workshop series, along with the Creating a Resume workshop. Customize the template as necessary to include *Room* and *Workshop* titles for each day of the week. The computer skills workshops are held in the Lab, the others are held in Room 104. The trainer always schedules the hour before each workshop for preparation. Fill out the workshop schedule and use your choice of formatting to indicate that the workshops cover a two-hour period. Add appropriate information to the Document Panel. Save the document as **Lastname_Firstname_2M_Planner** and submit it as directed.

End **You have completed Project 5M**

Outcomes-Based Assessments

Apply a combination of the 5A and 5B skills.

You and GO! | Project 5N Personal Resume

Project Files

For Project 5N, you will need the following file:

New blank Word document

You will save your documents as

Lastname_Firstname_2N_Personal_Resume
Lastname_Firstname_2N_Cover_Letter

Locate and print the information for a job for which you would like to apply, and then create your own personal resume using a table and a cover letter. Include any information that is appropriate, including your objective for a specific job, your experience, skills, education, honors, or awards. Create your own letterhead and cover letter, using the cover letter you created in Project 3B as a guide.

To complete the assignment, be sure to format the text appropriately, resize the table columns in the resume to best display the information, and check both documents for spelling and grammar errors.

Save the resume as **Lastname_Firstname_2N_Personal_Resume** and the cover letter as **Lastname_Firstname_2N_Personal_Cover_Letter** Add the file name to the footer, and add your name, your course name and section number, and the keywords **my resume** and **cover letter** to the Properties area. Submit your file as directed.

You have completed Project 3N

Apply a combination of the 5A and 5B skills.

GO! Collaborate | Project 5O Bell Orchid Hotels Group Running Case

Your instructor may assign this group case project to your class. If your instructor assigns this project, he or she will provide you with information and instructions to work as part of a group. The group will apply the skills gained thus far to help the Bell Orchid Hotel Group achieve its business goals.

End **You have completed Project 5O**

Creating Research Papers, Newsletters, and Merged Mailing Labels

OUTCOMES

At the end of this chapter you will be able to:

OBJECTIVES

Mastering these objectives will enable you to:

PROJECT 6A

Create a research paper that includes citations and a bibliography.

1. Create a Research Paper (p. 275)
2. Insert Footnotes in a Research Paper (p. 277)
3. Create Citations and a Bibliography in a Research Paper (p. 282)

PROJECT 6B

Create a multiple-column newsletter and merged mailing labels.

4. Format a Multiple-Column Newsletter (p. 291)
5. Use Special Character and Paragraph Formatting (p. 296)
6. Create Mailing Labels Using Mail Merge (p. 299)

Shutterstock

In This Chapter

Microsoft Word provides many tools for creating complex documents. For example, Word has tools that enable you to create a research paper that includes citations, footnotes, and a bibliography. You can also create multiple-column newsletters, format the nameplate at the top of the newsletter, use special character formatting to create distinctive title text, and add borders and shading to paragraphs to highlight important information.

In this chapter, you will edit and format a research paper, create a two-column newsletter, and then create a set of mailing labels to mail the newsletter to multiple recipients.

The projects in this chapter relate to **Memphis Primary Materials** located in the Memphis area. In addition to collecting common recyclable materials, the company collects and recycles computers, monitors, copiers and fax machines, cell phones, wood pallets, and compostable materials. The company's name comes from the process of capturing the "primary materials" of used items for reuse. Memphis Primary Materials ensures that its clients comply with all state and local regulations. They also provide training to clients on the process and benefits of recycling.

Project 6A Research Paper

Project Activities

In Activities 6.01 through 6.07, you will edit and format a research paper that contains an overview of recycling activities in which businesses can engage. This paper was created by Elizabeth Freeman, a student intern working for Memphis Primary Metals, and will be included in a customer information packet. Your completed document will look similar to Figure 6.1.

Project Files

For Project 6A, you will need the following file:

w03A_Green_Business

You will save your document as:

Lastname_Firstname_3A_Green_Business

Project Results

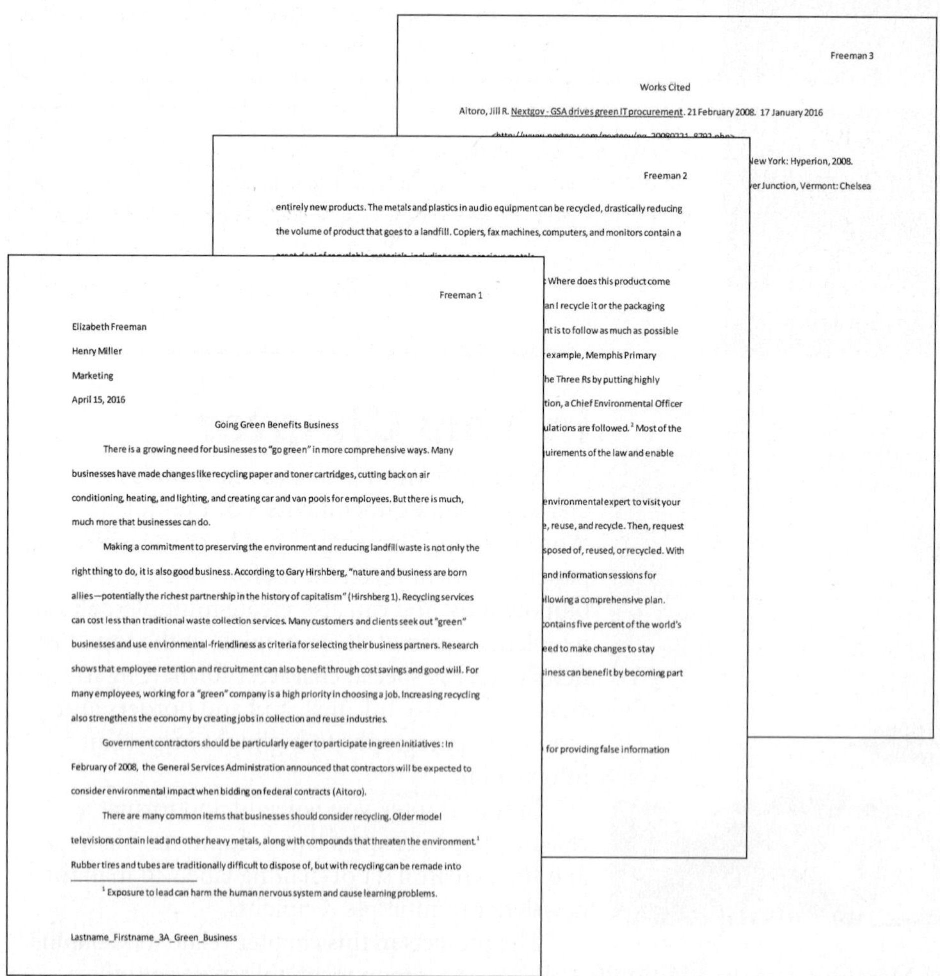

Freeman 3

Works Cited

Aitoro, Jill R. Nextgov - GSA drives green IT procurement. 21 February 2008. 17 January 2016

Freeman 2

entirely new products. The metals and plastics in audio equipment can be recycled, drastically reducing the volume of product that goes to a landfill. Copiers, fax machines, computers, and monitors contain a

Freeman 1

Elizabeth Freeman

Henry Miller

Marketing

April 15, 2016

Going Green Benefits Business

There is a growing need for businesses to "go green" in more comprehensive ways. Many businesses have made changes like recycling paper and toner cartridges, cutting back on air conditioning, heating, and lighting, and creating car and van pools for employees. But there is much, much more that businesses can do.

Making a commitment to preserving the environment and reducing landfill waste is not only the right thing to do, it is also good business. According to Gary Hirshberg, "nature and business are born allies—potentially the richest partnership in the history of capitalism" (Hirshberg 1). Recycling services can cost less than traditional waste collection services. Many customers and clients seek out "green" businesses and use environmental-friendliness as criteria for selecting their business partners. Research shows that employee retention and recruitment can also benefit through cost savings and good will. For many employees, working for a "green" company is a high priority in choosing a job. Increasing recycling also strengthens the economy by creating jobs in collection and reuse industries.

Government contractors should be particularly eager to participate in green initiatives: In February of 2008, the General Services Administration announced that contractors will be expected to consider environmental impact when bidding on federal contracts (Aitoro).

There are many common items that businesses should consider recycling. Older model televisions contain lead and other heavy metals, along with compounds that threaten the environment.[1] Rubber tires and tubes are traditionally difficult to dispose of, but with recycling can be remade into

[1] Exposure to lead can harm the human nervous system and cause learning problems.

Lastname_Firstname_3A_Green_Business

Figure 6.1
Project 6A Green Business

Objective 1 | Create a Research Paper

When you write a research paper or a report for college or business, follow a format prescribed by one of the standard ***style guides***—a manual that contains standards for the design and writing of documents. The two most commonly used styles for research papers are those created by the ***Modern Language Association (MLA)*** and the ***American Psychological Association (APA)***; there are several others.

Activity 6.01 | Formatting Text and Page Numbers in a Research Paper

When formatting the text for your research paper, refer to the standards for the style guide that you have chosen. In this activity, you will create a research paper using the MLA style. The MLA style uses 1-inch margins, a 0.5″ first line indent, and double spacing throughout the body of the document, with no extra space above or below paragraphs.

1. **Start** Word. From your student files, locate and open the document **w03A_Green_Business.** If necessary, display the formatting marks and rulers. In the location where you are storing your projects for this chapter, create a new folder named **Word Chapter 6** and then save the file in the folder as **Lastname_Firstname_3A_Green_Business**

2. Press Ctrl + A to select the entire document. On the **Home tab**, in the **Paragraph group**, click the **Line and Paragraph Spacing** button, and then change the line spacing to **2.0.** On the **Page Layout tab**, in the **Paragraph group**, change the **Spacing After** to **0 pt**.

3. Press Ctrl + Home to deselect and move to the top of the document. Press Enter one time to create a blank line at the top of the document, and then click to position the insertion point in the blank line. Type **Elizabeth Freeman** and press Enter.

4. Type **Henry Miller** and press Enter. Type **Marketing** and press Enter. Type **April 15, 2016** and press Enter. Type **Going Green Benefits Business** Right-click anywhere in the line you just typed, and then on the Mini toolbar, click the **Center** button. Compare your screen with Figure 6.2.

Figure 6.2

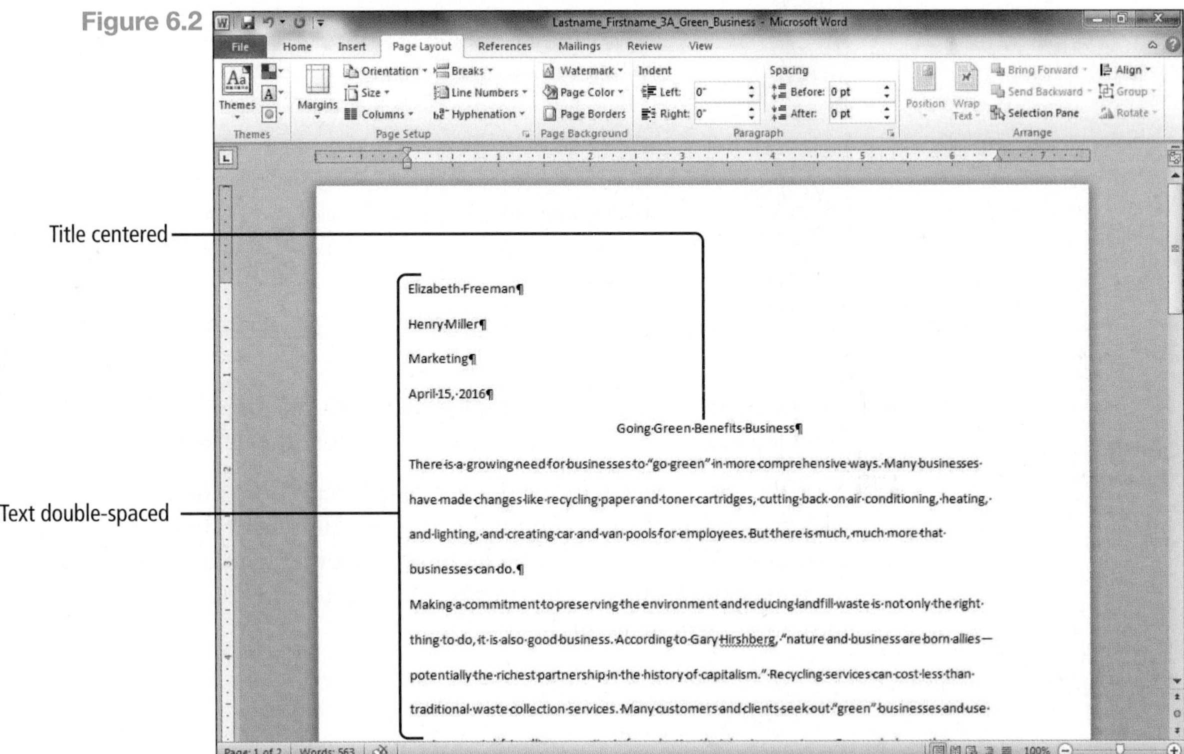

More Knowledge | Creating a Document Heading for a Research Paper

On the first page of an MLA-style research paper, on the first line, type the report author. On the second line, type the person for whom the report is prepared—for example, your professor or supervisor. On the third line, type the name of the class or department or organization. On the fourth line, type the date. On the fifth line type the report title and center it.

5 At the top of the **Page 1**, point anywhere in the white top margin area, right-click, and then click **Edit Header**. In the header area, type **Freeman** and then press Spacebar.

Recall that the text you insert into a header or footer displays on every page of a document. Within a header or footer, you can insert many different types of information; for example, automatic page numbers, the date, the time, the file name, or pictures.

6 On the **Design tab**, in the **Header & Footer group**, click the **Page Number** button, and then point to **Current Position**. In the displayed gallery, under **Simple**, click **Plain Number**. Compare your screen with Figure 6.3.

Word will automatically number the pages using this number format.

Figure 6.3

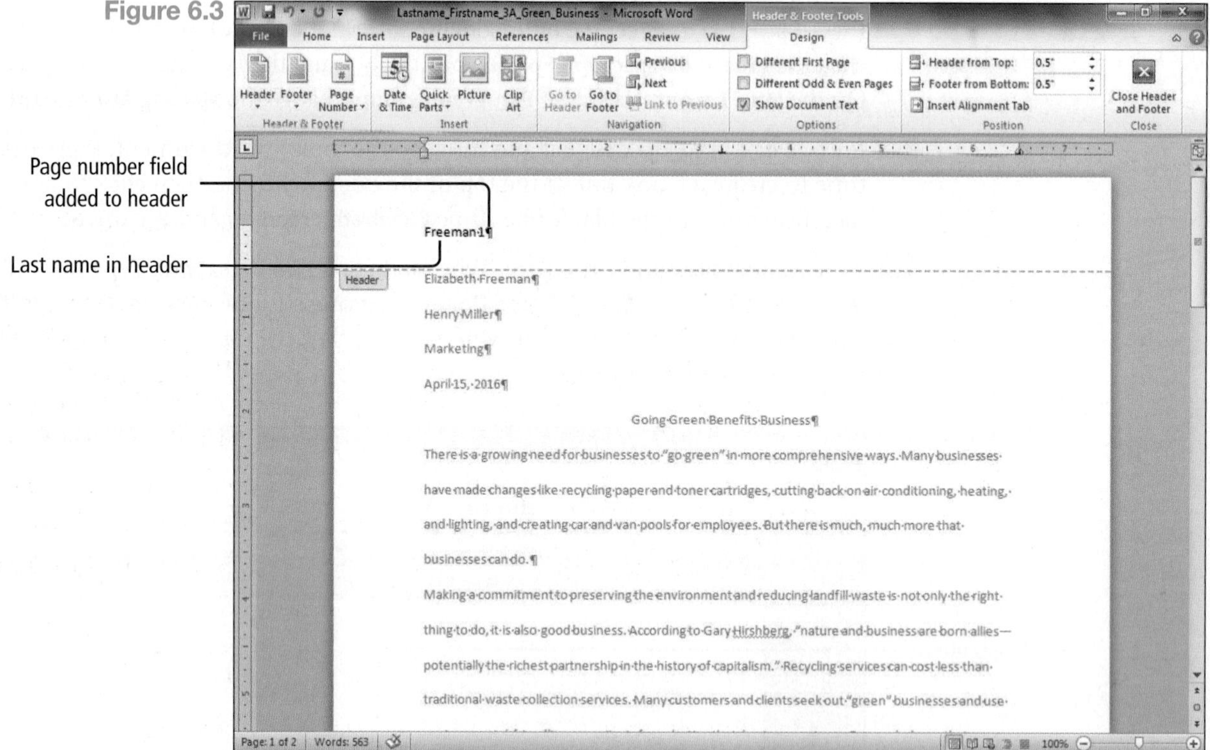

7 On the **Home tab**, in the **Paragraph group**, click the **Align Text Right** button. Double-click anywhere in the document to close the header area.

8 Near the top of **Page 1**, locate the paragraph beginning *There is a growing*, and then click to position the insertion point at the beginning of the paragraph. By moving the vertical scroll bar, scroll to the end of the document, hold down Shift, and then click to right of the last paragraph mark to select all of the text from the insertion point to the end of the document. Release Shift.

Another Way

Right-click the selected text, click Paragraph, on the Indents and Spacing tab, under Indentation, click the Special arrow, and then click First line. Under Indentation, in the By box, be sure 0.5" displays.

9 With the text selected, on the ruler, point to the **First Line Indent** button, and then drag the button to **0.5" on the horizontal ruler**. Compare your screen with Figure 6.4.

The MLA style uses 0.5-inch indents at the beginning of the first line of every paragraph. Indenting—moving the beginning of the first line of a paragraph to the right or left of the rest of the paragraph—provides visual cues to the reader to help divide the document text and make it easier to read.

Figure 6.4

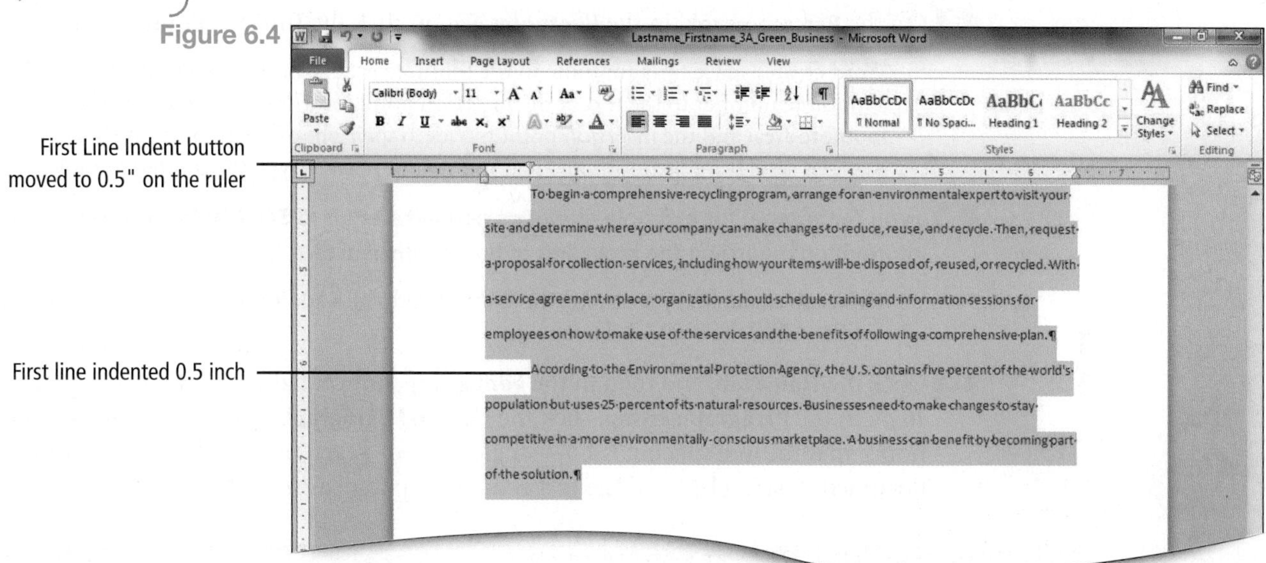

10 Click anywhere to deselect the text. Scroll to view the bottom of **Page 1**, point anywhere in the bottom white margin area, right-click, and then click **Edit Footer**. On the **Design tab**, in the **Insert group**, click the **Quick Parts** button, and then click **Field**. In the **Field** dialog box, under **Field names**, locate and click **FileName**, and then click **OK**.

The file name in the footer is *not* part of the research report format, but it is included in projects in this textbook so that you and your instructor can identify your work.

11 Double-click anywhere in the document to close the Footer area, and then **Save** your document.

More Knowledge | Suppressing the Page Number on the First Page

Some style guidelines require that the page number and other header and footer information on the first page be hidden from view—*suppressed*. To hide the information contained in the header and footer areas on Page 1 of a document, double-click in the header or footer area. Then, on the Design tab, in the Options group, select the Different First Page check box.

Objective 2 | Insert Footnotes in a Research Paper

Reports and research papers typically include information that you find in other sources, and these must be credited. Within report text, numbers mark the location of ***notes***—information that expands on the topic being discussed but that does not fit well in the document text. The numbers refer to ***footnotes***—notes placed at the bottom of the page containing the note, or to ***endnotes***—notes placed at the end of a document or chapter.

Activity 6.02 | Inserting Footnotes

Footnotes can be added as you type the document or after the document is complete. Word renumbers the footnotes automatically, so footnotes do not need to be entered in order, and if one footnote is removed, the remaining footnotes renumber automatically.

1 Scroll to view the top of **Page 2**. Locate the paragraph that begins *Consumers and businesses*. In the seventh line of text, toward the end of the line, click to position the insertion point to the right of the period after *followed*.

2 On the **References tab**, in the **Footnotes group**, click the **Insert Footnote** button.

Word creates space for a footnote in the footnote area at the bottom of the page and adds a footnote number to the text at the insertion point location. Footnote *1* displays in the footnote area, and the insertion point moves to the right of the number. A short black line is added just above the footnote area. You do not need to type the footnote number.

3 Type **Tennessee, for example, imposes penalties of up to $10,000 for providing false information regarding the recycling of hazardous waste.**

This is an explanatory footnote; the footnote provides additional information that does not fit well in the body of the report.

4 Click the **Home tab**, and then in the **Font group**, notice that the font size of the footer is *10 pt*. In the **Paragraph group**, click the **Line and Paragraph Spacing** button, and notice that the line spacing is *1.0*—single-spaced—even though the font size of the document text is 11 pt and the text is double spaced, as shown in Figure 6.5.

Figure 6.5

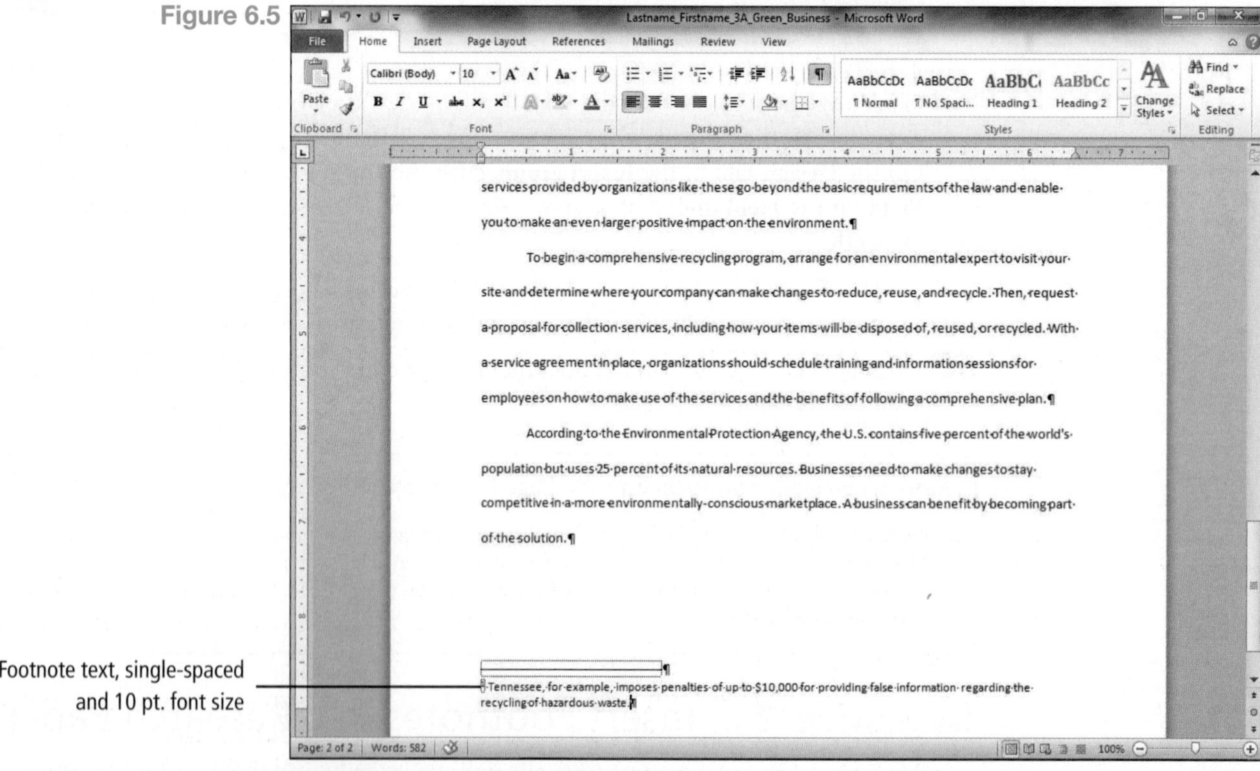

5 Scroll to view the bottom of **Page 1**, and then locate the paragraph that begins *There are many common*. At the end of the second line of text, click to position the insertion point to the right of the period following *environment*.

6 On the **References tab**, in the **Footnotes group**, click the **Insert Footnote** button. Type **Exposure to lead can harm the human nervous system and cause learning problems.** Notice that the footnote you just added becomes the new footnote *1*, as shown in Figure 6.6.

The first footnote is renumbered as footnote *2*.

Figure 6.6

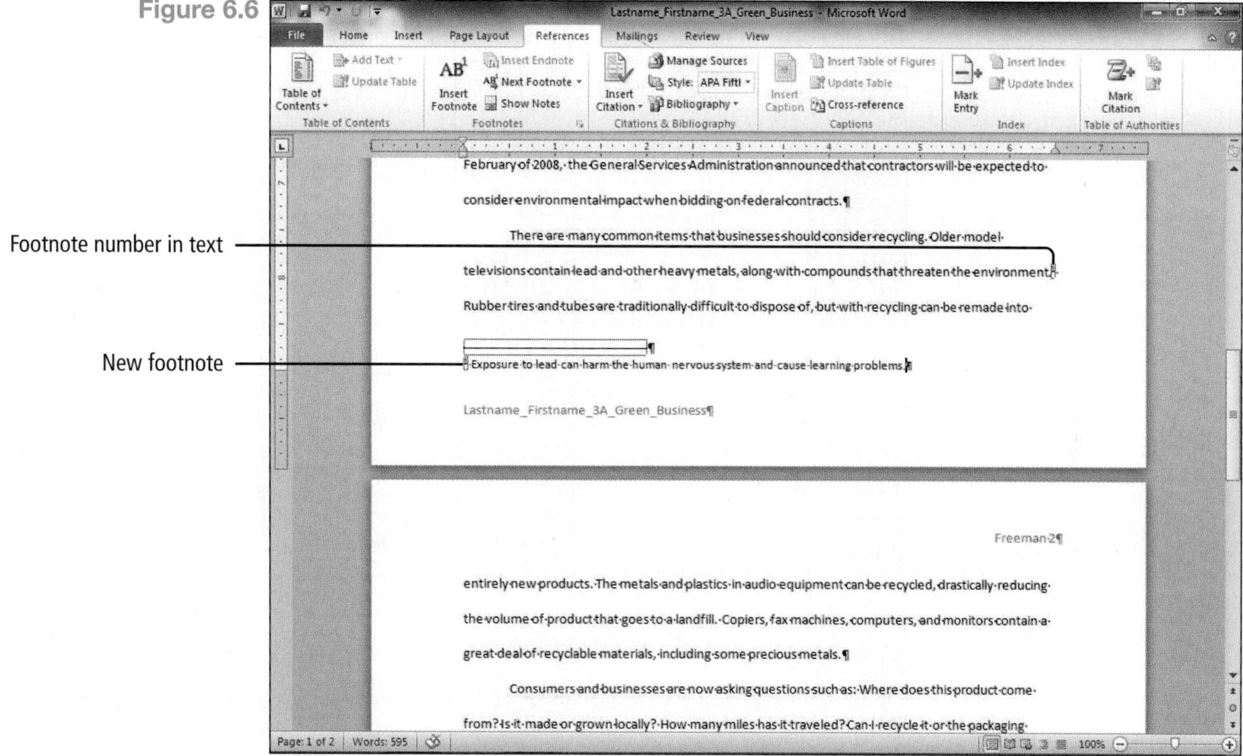

7 **Save** your document.

> **More Knowledge | Using Symbols Rather Than Numbers for Notes**
>
> Instead of using numbers to designate footnotes, you can use standard footnote symbols. The seven traditional symbols, available from the Footnote and Endnote dialog box, in order, are * (asterisk), † (dagger), ‡ (double dagger), § (section mark), || (parallels), ¶ (paragraph mark), and # (number or pound sign). This sequence can be continuous (this is the default setting), or can begin anew with each page.

Activity 6.03 | Modifying a Footnote Style

Microsoft Word contains built-in paragraph formats called ***styles***—groups of formatting commands, such as font, font size, font color, paragraph alignment, and line spacing—which can be applied to a paragraph with one command.

The default style for footnote text is a single-spaced paragraph that uses a 10-point Calibri font and no paragraph indents. MLA style specifies double-spaced text in all areas of a research paper—including footnotes. According to the MLA style, first lines of footnotes must also be indented 0.5 inch and use the same font size as the report text.

1 Scroll to view the bottom of **Page 2**. Point anywhere in the footnote text and right-click, and then from the shortcut menu, click **Style**. Compare your screen with Figure 6.7.

The Style dialog box displays, listing the styles currently in use in the document, in addition to some of the word processing elements that come with special built-in styles. Because you right-clicked on the footnote text, the selected style is the Footnote Text style.

Figure 6.7

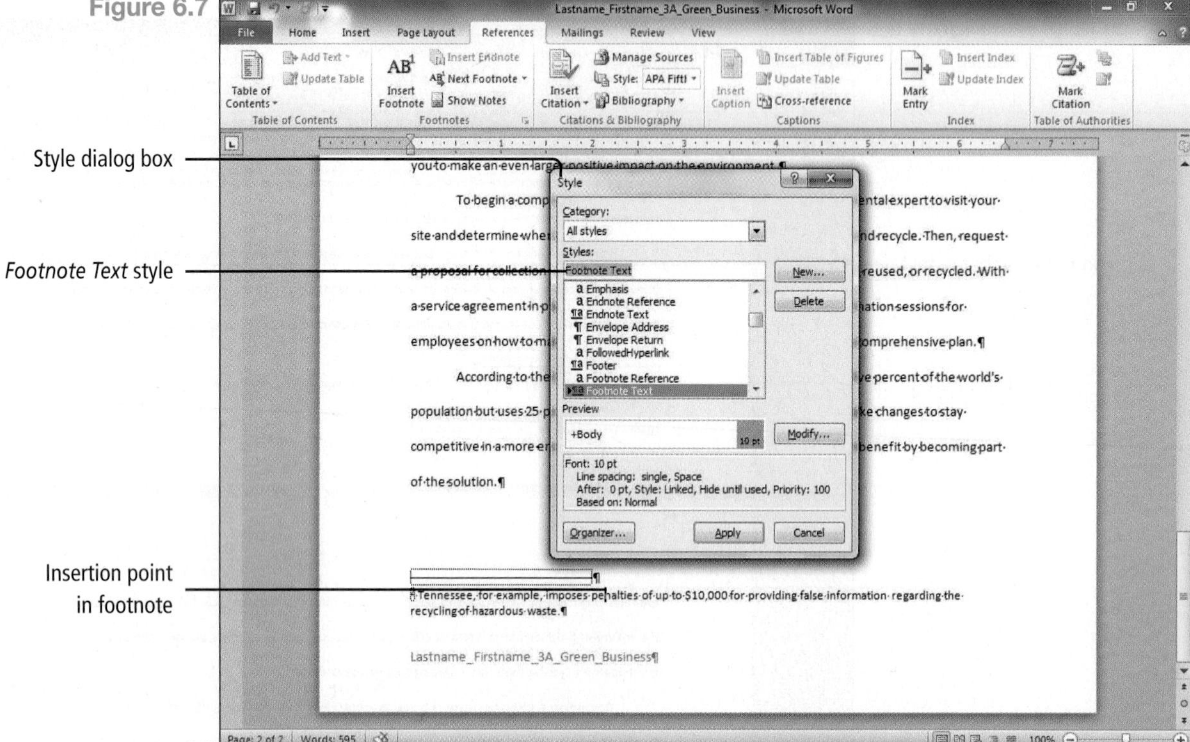

2 In the **Style** dialog box, click the **Modify** button to display the **Modify Style** dialog box.

3 In the **Modify Style** dialog box, locate the small **Formatting** toolbar in the center of the dialog box, click the **Font Size button arrow**, click **11**, and then compare your screen with Figure 6.8.

Figure 6.8

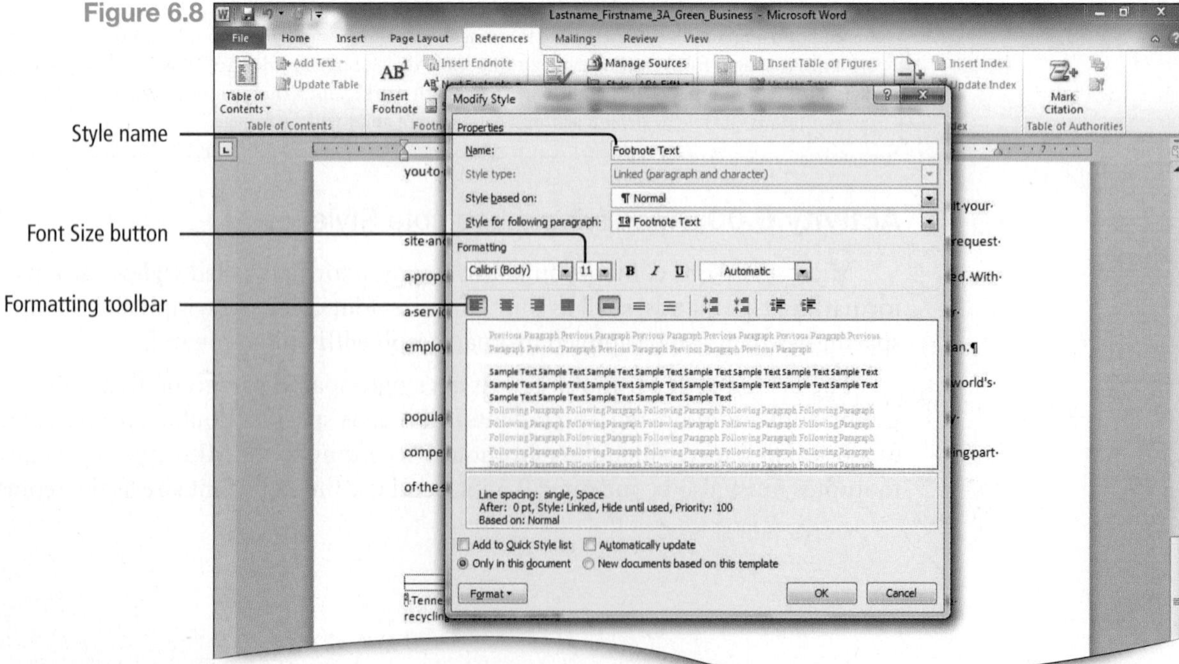

4 In the lower left corner of the dialog box, click the **Format** button, and then click **Paragraph**. In the **Paragraph** dialog box, under **Indentation**, click the **Special arrow**, and then click **First line**.

5 Under **Spacing**, click the **Line spacing** button arrow, and then click **Double**. Compare your dialog box with Figure 6.9.

Figure 6.9

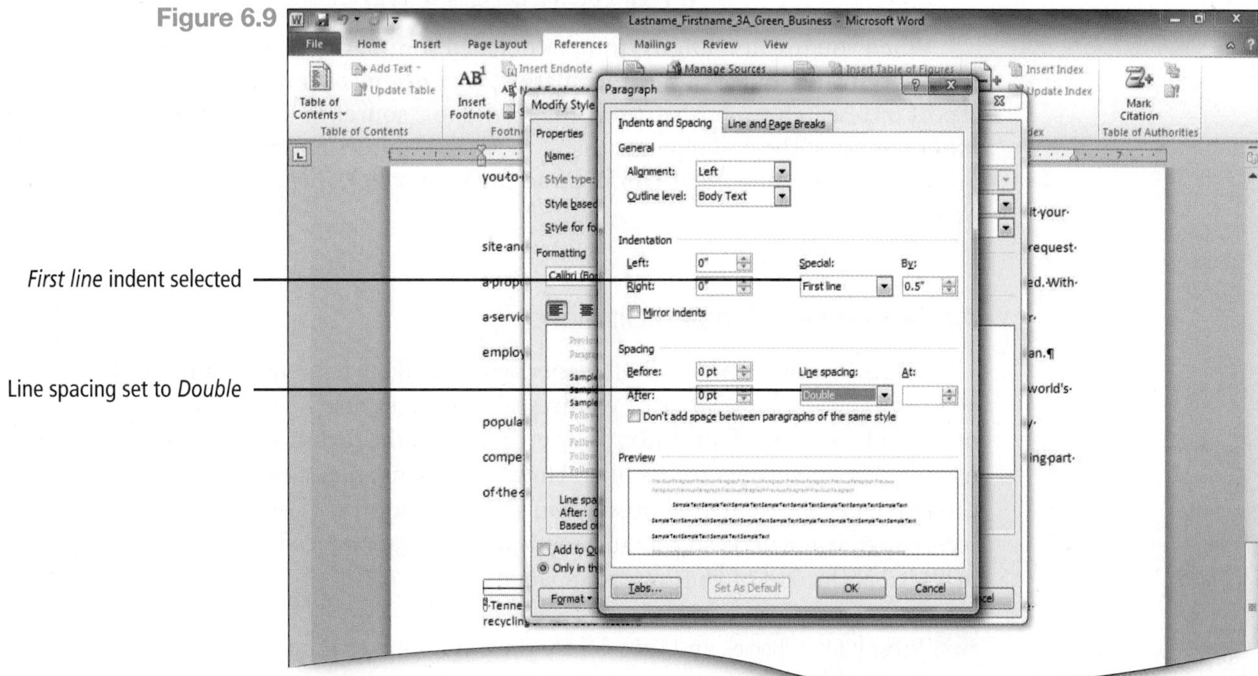

6 Click **OK** to close the **Paragraph** dialog box, click **OK** to close the **Modify Style** dialog box, and then click **Apply** to apply the new style. Notice that when you click Apply, the Style dialog box closes. Compare your screen with Figure 6.10.

Your inserted footnotes are formatted with the new Footnote Text paragraph style; any new footnotes that you insert will also use this format.

Figure 6.10

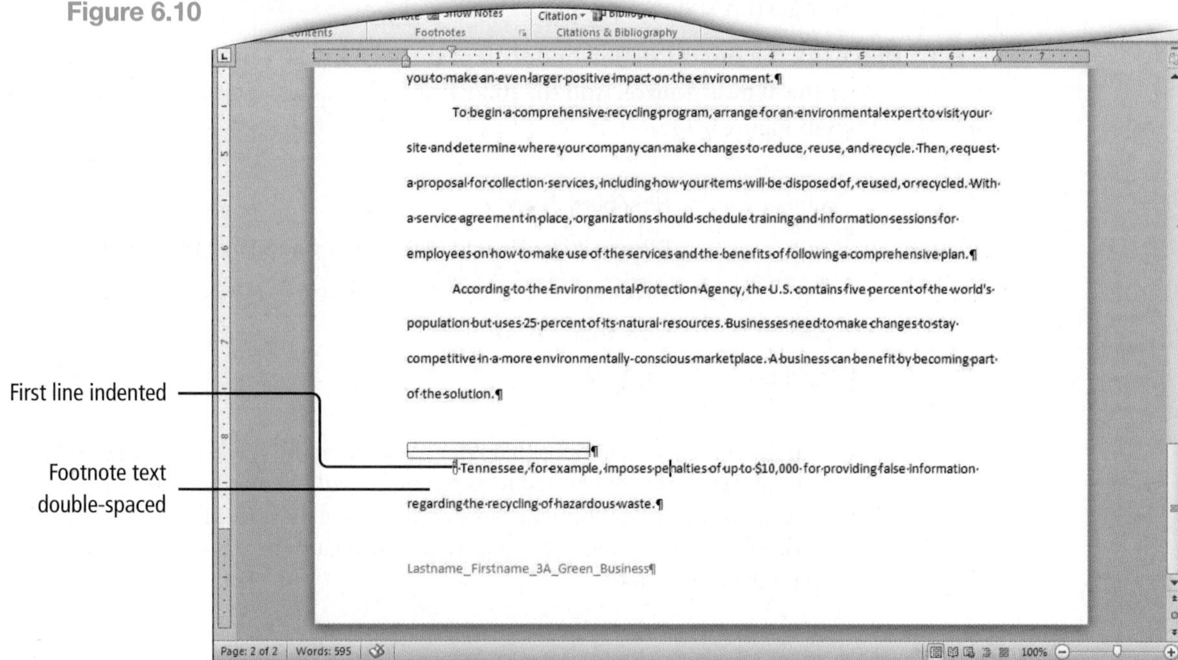

7 Scroll to view the bottom of **Page 1** to confirm that the new format was also applied to the first footnote, and then **Save** your document.

Objective 3 | Create Citations and a Bibliography in a Research Paper

When you use quotations from, or detailed summaries of, other people's work, you must specify the source of the information. A ***citation*** is a note inserted into the text of a report or research paper that refers the reader to a source in the bibliography. Create a ***bibliography*** at the end of a document to list the sources referred to in the document. Such a list is typically titled ***Works Cited*** (in MLA style), *Bibliography*, *Sources*, or *References*.

Activity 6.04 | Adding Citations

When writing a long research paper, you will likely reference numerous books, articles, and Web sites. Some of your research sources may be referenced many times, others only one time. References to sources within the text of your research paper are indicated in an *abbreviated* manner. However, as you enter a citation for the first time, you can also enter the *complete* information about the source. Then, when you have finished your paper, you will be able to automatically generate the list of sources that must be included at the end of your research paper.

1 Press Ctrl + Home, and then locate the paragraph that begins *Making a commitment*. In the third line, following the word *capitalism*, click to position the insertion point to the right of the quotation mark.

The citation in the document points to the full source information in the bibliography, which typically includes the name of the author, the full title of the work, the year of publication, and other publication information.

2 On the **References tab**, in the **Citations & Bibliography group**, click the **Style button arrow**, and then click **MLA Sixth Edition** (or the latest edition) to insert a reference using MLA style.

3 Click the **Insert Citation** button, and then click **Add New Source**. Be sure *Book* is selected as the **Type of Source**. Add the following information, and then compare your screen with Figure 6.11:

Author:	**Hirshberg, Gary**
Title:	**Stirring it Up: How to Make Money and Save the World**
Year:	**2008**
City:	**New York**
Publisher:	**Hyperion**

In the MLA style, citations that refer to items on the *Works Cited* page are placed in parentheses and are referred to as ***parenthetical references***—references that include the last name of the author or authors and the page number in the referenced source, which you add to the reference. No year is indicated, and there is no comma between the name and the page number.

Figure 6.11

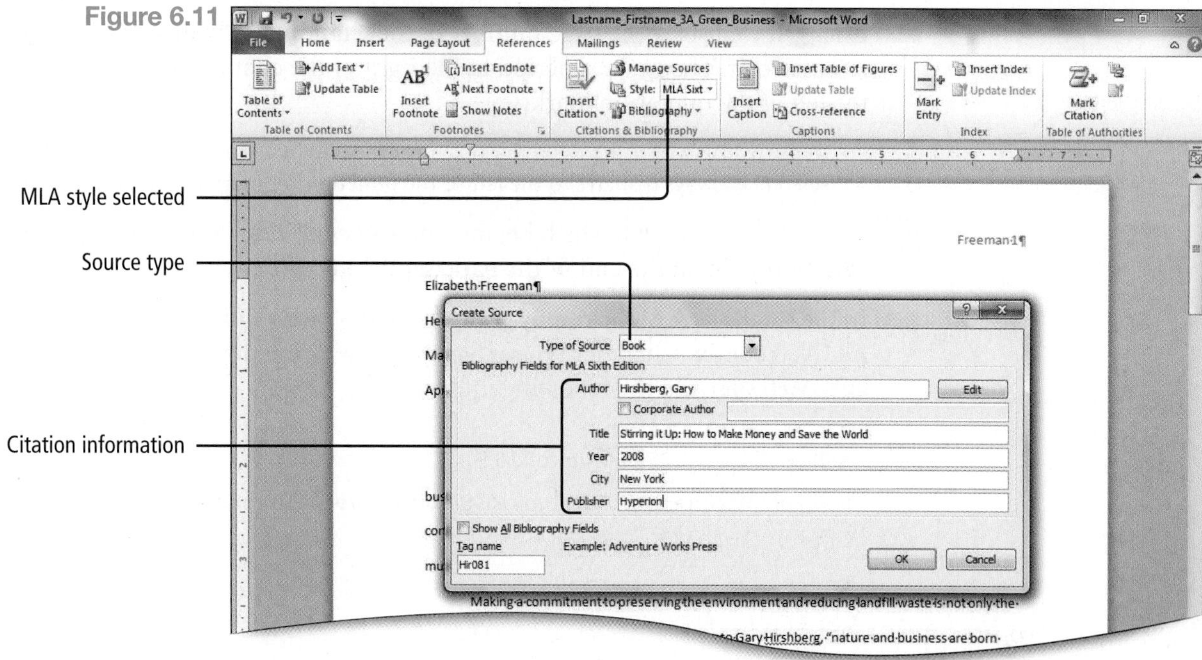

Note | Citing Corporate Authors

If the author of a document is identified as the name of an organization only, select the Corporate Author check box and type the name of the organization in the Corporate Author box.

4 Click **OK** to insert the citation. In the paragraph, point to *(Hirshberg)* and click one time to select the citation.

5 In the lower right corner of the box that surrounds the reference, point to the small arrow to display the ScreenTip *Citation Options*. Click this **Citation Options arrow**, and then from the list of options, click **Edit Citation**.

6 In the **Edit Citation** dialog box, under **Add**, in the **Pages** box, type **1** to indicate that you are citing from page 1 of this source. Compare your screen with Figure 6.12.

Figure 6.12

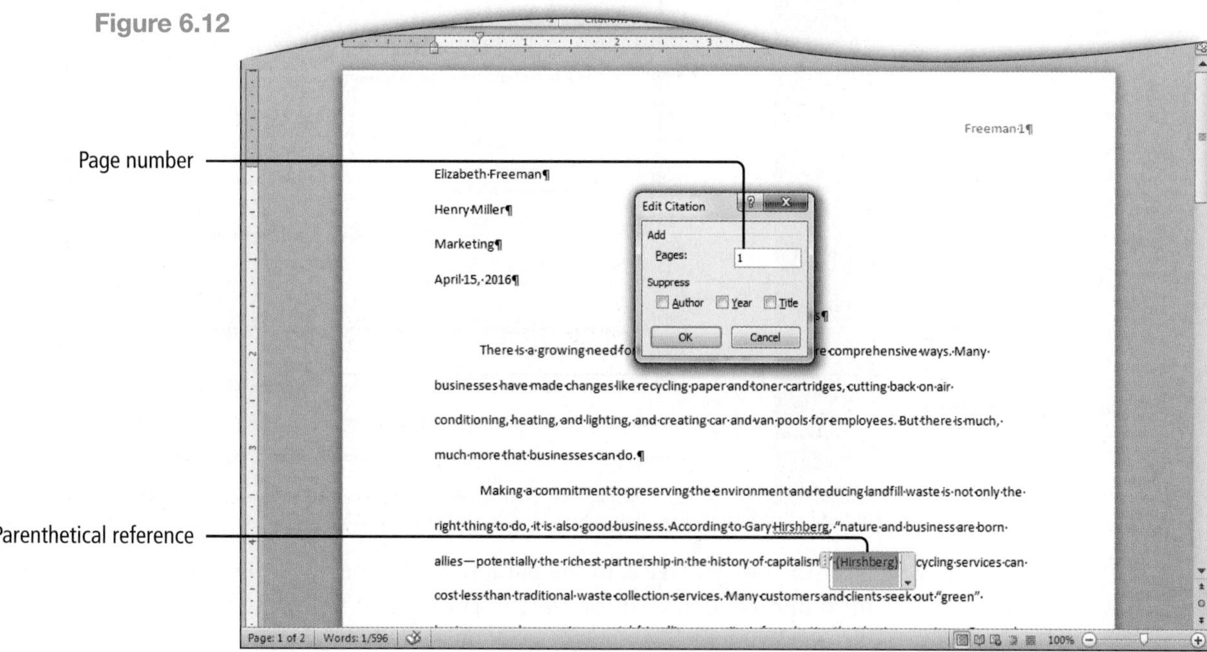

7 Click **OK** to display the page number of the citation. Click outside of the citation box to deselect it. Then type a period to the right of the citation, and delete the period to the left of the quotation mark.

In the MLA style, if the reference occurs at the end of a sentence, the parenthetical reference always displays to the left of the punctuation mark that ends the sentence.

8 In the next paragraph, which begins *Government contractors*, click to position the insertion point at the end of the paragraph, but before the period.

9 In the **Citations & Bibliography group**, click the **Insert Citation** button, and then click **Add New Source**. Click the **Type of Source arrow**, scroll down as necessary, and then click **Web site**. Add the following information:

Author:	**Aitoro, Jill R.**
Name of Web Page:	**Nextgov - GSA drives green IT procurement**
Year:	**2008**
Month:	**February**
Day:	**21**
Year Accessed:	**2016**
Month Accessed:	**January**
Day Accessed:	**17**
URL:	**http://www.nextgov.com/nextgov/ng_20080221_8792.php**

10 Compare your screen with Figure 6.13, and then click **OK** to close the **Create Source** dialog box and add the citation.

A parenthetical reference is added. Because the cited Web page has no page numbers, only the author name is used in the parenthetical reference.

Figure 6.13

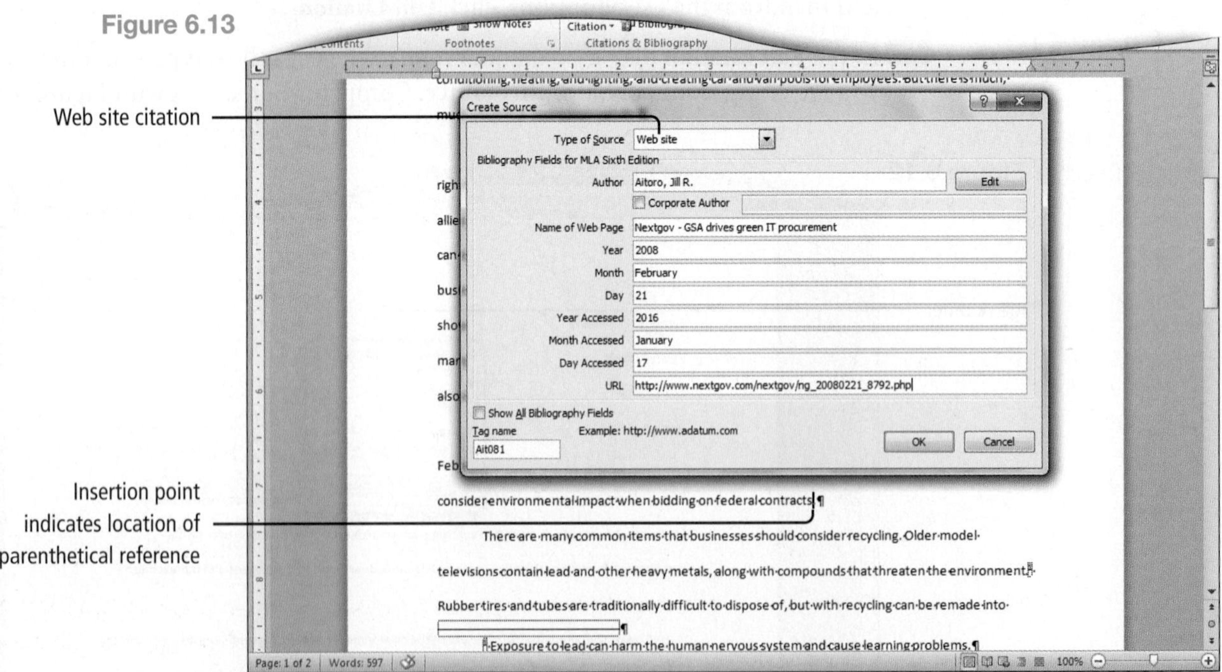

11 Near the top of **Page 2**, in the paragraph that begins *Consumers and businesses*, in the third line, click to position the insertion point following the word *toxic* to the left of the question mark.

12 In the **Citations & Bibliography group**, click the **Insert Citation** button, and then click **Add New Source**. Click the **Type of Source arrow**, if necessary scroll to the top of the list, click **Book**, and then add the following information:

Author:	**Scott, Nicky**
Title:	**Reduce, Reuse, Recycle: An Easy Household Guide**
Year:	**2007**
City:	**White River Junction, Vermont**
Publisher:	**Chelsea Green Publishing**

13 Click **OK**. Click the inserted citation to select it, click the **Citation Options arrow**, and then click **Edit Citation**.

14 In the **Edit Citation** dialog box, under **Add**, in the **Pages** box, type **7** to indicate that you are citing from page 7 of this source. Click **OK**.

15 On the **References tab**, in the **Citations & Bibliography group**, click the **Manage Sources** button. In the **Source Manager** dialog box, under **Current List**, click the third source and then compare your screen with Figure 6.14.

The Source Manager dialog box displays. Other citations on your computer display in the Master List box. The citations for the current document display in the Current List box. Word maintains the Master List so that if you use the same sources regularly, you can copy sources from your Master List to the current document. A preview of the selected bibliography entry also displays at the bottom of the dialog box.

Figure 6.14

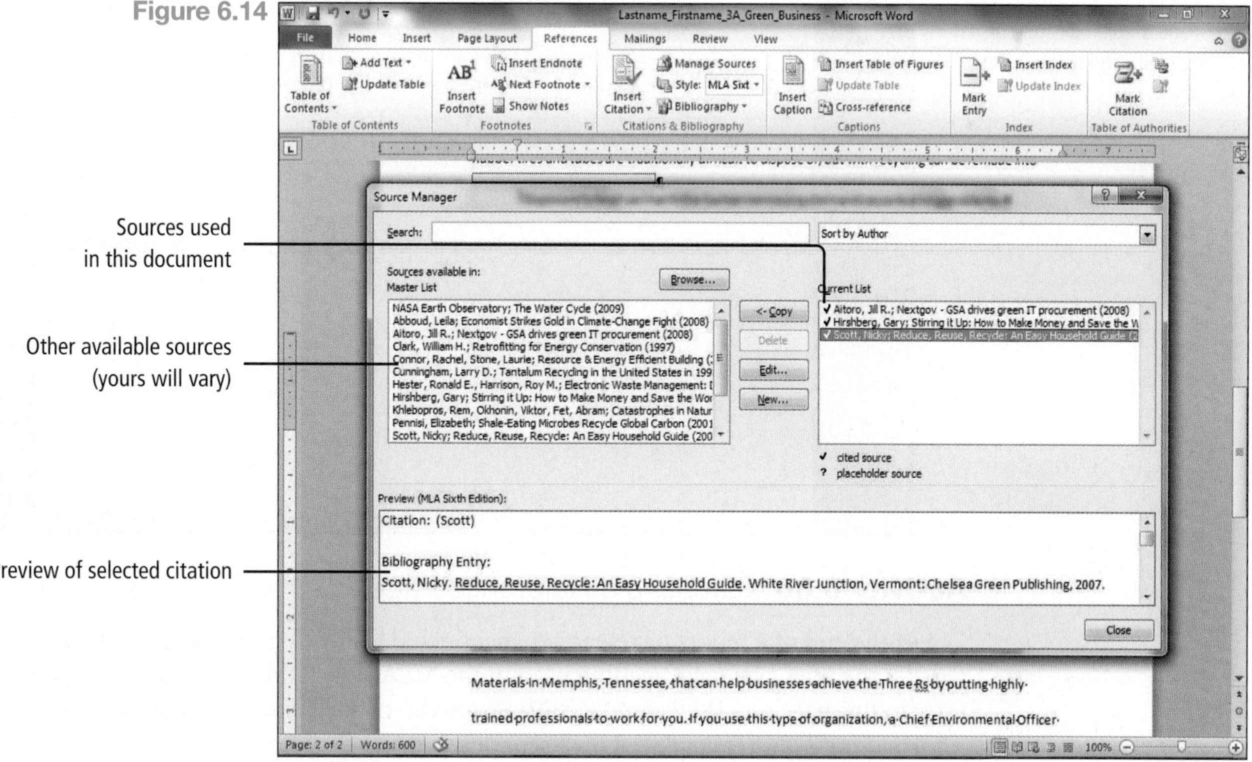

16 At the bottom of the **Source Manager** dialog box, click **Close**. Click anywhere in the document to deselect the parenthetical reference, and then **Save** your document.

Activity 6.05 | Inserting Page Breaks

In this activity you will insert a manual page break so that you can begin your bibliography on a new page.

1 Press Ctrl + End to move the insertion point to the end of the document. Notice that the insertion point displays at the end of the final paragraph, but above the footnote—the footnote is always associated with the page that contains the citation.

2 Press Ctrl + Enter to insert a manual page break.

A ***manual page break*** forces a page to end at the insertion point location, and then places any subsequent text at the top of the next page. Recall that the new paragraph retains the formatting of the previous paragraph, so the first line is indented.

3 On the ruler, point to the **First Line Indent** button, and then drag the **First Line Indent** button to the left to **0 inches on the horizontal ruler**.

4 Scroll as necessary to position the bottom of **Page 2** and the top of **Page 3** on your screen.

5 Compare your screen with Figure 6.15, and then **Save** your document.

A ***page break indicator***, which shows where a manual page break was inserted, displays at the bottom of the Page 2, and the footnote remains on the page that contains the citation, even though it displays below the page break indicator.

Figure 6.15

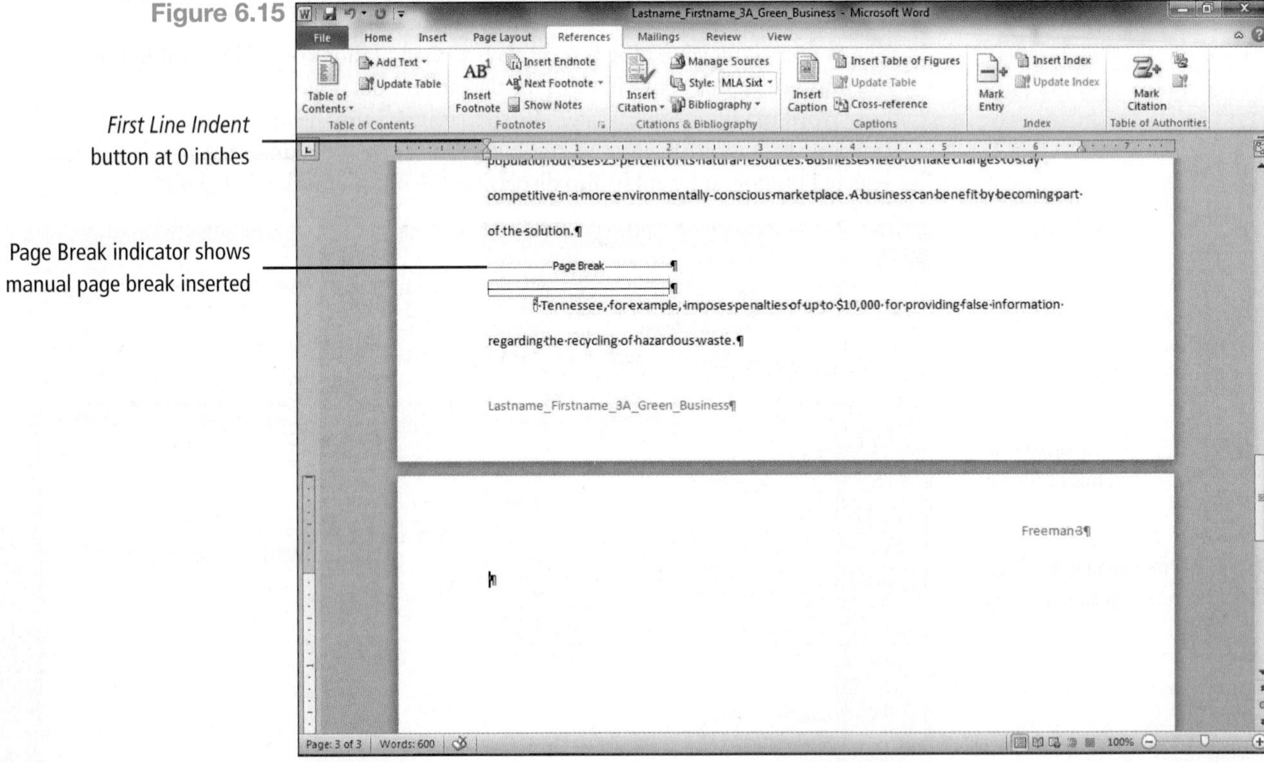

Activity 6.06 | Creating a Reference Page

At the end of a report or research paper, include a list of each source referenced. *Works Cited* is the reference page heading used in the MLA style guidelines. Other styles may refer to this page as a *Bibliography* (Business Style) or *References* (APA Style). This information is always displayed on a separate page.

1 With the insertion point blinking in the first line of **Page 3**, type **Works Cited** and then press Enter. On the **References tab**, in the **Citations & Bibliography group**, in the **Style** box, be sure *MLA* displays.

2 In the **Citations & Bibliography group**, click the **Bibliography** button, and then near the bottom of the list, click **Insert Bibliography**.

3 Scroll as necessary to view the entire list of three references, and then click anywhere in the inserted text.

The bibliography entries that you created display as a field, which is indicated by the gray shading when you click in the text. The field links to the Source Manager for the citations. The references display alphabetically by the author's last name.

4 In the bibliography, point to the left of the first entry—beginning *Aitoro, Jill*—to display the [pointer] pointer. Drag down to select all three references.

> **Another Way**
>
> Display the Paragraph dialog box. Under Spacing, click the Line spacing arrow, and then click Double. Under Spacing, in the After box, type **0**.

5 On the **Home tab**, in the **Paragraph group**, change the **Line spacing** to **2.0**, and then on the **Page Layout tab**, in the **Paragraph group**, change the **Spacing After** to **0 pt**.

The entries display according to MLA guidelines; the text is double-spaced, the extra space between paragraphs is removed, and each entry uses a ***hanging indent***—the first line of each entry extends 0.5 inch to the left of the remaining lines of the entry.

6 At the top of **Page 3**, right-click the *Works Cited* title, and then click the **Center** button [Center]. Compare your screen with Figure 6.16, and then **Save** [Save] your document.

In MLA style, the *Works Cited* title is centered.

Figure 6.16

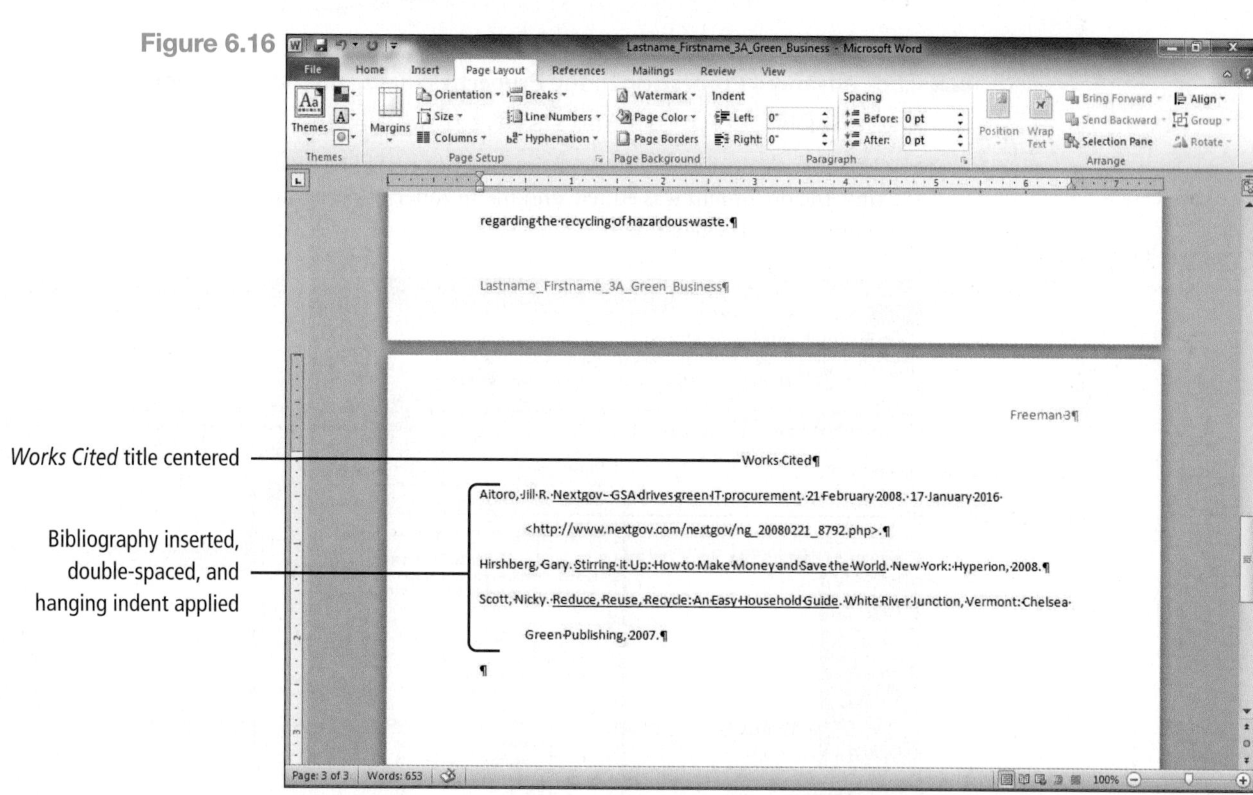

Activity 6.07 | Managing Document Properties

Recall that document property information is stored in the Document Panel. An additional group of property categories is also available.

1 Display **Backstage** view. On the right, under the document thumbnail, click **Properties**, and then click **Show Document Panel** to display the **Document Panel**.

2 Type your name and course information, and then add the keywords **green business, research paper**

3 In the upper left corner of the **Document Panel**, click the **Document Properties** button, and then compare your screen with Figure 6.17.

Figure 6.17

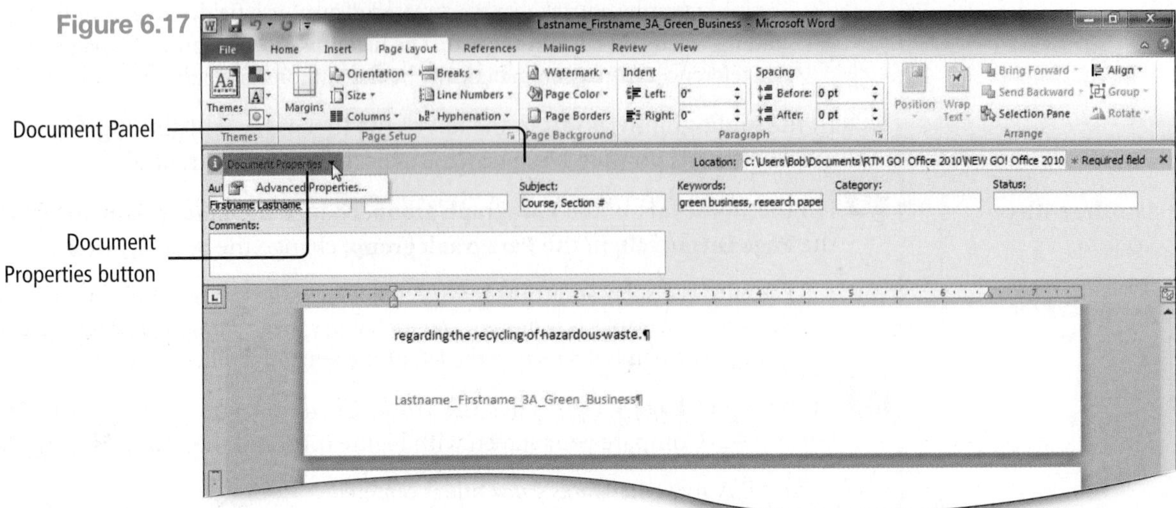

4 Click **Advanced Properties**. In the **Properties** dialog box, click the **Statistics tab**, and then compare your screen with Figure 6.18.

The document statistics show the number of revisions made to the document, the last time the document was edited, and the number of paragraphs, lines, words, and characters in the document.

Figure 6.18

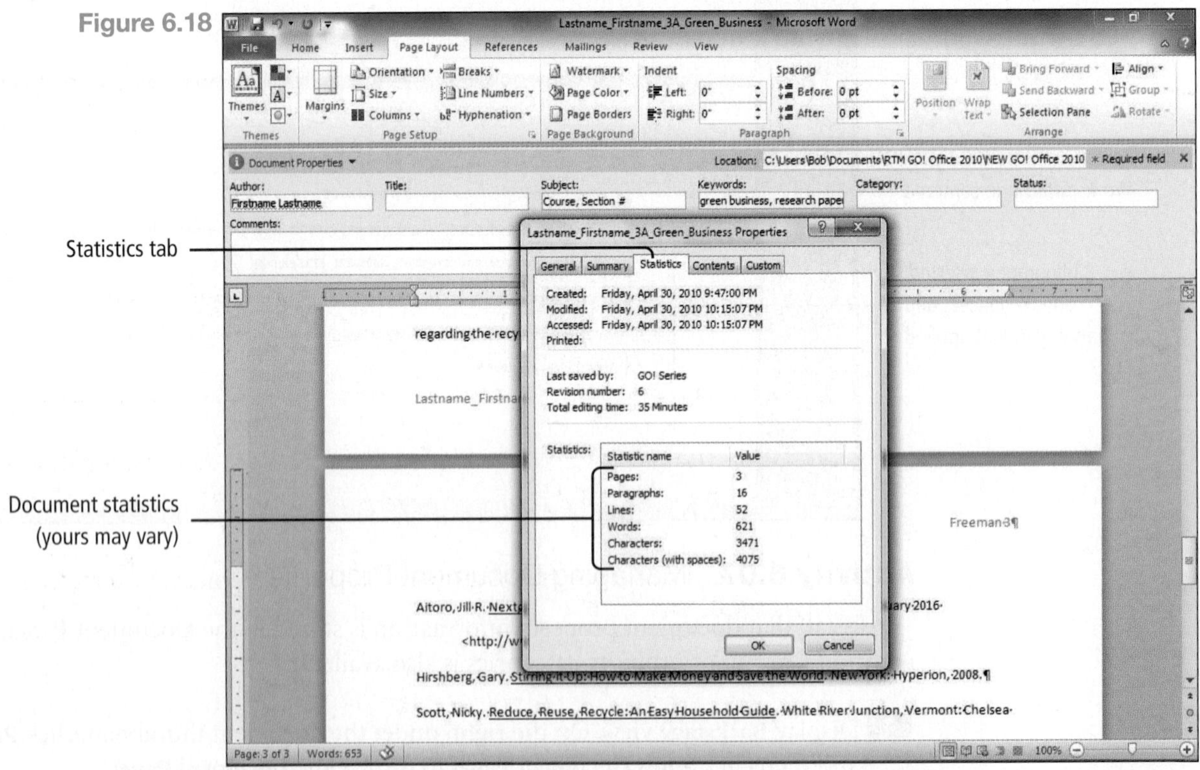

5 In the **Properties** dialog box, click the **Summary tab**. Notice that not all of the categories are filled in, and also notice that there are categories on this tab that are not found in the Document Panel.

Some of the boxes may contain information from your computer system.

6 In the **Properties** dialog box, click in the **Title** box and type **Going Green Benefits Business**

7 Click in the **Manager** box and type **Henry Miller**

8 In the **Company** box, select and delete any existing text, and then type **Memphis Primary Materials**

9 Click in the **Category** box and type **Marketing Documents**

10 Click in the **Comments** box and type **Draft copy of a research report that will be included in the marketing materials packet**

Additional information categories are available by clicking the Custom tab.

11 Compare your screen with Figure 6.19, and then at the bottom of the **Properties** dialog box, click **OK**.

Figure 6.19

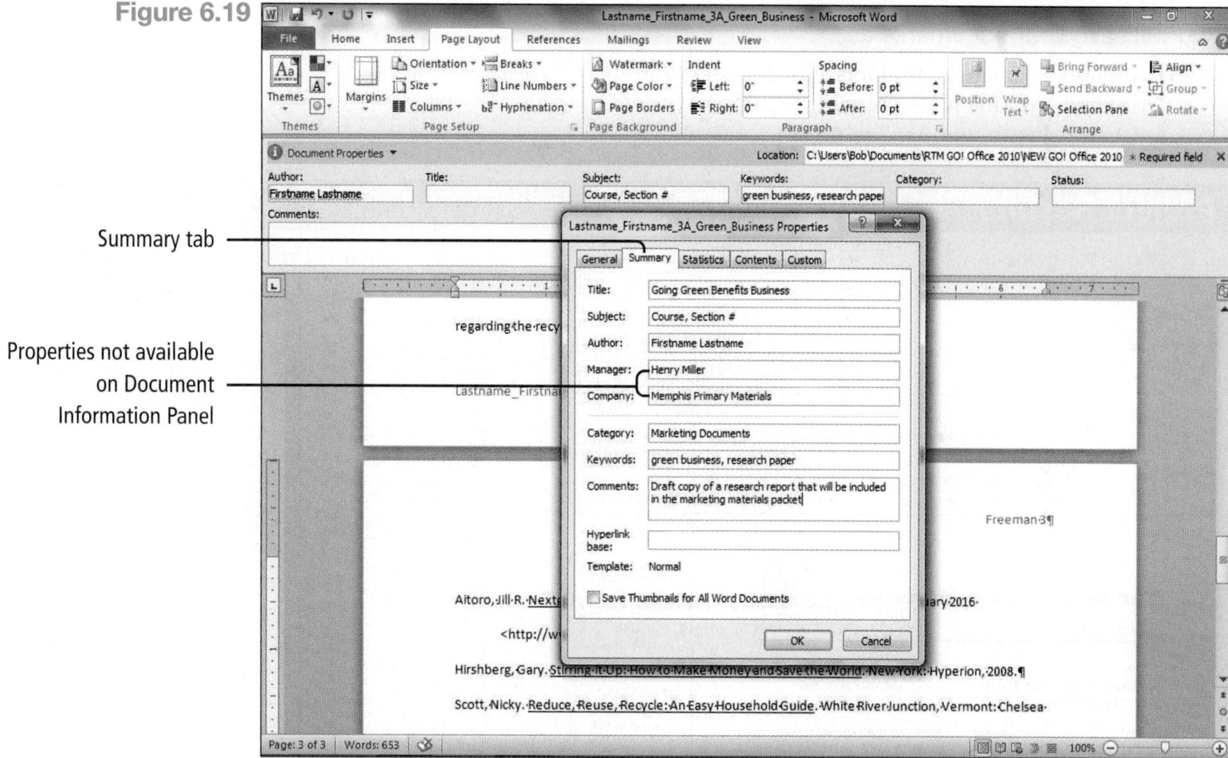

12 **Close** the **Document Panel**. Press Ctrl + F2, and then examine the three pages of your document in **Print Preview**. Redisplay your document. If necessary, make any corrections or adjustments.

13 **Save** your document, and then print or submit electronically as directed by your instructor. **Exit** Word.

End **You have completed Project 6A**

Project 6B Newsletter with Mailing Labels

Project Activities

In Activities 6.08 through 6.17, you will edit a newsletter that Memphis Primary Materials sends to its list of customers and subscribers. Your completed documents will look similar to Figure 6.20.

Project Files

For Project 6B, you will need the following files:

New blank Word document
w03B_Memphis_Newsletter
w03B_Addresses

You will save your documents as:

Lastname_Firstname_3B_Memphis_Newsletter
Lastname_Firstname_3B_Mailing_Labels
Lastname_Firstname_3B_Addresses

Project Results

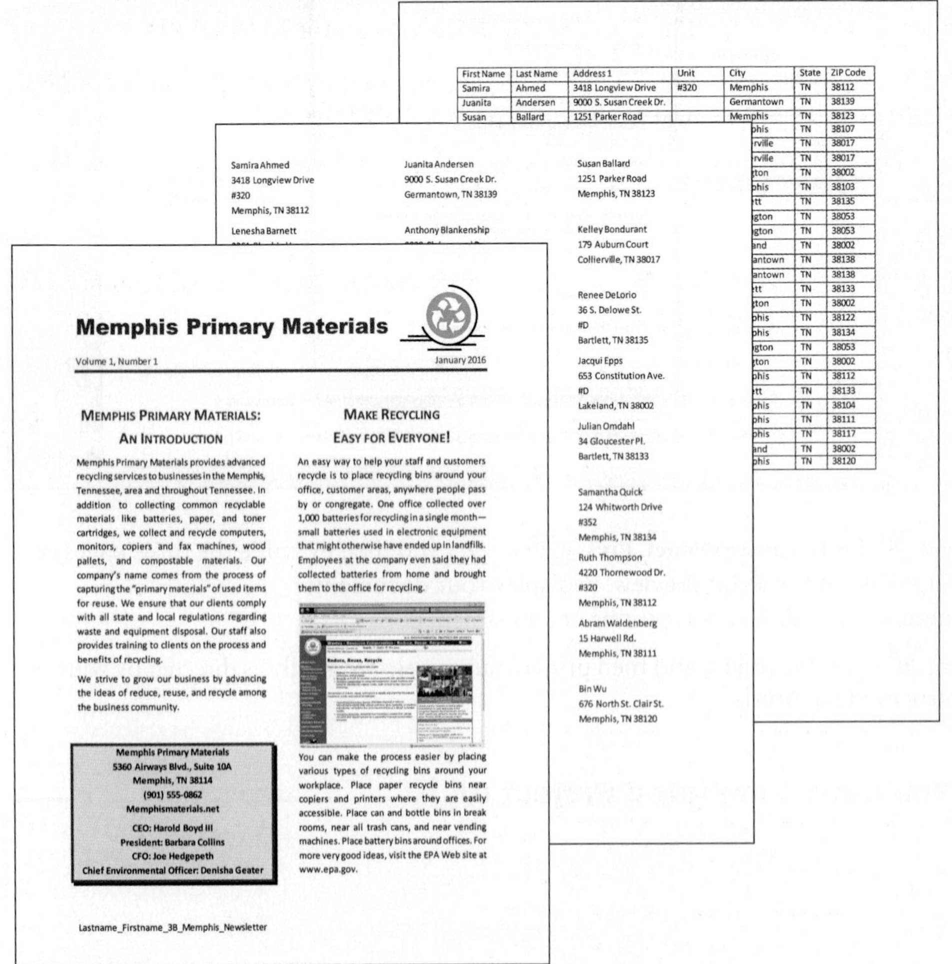

First Name	Last Name	Address 1	Unit	City	State	ZIP Code
Samira	Ahmed	3418 Longview Drive	#320	Memphis	TN	38112
Juanita	Andersen	9000 S. Susan Creek Dr.		Germantown	TN	38139
Susan	Ballard	1251 Parker Road		Memphis	TN	38123
				phis	TN	38107
				rville	TN	38017
				rville	TN	38017
				gton	TN	38002
				phis	TN	38103
				tt	TN	38135
				gton	TN	38053
				gton	TN	38053
				and	TN	38002
				antown	TN	38138
				antown	TN	38138
				tt	TN	38133
				ton	TN	38002
				phis	TN	38122
				phis	TN	38134
				gton	TN	38053
				ton	TN	38002
				phis	TN	38112
				tt	TN	38133
				phis	TN	38104
				phis	TN	38111
				phis	TN	38117
				and	TN	38002
				phis	TN	38120

Samira Ahmed
3418 Longview Drive
#320
Memphis, TN 38112

Juanita Andersen
9000 S. Susan Creek Dr.
Germantown, TN 38139

Susan Ballard
1251 Parker Road
Memphis, TN 38123

Lenesha Barnett

Anthony Blankenship

Kelley Bondurant
179 Auburn Court
Collierville, TN 38017

Renee DeLorio
36 S. Delowe St.
#D
Bartlett, TN 38135

Jacqui Epps
653 Constitution Ave.
#D
Lakeland, TN 38002

Julian Omdahl
34 Gloucester Pl.
Bartlett, TN 38133

Samantha Quick
124 Whitworth Drive
#352
Memphis, TN 38134

Ruth Thompson
4220 Thornewood Dr.
#320
Memphis, TN 38112

Abram Waldenberg
15 Harwell Rd.
Memphis, TN 38111

Bin Wu
676 North St. Clair St.
Memphis, TN 38120

Memphis Primary Materials

Volume 1, Number 1 — January 2016

Memphis Primary Materials: An Introduction

Memphis Primary Materials provides advanced recycling services to businesses in the Memphis, Tennessee, area and throughout Tennessee. In addition to collecting common recyclable materials like batteries, paper, and toner cartridges, we collect and recycle computers, monitors, copiers and fax machines, wood pallets, and compostable materials. Our company's name comes from the process of capturing the "primary materials" of used items for reuse. We ensure that our clients comply with all state and local regulations regarding waste and equipment disposal. Our staff also provides training to clients on the process and benefits of recycling.

We strive to grow our business by advancing the ideas of reduce, reuse, and recycle among the business community.

Memphis Primary Materials
5360 Airways Blvd., Suite 10A
Memphis, TN 38114
(901) 555-0862
Memphismaterials.net
CEO: Harold Boyd III
President: Barbara Collins
CFO: Joe Hedgepeth
Chief Environmental Officer: Denisha Geater

Make Recycling Easy for Everyone!

An easy way to help your staff and customers recycle is to place recycling bins around your office, customer areas, anywhere people pass by or congregate. One office collected over 1,000 batteries for recycling in a single month—small batteries used in electronic equipment that might otherwise have ended up in landfills. Employees at the company even said they had collected batteries from home and brought them to the office for recycling.

You can make the process easier by placing various types of recycling bins around your workplace. Place paper recycle bins near copiers and printers where they are easily accessible. Place can and bottle bins in break rooms, near all trash cans, and near vending machines. Place battery bins around offices. For more very good ideas, visit the EPA Web site at www.epa.gov.

Lastname_Firstname_3B_Memphis_Newsletter

Figure 6.20
Project 6B Memphis Newsletter

Objective 4 | Format a Multiple-Column Newsletter

All newspapers and most magazines and newsletters use multiple columns for articles because text in narrower columns is easier to read than text that stretches across a page. Word has a tool with which you can change a single column of text into two or more columns, and then format the columns. If a column does not end where you want it to, you can end the column at a location of your choice by inserting a ***manual column break***.

Activity 6.08 | Changing One Column of Text to Two Columns

Newsletters are usually two or three columns wide. When using 8.5 × 11-inch paper in portrait orientation, avoid creating four or more columns because they are so narrow that word spacing looks awkward, often resulting in one long word on a line by itself.

1. **Start** Word. From your student files, locate and open the document **w03B_Memphis_Newsletter**. If necessary, display the formatting marks and rulers. **Save** the file in your **Word Chapter 6** folder as **Lastname_Firstname_3B_Memphis_Newsletter** and then add the file name to the footer.

2. Select the first paragraph of text—*Memphis Primary Materials*. From the Mini toolbar, change the **Font** to **Arial Black** and the **Font Size** to **24**.

3. Select the first two paragraphs—the title and the Volume information and date. From the Mini toolbar, click the **Font Color button arrow**, and then under **Theme Colors**, in the fifth column, click the last color—**Blue, Accent 1, Darker 50%**.

4. With the text still selected, on the **Home tab**, in the **Paragraph group**, click the **Borders button arrow**, and then at the bottom, click **Borders and Shading**.

5. In the **Borders and Shading** dialog box, on the **Borders tab**, click the **Color arrow**, and then under **Theme Colors**, in the fifth column, click the last color—**Blue, Accent 1, Darker 50%**.

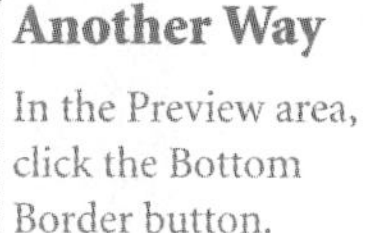

6. Click the **Width arrow**, and then click **3 pt**. In the **Preview** box at the right, point to the *bottom* border of the small preview and click one time. Compare your screen with Figure 6.21.

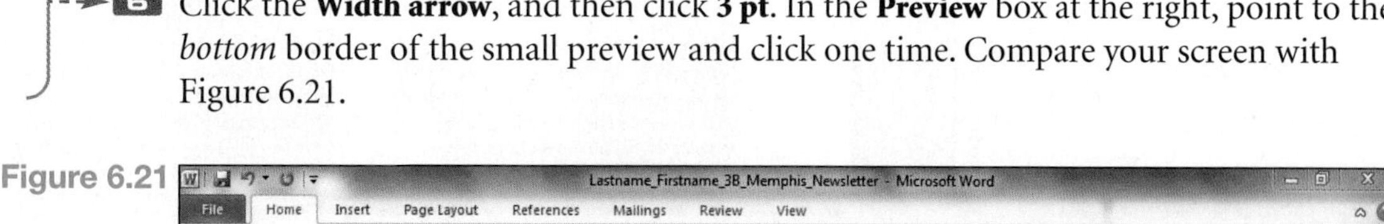

Figure 6.21

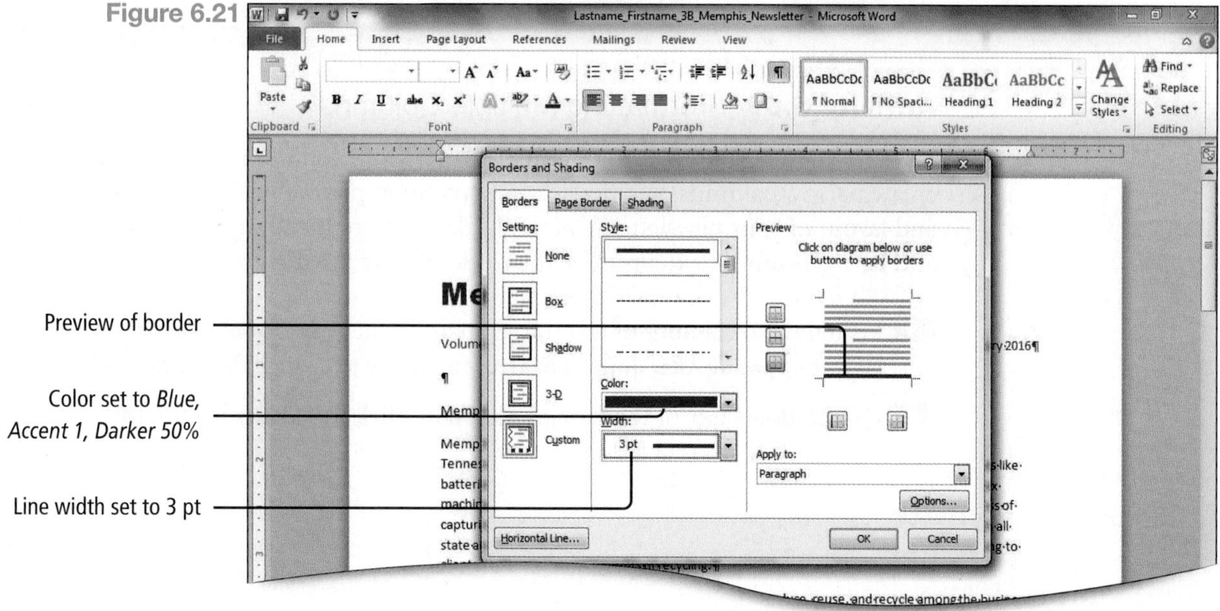

7 In the **Borders and Shading** dialog box, click **OK**.

The line visually defines the newsletter ***nameplate***—the banner on the front page of a newsletter that identifies the publication.

8 Below the nameplate, beginning with the paragraph *Memphis Primary Materials: An Introduction*, select all of the text to the end of the document, which extends to two pages.

9 On the **Page Layout tab**, in the **Page Setup group**, click the **Columns** button. From the **Columns** gallery, click **Two**.

10 Scroll up to view the top of **Page 1**, and then compare your screen with Figure 6.22, and then **Save** the document.

Word divides the text into two columns, and inserts a ***section break*** below the nameplate, dividing the one-column section of the document from the two-column section of the document. A ***section*** is a portion of a document that can be formatted differently from the rest of the document. A section break marks the end of one section and the beginning of another section. Do not be concerned if your columns do not break at the same line as shown in the figure.

Figure 6.22

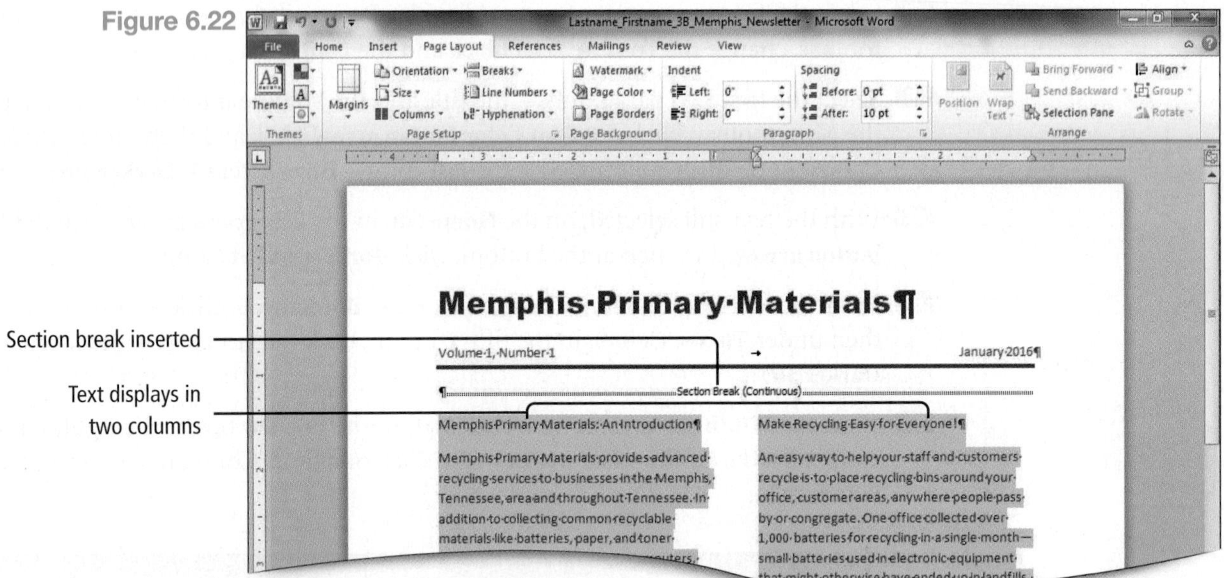

Activity 6.09 | Formatting Multiple Columns

The uneven right margin of a single page-width column is easy to read. When you create narrow columns, justified text is sometimes preferable. Depending on the design and layout of your newsletter, you might decide to reduce extra space between paragraphs and between columns to improve the readability of the document.

1 With the two columns of text still selected, on the **Page Layout tab**, in the **Paragraph group**, click the **Spacing After down spin arrow** one time to change the spacing after to **6 pt**.

2 On the **Home tab**, in the **Paragraph group**, click the **Justify** button.

3 Click anywhere in the document to deselect the text, and then compare your screen with Figure 6.23. **Save** the document.

Figure 6.23

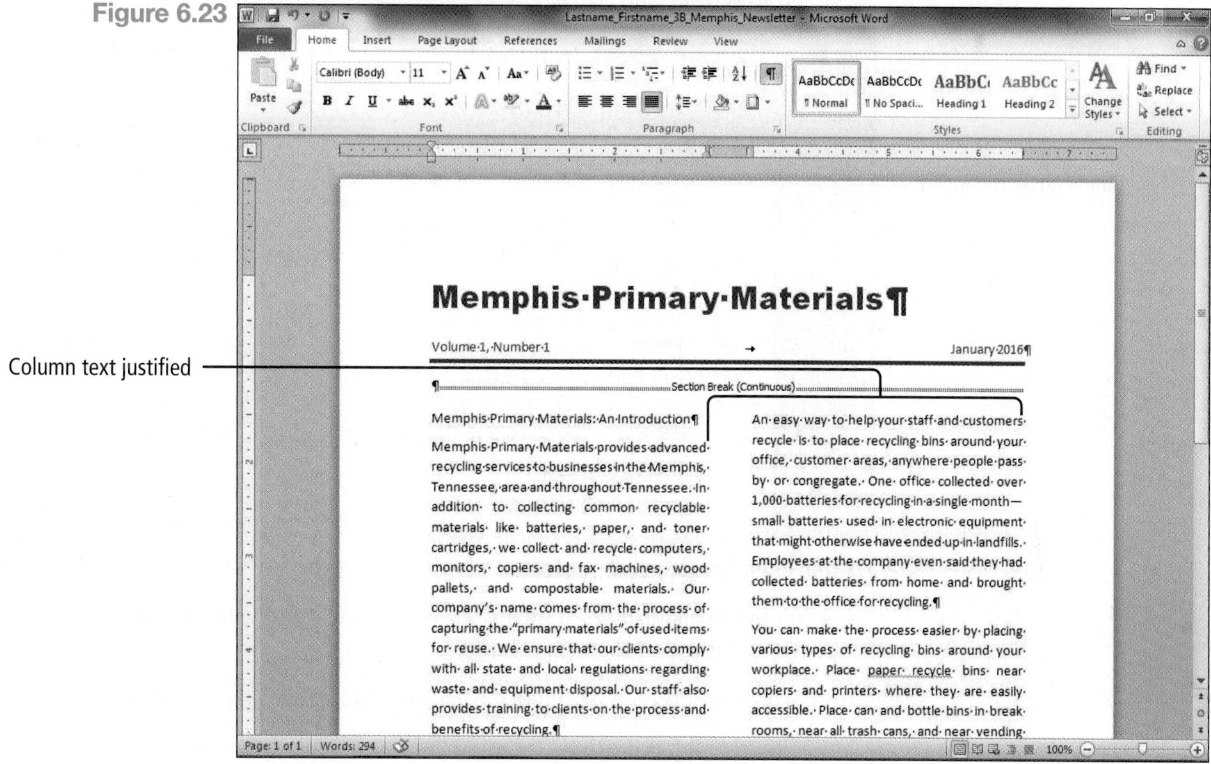

> **More Knowledge | Justifying Column Text**
>
> Although many magazines and newspapers still justify text in columns, there are a variety of opinions about whether to justify the columns, or to use left alignment and leave the right edge uneven. Justified text tends to look more formal and cleaner, but in a word processing document, it also results in uneven spacing between words. It is the opinion of some authorities that justified text is more difficult to read, especially in a page-width document. Let the overall look and feel of your newsletter be your guide.

Activity 6.10 | Inserting a Column Break

1 Scroll down to view the lower portion of the page. In the first column, locate the company address that begins with the paragraph *Memphis Primary Materials*, and then select that paragraph and the three following paragraphs, ending with the telephone number.

2 On the **Page Layout tab**, in the **Paragraph group**, click the **Spacing After down spin arrow** one time to change the spacing after to **0 pt**.

3 Select the three paragraphs that begin with *CEO* and end with *CFO*, and then in the **Paragraph group**, change the **Spacing After** to **0 pt**.

4 Near the bottom of the first column, click to position the insertion point at the beginning of the line that begins *Make Recycling*.

5 On the **Page Layout tab**, in the **Page Setup group**, click the **Breaks** button to display the gallery of Page Breaks and Section Breaks. Compare your screen with Figure 6.24.

Figure 6.24

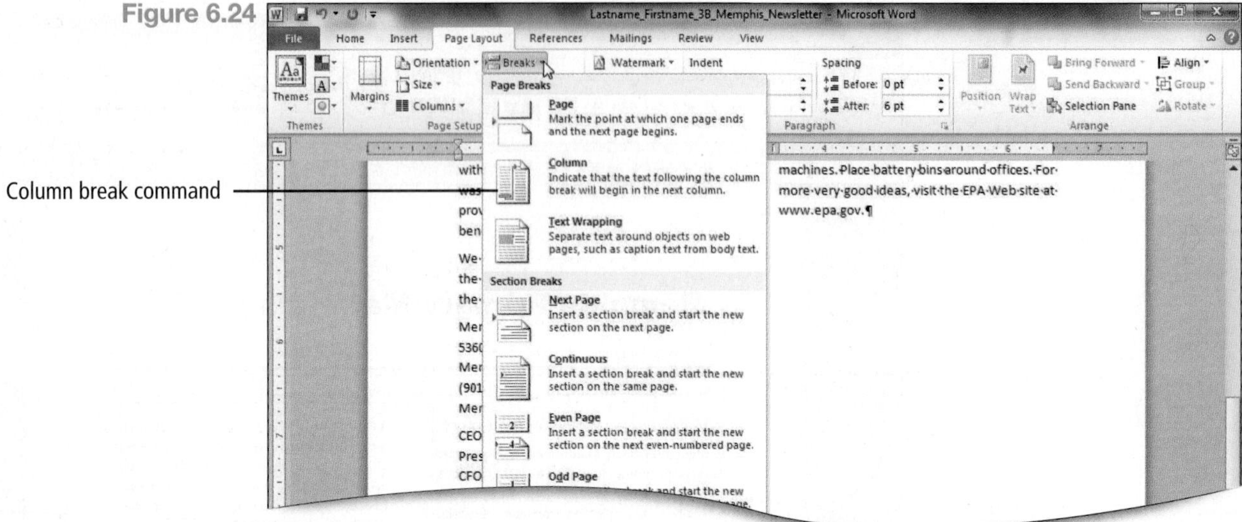

6 Under **Page Breaks**, click **Column**. Scroll to view the bottom of the first column.

A column break displays at the insertion point; text to the right of the insertion point moves to the top of the next column.

7 Compare your screen with Figure 6.25, and then **Save** the document.

A ***column break indicator***—a dotted line containing the words *Column Break*—displays at the bottom of the column.

Figure 6.25

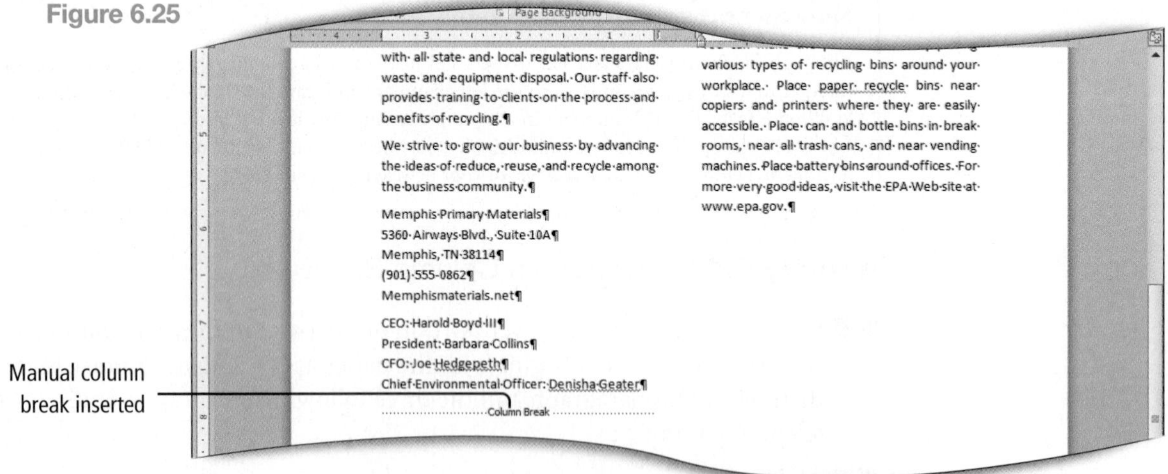

Activity 6.11 | Inserting a ClipArt Image

Clip art images—predefined graphics included with Microsoft Office or downloaded from the Web—can make your document visually appealing and more interesting.

1 Press Ctrl + Home. On the **Insert tab**, in the **Illustrations group**, click the **Clip Art** button to display the **Clip Art** task pane on the right of your screen.

2 In the **Clip Art** task pane, click in the **Search for** box, and then replace any existing text with **environmental awareness** so that Word can search for images that contain the keywords *environmental* and *awareness*.

3 In the **Clip Art** task pane, click the **Results should be arrow**. Be sure the **Illustrations** check box is selected, and then click as necessary to clear the *Photographs*, *Videos*, and *Audio* check boxes. Click the **Results should be** arrow again to collapse the list. Be sure the **Include Office.com content** check box is selected.

4 In the **Clip Art** task pane, click the **Go** button. Locate the image of the three white arrows in a blue circle. Click on the image to insert it, and then compare your screen with Figure 6.26.

Recall that when you insert a graphic, it is inserted as an inline object; that is, it is treated as a character in a line of text. Here, the inserted clip art becomes the first character in the nameplate.

Figure 6.26

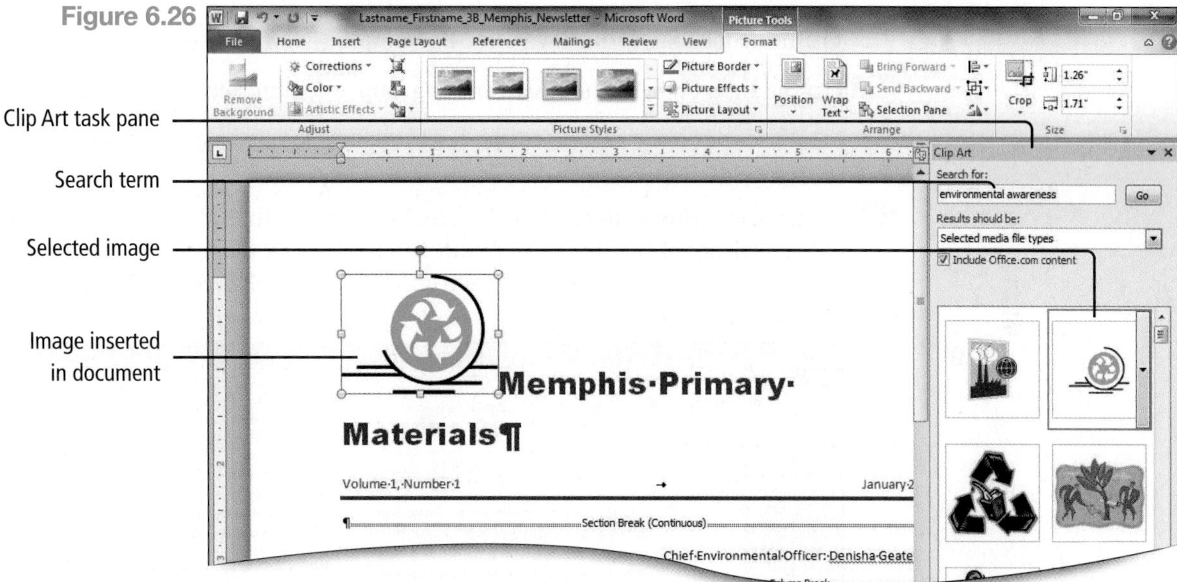

5 **Close** [X] the **Clip Art** task pane. With the image still selected, on the **Format tab**, in the **Size group**, click in the **Shape Height** box, type **1** and then press Enter. In the **Arrange group**, click the **Wrap Text** button, and then click **Square**.

6 Point to the image to display the [move] pointer, and then drag the image to the right so that the bottom edge aligns slightly above *January 2016*, and the right side aligns with the right margin. Recall that you can press the arrow keys as necessary to move the image in small, precise increments.

7 Compare your screen with Figure 6.27, and then **Save** [save] the document.

Figure 6.27

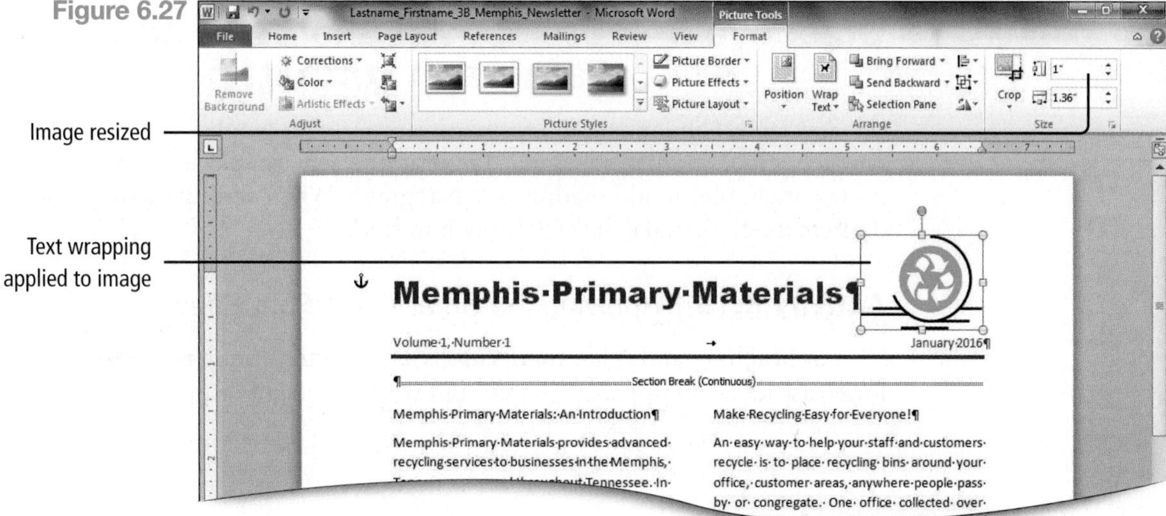

Activity 6.12 | Inserting a Screenshot

A ***screenshot*** is an image of an active window on your computer that you can paste into a document. Screenshots are especially useful when you want to insert an image of a Web site into a document you are creating in Word. You can insert a screenshot of any open window on your computer.

1 In the second column, click to position the insertion point at the beginning of the paragraph that begins *You can make*. Open your Internet browser, and then in the address bar type **www.epa.gov/osw/conserve/rrr** and press Enter. Maximize the browser window, if necessary.

2 From the taskbar, redisplay your **3B_Memphis_Newletter** document.

3 On the **Insert tab**, in the **Illustrations group**, click the **Screenshot** button.

All of your open windows display in the Available Windows gallery and are available to paste into the document.

4 In the **Screenshot** gallery, click the browser window that contains the EPA site to insert the screenshot at the insertion point, and notice that the image resizes to fit between the column margins. Compare your screen with Figure 6.28. **Save** the document.

Figure 6.28

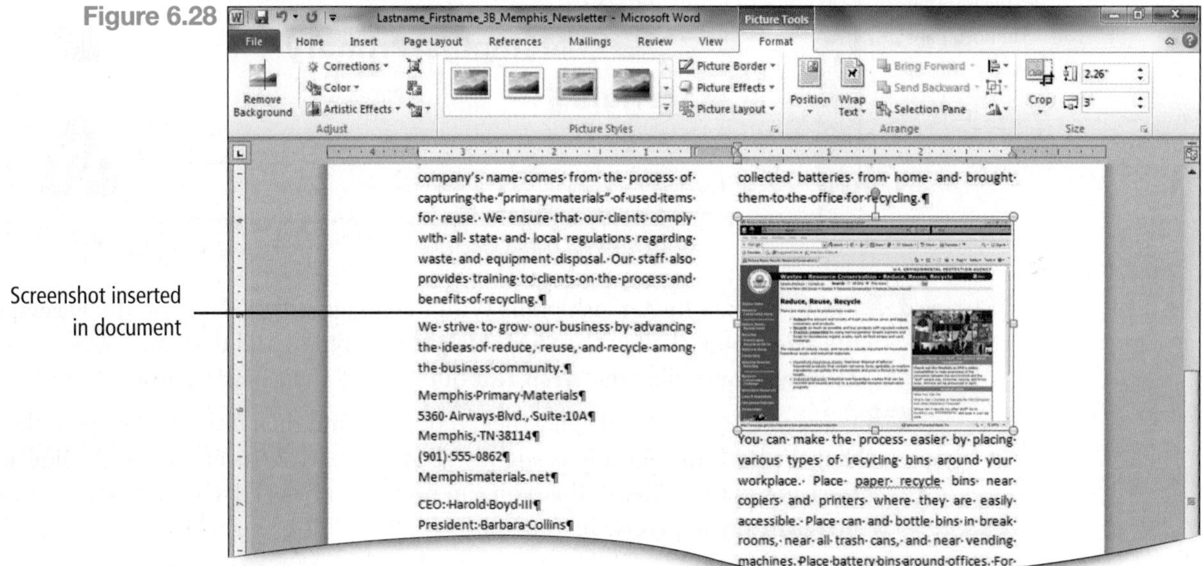

Objective 5 | Use Special Character and Paragraph Formatting

Special text and paragraph formatting is useful to emphasize text, and it makes your newsletter look more professional. For example, you can place a border around one or more paragraphs or add shading to a paragraph. When adding shading, use light colors; dark shading can make the text difficult to read.

Activity 6.13 | Applying the Small Caps Font Effect

For headlines and titles, ***small caps*** is an attractive font effect. The effect changes lowercase letters to uppercase letters, but with the height of lowercase letters.

1. At the top of the first column, select the paragraph *Memphis Primary Materials: An Introduction* including the paragraph mark.
2. Right-click the selected text, and then from the shortcut menu, click **Font**. In the **Font** dialog box, click the **Font color arrow**, and then under **Theme Colors**, in the fifth column, click the last color—**Blue, Accent 1, Darker 50%**.
3. Under **Font style**, click **Bold**. Under **Size**, click **18**. Under **Effects**, select the **Small caps** check box. Compare your screen with Figure 6.29.

   The Font dialog box provides more options than are available on the Ribbon and enables you to make several changes at the same time. In the Preview box, the text displays with the selected formatting options applied.

Figure 6.29

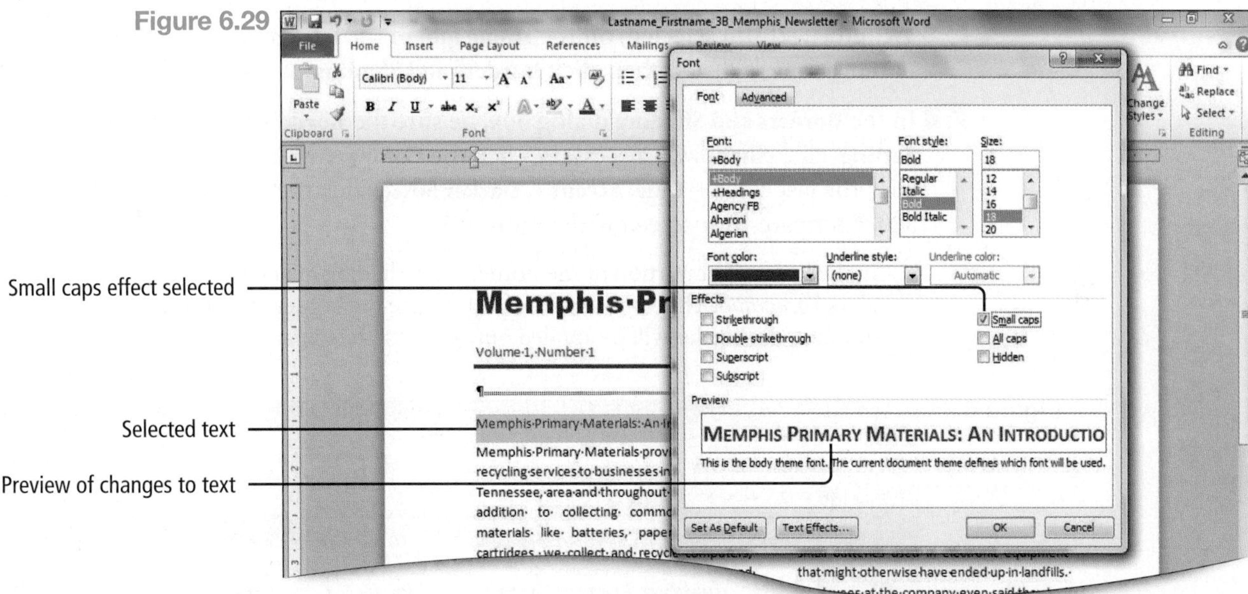

4. Click **OK**. Right-click the selected text, and then on the Mini toolbar, click **Center**.
5. With the text still selected, right-click, and then on the Mini toolbar, click the **Format Painter** button. Then, with the pointer, at the top of the second column, select the paragraph *Make Recycling Easy for Everyone!* to apply the same formats. Notice that the column title wraps placing a single word on the second line.
6. Position the insertion point to the right of the word *Recycling*, and then press Del to remove the space. Hold down Shift and then press Enter.

   Holding down Shift while pressing Enter inserts a ***manual line break***, which moves the text to the right of the insertion point to a new line while keeping the text in the same paragraph. A ***line break indicator***, in the shape of a bent arrow, indicates that a manual line break was inserted.
7. Compare your screen with Figure 6.30, and then **Save** the document.

Figure 6.30

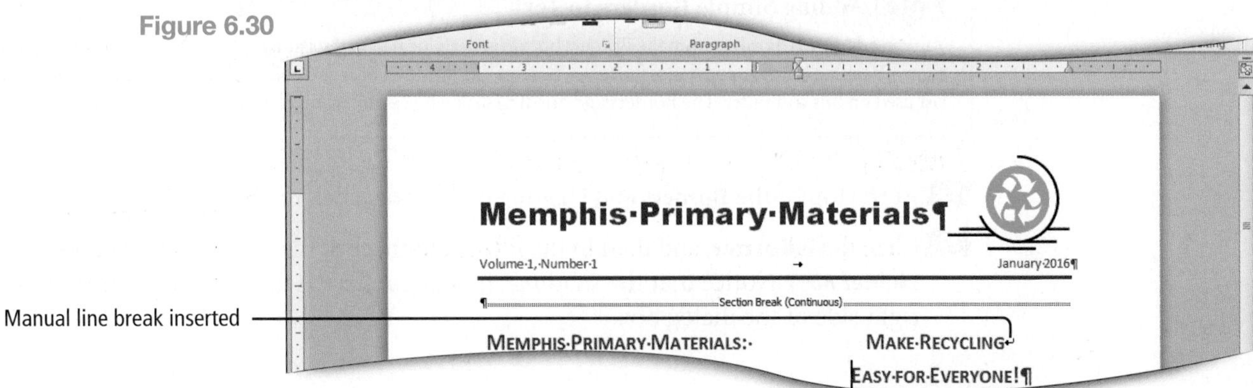

Activity 6.14 | Adding a Border and Shading to a Paragraph

Paragraph borders provide strong visual cues to the reader. Paragraph shading can be used with or without borders. When used with a border, light shading can be very effective in drawing the reader's eye to the text.

1. In the first column, in the paragraph that begins *We strive to grow*, click to position the insertion point at the end of the paragraph, and then press Enter one time.

2. At the bottom of the column, select the nine lines of company information, beginning with *Memphis Primary Materials* and ending with the paragraph that begins *Chief Environmental*. On the Mini toolbar, apply **Bold** and **Center**.

3. With the text still selected, on the **Home tab**, in the **Paragraph group**, click the **Borders button arrow**, and then click **Borders and Shading**.

4. In the **Borders and Shading** dialog box, be sure the **Borders tab** is selected. Under **Setting**, click **Shadow**. If necessary, click the **Color arrow**, and then in the fifth column, click the last color—**Blue, Accent 1, Darker 50%**. Click the **Width arrow**, and then click **3 pt**. Compare your screen with Figure 6.31.

   In the lower right portion of the Borders and Shading dialog box, the *Apply to* box displays *Paragraph*. The *Apply to* box directs where the border will be applied—in this instance, the border will be applied only to the selected paragraphs.

Figure 6.31

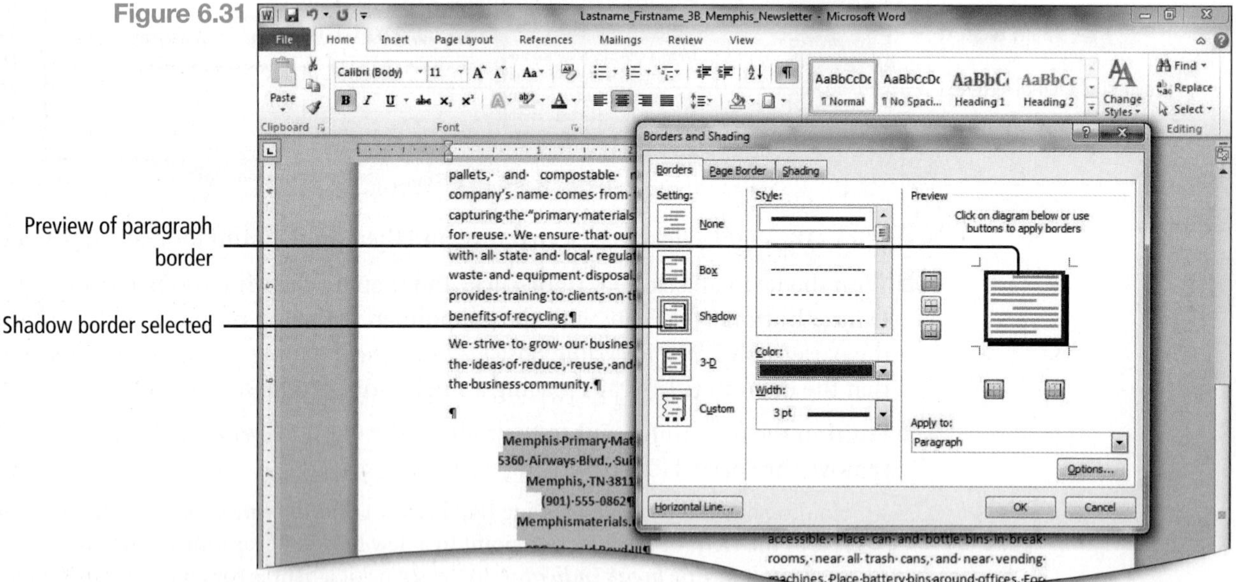

> **Note | Adding Simple Borders to Text**
>
> You can add simple borders from the Borders button gallery, located in the Paragraph group. This button offers less control over the border appearance, however, because the line thickness and color applied will match whatever was last used on this computer. The Borders and Shading dialog box enables you to make your own custom selections.

5. At the top of the **Borders and Shading** dialog box, click the **Shading tab**.

6. Click the **Fill arrow**, and then in the fifth column, click the second color—**Blue, Accent 1, Lighter 80%**. Notice that the shading change is reflected in the Preview area on the right side of the dialog box.

7 At the bottom of the **Borders and Shading** dialog box, click **OK**. Click anywhere in the document to deselect the text, and then compare your screen with Figure 6.32.

Figure 6.32

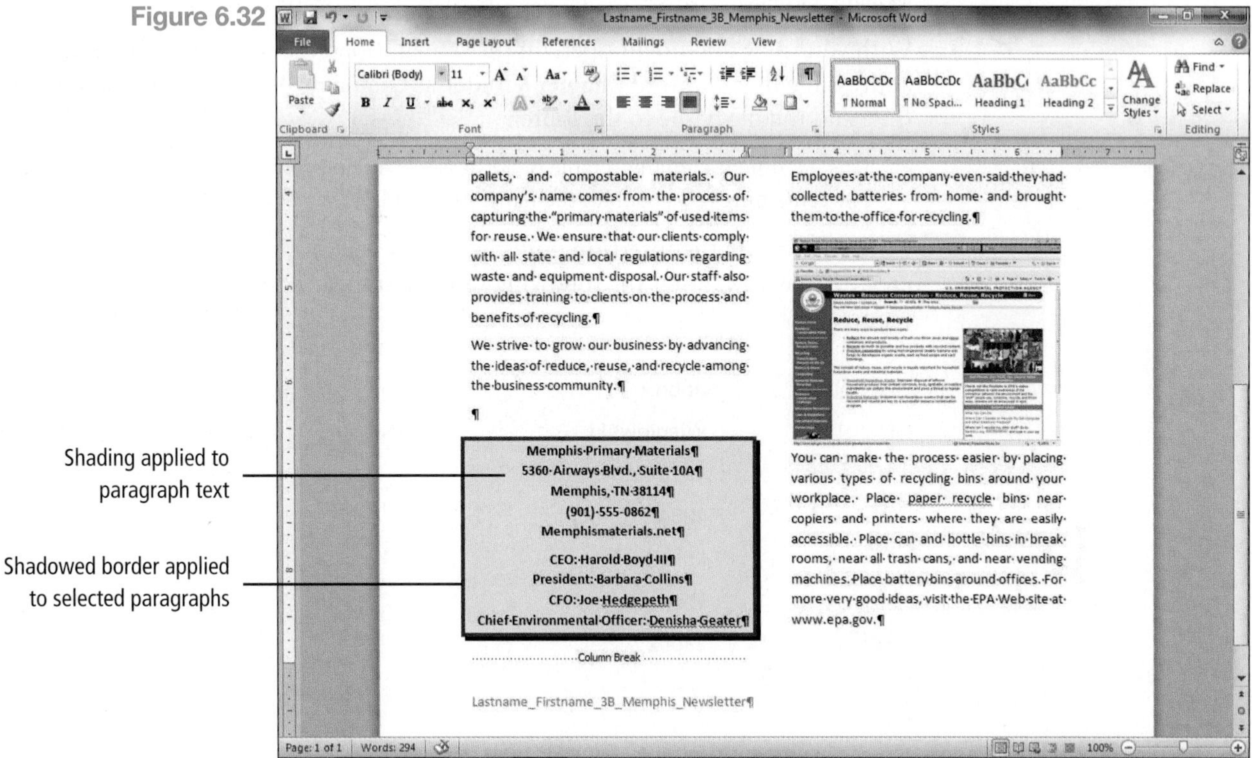

8 From **Backstage** view, display the **Document Panel**.

9 In the **Author** box, delete any text and then type your firstname and lastname. In the **Subject** box, type your course name and section number, and in the **Keywords** box, type **newsletter, January Close** [X] the **Document Panel**.

10 Press Ctrl + F2 to view the **Print Preview**. **Close** the preview, make any necessary corrections, and then click **Save** [Save]. **Exit** Word; hold this file until you complete this Project.

Objective 6 | Create Mailing Labels Using Mail Merge

Word's ***mail merge*** feature joins a ***main document*** and a ***data source*** to create customized letters or labels. The main document contains the text or formatting that remains constant. For labels, the main document contains the formatting for a specific label size. The data source contains information including the names and addresses of the individuals for whom the labels are being created. Names and addresses in a data source might come from a Word table, an Excel spreadsheet, or an Access database.

The easiest way to perform a mail merge is to use the Mail Merge Wizard, which asks you questions and, based on your answers, walks you step by step through the mail merge process.

Activity 6.15 | Opening the Mail Merge Wizard Template

In this activity, you will open the data source for the mail merge, which is a Word table containing names and addresses.

1 **Start** Word and display a new blank document. Display formatting marks and rulers. **Save** the document in your **Word Chapter 6** folder as **Lastname_Firstname_3B_ Mailing_Labels**

2 With your new document open on the screen, **Open** the file **w03B_Addresses. Save** the address file in your **Word Chapter 6** folder as **Lastname_Firstname_3B_Addresses** and then add the file name to the footer.

This document contains a table of addresses. The first row contains the column names. The remaining rows contain the names and addresses.

3 Click to position the insertion point in the last cell in the table, and then press Tab to create a new row. Enter the following information, and then compare your table with Figure 6.33:

First Name	**John**
Last Name	**Wisniewski**
Address 1	**1226 Snow Road**
Address 2	**#234**
City	**Lakeland**
State	**TN**
ZIP Code	**38002**

Figure 6.33

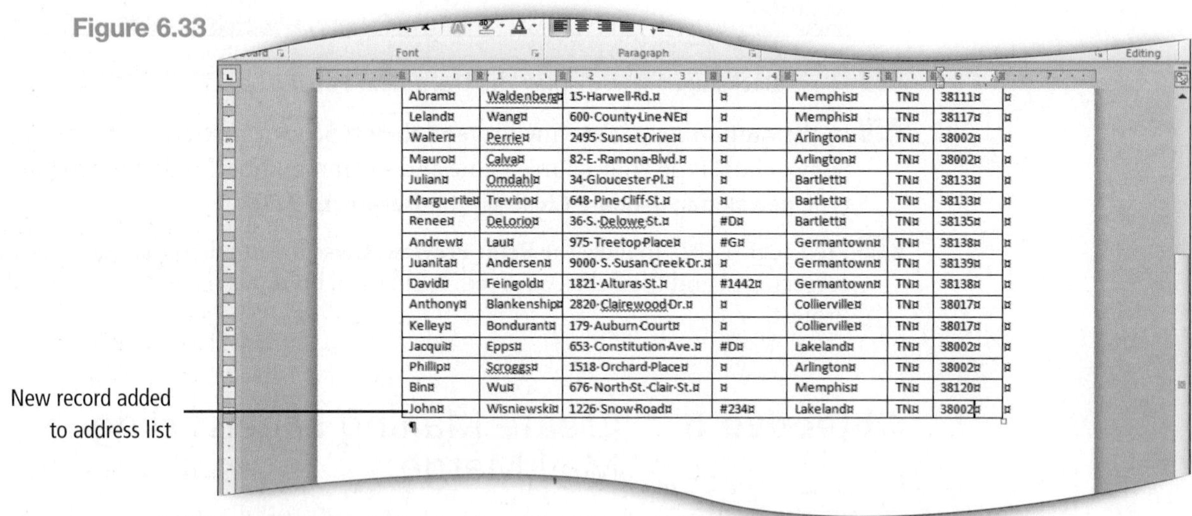

Abram	Waldenberg	15 Harwell Rd.		Memphis	TN	38111
Leland	Wang	600 County Line NE		Memphis	TN	38117
Walter	Perrie	2495 Sunset Drive		Arlington	TN	38002
Mauro	Calva	82 E. Ramona Blvd.		Arlington	TN	38002
Julian	Omdahl	34 Gloucester Pl.		Bartlett	TN	38133
Marguerite	Trevino	648 Pine Cliff St.		Bartlett	TN	38133
Renee	DeLorio	36 S. Delowe St.	#D	Bartlett	TN	38135
Andrew	Lau	975 Treetop Place	#G	Germantown	TN	38138
Juanita	Andersen	9000 S. Susan Creek Dr.		Germantown	TN	38139
David	Feingold	1821 Alturas St.	#1442	Germantown	TN	38138
Anthony	Blankenship	2820 Clairewood Dr.		Collierville	TN	38017
Kelley	Bondurant	179 Auburn Court		Collierville	TN	38017
Jacqui	Epps	653 Constitution Ave.	#D	Lakeland	TN	38002
Phillip	Scroggs	1518 Orchard Place		Arlington	TN	38002
Bin	Wu	676 North St. Clair St.		Memphis	TN	38120
John	Wisniewski	1226 Snow Road	#234	Lakeland	TN	38002

4 **Save**, and then **Close** the table of addresses. Be sure your blank **Lastname_ Firstname_3B_Mailing_Labels** document displays.

5 Click the **Mailings tab**. In the **Start Mail Merge group**, click the **Start Mail Merge** button, and then click **Step by Step Mail Merge Wizard** to display the **Mail Merge** task pane.

6 Under **Select document type**, click the **Labels** option button. At the bottom of the task pane, click **Next: Starting document** to display Step 2 of 6 of the Mail Merge Wizard.

7 Under **Select starting document**, be sure **Change document layout** is selected, and then under **Change document layout**, click **Label options**.

8 In the **Label Options** dialog box, under **Printer information**, click the **Tray arrow**, and then click **Default tray (Automatically Select)**—the exact wording may vary depending on your printer, but select the *Default* or *Automatic* option—to print the labels on regular paper rather than manually inserting labels in the printer.

9 Under **Label information**, click the **Label vendors arrow**, and then click **Avery US Letter**. Under **Product number**, scroll about halfway down the list, and then click **5160 Easy Peel Address Labels**. Compare your screen with Figure 6.34.

The Avery 5160 address label is a commonly used label. The precut sheets contain three columns of 10 labels each—for a total of 30 labels per sheet.

Figure 6.34

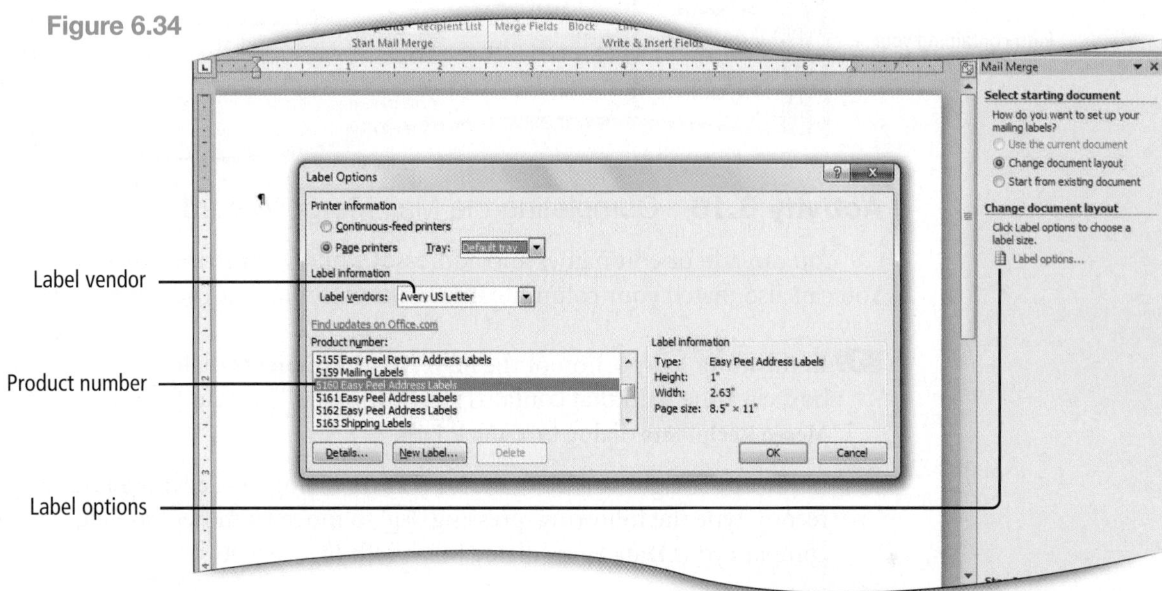

10 At the bottom of the **Label Options** dialog box, click **OK**. If a message box displays, click OK to set up the labels. At the bottom of the task pane, click **Next: Select recipients**.

The label page is set up with three columns and ten rows. The label borders may or may not display on your screen, depending on your settings. Here in Step 3 of the Mail Merge Wizard, you must identify the recipients—the data source. For your recipient data source, you can choose to use an existing list—for example, a list of names and addresses that you have in an Access database, an Excel worksheet, a Word table, or your Outlook contacts list. If you do not have an existing data source, you can type a new list at this point in the wizard.

11 If gridlines do not display, click the **Layout tab**. In the **Table group**, click the **View Gridlines** button, and then notice that each label is outlined with a dashed line. If you cannot see the right and left edges of the page, in the status bar, click the **Zoom Out** button as necessary to see the right and left edges of the label sheet on your screen.

12 Under **Select recipients**, be sure the **Use an existing list** option button is selected. Under **Use an existing list**, click **Browse**.

13 Navigate to your **Word Chapter 6** folder, select your **Lastname_Firstname_3B_Addresses** file, and then click **Open** to display the **Mail Merge Recipients** dialog box.

In the Mail Merge Recipients dialog box, the column headings are formed from the text in the first row of your Word table of addresses. Each row of information that contains data for one person is referred to as a ***record***. The column headings—for example, *Last_Name* and *First_Name*—are referred to as ***fields***. An underscore replaces the spaces between words in the field name headings.

14 Compare your screen with Figure 6.35.

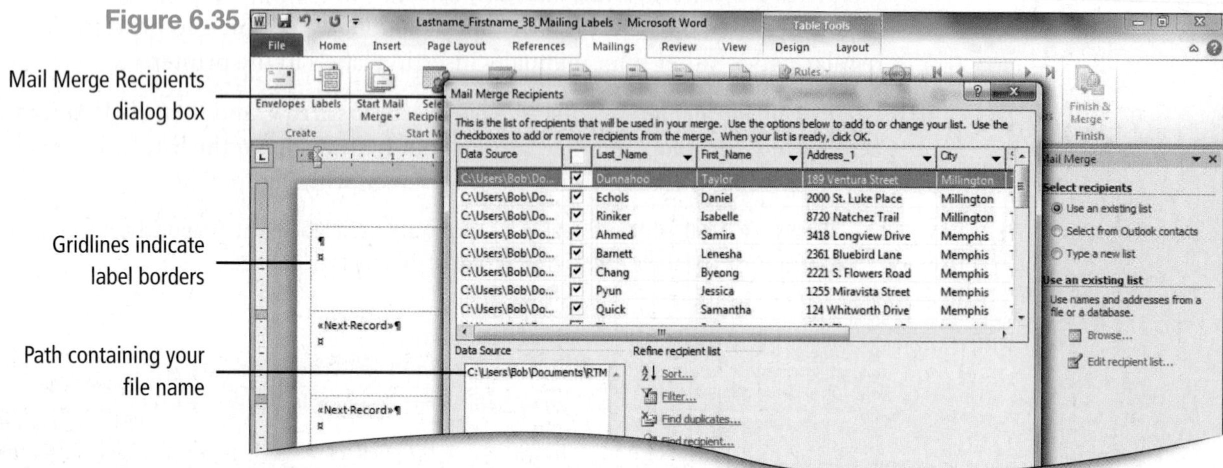

Activity 6.16 | Completing the Mail Merge Wizard

You can add or edit names and addresses while completing the Mail Merge Wizard. You can also match your column names with preset names used in Mail Merge.

1 In the lower left portion of the **Mail Merge Recipients** dialog box, in the **Data Source** box, click the path that contains your file name. Then, at the bottom of the **Mail Merge Recipients** dialog box, click **Edit**.

2 In the upper right corner of the **Data Form** dialog box, click **Add New**. In the blank record, type the following, pressing Tab to move from field to field, and then compare your **Data Form** dialog box wi0th Figure 6.36.

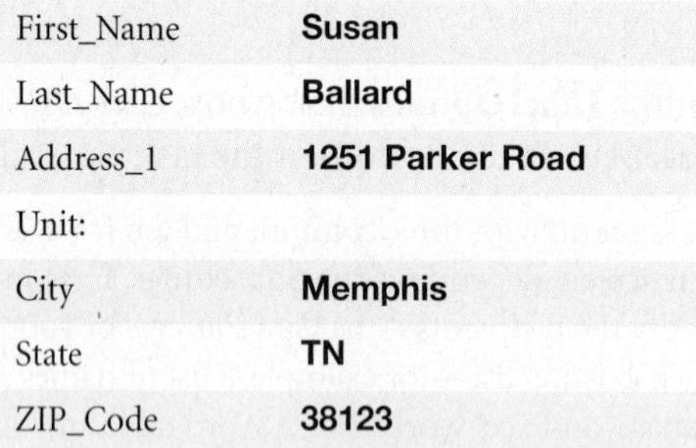

First_Name	**Susan**
Last_Name	**Ballard**
Address_1	**1251 Parker Road**
Unit:	
City	**Memphis**
State	**TN**
ZIP_Code	**38123**

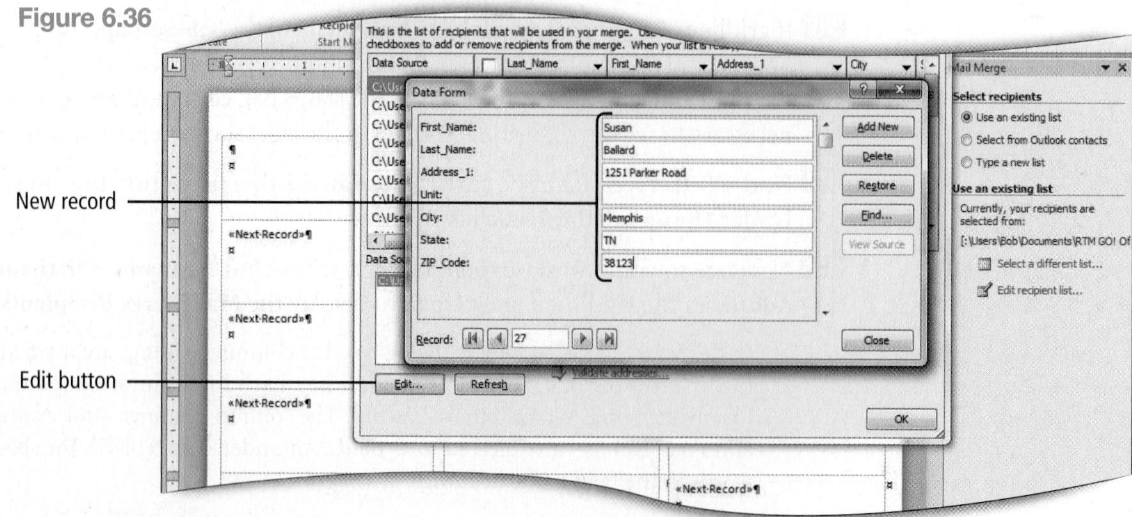

3 In the lower right corner of the **Data Form** dialog box, click **Close**. Scroll to the end of the recipient list to confirm that the record for *Susan Ballard* that you just added is in the list. At the bottom of the **Mail Merge Recipients** dialog box, click **OK**.

4 At the bottom of the **Mail Merge** task pane, click **Next: Arrange your labels**.

5 Under **Arrange your labels**, click **Address block**. In the **Insert Address Block** dialog box, under **Specify address elements**, examine the various formats for names. If necessary, under *Insert recipient's name in this format*, select the *Joshua Randall Jr.* format. Compare your dialog box with Figure 6.37.

Figure 6.37

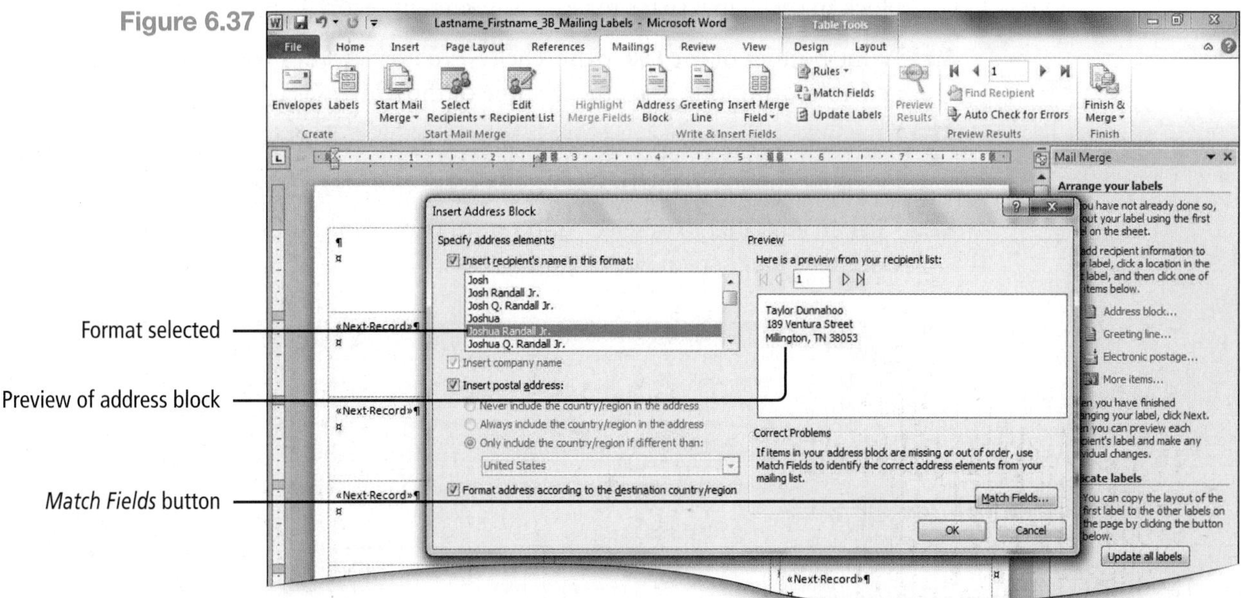

6 In the lower right corner of the **Insert Address Block** dialog box, click **Match Fields**.

If your field names are descriptive, the Mail Merge program will identify them correctly, as is the case with most of the information in the *Required for Address Block* section. However, the Address 2 field is unmatched—in the source file, this column is named *Unit*.

7 Scroll down and examine the dialog box, and then compare your screen with Figure 6.38.

Figure 6.38

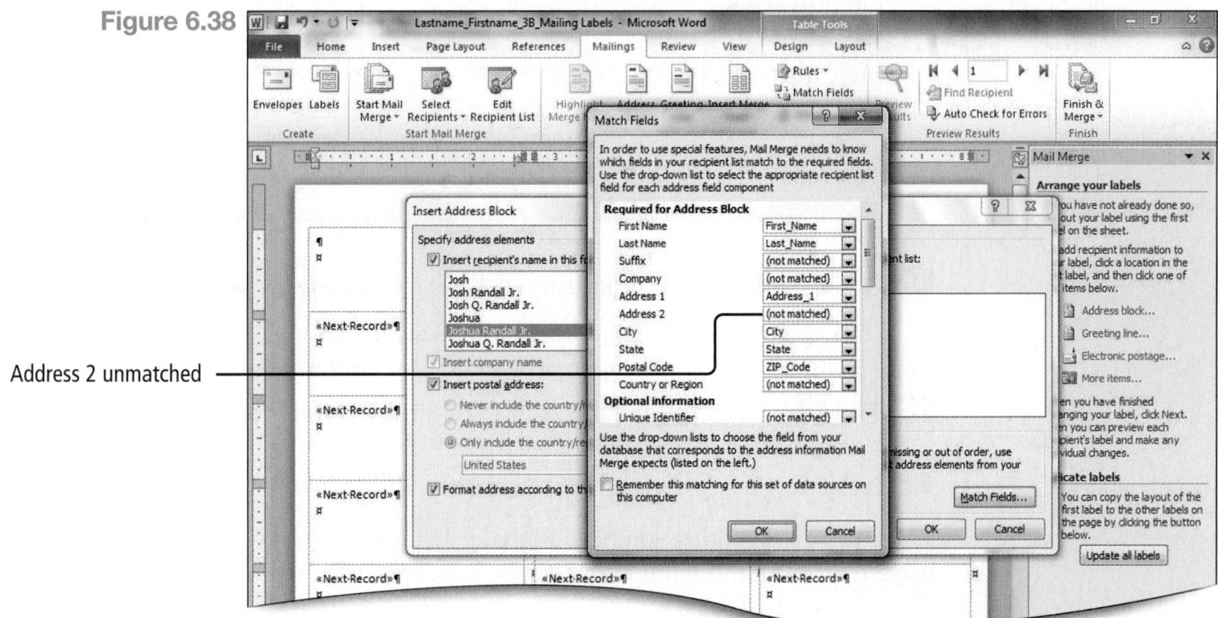

8 Click the **Address 2 arrow**, and then from the list of available fields, click **Unit** to match the Mail Merge field with the field in your data source.

9 At the bottom of the **Match Fields** dialog box, click **OK**. At the bottom of the **Insert Address Block** dialog box, click **OK**.

Word inserts the Address block in the first label space surrounded by double angle brackets. The *AddressBlock* field name displays, which represents the address block you saw in the Preview area of the Insert Address Block dialog box.

10 In the task pane, under **Replicate labels**, click **Update all labels** to insert an address block in each label space for each subsequent record.

11 At the bottom of the task pane, click **Next: Preview your labels**. Notice that for addresses with four lines, the last line of the address is cut off.

12 Press Ctrl + A to select all of the label text, click the **Page Layout tab**, and then in the **Paragraph group**, click in the **Spacing Before** box. Type **3** and press Enter.

13 Click in any label to deselect, and notice that 4-line addresses are no longer cut off. Compare your screen with Figure 6.39.

Figure 6.39

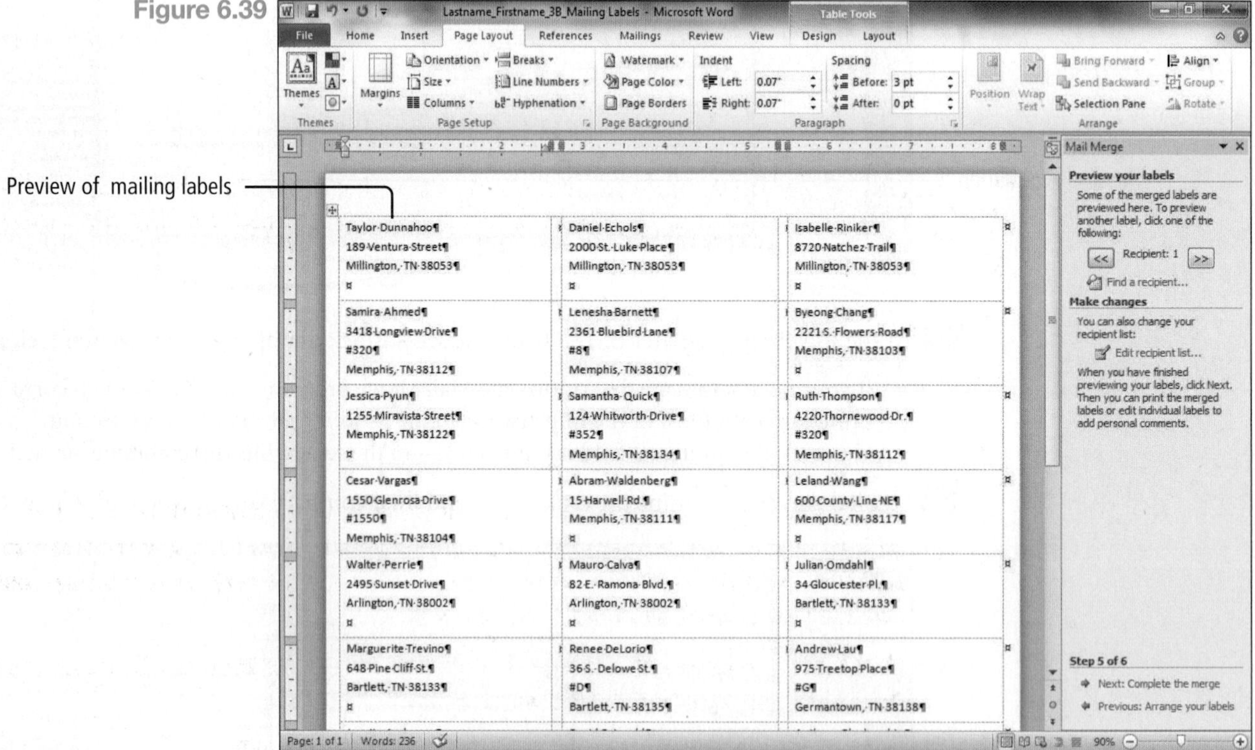

14 At the bottom of the task pane, click **Next: Complete the merge**.

Step 6 of the Mail Merge task pane displays. At this point you can print or edit your labels, although this is done more easily in the document window.

15 **Save** your labels, and then **Close** the **Mail Merge** task pane.

Activity 6.17 | Previewing and Printing the Mail Merge Document

If you discover that you need to make further changes to your labels, you can still make them even though the Mail Merge task pane is closed.

1 Add the file name to the footer, close the footer area, and then move to the top of Page 2. Click anywhere in the empty table row, click the **Layout tab**, in the **Rows & Columns group**, click the **Delete** button, and then click **Delete Rows**.

Adding footer text to a label sheet replaces the last row of labels on a page with the footer text, and moves the last row of labels to the top of the next page. In this instance, a blank second page is created, which you can delete by deleting the blank row.

2 Press Ctrl + F2 to display the **Print Preview**. Notice that the labels do not display in alphabetical order.

3 Click the **Mailings tab**, and then in the **Start Mail Merge group**, click the **Edit Recipient List** button to display the list of names and addresses.

4 In the **Mail Merge Recipients** dialog box, click the **Last_Name** field heading, and notice that the names are sorted alphabetically by the recipient's last name.

Mailing labels are often sorted by either last name or by ZIP Code.

5 Click the **Last_Name** field heading again, and notice that the last names are sorted in descending order. Click the **Last_Name** field one more time to return to ascending order, and then click **OK**. Press Ctrl + Home, and then compare your screen with Figure 6.40.

Figure 6.40

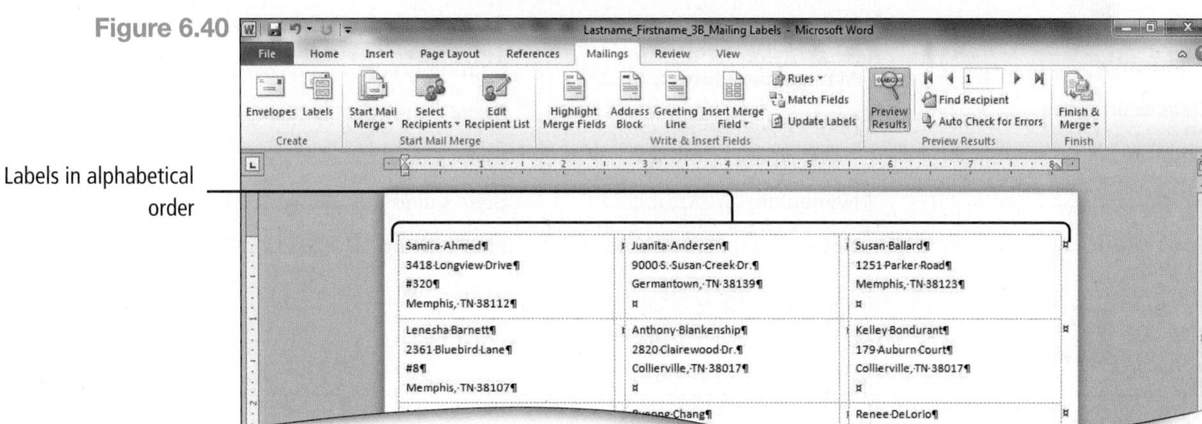

6 From **Backstage** view, display the **Document Panel**. In the **Author** box, delete any text and then type your firstname and lastname. In the **Subject** box, type your course name and section number, and in the **Keywords** box type **newsletter mailing labels** **Close** the **Document Panel**.

7 Click **Save**. Display **Backstage** view, and then click the **Print tab**. Examine the **Print Preview** on the right side of the window.

8 As directed by your instructor, print or submit electronically.

If you print, the labels will print on whatever paper is in the printer; unless you have preformatted labels available, the labels will print on a sheet of paper. Printing the labels on plain paper enables you to proofread the labels before you print them on more expensive label sheets.

9 **Close** the document, click **Yes** to save the data source, and then if necessary, click **Save** to save the labels.

10 In addition to your labels and address document, print or submit your **3B_Memphis_Newsletter** document as directed. **Exit** Word.

End **You have completed Project 6B**

Content-Based Assessments

Summary

In this chapter, you created a research paper using the MLA style. You added a header, footnotes, citations, and a bibliography, and changed the footnote style. You created a newsletter that used multiple columns. You added a column break, a page break, and a manual line break. You added special font effects, and added a border and shading to a paragraph. Finally, you used the Mail Merge Wizard to create a set of mailing labels for the newsletter.

Key Terms

American Psychological Association (APA) 275
Bibliography 282
Citation 282
Clip Art 294
Column break indicator 294
Data source 299
Endnote 277
Fields 301
Footnote 277
Hanging indent 287
Line break indicator 297
Mail merge 299
Main document 299
Manual column break ..291
Manual line break 297
Manual page break 286
Modern Language Association (MLA) 275
Nameplate 292
Note 277
Page break indicator 286
Parenthetical reference 282
Record 301
Screenshot 296
Section 292
Section break 292
Small caps 296
Style 279
Style guide 275
Works Cited 282

Matching

Match each term in the second column with its correct definition in the first column by writing the letter of the term on the blank line in front of the correct definition.

____ 1. A manual that contains standards for the design and writing of documents.

____ 2. One of two commonly used style guides for formatting research papers.

____ 3. An image of an active window on your computer that you can paste into a document.

____ 4. In a research paper, information that expands on the topic, but that does not fit well in the document text.

____ 5. In a research paper, a note placed at the bottom of the page.

____ 6. In a research paper, a note placed at the end of a document or chapter.

____ 7. A list of cited works in a report or research paper, also referred to as *Works Cited*, *Sources*, or *References*, depending upon the report style.

____ 8. In the MLA style, a list of cited works placed at the end of a research paper or report.

____ 9. A group of formatting commands, such as font, font size, font color, paragraph alignment, and line spacing that can be applied to a paragraph with one command.

____ 10. A note, inserted into the text of a research paper that refers the reader to a source in the bibliography.

____ 11. In the MLA style, a citation that refers to items on the *Works Cited* page, and which is placed in parentheses; the citation includes the last name of the author or authors, and the page number in the referenced source.

A American Psychological Association (APA)
B Bibliography
C Citation
D Endnote
E Footnote
F Hanging indent
G Manual column break
H Manual page break
I Note
J Page break indicator
K Parenthetical reference
L Screenshot
M Style
N Style guide
O Works Cited

_____ 12. The action of forcing a page to end and placing subsequent text at the top of the next page.

_____ 13. A dotted line with the text *Page Break* that indicates where a manual page break was inserted.

_____ 14. An indent style in which the first line of a paragraph extends to the left of the remaining lines, and that is commonly used for bibliographic entries.

_____ 15. An artificial end to a column to balance columns or to provide space for the insertion of other objects.

Multiple Choice

Circle the correct answer.

1. Column text that is aligned to both the left and right margins is referred to as:
A. centered **B.** justified **C.** indented

2. The banner on the front page of a newsletter that identifies the publication is the:
A. heading **B.** nameplate **C.** title

3. A portion of a document that can be formatted differently from the rest of the document is a:
A. tabbed list **B.** paragraph **C.** section

4. A font effect, commonly used in titles, that changes lowercase text into uppercase letters using a reduced font size is:
A. Small Caps **B.** Level 2 Head **C.** Bevel

5. To end a line before the normal end of the line, without creating a new paragraph, hold down the Shift key while pressing the:
A. Enter key **B.** Ctrl key **C.** Alt key

6. The nonprinting symbol that displays where a manual line break is inserted is the:
A. short arrow **B.** bent arrow **C.** anchor

7. In mail merge, the document that contains the text or formatting that remains constant is the:
A. data source **B.** mailing list **C.** main document

8. In mail merge, the list of variable information, such as names and addresses, that is merged with a main document to create customized form letters or labels is the:
A. data source **B.** mailing list **C.** main document

9. In mail merge, a row of information that contains data for one person is a:
A. record **B.** field **C.** label

10. To perform a mail merge using Word's step-by-step guided process, use the:
A. Mail Merge Template **B.** Mail Merge Management Source **C.** Mail Merge Wizard

Content-Based Assessments

Apply 6A skills from these Objectives:

1 Create a Research Paper
2 Insert Footnotes in a Research Paper
3 Create Citations and a Bibliography in a Research Paper

Skills Review | Project 6C Recycling Report

In the following Skills Review, you will format and edit a research paper for Memphis Primary Materials. The research topic is recycling in the natural environment. Your completed document will look similar to Figure 6.41.

Project Files

For Project 6C, you will need the following file:

w03C_Recycling_Report

You will save your document as:

Lastname_Firstname_3C_Recycling_Report

Project Results

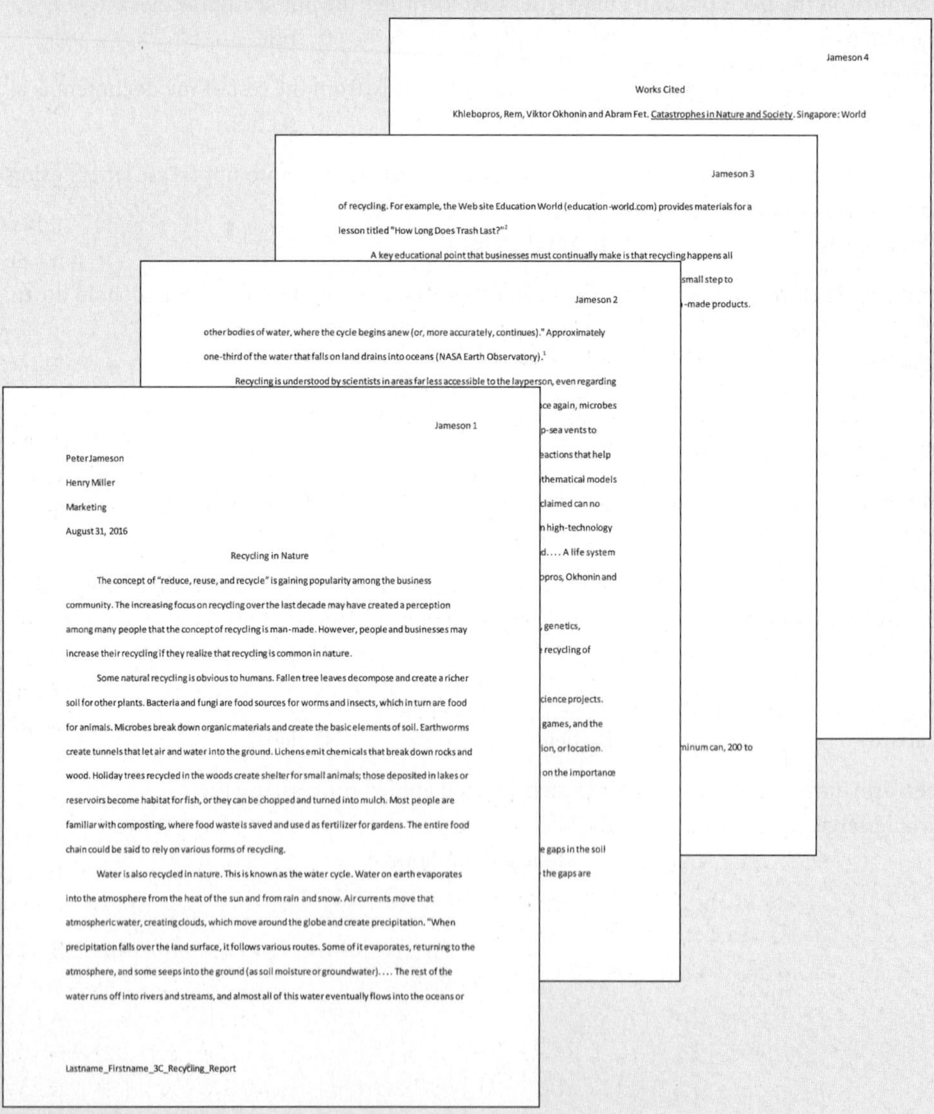

Figure 6.41

(Project 6C Recycling Report continues on the next page)

Skills Review | Project 6C Recycling Report (continued)

1 **Start** Word. From your student files, locate and open the document **w03C_Recycling_Report**. Display the formatting marks and rulers. **Save** the file in your **Word Chapter 6** folder as **Lastname_Firstname_3C_Recycling_Report**

a. Press Ctrl + A. On the **Home tab**, in the **Paragraph group**, click the **Line spacing** button, and then change the line spacing to **2.0**. On the **Page Layout tab**, in the **Paragraph group**, change the **Spacing After** to **0 pt**.

b. Press Ctrl + Home, press Enter to create a blank line at the top of the document, and then click to position the insertion point in the blank line. Type **Peter Jameson** and then press Enter. Type **Henry Miller** and then press Enter. Type **Marketing** and then press Enter. Type **August 31, 2016** and then press Enter.

c. Type **Recycling in Nature** and then right-click anywhere in the title you just typed. From the Mini toolbar, **Center** the title.

d. Near the top of **Page 1**, locate the paragraph beginning *The concept of*, and then click to position the insertion point at the beginning of the paragraph. Scroll to the end of the document, hold down Shift, and then click to the right of the last paragraph mark to select all of the text from the insertion point to the end of the document. On the horizontal ruler, drag the **First Line Indent** button to **0.5″**.

e. On **Page 1**, point to the top margin area and right-click. Click **Edit Header**. In the header area, type **Jameson** and then press Spacebar.

f. On the **Design tab**, in the **Header & Footer group**, click the **Page Number** button, and then point to **Current Position**. In the displayed gallery, under **Simple**, click **Plain Number**. On the **Home tab**, in the **Paragraph group**, click the **Align Text Right** button.

g. Click the **Design tab**, and then in the **Navigation group**, click the **Go to Footer** button. In the **Insert group**, click the **Quick Parts** button, and then click **Field**. In the **Field** dialog box, under **Field names**, locate and click **FileName**, and then click **OK**.

h. Double-click anywhere outside the footer area. **Save** your document.

2 Scroll to view the top of **Page 2**, locate the paragraph that ends *drains into oceans*, and then click to position the insertion point to the right of the period following *oceans*. On the **References tab**, in the **Footnotes group**, click the **Insert Footnote** button.

a. Type **Groundwater is found in two layers of the soil, the "zone of aeration," where gaps in the soil are filled with both air and water, and, further down, the "zone of saturation," where the gaps are completely filled with water.**

b. In the lower half of **Page 2**, locate the paragraph that begins *School students*. Click to position the insertion point at the end of the paragraph and insert a footnote.

c. As the footnote text, type **A wool sock will last one year in a landfill; a soup can, 80 to 100 years; an aluminum can, 200 to 500 years; and plastic rings from a six-pack of cans, 450 years. Save** your document.

d. At the bottom of **Page 2**, right-click anywhere in either footnote. From the shortcut menu, click **Style**. In the **Style** dialog box, click the **Modify** button. In the **Modify Style** dialog box, locate the small Formatting toolbar in the center of the dialog box, click the **Font Size button arrow**, and then click **11**.

e. In the lower left corner of the dialog box, click the **Format** button, and then click **Paragraph**. In the **Paragraph** dialog box, under **Indentation**, click the **Special arrow**, and then click **First line**. Under **Spacing**, click the **Line spacing button arrow**, and then click **Double**.

f. Click **OK** to close the **Paragraph** dialog box, click **OK** to close the **Modify Style** dialog box, and then click **Apply** to apply the new style. Notice that the second footnote moves to **Page 3**. **Save** your document.

3 Scroll to view the top of **Page 2**, and then locate the footnote marker at the end of the second line of text. Click to position the insertion point to the left of the period at the end of the paragraph.

a. On the **References tab**, in the **Citations & Bibliography group**, click the **Style button arrow**, and then click **MLA** to insert a reference using MLA style. Click the **Insert Citation** button, and then click **Add New Source**. Click the **Type of Source arrow**,

(Project 6C Recycling Report continues on the next page)

Skills Review | Project 6C Recycling Report (continued)

and then click **Web site**. Select the **Corporate Author** check box, and then add the following information (type the URL on one line):

Corporate Author:	**NASA Earth Observatory**
Name of Web Page:	**The Water Cycle**
Year:	**2009**
Month:	**March**
Day:	**3**
Year Accessed:	**2016**
Month Accessed:	**May**
Day Accessed:	**24**
URL:	**http://earthobservatory.nasa.gov/Features/Water/water_2.php**

b. Click **OK** to insert the citation. In the next paragraph, which begins *Recycling is understood,* in the fifth line, click to position the insertion point to the right of the quotation mark. In the **Citations & Bibliography group**, click the **Insert Citation** button, and then click **Add New Source**. Click the **Type of Source arrow**, click **Journal Article**, and then add the following information (type the Title on one line):

Author:	**Pennisi, Elizabeth**
Title:	**Shale-Eating Microbes Recycle Global Carbon**
Journal Name:	**Science**
Year:	**2001**
Pages:	**1043**

c. Click **OK**. In the text, click to select the citation, click the **Citation Options arrow**, and then click **Edit Citation**. In the **Edit Citation** dialog box, under **Add**, in the **Pages** box, type **1043** and then click **OK**. Add a period to the right of the citation and delete the period to the left of the quotation mark.

d. In the same paragraph, position the insertion point at the end of the paragraph. In the **Citations & Bibliography group**, click the **Insert Citation** button, and then click **Add New Source**. Click the **Type of Source arrow**, click **Book**, and then add the following information (type the Author information on one line):

Author:	**Khlebopros, Rem; Okhonin, Viktor; Fet, Abram**
Title:	**Catastrophes in Nature and Society**
Year:	**2007**
City:	**Singapore**
Publisher:	**World Scientific Publishing Company**

e. Click **OK**. Click to select the citation, click the **Citation Options arrow**, and then click **Edit Citation**. In the **Edit Citation** dialog box, under **Add**, in the **Pages** box, type **111** Click **OK**. Add a period to the right of the citation and delete the period to the left of the quotation mark.

f. Press Ctrl + End to move the insertion point to the end of the document. Press Ctrl + Enter to insert a manual page break. On the ruler, drag the **First Line Indent** button to the left to **0 inches on the horizontal ruler**.

g. Type **Works Cited** and then press Enter. On the **References tab**, in the **Citations & Bibliography group**, be sure **MLA** displays in the **Style** box. In the **Citations & Bibliography group**, click the **Bibliography** button, and then click **Insert Bibliography**.

h. In the bibliography, move the pointer to the left of the first entry—beginning *Khlebopros*—to display the pointer. Drag down to select all three references. On the **Home tab**, in the **Paragraph group**, set the **Line spacing** to **2.0**. On the **Page Layout tab**, set the **Spacing After** to **0 pt**.

i. Right-click the *Works Cited* title, and then from the Mini toolbar, click the **Center** button. **Save** your document.

4 From **Backstage** view, display the **Document Panel**, type your name and course information, and then add the keywords **recycling, nature, research paper** In the upper left corner of the panel, click the **Document Properties** button, and then click **Advanced Properties**.

(Project 6C Recycling Report continues on the next page)

Skills Review | Project 6C Recycling Report (continued)

a. In the **Properties** dialog box, click the **Summary tab**. In the **Properties** dialog box, fill in the following information:

Title:	**Recycling in Nature**
Manager:	**Henry Miller**
Company:	**Memphis Primary Materials**
Comments:	**Draft of a new white paper research report on recycling**

b. At the bottom of the **Properties** dialog box, click **OK**. **Close** the **Document Panel**. **Save** your document. View the Print Preview, and then print or submit electronically as directed by your instructor. **Exit** Word.

End **You have completed Project 6C**

Content-Based Assessments

Apply 6B skills from these Objectives:

4 Format a Multiple-Column Newsletter

5 Use Special Character and Paragraph Formatting

6 Create Mailing Labels Using Mail Merge

Skills Review | Project 6D Company Newsletter

In the following Skills Review, you will format a newsletter for Memphis Primary Materials, and then create a set of mailing labels for the newsletter. Your completed documents will look similar to Figure 6.42.

Project Files

For Project 6D, you will need the following files:

New blank Word document
w03D_Company_Newsletter
w03D_Addresses

You will save your documents as:

Lastname_Firstname_3D_Company_Newsletter
Lastname_Firstname_3D_Addresses
Lastname_Firstname_3D_Labels

Project Results

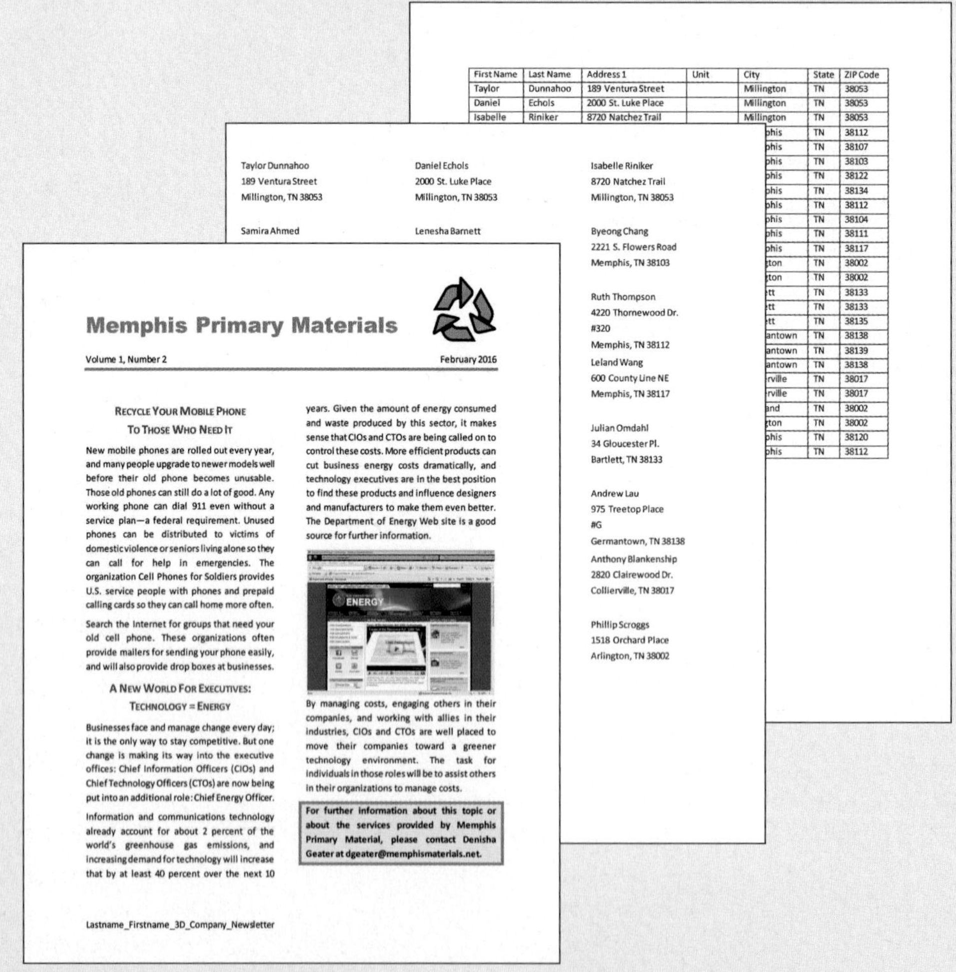

Figure 6.42

(Project 6D Company Newsletter continues on the next page)

Skills Review | Project 6D Company Newsletter (continued)

1 **Start** Word. From your student files, open the document **w03D_Company_Newsletter**. **Save** the file in your **Word Chapter 6** folder as **Lastname_Firstname_3D_Company_Newsletter** and then add the file name to the footer.

a. Select the first paragraph of text—*Memphis Primary Materials*. From the Mini toolbar, change the **Font** to **Arial Black** and the **Font Size** to **24**. Select the title you just formatted. Click the **Font Color button arrow**, and then under **Theme Colors**, in the seventh column, click the fifth color—**Olive Green, Accent 3, Darker 25%**.

b. Select the second paragraph. On the **Home tab**, in the **Paragraph group**, click the **Borders button arrow**, and then click **Borders and Shading**. In the **Borders and Shading** dialog box, click the **Color arrow**, and then under **Theme Colors**, in the seventh column, click the fifth color—**Olive Green, Accent 3, Darker 25%**. Click the **Width arrow**, and then click **3 pt**. In the **Preview** area, click the *bottom* border of the Preview and then click **OK**.

c. Below the nameplate, locate the paragraph that begins *Recycle Your Mobile*, and then select all of the text from that point to the end of the document. On the **Page Layout tab**, in the **Page Setup group**, click the **Columns** button, and then click **Two**.

d. With the text still selected, in the **Paragraph group**, set **Spacing After** to **6 pt**. On the **Home tab**, in the **Paragraph group**, click the **Justify** button. Click anywhere in the document to deselect the text, and then **Save** the newsletter.

e. Press Ctrl + Home. On the **Insert tab**, in the **Illustrations group**, click the **Clip Art** button. In the **Clip Art** task pane, click in the **Search for** box, and then type **conservation**

f. In the **Clip Art** task pane, click the **Results should be arrow**, and be sure that only the **Illustrations** check box is selected. Be sure the **Include Office.com content** check box is selected, and then click **Go**. Locate the image of three green arrows, as shown in Figure 6.42, and then click on the image.

g. On the **Format tab**, in the **Size group**, click in the **Shape Height** box, type **1** and then press Enter. In the **Arrange group**, click the **Wrap Text** button, and then click **Square**. **Close** the Clip Art task pane, and then drag the image to the location shown in Figure 6.42.

h. In the second column, position the insertion point at the beginning of the paragraph that begins *By managing costs*. Open your Web browser. In the address bar, type **www.energy.gov** and then press Enter. Maximize the browser window. Use the taskbar to return to your Word document.

i. On the **Insert tab**, in the **Illustrations group**, click the **Screenshot** button. In the gallery, click the DOE screenshot to insert it. **Close** your Web browser, and then **Save** your document.

2 At the top of the first column, select the paragraph that begins *Recycle Your Mobile*. Be sure to include the paragraph mark. Right-click the selected text, and then click **Font**. In the **Font** dialog box, click the **Font color arrow**, and then under **Theme Colors**, in the seventh column, click the last color—**Olive Green, Accent 3, Darker 50%**. Under **Font style**, click **Bold**. Under **Size**, click **14**. Under **Effects**, select the **Small caps** check box.

a. In the **Font** dialog box, click **OK**. Right-click the selected text, and then click the **Center** button. In the title you just formatted, click to position the insertion point to the right of *Phone*, and then press Del to remove the space. Hold down Shift, and then press Enter to insert a manual line break.

b. Select and right-click the title you just formatted, and then on the Mini toolbar, click the **Format Painter** button. Near the middle of the first column, select the paragraph that begins *A New World* to apply the same formatting.

c. At the bottom of the second column, in the paragraph that begins *For further*, select the entire paragraph. On the Mini toolbar, apply **Bold**.

d. With the text still selected, on the **Home tab**, in the **Paragraph group**, click the **Borders button arrow**, and then click **Borders and Shading**. In the **Borders and Shading** dialog box, be sure the **Borders tab** is selected. Under **Setting**, click **Box**. Click the **Width arrow**, and then click **3 pt**. If necessary, click the **Color arrow**, and then in the seventh column, click the fifth color—**Olive Green, Accent 3, Darker 25%**.

e. At the top of the **Borders and Shading** dialog box, click the **Shading tab**. Click the **Fill arrow**, and then in the seventh column, click the second color—**Olive Green, Accent 3, Lighter 80%**. At the bottom of the **Borders and Shading** dialog box, click **OK**. Click anywhere in the document to deselect the text.

(Project 6D Company Newsletter continues on the next page)

Content-Based Assessments

Skills Review | Project 6D Company Newsletter (continued)

f. Near the bottom of the first column, in the paragraph that begins *Information and communications*, click to position the insertion point at the beginning of the sixth line. On the **Page Layout tab**, in the **Page Setup group**, click the **Breaks** button. Under **Page Breaks**, click **Column**.

g. From **Backstage** view, display the **Document Panel**, type your name and course information. Add the keywords **newsletter, energy** and then **Close** the **Document Panel**. **Save** the document, view the Print Preview, and then **Exit** Word. Hold this file until you complete this project.

3 **Start** Word and display a new blank document. Display formatting marks and rulers. **Save** the document in your **Word Chapter 6** folder as **Lastname_Firstname_3D_Labels Open** the file **w03D_Addresses Save** the address file in your **Word Chapter 6** folder as **Lastname_Firstname_3D_Addresses** and then add the file name to the footer.

a. Click to position the insertion point in the last cell in the table, and then press Tab to create a new row. Enter the following new record:

First Name	**Eldon**
Last Name	**Aarons**
Address 1	**5354 Thornewood Dr.**
Unit	**#2B**
City	**Memphis**
State	**TN**
ZIP Code	**38112**

b. **Save**, and then **Close** the table of addresses; be sure your blank **Lastname_Firstname_3D_Labels** document displays. Click the **Mailings tab**. In the **Start Mail Merge group**, click the **Start Mail Merge** button, and then click **Step by Step Mail Merge Wizard**. Under **Select document type**, click the **Labels** option button.

c. At the bottom of the task pane, click **Next: Starting document**. Under **Select starting document**, be sure **Change document layout** is selected, and then under **Change document layout**, click **Label options**.

d. In the **Label Options** dialog box, under **Printer information**, click the **Tray arrow**, and then click **Default tray (Automatically Select)**.

e. Under **Label information**, click the **Label vendors arrow**, and then click **Avery US Letter**. Under **Product number**, scroll about halfway down the list, and then click **5160**. At the bottom of the **Label Options** dialog box, click **OK**. At the bottom of the task pane, click **Next: Select recipients**.

f. Under **Select recipients**, be sure the **Use an existing list** option button is selected. Under **Use an existing list**, click **Browse**. Navigate to your **Word Chapter 6** folder, select your **Lastname_Firstname_3D_Addresses** file, and then click **Open**. At the bottom of the **Mail Merge Recipients** dialog box, click **OK**, and then in the **Mail Merge** task pane, click **Next: Arrange your labels**.

g. Under **Arrange your labels**, click **Address block**. If necessary, in the **Insert Address Block** dialog box, under **Insert recipient's name in this format**, select the **Joshua Randall Jr.** format.

h. Click **Match Fields**. Click the **Address 2 arrow**, and then click **Unit**. Click **OK** two times.

i. In the task pane, under **Replicate labels**, click **Update all labels**. Click **Next: Preview your labels**. Press Ctrl + A to select all of the label text, and then on the **Page Layout tab**, click in the **Spacing Before** box, type **4** and press Enter to ensure that the four-line addresses will fit on the labels. **Save** your labels, and then **Close** the **Mail Merge** task pane.

4 Add the file name to the footer, and then close the footer area. Click in the bottom empty row of the table, click the **Layout tab**, in the **Rows & Columns group**, click **Delete**, and then click **Delete Rows**. From **Backstage** view, display the **Document Panel**, type your name and course information, and then add the keywords **newsletter mailing labels Close** the **Document Panel**.

a. Print or submit electronically your 3D_Company_Newsletter, 3D_Addresses, and 3D_Labels documents.

b. **Close** the document, click **Save** to save the labels, and then **Exit** Word.

End You have completed Project 6D

Apply 6A skills from these Objectives:

1. Create a Research Paper
2. Insert Footnotes in a Research Paper
3. Create Citations and a Bibliography in a Research Paper

Mastering Word | Project 6E Hazards

In the following Mastering Word project, you will edit and format a research paper for Memphis Primary Materials, the topic of which is hazardous materials in electronic waste. Your completed document will look similar to Figure 6.43.

Project Files

For Project 6E, you will need the following file:

w03E_Hazards

You will save your document as:

Lastname_Firstname_3E_Hazards

Project Results

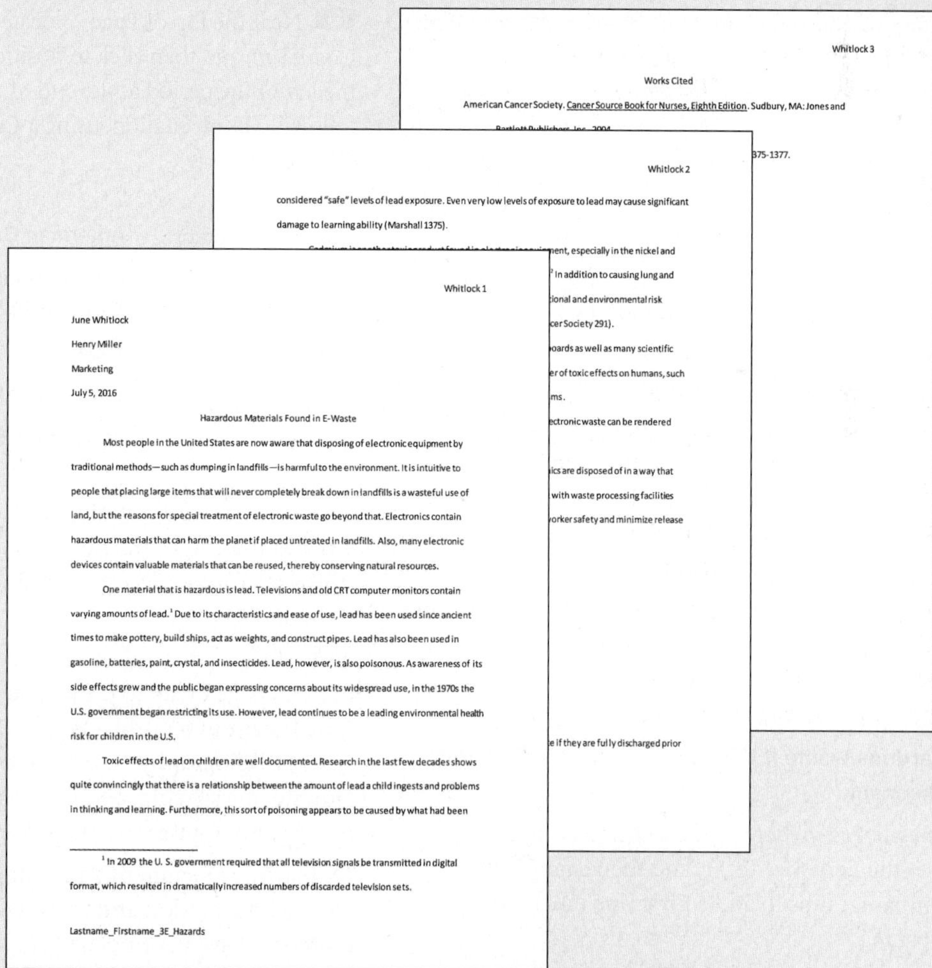

Whitlock 3

Works Cited

American Cancer Society. Cancer Source Book for Nurses, Eighth Edition. Sudbury, MA: Jones and

375-1377.

Whitlock 2

considered "safe" levels of lead exposure. Even very low levels of exposure to lead may cause significant damage to learning ability (Marshall 1375).

ment, especially in the nickel and

In addition to causing lung and

ional and environmental risk

cer Society 291).

oards as well as many scientific

er of toxic effects on humans, such

ms.

ctronic waste can be rendered

ics are disposed of in a way that

with waste processing facilities

orker safety and minimize release

e if they are fully discharged prior

Whitlock 1

June Whitlock

Henry Miller

Marketing

July 5, 2016

Hazardous Materials Found in E-Waste

Most people in the United States are now aware that disposing of electronic equipment by traditional methods—such as dumping in landfills—is harmful to the environment. It is intuitive to people that placing large items that will never completely break down in landfills is a wasteful use of land, but the reasons for special treatment of electronic waste go beyond that. Electronics contain hazardous materials that can harm the planet if placed untreated in landfills. Also, many electronic devices contain valuable materials that can be reused, thereby conserving natural resources.

One material that is hazardous is lead. Televisions and old CRT computer monitors contain varying amounts of lead.[1] Due to its characteristics and ease of use, lead has been used since ancient times to make pottery, build ships, act as weights, and construct pipes. Lead has also been used in gasoline, batteries, paint, crystal, and insecticides. Lead, however, is also poisonous. As awareness of its side effects grew and the public began expressing concerns about its widespread use, in the 1970s the U.S. government began restricting its use. However, lead continues to be a leading environmental health risk for children in the U.S.

Toxic effects of lead on children are well documented. Research in the last few decades shows quite convincingly that there is a relationship between the amount of lead a child ingests and problems in thinking and learning. Furthermore, this sort of poisoning appears to be caused by what had been

[1] In 2009 the U. S. government required that all television signals be transmitted in digital format, which resulted in dramatically increased numbers of discarded television sets.

Lastname_Firstname_3E_Hazards

Figure 6.43

(Project 6E Hazards continues on the next page)

Content-Based Assessments

Mastering Word | Project 6E Hazards (continued)

1 **Start** Word. From your student files open the document **w03E_Hazards. Save** the document in your **Word Chapter 6** folder as **Lastname_Firstname_3E_ Hazards** Display the header area, type **Whitlock** and then press Spacebar. Display the **Page Number gallery**, and then in the **Current Position**, add the **Plain Number** style. Apply **Align Text Right** formatting to the header. Add the file name to the footer.

2 Return to the beginning of the document, press Enter to insert a blank line, click in the blank line, type **June Whitlock** and then press Enter. Type **Henry Miller** and press Enter. Type **Marketing** and press Enter. Type **July 5, 2016**

3 Select all of the text in the document. Change the **Line Spacing** to **2.0**, and change the **Spacing After** to **0 pt**. Deselect the text, right-click anywhere in the title *Hazardous Materials Found in E-Waste*, and then **Center** the title.

Starting with the paragraph that begins *Most people*, select the text from that point to the end of the document, and then set the **First Line Indent** to **0.5"**.

4 Near the middle of **Page 1**, in the paragraph that begins *One material*, in the second line, click to position the insertion point to the right of the period following *lead*, and then add the following footnote:

> **In 2009 the U.S. government required that all television signals be transmitted in digital format, which resulted in dramatically increased numbers of discarded television sets.**

On **Page 2**, in the paragraph that begins *Cadmium is another*, in the second line, click to position the insertion point to the right of the period following *devices*, and then add the following footnote:

> **Newer lithium batteries are not considered hazardous waste if they are fully discharged prior to disposal.**

5 Right-click anywhere in the footnote, modify the **Style** to set the **Font Size** to **11**, and then change the **Format** of paragraphs to add a **First line** indent and use double-spacing.

Near the bottom of **Page 1**, locate the paragraph that begins *Toxic effects*, and then click position the insertion point to the left of the period at the end of the paragraph, which displays at the top of **Page 2**. In the **MLA** format, add the following **Journal Article** citation (type the Title on one line):

Author:	**Marshall, Eliot**
Title:	**EPA May Allow More Lead in Gasoline**
Journal Name:	**Science**
Year:	**1982**
Pages:	**1375–1377**

6 Near the top of **Page 2**, locate the paragraph that begins *Cadmium*, and then click to position the insertion point to the left of the period at the end of the paragraph. Add the following **Book** citation, using a **Corporate Author** (type the Title on one line):

Corporate Author:	**American Cancer Society**
Title:	**Cancer Source Book for Nurses, Eighth Edition**
Year:	**2004**
City:	**Sudbury, MA**
Publisher:	**Jones and Bartlett Publishers, Inc.**

Select the *Marshall* citation and add the page number **1375** At the end of the next paragraph, select the *American Cancer Society* citation and add the page number **291**

7 Move to the end of the document, and then insert a manual page break to create a new page. Change the **First Line Indent** to **0"**. Add a **Works Cited** title, and then **Insert Bibliography**. Select the two references, apply **Double** line spacing, and then remove spacing after the paragraphs. **Center** the *Works Cited* title.

Display the **Document Panel** and add your name and course information and the keywords **hazardous materials Save** your document. Display the Print Preview, make any necessary adjustments, and then print or submit electronically as directed. **Exit** Word.

You have completed Project 6E

Content-Based Assessments

Apply 6B skills from these Objectives:

4 Format a Multiple-Column Newsletter

5 Use Special Character and Paragraph Formatting

6 Create Mailing Labels Using Mail Merge

Mastering Word | Project 6F Spring Newsletter

In the following Mastering Word project, you will format a newsletter for Memphis Primary Materials, and then create a set of mailing labels for the newsletter. Your completed documents will look similar to Figure 6.44.

Project Files

For Project 6F, you will need the following files:

New blank Word document
w03F_Spring_Newsletter
w03F_Addresses

You will save your documents as:

Lastname_Firstname_3F_Spring_Newsletter
Lastname_Firstname_3F_Labels

Project Results

Jessica Pyun
1255 Miravista Street
Memphis, TN 38122

Samantha Quick
124 Whitworth Drive
#352
Memphis, TN 38134

Ruth Thompson
4220 Thornewood Dr.
#320
Memphis, TN 38112

Leland Wang
600 County Line NE
Memphis, TN 38117

Julian Omdahl
34 Gloucester Pl.
Bartlett, TN 38133

Andrew Lau
975 Treetop Place
#G
Germantown, TN 38138

Anthony Blankenship
2820 Clairewood
Collierville, TN 38017

Phillip Scroggs
1518 Orchard Place
Arlington, TN 38002

Alicia Hernandez
888 Dell Court
Lakeland, TN 38002

Michelle Norris
One Charleston Way
Memphis, TN 38120

Memphis Primary Materials

Volume 1, Number 3 March 2016

CARE ENOUGH TO RECYCLE

Carpet America Recovery Effort (CARE) is a joint effort between the carpet industry and the US Government to reduce the amount of carpet and padding being disposed of in landfills. Billions of pounds of carpet are disposed of each year.

Fortunately, carpet and padding can be recycled into new padding fiber, home accessories, erosion control products, and construction products. The CARE initiative combines the resources of manufacturers and local governments to find new ideas for old carpet and to overcome barriers to recycling.

For information on companies participating in the program and to find out if you are near a carpet reclamation center, please visit http://www.carpetrecovery.org

HAZARDS OF OLD HOME APPLIANCES

In 2006, the Environmental Protection Agency created a voluntary partnership effort to recover ozone-depleting materials from appliances like old refrigerators, freezers, air conditioners, and humidifiers. The program outlines best practices for recovering or destroying refrigerant and foam, recycling metals, plastic, and glass, and proper disposal of hazards like PCBs, oil, and mercury.

This initiative creates opportunities for for-profit companies like Memphis Primary Materials. We provide appliance recycling services to our business clients that include picking up old products, advising on the most energy-efficient new products, and processing discarded items for optimum safety and minimal environmental impact.

Memphis Primary Materials also completes the EPA RAD (Responsible Appliance Disposal) worksheet, which calculates how much energy usage and carbon-equivalent emissions were reduced as a result of their efforts.

For more information on the EPA programs for appliance recycling, see their Web site at http://www.epa.gov/ozone/partnerships/rad/index.html

The EPA's RAD Annual Report is online at http://www.epa.gov/ozone/partnerships/rad

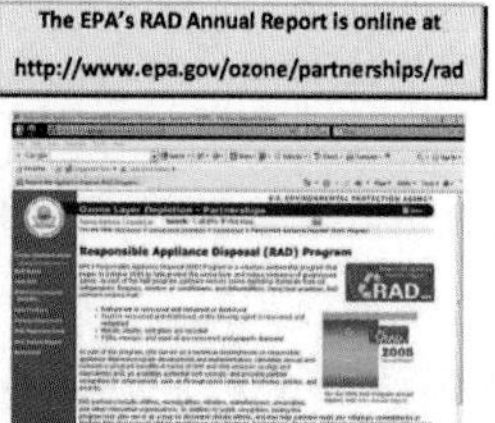

Lastname_Firstname_3F_Spring_Newsletter

Figure 6.44

(Project 6F Spring Newsletter continues on the next page)

Mastering Word | Project 6F Spring Newsletter (continued)

1 **Start** Word. Open **w03F_Spring_Newsletter**, and then save it in your **Word Chapter 6** folder as **Lastname_Firstname_3F_Spring_Newsletter** Add the file name to the footer. Display the rulers and formatting marks.

Select the first line of text—*Memphis Primary Materials*. Change the **Font** to **Arial Black**, the **Font Size** to **24**, and the **Font Color** to **Orange, Accent 6, Darker 25%**.

Select the second line of text—the date and volume. Change the **Font Color** to **Orange, Accent 6, Darker 25%**. Display the **Borders and Shading** dialog box, and then add an **Orange, Accent 6, Darker 25%**, **3 pt** line below the selected text.

2 Click at the beginning of the newsletter title. Display the **Clip Art** task pane, search for **recycle earth** and then insert the image of the orange and tan recycle arrows. Change the **Height** to **1** and then apply **Square** text wrapping. Close the **Clip Art** task pane. Drag the image to the location shown in Figure 6.44.

Starting with the paragraph that begins *CARE enough*, select all of the text from that point to the end of the document. Change the **Spacing After** to **6 pt**, format the text in two columns, and apply the **Justify** alignment.

3 At the top of the first column, select the paragraph *CARE Enough to Recycle*. From the **Font** dialog box, change the **Font Size** to **20**, apply **Bold**, add the **Small caps** effect, and change the **Font color** to **Orange, Accent 6, Darker 25%**. **Center** the paragraph. Near the bottom of the same column, apply the same formatting to the paragraph that begins *Hazards of Old*. Add a manual line break between *Old* and *Home*.

Move to the blank line at the bottom of the second column. Open your Web browser and open the **www.epa.gov/ozone/partnerships/rad/** Web site. Maximize the browser window and return to your Word document. Insert a **Screenshot** of the EPA Web page. **Close** your Web browser.

4 Select the two lines of text above the inserted screenshot. **Center** the text and apply **Bold**. Add a **Shadow** border, change the **Color** to **Tan, Background 2, Darker 25%**, the **Width** to **1 1/2 pt**, and then on the **Shading tab** of the dialog box, apply a **Fill** of **Tan, Background 2** shading—in the third column, the first color.

Display the **Document Panel** and add your name, course information, and the **Keywords Spring newsletter** Display the **Print Preview**, return to your document and make any necessary corrections, and then **Save** and **Close** the document. Hold this document until you complete the project.

5 Display a **New** blank document. **Save** the document in your **Word Chapter 6** folder as **Lastname_Firstname_3F_Labels** On the **Mailings tab**, start the **Step by Step Mail Merge Wizard.**

In **Step 1**, select **Labels** as the document type. In **Step 2**, set **Label options** to use the **Auto default** tray (yours may vary) and **Avery US Letter 5160**.

In **Step 3**, use an existing list, browse to select **w03F_Addresses**. In **Step 4**, add an **Address block** to the labels, use the *Joshua Randall Jr.* format, and then **Match Fields** by matching *Address 2* to *Unit*.

Update all labels and **Preview**. Select all of the label text, and then on the **Page Layout tab**, click in the **Spacing Before** box, type **4** and press Enter to ensure that the four-line addresses will fit on the labels. On the **Layout tab**, in the **Table group**, if necessary click **View Gridlines** to check the alignment of the labels.

Complete the merge, and then **Close** the **Mail Merge** task pane. Delete the last two empty rows of the table, and then add the file name to the footer.

6 Display the **Document Panel**, and then add your name and course information and the keywords **mailing labels** Display the **Print Preview**, return to your document and make any necessary corrections, and then **Save**. Print or submit electronically your two files that are the results of this project—3F_Spring_Newsletter and 3F_Labels. **Exit** Word.

End **You have completed Project 6F**

Apply 6A and 6B skills from these Objectives:

1. Create a Research Paper
2. Insert Footnotes in a Research Paper
3. Create Citations and a Bibliography in a Research Paper
4. Format a Multiple-Column Newsletter
5. Use Special Character and Paragraph Formatting
6. Create Mailing Labels Using Mail Merge

Mastering Word | Project 6G Economics

In the following Mastering Word project, you will edit and format a newsletter and a research paper for Memphis Primary Materials on the topic of environmental economics. Your completed documents will look similar to Figure 6.45.

Project Files

For Project 6G, you will need the following files:

New blank Word document
w03G_Economics
w03G_Addresses
w03G_April_Newsletter

You will save your documents as:

Lastname_Firstname_3G_Economics
Lastname_Firstname_3G_April_Newsletter
Lastname_Firstname_3G_Labels

Project Results

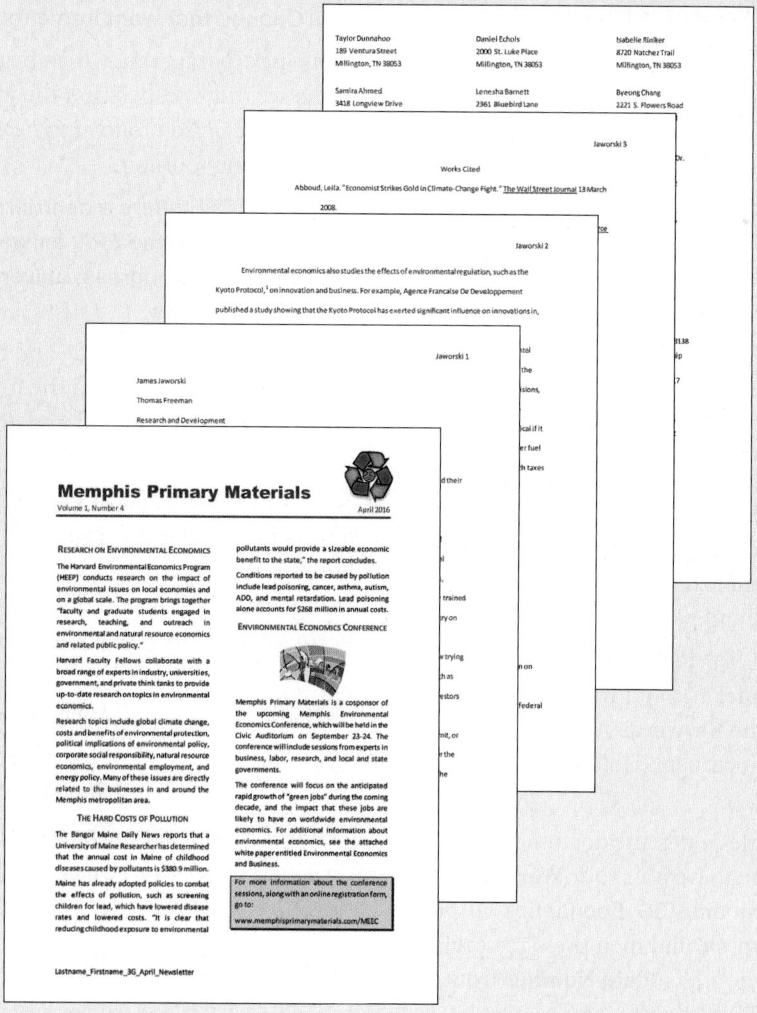

Figure 6.45

(Project 6G Economics continues on the next page)

Mastering Word | Project 6G Economics (continued)

1 **Start** Word. Open the document **w03G_April_Newsletter**, and then save the document in your **Word Chapter 6** folder as **Lastname_Firstname_3G_April_Newsletter** Add the file name to the footer. Starting with the paragraph that begins *Research on Environmental Economics*, select all of the text from that point to the end of the document—the document text extends to two pages. Set the **Spacing After** to **6 pt**, format the selected text as two columns, and set the alignment to **Justify**.

2 Near the bottom of the first column, in the paragraph that begins *Maine has already*, click to position the insertion point to the left of the sixth line, which begins *pollutants would*. Insert a column break. At the top of the first column, select the paragraph *Research on Environmental Economics*.

Display the **Font** dialog box, set the **Font Size** to **14**, apply **Bold**, set the **Font color** to **Dark Blue, Text 2**, and then add the **Small caps** effect. **Center** the paragraph. Use the Format Painter to copy the formatting and then apply the same formatting to the paragraph *The Hard Costs of Pollution* located near the bottom of the first column and to *Environmental Economics Conference* in the second column.

3 At the bottom of the second column, select the last two paragraphs of text. From the **Borders and Shading** dialog box, apply a **1 1/2 pt**, **Shadow** border using the **Dark Blue, Text 2** color, and then on the **Shading tab**, apply a **Fill** of **Dark Blue, Text 2, Lighter 80%**.

In the second column, click to position the insertion point at the beginning of the paragraph that begins *Memphis Primary Materials is a cosponsor*. Display the **Clip Art** task pane. Search for **conference** and limit your search to **Illustrations**. **Insert** the image shown in Figure 6.45, apply **Top and Bottom** text wrapping, decrease the **Height** of the image to **1″**, and position the image as shown. **Close** the Clip Art task pane.

Display the **Document Panel** and add your name and course information and the **Keywords April newsletter** **Save** and then **Close** the document. Hold this file until you complete this project.

4 From your student files, open the document **w03G_Economics**, and then save it in your **Word Chapter 6** folder as **Lastname_Firstname_3G_Economics** Display the header area, type **Jaworski** and then press Spacebar. In the **Header & Footer group**, add a **Plain Number** from the **Current Position** gallery. Apply **Align Text Right** formatting to the header. Move to the footer area and add the file name to the footer.

Select all of the text in the document. Change the **Line Spacing** to **2.0**, and change the **Spacing After** to **0**. Near the top of the document, **Center** the title *Environmental Economics and Business*. Beginning with the text below the centered title, select the text from that point to the end of the document, and then set a **First Line Indent** at **0.5″**.

5 At the bottom of **Page 1**, in the paragraph that begins *Environmental economics also*, in the second line, click to position the insertion point to the right of the comma following *Protocol*, and then insert the following footnote:

> **The Kyoto Protocol is an international agreement under the UN Framework Convention on Climate Change that went into effect in 2005.**

In the next paragraph, which begins *In the United States*, in the second line, position the insertion point to the right of the period following *Economics*, and then insert the following footnote:

> **The NCEE offers a centralized source of technical expertise to the EPA, as well as other federal agencies, Congress, universities, and other organizations.**

Right-click in the footnote, and then modify the style to set the **Font Size** to **11** and the format of the paragraph to include a **First line** indent and double-spacing. **Save** your document.

6 Near the bottom of **Page 1**, in the paragraph that begins *Environmental economists*, position the insertion point to the left of the period at the end of the paragraph. Using **MLA** format, add the following **Article in a Periodical** citation (type the Title on one line):

Author:	**Abboud, Leila**
Title:	**Economist Strikes Gold in Climate-Change Fight**
Periodical Title:	**The Wall Street Journal**
Year:	**2008**
Month:	**March**
Day:	**13**

(Project 6G Economics continues on the next page)

Mastering Word | Project 6G Economics (continued)

Select the *Abboud* citation and add the page number **A1** Near the middle of **Page 2**, in the paragraph that begins *In the United States*, click to position the insertion point to the left of the period at the end of the paragraph. Add the following **Book** citation in **MLA** format (type the Title on one line):

Author:	**Tietenberg, Tom; Folmer, Henk, Editors**
Title:	**The International Yearbook of Environmental Resource Economics, 2006/2007**
Year:	**2006**
City:	**Northampton, MA**
Publisher:	**Edward Elgar Publishers**

7 Select the *Tietenberg* citation and add the page number **1** Insert a manual page break at the end of the document. On the new **Page 3**, on the ruler, set the **First Line Indent** to **0"**. Type **Works Cited** and then press Enter.

On the **References tab**, in the **Citations & Bibliography group**, be sure *MLA* displays in the **Style** box. Insert the bibliography. Select the inserted references, set the **Line Spacing** to **2.0**, and then set **Spacing After** to **0 pt**. **Center** the *Works Cited* title.

Display the **Document Panel** and add your name and course information and the **Keywords environmental economics** Display the **Print Preview** to check your document, make any necessary adjustments, **Save**, and then **Close** the document. Hold this file until you complete this project.

8 Display a **New** blank document. **Save** the document in your **Word Chapter 6** folder as **Lastname_Firstname_3G_Labels** On the **Mailings tab**, start the **Step by Step Mail Merge Wizard**. In **Step 1**, select **Labels** as the document type. In **Step 2**, set **Label options** to use the **Auto default** tray (yours may vary) and **Avery US Letter 5160**. If you cannot see the gridlines, on the **Layout tab**, in the **Table group**, click **View Gridlines**. In **Step 3**, use an existing list, browse to select **w03G_Addresses**, and then click **OK**.

In **Step 4**, add an **Address block** to the labels, use the *Joshua Randall Jr.* format, and then **Match Fields** by matching *Address 2* to *Unit*. **Update all labels** and then **Preview**. Select all of the label text, and then on the **Page Layout tab**, click in the **Spacing Before** box, type **4** and press Enter. Complete the merge, and then **Close** the **Mail Merge** task pane. Delete the last two empty rows of the table, and then add the file name to the footer, which adds an additional page.

Display the **Document Panel**, and then add your name, course information, and the keywords **mailing labels** Click **Save**. Print or submit electronically your three files that are the results of this project—3G_Economics, 3G_April_Newsletter, and 3G_Labels. **Exit** Word.

End **You have completed Project 6G**

Apply a combination of the **6A** and **6B** skills.

GO! Fix It | Project **6H** Metals Report

Project Files

For Project 6H, you will need the following file:

w03H_Metals_Report

You will save your document as:

Lastname_Firstname_3H_Metals_Report

From the student files that accompany this textbook, locate and open the file w03H_Metals_Report, and then save the file in your Word Chapter 6 folder as **Lastname_Firstname_3H_Metals_Report**

This document contains errors that you must find and correct. Read and examine the document, and then edit to correct any errors that you find and to improve the overall document format. Types of errors could include, but are not restricted to:

- Formatting does not match MLA style guidelines that you practiced in the chapter
- Incorrect header format
- Incorrect spacing between paragraphs
- Incorrect paragraph indents
- Incorrect line spacing
- Incorrect footnote format
- Incorrectly formatted reference page

Things you should know to complete this project:

- Displaying formatting marks will assist in locating spacing errors.
- There are no errors in the parenthetical references in the document.
- There are no errors in the information in the footnotes or bibliographical references.

Save your document and add the file name to the footer. In the Document Panel, add your name, course information, and the keywords **valuable metals, recycling** Save your document and submit as directed.

You have completed Project 6H

Apply a combination of the 6A and 6B skills.

GO! Make It | Project 6I Green Newsletter

Project Files

For Project 6I, you will need the following files:

New blank Word document
w03I_Competition
w03I_Kids

You will save your document as:

Lastname_Firstname_3I_Green_Newsletter

Start with a new Word document, and then save the file in your chapter folder as **Lastname_Firstname_3I_Green_Newsletter** Create the document shown in Figure 6.46. Create a nameplate, and then insert the files w03I_Competition and w03I_Kids. The title is Arial Black, 24 pt, Dark Blue, Text 2. Other titles and borders are Dark Blue, Text 2. The two titles in the columns are Calibri, 16 pt. The clip art image can be found by using the search term **recycle** and the screenshot can be found at the Web address in the last line of the newsletter.

Add the file name to the footer; in the Document Panel, add your name and course information and the Keywords **green, campuses, kids** Save your document and submit as directed.

Project Results

Memphis Primary Materials

Volume 1, Number 4 April 2016

THE COMPETITIVE SPIRIT OF GREEN

One way to increase people's willingness to reuse and recycle is to invoke their spirit of competition—and prizes do not hurt either. College campuses are proving this by participating in the America's Greenest Campus competition.

America's Greenest Campus is a nationwide contest, with the goal of reducing the carbon footprint of entire campus populations across the country.

Partnering with Smart Power and the U.S. Department of Energy, the winning campus will receive a donation of $10,000. As of February 2009, the University of Maryland has reduced its CO2 emissions by 2% and George Mason University by 3%.

Students, faculty, and staff are encouraged to recycle, turn off lights, reduce heating and air conditioning, and engage in many other small and large changes that can help the environment. Treehugger.com calls the contest, "the NCAA of sustainability."

Another college competition for environmentalism is RecycleMania. Designed to encourage colleges and universities to reduce waste, the competition collects reports on recycling and trash over a 10-week period. This competition thinks of colleges and universities as small cities that consume large amounts of resources and generate a lot of solid waste. Participating campuses are ranked by categories such as "least amount of waste per capita." Weekly results are distributed to the participants so they can benchmark against their competition and step up their efforts.

With growing awareness of the need to reduce, reuse, and recycle among students, expect some competition if you are part of a campus community!

CLEANUP IS FOR KIDS

Cleaning up the planet isn't just for college students. Younger students often have a desire to get involved with environmental activities, and there is no shortage of resources.

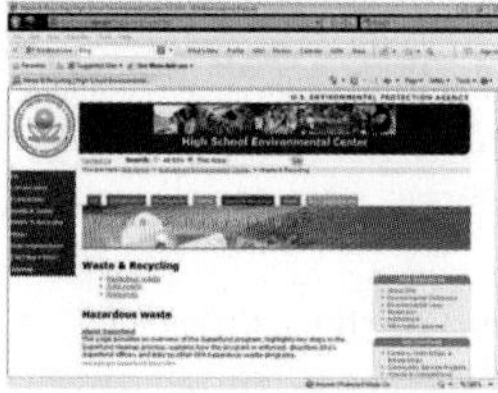

Start at the website of the Environmental Protection Agency. They provide resources like Cleanup for Kids, a Web site of the National Oceanic and Atmospheric Administration (NOAA), which makes the hazards of oil spills real through science demonstrations. The brochure, *Environmental Protection Begins With You*, outlines examples of community volunteer projects in which students can participate.

Learn more at the EPA website:
http://www.epa.gov/highschool/waste.htm

Lastname_Firstname_3I_Green_Newsletter

Figure 6.46

End You have completed Project 6I

Content-Based Assessments

Apply a combination of the 6A and 6B skills.

GO! Solve It | Project 6J Municipal Newsletter

Project Files

For Project 6J, you will need the following file:

New blank Word document

You will save your document as:

Lastname_Firstname_3J_Municipal_Newsletter

Memphis Primary Materials writes an informational newsletter for customers. Create a new document and save it in your Word Chapter 6 folder as **Lastname_Firstname_3J_Municipal_Newsletter** Use the following information to create a newsletter that includes a nameplate, multiple columns, at least two articles with article titles formatted so that they stand out, at least one clip art image, one screenshot, and one paragraph that includes a border and shading.

This issue (Volume 1, Number 6—June 2016) will focus on municipal solid waste—the waste generated by householders and small businesses. This category of waste does not include hazardous, industrial, or construction waste. The articles you write can be on any topic regarding municipal waste, and might include an introduction to the topic and a discussion of recycling in the U.S. or in the Memphis community. You will need to research this topic on the Web. A good place to start is www.epa.gov, which has many articles on solid municipal waste, and also provides links to further articles on the topic. You might also consider doing a Web search for the term **municipal solid waste recycling**

Add the file name to the footer. To the Document Panel, add your name, your course name and section number, and the keywords **municipal solid waste recycling**

		Performance Level	
	Exemplary: You consistently applied the relevant skills	**Proficient:** You sometimes, but not always, applied the relevant skills	**Developing:** You rarely or never applied the relevant skills
Performance Element: Create and format nameplate	The nameplate includes both the company name and the date and volume information, and is formatted attractively.	One or more of the nameplate elements are done correctly, but other items are either omitted or not formatted properly.	The newsletter does not include a nameplate.
Insert at least two articles in multiple-column format	The newsletter contains at least two articles, displayed in multiple columns that are well written and are free of grammar and spelling errors.	The newsletter contains only one article, or the text is not divided into two columns, or there are spelling and grammar errors in the text.	The newsletter contains only one article, the article is not divided into multiple columns, and there are spelling and grammar errors.
Insert and format at least one clip art image	An appropriate clip art image is included. The image is sized and positioned appropriately.	A clip art image is inserted, but is either inappropriate, or is formatted or positioned poorly.	No clip art image is included.
Border and shading added to a paragraph	One or more paragraphs display an attractive border with shading that enables the reader to read the text.	A border or shading is displayed, but not both; or, the shading is too dark to enable the reader to easily read the text.	No border or shading is added to a paragraph.
Insert a screenshot	A screenshot is inserted in one of the columns; the screenshot is related to the content of the article.	A screenshot is inserted in the document, but does not relate to the content of the article.	No screenshot is inserted.

End You have completed Project 6J

Apply a combination of the 6A and 6B skills.

GO! Solve It | Project 6K Paper Report

Project Files

For Project 6K, you will need the following file:

New blank Word document

You will save your document as:

Lastname_Firstname_3K_Paper_Report

Create a new file and save it as **Lastname_Firstname_3K_Paper_Report** Use the following information to create a report written in the MLA format. The report should include at least two footnotes, at least two citations, and should include a *Works Cited* page.

Memphis Primary Materials writes and distributes informational reports on topics of interest to the people of Memphis. This report will be written by Sarah Stanger for the head of Marketing, Henry Miller. Information reports are provided as a public service of the company, and are distributed free of charge.

The topic of the report is recycling and reuse of paper and paper products. The report should contain an introduction, and then details about how much paper is used, what it is used for, the increase of paper recycling over time, and how paper products can be recycled or reused. A good place to start is www.epa.gov, which has many articles on paper use and recycling, and also provides links to further articles on the topic. You might also consider doing a Web search for the terms **paper recycling**

Add the file name to the footer, and add your name, your course name and section number, and the keywords **paper products, recycling** to the Document Panel.

Performance Element	Performance Level: Exemplary: You consistently applied the relevant skills	Proficient: You sometimes, but not always, applied the relevant skills	Developing: You rarely or never applied the relevant skills
Format the header and heading	The last name and page number are right-aligned in the header, and the report has a four-line heading and a centered title.	The header and heading are included, but are not formatted according to MLA style guidelines.	The header or heading is missing or incomplete.
Format the body of the report	The report is double-spaced, with no space after paragraphs. The first lines of paragraphs are indented 0.5″.	Some, but not all, of the report formatting is correct.	The majority of the formatting does not follow MLA guidelines.
Footnotes are included and formatted correctly	Two or more footnotes are included, and the footnote text is 11 pt, double-spaced, and the first line of each footnote is indented.	The correct number of footnotes is included, but the footnotes are not formatted properly.	No footnotes are included.
Citations and bibliography are included and formatted according to MLA guidelines	At least two citations are included in parenthetical references, with page numbers where appropriate, and the sources are included in a properly formatted Works Cited page.	Only one citation is included, or the citations and sources are not formatted correctly.	No citations or Works Cited page are included.

End You have completed Project 6K

Outcomes-Based Assessments

Rubric

The following outcomes-based assessments are *open-ended assessments*. That is, there is no specific correct result; your result will depend on your approach to the information provided. Make *Professional Quality* your goal. Use the following scoring rubric to guide you in *how* to approach the problem, and then to evaluate *how well* your approach solves the problem.

The *criteria*—Software Mastery, Content, Format and Layout, and Process—represent the knowledge and skills you have gained that you can apply to solving the problem. The *levels of performance*—Professional Quality, Approaching Professional Quality, or Needs Quality Improvements—help you and your instructor evaluate your result.

	Your completed project is of Professional Quality if you:	**Your completed project is Approaching Professional Quality if you:**	**Your completed project Needs Quality Improvements if you:**
1-Software Mastery	Choose and apply the most appropriate skills, tools, and features and identify efficient methods to solve the problem.	Choose and apply some appropriate skills, tools, and features, but not in the most efficient manner.	Choose inappropriate skills, tools, or features, or are inefficient in solving the problem.
2-Content	Construct a solution that is clear and well organized, contains content that is accurate, appropriate to the audience and purpose, and is complete. Provide a solution that contains no errors in spelling, grammar, or style.	Construct a solution in which some components are unclear, poorly organized, inconsistent, or incomplete. Misjudge the needs of the audience. Have some errors in spelling, grammar, or style, but the errors do not detract from comprehension.	Construct a solution that is unclear, incomplete, or poorly organized; contains some inaccurate or inappropriate content; and contains many errors in spelling, grammar, or style. Do not solve the problem.
3-Format and Layout	Format and arrange all elements to communicate information and ideas, clarify function, illustrate relationships, and indicate relative importance.	Apply appropriate format and layout features to some elements, but not others. Overuse features, causing minor distraction.	Apply format and layout that does not communicate information or ideas clearly. Do not use format and layout features to clarify function, illustrate relationships, or indicate relative importance. Use available features excessively, causing distraction.
4-Process	Use an organized approach that integrates planning, development, self-assessment, revision, and reflection.	Demonstrate an organized approach in some areas, but not others; or, use an insufficient process of organization throughout.	Do not use an organized approach to solve the problem.

Outcomes-Based Assessments

Apply a combination of the 6A and 6B skills.

GO! Think | Project 6L Jobs Newsletter

Project Files

For Project 6L, you will need the following file:

New blank Word document

You will save your document as:

Lastname_Firstname_3L_Jobs_Newsletter

The marketing manager of Memphis Primary Materials needs to create the next issue of the company's monthly newsletter (Volume 1, Number 7—July 2016), which will focus on "green jobs." Green jobs are jobs associated with environmentally friendly companies or are positions with firms that manufacture, sell, or install energy-saving or resource-saving products.

Use the following information to create a newsletter that includes a nameplate, multiple columns, at least two articles with article titles formatted so that they stand out, at least one clip art image, one screenshot, and one paragraph that includes a border and shading.

The articles you write can be on any topic regarding green jobs, and might include an introduction to the topic, information about a recent (or future) green job conference, and a discussion of green jobs in the United States. You will need to research this topic on the Web. A good place to start is www.epa.gov. You might also consider doing a Web search for the terms **green jobs** or **green jobs conference**

Add the file name to the footer. Add appropriate information to the Document Panel. Save the document as **Lastname_Firstname_3L_Jobs_Newsletter** and submit it as directed.

End You have completed Project 6L

Apply a combination of the 6A and 6B skills.

GO! Think | Project 6M Construction Report

Project Files

For Project 6M, you will need the following file:

New blank Word document

You will save your document as:

Lastname_Firstname_3M_Construction_Report

As part of the ongoing research provided on environment topics by the staff of Memphis Primary Materials, the Marketing Director, Henry Miller, has asked a summer intern, James Bodine, to create a report on recycling and reuse in the construction and demolition of buildings.

Create a new file and save it as **Lastname_Firstname_3M_Construction_Report** Use the following information to create a report written in the MLA format. The report should include at least two footnotes, at least two citations, and should include a *Works Cited* page.

The report should contain an introduction, and then details about, for example, how much construction material can be salvaged from existing buildings, how these materials can be reused in future buildings, and how materials can be saved and recycled on new building projects. A good place to start is www.epa.gov, which has a number of articles on recycling and reuse of materials during construction and demolition. You might also consider doing a Web search for the terms **construction recycling** or **demolition recycling** or **construction and demolition**

Add the file name to the footer. Add appropriate information to the Document Panel and submit it as directed.

End You have completed Project 6M

Outcomes-Based Assessments

Apply a combination of the **6B** skills.

You and GO! | Project 6N College Newsletter

Project Files

For Project 6N, you will need the following file:

New blank Word document

You will save your document as

Lastname_Firstname_3N_College_Newsletter

In this project, you will create a one-page newsletter. The newsletter should include at least one article describing your college and one article about an academic or athletic program at your college.

Be sure to include a nameplate, at least two articles, at least one clip art or screenshot image, and a bordered paragraph or paragraphs. Before you submit the newsletter, be sure to check it for grammar and spelling errors, and also be sure to format the newsletter in an attractive manner by using the skills you practiced in this chapter.

Save the file as **Lastname_Firstname_3N_College_Newsletter** Add the file name to the footer, and add your name, your course name and section number, and the keywords **newsletter** and **college** to the Document Panel. Save and submit your file as directed.

 **You have completed Project 6N**

Apply a combination of the **6A** and **6B** skills.

GO! Collaborate | Project 6O Bell Orchid Hotels Group Running Case

Your instructor may assign this group case project to your class. If your instructor assigns this project, he or she will provide you with information and instructions to work as part of a group. The group will apply the skills gained thus far to help the Bell Orchid Hotel Group achieve its business goals.

 **You have completed Project 6O**

Business Running Case

Razvan CHIRNOAGA/Shutterstock

This project relates to **Front Range Action Sports**, which is one of the country's largest retailers of sports gear and outdoor recreation merchandise. The company has large retail stores in Colorado, Washington, Oregon, California, and New Mexico, in addition to a growing online business. Major merchandise categories include fishing, camping, rock climbing, winter sports, action sports, water sports, team sports, racquet sports, fitness, golf, apparel, and footwear.

In this project, you will apply skills you practiced from the Objectives in Word Chapters 4-6. You will assist Irene Shviktar, the Vice President of Marketing, to edit and create documents for a National Sales Meeting that will precede a Winter Sports Expo sponsored by Front Range Action Sports. The first document is a cover letter from the vice president to the company president. The letter will accompany a packet of materials for the meeting and the expo, which includes a brief resume for the guest speaker, a flyer that will announce the expo, a newsletter for employees, a research paper on the history and development of skis, and a set of name tags for a group of employees attending the national sales meeting. Your completed documents will look similar to Figure 2.1.

Project Files

For Project BRC1, you will need the following files:

New blank Word document
wBRC1_Cover_Letter_Text
wBRC1_Newsletter
wBRC1_Career_Text
wBRC1_Ski_Research
wBRC1_Addresses
wBRC1_Flyer_Text
wBRC1_Downhill_Racing
wBRC1_Powder_Skiing

You will save your documents as:

Lastname_Firstname_BRC1_Cover_Letter
Lastname_Firstname_BRC1_Newsletter
Lastname_Firstname_BRC1_Resume
Lastname_Firstname_BRC1_Ski_Research
Lastname_Firstname_BRC1_Name_Tags
Lastname_Firstname_BRC1_Flyer

Project Results

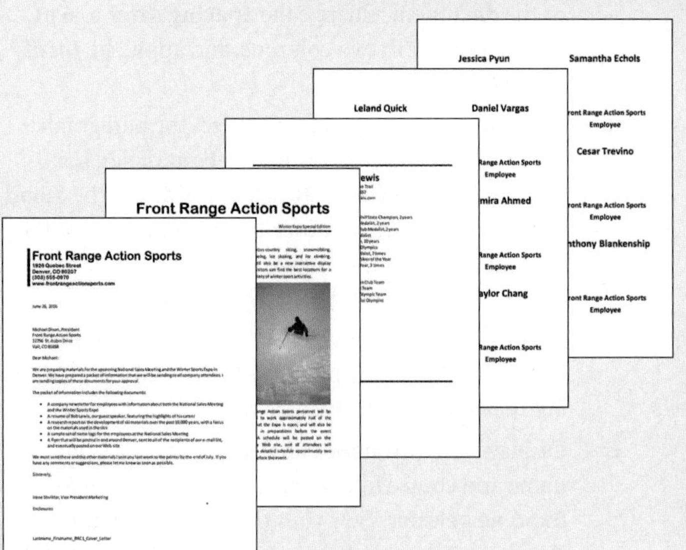

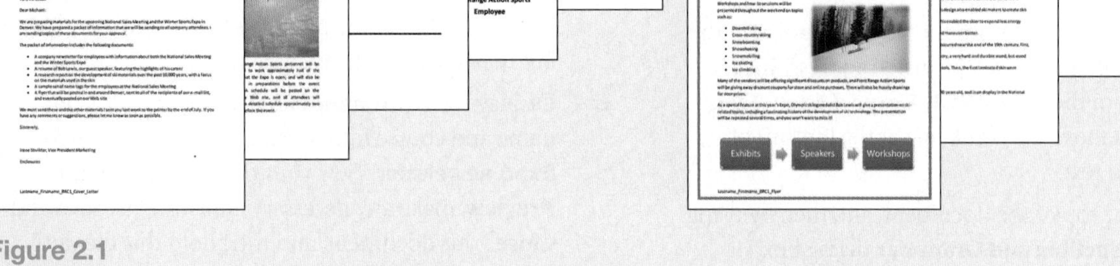

Figure 2.1

Business Running Case

Front Range Action Sports

1 **Start** Word and display a new document. Display rulers and formatting marks. In the location where you are storing your projects, create a new folder named **Front Range Action Sports** or navigate to this folder if you have already created it. **Save** the new document as **Lastname_Firstname_BRC1_Cover_Letter** Add the file name to the footer. Apply the **No Spacing** style to the document, and then type the following to form a letterhead:

Front Range Action Sports

1926 Quebec Street

Denver, CO 80207

(303) 555-0970

www.frontrangeactionsports.com

a. Press Enter to create a blank line below the letterhead. If the Web address changes to blue, right-click the address, and then from the shortcut menu, remove the hyperlink.

b. Select the letterhead text, but not the blank line. Change the **Font** to **Arial Rounded MT Bold**. Select the first line, and increase the **Font Size** to **28 pt** Change the **Font Size** of the remaining four lines to **12 pt**. Select all five lines of the letterhead, display the **Borders and Shading** dialog box, and then create a **6 pt**, **Black** border on the left side of the selected text.

c. Enter the following information using business letter format:

June 26, 2016

Michael Dixon, President

Front Range Action Sports

12756 St. Aubin Drive

Vail, CO 81658

d. Press Enter two times. With the insertion point in the second blank line below the inside address, **Insert** the text from the file **wBRC1_Cover_Letter_Text**, and then remove the blank line at the bottom of the selected text.

e. Move to the top of the document, and then by using either the **Spelling and Grammar** dialog box, or by right-clicking selected words, correct the *three* spelling, grammar, and word usage errors. Ignore proper names. In the paragraph that begins *If you have any*, select the first sentence and move it to the end of the paragraph.

f. In the middle of the document, select the five paragraphs beginning with *A company newsletter*, and create a bulleted list. In the fourth bullet, select the text *national sales meeting*, and then on the **Home tab**, in the **Font group**, click the **Change Case** button Aa, and then click **Capitalize Each Word**.

g. Display the **Document Panel**, add your name, course information, and the **Keywords expo, national sales meeting** View your document in **Print Preview,** make any necessary adjustments, **Save** and **Close** your document, and then hold this file until you complete the project.

2 From your student files, open **wBRC1_Newsletter**, and then **Save** it in your **Front Range Action Sports** folder as **Lastname_Firstname_BRC1_Newsletter** Add the file name to the footer.

a. Select the first paragraph of text—*Front Range Action Sports*. Change the **Font** to **Arial Rounded MT Bold**, the **Font Size** to **36**, and **Center** the text. Select the second paragraph of text, display the **Borders and Shading** dialog box, and then add a **Black**, **3 pt** line below the selected text.

b. Starting with the paragraph that begins *National Sales*, select all of the text from that point to the end of the document. Change the **Spacing After** to **6 pt**, format the text in two columns, and apply the **Justify** alignment.

c. At the top of the first column, select the paragraph *National Sales Meeting*. From the **Font** dialog box, change the **Font Size** to **20**, apply **Bold**, add the **Small caps** effect, and then **Center** the paragraph. Near the bottom of the same column, apply the same formatting to the paragraph *Winter Sports Expo*.

d. In the blank line above the last paragraph of the newsletter, **Insert** the picture **wBRC1_Powder_Skiing**. Set the **Width** of the picture to **3"**.

e. Display the **Document Panel**, and then add your name and course information and the **Keywords Expo newsletter** View your document in **Print Preview,** make any necessary adjustments, **Save** and **Close** your document, and then hold this file until you complete the project.

3 Display a new blank document and **Save** it in your **Front Range Action Sports** folder as **Lastname_Firstname_BRC1_Resume** Add the file name to the footer. **Insert** a **2 × 3** table.

(Business Running Case: Front Range Action Sports continues on the next page)

Front Range Action Sports (continued)

a. In the first cell of the table, type on four lines:

Robert Lewis

1227 Aspen Lake Trail

Vail, CO 81657

www.boblewisskis.com

b. In the second row, in the first cell, type **CAREER HIGHLIGHTS** In the cell to the immediate right, **Insert** the text from the file **wBRC1_Career_Text**, and then press Backspace to remove the blank line at the bottom of the inserted text.

c. In the third row, in the first cell, type **EDUCATION** In the cell to the right, type Mr. Lewis' educational information as follows:

University of Colorado

Ph.D. in Psychology

University of Colorado

M.S. in Psychology

University of Minnesota

B.S. in Psychology

d. Insert a new row at the bottom of the table. In the first cell of the new row, type **CONSULTANT** and then in the cell to the right, type the following:

U.S. Junior Ski Team

U.S. National Ski Team

Special Olympics

e. Apply **Bold** to the headings *CAREER HIGHLIGHTS*, *EDUCATION*, and *CONSULTANT*. Drag the vertical border between the two columns to approximately **1.5 inches on the horizontal ruler**.

f. In the first row, **Merge** the two cells, and then **Center** the text. Select *Robert Lewis*, increase the font size to **24 pt**, apply **Bold**, and then add **12 pt** spacing **Before** the text. If necessary, remove the hyperlink from the Web address. Select the Web address and add **18 pt** spacing after the text.

g. Create a bulleted list for the items below *SKIING* and below *COACHING*. In the cells to the right of *EDUCATION* and *CONSULTANT*, add **12 pt** spacing **After** the last item in each cell. Add **12 pt** spacing **After** *Ph.D. in Psychology* and *M.S. in Psychology*. Apply **Bold** to the three paragraphs that begin *University*.

h. Select the table, and then remove all borders. From the **Borders and Shading** dialog box, add a **3 pt** border to the top and bottom of the table. Change the top margin to **1.5"**. To the **Document Panel**, add your name, course information, and the **Keywords Robert Lewis resume** View your document in **Print Preview,** make any necessary adjustments, **Save** and then **Close** your document. Hold this file until you complete the project.

4 From your student files, open the document **wBRC1_Ski_Research**. **Save** the document in your **Front Range Action Sports** folder as **Lastname_Firstname_BRC1_Ski_Research** Display the header area, type **Johnson** and then press Spacebar. Display the **Page Number gallery**, and then in the **Current Position**, add the **Plain Number** style. Apply **Align Text Right** formatting to the header. Add the file name to the footer.

a. In the blank line at the beginning of the document, type **Walter Johnson** and then press Enter. Type **Irene Shviktar** and press Enter. Type **Marketing** and press Enter. Type **June 5, 2016**

b. Select all of the text in the document. Change the **Line Spacing** to **2.0**, and then change the **Spacing After** to **0 pt**. Click anywhere in the title that begins *The Evolution* and then **Center** the title.

c. Beginning with the paragraph that begins *The use of skis*, select the text from that point to the end of the document. Indent the first line of each selected paragraph to **0.5"**.

d. Near the top of **Page 1**, in the paragraph that begins *The use of skis*, in the third line, position the insertion point to the right of the period following *wood*, and then insert the following footnote:

The oldest known ski and pole is more than 4,000 years old, and is on display in the National Ski Hall of Fame and Museum in Ishpeming, Michigan.

e. Select the footnote text, change the **Font Size** to **11 pt**, add a **First Line Indent** of **0.5"**, and set **Line spacing** to **2.0"**.

f. In the paragraph that begins *The use of skis*, position the insertion point to the left of the period at the end of the paragraph. Using the **MLA** format, insert the following **Book** citation:

Author: **Huntford, Roland**

Title: **Two Planks and a Passion: The Dramatic History of Skiing**

Year: **2008**

City: **New York**

Publisher: **Continuum Press**

(Business Running Case: Front Range Action Sports continues on the next page)

Business Running Case

Front Range Action Sports (continued)

g. In the text, select the *Huntford* citation and insert the page numbers **4-6** Position the insertion point to the left of the period at the end of the document. Add the following **Web site** citation:

Author:	**Lund, Morten; Masia, Seth**
Name of Web Page:	**A Short History of Skis**
Year Accessed:	**2016**
Month Accessed:	**May**
Day Accessed:	**25**
URL:	**www.skiinghistory.org**

h. At the end of the document, insert a manual page break to create a new page. Change the **First Line Indent** to **0"**. Add a **Works Cited** title, display the **Bibliography** gallery, and then at the bottom of the gallery, click **Insert Bibliography**. Select the two references, remove the space after the paragraphs, and change the line spacing to **2.0**. **Center** the *Works Cited* title.

i. Press Ctrl + A to move to the top of the document, and then on the **Review tab**, in the **Proofing group**, click **Spelling & Grammar**. Ignore proper names, change *polyethelene* to *polyethylene*, and correct the subject-verb agreement between *have* and *has* in the last paragraph. Display the **Document Panel** and add your name and course information and the **Keywords ski history, ski research** View your document in **Print Preview** and make any necessary adjustments. **Save** and **Close** your document, and hold this file until you complete the project.

5 Display a **New** blank document. Start the **Step by Step Mail Merge Wizard** and select **Labels** as the document type. In **Step 2**, set **Label options** to use the **Auto default** tray (yours may vary) and **Avery US Letter 74541 Clip Style Name Badges**. In **Step 3**, **Use an existing list**, browse to select **wBRC1_Addresses**, click **Open**, and then click **OK**. This is a Name Badge label, and the steps differ slightly from the steps for creating mailing labels.

a. In **Step 4**, on the Ribbon, in the **Write & Insert Fields group**, click the **Insert Merge Field button arrow**, click **First_Name** field, press Spacebar, and then repeat for the **Last_Name** field. Press Enter six times.

b. Type **Front Range Action Sports** and press Enter. Type **Employee** Select the first line of the label—*<<First_Name>> <<Last_Name>>*. Change the **Font Size** to **24**, apply **Bold**, and then **Center** the text. Select the last two lines of text, change the **Font Size** to **18**, apply **Bold**, and then **Center** the text. In the **Mail Merge** task pane, click **Update all labels**, and then move to step 5—**Preview your labels.**

c. **Complete the merge**. On the **Mailings tab**, in the **Finish group**, click the **Finish & Merge** button, and then click **Edit Individual Documents**. Merge **All** of the records. **Save** the resulting document in your **Front Range Action Sports** folder as **Lastname_Firstname_BRC1_Name_Tags** and then if necessary, close the Mail Merge task pane. Add the file name to the footer. Preview the labels in **Print Preview** and make any necessary adjustments.

d. Display the **Document Panel**, and then add your name and course information and the **Keywords name tags, expo Save** and close your label document. **Close** the original document without saving. Hold this file until you complete the project.

6 From your student files, open **wBRC1_Flyer_Text**, and then **Save** it in your **Front Range Action Sports** folder as **Lastname_Firstname_BRC1_Flyer** Add the file name to the footer.

a. Select the title *Winter Sports Expo*, and apply a **Gradient Fill - Blue, Accent 1 Text Effect**—in the third row, the fourth effect. Increase the **Font Size** to **56** point, and then **Center** the title. Select the two paragraphs below the title that begin *Friday* and *Saturday*, and then change the **Spacing After** to **0**. Select the three paragraphs below the title—the three days and times—and then **Center** and apply **Bold**.

b. With the three paragraphs still selected, display the **Borders and Shading** dialog box. Apply a **Box** border using theme color **Blue, Accent 1** and a **3 pt** border, and add **Shading** using theme color **Blue, Accent 1, Lighter 80%**. Apply a **Page Border** using the **Box** setting, and the theme color **Blue, Accent 1** with a **Weight** of **6 pt**.

c. Format the seven sport topics—beginning with *Downhill skiing*—as a bulleted list, and then click anywhere to deselect the bulleted list. **Insert** the picture **wBRC1_Downhill_Racing**. Change the **Width** of the picture to **3.5"**, and then set **Wrap Text** to **Square**. Move the picture so that the right edge

(Business Running Case: Front Range Action Sports continues on the next page)

Front Range Action Sports (continued)

aligns with the right margin, and the top edge aligns with the top edge of the text that begins *Workshops and how-to*. Apply a **Picture Effect** using the **Soft Edge** of **10 point**.

d. Move to the end of the document and press Enter two times. Display the **Choose a SmartArt Graphic** dialog box, select **Process**, and then choose the first style—**Basic Process**. Click the border of the SmartArt graphic to deselect the first box. On the **Format tab**, set the **Width** of the SmartArt graphic to **6.5"** and the **Height** to **1"**; or, drag the SmartArt graphic sizing handles to change the width to **6.5"** and the height to **1"**. In the three boxes, add the following text in this order: **Exhibits** and **Speakers** and **Workshops** On the **Design tab**, apply the **3-D Polished** style. Click anywhere outside of the SmartArt to deselect it. Display your document in **Print Preview** and make any necessary adjustments.

e. Display the **Document Panel** and add your name and course information and the **Keywords expo, flyer** **Save** and **Close** the document. Submit the six files that you created in this project—the cover letter, newsletter, resume, research paper, name tag labels, and flyer—as directed by your instructor. **Exit** Word.

End **You have completed Business Running Case 1**

Creating a Worksheet and Charting Data

OUTCOMES

At the end of this chapter you will be able to:

OBJECTIVES

Mastering these objectives will enable you to:

PROJECT 7A

Create a sales report with an embedded column chart and sparklines.

1. Create, Save, and Navigate an Excel Workbook (p. 337)
2. Enter Data in a Worksheet (p. 340)
3. Construct and Copy Formulas and Use the SUM Function (p. 346)
4. Format Cells with Merge & Center and Cell Styles (p. 350)
5. Chart Data to Create a Column Chart and Insert Sparklines (p. 352)
6. Print, Display Formulas, and Close Excel (p. 357)

PROJECT 7B

Calculate the value of an inventory.

7. Check Spelling in a Worksheet (p. 363)
8. Enter Data by Range (p. 365)
9. Construct Formulas for Mathematical Operations (p. 366)
10. Edit Values in a Worksheet (p. 371)
11. Format a Worksheet (p. 372)

Shutterstock

In This Chapter

In this chapter, you will use Microsoft Excel 2010 to create and analyze data organized into columns and rows. After entering data in a worksheet, you can perform calculations, analyze the data to make logical decisions, and create charts.

In this chapter, you will create and modify Excel workbooks. You will practice the basics of worksheet design, create a footer, enter and edit data in a worksheet, chart data, and then save, preview, and print workbooks. You will also construct formulas for mathematical operations.

The projects in this chapter relate to **Texas Spectrum Wireless**, which provides accessories and software for all major brands of cell phones, smart phones, PDAs, mp3 players, and portable computers. The company sells thousands of unique products in their retail stores, which are located throughout Texas and the southern United States. They also sell thousands of items each year through their Web site, and offer free shipping and returns to their customers. The company takes pride in offering unique categories of accessories such as waterproof and ruggedized gear.

Project 7A Sales Report with Embedded Column Chart and Sparklines

Project Activities

In Activities 7.01 through 7.16, you will create an Excel worksheet for Roslyn Thomas, the President of Texas Spectrum Wireless. The worksheet displays the first quarter sales of wireless accessories for the current year, and includes a chart to visually represent the data. Your completed worksheet will look similar to Figure 7.1.

Project Files

For Project 7A, you will need the following file:

New blank Excel workbook

You will save your workbook as:

Lastname_Firstname_1A_Quarterly_Sales

Project Results

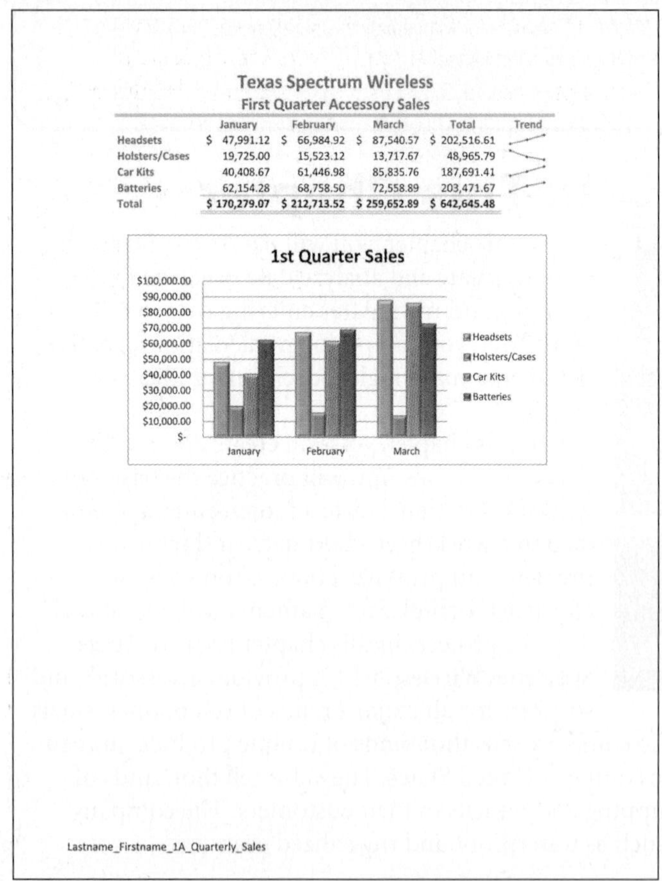

Texas Spectrum Wireless
First Quarter Accessory Sales

	January	February	March	Total	Trend
Headsets	$ 47,991.12	$ 66,984.92	$ 87,540.57	$ 202,516.61	
Holsters/Cases	19,725.00	15,523.12	13,717.67	48,965.79	
Car Kits	40,408.67	61,446.98	85,835.76	187,691.41	
Batteries	62,154.28	68,758.50	72,558.89	203,471.67	
Total	$ 170,279.07	$ 212,713.52	$ 259,652.89	$ 642,645.48	

Figure 7.1
Project 7A Quarterly Sales

Objective 1 | Create, Save, and Navigate an Excel Workbook

On startup, Excel displays a new blank ***workbook***—the Excel document that stores your data—which contains one or more pages called a ***worksheet***. A worksheet—or ***spreadsheet***—is stored in a workbook, and is formatted as a pattern of uniformly spaced horizontal rows and vertical columns. The intersection of a column and a row forms a box referred to as a ***cell***.

Activity 7.01 | Starting Excel and Naming and Saving a Workbook

1 **Start** Excel. In the lower right corner of the window, if necessary, click the Normal button, and then to the right, locate the zoom—magnification—level.

Your zoom level should be 100%, although some figures in this textbook may be shown at a higher zoom level.

Another Way

Use the keyboard shortcut F12 to display the Save As dialog box.

2 In the upper left corner of your screen, click the **File tab** to display **Backstage** view, click **Save As**, and then in the **Save As** dialog box, navigate to the location where you will store your workbooks for this chapter.

3 In your storage location, create a new folder named **Excel Chapter 7** Open the new folder to display its folder window, and then in the **File name** box, notice that *Book1* displays as the default file name.

4 In the **File name** box, click *Book1* to select it, and then using your own name, type **Lastname_Firstname_1A_Quarterly_Sales** being sure to include the underscore (Shift + -) instead of spaces between words. Compare your screen with Figure 7.2.

Figure 7.2

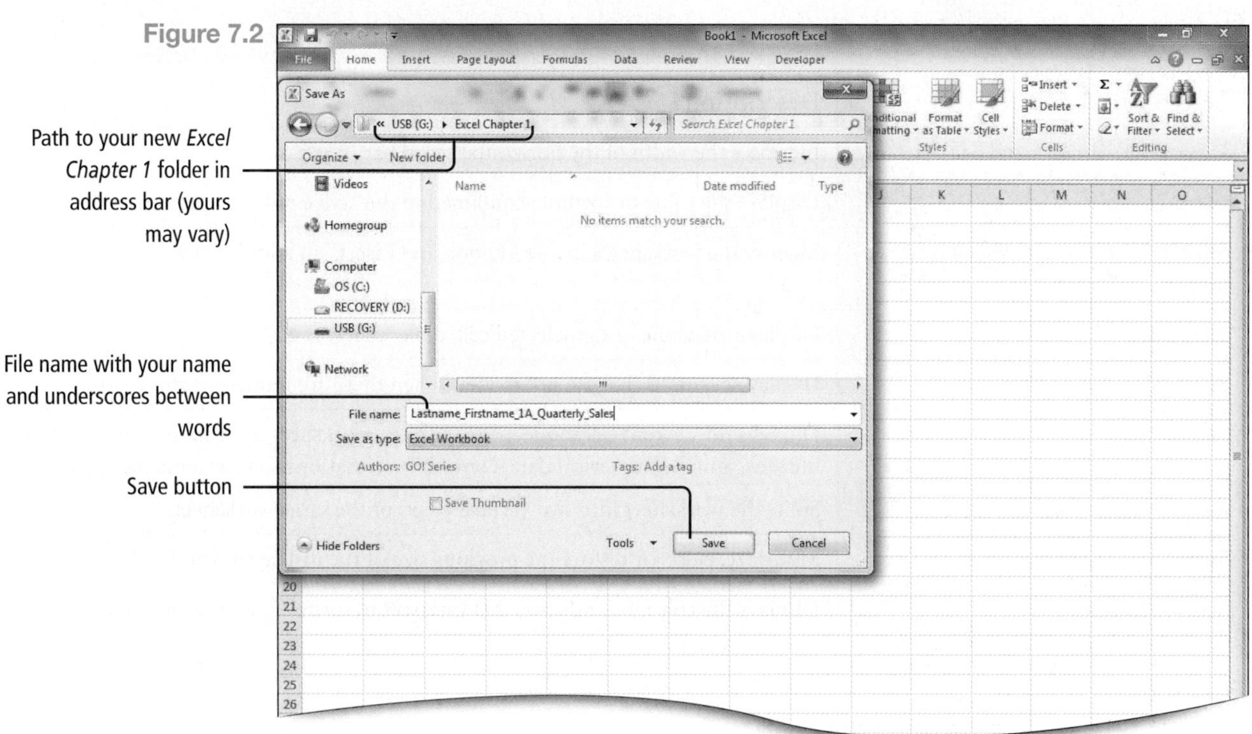

5 Click **Save**. Compare your screen with Figure 7.3, and then take a moment to study the Excel window parts in the table in Figure 7.4.

Figure 7.3

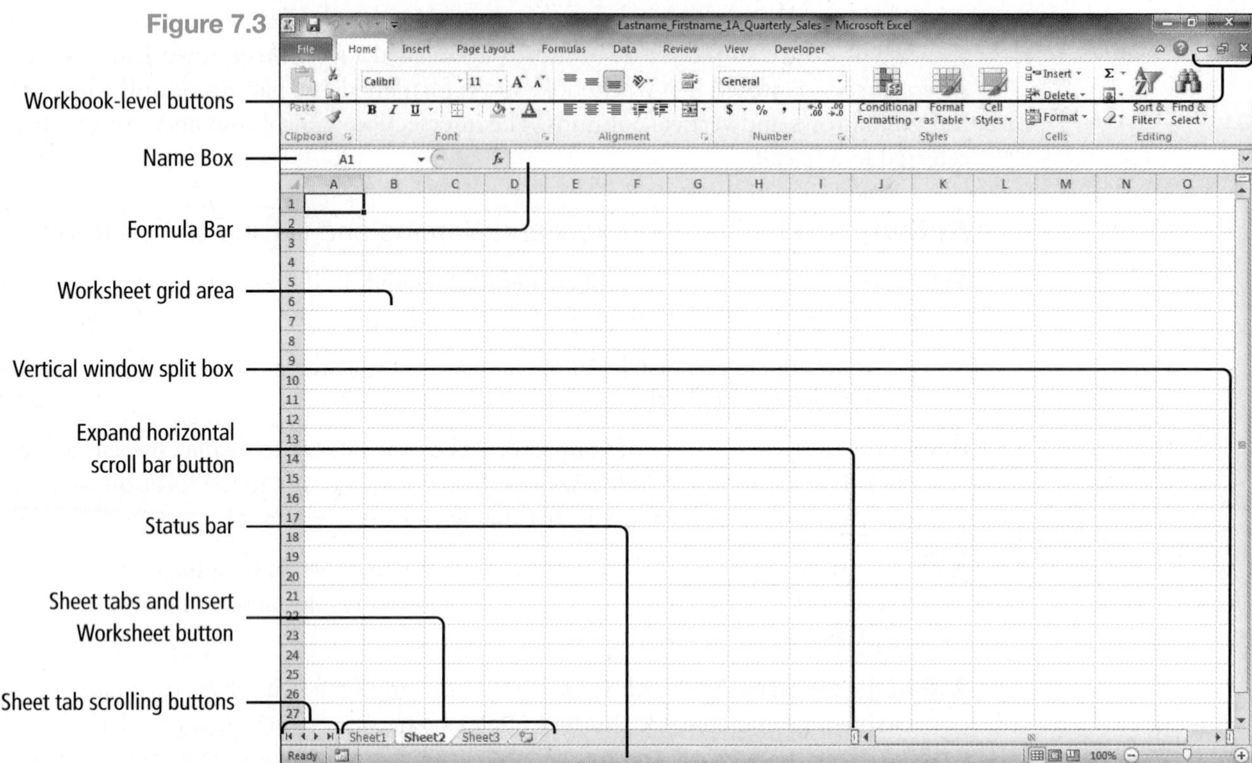

Parts of the Excel Window	
Screen Part	**Description**
Expand horizontal scroll bar button	Increases the width of the horizontal scroll bar.
Formula Bar	Displays the value or formula contained in the active cell; also permits entry or editing.
Sheet tabs and Insert Worksheet button	Identify the worksheets in a workbook and inserts an additional worksheet.
Name Box	Displays the name of the selected cell, table, chart, or object.
Sheet tab scrolling buttons	Display sheet tabs that are not in view when there are numerous sheet tabs.
Status bar	Displays the current cell mode, page number, worksheet information, view and zoom buttons, and for numerical data, common calculations such as Sum and Average.
Vertical window split box	Splits the worksheet into two vertical views of the same worksheet.
Workbook-level buttons	Minimize, close, or restore the previous size of the displayed workbook.
Worksheet grid area	Displays the columns and rows that intersect to form the worksheet's cells.

Figure 7.4

Activity 7.02 | Navigating a Worksheet and a Workbook

1 Take a moment to study Figure 7.5 and the table in Figure 7.6 to become familiar with the Excel workbook window.

Figure 7.5

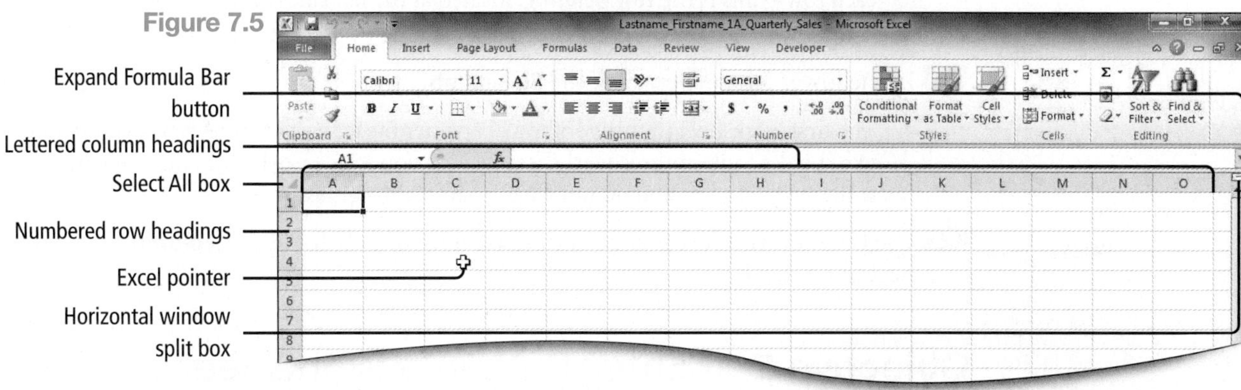

Excel Workbook Window Elements

Workbook Window Element	Description
Excel pointer	Displays the pointer in Excel.
Expand Formula Bar button	Increases the height of the Formula Bar to display lengthy cell content.
Horizontal window split box	Splits the worksheet into two horizontal views of the same worksheet.
Lettered column headings	Indicate the column letter.
Numbered row headings	Indicate the row number.
Select All box	Selects all the cells in a worksheet.

Figure 7.6

2 In the lower right corner of the screen, in the horizontal scroll bar, click the **right scroll arrow** one time to shift **column A** out of view.

A ***column*** is a vertical group of cells in a worksheet. Beginning with the first letter of the alphabet, *A*, a unique letter identifies each column—this is called the ***column heading***. Clicking one of the horizontal scroll bar arrows shifts the window either left or right one column at a time.

3 Point to the **right scroll arrow**, and then hold down the left mouse button until the columns begin to scroll rapidly to the right; release the mouse button when you begin to see pairs of letters as the column headings.

4 Slowly drag the horizontal scroll box to the left, and notice that just above the scroll box, ScreenTips with the column letters display as you drag. Drag the horizontal scroll box left or right—or click the left or right scroll arrow—as necessary to position **column Z** near the center of your screen.

Column headings after column Z use two letters starting with AA, AB, and so on through ZZ. After that, columns begin with three letters beginning with AAA. This pattern provides 16,384 columns. The last column is XFD.

5 In the lower left portion of your screen, click the **Sheet2 tab**.

The second worksheet displays and is the active sheet. Column A displays at the left.

6 In the vertical scroll bar, click the **down scroll arrow** one time to move **Row 1** out of view.

A ***row*** is a horizontal group of cells. Beginning with number 1, a unique number identifies each row—this is the ***row heading***, located at the left side of the worksheet. A single worksheet has 1,048,576 rows.

7 In the lower left corner, click the **Sheet1 tab**.

The first worksheet in the workbook becomes the active worksheet. By default, new workbooks contain three worksheets. When you save a workbook, the worksheets are contained within it and do not have separate file names.

8 Use the skills you just practiced to scroll horizontally to display **column A**, and if necessary, **row 1**.

Objective 2 | Enter Data in a Worksheet

Cell content, which is anything you type in a cell, can be one of two things: either a ***constant value***—referred to simply as a ***value***—or a ***formula***. A formula is an equation that performs mathematical calculations on values in your worksheet. The most commonly used values are ***text values*** and ***number values***, but a value can also include a date or a time of day.

Activity 7.03 | Entering Text and Using AutoComplete

A text value, also referred to as a ***label***, usually provides information about number values in other worksheet cells. For example, a title such as First Quarter Accessory Sales gives the reader an indication that the data in the worksheet relates to information about sales of accessories during the three-month period January through March.

1 Click the **Sheet1 tab** to make it the active sheet. Point to and then click the cell at the intersection of **column A** and **row 1** to make it the ***active cell***—the cell is outlined in black and ready to accept data.

The intersecting column letter and row number form the ***cell reference***—also called the ***cell address***. When a cell is active, its column letter and row number are highlighted. The cell reference of the selected cell, *A1*, displays in the Name Box.

2 With cell **A1** as the active cell, type the worksheet title **Texas Spectrum Wireless** and then press Enter. Compare your screen with Figure 7.7.

Text or numbers in a cell are referred to as ***data***. You must confirm the data you type in a cell by pressing Enter or by some other keyboard movement, such as pressing Tab or an arrow key. Pressing Enter moves the selection to the cell below.

Figure 7.7

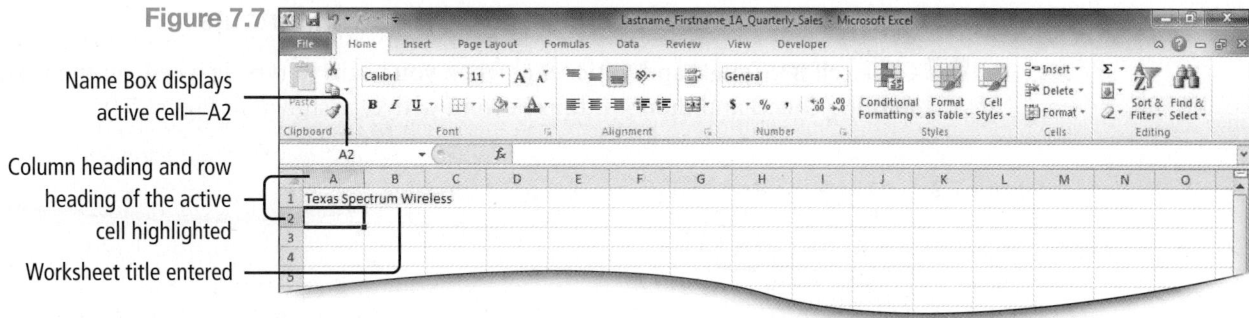

3 In cell **A1**, notice that the text does not fit; the text spills over and displays in cells **B1** and **C1** to the right.

If text is too long for a cell and cells to the right are empty, the text will display. If the cells to the right contain other data, only the text that will fit in the cell displays.

4 In cell **A2**, type the worksheet subtitle **First Quarter Accessory Sales** and then press Enter. Compare your screen with Figure 7.8.

Figure 7.8

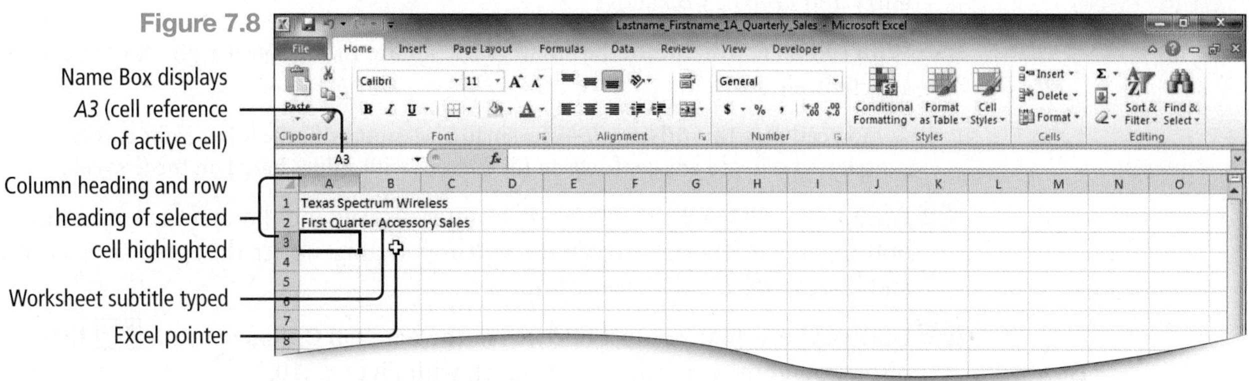

5 Press Enter again to make cell **A4** the active cell. In cell **A4**, type **Headsets** which will form the first row title, and then press Enter.

The text characters that you typed align at the left edge of the cell—referred to as ***left alignment***—and cell A5 becomes the active cell. Left alignment is the default for text values.

6 In cell **A5**, type **H** and notice the text from the previous cell displays.

If the first characters you type in a cell match an existing entry in the column, Excel fills in the remaining characters for you. This feature, called ***AutoComplete***, assists only with alphabetic values.

7 Continue typing the remainder of the row title **olsters/Cases** and press Enter.

The AutoComplete suggestion is removed when the entry you are typing differs from the previous value.

> **Another Way**
>
> Use the keyboard shortcut Ctrl + S to Save changes to your workbook.

8 In cell **A6**, type **Car Kits** and press Enter. In cell **A7**, type **Batteries** and press Enter. In cell **A8**, type **Total** and press Enter. On the Quick Access Toolbar, click **Save**.

Activity 7.04 | Using Auto Fill and Keyboard Shortcuts

1. Click cell **B3**. Type **J** and notice that when you begin to type in a cell, on the **Formula Bar**, the **Cancel** and **Enter** buttons become active, as shown in Figure 7.9.

Figure 7.9

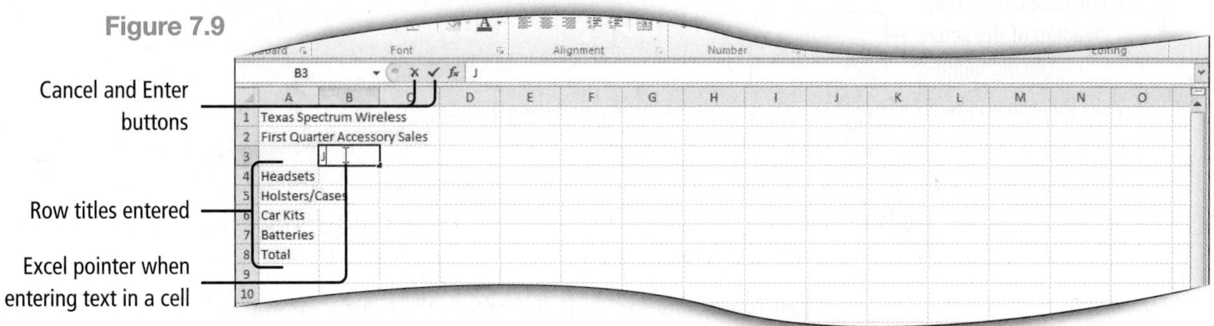

2. Continue to type **anuary** On the **Formula Bar**, notice that values you type in a cell also display there. Then, on the **Formula Bar**, click the **Enter** button to confirm the entry and keep cell **B3** active.

3. With cell **B3** active, locate the small black square in the lower right corner of the selected cell.

   You can drag this ***fill handle***—the small black square in the lower right corner of a selected cell—to adjacent cells to fill the cells with values based on the first cell.

4. Point to the **fill handle** until the + pointer displays, hold down the left mouse button, drag to the right to cell **D3**, and as you drag, notice the ScreenTips *February* and *March*. Release the mouse button.

5. Under the text that you just filled, click the **Auto Fill Options** button that displays, and then compare your screen with Figure 7.10.

   Auto Fill generates and extends a ***series*** of values into adjacent cells based on the value of other cells. A series is a group of things that come one after another in succession; for example, *January*, *February*, *March*.

   The Auto Fill Options button displays options to fill the data; options vary depending on the content and program from which you are filling, and the format of the data you are filling.

   Fill Series is selected, indicating the action that was taken. Because the options are related to the current task, the button is referred to as being ***context sensitive***.

Figure 7.10

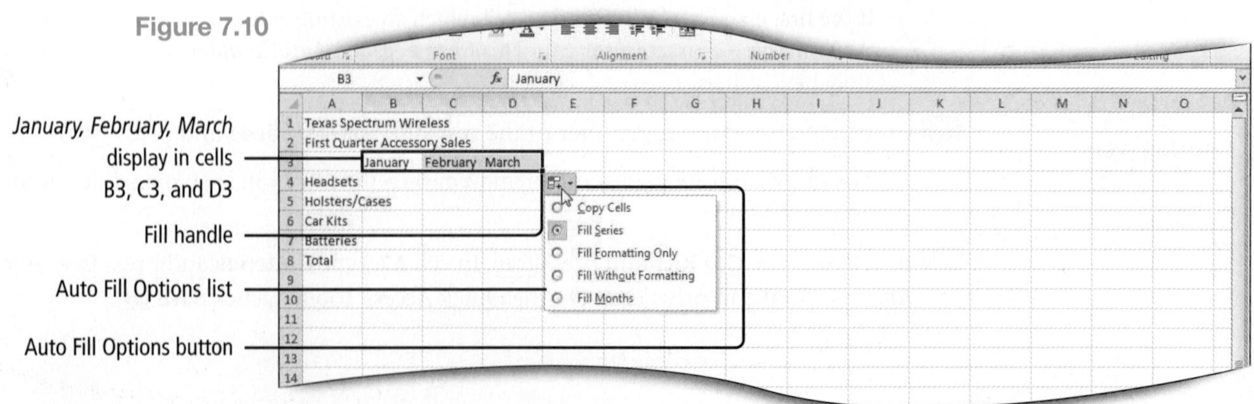

6. Click in any cell to cancel the display of the Auto Fill Options list.

   The list no longer displays; the button will display until you perform some other screen action.

7 Press Ctrl + Home, which is the keyboard shortcut to make cell **A1** active.

8 On the Quick Access Toolbar, click **Save** to save the changes you have made to your workbook, and then take a moment to study the table in Figure 7.11 to become familiar with additional keyboard shortcuts with which you can navigate the Excel worksheet.

Keyboard Shortcuts to Navigate the Excel Window

To Move the Location of the Active Cell:	**Press:**
Up, down, right, or left one cell	↑, ↓, →, ←
Down one cell	Enter
Up one cell	Shift + Enter
Up one full screen	Page Up
Down one full screen	PageDown
To column A of the current row	Home
To the last cell in the last column of the active area (the rectangle formed by all the rows and columns in a worksheet that contain entries)	Ctrl + End
To cell A1	Ctrl + Home
Right one cell	Tab
Left one cell	Shift + Tab

Figure 7.11

Activity 7.05 | Aligning Text and Adjusting the Size of Columns

1 In the **column heading area**, point to the vertical line between **column A** and **column B** to display the pointer, press and hold down the left mouse button, and then compare your screen with Figure 7.12.

A ScreenTip displays information about the width of the column. The default width of a column is 64 ***pixels***. A pixel, short for ***picture element***, is a point of light measured in dots per square inch. Sixty-four pixels equal 8.43 characters, which is the average number of digits that will fit in a cell using the default font. The default font in Excel is Calibri and the default font size is 11.

Figure 7.12

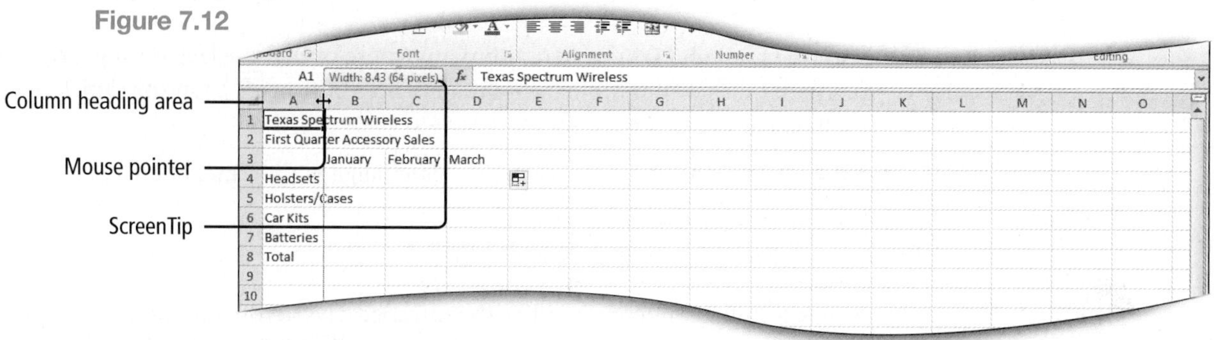

2 Drag to the right, and when the number of pixels indicated in the ScreenTip reaches **100 pixels**, release the mouse button. If you are not satisfied with your result, click Undo on the Quick Access Toolbar and begin again.

This width accommodates the longest row title in cells A4 through A8—*Holsters/Cases*. The worksheet title and subtitle in cells A1 and A2 span more than one column and still do not fit in column A.

3 Point to cell **B3** and then drag across to select cells **B3**, **C3**, and **D3**. Compare your screen with Figure 7.13; if you are not satisfied with your result, click anywhere and begin again.

The three cells, B3 through D3, are selected and form a ***range***—two or more cells on a worksheet that are adjacent (next to each other) or nonadjacent (not next to each other). This range of cells is referred to as *B3:D3*. When you see a colon (:) between two cell references, the range includes all the cells between the two cell references.

A range of cells that is selected in this manner is indicated by a dark border, and Excel treats the range as a single unit so you can make the same changes to more than one cell at a time. The selected cells in the range are highlighted except for the first cell in the range, which displays in the Name Box.

Figure 7.13

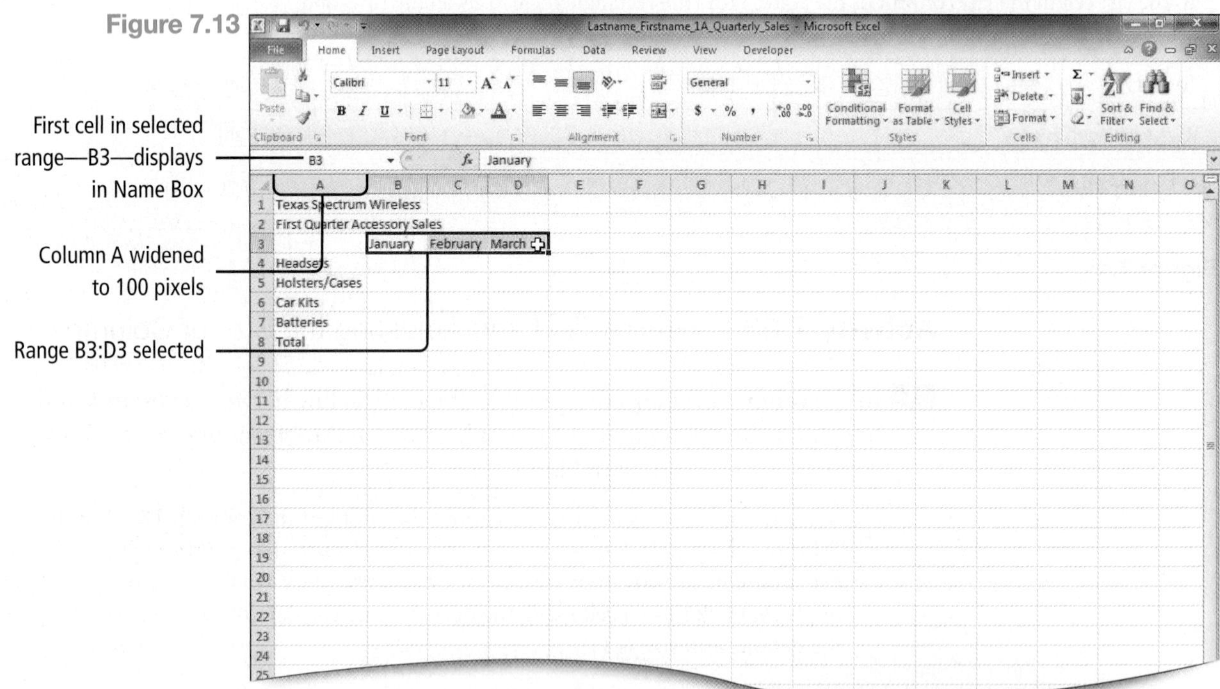

4 With the range **B3:D3** selected, point anywhere over the selected range, right-click, and then on the Mini toolbar, click the **Center** button. On the Quick Access Toolbar, click **Save**.

The column titles *January*, *February*, *March* align in the center of each cell.

Activity 7.06 | Entering Numbers

To type number values, use either the number keys across the top of your keyboard or the numeric keypad if you have one—laptop computers may not have a numeric keypad.

1 Under *January*, click cell **B4**, type **47991.12** and then on the **Formula Bar**, click the **Enter** button [✓] to maintain cell **B4** as the active cell. Compare your screen with Figure 7.14.

By default, *number* values align at the right edge of the cell. The default ***number format***—a specific way in which Excel displays numbers—is the ***general format***. In the default general format, whatever you type in the cell will display, with the exception of trailing zeros to the right of a decimal point. For example, in the number 237.50 the *0* following the *5* is a trailing zero.

Data that displays in a cell is the ***displayed value***. Data that displays in the Formula Bar is the ***underlying value***. The number of digits or characters that display in a cell—the displayed value—depends on the width of the column. Calculations on numbers will always be based on the underlying value, not the displayed value.

Figure 7.14

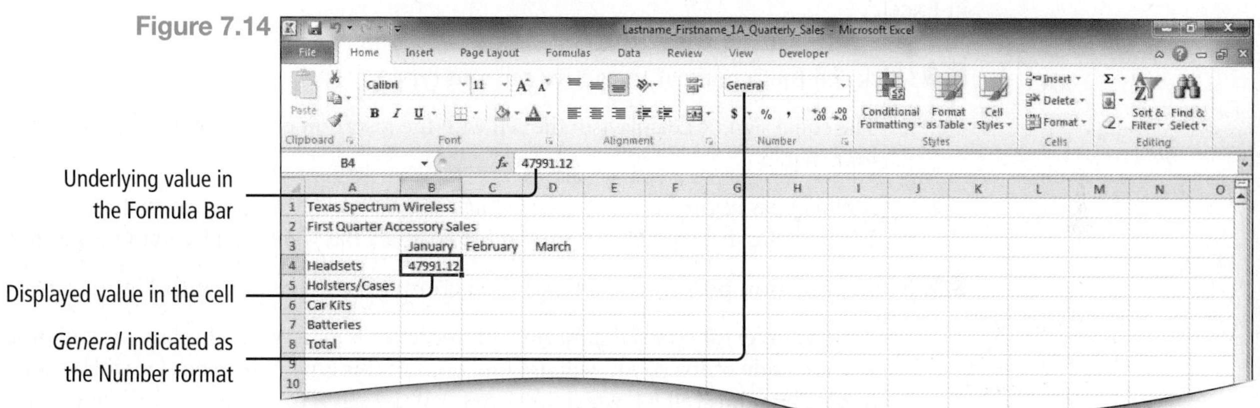

2 Press [Tab] to make cell **C4** active. Then, enter the remaining sales numbers as shown by using the following technique: Press [Tab] to confirm your entry and move across the row, and then press [Enter] at the end of a row to move to the next row.

	January	February	March
Headsets	47991.12	**66984.92**	**87540.57**
Holsters/Cases	**19725**	**15523.12**	**13717.67**
Car Kits	**40408.67**	**61446.98**	**85835.76**
Batteries	**62154.28**	**68758.50**	**72558.89**

3 Compare the numbers you entered with Figure 7.15 and then **Save** [💾] your workbook.

In the default general format, trailing zeros to the right of a decimal point will not display. For example, when you type *68758.50*, the cell displays 68758.5 instead.

Figure 7.15

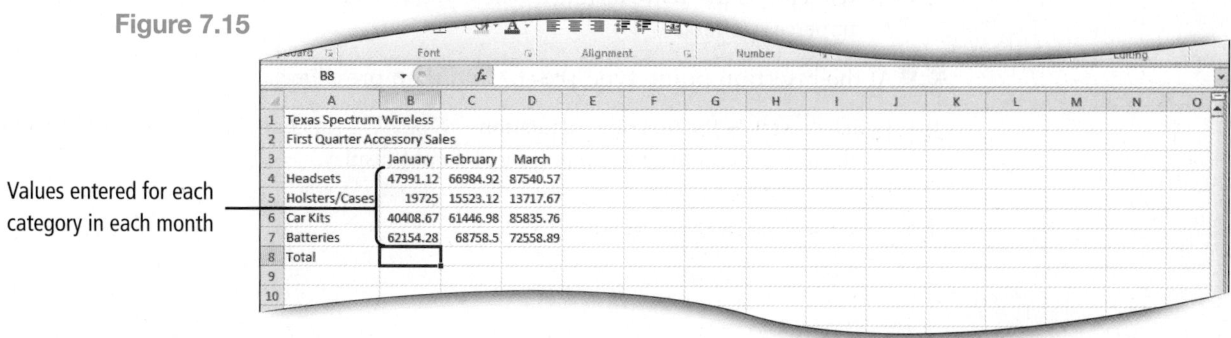

Objective 3 | Construct and Copy Formulas and Use the SUM Function

A cell contains either a constant value (text or numbers) or a formula. A formula is an equation that performs mathematical calculations on values in other cells, and then places the result in the cell containing the formula. You can create formulas or use a ***function***—a prewritten formula that looks at one or more values, performs an operation, and then returns a value.

Activity 7.07 | Constructing a Formula and Using the SUM Function

In this activity, you will practice three different ways to sum a group of numbers in Excel.

1 Click cell **B8** to make it the active cell and type **=**

The equal sign (=) displays in the cell with the insertion point blinking, ready to accept more data.

All formulas begin with the = sign, which signals Excel to begin a calculation. The Formula Bar displays the = sign, and the Formula Bar Cancel and Enter buttons display.

2 At the insertion point, type **b4** and then compare your screen with Figure 7.16.

A list of Excel functions that begin with the letter *B* may briefly display—as you progress in your study of Excel, you will use functions of this type. A blue border with small corner boxes surrounds cell B4, which indicates that the cell is part of an active formula. The color used in the box matches the color of the cell reference in the formula.

Figure 7.16

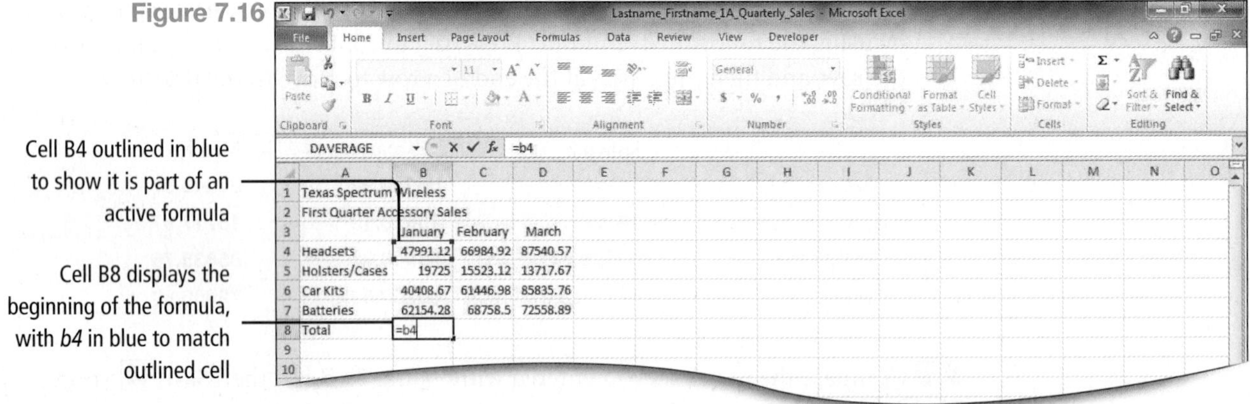

3 At the insertion point, type **+** and then type **b5**

A border of another color surrounds cell B5, and the color matches the color of the cell reference in the active formula. When typing cell references, it is not necessary to use uppercase letters.

4 At the insertion point, type **+b6+b7** and then press Enter.

The result of the formula calculation—*170279.1*—displays in the cell. Recall that in the default General format, trailing zeros do not display.

5 Click cell **B8** again, look at the **Formula Bar**, and then compare your screen with Figure 7.17.

The formula adds the values in cells B4 through B7, and the result displays in cell B8. In this manner, you can construct a formula by typing. Although cell B8 displays the *result* of the formula, the formula itself displays in the Formula Bar. This is referred to as the ***underlying formula***.

Always view the Formula Bar to be sure of the exact content of a cell—*a displayed number may actually be a formula*.

Figure 7.17

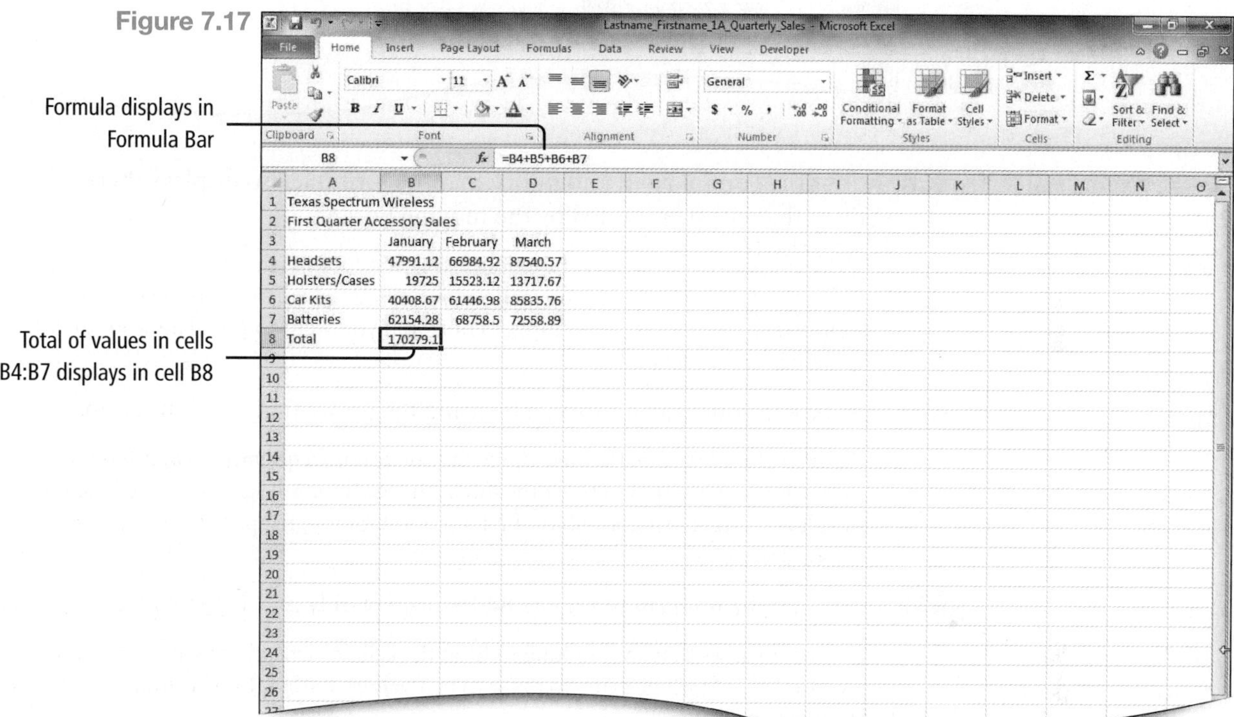

6 Click cell **C8** and type = to signal the beginning of a formula. Then, point to cell **C4** and click one time.

The reference to the cell C4 is added to the active formula. A moving border surrounds the referenced cell, and the border color and the color of the cell reference in the formula are color coded to match.

7 At the insertion point, type **+** and then click cell **C5**. Repeat this process to complete the formula to add cells **C4** through **C7**, and then press Enter.

The result of the formula calculation—*212713.5*—displays in the cell. This method of constructing a formula is the ***point and click method***.

Another Way

Use the keyboard shortcut Alt + =; or, on the Formulas tab, in the Function Library group, click the AutoSum button.

8 Click cell **D8**. On the **Home tab**, in the **Editing group**, click the **Sum** button Σ, and then compare your screen with Figure 7.18.

SUM is an Excel function—a prewritten formula. A moving border surrounds the range D4:D7 and *=SUM(D4:D7)* displays in cell D8.

The = sign signals the beginning of a formula, *SUM* indicates the type of calculation that will take place (addition), and *(D4:D7)* indicates the range of cells on which the sum calculation will be performed. A ScreenTip provides additional information about the action.

Figure 7.18

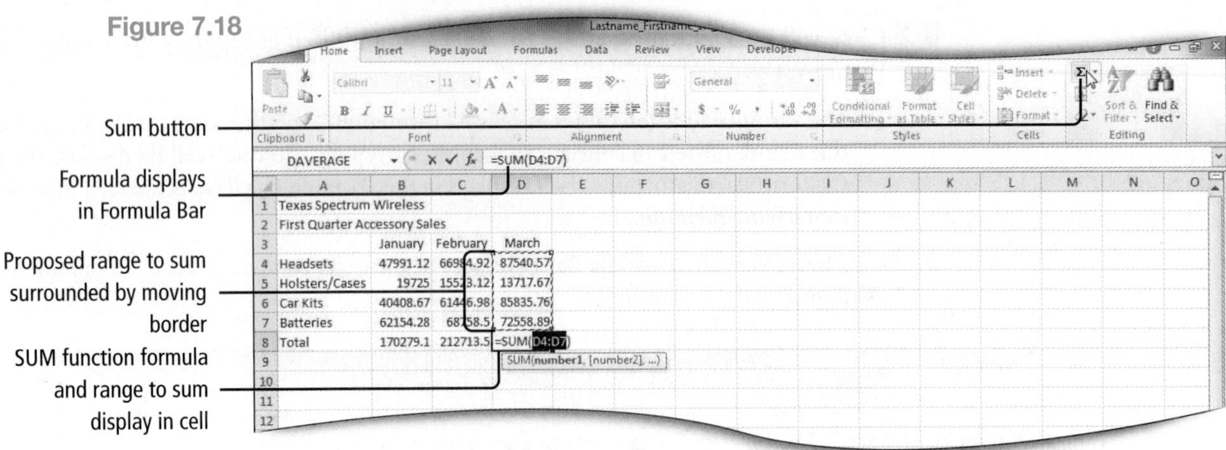

9 Look at the **Formula Bar**, and notice that the formula also displays there. Then, look again at the cells surrounded by the moving border.

When you activate the Sum function, Excel first looks *above* the active cell for a range of cells to sum. If no range is above the active cell, Excel will look to the *left* for a range of cells to sum. If the proposed range is not what you want to calculate, you can select a different group of cells.

10 Press Enter to construct a formula by using the prewritten SUM function.

Your total is *259652.9*. Because the Sum function is frequently used, it has its own button in the Editing group on the Home tab of the Ribbon. A larger version of the button also displays on the Formulas tab in the Function Library group. This button is also referred to as ***AutoSum***.

11 Notice that the totals in the range **B8:D8** display only *one* decimal place. Click **Save**.

Number values that are too long to fit in the cell do *not* spill over into the unoccupied cell to the right in the same manner as text values. Rather, Excel rounds the number to fit the space.

Rounding is a procedure that determines which digit at the right of the number will be the last digit displayed and then increases it by one if the next digit to its right is 5, 6, 7, 8, or 9.

Activity 7.08 | Copying a Formula by Using the Fill Handle

You have practiced three ways to create a formula—by typing, by using the point-and-click technique, and by using a Function button from the Ribbon. You can also copy formulas. When you copy a formula from one cell to another, Excel adjusts the cell references to fit the new location of the formula.

1 Click cell **E3**, type **Total** and then press Enter.

The text in cell E3 is centered because the centered format continues from the adjacent cell.

2 With cell **E4** as the active cell, hold down Alt, and then press =. Compare your screen with Figure 7.19.

Alt + = is the keyboard shortcut for the Sum function. Recall that Excel first looks above the selected cell for a proposed range of cells to sum, and if no data is detected, Excel looks to the left and proposes a range of cells to sum.

Figure 7.19

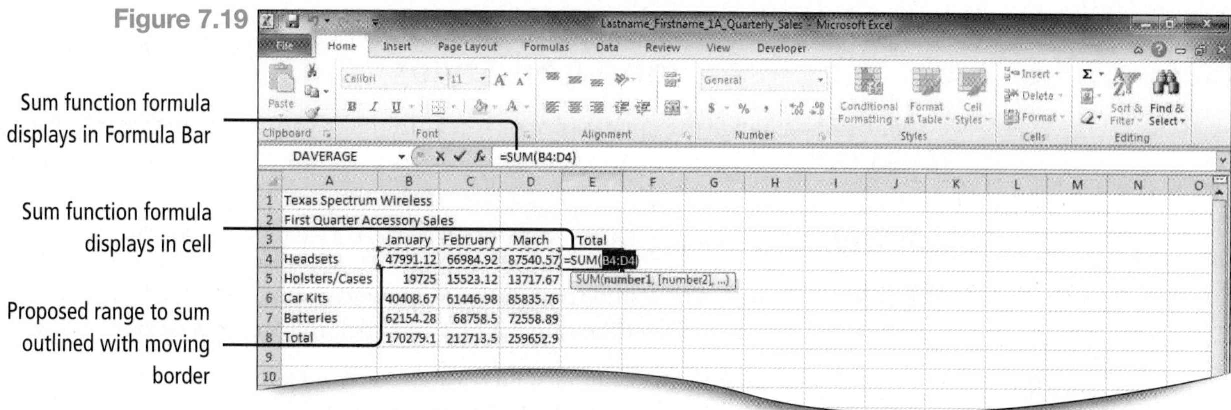

3 On the **Formula Bar**, click the **Enter** button [✓] to display the result and keep cell **E4** active.

The total dollar amount of *Headsets* sold in the quarter is *202516.6*. In cells E5:E8, you can see that you need a formula similar to the one in E4, but formulas that refer to the cells in row 5, row 6, and so on.

4 With cell **E4** active, point to the fill handle in the lower right corner of the cell until the [+] pointer displays. Then, drag down through cell **E8**; if you are not satisfied with your result, on the Quick Access Toolbar, click Undo [↶] and begin again. Compare your screen with Figure 7.20.

Figure 7.20

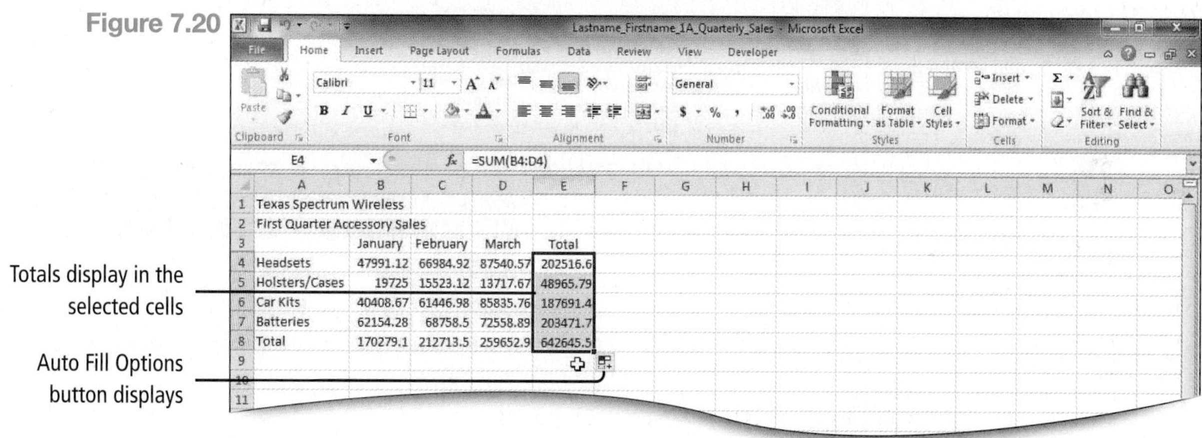

5 Click cell **E5**, look at the **Formula Bar**, and notice the formula *=SUM(B5:D5)*. Click cell **E6**, look at the **Formula Bar**, and then notice the formula *=SUM(B6:D6)*.

In each row, Excel copied the formula but adjusted the cell references *relative to* the row number. This is called a ***relative cell reference***—a cell reference based on the relative position of the cell that contains the formula and the cells referred to.

The calculation is the same, but it is performed on the cells in that particular row. Use this method to insert numerous formulas into spreadsheets quickly.

6 Click cell **F3,** type **Trend** and then press [Enter]. **Save** [💾] your workbook.

Objective 4 | Format Cells with Merge & Center and Cell Styles

Format—change the appearance of—cells to make your worksheet attractive and easy to read.

Activity 7.09 | Using Merge & Center and Applying Cell Styles

> **Another Way**
>
> Select the range, right-click over the selection, and then on the Mini toolbar, click the Merge & Center button.

1. Select the range **A1:F1**, and then in the **Alignment group**, click the **Merge & Center** button. Then, select the range **A2:F2** and click the **Merge & Center** button.

   The ***Merge & Center*** command joins selected cells into one larger cell and centers the contents in the new cell; individual cells in the range B1:F1 and B2:F2 can no longer be selected—they are merged into cell A1 and A2 respectively.

2. Click cell **A1**. In the **Styles group**, click the **Cell Styles** button, and then compare your screen with Figure 7.21.

   A ***cell style*** is a defined set of formatting characteristics, such as font, font size, font color, cell borders, and cell shading.

Figure 7.21

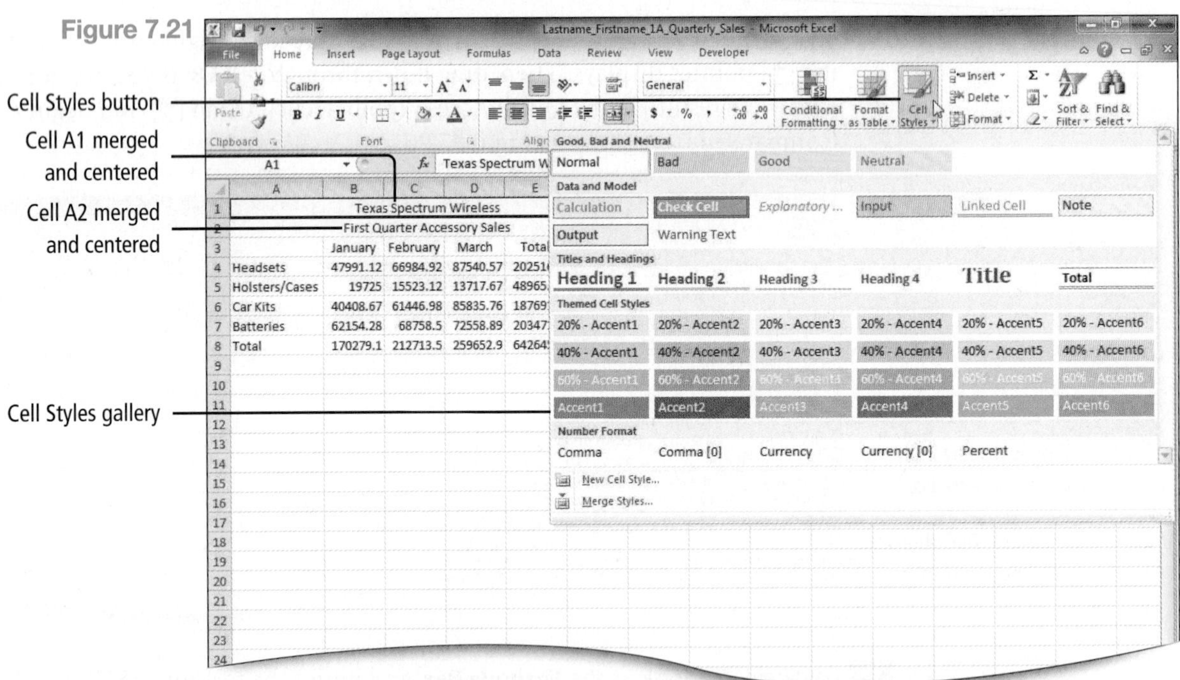

3. In the displayed gallery, under **Titles and Headings**, click **Title** and notice that the row height adjusts to accommodate this larger font size.

4. Click cell **A2**, display the **Cell Styles** gallery, and then under **Titles and Headings**, click **Heading 1**.

   Use cell styles to maintain a consistent look in a worksheet and across worksheets in a workbook.

5. Select the range **B3:F3**, hold down Ctrl, and then select the range **A4:A8** to select the column titles and the row titles.

   Use this technique to select two or more ranges that are nonadjacent—not next to each other.

6 Display the **Cell Styles** gallery, click **Heading 4** to apply this cell style to the column titles and row titles, and then **Save** your workbook.

> **Another Way**
> In the Name Box type b4:e4,b8:e8 and then press Enter.

Activity 7.10 | Formatting Financial Numbers

1 Select the range **B4:E4**, hold down Ctrl, and then select the range **B8:E8**.

This range is referred to as *b4:e4,b8:e8* with a comma separating the references to the two nonadjacent ranges.

> **Another Way**
> Display the Cell Styles gallery, and under Number Format, click Currency.

2 On the **Home tab**, in the **Number group**, click the **Accounting Number Format** button $. Compare your screen with Figure 7.22.

The ***Accounting Number Format*** applies a thousand comma separator where appropriate, inserts a fixed U.S. dollar sign aligned at the left edge of the cell, applies two decimal places, and leaves a small amount of space at the right edge of the cell to accommodate a parenthesis when negative numbers are present. Excel widens the columns to accommodate the formatted numbers.

Figure 7.22

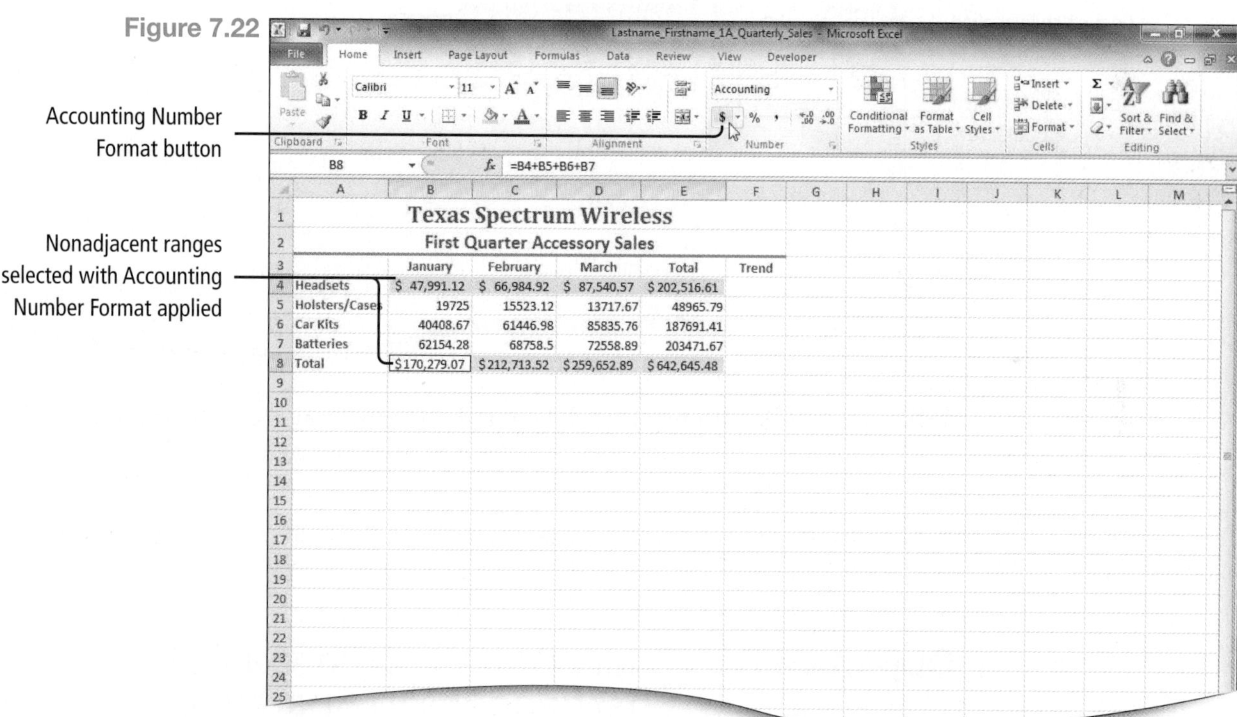

3 Select the range **B5:E7**, and then in the **Number group**, click the **Comma Style** button ,.

The ***Comma Style*** inserts thousand comma separators where appropriate and applies two decimal places. Comma Style also leaves space at the right to accommodate a parenthesis when negative numbers are present.

When preparing worksheets with financial information, the first row of dollar amounts and the total row of dollar amounts are formatted in the Accounting Number Format; that is, with thousand comma separators, dollar signs, two decimal places, and space at the right to accommodate a parenthesis for negative numbers, if any. Rows that are *not* the first row or the total row should be formatted with the Comma Style.

4 Select the range **B8:E8**. From the **Styles group**, display the **Cell Styles** gallery, and then under **Titles and Headings**, click **Total**. Click any blank cell to cancel the selection, and then compare your screen with Figure 7.23.

This is a common way to apply borders to financial information. The single border indicates that calculations were performed on the numbers above, and the double border indicates that the information is complete. Sometimes financial documents do not display values with cents; rather, the values are rounded up. You can do this by selecting the cells, and then clicking the Decrease Decimal button two times.

Figure 7.23

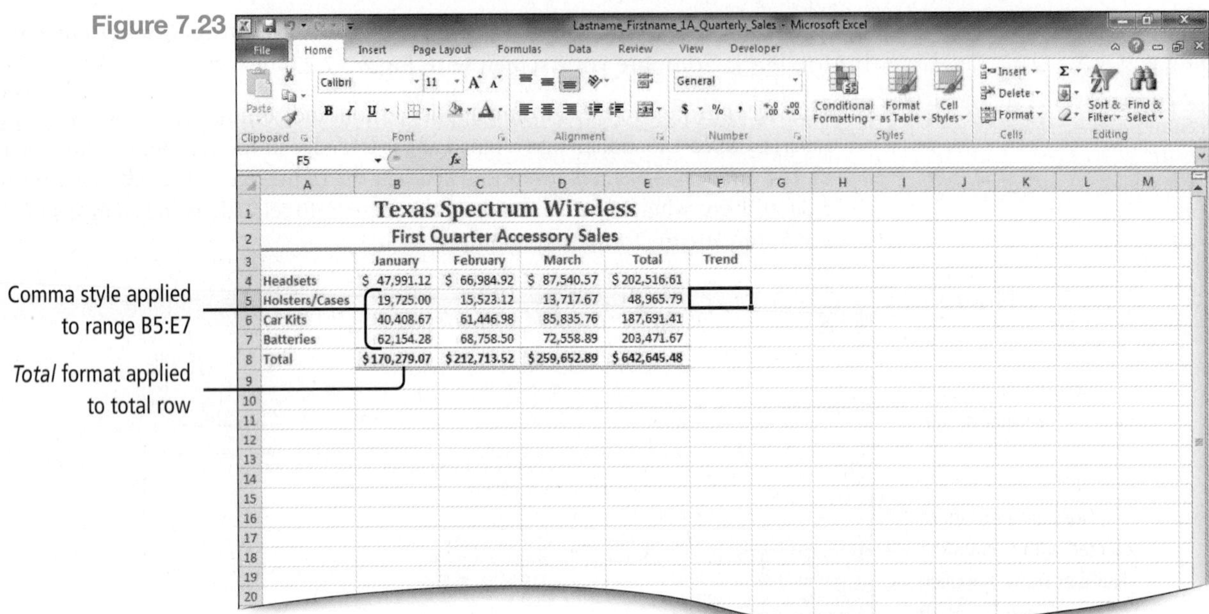

5 Click the **Page Layout tab**, and then in the **Themes group**, click **Themes**. Click the **Composite** theme, and notice that the cell styles change to match the new theme. Click **Save**.

Recall that a theme is a predefined set of colors, fonts, lines, and fill effects that look good together.

Objective 5 | Chart Data to Create a Column Chart and Insert Sparklines

A ***chart*** is a graphic representation of data in a worksheet. Data presented as a chart is easier to understand than a table of numbers. ***Sparklines*** are tiny charts embedded in a cell and give a visual trend summary alongside your data. A sparkline makes a pattern more obvious to the eye.

Activity 7.11 | Charting Data in a Column Chart

In this activity, you will create a ***column chart*** showing the monthly sales of accessories by category during the first quarter. A column chart is useful for illustrating comparisons among related numbers. The chart will enable the company president, Rosalyn Thomas, to see a pattern of overall monthly sales.

1 Select the range **A3:D7**. Click the **Insert tab**, and then in the **Charts group**, click **Column** to display a gallery of Column chart types.

When charting data, typically you should *not* include totals—include only the data you want to compare. By using different ***chart types***, you can display data in a way that is meaningful to the reader—common examples are column charts, pie charts, and line charts.

2 On the gallery of column chart types, under **2-D Column**, point to the first chart to display the ScreenTip *Clustered Column*, and then click to select it. Compare your screen with Figure 7.24.

A column chart displays in the worksheet, and the charted data is bordered by colored lines. Because the chart object is selected—surrounded by a border and displaying sizing handles—contextual tools named *Chart Tools* display and add contextual tabs next to the standard tabs on the Ribbon.

Figure 7.24

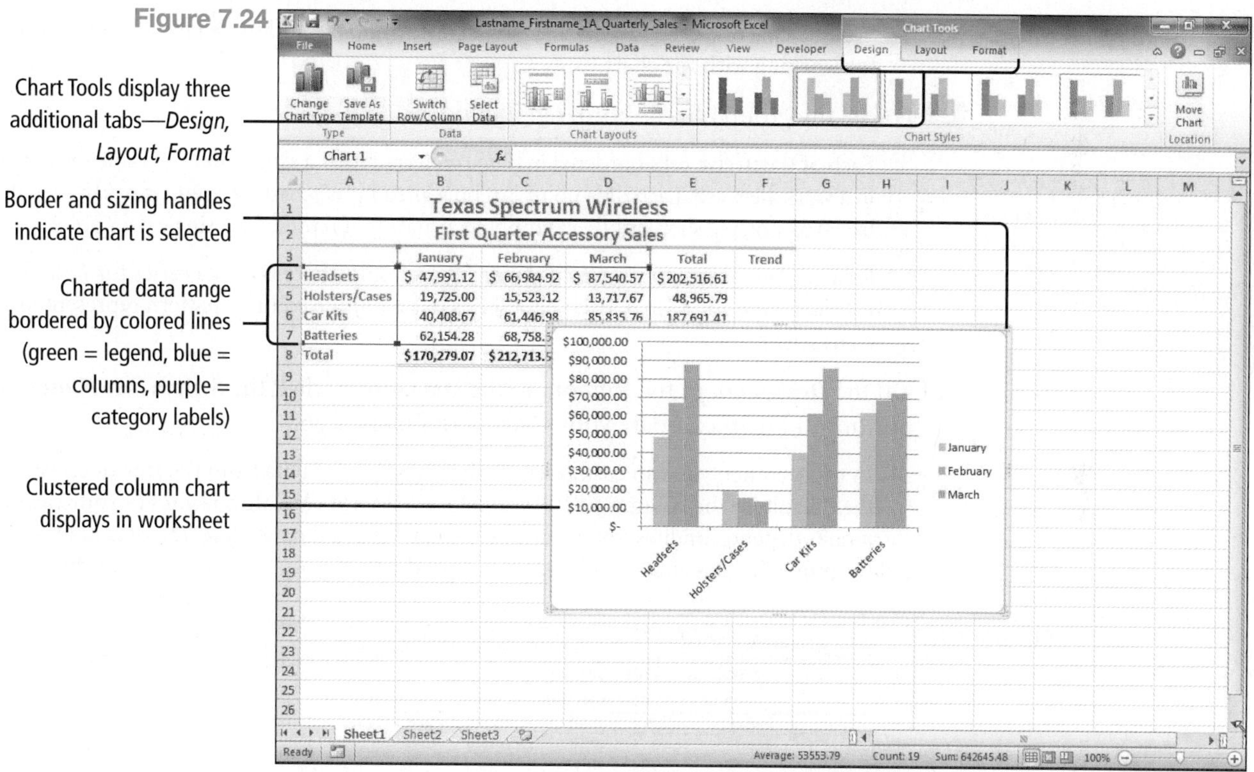

3 Point to the top border of the chart to display the [pointer icon] pointer, and then drag the upper left corner of the chart just inside the upper left corner of cell **A10**, approximately as shown in Figure 7.25.

Based on the data you selected in your worksheet, Excel constructs a column chart and adds ***category labels***—the labels that display along the bottom of the chart to identify the category of data. This area is referred to as the ***category axis*** or the ***x-axis***. Excel uses the row titles as the category names.

On the left, Excel includes a numerical scale on which the charted data is based; this is the ***value axis*** or the ***y-axis***. On the right, a ***legend***, which identifies the patterns or colors that are assigned to the categories in the chart, displays.

Figure 7.25

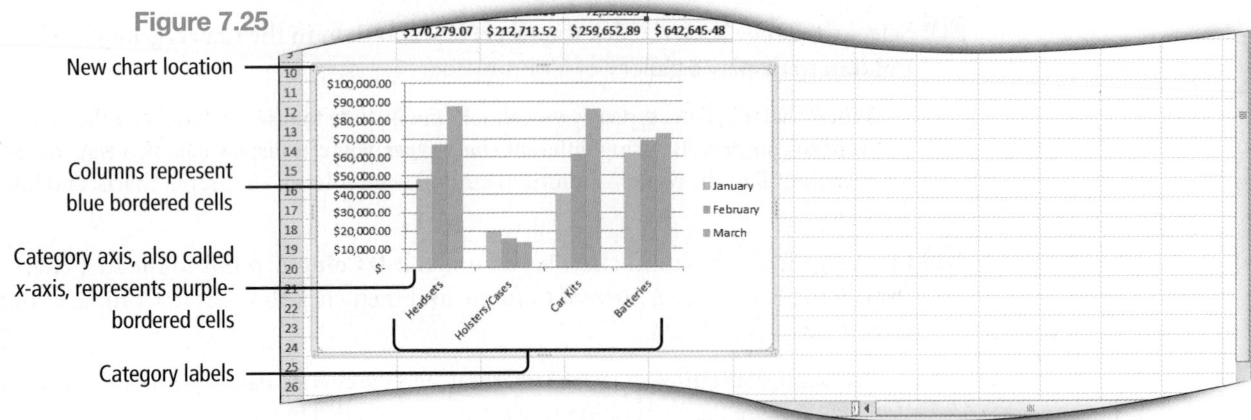

4 On the Ribbon, locate the contextual tabs under **Chart Tools—Design**, **Layout**, and **Format**.

When a chart is selected, Chart Tools become available and three tabs provide commands for working with the chart.

5 Locate the group of cells bordered in blue.

Each of the twelve cells bordered in blue is referred to as a ***data point***—a value that originates in a worksheet cell. Each data point is represented in the chart by a ***data marker***—a column, bar, area, dot, pie slice, or other symbol in a chart that represents a single data point.

Related data points form a ***data series***; for example, there is a data series for *January*, for *February*, and for *March*. Each data series has a unique color or pattern represented in the chart legend.

6 On the **Design tab** of the Ribbon, in the **Data group**, click the **Switch Row/Column** button, and then compare your chart with Figure 7.26.

In this manner, you can easily change the categories of data from the row titles, which is the default, to the column titles. Whether you use row or column titles as your category names depends on how you want to view your charted data. Here, the president wants to see monthly sales and the breakdown of product categories within each month.

Figure 7.26

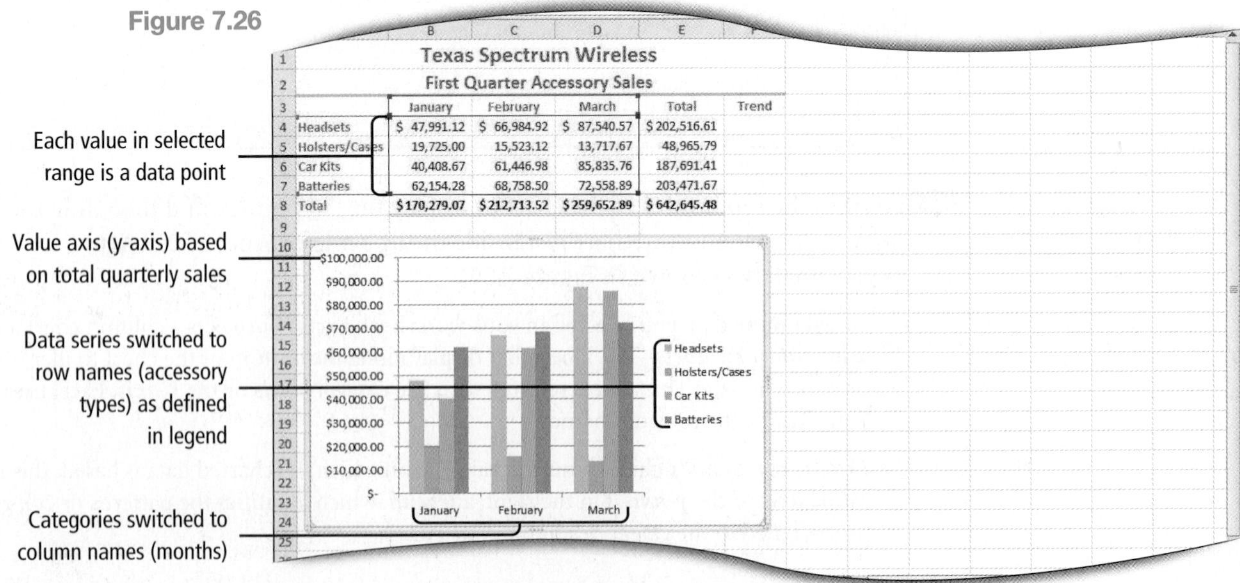

7 On the **Design tab**, in the **Chart Layouts group**, locate and click the **More** button. Compare your screen with Figure 7.27.

In the ***Chart Layouts gallery***, you can select a predesigned ***chart layout***—a combination of chart elements, which can include a title, legend, labels for the columns, and the table of charted cells.

Figure 7.27

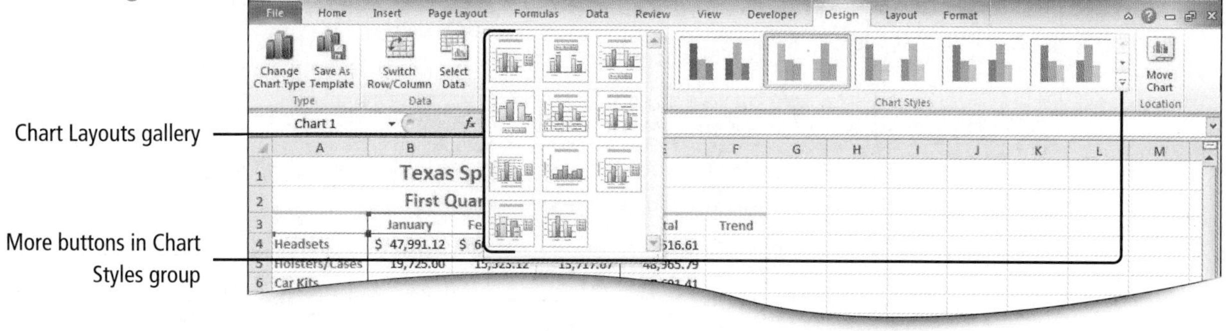

Chart Layouts gallery

More buttons in Chart Styles group

8 Click several different layouts to see the effect on your chart, and then using the ScreenTips as your guide, locate and click **Layout 1**.

9 In the chart, click anywhere in the text *Chart Title* to select the title box, watch the **Formula Bar** as you type **1st Quarter Sales** and then press Enter to display the new chart title.

10 Click in a white area just slightly *inside* the chart border to deselect the chart title. On the **Design tab**, in the **Chart Styles group**, click the **More** button. Compare your screen with Figure 7.28.

The ***Chart Styles gallery*** displays an array of pre-defined ***chart styles***—the overall visual look of the chart in terms of its colors, backgrounds, and graphic effects such as flat or beveled columns.

Figure 7.28

11 Using the ScreenTips as your guide, locate and click **Style 26**.

This style uses a white background, formats the columns with theme colors, and applies a beveled effect. With this clear visual representation of the data, the president can see the sales of all product categories in each month, and can see that the sale of headsets and car kits has risen quite markedly during the quarter.

12 Click any cell to deselect the chart, and notice that the *Chart Tools* no longer display in the Ribbon. Click **Save**, and then compare your screen with Figure 7.29.

Contextual tabs display when an object is selected, and then are removed from view when the object is deselected.

Figure 7.29

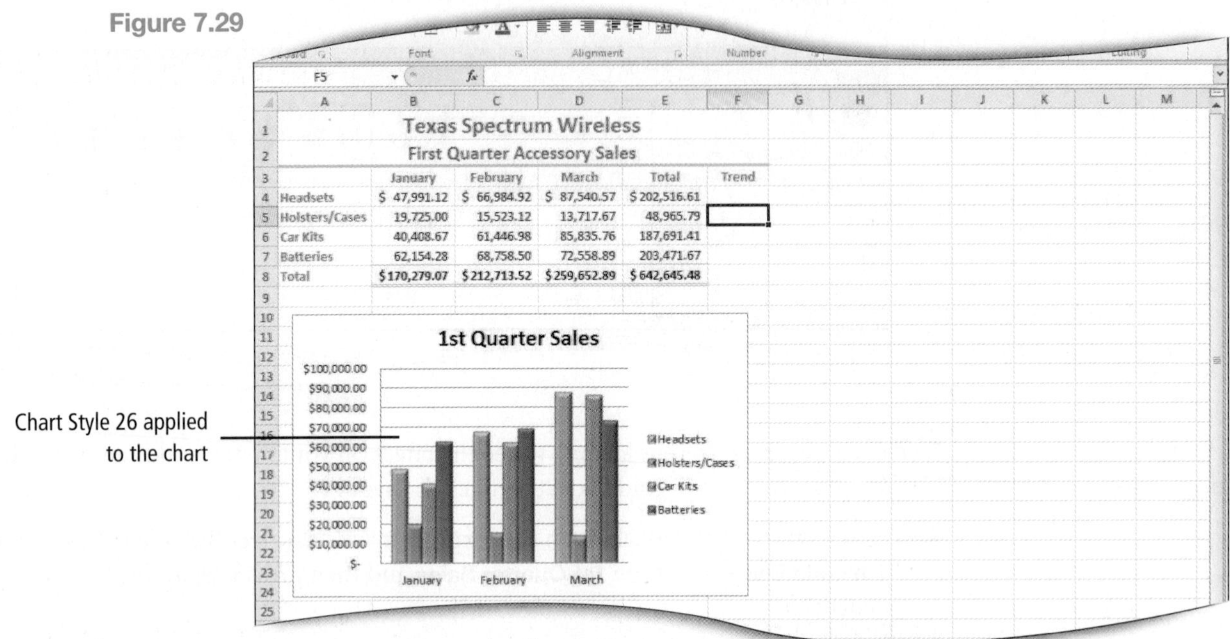

Activity 7.12 | Creating and Formatting Sparklines

By creating sparklines, you provide a context for your numbers. Your readers will be able to see the relationship between a sparkline and its underlying data quickly.

> **Another Way**
>
> In the worksheet, select the range F4:F7 to insert it into the Location Range box.

1 Select the range **B4:D7**. Click the **Insert tab**, and then in the **Sparklines group**, click **Line.** In the displayed **Create Sparklines** dialog box, notice that the selected range *B4:D7* displays.

2 With the insertion point blinking in the **Location Range** box, type **f4:f7** Compare your screen with Figure 7.30.

Figure 7.30

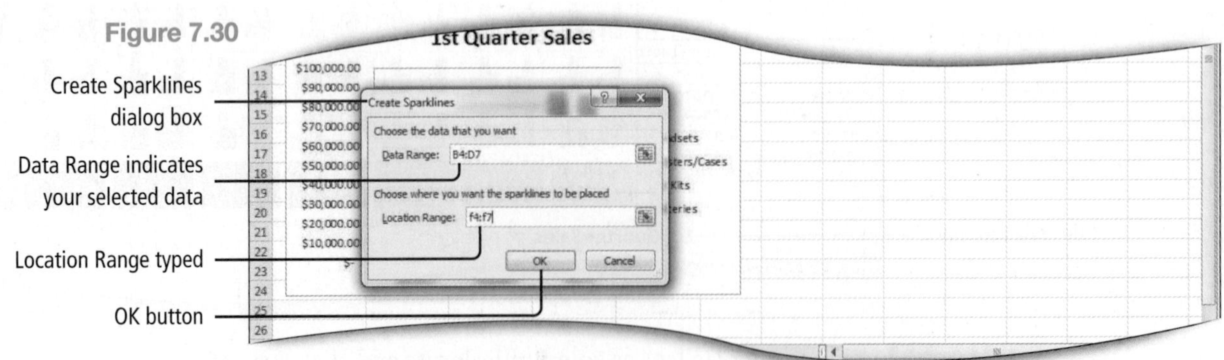

3 Click **OK** to insert the trend lines in the range F4:F7, and then on the **Design tab**, in the **Show group**, click the **Markers** check box to select it.

Alongside each row of data, the sparkline provides a quick visual trend summary for sales of each accessory item over the three-month period. For example, you can see instantly that of the four items, only Holsters/Cases had declining sales for the period.

4 In the **Style group**, click the **More** button. In the second row, click the fourth style—**Sparkline Style Accent 4, Darker 25%**. Click cell **A1** to deselect the range. Click **Save**. Compare your screen with Figure 7.31.

Use markers, colors, and styles in this manner to further enhance your sparklines.

Figure 7.31

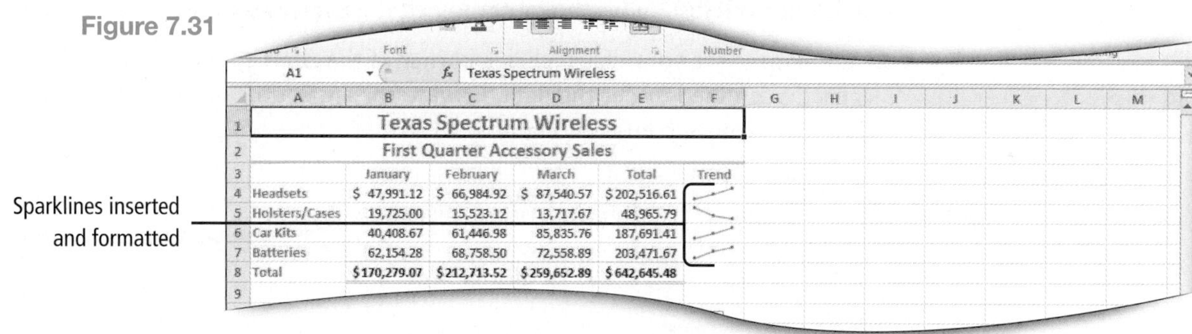

Objective 6 | Print, Display Formulas, and Close Excel

Use ***Page Layout view*** and the commands on the Page Layout tab to prepare for printing.

Activity 7.13 | Changing Views, Creating a Footer, and Using Print Preview

For each Excel project in this textbook, you will create a footer containing your name and the project name.

1 Be sure the chart is *not* selected. Click the **Insert tab**, and then in the **Text group**, click the **Header & Footer** button to switch to Page Layout view and open the **Header area**. Compare your screen with Figure 7.32.

In Page Layout view, you can see the edges of the paper of multiple pages, the margins, and the rulers. You can also insert a header or footer by typing in the areas indicated and use the Header & Footer Tools.

Figure 7.32

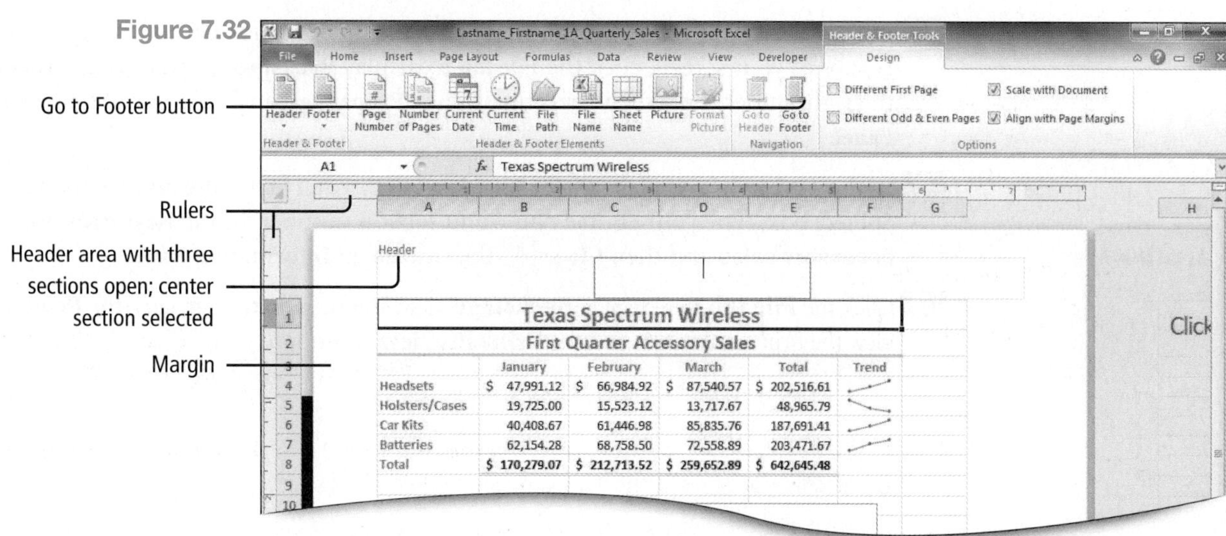

2 On the **Design tab**, in the **Navigation group**, click **Go to Footer** to open the **Footer area**, and then click just above the word *Footer* to place the insertion point in the **left section** of the **Footer area**.

3 In the **Header & Footer Elements group**, click the **File Name** button to add the name of your file to the footer—*&[File]* displays in the left section of the **Footer area**. Then, click in a cell just above the footer to exit the **Footer area** and view your file name.

4 Scroll up to see your chart, click a corner of the chart to select it, and then see if the chart is centered under the data. *Point* to the small dots on the right edge of the chart; compare your screen with Figure 7.33.

Figure 7.33

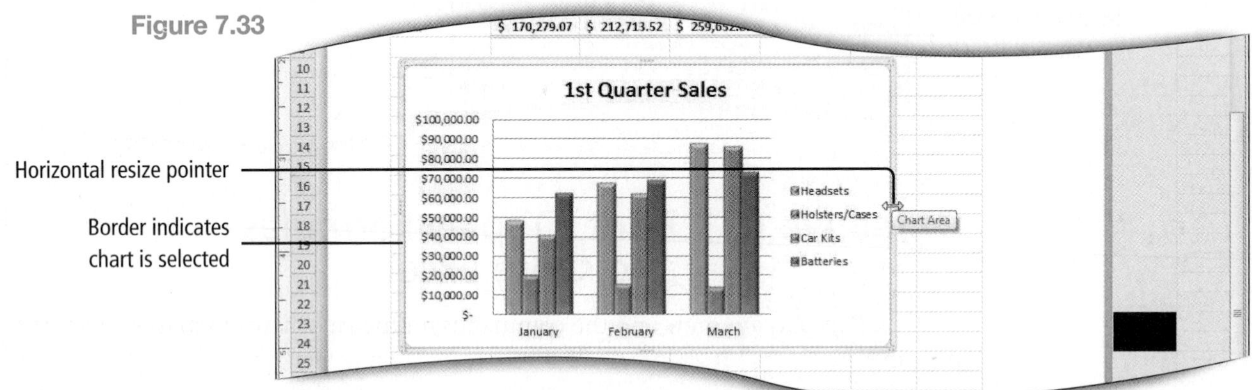

5 Drag the ⇔ pointer to the right so that the right border of the chart is just inside the right border of **column F**. Be sure the left and right borders of the chart are just slightly **inside** the left border of **column A** and the right border of **column F**—adjust as necessary.

6 Click any cell to deselect the chart. Click the **Page Layout tab**, in the **Page Setup group**, click the **Margins** button, and then at the bottom of the **Margins** gallery, click **Custom Margins**. In the **Page Setup** dialog box, under **Center on page**, select the **Horizontally** check box.

This action will center the data and chart horizontally on the page, as shown in the Preview area.

7 In the lower right corner of the **Page Setup** dialog box, click **OK**. In the upper left corner of your screen, click the **File tab** to display **Backstage** view. On the **Info tab**, on the right under the screen thumbnail, click **Properties**, and then click **Show Document Panel**.

8 In the **Author** box, replace the existing text with your firstname and lastname. In the **Subject** box, type your course name and section number. In the **Keywords** box type **accessory sales** and then **Close** [×] the **Document Information Panel**.

Another Way

Press Ctrl + F2 to view the Print Preview.

9 Click the **File tab** to redisplay **Backstage** view, and then on the left, click the **Print tab** to view the Print commands and the **Print Preview**. Compare your screen with Figure 7.34.

Figure 7.34

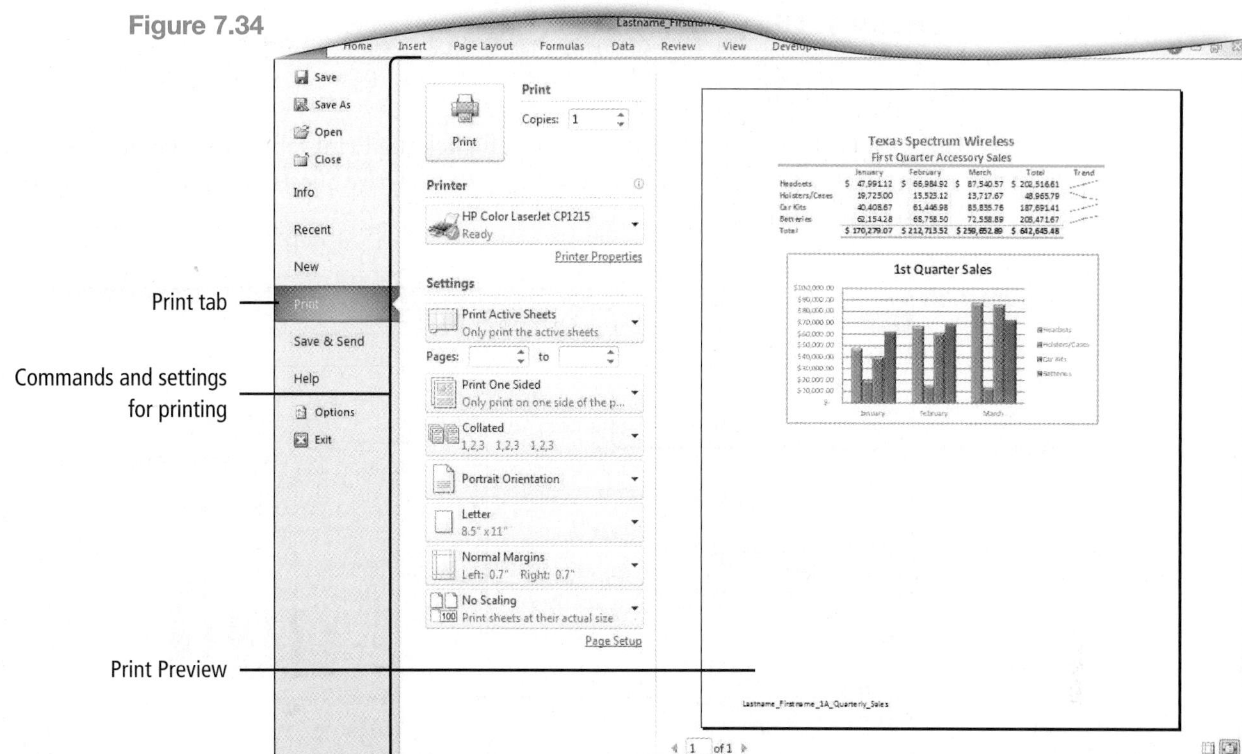

10 Note any adjustments that need to be made, and then on the Ribbon, click the **Home tab** to close Backstage view and return to the worksheet. In the lower right corner of your screen, click the **Normal** button to return to the Normal view, and then press Ctrl + Home to return to cell **A1**.

The ***Normal view*** maximizes the number of cells visible on your screen and keeps the column letters and row numbers closer. The vertical dotted line between columns indicates that as currently arranged, only the columns to the left of the dotted line will print on the first page. The exact position of the vertical line may depend on your default printer setting.

11 Make any necessary adjustments, and then **Save** your workbook.

Activity 7.14 | Deleting Unused Sheets in a Workbook

A new Excel workbook contains three blank worksheets. It is not necessary to delete unused sheets, but doing so saves storage space and removes any doubt that additional information is in the workbook.

1 At the bottom of your worksheet, click the **Sheet2 tab** to display the second worksheet in the workbook and make it active.

> **Another Way**
> On the Home tab, in the Cells group, click the Delete button arrow, and then click Delete Sheet.

2 Hold down Ctrl, and then click the **Sheet3 tab**. Release Ctrl, and then with both sheets selected (the tab background is white), point to either of the selected sheet tabs, right-click, and then on the shortcut menu, click **Delete**.

Excel deletes the two unused sheets from your workbook. If you attempt to delete a worksheet with data, Excel will display a warning and permit you to cancel the deletion. ***Sheet tabs*** are labels along the lower border of the Excel window that identify each worksheet.

Activity 7.15 | Printing a Worksheet

1 Click **Save** [icon].

2 Display **Backstage** view and on the left click the Print tab. Under **Print**, be sure **Copies** indicates *1*. Under **Settings**, verify that *Print Active Sheets* displays. Compare your screen with Figure 7.35.

Figure 7.35

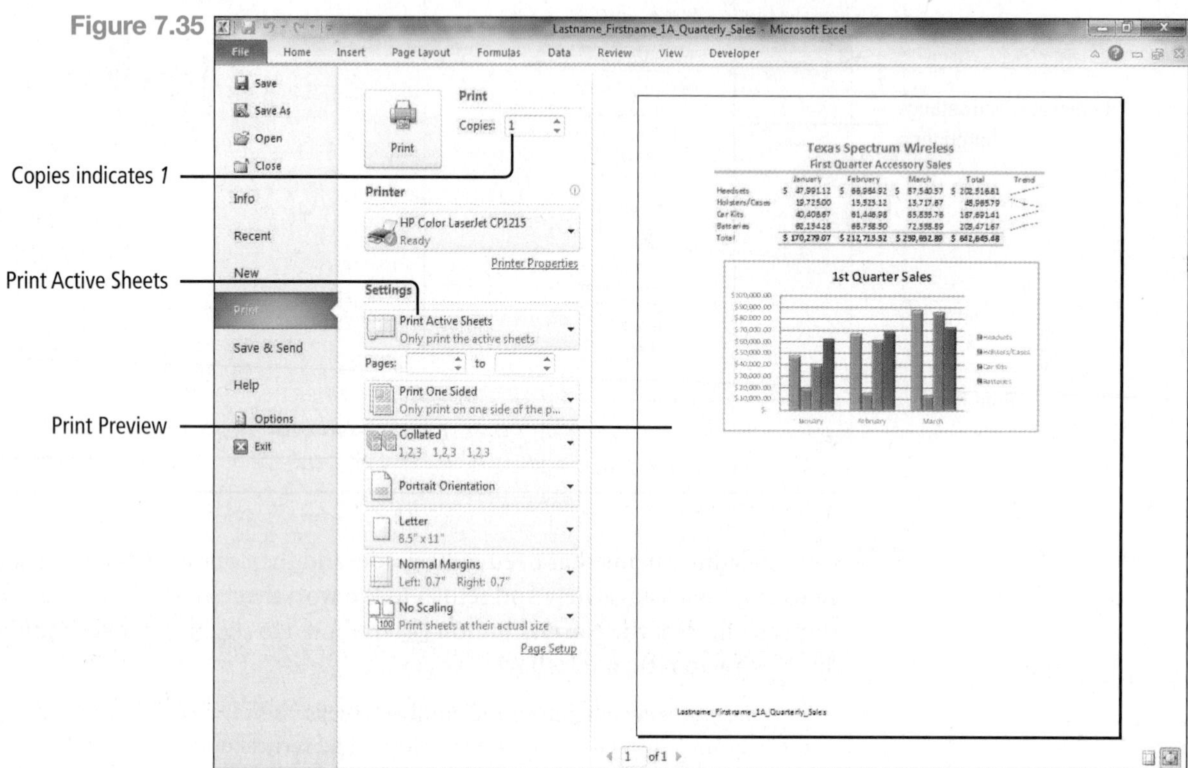

3 To print on paper, be sure that a printer is available to your system, and then in the **Print group**, click the **Print** button. To create an electronic printout, on the Backstage tabs, click the **Save & Send tab**, under **File Types** click **Create PDF/XPS Document**, and then on the right, click **Create PDF/XPS**. In the **Publish as PDF or XPS** dialog box, navigate to your storage location, and then click the **Publish** button to create the PDF file. Close the Adobe window.

Activity 7.16 | Displaying, Printing, and Hiding Formulas

When you type a formula in a cell, the cell displays the *results* of the formula calculation. Recall that this value is called the displayed value. You can view and print the underlying formulas in the cells. When you do so, a formula often takes more horizontal space to display than the result of the calculation.

1 If necessary, redisplay your worksheet. Because you will make some temporary changes to your workbook, on the Quick Access Toolbar, click **Save** [icon] to be sure your work is saved up to this point.

Another Way

Hold down Ctrl, and then press ` (usually located below Esc).

2 On the **Formulas tab**, in the **Formula Auditing group**, click the **Show Formulas** button. Then, in the **column heading area**, point to the **column A** heading to display the [↓] pointer, hold down the left mouse button, and then drag to the right to select columns **A:F**. Compare your screen with Figure 7.36.

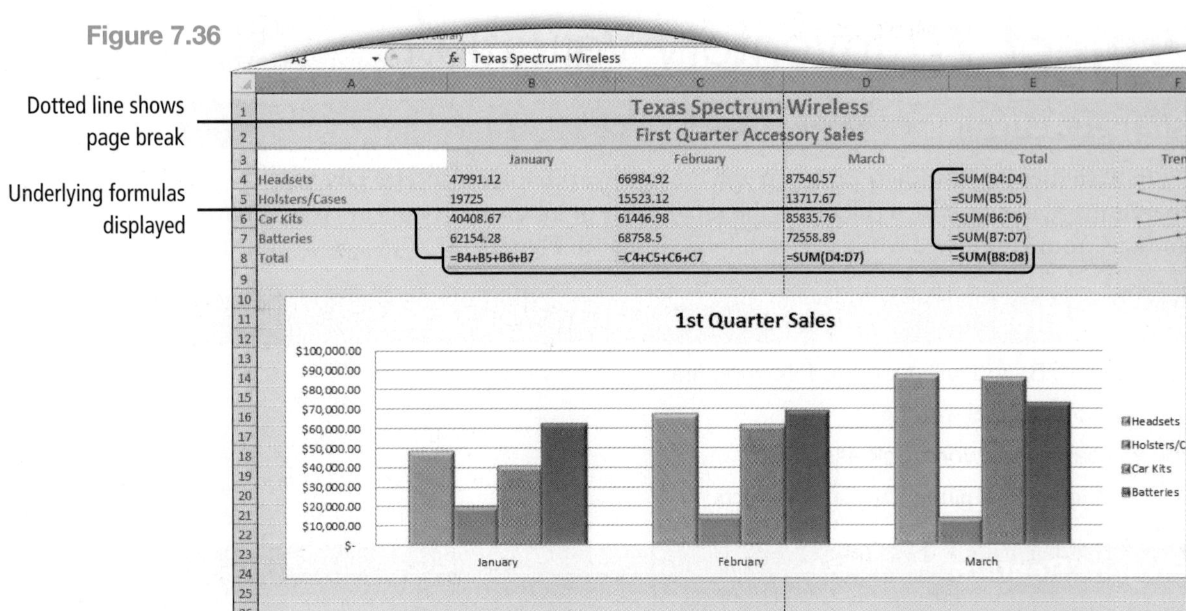

Figure 7.36

> **Note | Turning the Display of Formulas On and Off**
>
> The Show Formulas button is a toggle button. Clicking it once turns the display of formulas on—the button will glow orange. Clicking the button again turns the display of formulas off.

3 Point to the column heading boundary between any two of the selected columns to display the [+] pointer, and then double-click to AutoFit the selected columns.

AutoFit adjusts the width of a column to fit the cell content of the *widest* cell in the column.

> **Another Way**
>
> In the Scale to Fit group, click the Dialog Box Launcher button to display the Page tab of the Page Setup dialog box. Then, under Scaling, click the Fit to option button.

4 On the **Page Layout tab**, in the **Page Setup group**, click **Orientation**, and then click **Landscape**. In the **Scale to Fit** group, click the **Width arrow**, and then click **1 page** to scale the data to fit onto one page.

Scaling shrinks the width (or height) of the printed worksheet to fit a maximum number of pages, and is convenient for printing formulas. Although it is not always the case, formulas frequently take up more space than the actual data.

> **Another Way**
>
> In the Page Setup group, click the Dialog Box Launcher button to display the Page tab of the Page Setup dialog box. Then, under Orientation, click the Landscape option button.

5 In the **Page Setup group**, click the **Dialog Box Launcher** button. In the **Page Setup** dialog box, click the **Margins tab**, and then under **Center on page**, if necessary, click to select the **Horizontally** check box.

6 Click **OK** to close the dialog box. Check to be sure your chart is centered below the data and the left and right edges are slightly inside column A and column F—drag a chart edge and then deselect the chart if necessary. Display the **Print Preview**, and then submit your worksheet with formulas displayed, either printed or electronically, as directed by your instructor.

7 Click the **File tab** to display **Backstage** view, click **Close**, and when prompted, click **Don't Save** so that you do *not* save the changes you made—displaying formulas, changing column widths and orientation, and scaling—to print your formulas.

8 In the upper right corner of your screen, click the **Close** button to exit Excel.

End You have completed Project 7A

Project 7B Inventory Valuation

Project Activities

In Activities 7.17 through 7.24, you will create a workbook for Josette Lovrick, Operations Manager, which calculates the retail value of an inventory of car convenience products. Your completed worksheet will look similar to Figure 7.37.

Project Files

For Project 7B, you will need the following file:

New blank Excel workbook

You will save your workbook as:

Lastname_Firstname_1B_Car_Products

Project Results

Texas Spectrum Wireless

Car Products Inventory Valuation

As of December 31

	Warehouse Location	Quantity In Stock	Retail Price	Total Retail Value	Percent of Total Retail Value
Antenna Signal Booster	Dallas	1,126	$ 19.99	$ 22,508.74	8.27%
Car Power Port Adapter	Dallas	3,546	19.49	69,111.54	25.39%
Repeater Antenna	Houston	1,035	39.99	41,389.65	15.21%
SIM Card Reader and Writer	Houston	2,875	16.90	48,587.50	17.85%
Sticky Dash Pad	Houston	3,254	11.99	39,015.46	14.33%
Window Mount GPS Holder	Dallas	2,458	20.99	51,593.42	18.95%
Total Retail Value for All Products				$ 272,206.31	

Lastname_Firstname_1B_Car_Products

Figure 7.37
Project 7B Car Products

Objective 7 | Check Spelling in a Worksheet

In Excel, the spelling checker performs similarly to the other Microsoft Office programs.

Activity 7.17 | Checking Spelling in a Worksheet

1 **Start** Excel and display a new blank workbook. In cell **A1**, type **Texas Spectrum Wireless** and press Enter. In cell **A2**, type **Car Products Inventory** and press Enter.

2 On the Ribbon, click the **File tab** to display **Backstage** view, click **Save As**, and then in the **Save As** dialog box, navigate to your **Excel Chapter 7** folder. As the **File name**, type **Lastname_Firstname_1B_Car_Products** and then click **Save**.

3 Press Tab to move to cell **B3**, type **Quantity** and press Tab. In cell **C3**, type **Average Cost** and press Tab. In cell **D3**, type **Retail Price** and press Tab.

4 Click cell **C3**, and then look at the **Formula Bar**. Notice that in the cell, the displayed value is cut off; however, in the **Formula Bar**, the entire text value—the underlying value—displays. Compare your screen with Figure 7.38.

Text that is too long to fit in a cell spills over to cells on the right only if they are empty. If the cell to the right contains data, the text in the cell to the left is truncated. The entire value continues to exist, but is not completely visible.

Figure 7.38

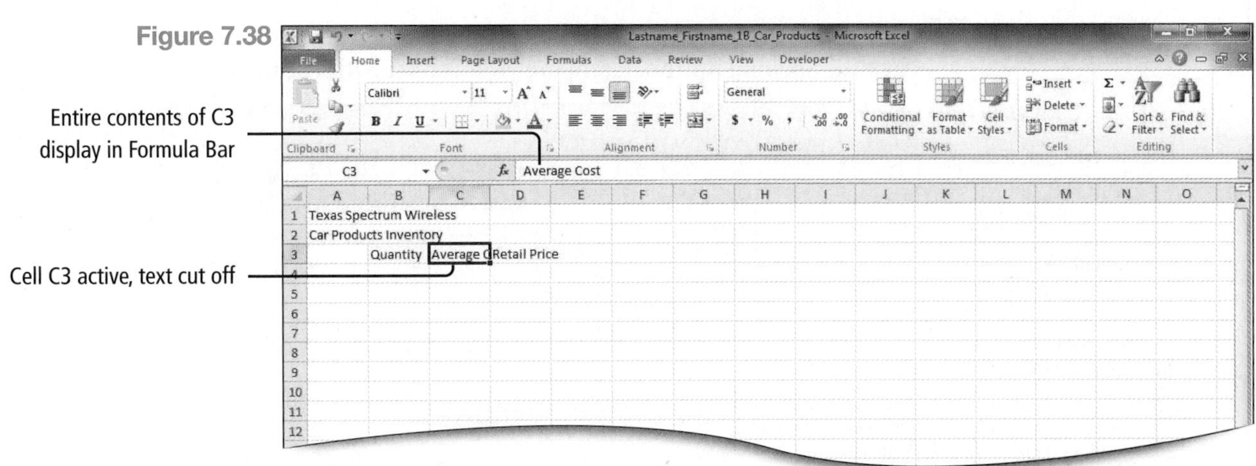

5 Click cell **E3**, type **Total Retail Value** and press Tab. In cell **F3**, type **Percent of Total Retail Value** and press Enter.

6 Click cell **A4**. *Without* correcting the spelling error, type **Antena Signal Booster** Press Enter. In the range **A5:A10**, type the remaining row titles shown below. Then compare your screen with Figure 7.39.

Car Power Port Adapter

Repeater Antenna

SIM Card Reader and Writer

Sticky Dash Pad

Window Mount GPS Holder

Total Retail Value for All Products

Figure 7.39

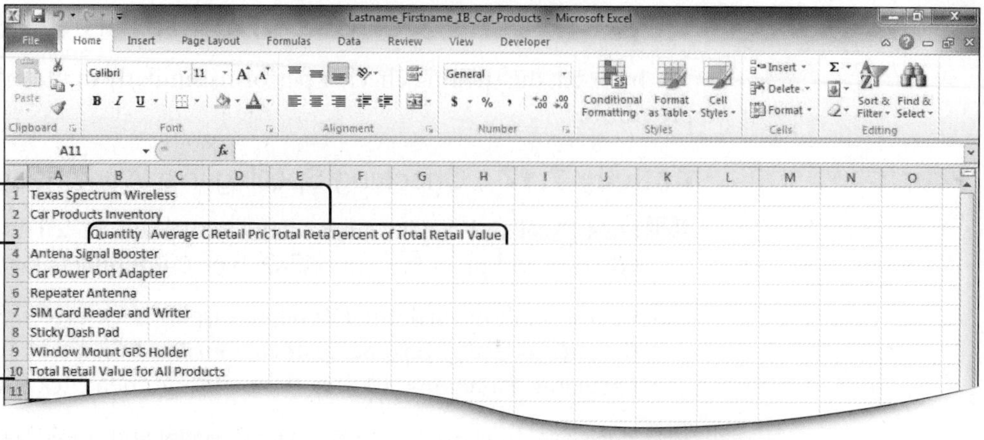

Column titles

Row titles

7 In the **column heading area**, point to the right boundary of **column A** to display the [+] pointer, and then drag to the right to widen **column A** to **215** pixels.

8 Select the range **A1:F1**, **Merge & Center** the text, and then from the **Cell Styles** gallery, apply the **Title** style.

9 Select the range **A2:F2**, **Merge & Center** the text, and then from the **Cell Styles** gallery, apply the **Heading 1** style. Press Ctrl + Home to move to the top of your worksheet.

> **Another Way**
>
> Press F7, which is the keyboard shortcut for the Spelling command.

10 With cell **A1** as the active cell, click the **Review tab**, and then in the **Proofing group**, click the **Spelling** button. Compare your screen with Figure 7.40.

Figure 7.40

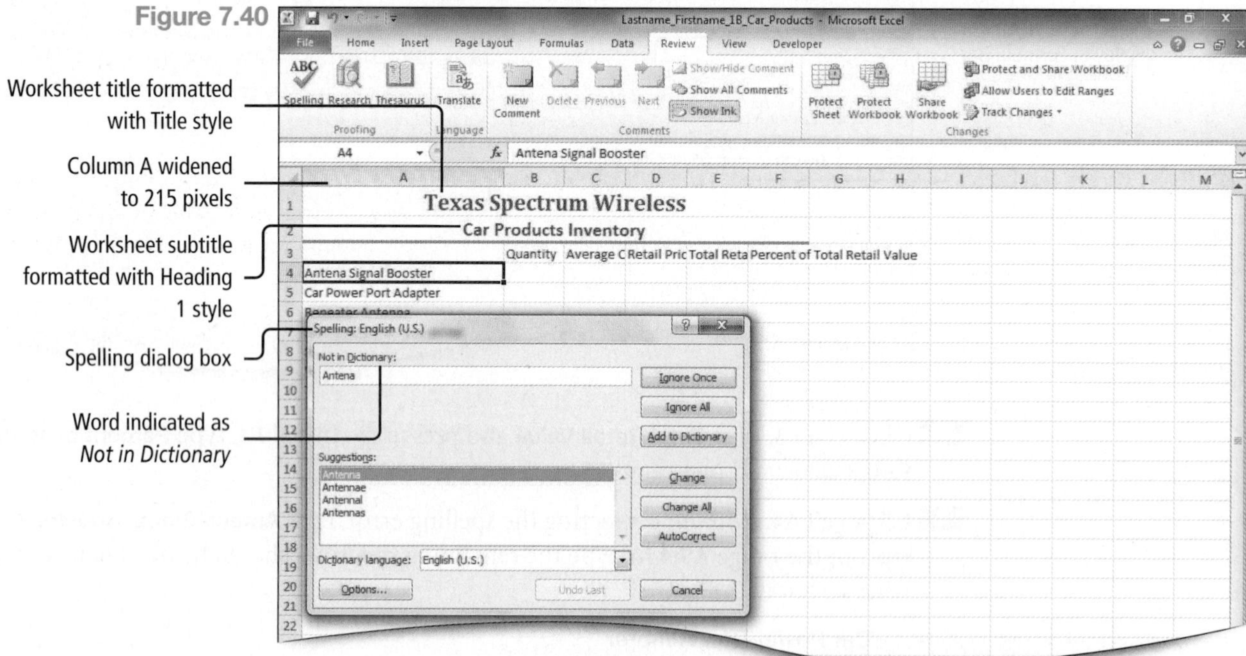

> **Alert! | Does a Message Display Asking if You Want to Continue Checking at the Beginning of the Sheet?**
>
> If a message displays asking if you want to continue checking at the beginning of the sheet, click Yes. The Spelling command begins its checking process with the currently selected cell and moves to the right and down. Thus, if your active cell was a cell after A4, this message may display.

11 In the **Spelling** dialog box, under **Not in Dictionary**, notice the word *Antena*.

The spelling tool does not have this word in its dictionary. Under *Suggestions*, Excel provides a list of suggested spellings.

12 Under **Suggestions**, click **Antenna**, and then click the **Change** button.

Antena, a typing error, is changed to *Antenna*. A message box displays *The spelling check is complete for the entire sheet*—unless you have additional unrecognized words. Because the spelling check begins its checking process starting with the currently selected cell, it is good practice to return to cell A1 before starting the Spelling command.

13 Correct any other errors you may have made. When the message displays, *The spelling check is complete for the entire sheet*, click **OK**. **Save** your workbook.

Objective 8 | Enter Data by Range

You can enter data by first selecting a range of cells. This is a time-saving technique, especially if you use the numeric keypad to enter the numbers.

Activity 7.18 | Entering Data by Range

1 Select the range **B4:D9**, type **1126** and then press Enter.

The value displays in cell B4, and cell B5 becomes the active cell.

2 With cell **B5** active in the range, and pressing Enter after each entry, type the following, and then compare your screen with Figure 7.41:

4226
1035
2875
3254
2458

After you enter the last value and press Enter, the active cell moves to the top of the next column within the selected range. Although it is not required to enter data in this manner, you can see that selecting the range before you enter data saves time because it confines the movement of the active cell to the selected range.

Figure 7.41

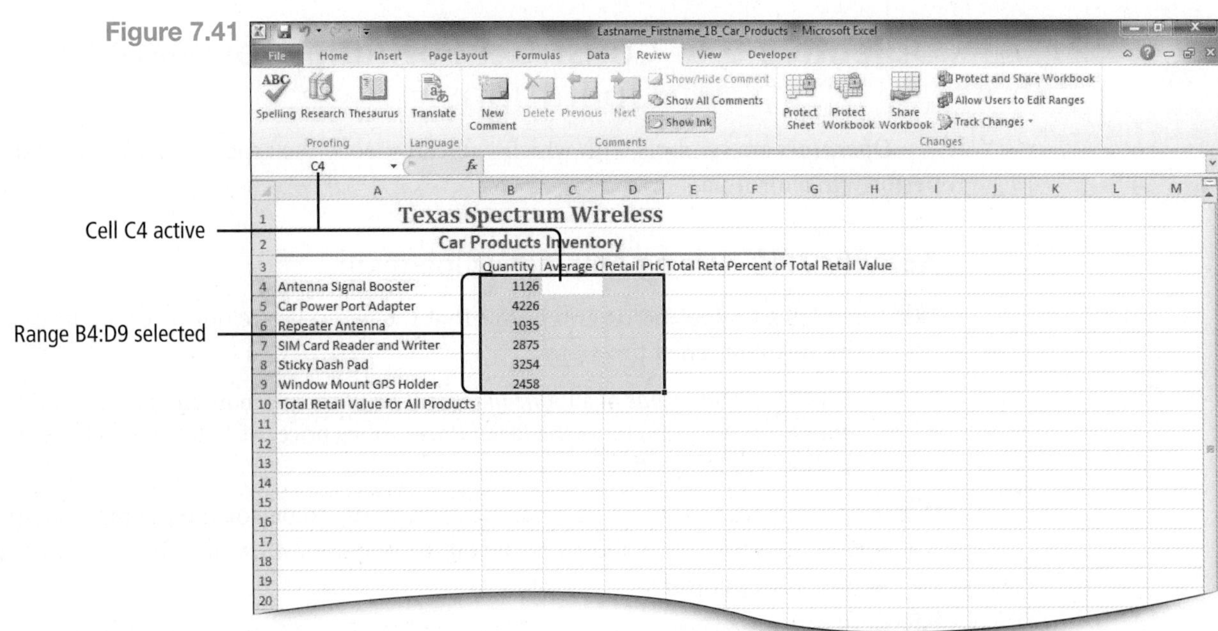

3 With the selected range still active, from the following table, beginning in cell **C4** and pressing Enter after each entry, enter the data for the **Average Cost** column and then the **Retail Price** column. If you prefer, deselect the range to enter the values—typing in a selected range is optional.

Average Cost	Retail Price
9.75	19.99
9.25	19.49
16.90	39.99
9.55	16.90
4.20	12.99
10.45	20.99

Recall that the default number format for cells is the *General* number format, in which numbers display exactly as you type them and trailing zeros do not display, even if you type them.

4 Click any blank cell, and then compare your screen with Figure 7.42. Correct any errors you may have made while entering data, and then click **Save**.

Figure 7.42

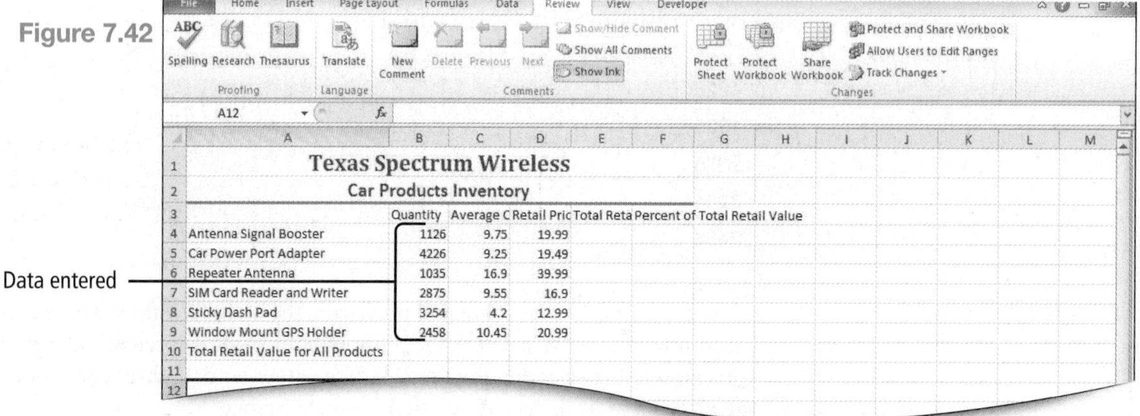

Objective 9 | Construct Formulas for Mathematical Operations

Operators are symbols with which you can specify the type of calculation you want to perform in a formula.

Activity 7.19 | Using Arithmetic Operators

1 Click cell **E4**, type **=b4*d4** and notice that the two cells are outlined as part of an active formula. Then press Enter.

The *Total Retail Value* of all *Antenna Signal Booster* items in inventory—*22508.74*—equals the *Quantity* (1,126) times the *Retail Price* (selling price) of 19.99. In Excel, the asterisk (*) indicates multiplication.

2 Take a moment to study the symbols you will use to perform basic mathematical operations in Excel, as shown in the table in Figure 7.43, which are referred to as ***arithmetic operators***.

Symbols Used in Excel for Arithmetic Operators	
Operator Symbol	**Operation**
+	Addition
-	Subtraction (also negation)
*	Multiplication
/	Division
%	Percent
^	Exponentiation

Figure 7.43

3 Click cell **E4**.

You can see that in cells E5:E9, you need a formula similar to the one in E4, but one that refers to the cells in row 5, row 6, and so forth. Recall that you can copy formulas and the cell references will change *relative to* the row number.

4 With cell **E4** selected, position your pointer over the fill handle in the lower right corner of the cell until the + pointer displays. Then, drag down through cell **E9** to copy the formula.

Another Way

Select the range, display the Cell Styles gallery, and then under Number Format, click Comma [0].

5 Select the range **B4:B9**, and then on the **Home tab**, in the **Number group**, click the **Comma Style** button ,. Then, in the **Number group**, click the **Decrease Decimal** button two times to remove the decimal places from these values.

Comma Style formats a number with two decimal places; because these are whole numbers referring to quantities, no decimal places are necessary.

6 Select the range **E4:E9**, and then at the bottom of your screen, in the status bar, notice the displayed values for **Average**, **Count**, and **Sum**—*48118.91833*, *6* and *288713.51*.

When you select numerical data, three calculations display in the status bar by default—Average, Count, and Sum. Here, Excel indicates that if you averaged the selected values, the result would be *48118.91833*, there are 6 cells in the selection that contain values, and that if you added the values the result would be 288713.51.

7 Click cell **E10**, in the **Editing group**, click the **Sum** button Σ, notice that Excel selects a range to sum, and then press Enter to display the total *288713.5*.

8 Select the range **C5:E9** and apply the **Comma Style** ,; notice that Excel widens **column E**.

9 Select the range **C4:E4**, hold down Ctrl, and then click cell **E10**. Release Ctrl and then apply the **Accounting Number Format** $. Notice that Excel widens the columns as necessary.

10 Click cell **E10**, and then from the **Cell Styles** gallery, apply the **Total** style. Click any blank cell, and then compare your screen with Figure 7.44.

Figure 7.44

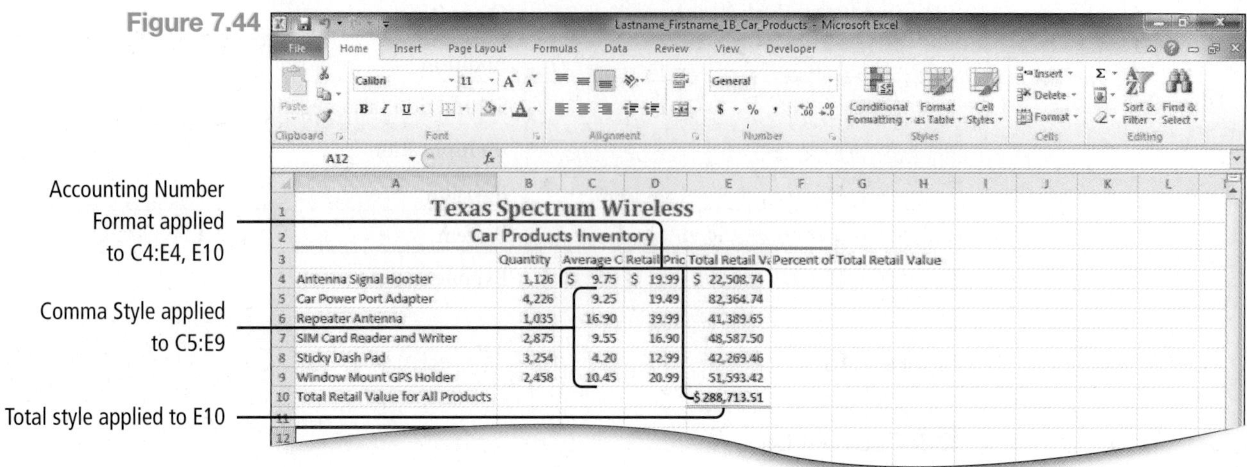

11 **Save** your workbook.

> **More Knowledge | Multiple Status Bar Calculations**
>
> You can display a total of six calculations on the status bar. To add additional calculations—Minimum, Maximum, and Numerical Count (the number of selected cells that contain a number value)—right-click on the status bar, and then click the additional calculations that you want to display.

Activity 7.20 | Copying Formulas Containing Absolute Cell References

In a formula, a relative cell reference refers to a cell by its position *in relation to* the cell that contains the formula. An ***absolute cell reference***, on the other hand, refers to a cell by its *fixed* position in the worksheet, for example, the total in cell E10.

A relative cell reference automatically adjusts when a formula is copied. In some calculations, you do *not* want the cell reference to adjust; rather, you want the cell reference to remain the same when the formula is copied.

1 Click cell **F4**, type = and then click cell **E4**. Type **/** and then click cell **E10**.

The formula *=E4/E10* indicates that the value in cell E4 will be *divided* by the value in cell E10. Why? Because Ms. Lovrick wants to know the percentage by which each product's Total Retail Value makes up the Total Retail Value for All Products.

Arithmetically, the percentage is computed by dividing the *Total Retail Value* for each product by the *Total Retail Value for All Products*. The result will be a percentage expressed as a decimal.

2 Press Enter. Click cell **F4** and notice that the formula displays in the **Formula Bar**. Then, point to cell **F4** and double-click.

The formula, with the two referenced cells displayed in color and bordered with the same color, displays in the cell. This feature, called the ***range finder***, is useful for verifying formulas because it visually indicates which workbook cells are included in a formula calculation.

3 Press Enter to redisplay the result of the calculation in the cell, and notice that approximately 8% of the total retail value of the inventory is made up of Antenna Signal Boosters.

4 Click cell **F4** again, and then drag the fill handle down through cell **F9**. Compare your screen with Figure 7.45.

Each cell displays an error message—*#DIV/0!* and a green triangle in the upper left corner of each cell indicates that Excel detects an error.

Like a grammar checker, Excel uses rules to check for formula errors and flags errors in this manner. Additionally, the Auto Fill Options button displays, from which you can select formatting options for the copied cells.

Figure 7.45

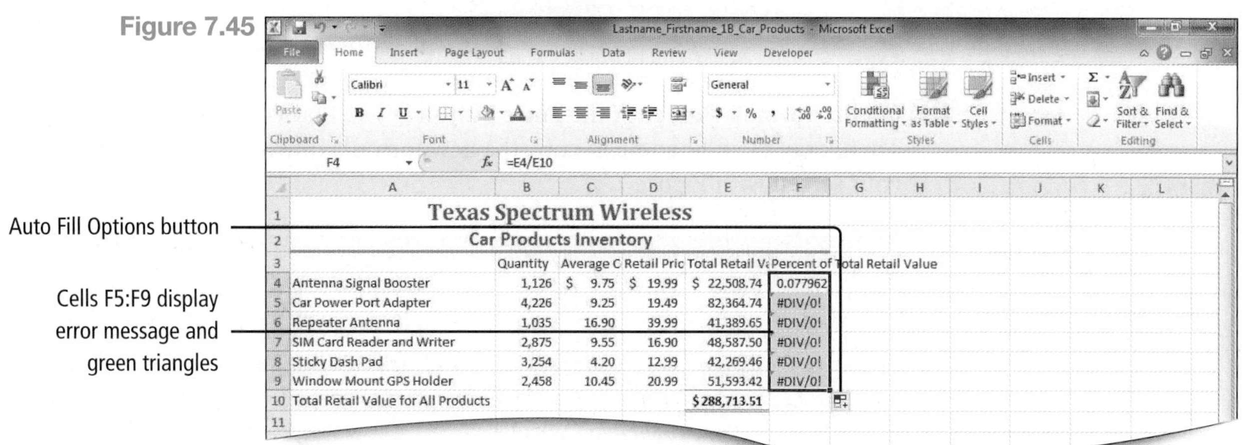

5 Click cell **F5**, and to the left of the cell, point to the **Error Checking** button to display its ScreenTip—*The formula or function used is dividing by zero or empty cells.*

In this manner, Excel suggests the cause of an error.

6 Look at the **Formula Bar** and examine the formula.

The formula is *=E5/E11*. The cell reference to *E5* is correct, but the cell reference following the division operator (/) is *E11*, and E11 is an *empty* cell.

7 Click cell **F6**, point to the **Error Checking** button, and in the **Formula Bar** examine the formula.

Because the cell references are relative, Excel builds the formulas by increasing the row number for each equation. But in this calculation, the divisor must always be the value in cell E10—the *Total Retail Value for All Products.*

8 Point to cell **F4**, and then double-click to place the insertion point within the cell.

> **Another Way**
>
> Edit the formula so that it indicates *=E4/E10*

9 Within the cell, use the arrow keys as necessary to position the insertion point to the left of *E10*, and then press F4. Compare your screen with Figure 7.46.

Dollar signs ($) display, which changes the reference to cell E10 to an absolute cell reference. The use of the dollar sign to denote an absolute reference is not related in any way to whether or not the values you are working with are currency values. It is simply the symbol that Excel uses to denote an absolute cell reference.

Figure 7.46

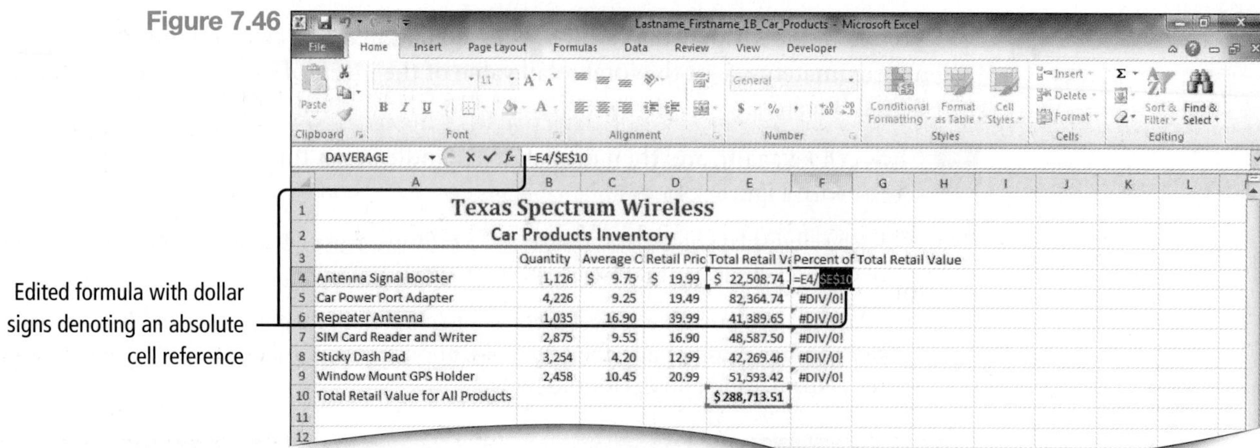

10 On the **Formula Bar**, click the **Enter** button so that **F4** remains the active cell. Then, drag the fill handle to copy the new formula down through cell **F9**. Compare your screen with Figure 7.47.

Figure 7.47

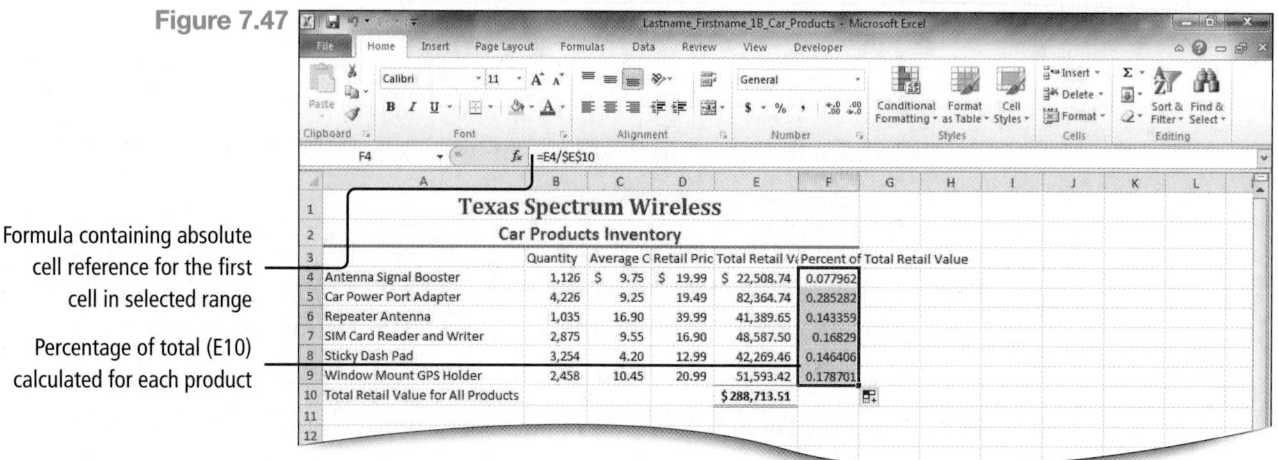

11 Click cell **F5**, examine the formula in the **Formula Bar**, and then examine the formulas for cells **F6**, **F7**, **F8**, and **F9**.

For each formula, the cell reference for the *Total Retail Value* of each product changed relative to its row; however, the value used as the divisor—*Total Retail Value for All Products* in cell F10—remained absolute. Thus, using either relative or absolute cell references, it is easy to duplicate formulas without typing them.

12 **Save** your workbook.

> **More Knowledge | Calculate a Percentage if You Know the Total and the Amount**
>
> Using the equation *amount/total = percentage*, you can calculate the percentage by which a part makes up a total—with the percentage formatted as a decimal. For example, if on a test you score 42 points correctly out of 50, your percentage of correct answers is 42/50 = 0.84 or 84%.

Objective 10 | Edit Values in a Worksheet

Excel performs calculations on numbers; that is why you use Excel. If you make changes to the numbers, Excel automatically *re*-calculates. This is one of the most powerful and valuable features of Excel.

Activity 7.21 | Editing Values in a Worksheet

You can edit text and number values directly within a cell or on the Formula Bar.

1 In cell **E10**, notice the column total *$288,713.51*. Then, click cell **B5**, and to change its value type **3546** Watch cell **E5** and press Enter.

Excel formulas *re-calculate* if you change the value in a cell that is referenced in a formula. It is not necessary to delete the old value in a cell; selecting the cell and typing a new value replaces the old value with your new typing.

The *Total Retail Value* of all *Car Power Port Adapters* items recalculates to *69,111.54* and the total in cell E10 recalculates to *$275,460.31*. Additionally, all of the percentages in column F recalculate.

2 Point to cell **D8**, and then double-click to place the insertion point within the cell. Use the arrow keys to move the insertion point to left or right of *2*, and use either Del or Backspace to delete *2* and then type **1** so that the new Retail Price is *11.99*.

3 Watch cell **E8** and **E10** as you press Enter, and then notice the recalculation of the formulas in those two cells.

Excel recalculates the value in cell E8 to *39,015.46* and the value in cell E10 to *$272,206.31*. Additionally, all of the percentages in column F recalculate because the *Total Retail Value for All Products* recalculated.

4 Point to cell **A2** so that the pointer is positioned slightly to the right of the word *Inventory*, and then double-click to place the insertion point in the cell. Edit the text to add the word **Valuation** pressing Spacebar as necessary, and then press Enter.

5 Click cell **B3**, and then in the **Formula Bar**, click to place the insertion point after the letter *y*. Press Spacebar one time, type **In Stock** and then on the **Formula Bar**, click the **Enter** button. Click **Save**, and then compare your screen with Figure 7.48.

Recall that if text is too long to fit in the cell and the cell to the right contains data, the text is truncated—cut off—but the entire value still exists as the underlying value.

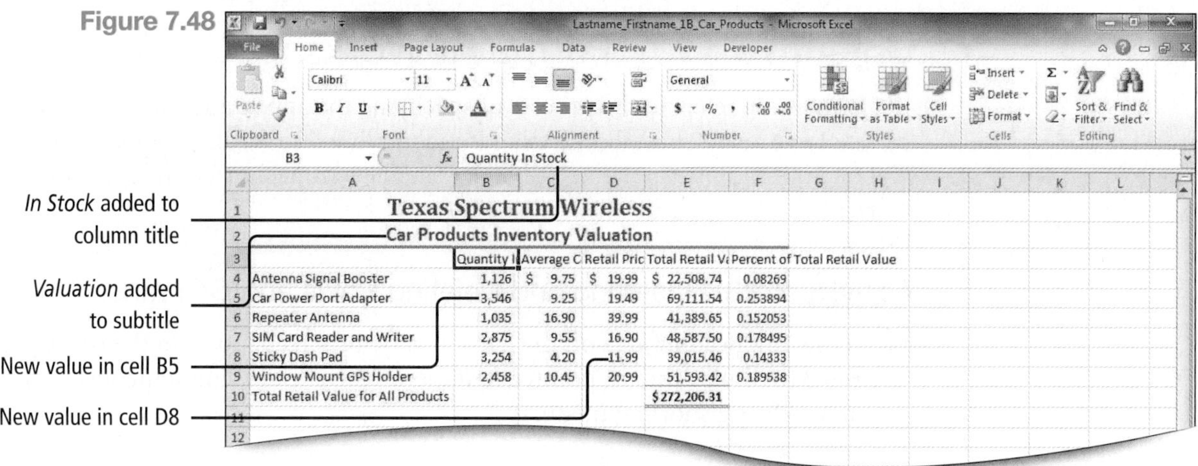

Figure 7.48

Activity 7.22 | Formatting Cells with the Percent Style

A percentage is part of a whole expressed in hundredths. For example, 75 cents is the same as 75 percent of one dollar. The Percent Style button formats the selected cell as a percentage rounded to the nearest hundredth.

1 Click cell **F4**, and then in the **Number group**, click the **Percent Style** button [%].

Your result is 8%, which is *0.08269* rounded to the nearest hundredth and expressed as a percentage. Percent Style displays the value of a cell as a percentage.

2 Select the range **F4:F9**, right-click over the selection, and then on the Mini toolbar, click the **Percent Style** button [%], click the **Increase Decimal** button [.00] two times, and then click the **Center** [≡] button.

Percent Style may not offer a percentage precise enough to analyze important financial information—adding additional decimal places to a percentage makes data more precise.

3 Click any cell to cancel the selection, **Save** [💾] your workbook, and then compare your screen with Figure 7.49.

Figure 7.49

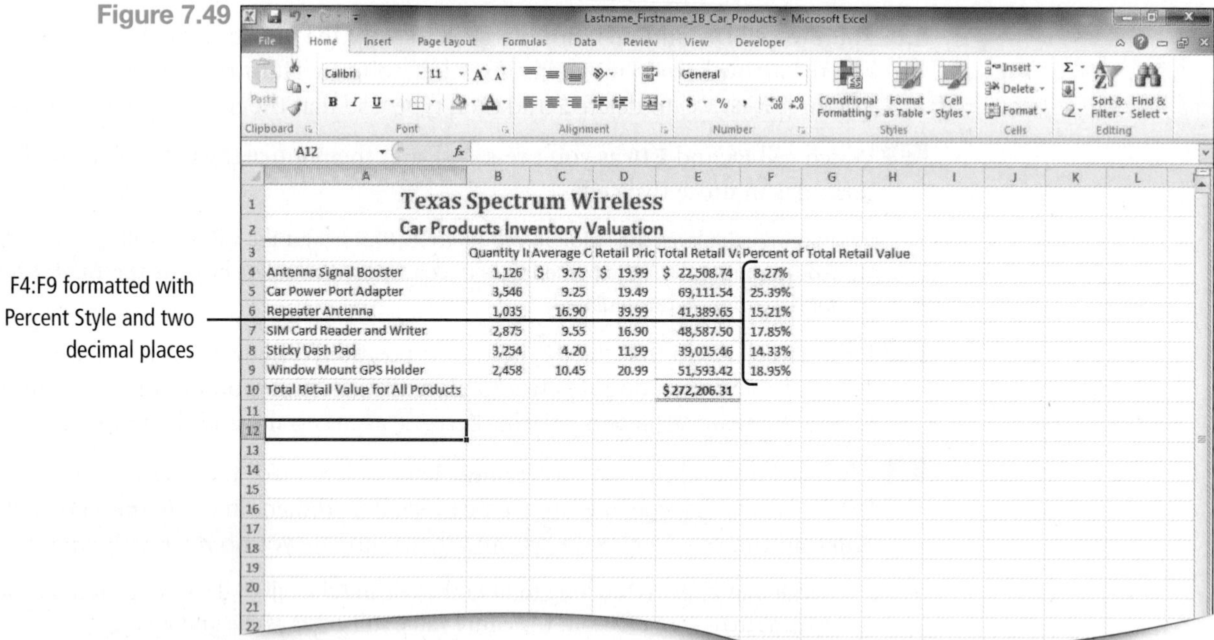

Objective 11 | Format a Worksheet

Formatting refers to the process of specifying the appearance of cells and the overall layout of your worksheet. Formatting is accomplished through various commands on the Ribbon, for example, applying Cell Styles, and also from shortcut menus, keyboard shortcuts, and the Format Cells dialog box.

Activity 7.23 | Inserting and Deleting Rows and Columns

1 In the **row heading area** on the left side of your screen, point to the row heading for **row 3** to display the [→] pointer, and then right-click to simultaneously select the row and display a shortcut menu.

> **Another Way**
>
> Select the row, on the Home tab, in the Cells group, click the Insert button arrow, and then click Insert Sheet Rows. Or, select the row and click the Insert button—the default setting of the button inserts a new sheet row above the selected row.

2. On the displayed shortcut menu, click **Insert** to insert a new **row 3**.

   The rows below the new row 3 move down one row, and the Insert Options button displays. By default, the new row uses the formatting of the row *above*.

3. Click cell **E11**. On the **Formula Bar**, notice that the range changed to sum the new range **E5:E10**. Compare your screen with Figure 7.50.

   If you move formulas by inserting additional rows or columns in your worksheet, Excel automatically adjusts the formulas. Excel adjusted all of the formulas in the worksheet that were affected by inserting this new row.

Figure 7.50

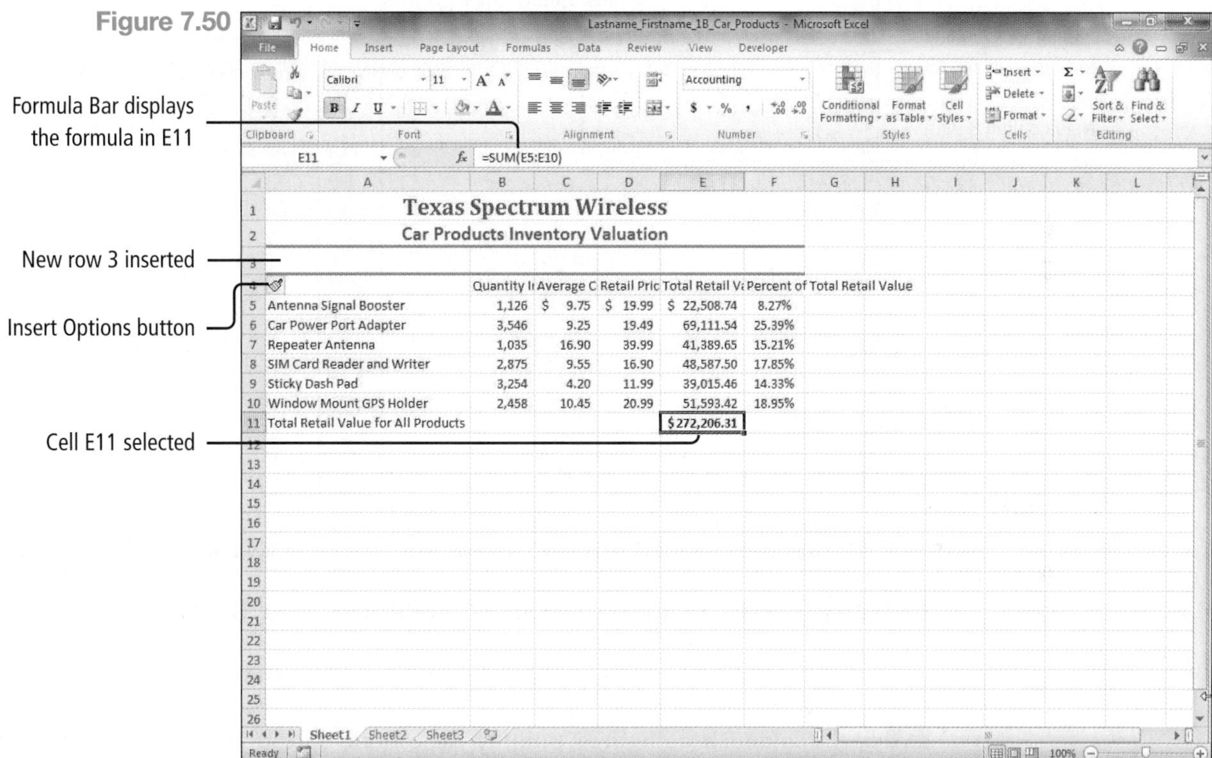

> **Another Way**
>
> Select the column, on the Home tab, in the Cells group, click the Insert button arrow, and then click Insert Sheet Columns. Or, select the column and click the Insert button—the default setting of the button inserts a new sheet column to the right of the selected column.

4. Click cell **A3**, type **As of December 31** and then on the **Formula Bar**, click the **Enter** button to maintain **A3** as the active cell. **Merge & Center** the text across the range **A3:F3**, and then apply the **Heading 2** cell style.

5. In the **column heading area**, point to **column B** to display the pointer, right-click, and then click **Insert**.

   By default, the new column uses the formatting of the column to the *left*.

6. Click cell **B4**, type **Warehouse Location** and then press Enter.

7. In cell **B5**, type **Dallas** and then type **Dallas** again in cells **B6** and **B10**. Use AutoComplete to speed your typing by pressing Enter as soon as the AutoComplete suggestion displays. In cells **B7**, **B8**, and **B9**, type **Houston**

8 In the **column heading area**, point to **column D**, right-click, and then click **Delete**.

The remaining columns shift to the left, and Excel adjusts all the formulas in the worksheet accordingly. You can use a similar technique to delete a row in a worksheet.

9 Compare your screen with Figure 7.51, and then **Save** your workbook.

Figure 7.51

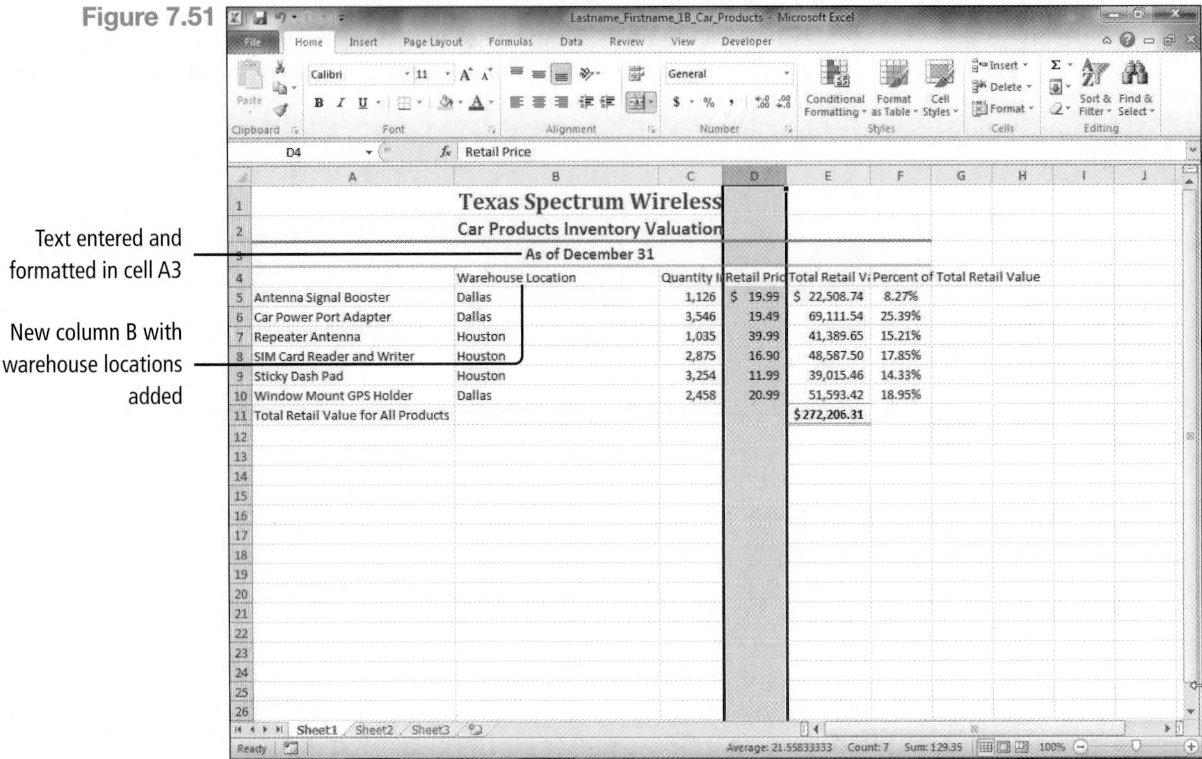

Activity 7.24 | Adjusting Column Widths and Wrapping Text

Use the Wrap Text command to display the contents of a cell on multiple lines.

1 In the **column heading area**, point to the **column B** heading to display the pointer, and then drag to the right to select **columns B:F**.

2 With the columns selected, in the **column heading area**, point to the right boundary of any of the selected columns to display the pointer, and then drag to set the width to **90 pixels**.

Use this technique to format multiple columns or rows simultaneously.

3 Select the range **B4:F4** that comprises the column headings, and then on the **Home tab**, in the **Alignment group**, click the **Wrap Text** button. Notice that the row height adjusts.

4 With the range **B4:F4** still selected, in the **Alignment group**, click the **Center** button and the **Middle Align** button. With the range **B4:F4** still selected, apply the **Heading 4** cell style.

The Middle Align command aligns text so that it is centered between the top and bottom of the cell.

5 Select the range **B5:B10**, right-click, and then on the shortcut menu, click the **Center** button [≡]. Click cell **A11**, and then from the **Cell Styles** gallery, under **Themed Cell Styles**, click **40% - Accent1**. Click any blank cell, and then compare your screen with Figure 7.52.

Figure 7.52

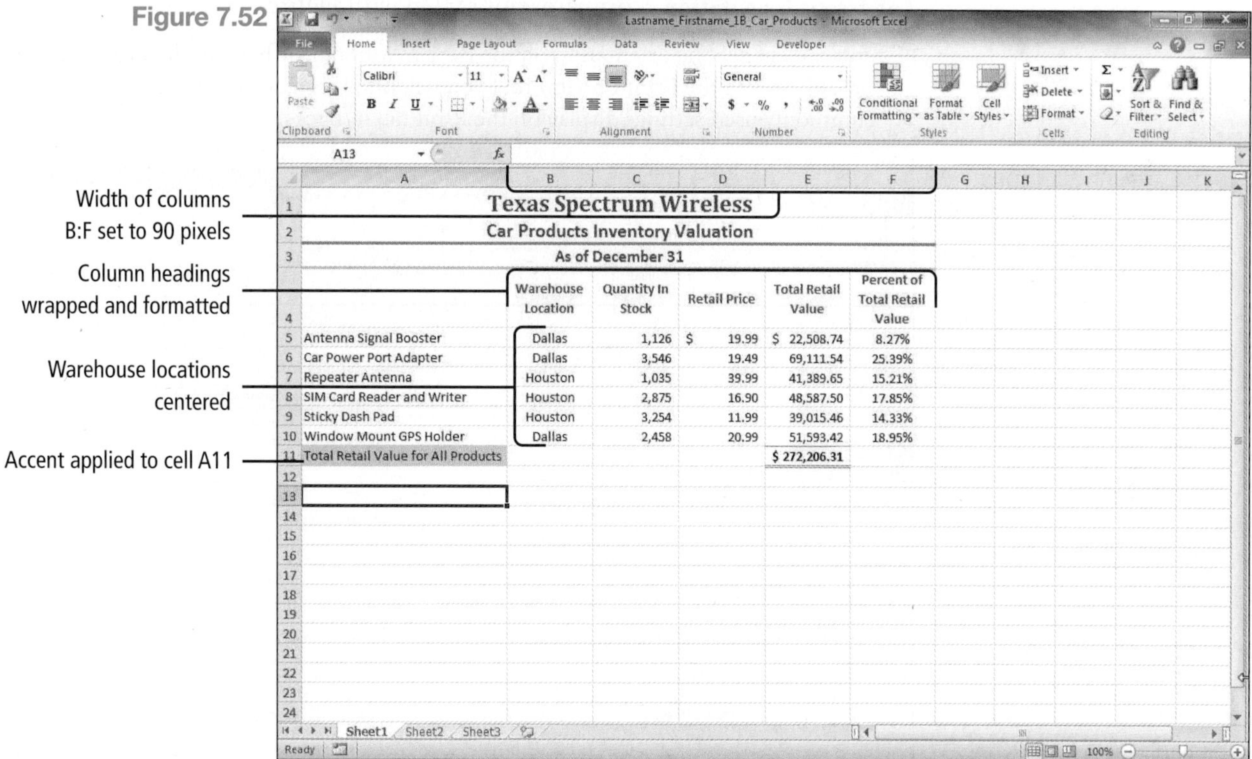

6 Click the **Insert tab**, and then in the **Text group**, click **Header & Footer** to switch to Page Layout view and open the **Header area**.

7 In the **Navigation group**, click the **Go to Footer** button to move to the bottom of the page and open the **Footer area**, and then click just above the word *Footer* to place the insertion point in the **left section** of the **Footer area**.

8 In the **Header & Footer Elements group**, click the **File Name** button to add the name of your file to the footer—*&[File]* displays in the left section of the **Footer area**. Then, click in a cell above the footer to exit the **Footer area** and view your file name.

9 Click the **Page Layout tab**, in the **Page Setup group**, click the **Margins** button, and then at the bottom of the **Margins gallery**, click **Custom Margins**. In the **Page Setup** dialog box, under **Center on page**, select the **Horizontally** check box; click **OK**.

10 In the upper left corner of your screen, click **File** to display **Backstage** view. On the **Info tab**, on the right under the screen thumbnail, click **Properties**, and then click **Show Document Panel**.

11 In the **Author** box, replace the existing text with your firstname and lastname. In the **Subject** box, type your course name and section number. In the **Keywords** box, type **car products, inventory** and then **Close** [×] the **Document Information Panel**.

12 Press Ctrl + F2 to view the **Print Preview**. At the bottom of the **Print Preview**, click the **Next Page** button ▶, and notice that as currently formatted, the worksheet occupies two pages.

13 In the center panel, under **Settings**, click **Portrait Orientation**, and then click **Landscape Orientation**. Compare your screen with Figure 7.53.

You can change the orientation on the Page Layout tab, or here, in the Print Preview. Because it is in the Print Preview that you will often see adjustments that need to be made, commonly used settings display on the Print tab in Backstage view.

Figure 7.53

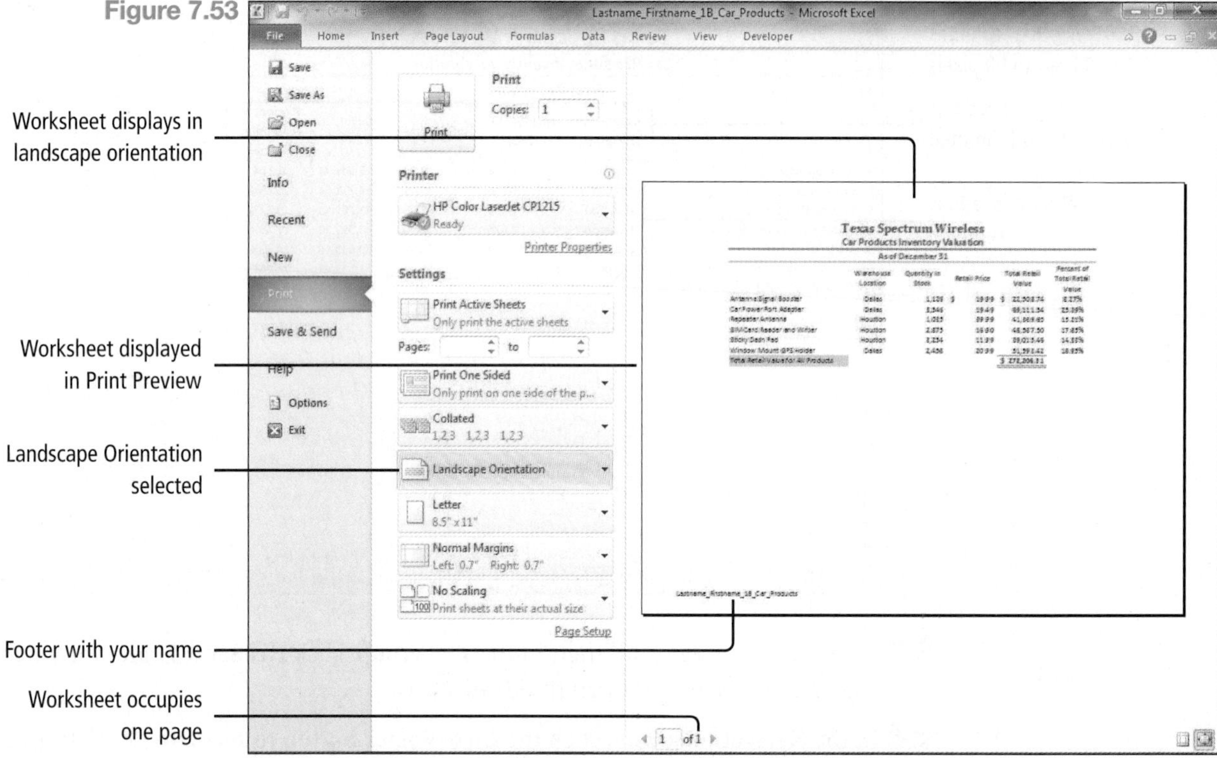

14 Note any additional adjustments or corrections that need to be made, and then on the Ribbon, click **Home** to redisplay your worksheet. In the lower right corner of your screen, on the right side of the status bar, click the **Normal** button to return to the Normal view, and then press Ctrl + Home to return to cell **A1**.

15 Make any necessary corrections. Then, at the bottom of your worksheet, click the **Sheet2 tab** to make it the active worksheet. Hold down Ctrl, and then click the **Sheet3 tab**. Release Ctrl, and then with both sheets selected (tab background is white), point to either of the selected sheet tabs, right-click, and click **Delete** to delete the unused sheets in the workbook.

16 **Save** your workbook.

17 Print or submit your worksheet electronically as directed by your instructor. If required by your instructor, print or create an electronic version of your worksheet with formulas displayed using the instructions in Activity 7.16 in Project 7A.

18 Close your workbook and close Excel.

End You have completed Project 7B

Content-Based Assessments

Summary

In this chapter, you used Microsoft Excel 2010 to create and analyze data organized into columns and rows and to chart and perform calculations on the data. By organizing your data with Excel, you will be able to make calculations and create visual representations of your data in the form of charts.

Key Terms

Absolute cell reference 368
Accounting Number Format 351
Active cell 340
Arithmetic operators 366
AutoComplete 341
Auto Fill 342
AutoFit 361
AutoSum 348
Category axis 353
Category labels 353
Cell 337
Cell address 340
Cell content 340
Cell reference 340
Cell style 350
Chart 352
Chart layout 355
Chart Layouts gallery 355
Chart styles 355
Chart Styles gallery 355
Chart types 353
Column 339
Column chart 352
Column heading 339
Comma Style 351
Constant value 340
Context sensitive 342
Data 340
Data marker 354
Data point 354
Data series 354
Displayed value 345
Expand Formula Bar button 339
Expand horizontal scroll bar button 338
Fill handle 342
Format 350
Formula 340
Formula Bar 338
Function 346
General format 345
Horizontal window split box 339
Insert Worksheet button 338
Label 340
Left alignment 341
Legend 353
Lettered column headings 339
Merge & Center 350
Name Box 338
Normal view 359
Number format 345
Number values 340
Numbered row headings 339
Operators 366
Page Layout view 357
Picture element 343
Pixels 343
Point and click method 347
Range 344
Range finder 368
Relative cell reference 349
Rounding 348
Row 340
Row heading 340
Scaling 361
Select All box 339
Series 342
Sheet tab scrolling buttons 338
Sheet tabs 338
Sparklines 352
Status bar 338
SUM function 347
Spreadsheet 337
Text values 340
Underlying formula 347
Underlying value 345
Value 340
Value axis 353
Vertical window split box 338
Workbook 337
Workbook-level buttons 338
Worksheet 337
X-axis 353
Y-axis 353

Matching

Match each term in the second column with its correct definition in the first column by writing the letter of the term on the blank line in front of the correct definition.

____ 1. An Excel file that contains one or more worksheets.

____ 2. Another name for a worksheet.

____ 3. The intersection of a column and a row.

A Cell
B Cell address
C Cell content

_____	4.	The labels along the lower border of the Excel window that identify each worksheet.	**D** Chart
_____	5.	A vertical group of cells in a worksheet.	**E** Column
_____	6.	A horizontal group of cells in a worksheet.	**F** Constant value
_____	7.	Anything typed into a cell.	**G** Data
_____	8.	Information such as numbers, text, dates, or times of day that you type into a cell.	**H** Fill handle
_____	9.	Text or numbers in a cell that are not a formula.	**I** Formula
_____	10.	An equation that performs mathematical calculations on values in a worksheet.	**J** Number value
_____	11.	A constant value consisting of only numbers.	**K** Row
_____	12.	Another name for a cell reference.	**L** Sheet tabs
_____	13.	Another name for a constant value.	**M** Spreadsheet
_____	14.	The small black square in the lower right corner of a selected cell.	**N** Value
_____	15.	The graphic representation of data in a worksheet.	**O** Workbook

Multiple Choice

Circle the correct answer.

1. On startup, Excel displays a new blank:
A. document **B.** workbook **C.** grid

2. An Excel window element that displays the value or formula contained in the active cell is the:
A. name box **B.** status bar **C.** formula bar

3. An Excel window element that displays the name of the selected cell, table, chart, or object is the:
A. name box **B.** status bar **C.** formula bar

4. A box in the upper left corner of the worksheet grid that selects all the cells in a worksheet is the:
A. name box **B.** select all box **C.** split box

5. A cell surrounded by a black border and ready to receive data is the:
A. active cell **B.** address cell **C.** reference cell

6. The feature that generates and extends values into adjacent cells based on the values of selected cells is:
A. AutoComplete **B.** Auto Fill **C.** fill handle

7. The default format that Excel applies to numbers is the:
A. comma format **B.** accounting format **C.** general format

8. The data that displays in the Formula Bar is referred to as the:
A. constant value **B.** formula **C.** underlying value

9. The type of cell reference that refers to cells by their fixed position in a worksheet is:
A. absolute **B.** relative **C.** exponentiation

10. Tiny charts embedded in a cell that give a visual trend summary alongside your data are:
A. embedded charts **B.** sparklines **C.** chart styles

Content-Based Assessments

Apply 7A skills from these Objectives:

1. Create, Save, and Navigate an Excel Workbook
2. Enter Data in a Worksheet
3. Construct and Copy Formulas and Use the Sum Function
4. Format Cells with Merge & Center and Cell Styles
5. Chart Data to Create a Column Chart and Insert Sparklines
6. Print, Display Formulas, and Close Excel

Skills Review | Project 7C GPS Sales

In the following Skills Review, you will create a new Excel worksheet with a chart that summarizes the first quarter sales of GPS (Global Positioning System) navigation devices. Your completed worksheet will look similar to Figure 7.54.

Project Files

For Project 7C, you will need the following file:

New blank Excel workbook

You will save your workbook as:

Lastname_Firstname_1C_GPS_Sales

Project Results

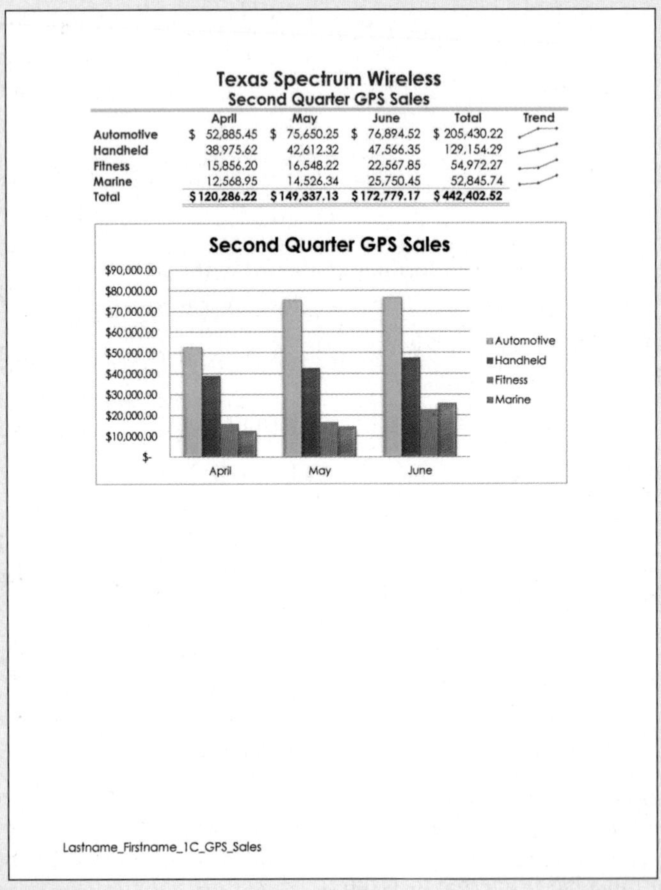

Texas Spectrum Wireless

Second Quarter GPS Sales

	April	May	June	Total	Trend
Automotive	$ 52,885.45	$ 75,650.25	$ 76,894.52	$ 205,430.22	
Handheld	38,975.62	42,612.32	47,566.35	129,154.29	
Fitness	15,856.20	16,548.22	22,567.85	54,972.27	
Marine	12,568.95	14,526.34	25,750.45	52,845.74	
Total	$ 120,286.22	$ 149,337.13	$ 172,779.17	$ 442,402.52	

Lastname_Firstname_1C_GPS_Sales

Figure 7.54

(Project 7C GPS Sales continues on the next page)

Skills Review | Project 7C GPS Sales (continued)

1 **Start** Excel. Click the **File tab** to display **Backstage** view, click **Save As**, and then in the **Save As** dialog box, navigate to your **Excel Chapter 7** folder. In the **File name** box, using your own name, type **Lastname_Firstname_1C_GPS_Sales** and then press Enter.

a. With cell **A1** as the active cell, type the worksheet title **Texas Spectrum Wireless** and then press Enter. In cell **A2**, type the worksheet subtitle **Second Quarter GPS Sales** and then press Enter.

b. Click in cell **A4**, type **Automotive** and then press Enter. In cell **A5**, type **Handheld** and then press Enter. In cell **A6**, type **Fitness** and then press Enter. In cell **A7**, type **Marine** and then press Enter. In cell **A8**, type **Total** and then press Enter.

c. Click cell **B3**. Type **April** and then in the **Formula Bar**, click the **Enter** button to keep cell **B3** the active cell. With **B3** as the active cell, point to the fill handle in the lower right corner of the selected cell, drag to the right to cell **D3**, and then release the mouse button to enter the text *May* and *June*.

d. Press Ctrl + Home, to make cell **A1** the active cell. In the **column heading area**, point to the vertical line between **column A** and **column B** to display the pointer, hold down the left mouse button and drag to the right to increase the column width to **100 pixels**.

e. Point to cell **B3**, and then drag across to select cells **B3** and **C3** and **D3**.With the range **B3:D3** selected, point anywhere over the selected range, right-click, and then on the Mini toolbar, click the **Center** button.

f. Click cell **B4**, type **52885.45** and press Tab to make cell **C4** active. Enter the remaining values, as shown in **Table 1**, pressing Tab to move across the rows and Enter to move down the columns.

2 Click cell **B8** to make it the active cell and type =

a. At the insertion point, type **b4** and then type **+** Type **b5** and then type **+b6+b7** Press Enter. Your result is *120286.2*.

b. Click in cell **C8**. Type = and then click cell **C4**. Type **+** and then click cell **C5**. Repeat this process to complete the formula to add cells **C4** through **C7**, and then press Enter. Your result is *149337.1*.

c. Click cell **D8**. On the **Home tab**, in the **Editing group**, click the **Sum** button, and then press Enter to construct a formula by using the SUM function. Your result is *172779.2*. You can use any of these methods to add values; the Sum button is the most efficient.

d. In cell **E3** type **Total** and press Enter. With cell **E4** as the active cell, hold down Alt, and then press =. On the **Formula Bar**, click the **Enter** button to display the result and keep cell **E4** active.

e. With cell **E4** active, point to the fill handle in the lower right corner of the cell. Drag down through cell **E8**, and then release the mouse button to copy the formula with relative cell references down to sum each row.

3 Click cell **F3**. Type **Trend** and then press Enter.

a. Select the range **A1:F1**, and then on the **Home tab**, in the **Alignment group**, click the **Merge & Center** button. Select the range **A2:F2**, and then click the **Merge & Center** button.

b. Click cell **A1**. In the **Styles group**, click the **Cell Styles** button. Under **Titles and Headings**, click **Title**. Click cell **A2**, display the **Cell Styles** gallery, and then click **Heading 1**.

c. Select the range **B3:F3**, hold down Ctrl, and then select the range **A4:A8**. From the **Cell Styles** gallery, click **Heading 4** to apply this cell style to the column and row titles.

d. Select the range **B4:E4**, hold down Ctrl, and then select the range **B8:E8**. On the **Home tab**, in the **Number group**, click the **Accounting Number Format** button. Select the range **B5:E7**, and then in the **Number group**, click the **Comma Style** button. Select the range **B8:E8**. From the **Styles group**, display the **Cell Styles** gallery, and then under **Titles and Headings**, click **Total**.

Table 1

	April	May	June
Automotive	52885.45	75650.25	76894.52
Handheld	38975.62	42612.32	47566.35
Fitness	15856.20	16548.22	22567.85
Marine	12568.95	14526.34	25750.45

---► (Return to Step 2)

(Project 7C GPS Sales continues on the next page)

Skills Review | Project 7C GPS Sales (continued)

e. On the Ribbon, click the **Page Layout tab**, and then from the **Themes group**, click the **Themes** button to display the **Themes** gallery. Click the **Austin** theme.

4 Select the range **A3:D7**. Click the **Insert tab**, and then in the **Charts group**, click **Column**. From the gallery of column chart types, under **2-D Column**, click the first chart—**Clustered Column**.

a. On the Quick Access Toolbar, click the **Save** button to be sure that you have saved your work up to this point. Point to the top border of the chart to display the pointer, and then drag to position the chart inside the upper left corner of cell **A10**.

b. On the **Design tab**, in the **Data group**, click the **Switch Row/Column** button so that the months display on the Horizontal (Category) axis and the types of GPS equipment display in the legend.

c. On the **Design tab**, in the **Chart Layouts group**, click the first layout—**Layout 1**.

d. In the chart, click anywhere in the text *Chart Title* to select the text box. Type **Second Quarter GPS Sales** and then press Enter.

e. Click anywhere in the chart so that the chart title text box is not selected. On the **Design tab**, in the **Chart Styles group**, click the **More** button. Using the ScreenTips as your guide, locate and click **Style 18**.

f. Point to the lower right corner of the chart to display the pointer, and then drag down and to the right so that the lower right border of the chart is positioned just inside the lower right corner of cell **F26**.

5 Select the range **B4:D7**. Click the **Insert tab**, and then in the **Sparklines group**, click **Line**. In the **Create Sparklines** dialog box, in the **Location Range** box, type **f4:f7** and then click **OK** to insert the sparklines.

a. On the **Design tab**, in the **Show group**, select the **Markers** check box to display markers in the sparklines.

b. On the **Design tab**, in the **Style group**, click the **More** button, and then in the second row, click the fourth style—**Sparkline Style Accent 4, Darker 25%**.

6 On the **Insert tab**, in the **Text group**, click **Header & Footer** to switch to **Page Layout** view and open the **Header** area.

a. In the **Navigation group**, click the **Go to Footer** button to open the Footer area. Click just above the word *Footer* to place the insertion point in the **left section** of the Footer.

b. In the **Header & Footer Elements group**, click the **File Name** button, and then click in a cell just above the footer to exit the Footer area.

7 On the right side of the status bar, click the **Normal** button to return to Normal view, and then press Ctrl + Home to make cell **A1** active.

a. Click the **File tab**, and then on the right, click **Properties**. Click **Show Document Panel**, and then in the **Author** box, delete any text and type your firstname and lastname. In the **Subject** box, type your course name and section number, and in the **Keywords** box, type **GPS sales Close** the Document Information Panel.

b. At the bottom of your worksheet, click the **Sheet2** tab. Hold down Ctrl, and then click the **Sheet3** tab. With both sheets selected, point to either of the selected sheet tabs, right-click, and then click **Delete** to delete the sheets.

c. Click the **Page Layout tab**. In the **Page Setup group**, click the **Margins** button, and then at the bottom of the **Margins** gallery, click **Custom Margins**. In the **Page Setup** dialog box, under **Center on page**, select the **Horizontally** check box.

d. In the lower right corner of the **Page Setup** dialog box, click **OK**. On the **File tab**, click **Print** to view the **Print Preview**. Click the **Home tab** to return to Normal view and if necessary, make any necessary corrections and resize and move your chart so that it is centered under the worksheet.

e. On the Quick Access Toolbar, click the **Save** button to be sure that you have saved your work up to this point.

f. Print or submit your workbook electronically as directed by your instructor. If required by your instructor, print or create an electronic version of your worksheets with formulas displayed by using the instructions in Activity 7.16. **Exit** Excel without saving so that you do not save the changes you made to print formulas.

You have completed Project 7C

Apply 7B skills from these Objectives:

- 7 Check Spelling in a Worksheet
- 8 Enter Data by Range
- 9 Construct Formulas for Mathematical Operations
- 10 Edit Values in a Worksheet
- 11 Format a Worksheet

Skills Review | Project 7D Charger Inventory

In the following Skills Review, you will create a worksheet that summarizes the inventory of cell phone chargers. Your completed worksheet will look similar to Figure 7.55.

Project Files

For Project 7D, you will need the following file:

New blank Excel workbook

You will save your workbook as:

Lastname_Firstname_1D_Charger_Inventory

Project Results

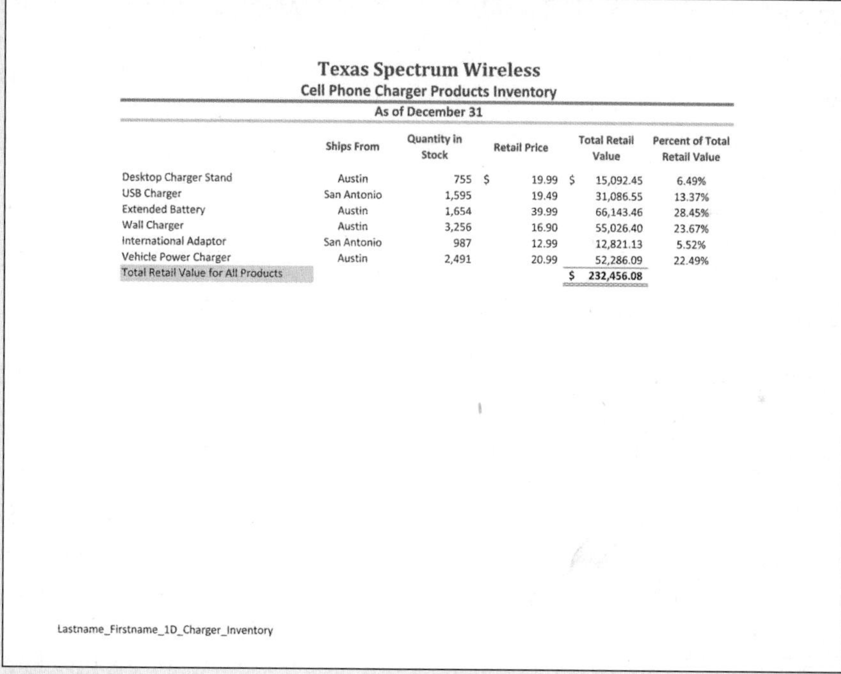

Texas Spectrum Wireless

Cell Phone Charger Products Inventory

As of December 31

	Ships From	Quantity in Stock	Retail Price	Total Retail Value	Percent of Total Retail Value
Desktop Charger Stand	Austin	755	$ 19.99	$ 15,092.45	6.49%
USB Charger	San Antonio	1,595	19.49	31,086.55	13.37%
Extended Battery	Austin	1,654	39.99	66,143.46	28.45%
Wall Charger	Austin	3,256	16.90	55,026.40	23.67%
International Adaptor	San Antonio	987	12.99	12,821.13	5.52%
Vehicle Power Charger	Austin	2,491	20.99	52,286.09	22.49%
Total Retail Value for All Products				$ 232,456.08	

Lastname_Firstname_1D_Charger_Inventory

Figure 7.55

(Project 7D Charger Inventory continues on the next page)

Skills Review | Project 7D Charger Inventory (continued)

1 **Start** Excel and display a new blank workbook. **Save** the workbook in your **Excel Chapter 7** folder, as **Lastname_Firstname_1D_Charger_Inventory** In cell **A1** type **Texas Spectrum Wireless** and in cell **A2** type **Cell Phone Charger Products Inventory**

a. Click cell **B3**, type **Quantity in Stock** and press Tab. In cell **C3** type **Average Cost** and press Tab. In cell **D3**, type **Retail Price** and press Tab. In cell **E3**, type **Total Retail Value** and press Tab. In cell **F3** type **Percent of Total Retail Value** and press Enter.

b. Click cell **A4**, type **Desktop Charger Stand** and press Enter. In the range **A5:A10**, type the remaining row titles as shown, including the misspelled words.

USB Charger

Extended Battery

Wall Charger

International Adaptor

Vehicle Powr Charger

Total Retail Value for All Products

c. Press Ctrl + Home to move to the top of your worksheet. On the **Review tab**, in the **Proofing group**, click the **Spelling** button. Correct *Powr* to **Power** and any other spelling errors you may have made, and then when the message displays, *The spelling check is complete for the entire sheet*, click **OK**.

d. In the **column heading area**, point to the right boundary of **column A** to display the ✛ pointer, and then drag to the right to widen **column A** to **225** pixels.

e. In the **column heading area**, point to the **column B** heading to display the ↓ pointer, and then drag to the right to select **columns B:F**. With the columns selected, in the **column heading area**, point to the right boundary of any of the selected columns, and then drag to the right to set the width to **100 pixels**.

f. Select the range **A1:F1.** On the **Home tab**, in the **Alignment group**, click the **Merge & Center** button, and then from the **Cell Styles** gallery, apply the **Title** style. Select the range **A2:F2. Merge & Center** the text across the selection, and then from the **Cell Styles** gallery, apply the **Heading 1** style.

2 Select the empty range **B4:D9**. With cell B4 active in the range, type **755** and then press Enter.

a. With cell **B5** active in the range, and pressing Enter after each entry, type the following data in the *Quantity in Stock* column:

1595

2654

3256

987

2491

b. With the selected range still active, from the following table, beginning in cell **C4** and pressing Enter after each entry, enter the following data for the **Average Cost** column and then the **Retail Price** column. If you prefer, type without selecting the range first; recall that this is optional.

Average Cost	Retail Price
9.75	19.99
9.25	19.49
16.90	39.99
9.55	16.90
14.20	12.99
10.45	20.99

3 In cell **E4**, type **=b4*d4** and then press Enter to construct a formula that calculates the *Total Retail Value* of the *Desktop Charger Stands* (Quantity × Retail Price).

a. Click cell **E4**, position your pointer over the fill handle, and then drag down through cell **E9** to copy the formula.

b. Select the range **B4:B9**, and then on the **Home tab**, in the **Number group**, click the **Comma Style** button. Then, in the **Number group**, click the **Decrease Decimal** button two times to remove the decimal places from these non-currency values.

c. Click cell **E10**, in the **Editing group**, click the **Sum** button, and then press Enter to calculate the *Total Retail Value for All Products*. Your result is *272446.1*.

d. Select the range **C5:E9** and apply the **Comma Style**. Select the range **C4:E4**, hold down Ctrl, and then click cell **E10**. With the nonadjacent cells selected, apply the **Accounting Number Format**. Click cell **E10**, and then from the **Cell Styles** gallery, apply the **Total** style.

(Project 7D Charger Inventory continues on the next page)

Skills Review | Project 7D Charger Inventory (continued)

e. Click cell **F4**, type = and then click cell **E4**. Type / and then click cell **E10**. Press F4 to make the reference to cell *E10* absolute, and then on the **Formula Bar**, click the **Enter** button so that **F4** remains the active cell. Drag the fill handle to copy the formula down through cell **F9**.

f. Point to cell **B6**, and then double-click to place the insertion point within the cell. Use the arrow keys to move the insertion point to left or right of *2*, and use either Del or Backspace to delete 2, and then type **1** and press Enter so that the new *Quantity in Stock* is *1654*. Notice the recalculations in the worksheet.

4 Select the range **F4:F9**, right-click over the selection, and then on the Mini toolbar, click the **Percent Style** button. Click the **Increase Decimal** button two times, and then **Center** the selection.

a. In the **row heading area** on the left side of your screen, point to **row 3** to display the ➡ pointer, and then right-click to simultaneously select the row and display a shortcut menu. On the displayed shortcut menu, click **Insert** to insert a new **row 3**.

b. Click cell **A3**, type **As of December 31** and then on the **Formula Bar**, click the **Enter** button to keep cell **A3** as the active cell. **Merge & Center** the text across the range **A3:F3**, and then apply the **Heading 2** cell style.

5 In the **column heading area**, point to **column B**. When the ⬇ pointer displays, right-click, and then click **Insert** to insert a new column.

a. Click cell **B4**, and type **Ships From** and press Enter. In cell **B5**, type **Austin** and then press Enter. In cell **B6**, type **San Antonio** and then press Enter

b. Using AutoComplete to speed your typing by pressing Enter as soon as the AutoComplete suggestion displays, in cells **B7**, **B8**, and **B10** type **Austin** and in cell **B9** type **San Antonio**

c. In the **column heading area**, point to the right boundary of **column B**, and then drag to the left and set the width to **90 pixels**. From the **column heading area**, point to **column D**, right-click, and then click **Delete**.

d. Select the range **B4:F4**, and then on the **Home tab**, in the **Alignment group**, click the **Wrap Text** button, the **Center** button, and the **Middle Align** button. With the range still selected, apply the **Heading 4** cell style.

e. Select the range **B5:B10**, right-click, and then click the **Center** button. Click cell **A11**, and then from the **Cell Styles** gallery, under **Themed Cell Styles**, click **40% - Accent1**.

6 On the **Insert tab**, in the **Text group**, click **Header & Footer**. In the **Navigation group**, click the **Go To Footer** button, and then click just above the word *Footer*. In the **Header & Footer Elements group**, click the **File Name** button to add the name of your file to the footer. Click in a cell just above the footer to exit the **Footer area**, and then return the worksheet to **Normal** view.

a. Press Ctrl + Home to move the insertion point to cell **A1**. On the **Page Layout tab**, in the **Page Setup group**, click **Orientation**, and then click **Landscape**.

b. In the **Page Setup group**, click the **Margins** button, and then at the bottom of the **Margins gallery**, click **Custom Margins**. In the **Page Setup** dialog box, under **Center on page**, select the **Horizontally** check box, and then click **OK**.

c. Click the **File tab** to display **Backstage** view, and then on the right, click **Properties**. Click **Show Document Panel**, and then in the **Author** box, delete any text and type your firstname and lastname. In the **Subject** box type your course name and section number, in the **Keywords** box type **cell phone chargers** and then **Close** the **Document Information Panel**.

d. Select **Sheet2** and **Sheet3**, and then **Delete** both sheets.

e. **Save** your file and then print or submit your workbook electronically as directed by your instructor. If required by your instructor, print or create an electronic version of your worksheet with formulas displayed by using the instructions in Activity 7.16. **Exit** Excel without saving so that you do not save the changes you made to print formulas.

End **You have completed Project 7D**

Content-Based Assessments

Apply 7A skills from these Objectives:

1. Create, Save, and Navigate an Excel Workbook
2. Enter Data in a Worksheet
3. Construct and Copy Formulas and Use the SUM Function
4. Format Cells with Merge & Center and Cell Styles
5. Chart Data to Create a Column Chart and Insert Sparklines
6. Print, Display Formulas, and Close Excel

Mastering Excel | Project 7E Hard Drives

In the following Mastering Excel project, you will create a worksheet comparing the sales of different types of external hard drives sold in the second quarter. Your completed worksheet will look similar to Figure 7.56.

Project Files

For Project 7E, you will need the following file:

New blank Excel workbook

You will save your workbook as:

Lastname_Firstname_1E_Hard_Drives

Project Results

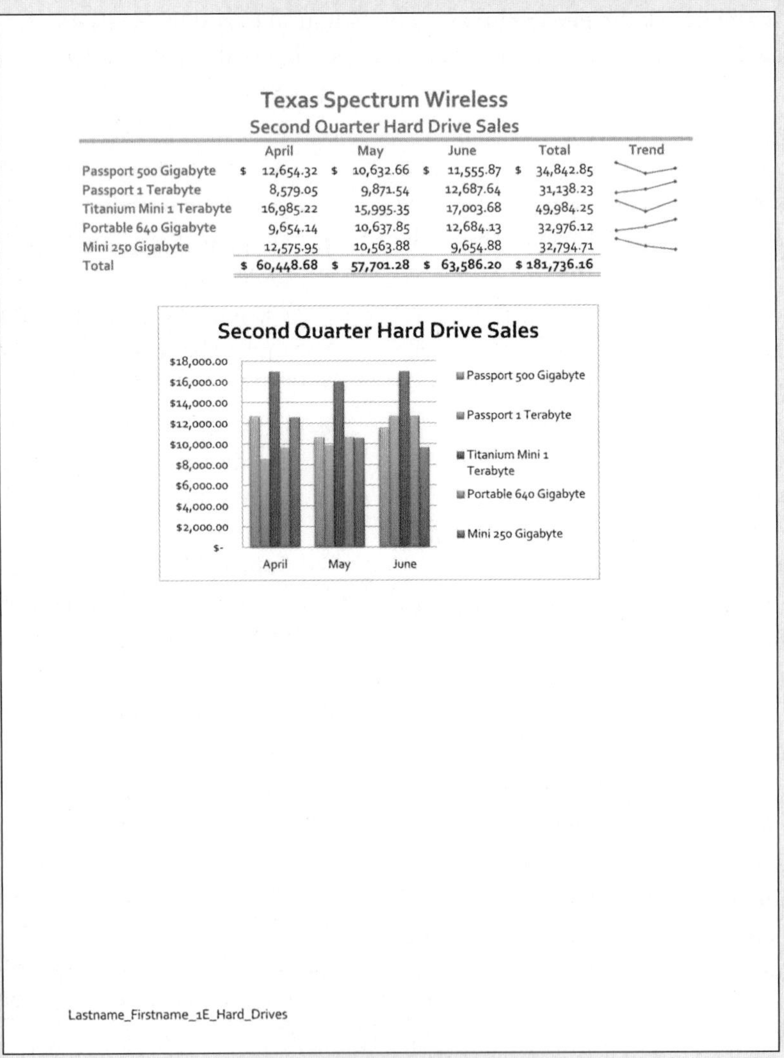

Texas Spectrum Wireless

Second Quarter Hard Drive Sales

	April	May	June	Total	Trend
Passport 500 Gigabyte	$ 12,654.32	$ 10,632.66	$ 11,555.87	$ 34,842.85	
Passport 1 Terabyte	8,579.05	9,871.54	12,687.64	31,138.23	
Titanium Mini 1 Terabyte	16,985.22	15,995.35	17,003.68	49,984.25	
Portable 640 Gigabyte	9,654.14	10,637.85	12,684.13	32,976.12	
Mini 250 Gigabyte	12,575.95	10,563.88	9,654.88	32,794.71	
Total	$ 60,448.68	$ 57,701.28	$ 63,586.20	$ 181,736.16	

Figure 7.56

(Project 7E Hard Drives continues on the next page)

Mastering Excel | Project 7E Hard Drives (continued)

1 **Start** Excel. In cell **A1**, type **Texas Spectrum Wireless** and in cell **A2**, type **Second Quarter Hard Drive Sales** Change the **Theme** to **Module**, and then **Save** the workbook in your **Excel Chapter 7** folder as **Lastname_Firstname_1E_Hard_Drives**

2 In cell **B3**, type **April** and then use the fill handle to enter the months *May* and *June* in the range **C3:D3**. In cell **E3**, type **Total** and in cell **F3**, type **Trend**

3 **Center** the column titles in the range **B3:F3**. **Merge & Center** the title across the range **A1:F1**, and apply the **Title** cell style. **Merge & Center** the subtitle across the range **A2:F2**, and apply the **Heading 1** cell style.

4 Widen **column A** to **170 pixels**, and then in the range **A4:A9**, type the following row titles:

Passport 500 Gigabyte

Passport 1 Terabyte

Titanium Mini 1 Terabyte

Portable 640 Gigabyte

Mini 250 Gigabyte

Total

5 Widen columns **B:F** to **100 pixels**, and then in the range **B4:D8**, enter the monthly sales figures for each type of hard drive, as shown in **Table 1** at the bottom of the page.

6 In cell **B9**, **Sum** the *April* hard drive sales, and then copy the formula across to cells **C9:D9**. In cell **E4**, **Sum** the *Passport 500 Gigabyte sales*, and then copy the formula down to cells **E5:E9**.

7 Apply the **Heading 4** cell style to the row titles and the column titles. Apply the **Total** cell style to the totals in the range **B9:E9**. Apply the **Accounting Number Format** to the first row of sales figures and to the total row. Apply the **Comma Style** to the remaining sales figures.

8 To compare the monthly sales of each product visually, select the range that represents the sales figures for the three months, including the month names, and for each product name—do not include any totals in the range. With this data selected, **Insert** a **2-D Clustered Column** chart. Switch the Row/Column data so that the months display on the category axis and the types of hard drives display in the legend.

9 Position the upper left corner of the chart in the approximate center of cell **A11** so that the chart is visually centered below the worksheet, as shown in Figure 7.56. Apply **Chart Style 26**, and then modify the **Chart Layout** by applying **Layout 1**. Change the **Chart Title** to **Second Quarter Hard Drive Sales**

10 In the range **F4:F8**, insert **Line** sparklines that compare the monthly data. Do not include the totals. Show the sparkline **Markers** and apply **Sparkline Style Accent 2, Darker 50%**—in the first row, the second style.

11 Insert a **Footer** with the **File Name** in the **left section**, and then return the worksheet to **Normal** view. Display the **Document Panel**, add your name, your course name and section, and the keywords **hard drives, sales** Delete the unused sheets, and then center the worksheet **Horizontally** on the page. Check your worksheet by previewing it in **Print Preview**, and then make any necessary corrections.

12 **Save** your workbook, and then print or submit electronically as directed. If required by your instructor, print or create an electronic version of your worksheets with formulas displayed by using the instructions in Activity 7.16. **Exit** Excel without saving so that you do not save the changes you made to print formulas.

Table 1

	April	May	June
Passport 500 Gigabyte	12654.32	10632.66	11555.87
Passport 1 Terabyte	8579.05	9871.54	12687.64
Titanium Mini 1 Terabyte	16985.22	15995.35	17003.68
Portable 640 Gigabyte	9654.14	10637.85	12684.13
Mini 250 Gigabyte	12575.95	10563.88	9654.88

(Return to Step 6)

End **You have completed Project 7E**

Content-Based Assessments

Apply **7B** skills from these Objectives:

- 7 Check Spelling in a Worksheet
- 8 Enter Data by Range
- 9 Construct Formulas for Mathematical Operations
- 10 Edit Values in a Worksheet
- 11 Format a Worksheet

Mastering Excel | Project 7F Camera Accessories

In the following Mastering Excel project, you will create a worksheet that summarizes the sale of digital camera accessories. Your completed worksheet will look similar to Figure 7.57.

Project Files

For Project 7F, you will need the following file:

New blank Excel workbook

You will save your workbook as:

Lastname_Firstname_1F_Camera_Accessories

Project Results

Texas Spectrum Wireless

Digital Camera Accessories Sales

Month Ending August 31

	Quantity Sold	Retail Price	Total Sales	Percent of Total Sales
Small Cloth Gear Bag	254	$ 19.99	$ 5,077.46	10.69%
Large Cloth Gear Bag	182	24.99	4,548.18	9.58%
Lens Cap	351	6.99	2,453.49	5.17%
Lens Hood	125	5.49	686.25	1.44%
Remote Switch	750	22.50	16,875.00	35.53%
Mini Tripod	554	24.99	13,844.46	29.15%
Cleaning Kit	365	10.99	4,011.35	8.45%
Total Sales for All Products			$ 47,496.19	

Lastname_Firstname_1F_Camera_Accessories

Figure 7.57

(Project 7F Camera Accessories continues on the next page)

Mastering Excel | Project 7F Camera Accessories (continued)

1 **Start** Excel and display a new blank workbook. **Save** the workbook in your **Excel Chapter 7** folder as **Lastname_Firstname_1F_Camera_Accessories** In cell **A1**, type **Texas Spectrum Wireless** In cell **A2**, type **Digital Camera Accessories Sales** and then **Merge & Center** the title and the subtitle across **columns A:F**. Apply the **Title** and **Heading 1** cell styles respectively.

2 Beginning in cell **B3**, type the following column titles: **Product Number** and **Quantity Sold** and **Retail Price** and **Total Sales** and **Percent of Total Sales**

3 Beginning in cell **A4**, type the following row titles, including misspelled words:

- **Small Cloth Gear Bag**
- **Large Cloth Gear Bag**
- **Lens Cap**
- **Lens Hood**
- **Remote Switch**
- **Mini Tripod**
- **Cleening Kit**
- **Total Sales for All Products**

4 Make cell **A1** the active cell, and then check spelling in your worksheet. Correct *Cleening* to **Cleaning**, and make any other necessary corrections. Widen **column A** to **180 pixels** and **columns B:F** to **90 pixels**.

5 In the range **B4:D10**, type the data shown in **Table 1** at the bottom of the page.

6 In cell **E4**, construct a formula to calculate the *Total Sales* of the *Small Cloth Gear Bags* by multiplying the *Quantity Sold* times the *Retail Price*. Copy the formula down for the remaining products. In cell **E11**, use the **SUM** function to calculate the *Total Sales for All Products*, and then apply the **Total** cell style to the cell.

7 Using absolute cell references as necessary so that you can copy the formula, in cell **F4**, construct a formula to calculate the *Percent of Total Sales* for the first product by dividing the *Total Sales* of the *Small Cloth Gear Bags* by the *Total Sales for All Products*. Copy the formula down for the remaining products. To the computed percentages, apply **Percent Style** with two decimal places, and then **Center** the percentages.

8 Apply the **Comma Style** with no decimal places to the *Quantity Sold* figures. To cells **D4**, **E4**, and **E11** apply the **Accounting Number Format**. To the range **D5:E10**, apply the **Comma Style**.

9 Change the *Retail Price* of the *Mini Tripod* to **24.99** and the *Quantity Sold* of the *Remote Switch* to **750** Delete **column B**, and then **Insert** a new **row 3**. In cell **A3**, type **Month Ending August 31** and then **Merge & Center** the text across the range **A3:E3**. Apply the **Heading 2** cell style. To cell **A12**, apply the **Accent1** cell style. Select the four column titles, apply **Wrap Text**, **Middle Align**, and **Center** formatting, and then apply the **Heading 3** cell style.

10 Insert a **Footer** with the **File Name** in the **left section**, and then return to **Normal** view. Display the **Document Panel**, add your name, your course name and section, and the keywords **digital camera accessories, sales**

11 Delete the unused sheets, and then center the worksheet **Horizontally** on the page. Preview the worksheet in **Print Preview**, and make any necessary corrections.

12 **Save** your workbook, and then print or submit electronically as directed. If required by your instructor, print or create an electronic version of your worksheets with formulas displayed by using the instructions in Activity 7.16. **Exit** Excel without saving so that you do not save the changes you made to print formulas.

Table 1

	Product Number	Quantity Sold	Retail Price
Small Cloth Gear Bag	CGB-3	254	19.99
Large Cloth Gear Bag	CGB-8	182	24.99
Lens Cap	LC-2	351	6.99
Lens Hood	LH-4	125	5.49
Remote Switch	RS-5	677	22.50
Mini Tripod	MTP-6	554	29.99
Cleaning Kit	CK-8	365	10.99

(Return to Step 6)

End **You have completed Project 7F**

Content-Based Assessments

Apply **7A** and **7B** skills from these Objectives:

1. Create, Save, and Navigate an Excel Workbook
2. Enter Data in a Worksheet
3. Construct and Copy Formulas and Use the SUM Function
4. Format Cells with Merge & Center and Cell Styles
5. Chart Data to Create a Column Chart and Insert Sparklines
6. Print, Display Formulas, and Close Excel
7. Check Spelling in a Worksheet
8. Enter Data by Range
9. Construct Formulas for Mathematical Operations
10. Edit Values in a Worksheet
11. Format a Worksheet

Mastering Excel | Project 7G Sales Comparison

In the following Mastering Excel project, you will create a new worksheet that compares annual laptop sales by store location. Your completed worksheet will look similar to Figure 7.58.

Project Files

For Project 7G, you will need the following file:

New blank Excel workbook

You will save your workbook as:

Lastname_Firstname_1G_Sales_Comparison

Project Results

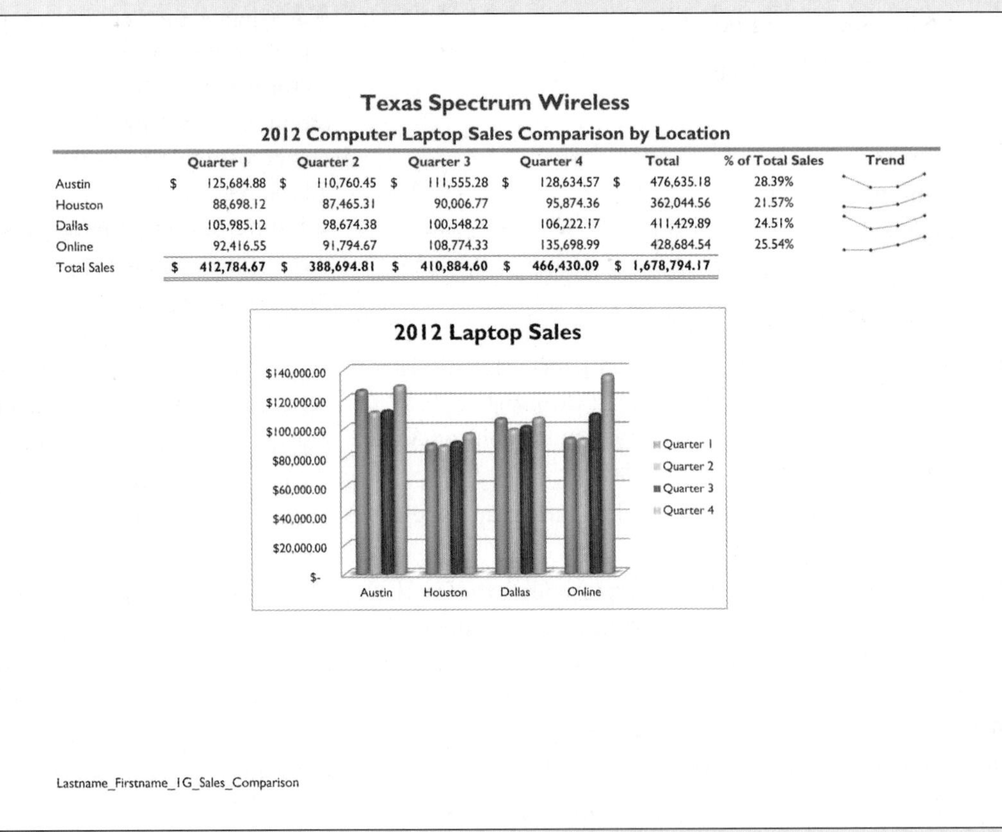

Texas Spectrum Wireless

2012 Computer Laptop Sales Comparison by Location

	Quarter 1	Quarter 2	Quarter 3	Quarter 4	Total	% of Total Sales	Trend
Austin	$ 125,684.88	$ 110,760.45	$ 111,555.28	$ 128,634.57	$ 476,635.18	28.39%	
Houston	88,698.12	87,465.31	90,006.77	95,874.36	362,044.56	21.57%	
Dallas	105,985.12	98,674.38	100,548.22	106,222.17	411,429.89	24.51%	
Online	92,416.55	91,794.67	108,774.33	135,698.99	428,684.54	25.54%	
Total Sales	**$ 412,784.67**	**$ 388,694.81**	**$ 410,884.60**	**$ 466,430.09**	**$ 1,678,794.17**		

Figure 7.58

(Project 7G Sales Comparison continues on the next page)

Mastering Excel | Project 7G Sales Comparison (continued)

1 **Start** Excel. In a new blank workbook, as the worksheet title, in cell **A1**, type **Texas Spectrum Wireless** As the worksheet subtitle, in cell **A2**, type **2012 Computer Laptop Sales Comparison by Location** and then **Save** the workbook in your **Excel Chapter 7** folder as **Lastname_Firstname_1G_Sales_Comparison**

2 In cell **B3**, type **Quarter 1** and then use the fill handle to enter *Quarter 2*, *Quarter 3*, and *Quarter 4* in the range **C3:E3**. In cell **F3**, type **Total** In cell **G3**, type **% of Total Sales** In cell **H3**, type **Trend**

3 In the range **A4:A7**, type the following row titles: **Austin** and **Houston** and **Online** and **Total Sales**

4 Widen columns **A:H** to **115 pixels**. **Merge & Center** the title across the range **A1:H1**, and then apply the **Title** cell style. **Merge & Center** the subtitle across the range **A2:H2**, and then apply the **Heading 1** cell style. Select the seven column titles, apply **Center** formatting, and then apply the **Heading 4** cell style.

5 In the range **B4:E6**, enter the sales values for each Quarter as shown in **Table 1** at the bottom of the page.

6 **Sum** the *Quarter 1* sales, and then copy the formula across for the remaining Quarters. **Sum** the sales for the *Austin* location, and then copy the formula down through cell **F7**. Apply the **Accounting Number Format** to the first row of sales figures and to the total row, and the **Comma Style** to the remaining sales figures. Format the totals in **row 7** with the **Total** cell style.

7 **Insert** a new **row 6** with the row title **Dallas** and the following sales figures for each quarter: **105985.12** and **98674.38** and **100548.22** and **106222.17** Copy the formula in cell **F5** down to cell **F6** to sum the new row.

8 Using absolute cell references as necessary so that you can copy the formula, in cell **G4** construct a formula to calculate the *Percent of Total Sales* for the first location by dividing the *Total* for the *Austin* location by the *Total Sales* for all Quarters. Copy the formula down for the remaining locations. To the computed percentages, apply **Percent Style** with two decimal places, and then **Center** the percentages.

9 Insert **Line** sparklines in the range **H4:H7** that compare the quarterly data. Do not include the totals. Show the sparkline **Markers** and apply the second style in the second row—**Sparkline Style Accent 2, Darker 25%.**

10 **Save** your workbook. To compare the quarterly sales of each location visually, select the range that represents the sales figures for the four quarters, including the quarter names and each location—do not include any totals in the range. With this data selected, **Insert** a **Column**, **Clustered Cylinder** chart.

11 Switch the row/column data so that the locations display on the category axis. Position the top edge of the chart in **row 10** and visually center it below the worksheet data. Apply **Chart Style 26**, and then modify the **Chart Layout** by applying **Layout 1**. Change the **Chart Title** to **2012 Laptop Sales**

12 Deselect the chart. Change the **Orientation** to **Landscape**, center the worksheet **Horizontally** on the page, and then change the **Theme** to **Solstice**. Scale the worksheet so that the **Width** fits to **1 page**. Insert a **Footer** with the **File Name** in the **left section**. Return the worksheet to **Normal** view and make **A1** the active cell so that you can view the top of your worksheet.

13 Display the **Document Panel**, add your name, your course name and section, and the keywords **laptops, sales** Delete the unused sheets, preview your worksheet in **Print Preview**, and then make any necessary corrections.

14 **Save** your workbook, and then print or submit electronically as directed. If required by your instructor, print or create an electronic version of your worksheets with formulas displayed by using the instructions in Activity 7.16. **Exit** Excel without saving so that you do not save the changes you made to print formulas.

Table 1

	Quarter 1	Quarter 2	Quarter 3	Quarter 4
Austin	125684.88	110760.45	111555.28	128634.57
Houston	88698.12	87465.31	90006.77	95874.36
Online	92416.55	91794.67	108774.33	135698.99

(Return to Step 6)

You have completed Project 7G

Apply a combination of the 7A and 7B skills.

GO! Fix It | Project 7H Team Sales

Project Files

For Project 7H, you will need the following file:

e01H_Team_Sales

You will save your workbook as:

Lastname_Firstname_1H_Team_Sales

In this project, you will edit a worksheet that summarizes sales by each sales team member at the Texas Spectrum Wireless San Antonio location for the month of February. From the student files that accompany this textbook, open the file e01H_Team_Sales, and then save the file in your Excel Chapter 7 folder as **Lastname_Firstname_1H_Team_Sales**

To complete the project, you must find and correct errors in formulas and formatting. View each formula in the Formula Bar and edit as necessary. In addition to errors that you find, you should know:

- There are two spelling errors.
- Worksheet titles should be merged and centered and appropriate cell styles should be applied.
- Appropriate number and accounting format with zero decimals should be applied to the data and text should be wrapped where necessary. Percent style formatting should be applied appropriately where necessary.
- Column headings should be formatted with the Heading 4 style.
- In the chart, the team member names should display on the Horizontal (Category) axis and the week names should display in the legend.
- The chart should include the title **February Team Member Sales**
- The worksheet should be centered horizontally on one page in Landscape orientation. Remove unused sheets.
- A footer should be inserted that includes the file name, and document properties should include the keywords **team sales, San Antonio**

Save your workbook, and then print or submit electronically as directed. If required by your instructor, print or create an electronic version of your worksheets with formulas displayed by using the instructions in Activity 7.16. Exit Excel without saving so that you do not save the changes you made to print formulas.

End You have completed Project 7H

Apply a combination of the 7A and 7B skills.

GO! Make It | Project 7I Printer Sales

Project Files

For Project 7I, you will need the following file:

New blank Excel workbook

You will save your workbook as:

Lastname_Firstname_1I_Printer_Sales

Create the worksheet shown in Figure 7.59. Use the Pushpin theme and change the Orientation to Landscape. Construct formulas in the Total Sold, Total Sales, and Percent of Total Sales columns, and in the Total row. Apply cell styles and number formatting as shown. Use Style 26 for the chart. Insert sparklines for the monthly data using the first style in the second row—Sparkline Style Accent 1, Darker 25%. Add your name, your course name and section, and the keywords **inkjet, printer, sales** to the document properties. Save the file in your Excel Chapter 7 folder as **Lastname_Firstname_1I_Printer_Sales**

Project Results

Texas Spectrum Wireless

First Quarter Inkjet Printer Sales

Model	April	May	June	Total Sold	Retail Price	Total Sales	Percent of Total Sales	Trend
Lear 200	390	224	421	1,035	$ 79.99	$ 82,789.65	8.50%	
Lear 355	168	186	153	507	169.99	86,184.93	8.85%	
Prima X50	250	379	339	968	199.99	193,590.32	19.88%	
Prima X90	386	423	482	1,291	249.99	322,737.09	33.15%	
Prima Z25	261	244	307	812	354.99	288,251.88	29.61%	
Total	1,455	1,456	1,702	4,613		$ 973,553.87		

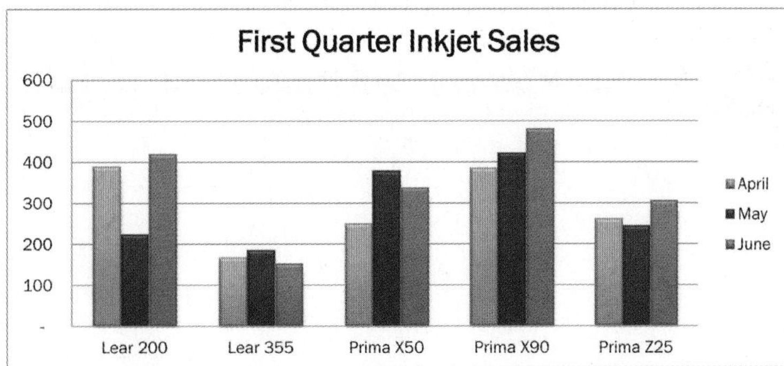

Lastname_Firstname_1I_Printer_Sales

Figure 7.59

End You have completed Project 7I

Content-Based Assessments

Apply a combination of the 7A and 7B skills.

GO! Solve It | Project 7J Warranty Sales

Project Files

For Project 7J, you will need the following file:

e01J_Warranty_Sales

You will save your workbook as:

Lastname_Firstname_1J_Warranty_Sales

Open the file e01J_Warranty_Sales and save it as **Lastname_Firstname_1J_Warranty_Sales** Complete the worksheet by using Auto Fill to enter the Quarter headings, and then calculating *Total Sold*, *Total Sales*, *Total For All Products*, and *Percent of Total Sales*. Format the worksheet attractively, and apply appropriate financial formatting. Insert a chart that compares the total number of warranties sold for each item across Quarters, and format the chart to display the information appropriately. Include the file name in the footer, add appropriate document properties, and submit as directed.

	Performance Level		
Performance Element	Exemplary: You consistently applied the relevant skills	Proficient: You sometimes, but not always, applied the relevant skills	Developing: You rarely or never applied the relevant skills
Create formulas	All formulas are correct and are efficiently constructed.	Formulas are correct but not always constructed in the most efficient manner.	One or more formulas are missing or incorrect; or only numbers were entered.
Create a chart	Chart created properly.	Chart was created but incorrect data was selected.	No chart was created.
Format attractively and appropriately	Formatting is attractive and appropriate.	Adequately formatted but difficult to read or unattractive.	Inadequate or no formatting.

End **You have completed Project 7J**

Content-Based Assessments

Apply a combination of the 7A and 7B skills.

GO! Solve It | Project 7K Service Receipts

Project Files

For Project 7K, you will need the following file:

e01K_Service_Receipts

You will save your workbook as:

Lastname_Firstname_1K_Service_Receipts

Open the file e01K_Service_Receipts and save it as **Lastname_Firstname_1K_Service_Receipts** Complete the worksheet by using Auto Fill to complete the month headings, and then calculating the Total Receipts for each month and for each product. Insert and format appropriate sparklines in the Trend column. Format the worksheet attractively with a title and subtitle, check spelling, adjust column width, and apply appropriate financial formatting. Insert a chart that compares the total sales receipts for each product with the months displaying as the categories, and format the chart attractively. Include the file name in the footer, add appropriate properties, and submit as directed.

Performance Element	Performance Level: Exemplary: You consistently applied the relevant skills	Proficient: You sometimes, but not always, applied the relevant skills	Developing: You rarely or never applied the relevant skills
Create formulas	All formulas are correct and are efficiently constructed.	Formulas are correct but not always constructed in the most efficient manner.	One or more formulas are missing or incorrect; or only numbers were entered.
Create a chart	Chart created properly.	Chart was created but incorrect data was selected.	No chart was created.
Insert and format sparklines	Sparklines inserted and formatted properly.	Sparklines were inserted but incorrect data was selected or sparklines were not formatted.	No sparklines were inserted.
Format attractively and appropriately	Formatting is attractive and appropriate.	Adequately formatted but difficult to read or unattractive.	Inadequate or no formatting.

End You have completed Project 7K

Outcomes-Based Assessments

Rubric

The following outcomes-based assessments are *open-ended assessments*. That is, there is no specific correct result; your result will depend on your approach to the information provided. Make *Professional Quality* your goal. Use the following scoring rubric to guide you in *how* to approach the problem, and then to evaluate *how well* your approach solves the problem.

The *criteria*—Software Mastery, Content, Format and Layout, and Process—represent the knowledge and skills you have gained that you can apply to solving the problem. The *levels of performance*—Professional Quality, Approaching Professional Quality, or Needs Quality Improvements—help you and your instructor evaluate your result.

	Your completed project is of Professional Quality if you:	**Your completed project is Approaching Professional Quality if you:**	**Your completed project Needs Quality Improvements if you:**
1-Software Mastery	Choose and apply the most appropriate skills, tools, and features and identify efficient methods to solve the problem.	Choose and apply some appropriate skills, tools, and features, but not in the most efficient manner.	Choose inappropriate skills, tools, or features, or are inefficient in solving the problem.
2-Content	Construct a solution that is clear and well organized, contains content that is accurate, appropriate to the audience and purpose, and is complete. Provide a solution that contains no errors in spelling, grammar, or style.	Construct a solution in which some components are unclear, poorly organized, inconsistent, or incomplete. Misjudge the needs of the audience. Have some errors in spelling, grammar, or style, but the errors do not detract from comprehension.	Construct a solution that is unclear, incomplete, or poorly organized; contains some inaccurate or inappropriate content; and contains many errors in spelling, grammar, or style. Do not solve the problem.
3-Format and Layout	Format and arrange all elements to communicate information and ideas, clarify function, illustrate relationships, and indicate relative importance.	Apply appropriate format and layout features to some elements, but not others. Overuse features, causing minor distraction.	Apply format and layout that does not communicate information or ideas clearly. Do not use format and layout features to clarify function, illustrate relationships, or indicate relative importance. Use available features excessively, causing distraction.
4-Process	Use an organized approach that integrates planning, development, self-assessment, revision, and reflection.	Demonstrate an organized approach in some areas, but not others; or, use an insufficient process of organization throughout.	Do not use an organized approach to solve the problem.

Outcomes-Based Assessments

Apply a combination of the 7A and 7B skills.

GO! Think | Project 7L Phone Plans

Project Files

For Project 7L, you will need the following file:

New blank Excel workbook

You will save your workbook as:

Lastname_Firstname_1L_Phone_Plans

Roslyn Thomas, President of Texas Spectrum Wireless, needs a worksheet that summarizes the following data regarding the first quarter sales of cell phone calling plans that the company is offering for domestic and international calls. Roslyn would like the worksheet to include a calculation of the total sales for each plan and a total of the sales of all of the plans. She would also like to know each plan's percentage of total sales.

	Number Sold	Price
Domestic Standard	2556	29.99
Domestic Premium	3982	49.99
Domestic Platinum	1647	64.99
International Standard	582	85.99
International Premium	365	102.99

Create a worksheet that provides Roslyn with the information needed. Include appropriate worksheet, column, and row titles. Using the formatting skills that you practiced in this chapter, format the worksheet in a manner that is professional and easy to read and understand. Insert a footer with the file name and add appropriate document properties. Save the file as **Lastname_Firstname_1L_Phone_Plans** and print or submit as directed by your instructor.

End **You have completed Project 7L**

Outcomes-Based Assessments

Apply a combination of the 7A and 7B skills.

GO! Think | Project **7M** Advertising

Project Files

For Project 7M, you will need the following file:

New blank Excel workbook

You will save your workbook as:

Lastname_Firstname_1M_Advertising

Eliott Verschoren, Vice President of Marketing for Texas Spectrum Wireless, is conducting an analysis of the advertising expenditures at the company's four retail locations based on the following data:

	Quarter 1	Quarter 2	Quarter 3	Quarter 4
Austin	22860	25905	18642	28405
Dallas	18557	17963	22883	25998
Houston	32609	28462	25915	31755
San Antonio	12475	15624	13371	17429

Using this information, create a workbook that includes totals by quarter and by location, sparklines to demonstrate the quarterly trends, and a column chart that compares the quarterly data across locations. Include appropriate worksheet, row, and column titles. Using the formatting skills that you practiced in this chapter, format the worksheet in a manner that is professional and easy to read and understand. Insert a footer with the file name and add appropriate document properties. Save the file as **Lastname_Firstname_1M_Advertising** and print or submit as directed by your instructor.

End You have completed Project 7M

Outcomes-Based Assessments

Apply a combination of the 7A and 7B skills.

You and GO! | Project 7N Personal Expenses

Project Files

For Project 7N, you will need the following file:

New blank Excel workbook

You will save your workbook as:

Lastname_Firstname_1N_Personal_Expenses

Develop a worksheet that details your personal expenses from the last three months. Some of these expenses might include, but are not limited to, Mortgage, Rent, Utilities, Phone, Food, Entertainment, Tuition, Childcare, Clothing, and Insurance. Include a total for each month and for each category of expense. Insert a column with a formula that calculates the percent that each expense category is of the total expenditures. Format the worksheet by adjusting column widths and wrapping text, and by applying appropriate financial number formatting and cell styles. Insert a column chart that compares your expenses by month and modify the chart layout and style. Insert a footer with the file name and center the worksheet horizontally on the page. Save your file as **Lastname_Firstname_1N_Personal_Expenses** and submit as directed.

End **You have completed Project 7N**

Apply a combination of the 7A and 7B skills.

GO! Collaborate | Project 7O Bell Orchid Hotels Group Running Case

This project relates to the **Bell Orchid Hotels**. Your instructor may assign this group case project to your class. If your instructor assigns this project, he or she will provide you with information and instructions to work as part of a group. The group will apply the skills gained thus far to help the Bell Orchid Hotels achieve their business goals.

End **You have completed Project 7O**

Using Functions, Creating Tables, and Managing Large Workbooks

OUTCOMES

At the end of this chapter you will be able to:

OBJECTIVES

Mastering these objectives will enable you to:

PROJECT 8A

Analyze inventory by applying statistical and logical calculations to data and by sorting and filtering data.

1. Use the SUM, AVERAGE, MEDIAN, MIN, and MAX Functions (p. 403)
2. Move Data, Resolve Error Messages, and Rotate Text (p. 407)
3. Use COUNTIF and IF Functions and Apply Conditional Formatting (p. 409)
4. Use Date & Time Functions and Freeze Panes (p. 414)
5. Create, Sort, and Filter an Excel Table (p. 416)
6. Format and Print a Large Worksheet (p. 419)

PROJECT 8B

Summarize the data on multiple worksheets.

7. Navigate a Workbook and Rename Worksheets (p. 424)
8. Enter Dates, Clear Contents, and Clear Formats (p. 425)
9. Copy and Paste by Using the Paste Options Gallery (p. 429)
10. Edit and Format Multiple Worksheets at the Same Time (p. 430)
11. Create a Summary Sheet with Column Sparklines (p. 436)
12. Format and Print Multiple Worksheets in a Workbook (p. 440)

Shutterstock

In This Chapter

In this chapter, you will use the Statistical functions to calculate the average of a group of numbers, and use other Logical and Date & Time functions. You will use the counting functions and apply conditional formatting to make data easy to visualize. In this chapter, you will also create a table and analyze the table's data by sorting and filtering the data. You will summarize a workbook that contains multiple worksheets.

The projects in this chapter relate to **Laurales Herbs and Spices**. After ten years as an Executive Chef, Laura Morales started her own business, which offers quality products for cooking, eating, and entertaining in retail stores and online. In addition to herbs and spices, there is a wide variety of condiments, confections, jams, sauces, oils, and vinegars. Later this year, Laura will add a line of tools, cookbooks, and gift baskets. The company name is a combination of Laura's first and last names, and also the name of an order of plants related to cinnamon.

Project 8A Inventory Status Report

Project Activities

In Activities 8.01 through 8.15, you will edit a worksheet for Laura Morales, President, detailing the current inventory of flavor products at the Oakland production facility. Your completed worksheet will look similar to Figure 8.1.

Project Files

For Project 8A, you will need the following file:

e02A_Flavor_Inventory

You will save your workbook as:

Lastname_Firstname_2A_Flavor_Inventory

Project Results

Oakland Facility: Inventory Status of Flavor Products
As of June 30

Flavor Statistics

Total Items in Stock	11,015
Average Price	$ 8.72
Median Price	$ 7.85
Lowest Price	$ 2.55
Highest Price	$ 31.95

Seasoning Types 20
Extract Types: 8 (2,190 total items in stock)

Quantity in Stock	Item #	Product Name	Retail Price	Size	Packaging	Category	Stock Level
228	13189	Pepper, Florida	8.75	8 oz.	Jar	Seasoning	OK
110	13558	French Four Spice	6.56	2 oz.	Foil Packet	Seasoning	*Order*
135	15688	Pepper, Lemon	6.25	4 oz.	Jar	Seasoning	OK
95	16555	Tuscan Sunset	4.55	2 oz.	Foil Packet	Seasoning	*Order*
125	21683	Galena Street Rub	3.95	4 oz.	Jar	Rub	OK
135	22189	Northwoods Fire	9.85	16 oz.	Jar	Seasoning	OK
143	23677	Marjoram	7.89	8 oz.	Foil Packet	Herb	OK
146	23688	Curry Powder, Hot	9.99	8 oz.	Jar	Spice	OK
234	24896	Butcher's Pepper	5.29	4 oz.	Foil Packet	Rub	OK
135	25678	Curry Powder, Sweet	9.99	8 oz.	Jar	Spice	OK
254	25844	Herbes De Provence	10.25	4 oz.	Foil Packet	Herb	OK
165	26787	Creole Dip Seasoning	8.75	8 oz.	Foil Packet	Seasoning	OK
156	32544	Mint, Spearmint	10.29	8 oz.	Foil Packet	Herb	OK
156	34266	Basil, French	10.19	8 oz.	Foil Packet	Herb	OK
188	34793	Onion Salt	3.55	2 oz.	Jar	Seasoning	OK
266	34878	Ginger, Cracked	7.89	8 oz.	Foil Packet	Spice	OK
177	34982	Jerk, Chicken and Fish	5.45	4 oz.	Foil Packet	Seasoning	OK
245	35677	Jerk, Pork	9.85	8 oz.	Foil Packet	Seasoning	OK
245	35690	Jerk, Jamaican	7.99	8 oz.	Jar	Rub	OK
145	35988	Basil, California	11.95	8 oz.	Foil Packet	Herb	OK
167	36820	Mint, Peppermint	10.39	8 oz.	Foil Packet	Herb	OK
248	37803	Chili Powder, Hot	3.39	2 oz.	Jar	Seasoning	OK
188	37845	Coffee	17.29	8 oz.	Bottle	Extract	OK
150	38675	Paprika, Hungarian Sweet	2.99	4 oz.	Jar	Seasoning	OK
168	38700	Chili Powder, Mild	3.39	2 oz.	Jar	Seasoning	OK
45	38744	Bicentennial Beef	4.49	4 oz.	Jar	Rub	*Order*
133	39704	Paprika, Californian	5.79	8 oz.	Jar	Seasoning	OK
165	42599	Ginger, Crystallized	9.85	8 oz.	Foil Packet	Spice	OK

Lastname_Firstname_2A_Flavor_Inventory

Quantity in Stock	Item #	Product Name	Retail Price	Size	Packaging	Category	Stock Level
425	43153	Cinnamon, Chinese	4.09	2 oz.	Foil Packet	Spice	OK
95	43625	Orange Peel	8.19	4 oz.	Tin	Seasoning	*Order*
211	43633	Peppermint	5.65	4 oz.	Bottle	Extract	OK
244	43813	Marjoram	4.45	4 oz.	Jar	Herb	OK
168	44482	Garlic Powder	5.89	6 oz.	Jar	Seasoning	OK
75	44587	Tandoori	16.85	8 oz.	Foil Packet	Spice	*Order*
235	44589	Garlic, Californian Flakes	11.25	2 oz.	Jar	Seasoning	OK
160	44879	Ginger	7.95	8 oz.	Jar	Spice	OK
165	45265	Pickling Spice	6.49	2 oz.	Jar	Spice	OK
100	45688	Nutmeg	7.85	8 oz.	Jar	Spice	*Order*
265	46532	Oregano	10.19	8 oz.	Jar	Herb	OK
73	49652	Rojo Taco	5.29	4 oz.	Foil Packet	Seasoning	*Order*
185	52164	Cloves, Whole	18.70	8 oz.	Jar	Spice	OK
165	53634	Vanilla, Double Strength	16.75	8 oz.	Bottle	Extract	OK
325	54635	Dill Weed	2.65	4 oz.	Foil Packet	Herb	OK
195	55255	Sea Salt, Pacific	2.55	8 oz.	Tin	Seasoning	OK
312	56853	Peppercorns, Indian	4.59	2 oz.	Jar	Spice	OK
152	64525	Onion Powder	4.85	4 oz.	Jar	Seasoning	OK
215	78655	Garlic Salt	2.58	6 oz.	Jar	Seasoning	OK
540	85655	Peppercorns, Red	3.69	2 oz.	Tin	Spice	OK
225	92258	Vanilla	15.95	4 oz.	Bottle	Extract	OK
368	93157	Almond	7.33	4 oz.	Bottle	Extract	OK
285	93553	Lemon	24.90	6 oz.	Bottle	Extract	OK
126	94236	Cumin	3.55	4 oz.	Foil Packet	Spice	OK
423	96854	Vanilla	31.95	6 oz.	Bottle	Extract	OK
325	98225	Orange	24.19	6 oz.	Bottle	Extract	OK
211	98655	Cloves, Ground	4.55	6 oz.	Jar	Spice	OK

Edited by Frank Barnes
5/2/2010 10:27

Lastname_Firstname_2A_Flavor_Inventory

Figure 8.1
Project 8A Flavor Inventory

Objective 1 | Use the SUM, AVERAGE, MEDIAN, MIN, and MAX Functions

A ***function*** is a predefined formula—a formula that Excel has already built for you—that performs calculations by using specific values in a particular order or structure. ***Statistical functions***, which include the AVERAGE, MEDIAN, MIN, and MAX functions, are useful to analyze a group of measurements.

Activity 8.01 | Using the SUM and AVERAGE Functions

Laura has a worksheet with information about the inventory of flavor product types currently in stock at the Oakland facility. In this activity, you will use the SUM and AVERAGE functions to gather information about the product inventory.

1 **Start** Excel. From **Backstage** view, display the **Open** dialog box, and then from the student files that accompany this textbook, locate and open **e02A_Flavor_Inventory**. Click the **File tab** to redisplay **Backstage** view, and then click **Save As**. In the **Save As** dialog box, navigate to the location where you are storing your projects for this chapter.

2 Create a new folder named **Excel Chapter 2** open the new folder, and then in the **File name** box, type **Lastname_Firstname_2A_Flavor_Inventory** Click **Save** or press Enter.

3 Scroll down. Notice that the worksheet contains data related to types of flavor products in inventory, including information about the *Quantity in Stock*, *Item #*, *Product Name*, *Retail Price*, *Size*, *Packaging*, and *Category*.

4 Leave row 3 blank, and then in cell **A4**, type **Total Items in Stock** In cell **A5**, type **Average Price** In cell **A6**, type **Median Price**

5 Click cell **B4**. Click the **Formulas tab**, and then in the **Function Library group**, click the **AutoSum** button. Compare your screen with Figure 8.2.

The ***SUM function*** that you have used is a predefined formula that adds all the numbers in a selected range of cells. Because it is frequently used, there are several ways to insert the function.

For example, you can insert the function from the Home tab's Editing group, by using the keyboard shortcut Alt + =, from the Function Library group on the Formulas tab, and also from the Math & Trig button in that group.

Figure 8.2

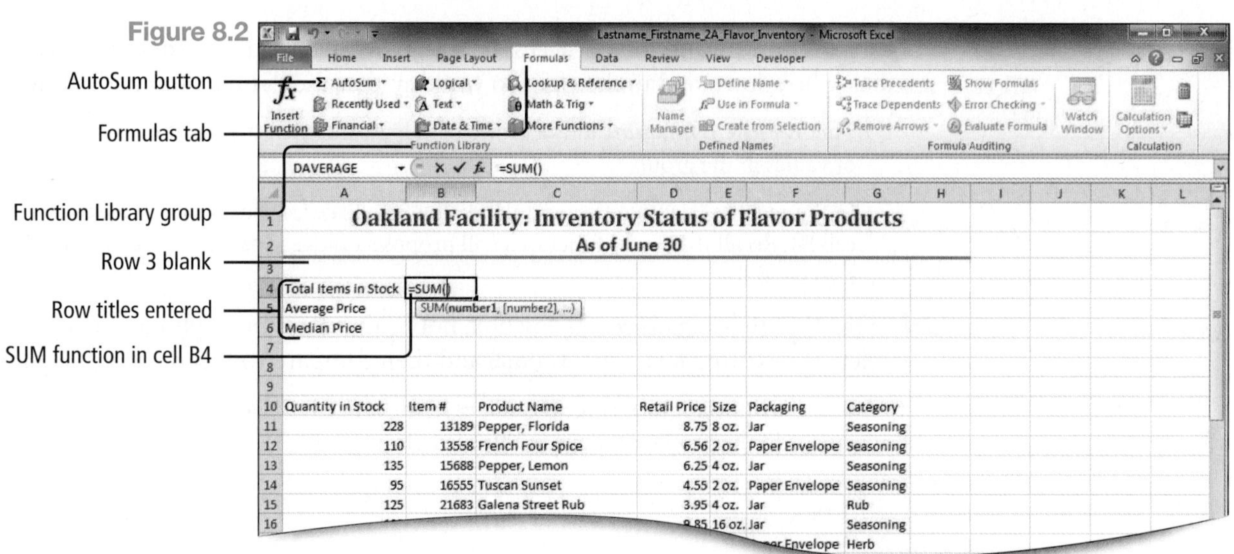

6 With the insertion point blinking in the function, select the range **A11:A65**, dragging down as necessary, and then press Enter. Scroll up to view the top of your worksheet, and notice your result in cell **B4**, *11015*.

7 Click cell **B4** and look at the **Formula Bar**: Compare your screen with Figure 8.3.

SUM is the name of the function. The values in parentheses are the ***arguments***—the values that an Excel function uses to perform calculations or operations. In this instance, the argument consists of the values in the range A11:A65.

Figure 8.3

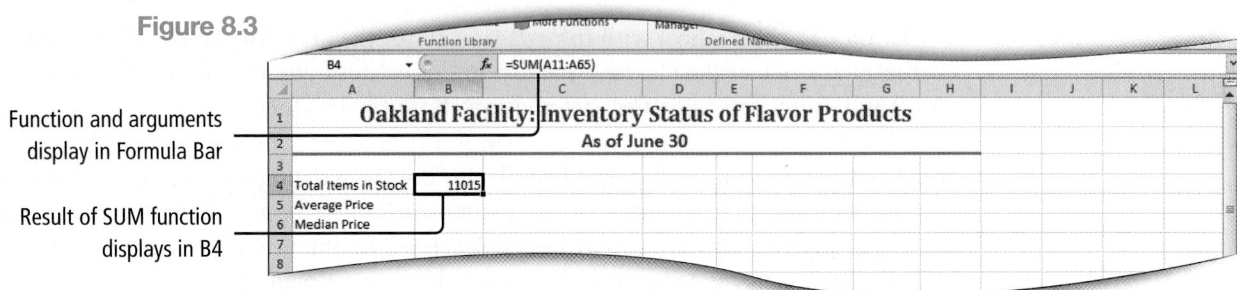

8 Click cell **B5**. In the **Function Library group**, click the **More Functions** button, point to **Statistical**, point to **AVERAGE**, and notice the ScreenTip. Compare your screen with Figure 8.4.

The ScreenTip describes how the AVERAGE function will compute the calculation.

Figure 8.4

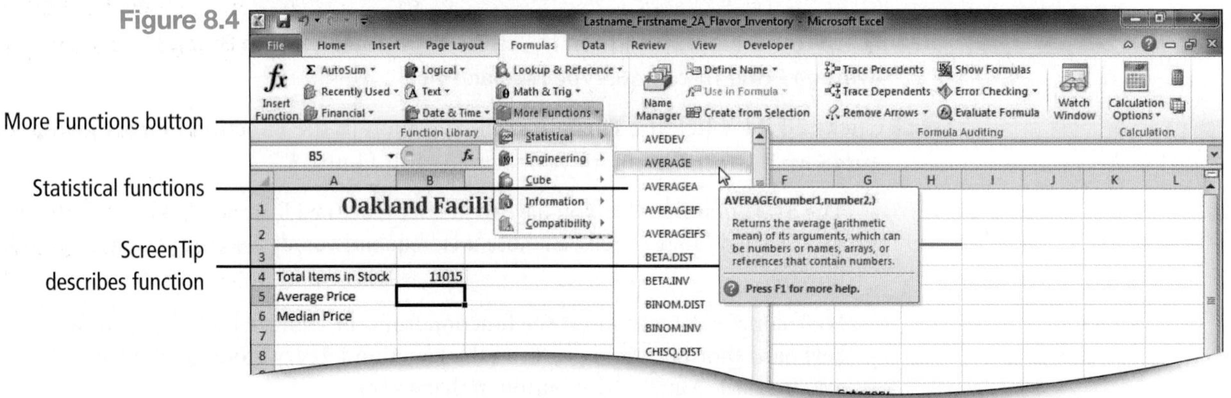

9 Click **AVERAGE**, and then if necessary, drag the title bar of the **Function Arguments** dialog box down and to the right so you can view the **Formula Bar** and cell **B5**.

The ***AVERAGE function*** adds a group of values, and then divides the result by the number of values in the group.

In the cell, the Formula Bar, and the dialog box, Excel proposes to average the value in cell B4. Recall that Excel functions will propose a range if data is above or to the left of a selected cell.

Another Way

Alternatively, with the existing text selected, select the range D11:D65 and press Enter.

10 In the **Function Arguments** dialog box, notice that *B4* is highlighted. Press Del to delete the existing text, type **d11:d65** and then compare your screen with Figure 8.5.

Because you want to average the values in the range D11:D65—and not cell B4—you must edit the proposed range in this manner.

Figure 8.5

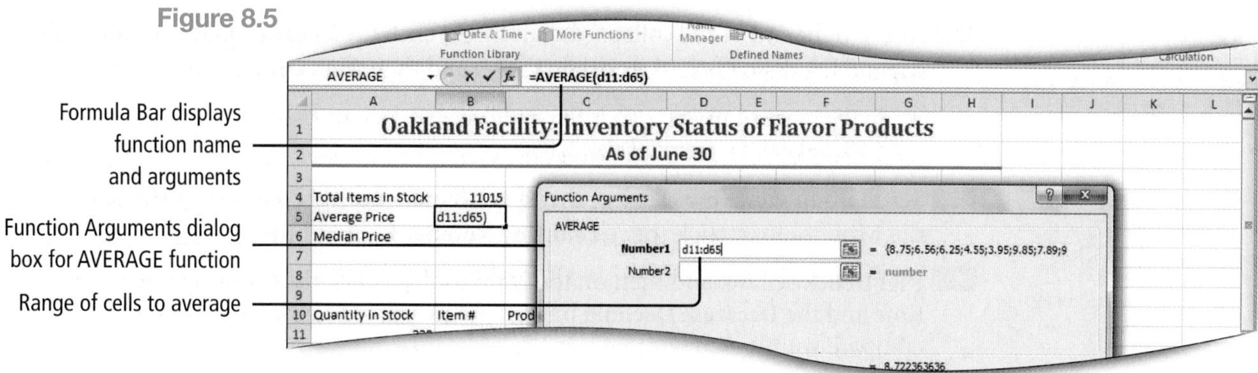

11 In the **Function Arguments** dialog box, click **OK**, and then **Save**.

The result indicates that the average Retail Price of all products is *8.72*.

Activity 8.02 | Using the MEDIAN Function

The ***MEDIAN function*** is a statistical function that describes a group of data—you may have seen it used to describe the price of houses in a particular geographical area. The MEDIAN function finds the middle value that has as many values above it in the group as are below it. It differs from AVERAGE in that the result is not affected as much by a single value that is greatly different from the others.

1 Click cell **B6**. In the **Function Library group**, click the **More Functions** button, display the list of **Statistical** functions, scroll down as necessary, and then click **MEDIAN**.

2 In the **Function Arguments** dialog box, to the right of the **Number 1** box, click the **Collapse Dialog** button.

The dialog box collapses to a small size with space only for the first argument so you can see more of your data.

3 Select the range **D11:D65**, and then compare your screen with Figure 8.6.

When indicating which cells you want to use in the function's calculation—known as *defining the arguments*—you can either select the values with your mouse or type the range of values, whichever you prefer.

Figure 8.6

	A	B	C	D	E	F	G
40	95	43625	Orange Peel	8.19	4 oz.	Tin	Seasoning
41	211	43633	Peppermint	5.65	4 oz.	Bottle	Extract
42	244	43813	Marjoram	4.45	4 oz.	Jar	Herb
43	168	44482	Garlic Powder	5.89	6 oz.	Jar	Seasoning
44	75	44587	Tand				
45	235	44589	Garli				
46	160	44879	Ging				
47	165	45265	Pickling Spice	6.49	2 oz.	Jar	Spice
48	100	45688	Nutmeg	7.85	8 oz.	Jar	Spice
49	265	46532	Oregano	10.19	8 oz.	Jar	Herb
50	73	49652	Rojo Taco	5.29	4 oz.	Paper Envelope	Seasoning
51	185	52164	Cloves, Whole	18.70	8 oz.	Jar	Spice
52	165	53634	Vanilla, Double Strength	16.75	8 oz.	Bottle	Extract
53	325	54635	Dill Weed	2.65	4 oz.	Paper Envelope	Herb
54	195	55255	Sea Salt, Pacific	2.55	8 oz.	Tin	Seasoning
55	312	56853	Peppercorns, Indian	4.59	2 oz.	Jar	Spice
56	152	64525	Onion Powder	4.85	4 oz.	Jar	Seasoning
57	215	78655	Garlic Salt	2.58	6 oz.	Jar	Seasoning
58	540	85655	Peppercorns, Red	3.69	2 oz.	Tin	Spice
59	225	92258	Vanilla	15.95	4 oz.	Bottle	Extract
60	368	93157	Almond	7.33	4 oz.	Bottle	Extract
61	285	93553	Lemon	24.90	6 oz.	Bottle	Extract
62	126	94236	Cumin	3.55	4 oz.	Paper Envelope	Spice
63	423	96854	Vanilla	31.95	6 oz.	Bottle	Extract
64	325	98225	Orange	24.19	6 oz.	Bottle	Extract
65	211	98655	Cloves, Ground	4.55	6 oz.	Jar	Spice
66							

Excel | Chapter 8

Another Way

Press Enter to expand the dialog box.

4. At the right end of the collapsed dialog box, click the **Expand Dialog** button to expand the dialog box to its original size, and then click **OK** to display *7.85*.

   In the range of prices, 7.85 is the middle value. Half of all flavor products are priced *above* 7.85 and half are priced *below* 7.85.

5. Scroll up to view **row 1**. Select the range **B5:B6** and right-click over the selection. On the Mini toolbar, click the **Accounting Number Format** button.

6. Right-click cell **B4**, and then on the Mini toolbar, click the **Comma Style** button one time and the **Decrease Decimal** button two times. Click **Save** and compare your screen with Figure 8.7.

Figure 8.7

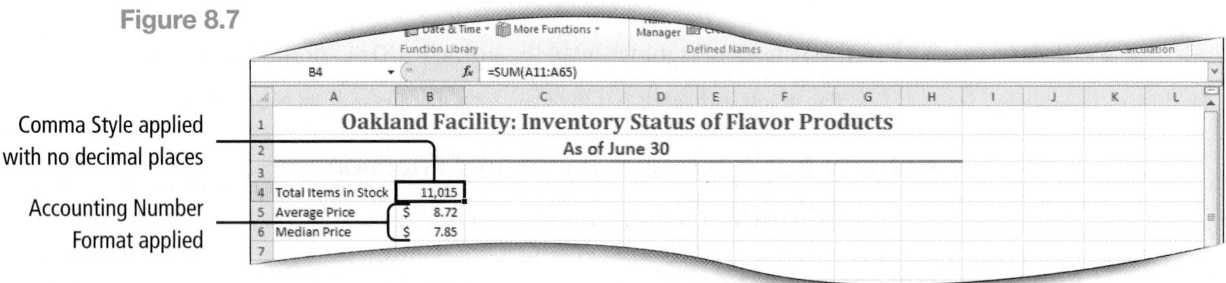

Activity 8.03 | Using the MIN and MAX Functions

The statistical ***MIN function*** determines the smallest value in a selected range of values. The statistical ***MAX function*** determines the largest value in a selected range of values.

1. In cell **A7**, type **Lowest Price** and then in cell **A8**, type **Highest Price**

2. Click cell **B7**. On the **Formulas tab**, in the **Function Library group**, click the **More Functions** button, display the list of **Statistical** functions, scroll as necessary, and then click **MIN**.

3. At the right end of the **Number1** box, click the **Collapse Dialog** button, select the range **D11:D65**, and then click the **Expand Dialog** button. Click **OK**.

   The lowest Retail Price is *2.55*.

4. Click cell **B8**, and then by using a similar technique, insert the **MAX** function to determine the highest **Retail Price**—*31.95*.

5. Select the range **B7:B8** and apply the **Accounting Number Format**, click **Save**, and then compare your screen with Figure 8.8.

Figure 8.8

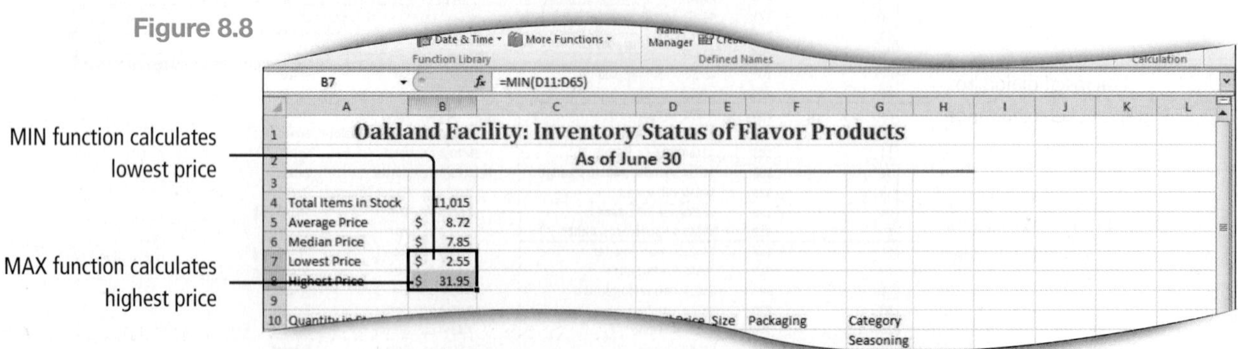

Objective 2 | Move Data, Resolve Error Messages, and Rotate Text

When you move a formula, the cell references within the formula do not change, no matter what type of cell reference you use.

If you move cells into a column that is not wide enough to display number values, Excel will display a message so that you can adjust as necessary.

You can reposition data within a cell at an angle by rotating the text.

Activity 8.04 | Moving Data and Resolving a # # # # # Error Message

1 Select the range **A4:B8**. Point to the right edge of the selected range to display the pointer, and then compare your screen with Figure 8.9.

Figure 8.9

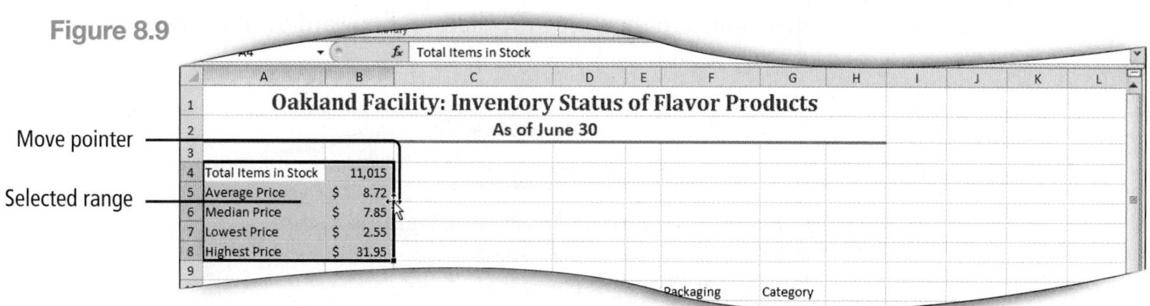

2 Drag the selected range to the right until the ScreenTip displays *D4:E8*, release the mouse button, and then notice that a series of # symbols displays in **column E**. Point to any of the cells that display # symbols, and then compare your screen with Figure 8.10.

Using this technique, cell contents can be moved from one location to another; this is referred to as ***drag and drop***.

If a cell width is too narrow to display the entire number, Excel displays the ##### error, because displaying only a portion of a number would be misleading. The underlying values remain unchanged and are displayed in the Formula Bar for the selected cell. An underlying value also displays in the ScreenTip if you point to a cell containing # symbols.

Figure 8.10

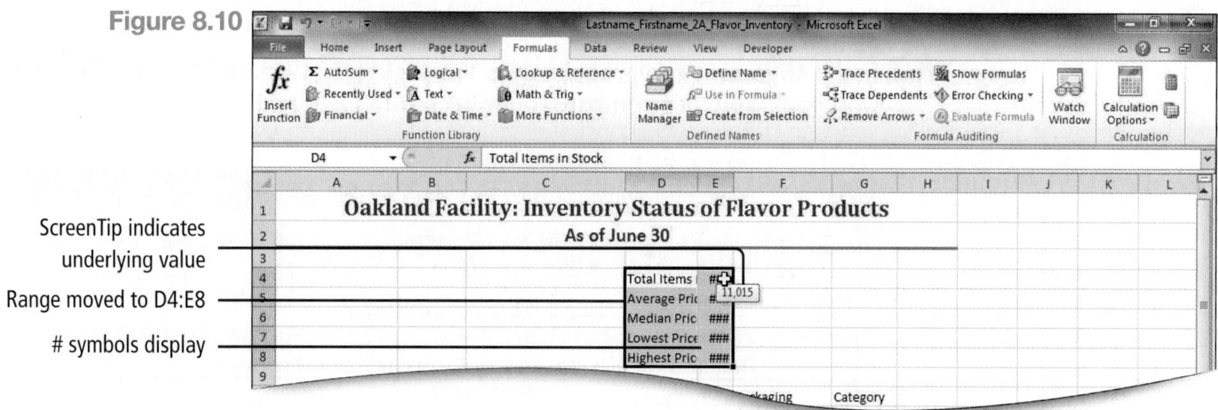

3 Select **column E** and widen it to **50** pixels, and notice that two cells are still not wide enough to display the cell contents.

4 In the **column heading area**, point to the right boundary of **column E** to display the pointer. Double-click to AutoFit the column to accommodate the widest entry.

5 Using the same technique, AutoFit **column D** to accommodate the widest text entry.

6 Select the range **D4:E8**. On the **Home tab**, in the **Styles group**, display the **Cell Styles** gallery. Under **Themed Cell Styles**, click **20%-Accent1**. Click **Save**.

Activity 8.05 | Rotating Text

Rotated text is useful to draw attention to data on your worksheet.

> **Another Way**
>
> Type the number of degrees directly into the Degrees box or use the spin box arrows to set the number.

1 In cell **C6**, type **Flavor Statistics** Select the range **C4:C8**, right-click over the selection, and then on the shortcut menu, click **Format Cells**. In the **Format Cells** dialog box, click the **Alignment tab**. Under **Text control**, select the **Merge cells** check box.

2 In the upper right portion of the dialog box, under **Orientation**, point to the **red diamond**, and then drag the diamond upward until the **Degrees** box indicates **30**. Compare your screen with Figure 8.11.

Figure 8.11

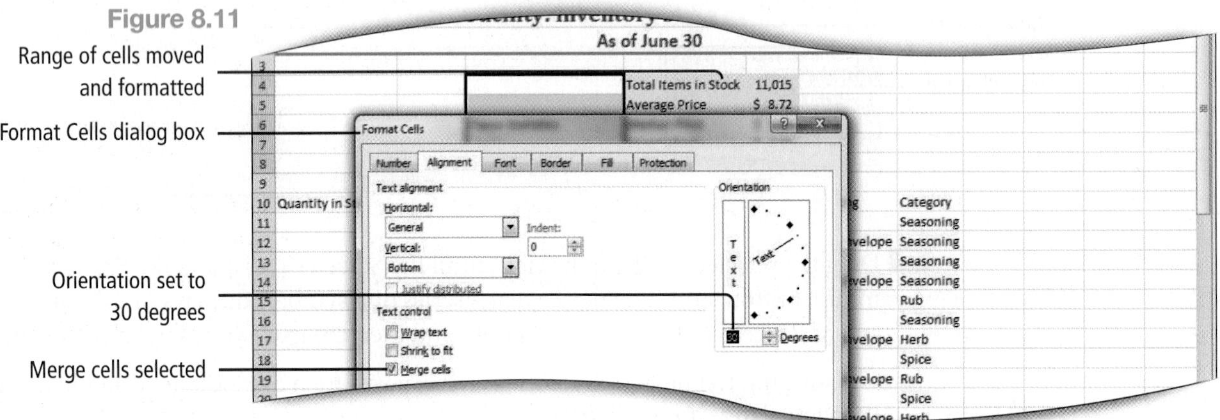

3 In the lower right corner of the **Format Cells** dialog box, click **OK**.

4 With the merged cell still selected, on the **Home tab**, in the **Font group**, change the **Font Size** to **14**, and then apply **Bold** and **Italic**. Click the **Font Color arrow**, and then in the fourth column, click the first color—**Dark Blue, Text 2**.

5 In the **Alignment group**, apply **Align Text Right**. Click cell **A1**, **Save** your workbook, and then compare your screen with Figure 8.12.

Figure 8.12

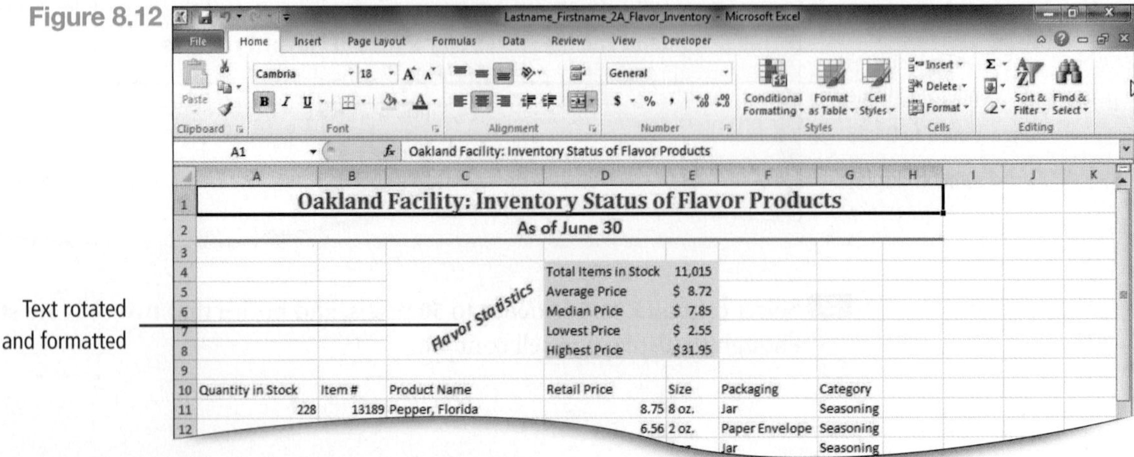

Objective 3 | Use COUNTIF and IF Functions and Apply Conditional Formatting

Recall that statistical functions analyze a group of measurements. Another group of Excel functions, referred to as ***logical functions***, test for specific conditions. Logical functions typically use conditional tests to determine whether specified conditions—called ***criteria***—are true or false.

Activity 8.06 | Using the COUNTIF Function

The ***COUNTIF function*** is a statistical function that counts the number of cells within a range that meet the given condition—the criteria that you provide. The COUNTIF function has two arguments—the range of cells to check and the criteria.

The seasonings of Laurales Herbs and Spices will be featured on an upcoming segment of a TV shopping channel. In this activity, you will use the COUNTIF function to determine the number of *seasoning* products currently available in inventory.

1. In the **row heading area**, point to **row 9** and right-click to select the row and display the shortcut menu. Click **Insert**, and then press F4 two times to repeat the last action and thus insert three blank rows.

   F4 is useful to repeat commands in Microsoft Office programs. Most commands can be repeated in this manner.

2. From the **row heading area**, select **rows 9:11**. On the **Home tab**, in the **Editing group**, click the **Clear** button, and then click **Clear Formats** to remove the blue accent color in columns D and E from the new rows.

   When you insert rows or columns, formatting from adjacent rows or columns repeats in the new cells.

3. Click cell **E4**, look at the **Formula Bar**, and then notice that the arguments of the **SUM** function adjusted and refer to the appropriate cells in rows 14:68.

   The referenced range updates to *A14:A68* after you insert the three new rows. In this manner, Excel adjusts the cell references in a formula relative to their new locations.

4. In cell **A10**, type **Seasoning Types:** and then press Tab.

5. With cell **B10** as the active cell, on the **Formulas tab**, in the **Function Library group**, click the **More Functions** button, and then display the list of **Statistical** functions. Click **COUNTIF**.

   Recall that the COUNTIF function counts the number of cells within a range that meet the given condition.

6 In the **Range** box, click the **Collapse Dialog** button, select the range **G14:G68**, and then at the right end of the collapsed dialog box, click the **Expand Dialog** button. Click in the **Criteria** box, type **Seasoning** and then compare your screen with Figure 8.13.

Figure 8.13

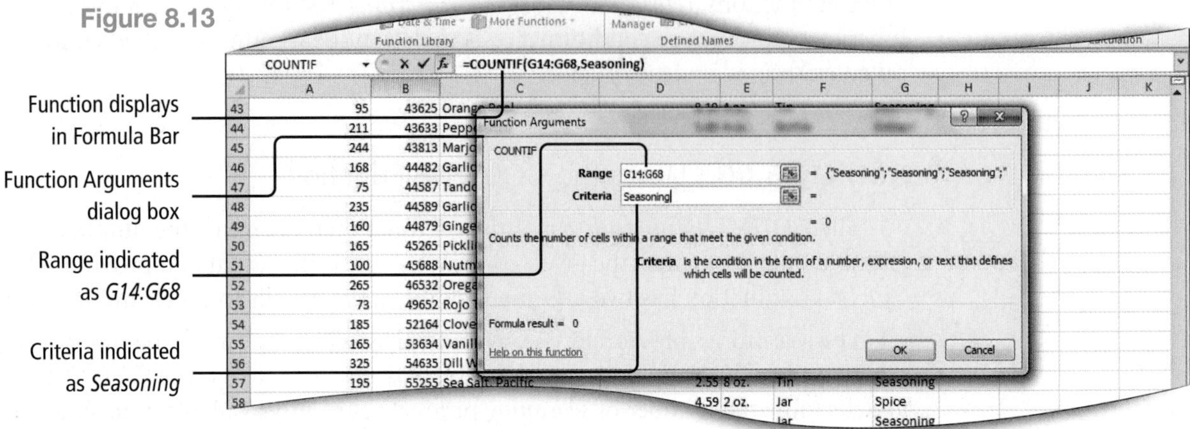

7 In the lower right corner of the **Function Arguments** dialog box, click **OK**.

There are *20* different *Seasoning* products available to feature on the TV show.

8 On the **Home tab**, in the **Alignment group**, click **Align Text Left** to place the result closer to the row title. **Save** your workbook.

Activity 8.07 | Using the IF Function

A ***logical test*** is any value or expression that you can evaluate as being true or false. The ***IF function*** uses a logical test to check whether a condition is met, and then returns one value if true, and another value if false.

For example, *C14=228* is an expression that can be evaluated as true or false. If the value in cell C14 is equal to 228, the expression is true. If the value in cell C14 is not 228, the expression is false.

In this activity, you will use the IF function to determine the inventory levels and determine if more products should be ordered.

1 Click cell **H13**, type **Stock Level** and then press Enter.

2 In cell **H14**, on the **Formulas tab**, in the **Function Library group**, click the **Logical** button, and then in the list, click **IF**. Drag the title bar of the **Function Arguments** dialog box up or down to view **row 14** on your screen.

3 With the insertion point in the **Logical_test** box, click cell **A14**, and then type **<125**

This logical test will look at the value in cell A14, which is *228*, and then determine if the number is less than 125. The expression *<125* includes the < ***comparison operator***, which means *less than*. Comparison operators compare values.

4 Examine the table in Figure 8.14 for a list of comparison operator symbols and their definitions.

Comparison Operators

Comparison Operator	Symbol Definition
=	Equal to
>	Greater than
<	Less than
>=	Greater than or equal to
<=	Less than or equal to
<>	Not equal to

Figure 8.14

5 Press Tab to move the insertion point to the **Value_if_true** box, and then type **Order**

If the result of the logical test is true—the Quantity in Stock is less than 125—cell H14 will display the text *Order* indicating that additional product must be ordered.

6 Click in the **Value_if_false** box, type **OK** and then compare your dialog box with Figure 8.15.

If the result of the logical test is false—the Quantity in Stock is *not* less than 125—then Excel will display *OK* in the cell.

Figure 8.15

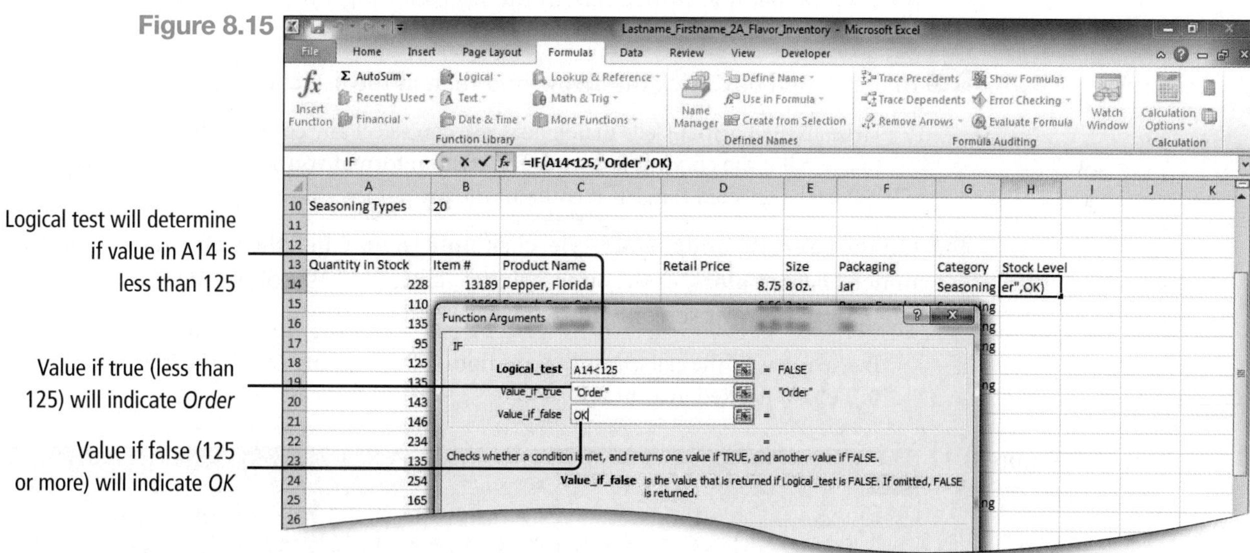

7 Click **OK** to display the result *OK* in cell **H14**.

8 Using the fill handle, copy the function in cell **H14** down through cell **H68**. Then scroll as necessary to view cell **A18**, which indicates *125*. Look at cell **H18** and notice that the **Stock Level** is indicated as *OK*. **Save** your workbook. Compare your screen with Figure 8.16.

The comparison operator indicated <125 (less than 125) and thus a value of *exactly* 125 is indicated as OK.

Figure 8.16

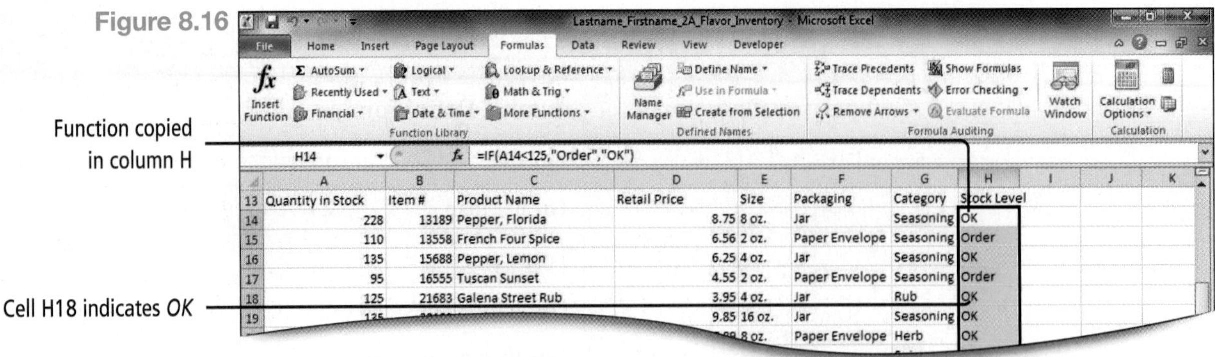

Activity 8.08 | Applying Conditional Formatting by Using Highlight Cells Rules and Data Bars

A ***conditional format*** changes the appearance of a cell based on a condition—a criteria. If the condition is true, the cell is formatted based on that condition; if the condition is false, the cell is *not* formatted. In this activity, you will use conditional formatting as another way to draw attention to the Stock Level of products.

1 Be sure the range **H14:H68** is selected. On the **Home tab**, in the **Styles group**, click the **Conditional Formatting** button. In the list, point to **Highlight Cells Rules**, and then click **Text that Contains.**

2 In the **Text That Contains** dialog box, with the insertion point blinking in the first box, type **Order** and notice that in the selected range, the text *Order* displays with the default format—Light Red Fill with Dark Red Text.

3 In the second box, click the **arrow**, and then in the list, click **Custom Format.**

Here, in the Format Cells dialog box, you can select any combination of formats to apply to the cell if the condition is true. The custom format you specify will be applied to any cell in the selected range if it contains the text *Order*.

4 On the **Font tab**, under **Font style**, click **Bold Italic**. Click the **Color arrow**, and then under **Theme Colors**, in the sixth column, click the first color—**Red, Accent 2.** Click **OK**. Compare your screen with Figure 8.17.

In the range, if the cell meets the condition of containing *Order*, the font color will change to Bold Italic, Red, Accent 2.

Figure 8.17

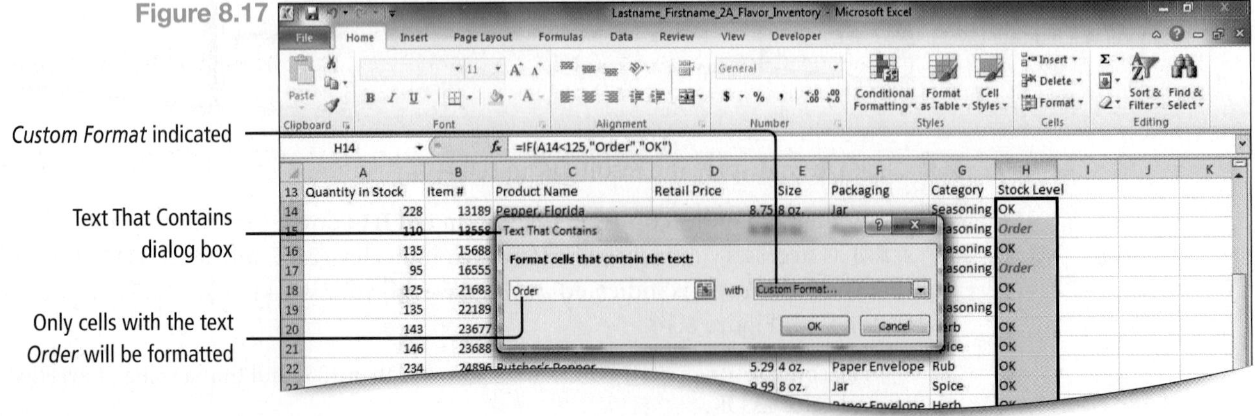

5 In the **Text That Contains** dialog box, click **OK**.

6 Select the range **A14:A68**. In the **Styles group**, click the **Conditional Formatting** button. Point to **Data Bars**, and then under **Gradient Fill**, click **Orange Data Bar**. Click anywhere to cancel the selection; click [Save]. Compare your screen with Figure 8.18.

A ***data bar*** provides a visual cue to the reader about the value of a cell relative to other cells. The length of the data bar represents the value in the cell. A longer bar represents a higher value and a shorter bar represents a lower value. Data bars are useful for identifying higher and lower numbers quickly within a large group of data, such as very high or very low levels of inventory.

Figure 8.18

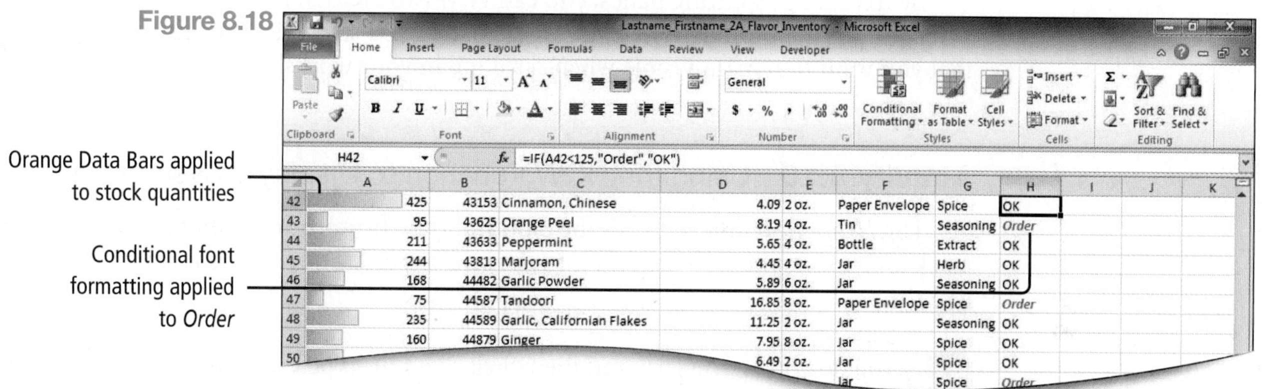

Activity 8.09 | Using Find and Replace

The ***Find and Replace*** feature searches the cells in a worksheet—or in a selected range—for matches, and then replaces each match with a replacement value of your choice.

Comments from customers on the company's blog indicate that, for dried herbs and seasonings, customers prefer a sealable foil packet rather than a paper envelope. Thus, all products of this type have been repackaged. In this activity, you will replace all occurrences of *Paper Envelope* with *Foil Packet.*

1 Select the range **F14:F68.**

Restrict the find and replace operation to a specific range in this manner, especially if there is a possibility that the name occurs elsewhere.

2 On the **Home tab**, in the **Editing group**, click the **Find & Select** button, and then click **Replace**.

3 Type **Paper Envelope** to fill in the **Find what** box. In the **Replace with** box, type **Foil Packet** and then compare your screen with Figure 8.19.

Figure 8.19

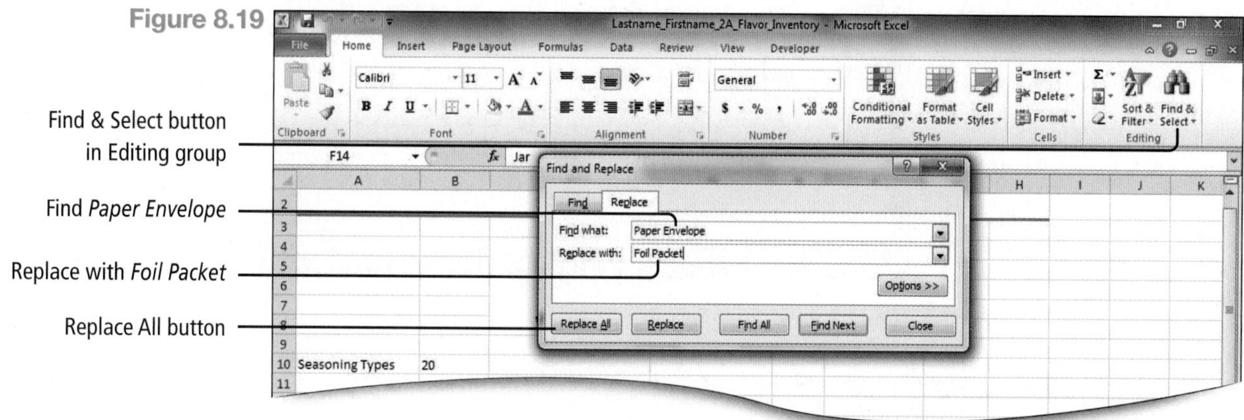

4. Click the **Replace All** button. In the message box, notice that 19 replacements were made, and then click **OK**. In the lower right corner of the **Find and Replace** dialog box, click the **Close** button. Click **Save** .

Objective 4 | Use Date & Time Functions and Freeze Panes

Excel can obtain the date and time from your computer's calendar and clock and display this information on your worksheet.

By freezing or splitting panes, you can view two areas of a worksheet and lock rows and columns in one area. When you freeze panes, you select the specific rows or columns that you want to remain visible when scrolling in your worksheet.

Activity 8.10 | Using the NOW Function to Display a System Date

The ***NOW function*** retrieves the date and time from your computer's calendar and clock and inserts the information into the selected cell. The result is formatted as a date and time.

1. Scroll down as necessary, and then click cell **A70**. Type **Edited by Frank Barnes** and then press Enter.

2. With cell **A71** as the active cell, on the **Formulas tab**, in the **Function Library group**, click the **Date & Time** button. In the list of functions, click **NOW**. Compare your screen with Figure 8.20.

Figure 8.20

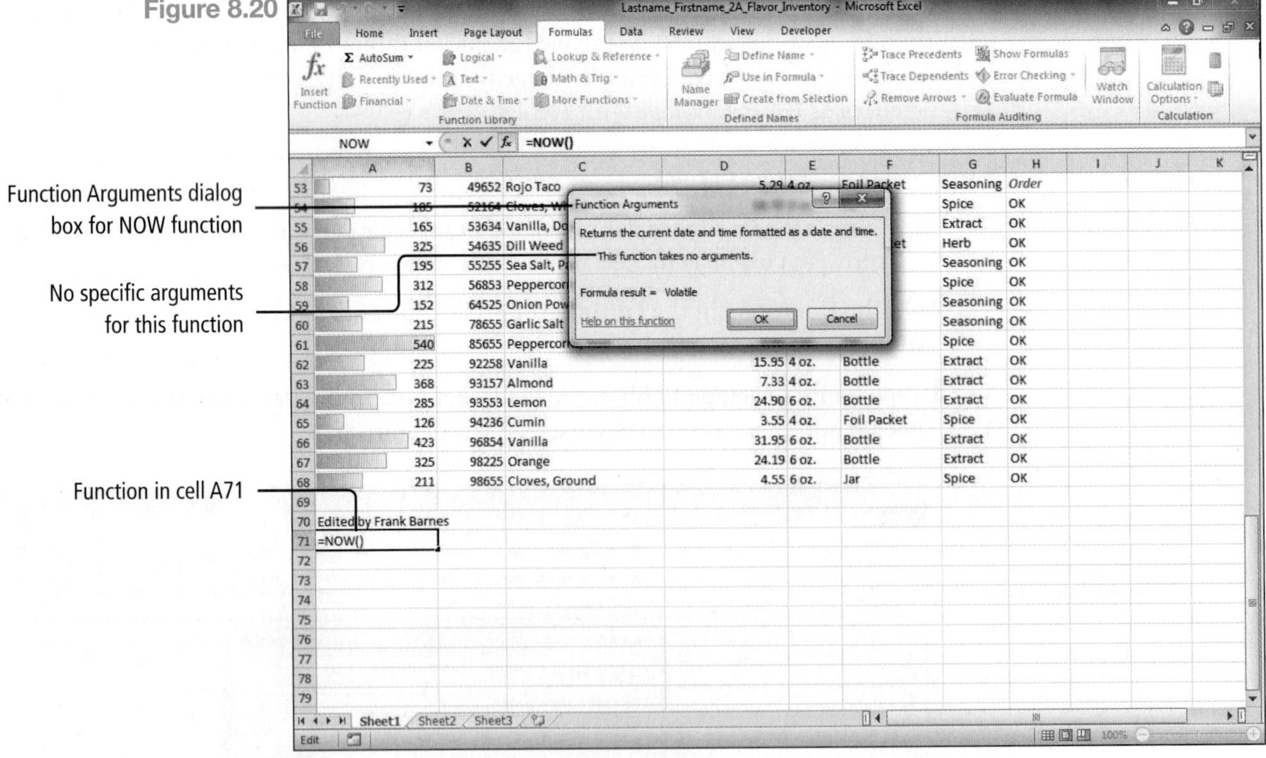

3 Read the description in the **Function Arguments** dialog box, and notice that this result is *Volatile*.

The Function Arguments dialog box displays a message indicating that this function does not require an argument. It also states that this function is ***volatile***, meaning the date and time will not remain as entered, but rather the date and time will automatically update each time you open this workbook.

4 In the **Function Arguments** dialog box, click **OK** to close the dialog box to display the current date and time in cell **A71**. **Save** your workbook.

More Knowledge | NOW Function Recalculates Each Time a Workbook Opens

The NOW function updates each time the workbook is opened. With the workbook open, you can force the NOW function to update by pressing F9, for example, to update the time.

Activity 8.11 | Freezing and Unfreezing Panes

In a large worksheet, if you scroll down more than 25 rows or scroll beyond column O (the exact row number and column letter varies, depending on your screen resolution), you will no longer see the top rows or first column of your worksheet where identifying information about the data is usually placed. You will find it easier to work with your data if you can always view the identifying row or column titles.

The ***Freeze Panes*** command enables you to select one or more rows or columns and then freeze (lock) them into place. The locked rows and columns become separate panes. A ***pane*** is a portion of a worksheet window bounded by and separated from other portions by vertical or horizontal bars.

1 Press Ctrl + Home to make cell **A1** the active cell. Scroll down until **row 40** displays at the top of your Excel window, and notice that all of the identifying information in the column titles is out of view.

2 Press Ctrl + Home again, and then from the **row heading area**, select **row 14**. Click the **View tab**, and then in the **Window group**, click the **Freeze Panes** button. In the list, click **Freeze Panes**. Click any cell to deselect the row, and then notice that a line displays along the upper border of **row 14**.

By selecting row 14, the rows above—rows 1 - 13—are frozen in place and will not move as you scroll down.

3 Watch the row numbers below **row 13**, and then begin to scroll down to bring **row 40** into view again. Notice that rows 1:13 are frozen in place. Compare your screen with Figure 8.21.

The remaining rows of data continue to scroll. Use this feature when you have long or wide worksheets.

Figure 8.21

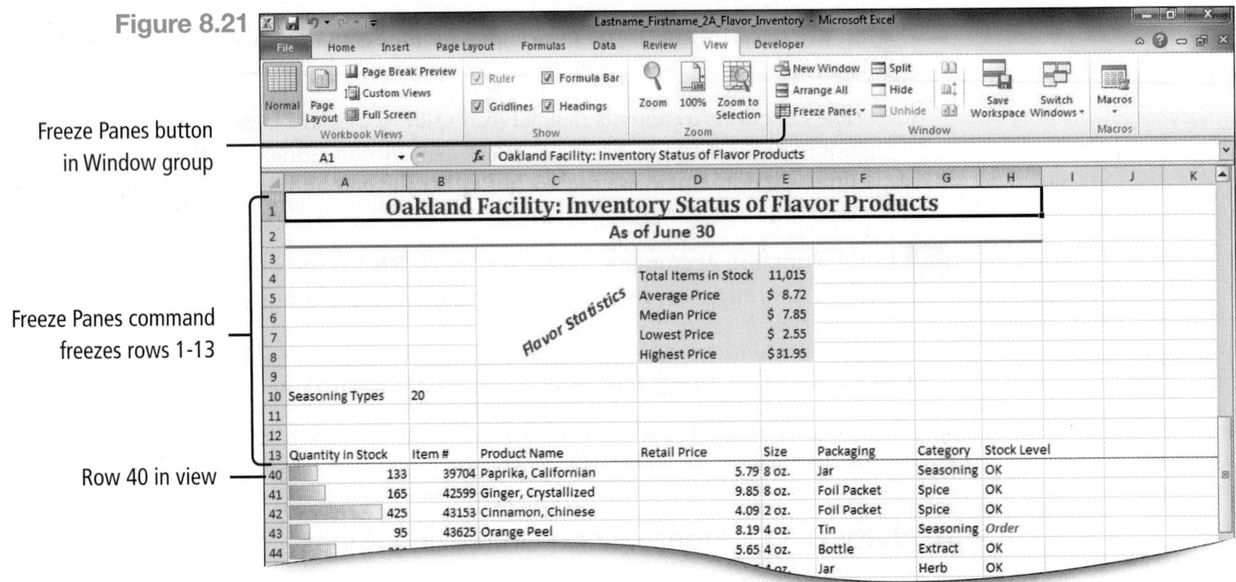

4 In the **Window group**, click the **Freeze Panes** button, and then click **Unfreeze Panes** to unlock all rows and columns. **Save** your workbook.

> **More Knowledge | Freeze Columns or Freeze both Rows and Columns**
>
> You can freeze columns that you want to remain in view on the left. Select the column to the right of the column(s) that you want to remain in view while scrolling to the right, and then click the Freeze Panes command. You can also use the command to freeze both rows and columns; click a *cell* to freeze the rows *above* the cell and the columns to the *left* of the cell.

Objective 5 | Create, Sort, and Filter an Excel Table

To analyze a group of related data, you can convert a range of cells to an ***Excel table***. An Excel table is a series of rows and columns that contains related data that is managed independently from the data in other rows and columns in the worksheet.

Activity 8.12 | Creating an Excel Table

1 Be sure that you have applied the Unfreeze Panes command—no rows on your worksheet are locked. Then, click any cell in the data below row 13.

> **Another Way**
>
> Select the range of cells that make up the table, including the header row, and then click the Table button.

2 Click the **Insert tab**. In the **Tables group**, click the **Table** button. In the **Create Table** dialog box, if necessary, click to select the **My table has headers** check box, and then compare your screen with Figure 8.22.

The column titles in row 13 will form the table headers. By clicking in a range of contiguous data, Excel will suggest the range as the data for the table. You can adjust the range if necessary.

Figure 8.22

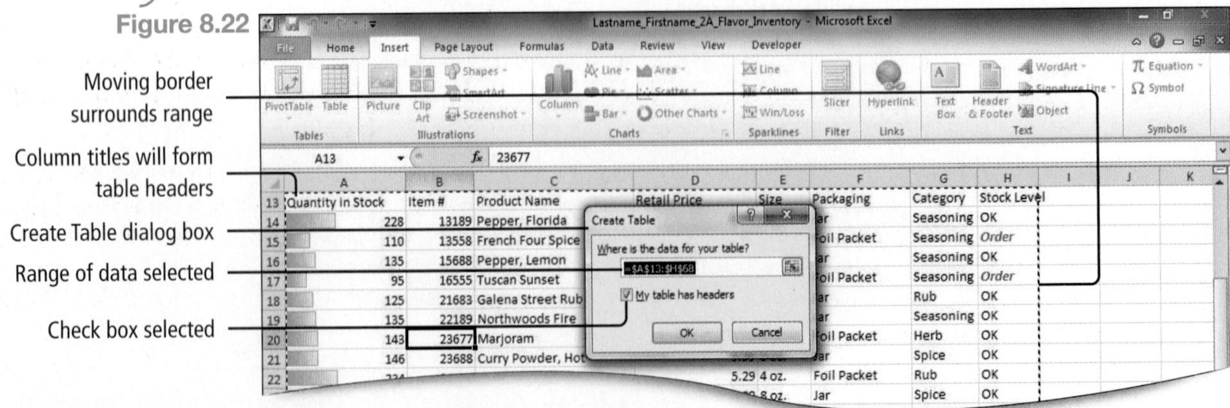

3 Click **OK**. With the range still selected, on the Ribbon notice that the **Table Tools** are active.

4 On the **Design tab**, in the **Table Styles group**, click the **More** button, and then under **Light**, locate and click **Table Style Light 16.**

5 Press Ctrl + Home. Click **Save**, and then compare your screen with Figure 8.23.

Sorting and filtering arrows display in the table's header row.

Figure 8.23

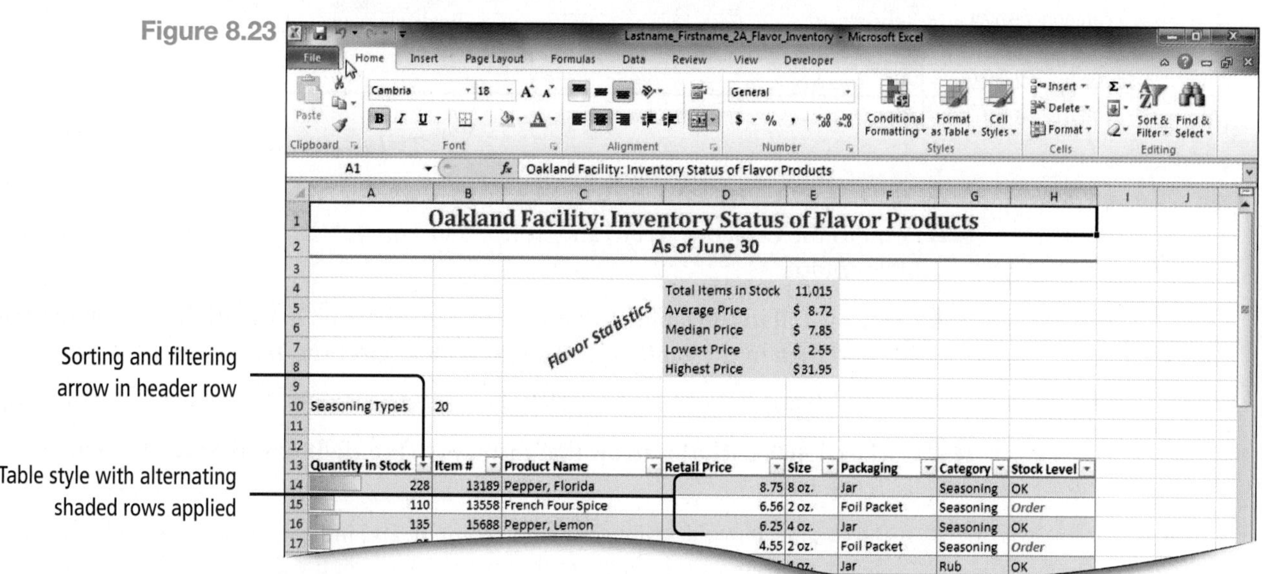

Activity 8.13 | Sorting and Filtering an Excel Table

You can ***sort*** tables—arrange all the data in a specific order—in ascending or descending order. You can ***filter*** tables—display only a portion of the data based on matching a specific value—to show only the data that meets the criteria that you specify.

1 In the header row of the table, click the **Retail Price arrow**, and then on the menu, click **Sort Smallest to Largest**. Next to the arrow, notice the small **up arrow** indicating an ascending (smallest to largest) sort.

The rows in the table are sorted from the lowest retail price to highest retail price.

2 In the table's header row, click the **Category arrow**. On the menu, click **Sort A to Z.** Next to the arrow, notice the small **up arrow** indicating an ascending (A to Z) sort.

The rows in the table are sorted alphabetically by Category.

3 Click the **Category arrow** again, and then sort from **Z to A.**

The rows in the table are sorted in reverse alphabetic order by Category name, and the small arrow points downward, indicating a descending (Z to A) sort.

4 Click the **Category arrow** again. On the menu, click the **(Select All)** check box to clear all the check boxes. Click to select only the **Extract** check box, and then click **OK.** Compare your screen with Figure 8.24.

Only the rows containing *Extract* in the Category column display—the remaining rows are hidden from view. A small funnel—the filter icon—indicates that a filter is applied to the data in the table. Additionally, the row numbers display in blue to indicate that some rows are hidden from view. A filter hides entire rows in the worksheet.

Figure 8.24

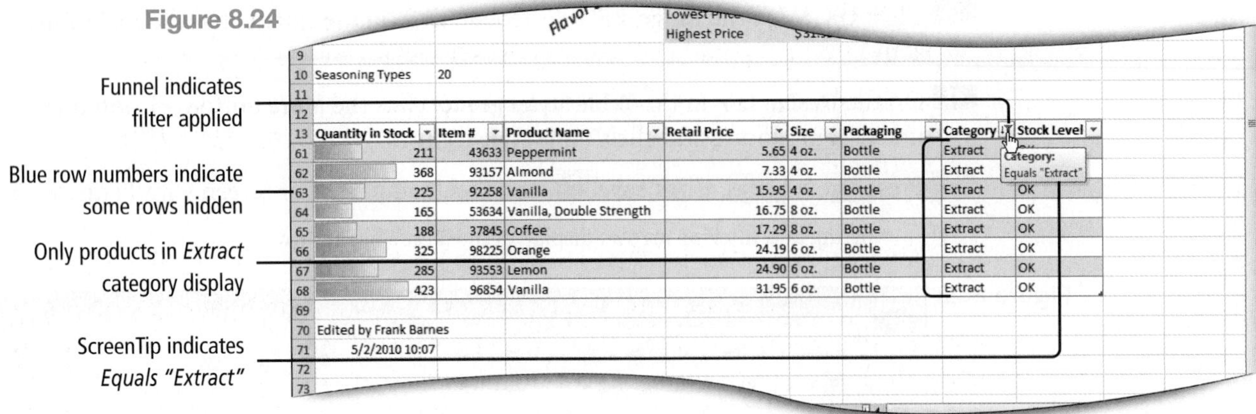

5 Point to the **Category arrow**, and notice that *Equals "Extract"* displays to indicate the filter criteria.

6 Click any cell in the table so that the table is selected. On the Ribbon, click the **Design tab**, and then in the **Table Style Options group**, select the **Total Row** check box.

Total displays in cell A69. In cell H69, the number *8* indicates that eight rows currently display.

7 Click cell **A69**, click the **arrow** that displays to the right of cell **A69**, and then in the list, click **Sum**.

Excel sums only the visible rows in Column A, and indicates that 2190 products in the Extract category are in stock. In this manner, you can use an Excel table to quickly find information about a group of data.

8 Click cell **A11**, type **Extract Types:** and press Tab. In cell **B11**, type **8 (2,190 total items in stock)** and then press Enter.

9 In the table header row, click the **Category arrow**, and then on the menu, click **Clear Filter From "Category"**.

All the rows in the table redisplay. The Z to A sort on Category remains in effect.

10 Click the **Packaging arrow**, click the **(Select All)** check box to clear all the check boxes, and then click to select the **Foil Packet** check box. Click **OK**.

11 Click the **Category arrow**, click the **(Select All)** check box to clear all the check boxes, and then click the **Herb** check box. Click **OK**, and then compare your screen with Figure 8.25.

By applying multiple filters, Laura can quickly determine that seven items in the Herb category are packaged in foil packets with a total of 1,346 such items in stock.

Figure 8.25

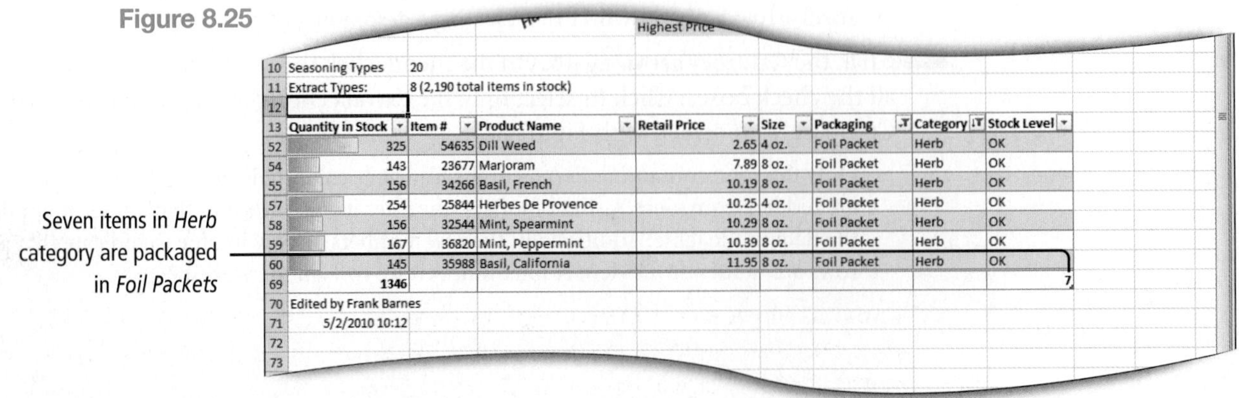

12 Click the **Category arrow**, and then click **Clear Filter From "Category"**. Use the same technique to remove the filter from the **Packaging** column.

13 In the table header row, click the **Item# arrow**, and then click **Sort Smallest to Largest**, which will apply an ascending sort to the data using the *Item#* column. **Save** your workbook.

Activity 8.14 | Converting a Table to a Range of Data

When you are finished answering questions about the data in a table by sorting, filtering, and totaling, you can convert the table into a normal range. Doing so is useful if you want to use the feature only to apply an attractive Table Style to a range of cells. For example, you can insert a table, apply a Table Style, and then convert the table to a normal range of data but keep the formatting.

> **Another Way**
>
> With any table cell selected, right-click, point to Table, and then click Convert to Range.

1 Click anywhere in the table to activate the table and display the **Table Tools** on the Ribbon. On the **Design tab**, in the **Table Style Options group**, click the **Total Row** check box to clear the check mark and remove the Total row from the table.

2 On the **Design tab**, in the **Tools group**, click the **Convert to Range** button. In the message box, click **Yes**. Click **Save**, and then compare your screen with Figure 8.26.

Figure 8.26

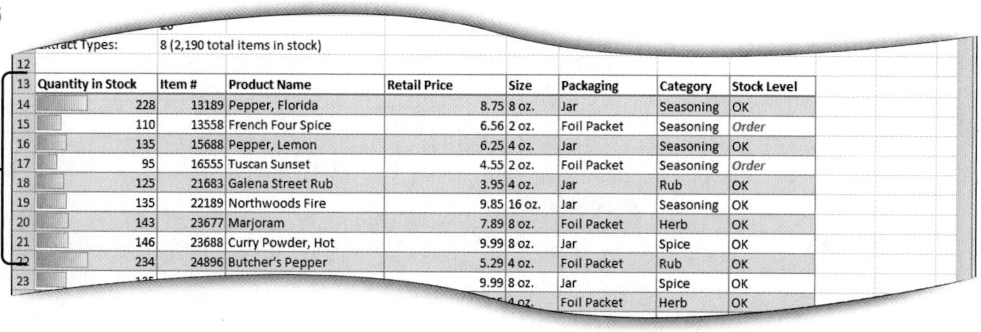

...ract Types: 8 (2,190 total items in stock)

Quantity in Stock	Item #	Product Name	Retail Price	Size	Packaging	Category	Stock Level
228	13189	Pepper, Florida	8.75	8 oz.	Jar	Seasoning	OK
110	13558	French Four Spice	6.56	2 oz.	Foil Packet	Seasoning	Order
135	15688	Pepper, Lemon	6.25	4 oz.	Jar	Seasoning	OK
95	16555	Tuscan Sunset	4.55	2 oz.	Foil Packet	Seasoning	Order
125	21683	Galena Street Rub	3.95	4 oz.	Jar	Rub	OK
135	22189	Northwoods Fire	9.85	16 oz.	Jar	Seasoning	OK
143	23677	Marjoram	7.89	8 oz.	Foil Packet	Herb	OK
146	23688	Curry Powder, Hot	9.99	8 oz.	Jar	Spice	OK
234	24896	Butcher's Pepper	5.29	4 oz.	Foil Packet	Rub	OK
			9.99	8 oz.	Jar	Spice	OK
				4 oz.	Foil Packet	Herb	OK

Table converted to a normal range, color and shading formats remain

Objective 6 | Format and Print a Large Worksheet

A worksheet might be too wide, too long—or both—to print on a single page. Use Excel's ***Print Titles*** and ***Scale to Fit*** commands to create pages that are attractive and easy to read.

The Print Titles command enables you to specify rows and columns to repeat on each printed page. Scale to Fit commands enable you to stretch or shrink the width, height, or both, of printed output to fit a maximum number of pages.

Activity 8.15 | Printing Titles and Scaling to Fit

1 Press Ctrl + Home to display the top of your worksheet. Select the range **A13:H13**. On the **Home tab**, from the **Styles group**, apply the **Heading 4** cell style, and then apply **Center**.

2 On the **Insert tab**, in the **Text group**, click **Header & Footer**. In the **Navigation group**, click the **Go to Footer** button, and then click just above the word *Footer*.

3 In the **Header & Footer Elements group**, click the **File Name** button to add the name of your file to the footer—*&[File]* displays. Then, click in a cell just above the footer to exit the Footer and view your file name.

4 Delete the unused sheets **Sheet2** and **Sheet3**. On the right edge of the status bar, click the **Normal** button, and then press Ctrl + Home to display the top of your worksheet.

Dotted lines indicate where the pages would break if printed as currently formatted; these dotted lines display when you switch from Page Layout view to Normal view.

5 On the **Page Layout tab**, in the **Themes group**, click the **Themes** button, and then click **Concourse**.

6 In the **Page Setup group**, click **Margins**, and then at the bottom, click **Custom Margins**. In the **Page Setup** dialog box, under **Center on page**, select the **Horizontally** check box, and then click **OK**.

7 In the **Page Setup group**, click **Orientation**, and then click **Landscape**. Press Ctrl + F2 to display the **Print Preview**. At the bottom of the **Print Preview**, click the **Next Page** button ▶. Compare your screen with Figure 8.27.

As currently formatted, the worksheet will print on five pages, and the columns will span multiple pages. Additionally, after Page 1, no column titles are visible to identify the data in the columns.

Figure 8.27

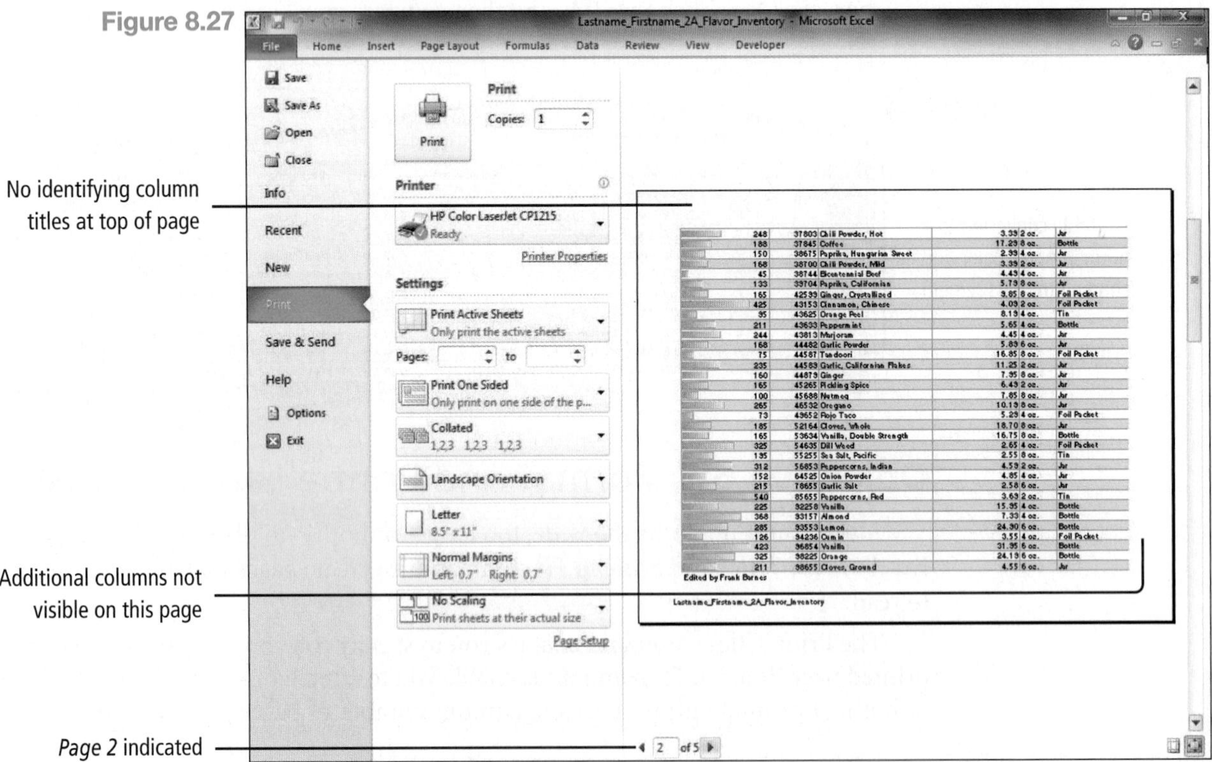

8 Click **Next Page** [▶] two times to display **Page 4**, and notice that two columns move to an additional page.

9 On the Ribbon, click **Page Layout** to redisplay the worksheet. In the **Page Setup group**, click the **Print Titles** button. Under **Print titles**, click in the **Rows to repeat at top** box, and then at the right, click the **Collapse Dialog** button [icon].

10 From the **row heading area**, select **row 13**, and then click the **Expand Dialog** button [icon]. Click **OK** to print the column titles in row 13 at the top of every page.

Adding the titles on each page increases the number of pages to 6.

> **Another Way**
>
> With the worksheet displayed, on the Page Layout tab, in the Scale to Fit group, click the Width button arrow, and then click 1 page.

11 Press Ctrl + F2 to display the **Print Preview**. In the center panel, at the bottom of the **Settings group**, click the **Scaling** button, and then on the displayed list, point to **Fit All Columns on One Page**. Compare your screen with Figure 8.28.

This action will shrink the width of the printed output to fit all the columns on one page. You can make adjustments like this on the Page Layout tab, or here, in the Print Preview.

Figure 8.28

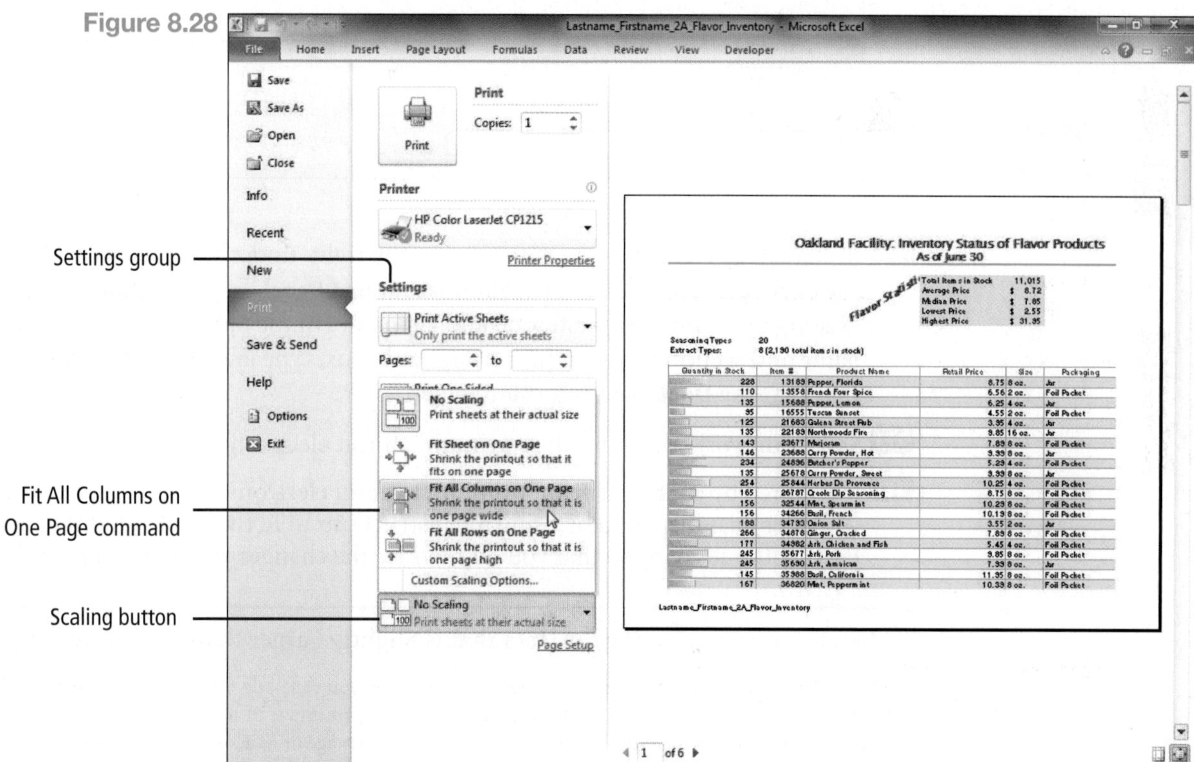

12 Click **Fit All Columns on One Page**. Notice in the **Print Preview** that all the columns display on one page.

13 At the bottom of the **Print Preview**, click the **Next Page** button [▶] one time. Notice that the output will now print on two pages and that the column titles display at the top of **Page 2**. Compare your screen with Figure 8.29.

Figure 8.29

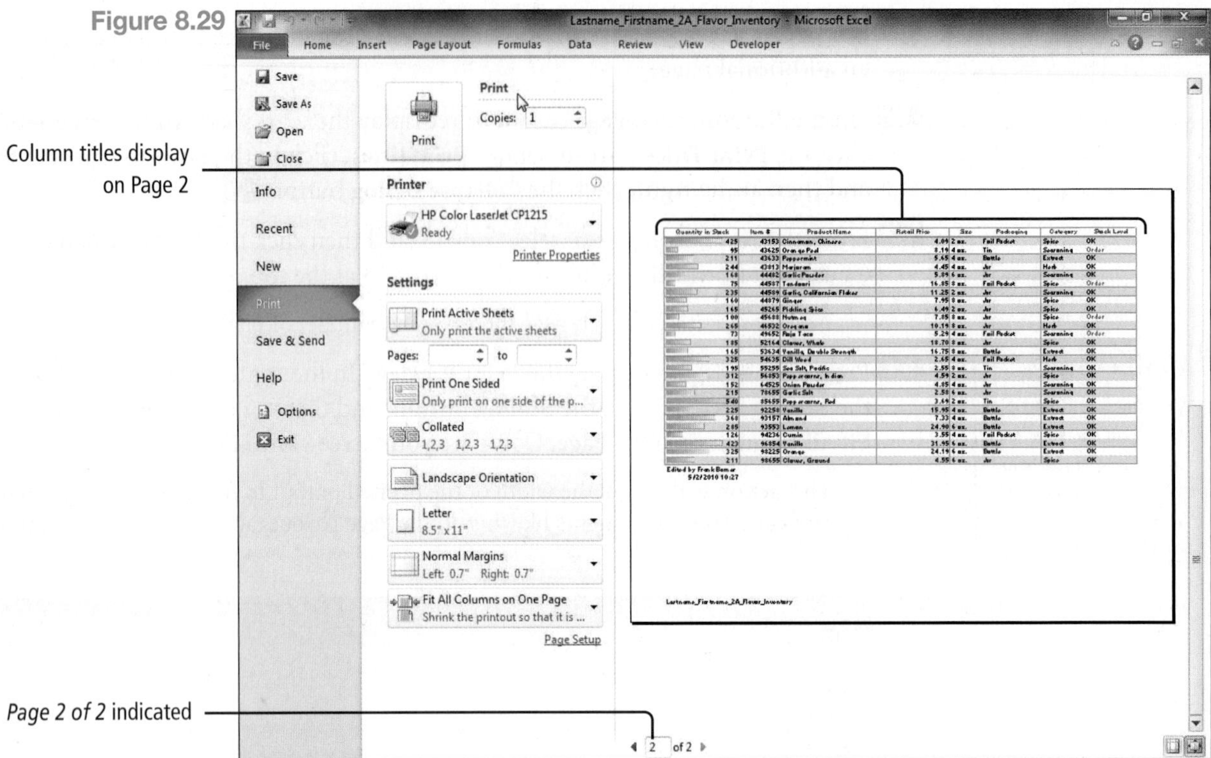

14 In **Backstage** view, click the **Info tab**. On the right, under the document thumbnail, click **Properties**, and then click **Show Document Panel**. In the **Author** box, replace the existing text with your firstname and lastname. In the **Subject** box, type your course name and section number. In the **Keywords** box, type **inventory, Oakland** and then **Close** [×] the **Document Information Panel**.

15 **Save** your workbook, and then print or submit electronically as directed.

16 If required by your instructor, print or create an electronic version of your worksheets with formulas displayed by using the instructions in Activity 1.16, and then **Close** [×] Excel without saving so that you do not save the changes you made to print formulas.

More Knowledge | Scaling for Data that is Slightly Larger than the Printed Page

If your data is just a little too large to fit on a printed page, you can scale the worksheet to make it fit. Scaling reduces both the width and height of the printed data to a percentage of its original size or by the number of pages that you specify. To adjust the printed output to a percentage of its actual size, for example to 80%, on the Page Layout tab, in the Scale to Fit group, click the Scale arrows to select a percentage.

End You have completed Project 8A

Project 8B Weekly Sales Summary

Project Activities

In Activities 8.16 through 8.26, you will edit an existing workbook for Laura Morales. The workbook summarizes the online and in-store sales of products during a one-week period in July. The worksheets of your completed workbook will look similar to Figure 8.30.

Project Files

For Project 8B, you will need the following file:

e02B_Weekly_Sales

You will save your workbook as:

Lastname_Firstname_2B_Weekly_Sales

Project Results

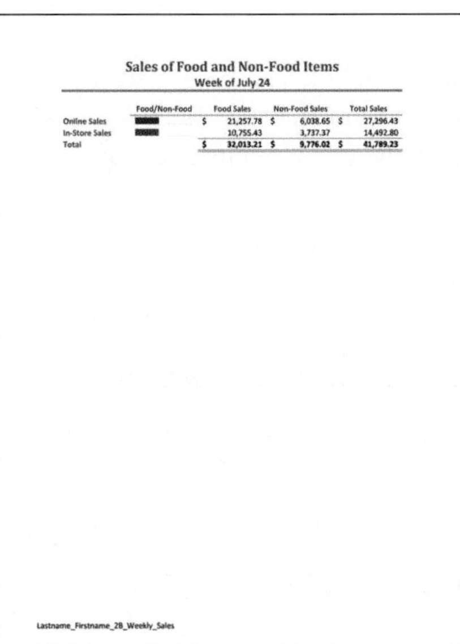

Sales of Food and Non-Food Items

Week of July 24

	Food/Non-Food	Food Sales	Non-Food Sales	Total Sales
Online Sales		$ 21,257.78	$ 6,038.65	$ 27,296.43
In-Store Sales		10,755.43	3,737.37	14,492.80
Total		$ 32,013.21	$ 9,776.02	$ 41,789.23

Lastname_Firstname_2B_Weekly_Sales

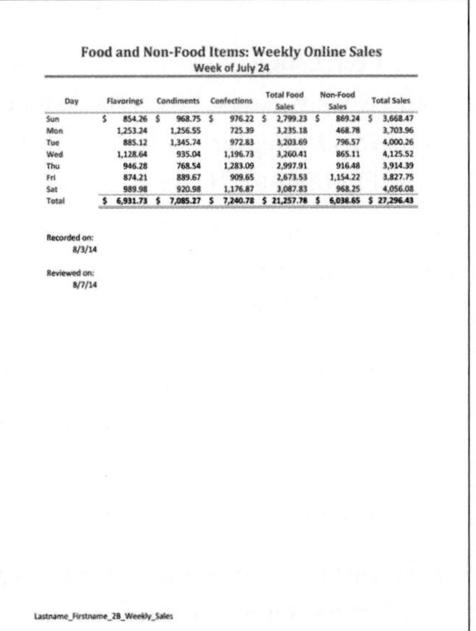

Food and Non-Food Items: Weekly Online Sales

Week of July 24

Day	Flavorings	Condiments	Confections	Total Food Sales	Non-Food Sales	Total Sales
Sun	$ 854.26	$ 968.75	$ 976.22	$ 2,799.23	$ 869.24	$ 3,668.47
Mon	1,253.24	1,256.55	725.39	3,235.18	468.78	3,703.96
Tue	885.12	1,345.74	972.83	3,203.69	796.57	4,000.26
Wed	1,128.64	935.04	1,196.73	3,260.41	865.11	4,125.52
Thu	946.28	768.54	1,283.09	2,997.91	916.48	3,914.39
Fri	874.21	889.67	909.65	2,673.53	1,154.22	3,827.75
Sat	989.98	920.98	1,176.87	3,087.83	968.25	4,056.08
Total	$ 6,931.73	$ 7,085.27	$ 7,240.78	$ 21,257.78	$ 6,038.65	$ 27,296.43

Recorded on:
8/3/14

Reviewed on:
8/7/14

Lastname_Firstname_2B_Weekly_Sales

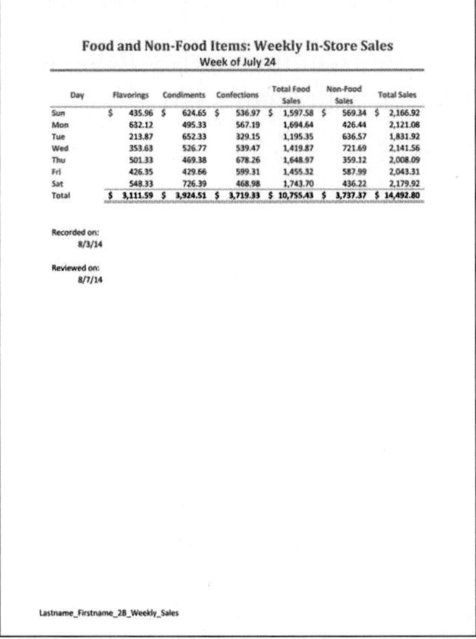

Food and Non-Food Items: Weekly In-Store Sales

Week of July 24

Day	Flavorings	Condiments	Confections	Total Food Sales	Non-Food Sales	Total Sales
Sun	$ 435.96	$ 624.65	$ 536.97	$ 1,597.58	$ 569.34	$ 2,166.92
Mon	632.12	495.33	567.19	1,694.64	426.44	2,121.08
Tue	213.87	652.33	329.15	1,195.35	636.57	1,831.92
Wed	353.63	526.77	539.47	1,419.87	721.69	2,141.56
Thu	501.33	469.38	678.26	1,648.97	359.12	2,008.09
Fri	426.35	429.66	599.31	1,455.32	587.99	2,043.31
Sat	548.33	726.39	468.98	1,743.70	436.22	2,179.92
Total	$ 3,111.59	$ 3,924.51	$ 3,719.33	$ 10,755.43	$ 3,737.37	$ 14,492.80

Recorded on:
8/3/14

Reviewed on:
8/7/14

Lastname_Firstname_2B_Weekly_Sales

Figure 8.30
Project 8B Weekly Sales

Objective 7 | Navigate a Workbook and Rename Worksheets

Use multiple worksheets in a workbook to organize data in a logical arrangement. When you have more than one worksheet in a workbook, you can ***navigate*** (move) among worksheets by clicking the ***sheet tabs***. Sheet tabs identify each worksheet in a workbook and are located along the lower left edge of the workbook window. When you have more worksheets in the workbook than can be displayed in the sheet tab area, use the four sheet tab scrolling buttons to move sheet tabs into and out of view.

Activity 8.16 | Navigating Among Worksheets, Renaming Worksheets, and Changing the Tab Color of Worksheets

Excel names the first worksheet in a workbook *Sheet1* and each additional worksheet in order—*Sheet2*, *Sheet3*, and so on. Most Excel users rename the worksheets with meaningful names. In this activity, you will navigate among worksheets, rename worksheets, and change the tab color of sheet tabs.

> **Another Way**
>
> Press Ctrl + F12 to display the Open dialog box. Press F12 to display the Save As dialog box.

1. **Start** Excel. From **Backstage** view, display the **Open** dialog box. From your student files, open **e02B_Weekly_Sales**. From **Backstage** view, display the **Save As** dialog box, navigate to your **Excel Chapter 2** folder, and then using your own name, save the file as **Lastname_Firstname_2B_Weekly_Sales**

   In the displayed workbook, there are two worksheets into which some data has already been entered. For example, on the first worksheet, the days of the week and sales data for the one-week period displays.

2. Along the bottom of the Excel window, point to and then click the **Sheet2 tab**.

   The second worksheet in the workbook displays and becomes the active worksheet. *Sheet2* displays in bold.

3. In cell **A1**, notice the text *In-Store*—this worksheet will contain data for in-store sales.

4. Click the **Sheet1 tab**. Then, point to the **Sheet1 tab**, and double-click to select the sheet tab name. Type **Online Sales** and press Enter.

   The first worksheet becomes the active worksheet, and the sheet tab displays *Online Sales*.

5. Point to the **Sheet2 tab**, right-click, and then from the shortcut menu, click **Rename**. Type **In-Store Sales** and press Enter. Compare your screen with Figure 8.31.

   You can use either of these methods to rename a sheet tab.

Figure 8.31

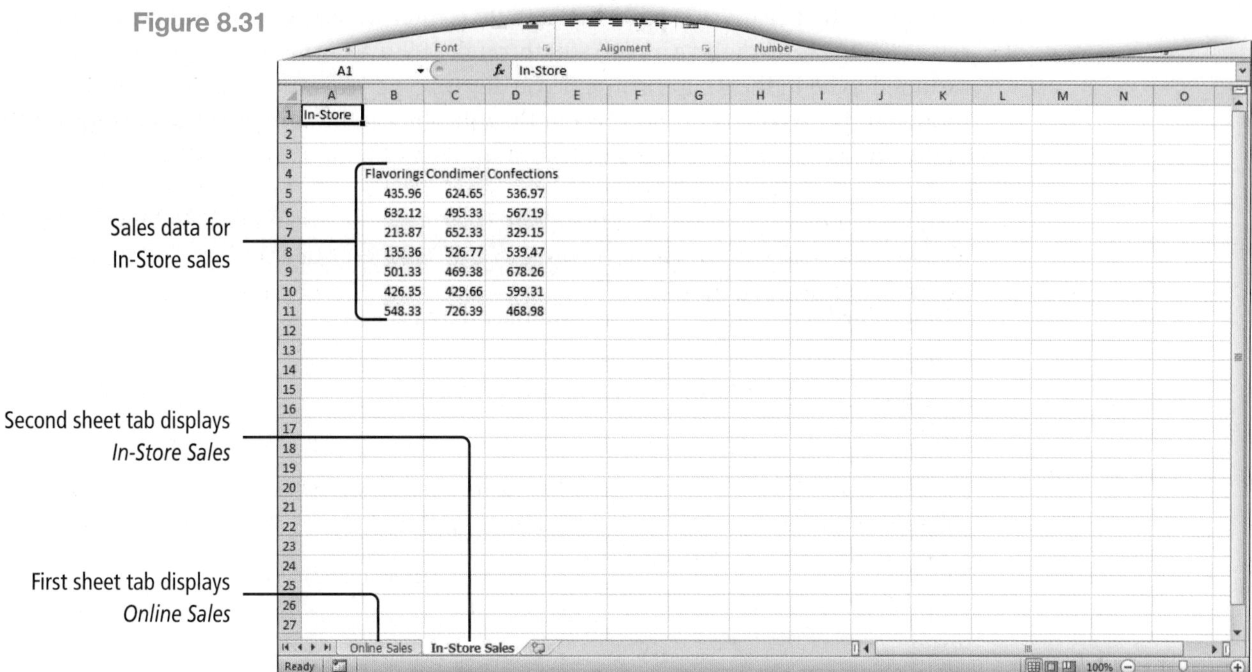

> **Another Way**
> Alternatively, on the Home tab, in the Cells group, click the Format button, and then on the displayed list, point to Tab Color.

6. Point to the **In-Store Sales sheet tab** and right-click. On the shortcut menu, point to **Tab Color**, and then in the last column, click the first color—**Orange, Accent 6**.

7. Using the technique you just practiced, change the tab color of the **Online Sales sheet tab** to **Aqua, Accent 5**—in the next to last column, the first color. **Save** your workbook.

Objective 8 | Enter Dates, Clear Contents, and Clear Formats

Dates represent a type of value that you can enter in a cell. When you enter a date, Excel assigns a serial value—a number—to the date. This makes it possible to treat dates like other numbers. For example, if two cells contain dates, you can find the number of days between the two dates by subtracting the older date from the more recent date.

Activity 8.17 | Entering and Formatting Dates

In this activity, you will examine the various ways that Excel can format dates in a cell. Date values entered in any of the following formats will be recognized by Excel as a date:

Format	Example
m/d/yy	7/4/12
d-mmm	4-Jul
d-mmm-yy	4-Jul-12
mmm-yy	Jul-12

On your keyboard, - (the hyphen key) and / (the forward slash key) function identically in any of these formats and can be used interchangeably. You can abbreviate the month name to three characters or spell it out. You can enter the year as two digits, four digits, or even leave it off. When left off, the current year is assumed but does not display in the cell.

A two-digit year value of 30 through 99 is interpreted by the Windows operating system as the four-digit years of 1930 through 1999. All other two-digit year values are assumed to be in the 21st century. If you always type year values as four digits, even though only two digits may display in the cell, you can be sure that Excel interprets the year value as you intended. Examples are shown in Figure 8.32.

How Excel Interprets Dates	
Date Typed As:	**Completed by Excel As:**
7/4/12	7/4/2012
7-4-98	7/4/1998
7/4	4-Jul (current year assumed)
7-4	4-Jul (current year assumed)
July 4	4-Jul (current year assumed)
Jul 4	4-Jul (current year assumed)
Jul/4	4-Jul (current year assumed)
Jul-4	4-Jul (current year assumed)
July 4, 1998	4-Jul-98
July 2012	Jul-12 (first day of month assumed)
July 1998	Jul-98 (first day of month assumed)

Figure 8.32

1. On the **Online Sales** sheet, click cell **A16** and notice that the cell indicates *8/3* (August 3). In the **Formula Bar**, notice that the full date of August 3, 2014 displays in the format *8/3/2014*.

2. With cell **A16** selected, on the **Home tab**, in the **Number group**, click the **Number Format arrow**. At the bottom of the menu, click **More Number Formats** to display the **Number tab** of the **Format Cells** dialog box.

   Under Category, *Date* is selected, and under Type, *3/14* is selected. Cell A16 uses this format type; that is, only the month and day display in the cell.

3. In the displayed dialog box, under **Type**, click several other date types and watch the **Sample** area to see how applying the selected date format would format your cell. When you are finished, click the **3/14/01** type, and then compare your screen with Figure 8.33.

Figure 8.33

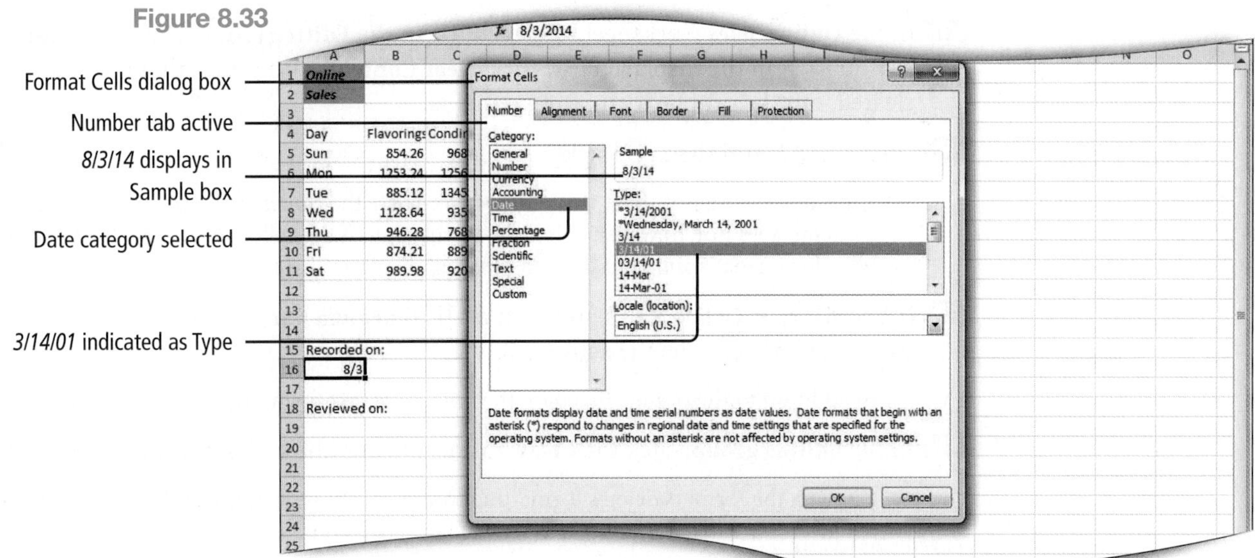

4 At the bottom of the dialog box, click **OK**. Click cell **A19**, type **8-7-14** and then press Enter.

Cell A19 has no special date formatting applied, and thus displays in the default date format *8/7/2014*.

> **Alert! | The Date Does Not Display as 8/7/2014?**
>
> Settings in your Windows operating system determine the default format for dates. If your result is different, it is likely that the formatting of the default date was adjusted on the computer at which you are working.

5 Click cell **A19** again. Hold down Ctrl and press ; (semicolon) on your keyboard. Press Enter to confirm the entry.

Excel enters the current date, obtained from your computer's internal calendar, in the selected cell using the default date format. Ctrl + ; is a quick method to enter the current date.

6 Click cell **A19** again, type **8/7/14** and then press Enter.

Because the year *14* is less than 30, Excel assumes a 21st century date and changes *14* to *2014* to complete the four-digit year. Typing *98* would result in *1998*. For two-digit years that you type that are between 30 and 99, Excel assumes a 20th century date.

7 Click cell **A16**, and then on the **Home tab**, in the **Clipboard group**, click the **Format Painter** button. Click cell **A19**, and notice that the date format from cell **A16** is copied to cell **A19**. **Save** your workbook.

Activity 8.18 | Clearing Cell Contents and Formats

A cell has *contents*—a value or a formula—and a cell may also have one or more *formats* applied, for example bold and italic font styles, fill color, font color, and so on. You can choose to clear—delete—the *contents* of a cell, the *formatting* of a cell, or both.

Clearing the contents of a cell deletes the value or formula typed there, but it does *not* clear formatting applied to a cell. In this activity, you will clear the contents of a cell and then clear the formatting of a cell that contains a date to see its underlying content.

1. In the **Online Sales** worksheet, click cell **A1**. In the **Editing group**, click the **Clear** button. On the displayed list, click **Clear Contents** and notice that the text is cleared, but the orange formatting remains.

2. Click cell **A2**, and then press Del.

   You can use either of these two methods to delete the *contents* of a cell. Deleting the contents does not, however, delete the formatting of the cell; you can see that the orange fill color format applied to the two cells still displays.

3. In cell **A1**, type **Online Sales** and then on the **Formula Bar**, click the **Enter** button so that cell **A1** remains the active cell.

   In addition to the orange fill color, the bold italic text formatting remains with the cell.

4. In the **Editing group**, click the **Clear** button, and then click **Clear Formats.**

   Clearing the formats deletes formatting from the cell—the orange fill color and the bold and italic font styles—but does not delete the cell's contents.

5. Use the same technique to clear the orange fill color from cell **A2**. Click cell **A16**, click the **Clear** button, and then click **Clear Formats**. In the **Number group**, notice that *General* displays as the number format of the cell.

   The box in the Number group indicates the current Number format of the selected cell. Clearing the date formatting from the cell displays the date's serial number. The date, August 3, 2014, is stored as a serial number that indicates the number of days since January 1, 1900. This date is the 41,854th day since the reference date of January 1, 1900.

6. On the Quick Access Toolbar, click the **Undo** button to restore the date format. **Save** your workbook, and then compare your screen with Figure 8.34.

Figure 8.34

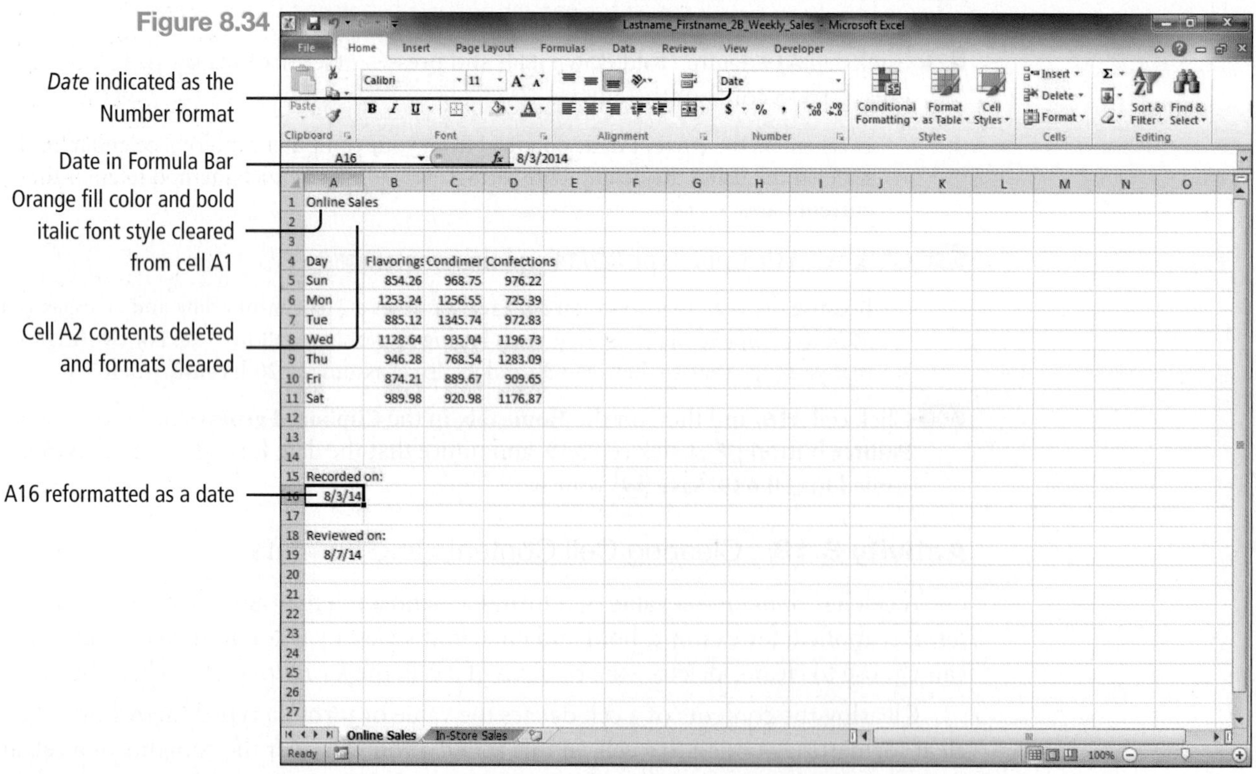

Objective 9 | Copy and Paste by Using the Paste Options Gallery

Data in cells can be copied to other cells in the same worksheet, to other sheets in the same workbook, or to sheets in another workbook. The action of placing cell contents that have been copied or moved to the Office Clipboard into another location is called ***paste***.

Activity 8.19 | Copying and Pasting by Using the Paste Options Gallery

Recall that the Office Clipboard is a temporary storage area maintained by your Windows operating system. When you select one or more cells, and then perform the Copy command or the Cut command, the selected data is placed on the Office Clipboard. From the Office Clipboard storage area, the data is available for pasting into other cells, other worksheets, other workbooks, and even into other Office programs. When you paste, the ***Paste Options gallery*** displays, which includes Live Preview to preview the Paste formatting that you want.

1 With the **Online Sales** worksheet active, select the range **A4:A19**.

A range of cells identical to this one is required for the *In-Store Sales* worksheet.

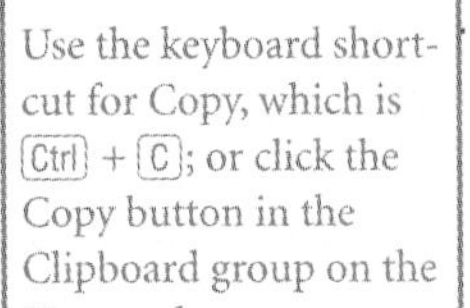

Another Way

Use the keyboard shortcut for Copy, which is Ctrl + C; or click the Copy button in the Clipboard group on the Home tab.

2 Right-click over the selection, and then click **Copy** to place a copy of the cells on the Office Clipboard. Notice that the copied cells display a moving border.

3 At the bottom of the workbook window, click the **In-Store Sales sheet tab** to make it the active worksheet. Point to cell **A4**, right-click, and then on the shortcut menu, under **Paste Options**, *point* to the first button—**Paste**. Compare your screen with Figure 8.35.

Live Preview displays how the copied cells will be placed in the worksheet if you click the Paste button. In this manner, you can experiment with different paste options, and then be sure you are selecting the paste operation that you want. When pasting a range of cells, you need only point to or select the cell in the upper left corner of the ***paste area***—the target destination for data that has been cut or copied using the Office Clipboard.

Figure 8.35

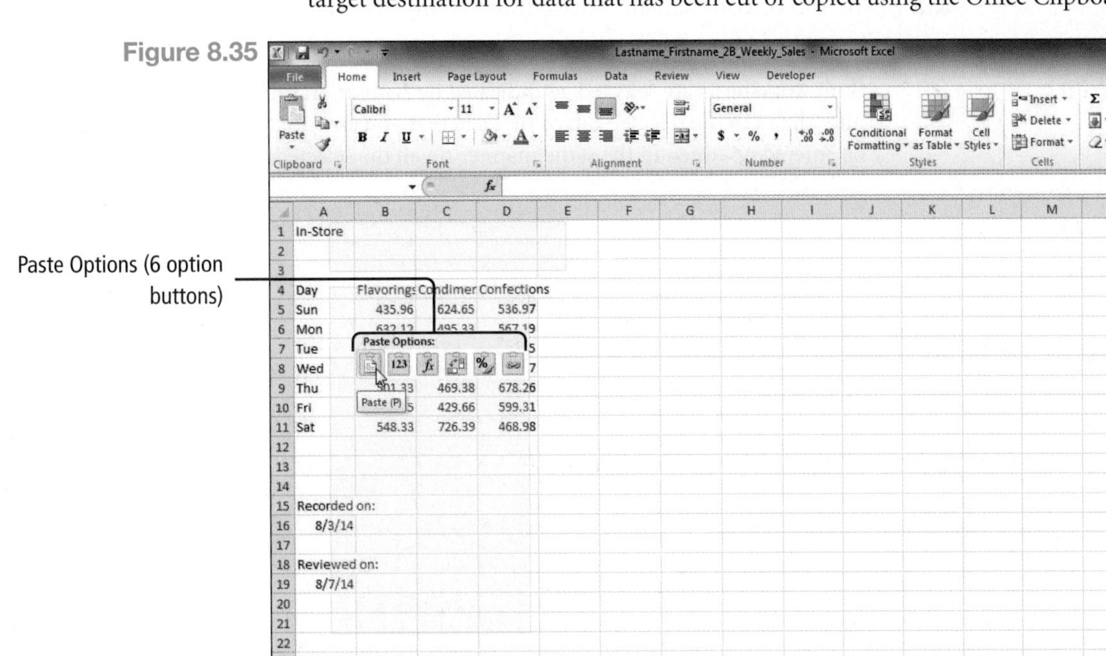

Another Way

Use the keyboard shortcut for Paste, which is Ctrl + V; or click the Paste button in the Clipboard group on the Home tab.

4 Click the first button, **Paste**. In the status bar, notice that the message still displays, indicating that your selected range remains available on the Office Clipboard.

5 Display the **Online Sales** worksheet. Press Esc to cancel the moving border. **Save** your workbook.

The status bar no longer displays the message.

Note | Pressing Enter to Complete a Paste Action

If you want to paste the same text more than one time, click the Paste button so that the copied text remains available on the Office Clipboard. Otherwise, you can press Enter to complete the Paste command.

Objective 10 | Edit and Format Multiple Worksheets at the Same Time

You can enter or edit data on several worksheets at the same time by selecting and grouping multiple worksheets. Data that you enter or edit on the active sheet is reflected in all selected sheets. If you apply color to the sheet tabs, the name of the sheet tab will be underlined in the color you selected. If the sheet tab displays with a background color, you know the sheet is not selected.

Activity 8.20 | Grouping Worksheets for Editing

In this activity, you will group the two worksheets, and then format both worksheets at the same time.

1 With the **Online Sales** sheet active, press Ctrl + Home to make cell **A1** the active cell. Point to the **Online Sales sheet tab**, right-click, and then from the shortcut menu, click **Select All Sheets**.

2 At the top of your screen, notice that *[Group]* displays in the title bar. Compare your screen with Figure 8.36.

Both worksheets are selected, as indicated by *[Group]* in the title bar and the sheet tab names underlined in the selected tab color. Data that you enter or edit on the active sheet will also be entered or edited in the same manner on all the selected sheets in the same cells.

Figure 8.36

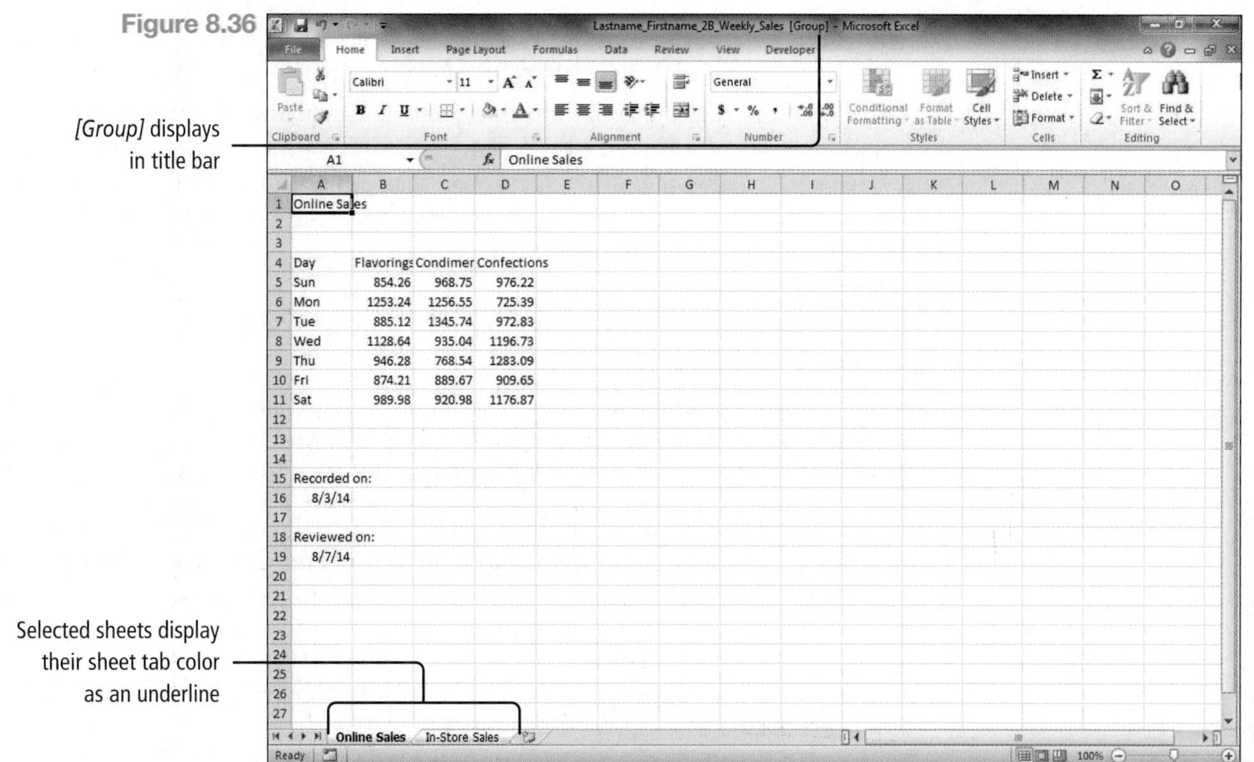

3 Select **columns A:G**, and then set their width to **85 pixels**.

4 Click cell **A2**, type **Week of July 24** and then on the **Formula Bar**, click the **Enter** button to keep cell **A2** as the active cell. **Merge & Center** the text across the range **A2:G2**, and then apply the **Heading 1** cell style.

5 Click cell **E4**, type **Total Food Sales** and then press Tab. In cell **F4**, type **Non-Food Sales** and then press Tab. In cell **G4**, type **Total Sales** and then press Enter.

6 Select the range **A4:G4**, and then apply the **Heading 3** cell style. In the **Alignment group**, click the **Center**, **Middle Align**, and **Wrap Text** buttons. **Save** your workbook.

Another Way

Right-click any sheet tab, and then click Ungroup Sheets.

7 Display the **In-Store Sales** worksheet to cancel the grouping, and then compare your screen with Figure 8.37.

As soon as you select a single sheet, the grouping of the sheets is canceled and *[Group]* no longer displays in the title bar. Because the sheets were grouped, the same new text and formatting was applied to both sheets. In this manner, you can make the same changes to all the sheets in a workbook at one time.

Figure 8.37

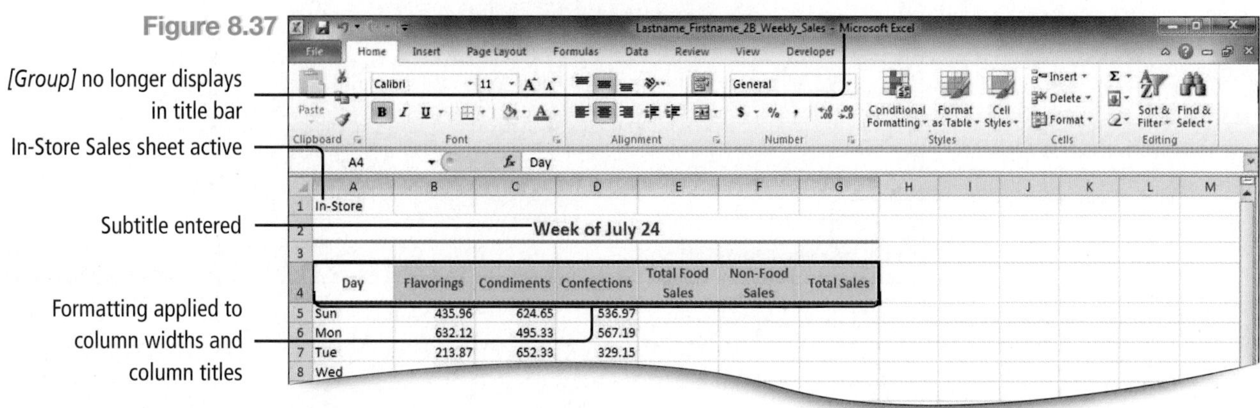

Activity 8.21 | Formatting and Constructing Formulas on Grouped Worksheets

Recall that formulas are equations that perform calculations on values in your worksheet and that a formula starts with an equal sign (=). Operators are the symbols with which you specify the type of calculation that you want to perform on the elements of a formula. In this activity, you will enter sales figures for Non-Food items from both Online and In-Store sales, and then calculate the total sales.

1. Display the **Online Sales** worksheet. Verify that the sheets are not grouped—*[Group]* does *not* display in the title bar.

2. Click cell **A1**, type **Food and Non-Food Items: Weekly Online Sales** and then on the **Formula Bar**, click the **Enter** button to keep cell **A1** as the active cell. **Merge & Center** the text across the range **A1:G1**, and then apply the **Title** cell style.

3. In the column titled *Non-Food Sales*, click cell **F5**, in the range **F5:F11**, type the following data for Non-Food Sales, and then compare your screen with Figure 8.38.

	Non-Food Sales
Sun	**869.24**
Mon	**468.78**
Tue	**796.57**
Wed	**865.11**
Thu	**916.48**
Fri	**1154.22**
Sat	**968.25**

Figure 8.38

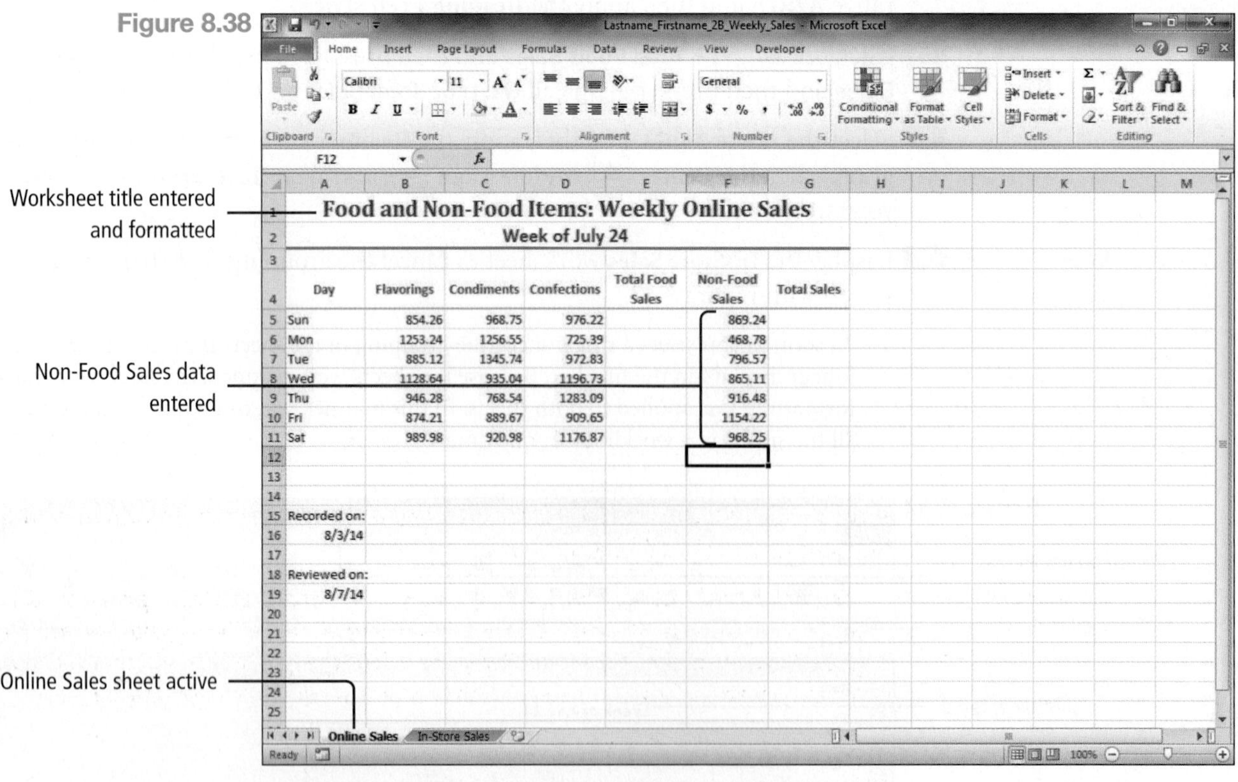

4 Display the **In-Store Sales** sheet. In cell **A1**, replace *In-Store* by typing **Food and Non-Food Items: Weekly In-Store Sales** and then on the **Formula Bar**, click the **Enter** button to keep cell **A1** as the active cell. **Merge & Center** the text across the range **A1:G1**, and then apply the **Title** cell style.

5 In the column titled *Non-Food Sales*, click cell **F5**, in the range **F5:F11**, type the following data for Non-Food Sales, and then compare your screen with Figure 8.39.

	Non-Food Sales
Sun	**569.34**
Mon	**426.44**
Tue	**636.57**
Wed	**721.69**
Thu	**359.12**
Fri	**587.99**
Sat	**436.22**

Figure 8.39

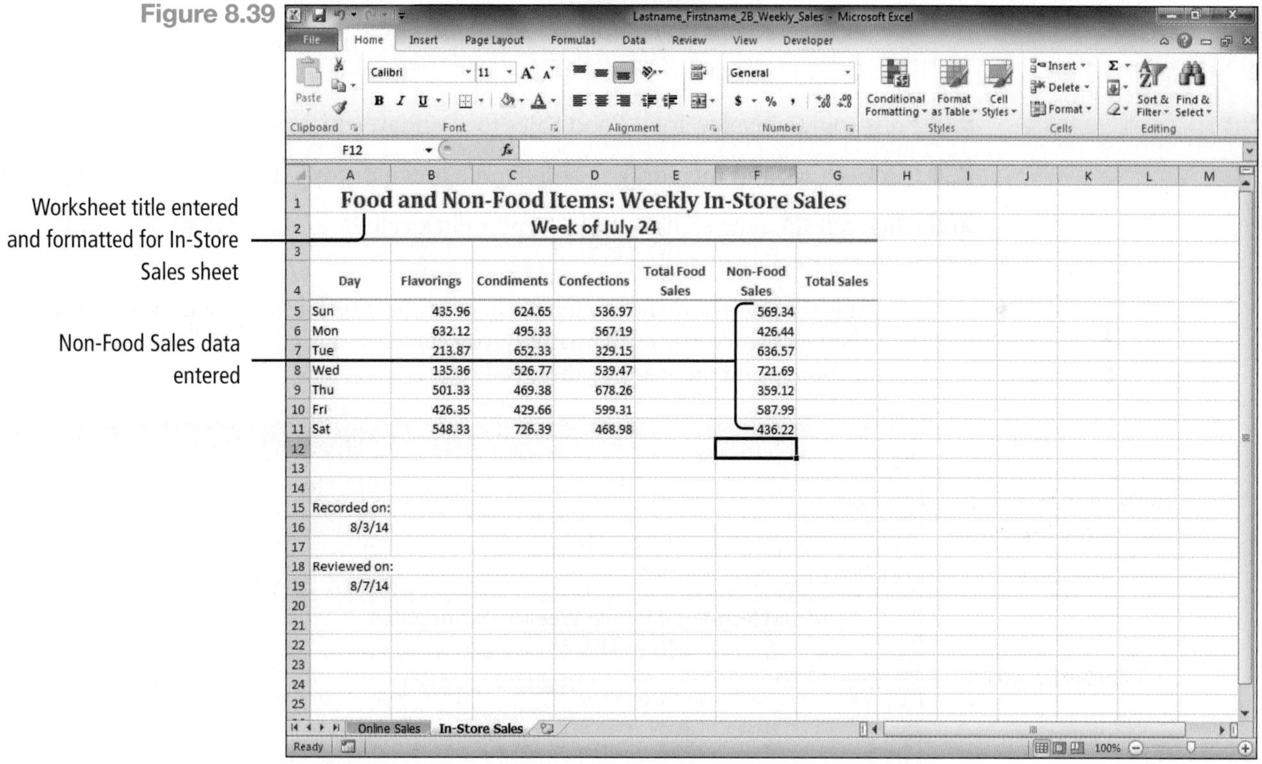

Worksheet title entered and formatted for In-Store Sales sheet

Non-Food Sales data entered

6 **Save** your workbook. Right-click the **Online Sales sheet tab**, and then from the shortcut menu, click **Select All Sheets**.

The first worksheet becomes the active sheet, and the worksheets are grouped. *[Group]* displays in the title bar, and the sheet tabs are underlined in the tab color to indicate they are selected as part of the group. Recall that when grouped, any action that you perform on the active worksheet is *also* performed on any other selected worksheets.

7 With the sheets *grouped* and the **Online Sales** sheet active, click cell **E5**. On the **Home tab**, in the **Editing group**, click the **Sum** button [Σ]. Compare your screen with Figure 8.40.

Recall that when you enter the SUM function, Excel looks first above and then left for a proposed range of cells to sum.

Figure 8.40

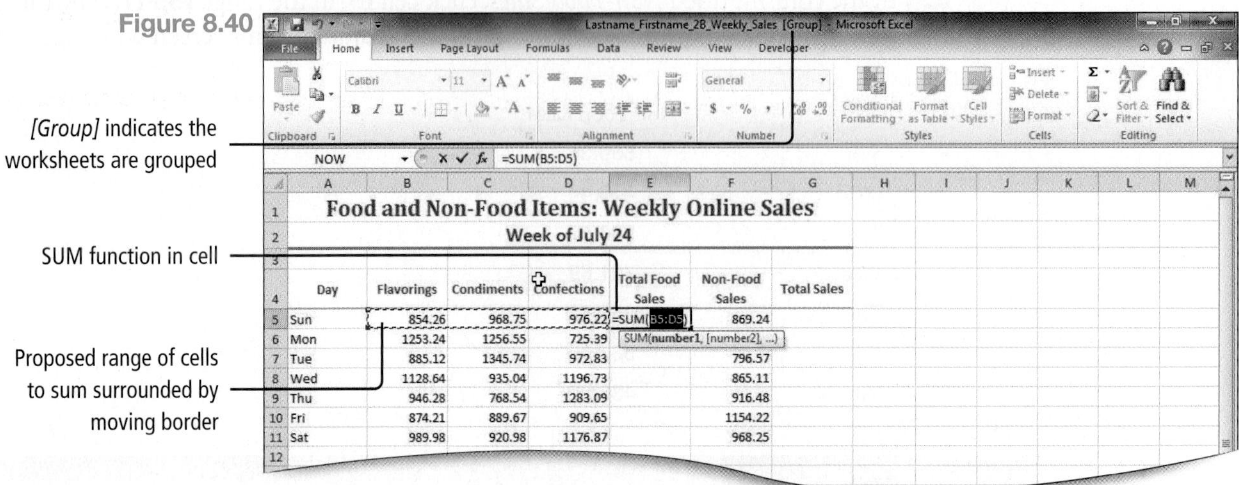

8 Press Enter to display Total Food Sales for Sunday, which is *2799.23*.

9 Click cell **E5**, and then drag the fill handle down to copy the formula through cell **E11**.

10 Click cell **G5**, type **=** click cell **E5**, type **+** click cell **F5**, and then compare your screen with Figure 8.41.

Using the point-and-click technique to construct this formula is only one of several techniques you can use. Alternatively, you could use any other method to enter the SUM function to add the values in these two cells.

Figure 8.41

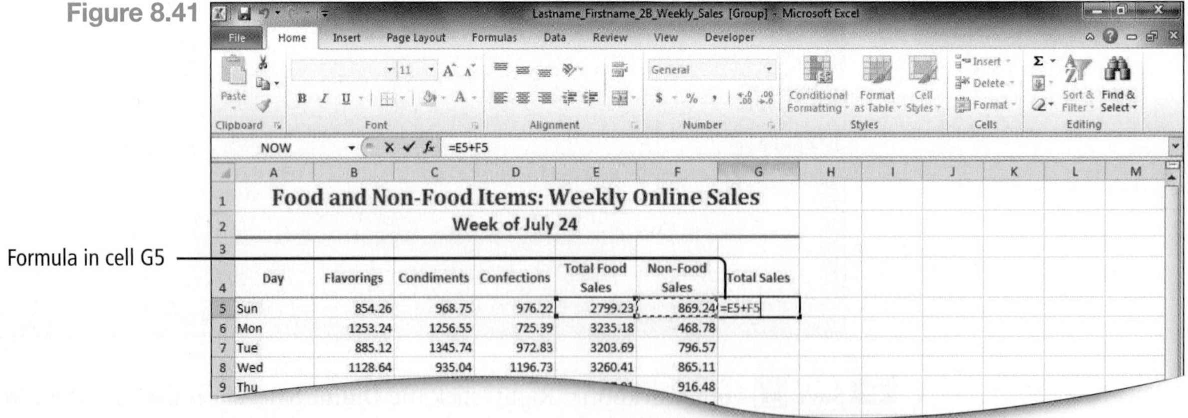

11 Press Enter to display the result *3668.47*, and then copy the formula down through cell **G11**.

12 In cell **A12**, type **Total** and then select the range **B5:G12**, which is all of the sales data and the empty cells at the bottom of each column of sales data.

13 With the range **B5:G12** selected, hold down Alt and press = to enter the **SUM** function in each empty cell.

Selecting a range in this manner will place the Sum function in the empty cells at the bottom of each column.

14 Select the range **A5:A12**, and then apply the **Heading 4** cell style.

15 To apply financial formatting to the worksheets, select the range **B5:G5**, hold down Ctrl, and then select the range **B12:G12**. With the nonadjacent ranges selected, apply the **Accounting Number Format** [$ ▾].

16 Select the range **B6:G11** and apply **Comma Style** [,]. Select the range **B12:G12** and apply the **Total** cell style.

17 Press Ctrl + Home to move to the top of the worksheet; compare your screen with Figure 8.42.

Figure 8.42

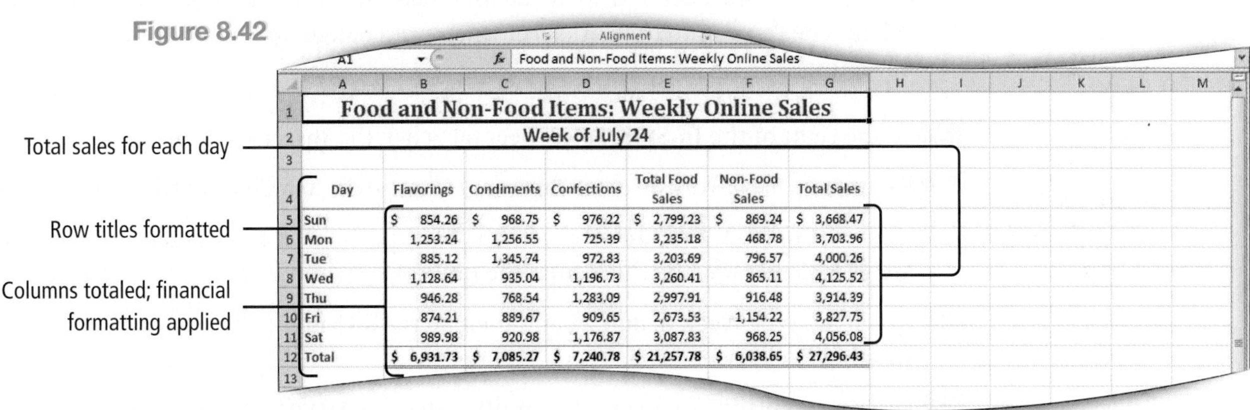

Day	Flavorings	Condiments	Confections	Total Food Sales	Non-Food Sales	Total Sales
Sun	$ 854.26	$ 968.75	$ 976.22	$ 2,799.23	$ 869.24	$ 3,668.47
Mon	1,253.24	1,256.55	725.39	3,235.18	468.78	3,703.96
Tue	885.12	1,345.74	972.83	3,203.69	796.57	4,000.26
Wed	1,128.64	935.04	1,196.73	3,260.41	865.11	4,125.52
Thu	946.28	768.54	1,283.09	2,997.91	916.48	3,914.39
Fri	874.21	889.67	909.65	2,673.53	1,154.22	3,827.75
Sat	989.98	920.98	1,176.87	3,087.83	968.25	4,056.08
Total	$ 6,931.73	$ 7,085.27	$ 7,240.78	$ 21,257.78	$ 6,038.65	$ 27,296.43

18 Click the **In-Store Sales sheet tab** to cancel the grouping and display the second worksheet. Click **Save**, and then compare your screen with Figure 8.43.

With your worksheets grouped, the calculations on the first worksheet were also performed on the second worksheet.

Figure 8.43

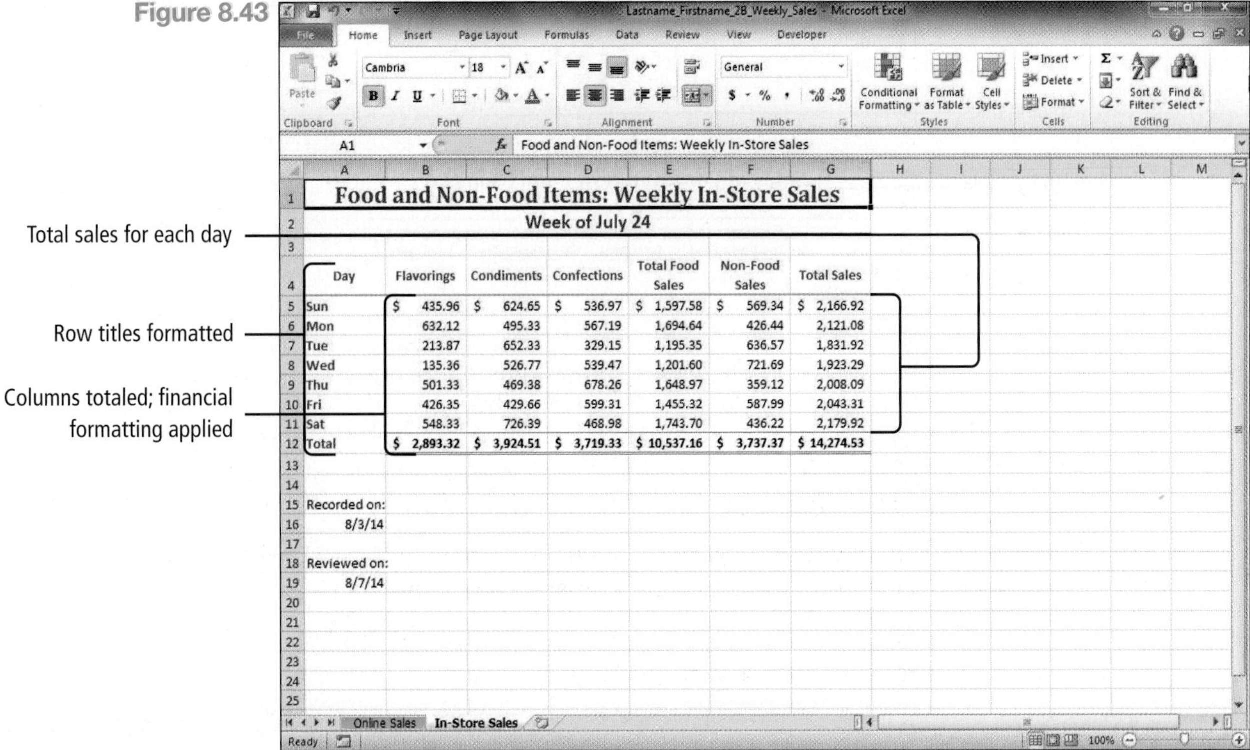

Day	Flavorings	Condiments	Confections	Total Food Sales	Non-Food Sales	Total Sales
Sun	$ 435.96	$ 624.65	$ 536.97	$ 1,597.58	$ 569.34	$ 2,166.92
Mon	632.12	495.33	567.19	1,694.64	426.44	2,121.08
Tue	213.87	652.33	329.15	1,195.35	636.57	1,831.92
Wed	135.36	526.77	539.47	1,201.60	721.69	1,923.29
Thu	501.33	469.38	678.26	1,648.97	359.12	2,008.09
Fri	426.35	429.66	599.31	1,455.32	587.99	2,043.31
Sat	548.33	726.39	468.98	1,743.70	436.22	2,179.92
Total	$ 2,893.32	$ 3,924.51	$ 3,719.33	$ 10,537.16	$ 3,737.37	$ 14,274.53

Objective 11 | Create a Summary Sheet with Column Sparklines

A ***summary sheet*** is a worksheet where totals from other worksheets are displayed and summarized. Recall that sparklines are tiny charts within a single cell that show a data trend.

Activity 8.22 | Constructing Formulas that Refer to Cells in Another Worksheet

In this activity, you will insert a new worksheet in which you will place the totals from the Online Sales worksheet and the In-Store Sales worksheet. You will construct formulas in the Summary worksheet to display the total sales for both online sales and in-store sales that will update the Summary worksheet whenever changes are made to the other worksheet totals.

1. To the right of the **In-Store Sales** sheet tab, click the **Insert Worksheet** button.
2. Rename the new worksheet tab **Summary** Change the **Tab Color** to **Olive Green, Accent 3**.
3. Widen **columns A:E** to **110** pixels. In cell **A1**, type **Sales of Food and Non-Food Items** **Merge & Center** the title across the range **A1:E1**, and then apply the **Title** cell style.
4. In cell **A2**, type **Week of July 24** and then **Merge & Center** across **A2:E2**; apply the **Heading 1** cell style.
5. Leave **row 3** blank. To form column titles, in cell **B4**, type **Food/Non-Food** and press Tab. In cell **C4**, type **Food Sales** and press Tab. In cell **D4**, type **Non-Food Sales** and press Tab. In cell **E5**, type **Total Sales** Press Enter. Select the range **B4:E4**. Apply the **Heading 3** cell style and **Center**.
6. To form row titles, in cell **A5**, type **Online Sales** In cell **A6**, type **In-Store Sales** and then compare your screen with Figure 8.44.

Figure 8.44

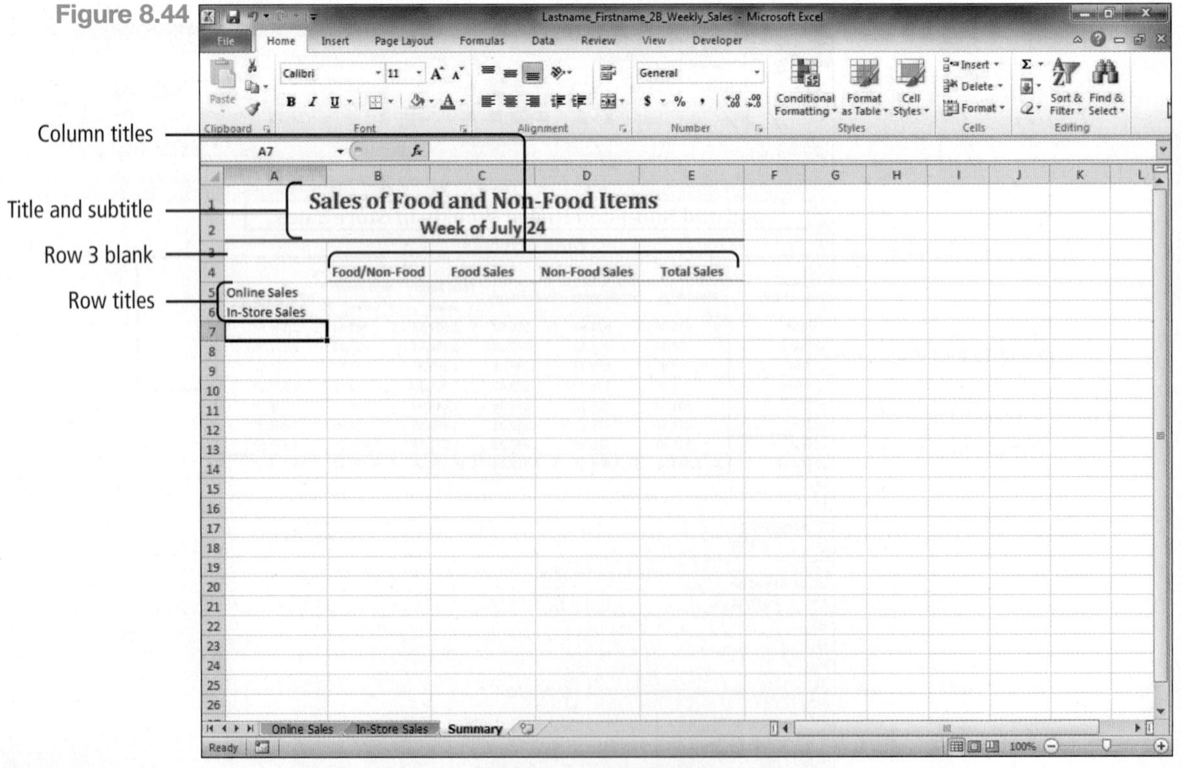

7 Click cell **C5**. Type = Click the **Online Sales sheet tab**. On the **Online Sales** worksheet, click cell **E12**, and then press Enter to redisplay the **Summary** worksheet and insert the total **Food Sales** amount of *$21,257.78*.

8 Click cell **C5** to select it again. Look at the **Formula Bar**, and notice that instead of a value, the cell contains a formula that is equal to the value in another cell in another worksheet. Compare your screen with Figure 8.45.

The value in this cell is equal to the value in cell E12 of the *Online Sales* worksheet. The Accounting Number Format applied to the referenced cell is carried over. By using a formula of this type, changes in cell E12 on the *Online Sales* worksheet will be automatically updated in this *Summary* worksheet.

Figure 8.45

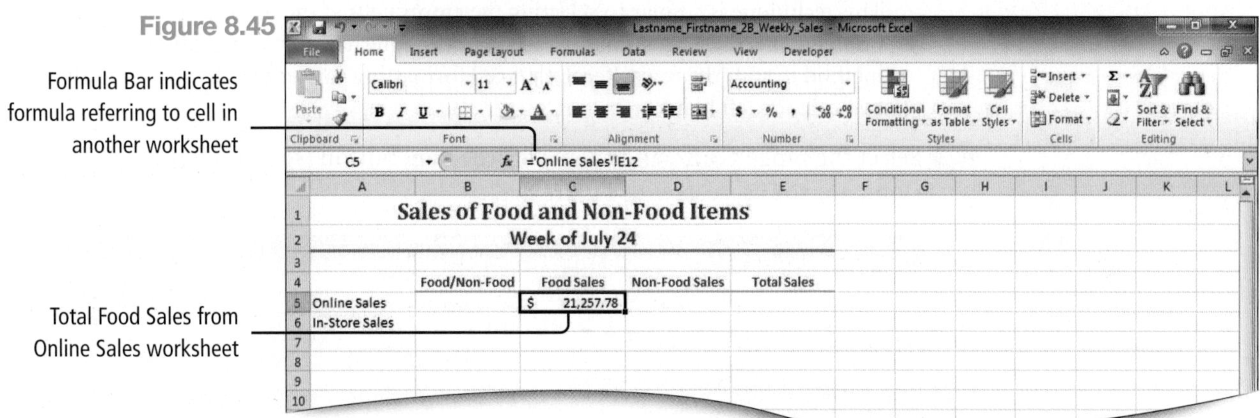

9 Click cell **D5**. Type = and then click the **Online Sales sheet tab**. Click cell **F12**, and then press Enter to redisplay the **Summary** worksheet and insert the total **Non-Food Sales** amount of *$6,038.65*.

10 By using the techniques you just practiced, in cells **C6** and **D6** insert the total **Food Sales** and **Non-Food Sales** data from the **In-Store Sales** worksheet. Click **Save**, and then compare your screen with Figure 8.46.

Figure 8.46

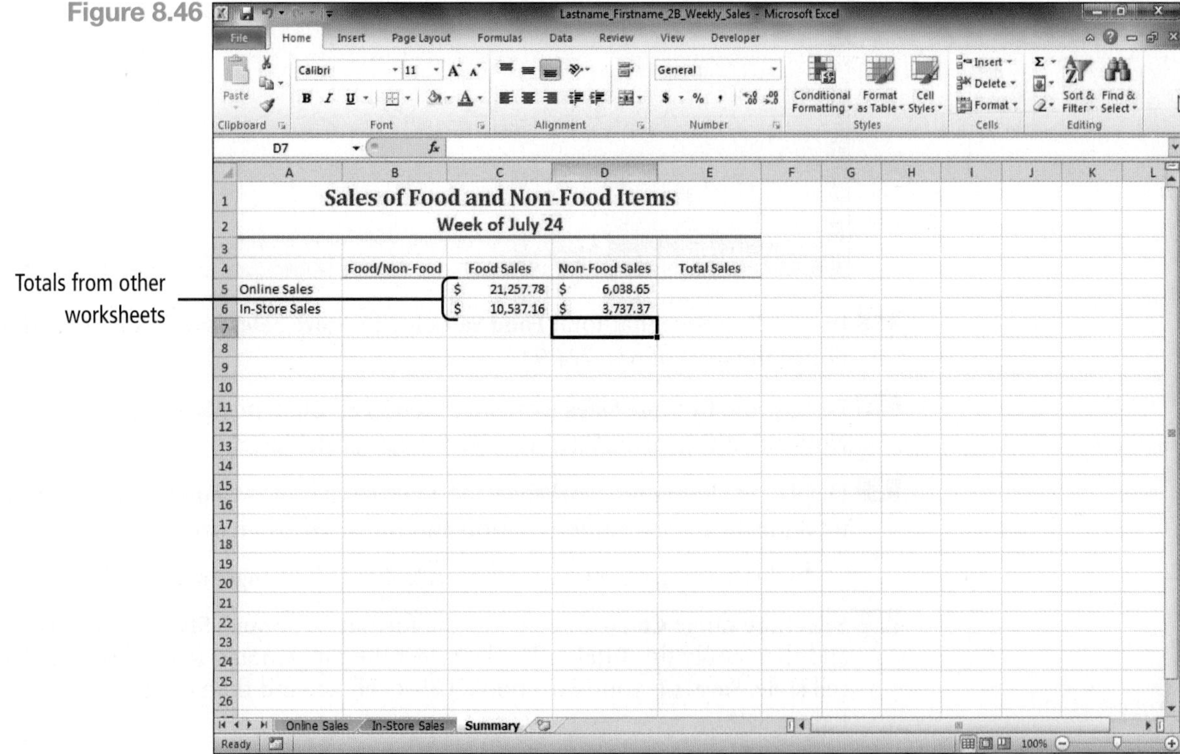

Activity 8.23 | Changing Values in a Detail Worksheet to Update a Summary Worksheet

The formulas in cells C5:D6 display the totals from the other two worksheets. Changes made to any of the other two worksheets—sometimes referred to as ***detail sheets*** because the details of the information are contained there—that affect their totals will display on this Summary worksheet. In this manner, the Summary worksheet accurately displays the current totals from the other worksheets.

1. In cell **A7**, type **Total** Select the range **C5:E6**, and then click the **Sum** button [Σ] to total the two rows.

   This technique is similar to selecting the empty cells at the bottom of columns and then inserting the SUM function for each column. Alternatively, you could use any other method to sum the rows. Recall that cell formatting carries over to adjacent cells unless two cells are left blank.

2. Select the range **C5:E7**, and then click the **Sum** button [Σ] to total the three columns. Compare your screen with Figure 8.47.

Figure 8.47

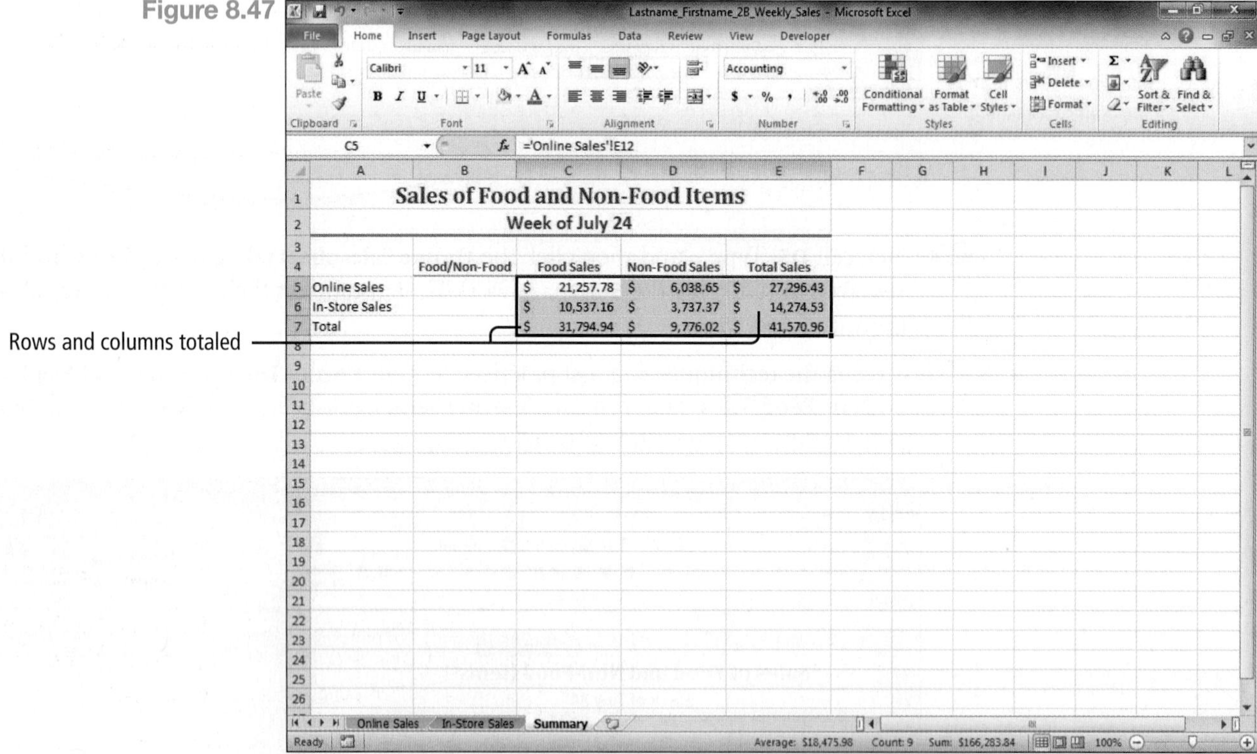

	B	C	D	E
4	Food/Non-Food	Food Sales	Non-Food Sales	Total Sales
5 Online Sales		$ 21,257.78	$ 6,038.65	$ 27,296.43
6 In-Store Sales		$ 10,537.16	$ 3,737.37	$ 14,274.53
7 Total		$ 31,794.94	$ 9,776.02	$ 41,570.96

3. In cell **C6**, notice that total **Food Sales** for **In-Store Sales** is *$10,537.16*, and in cell **C7**, notice the total of *$31,794.94*.

4. Display the **In-Store Sales** worksheet, click cell **B8**, type **353.63** and then press [Enter]. Notice that the formulas in the worksheet recalculate.

5. Display the **Summary** worksheet, and notice that in the **Food Sales** column, both the total for the *In-Store Sales* location and the *Total* also recalculated.

   In this manner, a Summary sheet recalculates any changes made in the other worksheets.

6. Select the range **C6:E6** and change the format to **Comma Style**. Select the range **C7:E7**, and then apply the **Total** cell style. Select the range **A5:A7** and apply the **Heading 4** cell style. **Save** [save icon] your workbook. Click cell **A1**, and then compare your screen with Figure 8.48.

Figure 8.48

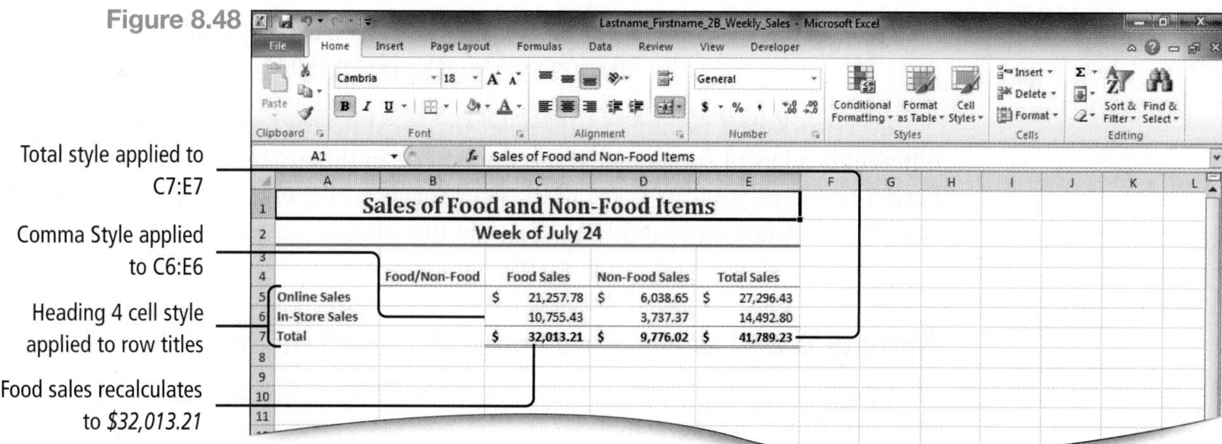

Activity 8.24 | Inserting Sparklines

In this activity, you will insert column sparklines to visualize the ratio of Food to Non-Food sales for both Online and In-Store.

1 Click cell **B5**. On the **Insert tab**, in the **Sparklines group**, click **Column**. In the **Create Sparklines** dialog box, with the insertion point blinking in the **Data Range** box, select the range **C5:D5**. Compare your screen with Figure 8.49.

Figure 8.49

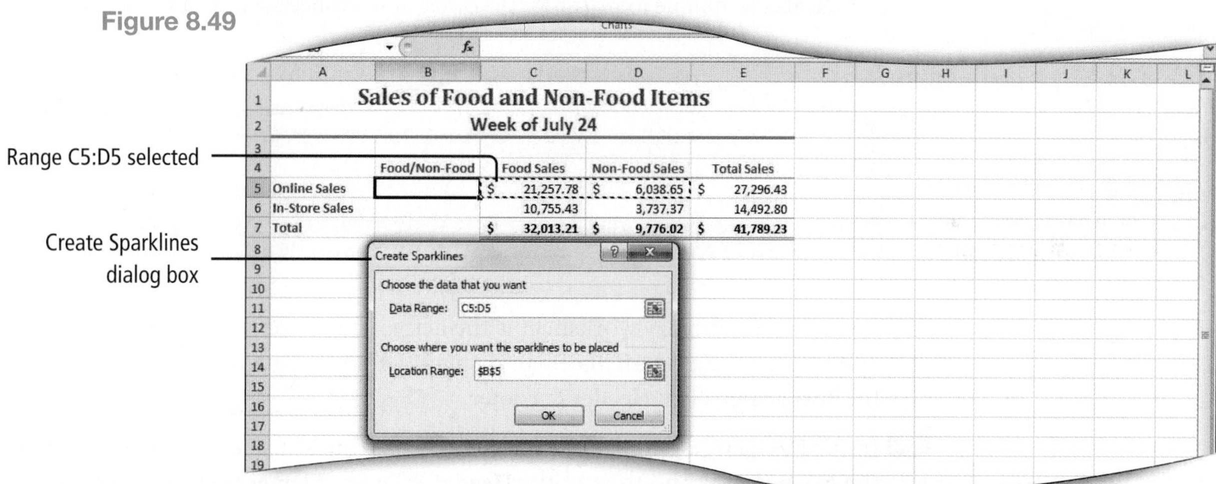

2 Click **OK**. Click cell **B6**, and then **Insert** a **Column Sparkline** for the range **C6:D6**. In the **Style group**, apply **Sparkline Style Accent 2, Darker 25%**—in the second row, the second style. Press Ctrl + Home, click **Save**, and then compare your screen with Figure 8.50.

You can see, at a glance, that for both Online and In-Store sales, Food sales are much greater than Non-Food sales.

Figure 8.50

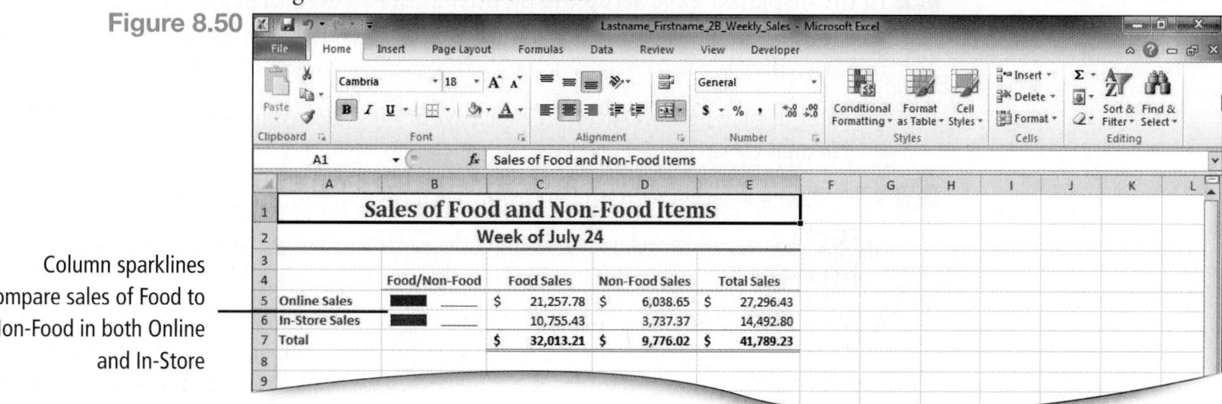

Objective 12 | Format and Print Multiple Worksheets in a Workbook

Each worksheet within a workbook can have different formatting, for example different headers or footers. If all the worksheets in the workbook will have the same header or footer, you can select all the worksheets and apply formatting common to all of the worksheets; for example, you can set the same footer in all of the worksheets.

Activity 8.25 | Moving and Formatting Worksheets in a Workbook

In this activity, you will move the Summary sheet to become the first worksheet in the workbook. Then you will format and prepare your workbook for printing. The three worksheets containing data can be formatted simultaneously.

1. Point to the **Summary sheet tab**, hold down the left mouse button to display a small black triangle—a caret—and then notice that a small paper icon attaches to the mouse pointer.
2. Drag to the left until the caret and mouse pointer are to the left of the **Online Sales sheet tab**, as shown in Figure 8.51, and then release the left mouse button.

   Use this technique to rearrange the order of worksheets within a workbook.

Figure 8.51

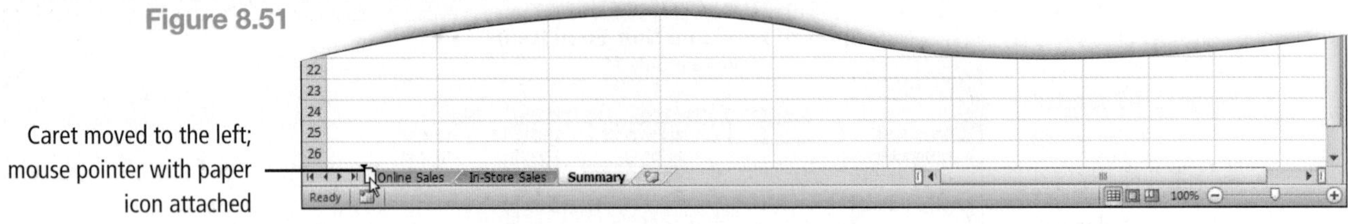

3. Be sure the **Summary** worksheet is the active sheet, point to its sheet tab, right-click, and then click **Select All Sheets** to display *[Group]* in the title bar. On the **Insert tab**, in the **Text group**, click **Header & Footer**.
4. In the **Navigation group**, click the **Go to Footer** button, click in the **left section** above the word *Footer*, and then in the **Header & Footer Elements group**, click the **File Name** button.
5. Click in a cell above the footer to deselect the **Footer area**. On the **Page Layout tab**, in the **Page Setup group**, click the **Margins** button, and then at the bottom of the **Margins** gallery, click **Custom Margins**.
6. In the displayed **Page Setup** dialog box, under **Center on page**, select the **Horizontally** check box. Click **OK**, and then on the status bar, click the **Normal** button to return to Normal view.

   After displaying worksheets in Page Layout View, dotted lines indicate the page breaks in Normal view.
7. Press Ctrl + Home; verify that *[Group]* still displays in the title bar.

   By selecting all sheets, you can apply the same formatting to all the worksheets at the same time.

8 Display **Backstage** view, show the **Document Panel**, type your firstname and lastname in the Author box, and then type your course name and section number in the **Subject** box. As the **Keywords** type **weekly sales, online, in-store** and then **Close** [×] the **Document Information Panel**.

9 Press Ctrl + F2; compare your screen with Figure 8.52.

By grouping, you can view all sheets in Print Preview. If you do not see *1 of 3* at the bottom of the Preview, click the Home tab, select all the sheets again, and then redisplay Print Preview.

Figure 8.52

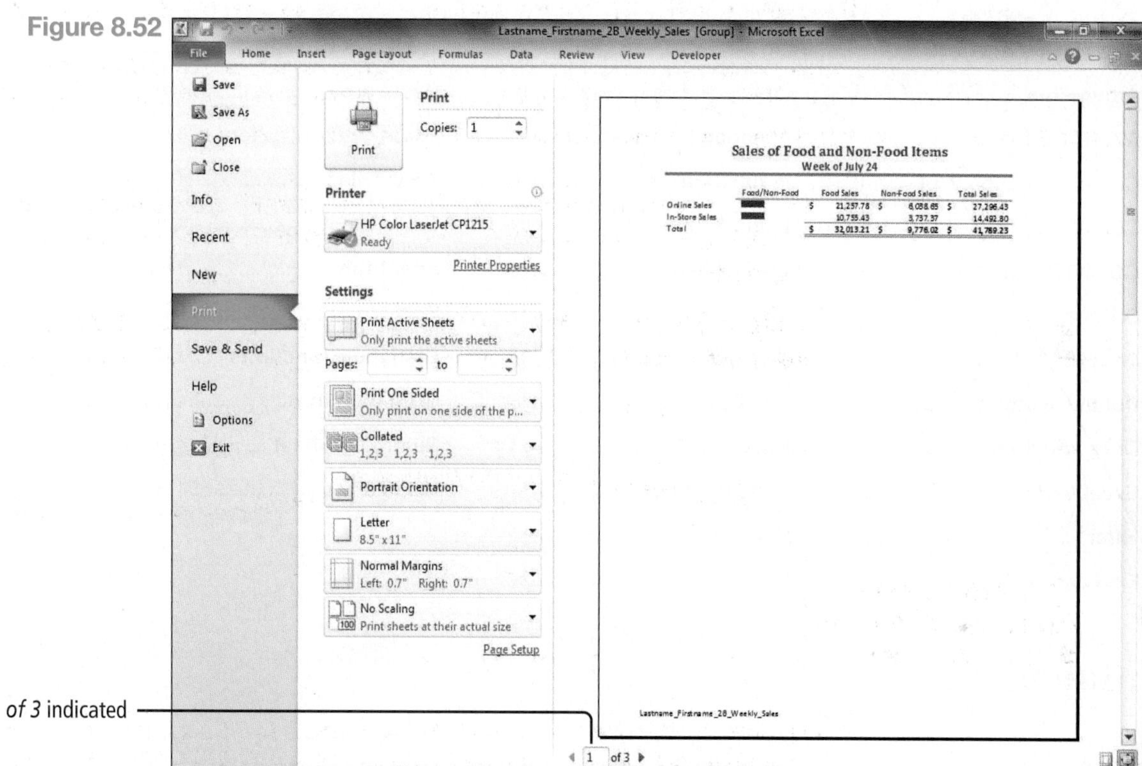

10 At the bottom of the **Print Preview**, click the **Next Page** [▶] button as necessary and take a moment to view each page of your workbook.

Activity 8.26 | Printing All the Worksheets in a Workbook

1 In **Backstage** view, click the **Save** button to save your workbook before printing. To submit your workbook electronically, follow the instructions provided by your instructor. To print your workbook, continue to Step 2.

2 Display **Backstage** view, click the **Print tab**, verify that the worksheets in your workbook are still grouped—*[Group]* displays in the title bar—and then in the center panel, in the **Print group**, click the **Print** button.

3 If required, print or create an electronic version of your worksheets with formulas displayed by using the instructions in Activity 1.16, and then **Close** [×] Excel without saving so that you do not save the changes you made to print formulas.

End **You have completed Project 8B**

Content-Based Assessments

Summary

In this chapter, you used the Statistical, Logical, and Date & Time functions from the Function Library. You created a table and analyzed the table's data by sorting and filtering. You also created a workbook with multiple worksheets, and then summarized all the worksheets on a summary worksheet.

Key Terms

Arguments 404
AVERAGE function 404
Comparison operator ..410
Conditional format 412
COUNTIF function 409
Criteria 409
Data bar 413
Detail sheets 438
Drag and drop 407
Excel table 416
Filter 417
Find and replace 413
Freeze Panes 415
Function 403
IF function 410
Logical functions 409
Logical test 410
MAX function 406
MEDIAN function 405
MIN function 406
Navigate 424
NOW function 414
Pane 415
Paste 429
Paste area 429
Paste Options gallery 429
Print Titles 419
Scale to Fit 419
Sheet tab 424
Sort 417
Statistical functions 403
SUM function 403
Summary Sheet 439
Volatile 415

Matching

Match each term in the second column with its correct definition in the first column by writing the letter of the term on the blank line in front of the correct definition.

____ 1. A predefined formula that performs calculations by using specific values in a particular order or structure.
____ 2. Excel functions such as AVERAGE that are useful to analyze a group of measurements.
____ 3. A predefined formula that adds all the numbers in a selected range.
____ 4. A function that adds a group of values, and then divides the result by the number of values in the group.
____ 5. A function that finds the middle value that has as many values above it in the group as are below it.
____ 6. A function that determines the smallest value in a range.
____ 7. A function that determines the largest value in a range.
____ 8. The action of moving a selection by dragging it to a new location.
____ 9. A group of functions that tests for specific conditions, and which typically use conditional tests to determine whether specified conditions are true or false.
____ 10. Conditions that you specify in a logical function.
____ 11. A statistical function that counts the number of cells within a range that meet the given condition and which has two arguments—the range of cells to check and the criteria.
____ 12. Any value or expression that can be evaluated as being true or false.

A AVERAGE function
B Comparison operators
C Conditional format
D COUNTIF function
E Criteria
F Drag and drop
G Function
H IF function
I Logical functions
J Logical test
K MAX function
L MEDIAN function
M MIN function
N Statistical functions
O SUM function

_____ 13. A function that uses a logical test to check whether a condition is met, and then returns one value if true, and another value if false.

_____ 14. Symbols that evaluate each value to determine if it is the same (=), greater than (>), less than (<), or in between a range of values as specified by the criteria.

_____ 15. A format that changes the appearance of a cell based on a condition.

Multiple Choice

Circle the correct answer.

1. A shaded bar that provides a visual cue about the value of a cell relative to other cells is a:
   A. data bar **B.** detail bar **C.** filter
2. The function that retrieves and then displays the date and time from your computer is the:
   A. DATE function **B.** NOW function **C.** CALENDAR function
3. The command that enables you to select one or more rows or columns and lock them into place is:
   A. drag and drop **B.** scale to fit **C.** freeze panes
4. A series of rows and columns with related data that is managed independently from other data is a:
   A. table **B.** pane **C.** detail sheet
5. The process of arranging data in a specific order based on the value in each field is called:
   A. filtering **B.** sorting **C.** scaling
6. The process of displaying only a portion of the data based on matching a specific value to show only the data that meets the criteria that you specify is called:
   A. filtering **B.** sorting **C.** scaling
7. The Excel command that enables you to specify rows and columns to repeat on each printed page is:
   A. navigate **B.** print titles **C.** conditional format
8. The labels along the lower border of the workbook window that identify each worksheet are the:
   A. data bars **B.** sheet tabs **C.** detail sheets
9. A worksheet where totals from other worksheets are displayed and summarized is a:
   A. summary sheet **B.** detail sheet **C.** table
10. The worksheets that contain the details of the information summarized on a summary sheet are called:
    A. summary sheets **B.** detail sheets **C.** tables

Apply 8A skills from these Objectives:

1. Use the SUM, AVERAGE, MEDIAN, MIN, and MAX Functions
2. Move Data, Resolve Error Messages, and Rotate Text
3. Use COUNTIF and IF Functions and Apply Conditional Formatting
4. Use Date & Time Functions and Freeze Panes
5. Create, Sort, and Filter an Excel Table
6. Format and Print a Large Worksheet

Skills Review | Project 8C Sauces Inventory

In the following Skills Review, you will edit a worksheet for Laura Morales, President, detailing the current inventory of sauces at the Portland facility. Your completed workbook will look similar to Figure 8.53.

Project Files

For Project 8C, you will need the following file:

e02C_Sauces_Inventory

You will save your workbook as:

Lastname_Firstname_2C_Sauces_Inventory

Project Results

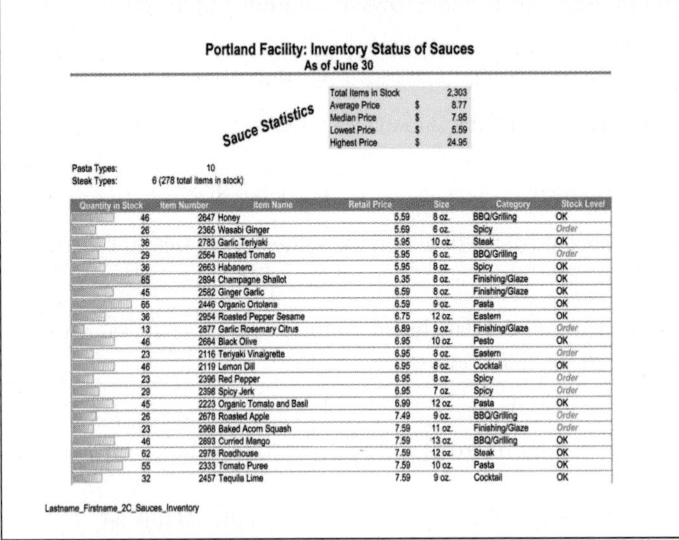

Portland Facility: Inventory Status of Sauces
As of June 30

Sauce Statistics

Total Items in Stock		2,303
Average Price	$	8.77
Median Price	$	7.95
Lowest Price	$	5.59
Highest Price	$	24.95

Pasta Types: 10
Steak Types: 6 (278 total items in stock)

Quantity in Stock	Item Number	Item Name	Retail Price	Size	Category	Stock Level
46	2647	Honey	5.59	8 oz.	BBQ/Grilling	OK
26	2365	Wasabi Ginger	5.69	6 oz.	Spicy	Order
36	2783	Garlic Teriyaki	5.95	10 oz.	Steak	OK
29	2564	Roasted Tomato	5.95	6 oz.	BBQ/Grilling	Order
36	2663	Habanero	5.95	8 oz.	Spicy	OK
85	2894	Champagne Shallot	6.35	8 oz.	Finishing/Glaze	OK
45	2582	Ginger Garlic	6.59	8 oz.	Finishing/Glaze	OK
65	2446	Organic Ortolana	6.59	9 oz.	Pasta	OK
36	2954	Roasted Pepper Sesame	6.75	12 oz.	Eastern	OK
13	2877	Garlic Rosemary Citrus	6.89	9 oz.	Finishing/Glaze	Order
46	2684	Black Olive	6.95	10 oz.	Pesto	OK
23	2116	Teriyaki Vinaigrette	6.95	8 oz.	Eastern	Order
46	2119	Lemon Dill	6.95	8 oz.	Cocktail	OK
23	2396	Red Pepper	6.95	8 oz.	Spicy	Order
29	2398	Spicy Jerk	6.95	7 oz.	Spicy	Order
45	2223	Organic Tomato and Basil	6.99	12 oz.	Pasta	OK
26	2678	Roasted Apple	7.49	9 oz.	BBQ/Grilling	Order
23	2968	Baked Acorn Squash	7.59	11 oz.	Finishing/Glaze	Order
46	2893	Curried Mango	7.59	13 oz.	BBQ/Grilling	OK
62	2978	Roadhouse	7.59	12 oz.	Steak	OK
55	2333	Tomato Puree	7.59	10 oz.	Pasta	OK
32	2457	Tequila Lime	7.59	9 oz.	Cocktail	OK

Lastname_Firstname_2C_Sauces_Inventory

Quantity in Stock	Item Number	Item Name	Retail Price	Size	Category	Stock Level
46	2455	Jalapeno	7.59	10 oz.	Spicy	OK
46	2554	Mesquite	7.75	12 oz.	Steak	OK
37	2616	Honey Ginger Teriyaki	7.89	10 oz.	BBQ/Grilling	OK
62	2934	Ginger Garlic	7.95	8 oz.	Eastern	OK
39	2312	Chimichurri	7.95	12 oz.	Steak	OK
56	2225	Organic Arrabbiata	7.95	14 oz.	Pasta	OK
46	2534	Mushroom Sage	8.35	12 oz.	Steak	OK
49	2999	Garlic Spread	8.49	8 oz.	Cocktail	OK
49	2642	Vidalia Onion Fig	8.59	12 oz.	Spicy	OK
36	2696	Basil	8.59	10 oz.	Pesto	OK
46	2553	Sun Dried Tomato	8.59	9 oz.	Pesto	OK
56	2841	Sun Dried Tomato and Olive	8.59	7 oz.	Pesto	OK
49	2489	Spicy Horseradish	8.59	10 oz.	Cocktail	OK
48	2288	Sweet Pepper and Tomato	8.59	14 oz.	Pasta	OK
49	2221	Vodka Tomato	8.59	12 oz.	Pasta	OK
43	2493	Sesame Ginger Teriyaki	8.95	12 oz.	Eastern	OK
45	2336	Genovese	8.95	8 oz.	Pesto	OK
26	2892	Roasted Garlic Peanut	9.59	14 oz.	Eastern	Order
28	2895	Citrus Teriyaki	9.59	15 oz.	Eastern	Order
36	2444	Pomegranate	9.59	10 oz.	BBQ/Grilling	OK
46	2698	Artichoke	9.59	8 oz.	Pesto	OK
26	2897	Maple Chipotle	9.59	13 oz.	BBQ/Grilling	Order
28	2345	New England Cranberry	9.59	12 oz.	Cocktail	Order
37	2598	Wild Mushroom	9.59	8 oz.	Finishing/Glaze	OK
49	2346	Sweet Chipotle	9.59	12 oz.	Spicy	OK
65	2347	Grandma Jones	9.65	12 oz.	Cocktail	OK
49	2485	Maple Chipotle	9.69	15 oz.	Steak	OK
42	2465	Organic Carli	9.95	8 oz.	Pesto	OK
42	2668	Black Truffles	10.95	6 oz.	Finishing/Glaze	OK
65	2556	Porcini Tomato	12.59	12 oz.	Pasta	OK
28	2113	Mushroom Cream	16.95	16 oz.	Pasta	Order
29	2433	Artichoke Heart	19.59	16 oz.	Pasta	Order
32	2963	Asparagus Tip	24.95	16 oz.	Pasta	OK

Edited by Michelle Albright
5/1/2010 18:28

Lastname_Firstname_2C_Sauces_Inventory

Figure 8.53

(Project 8C Sauces Inventory continues on the next page)

Content-Based Assessments

Skills Review | Project 8C Sauces Inventory (continued)

1 **Start** Excel. From your student files, locate and open **e02C_Sauces_Inventory**. From **Backstage** view, display the **Save As** dialog box, navigate to your **Excel Chapter 2** folder, and then save the workbook as **Lastname_Firstname_2C_Sauces_Inventory**

a. Click cell **B4**. Click the **Formulas tab**, and then in the **Function Library group**, click the **AutoSum** button. Select the range **A14:A68**, and then press Enter.

b. With cell **B5** active, in the **Function Library group**, click the **More Functions** button. Point to **Statistical**, click **AVERAGE**, and then in the **Number1** box, type **d14:d68** Click **OK**.

c. Click cell **B6**. In the **Function Library group**, click the **More Functions** button, point to **Statistical**, and then click **MEDIAN**. In the **Function Arguments** dialog box, to the right of the **Number1** box, click the **Collapse Dialog** button. Select the range **D14:D68**, click the **Expand Dialog** button, and then click **OK**.

d. Click cell **B7**, and then by using a similar technique to insert a statistical function, insert the **MIN** function to determine the lowest **Retail Price**. Click cell **B8**, and then insert the **MAX** function to determine the highest **Retail Price**.

2 Right-click cell **B4**. On the Mini toolbar, click the **Comma Style** button, and then click the **Decrease Decimal** button two times. Select the range **B5:B8**, and apply the **Accounting Number Format**.

a. Select the range **A4:B8**. Point to the right edge of the selected range to display the [pointer icon] pointer. Drag the selected range to the right until the ScreenTip displays *D4:E8*, and then release the mouse button.

b. With the range **D4:E8** selected, on the **Home tab**, in the **Styles group**, display the **Cell Styles** gallery, and then under **Themed Cell Styles**, click **20% - Accent1**.

c. In cell **C6**, type **Sauce Statistics** Select the range **C4:C8**, right-click over the selection, and then click **Format Cells**. In the **Format Cells** dialog box, click the **Alignment tab**. Under **Text control**, select the **Merge cells** check box.

d. In the upper right portion of the dialog box, under **Orientation**, point to the **red diamond**, and then drag the diamond upward until the **Degrees** box indicates *20*. Click **OK**.

e. With the merged cell still selected, on the **Home tab**, in the **Font group**, change the **Font Size** to **18**, and then apply **Bold** and **Italic**. Click the **Font Color button arrow**, and then in the fourth column, click the first color—**Dark Blue, Text 2**.

3 Click cell **B10**. On the **Formulas tab**, in the **Function Library group**, click the **More Functions** button, and then display the list of **Statistical** functions. Click **COUNTIF**.

a. At the right edge of the **Range** box, click the **Collapse Dialog** button, select the range **F14:F68**, and then press Enter. Click in the **Criteria** box, type **Pasta** and then click **OK** to calculate the number of *Pasta* types.

b. Click cell **G14**. On the **Formulas tab**, in the **Function Library group**, click the **Logical** button, and then in the list, click **IF**. If necessary, drag the title bar of the **Function Arguments** dialog box up so that you can view **row 14** on your screen.

c. With the insertion point in the **Logical_test** box, click cell **A14**, and then type **<30** Press Tab to move the insertion point to the **Value_if_true** box, and then type **Order** Press Tab to move the insertion point to the **Value_if_false** box, type **OK** and then click **OK**. Using the fill handle, copy the function in cell **G14** down through cell **G68**.

4 With the range **G14:G68** selected, on the **Home tab**, in the **Styles group**, click the **Conditional Formatting** button. In the list, point to **Highlight Cells Rules**, and then click **Text that Contains**.

a. In the **Text That Contains** dialog box, with the insertion point blinking in the first box, type **Order** and then in the second box, click the **arrow**. In the list, click **Custom Format**.

b. In the **Format Cells** dialog box, on the **Font tab**, under **Font style**, click **Bold Italic**. Click the **Color arrow**, and then under **Theme Colors**, in the sixth column, click the first color—**Red, Accent 2**. In the lower right corner of the **Format Cells** dialog box, click **OK**. In the **Text That Contains** dialog box, click **OK** to apply the font color, bold, and italic to the cells that contain the word *Order*.

c. Select the range **A14:A68**. In the **Styles group**, click the **Conditional Formatting** button. In the list, point to **Data Bars**, and then under **Gradient Fill**, click **Orange Data Bar**. Click anywhere to cancel the selection.

d. Select the range **F14:F68**. On the **Home tab**, in the **Editing group**, click the **Find & Select** button, and then click **Replace**. In the **Find and Replace** dialog box, in the **Find what** box, type **Hot** and then in the

(Project 8C Sauces Inventory continues on the next page)

Skills Review | Project 8C Sauces Inventory (continued)

Replace with box type **Spicy** Click the **Replace All** button and then click **OK**. In the lower right corner of the **Find and Replace** dialog box, click the **Close** button.

e. Scroll down as necessary, and then click cell **A70**. Type **Edited by Michelle Albright** and then press Enter. With cell **A71** as the active cell, on the **Formulas tab**, in the **Function Library group**, click the **Date & Time** button. In the list of functions, click **NOW**, and then click **OK** to enter the current date and time.

5 Select the range **A13:G68**. Click the **Insert tab**, and then in the **Tables group**, click the **Table** button. In the **Create Table** dialog box, if necessary, select the My table has headers check box, and then click **OK**. On the **Design tab**, in the **Table Styles group**, click the **More** button, and then under **Light**, locate and click **Table Style Light 9**.

a. In the header row of the table, click the **Retail Price arrow**, and then from the menu, click **Sort Smallest to Largest**. Click the **Category arrow**. On the menu, click the **(Select All)** check box to clear all the check boxes. Scroll as necessary and then click to select only the **Steak** check box. Click **OK**.

b. On the **Design tab**, in the **Table Style Options group**, select the **Total Row** check box. Click cell **A69**, click the **arrow** that displays to the right of cell **A69**, and then in the list, click **Sum**. In cell **B11**, type the result **6 (278 total items in stock)** and then press Enter.

c. In the header row of the table, click the **Category arrow** and then click **Clear Filter From "Category"** to redisplay all of the data. Click anywhere in the table. Click the **Design tab**, in the **Table Style Options group**, clear the **Total Row** check box, and then in the **Tools group**, click the **Convert to Range** button. Click **Yes**.

d. On the **Page Layout tab**, in the **Themes group**, click the **Themes** button, and then click **Horizon**.

6 On the **Page Layout tab**, click the **Margins** button, and then click **Custom Margins**. On the **Margins tab**, under **Center on page**, select the **Horizontally** check box. Click **OK**. On the **Page Layout tab**, in the **Scale to Fit group**, click the **Width button arrow**, and then click **1 page**.

a. In the **Page Setup group**, click the **Print Titles** button. Under **Print titles**, click in the **Rows to repeat at top** box, and then to the right, click the **Collapse Dialog** button. From the **row heading area**, select **row 13**, and then click the **Expand Dialog** button. Click **OK**.

b. On the **Insert tab**, in the **Text group**, click the **Header & Footer** button. Insert the **File Name** in the **left section** of the footer. Return to **Normal** view, make cell **A1** the active cell, and then delete the unused sheets.

c. Display the **Document Panel**, and then add your name, your course name and section, and the keywords **inventory, Portland Close** the **Document Information Panel**.

d. **Save** your workbook. Print or submit electronically as directed by your instructor. If required by your instructor, print or create an electronic version of your worksheets with formulas displayed by using the instructions in Activity 1.16, and then **Close** Excel without saving so that you do not save the changes you made to print formulas.

End You have completed Project 8C

Content-Based Assessments

Apply **8B** skills from these Objectives:

- **7** Navigate a Workbook and Rename Worksheets
- **8** Enter Dates, Clear Contents, and Clear Formats
- **9** Copy and Paste by Using the Paste Options Gallery
- **10** Edit and Format Multiple Worksheets at the Same Time
- **11** Create a Summary Sheet with Column Sparklines
- **12** Format and Print Multiple Worksheets in a Workbook

Skills Review | Project **8D** February Sales

In the following Skills Review, you will edit a workbook that summarizes in-store and online sales in the California and Oregon retail locations. Your completed workbook will look similar to Figure 8.54.

Project Files

For Project 8D, you will need the following file:

e02D_February_Sales

You will save your workbook as:

Lastname_Firstname_2D_February_Sales

Project Results

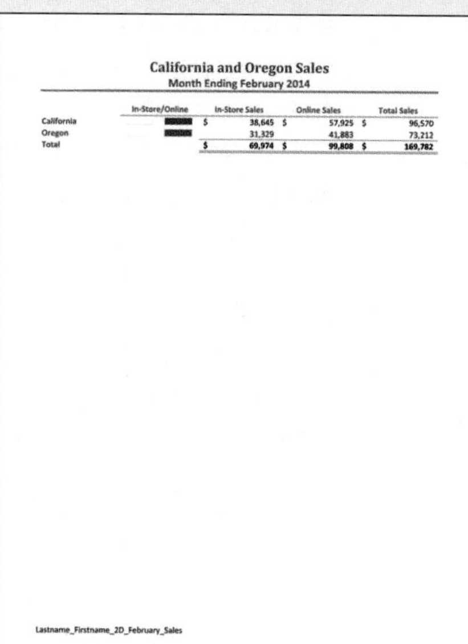

California and Oregon Sales
Month Ending February 2014

	In-Store/Online	In-Store Sales	Online Sales	Total Sales
California		$ 38,645	$ 57,925	$ 96,570
Oregon		31,329	41,883	73,212
Total		$ 69,974	$ 99,808	$ 169,782

Lastname_Firstname_2D_February_Sales

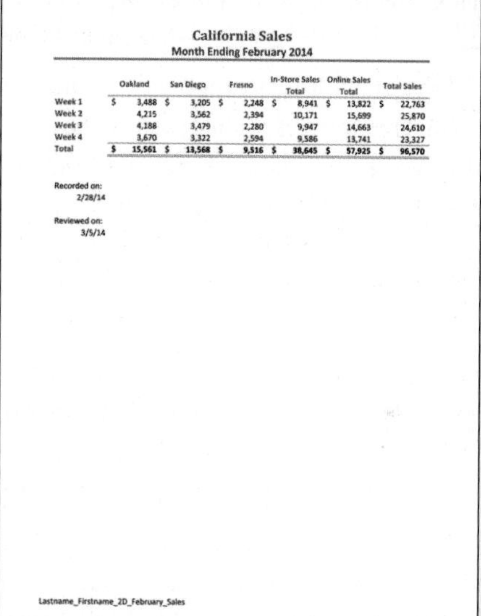

California Sales
Month Ending February 2014

	Oakland	San Diego	Fresno	In-Store Sales Total	Online Sales Total	Total Sales
Week 1	$ 3,488	$ 3,205	$ 2,248	$ 8,941	$ 13,822	$ 22,763
Week 2	4,215	3,562	2,394	10,171	15,699	25,870
Week 3	4,188	3,479	2,280	9,947	14,663	24,610
Week 4	3,670	3,322	2,594	9,586	13,741	23,327
Total	$ 15,561	$ 13,568	$ 9,516	$ 38,645	$ 57,925	$ 96,570

Recorded on:
2/28/14

Reviewed on:
3/5/14

Lastname_Firstname_2D_February_Sales

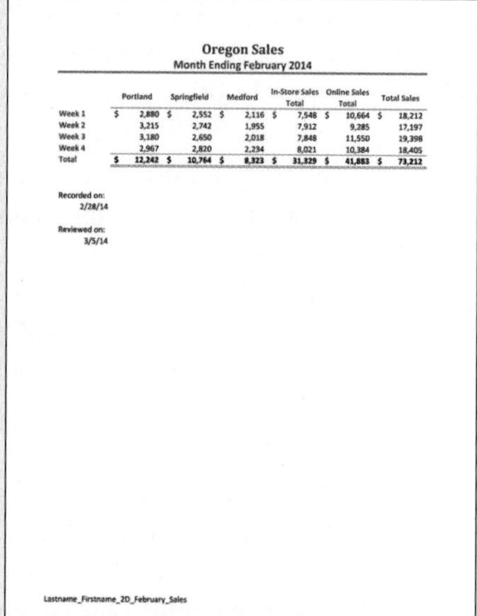

Oregon Sales
Month Ending February 2014

	Portland	Springfield	Medford	In-Store Sales Total	Online Sales Total	Total Sales
Week 1	$ 2,880	$ 2,552	$ 2,116	$ 7,548	$ 10,664	$ 18,212
Week 2	3,215	2,742	1,955	7,912	9,285	17,197
Week 3	3,180	2,650	2,018	7,848	11,550	19,398
Week 4	2,967	2,820	2,234	8,021	10,384	18,405
Total	$ 12,242	$ 10,764	$ 8,323	$ 31,329	$ 41,883	$ 73,212

Recorded on:
2/28/14

Reviewed on:
3/5/14

Lastname_Firstname_2D_February_Sales

Figure 8.54

(Project 8D February Sales continues on the next page)

Content-Based Assessments

Skills Review | Project 8D February Sales (continued)

1 **Start** Excel. From your student files, locate and open **e02D_February_Sales**. Click the **File tab**, click **Save As**, navigate to your **Excel Chapter 2** folder, and then using your own name, save the file as **Lastname_Firstname_ 2D_February_Sales**

a. Point to the **Sheet1 tab**, and then double-click to select the sheet tab name. Type **California Sales** and then press Enter.

b. Point to the **Sheet2 tab**, right-click, and then from the shortcut menu, click **Rename**. Type **Oregon Sales** and press Enter.

c. Point to the **California Sales sheet tab** and right-click. On the shortcut menu, point to **Tab Color**, and then in the last column, click the first color—**Orange, Accent 6**.

d. Using the technique you just practiced, change the tab color of the **Oregon Sales sheet tab** to **Aqua, Accent 5**—in the next to last column, the first color.

e. Click the **California Sales sheet tab**, and then click cell **A13**. On the **Home tab**, in the **Number group**, click the **Number Format arrow**. From the bottom of the displayed menu, click **More Number Formats** to display the **Number tab** of the **Format Cells** dialog box. Click the **3/14/01** type, and then at the bottom of the dialog box, click **OK**.

f. Click cell **A16**, type **3/5/14** and then press Enter. Click cell **A13**, and then on the **Home tab**, in the **Clipboard group**, click the **Format Painter** button. Click cell **A16** to copy the date format from cell **A13** to cell **A16**.

g. Click cell **A1**. In the **Editing group**, click the **Clear** button. From the displayed list, click **Clear Formats**.

h. Select the range **A4:A16**. On the **Home tab**, in the **Clipboard group**, click the **Copy** button. At the bottom of the workbook window, click the **Oregon Sales sheet tab** to make it the active worksheet. Right-click cell **A4**, and then under **Paste Options**, click the first button—**Paste**. Display the **California Sales** sheet. Press Esc to cancel the moving border.

2 With the **California Sales** sheet active, press Ctrl + Home to make cell **A1** the active cell. Point to the sheet tab, right-click, and then on the shortcut menu, click **Select All Sheets**. Verify that *[Group]* displays in the title bar.

a. **Merge & Center** the text in cell A1 across the range **A1:G1**, and then apply the **Title** cell style. Select **columns A:G**, and then set their widths to **85 pixels**.

b. Click cell **A2**, type **Month Ending February 2014** and then on the **Formula Bar**, click the **Enter** button to keep cell **A2** as the active cell. **Merge & Center** the text across the range **A2:G2**, and then apply the **Heading 1** cell style.

c. Select the range **B4:G4**, and then apply the **Heading 3** cell style. In the **Alignment group**, click the **Center**, **Middle Align**, and **Wrap Text** buttons.

d. With the sheets still *grouped* and the **California Sales** sheet active, click cell **E5**. On the **Home tab**, in the **Editing group**, click the **Sum** button, and then press Enter. Click cell **E5**, and then drag the fill handle down to copy the formula through cell **E8**.

e. Click cell **G5**, type **=** click cell **E5**, type **+** click cell **F5**, and then press Enter. Copy the formula down through cell **G8**. In cell **A9**, type **Total** Select the range **B5:G9**, and then press Alt + = to enter the SUM function for all the columns. Select the range **A5:A9**, and then apply the **Heading 4** cell style.

f. Select the range **B5:G5**, hold down Ctrl, and then select the range **B9:G9**. Apply the **Accounting Number Format** and decrease the decimal places to zero. Select the range **B6:G8**, and then apply **Comma Style** with zero decimal places. Select the range **B9:G9** and apply the **Total** cell style.

3 Click the **Oregon Sales sheet tab** to cancel the grouping and display the second worksheet.

a. To the right of the **Oregon Sales** sheet tab, click the **Insert Worksheet** button. Rename the new worksheet tab **Summary** and then change the **Tab Color** to **Olive Green, Accent 3**—in the seventh column, the first color.

b. Widen **columns A:E** to **125** pixels. In cell **A1**, type **California and Oregon Sales** and then **Merge & Center** the title across the range **A1:E1**. Apply the **Title** cell style. In cell **A2**, type **Month Ending February 2014** and then **Merge & Center** the text across the range **A2:E2**. Apply the **Heading 1** cell style. In cell **A5**, type **California** and in cell **A6**, type **Oregon**

c. In cell **B4**, type **In-Store/Online** and press Tab. In cell **C4**, type **In-Store Sales** and press Tab. In cell **D4**, type **Online Sales** and press Tab. In cell **E4**, type **Total Sales** Select the range **B4:E4**, apply the **Heading 3** cell style, and then **Center** these column titles.

(Project 8D February Sales continues on the next page)

Skills Review | Project 8D February Sales (continued)

d. Click cell **C5**. Type = and then click the **California Sales sheet tab**. In the **California Sales** worksheet, click cell **E9**, and then press Enter. Click cell **D5**. Type = and then click the **California Sales sheet tab**. Click cell **F9**, and then press Enter.

e. By using the techniques you just practiced, in cells **C6** and **D6**, insert the total **In-Store Sales** and **Online Sales** data from the **Oregon Sales** worksheet.

f. Select the range **C5:E6**, and then click the **Sum** button to total the two rows. In cell **A7**, type **Total** and then select the range **C5:E7**. Click the **Sum** button to total the three columns. Select the nonadjacent ranges **C5:E5** and **C7:E7**, and then apply **Accounting Number Format** with zero decimal places. Select the range **C6:E6**, and then apply **Comma Style** with zero decimal places. Select the range **C7:E7**, and then apply the **Total** cell style. Select the range **A5:A7** and apply the **Heading 4** cell style.

g. Click cell **B5**. On the **Insert tab**, in the **Sparklines group**, click **Column**. In the **Create Sparklines** dialog box, with the insertion point blinking in the **Data Range** box, select the range **C5:D5** and then click **OK**.

h. Click cell **B6**, and then **Insert** a **Column Sparkline** for the range **C6:D6**. In the **Style group**, apply the second style in the second row—**Sparkline Style Accent 2, Darker 25%** to this sparkline.

4 Point to the **Summary sheet tab**, hold down the left mouse button to display a small black triangle, and drag to the left until the triangle and mouse pointer are to the left of the **California Sales sheet tab**, and then release the left mouse button.

a. Be sure the **Summary** worksheet is the active sheet, point to its sheet tab, right-click, and then click **Select All Sheets** to display *[Group]* in the title bar. On the **Insert tab**, in the **Text group**, click the **Header & Footer** button. Display the **Footer** area, and then in the **left section**, insert the **File Name**. Center the worksheets **Horizontally** on the page, return to **Normal** view, and make cell **A1** active.

b. Display the **Document Panel**, and then add your name, your course name and section, and the keywords **February sales Close** the **Document Information Panel**.

c. **Save** your workbook. To submit your workbook electronically, follow the instructions provided by your instructor. To print your workbook, continue to Step d.

d. Display **Backstage** view, verify that the worksheets in your workbook are still grouped—*[Group]* displays in the title bar—and then on the left click **Print**. Under **Settings**, verify that **Print Active Sheets** displays. At the top of the screen, verify that the **Number of Copies** is **1**. Click the **Print** button.

e. If required by your instructor, print or create an electronic version of your worksheets with formulas displayed by using the instructions in Activity 1.16, and then **Close** Excel without saving so that you do not save the changes you made to print formulas.

End **You have completed Project 8D**

Content-Based Assessments

Apply 8A skills from these Objectives:

1. Use the SUM, AVERAGE, MEDIAN, MIN, and MAX Functions
2. Move Data, Resolve Error Messages, and Rotate Text
3. Use COUNTIF and IF Functions and Apply Conditional Formatting
4. Use Date & Time Functions and Freeze Panes
5. Create, Sort, and Filter an Excel Table
6. Format and Print a Large Worksheet

Mastering Excel | Project 8E Desserts

In the following Mastery project, you will edit a worksheet for Laura Morales, President, detailing the current inventory of desserts produced at the San Diego facility. Your completed worksheet will look similar to Figure 8.55.

Project Files

For Project 8E, you will need the following file:

e02E_Desserts

You will save your workbook as:

Lastname_Firstname_2E_Desserts

Project Results

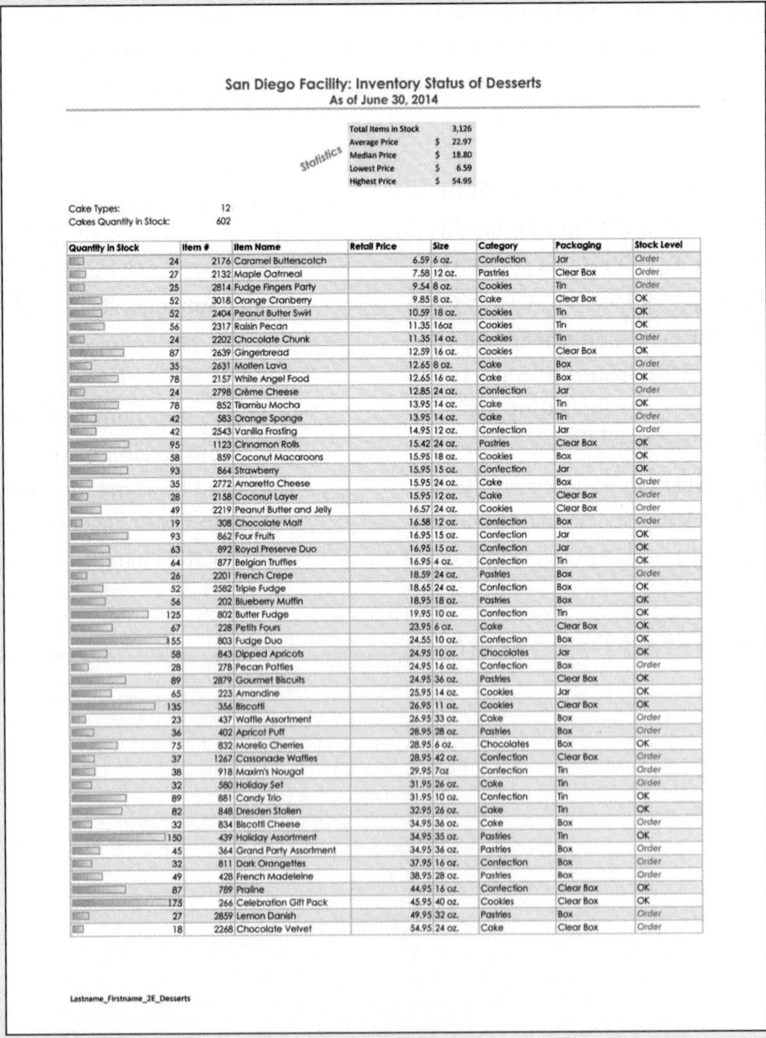

San Diego Facility: Inventory Status of Desserts
As of June 30, 2014

Statistics

Total Items in Stock		3,126
Average Price	$	22.97
Median Price	$	18.80
Lowest Price	$	6.59
Highest Price	$	54.95

Cake Types: 12
Cakes Quantity in Stock: 602

Quantity in Stock	Item #	Item Name	Retail Price	Size	Category	Packaging	Stock Level
24	2176	Caramel Butterscotch	6.59	6 oz.	Confection	Jar	Order
27	2132	Maple Oatmeal	7.58	12 oz.	Pastries	Clear Box	Order
25	2814	Fudge Fingers Party	9.54	8 oz.	Cookies	Tin	Order
52	3018	Orange Cranberry	9.85	8 oz.	Cake	Clear Box	OK
52	2404	Peanut Butter Swirl	10.59	18 oz.	Cookies	Tin	OK
56	2317	Raisin Pecan	11.35	16oz	Cookies	Tin	OK
24	2202	Chocolate Chunk	11.35	14 oz.	Cookies	Tin	Order
87	2639	Gingerbread	12.59	16 oz.	Cookies	Clear Box	OK
35	2631	Molten Lava	12.65	8 oz.	Cake	Box	Order
78	2157	White Angel Food	12.65	16 oz.	Cake	Box	OK
24	2798	Crème Cheese	12.85	24 oz.	Confection	Jar	Order
78	852	Tiramisu Mocha	13.95	14 oz.	Cake	Tin	OK
42	583	Orange Sponge	13.95	14 oz.	Cake	Tin	Order
42	2543	Vanilla Frosting	14.95	12 oz.	Confection	Jar	Order
95	1123	Cinnamon Rolls	15.42	24 oz.	Pastries	Clear Box	OK
58	859	Coconut Macaroons	15.95	18 oz.	Cookies	Box	OK
93	864	Strawberry	15.95	15 oz.	Confection	Jar	OK
35	2772	Amaretto Cheese	15.95	24 oz.	Cake	Box	Order
28	2158	Coconut Layer	15.95	12 oz.	Cake	Clear Box	Order
49	2219	Peanut Butter and Jelly	16.57	24 oz.	Cookies	Clear Box	Order
19	308	Chocolate Malt	16.58	12 oz.	Confection	Box	Order
93	862	Four Fruits	16.95	15 oz.	Confection	Jar	OK
63	892	Royal Preserve Duo	16.95	15 oz.	Confection	Jar	OK
64	877	Belgian Truffles	16.95	4 oz.	Confection	Tin	OK
26	2201	French Crepe	18.59	24 oz.	Pastries	Box	Order
52	2582	Triple Fudge	18.65	24 oz.	Confection	Box	OK
56	202	Blueberry Muffin	18.95	18 oz.	Pastries	Box	OK
125	802	Butter Fudge	19.95	10 oz.	Confection	Tin	OK
67	228	Petits Fours	23.95	6 oz.	Cake	Clear Box	OK
155	803	Fudge Duo	24.55	10 oz.	Confection	Box	OK
58	843	Dipped Apricots	24.95	10 oz.	Chocolates	Jar	OK
28	278	Pecan Patties	24.95	16 oz.	Confection	Box	Order
89	2879	Gourmet Biscuits	24.95	36 oz.	Pastries	Clear Box	OK
65	223	Amandine	25.95	14 oz.	Cookies	Jar	OK
135	356	Biscotti	26.95	11 oz.	Cookies	Clear Box	OK
23	437	Waffle Assortment	26.95	33 oz.	Cake	Box	Order
36	402	Apricot Puff	28.95	28 oz.	Pastries	Box	Order
75	832	Morello Cherries	28.95	6 oz.	Chocolates	Box	OK
37	1267	Cassonade Waffles	28.95	42 oz.	Confection	Clear Box	Order
38	918	Maxim's Nougat	29.95	7oz	Confection	Tin	Order
32	580	Holiday Set	31.95	26 oz.	Cake	Tin	Order
89	881	Candy Trio	31.95	10 oz.	Confection	Tin	OK
82	848	Dresden Stollen	32.95	26 oz.	Cake	Tin	OK
32	834	Biscotti Cheese	34.95	36 oz.	Cake	Box	Order
150	439	Holiday Assortment	34.95	35 oz.	Pastries	Tin	OK
45	364	Grand Party Assortment	34.95	36 oz.	Pastries	Box	Order
32	811	Dark Orangettes	37.95	16 oz.	Confection	Box	Order
49	428	French Madeleine	38.95	28 oz.	Pastries	Box	Order
87	789	Praline	44.95	16 oz.	Confection	Clear Box	OK
175	266	Celebration Gift Pack	45.95	40 oz.	Cookies	Clear Box	OK
27	2859	Lemon Danish	49.95	32 oz.	Pastries	Box	Order
18	2268	Chocolate Velvet	54.95	24 oz.	Cake	Clear Box	Order

Lastname_Firstname_2E_Desserts

Figure 8.55

(Project 8E Desserts continues on the next page)

Mastering Excel | Project 8E Desserts (continued)

1 **Start** Excel, from your student files, locate and open **e02E_Desserts**, and then **Save** the file in your **Excel Chapter 2** folder as **Lastname_Firstname_2E_Desserts**

2 In cell **B4**, calculate the **Total Items in Stock** by summing the **Quantity in Stock** data, and then apply **Comma Style** with zero decimal places to the result. In each cell in the range **B5:B8**, insert formulas to calculate the Average, Median, Lowest, and Highest retail prices, and then apply the **Accounting Number Format** to each result.

3 Move the range **A4:B8** to the range **D4:E8**, and then apply the **20% - Accent1** cell style. Widen **column D** to **130 pixels**. In cell **C6**, type **Statistics** select the range **C4:C8**, and then from the **Format Cells** dialog box, merge the selected cells. Change the text **Orientation** to **25 Degrees**, and then apply **Bold** and **Italic**. Change the **Font Size** to **14** and the **Font Color** to **Pink, Accent 1, Darker 25%**. Apply **Middle Align** and **Align Text Right**.

4 In cell **B10**, use the **COUNTIF** function to count the number of **Cake** items. In the **Packaging** column, **Replace All** occurrences of **Cellophane** with **Clear Box**

5 In cell **H14**, enter an **IF** function to determine the items that must be ordered. If the **Quantity in Stock** is less than **50** the **Value_if_true** is **Order** Otherwise the **Value_if_false** is **OK** Fill the formula down through cell **H65**. Apply **Conditional Formatting** to the **Stock Level** column so that cells that contain the text *Order* are formatted with **Bold Italic** and with a **Color** of **Blue, Accent 5**. Apply conditional formatting to the **Quantity in Stock** column by applying a **Gradient Fill Orange Data Bar**.

6 Format the range **A13:H65** as a **Table** with headers, and apply the **Table Style Light 16** style. Sort the table from smallest to largest by **Retail Price**, and then filter on the **Category** column to display the **Cake** types. Display a **Total Row** in the table and then in cell **A66**, **Sum** the **Quantity in Stock** for the **Cake** items. Type the result in cell **B11**, and apply appropriate number formatting. Click in the table, and then on the **Design tab**, remove the total row from the table. Clear the **Category** filter and convert the table to a range.

7 Change the theme to **Composite**. Display the footer area, and insert the **File Name** in the **left section**. Center the worksheet **Horizontally**, and then use the **Scale to Fit** option to change the **Width** to **1 page**. Return to **Normal** view and make cell **A1** the active cell. In **Backstage** view, display the **Print Preview**, and then make any necessary corrections.

8 Add your name, your course name and section, and the keywords **desserts inventory, San Diego** to the Document Panel. **Save**, and then print or submit electronically as directed. If required by your instructor, print or create an electronic version of your worksheets with formulas displayed by using the instructions in Activity 1.16, and then **Close** Excel without saving so that you do not save the changes you made to print formulas.

End **You have completed Project 8E**

Apply 8B skills from these Objectives:

- 7 Navigate a Workbook and Rename Worksheets
- 8 Enter Dates, Clear Contents, and Clear Formats
- 9 Copy and Paste by Using the Paste Options Gallery
- 10 Edit and Format Multiple Worksheets at the Same Time
- 11 Create a Summary Sheet with Column Sparklines
- 12 Format and Print Multiple Worksheets in a Workbook

Mastering Excel | Project 8F Compensation

In the following Mastery project, you will edit a workbook that summarizes the Laurales Herb and Spices salesperson compensation for the month of November. Your completed worksheet will look similar to Figure 8.56.

Project Files

For Project 8F, you will need the following file:

e02F_Compensation

You will save your workbook as:

Lastname_Firstname_2F_Compensation

Project Results

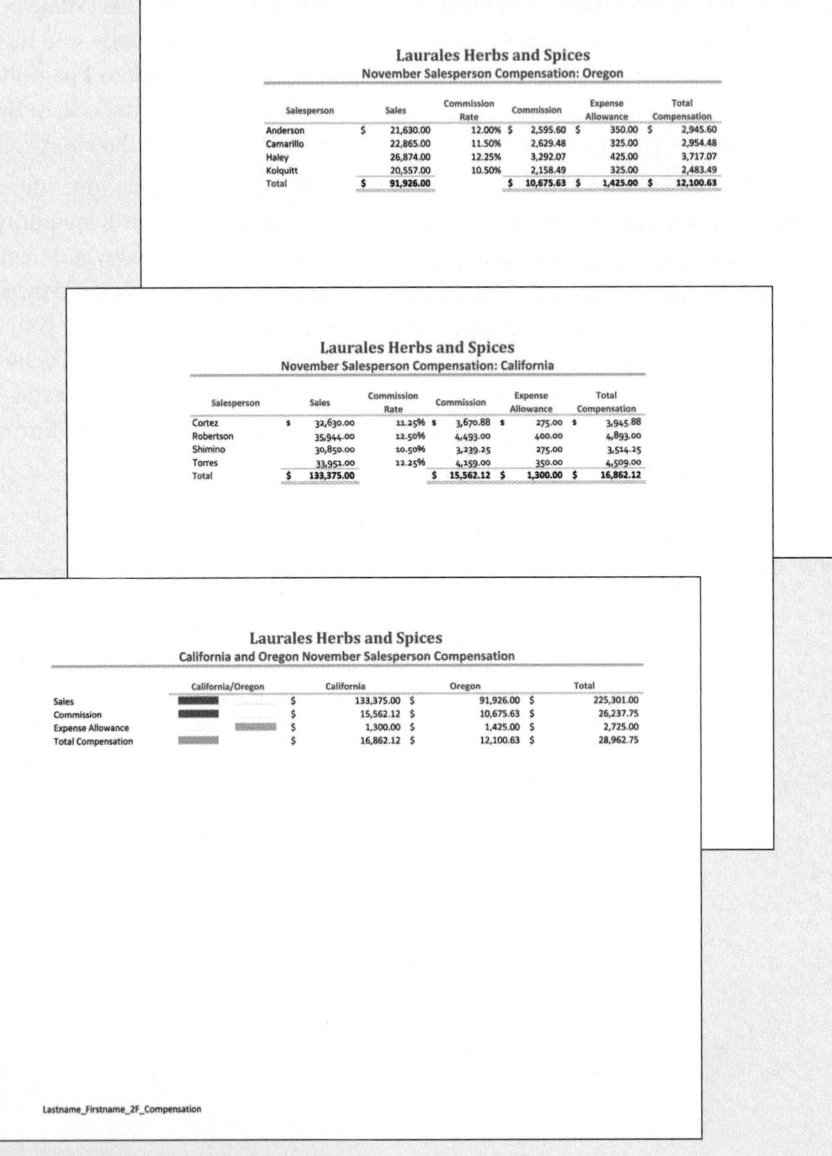

Laurales Herbs and Spices
November Salesperson Compensation: Oregon

Salesperson	Sales	Commission Rate	Commission	Expense Allowance	Total Compensation
Anderson	$ 21,630.00	12.00%	$ 2,595.60	$ 350.00	$ 2,945.60
Camarillo	22,865.00	11.50%	2,629.48	325.00	2,954.48
Haley	26,874.00	12.25%	3,292.07	425.00	3,717.07
Kolquitt	20,557.00	10.50%	2,158.49	325.00	2,483.49
Total	$ 91,926.00		$ 10,675.63	$ 1,425.00	$ 12,100.63

Laurales Herbs and Spices
November Salesperson Compensation: California

Salesperson	Sales	Commission Rate	Commission	Expense Allowance	Total Compensation
Cortez	$ 32,630.00	11.25%	$ 3,670.88	$ 275.00	$ 3,945.88
Robertson	35,944.00	12.50%	4,493.00	400.00	4,893.00
Shimino	30,850.00	10.50%	3,239.25	275.00	3,514.25
Torres	33,951.00	12.25%	4,159.00	350.00	4,509.00
Total	$ 133,375.00		$ 15,562.12	$ 1,300.00	$ 16,862.12

Laurales Herbs and Spices
California and Oregon November Salesperson Compensation

	California/Oregon	California	Oregon	Total
Sales		$ 133,375.00	$ 91,926.00	$ 225,301.00
Commission		$ 15,562.12	$ 10,675.63	$ 26,237.75
Expense Allowance		$ 1,300.00	$ 1,425.00	$ 2,725.00
Total Compensation		$ 16,862.12	$ 12,100.63	$ 28,962.75

Lastname_Firstname_2F_Compensation

Figure 8.56

(Project 8F Compensation continues on the next page)

Mastering Excel | Project 8F Compensation (continued)

1 **Start** Excel, from your student files, open **e02F_ Compensation**, and then save the file in your **Excel Chapter 2** folder as **Lastname_Firstname_2F_ Compensation**

2 Rename **Sheet1** as **California** and change the **Tab Color** to **Green, Accent 1**. Rename **Sheet2** as **Oregon** and change the **Tab Color** to **Gold, Accent 3**.

3 Click the **California sheet tab** to make it the active sheet, and then group the worksheets. In cell **A1**, type **Laurales Herbs and Spices** and then **Merge & Center** the text across the range **A1:F1**. Apply the **Title** cell style. **Merge & Center** the text in cell **A2** across the range **A2:F2**, and then apply the **Heading 1** cell style.

4 With the sheets still grouped, in cell **D5** calculate **Commission** for *Cortez* by multiplying the **Sales** by the **Commission Rate**. Copy the formula down through cell **D8**. In cell **F5**, calculate **Total Compensation** by summing the **Commission** and **Expense Allowance** for *Cortez*. Copy the formula down through the cell **F8**.

5 In **row 9**, sum the **Sales**, **Commission**, **Expense Allowance**, and **Total Compensation** columns. Apply the **Accounting Number Format** with two decimal places to the appropriate cells in **row 5** and **row 9** (do not include the percentages). Apply the **Comma Style** with two decimal places to the appropriate cells in **rows 6:8** (do not include the percentages). Apply the **Total** cell style to the appropriate cells in the Total row.

6 Insert a new worksheet. Change the sheet name to **Summary** and then change the **Tab Color** to **Periwinkle, Accent 5**. Widen **columns A:E** to **165** pixels, and then move the **Summary** sheet so that it is the first sheet in the workbook. In cell **A1**, type **Laurales Herbs and Spices** **Merge & Center** the title across the range **A1:E1**, and then apply the **Title** cell style. In cell **A2**, type **California and Oregon November Salesperson Compensation** and then **Merge & Center** the text across the range **A2:E2**. Apply the **Heading 1** cell style.

7 In the range **A5:A8**, type the following row titles and then apply the **Heading 4** cell style:

Sales

Commission

Expense Allowance

Total Compensation

8 In the range **B4:E4**, type the following column titles, and then **Center** and apply the **Heading 3** cell style.

California/Oregon

California

Oregon

Total

9 In cell **C5**, enter a formula that references cell **B9** in the **California** worksheet so that the total sales for California displays in **C5**. Create similar formulas to enter the total **Commission**, **Expense Allowance** and **Total Compensation** for California in the range **C6:C8**. Using the same technique, enter formulas in the range **D5:D8** so that the **Oregon** totals display.

10 Sum the **Sales**, **Commission**, **Expense Allowance**, and **Total Compensation** rows.

11 In cell **B5**, insert a **Column Sparkline** for the range **C5:D5**. In cells **B6**, **B7**, and **B8**, insert **Column** sparklines for the appropriate ranges to compare California totals with Oregon totals. To the sparkline in **B6**, apply the second style in the third row—**Sparkline Style Accent 2, (no dark or light)**. In **B7** apply the third style in the third row—**Sparkline Style Accent 3, (no dark or light)**. In **B8** apply the fourth style in the third row—**Sparkline Style Accent 4, (no dark or light)**.

12 **Group** the three worksheets, and then insert a footer in the left section with the **File Name**. Center the worksheets **Horizontally** on the page, and then change the **Orientation** to **Landscape**. Return the document to **Normal** view.

13 Display the **Document Panel**. Add your name, your course name and section, and the keywords **November sales** **Save** your workbook, and then print or submit electronically as directed. If required by your instructor, print or create an electronic version of your worksheets with formulas displayed by using the instructions in Activity 1.16, and then **Close** Excel without saving so that you do not save the changes you made to print formulas.

End **You have completed Project 8F**

Content-Based Assessments

Apply 8A and 8B skills from these Objectives:

1. Use the SUM, AVERAGE, MEDIAN, MIN, and MAX Functions
2. Move Data, Resolve Error Messages, and Rotate Text
3. Use COUNTIF and IF Functions and Apply Conditional Formatting
4. Use Date & Time Functions and Freeze Panes
5. Create, Sort, and Filter an Excel Table
6. Format and Print a Large Worksheet
7. Navigate a Workbook and Rename Worksheets
8. Enter Dates, Clear Contents, and Clear Formats
9. Copy and Paste by Using the Paste Options Gallery
10. Edit and Format Multiple Worksheets at the Same Time
11. Create a Summary Sheet with Column Sparklines
12. Format and Print Multiple Worksheets in a Workbook

Mastering Excel | Project 8G Inventory Summary

In the following Mastery project, you will edit a worksheet that summarizes the inventory status at the Petaluma production facility. Your completed workbook will look similar to Figure 8.57.

Project Files

For Project 8G, you will need the following file:

e02G_Inventory_Summary

You will save your workbook as:

Lastname_Firstname_2G_Inventory_Summary

Project Results

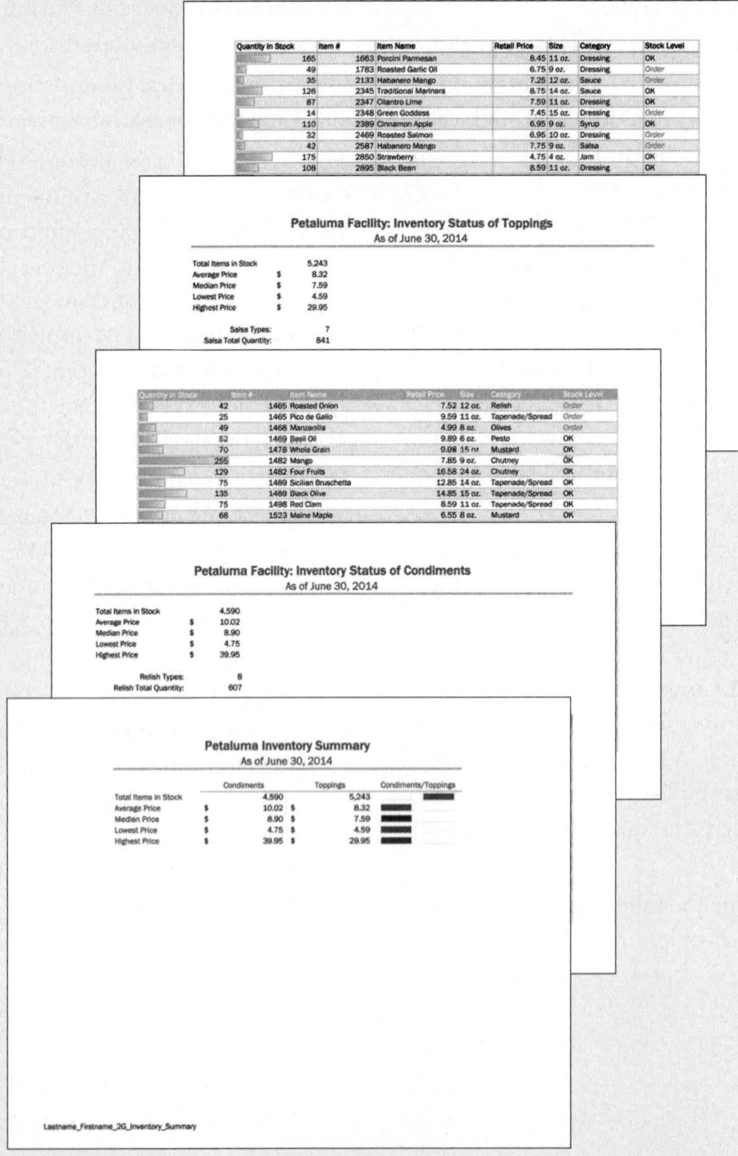

Figure 8.57

(Project 8G Inventory Summary continues on the next page)

Content-Based Assessments

Mastering Excel | Project 8G Inventory Summary (continued)

1 **Start** Excel. From your student files, open **e02G_Inventory_Summary**. Save the file in your **Excel Chapter 2** folder as **Lastname_Firstname_2G_Inventory_Summary**

2 Rename **Sheet1** as **Condiments** and **Sheet2** as **Toppings** Make the following calculations in each of the two worksheets *without* grouping the sheets:

- In cell **B4**, enter a formula to sum the **Quantity in Stock** data, and then apply **Comma Style** with zero decimal places to the result.
- In cells **B5:B8**, enter formulas to calculate the Average, Median, Lowest, and Highest retail prices, and then apply the **Accounting Number Format**.

3 In each of the two worksheets, make the following calculations *without* grouping the sheets:

- In cell **B10**, enter a COUNTIF function to determine how many different types of **Relish** products are in stock on the **Condiments** sheet and how many different types of **Salsa** products are in stock on the **Toppings** worksheet.
- In cell **G15**, enter an **IF** function to determine the items that must be ordered. If the **Quantity in Stock** is less than **50** the **Value_if_true** is **Order** Otherwise the **Value_if_false** is **OK** Fill the formula down through all the rows.
- Apply **Conditional Formatting** to the **Stock Level** column so that cells that contain the text *Order* are formatted with **Bold Italic** with a **Font Color** of **Gold, Accent 1, Darker 25%**. Apply **Gradient Fill Green Data Bars** to the **Quantity in Stock** column.

4 In the **Condiments** sheet, format the range **A14:G64** as a table with headers and apply **Table Style Medium 2**. Insert a **Total Row**, filter by **Category** for **Relish**, and then **Sum** the **Quantity in Stock** column. Record the result in cell **B11**.

5 Select the table, clear the filter, **Sort** the table on the **Item #** column from **Smallest to Largest**, remove the **Total Row**, and then convert the table to a range. On the **Page Layout tab**, set **Print Titles** so that **row 14** repeats at the top of each page.

6 In the **Toppings** sheet, format the range **A14:G61** as a table with headers and apply **Table Style Light 16**. Insert a **Total Row**, filter by **Category** for **Salsa**, and then **Sum** the **Quantity in Stock** column. Record the result in cell **B11**.

7 Select the table, clear the filter, **Sort** the table on the **Item #** column from **Smallest to Largest**, remove the **Total Row**, and then convert the table to a range.

8 On the **Page Layout tab**, set **Print Titles** so that **row 14** repeats at the top of each page, and then **Save** your workbook. **Group** the two worksheets. **Center** the worksheets **Horizontally**, and then use the **Scale to Fit** option to change the **Width** to **1 page**.

9 Insert a new worksheet. Change the sheet name to **Summary** and then widen **columns A:D** to **170** pixels. Move the **Summary** sheet so that it is the first sheet in the workbook. In cell **A1**, type **Petaluma Inventory Summary** **Merge & Center** the title across the range **A1:D1**, and then apply the **Title** cell style. In cell **A2**, type **As of June 30, 2014** and then **Merge & Center** the text across the range **A2:D2**. Apply the **Heading 1** cell style.

10 On the **Condiments sheet**, **Copy** the range **A4:A8**. Display the **Summary sheet** and **Paste** the selection to cell **A5**. Apply the **Heading 4** cell style to the selection. In the **Summary sheet**, in cell **B4**, type **Condiments** In cell **C4**, type **Toppings** and in cell **D4**, type **Condiments/Toppings** **Center** the column titles, and then apply the **Heading 3** cell style.

11 In cell **B5**, enter a formula that references cell **B4** in the **Condiments sheet** so that the **Condiments Total Items in Stock** displays in **B5**. Create similar formulas to enter the **Average Price**, **Median Price**, **Lowest Price**, and **Highest Price** from the **Condiments sheet** into the **Summary** sheet in the range **B6:B9**.

12 Enter formulas in the range **C5:C9** that reference the appropriate cells in the **Toppings** worksheet. To the range **B5:C5**, apply **Comma Style** with zero decimal places. In cells **D5**, **D6**, **D7**, **D8**, and **D9**, insert **Column** sparklines using the values in the *Condiments* and *Toppings* columns. Format each sparkline using the first five Sparkline styles in the first row.

13 Center the **Summary** worksheet **Horizontally** and change the **Orientation** to **Landscape**. **Group** the worksheets and insert a footer in the left section with the **File Name**. In **Normal** view, make cell **A1** the active cell. Display the **Document Panel**. Add your name, your course name and section, and the keywords **Petaluma inventory**

14 **Save** your workbook, and then print or submit electronically as directed. If required by your instructor, print or create an electronic version of your worksheets with formulas displayed by using the instructions in Activity 1.16, and then **Close** Excel without saving so that you do not save the changes you made to print formulas.

End **You have completed Project 8G**

Excel | Chapter 8

Apply a combination of the 8A and 8B skills.

GO! Fix It | Project 8H Confections

Project Files

For Project 8H, you will need the following file:

e02H_Confections

You will save your workbook as:

Lastname_Firstname_2H_Confections

In this project, you will correct a worksheet that contains the confection inventory for the month of June at the Laurales Herb and Spices Petaluma production facility. From the student files that accompany this textbook, open the file e02H_Confections, and then save the file in your chapter folder as **Lastname_Firstname_2H_Confections**

To complete the project, you must find and correct errors in formulas and formatting. View each formula in cells B4:B8 and edit as necessary. In addition to errors that you find, you should know:

- The table should be sorted smallest to largest by Item #.
- New stock should be ordered when the Quantity in Stock is less than 50, and the word *Order* should be formatted with bold, italic, in font color Red, Accent 3.
- The table should be converted to a range.
- Gradient fill red data bars should be applied to the Quantity in Stock column.

Insert the file name in the left section of the footer, center the worksheet horizontally, and repeat the table column titles on each page. Edit the document properties with your name, course and section, and the keywords **Petaluma, confections** Save your file, and then print or submit your worksheet electronically as directed by your instructor. If required by your instructor, print or create an electronic version of your worksheets with formulas displayed by using the instructions in Activity 1.16, and then Close Excel without saving so that you do not save the changes you made to print formulas.

End **You have completed Project 8H**

Apply a combination of the 8A and 8B skills.

GO! Make It | Project 8I Salary Summary

Project Files

For Project 8I, you will need the following file:

e02I_Salary_Summary

You will save your workbook as:

Lastname_Firstname_2I_Salary_Summary

Open e02I_Salary_Summary and save the file in your Excel Chapter 2 folder as **Lastname_Firstname_2I_Salary_Summary** Edit the worksheet as shown in Figure 8.58. To calculate Commission for each salesperson, multiply the Sales by the Commission Rate, using absolute cell references as necessary. To determine the Bonus, construct an IF function where the Logical Test determines if Sales are greater than 21,500, the Value_if_true is 500, and the Value_if_false is 0. Calculate Total Compensation by adding the Commission and the Bonus for each salesperson. Determine the Sales and Compensation totals, averages, medians, and highest and lowest amounts. Insert a table, apply Table Medium Style 16, sort the table as shown in Figure 8.58, apply cell styles and number formatting as indicated, and convert the table to a range. Insert a footer with the file name in the left section, center the worksheet horizontally, and add your name, your course name and section, and the keywords **commission, sales** to the document properties. Print or submit electronically as directed by your instructor.

Project Results

Laurales Herbs and Spices

January Sales and Compensation

	Sales	Compensation
Total	$ 394,393.00	$ 64,658.95
Average	$ 23,199.59	$ 3,803.47
Median	$ 22,924.00	$ 3,938.60
Highest	$ 33,909.00	$ 5,586.35
Lowest	$ 12,320.00	$ 1,848.00

Commission Rate 15%

Name	Sales	Commission	Bonus	Total Compensation
Anderson	12,320	1,848	-	1,848
Antonetti	22,299	3,345	500	3,845
Belitti	12,523	1,878	-	1,878
Caprio	12,932	1,940	-	1,940
Chiu	33,909	5,086	500	5,586
Cloutier	30,550	4,583	500	5,083
Fernandez	21,345	3,202	-	3,202
Hernandez	22,045	3,307	500	3,807
Hutchins	31,309	4,696	500	5,196
Jackson	29,505	4,426	500	4,926
Johnson	25,340	3,801	500	4,301
Lee	13,500	2,025	-	2,025
Lin	32,950	4,943	500	5,443
Maya	23,950	3,593	500	4,093
Nguyen	22,924	3,439	500	3,939
Ochoa	25,900	3,885	500	4,385
Patel	21,092	3,164	-	3,164

Lastname_Firstname_2I_Salary Summary

Figure 8.58

End You have completed Project 8I

Content-Based Assessments

Apply a combination of the 8A and 8B skills.

GO! Solve It | Project 8J Toppings

Project Files

For Project 8J, you will need the following file:

e02J_Toppings

You will save your workbook as:

Lastname_Firstname_2J_Toppings

Open the file e02J_Toppings and save it as **Lastname_Firstname_2J_Toppings** Complete the worksheet by entering appropriate formulas in cells B5 and B6. In the Stock Level column, enter an IF function that determines whether the quantity in stock is greater than 65. If the Quantity in Stock is greater than 65, then the Stock Level should display the text **OK** Otherwise the Stock Level should display the text **Order** Insert a Table with a total row and apply an attractive table style. Sort the table by Item #, calculate the values for B7 and B8, and then clear all filters and remove the total row from the table. Convert the table to a range. Format the worksheet attractively, and apply appropriate Data Bars to the Quantity in Stock column and conditional formatting to the Stock Level column so that items that need to be ordered are easily identified. Include the file name in the footer, add appropriate properties, and submit as directed.

Performance Element	Performance Level		
	Exemplary: You consistently applied the relevant skills	Proficient: You sometimes, but not always, applied the relevant skills	Developing: You rarely or never applied the relevant skills
Create formulas	All formulas are correct and are efficiently constructed.	Formulas are correct but not always constructed in the most efficient manner.	One or more formulas are missing or incorrect; or only numbers were entered.
Insert and format a table	Table was created and formatted properly.	Table was created but incorrect data was selected or the table was not formatted.	No table was created.
Format worksheet data attractively and appropriately	Formatting is attractive and appropriate.	Adequately formatted but difficult to read or unattractive.	Inadequate or no formatting.

End You have completed Project 8J

Apply a combination of the 8A and 8B skills.

GO! Solve It | Project 8K First Quarter Summary

Project Files

For Project 8K, you will need the following file:

e02K_First_Quarter

You will save your workbook as:

Lastname_Firstname_2K_First_Quarter

Open the file e02K_First_Quarter and save it as **Lastname_Firstname_2K_First_Quarter** This workbook contains two worksheets; one that includes California sales data by product and one that includes Oregon sales data by product. Complete the two worksheets by calculating totals by product and by month. Then calculate the Percent of Total by dividing the Product Total by the Monthly Total, using absolute cell references as necessary. Format the worksheets attractively with a title and subtitle, and apply appropriate financial formatting. Insert a new worksheet that summarizes the monthly totals by state. Enter the months as the column titles and the states as the row titles. Include a Product Total column and a column for sparklines titled **Jan./Feb./March** Format the Summary worksheet attractively with a title and subtitle, insert column sparklines that compare the months, and apply appropriate financial formatting. Include the file name in the footer, add appropriate document properties, and submit as directed.

Performance Element	Performance Level: Exemplary: You consistently applied the relevant skills	Proficient: You sometimes, but not always, applied the relevant skills	Developing: You rarely or never applied the relevant skills
Create formulas	All formulas are correct and are efficiently constructed.	Formulas are correct but not always constructed in the most efficient manner.	One or more formulas are missing or incorrect; or only numbers were entered.
Create Summary worksheet	Summary worksheet created properly.	Summary worksheet was created but the data, sparklines, or formulas were incorrect.	No Summary worksheet was created.
Format attractively and appropriately	Formatting is attractive and appropriate.	Adequately formatted but difficult to read or unattractive.	Inadequate or no formatting.

End **You have completed Project 8K**

Outcomes-Based Assessments

Rubric

The following outcomes-based assessments are *open-ended assessments*. That is, there is no specific correct result; your result will depend on your approach to the information provided. Make *Professional Quality* your goal. Use the following scoring rubric to guide you in *how* to approach the problem, and then to evaluate *how well* your approach solves the problem.

The *criteria*—Software Mastery, Content, Format and Layout, and Process—represent the knowledge and skills you have gained that you can apply to solving the problem. The *levels of performance*—Professional Quality, Approaching Professional Quality, or Needs Quality Improvements—help you and your instructor evaluate your result.

	Your completed project is of Professional Quality if you:	**Your completed project is Approaching Professional Quality if you:**	**Your completed project Needs Quality Improvements if you:**
1-Software Mastery	Choose and apply the most appropriate skills, tools, and features and identify efficient methods to solve the problem.	Choose and apply some appropriate skills, tools, and features, but not in the most efficient manner.	Choose inappropriate skills, tools, or features, or are inefficient in solving the problem.
2-Content	Construct a solution that is clear and well organized, contains content that is accurate, appropriate to the audience and purpose, and is complete. Provide a solution that contains no errors in spelling, grammar, or style.	Construct a solution in which some components are unclear, poorly organized, inconsistent, or incomplete. Misjudge the needs of the audience. Have some errors in spelling, grammar, or style, but the errors do not detract from comprehension.	Construct a solution that is unclear, incomplete, or poorly organized; contains some inaccurate or inappropriate content; and contains many errors in spelling, grammar, or style. Do not solve the problem.
3-Format and Layout	Format and arrange all elements to communicate information and ideas, clarify function, illustrate relationships, and indicate relative importance.	Apply appropriate format and layout features to some elements, but not others. Overuse features, causing minor distraction.	Apply format and layout that does not communicate information or ideas clearly. Do not use format and layout features to clarify function, illustrate relationships, or indicate relative importance. Use available features excessively, causing distraction.
4-Process	Use an organized approach that integrates planning, development, self-assessment, revision, and reflection.	Demonstrate an organized approach in some areas, but not others; or, use an insufficient process of organization throughout.	Do not use an organized approach to solve the problem.

Outcomes-Based Assessments

Apply a combination of the 8A and 8B skills.

GO! Think | Project 8L Seasonings

Project Files

For Project 8L, you will need the following file:

e02L_Seasonings

You will save your workbook as:

Lastname_Firstname_2L_Seasonings

Laura Morales, President of Laurales Herbs and Spices, has requested a worksheet that summarizes the seasonings inventory data for the month of March. Laura would like the worksheet to include the total Quantity in Stock and Number of Items for each category of items and she would like the items to be sorted from lowest to highest retail price.

Edit the workbook to provide Laura with the information requested. Format the worksheet titles and data and include an appropriately formatted table so that the worksheet is professional and easy to read and understand. Insert a footer with the file name and add appropriate document properties. Save the file as **Lastname_Firstname_2L_Seasonings** and print or submit as directed by your instructor.

End **You have completed Project 8L**

Apply a combination of the 8A and 8B skills.

GO! Think | Project 8M Expense Summary

Project Files

For Project 8M, you will need the following file:

e02M_Expense_Summary

You will save your workbook as:

Lastname_Firstname_2M_Expense_Summary

Sara Lopez, Director of the San Diego production facility, has requested a summary analysis of the administrative expenses the facility incurred in the last fiscal year. Open e02M_Expense_Summary and then complete the calculation in the four worksheets containing the quarterly data. Summarize the information in a new worksheet that includes formulas referencing the totals for each expense category for each quarter. Sum the expenses to display the yearly expense by quarter and expense category. Format the worksheets in a manner that is professional and easy to read and understand. Insert a footer with the file name and add appropriate document properties. Save the file as **Lastname_Firstname_2M_Expense_Summary** and print or submit as directed by your instructor.

End **You have completed Project 8M**

Outcomes-Based Assessments

Apply a combination of the 8A and 8B skills.

You and GO! | Project 8N Annual Expenses

Project Files

For Project 8N, you will need the following file:

New blank Excel workbook

You will save your workbook as:

Lastname_Firstname_2N_Annual_Expenses

Develop a workbook that details the expenses you expect to incur during the current year. Create four worksheets, one for each quarter of the year and enter your expenses by month. For example, the Quarter 1 sheet will contain expense information for January, February, and March. Some of these expenses might include, but are not limited to, Mortgage, Rent, Utilities, Phone, Food, Entertainment, Tuition, Childcare, Clothing, and Insurance. Include monthly and quarterly totals for each category of expense. Insert a worksheet that summarizes the total expenses for each quarter. Format the worksheet by adjusting column width and wrapping text, and by applying appropriate financial number formatting and cell styles. Insert a footer with the file name and center the worksheet horizontally on the page. Save your file as **Lastname_Firstname_2N_Annual_Expenses** and submit as directed.

End You have completed Project 8N

Apply a combination of the 8A and 8B skills.

GO! Collaborate | Project 8O Bell Orchid Hotels Group Running Case

This project relates to the Bell Orchid Hotels. Your instructor may assign this group case project to your class. If your instructor assigns this project, he or she will provide you with information and instructions to work as part of a group. The group will apply the skills gained thus far to help the Bell Orchid Hotels achieve their business goals.

End You have completed Project 8O

Analyzing Data with Pie Charts, Line Charts, and What-If Analysis Tools

OUTCOMES

At the end of this chapter you will be able to:

OBJECTIVES

Mastering these objectives will enable you to:

PROJECT 9A

Present budget data in a pie chart.

1. Chart Data with a Pie Chart (p. 465)
2. Format a Pie Chart (p. 468)
3. Edit a Workbook and Update a Chart (p. 474)
4. Use Goal Seek to Perform What-If Analysis (p. 475)

PROJECT 9B

Make projections using what-if analysis and present projections in a line chart.

5. Design a Worksheet for What-If Analysis (p. 481)
6. Answer What-If Questions by Changing Values in a Worksheet (p. 488)
7. Chart Data with a Line Chart (p. 491)

Shutterstock

In This Chapter

In this chapter, you will work with two different types of commonly used charts that make it easy to visualize data. You will create a pie chart in a separate chart sheet to show how the parts of a budget contribute to a total budget. You will also practice using parentheses in a formula, calculate the percentage rate of an increase, answer what-if questions, and then chart data in a line chart to show the flow of data over time. In this chapter you will also practice formatting the axes in a line chart.

The projects in this chapter relate to **The City of Orange Blossom Beach**, a coastal city located between Fort Lauderdale and Miami. The city's access to major transportation provides both residents and businesses an opportunity to compete in the global marketplace. Each year the city welcomes a large number of tourists who enjoy the warm climate and beautiful beaches, and who embark on cruises from this major cruise port. The city encourages best environmental practices and partners with cities in other countries to promote sound government at the local level.

Project 9A Budget Pie Chart

Project Activities

In Activities 9.01 through 9.11, you will edit a worksheet for Lila Darius, City Manager, that projects expenses from the city's general fund for the next fiscal year, and then present the data in a pie chart. Your completed worksheet will look similar to Figure 9.1.

Project Files

For Project 9A, you will need the following file:

e03A_Fund_Expenses

You will save your workbook as:

Lastname_Firstname_3A_Fund_Expenses

Project Results

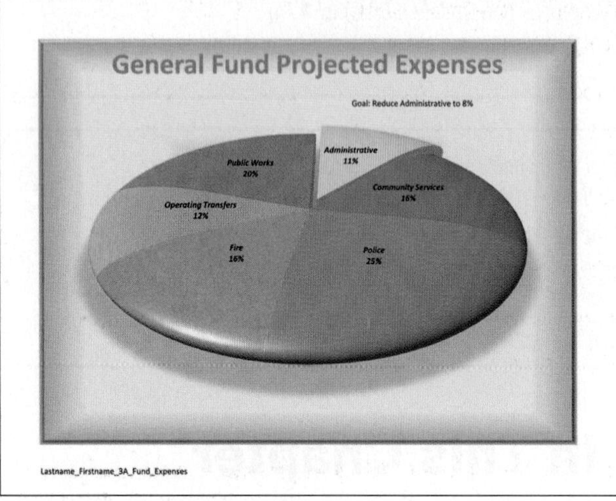

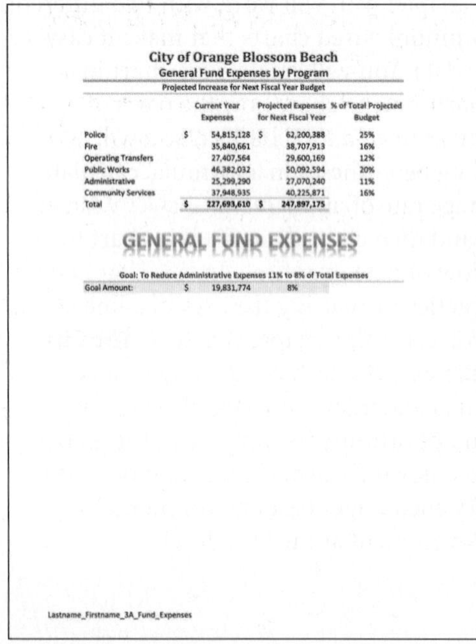

City of Orange Blossom Beach
General Fund Expenses by Program
Projected Increase for Next Fiscal Year Budget

	Current Year Expenses	Projected Expenses for Next Fiscal Year	% of Total Projected Budget
Police	$ 54,815,128	$ 62,200,388	25%
Fire	35,840,661	38,707,913	16%
Operating Transfers	27,407,564	29,600,169	12%
Public Works	46,382,032	50,092,594	20%
Administrative	25,299,290	27,070,240	11%
Community Services	37,948,935	40,225,871	16%
Total	$ 227,693,610	$ 247,897,175	

GENERAL FUND EXPENSES

Goal: To Reduce Administrative Expenses 11% to 8% of Total Expenses

Goal Amount:	$ 19,831,774	8%

Lastname_Firstname_3A_Fund_Expenses

Figure 9.1
Project 9A Fund Expenses

Objective 1 | Chart Data with a Pie Chart

A ***pie chart*** shows the relationship of each part to a whole. The size of each pie slice is equal to its value compared to the total value of all the slices. The pie chart style charts data that is arranged in a single column or single row, and shows the size of items in a single data series proportional to the sum of the items. Whereas a column or bar chart can have two or more data series in the chart, a pie chart can have only one data series.

Consider using a pie chart when you have only one data series to plot, you do not have more than seven categories, and the categories represent parts of a total value.

Activity 9.01 | Creating a Pie Chart and a Chart Sheet

A ***fund*** is a sum of money set aside for a specific purpose. In a municipal government like the City of Orange Blossom Beach, the ***general fund*** is money set aside for the normal operating activities of the city, such as police, fire, and administering the everyday functions of the city.

1 **Start** Excel. From the student files that accompany this textbook, open **e03A_Fund_Expenses.** From **Backstage view**, display the **Save As** dialog box. Navigate to the location where you are storing projects for this chapter.

2 Create a new folder named **Excel Chapter 3** and open the new folder. In the **File name** box, type **Lastname_Firstname_3A_Fund_Expenses** Click **Save** or press Enter.

The worksheet indicates the expenses for the current year and the projected expenses for the next fiscal year.

3 Click cell **D5**, and then type **=** to begin a formula.

4 Click cell **C5**, which is the first value that is part of the total Projected Expenses, to insert it into the formula. Type **/** to indicate division, and then click cell **C11**, which is the total Projected Expenses.

Recall that to determine the percentage by which a value makes up a total, you must divide the value by the total. The result will be a percentage expressed as a decimal.

5 Press F4 to make the reference to the value in cell **C11** absolute, which will enable you to copy the formula. Compare your screen with Figure 9.2.

Recall that an ***absolute cell reference*** refers to a cell by its fixed position in the worksheet. The reference to cell C5 is a ***relative cell reference***, because when you copy the formula, you want the reference to change *relative* to its row.

Recall also that dollar signs display to indicate that a cell reference is absolute.

Figure 9.2

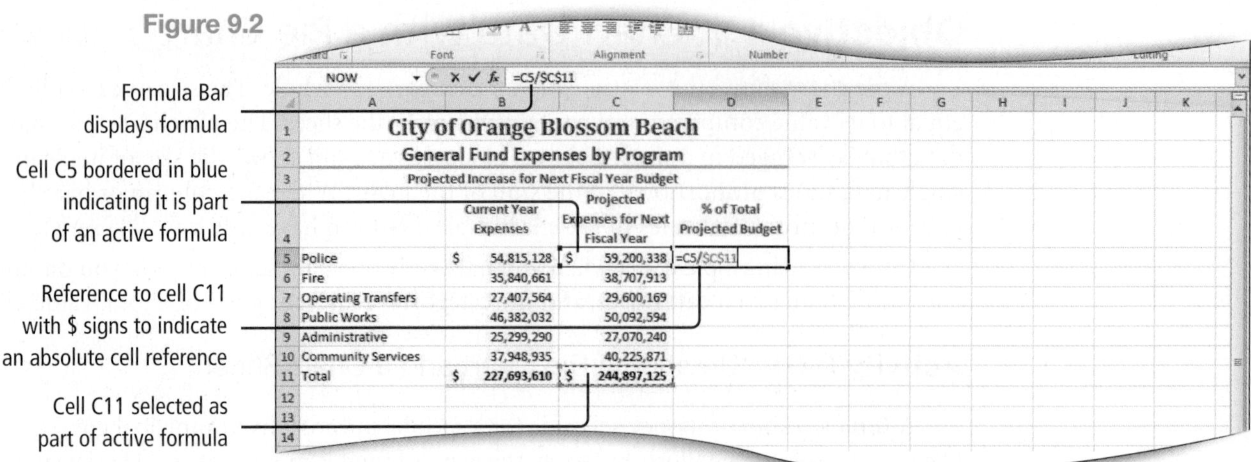

6 On the **Formula Bar**, click the **Enter** button [✓] to confirm the entry and to keep cell **D5** the active cell. Copy the formula down through cell **D10**, and then compare your screen with Figure 9.3.

Figure 9.3

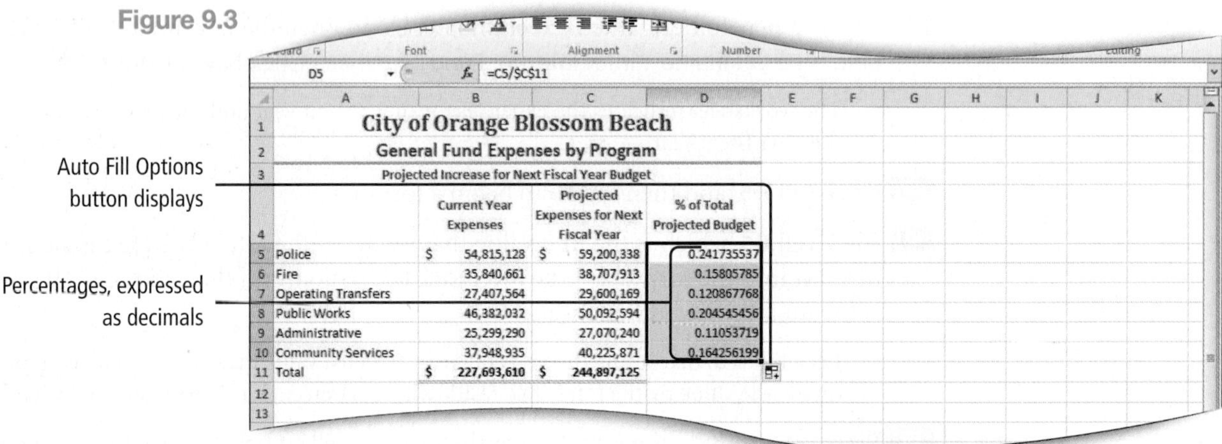

7 With the range **D5:D10** still selected, right-click over the selection, and then on the Mini toolbar, click the **Percent Style** button [%] and the **Center** [≡] button. Click cell **A1** to cancel the selection, and then **Save** [💾] your workbook. Compare your screen with Figure 9.4.

Figure 9.4

Percent of Total for each program calculated, expressed as percentages

A1 | City of Orange Blossom Beach

City of Orange Blossom Beach
General Fund Expenses by Program
Projected Increase for Next Fiscal Year Budget

	Current Year Expenses	Projected Expenses for Next Fiscal Year	% of Total Projected Budget
Police	$ 54,815,128	$ 59,200,338	24%
Fire	35,840,661	38,707,913	16%
Operating Transfers	27,407,564	29,600,169	12%
Public Works	46,382,032	50,092,594	20%
Administrative	25,299,290	27,070,240	11%
Community Services	37,948,935	40,225,871	16%
Total	$ 227,693,610	$ 244,897,125	

8 Select the range **A5:A10**, hold down Ctrl, and then select the range **C5:C10** to select the nonadjacent ranges with the program names and the projected expense for each program.

To create a pie chart, you must select two ranges. One range contains the labels for each slice of the pie chart, and the other range contains the values that add up to a total. The two ranges must have the same number of cells and the range with the values should *not* include the cell with the total.

The program names (Police, Fire, and so on) are the category names and will identify the slices of the pie chart. Each projected expense is a ***data point***—a value that originates in a worksheet cell and that is represented in a chart by a ***data marker***. In a pie chart, each pie slice is a data marker. Together, the data points form the ***data series***—related data points represented by data markers—and determine the size of each pie slice.

9 With the nonadjacent ranges selected, click the **Insert tab**, and then in the **Charts group**, click **Pie**. Under **3-D Pie**, click the first chart—**Pie in 3-D**—to create the chart on your worksheet.

10 On the **Design tab**, at the right end of the Ribbon in the **Location group**, click the **Move Chart** button. In the **Move Chart** dialog box, click the **New sheet** option button.

11 In the **New sheet** box, replace the highlighted text *Chart1* by typing **Projected Expenses Chart** and then click **OK** to display the chart on a separate worksheet in your workbook. Compare your screen with Figure 9.5.

The pie chart displays on a separate new sheet in your workbook, and a ***legend*** identifies the pie slices. Recall that a legend is a chart element that identifies the patterns or colors assigned to the categories in the chart.

A ***chart sheet*** is a workbook sheet that contains only a chart; it is useful when you want to view a chart separately from the worksheet data. The sheet tab indicates *Projected Expenses Chart*.

Figure 9.5

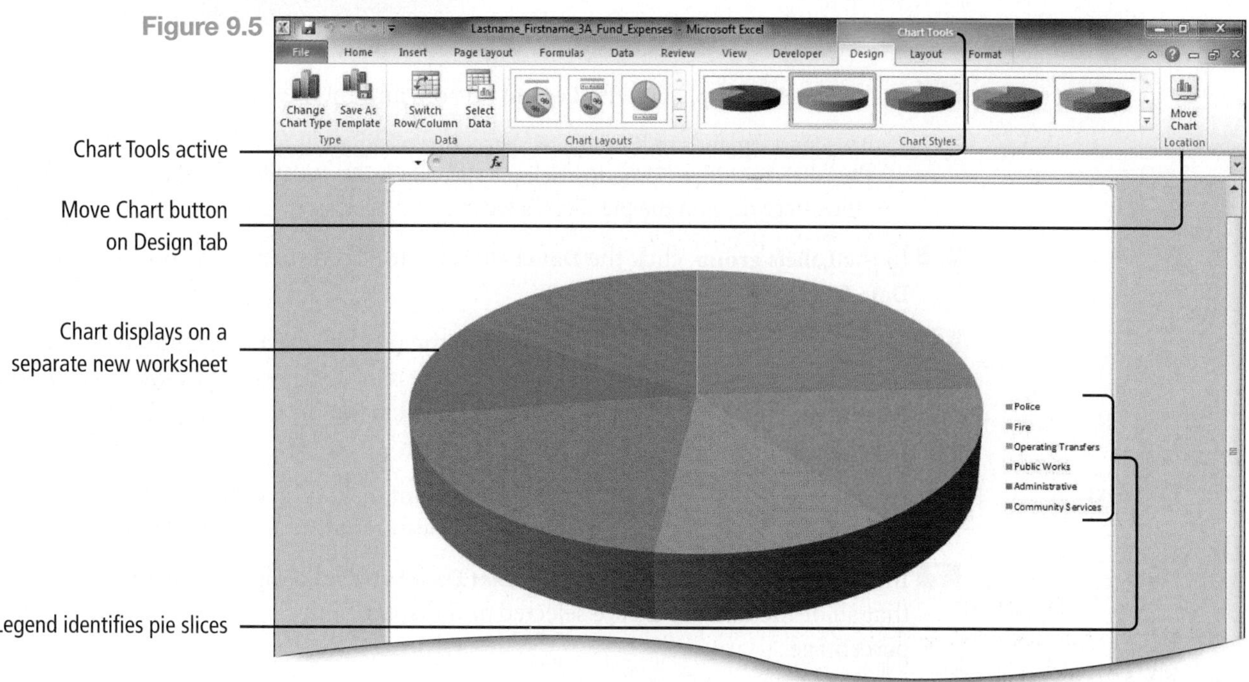

Objective 2 | Format a Pie Chart

Activity 9.02 | Applying Percentages to Labels in a Pie Chart

In your worksheet, for each expense, you calculated the percent of the total in column D. These percentages can also be calculated by the Chart feature and added to the pie slices as labels.

1. On the Ribbon under **Chart Tools**, click the **Layout tab**, and then in the **Labels group**, click the **Chart Title** button. On the displayed list, click **Above Chart**.
2. With the **Chart Title** box selected, watch the **Formula Bar** as you type **General Fund Projected Expenses** and then press Enter to create the new chart title in the box.
3. Point to the chart title text, right-click to display the Mini toolbar, and then change the **Font Size** to **36** and change the **Font Color** A to **Olive Green, Accent 1, Darker 25%**—in the fifth column, the fifth color. Compare your screen with Figure 9.6.

Figure 9.6

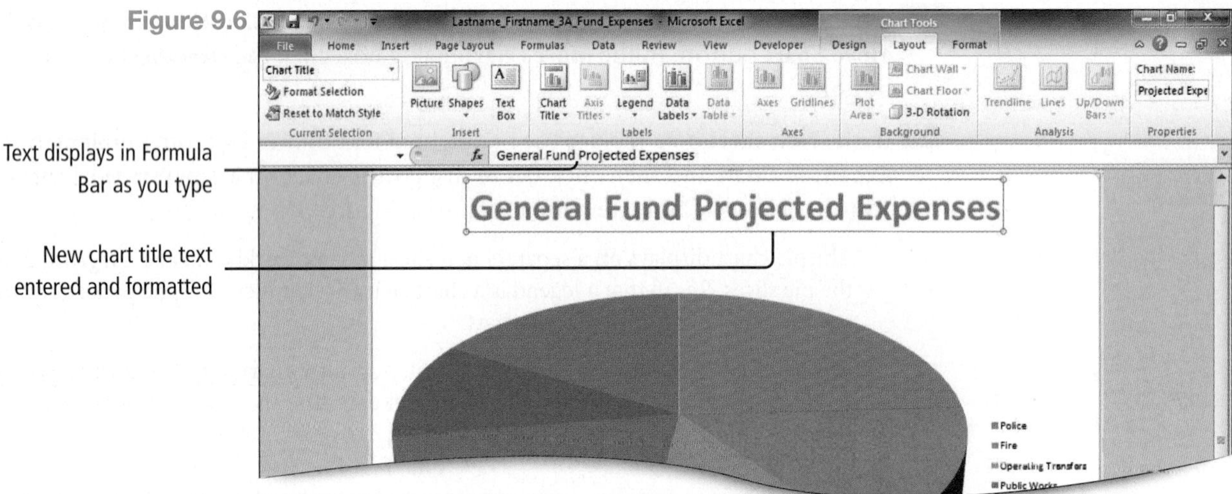

4. In the **Labels group**, click the **Legend** button, and then click **None**.

   The chart expands to fill the new space. In a pie chart, it is usually more effective to place the labels within, or close to, each pie slice. Because you will place the program names (the categories) on the pie slices, a legend is unnecessary.

5. In the **Labels group**, click the **Data Labels** button, and then at the bottom, click **More Data Label Options**.
6. In the **Format Data Labels** dialog box, on the left, be sure **Label Options** is selected. On the right, under **Label Contains**, click as necessary to select the **Category Name** and **Percentage** check boxes. *Clear* any other check boxes in this group. Under **Label Position**, click the **Center** option button.

   In the worksheet, you calculated the percent of the total in column D. Here, the percentage will be calculated by the Chart feature and added to the chart as a label.

7. In the lower right corner of the **Format Data Labels** dialog box, click **Close**, and notice that all of the data labels are selected and display both the category name and the percentage.

8 Point to any of the selected labels, right-click to display the Mini toolbar, and then change the **Font Size** to **11**, apply **Bold** [B], and apply **Italic** [I].

9 **Save** your workbook. Press Esc to deselect the labels, and then compare your screen with Figure 9.7.

Figure 9.7

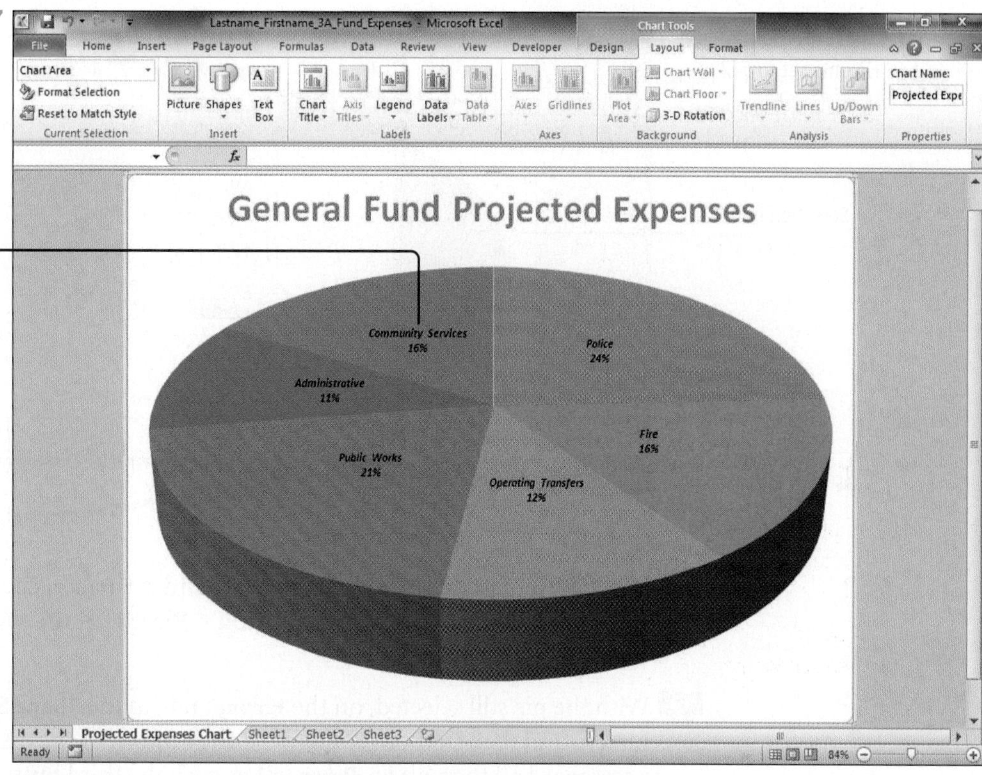

Data labels on pie slices replace legend; labels include category name and percentage; data labels centered in slice, 11 pt font, bold and italic

Activity 9.03 | Formatting a Pie Chart with 3-D

3-D, which is short for *three-dimensional*, refers to an image that appears to have all three spatial dimensions—length, width, and depth.

1 Click in any pie slice outside of the label to select the entire pie; notice that selection handles display on the outside corners of each slice.

2 Click the **Format tab**. In the **Shape Styles group**, click the **Shape Effects** button, point to **Bevel**, and then at the bottom of the gallery, click **3-D Options**.

3 In the **Format Data Series** dialog box, on the right, under **Bevel**, click the **Top** button. In the displayed gallery, under **Bevel**, point to the first button to display the ScreenTip *Circle*. Click the **Circle** button. Then click the **Bottom** button, and apply the **Circle** bevel.

Bevel is a shape effect that uses shading and shadows to make the edges of a shape appear to be curved or angled.

4 In the four **Width** and **Height** spin boxes, type **512 pt** and then compare your screen with Figure 9.8.

Excel | Chapter 9

Figure 9.8

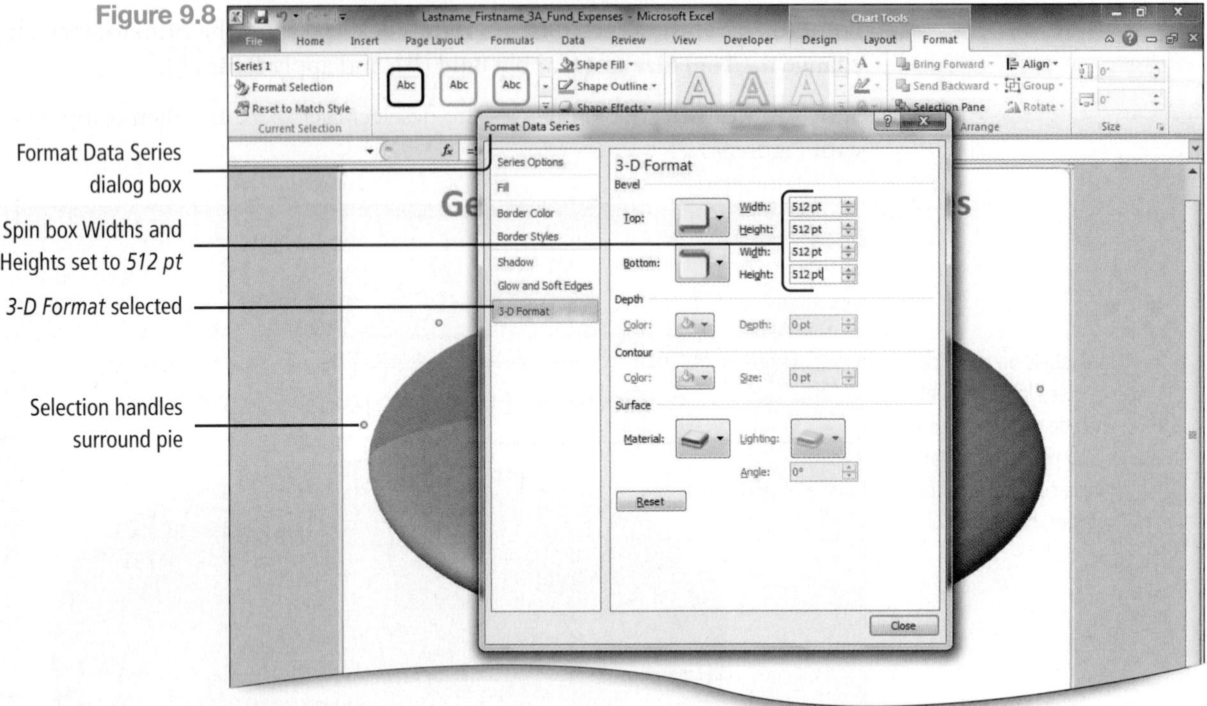

5 In the lower portion of the dialog box, under **Surface**, click the **Material** button. Under **Standard**, click the third button—**Plastic**. In the lower right corner, click **Close**.

6 With the pie still selected, on the **Format tab**, in the **Shape Styles group**, click **Shape Effects**, and then point to **Shadow**. At the bottom of the displayed gallery, scroll if necessary, and then under **Perspective**, click the third button, which displays the ScreenTip *Below* to display a shadow below the pie chart. Click **Save**.

Activity 9.04 | Rotating a Pie Chart

The order in which the data series in pie charts are plotted in Excel is determined by the order of the data on the worksheet. To gain a different view of the chart, you can rotate the chart within the 360 degrees of the circle of the pie shape to present a different visual perspective of the chart.

1 Notice the position of the **Fire** and **Police** slices in the chart. Then, with the pie chart still selected—sizing handles surround the pie—point anywhere in the pie and right-click. On the displayed shortcut menu, click **Format Data Series**.

Another Way
Drag the slider to 100.

2 In the **Format Data Series** dialog box, on the left, be sure **Series Options** is selected. On the right, under **Angle of first slice**, click in the box and type **100** to rotate the chart 100 degrees to the right.

3 Close the **Format Data Series** dialog box. Click **Save**, and then compare your screen with Figure 9.9.

Rotating the chart can provide a better perspective to the chart. Here, rotating the chart in this manner emphasizes that the Fire and Police programs represent a significant portion of the total expenses.

Figure 9.9

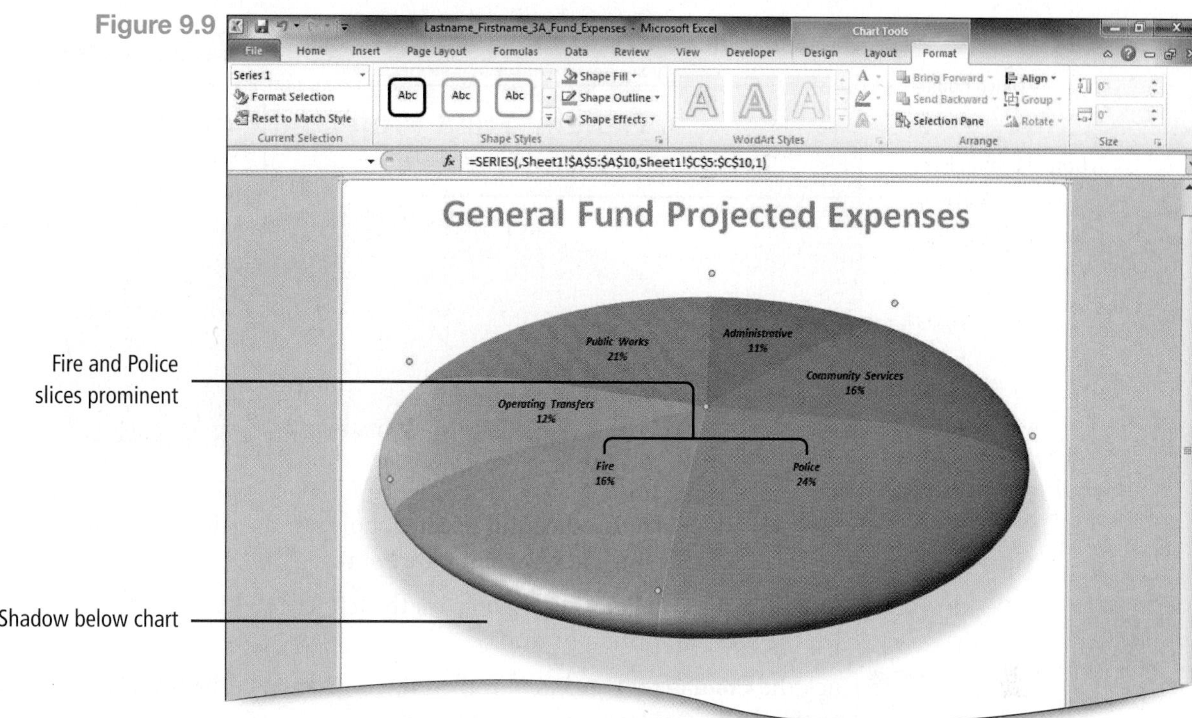

Activity 9.05 | Exploding and Coloring a Pie Slice

You can pull out—***explode***—one or more slices of a pie chart to emphasize a specific slice or slices. Additionally, there is a different chart type you can select if you want *all* the slices to explode and emphasize all the individual slices of a pie chart—the exploded pie or exploded pie in 3-D chart type. The exploded pie chart type displays the contribution of *each* value to the total, while at the same time emphasizing individual values.

1 Press Esc to deselect all chart elements. Click any slice to select the entire pie, and then click the **Administrative** slice to select only that slice. Compare your screen with Figure 9.10.

Figure 9.10

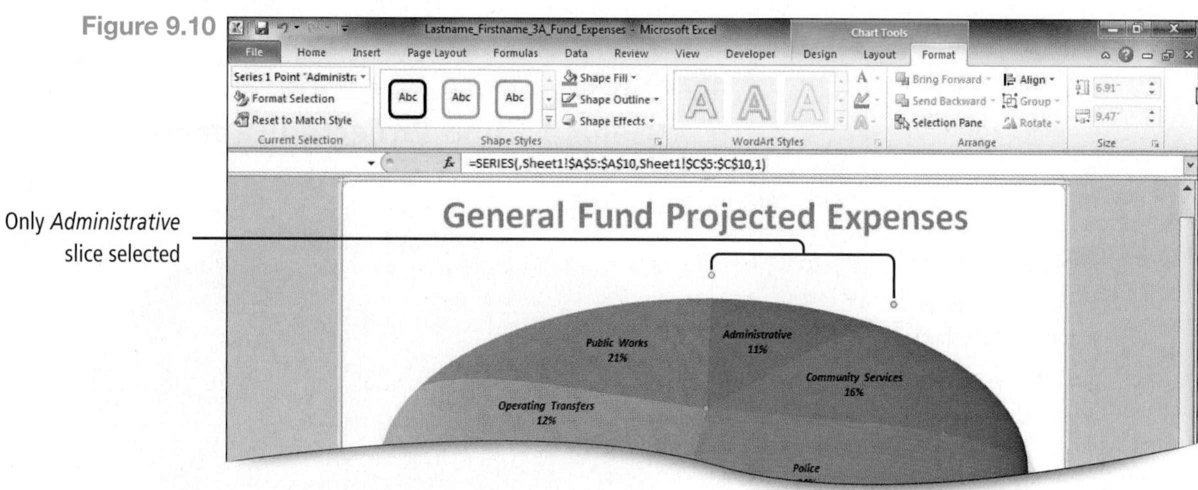

2 Point to the **Administrative** slice to display the pointer, and then drag the slice slightly upward and away from the center of the pie, as shown in Figure 9.11, and then release the mouse button.

Figure 9.11

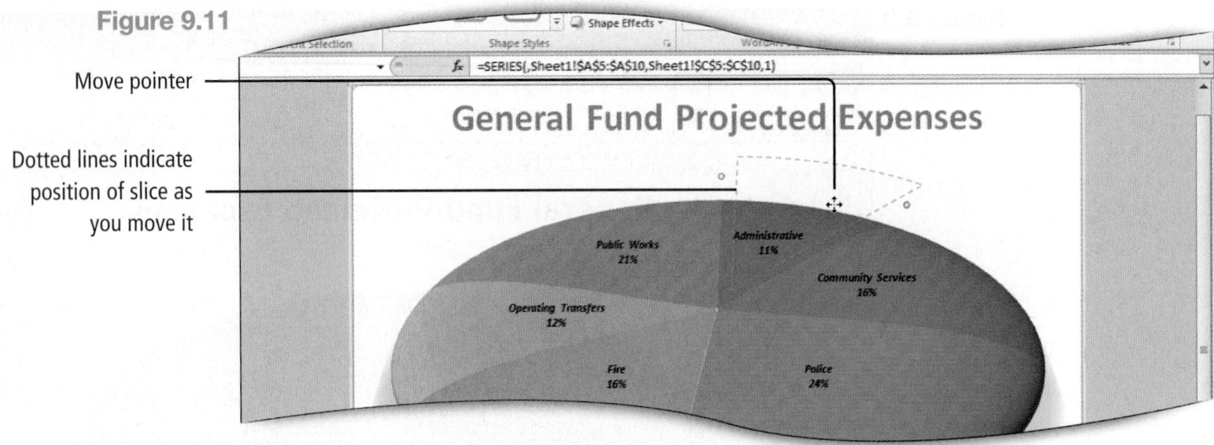

3 With the **Administrative** slice still selected, point to the slice and right-click, and then on the shortcut menu, click **Format Data Point.**

4 In the **Format Data Point** dialog box, on the left, click **Fill**. On the right, under **Fill**, click the **Solid fill** option button.

5 Click the **Color arrow**, and then under **Theme Colors**, in the seventh column, click the fourth color—**Gold, Accent 3, Lighter 40%**.

6 In the lower right corner of the **Format Data Point** dialog box, click the **Close** button.

Activity 9.06 | Formatting the Chart Area

The entire chart and all of its elements comprise the ***chart area***.

1 Point to the white area just inside the border of the chart to display the ScreenTip *Chart Area*. Click one time.

2 On the **Format tab**, in the **Shape Styles group**, click the **Shape Effects** button, point to **Bevel**, and then under **Bevel**, in the second row, click the third bevel—**Convex**.

3 Press Esc to deselect the chart element and view this effect—a convex beveled frame around your entire chart—and then compare your screen with Figure 9.12.

Figure 9.12

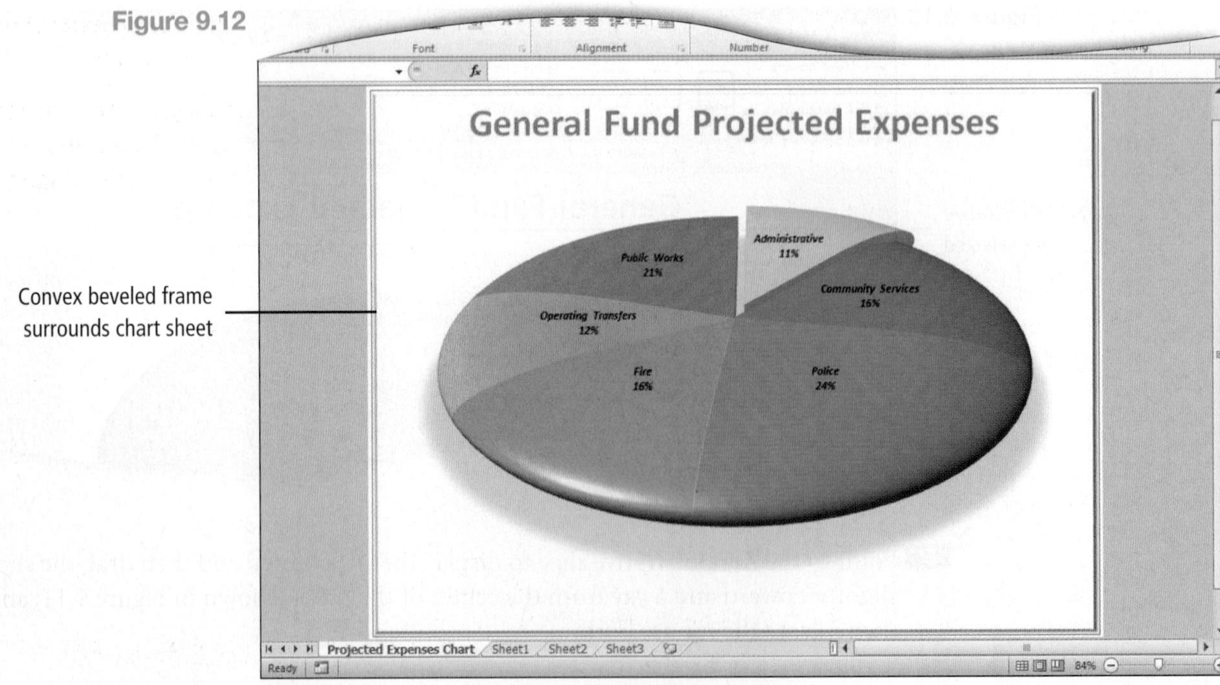

4. Point slightly inside the border of the chart to display the ScreenTip *Chart Area*, right-click, and then on the shortcut menu, click **Format Chart Area.**

5. In the **Format Chart Area** dialog box, on the left, be sure that **Fill** is selected. On the right, under **Fill**, click the **Gradient fill** option button.

6. Click the **Preset colors** arrow, and then in the second row, click the last preset, **Fog.** Click the **Type arrow**, and then click **Path**. Click the **Close** button.

7. Compare your screen with Figure 9.13, and then **Save** your workbook.

Figure 9.13

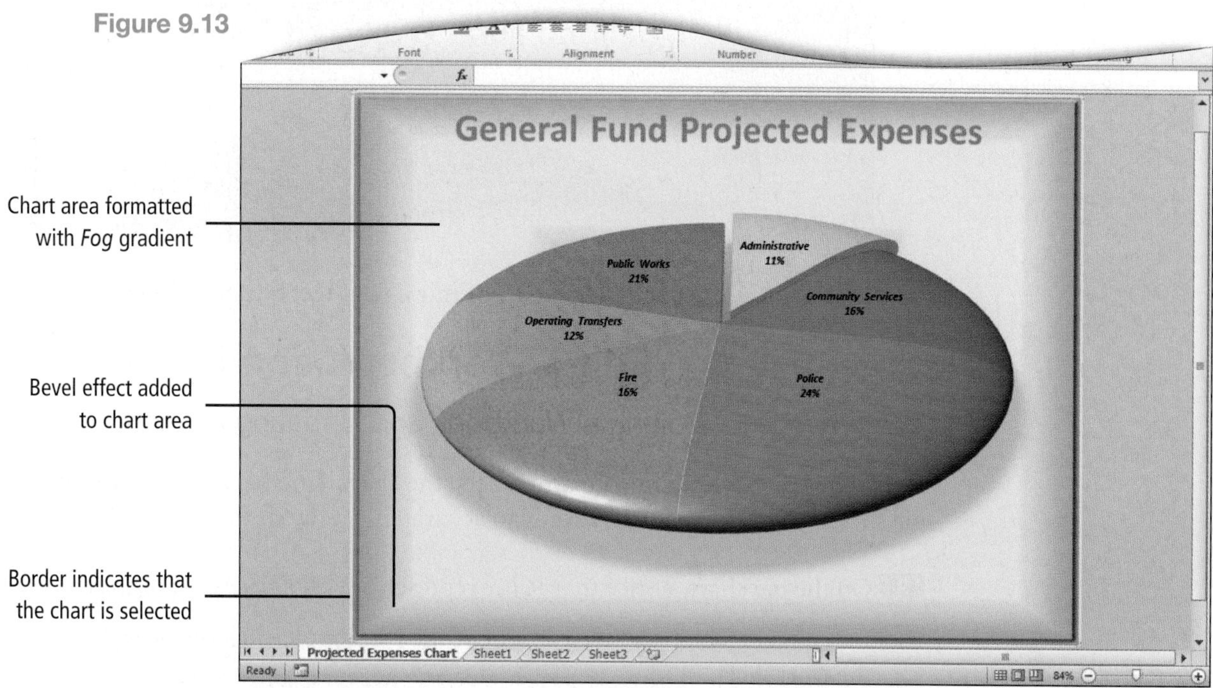

Activity 9.07 | Inserting a Text Box in a Chart

A ***text box*** is a movable, resizable container for text or graphics.

1. With the Chart Area still selected, click the **Layout tab**, and then in the **Insert group**, click the **Text Box** button, and then move the pointer into the chart area.

2. Position the displayed pointer under the *c* in *Projected* and about midway between the title and the pie—above the *Administrative* slice. Hold down the left mouse button, and then drag down and to the right approximately as shown in Figure 9.14; your text box need not be precise.

Figure 9.14

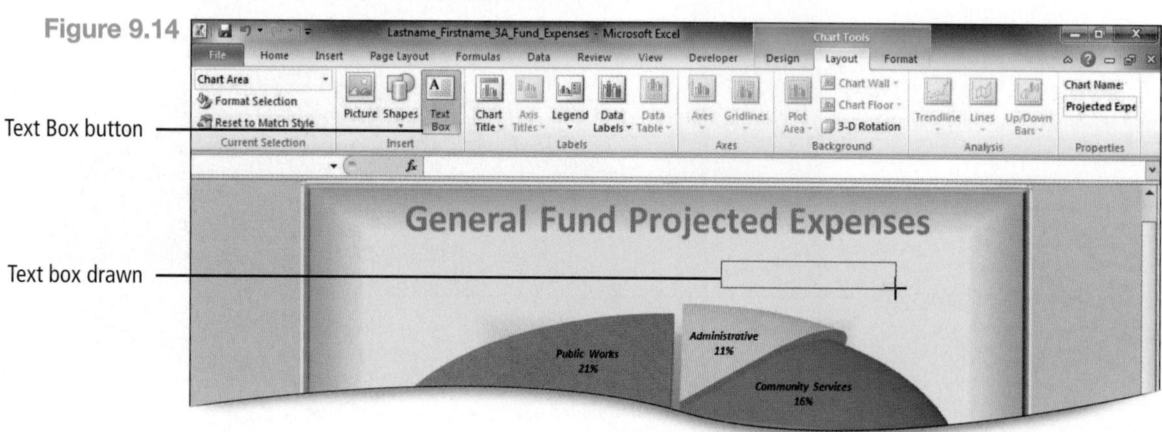

3 With the insertion point blinking inside the text box, type **Goal: Reduce Administrative to 8%** Press Esc or click outside the chart area to deselect the chart element, and then compare your screen with Figure 9.15.

Figure 9.15

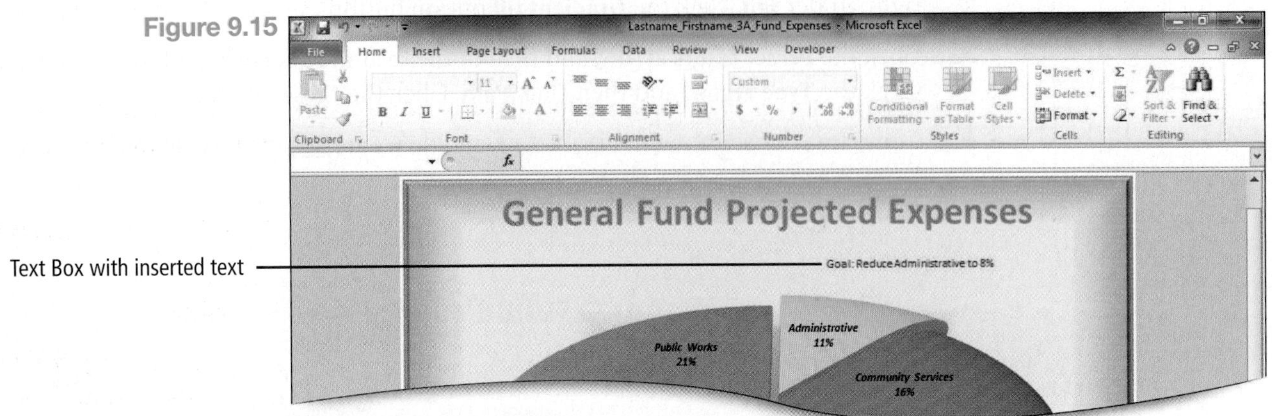

Text Box with inserted text

4 If necessary, select and then adjust or move your text box. **Save** your workbook.

Objective 3 | Edit a Workbook and Update a Chart

Activity 9.08 | Editing a Workbook and Updating a Chart

If you edit the data in your worksheet, the chart data markers—in this instance the pie slices—will adjust automatically to accurately represent the new values.

1 On the pie chart, notice that *Police* represents 24% of the total projected expenses.

2 In the sheet tab area at the bottom of the workbook, click the **Sheet1 tab** to redisplay the worksheet.

3 Click cell **C5**, and then in **Formula Bar**, change *59,200,338* to **62,200,388**

> **Another Way**
> Double-click the cell to position the insertion point in the cell and edit.

4 Press Enter, and notice that the total in cell **C11** recalculates to *$247,897,175* and the percentages in **column D** also recalculate.

5 Display the **Projected Expenses Chart** sheet. Notice that the pie slices adjust to show the recalculation—*Police* is now *25%* of the projected expenses. Click **Save**, and then compare your screen with Figure 9.16.

Figure 9.16

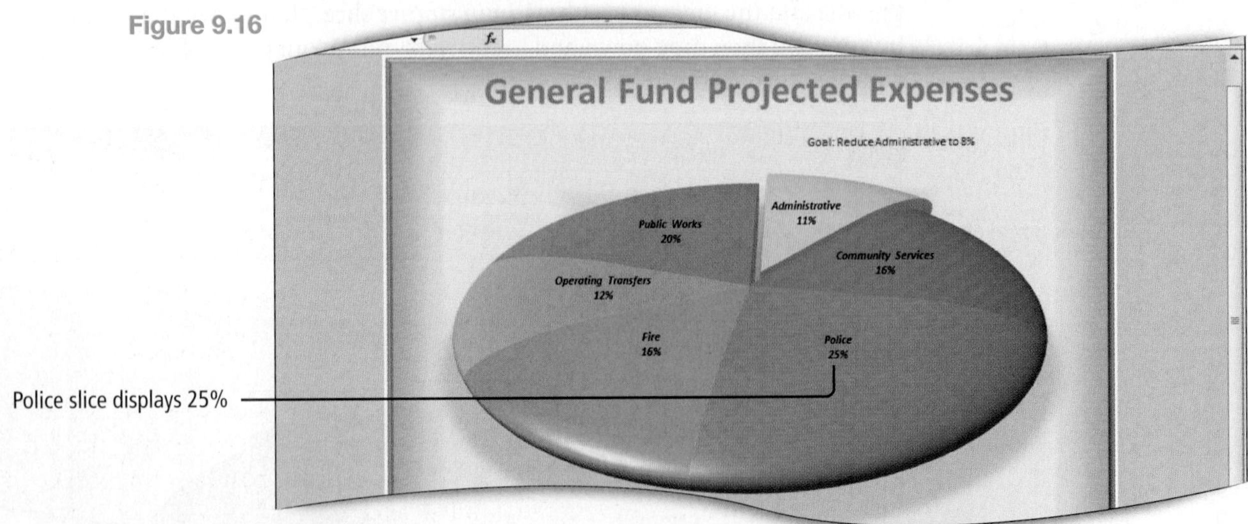

Police slice displays 25%

Activity 9.09 | Inserting WordArt in a Worksheet

WordArt is a gallery of text styles with which you can create decorative effects, such as shadowed or mirrored text. In an Excel worksheet, WordArt can be effective if you plan to display your worksheet in a PowerPoint presentation, or if readers will be viewing the worksheet data online.

1. In the sheet tab area at the bottom of the workbook, click the **Sheet1 tab** to redisplay the worksheet. Click the **Insert tab**, and then in the **Text group**, click the **WordArt** button.
2. In the WordArt gallery, in the last row, click the last style—**Fill – Olive Green, Accent 1, Metal Bevel, Reflection.**

   The WordArt indicating *YOUR TEXT HERE* displays in the worksheet.
3. With the WordArt selected, type **general fund expenses** and then point anywhere on the dashed border surrounding the WordArt object. Click the dashed border one time to change it to a solid border, indicating that all of the text is selected.
4. On the **Home tab**, in the **Font group**, change the **Font Size** to **28.**
5. Point to the WordArt border to display the [pointer icon] pointer, and then drag to position the upper left corner of the WordArt approximately as shown in Figure 9.17. If necessary, hold down [Ctrl] and press any of the arrow keys on your keyboard to move the WordArt object into position in small increments. Click any cell to deselect the WordArt, and then click **Save** [Save icon].

Figure 9.17

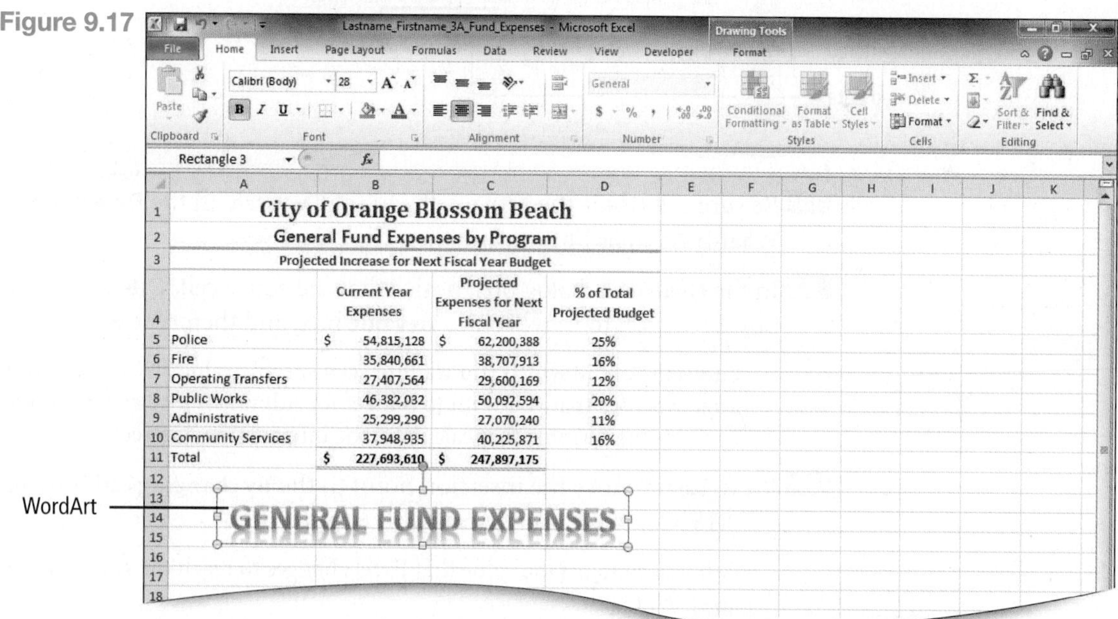

	A	B	C	D
1	City of Orange Blossom Beach			
2	General Fund Expenses by Program			
3	Projected Increase for Next Fiscal Year Budget			
4		Current Year Expenses	Projected Expenses for Next Fiscal Year	% of Total Projected Budget
5	Police	$ 54,815,128	$ 62,200,388	25%
6	Fire	35,840,661	38,707,913	16%
7	Operating Transfers	27,407,564	29,600,169	12%
8	Public Works	46,382,032	50,092,594	20%
9	Administrative	25,299,290	27,070,240	11%
10	Community Services	37,948,935	40,225,871	16%
11	Total	$ 227,693,610	$ 247,897,175	

Objective 4 | Use Goal Seek to Perform What-If Analysis

Activity 9.10 | Using Goal Seek to Perform What-If Analysis

The process of changing the values in cells to see how those changes affect the outcome of formulas in your worksheet is referred to as ***what-if analysis.*** A what-if analysis tool that is included with Excel is ***Goal Seek***, which finds the input needed in one cell to arrive at the desired result in another cell.

1 In cell **A17**, type **Goal: To Reduce Administrative Expenses from 11% to 8% of Total Expenses** Merge and center the text across the range **A17:D17**, and then apply the **Heading 3** Cell Style.

2 In cell **A18**, type **Goal Amount:** and press Enter.

3 Select the range **C9:D9**, right-click over the selection, and then click **Copy**. Point to cell **B18**, right-click, and then under **Paste Options**, click the **Paste** button.

4 Press Esc to cancel the moving border, click cell **C18**, and then compare your screen with Figure 9.18.

Figure 9.18

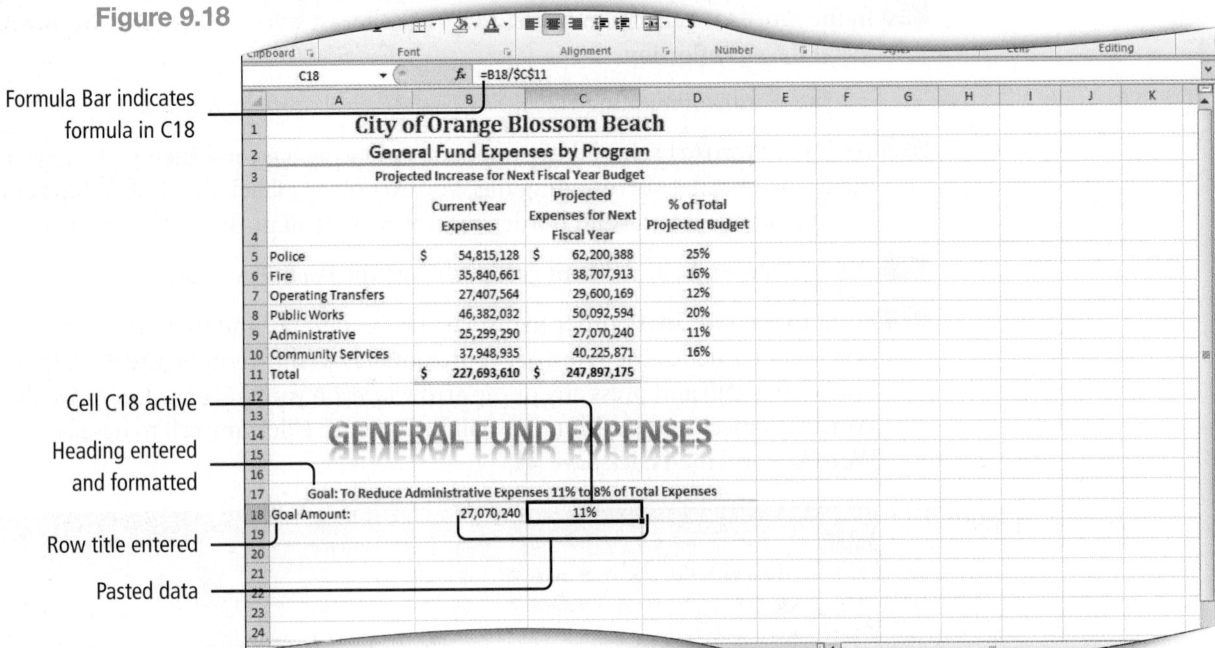

5 Be sure cell **C18** is the active cell. On the **Data tab**, in the **Data Tools group**, click the **What-If Analysis** button, and then click **Goal Seek**.

6 In the **Goal Seek** dialog box, notice that the active cell, **C18**, is indicated in the **Set cell** box. Press Tab to move to the **To value** box, and then type **8%**

C18 is the cell in which you want to set a specific value; 8% is the percentage of the total expenses that you want to budget for Administrative expenses. The Set cell box contains the formula that calculates the information you seek.

7 Press Tab to move the insertion point to the **By changing cell** box, and then click cell **B18**. Compare your screen with Figure 9.19.

Cell B18 contains the value that Excel changes to reach the goal. Excel formats this cell as an absolute cell reference.

Figure 9.19

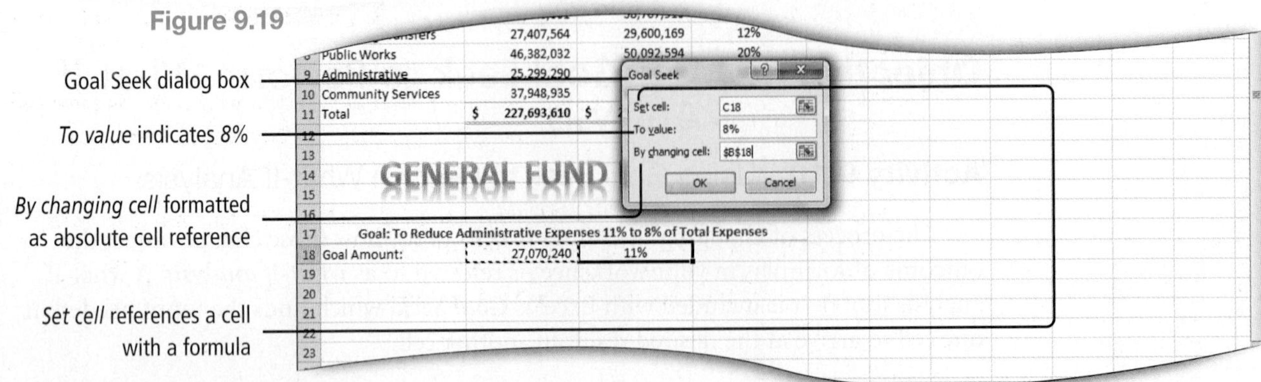

8 Click **OK**. In the displayed **Goal Seek Status** dialog box, click **OK**.

9 Select the range **A18:C18**. From the **Home tab**, display the **Cell Styles** gallery. Under **Themed Cell Styles**, apply **20% - Accent3**. Click cell **B18**, and then from the **Cell Styles** gallery, at the bottom of the gallery under **Number Format**, apply the **Currency [0]** cell style.

10 Press Ctrl + Home, click **Save**, and then compare your screen with Figure 9.20.

Excel calculates that the City must budget for *$19,831,774* in Administrative expenses in order for this item to become 8% of the total projected budget.

Figure 9.20

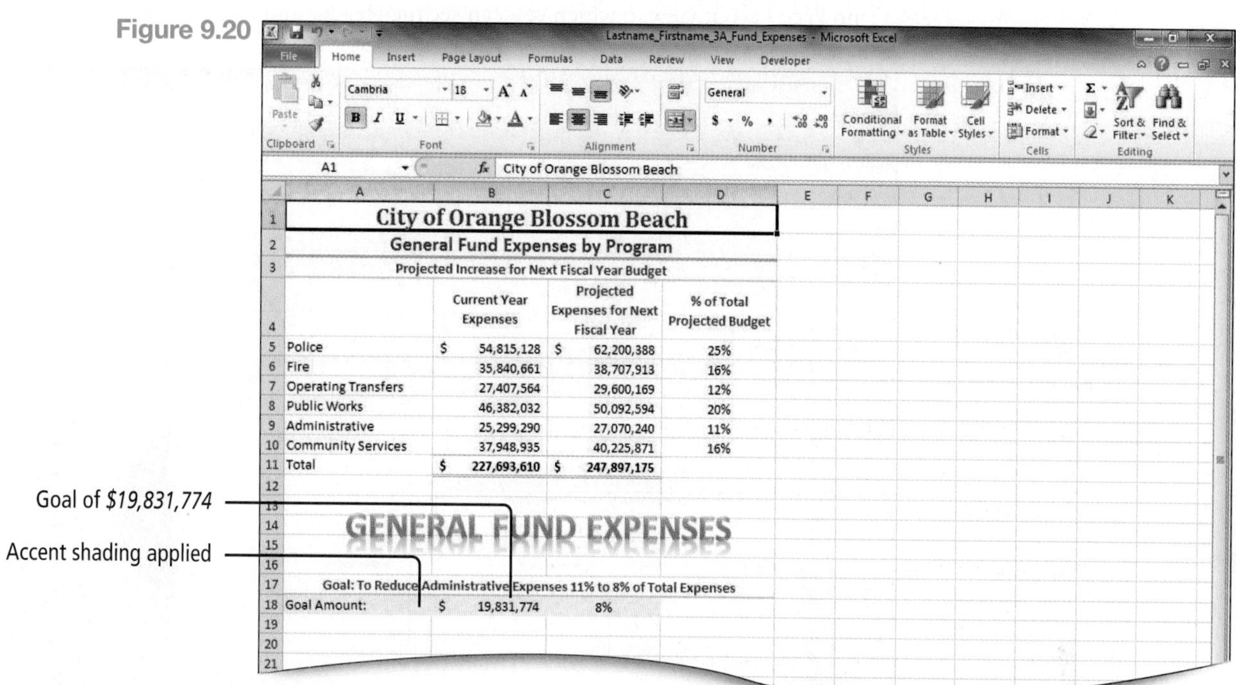

	Current Year Expenses	Projected Expenses for Next Fiscal Year	% of Total Projected Budget
Police	$ 54,815,128	$ 62,200,388	25%
Fire	35,840,661	38,707,913	16%
Operating Transfers	27,407,564	29,600,169	12%
Public Works	46,382,032	50,092,594	20%
Administrative	25,299,290	27,070,240	11%
Community Services	37,948,935	40,225,871	16%
Total	$ 227,693,610	$ 247,897,175	
Goal Amount:	$ 19,831,774	8%	

Activity 9.11 | Preparing and Printing a Workbook with a Chart Sheet

> **Another Way**
> Right-click the sheet tab, click Rename, type, and press Enter.

1 With your worksheet displayed, in the sheet tab area, double-click *Sheet1* to select the text, and then type **Projected Expenses Data** and press Enter.

2 Select **Sheet2** and **Sheet3**, right-click over the selected tabs, and then click **Delete** to delete the unused sheets.

3 On the **Insert tab**, click **Header & Footer**. In the **Navigation group**, click the **Go to Footer** button, click in the **left section** above the word *Footer*, and then in the **Header & Footer Elements group**, click the **File Name** button.

4 Click in a cell above the footer to deselect the **Footer area** and view your file name. On the **Page Layout tab**, in the **Page Setup group**, click the **Margins** button, and then at the bottom click **Custom Margins**.

5 In the displayed **Page Setup** dialog box, under **Center on page**, select the **Horizontally** check box. Click **OK**, and then on the status bar, click the **Normal** button to return to Normal view.

Recall that after displaying worksheets in Page Layout View, dotted lines display to indicate the page breaks when you return to Normal view.

6 Press Ctrl + Home to move to the top of the worksheet.

7 Click the **Projected Expenses Chart** sheet tab to display the chart sheet. On the **Insert tab**, in the **Text group**, click **Header & Footer** to display the **Header/Footer tab** of the **Page Setup** dialog box.

8 In the center of the **Page Setup** dialog box, click **Custom Footer**. With the insertion point blinking in the **Left section**, in the row of buttons in the middle of the dialog box, locate and click the **Insert File Name** button. Compare your screen with Figure 9.21.

Use the Page Setup dialog box in this manner to insert a footer on a chart sheet, which has no Page Layout view in which you can see the Header and Footer areas.

Figure 9.21

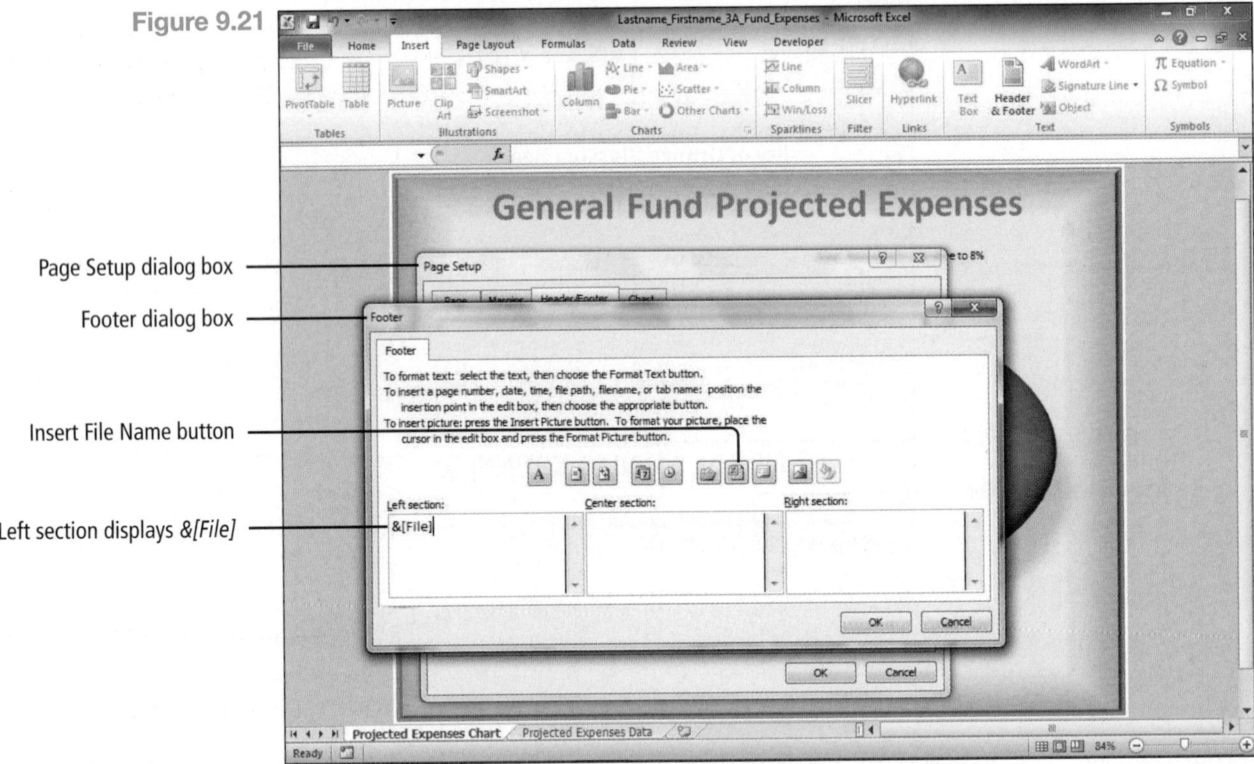

9 Click **OK** two times. Display **Backstage** view, on the right under the thumbnail, click **Properties**, and then click **Show Document Panel**. In the **Author** box, replace the existing text with your firstname and lastname. In the **Subject** box, type your course name and section number. In the **Keywords** box type **general fund, expenses, pie chart** and then **Close** the **Document Information Panel**.

10 Right-click either of the sheet tabs, and then click **Select All Sheets**. Verify that *[Group]* displays in the title bar.

Recall that by selecting all sheets, you can view all of the workbook pages in Print Preview.

11 Press Ctrl + F2 to display the **Print Preview**. Examine the first page, and then at the bottom of the **Print Preview**, click the **Next Page** button to view the second page of your workbook.

Note | Printing a Chart Sheet Uses More Toner

Printing a chart that displays on a chart sheet will use more toner or ink than a small chart that is part of a worksheet. If you are printing your work, check with your instructor to verify whether or not you should print the chart sheet.

12 Click **Save** to redisplay the workbook. Print or submit electronically as directed by your instructor.

13 If you are directed to submit printed formulas, refer to Activity 2.16 in Project 2A to do so.

14 If you printed your formulas, be sure to redisplay the worksheet by clicking the Show Formulas button to turn it off. **Close** the workbook. If you are prompted to save changes, click **No** so that you do not save the changes to the worksheet that you used for printing formulas. **Close** Excel.

More Knowledge | Setting the Default Number of Sheets in a New Workbook

By default, the number of new worksheets in a new workbook is three, but you can change this default number. From Backstage view, display the Excel Options dialog box, click the General tab, and then under When creating new workbooks, change the number in the Include this many sheets box.

End You have completed Project 9A

Project 9B Growth Projection with Line Chart

Project Activities

In Activities 9.12 through 9.19, you will assist Lila Darius, City Manager, in creating a worksheet to estimate future population growth based on three possible growth rates. You will also create a line chart to display past population growth. Your resulting worksheet and chart will look similar to Figure 9.22.

Project Files

For Project 9B, you will need the following files:

e03B_Population_Growth
e03B_Beach

You will save your workbook as:

Lastname_Firstname_3B_Population_Growth

Project Results

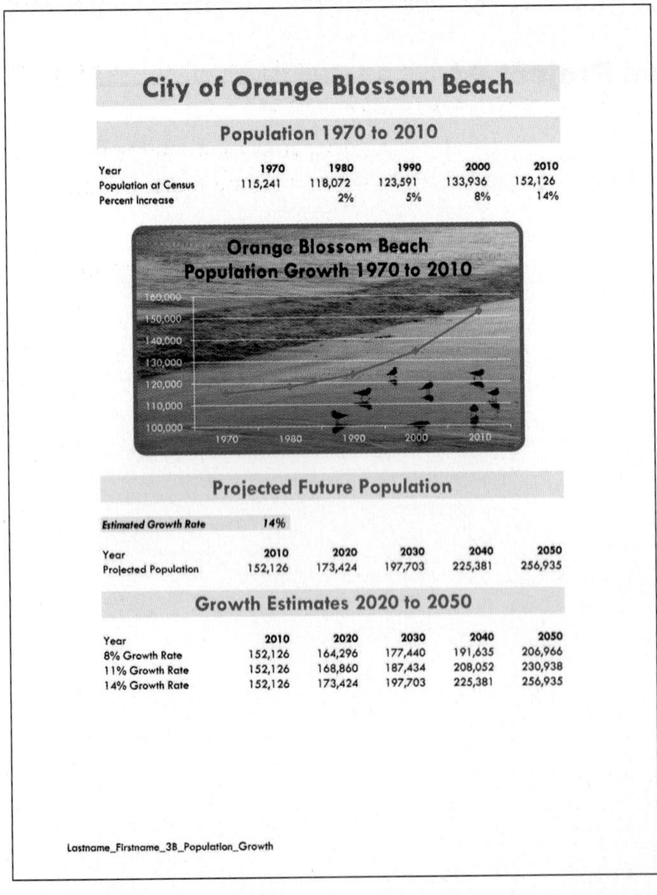

City of Orange Blossom Beach

Population 1970 to 2010

Year	1970	1980	1990	2000	2010
Population at Census	115,241	118,072	123,591	133,936	152,126
Percent Increase		2%	5%	8%	14%

Projected Future Population

Estimated Growth Rate	14%				
Year	2010	2020	2030	2040	2050
Projected Population	152,126	173,424	197,703	225,381	256,935

Growth Estimates 2020 to 2050

Year	2010	2020	2030	2040	2050
8% Growth Rate	152,126	164,296	177,440	191,635	206,966
11% Growth Rate	152,126	168,860	187,434	208,052	230,938
14% Growth Rate	152,126	173,424	197,703	225,381	256,935

Lastname_Firstname_3B_Population_Growth

Figure 9.22
Project 9B Population Growth

Objective 5 | Design a Worksheet for What-If Analysis

Excel recalculates; if you change the value in a cell referenced in a formula, Excel automatically recalculates the result of the formula. Thus, you can change cell values to see *what* would happen *if* you tried different values. Recall that this process of changing the values in cells to see how those changes affect the outcome of formulas in your worksheet is referred to as what-if analysis.

Activity 9.12 | Using Parentheses in a Formula to Calculate a Percentage Rate of Increase

Ms. Darius has the city's population figures for the past five 10-year census periods. In each 10-year census period, the population has increased. In this activity, you will construct a formula to calculate the ***percentage rate of increase***—the percent by which one number increases over another number—for each 10-year census period since 1970. From this information, future population growth can be estimated.

1. **Start** Excel. From your student files, open the file **e03B_Population_Growth**. From **Backstage** view, display the **Save As** dialog box. Navigate to your **Excel Chapter 3** folder, in the **File name** box, name the file **Lastname_Firstname_3B_Population_Growth** and then click **Save** or press Enter.

2. Leave **row 4** blank, and then click cell **A5**. Type **Year** and then press Tab. In cell **B5**, type **1970** and then press Tab.

3. In cell **C5**, type **1980** and then press Tab. Select the range **B5:C5**, and then drag the fill handle to the right through cell **F5** to extend the series to 2010.

   By establishing a pattern of 10-year intervals with the first two cells, you can use the fill handle to continue the series. The AutoFill feature will do this for any pattern that you establish with two or more cells.

4. With the range **B5:F5** still selected, right-click over the selection, and then on the Mini toolbar, click **Bold** B. Compare your screen with Figure 9.23.

Figure 9.23

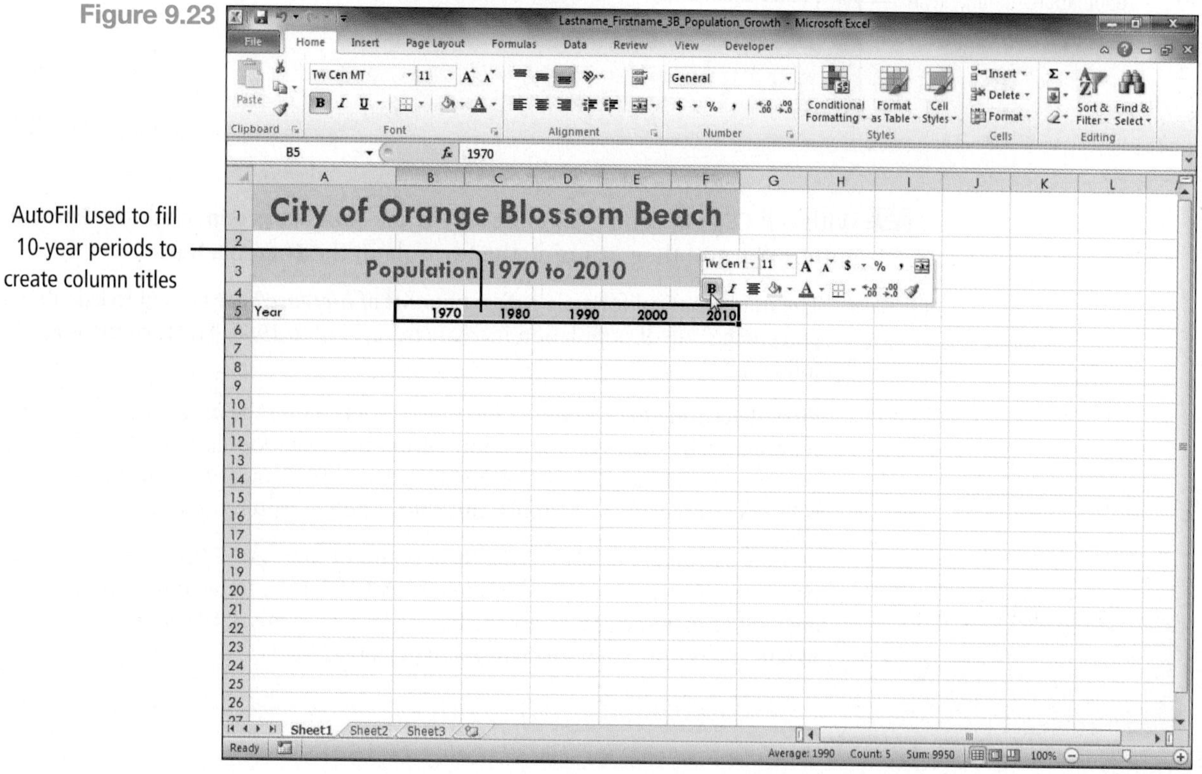

AutoFill used to fill 10-year periods to create column titles

Excel | Chapter 9

5 In cell **A6**, type **Population at Census** and press Enter. In cell **A7**, type **Percent Increase** and press Enter.

6 Click cell **B6**, and then beginning in cell **B6**, and pressing Tab to move across the row, enter the following values for the population in the years listed:

1970	1980	1990	2000	2010
115241	**118072**	**123591**	**133936**	**152126**

7 Select the range **B6:F6**, right-click, on the Mini toolbar, click **Comma Style** [,], and then click **Decrease Decimal** [.00 →.0] two times.

8 Click cell **C7**. Being sure to include the parentheses, type **=(c6-b6)/b6** and then on the **Formula Bar**, click the **Enter** button [✓] to keep cell **C7** active; your result is *0.02456591* (or *0.02*). Compare your screen with Figure 9.24.

Recall that as you type, a list of Excel functions that begin with the letter *C* and *B* may briefly display. This is ***Formula AutoComplete***, an Excel feature which, after typing an = (equal sign) and the beginning letter or letters of a function name, displays a list of function names that match the typed letter(s). In this instance, the letters represent cell references, *not* the beginning of a function name.

Figure 9.24

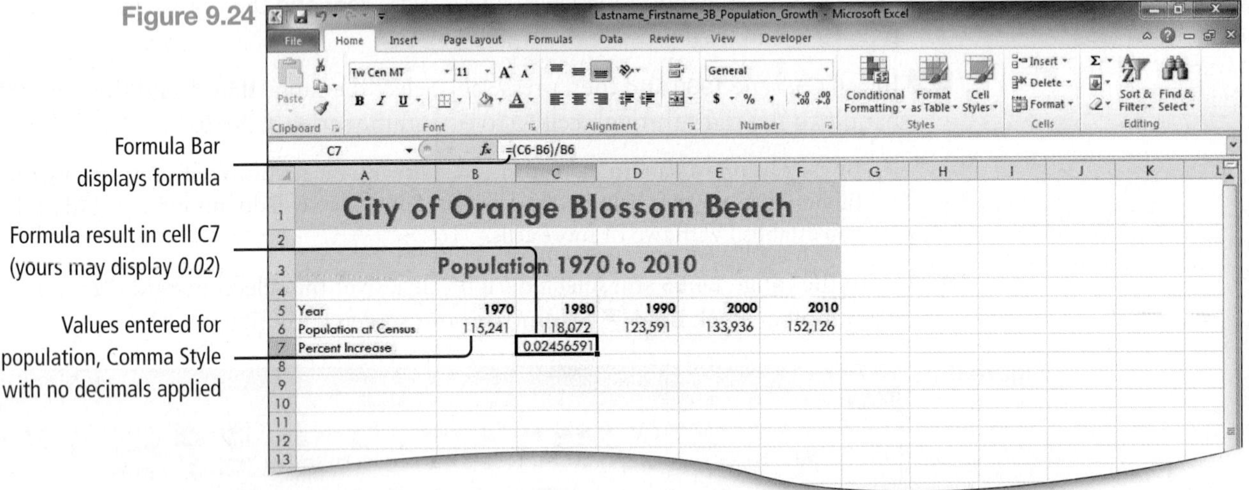

9 With cell **C7** active, on the **Home tab**, in the **Number group**, click the **Percent Style** button [%], and then examine the formula in the **Formula Bar**.

The mathematical formula ***rate = amount of increase/base*** is used to calculated the percentage rate of population increase from 1970 to 1980. The formula is applied as follows:

First, determine the *amount of increase* by subtracting the ***base***—the starting point represented by the 1970 population—from the 1980 population. Thus, the *amount of increase* = 118,072 – 115,241 or 2,831. Between 1970 and 1980, the population increased by 2,831 people. In the formula, this calculation is represented by *C6-B6*.

Second, calculate the *rate*—what the amount of increase (2,831) represents as a percentage of the base (1970's population of 115,241). Determine this by dividing the amount of increase (2,831) by the base (115,241). Thus, 2,831 divided by 115,241 is equal to 0.02456591 or, when formatted as a percent, 2%.

10 In the **Formula Bar**, locate the parentheses enclosing *C6-B6*.

Excel follows a set of mathematical rules called the ***order of operations***, which has four basic parts:

- Expressions within parentheses are processed first.
- Exponentiation, if present, is performed before multiplication and division.
- Multiplication and division are performed before addition and subtraction.
- Consecutive operators with the same level of precedence are calculated from left to right.

11 Click cell **D7**, type = and then by typing, or using a combination of typing and clicking cells to reference them, construct a formula similar to the one in cell **C7** to calculate the rate of increase in population from 1980 to 1990. Compare your screen with Figure 9.25.

Recall that the first step is to determine the *amount of increase*—1990 population minus 1980 population—and then to write the calculation so that Excel performs this operation first; that is, place it in parentheses.

The second step is to divide the result of the calculation in parentheses by the *base*—the population for 1980.

Figure 9.25

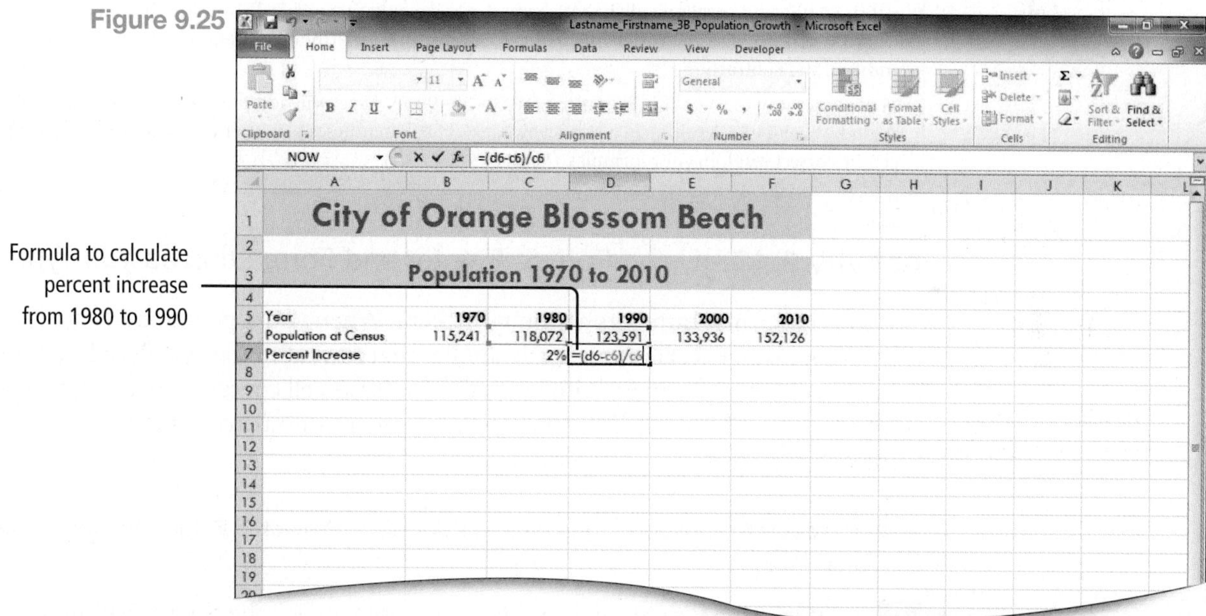

12 Press Enter; your result is *0.04674267* (or *0.05*). Format cell **D7** with the **Percent Style** %.

Your result is *5%*; Excel rounds up or down to format percentages.

13 With cell **D7** selected, drag the fill handle to the right through cell **F7**. Click any empty cell to cancel the selection, **Save** your workbook, and then compare your screen with Figure 9.26.

Because this formula uses relative cell references—that is, for each year, the formula is the same but the values used are relative to the formula's location—you can copy the formula in this manner. For example, the result for 1990 uses the 1980 population as the base, the result for 2000 uses the 1990 population as the base, and the result for 2010 uses the 2000 population as the base.

The formula results show the percent of increase for each 10-year period between 1970 and 2010. You can see that in each 10-year period, the population has grown as much as 14%—from 2000 to 2010—and as little as 2%—from 1970 to 1980.

Figure 9.26

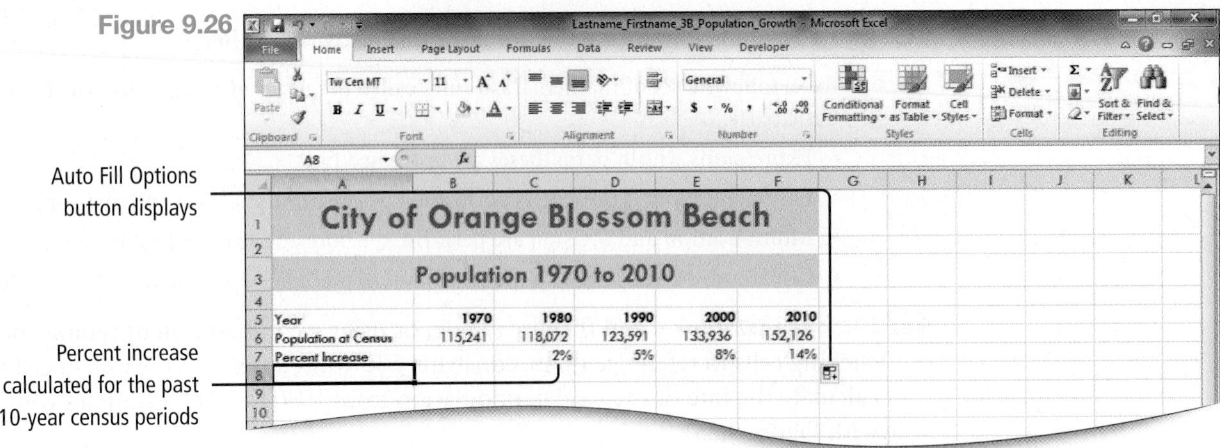

More Knowledge | Use of Parentheses in a Formula

When writing a formula in Excel, use parentheses to communicate the order in which the operations should occur. For example, to average three test scores of 100, 50, and 90 that you scored on three different tests, you would add the test scores and then divide by the number of test scores in the list. If you write this formula as =100+50+90/3, the result would be 180, because Excel would first divide 90 by 3 and then add 100+50+30. Excel would do so because the order of operations states that multiplication and division are calculated *before* addition and subtraction.

The correct way to write this formula is =(100+50+90)/3. Excel will add the three values, and then divide the result by 3, or 240/3 resulting in a correct average of 80. Parentheses play an important role in ensuring that you get the correct result in your formulas.

Activity 9.13 | Using Format Painter and Formatting as You Type

You can format numbers as you type them. When you type numbers in a format that Excel recognizes, Excel automatically applies that format to the cell. Recall that once applied, cell formats remain with the cell, even if the cell contents are deleted. In this activity, you will format cells by typing the numbers with percent signs and use Format Painter to copy text (non-numeric) formats.

1 Leave **row 8** blank, and then click cell **A9**. Type **Projected Future Population** and then press Enter.

Another Way

On the Home tab, in the Clipboard group, click the Format Painter button.

2 Point to cell **A3**, right-click, on the Mini toolbar click the **Format Painter** button, and then click cell **A9**.

The format of cell A3 is *painted*—applied to—cell A9, including the merging and centering of the text across the range A9:F9.

3 Leave **row 10** blank, and then click cell **A11**, type **Estimated Growth Rate** and then press Enter.

4 Leave **row 12** blank, and then click cell **A13**. Type **Year** and then in cell **A14**, type **Projected Population**

5 In cell **B13**, type **2010** and then press Tab. In cell **C13**, type **2020** and then press Tab.

6 Select the range **B13:C13**, and then drag the fill handle through cell **F13** to extend the pattern of years to *2050*. Apply **Bold** B to the selected range. Compare your screen with Figure 9.27.

Figure 9.27

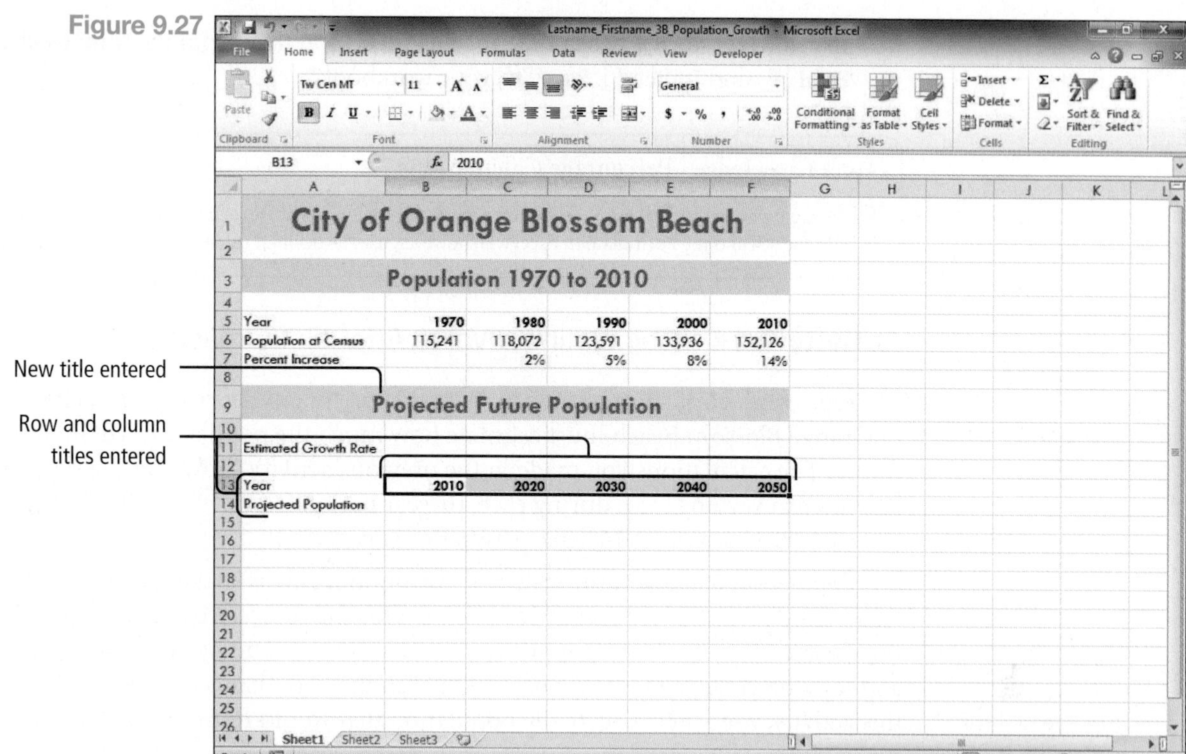

7 Click cell **B14**, and then on the **Home tab**, in the **Number group**, notice that the **Number Format** box indicates *General*. Then, being sure to type the comma, type **152,126**

8 On the **Formula Bar**, click the **Enter** button ✓ to keep the cell active, and then in the **Number group**, notice that the format changed to *Number*.

9 Press Del, and then in the **Number group**, notice that the *Number* format is still indicated.

Recall that deleting the contents of a cell does not delete the cell's formatting.

10 *Without* typing a comma, in cell **B14**, type **152126** and then press Enter.

The comma displays even though you did not type it. When you type a number and include a formatting symbol such as a comma or dollar sign, Excel applies the format to the cell. Thus, if you delete the contents of the cell and type in the cell again, the format you established remains applied to the cell. This is referred to as ***format as you type***.

11 Examine the format of the value in cell **B14**, and then compare it to the format in cell **B6** where you used the **Comma Style** button to format the cell. Notice that the number in cell **B14** is flush with the right edge of the cell, but the number in cell **B6** leaves a small amount of space on the right edge.

When you type commas as you enter numbers, Excel applies the *Number* format, which does *not* leave a space at the right of the number for a closing parenthesis in the event of a negative number. This is different from the format that is applied when you use the *Comma Style* button on the Ribbon or Mini toolbar, as you did for the numbers entered in row 6. Recall that the Comma Style format applied from either the Ribbon or the Mini toolbar leaves space on the right for a closing parenthesis in the event of a negative number.

12 In cell **B11**, type **8%** Select the range **A11:B11**, and then from the Mini toolbar, apply **Bold** [B] and **Italic** [I]. **Save** [Save] your workbook.

> **More Knowledge | Percentage Calculations**
>
> When you type a percentage into a cell—for example *8%*—the percentage format, without decimal points, displays in both the cell and the Formula Bar. Excel will, however, use the decimal value of *0.08* for actual calculations.

Activity 9.14 | Calculating a Value After an Increase

A growing population results in increased use of city services. Thus, city planners in Orange Blossom Beach must estimate how much the population will increase in the future. The calculations you made in the previous activity show that the population has increased at varying rates during each 10-year period from 1970 to 2010, ranging from a low of 2% to a high of 14% per 10-year census period.

Population data from the state and surrounding areas suggests that future growth will trend close to that of the recent past. To plan for the future, Ms. Darius wants to prepare three forecasts of the city's population based on the percentage increases in 2000, in 2010, and for a percentage increase halfway between the two; that is, for 8%, 11%, and 14%. In this activity, you will calculate the population that would result from an 8% increase.

1 Click cell **C14**. Type **=b14*(100%+b11)** and then on the **Formula Bar**, click the **Enter** [✓] button to display a result of *164296.08*. Compare your screen with Figure 9.28.

This formula calculates what the population will be in the year 2020 assuming an increase of 8% over 2010's population. Use the mathematical formula ***value after increase* = *base* × *percent for new value*** to calculate a value after an increase as follows:

First, establish the *percent for new value*. The ***percent for new value* = *base percent* + *percent of increase***. The *base percent* of 100% represents the base population and the *percent of increase* in this instance is 8%. Thus, the population will equal 100% of the base year plus 8% of the base year. This can be expressed as 108% or 1.08. In this formula, you will use 100% + the rate in cell B11, which is 8%, to equal 108%.

Second, enter a reference to the cell that contains the *base*—the population in 2010. The base value resides in cell B14—*152,126*.

Third, calculate the *value after increase*. Because in each future 10-year period the increase will be based on 8%—an absolute value located in cell B11—this cell reference can be formatted as absolute by typing dollar signs.

Figure 9.28

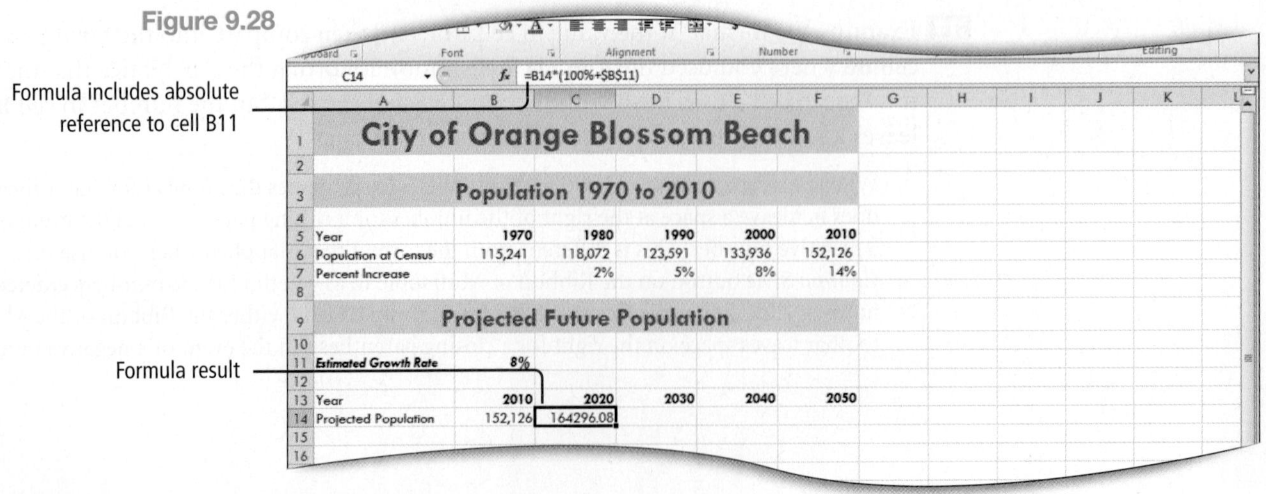

2 With cell **C14** as the active cell, drag the fill handle to copy the formula to the range **D14:F14**.

3 Point to cell **B14**, right-click, click the **Format Painter** button, and then select the range **C14:F14**. Click an empty cell to cancel the selection, click **Save** and then compare your screen with Figure 9.29.

This formula uses a relative cell address—B14—for the *base*; the population in the previous 10-year period is used in each of the formulas in cells D14:F14 as the *base* value. Because the reference to the *percent of increase* in cell B11 is an absolute reference, each *value after increase* is calculated with the value from cell B11.

The population projected for 2020—*164,296*—is an increase of 8% over the population in 2010. The projected population in 2030—*177,440*—is an increase of 8% over the population in 2020 and so on.

Figure 9.29

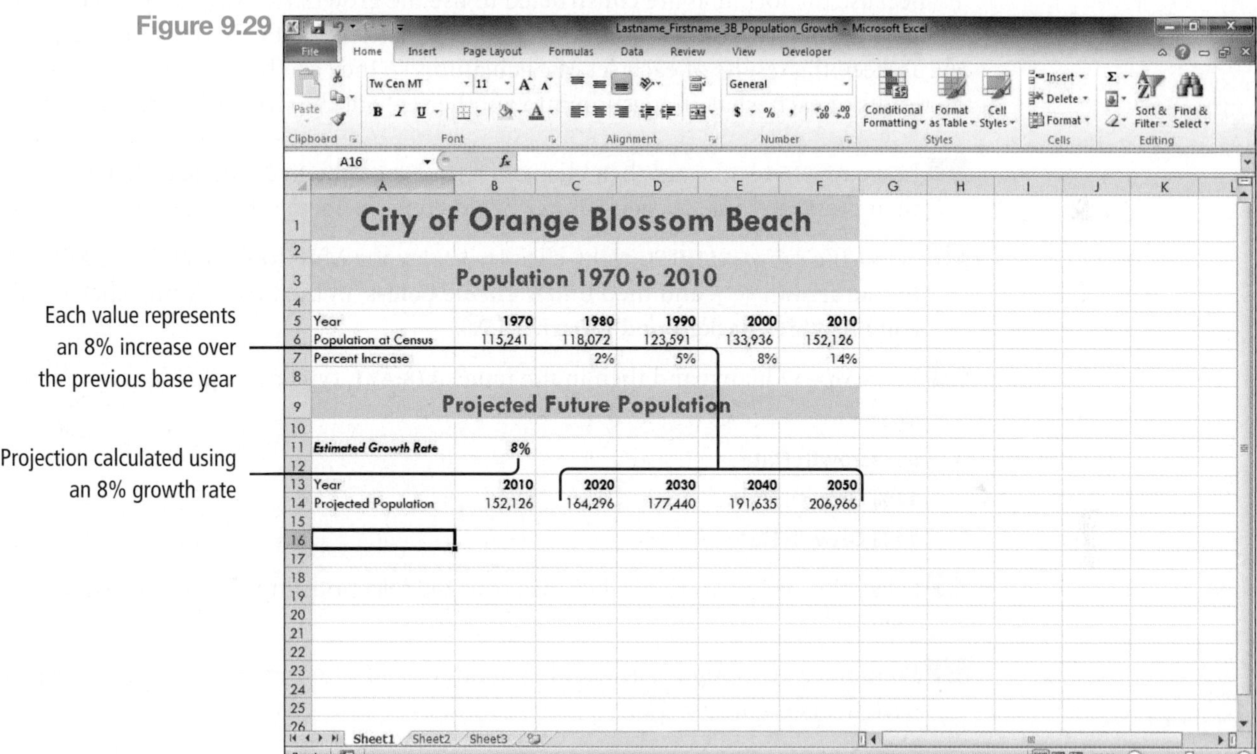

More Knowledge | Percent Increase or Decrease

The basic formula for calculating an increase or decrease can be done in two parts. First determine the percent by which the base value will be increased or decreased, and then add or subtract the results to the base. The formula can be simplified by using (1+amount of increase) or (1–amount of decrease), where 1, rather than 100%, represents the whole. Thus, the formula used in Step 1 of Activity 9.14 could also be written =b14*(1+b11), or =(b14*b11)+b14.

Objective 6 | Answer What-If Questions by Changing Values in a Worksheet

If a formula depends on the value in a cell, you can see what effect it will have if you change the value in that cell. Then, you can copy the value computed by the formula and paste it into another part of the worksheet where you can be compare it to other values.

Activity 9.15 | Answering What-If Questions and Using Paste Special

A growth rate of 8% in each 10-year period will result in a population of almost 207,000 people by 2050. The city planners will likely ask: *What if* the population grows at the highest rate (14%)? *What if* the population grows at a rate that is halfway between the 2000 and 2010 rates (11%)?

Because the formulas are constructed to use the growth rate displayed in cell B11, Ms. Darius can answer these questions quickly by entering different percentages into that cell. To keep the results of each set of calculations so they can be compared, you will paste the results of each what-if question into another area of the worksheet.

1 Leave **row 15** blank, and then click cell **A16**. Type **Growth Estimates 2020 to 2050** and then press Enter. Use **Format Painter** to copy the format from cell **A9** to cell **A16**.

2 Select the range **A11:B11**, right-click to display the Mini toolbar, click the **Fill Color button arrow**, and then under **Theme Colors**, in the first column, click the third color—**White, Background 1, Darker 15%**.

3 Leave **row 17** blank, and then in the range **A18:A21**, type the following row titles:

Year

8% Growth Rate

11% Growth Rate

14% Growth Rate

Another Way

Press Ctrl + C; or, on the Home tab, in the Clipboard group, click the Copy button.

4 Select the range **B13:F13**, right-click over the selection, and then on the shortcut menu, click **Copy**.

5 Point to cell **B18**, right-click, and then on the shortcut menu, under **Paste Options**, click the **Paste** button.

Recall that when pasting a group of copied cells to a target range, you need only point to or select the first cell of the range.

6 Select and **Copy** the range **B14:F14**, and then **Paste** it beginning in cell **B19**.

7 Click cell **C19**. On the **Formula Bar**, notice that the *formula* was pasted into the cell, as shown in Figure 9.30.

This is *not* the desired result. The actual *calculated values*—not the formulas—are needed in the range.

Figure 9.30

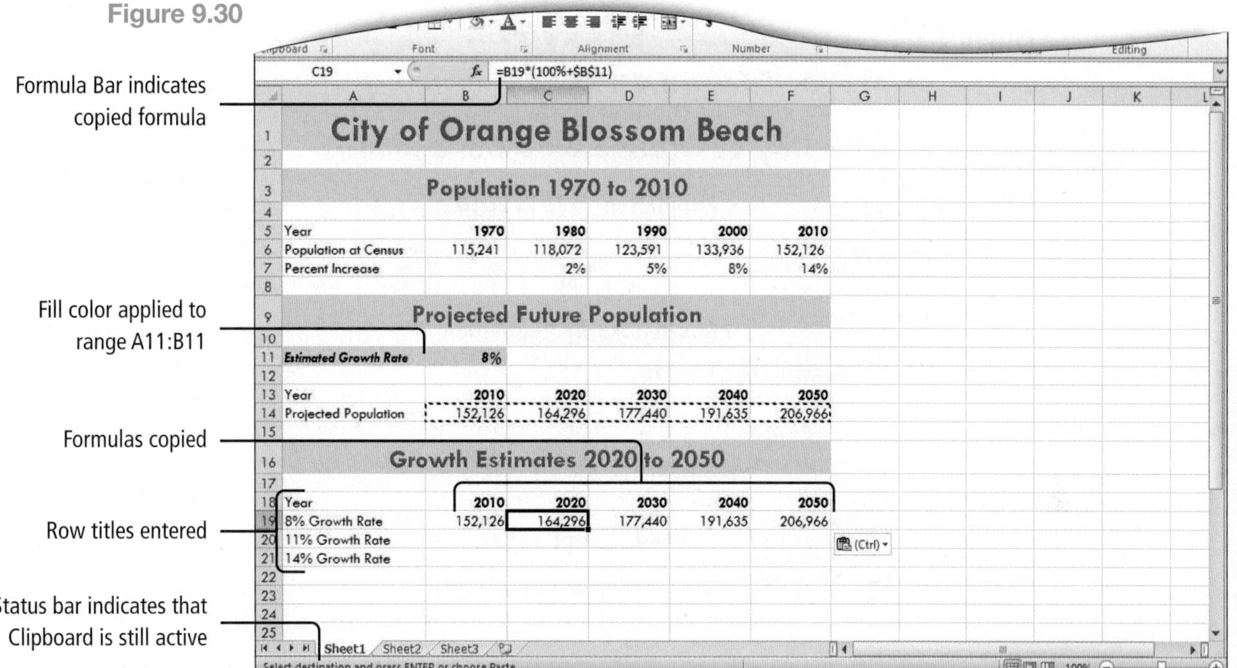

8 On the Quick Access Toolbar, click the **Undo** button. With the range **B14:F14** still copied to the Clipboard—as indicated by the message in the status bar and the moving border—point to cell **B19**, and then right-click to display the shortcut menu.

9 Under **Paste Options**, point to **Paste Special** to display another gallery, and then under **Paste Values**, point to the **Values & Number Formatting** button to display the ScreenTip as shown in Figure 9.31.

The ScreenTip *Values & Number Formatting (A)* indicates that you can paste the *calculated values* that result from the calculation of formulas along with the formatting applied to the copied cells. *(A)* is the keyboard shortcut for this command.

Figure 9.31

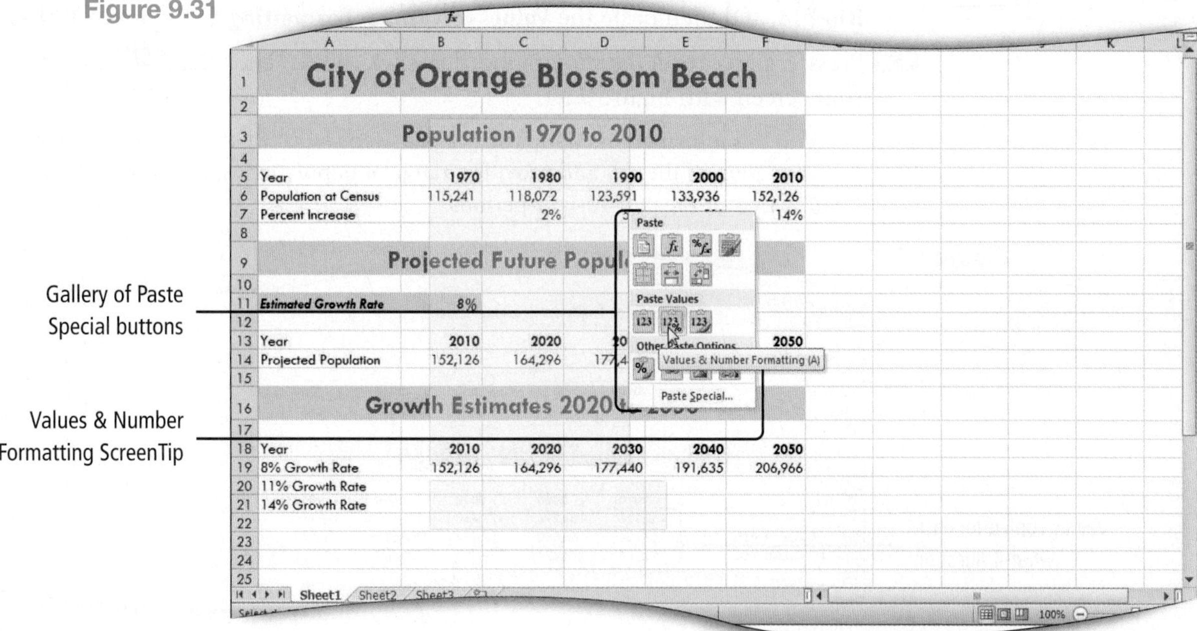

Excel | Chapter 9

10 Click the **Values & Number Formatting** button, click cell **C19** and notice on the **Formula Bar** that the cell contains a *value*, not a formula. Press Esc to cancel the moving border. Compare your screen with Figure 9.32.

The calculated estimates based on an 8% growth rate are pasted along with their formatting.

Figure 9.32

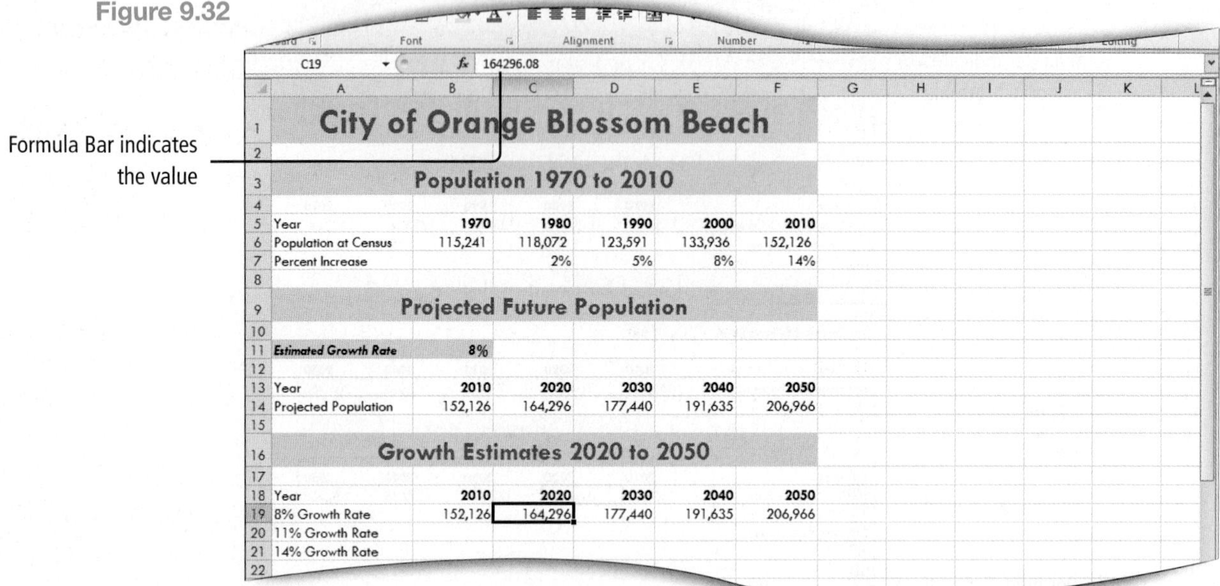

11 Click cell **B11**. Type **11** and then watch the values in **C14:F14** *recalculate* as, on the **Formula Bar**, you click the **Enter** button.

The value *11%* is halfway between 8% and 14%—the growth rates from the two most recent 10-year periods.

12 Select and **Copy** the new values in the range **B14:F14**. Point to cell **B20**, right-click, and then on the shortcut menu, point to **Paste Special**. Under **Paste Values**, click the **Values & Number Formatting** button.

13 In cell **B11**, change the percentage by typing **14** and then press Enter. Notice that the projected values in **C14:F14** recalculate.

14 Using the skills you just practiced, select and copy the recalculated values in the range **B14:F14**, and then paste the **Values & Number Formatting** to the range **B21:F21**.

15 Press Esc to cancel the moving border, click cell **A1**, click **Save**, and then compare your screen with Figure 9.33.

With this information, Ms. Darius can answer several what-if questions about the future population of the city and provide a range of population estimates based on the rates of growth over the past 10-year periods.

Figure 9.33

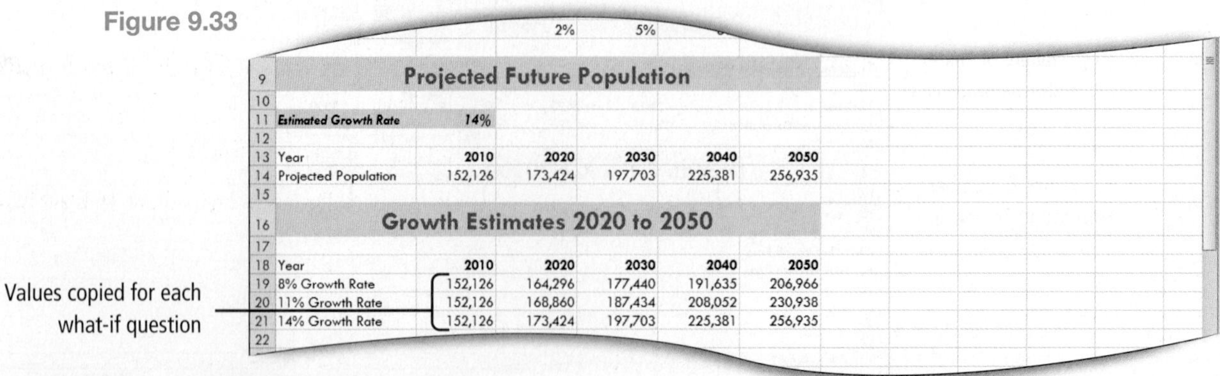

Objective 7 | Chart Data with a Line Chart

A ***line chart*** displays trends over time. Time is displayed along the bottom axis and the data point values connect with a line. The curve and direction of the line makes trends obvious to the reader.

Whereas the columns in a column chart and the pie slices in a pie chart emphasize the distinct values of each data point, the line in a line chart emphasizes the flow from one data point value to the next.

Activity 9.16 | Inserting Multiple Rows and Creating a Line Chart

So that city council members can see how the population has increased over the past five census periods, in this activity, you will chart the actual population figures from 1970 to 2010 in a line chart.

1. In the **row header area**, point to **row 8** to display the ➡ pointer, and then drag down to select **rows 8:24**. Right-click over the selection, and then click **Insert** to insert the same number of blank rows as you selected. Compare your screen with Figure 9.34.

   Use this technique to insert multiple rows quickly.

Figure 9.34

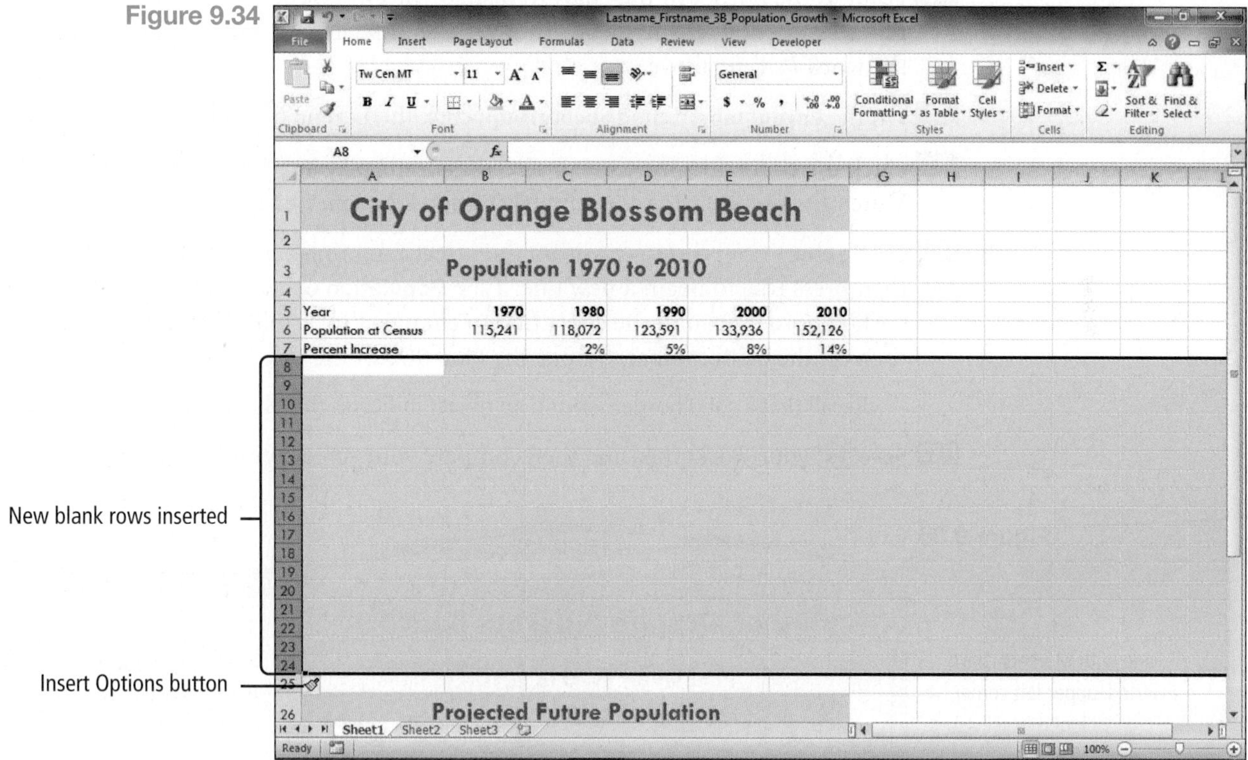

2. Near **row 25**, click the **Insert Options** button, and then click the **Clear Formatting** option button to clear any formatting from these rows.

   You will use this blank area in which to position your line chart.

3. Select the range **A6:F6**. On the **Insert tab**, in the **Charts group**, click the **Line** button.

4 In the displayed gallery of line charts, in the second row, point to the first chart type to display the ScreenTip *Line with Markers*. Compare your screen with Figure 9.35.

Figure 9.35

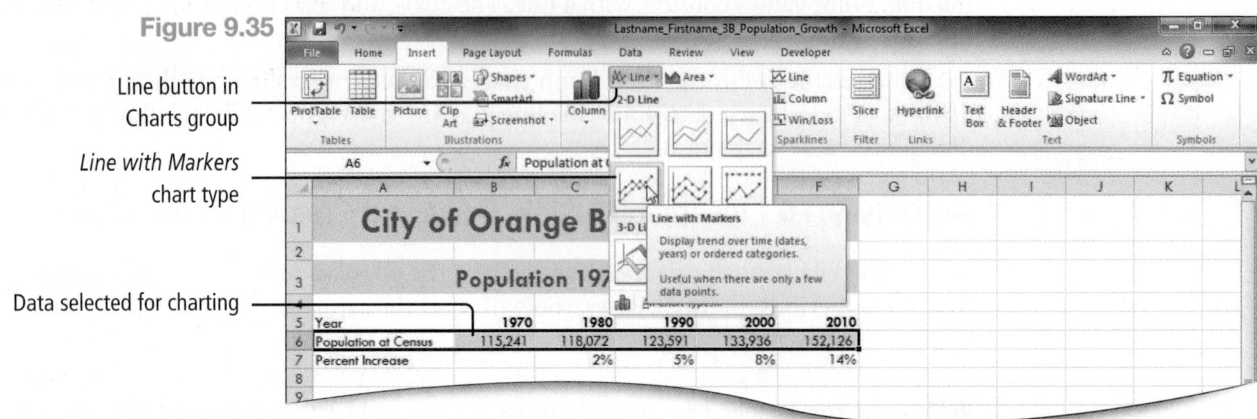

5 Click the **Line with Markers** chart type to create the chart as an embedded chart in the worksheet.

6 Point to the border of the chart to display the pointer, and then drag the chart so that its upper left corner is positioned in cell **A9**, aligned approximately under the *t* in the word *Percent* above.

7 On the **Layout tab**, in the **Labels group**, click the **Legend** button, and then click **None**.

8 Click the chart title one time to select it and display a solid border around the title. Watch the **Formula Bar** as you type **Orange Blossom Beach** and then press Enter.

9 In the chart title, click to position the insertion point following the *h* in *Beach*, and then press Enter to begin a new line. Type **Population Growth 1970 to 2010** Click the dashed border around the chart title to change it to a solid border, right-click, and then on the Mini toolbar, change the **Font Size** of the title to **20**.

Recall that a solid border around an object indicates that the entire object is selected.

10 **Save** your workbook, and then compare your screen with Figure 9.36.

Figure 9.36

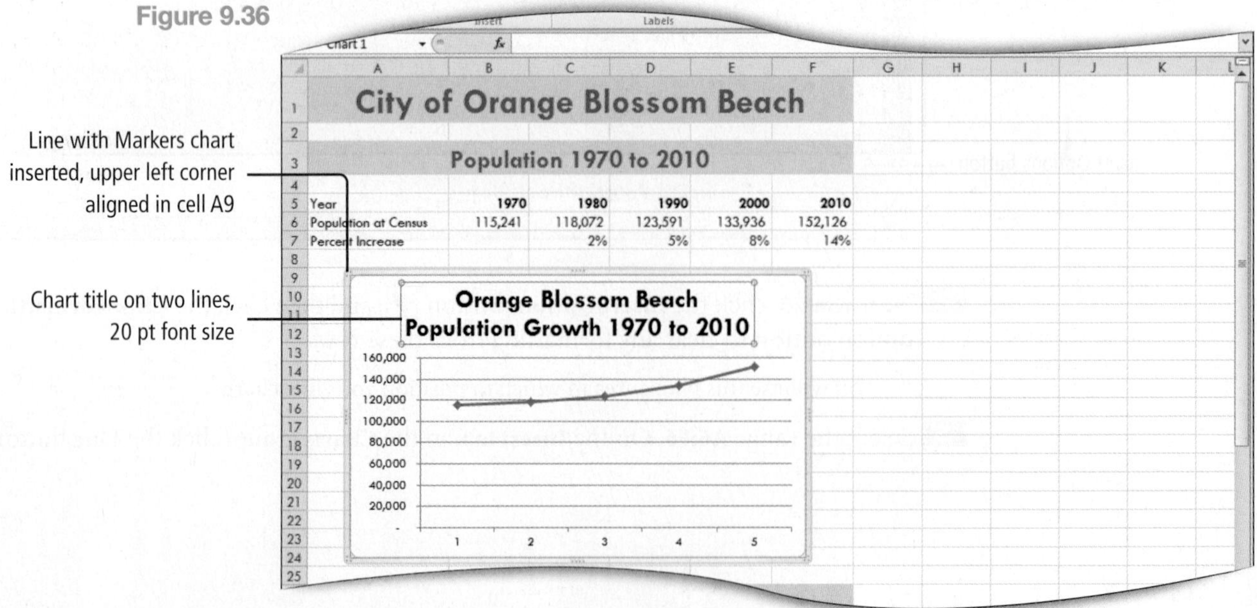

Activity 9.17 | Formatting Axes in a Line Chart

An ***axis*** is a line that serves as a frame of reference for measurement; it borders the chart ***plot area***. The plot area is the area bounded by the axes, including all the data series. Recall that the area along the bottom of a chart that identifies the categories of data is referred to as the ***category axis*** or the ***x-axis***. Recall also that the area along the left side of a chart that shows the range of numbers for the data points is referred to as the ***value axis*** or the ***y-axis***.

In this activity, you will change the category axis to include the names of the 10-year census periods and adjust the numeric scale of the value axis.

> **Another Way**
>
> At the bottom of the chart, point to any of the numbers 1 through 5 to display the ScreenTip *Horizontal (Category) Axis*. Right-click, and then from the shortcut menu, click Select Data.

1 Be sure the chart is still selected—a pale frame surrounds the chart area. Click the **Design tab**, and then in the **Data group**, click the **Select Data** button.

2 On the right side of the displayed **Select Data Source** dialog box, under **Horizontal (Category) Axis Labels**, locate the **Edit** button, as shown in Figure 9.37.

Figure 9.37

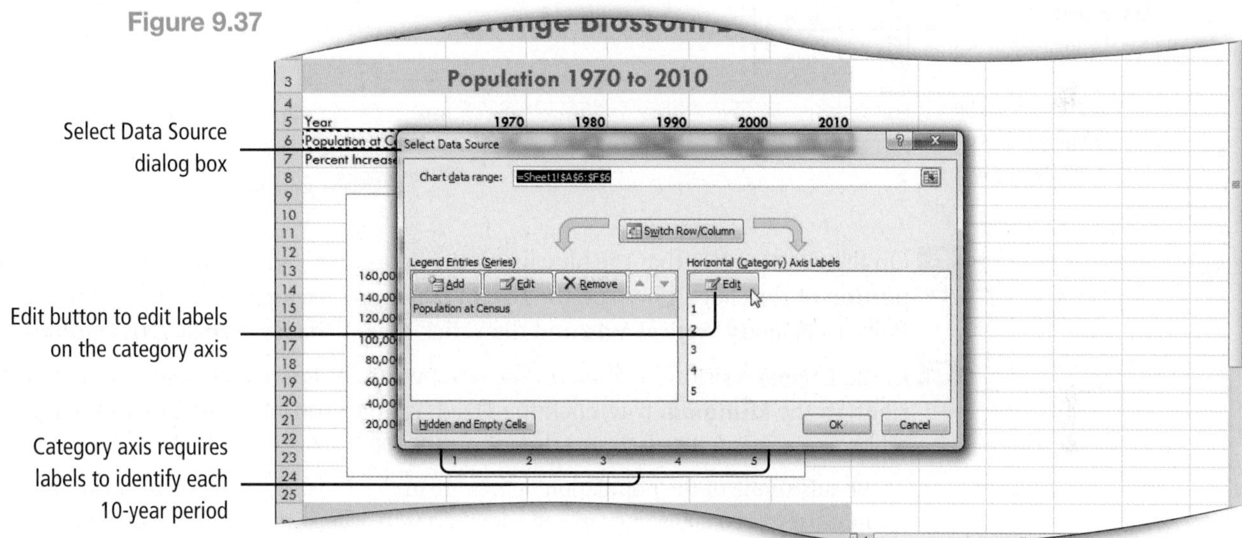

3 In the right column, click the **Edit** button. If necessary, drag the title bar of the **Axis Labels** dialog box to the right of the chart so that it is not blocking your view of the data, and then select the years in the range **B5:F5**. Compare your screen with Figure 9.38.

Figure 9.38

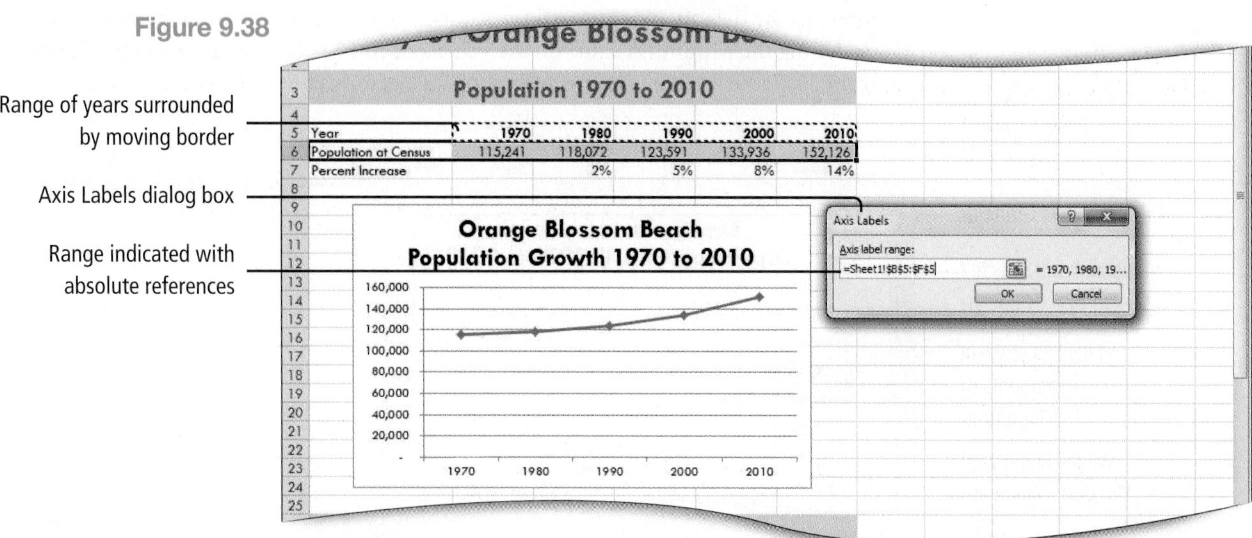

4 In the **Axis Labels** dialog box, click **OK**, and notice that in the right column of the **Select Data Source** dialog box, the years display as the category labels. Click **OK** to close the **Select Data Source** dialog box. Compare your screen with Figure 9.39.

Figure 9.39

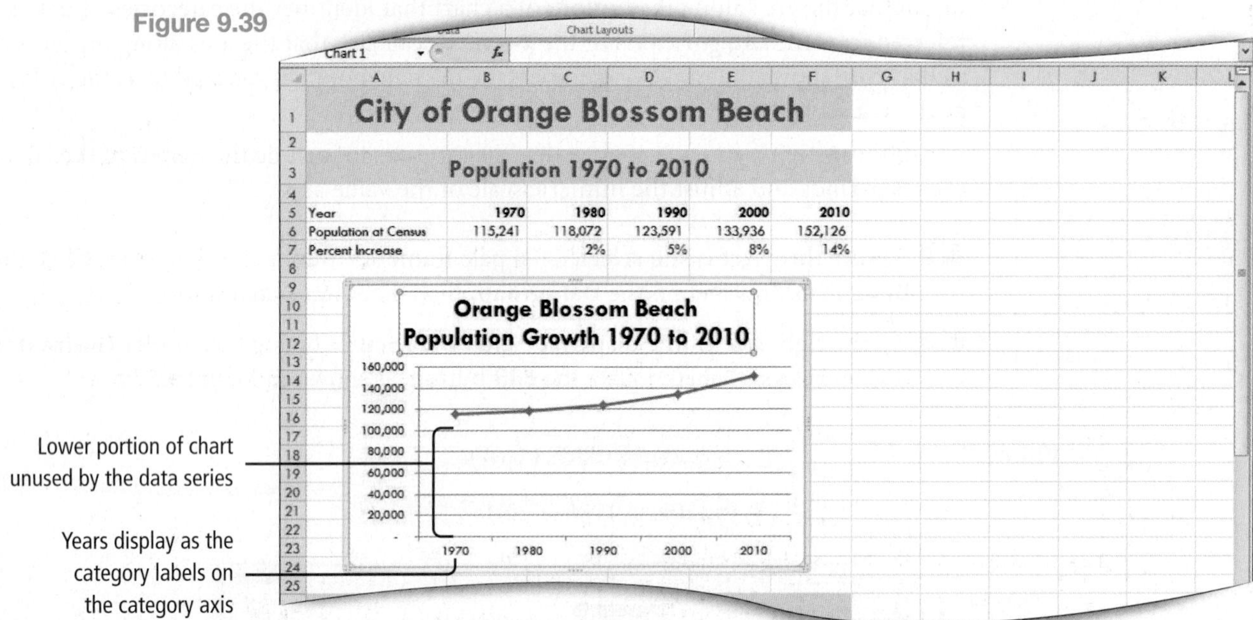

Another Way

On the left side of the chart, point to any of the numbers to display the ScreenTip *Vertical (Value) Axis*, and then right-click. From the shortcut menu, click Format Axis.

5 On the chart, notice that the blue line—the data series—does not display in the lower portion of the chart. Then, on the **Layout tab**, in the **Axes group**, click the **Axes** button. Point to **Primary Vertical Axis**, and then click **More Primary Vertical Axis Options**.

6 In the **Format Axis** dialog box, on the left, be sure **Axis Options** is selected. On the right, in the **Minimum** row, click the **Fixed** option button. In the box to the right, select the existing text *0.0*, and then type **100000**

Because none of the population figures are under 100,000, changing the Minimum number to 100,000 will enable the data series to occupy more of the plot area.

7 In the **Major unit** row, click the **Fixed** option button, select the text in the box to the right *20000.0*, and then type **10000** In the lower right corner, click **Close**. **Save** your workbook, and then compare your screen with Figure 9.40.

The ***Major unit*** value determines the spacing between ***tick marks*** and thus between the gridlines in the plot area. Tick marks are the short lines that display on an axis at regular intervals. By default, Excel started the values at zero and increased in increments of 20,000. By setting the Minimum value on the value axis to 100,000 and changing the Major unit from 20,000 to 10,000, the line chart shows a clearer trend in the population growth.

Figure 9.40

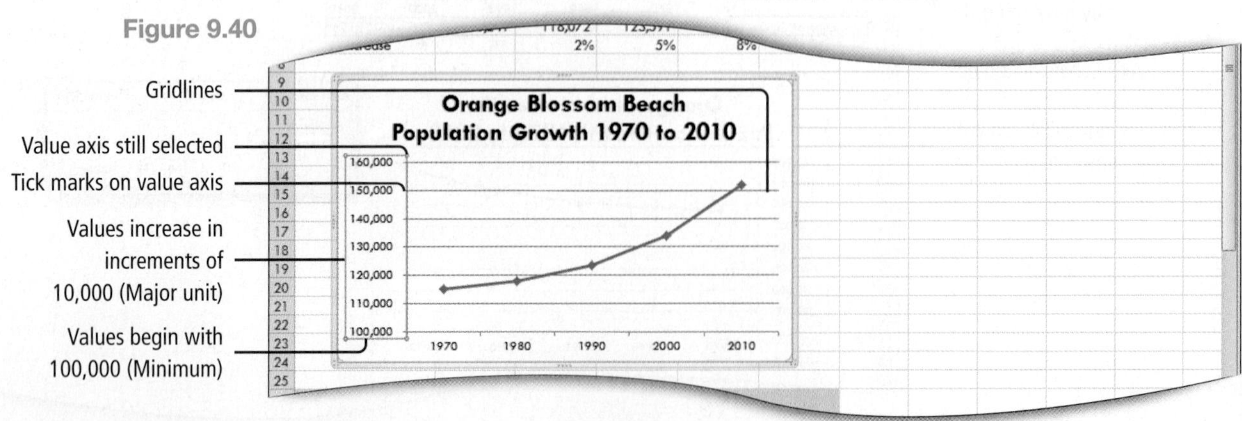

Activity 9.18 | Formatting the Chart and Plot Areas

An Excel chart has two background elements—the plot area and the chart area—which, by default display a single fill color. To add visual appeal to a chart, you can insert a graphic image as the background.

When formatting chart elements, there are several ways to display the dialog boxes that you need. You can right-click the area you want to format and choose a command on the shortcut menu. In this activity, you will use the Chart Elements box in the Current Selection group on the Format tab of the Ribbon, which is convenient if you are changing the format of a variety of chart elements.

1 Click the **Format tab**, and then in the **Current Selection group**, point to the small arrow to the right of the first item in the group to display the ScreenTip *Chart Elements*. Compare your screen with Figure 9.41.

From the ***Chart Elements box***, you can select a chart element so that you can format it.

Figure 9.41

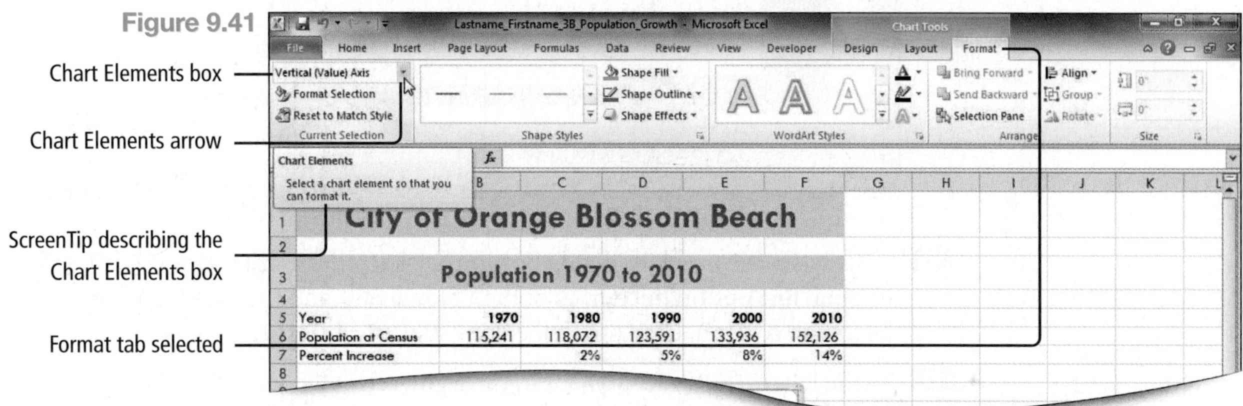

2 Click the **Chart Elements arrow**, and then from the displayed list, click **Chart Area**. Directly below the **Chart Elements** box, click the **Format Selection** button.

The Format Chart Area dialog box displays. Use this technique to select the chart element that you want to format, and then click the Format Selection button to display the appropriate dialog box.

3 In the **Format Chart Area** dialog box, on the left, be sure that **Fill** is selected.

4 On the right, under **Fill**, click the **Picture or texture fill** option button, and then under **Insert from**, click the **File** button. In the **Insert Picture** dialog box, navigate to your student files, and then insert the picture **e03B_Beach**. Leave the dialog box open, and then compare your screen with Figure 9.42.

Figure 9.42

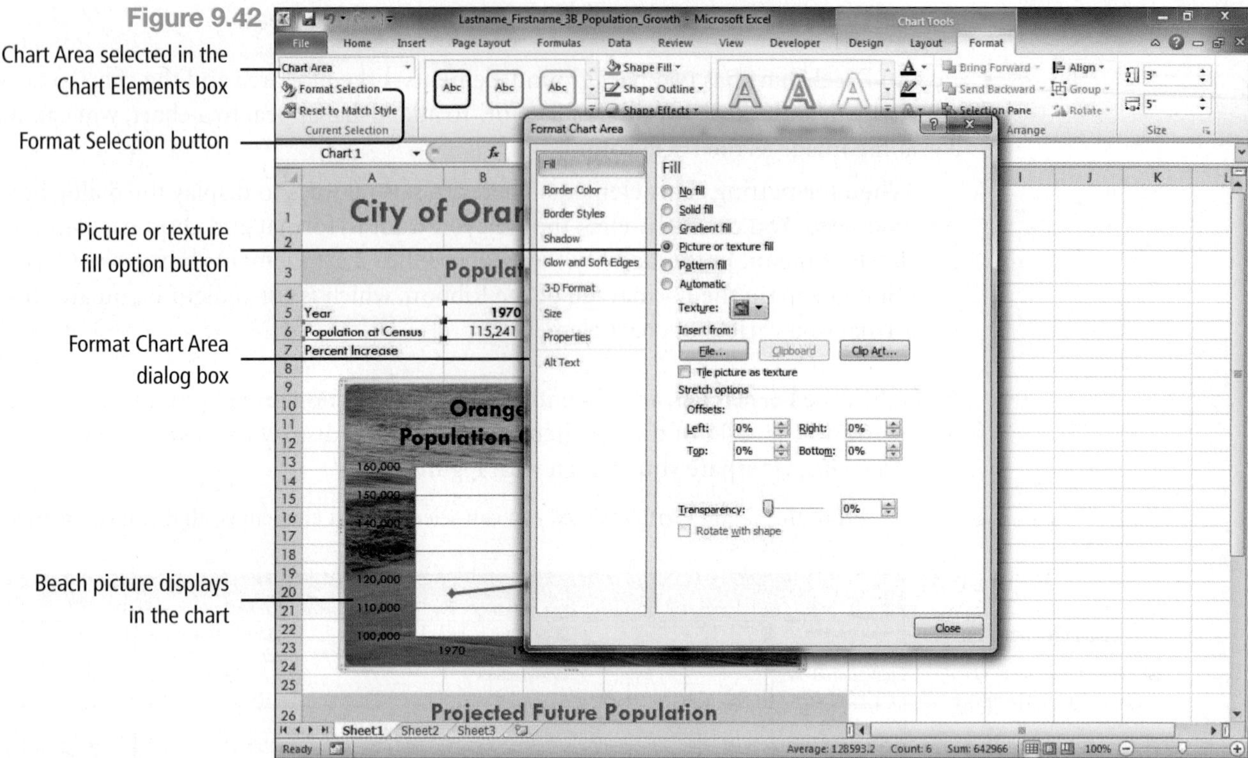

5 In the **Format Chart Area** dialog box, on the left, click **Border Color**, on the right click the **Solid line** option button, click the **Color arrow**, and then under **Theme Colors**, in the fourth column, click the first color—**Dark Teal, Text 2**.

6 On the left, click **Border Styles**. On the right, select the text in the **Width** box and type **4 pt** At the bottom select the **Rounded corners** check box, and then **Close** the dialog box.

A 4 pt teal border with rounded corners frames the chart.

7 In the **Current Selection group**, click the **Chart Elements arrow**, on the list click **Plot Area**, and then click the **Format Selection** button.

8 In the **Format Plot Area** dialog box, on the left, be sure that **Fill** is selected, and then on the right, click the **No fill** option button. **Close** the dialog box.

The fill is removed from the plot area so that the picture is visible as the background.

9 Click the **Chart Elements arrow**, on the list click **Vertical (Value) Axis**, and then click the **Format Selection** button.

10 In the **Format Axis** dialog box, on the left click **Line Color**, on the right click the **Solid line** option button, click the **Color arrow**, and then click the first color—**White, Background 1**. Compare your screen with Figure 9.43.

The vertical line with tick marks displays in white.

Figure 9.43

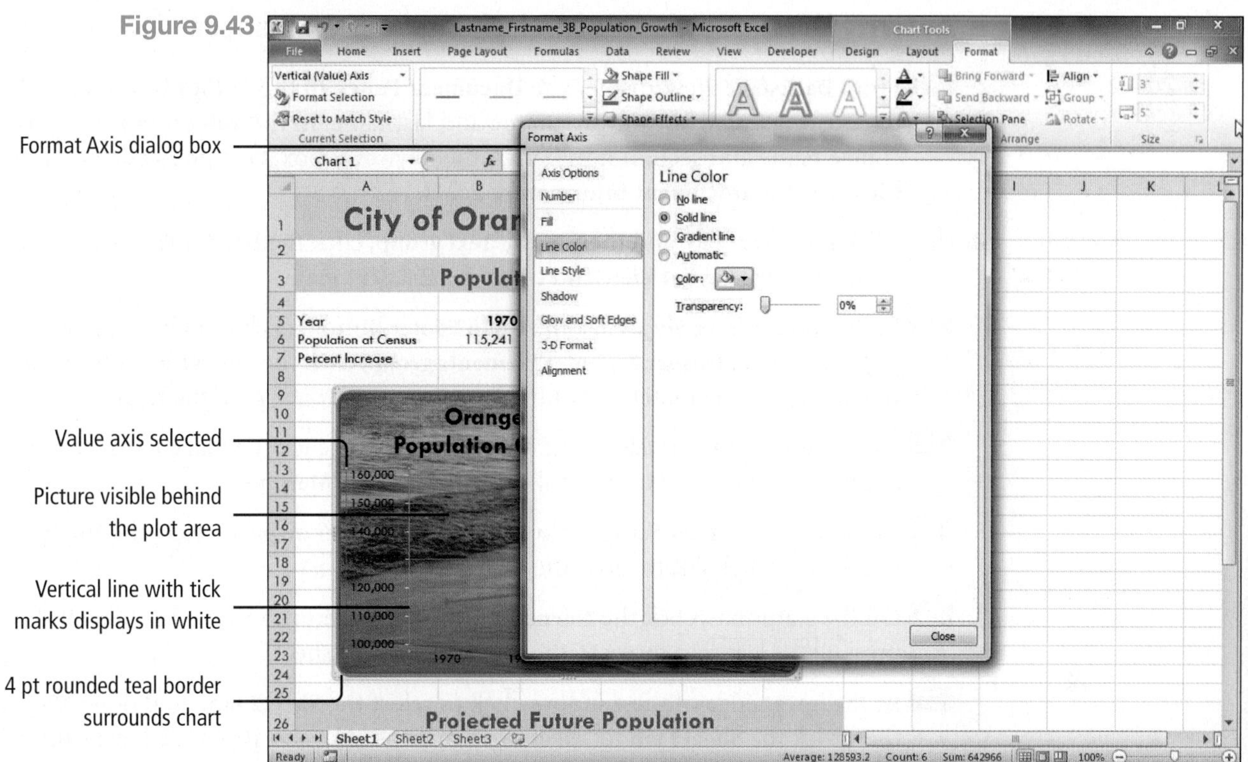

11 **Close** the dialog box. From the **Chart Elements** box, select the **Vertical (Value) Axis Major Gridlines**, and then click **Format Selection**. Change the **Line Color** to a **Solid line**, and then apply the **White, Background 1** color. **Close** the dialog box.

12 From the **Chart Elements** list, select the **Horizontal (Category) Axis**, and then click **Format Selection**. In the **Format Axis** dialog box, change the **Line Color** to a **Solid line**, and then apply the **White, Background 1** color. **Close** the dialog box.

13 Point to any of the numbers on the vertical value axis, right-click, and then on the Mini toolbar, change the **Font Color** to **White, Background 1**. Point to any of the years on the horizontal category axis, right-click, and then change the **Font Color** to **White, Background 1**.

For basic text-formatting changes—for example changing the size, font, style, or font color—you must leave the Chart Tools on the Ribbon and use commands from the Home tab or the Mini toolbar.

14 Click any cell to deselect the chart, press Ctrl + Home to move to the top of your worksheet, click **Save**, and then compare your screen with Figure 9.44.

Figure 9.44

Activity 9.19 | Preparing and Printing Your Worksheet

1 From **Backstage** view, display the **Document Panel.** In the **Author** box, replace the existing text with your firstname and lastname. In the **Subject** box, type your course name and section number. In the **Keywords** box, type **population** and then **Close** [×] the **Document Information Panel.**

2 Click the **Insert tab**, and then in the **Text group**, click the **Header & Footer** button to switch to **Page Layout View** and open the **Header area.**

3 In the **Navigation group**, click the **Go to Footer** button, click just above the word *Footer*, and then in the **Header & Footer Elements group**, click the **File Name** button. Click in a cell just above the footer to exit the **Footer area** and view your file name.

4 Click the **Page Layout tab.** In the **Page Setup group**, click the **Margins** button, and then at the bottom of the **Margins** gallery, click **Custom Margins.**

5 In the displayed **Page Setup** dialog box, under **Center on page**, select the **Horizontally** check box. Click **OK** to close the dialog box.

6 On the status bar, click the **Normal** button [▦] to return to Normal view, and then press Ctrl + Home to move to the top of your worksheet.

7 At the lower edge of the window, click to select the **Sheet2 tab**, hold down Ctrl, and then click the **Sheet3 tab** to select the two unused sheets. Right-click over the selected sheet tabs, and then on the displayed shortcut menu, click **Delete.**

8 **Save** [💾] your workbook before printing or submitting. Press Ctrl + F2 to display the **Print Preview** to check your worksheet. Compare your screen with Figure 9.45.

Figure 9.45

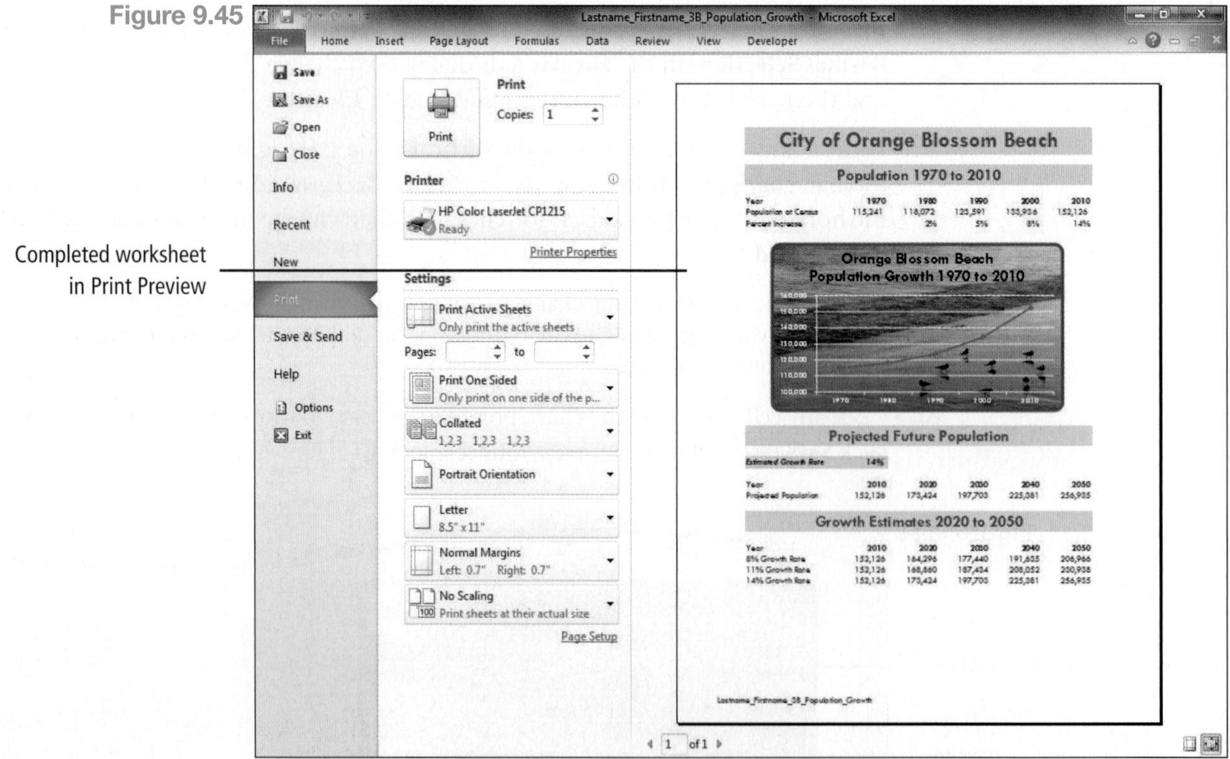

9. If necessary, return to the worksheet to make any necessary adjustments or corrections, and then **Save**.

10. Print or submit electronically as directed. If you are directed to submit printed formulas, refer to Activity 2.16 to do so.

11. If you printed your formulas, be sure to redisplay the worksheet by clicking the Show Formulas button to turn it off. From **Backstage** view, click **Close**. If the dialog box displays asking if you want to save changes, click **No** so that you do *not* save the changes you made for printing formulas. **Close** Excel.

 **You have completed Project 9B**

Content-Based Assessments

Summary

In this chapter, you created a pie chart to show how the parts of a budget contribute to a total budget. Then you formatted the pie chart attractively and used Goal Seek. You also practiced using parentheses in a formula, calculating the percentage rate of an increase, answering what-if questions, and charting data in a line chart to show the flow of data over time.

Key Terms

3-D 469
Absolute cell reference 465
Axis 493
Base 482
Bevel 469
Category axis 493
Chart area 472
Chart Elements box 495
Chart sheet 467
Data marker 467
Data point 467
Data series 467
Explode 471
Format as you type 485
Formula AutoComplete 482
Fund 465
General fund 465
Goal Seek 475
Legend 467
Line chart 491
Major unit 494
Order of operations 483
Percent for new value = base percent + percent of increase 486
Percentage rate of increase 481
Pie chart 465
Plot area 493
Rate = amount of increase/base 482
Relative cell reference 465
Text box 473
Tick marks 494
Value after increase = base × percent for new value 486
Value axis 493
What-if analysis 475
WordArt 475
x-axis 493
y-axis 493

Matching

Match each term in the second column with its correct definition in the first column by writing the letter of the term on the blank line in front of the correct definition.

____ 1. A chart that shows the relationship of each part to a whole.

____ 2. The term used to describe money set aside for the normal operating activities of a government entity such as a city.

____ 3. In a formula, the address of a cell based on the relative position of the cell that contains the formula and the cell referred to.

____ 4. A column, bar, area, dot, pie slice, or other symbol in a chart that represents a single data point.

____ 5. A workbook sheet that contains only a chart.

____ 6. A shape effect that uses shading and shadows to make the edges of a shape appear to be curved or angled.

____ 7. The entire chart and all of its elements.

____ 8. The process of changing the values in cells to see how those changes affect the outcome of formulas in a worksheet.

____ 9. The mathematical formula to calculate a rate of increase.

A Axis
B Bevel
C Category axis
D Chart area
E Chart sheet
F Data marker
G Format as you type
H General Fund
I Order of operations
J Pie chart
K Rate=amount of increase/base
L Relative cell reference
M Tick marks
N Value axis
O What-if analysis

_____ 10. The mathematical rules for performing multiple calculations within a formula.

_____ 11. The Excel feature by which a cell takes on the formatting of the number typed into the cell.

_____ 12. A line that serves as a frame of reference for measurement and that borders the chart plot area.

_____ 13. The area along the bottom of a chart that identifies the categories of data; also referred to as the x-axis.

_____ 14. A numerical scale on the left side of a chart that shows the range of numbers for the data points; also referred to as the y-axis.

_____ 15. The short lines that display on an axis at regular intervals.

Multiple Choice

Circle the correct answer.

1. A sum of money set aside for a specific purpose is a:
A. value axis **B.** fund **C.** rate

2. A cell reference that refers to a cell by its fixed position in a worksheet is referred to as being:
A. absolute **B.** relative **C.** mixed

3. A value that originates in a worksheet cell and that is represented in a chart by a data marker is a data:
A. point **B.** cell **C.** axis

4. Related data points represented by data markers are referred to as the data:
A. slices **B.** set **C.** series

5. The action of pulling out a pie slice from a pie chart is called:
A. extract **B.** explode **C.** plot

6. A gallery of text styles with which you can create decorative effects, such as shadowed or mirrored text is:
A. WordArt **B.** shape effects **C.** text fill

7. The percent by which one number increases over another number is the percentage rate of:
A. decrease **B.** change **C.** increase

8. A chart type that displays trends over time is a:
A. pie chart **B.** line chart **C.** column chart

9. The area bounded by the axes of a chart, including all the data series, is the:
A. chart area **B.** plot area **C.** axis area

10. The x-axis is also known as the:
A. category axis **B.** value axis **C.** data axis

Content-Based Assessments

Apply 9A skills from these Objectives:

1. Chart Data with a Pie Chart
2. Format a Pie Chart
3. Edit a Workbook and Update a Chart
4. Use Goal Seek to Perform What-If Analysis

Skills Review | Project 9C Fund Revenue

In the following Skills Review, you will edit a worksheet for Jennifer Carson, City Finance Manager, which details the City general fund revenue. Your completed worksheets will look similar to Figure 9.46.

Project Files

For Project 9C, you will need the following file:

e03C_Fund_Revenue

You will save your workbook as:

Lastname_Firstname_3C_Fund_Revenue

Project Results

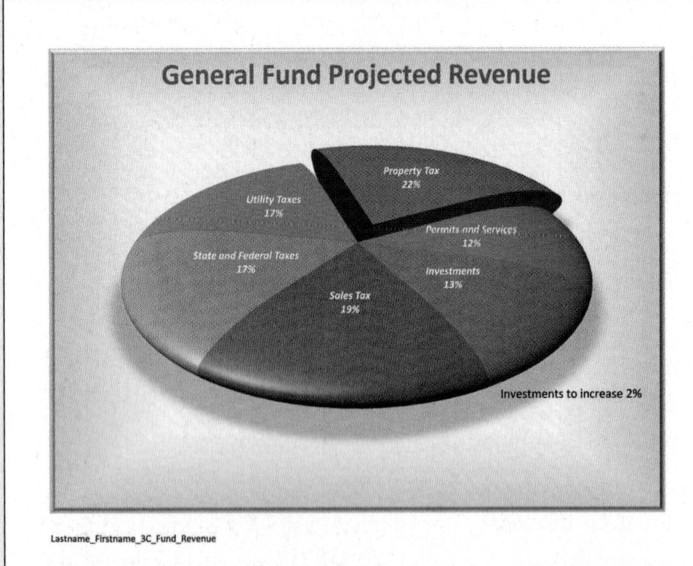

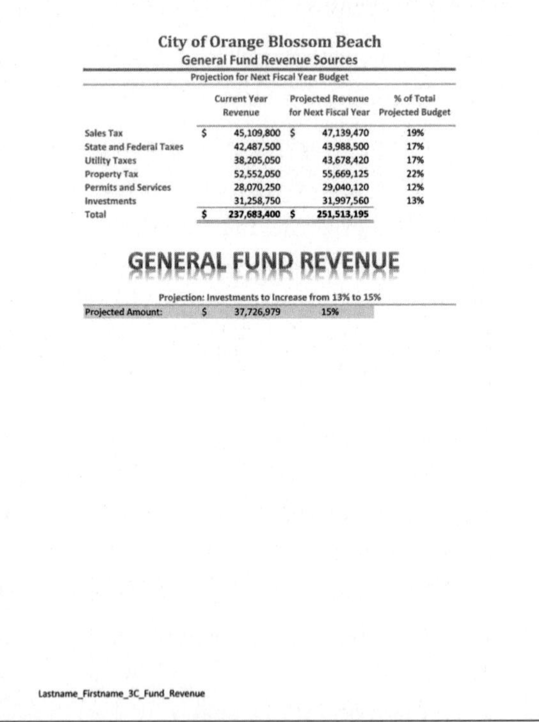

City of Orange Blossom Beach

General Fund Revenue Sources

Projection for Next Fiscal Year Budget

	Current Year Revenue	Projected Revenue for Next Fiscal Year	% of Total Projected Budget
Sales Tax	$ 45,109,800	$ 47,139,470	19%
State and Federal Taxes	42,487,500	43,988,500	17%
Utility Taxes	38,205,050	43,678,420	17%
Property Tax	52,552,050	55,669,125	22%
Permits and Services	28,070,250	29,040,120	12%
Investments	31,258,750	31,997,560	13%
Total	$ 237,683,400	$ 251,513,195	

GENERAL FUND REVENUE

Projection: Investments to Increase from 13% to 15%

Projected Amount:	$ 37,726,979	15%

Lastname_Firstname_3C_Fund_Revenue

Figure 9.46

(Project 9C Fund Revenue continues on the next page)

Skills Review | Project 9C Fund Revenue (continued)

1 **Start** Excel. From your student files, open the file **e03C_Fund_Revenue**. **Save** the file in your **Excel Chapter 3** folder as **Lastname_Firstname_3C_Fund_Revenue**

a. Click cell **D5**, and then type **=** to begin a formula. Click cell **C5**, type **/** and then click cell **C11**. Press F4 to make the reference to the value in cell **C11** absolute. On the **Formula Bar**, click the **Enter** button, and then fill the formula down through cell **D10**.

b. With the range **D5:D10** selected, right-click over the selection, and then on Mini toolbar, click the **Percent Style** button and the **Center** button.

2 Select the nonadjacent ranges **A5:A10** and **C5:C10** to select the revenue names and the projected revenue. Click the **Insert tab**, and then in the **Charts group**, click **Pie**. Under **3-D Pie**, click the first chart—**Pie in 3-D**.

a. On the **Design tab**, in the **Location group**, click the **Move Chart** button. In the **Move Chart** dialog box, click the **New sheet** option button. In the **New sheet** box, replace the highlighted text *Chart1* by typing **Projected Revenue Chart** and then click **OK**.

b. On the **Layout tab**, in the **Labels group**, click the **Chart Title** button, and then click **Above Chart**. With the **Chart Title** box selected, type **General Fund Projected Revenue** and then press Enter to create the new chart title.

c. Point to the chart title text, and then right-click to display the Mini toolbar. Change the **Font Size** to **32** and change the **Font Color** to **Blue-Gray, Text 2**—in the fourth column, the first color.

d. Click in a white area of the chart to deselect the chart title. On the **Layout tab**, in the **Labels group**, click the **Legend** button, and then click **None**.

e. In the **Labels group**, click the **Data Labels** button, and then click **More Data Label Options**. In the **Format Data Labels** dialog box, on the left, be sure **Label Options** is selected. On the right, under **Label Contains**, click as necessary to select the **Category Name** and **Percentage** check boxes. *Clear* any other check boxes in this group. Under **Label Position**, click the **Center** option button. Click **Close**.

f. Point to any of the selected labels, right-click to display the Mini toolbar, and then change the **Font Size** to **12**, the **Font Color** to **White, Background 1, Darker 5%**, and then apply **Bold** and **Italic**.

3 3. Click in any pie slice outside of the label to select the entire pie. Click the **Format tab**, and then in the **Shape Styles group**, click the **Shape Effects** button. Point to **Bevel**, and then at the bottom of the gallery, click **3-D Options**.

a. In the **Format Data Series** dialog box, on the right, under **Bevel**, click the **Top** button. In the gallery, under **Bevel**, in the first row, click the first button—**Circle**. Then click the **Bottom** button, and apply the **Circle** bevel. In the four **Width** and **Height** spin boxes, type **512**

b. In the lower portion of the dialog box, under **Surface**, click the **Material** button. Under **Standard**, click the third button—**Plastic**. In the lower right corner, click the **Close** button.

c. On the **Format tab**, in the **Shape Styles group**, click **Shape Effects**, and then point to **Shadow**. Under **Perspective**, click the third button—**Below**.

d. With the pie chart still selected, point anywhere in the pie and right-click. On the displayed shortcut menu, click **Format Data Series**. In the **Format Data Series** dialog box, on the left, be sure **Series Options** is selected. On the right, click in the box under **Angle of first slice**, change *0* to type **150** to move the largest slice—*Property Tax*—to the top of the pie. Click **Close**.

e. Click in the area outside of the chart sheet to deselect all chart elements. Then, on the pie chart, click the outer edge of the **Property Tax** slice one time to select the pie chart, and then click the **Property Tax** slice again to select only that slice.

f. Point to the **Property Tax** slice, and then explode the slice by dragging it slightly away from the center of the pie.

g. With the **Property Tax** slice still selected, point to the slice and right-click. On the shortcut menu, click **Format Data Point**. In the displayed **Format Data Point** dialog box, on the left, click **Fill**. On the right, under **Fill**, click the **Solid fill** option button. Click the **Color arrow**, and then under **Theme Colors**, in the sixth column, click the fifth color—**Dark Yellow, Accent 2, Darker 25%**. Click **Close**.

4 Point to the white area just inside the border of the chart to display the ScreenTip **Chart Area**, and then click one time.

a. On the **Format tab**, in the **Shape Styles group**, click the **Shape Effects** button, point to **Bevel**, and then under **Bevel**, in the second row, click the third bevel—**Convex**.

b. With the chart area still selected, right-click in a white area at the outer edge of the chart, and then

(Project 9C Fund Revenue continues on the next page)

Skills Review | Project 9C Fund Revenue (continued)

on the shortcut menu, click **Format Chart Area**. In the **Format Chart Area** dialog box, on the left, be sure that **Fill** is selected. On the right, under **Fill**, click the **Gradient fill** option button. Click the **Preset colors** arrow, and then in the third row, click the fourth preset, **Parchment**. Click the **Type arrow**, and then click **Path**. Click the **Close** button.

c. Click the **Layout tab**, and then in the **Insert group**, click the **Text Box** button. Position the pointer near the lower corner of the *Investments* slice. Hold down the left mouse button, and then drag down and to the right so that the text box extends to the end of the chart area and is approximately one-half inch high. With the insertion point blinking inside the text box, type **Investments to increase 2%** Select the text and then on the Mini toolbar, change the **Font Size** to **12**. If necessary, use the sizing handles to widen the text box so that the text displays on one line.

5 In the sheet tab area at the bottom of the workbook, click the **Sheet1 tab** to redisplay the worksheet.

a. Click the **Insert tab**, and then in the **Text group**, click the **WordArt** button.

b. In the **WordArt** gallery, in the last row, click the last style—**Fill – Red, Accent 1, Metal Bevel, Reflection**. Type **general fund revenue** and then point anywhere on the dashed border surrounding the WordArt object. Click the dashed border one time to change it to a solid border, indicating that all of the text is selected. Right-click the border to display the Mini toolbar, and then change the **Font Size** to **28**.

c. Drag to position the upper left corner of the WordArt in cell **A13**, centered below the worksheet.

6 In cell **A17**, type **Projection: Investments to Increase from 13% to 15%** and then **Merge & Center** the text across the range **A17:D17**. Apply the **Heading 3** cell style.

a. In cell **A18**, type **Projected Amount:** and press Enter. Select the range **C10:D10**, right-click over the selection, and then click **Copy**. Point to cell **B18**, right-click, and then under **Paste Options**, click the **Paste** button. Press Esc to cancel the moving border.

b. Click cell **C18**. On the **Data tab**, in the **Data Tools group**, click the **What-If Analysis** button, and then click **Goal Seek**. In the **Goal Seek** dialog box, press Tab to move to the **To value** box, and then type **15%**

c. Press Tab to move the insertion point to the **By changing cell** box, and then click cell **B18**. Click **OK**. In the displayed **Goal Seek Status** dialog box, click **OK**.

d. Select the range **A18:C18**. From the **Home tab**, display the **Cell Styles** gallery. Under **Themed Cell Styles**, apply **40% - Accent3**. Click cell **B18**, and then from the **Cell Styles** gallery, apply the **Currency [0]** cell style.

7 With your worksheet displayed, in the sheet tab area, double-click *Sheet1* to select the text, and then type **Projected Revenue Data** and press Enter.

a. On the **Insert tab**, in the **Text group**, click **Header & Footer**. In the **Navigation group**, click the **Go to Footer** button, click in the **left section** above the word *Footer*, and then in the **Header & Footer Elements group**, click the **File Name** button. Click in a cell above the footer to deselect the **Footer area** and view your file name.

b. On the **Page Layout tab**, in the **Page Setup group**, click the **Margins** button, and then at the bottom of the **Margins gallery**, click **Custom Margins**. In the **Page Setup** dialog box, under **Center on page**, select the **Horizontally** check box. Click **OK**, and then on the status bar, click the **Normal** button. Press Ctrl + Home to move to the top of your worksheet.

c. Click the **Projected Revenue Chart** sheet tab to display the chart sheet. On the **Insert tab**, click **Header & Footer**. In the center of the **Page Setup** dialog box, click **Custom Footer**. With the insertion point blinking in the **Left section**, in the row of buttons in the middle of the dialog box, locate and click the **Insert File Name** button. Click **OK** two times.

d. Right-click either of the sheet tabs, and then click **Select All Sheets**. From **Backstage** view, show the **Document Panel**. In the **Author** box, replace the existing text with your firstname and lastname. In the **Subject** box, type your course name and section number. In the **Keywords** box type **general fund, projected revenue** **Close** the **Document Information Panel**.

e. With the two sheets still grouped, press Ctrl + F2 to display the **Print Preview**, and then view the two pages of your workbook.

f. **Save** your workbook. Print or submit electronically as directed by your instructor. If required by your instructor, print or create an electronic version of your worksheets with formulas displayed by using the instructions in Activity 2.16, and then **Close** Excel without saving so that you do not save the changes you made to print formulas.

End You have completed Project 9C

Apply **9B** skills from these Objectives:

- **5** Design a Worksheet for What-If Analysis
- **6** Answer What-If Questions by Changing Values in a Worksheet
- **7** Chart Data with a Line Chart

Skills Review | Project 9D Revenue Projection

In the following Skills Review, you will edit a worksheet for Jennifer Carson, City Finance Manager, which forecasts the permit revenue that the City of Orange Blossom Beach expects to collect in the next five years. Your completed worksheet will look similar to Figure 9.47.

Project Files

For Project 9D, you will need the following files:

e03D_Revenue_Projection
e03D_Shoreline

You will save your workbook as:

Lastname_Firstname_3D_Revenue_Projection

Project Results

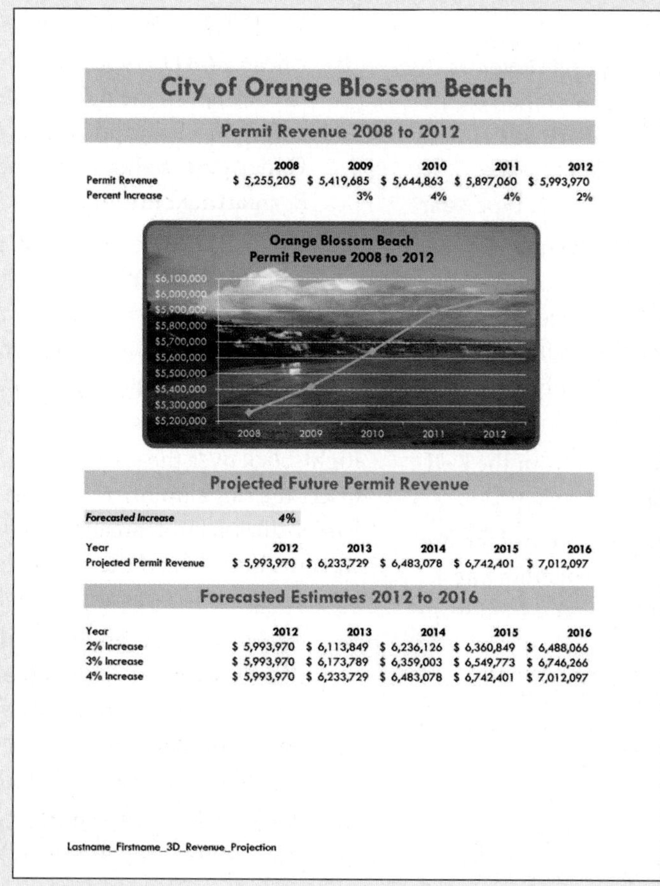

City of Orange Blossom Beach

Permit Revenue 2008 to 2012

	2008	2009	2010	2011	2012
Permit Revenue	$ 5,255,205	$ 5,419,685	$ 5,644,863	$ 5,897,060	$ 5,993,970
Percent Increase		3%	4%	4%	2%

Projected Future Permit Revenue

Forecasted Increase 4%

Year	2012	2013	2014	2015	2016
Projected Permit Revenue	$ 5,993,970	$ 6,233,729	$ 6,483,078	$ 6,742,401	$ 7,012,097

Forecasted Estimates 2012 to 2016

Year	2012	2013	2014	2015	2016
2% Increase	$ 5,993,970	$ 6,113,849	$ 6,236,126	$ 6,360,849	$ 6,488,066
3% Increase	$ 5,993,970	$ 6,173,789	$ 6,359,003	$ 6,549,773	$ 6,746,266
4% Increase	$ 5,993,970	$ 6,233,729	$ 6,483,078	$ 6,742,401	$ 7,012,097

Lastname_Firstname_3D_Revenue_Projection

Figure 9.47

(Project 9D Revenue Projection continues on the next page)

Skills Review | Project 9D Revenue Projection (continued)

1 **Start** Excel. From your student files, open the file **e03D_Revenue_Projection**. **Save** the file in your **Excel Chapter 3** folder with the file name **Lastname_Firstname_3D_Revenue_Projection**

a. Click cell **C7**. Being sure to include the parentheses, type **=(c6-b6)/b6** and then on the **Formula Bar**, click the **Enter** button. In the **Number group**, click the **Percent Style** button.

b. Click cell **D7**, type **=** and then by typing, or using a combination of typing and clicking cells to reference them, construct a formula similar to the one in cell **C7** to calculate the rate of increase in population from 2009 to 2010. Format cell **D7** with the **Percent Style**. With cell **D7** selected, drag the fill handle to the right through cell **F7**.

c. In cell **A9**, type **Projected Future Permit Revenue** and then press Enter. Point to cell **A3**, and then right-click. On the Mini toolbar, click the **Format Painter** button, and then click cell **A9**. In cell **A11**, type **Forecasted Increase** and then in cell **A13**, type **Year**

d. In cell **A14**, type **Projected Permit Revenue** and then in cell **B13**, type **2012** and press Tab. In cell **C13**, type **2013** and then press Tab. Select the range **B13:C13**, and then drag the fill handle through cell **F13** to extend the pattern of years to *2016*. Apply **Bold** to the selection.

e. Click cell **B14**, type **5993970** and then from the **Cell Styles** gallery, apply the **Currency [0]** style.

f. In cell **B11**, type **2%** which is the percent of increase from 2011 to 2012, and then on the **Formula Bar**, click **Enter**. Select the range **A11:B11**, and then from the Mini toolbar, apply **Bold** and **Italic**.

2 Click cell **C14**. Type **=b14*(100%+b11)** and then on the **Formula Bar**, click the **Enter** button. With cell **C14** as the active cell, drag the fill handle to copy the formula to the range **D14:F14**.

a. Point to cell **B14**, right-click, click the **Format Painter** button, and then select the range **C14:F14**.

b. Click cell **A16**. Type **Forecasted Estimates 2012 to 2016** and then press Enter. Use **Format Painter** to copy the format from cell **A9** to cell **A16**.

c. Select the range **A11:B11**, right-click to display the Mini toolbar, click the **Fill Color button arrow**, and then under **Theme Colors**, in the first column, click the third color—**White, Background 1, Darker 15%**.

d. In the range **A18:A21**, type the following row titles:

Year

2% Increase

3% Increase

4% Increase

3 Select the range **B13:F13**, right-click over the selection, and then on the shortcut menu, click **Copy**. **Paste** the selection to the range **B18:F18**.

a. Select the range **B14:F14**, right-click over the selection, and then on the shortcut menu, click **Copy**. Point to **B19**, right-click, and then from the shortcut menu, point to **Paste Special**. Under **Paste Values**, click the second button—**Values & Number Formatting**. Press Esc to cancel the moving border,

b. Click cell **B11**. Type **3** and then press Enter. **Copy** the new values in the range **B14:F14**. Point to cell **B20** and right-click, and then point to **Paste Special**. Under **Paste Values**, click the **Values & Number Formatting** button.

c. In cell **B11**, type **4** and then press Enter. Select and copy the range **B14:F14**, and then paste the values and number formats to the range **B21:F21**. Press Esc to cancel the moving border.

4 In the **row header area**, point to **row 8** to display the → pointer, and then drag down to select **rows 8:24**. Right-click over the selection, and then click **Insert** to insert the same number of blank rows as you selected. Under the selection area near cell **A25**, click the **Insert Options** button, and then click the **Clear Formatting** option button to clear any formatting from these rows.

a. Select the range **A6:F6**. On the **Insert tab**, in the **Charts group**, click the **Line** button. In the displayed gallery of line charts, in the second row, click the **Line with Markers** chart type to create the chart as an embedded chart in the worksheet.

b. Point to the border of the chart to display the ✥ pointer, and then drag the chart so that its upper left corner is positioned in cell **A9**, aligned approximately under the *r* in the word *Increase* above.

c. On the **Layout tab**, in the **Labels group**, click the **Legend** button, and then click **None**. Click the chart title one time to select it. Type **Orange Blossom Beach** and then press Enter.

(Project 9D Revenue Projection continues on the next page)

Skills Review | Project 9D Revenue Projection (continued)

d. In the chart title, click to position the insertion point following the *h* in *Beach*, and then press Enter to begin a new line. Type **Permit Revenue 2008 to 2012** Click the dashed border around the chart title to change it to a solid border, right-click the solid border, and then on the Mini toolbar, change the **Font Size** of the title to **14**.

5 With the chart selected, click the **Design tab**, and then in the **Data group**, click the **Select Data** button. On the right side of the **Select Data Source** dialog box, under **Horizontal (Category) Axis Labels**, in the right column, click the **Edit** button. If necessary, drag the title bar of the Axis Labels dialog box to the right of the chart so that it is not blocking your view of the data, and then select the years in the range **B5:F5**. Click **OK** two times to enter the years as the category labels.

a. On the **Layout tab**, in the **Axes group**, click the **Axes** button. Point to **Primary Vertical Axis**, and then click **More Primary Vertical Axis Options**. In the **Format Axis** dialog box, on the left, be sure **Axis Options** is selected. On the right, in the **Minimum** row, click the **Fixed** option button. In the box to the right, select the existing text, and then type **5200000**

b. In the **Major unit** row, click the **Fixed** option button, select the value *200000.0* in the box to the right, and then type **100000** In the lower right corner, click **Close**.

c. Click the **Format tab**, and then in the **Current Selection group**, click the **Chart Elements arrow**. From the displayed list, click **Chart Area**. Directly below the **Chart Elements** box, click the **Format Selection** button.

d. In the **Format Chart Area** dialog box, on the left, be sure that **Fill** is selected. On the right, under **Fill**, click the **Picture or texture fill** option button, and then under **Insert from**, click the **File** button. In the **Insert Picture** dialog box, navigate to your student files, and then insert the picture **e03D_Shoreline**. In the **Format Chart Area** dialog box, on the left, click **Border Color**. On the right click the **Solid line** option button, and then click the **Color arrow**. Under **Theme Colors**, in the fourth column, click the first color—**Brown, Text 2**.

e. On the left, click **Border Styles**. On the right, select the text in the **Width** box and type **4** Select the **Rounded corners** check box, and then **Close** the dialog box.

6 In the **Current Selection group**, click the **Chart Elements arrow**, on the list click **Plot Area**, and then click the **Format Selection** button. In the **Format Plot Area** dialog box, on the left, be sure that **Fill** is selected, and then on the right, click the **No fill** option button. **Close** the dialog box.

a. Click the **Chart Elements arrow**, on the list click **Vertical (Value) Axis**, and then click the **Format Selection** button. In the **Format Axis** dialog box, on the left, click **Line Color**. On the right, click the **Solid line** option button, click the **Color arrow**, and then click the first color—**White, Background 1**. **Close** the dialog box.

b. From the **Chart Elements** box, select the **Vertical (Value) Axis Major Gridlines**, and then click **Format Selection**. Change the **Line Color** to a **Solid line**, and then apply the **White, Background 1** color. **Close** the dialog box.

c. From the **Chart Elements** box, select the **Horizontal (Category) Axis**, and then click **Format Selection**. Change the **Line Color** to a **Solid line**, and then apply the **White, Background 1** color. **Close** the dialog box.

d. Point to any of the numbers on the **vertical value axis**, right-click, and then on the Mini toolbar, change the **Font Color** to **White, Background 1**. Point to any of the years on the **horizontal category axis**, right-click, and then change the **Font Color** to **White, Background 1**.

e. Click any cell to deselect the chart. Insert a **Header & Footer** with the **file name** in the **left section** of the footer, and then center the worksheet **Horizontally** on the page. Return to **Normal** view, and press Ctrl + Home. From **Backstage** view, show the **Document Panel**. In the **Author** box, replace the existing text with your firstname and lastname. In the **Subject** box, type your course name and section number. In the **Keywords** box type **permit revenue, forecast** **Close** the **Document Information Panel**.

f. **Save** your workbook. Print or submit electronically as directed by your instructor. If required by your instructor, print or create an electronic version of your worksheet with formulas displayed by using the instructions in Activity 2.16, and then **Close** Excel without saving so that you do not save the changes you made to print formulas.

End **You have completed Project 9D**

Excel | Chapter 9

Content-Based Assessments

Apply 9A skills from these Objectives:

1. Chart Data with a Pie Chart
2. Format a Pie Chart
3. Edit a Workbook and Update a Chart
4. Use Goal Seek to Perform What-If Analysis

Mastering Excel | Project 9E Investments

In the following project, you will you will edit a worksheet for Jennifer Carson, City Finance Manager, that summarizes the investment portfolio of the City of Orange Blossom Beach. Your completed worksheets will look similar to Figure 9.48.

Project Files

For Project 9E, you will need the following file:

e03E_Investments

You will save your workbook as:

Lastname_Firstname_3E_Investments

Project Results

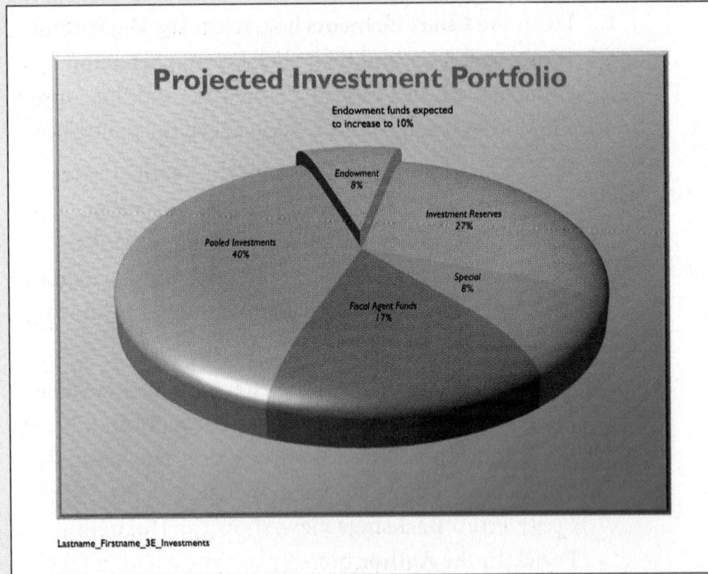

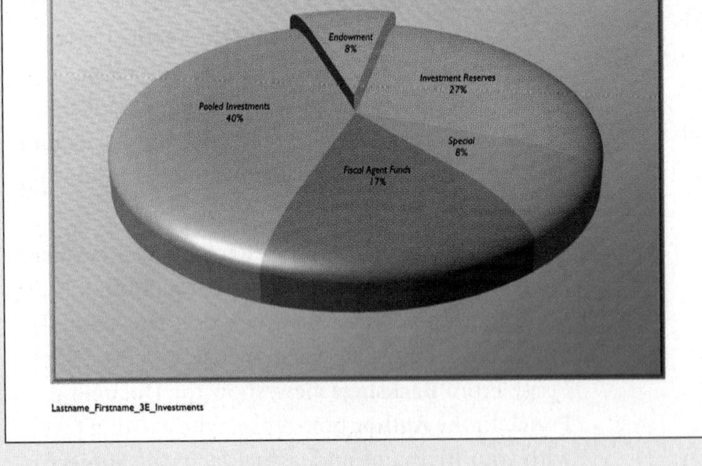

City of Orange Blossom Beach
Investment Portfolio
Projection for Next Fiscal Year Budget

	Current Year Investments	Projected Investments for Next Fiscal Year	% of Total Projected Investments
Pooled Investments	$ 28,809,800	$ 32,956,740	40%
Endowment	8,120,500	6,754,950	8%
Investment Reserves	13,786,400	22,712,600	27%
Special	4,007,520	6,874,325	8%
Fiscal Agent Funds	11,694,500	13,987,550	17%
Total	$ 66,418,720	$ 83,286,165	

GENERAL FUND INVESTMENTS

Goal: Increase Endowment Fund from 8% to 10%

Goal Amount	$ 8,328,617	10%

Lastname_Firstname_3E_Investments

Figure 9.48

(Project 9E Investments continues on the next page)

Mastering Excel | Project 9E Investments (continued)

1 **Start** Excel. From your student files, locate and open **e03E_Investments**. **Save** the file in your **Excel Chapter 3** folder as **Lastname_Firstname_3E_Investments**

2 In cells **B10** and **C10**, enter formulas to calculate totals for each column. Then, in cell **D5**, enter a formula to calculate the % of Total Projected Investments for Pooled Investments by dividing the **Projected Investments for Next Fiscal Year** for the **Pooled Investments** by the **Total Projected Investments for Next Fiscal Year**. Use absolute cell references as necessary, format the result in **Percent Style**, and **Center** the percentage. Fill the formula down through cell **D9**.

3 Select the nonadjacent ranges **A5:A9** and **C5:C9**, and then insert a **Pie in 3-D** chart. Move the chart to a **New sheet** named **Projected Investment Chart** Insert a **Chart Title** above the chart with the text **Projected Investment Portfolio** Change the chart title **Font Size** to **32** and change the **Font Color** to **Brown, Accent 6**—in the last column, the first color.

4 Remove the **Legend** from the chart, and then add **Data Labels** formatted so that only the **Category Name** and **Percentage** display positioned in the **Center**. Change the data labels **Font Size** to **11**, and then apply **Italic**.

5 Select the entire pie, display the **Shape Effects** gallery, point to **Bevel**, and then at the bottom of the gallery, click **3-D Options**. Change the **Top** and **Bottom** options to the last **Bevel** type—**Art Deco**. Set the **Top Width** and **Height** boxes to **256** and then set the **Bottom Width** and **Height** boxes to **0** Change the **Material** to the third **Standard** type—**Plastic**.

6 With the pie chart selected, display the shortcut menu, and then click **Format Data Series**. Change the **Angle of first slice** to **200** to move the *Endowment* slice to the top of the pie. Select the **Endowment** slice, and then explode the slice slightly.

7 Change the **Fill Color** of the **Pooled Investments** slice to **Gray-50%, Accent 1, Lighter 40%**. Format the **Chart Area** by applying a **Convex Bevel**. To the **Chart Area**, apply the **Moss, Preset Gradient fill**. In the **Angle** box, type **45** and then **Close** the **Format Chart Area** dialog box.

8 **Insert** a **Text Box** positioned approximately halfway between the *Endowment* pie slice and the *v* in the word *Investment* in the title. In the text box, type **Endowment funds expected to increase to 10%** Select the text and then on the Mini toolbar, change the **Font Size** to **12**. Size the text box as necessary so that the text displays on two lines as shown in Figure 9.48.

9 Display **Sheet1** and rename the sheet as **Projected Investment Data** Insert a **WordArt**—in the fifth row, insert the last WordArt style—**Fill – Gray-50%, Accent 1, Plastic Bevel, Reflection**. Type **General Fund Investments** and then change the **Font Size** to **20**. Drag to position the upper left corner of the WordArt in cell **A12**, centered below the worksheet.

10 In cell **A16**, type **Goal: Increase Endowment Fund from 8% to 10%** and then **Merge & Center** the text across the range **A16:D16**. Apply the **Heading 3** cell style. In cell **A17**, type **Goal Amount**

11 **Copy** the range **C6:D6** to cell **B17**. Click cell **C17**, and then use **Goal Seek** to determine the projected amount of endowment funds in cell **B17** if the value in **C17** is **10%**.

12 Select the range **A17:C17**, and then apply the **20% - Accent2** cell style. In **B17**, from the **Cell Styles** gallery, apply the **Currency [0]** cell style.

13 Insert a **Header & Footer** with the file name in the **left section** of the footer. In Page Layout view, check that the WordArt is centered under the worksheet data. Center the worksheet **Horizontally** on the page, and then return to **Normal** view. Display the **Projected Investment Chart** sheet and insert a **Custom Footer** with the file name in the **Left section**.

14 Group the sheets, and then display the **Document Panel**. Add your name, your course name and section, and the keywords **investment portfolio**

15 **Save** your workbook. Print or submit electronically as directed by your instructor. If required by your instructor, print or create an electronic version of your worksheets with formulas displayed by using the instructions in Activity 2.16, and then **Close** Excel without saving so that you do not save the changes you made to print formulas.

End **You have completed Project 9E**

Apply 9B skills from these Objectives:

5. Design a Worksheet for What-If Analysis
6. Answer What-If Questions by Changing Values in a Worksheet
7. Chart Data with a Line Chart

Mastering Excel | Project 9F Benefit Analysis

In the following project, you will edit a worksheet that Jeffrey Lovins, Human Resources Director, will use to prepare a five-year forecast of the annual cost of city employee benefits per employee. Your completed worksheet will look similar to Figure 9.49.

Project Files

For Project 9F, you will need the following file:

e03F_Benefit_Analysis

You will save your workbook as:

Lastname_Firstname_3F_Benefit Analysis

Project Results

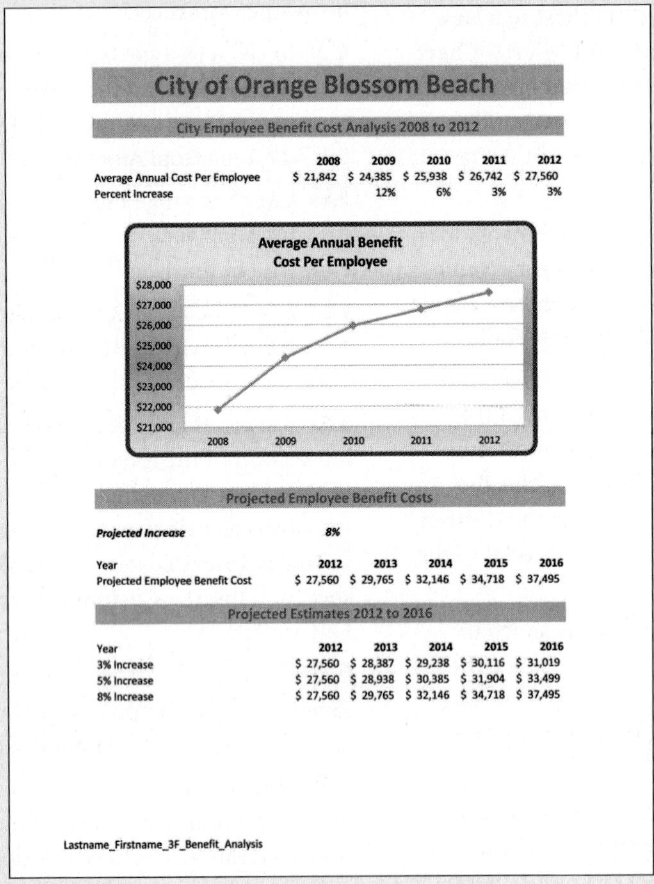

City of Orange Blossom Beach

City Employee Benefit Cost Analysis 2008 to 2012

	2008	2009	2010	2011	2012
Average Annual Cost Per Employee	$ 21,842	$ 24,385	$ 25,938	$ 26,742	$ 27,560
Percent Increase		12%	6%	3%	3%

Projected Employee Benefit Costs

Projected Increase 8%

Year	2012	2013	2014	2015	2016
Projected Employee Benefit Cost	$ 27,560	$ 29,765	$ 32,146	$ 34,718	$ 37,495

Projected Estimates 2012 to 2016

Year	2012	2013	2014	2015	2016
3% Increase	$ 27,560	$ 28,387	$ 29,238	$ 30,116	$ 31,019
5% Increase	$ 27,560	$ 28,938	$ 30,385	$ 31,904	$ 33,499
8% Increase	$ 27,560	$ 29,765	$ 32,146	$ 34,718	$ 37,495

Lastname_Firstname_3F_Benefit_Analysis

Figure 9.49

(Project 9F Benefit Analysis continues on the next page)

Mastering Excel | Project 9F Benefit Analysis (continued)

1 **Start** Excel. From your student files, open the file **e03F_Benefit_Analysis. Save** the file in your **Excel Chapter 3** folder as **Firstname_Lastname_3F_Benefit_Analysis**

2 In cell **C7**, construct a formula to calculate the percent of increase in employee annual benefit costs from 2008 to 2009. Format the result with the **Percent Style** and then fill the formula through cell **F7**.

3 In cell **A9**, type **Projected Employee Benefit Costs** and then use **Format Painter** to copy the formatting from cell **A3** to cell **A9**. In cell **A11**, type **Projected Increase** and then in cell **A13**, type **Year** In cell **A14**, type **Projected Employee Benefit Cost** and then in the range **B13:F13**, use the fill handle to enter the years 2012 through 2016. Apply **Bold** to the years. In cell **B14**, type **27560** and then from the **Cell Styles** gallery, apply the **Currency [0]** format. In cell **B11**, type **3%** which is the percent of increase from 2011 to 2012. To the range **A11:B11**, apply **Bold** and **Italic**.

4 In cell **C14**, construct a formula to calculate the annual cost of employee benefits for the year 2013 after the projected increase of 3% is applied. Fill the formula through cell **F14**, and then use **Format Painter** to copy the formatting from cell **B14** to the range **C14:F14**.

5 In cell **A16**, type **Projected Estimates 2012 to 2016** and then use **Format Painter** to copy the format from cell **A9** to cell **A16**. In cells **A18:A21**, type the following row titles:

Year
3% Increase
5% Increase
8% Increase

6 **Copy** the range **B13:F13**, and then **Paste** the selection to **B18:F18**. Copy the range **B14:F14** and then paste the **Values & Number Formatting** to the range **B19:F19**. Complete the Projected Estimates section of the worksheet by changing the *Projected Increase* in **B11** to **5%** and then to **8%** copying and pasting the **Values & Number Formatting** to the appropriate ranges in the worksheet.

7 Select **rows 8:24**, and then **Insert** the same number of blank rows as you selected. **Clear Formatting** from the inserted rows. By using the data in **A5:F6**, insert a **Line with Markers** chart in the worksheet. Move the chart so that its upper left corner is positioned in cell **A9** and centered under the data above. Remove the **Legend**, and then replace the existing chart title with the two-line title **Average Annual Benefit Cost Per Employee** The text *Cost per Employee* should display on the second line. Change the title **Font Size** to **14**.

8 Format the **Primary Vertical Axis** so that the **Minimum** is **21000** and the **Major unit** is **1000** Format the **Chart Area** with a **Gradient fill** by applying the third **Preset color** in the third row—**Wheat**. Change the **Border Color** by applying a **Solid line—Orange, Accent 1, Darker 50%**. Change the **Width** of the border to **4** and apply the **Rounded corners** option.

9 Deselect the chart, and then insert a **Header & Footer** with the file name in the **left section** of the footer; center the worksheet **Horizontally** on the page. In the **Document Panel**, add your name, your course name and section, and the keywords **employee benefits, forecast**

10 **Save** your workbook. Print or submit electronically as directed by your instructor. If required by your instructor, print or create an electronic version of your worksheets with formulas displayed by using the instructions in Activity 2.16, and then **Close** Excel without saving so that you do not save the changes you made to print formulas.

End **You have completed Project 9F**

Content-Based Assessments

Apply 9A and 9B skills from these Objectives:

1. Chart Data with a Pie Chart
2. Format a Pie Chart
3. Edit a Workbook and Update a Chart
4. Use Goal Seek to Perform What-If Analysis
5. Design a Worksheet for What-If Analysis
6. Answer What-If Questions by Changing Values in a Worksheet
7. Chart Data with a Line Chart

Mastering Excel | Project 9G Operations Analysis

In the following project, you will you will edit a workbook for Jennifer Carson, City Finance Manager, that summarizes the operations costs for the Public Works Department. Your completed worksheets will look similar to Figure 9.50.

Project Files

For Project 9G, you will need the following file:

e03G_Operations_Analysis

You will save your workbook as:

Lastname_Firstname_3G_Operations_Analysis

Project Results

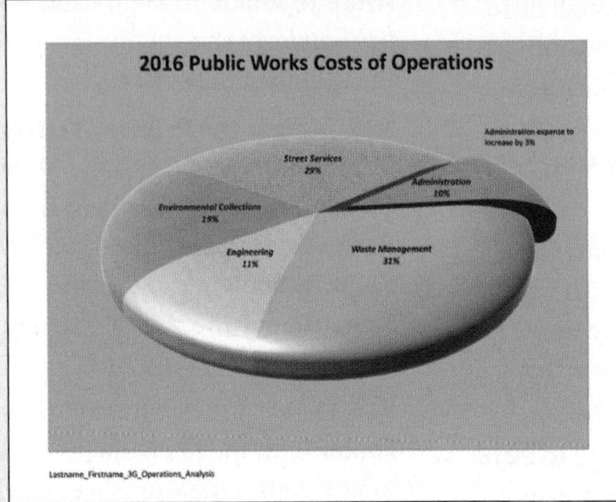

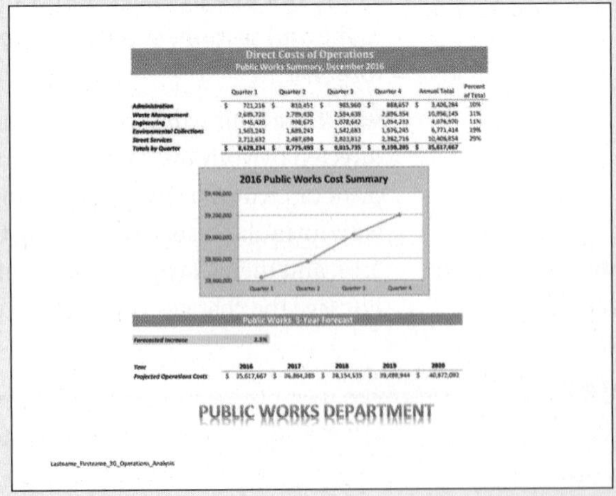

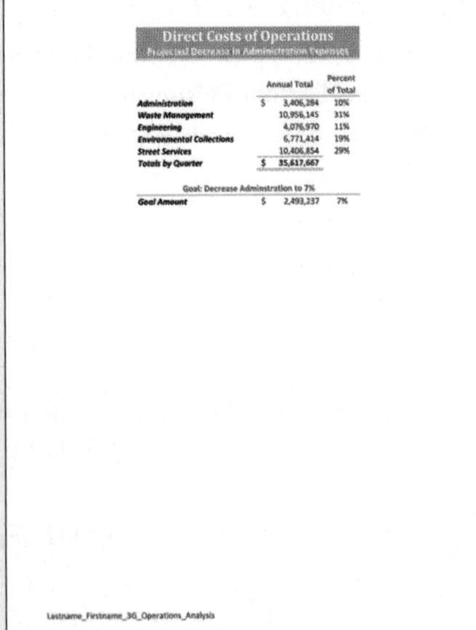

Direct Costs of Operations
Projected Decrease in Administration Expenses

	Annual Total	Percent of Total
Administration	$ 3,406,284	10%
Waste Management	10,956,145	31%
Engineering	4,076,970	11%
Environmental Collections	6,771,414	19%
Street Services	10,406,854	29%
Totals by Quarter	$ 35,617,667	

Goal: Decrease Administration to 7%

Goal Amount	$ 2,493,237	7%

Lastname_Firstname_3G_Operations_Analysis

Figure 9.50

(Project 9G Operations Analysis continues on the next page)

Mastering Excel | Project 9G Operations Analysis (continued)

1 **Start** Excel. From your student files, open **e03G_Operations_Analysis. Save** the file as in your **Excel Chapter 3** folder as **Lastname_Firstname_3G_Operations_Analysis**

2 In the **Public Works** sheet, calculate totals in the ranges **F5:F9** and **B10:F10**. In cell **G5**, construct a formula to calculate the **Percent of Total** by dividing the **Annual Total** for **Administration** in cell **F5** by the **Annual Total** for all quarters in cell **F10**. Use absolute cell references as necessary, format the result in **Percent Style**, and then **Center**. Fill the formula down through cell **G9**.

3 Select the nonadjacent ranges **A5:A9** and **F5:F9**, and then insert a **Pie in 3-D** chart. Move the chart to a **New sheet** with the name **Public Works Summary Chart** Insert a **Chart Title** above the chart with the text **2016 Public Works Costs of Operations** and then change the **Font Size** to **28**.

4 Remove the **Legend** from the chart and then add **Data Labels** formatted so that only the **Category Name** and **Percentage** displays positioned in the **Center**. Change the data labels **Font Size** to **12**, and apply **Bold** and **Italic**.

5 Select the chart, and then modify the pie chart **Shape Effects** by changing the **Bevel, 3-D Options**. Change the **Top** and **Bottom** options to the first **Bevel** type—**Circle.** Set the **Top Width** and **Height** boxes to **256 pt** and then set the **Bottom Width** and **Height** boxes to **50 pt** Change the **Material** to the fourth **Standard Effect** type—**Metal.**

6 In the displayed **Format Data Series** dialog box, on the left, click **Series Options**, and then change the **Angle of first** slice to **50** Explode the **Administration** slice slightly away from the pie. Format the **Chart Area** with a **Solid fill**—**Aqua, Accent 2**—in the sixth column, the first color.

7 Insert a **Text Box** positioned outside the upper corner of the **Administration** pie slice extending to the edge of the chart area and that is about one-half inch in height. In the text box, type **Administration expense to increase by 3%** Change the **Font Size** to **10.5**. Size the text box so that the text displays on two lines. On this chart sheet, insert a **Custom Footer** with the file name in the **left section**.

8 In the **Public Works** sheet, using the data in the nonadjacent ranges **B4:E4** and **B10:E10**, insert a **Line with Markers** chart in the worksheet. Move the chart so that its upper left corner is positioned in cell **A12**, aligned approximately under the *t* in the word *Collections* above. Remove the **Legend** and then add a **Chart Title** above the chart with the text **2016 Public Works Cost Summary** Edit the **Primary Vertical Axis** so that the **Minimum** is **Fixed** at **8600000** and the **Major unit** is **Fixed** at **200000** Format the **Chart Area** with a **Solid fill** by applying **Aqua, Accent 2, Lighter 40%**—in the sixth column, the fourth color.

9 In cell **B35**, type **35617667** and then apply the **Currency [0]** cell style. In cell **C35**, construct a formula to calculate the **Projected Operations Costs** after the forecasted increase is applied. Fill the formula through cell **F35**, and then use **Format Painter** to copy the formatting from cell **B35** to the range **C35:F35**.

10 Insert a **WordArt** using the last style—**Fill - Brown, Accent 1, Metal Bevel, Reflection** Type **Public Works Department** and then change the **Font Size** to **32**. Drag to position the WordArt in cell **A38**, centered below the worksheet.

11 Change the **Orientation** to **Landscape**, and then use the **Scale to Fit** options to fit the **Height** to **1 page**. Insert a **Header & Footer** with the **file name** in the left area of the footer. In **Page Layout** view, check and adjust if necessary the visual centering of the chart and the WordArt. Center the worksheet **Horizontally** on the page, and then return to **Normal** view.

12 Display the **Projected Decrease sheet.** In cell **C5**, calculate the **Percent of Total** by dividing the *Administration Annual Total* by the *Totals by Quarter*, using absolute cell references as necessary. Apply **Percent Style** and then fill the formula from **C5:C9**.

13 **Copy** cell **B5**, and then use **Paste Special** to paste the **Values & Number Formatting** to cell **B13**. **Copy** and **Paste** cell **C5** to **C13**. With cell **C13** selected, use **Goal Seek** to determine the goal amount of administration expenses in cell **B13** if the value in **C13** is set to **7%**

14 On the **Projected Decrease** sheet, insert a **Header & Footer** with the file name in the **left section** of the footer, and then center the worksheet **Horizontally** on the page. Show the **Document Panel**. Add your name, your course name and section, and the keywords **public works**

15 **Save** your workbook. Print or submit electronically as directed by your instructor. If required by your instructor, print or create an electronic version of your worksheets with formulas displayed by using the instructions in Activity 2.16, and then **Close** Excel without saving so that you do not save the changes you made to print formulas.

End **You have completed Project 9G**

Content-Based Assessments

Apply a combination of the 9A and 9B skills.

GO! Fix It | Project 9H Recreation

Project Files

For Project 9H, you will need the following file:

e03H_Recreation

You will save your workbook as:

Lastname_Firstname_3H_Recreation

In this project, you will correct a worksheet that contains the annual enrollment of residents in city-sponsored recreation programs. From the student files that accompany this textbook, open the file e03H_Recreation, and then save the file in your chapter folder as **Lastname_Firstname_3H_Recreation**

To complete the project, you must find and correct errors in formulas and formatting. View each formula in the worksheet and edit as necessary. Review the format and title of the pie chart and make corrections and formatting changes as necessary. In addition to errors that you find, you should know:

- The pie chart data should include the Age Group and the Total columns.
- The Chart Area should include a blue solid fill background and the title font color should be white.
- The pie chart should be in a separate worksheet named **Enrollment Analysis Chart**

Add a footer to both sheets, and add your name, your course name and section, and the keywords **Parks and Recreation, enrollment** to the document properties. Save your file and then print or submit your worksheet electronically as directed by your instructor. If required by your instructor, print or create an electronic version of your worksheets with formulas displayed by using the instructions in Activity 2.16, and then close Excel without saving so that you do not save the changes you made to print formulas.

End **You have completed Project 9H**

Apply a combination of the 9A and 9B skills.

GO! Make It | Project 9I Tax Projection

Project Files

For Project 9I, you will need the following file:

New blank Excel workbook

You will save your workbook as:

Lastname_Firstname_3I_Tax_Projection

Start a new blank Excel workbook and create the worksheet shown in Figure 9.51. In the range C7:F7, calculate the rate of increase from the previous year. In the range C31:F31, calculate the projected property tax for each year based on the forecasted increase. Complete the worksheet by entering in the range B36:F38, the projected property tax revenue for each year based on 2%, 3%, and 4% increases. Insert the chart as shown, using the 2010 through 2014 Property Tax Revenue data. Fill the chart area with the Daybreak gradient fill and change the chart title font size to 14. Scale the width to fit to one page, and then add your name, your course name and section, and the keywords **property tax** to the document properties. Save the file in your Excel Chapter 3 folder as **Lastname_Firstname_3I_Tax_Projection** and then print or submit electronically as directed by your instructor.

Project Results

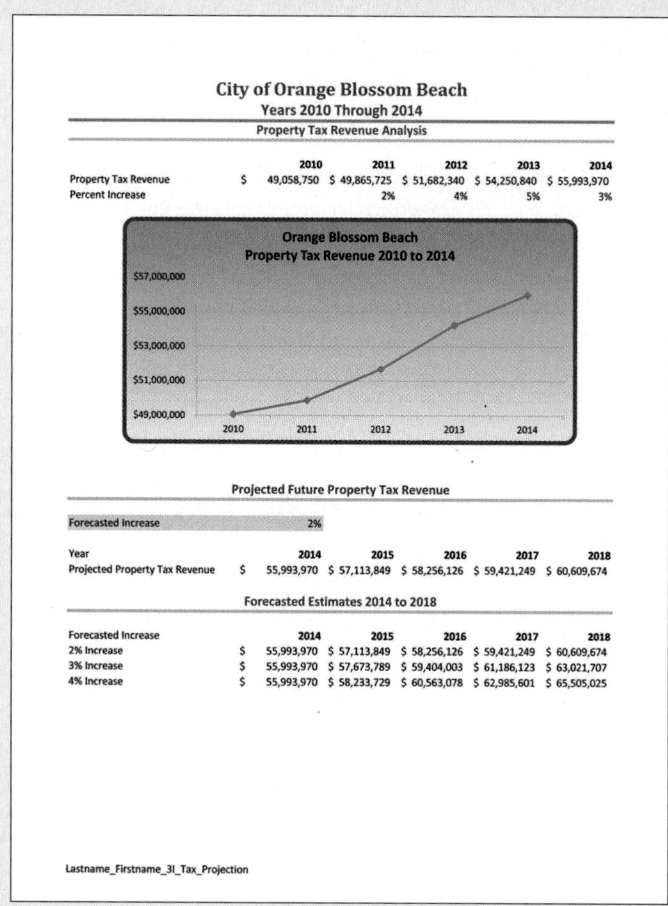

City of Orange Blossom Beach

Years 2010 Through 2014

Property Tax Revenue Analysis

	2010	2011	2012	2013	2014
Property Tax Revenue	$ 49,058,750	$ 49,865,725	$ 51,682,340	$ 54,250,840	$ 55,993,970
Percent Increase		2%	4%	5%	3%

Projected Future Property Tax Revenue

Forecasted Increase	2%				
Year	2014	2015	2016	2017	2018
Projected Property Tax Revenue	$ 55,993,970	$ 57,113,849	$ 58,256,126	$ 59,421,249	$ 60,609,674

Forecasted Estimates 2014 to 2018

Forecasted Increase	2014	2015	2016	2017	2018
2% Increase	$ 55,993,970	$ 57,113,849	$ 58,256,126	$ 59,421,249	$ 60,609,674
3% Increase	$ 55,993,970	$ 57,673,789	$ 59,404,003	$ 61,186,123	$ 63,021,707
4% Increase	$ 55,993,970	$ 58,233,729	$ 60,563,078	$ 62,985,601	$ 65,505,025

Lastname_Firstname_3I_Tax_Projection

Figure 9.51

End You have completed Project 9I

Content-Based Assessments

Apply a combination of the 9A and 9B skills.

GO! Solve It | Project 9J Staffing

Project Files

For Project 9J, you will need the following file:

e03J_Staffing

You will save your workbook as:

Lastname_Firstname_3J_Staffing

Open the file e03J_Staffing and save it as **Lastname_Firstname_3J_Staffing** Complete the worksheet by calculating totals and the % of Total Employees. Format the worksheet attractively including appropriate number formatting. Insert a pie chart in a separate sheet that illustrates the Two-Year Projection staffing levels by department and use the techniques that you practiced in this chapter to format the chart so that it is attractive and easy to understand. Change the angle of the first slice so that the Public Safety slice displays below the title. Then, insert a text box that indicates that the increase in Public Safety staffing is contingent upon City Council approval. Include the file name in the footer, add appropriate properties, save and submit as directed.

Performance Criteria	Performance Level: Exemplary: You consistently applied the relevant skills	Proficient: You sometimes, but not always, applied the relevant skills	Developing: You rarely or never applied the relevant skills
Create formulas	All formulas are correct and are efficiently constructed.	Formulas are correct but not always constructed in the most efficient manner.	One or more formulas are missing or incorrect; or only numbers were entered.
Chart inserted and formatted	Chart was inserted and formatted properly.	Chart was inserted but incorrect data was selected or the chart was not formatted.	No chart was inserted.
Format attractively and appropriately	Formatting is attractive and appropriate.	Adequately formatted but difficult to read or unattractive.	Inadequate or no formatting.

End **You have completed Project 9J**

Apply a combination of the 9A and 9B skills.

GO! Solve It | Project 9K Water Usage

Project Files

For Project 9K, you will need the following file:

New blank Excel workbook
e03K_Beach

You will save your workbook as:

Lastname_Firstname_3K_Water_Usage

The City of Orange Blossom Beach is a growing community and the City Council has requested an analysis of future resource needs. In this project, you will create a worksheet for the Department of Water and Power that lists residential water usage over the past ten years and that forecasts the amount of water that city residents will use in the next ten years. Create a worksheet with the following data:

	2008	2010	2012	2014	2016
Water Use in Acre Feet	62500	68903	73905	76044	80342

Calculate the percent increase for the years 2010 to 2016. Below the Percent Increase, insert a line chart that illustrates the city's water usage from 2008 to 2016. Below the chart, add a section to the worksheet to calculate the projected water usage for the years 2016 to 2024 in two-year increments based on a 4% annual increase. The 2016 amount is 80,342. Format the chart and worksheet attractively with a title and subtitle, and apply appropriate formatting. If you choose to format the chart area with a picture, you can use e03K_Beach located with your student files. Include the file name in the footer and enter appropriate document properties. Save the workbook as **Lastname_Firstname_3K_Water_Usage** and submit it as directed.

Performance Criteria	Performance Level: Exemplary: You consistently applied the relevant skills	Proficient: You sometimes, but not always, applied the relevant skills	Developing: You rarely or never applied the relevant skills
Create formulas	All formulas are correct and are efficiently constructed.	Formulas are correct but not always constructed in the most efficient manner.	One or more formulas are missing or incorrect or only numbers were entered.
Insert and format line chart	Line chart created correctly and is attractively formatted.	Line chart was created but the data was incorrect or the chart was not appropriately formatted.	No line chart was created.
Format attractively and appropriately	Formatting is attractive and appropriate.	Adequately formatted but difficult to read or unattractive.	Inadequate or no formatting.

End You have completed Project 9K

Outcomes-Based Assessments

Rubric

The following outcomes-based assessments are *open-ended assessments*. That is, there is no specific correct result; your result will depend on your approach to the information provided. Make *Professional Quality* your goal. Use the following scoring rubric to guide you in *how* to approach the problem, and then to evaluate *how well* your approach solves the problem.

The *criteria*—Software Mastery, Content, Format and Layout, and Process—represent the knowledge and skills you have gained that you can apply to solving the problem. The *levels of performance*—Professional Quality, Approaching Professional Quality, or Needs Quality Improvements—help you and your instructor evaluate your result.

	Your completed project is of Professional Quality if you:	**Your completed project is Approaching Professional Quality if you:**	**Your completed project Needs Quality Improvements if you:**
1-Software Mastery	Choose and apply the most appropriate skills, tools, and features and identify efficient methods to solve the problem.	Choose and apply some appropriate skills, tools, and features, but not in the most efficient manner.	Choose inappropriate skills, tools, or features, or are inefficient in solving the problem.
2-Content	Construct a solution that is clear and well organized, contains content that is accurate, appropriate to the audience and purpose, and is complete. Provide a solution that contains no errors in spelling, grammar, or style.	Construct a solution in which some components are unclear, poorly organized, inconsistent, or incomplete. Misjudge the needs of the audience. Have some errors in spelling, grammar, or style, but the errors do not detract from comprehension.	Construct a solution that is unclear, incomplete, or poorly organized; contains some inaccurate or inappropriate content; and contains many errors in spelling, grammar, or style. Do not solve the problem.
3-Format and Layout	Format and arrange all elements to communicate information and ideas, clarify function, illustrate relationships, and indicate relative importance.	Apply appropriate format and layout features to some elements, but not others. Overuse features, causing minor distraction.	Apply format and layout that does not communicate information or ideas clearly. Do not use format and layout features to clarify function, illustrate relationships, or indicate relative importance. Use available features excessively, causing distraction.
4-Process	Use an organized approach that integrates planning, development, self-assessment, revision, and reflection.	Demonstrate an organized approach in some areas, but not others; or, use an insufficient process of organization throughout.	Do not use an organized approach to solve the problem.

Outcomes-Based Assessments

Apply a combination of the 9A and 9B skills.

GO! Think | Project 9L School Enrollment

Project Files

For Project 9L, you will need the following file:

New blank Excel workbook

You will save your workbook as:

Lastname_Firstname_3L_School_Enrollment

Marcus Chavez, the Superintendent of Schools for the City of Orange Blossom Beach, has requested an enrollment analysis of students in the city public elementary schools in order to plan school boundary modifications resulting in more balanced enrollments. Enrollments in district elementary schools for the past two years are as follows:

School	2014 Enrollment	2015 Enrollment
Orange Blossom	795	824
Kittridge	832	952
Glenmeade	524	480
Hidden Trails	961	953
Beach Side	477	495
Sunnyvale	515	502

Create a workbook to provide Marcus with the enrollment information for each school and the total district enrollment. Insert a column to calculate the percent change from 2014 to 2015. Note that some of the results will be negative numbers. Format the percentages with two decimal places. Insert a pie chart in its own sheet that illustrates the 2015 enrollment figures for each school and format the chart attractively. Format the worksheet so that it is professional and easy to read and understand. Insert a footer with the file name and add appropriate document properties. Save the file as **Lastname_Firstname_3L_School_Enrollment** and print or submit as directed by your instructor.

End **You have completed Project 9L**

Outcomes-Based Assessments

Apply a combination of the 9A and 9B skills.

GO! Think | Project 9M Park Acreage

Project Files

For Project 9M, you will need the following files:

New blank Excel workbook
e03M_Park

You will save your workbook as:

Lastname_Firstname_3M_Park_Acreage

The City of Orange Blossom Beach wants to maintain a high ratio of parkland to residents and has established a goal of maintaining a minimum of 50 parkland acres per 1,000 residents. The following table contains the park acreage and the population, in thousands, since 1980. Start a new blank Excel workbook and then enter appropriate titles. Then, enter the following data in the worksheet and calculate the *Acres per 1,000 residents* by dividing the Park acreage by the Population in thousands.

	1980	1990	2000	2010
Population in thousands	118.4	123.9	133.5	152.6
Park acreage	5,800	6,340	8,490	9,200
Acres per 1,000 residents				

Create a line chart that displays the Park Acres Per 1,000 Residents for each year. Format the chart professionally and insert the picture e03M_Park from your student files in the chart fill area. Below the chart, create a new section titled **Park Acreage Analysis** and then copy and paste the Years and the Park acreage values to the new section. Calculate the *Percent increase* from the previous ten years for the 1990, 2000, and 2010 years. Below the Park Acreage Analysis section, create a new worksheet section titled **Park Acreage Forecast** and then enter the following values.

	2010	2020	2030	2040
Population in thousands	152.6	173.2	197.7	225.3
Park acreage necessary				
Percent increase				

Calculate the *Park acreage necessary* to reach the city's goal by multiplying the Population in thousands by 50. Then calculate the *Percent increase* from the previous ten years for the 2020, 2030, and 2040 years. Use techniques that you practiced in this chapter to format the worksheet professionally. Insert a footer with the file name and add appropriate document properties. Save the file as **Lastname_Firstname_3M_Park_Acreage** and print or submit as directed by your instructor.

End **You have completed Project 9M**

Outcomes-Based Assessments

Apply a combination of the 9A and 9B skills.

You and GO! | Project 9N Expense Analysis

Project Files

For Project 9N, you will need the following file:

New blank Excel workbook

You will save your workbook as:

Lastname_Firstname_3N_Expense_Analysis

Develop a worksheet that details the expenses you have incurred during the past two months and list the expenses for each month in separate columns. Calculate totals for each column and then add a column in which you can calculate the percent change from one month to the next. Insert and format a pie chart that illustrates the expenses that you incurred in the most recent month. After reviewing the pie chart, determine a category of expense in which you might be overspending, and then pull that slice out of the pie and insert a text box indicating how you might save money on that expense. Insert a footer with the file name and center the worksheet horizontally on the page. Save your file as **Lastname_Firstname_3N_Expense_Analysis** and submit as directed.

End You have completed Project 9N

Apply a combination of the 9A and 9B skills.

GO! Collaborate | Project 9O Bell Orchid Hotels Group Running Case

This project relates to the **Bell Orchid Hotels**. Your instructor may assign this group case project to your class. If your instructor assigns this project, he or she will provide you with information and instructions to work as part of a group. The group will apply the skills gained thus far to help the Bell Orchid Hotels achieve their business goals.

End You have completed Project 9O

Business Running Case

Razvan CHIRNOAGA/Shutterstock

This project relates to **Front Range Action Sports**, which is one of the country's largest retailers of sports gear and outdoor recreation merchandise. The company has large retail stores in Colorado, Washington, Oregon, California, and New Mexico, in addition to a growing online business. Major merchandise categories include fishing, camping, rock climbing, winter sports, action sports, water sports, team sports, racquet sports, fitness, golf, apparel, and footwear.

In this project, you will apply the skills you practiced from the Objectives in Excel Chapters 7 through 9. You will develop a workbook for Frank Osei, the Vice President of Finance, that contains year-end sales and inventory summary information. In the first two worksheets, you will summarize and chart net sales. In the next three worksheets, you will detail the ending inventory of the two largest company-owned production facilities in Seattle and Denver. Mr. Osei is particularly interested in data regarding the new line of ski equipment stocked at these two locations. In the last worksheet, you will summarize and chart annual expenses. Your completed worksheets will look similar to Figure 2.1.

Project Files

For Project BRC1, you will need the following files:

eBRC1_Annual_Report
eBRC1_Skiing

You will save your workbook as:

Lastname_Firstname_BRC1_Annual_Report

Project Results

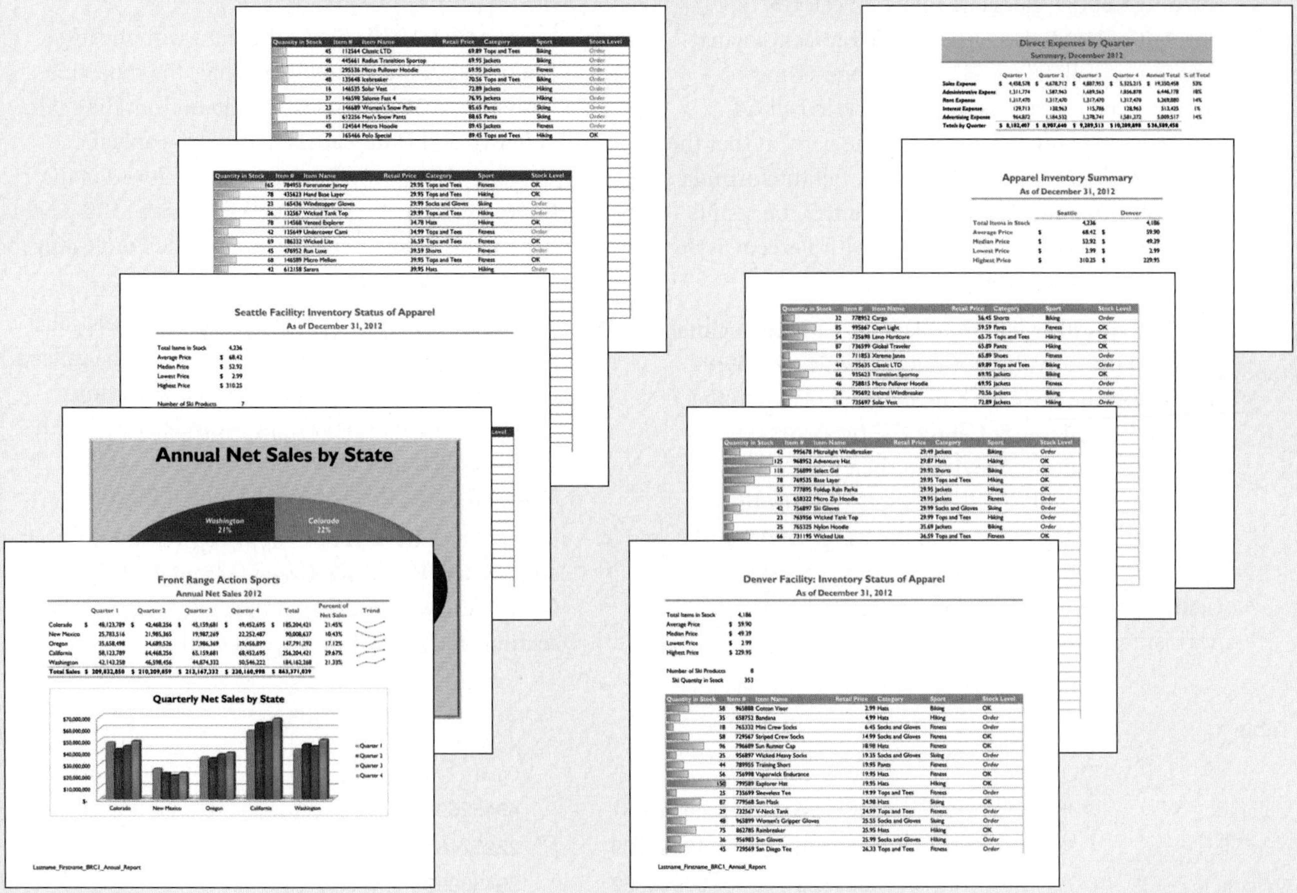

Figure 2.1

Business Running Case

Front Range Action Sports

1 **Start** Excel. From the student files that accompany this textbook, locate and open **eBRC1_Annual_Report**. In the location where you are storing your projects, create a new folder named **Front_Range_Action_Sports** or navigate to this folder if you have already created it. **Save** the new workbook as **Lastname_Firstname_BRC1_Annual_Report**

a. Familiarize yourself with the workbook by clicking each sheet tab, and then display the **Net Sales** worksheet. Click cell **B3**, and then use the fill handle to enter *Quarter 2*, *Quarter 3*, and *Quarter 4* in the range **C3:E3**. In the range **C4:E8**, enter the sales data for Quarter 2, Quarter 3, and Quarter 4 shown in **Table 1** at the bottom of the page.

b. Adjust the width of columns **B:F** to **125** pixels. Adjust the width of columns **G:H** to **100** pixels. In cell **F3**, type **Total** and then in the range **F4:F8**, calculate the annual total sales for each state. In the range **B9:F9**, calculate totals. In cell **G3**, type **Percent of Net Sales** and apply **Wrap Text** formatting to this cell. In cell **H3**, type **Trend** Using absolute cell references as necessary, in cell **G4**, construct a formula to calculate the percent that the *Colorado Total* is of the *Total Sales*. Fill the formula down through the range **G5:G8**. **Center** the results and then format the percentages with **Percent Style** and **two decimal places**.

c. Apply **Accounting Number Format** with **no decimal places** to the nonadjacent ranges **B4:F4** and **B9:F9**. Apply **Comma Style** with **no decimal** places to the range **B5:F8**. **Merge & Center** the two worksheet titles across columns **A:H**, and then to cell **A1**, apply the **Title** style and to cell **A2**, apply the **Heading 1** style. Apply the **Total** style to the range **B9:F9** and apply the **Heading 4** style to the range **B3:H3**. **Center** the column headings in **B3:H3** both horizontally and vertically.

d. In the range **H4:H8**, insert **Line** sparklines to represent the trend of each state across the four quarters. Add **Markers** and apply **Sparkline Style Accent 2 (no dark or light)**.

e. Select the range **A3:E8**, and then insert a **3-D Clustered Column** chart. Align the upper left corner of the chart inside the upper left corner of cell **A11**, and then size the chart so that its lower right corner is slightly inside cell **H24**. Apply chart **Style 26** and chart **Layout 1.** Replace the chart title text with **Quarterly Net Sales by State** Insert the file name in the **left section** of the footer, set the orientation to **Landscape**, and center the worksheet horizontally. Return to **Normal** view.

2 To show the percent that each state contributes to the total sales, select the nonadjacent ranges that represent the state names and state totals. Insert a **Pie in 3-D** chart and move the chart to a **New sheet**. Name the sheet **Net Sales by State** and then move the sheet so that it is the second sheet in the workbook.

a. Insert a **Chart Title** above the chart with the text **Annual Net Sales by State** Change the chart title **Font Size** to **36**. Remove the **Legend** from the chart, and then add **Data Labels** that display only the **Category Name** and **Percentage** positioned in the **Center**. Change the data labels **Font Size** to **14**, and then apply **Bold** and **Italic**. Change the **Font Color** to **White, Background 1**.

b. Select the entire pie, display the **Shape Effects** gallery, point to **Bevel**, and then at the bottom of the gallery, click **3-D Options**. Change the **Top** and **Bottom** options to the first **Bevel** type—**Circle**. Set all of the **Width** and **Height** boxes to **512** and then change the **Material** to the third **Standard** type—**Plastic**.

c. Format the **Chart Area** by applying a **Convex Bevel** and a **Solid fill—Dark Green, Accent 4, Lighter 60%**. Insert a **Custom Footer** with the **File Name** in the **left section**, and then **Save** the workbook.

Table 1

	Quarter 1	Quarter 2	Quarter 3	Quarter 4
Colorado	48123789	**42468256**	**45159681**	**49452695**
New Mexico	25783516	**21985365**	**19987269**	**22252487**
Oregon	35658498	**34689526**	**37986369**	**39456899**
California	58123789	**64468256**	**65159681**	**68452695**
Washington	42143258	**46598456**	**44874332**	**50546222**

(Return to Step 1-b)

(Business Running Case: Front Range Action Sports continues on the next page)

Front Range Action Sports (continued)

3 Display the **Seattle Inventory** worksheet, and then in cell **B4**, construct a formula to calculate the *Total Items in Stock* by summing the **Quantity in Stock** column. Format the result with **Comma Style** and **no decimal places**.

a. In cell **B5**, construct a formula to calculate the average of the **Retail Price** column. In the range **B6:B8**, construct similar formulas to calculate the median, lowest, and highest retail prices. Format the results in **B5:B8** with **Accounting Number Format**. In cell **B10**, use the **COUNTIF** function to count the number of **Skiing** items that the Seattle location stocks.

b. In cell **G14**, enter an **IF** function to determine the items that must be ordered. If the **Quantity in Stock** is less than **50** then **Value_if_true** is **Order** Otherwise the **Value_if_false** is **OK** Fill the formula down through cell **G87**. Apply **Conditional Formatting** to the **Stock Level** column so that cells that contain the text *Order* are formatted with **Bold Italic** and with a **Font Color** of **Orange, Accent 1**. Apply **Orange Gradient Fill Data Bars** to the **Quantity in Stock** column.

c. Insert a table with headers using the range **A13:G87**. Apply **Table Style Light 11**. **Sort** the table from smallest to largest on the **Retail Price** column, and then filter the table on the **Sport** column to display the **Skiing** types. Display a **Total Row** in the table, and then in cell **A88**, **Sum** the **Quantity in Stock** for the **Skiing** items. Type the result in cell **B11**. Remove the total row from the table, clear the **Sport** filter so that all of the data displays, and then convert the table to a range.

d. Change the **Print Titles** option so that **row 13** prints at the top of each page. Insert the file name in the **left section** of the footer, set the orientation to **Landscape**, and center the worksheet horizontally. Return to **Normal** view.

4 Display the **Denver Inventory** worksheet, and then in cell **B4**, construct a formula to calculate the *Total Items in Stock* by summing the **Quantity in Stock** column. Format the result with **Comma Style** and **no decimal places**.

a. In the range **B5:B8**, use the appropriate statistical functions to calculate the price data. Format the results with **Accounting Number Format**. In cell **B10**, use the **COUNTIF** function to count the number of **Skiing** items that the Denver location stocks.

b. In cell **G14**, enter an **IF** function to determine the items that must be ordered. If the **Quantity in Stock** is less than **50 Value_if_true** is **Order** Otherwise the **Value_if_false** is **OK** Fill the formula down through cell **G87**. Apply **Conditional Formatting** to the **Stock Level** column so that cells that contain the text *Order* are formatted with **Bold Italic** and with a **Font Color** of **Dark Blue, Accent 3**. Apply **Light Blue Gradient Fill Data Bars** to the **Quantity in Stock** column.

c. Create a table with headers using the range **A13:G87**. Apply **Table Style Light 9**. **Sort** the table from smallest to largest on the **Retail Price** column, and then filter the table on the **Sport** column to display the **Skiing** types. Display a **Total Row** in the table and then in cell **A88, Sum** the **Quantity in Stock** for the **Skiing** items. Type the result in cell **B11**. Remove the total row from the table, clear the **Sport** filter so that all of the data displays, and then convert the table to a range.

d. Change the **Print Titles** option so that **row 13** prints at the top of each page. Insert the file name in the **left section** of the footer, set the orientation to **Landscape**, and center the worksheet horizontally. Return to **Normal** view.

e. Display the **Inventory Summary** sheet. In cell **B5**, enter a formula that references cell **B4** in the **Seattle Inventory** sheet so that the Seattle *Total Items in Stock* displays in **B5**. Create similar formulas to enter the **Average Price**, **Median Price, Lowest Price,** and **Highest Price** in the range **B6:B9**. Enter similar formulas in the range **C5:C9** so that the **Denver** totals display. Be sure the range **B6:C9** is formatted with **Accounting Number Format**. Insert the file name in the **left section** of the footer, set the orientation to **Portrait**, and center the worksheet horizontally. Return to **Normal** view. **Save** the workbook.

5 Display the **Annual Expenses** worksheet. Construct formulas to calculate the *Totals by Quarter* in the range **B10:E10** and the *Annual Totals* in the range **F5:F10**.

a. Using absolute cell references as necessary, in cell **G5**, construct a formula to calculate the *% of Total* by dividing the **Sales Expense Annual Total** by the **Annual Totals by Quarter**. Apply **Percent Style**, fill the formula down through the range **G6:G9**, and **Center** the percentages.

(Business Running Case: Front Range Action Sports continues on the next page)

Front Range Action Sports (continued)

b. Apply appropriate financial formatting to the data using no decimal places, and apply the **Total** cell style to the *Totals by Quarter*. **Center** the column headings and apply the **Heading 4** cell style.

c. **Merge & Center** the worksheet title and subtitle across columns **A:G**, and then to cell **A1**, apply the **Title** style and to cell **A2**, apply the **Heading 1** style. To the range **A1:A2**, apply a **Fill Color** using **Dark Blue, Accent 3, Lighter 60%**.

d. Using the data in the nonadjacent ranges **B4:E4** and **B10:E10**, insert a **Line with Markers** chart. Position the upper left corner of the chart slightly inside cell **B12** and resize the chart so that the lower right corner is inside cell **F25**. Remove the **Legend** and then add a **Chart Title** above the chart with the text **2012 Direct Expenses**

e. Apply chart **Style 13**, and then format the **Chart Area** with the picture **eBRC1_Skiing** from your student files. Format the **Plot Area** by changing the **Fill** option to **No fill**. Edit the **Vertical (Value) Axis** so that the **Minimum** is **8000000** and the **Major unit** is **1000000**

6 Use **Format Painter** to copy the formatting from cell **A2** to **A27**. In cell **B32**, enter a formula that references the value in cell **F10**.

a. Using absolute cell references as necessary, in cell **C32**, construct a formula to calculate the projected expenses for 2013 after the *Forecasted increase* in cell **B29** is applied. Fill the formula through cell **F32**. If necessary, use Format Painter to copy the format in cell B32 to the remaining cells in the row.

b. On the **Page Layout tab**, in the **Scale to Fit group**, set both the **Width** and **Height** to scale to **1 page**. Insert the file name in the **left section** of the footer, set the orientation to **Landscape**, and center the worksheet horizontally. Return to **Normal** view. Display the **Document Properties**. Add your name, your course name and section, and the keywords **annual report**

c. **Save** your workbook. Select all the sheets, and then display and check the Print Preview. There are a total of 10 pages. Print or submit electronically as directed. If required by your instructor, print or create an electronic version of your worksheets with formulas displayed by using the instructions in Activity 2.16, and then **Close** Excel without saving so that you do not save the changes you made to print formulas.

End **You have completed Business Running Case 1**

Getting Started with Access Databases

OUTCOMES

At the end of this chapter you will be able to:

OBJECTIVES

Mastering these objectives will enable you to:

PROJECT 10A
Create a new database.

1. Identify Good Database Design (p. 529)
2. Create a Table and Define Fields in a New Database (p. 530
3. Change the Structure of Tables and Add a Second Table (p. 542)
4. Create and Use a Query, Form, and Report (p. 552)
5. Save and Close a Database (p. 558)

PROJECT 10B
Create a database from a template.

6. Create a Database Using a Template (p. 560)
7. Organize Objects in the Navigation Pane (p. 564)
8. Create a New Table in a Database Created with a Template (p. 566)
9. Print a Report and a Table in a Database Created with a Template (p. 568)

Joy Brown/Shutterstock

In This Chapter

In this chapter, you will use Microsoft Access 2010 to organize a collection of related information. Access is a powerful program that enables you to organize, search, sort, retrieve, and present information in a professional-looking manner. You will create new databases, enter data into Access tables, and create a query, form, and report—all of which are Access objects that make a database useful. In this chapter, you will also create a database from a template provided with the Access program. The template creates a complete database that you can use as provided, or you can modify it to suit your needs. Additional templates are available from the Microsoft Online Web site. For your first attempt at a database, consider using a template.

The projects in this chapter relate to **Capital Cities Community College**, which is located in the Washington D. C. metropolitan area. The college provides high-quality education and professional training to residents in the cities surrounding the nation's capital. Its four campuses serve over 50,000 students and offer more than 140 certificate programs and degrees at the associate's level. CapCCC has a highly acclaimed Distance Education program and an extensive Workforce Development program. The college makes positive contributions to the community through cultural and athletic programs and partnerships with businesses and non-profit organizations.

Project 10A Contact Information Database with Two Tables

Project Activities

In Activities 10.01 through 10.17, you will assist Dr. Justin Mitrani, Vice President of Instruction at Capital Cities Community College, in creating a new database for tracking the contact information for students and faculty members. Your completed database objects will look similar to Figure 10.1.

Project Files

For Project 10A, you will need the following files:

New blank Access database
a01A_Students (Excel workbook)
a01A_Faculty (Excel workbook)

You will save your database as:

Lastname_Firstname_1A_Contacts

Project Results

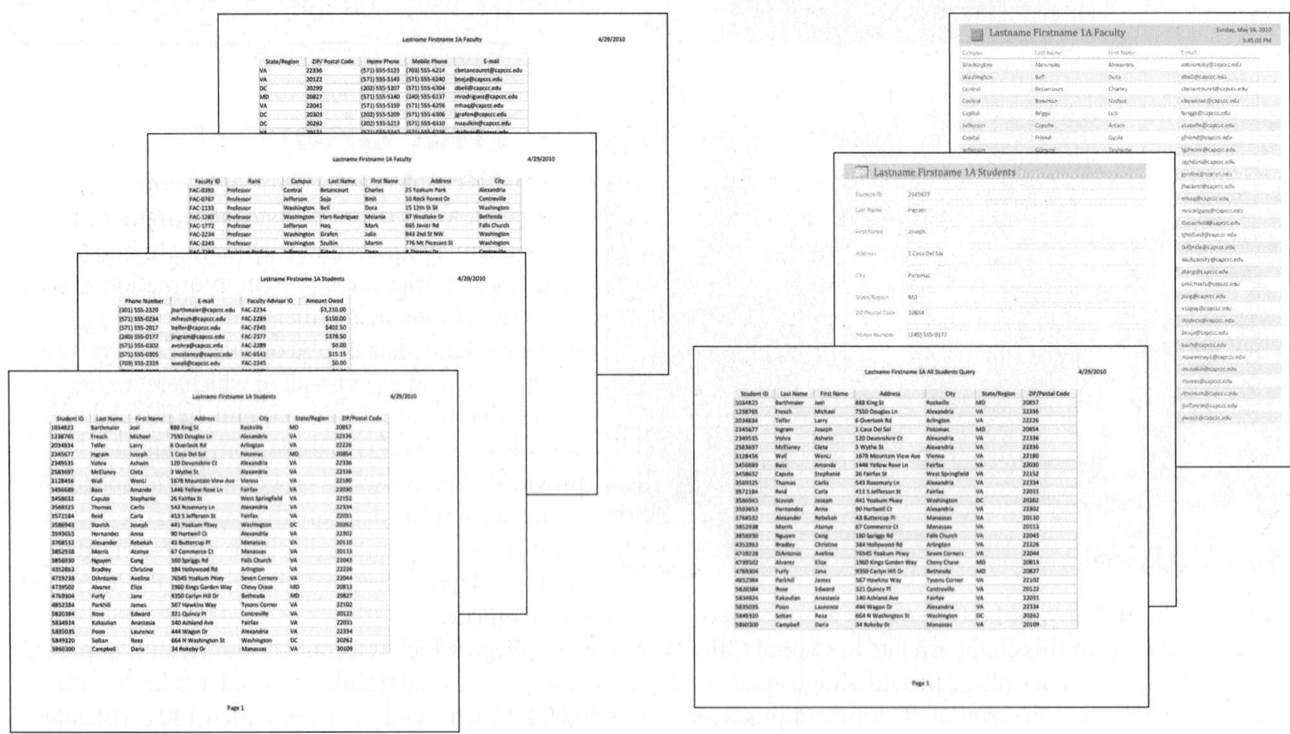

Figure 10.1
Project 10A Contacts

Objective 1 | Identify Good Database Design

A ***database*** is an organized collection of ***data***—facts about people, events, things, or ideas—related to a specific topic or purpose. ***Information*** is data that is organized in a useful manner. Your personal address book is a type of database, because it is a collection of data about one topic—the people with whom you communicate. A simple database of this type is called a ***flat database*** because it is not related or linked to any other collection of data. Another example of a simple database is a list of movie DVDs. You do not keep information about your DVDs in your address book because the data is not related to your addresses.

A more sophisticated type of database is a ***relational database***, because multiple collections of data in the database are related to one another; for example, data about the students, the courses, and the faculty members at a college. Microsoft Access 2010 is a relational ***database management system***—also referred to as a ***DBMS***—which is software that controls how related collections of data are stored, organized, retrieved, and secured.

Activity 10.01 | Using Good Design Techniques to Plan a Database

The first step in creating a new database is to determine the information you want to keep track of, and then ask yourself, *What questions should this database be able to answer for me?* The purpose of a database is to store the data in a manner that makes it easy for you to get the information you need by asking questions. For example, in the Contacts database for Capital Cities Community College, the questions to be answered might include:

How many students are enrolled at Capital Cities Community College?

How many faculty members teach in the Accounting Department?

Which and how many students live in Arlington, Virginia?

Which and how many students have a balance owed?

Which and how many students are majoring in Information Systems Technology?

Tables are the foundation of an Access database because all of the data is stored in one or more tables. A table is similar in structure to an Excel worksheet; that is, data is organized into rows and columns. Each table row is a ***record***—all of the categories of data pertaining to one person, place, thing, event, or idea. Each table column is a ***field***—a single piece of information for every record. For example, in a table storing student contact information, each row forms a record for only one student. Each column forms a field for a single piece of information for every record; for example, the student ID number for all students.

When organizing the fields of information in your database, break each piece of information into its smallest useful part. For example, create three fields for the name of a student—one field for the last name, one field for the first name, and one field for the middle name or initial.

The ***first principle of good database design*** is to organize data in the tables so that ***redundant***—duplicate—data does not occur. For example, record the contact information for students in only *one* table, because if the address for a student changes, the change can be made in just one place. This conserves space, reduces the likelihood of errors when recording the new data, and does not require remembering all of the different places where the address is stored.

The ***second principle of good database design*** is to use techniques that ensure the accuracy of data when it is entered into the table. Typically, many different people enter data into a database—think of all the people who enter data at your college. When entering a state in a contacts database, one person might enter the state as *Virginia* and another might enter the state as *VA*. Use design techniques to help those who enter data into a database do so in a consistent and accurate manner.

Normalization is the process of applying design rules and principles to ensure that your database performs as expected. Taking the time to plan and create a database that is well designed will ensure that you can retrieve meaningful information from the database.

The tables of information in a relational database are linked or joined to one another by a ***common field***—a field in one or more tables that stores the same data. For example, the Student Contacts table includes the Student ID, name, and address of every student. The Student Activities table includes the name of each club, and the Student ID—but not the name or address—of each student in each club. Because the two tables share a common field—Student ID—you can create a list of names and addresses of all the students in the Photography Club. The names and addresses are stored in the Student Contacts table, and the Student IDs of the Photography Club members are stored in the Student Activities table.

Objective 2 | Create a Table and Define Fields in a New Blank Database

There are two methods to create a new Access database: create a new database using a ***database template***—a preformatted database designed for a specific purpose—or create a new database from a blank database. A blank database has no data and has no database tools; you create the data and the tools as you need them.

Regardless of the method you use, you must name and save the database before you can create any ***objects*** in it. Objects are the basic parts of a database; you create objects to store your data and to work with your data. The most common database objects are tables, forms, and reports. Think of an Access database as a container for the objects that you will create.

Activity 10.02 | Starting with a New Database

1 **Start** Access. Take a moment to compare your screen with Figure 10.2 and study the parts of the Microsoft Access window described in the table in Figure 10.3.

From this Access starting point in Backstage view, you can open an existing database, create a new blank database, or create a new database from a template.

Figure 10.2

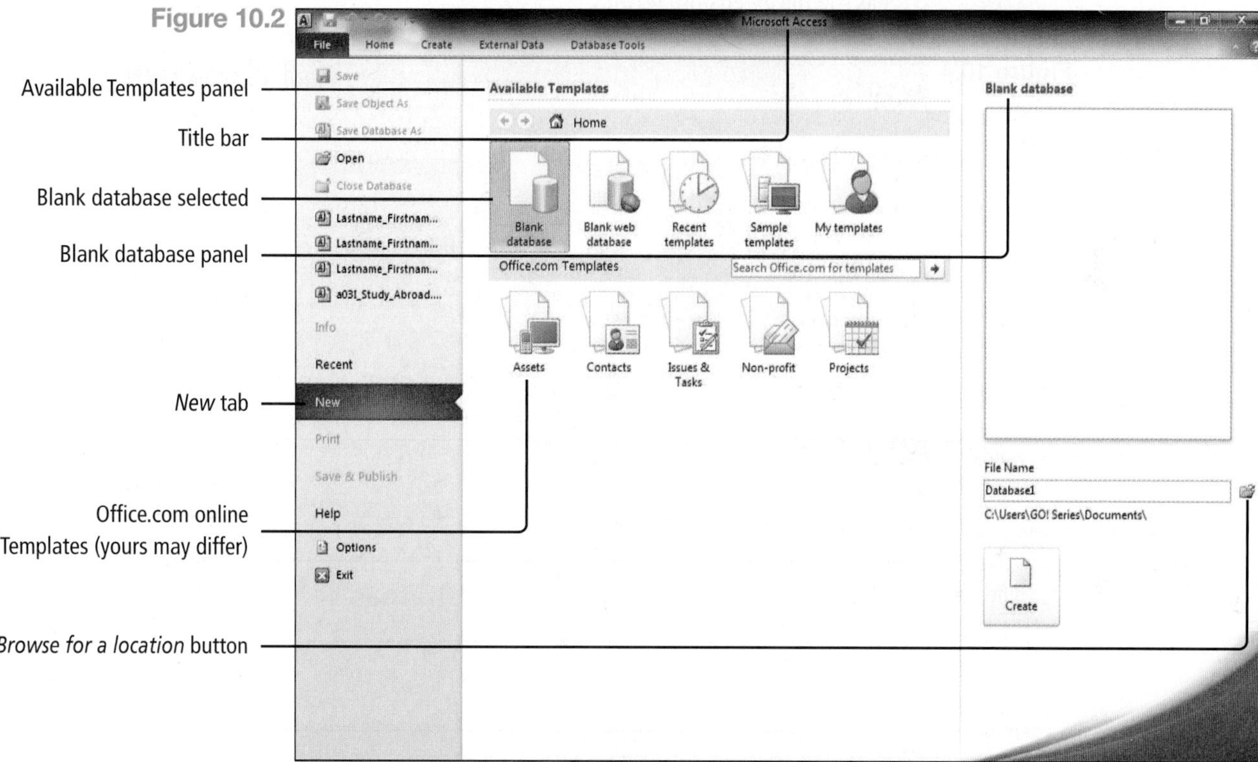

Microsoft Access Opening Window	
Window Part	**Description**
Available Templates panel	Displays alternative methods of creating a database.
Blank database	Starts a new blank database.
Blank database panel	Displays when *Blank database* button is selected under Available Templates.
Browse for location button	Enables you to select a storage location for the database.
New tab	Displays, when active in Backstage view, the various methods by which you can create a new database.
Office.com Templates	Displays template categories available from the Office.com Web site.
Title bar	Displays the Quick Access Toolbar, program name, and program-level buttons.

Figure 10.3

2 On the right, under **Blank database**, to the right of the **File Name** box, click the **Browse** button. In the **File New Database** dialog box, navigate to the location where you are saving your databases for this chapter, create a new folder named **Access Chapter 10** and then notice that *Database1* displays as the default file name—the number at the end of your file name might differ if you have saved a database previously with the default name. In the **File New Database** dialog box, click **Open**.

3 In the **File name** box, replace the existing text with **Lastname_Firstname_1A_Contacts** Press Enter, and then compare your screen with Figure 10.4.

On the right, the name of your database displays in the File Name box, and the drive and folder where the database is stored displays under the File Name box. An Access database has the file extension *.accdb*.

Figure 10.4

4 Under the **File Name** box, click the **Create** button, compare your screen with Figure 10.5, and then take a moment to study the screen elements described in the table in Figure 10.6.

Access creates the new database and opens *Table1*. Recall that a ***table*** is an Access object that stores your data in columns and rows, similar to the format of an Excel worksheet. Table objects are the foundation of a database because tables store the actual data.

Figure 10.5

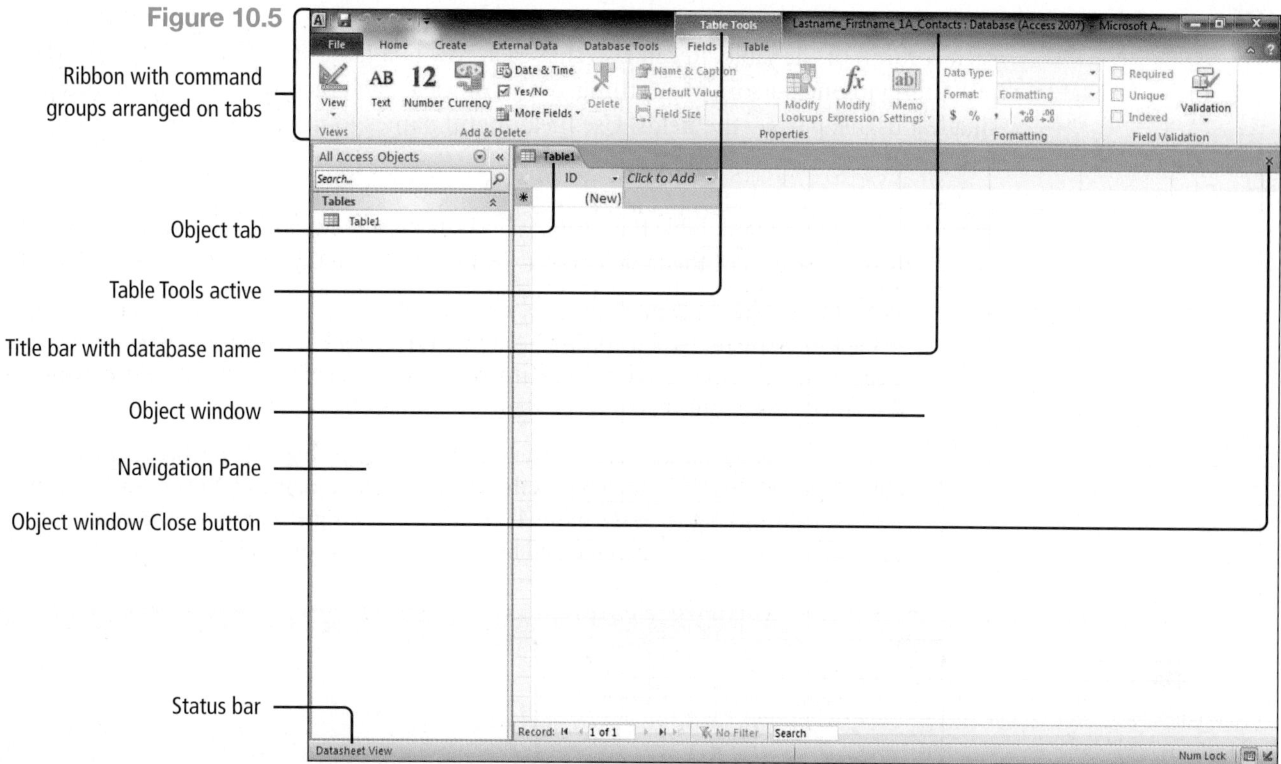

Parts of the Access Database Window

Window Part	Description
Navigation Pane	Displays the database objects; from here you open the database objects to display in the object window at the right.
Object tab	Identifies and enables you to select the open object.
Object window	Displays the active or open object (table, query, or other object).
Object window Close button	Closes the active object (table, query, or other object).
Ribbon with command groups arranged on tabs	Groups the commands for performing related database tasks on tabs.
Status bar	Indicates the active view and the status of actions occurring within the database on the left; provides buttons to switch between Datasheet view and Design view on the right.
Table Tools	Provides tools for working with a table object; Table Tools are available only when a table is displayed.
Title bar	Displays the name of your database.

Figure 10.6

Activity 10.03 | Assigning the Data Type and Name to Fields

After you have saved and named your database, the next step is to consult your database plan, and then create the tables in which to enter your data. Limit the data in each table to *one* subject. For example, in this project, your database will have two tables—one for student contact information and one for faculty contact information.

Recall that each column in a table is a field and that field names display at the top of each column of the table. Recall also that each row in a table is a record—all of the data pertaining to one person, place, thing, event, or idea. Each record is broken up into its smallest usable parts—the fields. Use meaningful names to name fields; for example, *Last Name.*

1 Notice the new blank table that displays in Datasheet view, and then take a moment to study the elements of the table's object window. Compare your screen with Figure 10.7.

The table displays in ***Datasheet view***, which displays the data as columns and rows similar to the format of an Excel worksheet. Another way to view a table is in ***Design view***, which displays the underlying design—the ***structure***—of the table's fields. The ***object window*** displays the open object—in this instance, the table object.

In a new blank database, there is only one object—a new blank table. Because you have not yet named this table, the object tab displays a default name of *Table1*. Access creates the first field and names it *ID*. In the ID field, Access assigns a unique sequential number—each number incremented by one—to each record as it is entered into the table.

Figure 10.7

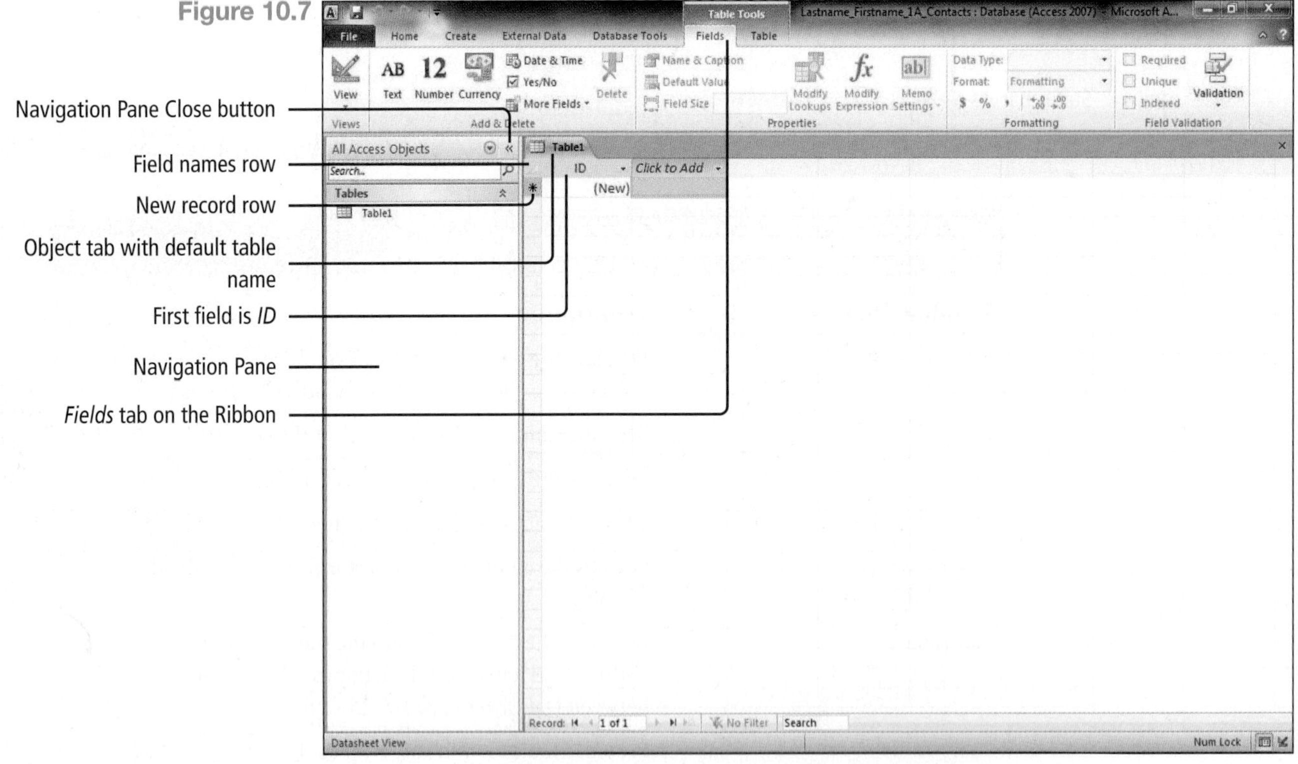

2 In the **Navigation Pane**, click the **Open/Close** button « to collapse the **Navigation Pane** to a narrow bar on the left and to display more of the table.

The ***Navigation Pane*** is an area of the Access window that displays and organizes the names of the objects in a database. From the Navigation Pane, you can open objects for use.

Another Way

To the right of *Click to Add*, click the arrow.

3 In the field names row, click anywhere in the text *Click to Add* to display a list of data types. Compare your screen with Figure 10.8.

Data type is the characteristic that defines the kind of data that you can type in a field, such as numbers, text, or dates. A field in a table can have only one data type. Part of your database design should include deciding on the data type of each field. After you have selected the data type, you can name the field.

Figure 10.8

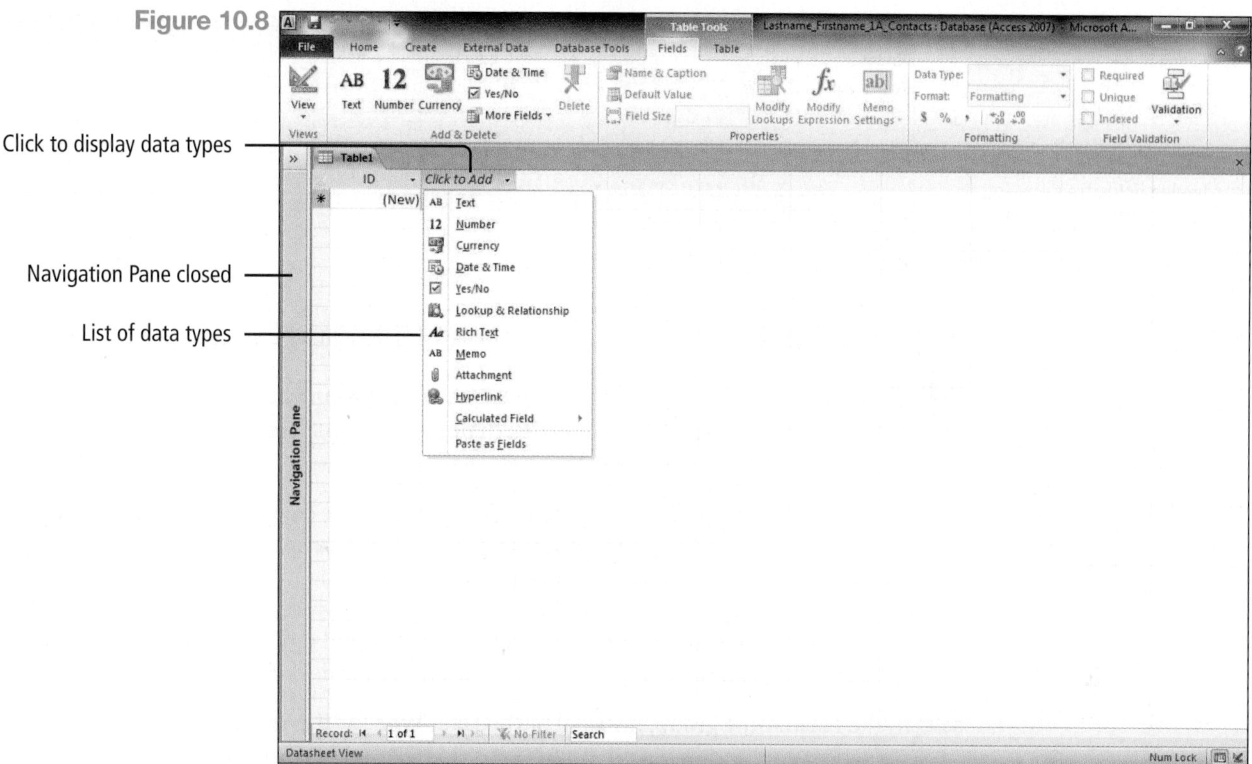

4 In the list of data types, click **Text**, and notice that in the second column, *Click to Add* changes to *Field1*, which is selected. Type **Last Name** and then press Enter.

The second column displays *Last Name* as the field name, and the data type list displays in the third column. The ***Text data type*** describes text, a combination of text and numbers, or numbers that are not used in calculations, such as a ZIP code.

Another Way

With the list of data types displayed, type *T* to select Text.

5 In the third field name box, click **Text**, type **First Name** and then press Enter. In the fourth field name box, click **Text**, type **Middle Initial** and then press Enter.

6 Using the technique you just practiced, create the remaining fields as follows by first selecting the data type, then typing the field name, and then pressing Enter. The field names in the table will display on one line.

The ZIP/Postal Code field is assigned a data type of Text because the number is never used in a calculation. The Amount Owed field is assigned a data type of Currency; the ***Currency data type*** describes monetary values and numeric data used in mathematical calculations involving data with one to four decimal places. Access automatically adds a U.S. dollar sign ($) and two decimal places to all of the numbers in the fields with a data type of *Currency*.

Data Type		Text	Text	Text	**Text**	**Text**	**Text**	**Text**	**Text**	**Text**	**Text**	**Currency**
Field Name	ID	Last Name	First Name	Middle Initial	**Address**	**City**	**State/ Region**	**ZIP/Postal Code**	**Phone Number**	**E-mail**	**Faculty Advisor ID**	**Amount Owed**

7 If necessary, by using the horizontal scroll bar at the bottom of the screen, scroll to the left to bring the first column into view. Compare your screen with Figure 10.9.

Access automatically created the ID field, and you created 11 additional fields in the table. The horizontal scroll bar indicates that there are additional fields that are not displayed on the screen—your screen width may vary.

Figure 10.9

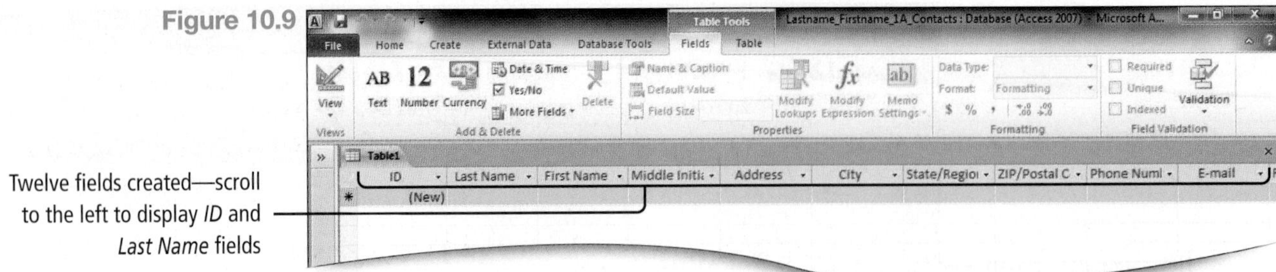

Activity 10.04 | Renaming Fields and Changing Data Types in a Table

Another Way

Right-click the field name, and then on the shortcut menu, click Rename Field.

1. Click anywhere in the text *ID*. In the **Properties group**, click the **Name & Caption** button. In the **Enter Field Properties** dialog box, in the **Name** box, change *ID* to **Student ID** and then click **OK**.

   The field name *Student ID* is a better description of the data in this field. In the Enter Field Properties dialog box, the ***Caption*** property is used to display a name for a field other than that listed as the field name. Many database designers do not use spaces in field names; instead, they might name a field LastName—with no spaces—and then create a caption for that field so it displays with spaces in tables, forms, and reports. In the Enter Field Properties dialog box, you can also provide a description for the field if you want to do so.

2. In the **Formatting group**, notice that the **Data Type** for the **Student ID** field is *AutoNumber*. Click the **Data Type arrow**, click **Text**, and then compare your screen with Figure 10.10.

   In the new record row, the Student ID field is selected. By default, Access creates an ID field for all new tables and sets the data type for the field to AutoNumber. The ***AutoNumber data type*** describes a unique sequential or random number assigned by Access as each record is entered. By changing the data type of this field from *AutoNumber* to *Text,* you can enter a custom student ID number.

   When records in a database have *no* unique value, for example the names in your address book, the AutoNumber data type is a useful way to automatically create a unique number so that you have a way to ensure that every record is different from the others.

Figure 10.10

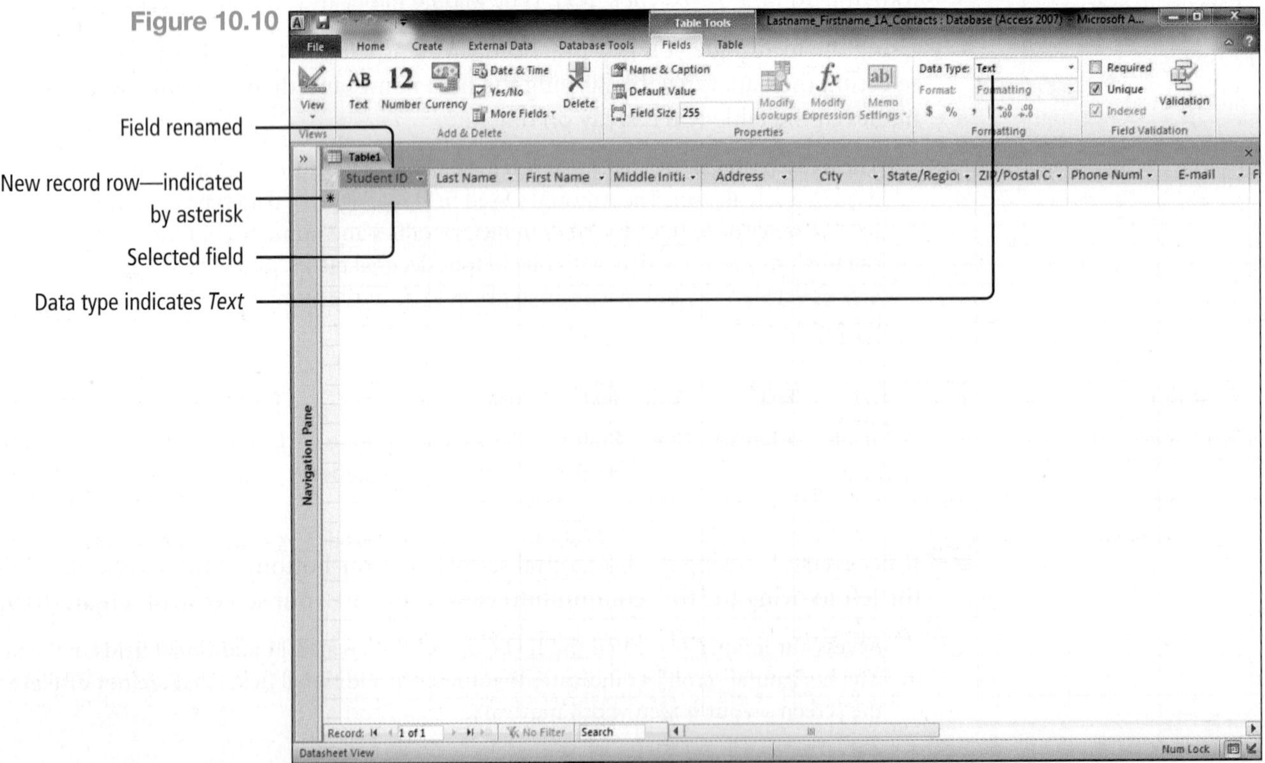

Activity 10.05 | Adding a Record to a Table

A new address book is not useful until you fill it with names, addresses, and phone numbers. Likewise, a new database is not useful until you ***populate*** it—fill one or more tables with data. You can populate a table with records by typing data directly into the table.

> **Another Way**
> Press Tab to move to the next field.

1 In the new record row, click in the **Student ID** field to display the insertion point, type **1238765** and then press Enter. Compare your screen with Figure 10.11.

The pencil icon in the ***record selector box***—the small box at the left of a record in Datasheet view that, when clicked, selects the entire record—indicates that a record is being entered or edited.

Figure 10.11

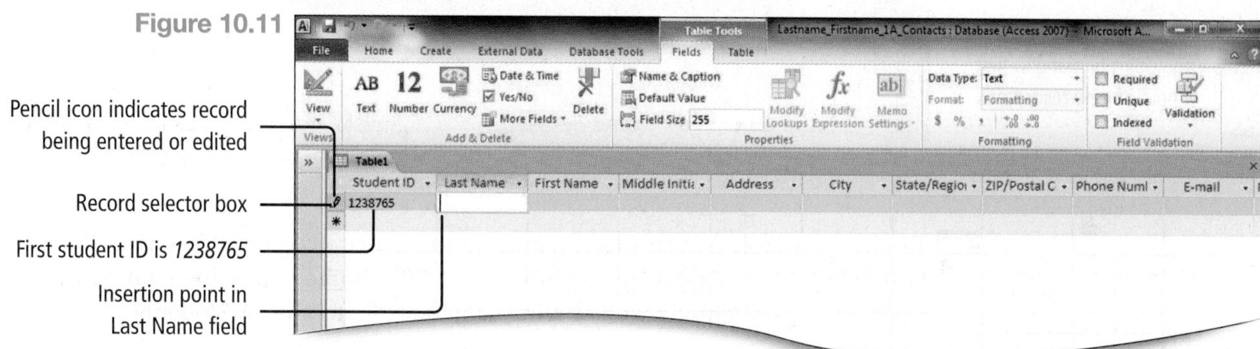

2 With the insertion point positioned in the **Last Name** field, type **Fresch** and then press Enter.

> **Note | Correct Typing Errors**
> Correct typing errors by using the techniques you have practiced in other Office applications. For example, use Backspace to remove characters to the left, Del to remove characters to the right, or select the text you want to replace and type the correct information. Press Esc to exit out of a record that has not been completely entered.

3 In the **First Name** field, type **Michael** and then press Enter.

4 In the **Middle Initial** field, type **B** and then press Enter.

5 In the **Address** field, type **7550 Douglas Ln** and then press Enter.

Do not be concerned if the data does not completely display in the column. As you progress in your study of Access, you will adjust the column widths so that you can view all of the data.

6 Continue entering data in the fields as indicated below, pressing Enter to move to the next field.

City	State/Region	ZIP/Postal Code	Phone Number	E-mail	Faculty Advisor ID
Alexandria	**VA**	**22336**	**(571) 555-0234**	**mfresch@capccc.edu**	**FAC-2289**

> **Note | Format for Typing Telephone Numbers in Access**
> Access does not require any specific format for typing telephone numbers in a database. The examples in this project use the format of Microsoft Outlook. Using such a format facilitates easy transfer of Outlook information to and from Access.

7 In the **Amount Owed** field, type **150** and then press Enter. Compare your screen with Figure 10.12.

Pressing Enter or Tab in the last field moves the insertion point to the next row to begin a new record. As soon as you move to the next row, Access saves the record—you do not have to take any specific action to save a record.

Figure 10.12

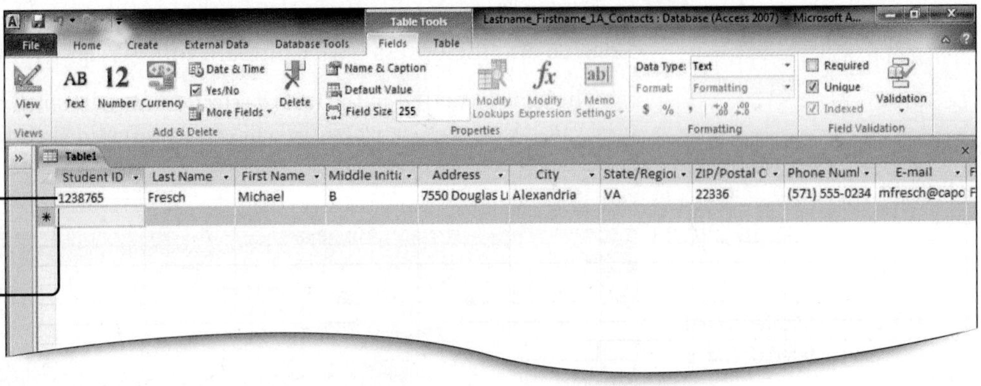

First record entered and saved

Insertion point blinking in first field of new record row

8 To give your table a meaningful name, on the Quick Access Toolbar, click the **Save** button. In the **Save As** dialog box, in the **Table Name** box, using your own name, replace the highlighted text by typing **Lastname Firstname 1A Students**

Save each database object with a name that identifies the data that it contains. When you save objects within a database, it is not necessary to use underscores. Your name is included as part of the object name so that you and your instructor can identify your printouts or electronic files.

9 In the **Save As** dialog box, click **OK**, and then notice that the object tab displays the new table name you just typed.

More Knowledge | Renaming a Table

To change the name of a table, close the table, display the Navigation Pane, right-click the table name, and then on the shortcut menu, click Rename. Type the new name or edit as you would any selected text.

Activity 10.06 | Adding Additional Records to a Table

1 In the new record row, click in the **Student ID** field, and then enter the contact information for the following two additional students, pressing Enter or Tab to move from field to field. The data in each field will display on one line in the table.

Student ID	Last Name	First Name	Middle Initial	Address	City	State/ Region	ZIP/ Postal Code	Phone Number	E-mail	Faculty Advisor ID	Amount Owed
2345677	**Ingram**	**Joseph**	**S**	**1 Casa Del Sol**	**Potomac**	**MD**	**20854**	**(240) 555-0177**	**jingram@ capccc.edu**	**FAC-2377**	**378.5**
3456689	**Bass**	**Amanda**	**J**	**1446 Yellow Rose Ln**	**Fairfax**	**VA**	**22030**	**(703) 555-0192**	**abass@ capccc.edu**	**FAC-9005**	**0**

2 Compare your screen with Figure 10.13.

Figure 10.13

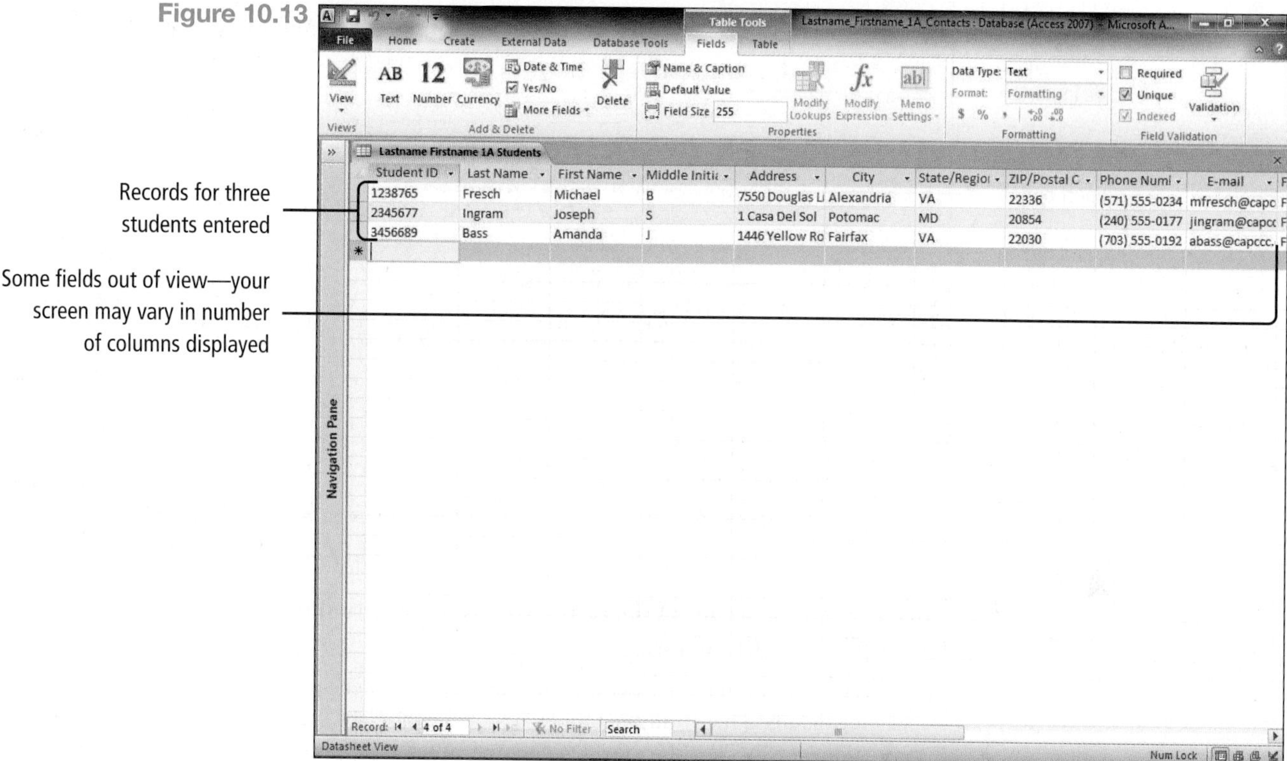

Activity 10.07 | Importing Data from an Excel Workbook into an Existing Access Table

When you create a database table, you can type the records directly into a table. You can also ***import*** data from a variety of sources. Importing is the process of copying data from one source or application to another application. For example, you can import data from a Word table or an Excel worksheet into an Access database because the data is arranged in columns and rows, similar to a table in Datasheet view.

In this activity, you will ***append***—add on—data from an Excel spreadsheet to your *1A Students* table. To append data, the table must already be created, and it must be closed.

1 In the upper right corner of the table, below the Ribbon, click the **Object Close** [X] button to close your **1A Students** table. Notice that no objects are open.

2 On the Ribbon, click the **External Data tab**. In the **Import & Link group**, click the **Excel** button. In the **Get External Data - Excel Spreadsheet** dialog box, click the **Browse** button.

> **Another Way**
> Select the file name, and in the lower right area of the dialog box, click Open.

3 In the **File Open** dialog box, navigate to your student files, locate and double-click the Excel file **a01A_Students**, and then compare your screen with Figure 10.14.

The path to the ***source file***—the file being imported—displays in the File name box. There are three options for importing data from an Excel workbook—import the data into a *new* table in the current database, append a copy of the records to an existing table, or link the data from Excel to a linked table. A ***link*** is a connection to data in another file. When linking, Access creates a table that maintains a link to the source data.

Figure 10.14

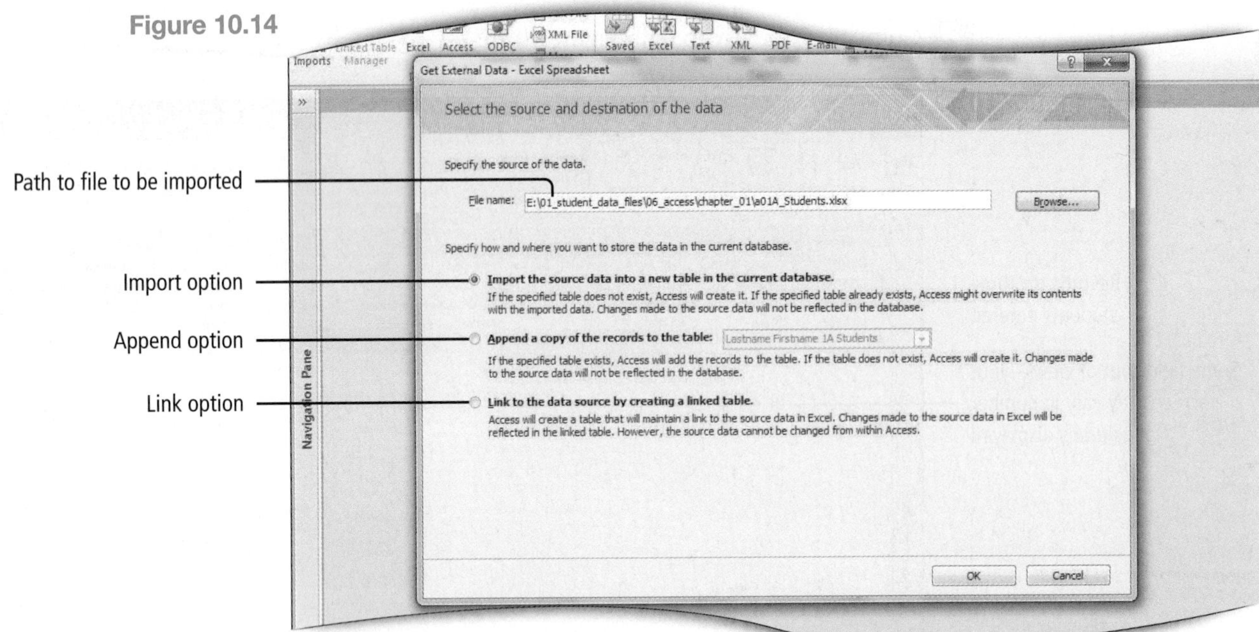

4 Click the **Append a copy of the records to the table** option button, and then in the box to its right, click the **arrow**.

Currently your database has only one table, so no other tables display on the list. However, when a database has multiple tables, here you can select the table to which you want to append records. The table into which you import or append data is referred to as the ***destination table***.

5 Press Esc to cancel the list, and then in the lower right corner of the dialog box, click **OK**. Compare your screen with Figure 10.15.

The first screen of the Import Spreadsheet Wizard displays, and the presence of scroll bars indicates that records and fields are out of view in this window. To append records from an Excel worksheet to an existing database table, the field names in the Excel worksheet must be identical to the field names in the table, and that is true in this table.

Figure 10.15

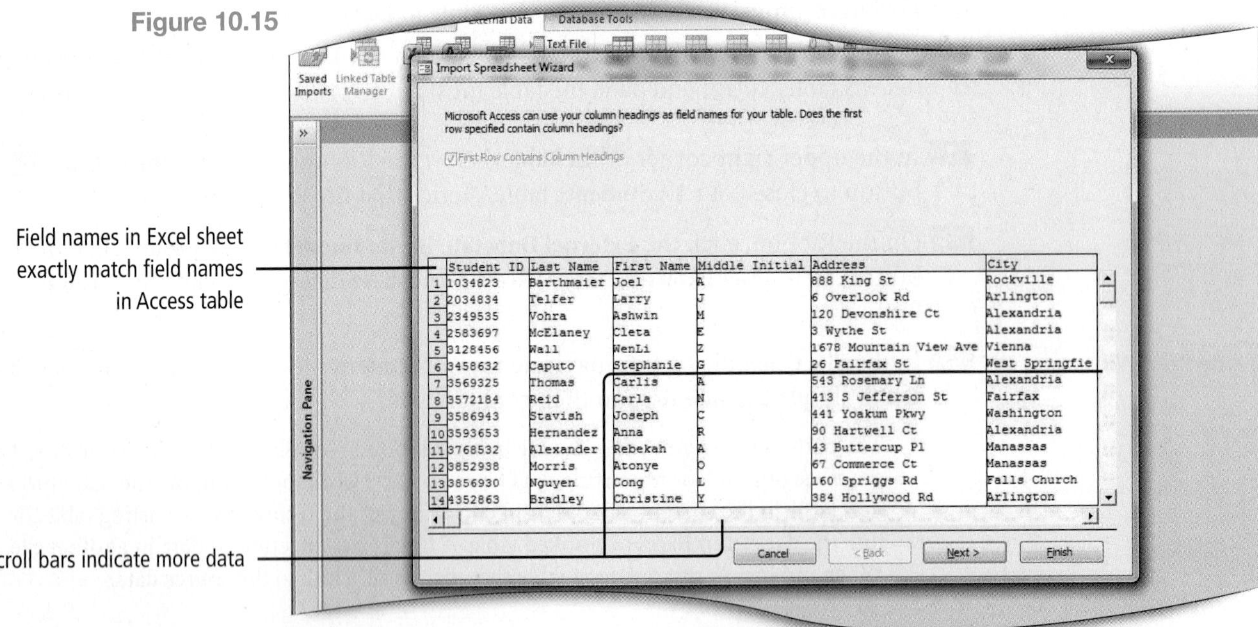

6 In the lower right corner, click **Next**. Notice that the name of your table displays under **Import to Table**. In the lower right corner, click **Finish**.

7 In the **Get External Data - Excel Spreadsheet** dialog box, click **Close**, and then **Open** [»] the **Navigation Pane**.

8 Point to the right edge of the **Navigation Pane** to display the [⇔] pointer. Drag to the right to widen the pane to display the entire table name, and then compare your screen with Figure 10.16.

Figure 10.16

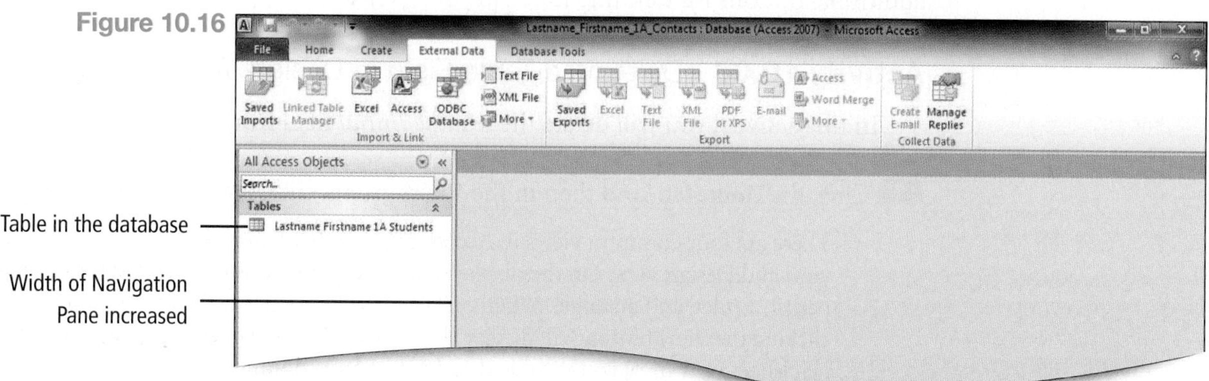

> **Another Way**
>
> To open an object from the Navigation Pane, right-click the object name, and then on the shortcut menu, click Open.

9 In the **Navigation Pane**, double-click your **1A Students** table to open the table in Datasheet view, and then **Close** [«] the **Navigation Pane**.

10 At the bottom left corner of your screen, locate the navigation area, and notice that there are a total of **26** records in the table—you created three records and imported 23 additional records. Compare your screen with Figure 10.17.

The records from the Excel worksheet display in your table, and the first record is selected. The ***navigation area*** indicates the number of records in the table and contains controls (arrows) with which you can navigate among the records.

Figure 10.17

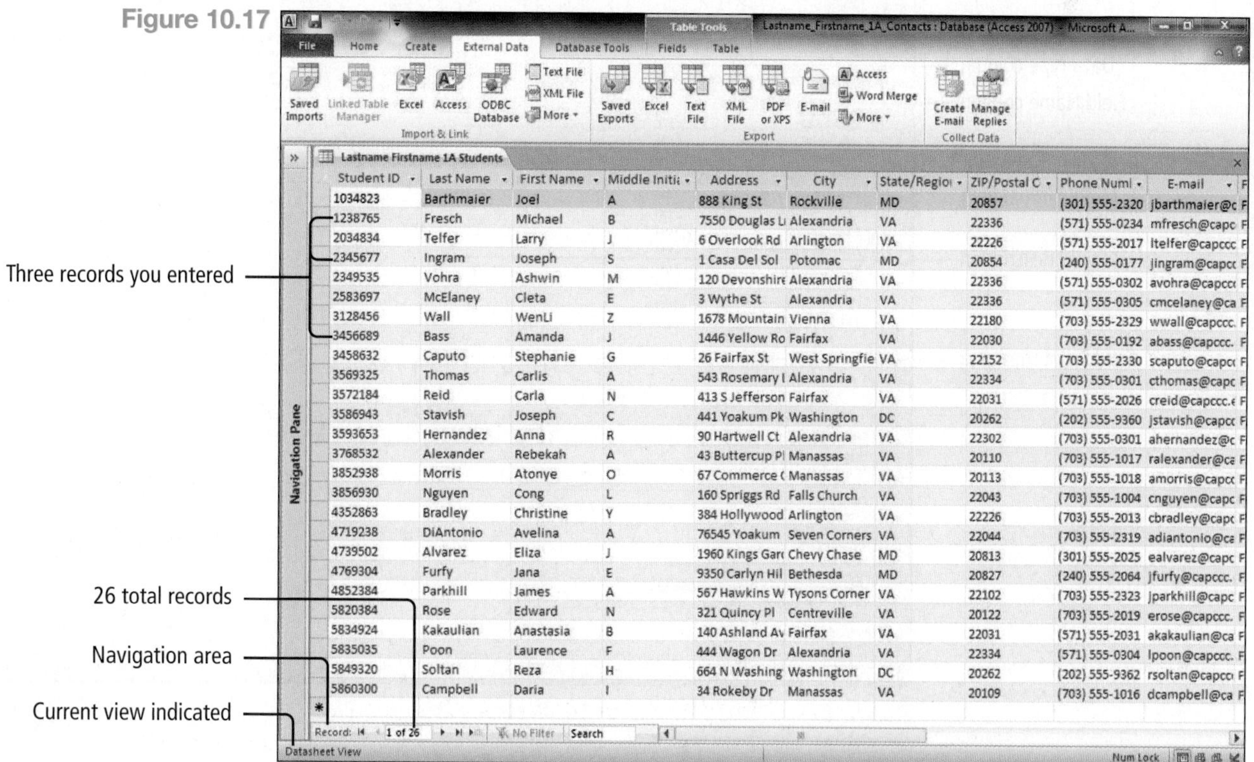

Access | Chapter 10

Objective 3 | Change the Structure of Tables and Add a Second Table

Recall that the structure of a table is the underlying design, including field names and data types. You can create a table or modify a table in Datasheet view. To define and modify fields, many database experts prefer to work in Design view, where you have many additional options for defining the fields in a table.

Activity 10.08 | Deleting a Table Field in Design View

In this activity, you will delete the *Middle Initial* field from the table.

1 Click the **Home tab**, and then in the **Views group**, click the **View button arrow**.

There are four common views in Access, but two that you will use often are Datasheet view and Design view. On the displayed list, Design view is represented by a picture of a pencil, a ruler, and an angle. When one of these four icons is displayed on the View button, clicking the View button will display the table in the view represented by the icon. Datasheet view displays the table data in rows and columns.

2 On the list, click **Design View**, and then compare your screen with Figure 10.18.

Design view displays the underlying design—the structure—of the table and its fields. In Design view, you cannot view the data; you can view only the information about each field's characteristics. Each field name is listed, along with its data type. A column to add a Description—information about the data in the field—is provided.

In the Field Properties area, you can make additional decisions about how each individual field looks and behaves. For example, you can set a specific field size.

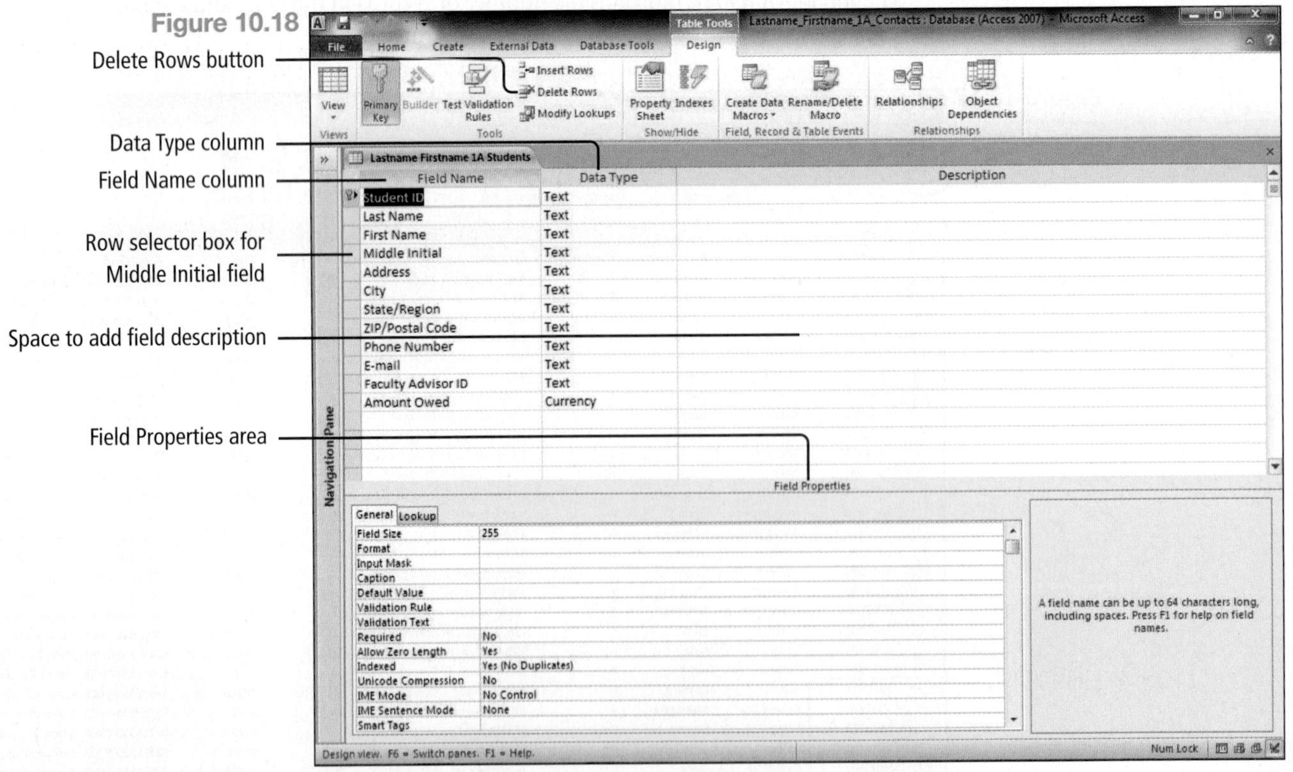

Figure 10.18

3 In the **Field Name** column, to the left of **Middle Initial**, point to the row selector box to display the ➡ pointer, and then click one time to select the entire row.

Another Way

Right-click the selected row and click Delete Rows.

4 On the **Design tab**, in the **Tools group**, click the **Delete Rows** button, read the message in the message box, and then click **Yes**.

Deleting a field deletes both the field and its data; you cannot undo this action. Thus, Access prompts you to be sure you want to proceed. If you change your mind after deleting a field, you must add the field back into the table and then reenter the data in that field for every record.

Activity 10.09 | Modifying a Field Size and Adding a Description

Typically, many individuals enter data into a table. For example, at your college many Registration Assistants enter and modify student and course information daily. Two ways to help reduce errors are to restrict what can be typed in a field and to add descriptive information.

1 With your table still displayed in **Design** view, in the **Field Name** column, click anywhere in the **State/Region** field name.

2 In the lower portion of the screen, under **Field Properties**, click **Field Size** to select the text *255*, type **2** and then compare your screen with Figure 10.19.

This action limits the size of the State/Region field to no more than two characters—the size of the two-letter state abbreviations provided by the United States Postal Service. ***Field properties*** control how the field displays and how data can be entered in the field. You can define properties for every field in the Field Properties area.

The default field size for a text field is 255. Limiting the field size property to 2 ensures that only two characters can be entered for each state. However, this does not prevent someone from entering two characters that are incorrect. Setting the proper data type for the field and limiting the field size are two ways to *help* to reduce errors.

Figure 10.19

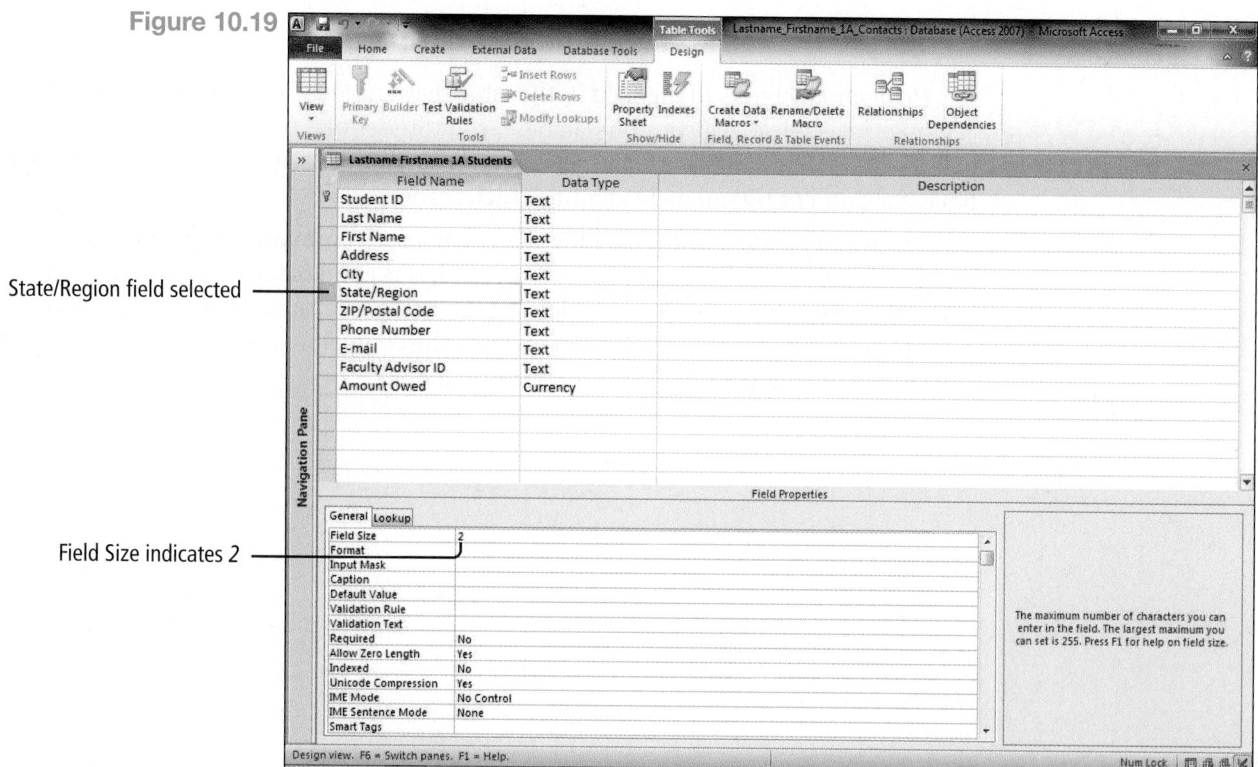

Access | Chapter 10

3 In the **State/Region** row, click in the **Description** box, type **Two-character state abbreviation** and then press Enter.

Descriptions for fields in a table are optional. Include a description if the field name does not provide an obvious explanation of the field. Information typed in the description area displays on the left side of the status bar in Datasheet view when the field is active, providing additional information to individuals who are entering data.

When you enter a description for a field, a Property Update Options button displays below the text you typed, which enables you to copy the description for the field to all other database objects that use this table as an underlying source.

4 Click in the **Student ID** field name box. Using the technique you practiced, in the **Field Properties** area, change the **Field Size** to **7**

By limiting the field size to seven characters, which is the maximum number of characters in a Student ID, you help to ensure the accuracy of the data.

5 In the **Student ID** row, click in the **Description** box, and then type **Seven-digit Student ID number**

6 Click in the **Faculty Advisor ID** field name box. In the **Field Properties** area, change the **Field Size** to **8** In the **Description** box for this field, type **Eight-character ID of faculty member assigned as advisor** and then press Enter.

7 On the Quick Access Toolbar, click the **Save** button to save the design changes to your table, and then notice the message.

The message indicates that the field size property of one or more fields has changed to a shorter size. If more characters are currently present in the Student ID, State/Region, or Faculty Advisor ID than you have allowed, the data could be ***truncated***—cut off or shortened—because the fields were not previously restricted to a specific number of characters.

8 In the message box, click **Yes**.

Activity 10.10 | Viewing a Primary Key in Design View

Primary key refers to the field in the table that uniquely identifies a record. For example, in a college registration database, your Student ID number uniquely identifies you—no other student at the college has your exact student number. In the 1A Students table, the Student ID uniquely identifies each student.

When you create a table using the Blank database command, by default Access designates the first field as the primary key field. It is good database design practice to establish a primary key for every table, because doing so ensures that you do not enter the same record more than once. You can imagine the confusion if another student at your college had the same Student ID number as you do.

1 With your table still displayed in Design view, in the **Field Name** column, click in the **Student ID** box. To the left of the box, notice the small icon of a key, as shown in Figure 10.20.

Access automatically designates the first field as the primary key field, but you can set any field as the primary key by clicking in the box to the left of the field name, and then clicking the Primary Key button.

Figure 10.20

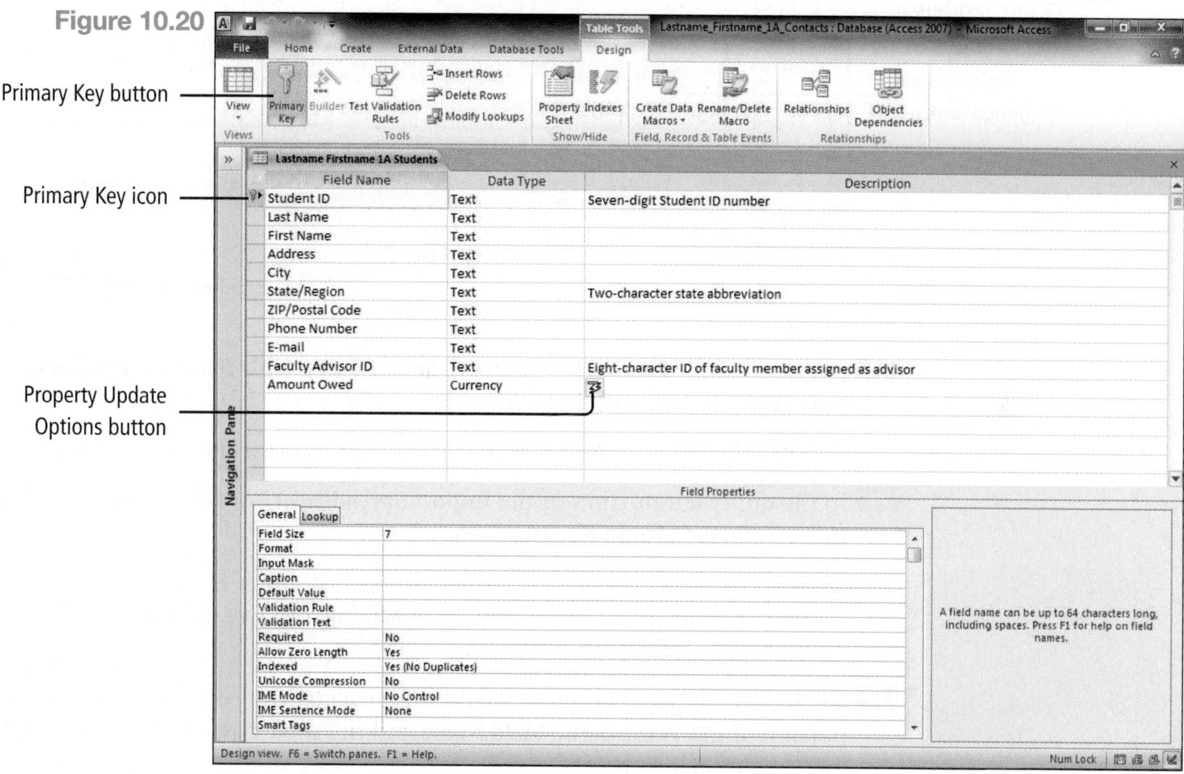

2 On the **Design tab**, in the **Views group**, notice that the **View** button contains a picture of a Datasheet, indicating that clicking the button will return you to Datasheet view. Click the **View** button.

Activity 10.11 | Adding a Second Table to a Database by Importing an Excel Spreadsheet

Many Microsoft Office users track data in an Excel spreadsheet. The sorting and filtering capabilities of Excel are useful for a simple database where all the information resides in one large Excel spreadsheet. However, Excel is limited as a database management tool because it cannot *relate* the information in multiple spreadsheets in a way in which you could ask a question and get a meaningful result. Data in an Excel spreadsheet can easily become an Access table by importing the spreadsheet, because Excel's format of columns and rows is similar to that of an Access table.

1 On the Ribbon, click the **External Data tab**, and then in the **Import & Link group**, click the **Excel** button. In the **Get External Data – Excel Spreadsheet** dialog box, to the right of the **File name** box, click **Browse**.

2 In the **File Open** dialog box, navigate to your student files, and then double-click **a01A_Faculty**. Compare your screen with Figure 10.21.

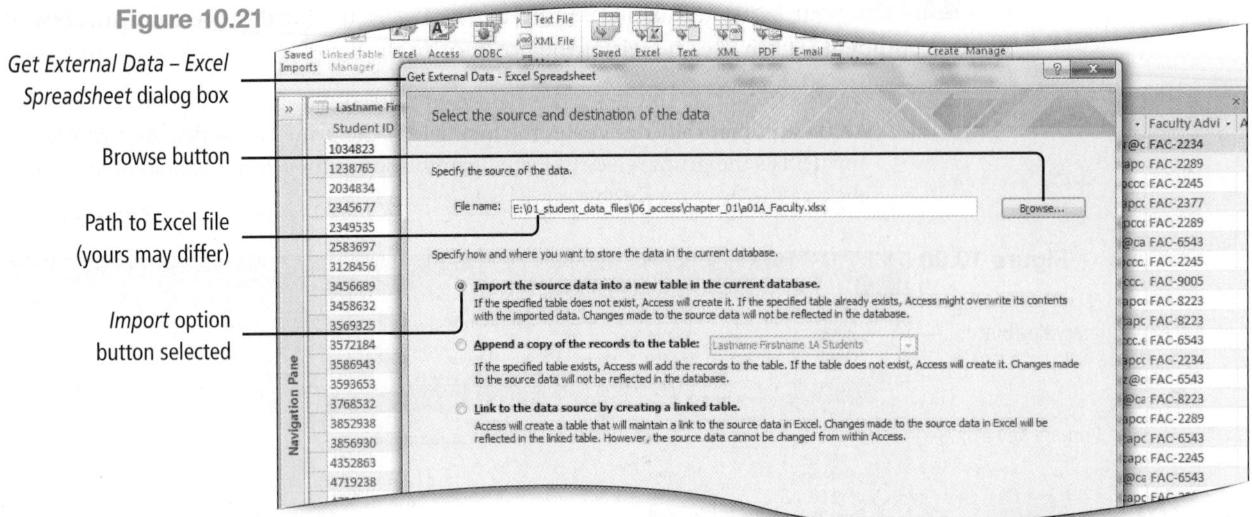

3 Be sure that the **Import the source data into a new table in the current database** option button is selected, and then click **OK**.

The Import Spreadsheet Wizard opens and displays the spreadsheet data.

4 In the upper left portion of the **Import Spreadsheet Wizard** dialog box, select the **First Row Contains Column Headings** check box.

The Excel data is framed, indicating that the first row of Excel column titles will become the Access table field names, and the remaining rows will become the individual records in the new Access table.

5 Click **Next**. Notice that the first column—*Faculty ID*—is selected, and in the upper portion of the Wizard, the **Field Name** and the **Data Type** display. Compare your screen with Figure 10.22.

Here you can review and change the field properties for each field (column). You can also identify fields in the spreadsheet that you do not want to import into the Access table by selecting the Do not import field (Skip) check box.

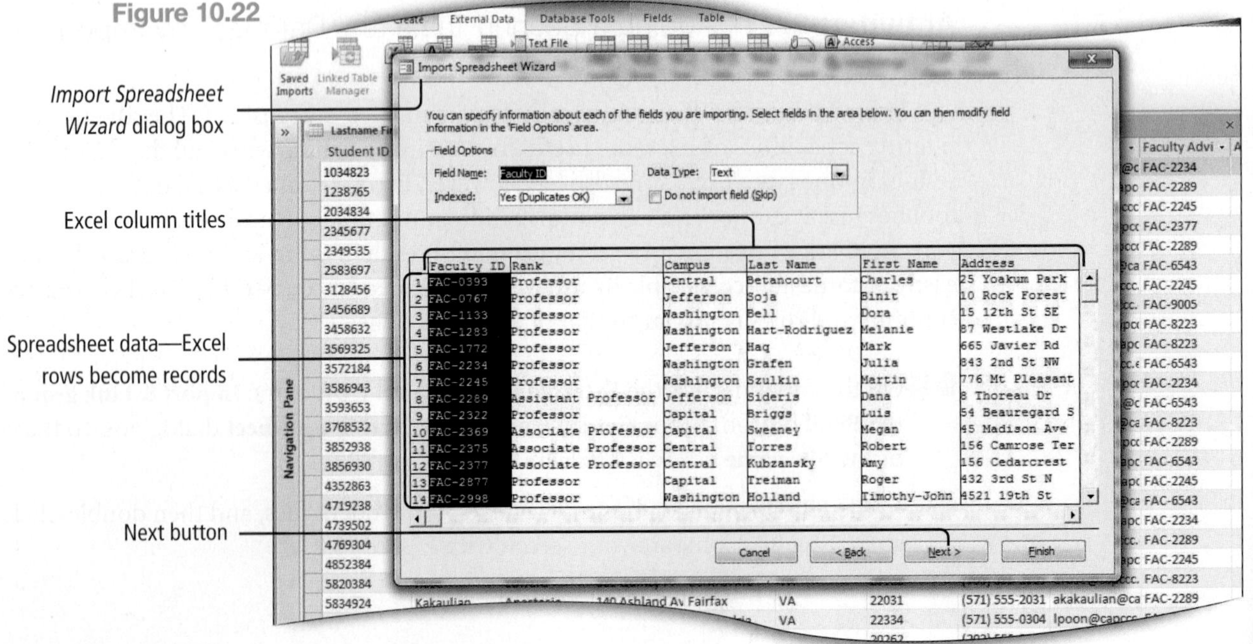

6 Click **Next**. In the upper portion of the Wizard, click the **Choose my own primary key** option button, and then be sure that **Faculty ID** displays.

In the new table, Faculty ID will be the primary key. No two faculty members have the same Faculty ID. By default, Access selects the first field as the primary key, but you can click the arrow to select a different field.

7 Click **Next**. In the **Import to Table** box, type **Lastname Firstname 1A Faculty** and then click **Finish**.

8 In the **Get External Data – Excel Spreadsheet** dialog box, click **Close**, and then **Open** [»] the **Navigation Pane**.

9 In the **Navigation Pane**, double-click your **1A Faculty** table to open it in Datasheet view, and then **Close** [«] the **Navigation Pane**.

10 Click in the **ZIP/Postal Code** field, and then on the Ribbon, click the **Fields tab**. In the **Formatting group**, change the **Data Type** to **Text**. Compare your screen with Figure 10.23.

The data from the *a01A_Faculty* worksheet displays in your *1A Faculty* table in the database. The navigation area indicates that there are 30 records in the table. Recall that if a field contains numbers that are not used in calculations, the data type should be set to Text. When you import data from an Excel spreadsheet, check the data types of all fields to ensure they are correct.

Figure 10.23

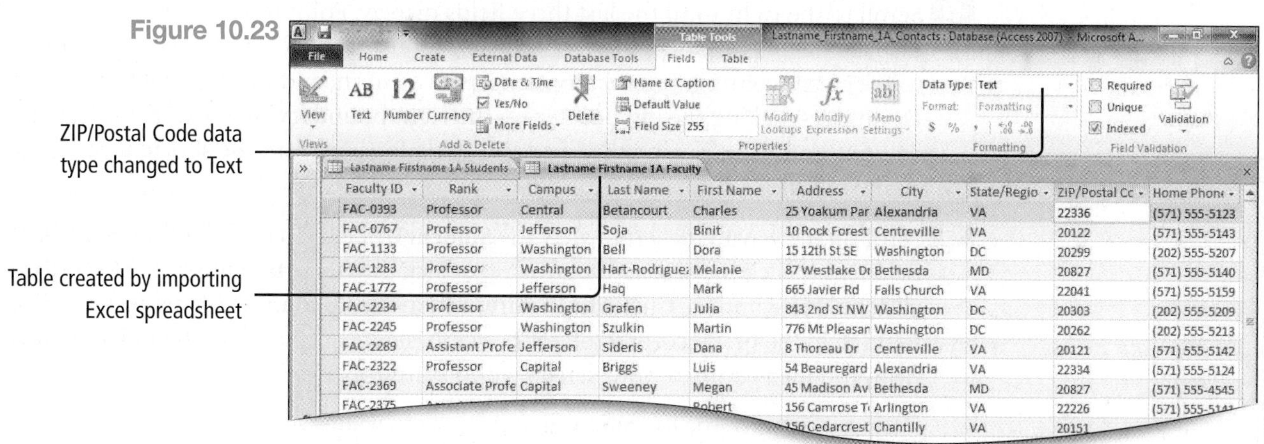

Activity 10.12 | Adjusting Column Widths

By using techniques similar to those you use for Excel worksheets, you can adjust the widths of Access fields that display in Datasheet view.

1 In the object window, click the **object tab** for your **1A Students** table.

Clicking the object tabs along the top of the object window enables you to display open objects to work with them. All of the columns are the same width regardless of the amount of data in the field, the field size that was set, or the length of the field name. If you print the table as currently displayed, some of the data or field names will not fully print until you adjust the column widths.

2 In the field names row, point to the right edge of the **Address** field to display the [+] pointer, and then compare your screen with Figure 10.24.

Figure 10.24

Pointer positioned on right edge of Address field

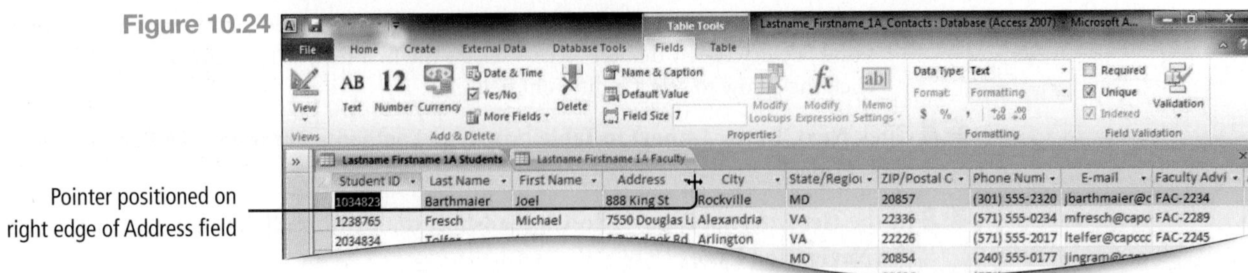

3 With your [+] pointer positioned as shown in Figure 10.24, double-click the right edge of the **Address** field.

The column width of the Address field widens to fully display the longest entry in the field. In this manner, the width of a column can be increased or decreased to fit its contents in the same manner as a column in an Excel worksheet. In Access this is referred to as ***Best Fit***.

4 Point to the **Phone Number** field name to display the [↓] pointer, right-click to select the entire column and display a shortcut menu, and then click **Field Width**. In the **Column Width** dialog box, click **Best Fit**.

5 Scroll to the right until the last three fields display. Point to the **E-mail** field name to display the [↓] pointer, hold down the left mouse button, and then drag to the right to select this column, the **Faculty Advisor ID** column, and the **Amount Owed** column. By double-clicking the [+] pointer on the right boundary of any of the selected columns, or by displaying the Field Width dialog box from the shortcut menu, apply **Best Fit** to the selected columns.

6 Scroll all the way to the left to view the **Student ID** field. To the left of the *Student ID* field name, click the **Select All** button [ ]. Click the **Home tab**, and in the **Records group**, click the **More** button. Click **Field Width**, and in the **Column Width** dialog box, click **Best Fit**. In the first record, scroll to the right as necessary, click in the **Amount Owed** field, and then compare your screen with Figure 10.25.

In this manner, you can adjust all of the column widths at one time. After applying Best Fit, be sure to click in any field to remove the selection from all of the records; otherwise, the layout changes will not be saved with the table. Adjusting the width of columns does not change the data in the table's records; it changes only the *display* of the data.

Figure 10.25

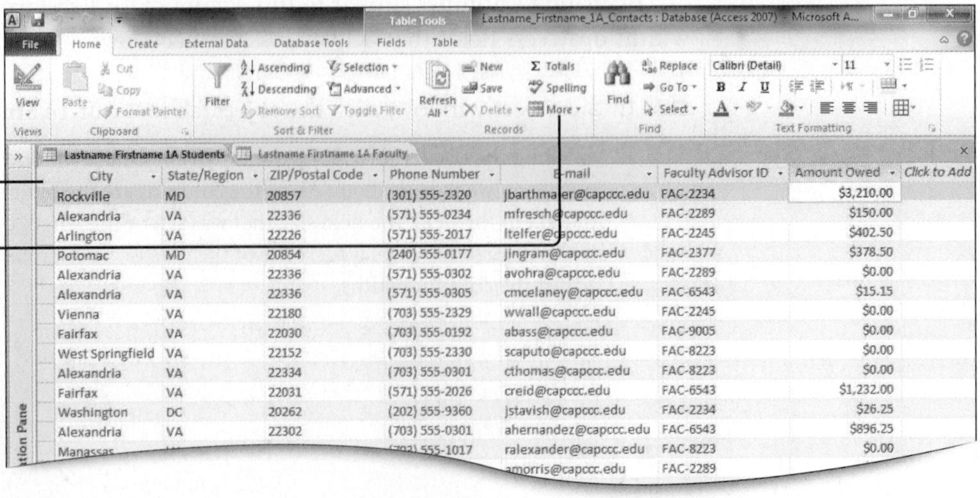

Select All button

More button

> **Note | Adjusting Column Widths**
>
> If you adjust column widths individually, scroll to the right and scroll down to be sure that all of the data displays in all of the fields. Access adjusts the column widths to fit the screen size based on the displayed data. If data is not displayed on the screen when you adjust a column width, the column may not be adjusted adequately to display all of the data in the field. For that reason, select all of the columns and apply Best Fit to be sure that all of the data displays when scrolling or printing. Click in any field after applying Best Fit to remove the selection, and then save the table before performing other tasks.

7 On the Quick Access Toolbar, click the **Save** button to save the table design changes—changing the column widths.

If you do not save the table after making design changes, Access will prompt you to save when you close the table.

Activity 10.13 | Printing a Table

Although a printed table does not look as professional as a printed report, there are times when you will want to print a table. For example, you may need a quick reference or want to proofread the data that has been entered.

1 On the Ribbon, click the **File tab** to display **Backstage** view, click the **Print** tab, click **Print Preview**, and then compare your screen with Figure 10.26.

Figure 10.26

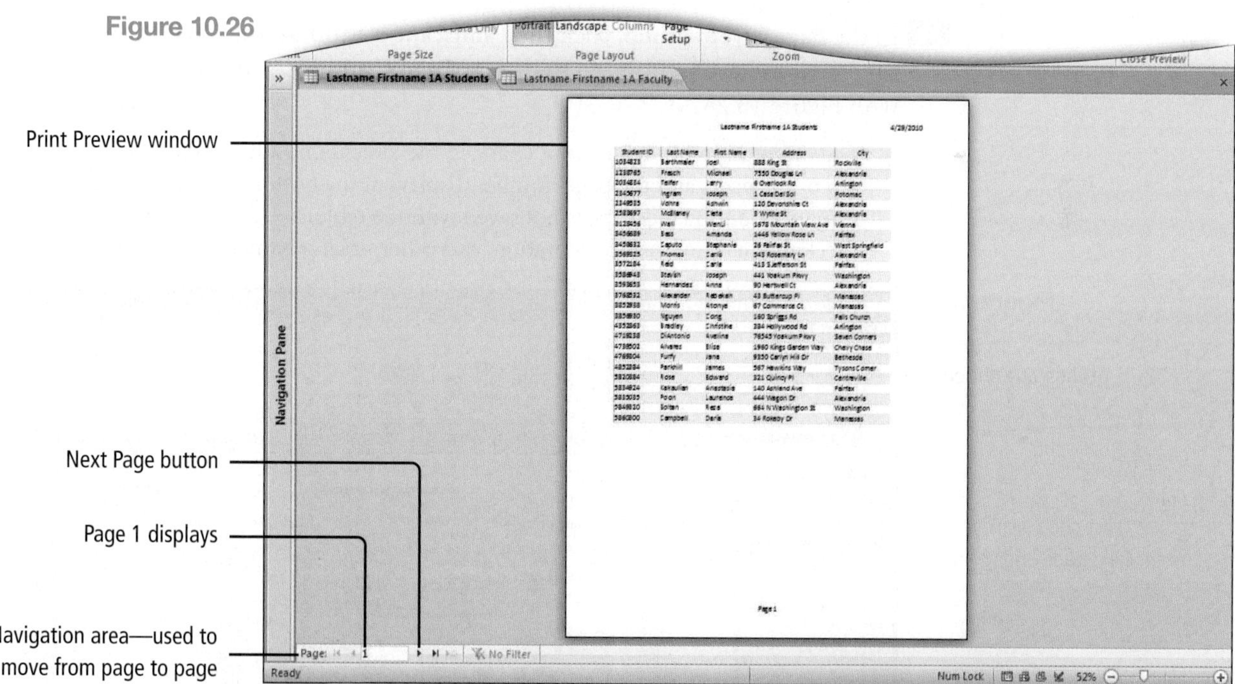

2 In the lower left corner, click the **Next Page** button two times. Point to the top of the page to display the pointer, click one time to zoom in, and then compare your screen with Figure 10.27.

The display enlarges, and the Zoom Out pointer displays. The third page of the table displays the last two field columns. The Next Page button is dimmed, indicating there are no more pages. The Previous Page button is darker, indicating that pages exist before this page.

Figure 10.27

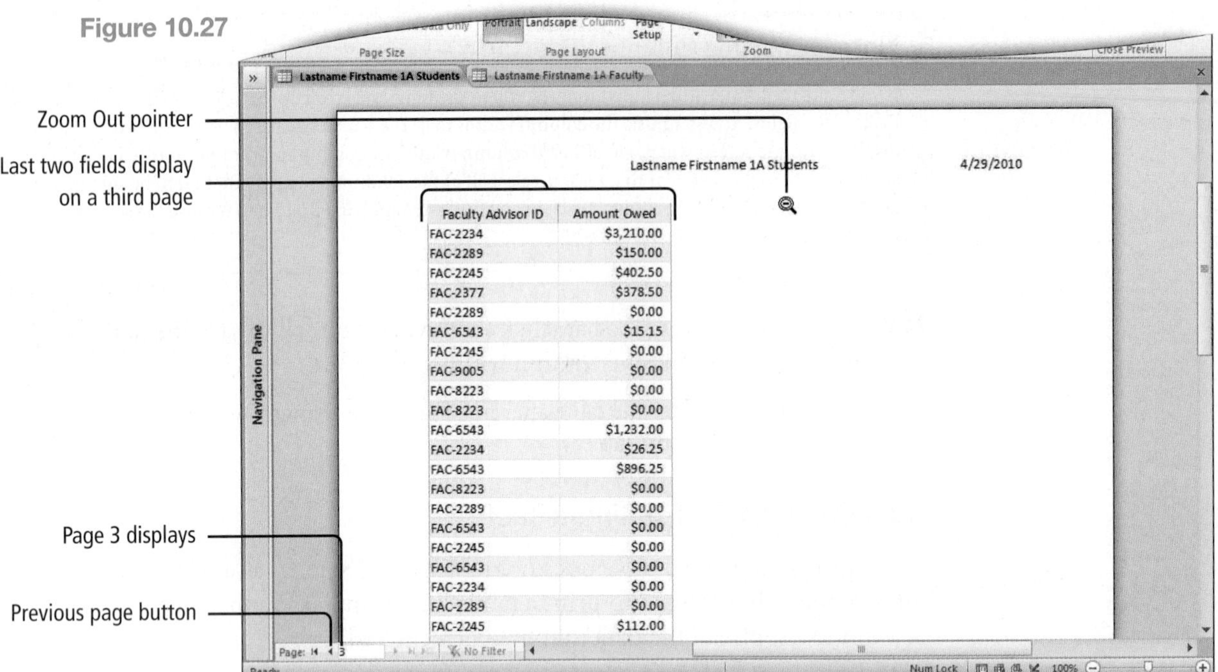

> **Another Way**
>
> Click the [Zoom Out] pointer to zoom back to Fit to Window view.

3. On the Ribbon, in the **Zoom group**, click the **Zoom** button to zoom back to Fit to Window view.

4. In the **Page Layout group**, click the **Landscape** button. In the navigation area, click the **Previous Page** button [◄] to display **Page 1**, and then compare your screen with Figure 10.28.

   The orientation of the printout changes, the table name and current date display at the top of the page, and the page number displays at the bottom. The change in orientation from portrait to landscape is not saved with the table. Each time you print, you must check the margins, page orientation, and other print parameters to print as you intend.

Figure 10.28

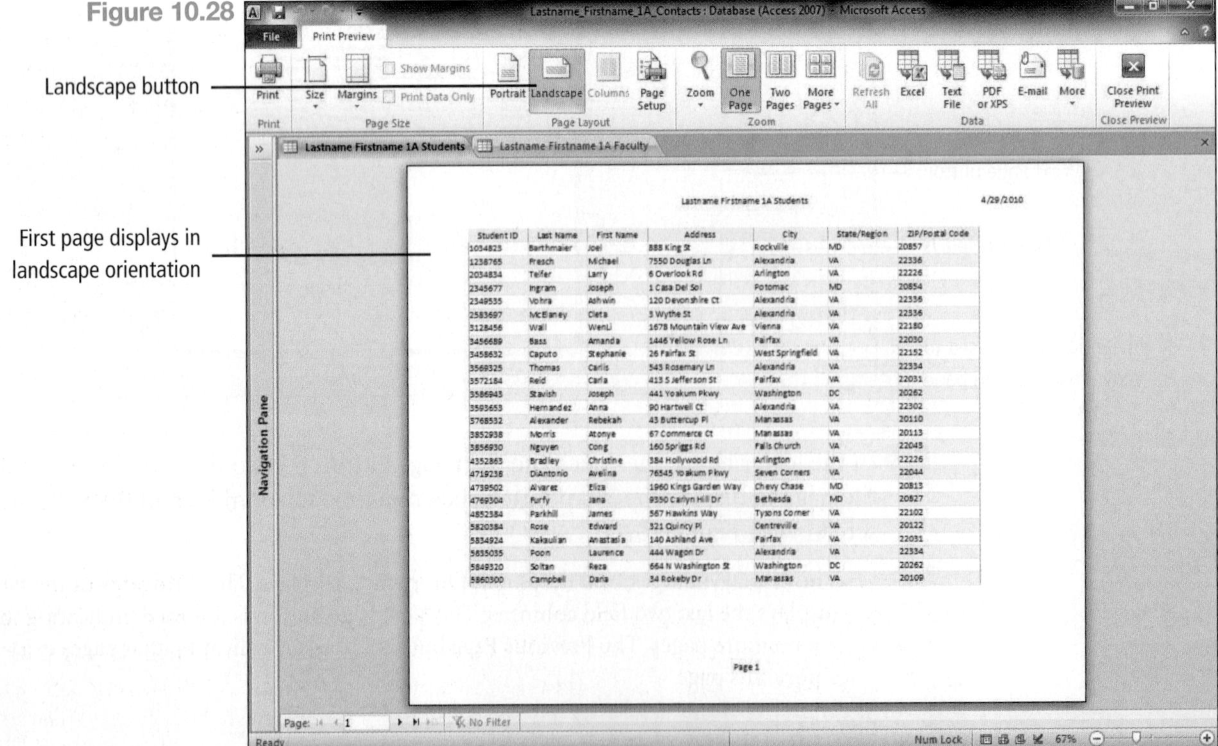

Note | Headers and Footers in Access Objects

The headers and footers in Access tables and queries are controlled by default settings; you cannot add additional information or edit the information. The object name displays in the center of the header area with the date on the right—that is why adding your own name to the object name is helpful to identify your paper or electronic results. The page number displays in the center of the footer area. The headers and footers in Access reports and forms, however, are more flexible; you can add to and edit the information.

5. On the **Print Preview tab**, in the **Print group**, click the **Print** button. In the **Print** dialog box, under **Print Range**, verify that the **All** option button is selected. Under **Copies**, verify that the **Number of Copies** is **1**. Compare your screen with Figure 10.29.

Figure 10.29

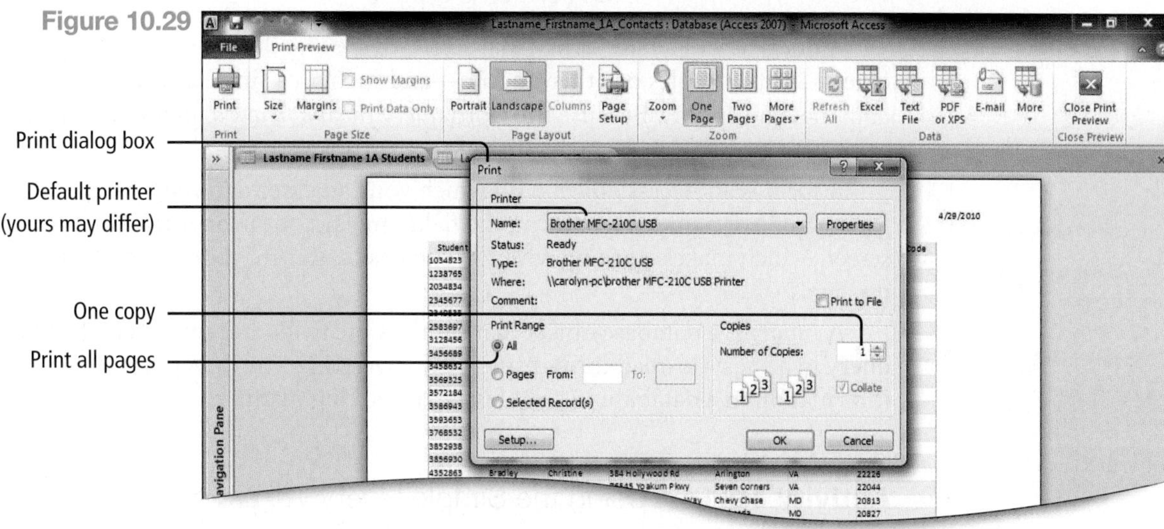

6. Determine how your instructor wants you to submit your work for this project—on paper or electronically. If submitting electronically, determine if, in addition to submitting your Access database, you are to create and submit electronic printouts of individual database objects.

7. To print on paper, in the **Print** dialog box, click **OK**, and then in the **Close Preview group**, click the **Close Print Preview** button. This printout will have two pages. To create an electronic PDF printout of this table object, in the Print dialog box, click Cancel, and then follow the steps in the following Note—or follow the specific directions provided by your instructor.

Note | To Create a PDF Electronic Printout of an Access Object

Display the object (table, report, and so on) in Print Preview and adjust margins and orientation as desired. On the Print Preview tab, in the Data group, click the PDF or XPS button. In the Publish as PDF or XPS dialog box, navigate to your chapter folder. Use the default file name, or follow your instructor's directions to name the object. In the lower right corner, click Publish—the default setting is PDF. If necessary, close the Adobe Acrobat/Reader window and the Export-PDF dialog box. Click the Close Print Preview button; your electronic printout is saved.

8. At the far right edge of the object window, click the **Close Object** button [X] to close the **1A Students** table.

9. With your **1A Faculty** table displayed, to the left of the **Faculty ID** field name, click the **Select All** button to select all of the columns. On the **Home tab**, in the **Records group**, click the **More** button. Click **Field Width**, and in the **Column Width** dialog box, click **Best Fit**. Click in any field in the table to remove the selection, and then **Save** the table.

10 Display the table in **Print Preview**. Change the **Orientation** to **Landscape**. If directed to do so by your instructor, create a paper or electronic printout, and then **Close Print Preview**—two pages result.

11 Click the **Close Object** button [×].

All of your database objects—the *1A Students* table and the *1A Faculty* table—are closed; the object window is empty.

Objective 4 | Create and Use a Query, Form, and Report

A ***query*** is a database object that retrieves specific data from one or more database objects—either tables or other queries—and then, in a single datasheet, displays only the data that you specify. Because the word *query* means *to ask a question*, think of a query as a question formed in a manner that Access can answer.

A ***form*** is an Access object with which you can enter data, edit data, or display data from a table or a query. In a form, the fields are laid out in an attractive format on the screen, which makes working with the database easier for those who must enter and look up data.

A ***report*** is a database object that displays the fields and records from a table or a query in an easy-to-read format suitable for printing. Create reports to *summarize* information in a database in a professional-looking manner.

Activity 10.14 | Using the Simple Query Wizard to Create a Query

A ***select query*** is one type of Access query. A select query, also called a ***simple select query***, retrieves (selects) data from one or more tables or queries and then displays the selected data in a datasheet. A select query creates subsets of data to answer specific questions; for example, *Which students live in Arlington, VA?*

The objects from which a query selects its data are referred to as the query's ***data source***. In this activity, you will create a simple select query using a ***wizard***. A wizard is a feature in Microsoft Office programs that walks you step by step through a process. The process involves choosing the data source, and then indicating the fields you want to include in the query result. The query—the question that you want to ask—is *What is the name, complete mailing address, and Student ID of every student?*

1 Click the **Create tab**, and then in the **Queries group**, click the **Query Wizard** button. In the **New Query** dialog box, click **Simple Query Wizard**, and then click **OK**. Compare your screen with Figure 10.30.

Figure 10.30

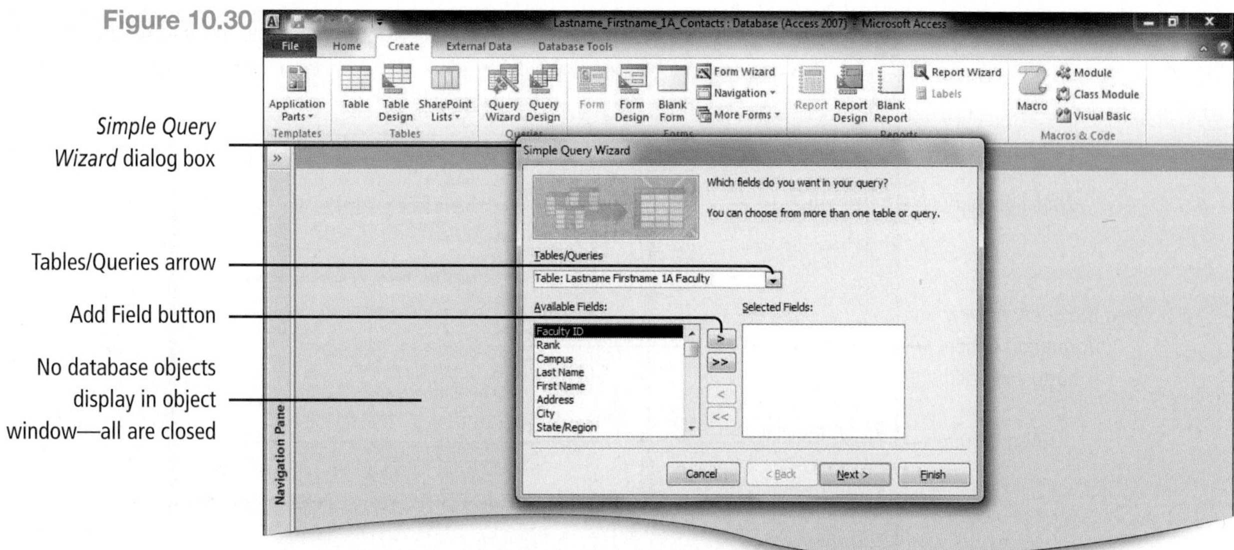

2 Click the **Tables/Queries arrow**, and then click your **Table: 1A Students.**

To create a query, first choose the data source—the object from which to select data. The name and complete mailing address of every student is stored in the 1A Students table, so this table will be your data source.

3 Under **Available Fields**, click **Student ID**, and then click the **Add Field** button **>** to move the field to the **Selected Fields** list on the right. Point to the **Last Name** field, and then double-click to add the field to the **Selected Fields** list.

Use either method to add fields to the Selected Fields list. Fields can be added in any order.

4 By using the **Add Field** button **>** or by double-clicking the field name, add the following fields to the **Selected Fields** list: **First Name**, **Address**, **City**, **State/Region**, and **ZIP/Postal Code**. Compare your screen with Figure 10.31.

Choosing these seven fields will answer the question, *What is the Student ID, name, and address of every student?*

Figure 10.31

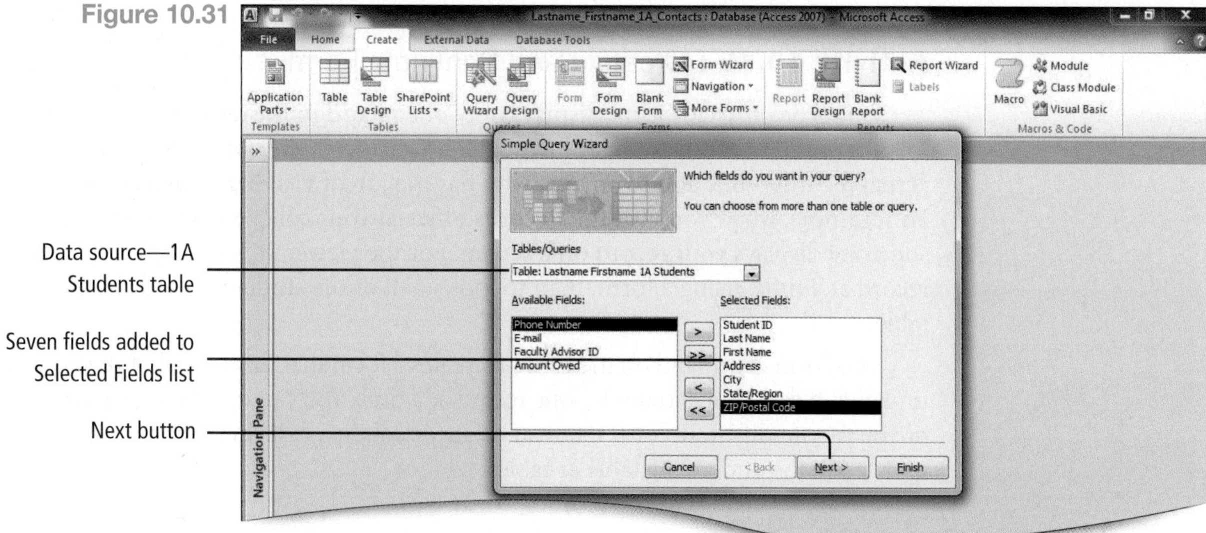

5 Click **Next**. In the **Simple Query Wizard** dialog box, click in the **What title do you want for your query?** box. Edit as necessary so that the query name, using your own last and first name, is **Lastname Firstname 1A All Students Query** and then compare your screen with Figure 10.32.

Figure 10.32

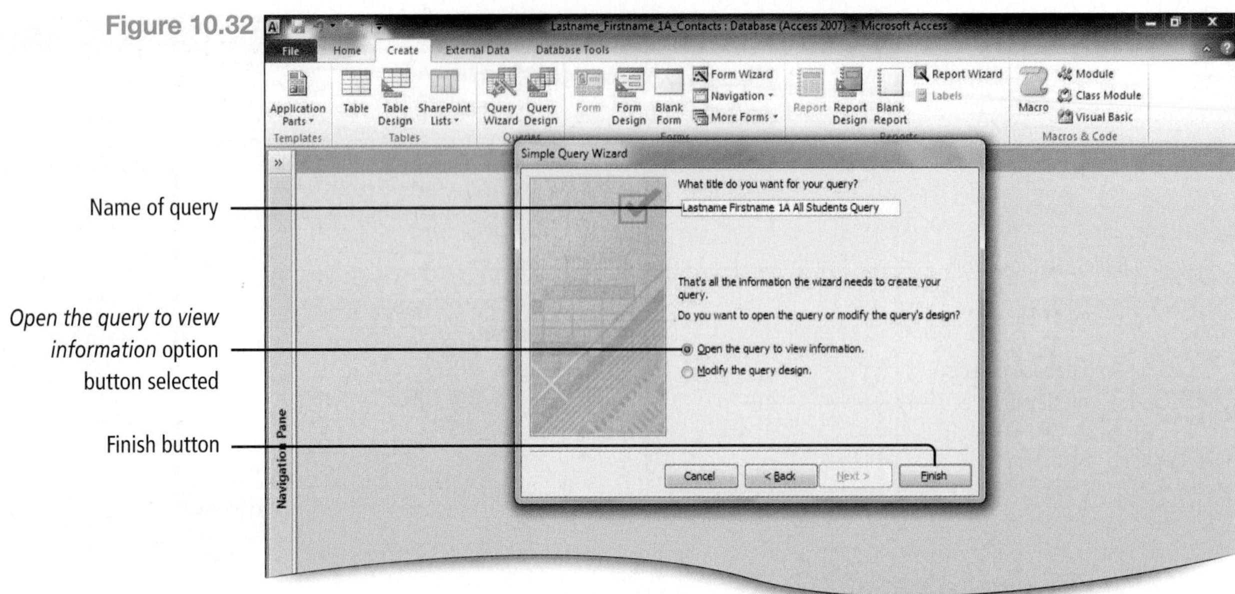

6 Click **Finish**.

Access ***runs*** the query—performs the actions indicated in your query design by searching the records in the data source you selected, and then finding the records that match specified criteria. The records that match the criteria display in a datasheet. A select query *selects*—pulls out and displays—*only* the information from the data source that you requested, including the specified fields.

In the object window, Access displays every student record in Datasheet view, but displays *only* the seven fields that you moved to the Selected Fields list in the Simple Query Wizard dialog box.

7 If necessary, apply Best Fit to the columns and then Save the query. Display the query in **Print Preview**. Change the **Orientation** to **Landscape**, and then create a paper or electronic printout as instructed. **Close** the **Print Preview**.

8 In the object window, click the **Close Object** button [X] to close the query.

Activity 10.15 | Creating and Printing a Form

One type of Access form displays only one record in the database at a time. Such a form is useful not only to the individual who performs the data entry—typing in the actual records—but also to anyone who has the job of viewing information in a database. For example, when you visit the Records office at your college to obtain a transcript, someone displays your record on a screen. For the viewer, it is much easier to look at one record at a time, using a form, than to look at all of the student records in the database table.

The Form command on the Ribbon creates a form that displays all of the *fields* from the underlying data source (table)—one record at a time. You can use this new form immediately, or you can modify it. Records that you create or edit in a form are automatically added to or updated in the underlying table or tables.

1 **Open** [»] the **Navigation Pane**. Increase the width of the **Navigation Pane** so that all object names display fully. Notice that a table displays a datasheet icon, and a query displays an icon of two overlapping datasheets. Right-click your **1A Students** table to display a menu as shown in Figure 10.33.

Figure 10.33

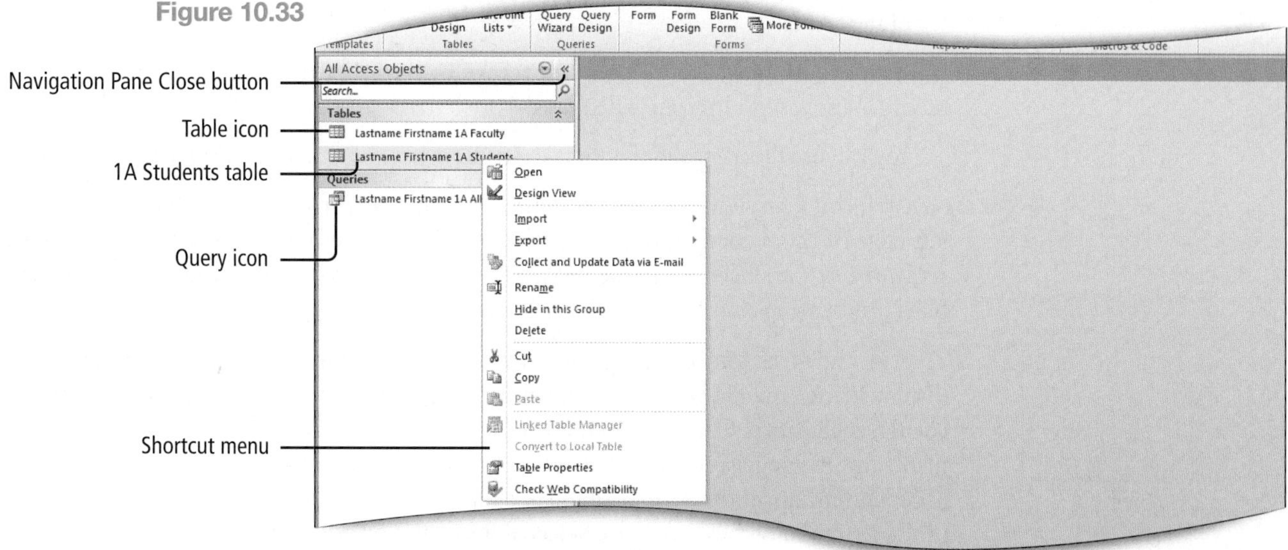

2 On the shortcut menu, click **Open** to display the table in the object window, and then **Close** [«] the **Navigation Pane** to maximize your object space.

3 Scroll to the right, and notice that there are 11 fields in the table. On the **Create tab**, in the **Forms group**, click the **Form** button. Compare your screen with Figure 10.34.

Access creates a form based on the currently selected object—the 1A Students table. Access creates the form in a simple top-to-bottom format, with all 11 fields in the record lined up in a single column.

The form displays in ***Layout view***—the Access view in which you can make changes to a form or to a report while the object is open. Each field displays the data for the first student record in the table—*Joel Barthmaier*.

Figure 10.34

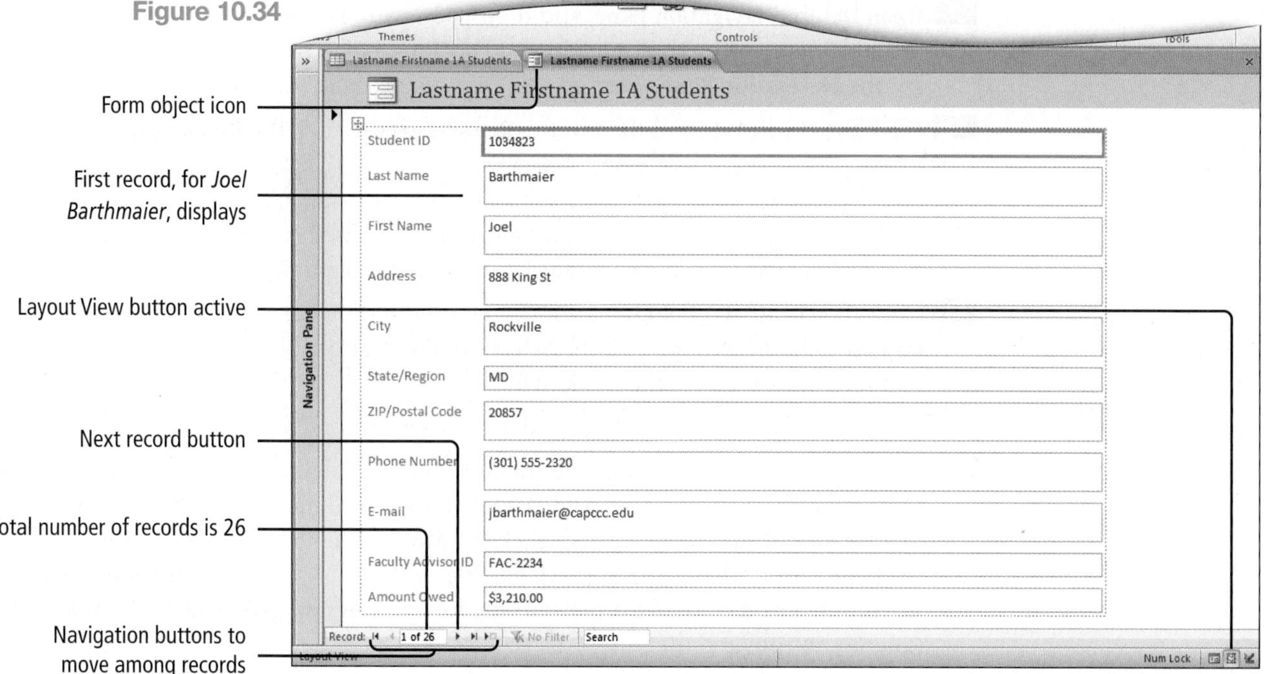

4 At the right edge of the status bar, notice that the **Layout View** button is active, indicating that the form is displayed in Layout view.

> **Another Way**
> On the Home tab, in the Views group, click the View button, which displays an icon of a form.

5 At the right edge of the status bar, click the **Form View** button.

In ***Form view***, you can view the records, but you cannot change the layout or design of the form.

6 In the navigation area, click the **Next record** button three times. The fourth record—for *Joseph Ingram*—displays.

You can use the navigation buttons to scroll among the records to display any single record.

7 **Save** the form with the default name—*Lastname Firstname 1A Students*. Along the left edge of the record, under ▶, click anywhere in the narrow gray bar—the ***record selector bar***—to select only the record for *Joseph Ingram*. Notice that the bar turns black, indicating that the record is selected.

8 To print the form for *Joseph Ingram* only, click the **File tab**, and then click **Print**—do *not* display Print Preview. Instead, click **Print**. In the **Print** dialog box, in the lower left corner, click **Setup**. Click the **Columns tab**, change the **Width** to **7.5** so that the form prints on one page, and then click **OK**. The maximum column width that you can enter is dependent upon the printer that is installed on your system. In the lower left corner of the **Print** dialog box, click the **Selected Record(s)** option button, and then click **OK**.

> **Note** | To Print a Single Form in PDF
> To create a PDF electronic printout of a single record in a form, change the column width to 7.5 as described in step 8 above, and then in the Print dialog box, click Cancel. On the left edge of the form, click the Record Selector bar so that it is black—selected. On the Ribbon click the External Data tab. In the Export group, click the PDF or XPS button. Navigate to your chapter folder, and then in the lower left corner of the dialog box, if necessary, select the Open file after publishing check box. In the lower right corner of the dialog box, click the Options button. In the Options dialog box, under Range, click the Selected records option button, click OK, and then click Publish. Close the Adobe Reader or Acrobat window.

9 **Close** the form. Notice that your **1A Students** table remains open.

Activity 10.16 | Creating, Modifying, and Printing a Report

1 **Open** the **Navigation Pane**, and then open your **1A Faculty** table by double-clicking the table name or by right-clicking and clicking Open from the shortcut menu. **Close** the **Navigation Pane.**

2 Click the **Create tab**, and then in the **Reports group**, click the **Report** button.

When you click the Report button, Access generates the report in Layout view and includes all of the fields and all of the records in the table, and does so in a format suitable for printing. Dotted lines indicate how the report would break across pages if you print it. In Layout view, you can make quick changes to the report layout.

> **Another Way**
> Right-click the field. From the shortcut menu, click Select Entire Column, and then press Del.

3 Click the **Faculty ID** field name, and then on the Ribbon, click the **Arrange tab**. In the **Rows & Columns group**, click the **Select Column** button, and then press Del. Using the same technique, delete the **Rank** field.

The Faculty ID and Rank fields and data are deleted, and the report readjusts the fields.

4 Click the **Address** field name, and then use the scroll bar at the bottom of the screen to scroll to the right to display the **Mobile Phone** field; be careful not to click in the report. Hold down Shift and then click the **Mobile Phone** field name to select all of the fields from *Address* through *Mobile Phone*. With all the field names selected—surrounded by a colored border—in the **Row & Columns group**, click the **Select Column** button, and then press Del.

Use this technique to select and delete multiple columns in Layout view.

5 Scroll to the left, and notice that you can see all of the remaining fields. In any record, click in the **E-mail** field. Point to the right edge of the field box to display the ↔ pointer. Drag to the right slightly to increase the width of the field so that all E-mail addresses display on one line.

6 Click the **Last Name** field name. On the Ribbon, click the **Home tab**. In the **Sort & Filter group**, click the **Ascending** button. Compare your screen with Figure 10.35.

By default, tables are sorted in ascending order by the primary key field, which is the Faculty ID field. You can change the default and sort any field in either ascending order or descending order. The sort order does not change in the underlying table, only in the report.

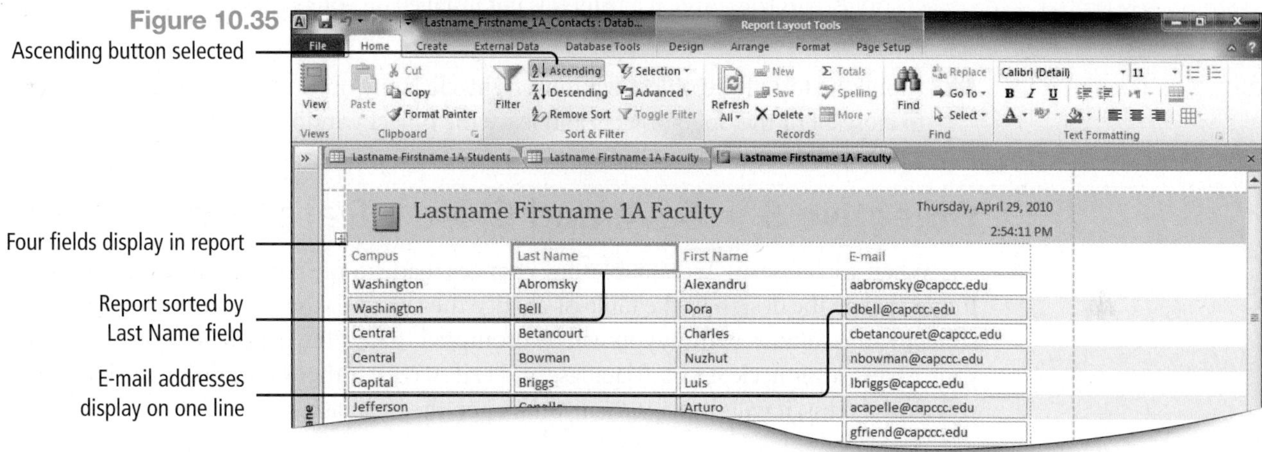

Figure 10.35

7 Click the **Save** button. In the **Report Name** box, add **Report** to the end of the suggested name, and then click **OK**.

8 Display the report in **Print Preview**. In the **Zoom group**, click the **Two Pages** button, and then compare your screen with Figure 10.36.

The report will print on two pages because the page number at the bottom of the report is located beyond the right margin of the report.

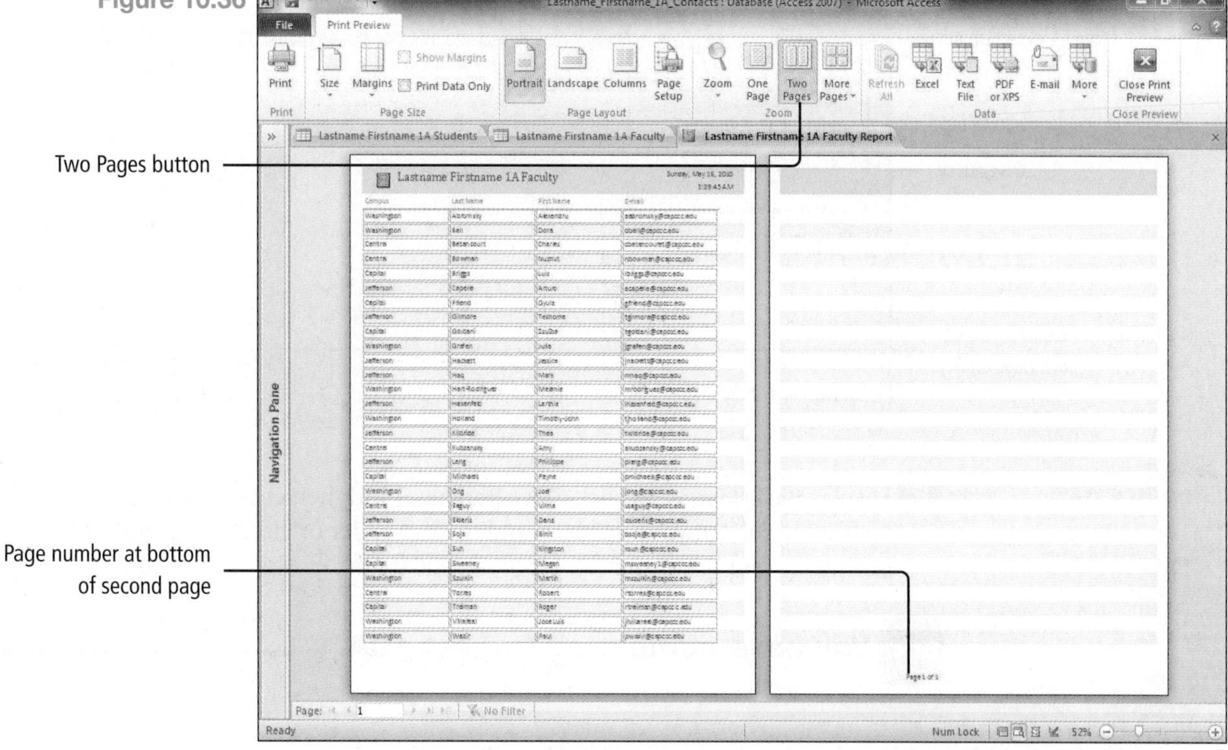

Figure 10.36

9 In the **Close Preview group**, click the **Close Print Preview button**. Scroll down to the bottom of the report, and then scroll to the right to display the page number. Click the page number—**Page 1 of 1**—and then press Del.

10 Display the report in **Print Preview** and notice that the report will print on one page. In the **Zoom group**, click the **One Page** button. **Save** the changes to the design of the report, and then create a paper or electronic printout as instructed. At the right end of the Ribbon, click the **Close Print Preview** button.

The default margins of a report created with the Report tool are 0.25 inch. Some printers require a greater margin so your printed report may result in two pages—you will learn to adjust this later. Also, if a printer is not installed on your system, the report may print on two pages.

11 Along the top of the object window, right-click any object tab, and then click **Close All** to close all of the open objects and leave the object window empty.

Objective 5 | Save and Close a Database

When you close an Access table, any changes made to the records are saved automatically. If you change the design of the table or change the layout of the Datasheet view, such as adjusting the column widths, you will be prompted to save the design changes. At the end of your Access session, close your database and exit Access. If the Navigation Pane is open when you close Access, it will display when you reopen the database.

Activity 10.17 | Closing and Saving a Database

1 **Open** » the **Navigation Pane**. Notice that your report object displays with a green report icon. Compare your screen with Figure 10.37.

Figure 10.37

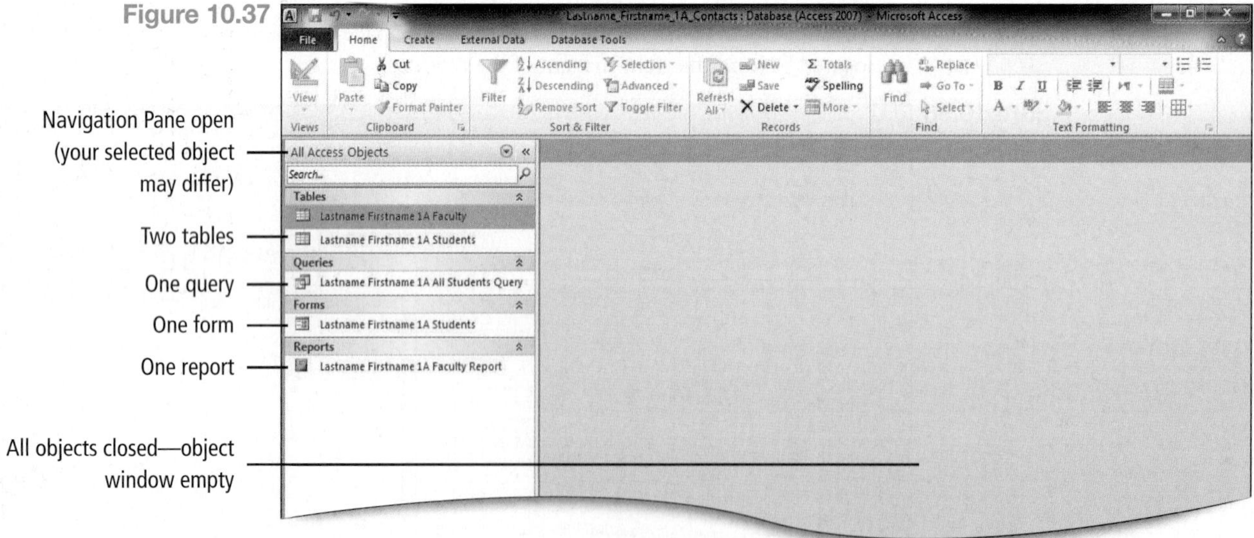

Another Way

In the upper right corner of the window, click the Close button.

2 Display **Backstage** view, click **Close Database**, and then click **Exit**. As directed by your instructor, submit your database and the five paper or electronic printouts—two tables, one query, one form, and one report—that are the results of this project.

End You have completed Project 10A

Project 10B Student Workshops Database

Project Activities

In Activities 10.18 through 10.23, you will assist Dr. Kirsten McCarty, Vice President of Student Services, by creating a database to store information about student workshops presented by Capital Cities Community College. You will use a database template that tracks event information, add workshop information to the database, and then print the results. Your completed report and table will look similar to Figure 10.38.

Project Files

For Project 10B, you will need the following files:

New Access database using the Events template
a01B_Workshops (Excel workbook)

You will save your database as:

Lastname_Firstname_1B_Student_Workshops

Project Results

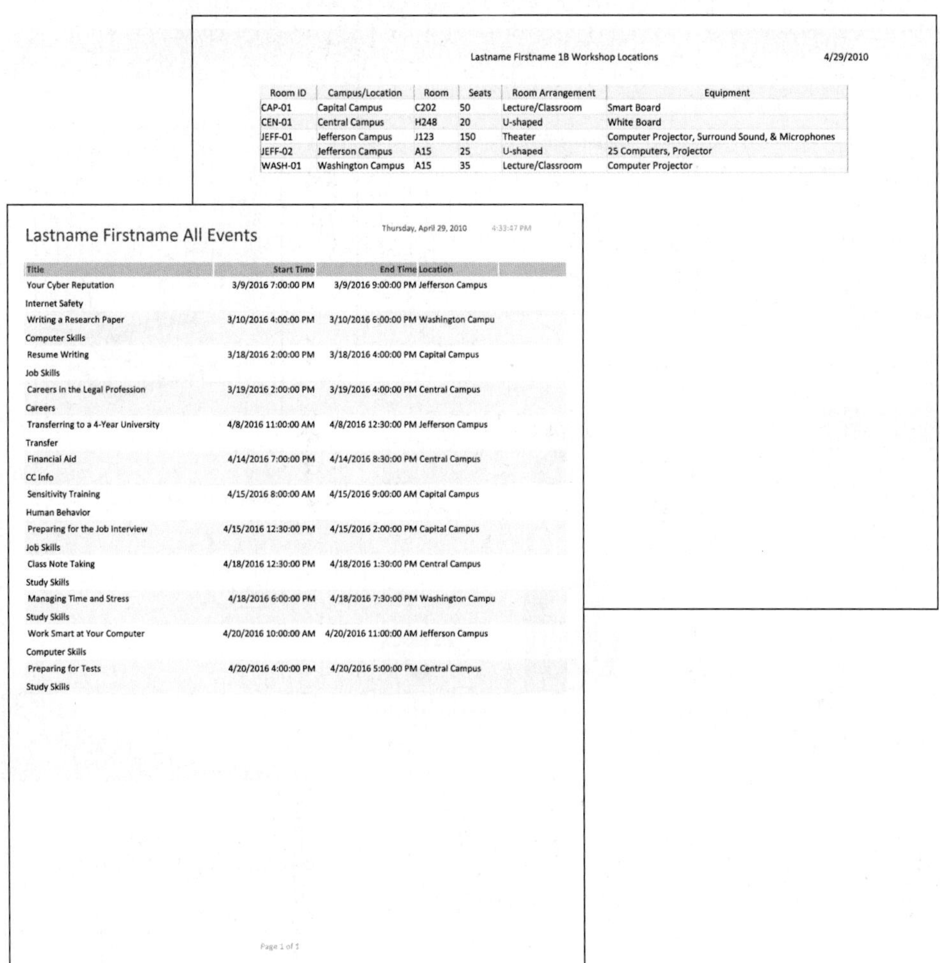

Lastname Firstname 1B Workshop Locations 4/29/2010

Room ID	Campus/Location	Room	Seats	Room Arrangement	Equipment
CAP-01	Capital Campus	C202	50	Lecture/Classroom	Smart Board
CEN-01	Central Campus	H248	20	U-shaped	White Board
JEFF-01	Jefferson Campus	J123	150	Theater	Computer Projector, Surround Sound, & Microphones
JEFF-02	Jefferson Campus	A15	25	U-shaped	25 Computers, Projector
WASH-01	Washington Campus	A15	35	Lecture/Classroom	Computer Projector

Lastname Firstname All Events — Thursday, April 29, 2010 4:33:47 PM

Title	Start Time	End Time	Location
Your Cyber Reputation	3/9/2016 7:00:00 PM	3/9/2016 9:00:00 PM	Jefferson Campus
Internet Safety			
Writing a Research Paper	3/10/2016 4:00:00 PM	3/10/2016 6:00:00 PM	Washington Campu
Computer Skills			
Resume Writing	3/18/2016 2:00:00 PM	3/18/2016 4:00:00 PM	Capital Campus
Job Skills			
Careers in the Legal Profession	3/19/2016 2:00:00 PM	3/19/2016 4:00:00 PM	Central Campus
Careers			
Transferring to a 4-Year University	4/8/2016 11:00:00 AM	4/8/2016 12:30:00 PM	Jefferson Campus
Transfer			
Financial Aid	4/14/2016 7:00:00 PM	4/14/2016 8:30:00 PM	Central Campus
CC Info			
Sensitivity Training	4/15/2016 8:00:00 AM	4/15/2016 9:00:00 AM	Capital Campus
Human Behavior			
Preparing for the Job Interview	4/15/2016 12:30:00 PM	4/15/2016 2:00:00 PM	Capital Campus
Job Skills			
Class Note Taking	4/18/2016 12:30:00 PM	4/18/2016 1:30:00 PM	Central Campus
Study Skills			
Managing Time and Stress	4/18/2016 6:00:00 PM	4/18/2016 7:30:00 PM	Washington Campu
Study Skills			
Work Smart at Your Computer	4/20/2016 10:00:00 AM	4/20/2016 11:00:00 AM	Jefferson Campus
Computer Skills			
Preparing for Tests	4/20/2016 4:00:00 PM	4/20/2016 5:00:00 PM	Central Campus
Study Skills			

Page 1 of 1

Figure 10.38
Project 10B Student Workshops

Objective 6 | Create a Database Using a Template

A ***database template*** contains pre-built tables, queries, forms, and reports to perform a specific task, such as tracking a large number of events. For example, your college may hold events such as athletic contests, plays, lectures, concerts, and club meetings. Using a predefined template, your college Activities Director can quickly create a database to manage these events. The advantage of using a template to start a new database is that you do not have to create the objects—all you need to do is enter your data and modify the pre-built objects to suit your needs.

The purpose of the database in this project is to track the student workshops offered by Capital Cities Community College. The questions to be answered might include:

What workshops will be offered and when will they be offered?

In what rooms and campus locations will the workshops be held?

Which workshop locations have a computer projector for PowerPoint presentations?

Activity 10.18 | Creating a New Database Using a Template

1 **Start** Access. Under **Available Templates**, click **Sample templates**. If necessary, scroll down to locate and then click **Events**. Compare your screen with Figure 10.39.

Sample templates are stored on your computer; they are included with the Access program.

Figure 10.39

2 On the right side of the screen, to the right of the **File Name** box, click the **Browse** button, and then navigate to your **Access Chapter 10** folder.

3 At the bottom of the **File New Database** dialog box, select the text in the **File name** box. Using your own name, type **Lastname_Firstname_1B_Student_Workshops** and then press Enter.

4 In the lower right corner of your screen, click the **Create** button.

Access creates the *1B Student Workshops* database, and the database name displays in the title bar. A predesigned *form*—Event List—displays in the object window. Although you can enter events for any date, when you open the database in the future, the Event List will display only those events for the current date and future dates.

5 Under the Ribbon, on the **Message Bar**, a Security Warning displays. On the **Message Bar**, click the **Enable Content** button.

Databases provided by Microsoft are safe to use on your computer.

Activity 10.19 | Building a Table by Entering Records in a Multiple Items Form

The purpose of a form is to simplify the entry of data into a table—either for you or for others who enter data. In Project 2A, you created a simple form that enabled you to display or enter records in a table one record at a time. The Events template creates a ***Multiple Items form***, a form that enables you to display or enter *multiple* records in a table, but still with an easier and simplified layout than typing directly into the table itself.

1 Click in the first empty **Title** field. Type **Your Cyber Reputation** and then press Tab. In the **Start Time** field, type **3/9/16 7p** and then press Tab.

Access formats the date and time. As you enter dates and times, a small calendar displays to the right of the field, which you can click to select a date instead of typing.

2 In the **End Time** field, type **3/9/16 9p** and then press Tab. In the **Description** field, type **Internet Safety** and then press Tab. In the **Location** field, type **Jefferson Campus** and then press Tab three times to move to the **Title** field in the new record row. Compare your screen with Figure 10.40.

Because the workshops have no unique value, Access uses the AutoNumber data type of the ID field to assign a unique, sequential number to each record. In the navigation area, each record is identified as a task, rather than a record or page.

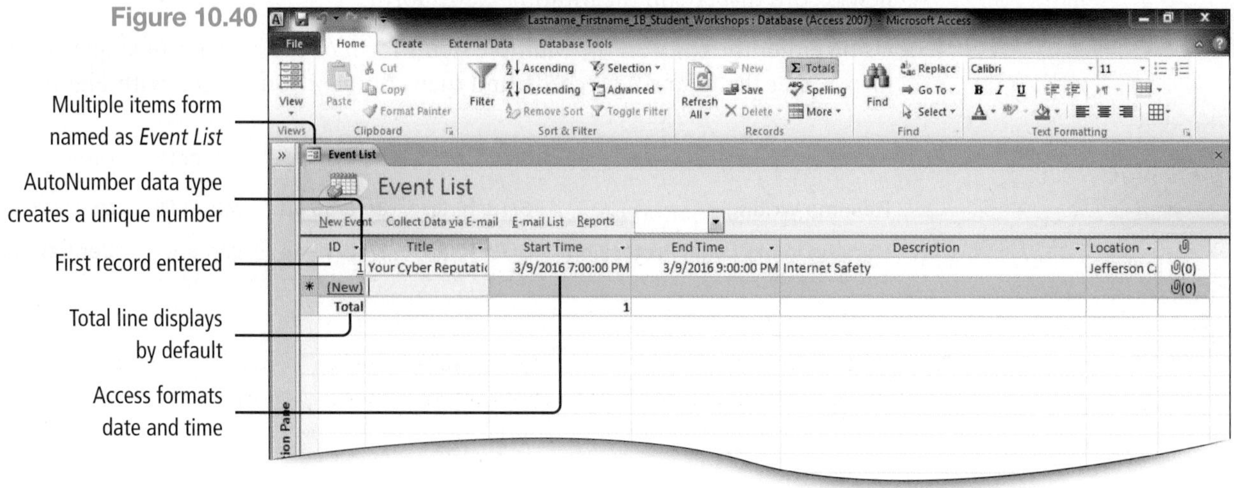

Figure 10.40

3 Directly above the field names row, click **New Event**.

A ***single-record form*** displays, similar to the simple form you created in Project 2A. A single-record form enables you to display or enter one record at a time into a table.

4 Using Tab to move from field to field, enter the following record—press Tab three times to move from the **End Time** field to the **Description** field. Compare your screen with Figure 10.41.

Title	Location	Start Time	End Time	Description
Writing a Research Paper	**Washington Campus**	**3/10/16 4p**	**3/10/16 6p**	**Computer Skills**

Figure 10.41

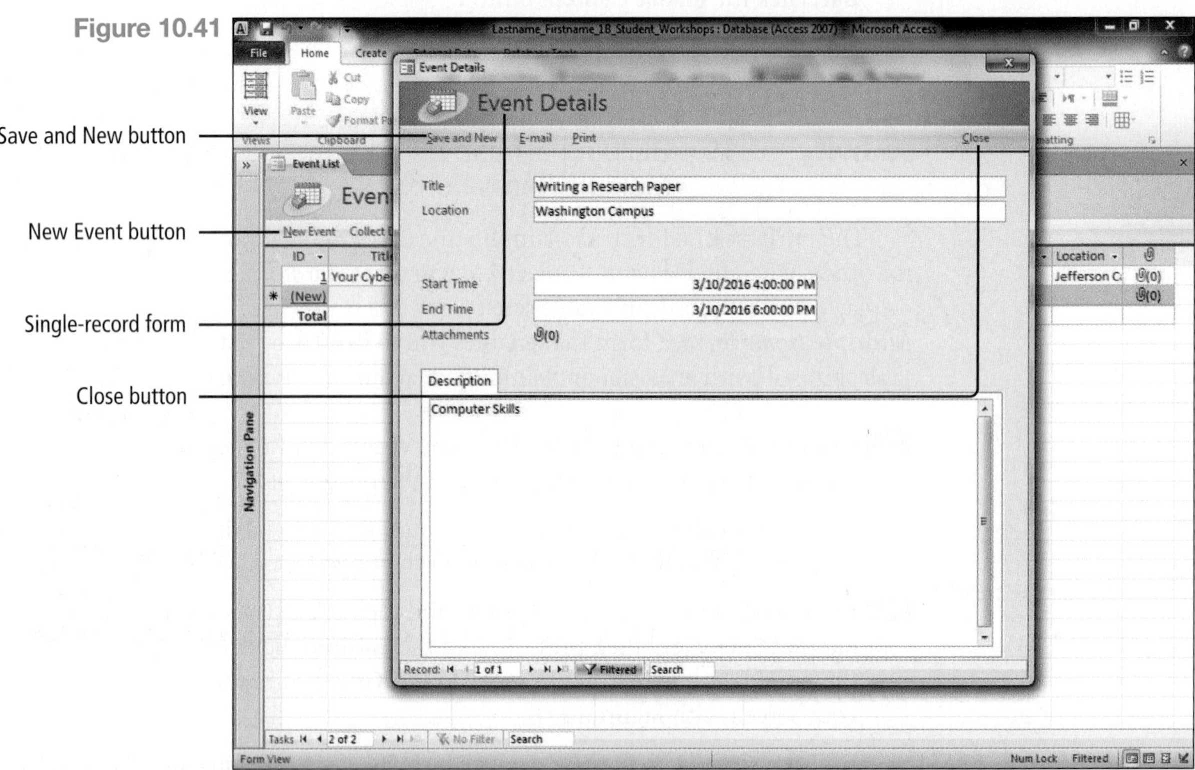

5 In the upper right corner of the single-record form, click **Close**, and notice that the new record displays in the Multiple Items form.

6 Using either the rows on the Multiple Items form or the New Event single-record form, enter the following records, and then compare your screen with Figure 10.42.

ID	Title	Start Time	End Time	Description	Location
3	**Resume Writing**	**3/18/16 2p**	**3/18/16 4p**	**Job Skills**	**Capital Campus**
4	**Careers in the Legal Profession**	**3/19/16 2p**	**3/19/16 4p**	**Careers**	**Central Campus**

> **Alert! | Does a Single Record Form Open?**
>
> In the Multiple Items form, pressing Enter three times at the end of a row to begin a new record may display the single-record New Event form. If you prefer to use the Multiple Items form, close the single-record form and continue entering records, using the Tab key to move from field to field.

Figure 10.42

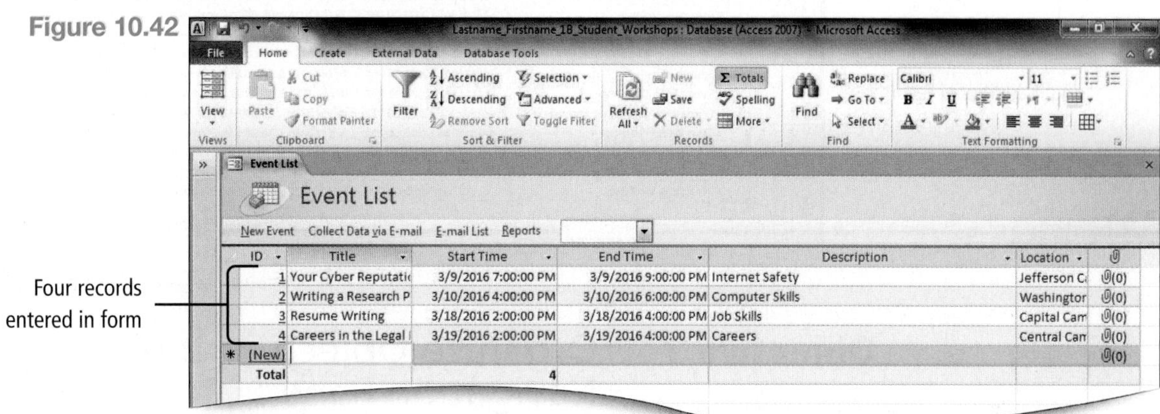

7 In the upper right corner of the object window, click **Close** [X] to close the **Event List** form.

8 On the Ribbon, click the **External Data tab**. In the **Import & Link group**, click the **Excel** button.

Recall that you can populate a table by importing data from an Excel workbook.

9 In the **Get External Data – Excel Spreadsheet** dialog box, click the **Browse** button. Navigate to your student files, and then double-click **a01B_Workshops**.

10 Click the second option button—**Append a copy of the records to the table**—and then click **OK**.

11 Click **Next**, click **Finish**, and then **Close** the dialog box.

12 **Open** [»] the **Navigation Pane**. Double-click **Event List** to open the form that displays data stored in the Events table, and then **Close** [«] the **Navigation Pane**.

13 To the left of the **ID** field name, click the **Select All** button to select all of the columns.

> **Another Way**
>
> With the columns selected, in the field heading row, point to the right edge of any of the selected columns, and then double-click to apply Best Fit to all of the selected columns.

14 In the field names row, point to any of the selected field names, right-click, and then click **Field Width**. In the **Column Width** dialog box, click **Best Fit**. Notice that the widths of all of the columns are adjusted to accommodate the longest entry in the column.

15 In the first record, click in the **Title** field to deselect the columns. **Save** the form, and then compare your screen with Figure 10.43.

Eight additional records display—those imported from the a01B_Workshops Excel workbook.

Figure 10.43

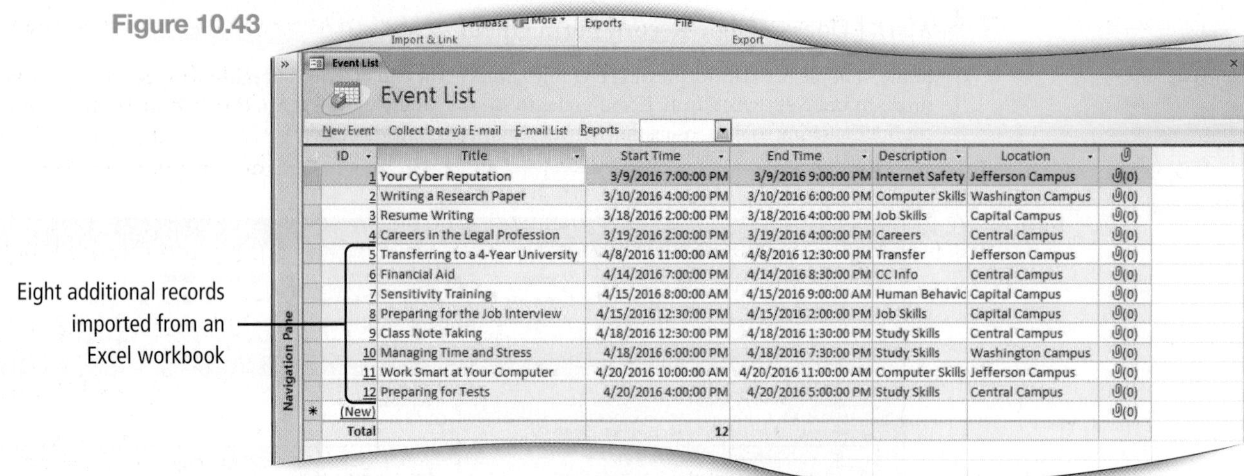

Objective 7 | Organize Objects in the Navigation Pane

Use the Navigation Pane to organize database objects, to open them, and to perform common tasks like renaming an object.

Activity 10.20 | Organizing Database Objects in the Navigation Pane

The Navigation Pane groups and displays your database objects and can do so in predefined arrangements. In this activity, you will group your database objects using the ***Tables and Related Views*** category, which groups objects by the table to which they are related. This grouping is useful because you can easily determine the data source table of queries, forms, and reports.

1 **Open** [»] the **Navigation Pane**. At the top of the **Navigation Pane**, click the **Navigation arrow** [▾]. In the list, under **Navigate To Category**, click **Tables and Related Views**.

2 Confirm that *Events* displays in the bar under the Search box at the top of the **Navigation Pane**. Compare your screen with Figure 10.44.

The icons to the left of the objects listed in the Navigation Pane indicate that the Events template created a number of objects for you—among them, one table titled *Events*, one query, two forms, and five reports. The Event List Multiple Items form, which is currently displayed in the object window, is included in the Navigation Pane. All of the objects were created using the underlying data source, which is the Events table.

Figure 10.44

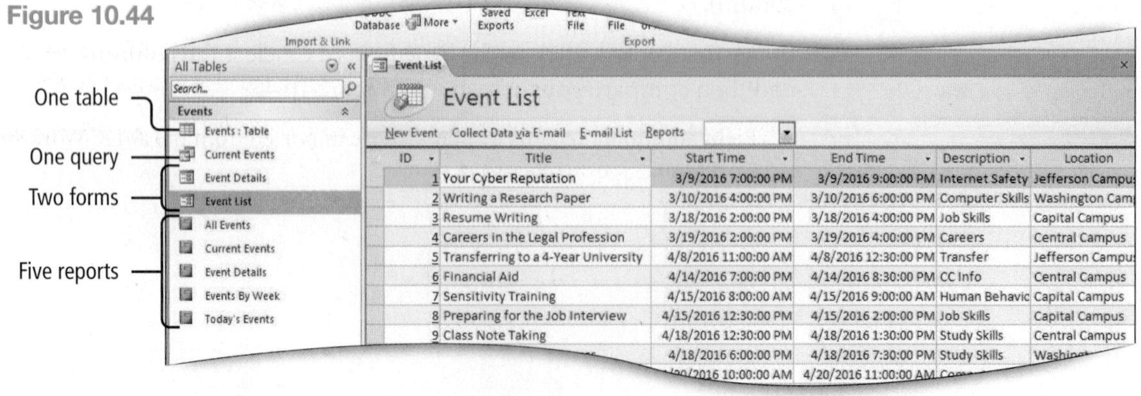

Another Way

Double-click the table name to open it in the object window.

3 In the **Navigation Pane**, point to the **Events** *table*, right-click, and then click **Open**.

The Events table is the active object in the object window. Use the Navigation Pane to open objects for use. The 12 records that you entered using the Multiple Items *form* and by importing from an Excel workbook display in the *table*. Tables are the foundation of your database because your data must be stored in a table. You can enter records directly into a table or you can use a form to enter records.

4 In the object window, click the **Event List tab** to bring the form into view and make it the active object.

Recall that a form presents a more user-friendly screen for entering records into a table.

Another Way

Double-click the report name to open it.

5 In the **Navigation Pane**, right-click the *report* (green icon) named **Current Events**, and then click **Open**. Compare your screen with Figure 10.45.

An advantage of using a template to begin a database is that many objects, such as attractively formatted reports, are already designed for you.

Figure 10.45

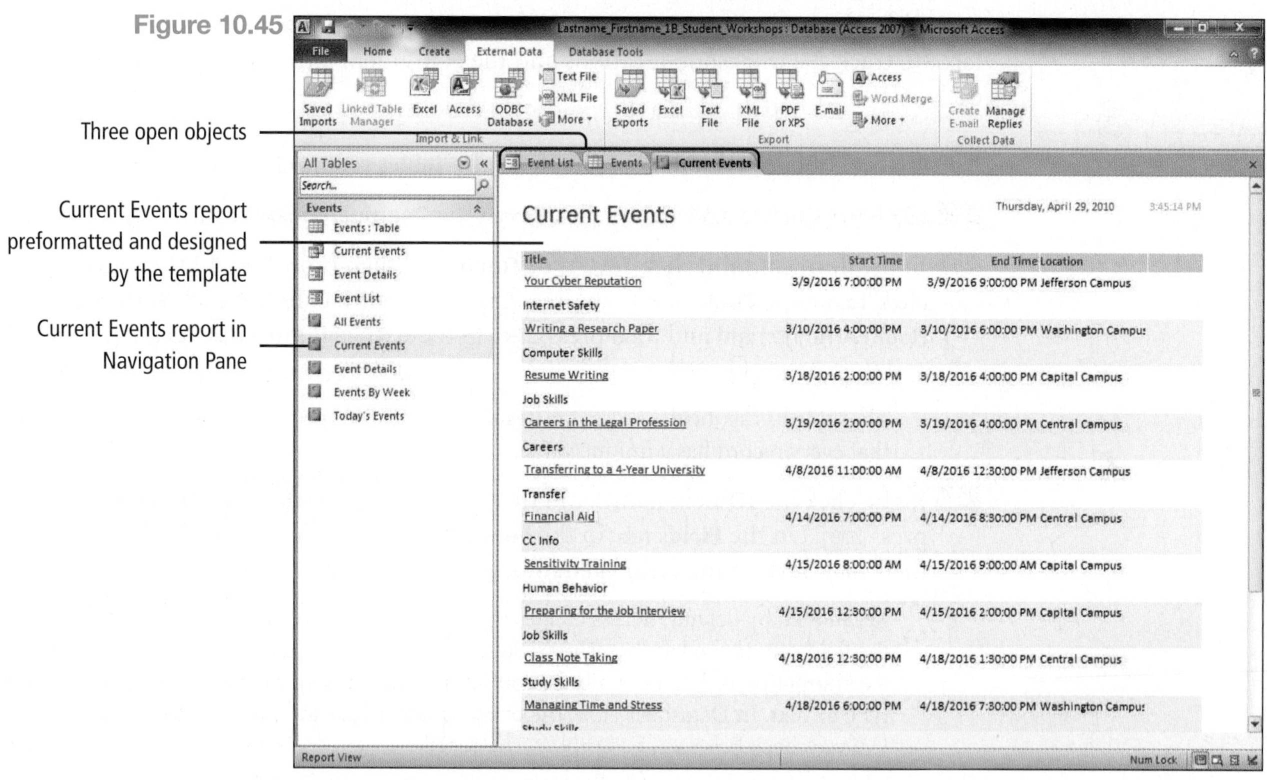

6 In the object window, **Close** [X] the **Current Events** report.

7 From the **Navigation Pane**, open the **Events By Week** report.

In this predesigned report, the events are displayed by week. After entering records in the form or table, the preformatted reports are updated with the records from the table.

8 **Close** [X] the **Events By Week** report, and then **Close** [X] the remaining two open objects. **Close** [«] the **Navigation Pane**.

Objective 8 | Create a New Table in a Database Created with a Template

The Events database template created only one table—the *Events* table. Although the database was started from a template and contains other objects, you can add additional objects as needed.

Activity 10.21 | Creating a New Table and Changing Its Design

Dr. McCarty has information about the various locations where workshops are held. For example, for the Jefferson campus, she has information about the room, seating arrangements, number of seats, and audio-visual equipment. In the Events table, workshops are scheduled in rooms at each of the four campuses. It would not make sense to store information about the campus rooms multiple times in the same table. It is *not* considered good database design to have duplicate information in a table.

When data in a table becomes redundant, it is usually an indication that you need a new table to contain the information about the topic. In this activity, you will create a table to track the workshop locations and the equipment and seating arrangements in each location.

1. On the Ribbon, click the **Create tab**. In the **Tables group**, click the **Table** button.

2. Click the **Click to Add arrow**, click **Text**, type **Campus/Location** and then press Enter.

3. In the third column, click **Text**, type **Room** and then press Enter. In the fourth column, click **Text**, type **Seats** and then press Enter. In the fifth column, click **Text**, type **Room Arrangement** and then press Enter. In the sixth column, click **Text**, type **Equipment** and then press ↓.

   The table has six fields. Access creates the first field in the table—the ID field—to ensure that every record has a unique value.

4. Right-click the **ID** field name, and then click **Rename Field**. Type **Room ID** and then press Enter. On the **Fields tab**, in the **Formatting group**, click the **Data Type arrow**, and then click **Text**. In the **Field Validation group**, notice that **Unique** is selected.

   Recall that, by default, Access creates the ID field with the AutoNumber data type so that the field can be used as the primary key. Here, this field will store a unique room ID that is a combination of letters, symbols, and numbers, so it is appropriate to change the data type to Text. In Datasheet view, the primary key field is identified by the selection of the Unique check box.

5 In the new record row, click in the **Room ID** field, type **JEFF-01** and then press Tab. In the **Campus/Location** field, type **Jefferson Campus** and then press Tab. In the **Room** field, type **J123** and then press Tab. In the **Seats** field, type **150** and then press Tab. In the **Room Arrangement** field, type **Theater** and then press Tab. In the **Equipment** field, type **Computer Projector, Surround Sound, & Microphones** and then press Tab to move to the new record row. Compare your screen with Figure 10.46.

Recall that Access saves the record when you move to another row within the table. You can press either Tab or Enter to move to another field in a table.

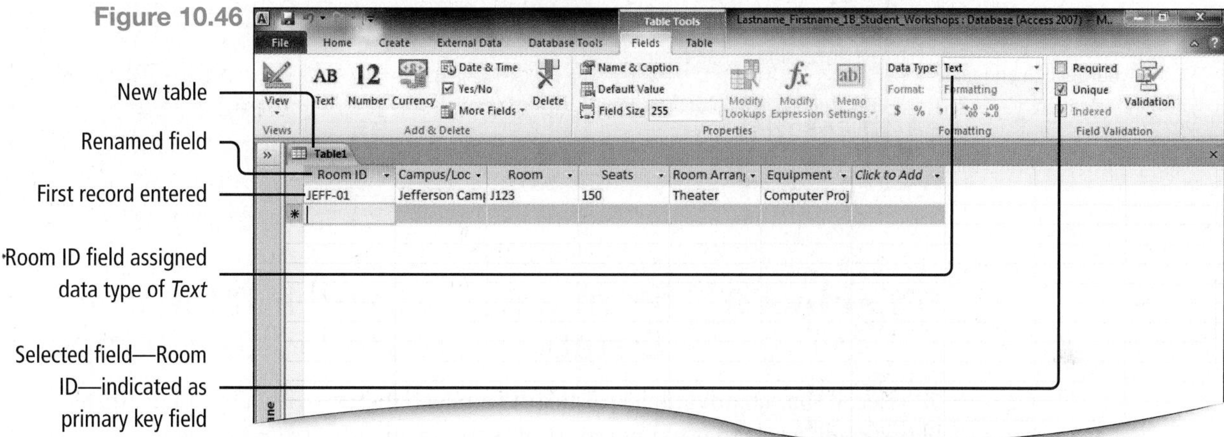

Figure 10.46

6 In the **Views group**, click the **View** button to switch to **Design** view. In the **Save As** dialog box, save the table as **Lastname Firstname 1B Workshop Locations** and then click **OK**.

7 In the **Field Name** column, to the left of the **Room ID** box, notice the key icon.

In Design view, the key icon indicates the field—Room ID—that is identified as the primary key.

8 In the **Views group**, click the **View** button to switch to **Datasheet** view.

9 Enter the following records in the table:

Room ID	Campus/Location	Room	Seats	Room Arrangement	Equipment
WASH-01	**Washington Campus**	**A15**	**35**	**Lecture/Classroom**	**Computer Projector**
CAP-01	**Capital Campus**	**C202**	**50**	**Lecture/Classroom**	**Smart Board**
CEN-01	**Central Campus**	**H248**	**20**	**U-shaped**	**White Board**
JEFF-02	**Jefferson Campus**	**A15**	**25**	**U-shaped**	**25 Computers, Projector**

10 To the left of the **Room ID** field name, click the **Select All** button to select all of the columns. On the **Home tab**, in the **Records group**, click the **More** button. Click **Field Width**, and in the **Column Width** dialog box, click **Best Fit**. Click in any field to remove the selection, and then **Save** the changes to the table. In the object window, **Close** the **1B Workshop Locations** table.

11 **Open** the **Navigation Pane**, and then locate the name of your new table. Point to the right edge of the **Navigation Pane** to display the pointer. Drag to the right to display the entire table name, and then compare your screen with Figure 10.47.

Recall that as currently arranged, the Navigation Pane organizes the objects by Tables and Related Views. In Figure 10.47, the Events table is listed first, followed by its related objects, and then the Workshop Locations table is listed. In its current view, the tables are sorted in ascending order by name; therefore, your table may be listed before the Events table depending on your last name.

Figure 10.47

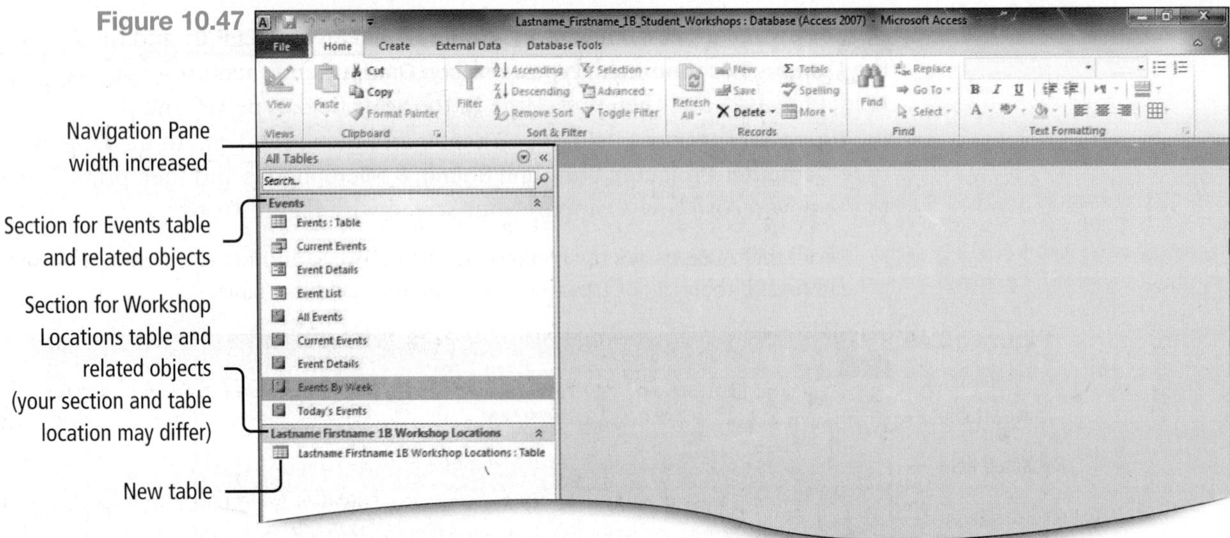

Objective 9 | Print a Report and a Table in a Database Created with a Template

Recall that an advantage to starting a new database with a template, instead of from a blank database, is that many report objects are already created for you.

Activity 10.22 | Viewing and Printing a Report

1 From the **Navigation Pane**, open the **Event Details** *report* (not the form).

The pre-built Event Details report displays in an attractively arranged format.

2 **Close** the **Event Details** report. Open the **All Events** report. In the lower right corner of the status bar, click the **Layout View** button. At the top of the report, click on the text *All Events* to display a colored border, and then click to the left of the letter *A* to place the insertion point there. Using your own name, type **Lastname Firstname** and then press Spacebar. Press Enter, and then **Save** the report.

Each report displays the records in the table in different useful formats.

> **Another Way**
> Right-click the object tab, and then click Print Preview.

3 Display **Backstage** view, click **Print**, and then click **Print Preview**. In the navigation area, notice that the navigation arrows are dimmed, which indicates that this report will print on one page.

4 Create a paper or electronic printout as instructed, **Close Print Preview**, and then **Close** the report.

Activity 10.23 | Printing a Table

When printing a table, use the Print Preview command to determine if the table will print on one page or if you need to adjust column widths, margins, or the orientation. Recall that there will be occasions when you want to print a table for a quick reference or for proofreading. For a more professional-looking format, and for more options to format the output, create and print a report.

1 From the **Navigation Pane**, open your **1B Workshop Locations** table. **Close** « the **Navigation Pane**. Display **Backstage** view, click **Print**, and then click **Print Preview**.

The table displays in the Print Preview window, showing how it will look when it is printed. The name of the table and the date the table is printed display at the top of the page. The navigation area displays *1* in the Pages box, and the right-pointing arrow—the Next Page arrow—is active. Recall that when a table is in the Print Preview window, the navigation arrows are used to navigate from one page to the next, rather than from one record to the next.

2 In the navigation area, click the **Next Page** button ▸.

The second page of the table displays the last field column. Whenever possible, try to print all of the fields horizontally on one page. Of course, if there are many records, more than one page may be needed to print all of the records.

3 On the **Print Preview tab**, in the **Page Layout group**, click the **Landscape** button, and then compare your screen with Figure 10.48. Notice that the entire table will print on one page.

Figure 10.48

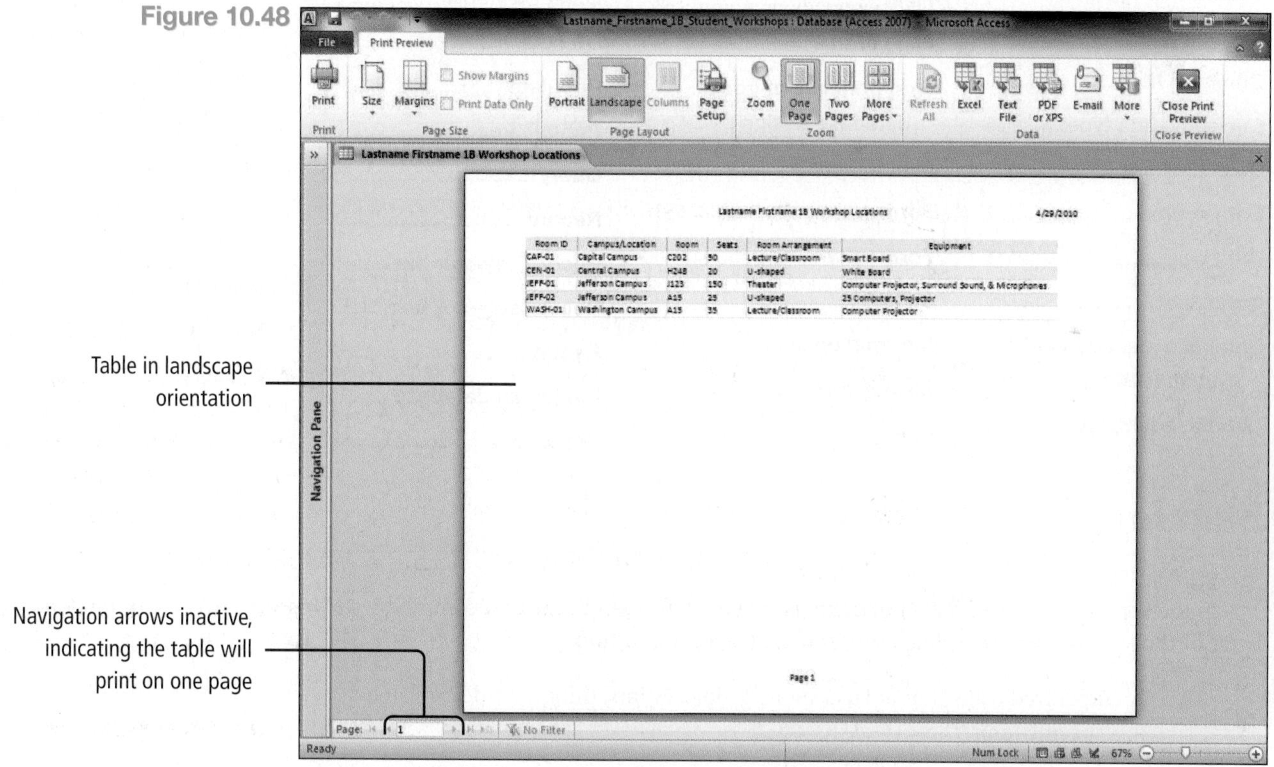

4 Create a paper or electronic printout if instructed to do so, and then **Close Print Preview**.

5 **Close** ✕ the **1B Workshop Locations** table. For the convenience of the next person opening the database, **Open** » the **Navigation Pane**. In **Backstage** view, click **Close Database**, and then click **Exit** to close the Access program. As directed by your instructor, submit your database and the two paper or electronic printouts—one report and one table—that are the results of this project.

End **You have completed Project 10B**

Content-Based Assessments

Summary

Microsoft Access 2010 is a database management system that uses various objects—tables, forms, queries, reports—to organize information. Data is stored in tables in which you establish fields, set the data type and field size, and create a primary key. Data from a database can be reported and printed.

Key Terms

- **Append** 539
- **AutoNumber data type** 536
- **Best Fit** 548
- **Blank database** 531
- **Caption** 536
- **Common field** 530
- **Currency data type** 535
- **Data** 529
- **Data source** 552
- **Data type** 534
- **Database** 529
- **Database management system (DBMS)** 529
- **Database template** 530
- **Datasheet view** 534
- **DBMS** 529
- **Design view** 534
- **Destination table** 540
- **Field** 529
- **Field properties** 543
- **First principle of good database design** 530
- **Flat database** 529
- **Form** 552
- **Form view** 556
- **Import** 539
- **Information** 529
- **Layout view** 555
- **Link** 539
- **Multiple Items form** 561
- **Navigation area** 541
- **Navigation Pane** 534
- **Normalization** 530
- **Object window** 534
- **Objects** 531
- **Populate** 537
- **Primary key** 544
- **Query** 552
- **Record** 529
- **Record selector bar** 556
- **Record selector box** 537
- **Redundant** 530
- **Relational database** 529
- **Report** 552
- **Run** 554
- **Second principle of good database design** 530
- **Select query** 552
- **Simple select query** 552
- **Single-record form** 562
- **Source file** 539
- **Structure** 534
- **Table** 529
- **Tables and Related Views** 546
- **Text data type** 535
- **Truncated** 544
- **Wizard** 552

Matching

Match each term in the second column with its correct definition in the first column by writing the letter of the term on the blank line in front of the correct definition.

A Common field
B Data
C Database
D Field
E First principle of good database design
F Flat database
G Information
H Navigation Pane
I Normalization
J Object window
K Objects
L Populate
M Record
N Second principle of good database design
O Table

____ 1. An organized collection of facts about people, events, things, or ideas related to a specific topic.

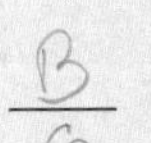

____ 2. Facts about people, events, things, or ideas.

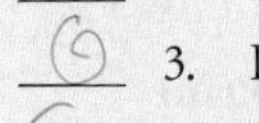

____ 3. Data that is organized in a useful manner.

____ 4. A simple database file that is not related or linked to any other collection of data.

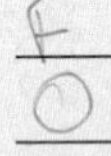

____ 5. The database object that stores the data, and which is the foundation of an Access database.

____ 6. A table row that contains all of the categories of data pertaining to one person, place, thing, event, or idea.

____ 7. A single piece of information that is stored in every record and represented by a column in a table.

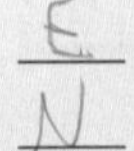

____ 8. A principle stating that data is organized in tables so that there is no redundant data.

____ 9. A principle stating that techniques are used to ensure the accuracy of data entered into a table.

Content-Based Assessments

____ 10. The process of applying design rules and principles to ensure that a database performs as expected.

____ 11. A field in one or more tables that stores the same data.

____ 12. The basic parts of a database; for example tables, forms, queries, and reports.

____ 13. The window area that organizes the database objects and from which you open objects.

____ 14. The window area that displays each open object on its own tab.

____ 15. The action of filling a database with records.

Multiple Choice

Circle the correct answer.

1. The Access view that displays data in columns and rows like an Excel worksheet is:
   A. Datasheet view **B.** Design view **C.** Layout view
2. The characteristic that defines the kind of data you can enter into a field is the:
   A. data source **B.** data type **C.** field property
3. The box at the left of a record in Datasheet view that you click to select an entire record is the:
   A. link **B.** navigation area **C.** record selector box
4. To add on to the end of an object, such as to add records to the end of an existing table, is to:
   A. append **B.** import **C.** run
5. Characteristics of a field that control how the field displays and how data is entered are:
   A. data sources **B.** data types **C.** field properties
6. The field that uniquely identifies a record in a table is known as the:
   A. attachments field **B.** common field **C.** primary key
7. The underlying design of a table is referred to as the:
   A. caption **B.** source file **C.** structure
8. The object that retrieves specific data and then displays only the data that you specify is a:
   A. form **B.** query **C.** report
9. The object that displays fields and records from a table or query in a printable format is a:
   A. form **B.** query **C.** report
10. Information repeated in a database in a manner that indicates poor design is said to be:
    A. relational **B.** redundant **C.** truncated

Content-Based Assessments

Apply 10A skills from these Objectives:

1. Identify Good Database Design
2. Create a Table and Define Fields in a New Database
3. Change the Structure of Tables and Add a Second Table
4. Create and Use a Query, Form, and Report
5. Save and Close a Database

Skills Review | Project 10C Work Study Students Database

In the following Skills Review, you will create a database to store information about the Work Study students and the divisions in which they are employed. Your completed database objects will look similar to Figure 10.49.

Project Files

For Project 10C, you will need the following files:

New blank Access database
a01C_Student_Workers (Excel workbook)
a01C_Divisions (Excel workbook)

You will save your database as:

Lastname_Firstname_1C_Student_Workers

Project Results

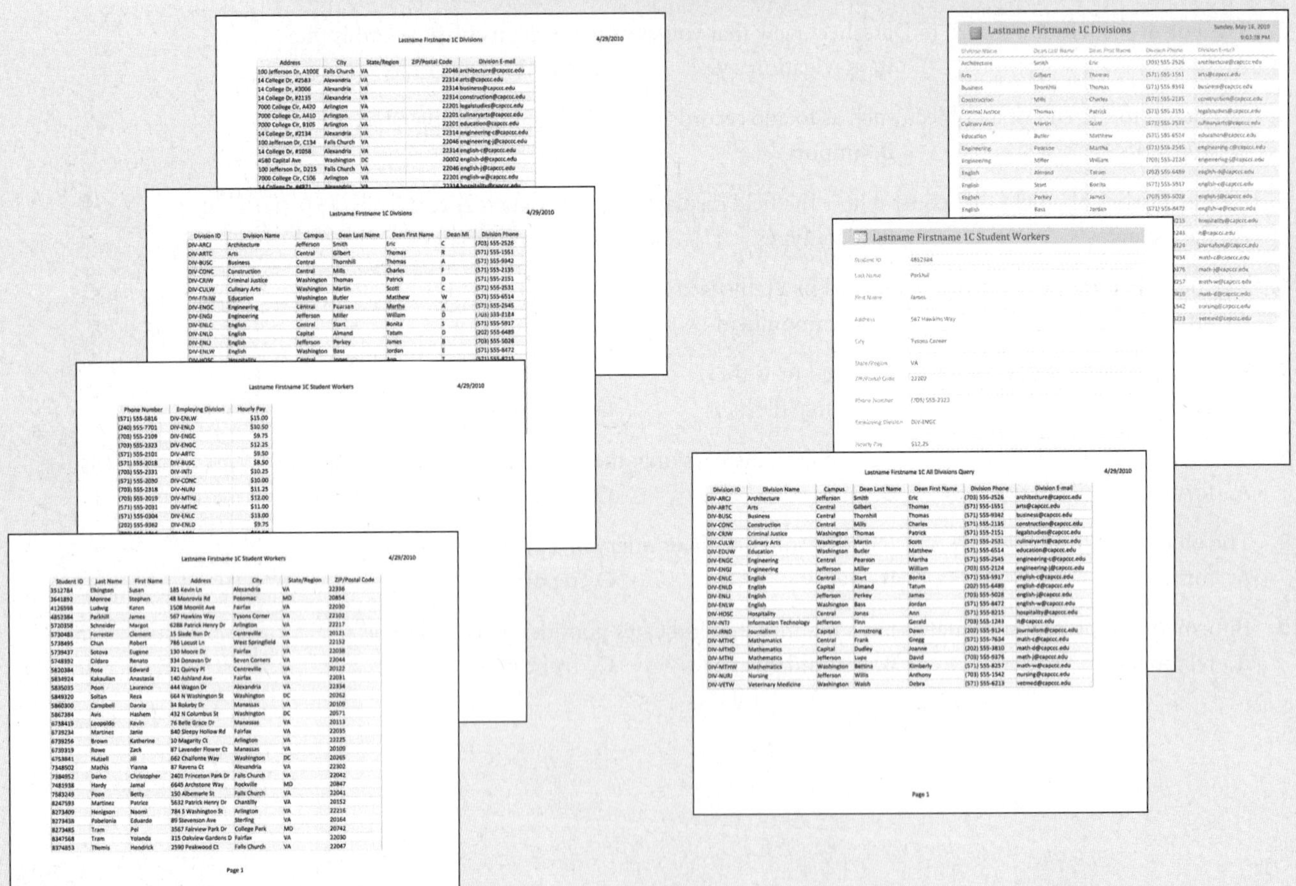

Figure 10.49

(Project 10C Work Study Students Database continues on the next page)

Skills Review | Project 10C Work Study Students Database (continued)

1 **Start** Access. Click **Blank database**, and then in the lower right corner, click the **Browse** button. In the **File New Database** dialog box, navigate to your **Access Chapter 10** folder, and then in the **File name** box, replace the existing text with **Lastname_Firstname_1C_Student_Workers** Press Enter, and then in the lower right corner, click **Create**.

a. **Close** the **Navigation Pane**. Click in the text *Click to Add*. Click **Text**, type **Last Name** and then press Enter.

b. In the third field name box, click **Text**, type **First Name** and then press Enter. In the fourth field name box, click **Text**, type **Middle Initial** and then press Enter. Create the remaining fields as shown in **Table 1**, pressing Enter after the last field name.

c. Scroll as necessary to view the first field. Click the **ID** field name. In the **Properties group**, click the **Name & Caption** button. In the **Enter Field Properties** dialog box, in the **Name** box, change *ID* to **Student ID** and then click **OK**. In the **Formatting group**, click the **Data Type arrow**, and then click **Text**.

d. In the first record row, click in the **Student ID** field, type **3512784** and press Enter. In the **Last Name** field, type **Elkington** In the **First Name** field, type **Susan** In the **Middle Initial** field, type **A** In the **Address** field, type **185 Kevin Ln**

e. Continue entering data in the fields as shown in **Table 2**, pressing Enter to move to the next field and to the next row.

f. Click **Save**, and then in the **Table Name** box, using your own name, replace the selected text by typing **Lastname Firstname 1C Student Workers** and then click **OK**.

2 Scroll, if necessary, to view the first field. In the new record row, click in the **Student ID** field, and then enter the information for two additional students as shown in **Table 3**, pressing Enter to move from field to field.

a. **Close** your **1C Student Workers** table. On the **External Data tab**, in the **Import & Link group**, click the **Excel** button. In the **Get External Data - Excel Spreadsheet** dialog box, click the **Browse** button. In the **File Open** dialog box, navigate to your student data files, and then double-click the **a01C_Student_Workers** Excel file.

b. **Append a copy of the records to the table**, and then click **OK**. Click **Next**, click **Finish**, and then click **Close**. **Open** the **Navigation Pane**, and then widen it so that you can view the entire table name. In the **Navigation Pane**, double-click your **1C Student Workers** table to open it, and then **Close** the **Navigation Pane**—30 total records display.

Table 1

Data Type					Text	Text	Text	Text	Text	Text	Currency
Field Name	ID	Last Name	First Name	Middle Initial	**Address**	**City**	**State/Region**	**ZIP/Postal Code**	**Phone Number**	**Employing Division**	**Hourly Pay**

(Return to Step 1-c)

Table 2

City	State/Region	ZIP/Postal Code	Phone Number	Employing Division	Hourly Pay
Alexandria	**VA**	**22336**	**(571) 555-5816**	**DIV-ENLW**	**15**

(Return to Step 1-f)

Table 3

Student ID	Last Name	First Name	Middle Initial	Address	City	State/Region	ZIP/Postal Code	Phone Number	Employing Division	Hourly Pay
3641892	**Monroe**	**Stephen**	**D**	**48 Monrovia Rd**	**Potomac**	**MD**	**20854**	**(240) 555-7701**	**DIV-ENLD**	**10.5**
4126598	**Ludwig**	**Karen**	**E**	**1508 Moonlit Ave**	**Fairfax**	**VA**	**22030**	**(703) 555-2109**	**DIV-ENGC**	**9.75**

(Return to Step 2-a)

(Project 10C Work Study Students Database continues on the next page)

Content-Based Assessments

Skills Review | Project 10C Work Study Students Database (continued)

3 Click the **Home tab**, and then in the **Views group**, click the **View** button to switch to **Design** view.

a. To the left of **Middle Initial**, point to the row selector box, and then click to select the entire row. On the **Design tab**, in the **Tools group**, click the **Delete Rows** button, and then click **Yes**.

b. Click anywhere in the **State/Region** field name, and then under **Field Properties**, set the **Field Size** to **2** In the **State/Region** row, click in the **Description** box, and then type **Two-character state abbreviation**

c. Click in the **Student ID** field name box, set the **Field Size** to **7** and in the **Description** box, type **Seven-digit Student ID** Then **Save** the design of your table; click **Yes**. On the **Design tab**, in the **Views group**, click the **View** button to switch to **Datasheet** view.

4 On the Ribbon, click the **External Data tab**, and then in the **Import & Link group**, click the **Excel** button. In the **Get External Data – Excel Spreadsheet** dialog box, click the **Browse** button. Navigate to your student data files, and then double-click **a01C_Divisions**. Be sure that the **Import the source data into a new table in the current database** option button is selected, and then click **OK**.

a. In the **Import Spreadsheet Wizard** dialog box, click to select the **First Row Contains Column Headings** check box, and then click **Next**.

b. Click **Next** again. Click the **Choose my own primary key** option button, and to the right, be sure that *Division ID* displays. Click **Next**. In the **Import to Table** box, type **Lastname Firstname 1C Divisions** and then click **Finish**. Click **Close**, **Open** the **Navigation Pane**, and then open your **1C Divisions** table. **Close** the **Navigation Pane**—22 records display.

c. At the top of the object window, click the **1C Student Workers tab**. To the left of the **Student ID** field name, click the **Select All** button. Click the **Home tab**, and in the **Records group**, click the **More** button. Click **Field Width**, and in the **Column Width** dialog box, click **Best Fit**. Click in any field, and then **Save** the table.

d. Display **Backstage** view, click **Print**, and then click **Print Preview**. In the **Page Layout group**, click the **Landscape** button. Create a paper or electronic printout as directed by your instructor; two pages result. Click **Close Print Preview**, and then **Close** your **1C Student Workers** table.

e. With your **1C Divisions** table displayed, to the left of the **Division ID** field name, click the **Select All** button, and then apply **Best Fit** to all of the columns. Click in any field, **Save** the table, and then display the table in **Print Preview**. Change the **Orientation** to **Landscape**. Create a paper or electronic printout as directed—two pages result. **Close Print Preview**, and then **Close** your **1C Divisions** table.

5 On the **Create tab**, in the **Queries group**, click the **Query Wizard** button. In the **New Query** dialog box, click **Simple Query Wizard**, and then click **OK**. Click the **Tables/Queries arrow**, and then be sure your **Table: 1C Divisions** is selected.

a. Under **Available Fields**, click **Division ID**, and then click the **Add Field** button to move the field to the **Selected Fields** list on the right. Using either the **Add Field** button or by double-clicking, add the following fields to the **Selected Fields** list: **Division Name**, **Campus**, **Dean Last Name**, **Dean First Name**, **Division Phone**, and **Division E-mail**. The query will answer the question, *What is the Division ID, Division Name, Campus, Dean's name, Division Phone number, and Division E-mail address of every division?*

b. Click **Next**. In the **Simple Query Wizard** dialog box, change the query title to **Lastname Firstname 1C All Divisions Query** and then click **Finish** to run the query.

c. Display the query in **Print Preview**. Change the **Orientation** to **Landscape**. In the **Page Size group**, click the **Margins** button, and then click **Normal**. Create a paper or electronic printout as directed—one page results. **Close Print Preview**, and then **Close** the query.

d. **Open** the **Navigation Pane**, open your **1C Student Workers** table, and then **Close** the **Navigation Pane**. The table contains 10 fields. On the **Create tab**, in the **Forms group**, click the **Form** button. Click **Save**, and then in the **Save As** dialog box, accept the default name for the form—*Lastname Firstname 1C Student Workers*—by clicking **OK**. In the navigation area, click the **Next record** button three times to display the record for *James Parkhill*. At the left edge of the form, click the gray **record selector bar** to select only this record. By using the instructions in Activity 10.15, print or create an electronic printout of this record as directed. **Close** the form object. Your **1C Student Workers** table object remains open.

(Project 10C Work Study Students Database continues on the next page)

Skills Review | Project 10C Work Study Students Database (continued)

6 **Open** the **Navigation Pane**, open your **1C Divisions** table, and then **Close** the **Navigation Pane**. On the **Create tab**, in the **Reports group**, click the **Report** button. In the field names row at the top of the report, click the **Division ID** field name. On the Ribbon, click the **Arrange tab**. In the **Rows & Columns group**, click the **Select Column** button, and then press Del. Using the same technique, delete the **Campus** field.

a. Scroll to position the **Dean MI** field at the left of your screen, and click the field name **Dean MI**. Hold down Ctrl, and then click the field names for **Address**, **City**, **State/Region**, and **ZIP/Postal Code**. On the **Arrange tab**, in the **Rows & Columns group**, click the **Select Column** button, and then press Del.

b. Scroll to the left, and then click in the **Dean Last Name** field name. By using the ↔ pointer, decrease the width of the field until there is about **0.25 inch** of space between the **Dean Last Name** field and the **Dean First Name** field. Decrease the widths of the **Dean First Name** and **Division Phone** fields in a similar manner. In the **Division E-mail** field, click in the first record—the data in the field displays on two lines. Increase the width of the field slightly so that each record's data in the field displays on one line. Be sure that the width of the report is within the dotted boundaries.

c. Click the **Division Name** field name. On the Ribbon, click the **Home tab**. In the **Sort & Filter group**, click the **Ascending** button to sort the report in alphabetic order by Division Name.

d. **Save** the report as **Lastname Firstname 1C Divisions Report** and then click **OK**. Display the report in **Print Preview**. In the **Zoom group**, click the **Two Pages** button, and notice that the report will print on two pages because the page number is beyond the right margin of the report. **Close Print Preview**. With the report displayed in **Layout** view, scroll down and to the right to display the page number—**Page 1 of 1**. Click the page number, press Del, and then **Save** the changes to the report.

e. Display the report in **Print Preview**, and notice that the report will print on one page. In the **Zoom group**, click the **One Page** button. Create a paper or electronic printout of the report as directed. Click **Close Print Preview**. Along the top of the object window, right click any **object tab**, and then click **Close All** to close all of the open objects, leaving the object window empty.

f. **Open** the **Navigation Pane**. If necessary, increase the width of the **Navigation Pane** so that all object names display fully. Display **Backstage** view, click **Close Database**, and then click **Exit**. As directed by your instructor, submit your database and the five paper or electronic printouts—two tables, one query, one form, and one report—that are the results of this project.

End **You have completed Project 10C**

Apply 10B skills from these Objectives:

6. Create a Database Using a Template
7. Organize Objects in the Navigation Pane
8. Create a New Table in a Database Created with a Template
9. Print a Report and a Table in a Database Created with a Template

Skills Review | Project 10D Benefits Events

In the following Skills Review, you will create a database to store information about Employee Benefit Events at Capital Cities Community College. Your completed report and table will look similar to Figure 10.50.

Project Files

For Project 10D, you will need the following files:

New Access database using the Events template
a01D_Benefits_Events (Excel workbook)

You will save your database as:

Lastname_Firstname_1D_Benefits_Events

Project Results

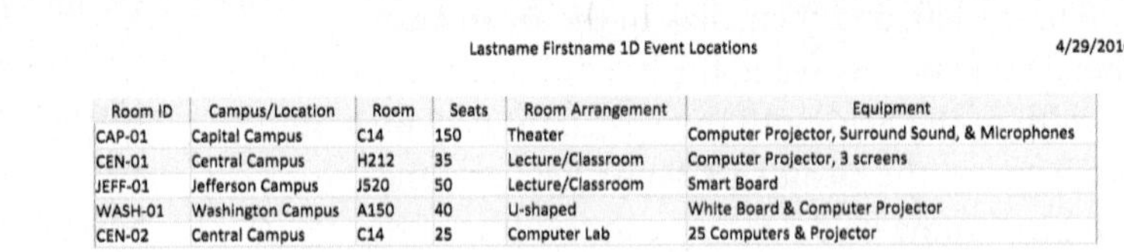

Lastname Firstname 1D Event Locations 4/29/2010

Room ID	Campus/Location	Room	Seats	Room Arrangement	Equipment
CAP-01	Capital Campus	C14	150	Theater	Computer Projector, Surround Sound, & Microphones
CEN-01	Central Campus	H212	35	Lecture/Classroom	Computer Projector, 3 screens
JEFF-01	Jefferson Campus	J520	50	Lecture/Classroom	Smart Board
WASH-01	Washington Campus	A150	40	U-shaped	White Board & Computer Projector
CEN-02	Central Campus	C14	25	Computer Lab	25 Computers & Projector

Page 1

Lastname Firstname All Events

Thursday, April 29, 2010 7:03:33 PM

Title	Start Time	End Time	Location
Medical Plan	5/2/2016 8:00:00 AM	5/2/2016 1:00:00 PM	Jefferson Campus
Health Benefits			
Eye Care Plan	5/2/2016 2:00:00 PM	5/2/2016 4:00:00 PM	Washington Campu
Health Benefits			
Prescription Plan	5/3/2016 8:00:00 AM	5/3/2016 10:00:00 AM	Capital Campus
Health Benefits			
Pension Plan	5/3/2016 2:00:00 PM	5/3/2016 4:00:00 PM	Central Campus
Retirement Benefits			
Life Insurance Plan	5/4/2016 10:00:00 AM	5/4/2016 12:00:00 PM	Capital Campus
Life Insurance Benefits			
Deferred Compensation Plan	5/4/2016 3:00:00 PM	5/4/2016 5:00:00 PM	Capital Campus
Compensation Benefits			
Dental Plan	5/5/2016 9:00:00 AM	5/5/2016 11:00:00 AM	Central Campus
Health Benefits			
Medical Plan	5/5/2016 1:00:00 PM	5/5/2016 3:00:00 PM	Central Campus
Health Benefits			
Medical Plan	5/6/2016 8:00:00 AM	5/6/2016 11:00:00 AM	Washington Campu
Health Benefits			
Long Term Disability	5/6/2016 10:00:00 AM	5/6/2016 11:30:00 AM	Jefferson Campus
Health Benefits			
Annuity Options	5/6/2016 2:00:00 PM	5/6/2016 4:00:00 PM	Jefferson Campus
Retirement Benefits			

Page 1 of 1

Figure 10.50

(Project 10D Benefits Events continues on the next page)

Skills Review | Project 10D Benefits Events (continued)

1 **Start** Access. Under **Available Templates**, click **Sample templates**, and then click **Events**. On the right, to the right of the **File Name** box, click the **Browse** button, and then navigate to your **Access Chapter 10** folder.

a. Select the text in the **File name** box, and then using your own information, type **Lastname_Firstname_1D_Benefits_Events** and then press Enter. In the lower right corner of your screen, click the **Create** button. If necessary, click Enable Content.

b. Click in the first empty **Title** field, type **Medical Plan** and then press Tab. In the **Start Time** field, type **5/2/16 8a** and then press Tab.

c. In the **End Time** field, type **5/2/16 1p** and then press Tab. In the **Description** field, type **Health Benefits** and then press Tab. In the **Location** field, type **Jefferson Campus** and then press Tab three times to move to the **Title** field in the new record row.

d. Directly above the field names row, click **New Event**, and then using Tab to move from field to field, enter the record shown in **Table 1** by using the single-record form, which is another way to enter records into a table.

e. **Close** the single-record form. Using either the rows on the Multiple Items form or the New Event single-record form, enter the records shown in **Table 2**.

f. **Close** the **Event List** form. On the Ribbon, click the **External Data tab**, and in the **Import & Link group**, click the **Excel** button. In the **Get External Data – Excel Spreadsheet** dialog box, click the **Browse** button. Navigate to your student data files, and then double-click **a01D_Benefits_Events**. Click the second option button—**Append a copy of the records to the table**—and then click **OK**.

g. Click **Next**, click **Finish**, and then **Close** the dialog box. **Open** the **Navigation Pane**, and then double-click **Event List** to open the form that displays data stored in the Events table—11 total records display.

2 At the top of the **Navigation Pane**, click the **Navigation arrow**. In the list, under **Navigate To Category**, click **Tables and Related Views**.

a. In the **Navigation Pane**, point to the **Events** *table*, right-click, and then click **Open** to display the records in the underlying table.

b. In the **Navigation Pane**, double-click the *report* named **Current Events** to view this predesigned report. From the **Navigation Pane**, open the **Events By Week** report to view this predesigned report.

c. **Close** the **Events By Week** report, and then **Close** the remaining three open objects. **Close** the **Navigation Pane**.

3 On the **Create tab**, in the **Tables group**, click the **Table** button.

a. Click the **Click to Add arrow**, click **Text**, type **Campus/Location** and then press Enter. In the third column, click **Text**, type **Room** and then press Enter. In the fourth column, click **Text**, type **Seats** and then press Enter. In the fifth column, click **Text**, type **Room Arrangement** and then press Enter. In the sixth column, click **Text**, type **Equipment** and then press ↓.

b. Right-click the **ID** field name, and then click **Rename Field**. Type **Room ID** and then press Enter. On the **Fields tab**, in the **Formatting group**, click the **Data Type arrow**, and then click **Text**.

c. In the new record row, click in the **Room ID** field, type **CAP-01** and then press Tab. In the **Campus/Location** field, type **Capital Campus** and then press Tab. In the **Room** field, type **C14** and then press Tab. In the **Seats** field, type **150** and then press Tab. In the **Room Arrangement** field, type **Theater** and then press Tab. In the **Equipment** field, type **Computer Projector, Surround Sound, & Microphones** and then press Tab to move to the new record row.

Table 1

Title	Location	Start Time	End Time	Description
Eye Care Plan	**Washington Campus**	**5/2/16 2p**	**5/2/16 4p**	**Health Benefits**

(Return to Step 1-e)

Table 2

ID	Title	Start Time	End Time	Description	Location
3	**Prescription Plan**	**5/3/16 8a**	**5/3/16 10a**	**Health Benefits**	**Capital Campus**
4	**Pension Plan**	**5/3/16 2p**	**5/3/16 4p**	**Retirement Benefits**	**Central Campus**

(Return to Step 1-f)

(Project 10D Benefits Events continues on the next page)

Skills Review | Project 10D Benefits Events (continued)

d. In the **Views group**, click the **View** button to switch to **Design** view. In the **Save As** dialog box, save the table as **Lastname Firstname 1D Event Locations** and then click **OK**. Notice that the **Room ID** field is the **Primary Key**.

e. On the **Design tab**, in the **Views group**, click the **View** button to switch to **Datasheet** view. Enter the records in the table as shown in **Table 3**.

f. To the left of the **Room ID** field name, click the **Select All** button to select all of the columns. On the **Home tab**, in the **Records group**, click the **More** button. In the **Column Size** dialog box, click **Best Fit**.

g. Click in any record to cancel the selection of the columns, and then **Save** the table. **Open** the **Navigation Pane**, and then widen the pane to view the full names of all objects.

4 **Open** the **All Events** report, and then **Close** the **Navigation Pane**. In the lower right corner, click the **Layout View** button. At the top of the report, click the text *All Events* to surround the title with a colored border, and then click to the left of the letter *A* to place the insertion point there. Using your own name, type **Lastname Firstname** and then press Spacebar and Enter. **Save** the report.

a. Display **Backstage** view, click **Print**, and then click **Print Preview**. Notice that the entire report will print on one page in portrait orientation. Create a paper or electronic printout if instructed to do so, and then click **Close Print Preview**. **Close** the **All Events** report.

b. With the **1D Event Locations** table open in **Datasheet** view, display **Backstage** view, click **Print**, and then click **Print Preview**. On the **Print Preview tab**, in the **Page Layout group**, click the **Landscape** button, and then notice that the entire table will print on one page.

c. Create a paper or electronic printout if instructed to do so, and then click **Close Print Preview**. **Close** the **1D Event Locations** table.

d. **Open** the **Navigation Pane**. Display **Backstage** view, click **Close Database**, and then click **Exit**. As directed by your instructor, submit your database and the two paper or electronic printouts—one report and one table—that are the results of this project.

Table 3

Room ID	Campus/Location	Room	Seats	Room Arrangement	Equipment
CEN-01	Central Campus	H212	35	Lecture/Classroom	Computer Projector, 3 screens
JEFF-01	Jefferson Campus	J520	50	Lecture/Classroom	Smart Board
WASH-01	Washington Campus	A150	40	U-shaped	White Board & Computer Projector
CEN-02	Central Campus	C14	25	Computer Lab	25 Computers & Projector

(Return to Step 3-f)

End **You have completed Project 10D**

Apply 10A skills from these Objectives:

1. Identify Good Database Design
2. Create a Table and Define Fields in a New Database
3. Change the Structure of Tables and Add a Second Table
4. Create and Use a Query, Form, and Report
5. Save and Close a Database

Mastering Access | Project 10E Kiosk Inventory

In the following Mastering Access project, you will create a database to track information about the inventory of items for sale in the kiosk located on the quad at the Central Campus of Capital Cities Community College. Your completed database objects will look similar to those in Figure 10.51.

Project Files

For Project 10E, you will need the following files:

New blank Access database
a01E_Inventory (Excel workbook)
a01E_Inventory_Storage (Excel workbook)

You will save your database as:

Lastname_Firstname_1E_Inventory

Project Results

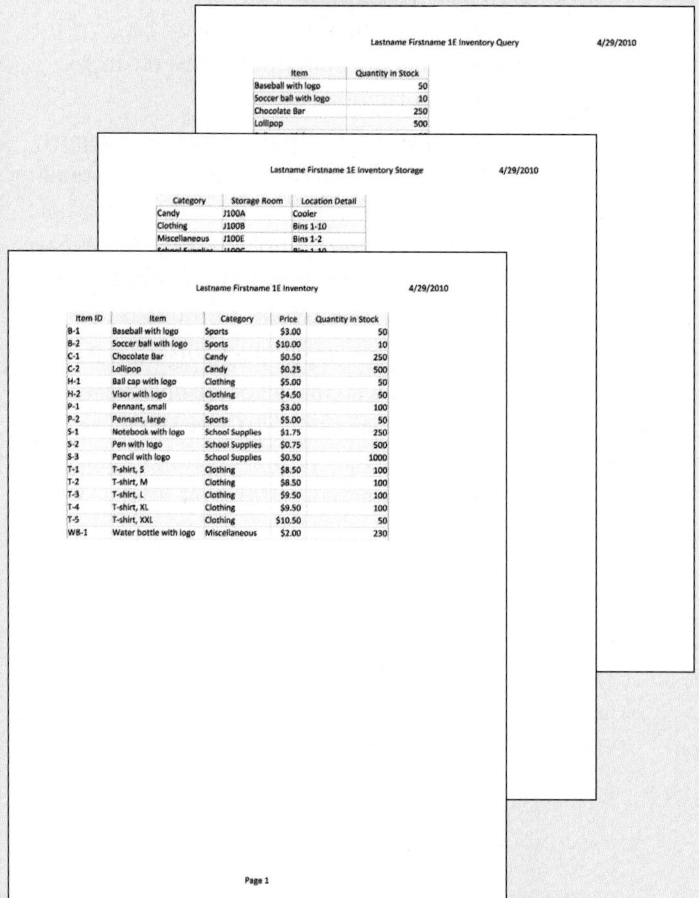

Lastname Firstname 1E Inventory Query 4/29/2010

Item	Quantity in Stock
Baseball with logo	50
Soccer ball with logo	10
Chocolate Bar	250
Lollipop	500

Lastname Firstname 1E Inventory Storage 4/29/2010

Category	Storage Room	Location Detail
Candy	J100A	Cooler
Clothing	J100B	Bins 1-10
Miscellaneous	J100E	Bins 1-2

Lastname Firstname 1E Inventory 4/29/2010

Item ID	Item	Category	Price	Quantity in Stock
B-1	Baseball with logo	Sports	$3.00	50
B-2	Soccer ball with logo	Sports	$10.00	10
C-1	Chocolate Bar	Candy	$0.50	250
C-2	Lollipop	Candy	$0.25	500
H-1	Ball cap with logo	Clothing	$5.00	50
H-2	Visor with logo	Clothing	$4.50	50
P-1	Pennant, small	Sports	$3.00	100
P-2	Pennant, large	Sports	$5.00	50
S-1	Notebook with logo	School Supplies	$1.75	250
S-2	Pen with logo	School Supplies	$0.75	500
S-3	Pencil with logo	School Supplies	$0.50	1000
T-1	T-shirt, S	Clothing	$8.50	100
T-2	T-shirt, M	Clothing	$8.50	100
T-3	T-shirt, L	Clothing	$9.50	100
T-4	T-shirt, XL	Clothing	$9.50	100
T-5	T-shirt, XXL	Clothing	$10.50	50
WB-1	Water bottle with logo	Miscellaneous	$2.00	230

Page 1

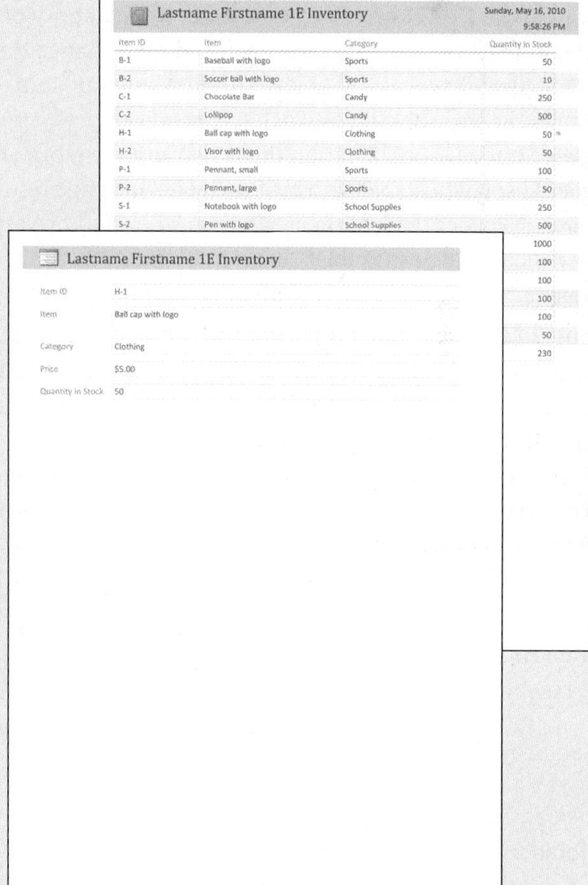

Lastname Firstname 1E Inventory Sunday, May 16, 2010 9:58:26 PM

Item ID	Item	Category	Quantity in Stock
B-1	Baseball with logo	Sports	50
B-2	Soccer ball with logo	Sports	10
C-1	Chocolate Bar	Candy	250
C-2	Lollipop	Candy	500
H-1	Ball cap with logo	Clothing	50
H-2	Visor with logo	Clothing	50
P-1	Pennant, small	Sports	100
P-2	Pennant, large	Sports	50
S-1	Notebook with logo	School Supplies	250
S-2	Pen with logo	School Supplies	500
			1000
			100
			100
			100
			100
			50
			230

Lastname Firstname 1E Inventory

Item ID	H-1
Item	Ball cap with logo
Category	Clothing
Price	$5.00
Quantity in Stock	50

Figure 10.51

(Project 10E Kiosk Inventory continues on the next page)

Mastering Access | Project 10E Kiosk Inventory (continued)

1 **Start** Access. Create a new **Blank database** in your **Access Chapter 10** folder. Name the database **Lastname_Firstname_1E_Inventory** and then **Close** the **Navigation Pane**. Create additional fields as shown in **Table 1**.

2 Change the **Data Type** of the **ID** field to **Text**, rename the field to **Item ID** and then enter the records as shown in **Table 2**.

3 **Save** the table as **Lastname Firstname 1E Inventory** and then **Close** the table. From your student data files, **Import** and then **Append** the **a01E_Inventory** Excel file to the **1E Inventory** table. Then, from the **Navigation Pane**, open your **1E Inventory** table—17 records display. Widen and then **Close** the **Navigation Pane**.

4 In **Design** view, delete the **Storage Location** field. Click in the **Category** field, change the **Field Size** to **25** and in the **Description** box, type **Enter the category of the Item** Click in the **Item ID** field, and then change the **Field Size** to **10** **Save** the changes to the design of your table, click **Yes**, and then switch to **Datasheet** view. Apply **Best Fit** to all of the fields in the table, **Save** the table, and then display the table in **Print Preview**—one page results. Create a paper or electronic printout as directed by your instructor. **Close** the table.

5 From your student data files, **Import** the **a01E_Inventory_Storage** Excel file into the database as a new table; use the first row as the column headings and the **Category** field as the primary key. As the last step in the Wizard, name the table **Lastname Firstname 1E Inventory Storage** and then **Open** the **Navigation Pane**. **Open** your **1E Inventory Storage** table, and then **Close** the **Navigation Pane**. Display the new table in **Design** view, click in the **Location Detail** field, change the **Field Size** to **30** and then as the **Description**, type **Enter room and bin numbers or alternate location of inventory item.** In **Datasheet** view, apply **Best Fit** to all of the fields, **Save** the table, and then display the table in **Print Preview**. Create a paper or electronic printout as directed—one page results. **Close** the table.

6 **Create**, by using the **Query Wizard**, a **Simple Query** based on your **1E Inventory** table. Include only the fields that will answer the question *For all Items, what is the Quantity in Stock?* **Save** the query with the default name. Create a paper or electronic printout as directed and then **Close** the query.

7 Display the **1E Inventory** table, and then **Create** a **Form** for this table. **Save** the form as **Lastname Firstname 1E Inventory Form** Display and then select the fifth record. By using the instructions in Activity 10.15, print or create an electronic printout of only this record as directed. **Close** the form object.

8 With the **1E Inventory** table open, **Create** a **Report**. **Delete** the **Price** field, and then sort the records in **Ascending** order by the **Item ID** field. Scroll down to the bottom of the report and delete the page number—**Page 1 of 1**. **Save** the report as **Lastname Firstname 1E Inventory Report** and then create a paper or electronic printout as directed.

9 **Close All** open objects. **Open** the **Navigation Pane**. If necessary, widen the pane so that all of the object names display fully. In **Backstage** view, click **Close Database** and then click **Exit**. As directed by your instructor, submit your database and the five paper or electronic printouts—two tables, one query, one form, and one report—that are the results of this project.

Table 1

Data Type		Text	Text	Text	Currency	Number
Field Name	ID	**Item**	**Category**	**Storage Location**	**Price**	**Quantity in Stock**

(Return to Step 2)

Table 2

Item ID	Item	Category	Storage Location	Price	Quantity in Stock
C-1	**Chocolate Bar**	**Candy**	**J100A**	**.5**	**250**
C-2	**Lollipop**	**Candy**	**J100A**	**.25**	**500**
T-1	**T-shirt, S**	**Clothing**	**J100B**	**8.5**	**100**

(Return to Step 3)

End **You have completed Project 10E**

Content-Based Assessments

Apply **10B** skills from these Objectives:

6. Create a Database Using a Template
7. Organize Objects in the Navigation Pane
8. Create a New Table in a Database Created with a Template
9. Print a Report and a Table in a Database Created with a Template

Mastering Access | Project **10F** Recruiting Events

In the following Mastering Access project, you will create a database to store information about the recruiting events that are scheduled to attract new students to Capital Cities Community College. Your completed report and table will look similar to those in Figure 10.52.

Project Files

For Project 10F, you will need the following files:

New Access database using the Events template
a01F_Recruiting_Events (Excel workbook)

You will save your database as:

Lastname_Firstname_1F_Recruiting_Events

Project Results

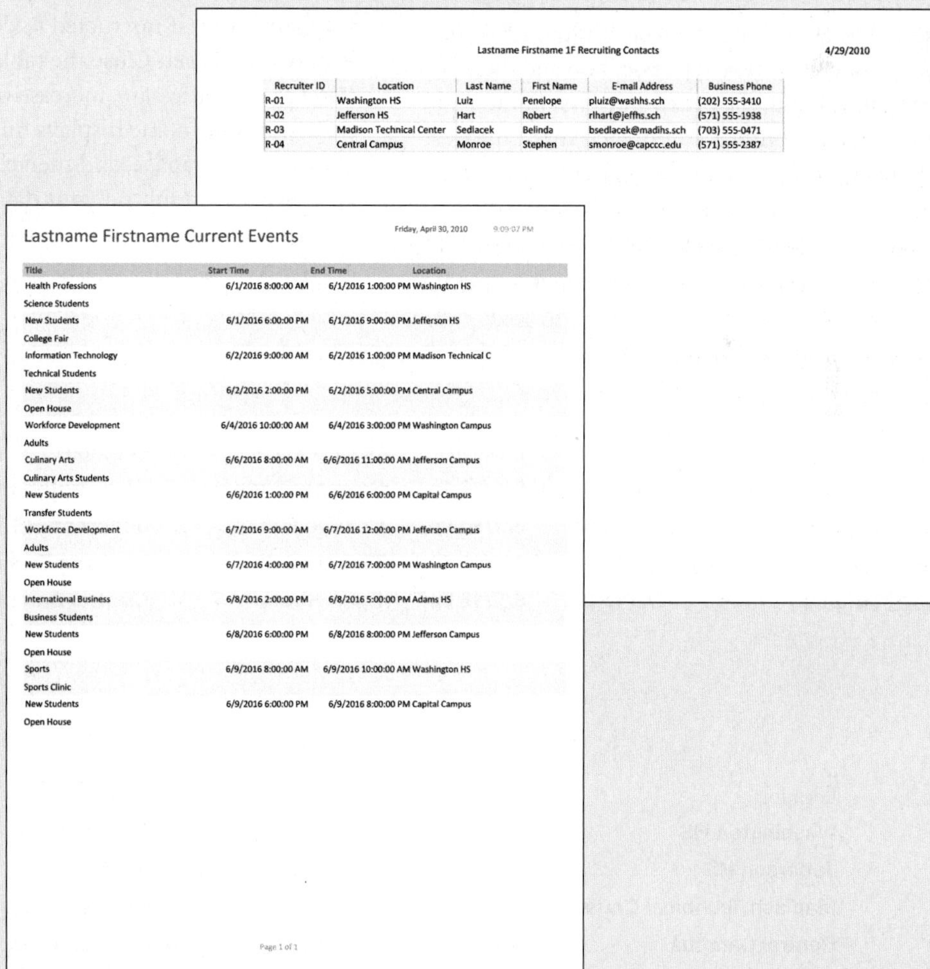

Lastname Firstname 1F Recruiting Contacts 4/29/2010

Recruiter ID	Location	Last Name	First Name	E-mail Address	Business Phone
R-01	Washington HS	Luiz	Penelope	pluiz@washhs.sch	(202) 555-3410
R-02	Jefferson HS	Hart	Robert	rlhart@jeffhs.sch	(571) 555-1938
R-03	Madison Technical Center	Sedlacek	Belinda	bsedlacek@madihs.sch	(703) 555-0471
R-04	Central Campus	Monroe	Stephen	smonroe@capccc.edu	(571) 555-2387

Lastname Firstname Current Events Friday, April 30, 2010 9:09:07 PM

Title	Start Time	End Time	Location
Health Professions Science Students	6/1/2016 8:00:00 AM	6/1/2016 1:00:00 PM	Washington HS
New Students College Fair	6/1/2016 6:00:00 PM	6/1/2016 9:00:00 PM	Jefferson HS
Information Technology Technical Students	6/2/2016 9:00:00 AM	6/2/2016 1:00:00 PM	Madison Technical C
New Students Open House	6/2/2016 2:00:00 PM	6/2/2016 5:00:00 PM	Central Campus
Workforce Development Adults	6/4/2016 10:00:00 AM	6/4/2016 3:00:00 PM	Washington Campus
Culinary Arts Culinary Arts Students	6/6/2016 8:00:00 AM	6/6/2016 11:00:00 AM	Jefferson Campus
New Students Transfer Students	6/6/2016 1:00:00 PM	6/6/2016 6:00:00 PM	Capital Campus
Workforce Development Adults	6/7/2016 9:00:00 AM	6/7/2016 12:00:00 PM	Jefferson Campus
New Students Open House	6/7/2016 4:00:00 PM	6/7/2016 7:00:00 PM	Washington Campus
International Business Business Students	6/8/2016 2:00:00 PM	6/8/2016 5:00:00 PM	Adams HS
New Students Open House	6/8/2016 6:00:00 PM	6/8/2016 8:00:00 PM	Jefferson Campus
Sports Sports Clinic	6/9/2016 8:00:00 AM	6/9/2016 10:00:00 AM	Washington HS
New Students Open House	6/9/2016 6:00:00 PM	6/9/2016 8:00:00 PM	Capital Campus

Page 1 of 1

Figure 10.52

(Project 10F Recruiting Events continues on the next page)

Mastering Access | Project 10F Recruiting Events (continued)

1 **Start** Access, click **Sample templates**, and then click **Events**. In your **Access Chapter 10** folder, save the database as **Lastname_Firstname_1F_Recruiting_Events** If necessary, enable the content.

2 In the Multiple Items form or the New Event single-record form, enter the records shown in **Table 1** into the Events table.

3 **Close** the **Event List** form, and then click the **External Data tab**. **Import** and **Append** the **Excel** file **a01F_Recruiting_Events** to the **Events** table. **Open** the **Navigation Pane**, organize the objects by **Tables and Related Views**, and then **Open** your **Events** table to view 13 records. **Close** the **Navigation Pane**. Apply **Best Fit** to all of the fields, **Save** the table, and then **Close** the table.

4 **Create** a new table using the **Table** button. Click the **Click to Add arrow**, click **Text**, type **Location** and then press Enter. In the third column, click **Text**, type **Last Name** and then press Enter. In the fourth column, click **Text**, type **First Name** and then press Enter. In the fifth column, click **Text**, type **E-mail Address** and then press Enter. In the sixth column, click **Text**, type **Business Phone** and then press ↓.

5 Right-click the **ID** field name, and then **Rename** the field to **Recruiter ID** Change the **Data Type** to **Text**, and then enter the records as shown in **Table 2**.

6 Apply **Best Fit** to all of the columns. **Save** the table as **Lastname Firstname 1F Recruiting Contacts** and then **Close** the table.

7 From the **Navigation Pane**, open the **Current Events Report**. In the lower right corner of the status bar, click the **Layout View** button, click the title *Current Events*, and then click to position your insertion point to the left of *C*. Type your own name in the format **Lastname Firstname** Display the report in **Print Preview**, and then create a paper or electronic printout if instructed to do so. **Close** the **Print Preview**. **Close** the report and save the changes.

8 From the **Navigation Pane**, open your **1F Recruiting Contacts** table. Display the table in **Print Preview**, change to **Landscape** orientation, and then create a paper or electronic printout if instructed to do so. **Close** the **Print Preview**, and then **Close** the table. **Open** the **Navigation Pane** and, if necessary, increase the width of the pane so that your table name displays fully. From **Backstage** view, click **Close Database**, and then click **Exit**. As directed by your instructor, submit your database and the two paper or electronic printouts—one report and one table—that are the results of this project.

Table 1

ID	Title	Start Time	End Time	Description	Location
	Health Professions	**6/1/16 8a**	**6/1/16 1p**	**Science Students**	**Washington HS**
2	**New Students**	**6/1/16 6p**	**6/1/16 9p**	**College Fair**	**Jefferson HS**
3	**Information Technology**	**6/2/16 9a**	**6/2/16 1p**	**Technical Students**	**Madison Technical Center**
4	**New Students**	**6/2/16 2p**	**6/2/16 5p**	**Open House**	**Central Campus**

(Return to Step 3)

Table 2

Recruiter ID	Location	Last Name	First Name	E-mail Address	Business Phone
R-01	**Washington HS**	**Luiz**	**Penelope**	**pluiz@washhs.sch**	**(202) 555-3410**
R-02	**Jefferson HS**	**Hart**	**Robert**	**rlhart@jeffhs.sch**	**(571) 555-1938**
R-03	**Madison Technical Center**	**Sedlacek**	**Belinda**	**bsedlacek@madihs.sch**	**(703) 555-0471**
R-04	**Central Campus**	**Monroe**	**Stephen**	**smonroe@capccc.edu**	**(571) 555-2387**

(Return to Step 6)

End **You have completed Project 10F**

Content-Based Assessments

Apply **10A** and **10B** skills from these Objectives:

1. Identify Good Database Design
2. Create a Table and Define Fields in a New Database
3. Change the Structure of Tables and Add a Second Table
4. Create and Use a Query, Form, and Report
5. Save and Close a Database
6. Create a Database Using a Template
7. Organize Objects in the Navigation Pane
8. Create a New Table in a Database Created with a Template
9. Print a Report and a Table in a Database Created with a Template

Mastering Access | Project 10G Campus Expansion

In the following Mastering Access project, you will create one database to store information about the campus expansion for Capital Cities Community College and a second database to store information about the public events related to the expansion projects. Your completed database objects will look similar to Figure 10.53.

Project Files

For Project 10G, you will need the following files:

New blank Access database
a01G_Projects (Excel workbook)
a01G_Contractors (Excel workbook)
New Access database using the Events template

You will save your databases as:

Lastname_Firstname_1G_Campus_Expansion
Lastname_Firstname_1G_Public_Events

Project Results

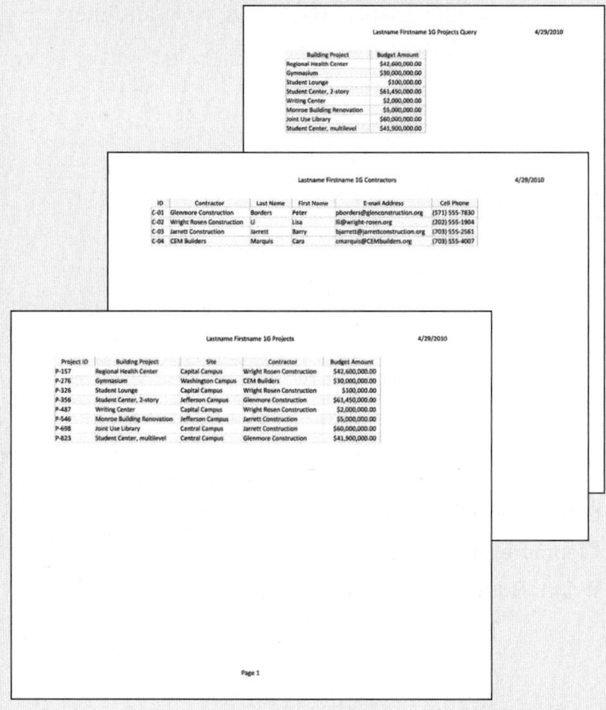

Lastname Firstname 1G Projects Query 4/29/2010

Building Project	Budget Amount
Regional Health Center	$42,600,000.00
Gymnasium	$30,000,000.00
Student Lounge	$100,000.00
Student Center, 2-story	$61,450,000.00
Writing Center	$2,000,000.00
Monroe Building Renovation	$5,000,000.00
Joint Use Library	$60,000,000.00
Student Center, multilevel	$41,900,000.00

Lastname Firstname 1G Contractors 4/29/2010

ID	Contractor	Last Name	First Name	E-mail Address	Cell Phone
C-01	Glenmore Construction	Borders	Peter	pborders@glenconstruction.org	(571) 555-7830
C-02	Wright Rosen Construction	Li	Lisa	lli@wright-rosen.org	(202) 555-1904
C-03	Jarrett Construction	Jarrett	Barry	bjarrett@jarrettconstruction.org	(703) 555-2561
C-04	CEM Builders	Marquis	Cara	cmarquis@CEMbuilders.org	(703) 555-4007

Lastname Firstname 1G Projects 4/29/2010

Project ID	Building Project	Site	Contractor	Budget Amount
P-157	Regional Health Center	Capital Campus	Wright Rosen Construction	$42,600,000.00
P-276	Gymnasium	Washington Campus	CEM Builders	$30,000,000.00
P-326	Student Lounge	Capital Campus	Wright Rosen Construction	$100,000.00
P-356	Student Center, 2-story	Jefferson Campus	Glenmore Construction	$61,450,000.00
P-487	Writing Center	Capital Campus	Wright Rosen Construction	$2,000,000.00
P-546	Monroe Building Renovation	Jefferson Campus	Jarrett Construction	$5,000,000.00
P-698	Joint Use Library	Central Campus	Jarrett Construction	$60,000,000.00
P-823	Student Center, multilevel	Central Campus	Glenmore Construction	$41,900,000.00

Page 1

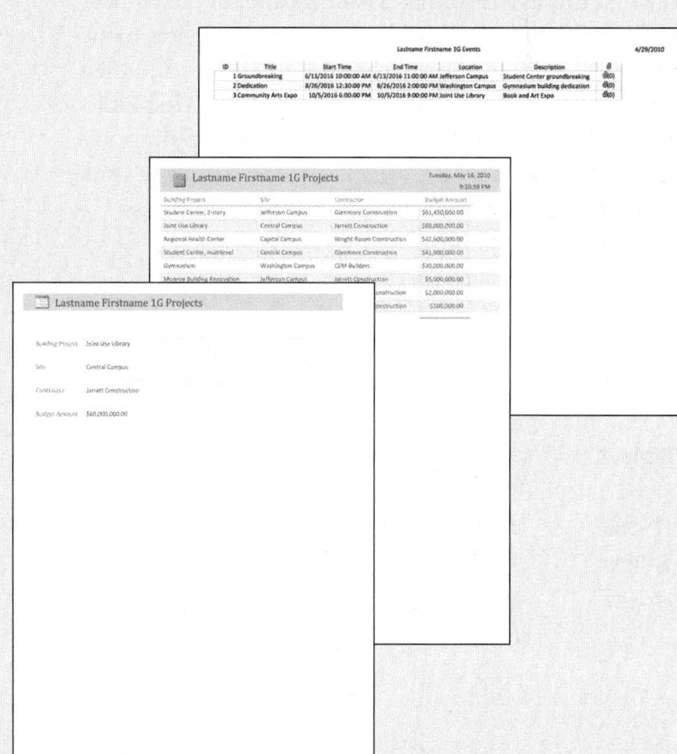

Lastname Firstname 1G Events 4/29/2010

ID	Title	Start Time	End Time	Location	Description	
1	Groundbreaking	6/13/2016 10:00:00 AM	6/13/2016 11:00:00 AM	Jefferson Campus	Student Center groundbreaking	(0)
2	Dedication	8/26/2016 12:30:00 PM	8/26/2016 2:00:00 PM	Washington Campus	Gymnasium building dedication	(0)
3	Community Arts Expo	10/5/2016 6:00:00 PM	10/5/2016 9:00:00 PM	Joint Use Library	Book and Art Expo	(0)

Lastname Firstname 1G Projects Tuesday, May 18, 2010 9:10:59 PM

Building Project	Site	Contractor	Budget Amount
Student Center, 2-story	Jefferson Campus	Glenmore Construction	$61,450,000.00
Joint Use Library	Central Campus	Jarrett Construction	$60,000,000.00
Regional Health Center	Capital Campus	Wright Rosen Construction	$42,600,000.00
Student Center, multilevel	Central Campus	Glenmore Construction	$41,900,000.00
Gymnasium	Washington Campus	CEM Builders	$30,000,000.00
Monroe Building Renovation	Jefferson Campus	Jarrett Construction	$5,000,000.00
		...onstruction	$2,000,000.00
		...nstruction	$100,000.00

Lastname Firstname 1G Projects

Building Project: Joint Use Library
Site: Central Campus
Contractor: Jarrett Construction
Budget Amount: $60,000,000.00

Figure 10.53

(Project 10G Campus Expansion continues on the next page)

Mastering Access | Project 10G Campus Expansion (continued)

1 **Start** Access. Create a new **Blank database** in your **Access Chapter 10** folder. Name the database **Lastname_Firstname_1G_Campus_Expansion** and then **Close** the **Navigation Pane**. Create the additional fields shown in **Table 1**.

2 Change the **ID** field name to **Project ID** and change its **Data Type** to **Text**. Add the three records shown in **Table 2**.

3 **Save** the table as **Lastname Firstname 1G Projects** and then **Close** the table. **Import** and **Append** the **Excel** file **a01G_Projects** to the **1G Projects** table. Then, from the **Navigation Pane**, open your **1G Projects** table—8 total records display. **Close** the **Navigation Pane**.

4 In **Design** view, click in the **Project ID** field, change the **Field Size** to **5** and as the **Description** type **Enter Project ID using the format P-###** Switch to **Datasheet** view, and save by clicking **Yes** two times. Apply **Best Fit** to all of the fields in the table, **Save** the table, and then display it in **Print Preview**. Set the orientation to **Landscape**—one page results. Create a paper or electronic printout as directed by your instructor, and then **Close** the table.

5 From the **External Data tab**, import the **Excel** file **a01G_Contractors** into the database as a new table; use the first row as the column headings and set the **ID** field as the primary key. In the final Wizard dialog box, name the table **Lastname Firstname 1G Contractors** and then **Open** the new table in **Datasheet** view. Apply **Best Fit** to all of the fields, **Save** the table, and then display the table in **Print Preview**. Set the orientation to **Landscape**—one page results. Create a paper or electronic printout as directed, and then **Close** the table.

6 **Create**, by using the **Query Wizard**, a **Simple Query** based on your **1G Projects** table. Include only the appropriate fields to answer the question *For every Building Project, what is the Budget Amount?* Create the query and save it with the default name. Create a paper or electronic printout as directed, and then **Close** the query.

7 Open your **1G Projects** table, and then **Create** a **Form** for this table. Save the form as **Lastname Firstname 1G Projects Form** Display and select the seventh record, and then by using the instructions in Activity 10.15, print or create an electronic printout of this record as directed. **Close** the form object, saving changes to it.

8 With the **1G Projects** table open and active, **Create** a **Report**. **Delete** the **Project ID** field. Sort the records in **Descending** order by the **Budget Amount** field—Access automatically totals this field. Adjust the field widths on the left and right as necessary so that the fields display within the margins of the report. At the bottom of the report, delete the **page number**, and then delete the total that displays in the **Budget Amount** column. **Save** the report as **Lastname Firstname 1G Projects Report** and then create a paper or electronic printout as directed.

9 **Close All** open objects. If necessary, **Open** the **Navigation Pane** and widen the pane so that all object names display fully. Display **Backstage** view, and then click **Close Database**. Do *not* exit Access.

Table 1

Data Type		Text	Text	Text	Currency
Field Name	ID	**Building Project**	**Site**	**Contractor**	**Budget Amount**

(Return to Step 2)

Table 2

Project ID	Building Project	Site	Contractor	Budget Amount
P-356	**Student Center, 2-story**	**Jefferson Campus**	**Glenmore Construction**	**61450000**
P-823	**Student Center, multilevel**	**Central Campus**	**Glenmore Construction**	**41900000**
P-157	**Regional Health Center**	**Capital Campus**	**Wright Rosen Construction**	**42600000**

(Return to Step 3)

(Project 10G Campus Expansion continues on the next page)

Mastering Access | Project 10G Campus Expansion (continued)

10 From **Sample templates**, create a new database using the **Events** template. **Save** the database in your **Access Chapter 10** folder, and as the file name, type **Lastname_Firstname_1G_Public_Events** If necessary, enable the content. Enter the records in **Table 3** by using the displayed Multiple Items Event List form or the single-record form, which is available by clicking New Event above the field names row.

11 **Close** the **Event List** form. Open the **Navigation Pane**, and then by using the **Navigation Pane arrow**, arrange the database objects by **Tables and Related Views**. Point to the **Events: Table** object, right-click, click **Rename**, and then using your own name, type **Lastname Firstname 1G Events** Press Enter and then widen the Navigation Pane if necessary.

12 **Open** the **1G Events** table, **Close** the **Navigation Pane**, and then apply **Best Fit** to all of the columns. **Save** the table, display it in **Print Preview**, change the orientation to **Landscape**, set the **Margins** to **Normal**, and then create a paper or electronic printout as directed. **Close** all open objects. **Open** the **Navigation Pane**, display **Backstage** view, click **Close Database**, and then click **Exit**. As directed by your instructor, submit your database and the six paper or electronic printouts—three tables, one query, one form, and one report—that are the results of this project.

Table 3

ID	Title	Start Time	End Time	Description	Location
1	**Groundbreaking**	**6/13/16 10a**	**6/13/16 11a**	**Student Center groundbreaking**	**Jefferson Campus**
2	**Dedication**	**8/26/16 12:30p**	**8/26/16 2p**	**Gymnasium building dedication**	**Washington Campus**
3	**Community Arts Expo**	**10/5/16 6p**	**10/5/16 9p**	**Book and Art Expo**	**Joint Use Library**

(Return to Step 11)

End **You have completed Project 10G**

Content-Based Assessments

Apply a combination of the **10A** and **10B** skills.

GO! Fix It | Project 10H Scholarships

Project Files

For Project 10H, you will need the following file:

a01H_Scholarships

You will save your database as:

Lastname_Firstname_1H_Scholarships

In this project, you will make corrections to and update an Access database that will store information about scholarships awarded to students. Start Access. In Backstage view, click Open, navigate to your student files, and then open the file a01H_Scholarships. With the database open, display Backstage view. Click Save Database As, and in the Save As dialog box, navigate to your Access Chapter 10 folder, name the file **Lastname_Firstname_1H_Scholarships** and then click Save. In the message bar, click the Enable Content button.

To complete the project you must find and correct errors in field names, data types, data design, and column widths. You should know:

- The table name should be renamed **Lastname Firstname 1H Scholarships**
- In the table, all of the data in the fields and the field names should display fully.
- Three fields in the table have incorrect data types.
- The field that represents the unique value for each record should be set as the primary key.
- In one of the records, there is a data entry error involving an athlete's name; after correcting the entry, be sure to click in another record so that the record you edit is saved.
- When open, the Navigation Pane should fully display the table name.
- A query should be created for the 1H Scholarships table that answers the question *What is the Amount, Sport, First Name, and Last Name of every athlete receiving a scholarship?* Apply Best Fit to the query results.
- Using the table, a report should be created that includes the Amount, Sport, Award Date, and the last and first name of the athlete. Sort the report in descending order by the amount and then adjust the column widths so that the fields display within the margins of the report. At the bottom of the report, delete the total for the Amount field, and then delete the page number and save with the default name.

If directed to do so, create a paper or electronic printout of the table, the query, and the report. The table should use Landscape orientation, and the query and report should use Portrait orientation. Be sure that the report prints on one page.

End **You have completed Project 10H**

Content-Based Assessments

Apply a combination of the 10A and 10B skills.

GO! Make It | Project 10I Theater Events

Project Files

For Project 10I, you will need the following file:

New Access database using the Events template

You will save your database as:

Lastname_Firstname_1I_Theater_Events

Using the Events database template, create the table of theater events shown in Figure 10.54 that the Performing Arts department will present or host for April. Name the database **Lastname_Firstname_1I_Theater_Events** Arrange the Navigation Pane by Tables and Related Views, rename the Events table **Lastname Firstname 1I Theater Events** and then widen the Navigation Pane so that all object names display fully. Open the table, apply Best Fit to all the columns, save the table, and then create a paper or electronic printout of the table as directed by your instructor. Use Landscape orientation and Normal margins.

Project Results

Lastname Firstname 1I Theater Events 4/29/2010

ID	Title	Start Time	End Time	Location	Description	📎
1	Symphony Orchestra Concert	4/2/2016 7:30:00 PM	4/2/2016 10:00:00 PM	Jefferson Campus	Opera soprano Barbara Botillini	(0)
2	The Big Band Concert	4/4/2016 7:30:00 PM	4/4/2016 9:00:00 PM	Capital Campus	The Ruth Mystic Big Band Concert	(0)
3	Chaos in the House	4/6/2016 3:00:00 PM	4/6/2016 5:00:00 PM	Central Campus	Gospel Show	(0)
4	Tom Sawyer	4/7/2016 7:00:00 PM	4/7/2016 10:00:00 PM	Washington Campus	CapCCC Players	(0)
5	Tom Sawyer	4/8/2016 3:00:00 PM	4/8/2016 6:00:00 PM	Washington Campus	CapCCC Players	(0)
6	Virginia Arts Festival	4/16/2016 8:00:00 PM	4/16/2016 10:00:00 PM	Jefferson Campus	Anika Shankar	(0)
7	Virginia Arts Festival	4/17/2016 7:00:00 PM	4/17/2016 9:00:00 PM	Central Campus	Music from the Crooked Elbow	(0)
8	College Awards Ceremony	4/22/2016 1:00:00 PM	4/22/2016 4:00:00 PM	Washington Campus	CapCCC Faculty and Staff Awards	(0)
9	Virginia Arts Festival	4/23/2016 7:30:00 PM	4/23/2016 10:00:00 PM	Capital Campus	Russian Folk Dance Spectacular	(0)
10	Music in Motion Dance	4/29/2016 1:00:00 PM	4/29/2016 3:00:00 PM	Central Campus	Dancing to Modern Music	(0)

Page 1

Figure 10.54

End You have completed Project 10I

Content-Based Assessments

Apply a combination of the 10A and 10B skills.

GO! Solve It | Project 10J Student Activities

Project Files

For Project 10J, you will need the following files:

New Access database using the Events template
a01J_Student_Activities (Word document)

You will save your database as:

Lastname_Firstname_1J_Student_Activities

Create a new database from the Events database template and name the database **Lastname_Firstname_1J_Student_Activities** Using the data in the a01J_Student_Activities Word document, enter the data into the Multiple Items form. Each event begins at 7 p.m. and ends at 9 p.m. After entering the records, close the form, arrange the Navigation Pane by Tables and Related Views, rename the table that stores the records as **Lastname Firstname 1J Activities** and then widen the Navigation Pane so that all object names display fully. Open the table, apply Best Fit to the columns, and then save the table. Display the table in Print Preview, and then use the proper commands to be sure that the table prints on one page with the table name at the top of the page. Print the table or submit electronically as directed.

Performance Elements	Performance Level		
	Exemplary: You consistently applied the relevant skills	**Proficient:** You sometimes, but not always, applied the relevant skills	**Developing:** You rarely or never applied the relevant skills
Create database and enter data	Database was created using the correct template and correct name. Data entered correctly.	Some but not all of the data was entered correctly.	Most of the data was entered incorrectly.
Rename table and format table	Table named correctly and Best Fit applied to all columns.	Table named incorrectly and/or Best Fit not properly applied.	Incorrect table name and inadequate formatting applied to all columns.
Create table printout	Printout displays on one page in Landscape orientation and the table name displays at the top.	The printout displays on two pages or the table name does not display at the top.	The printout displays on two pages and the table name does not display at the top of the page.

End You have completed Project 10J

Apply a combination of the 10A and 10B skills.

GO! Solve It | Project 10K Media Contacts

Project Files

For Project 10K, you will need the following files:

New blank Access database
a01K_Media_Contacts (Excel workbook)

You will save your database as:

Lastname_Firstname_1K_Media_Contacts

Create a new blank database and name the database **Lastname_Firstname_1K_Media_Contacts** Close the default Table1. Create a table by importing the a01K_Media_Contacts Excel workbook, use the first row as the column headings, and use Media ID as the Primary Key. Name the table **Lastname Firstname 1K Media Contacts** Modify the table design by creating separate fields for the Contact's first name and last name, and then adjust the data accordingly. Apply Best Fit to the columns, and then save the table. Display the table in Print Preview, and then use the Page Layout commands to display the table on one page, being sure the table name prints at the top of the page. Print the table or submit electronically as directed.

Create a simple query that answers the following question: *What are the Publication name, first name, last name, and E-mail address for all of the media contacts?* Accept the default name, apply Best Fit to all of the columns, and then create a paper or electronic printout on one page as directed.

Create a report and delete the Media ID column. Adjust the widths of the remaining fields so that all of the data displays within the margins of the report. Sort the report in ascending order by the Publication field. In Layout View, select the report title, and then on the Format tab, in the Font group, change the font of the title of the report to 14. At the bottom of the report, delete the page number. Save the report as **Lastname Firstname 1K Media Contacts Report** and then create a paper or electronic printout as directed. Arrange the Navigation Pane by Tables and Related Views, and then widen the Navigation Pane so that all object names display fully.

Performance Element	Performance Level: Exemplary: You consistently applied the relevant skills	Proficient: You sometimes, but not always, applied the relevant skills	Developing: You rarely or never applied the relevant skills
Create database, import data to create a table, and then modify the table design	Table created by importing from an Excel workbook, fields correctly modified, and primary key field identified.	Table created by importing from an Excel workbook, but fields are incorrect, or primary key field is incorrect.	Table created by importing from an Excel workbook, but both fields and primary key are incorrect.
Create query	Query created, named correctly, answers the question, formatted correctly.	Query created, but does not completely answer the question or formatted incorrectly.	Query does not answer the question and also includes errors in formatting.
Create report	Report created, Media ID field deleted, field sizes adjusted, sorted by Publication, correctly named, and formatted.	Report created with some errors in fields, report name, sorting, or formatting.	Report created with numerous errors in fields, report name, sorting, or formatting.

End **You have completed Project 10K**

Outcomes-Based Assessments

Rubric

The following outcomes-based assessments are *open-ended assessments*. That is, there is no specific correct result; your result will depend on your approach to the information provided. Make *Professional Quality* your goal. Use the following scoring rubric to guide you in *how* to approach the problem, and then to evaluate *how well* your approach solves the problem.

The *criteria*—Software Mastery, Content, Format and Layout, and Process—represent the knowledge and skills you have gained that you can apply to solving the problem. The *levels of performance*—Professional Quality, Approaching Professional Quality, or Needs Quality Improvements—help you and your instructor evaluate your result.

	Your completed project is of Professional Quality if you:	**Your completed project is Approaching Professional Quality if you:**	**Your completed project Needs Quality Improvements if you:**
1-Software Mastery	Choose and apply the most appropriate skills, tools, and features and identify efficient methods to solve the problem.	Choose and apply some appropriate skills, tools, and features, but not in the most efficient manner.	Choose inappropriate skills, tools, or features, or are inefficient in solving the problem.
2-Content	Construct a solution that is clear and well organized, contains content that is accurate, appropriate to the audience and purpose, and is complete. Provide a solution that contains no errors in spelling, grammar, or style.	Construct a solution in which some components are unclear, poorly organized, inconsistent, or incomplete. Misjudge the needs of the audience. Have some errors in spelling, grammar, or style, but the errors do not detract from comprehension.	Construct a solution that is unclear, incomplete, or poorly organized; contains some inaccurate or inappropriate content; and contains many errors in spelling, grammar, or style. Do not solve the problem.
3-Format and Layout	Format and arrange all elements to communicate information and ideas, clarify function, illustrate relationships, and indicate relative importance.	Apply appropriate format and layout features to some elements, but not others. Overuse features, causing minor distraction.	Apply format and layout that does not communicate information or ideas clearly. Do not use format and layout features to clarify function, illustrate relationships, or indicate relative importance. Use available features excessively, causing distraction.
4-Process	Use an organized approach that integrates planning, development, self-assessment, revision, and reflection.	Demonstrate an organized approach in some areas, but not others; or, use an insufficient process of organization throughout.	Do not use an organized approach to solve the problem.

Outcomes-Based Assessments

Apply a combination of the 10A and 10B skills.

GO! Think | Project 10L Student Clubs

Project Files

For Project 10L, you will need the following files:

New blank Access database
a01L_Clubs (Word file)
a01L_Student_Clubs (Excel file)
a01L_Club_Presidents (Excel file)

You will save your database as:

Lastname_Firstname_1L_Student_Clubs

Kirsten McCarty, Vice President of Student Services, needs a database that tracks information about student clubs. The database should contain two tables, one for club information and one for contact information for the club presidents.

Create a new blank database and name it **Lastname_Firstname_1L_Student_Clubs** Using the information provided in the a01L_Clubs Word document, create the first table with two records to store information about the clubs. Then import 23 records from the a01L_Student_Clubs Excel file. Create a second table by importing 25 records from the a0lL_Club_Presidents Excel file. Name the tables appropriately and include your name. Be sure the data types are correct and the records are entered correctly. Apply Best Fit to all of the columns.

Create a simple query based on the Clubs table that answers the following question: *What are the Club Name, Meeting Day, Meeting Time, and Room ID for all of the clubs?* Based on the Clubs table, create a form. Create a report based on the Presidents of the clubs that lists the Last Name (in ascending order), First Name, and Phone number of every president. Print the two tables, the seventh record in Form view, the query, and the report being sure that each object prints on one page, or submit electronically as directed. Group objects on the Navigation Pane by Tables and Related Views. On the Navigation Pane, be sure that all object names display fully.

End You have completed Project 10L

Apply a combination of the 10A and 10B skills.

GO! Think | Project 10M Faculty Training

Project Files

For Project 10M, you will need the following file:

New Access database using the Events template
a01M_Faculty_Training (Word file)

You will save your database as:

Lastname_Firstname_1M_Faculty_Training

Use the information provided in the a01M_Faculty_Training Word file to create a database using the Events database template. Name the database **Lastname_Firstname_1M_Faculty_Training** Use the information in the Word file to enter the records. Training times begin at 11:30 a.m. and end at 1 p.m. Arrange the Navigation Pane by Tables and Related Views, and rename the Events table appropriately to include your name. Display the All Events report in Layout View and insert your Lastname Firstname in front of the report title *All Events*. Print the table and the All Events report or submit electronically as directed.

End You have completed Project 10M

Apply a combination of the 10A and 10B skills.

You and GO! | Project 10N Personal Contacts

Project Files

For Project 10N, you will need the following file:

New blank Access database

You will save your database as:

Lastname_Firstname_1N_Personal_Contacts

Create a database that stores information about your personal contacts, such as friends and family members. Name the database **Lastname_Firstname_1N_Personal_Contacts** Include a field for a birthday. Enter at least 10 records in the table, and name the table **Lastname Firstname 1N Personal Contacts** Create a query that includes at least three of the fields in the table in the result; for example, a list of names and phone numbers. Create a report that includes the name and address for each contact. Print the table, query, and report, making sure that the data for each object prints on one page, or submit electronically as directed.

You have completed Project 10N

Apply a combination of the 10A and 10B skills.

GO! Collaborate | Project 10O Bell Orchid Hotels Group Running Case

This project relates to the **Bell Orchid Hotels.** Your instructor may assign this group case project to your class. If your instructor assigns this project, he or she will provide you with information and instructions to work as part of a group. The group will apply the skills gained thus far to help the Bell Orchid Hotels achieve their business goals.

You have completed Project 10O

Sort and Query a Database

OUTCOMES At the end of this chapter you will be able to:	**OBJECTIVES** Mastering these objectives will enable you to:
PROJECT 11A Sort and query a database.	1. Open an Existing Database (p. 595) 2. Create Table Relationships (p. 596) 3. Sort Records in a Table (p. 601) 4. Create a Query in Design View (p. 604) 5. Create a New Query from an Existing Query (p. 607) 6. Sort Query Results (p. 608) 7. Specify Criteria in a Query (p. 610)
PROJECT 11B Create complex queries.	8. Specify Numeric Criteria in a Query (p. 616) 9. Use Compound Criteria (p. 621) 10. Create a Query Based on More Than One Table (p. 623) 11. Use Wildcards in a Query (p. 625) 12. Use Calculated Fields in a Query (p. 627) 13. Calculate Statistics and Group Data in a Query (p. 630) 14. Create a Crosstab Query (p. 633)

Brendan Fisher/Shutterstock

In This Chapter

In this chapter, you will sort Access database tables and create and modify queries. To convert data into meaningful information, you must manipulate your data in a way that you can answer questions. One question might be: *Which students have a grade point average of 3.0 or higher?* With such information, you could send information about scholarships or internships to selected students.

Questions can be answered by sorting the data in a table or by creating a query. Queries enable you to isolate specific data in database tables by limiting the fields that display and by setting conditions that limit the records to those that match specified conditions. You can also use a query to create a new field that is calculated by using one or more existing fields.

The projects in this chapter relate to **Capital Cities Community College**, which is located in the Washington D. C. metropolitan area. The college provides high-quality education and professional training to residents in the cities surrounding the nation's capital. Its four campuses serve over 50,000 students and offer more than 140 certificate programs and degrees at the associate's level. CapCCC has a highly acclaimed Distance Education program and an extensive Workforce Development program. The college makes positive contributions to the community through cultural and athletic programs and partnerships with businesses and non-profit organizations.

Project 11A Instructors and Courses Database

Project Activities

In Activities 11.01 through 11.13, you will assist Carolyn Judkins, the Dean of the Business and Information Technology Division at the Jefferson Campus, in locating information about instructors and courses in the Division. Your results will look similar to Figure 11.1.

Project Files

For Project 3A, you will need the following file:

a02A_Instructors_Courses

You will save your database as:

Lastname_Firstname_2A_Instructors_Courses

Project Results

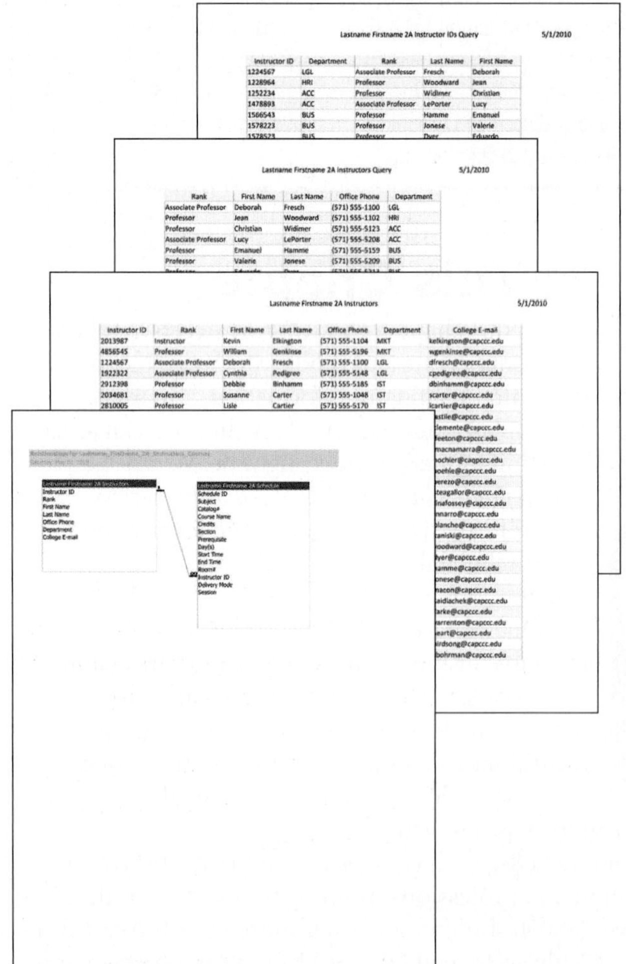

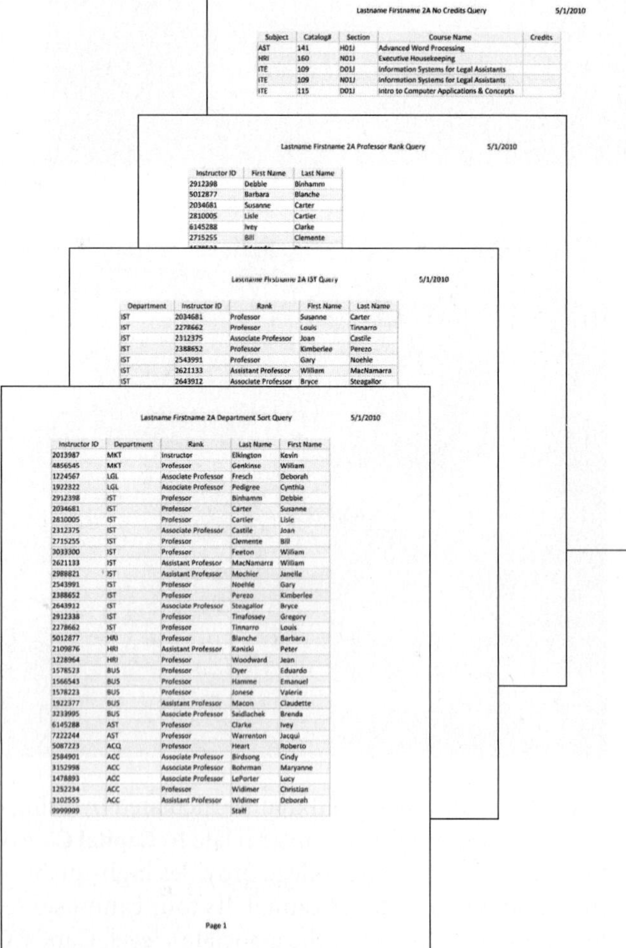

Figure 11.1

Project 11A Instructors and Courses

Objective 1 | Open an Existing Database

There will be instances in which you may want to work with a database and still keep the *original* version of the database. Like the other Microsoft Office 2010 applications, you can open a database file and save it with a new name.

Activity 11.01 | Opening and Renaming an Existing Database

1 Start **Access**. In **Backstage** view, click **Open**. Navigate to the student data files for this textbook, and then open the Access database **a02A_Instructors_Courses**.

2 Click the **File tab** to return to **Backstage** view, and then click **Save Database As.** In the **Save As** dialog box, navigate to the location where you are saving your databases for this chapter. Create a new folder named **Access Chapter 11** and then click **Open**.

3 In the **File name** box, select the file name, to which *1* has been added at the end. Edit as necessary to name the database **Lastname_Firstname_2A_Instructors_Courses** and then press Enter.

Use this technique when you want to keep a copy of the original database file.

4 On the **Message Bar**, notice the **Security Warning**. In the **Navigation Pane**, notice that this database contains two table objects. Compare your screen with Figure 11.2.

Figure 11.2

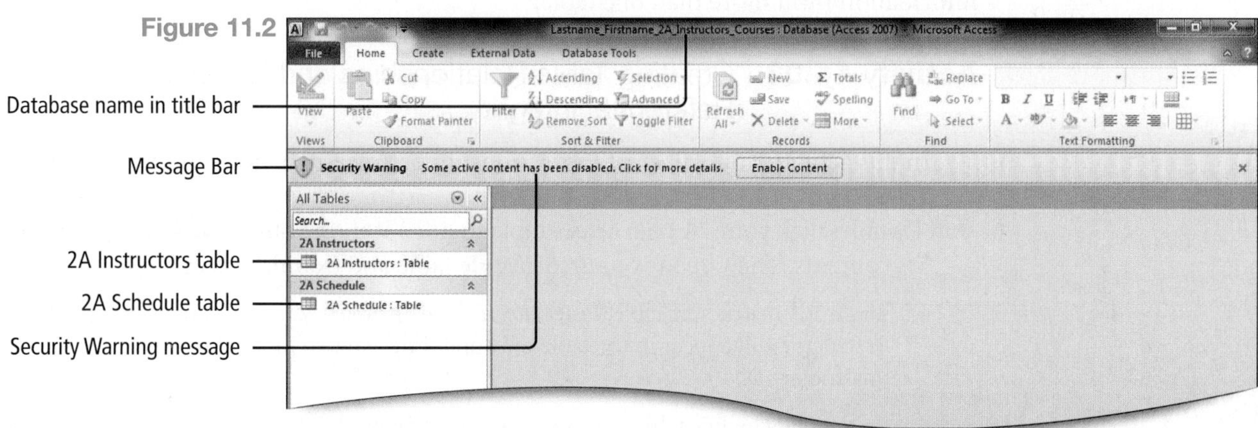

Activity 11.02 | Resolving Security Alerts and Renaming Tables

The ***Message Bar*** is the area below the Ribbon that displays information such as security alerts when there is potentially unsafe, active content in an Office document that you open. Settings that determine the alerts that display on your Message Bar are set in the Access ***Trust Center***, which is an area of Access where you can view the security and privacy settings for your Access installation.

You may or may not be able to change the settings in the Trust Center, depending upon decisions made within your organization's computing environment. You can display the Trust Center from Options, which is available in Backstage view.

1 On the **Message Bar**, click the **Enable Content** button.

When working with the student files that accompany this textbook, repeat these actions each time you see this security warning. Databases for this textbook are safe to use on your computer.

2 In the **Navigation Pane**, right-click the **2A Instructors** table, and then click **Rename**. With the table name selected and using your own name, type **Lastname Firstname 2A Instructors** and then press Enter to rename the table. Using the same technique, **Rename** the **2A Schedule** table to **Lastname Firstname 2A Schedule**

Including your name in the table enables you and your instructor to easily identify your work, because Access includes the table name in the header of printed and PDF pages.

3 Point to the right edge of the **Navigation Pane** to display the ⟺ pointer. Drag to the right to widen the pane until both table names display fully.

Objective 2 | Create Table Relationships

Access databases are relational databases because the tables in the database can relate—actually connect—to other tables through common fields. Recall that common fields are fields that contain the same data in more than one table.

After you have a table for each subject in your database, you must provide a way to connect the data in the tables when you need meaningful information. To do this, create common fields in related tables, and then define table relationships. A ***relationship*** is an association that you establish between two tables based on common fields. After the relationship is established, you can create a query, a form, or a report that displays information from more than one table.

Activity 11.03 | Creating Table Relationships and Enforcing Referential Integrity

In this activity, you will create a relationship between two tables in the database.

1 Double-click your **2A Instructors** table to open it in the object window and examine its contents. Then open your **2A Schedule** table and examine its contents.

In the 2A Instructors table, *Instructor ID* is the primary key field, which ensures that each instructor will appear in the table only one time. No two instructors have the same Instructor ID.

In the 2A Schedule table, *Schedule ID* is the primary key field. Every scheduled course section during an academic term has a unique Schedule ID. The 2A Schedule table includes the *Instructor ID* field, which is the common field between the 2A Schedule table and the 2A Instructors table.

2 In the **2A Schedule** table, scroll to the right to display the Instructor ID field, and then compare your screen with Figure 11.3.

Because *one* instructor can teach *many* different courses, *one* Instructor ID number can be present *many* times in the 2A Schedule table. This relationship between each instructor and the courses is known as a ***one-to-many relationship***. This is the most common type of relationship in Access.

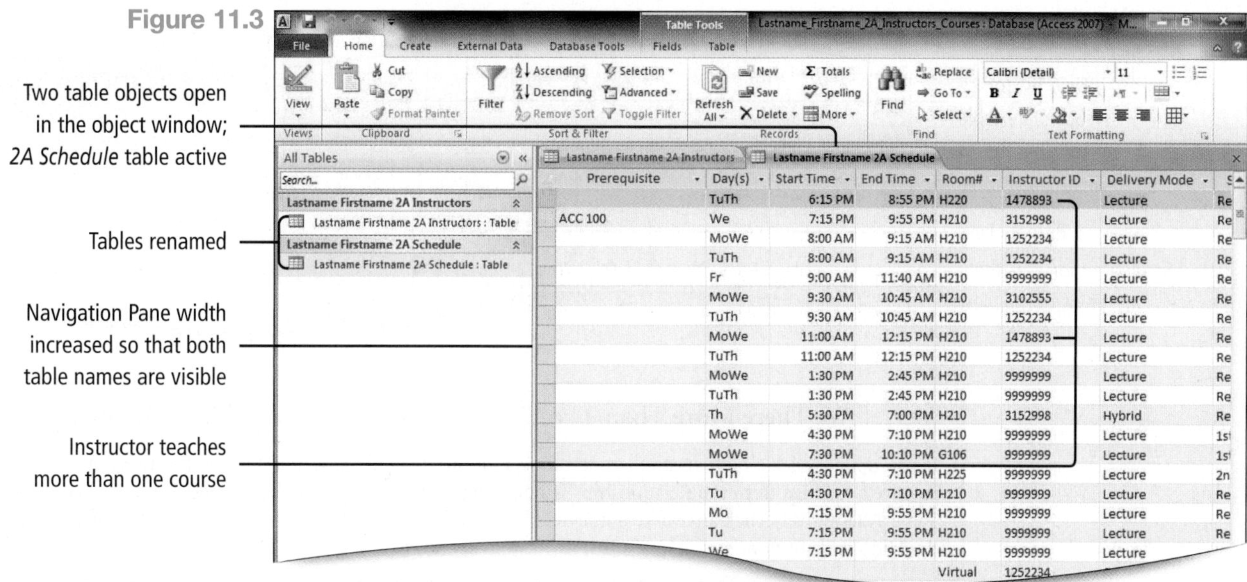

Figure 11.3

3 In the upper right corner of the object window, click **Close** two times to close each table. Click the **Database Tools tab**, and then in the **Relationships group**, click the **Relationships** button. Compare your screen with Figure 11.4.

The Show Table dialog box displays in the Relationships window. In the Show Table dialog box, the Tables tab displays all of the table objects in the database. Your two tables are listed.

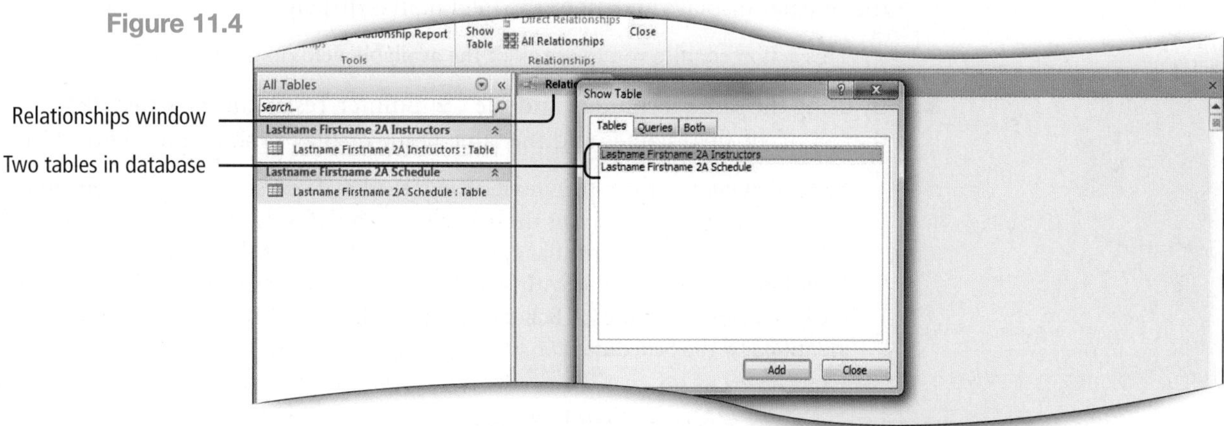

Figure 11.4

4 Point to the title bar of the **Show Table** dialog box, and then drag down and to the right slightly to move the **Show Table** dialog box away from the top of the **Relationships** window.

Moving the Show Table dialog box enables you to see the tables as they are added to the Relationships window.

5 In the **Show Table** dialog box, click your **2A Instructors** table, and then at the bottom of the dialog box, click **Add**. In the **Show Table** dialog box, double-click your **2A Schedule** table to add the table to the **Relationships** window. In the **Show Table** dialog box, click **Close**, and then compare your screen with Figure 11.5.

You can use either technique to add a table to the Relationships window. A ***field list***—a list of the field names in a table—for each of the two table objects displays, and each table's primary key is identified. Although this database currently has only two tables, larger databases can have many tables. Scroll bars in a field list indicate that there are fields that are not currently in view.

Access | Chapter 11

Figure 11.5

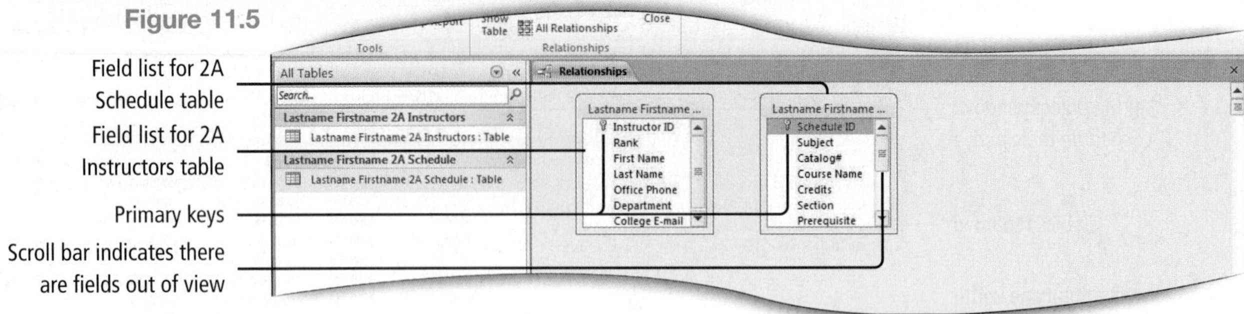

Alert! | Are There More Than Two Field Lists in the Relationships Window?

If you double-click a table more than one time, a duplicate field list displays in the Relationships window. To remove a field list from the Relationships window, right-click the title bar of the field list, and then click Hide Table. Alternatively, click anywhere in the field list, and then on the Design tab, in the Relationships group, click the Hide Table button.

6 In the **2A Schedule** field list—the field list on the right—point to the title bar to display the pointer. Drag the field list to the right until there is about 2 inches between the field lists.

7 In the **2A Instructors** field list—the field list on the left—point to the lower right corner of the field list to display the pointer, and then drag down and to the right to increase the height and width of the field list until the entire name of the table in the title bar displays and all of the field names display.

This action enables you to see all of the available fields and removes the vertical scroll bar.

8 By using the same technique and the pointer, resize the **2A Schedule** field list so that all of the field names and the table name display as shown in Figure 11.6.

Recall that *one* instructor can teach *many* scheduled courses. This arrangement of the tables on your screen displays the *one table* on the left side and the *many table* on the right side. Recall also that the primary key in each table is the field that uniquely identifies the record in each table. In the 2A Instructors table, each instructor is uniquely identified by the Instructor ID. In the 2A Schedule table, each scheduled course section is uniquely identified by the Schedule ID.

Figure 11.6

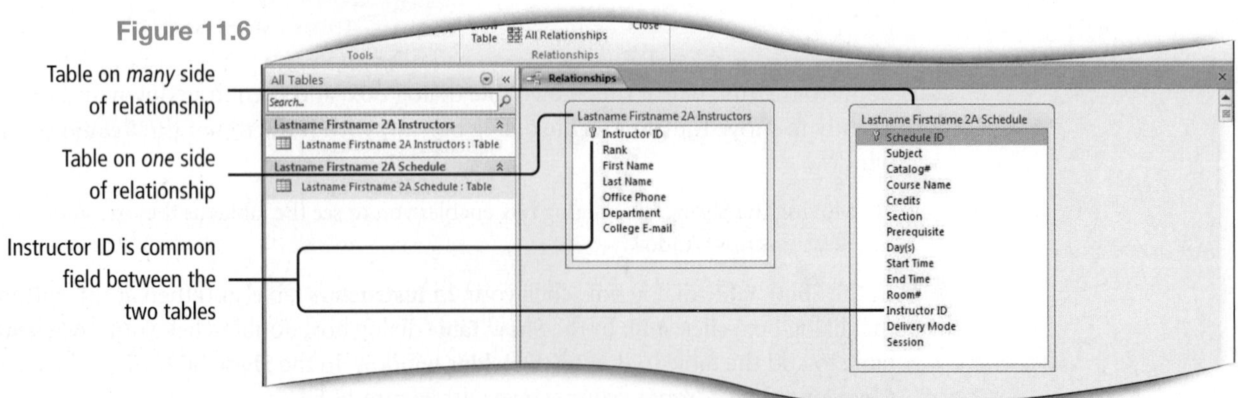

Note | The Field That Is Highlighted Does Not Matter

After you rearrange the two field lists in the Relationships window, the highlighted field indicates the active field list, which is the list you moved last. This is of no consequence for completing the activity.

Another Way

On the Design tab, in the Tools group, click the Edit Relationships button. In the Edit Relationships dialog box, click Create New, and then in the Create New dialog box, designate the tables and fields that will create the relationship.

9. In the **2A Instructors** field list, point to **Instructor ID**, hold down the left mouse button, and then drag down and to the right into the **2A Schedule** field list until the pointer's arrow is on top of **Instructor ID**. Then release the mouse button to display the **Edit Relationships** dialog box.

   As you drag, a small graphic displays to indicate that you are dragging a field from one field list to another. A table relationship works by matching data in two fields—the common field. In these two tables, the common field has the same name—*Instructor ID*. Common fields are not required to have the same names; however, they must have the same data type and field size.

10. Point to the title bar of the **Edit Relationships** dialog box, and then drag the dialog box below the two field lists as shown in Figure 11.7.

   Both tables include the Instructor ID field—the common field between the two tables. By dragging, you create the *one-to-many* relationship. In the 2A Instructors table, Instructor ID is the primary key. In the 2A Schedule table, Instructor ID is referred to as the ***foreign key*** field. The foreign key is the field in the related table used to connect to the primary key in another table. The field on the *one* side of the relationship is typically the primary key.

Figure 11.7

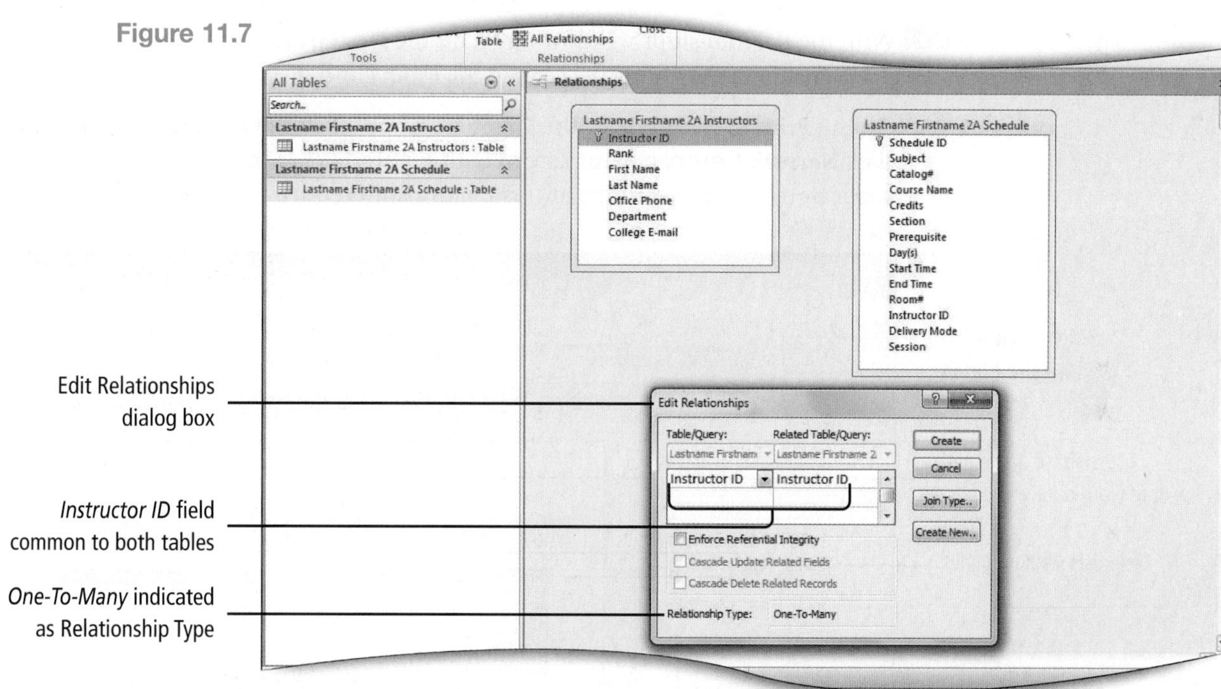

11. In the **Edit Relationships** dialog box, click to select the **Enforce Referential Integrity** check box.

   Referential integrity is a set of rules that Access uses to ensure that the data between related tables is valid. Enforcing referential integrity ensures that an instructor cannot be added to the 2A Schedules table if the Instructor ID is *not* included in the 2A Instructors table. Similarly, enforcing referential integrity ensures that you cannot delete an instructor from the 2A Instructors table if there is a course listed in the 2A Schedule table for that instructor.

12. In the **Edit Relationships** dialog box, click the **Create** button, and then compare your screen with Figure 11.8.

   A ***join line***—the line joining two tables—displays between the two tables. On the join line, *1* indicates the *one* side of the relationship, and the infinity symbol (∞) indicates the *many* side of the relationship. These symbols display when referential integrity is enforced.

Access | Chapter 11

Figure 11.8

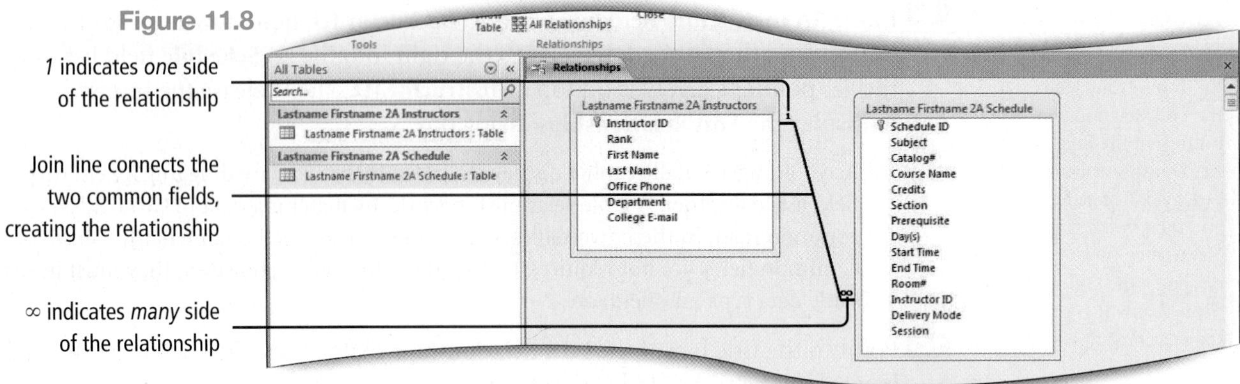

Activity 11.04 | Printing a Relationship Report and Displaying Subdatasheet Records

The Relationships window provides a map of how your database tables are related, and you can print this information as a report.

1. With the **Relationships** window open, on the **Design tab**, in the **Tools group**, click the **Relationship Report** button to create the report and display it in Print Preview.
2. On the **Print Preview tab**, in the **Page Size group**, click the **Margins** button, and then click **Normal**. Compare your screen with Figure 11.9. If instructed to do so, create a paper or electronic printout of this relationship report.

Figure 11.9

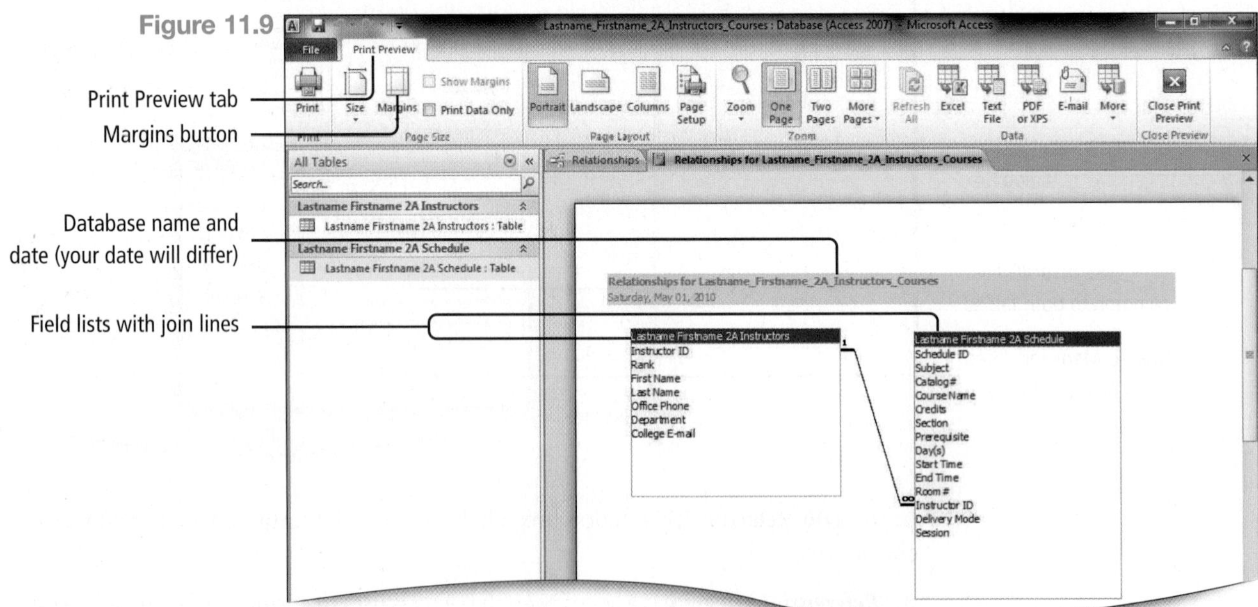

3. On the **Quick Access Toolbar**, click the **Save** button to save the report. In the **Save As** dialog box, click **OK** to accept the default name.

   The report name displays in the Navigation Pane under *Unrelated Objects*. Because the report is just a map of the relationships, and not a report containing actual records, it is not associated with any of the tables.

4. In the object window, **Close** the report, and then **Close** the **Relationships** window.

5 From the **Navigation Pane**, open your **2A Instructors** table, and then **Close** « the **Navigation Pane**. For the first record—*Instructor ID 1224567*—on the left side of the record, click the **plus sign** (+), and then compare your screen with Figure 11.10.

Plus signs to the left of a record in a table indicate that *related* records exist in another table. Clicking the plus sign displays the related records in a ***subdatasheet***. In the first record, for *Deborah Fresch*, you can see that related records exist in the 2A Schedule table—she is teaching five LGL courses that are listed in the schedule. The plus sign displays because you created a relationship between the two tables using the Instructor ID field—the common field.

Figure 11.10

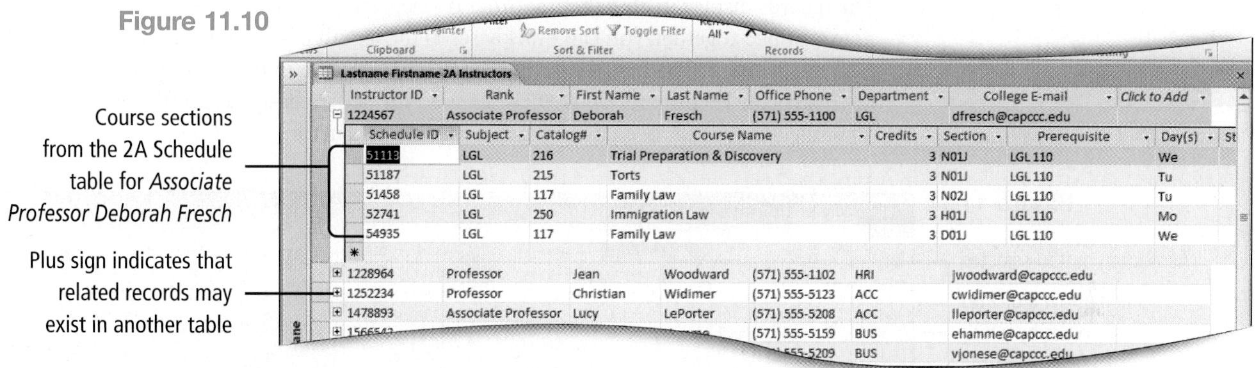

6 For the first record, click the **minus sign** (-) to collapse the subdatasheet.

> **More Knowledge | Other Types of Relationships: One-to-One and Many-to-Many**
>
> There are other relationships you can create using the same process in the Relationships window. The type of relationship is determined by the placement of the primary key field. A one-to-one relationship exists between two tables when a record in one table is related to a single record in a second table. In this case, both tables use the same field as the primary key. This is most often used when data is placed in a separate table because access to the information is restricted.
>
> You can also create a many-to-many relationship between tables, where many records in one table can be related to many records in another table. For example, many students can enroll in many courses. To create a many-to-many relationship, you must create a third table that contains the primary key fields from both tables. These primary key fields are then joined to their related fields in the other tables. In effect, you create multiple one-to-one relationships.

Objective 3 | Sort Records in a Table

Sorting is the process of arranging data in a specific order based on the value in a field. For example, you can sort the names in your address book alphabetically by each person's last name, or you can sort your DVD collection by the date of purchase. Initially, records in an Access table display in the order they are entered into the table. When a primary key is established, the records display in order based on the primary key field.

Activity 11.05 | Sorting Records in a Table in Ascending or Descending Order

In the following activity, you will determine the departments of the faculty in the Business and Information Technology Division by sorting the data. You can sort data in either ***ascending order*** or ***descending order***. Ascending order sorts text alphabetically (A to Z) and sorts numbers from the lowest number to the highest number. Descending order sorts text in reverse alphabetical order (Z to A) and sorts numbers from the highest number to the lowest number.

1 Notice that the records in the **2A Instructors** table are sorted in ascending order by **Instructor ID**, which is the primary key field.

> **Another Way**
>
> On the Home tab, in the Sort & Filter group, click the Ascending button.

2 In the field names row, click the **Department arrow**, click **Sort A to Z**, and then compare your screen with Figure 11.11.

To sort records in a table, click the arrow to the right of the field name in the column on which you want to sort, and then choose the sort order. After a field is sorted, a small arrow in the field name box indicates its sort order. The small arrow in the field name points up, indicating an ascending sort; and in the Ribbon, the Ascending button is selected.

The records display in alphabetical order by Department. Because the department names are now grouped together, you can quickly scroll the length of the table to see the instructors in each department. The first record in the table has no data in the Department field because the Instructor ID number *9999999* is reserved for Staff, a designation that is used until a scheduled course has been assigned to a specific instructor.

Figure 11.11

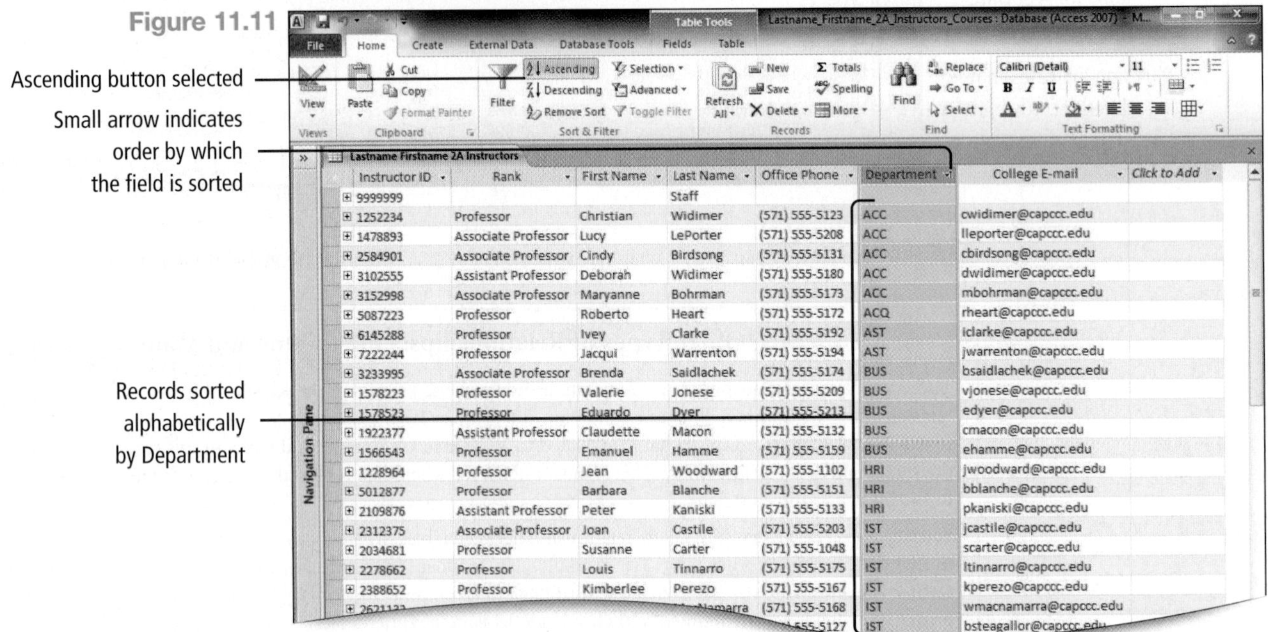

3 On the **Home tab**, in the **Sort & Filter group**, click the **Remove Sort** button to clear the sort and return the records to the default sort order, which is by the primary key field—*Instructor ID.*

4 Click the **Last Name arrow**, and then click **Sort Z to A**.

The records in the table are sorted by last name in reverse alphabetical order. The small arrow in the Field name box points down, indicating a descending sort. On the Ribbon, the Descending button is selected.

5 In the **Sort & Filter group**, click the **Remove Sort** button.

Activity 11.06 | Sorting Records in a Table on Multiple Fields

To sort a table on two or more fields, first identify the fields that will act as the ***outermost sort field*** and the ***innermost sort field***. The outermost sort field is the first level of sorting, and the innermost sort field is the second level of sorting. For example, you might want to sort first by the Last Name field, which would be the outermost sort field, and then by the First Name field, which would be the innermost sort field. After you identify your outermost and innermost sort fields, sort the innermost field first, and then sort the outermost field.

In this activity, you will sort the records in descending order by the department name. Within each department name, you will sort the records in ascending order by last name.

1 In the **Last Name** field, click any record. In the **Sort & Filter group**, click the **Ascending** button.

The records are sorted in ascending alphabetical order by Last Name—the innermost sort field.

2 Point anywhere in the **Department** field, and then right-click. From the shortcut menu, click **Sort Z to A**. Compare your screen with Figure 11.12.

The records are sorted in descending alphabetical order first by Department—the *outermost* sort field—and then within a specific Department grouping, the sort continues in ascending alphabetical order by Last Name—the *innermost* sort field. The records are sorted on multiple fields using both ascending and descending order.

Figure 11.12

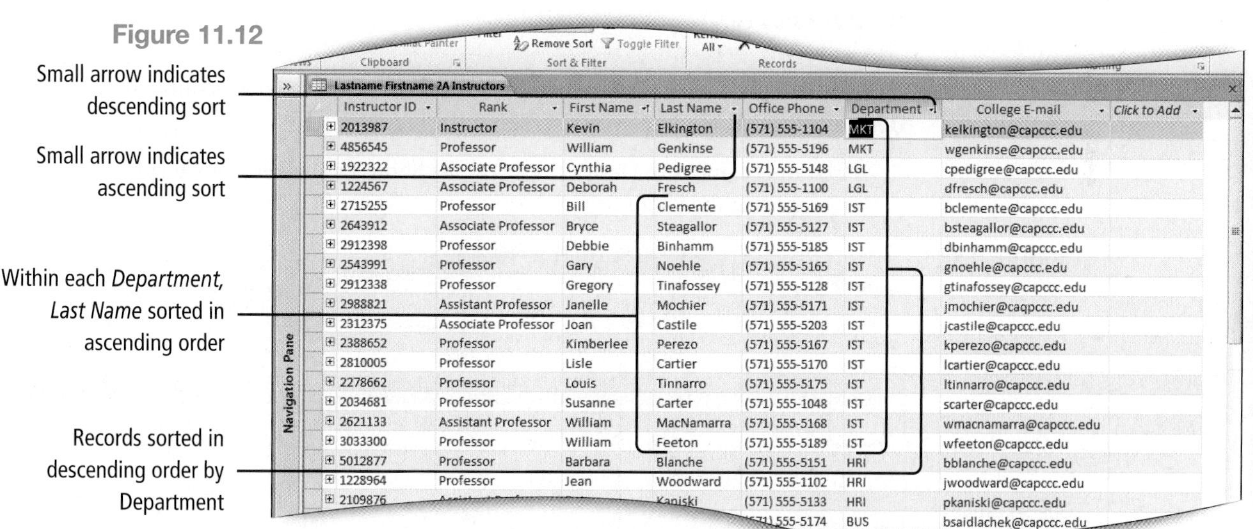

3 Display **Backstage** view, click **Print**, and then click **Print Preview**. In the **Page Layout** group, click the **Landscape** button. In the **Zoom group**, click the **Two Pages** button, and notice that the table will print on two pages.

4 On the **Print Preview tab**, in the **Print group**, click the **Print** button. Under **Print Range**, click the **Pages** option button. In the **From** box, type **1** and then in the **To** box, type **1** to print only the first page. If directed to submit a paper copy, click OK or create an electronic copy as instructed. To create a PDF of only the first page, in the Data group, click PDF or XPS, click the Options button, and then indicate *Page 1 to 1*. In the **Close Preview group**, click the **Close Print Preview** button.

5 In the object window, **Close** [×] the table. In the message box, click **Yes** to save the changes to the sort order.

6 **Open** [»] the **Navigation Pane**, and then open the **2A Instructors** table. Notice the table was saved with the sort order you specified.

7 In the **Sort & Filter group**, click the **Remove Sort** button. **Close** [×] the table, and in the message box, click **Yes** to save the table with the sort removed. **Close** [«] the **Navigation Pane**.

Generally, tables are not stored with the data sorted. Instead, queries are created that sort the data; and then reports are created to display the sorted data.

Objective 4 | Create a Query in Design View

Recall that a ***select query*** is a database object that retrieves (selects) specific data from one or more tables and then displays the specified data in Datasheet view. A query answers a question such as *Which instructors teach courses in the IST department?* Unless a query has already been set up to ask this question, you must create a new query.

Database users rarely need to see all of the records in all of the tables. That is why a query is so useful; it creates a ***subset*** of records—a portion of the total records—according to your specifications and then displays only those records.

Activity 11.07 | Creating a New Select Query in Design View

Previously, you created a query using the Query Wizard. To create complex queries, use Query Design view. The table or tables from which a query selects its data is referred to as the ***data source***.

1 On the Ribbon, click the **Create tab**, and then in the **Queries group**, click the **Query Design** button. Compare your screen with Figure 11.13.

A new query opens in Design view and the Show Table dialog box displays, which lists both tables in the database.

Figure 11.13

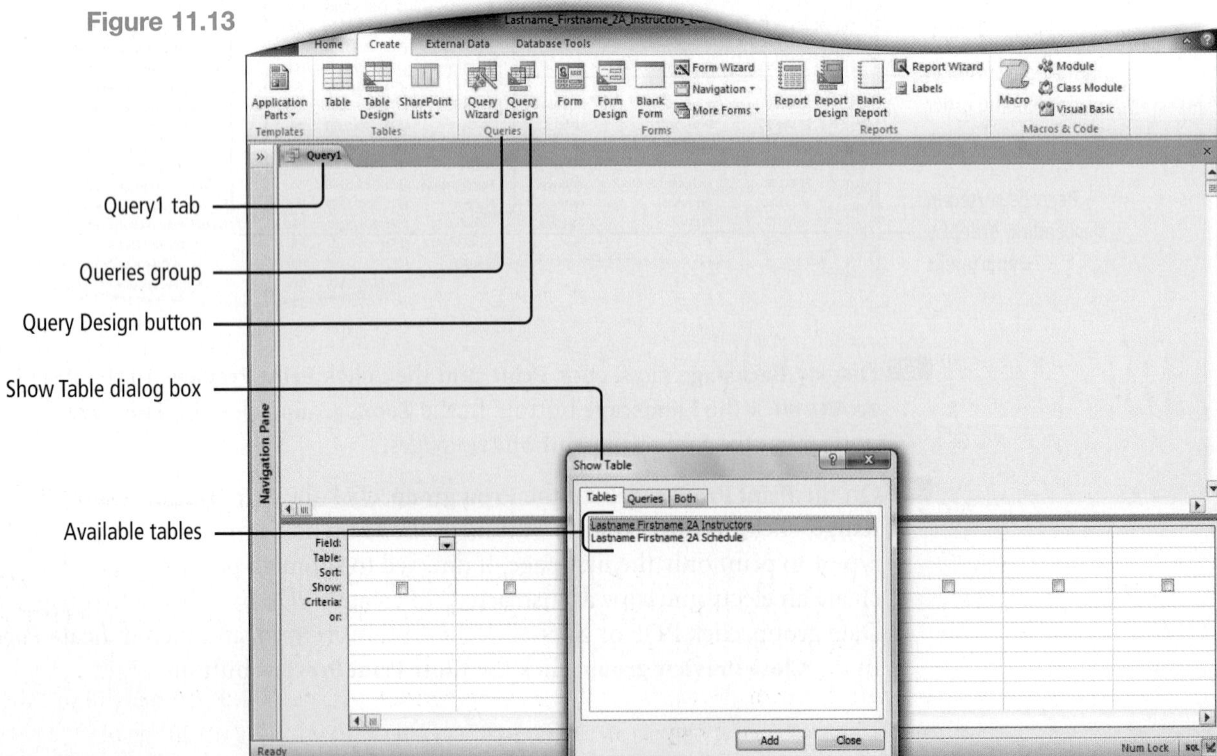

2 In the **Show Table** dialog box, double-click **2A Instructors**, and then **Close** the **Show Table** dialog box.

A field list for the 2A Instructors table displays in the upper area of the Query window. The Instructor ID field is the primary key field in this table. The Query window has two parts: the ***table area*** (upper area), which displays the field lists for tables that are used in the query, and the ***design grid*** (lower area), which displays the design of the query.

> **Alert! | Is There More Than One Field List in the Query Window?**
>
> If you double-click a table more than one time, a duplicate field list displays in the Query window. To remove a field list from the Query window, right-click the title bar of the field list, and then click Remove Table.

3 Point to the lower right corner of the field list to display the pointer, and then drag down and to the right to expand the field list, displaying all of the field names and the table name. In the **2A Instructors** field list, double-click **Rank**, and then look at the design grid.

The Rank field name displays in the design grid in the Field row. You limit the fields that display when the query is run by placing only the desired field names in the design grid.

4 In the **2A Instructors** field list, point to **First Name**, hold down the left mouse button, and then drag down into the design grid until the pointer displays in the **Field** row in the second column. Release the mouse button, and then compare your screen with Figure 11.14.

This is a second way to add field names to the design grid. As you drag the field, a small rectangular shape attaches to the mouse pointer. When you release the mouse button, the field name displays in the Field row.

Figure 11.14

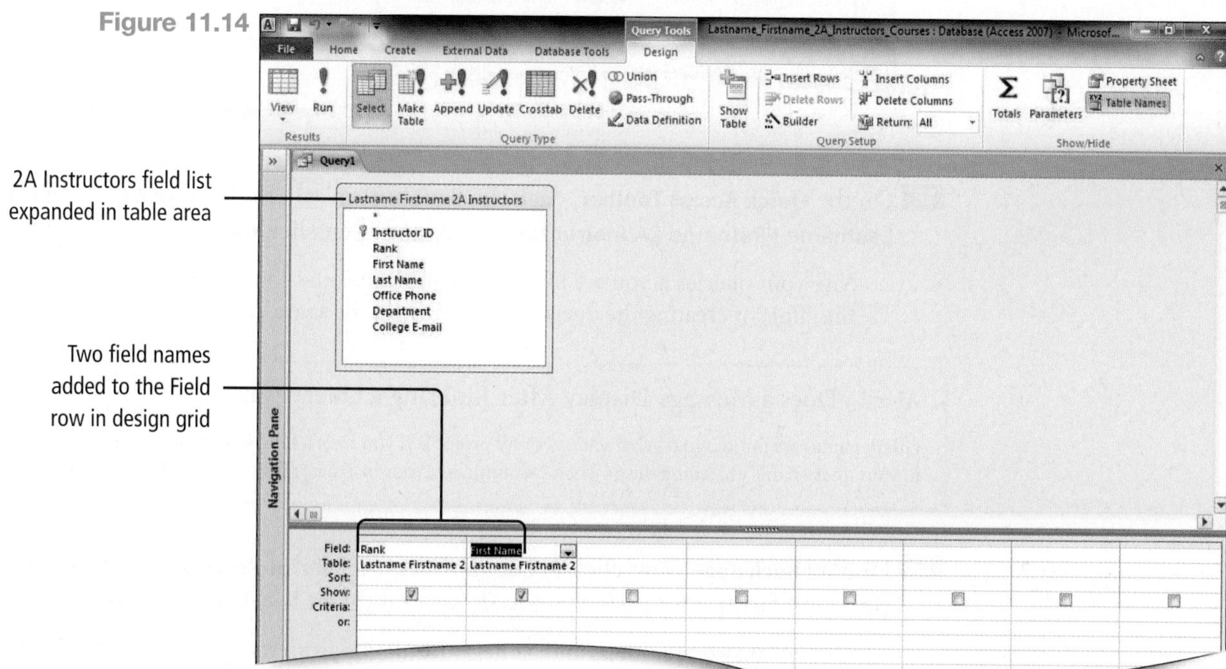

5 In design grid, in the **Field** row, click in the third column, and then click the **arrow** that displays. From the list, click **Last Name** to add the field to the design grid, which is a third way to add a field to the design grid.

6 Using one of the techniques you just practiced, add the **Office Phone** field to the fourth column and the **Department** field to the fifth column in the design grid.

Activity 11.08 | Running, Saving, Printing, and Closing a Query

After you create a query, you ***run*** it to display the results. When you run a query, Access looks at the records in the table (or tables) you have included in the query, finds the records that match the specified conditions (if any), and displays only those records in a datasheet. Only the fields that you have added to the design grid display in the query results. The query always runs using the current table or tables, presenting the most up-to-date information.

> **Another Way**
>
> On the Design tab, in the Results group, click the View button to automatically start the Run command.

1 On the **Design tab**, in the **Results group**, click the **Run** button, and then compare your screen with Figure 11.15.

This query answers the question, *What is the Rank, First Name, Last Name, Office Phone number, and Department of all of the instructors in the 2A Instructors table?* A query is a subset of the records in one or more tables, arranged in Datasheet view, using the fields and conditions that you specify. The five fields that you specified in the design grid display in columns, and the records from the 2A Instructors table display in rows.

Figure 11.15

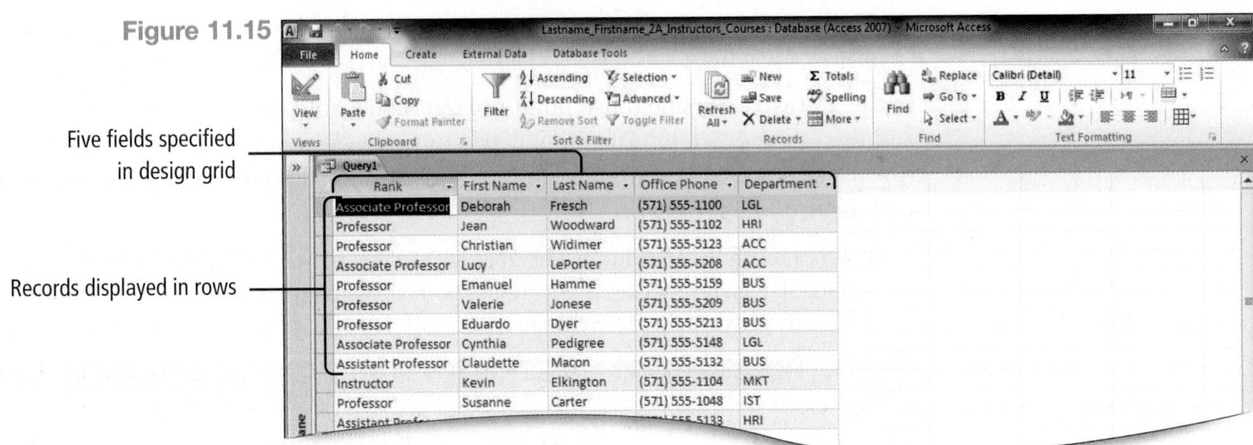

2 On the **Quick Access Toolbar**, click the **Save** button. In the **Save As** dialog box, type **Lastname Firstname 2A Instructors Query** and then click **OK**.

Save your queries if you are likely to ask the same question again; doing so will save you the effort of creating the query again to answer the same question.

> **Alert! | Does a Message Display After Entering a Query Name?**
>
> Query names are limited to 64 characters. For all projects, if you have a long last name or first name that results in your query name exceeding the 64-character limit, ask your instructor how you should abbreviate your name.

3 Display **Backstage** view, click **Print**, and then click **Print Preview**. Create a paper or electronic printout if instructed to do so, and then **Close Print Preview**.

Queries answer questions and gather information from the data in the tables. Queries are typically created as a basis for a report, but query results can be printed like any other table of data.

4 **Close** [X] the query. **Open** [»] the **Navigation Pane**, and then notice that the **2A Instructors Query** object displays under the **2A Instructors** table object.

The new query name displays in the Navigation Pane under the table with which it is related—the 2A Instructors table. Only the design of the query is saved. The records still reside in the table object. Each time you open the query, Access runs it again and displays the results based on the data stored in the related table(s). Thus, the results of a query always reflect the latest information in the related table(s).

Objective 5 | Create a New Query from an Existing Query

You can create a new query from scratch or you can open an existing query, save it with new name, and modify the design to suit your needs. Using an existing query saves you time if your new query uses all or some of the same fields and conditions in an existing query.

Activity 11.09 | Creating a New Query from an Existing Query

1 From the **Navigation Pane**, open your **2A Instructors Query** by either double-clicking the name or by right-clicking and clicking Open.

The query runs, opens in Datasheet view, and displays the records from the 2A Instructors table as specified in the query design grid.

2 Display **Backstage** view, and then click **Save Object As**. In the **Save As** dialog box, type **Lastname Firstname 2A Instructor IDs Query** and then click **OK**. Click the **Home tab**, and then in the **Views group**, click the **View** button to switch to **Design** view.

A new query, based on a copy of the 2A Instructors Query, is created and displays in the object window and in the Navigation Pane under its data source—the 2A Instructors table.

3 **Close** [«] the **Navigation Pane**. In the design grid, point to the thin gray selection bar above the **Office Phone** field name until the [↓] pointer displays. Click to select the **Office Phone** column, and then press [Del].

This action deletes the field from the query design only—it has no effect on the field in the underlying 2A Instructors table. The Department field moves to the left. Similarly, you can select multiple fields and delete them at one time.

4 From the gray selection bar, select the **First Name** column. In the selected column, point to the selection bar to display the pointer, and then drag to the right until a dark vertical line displays on the right side of the **Last Name** column. Release the mouse button to position the **First Name** field in the third column.

To rearrange fields in the query design, select the field to move, and then drag it to a new position in the design grid.

5 Using the technique you just practiced, move the **Department** field to the left of the **Rank** field.

6 From the field list, drag the **Instructor ID** field down to the first column in the design grid until the pointer displays, and then release the mouse button. Compare your screen with Figure 11.16.

The Instructor ID field displays in the first column, and the remaining four fields move to the right. Use this method to insert a field to the left of a field already displayed in the design grid.

Figure 11.16

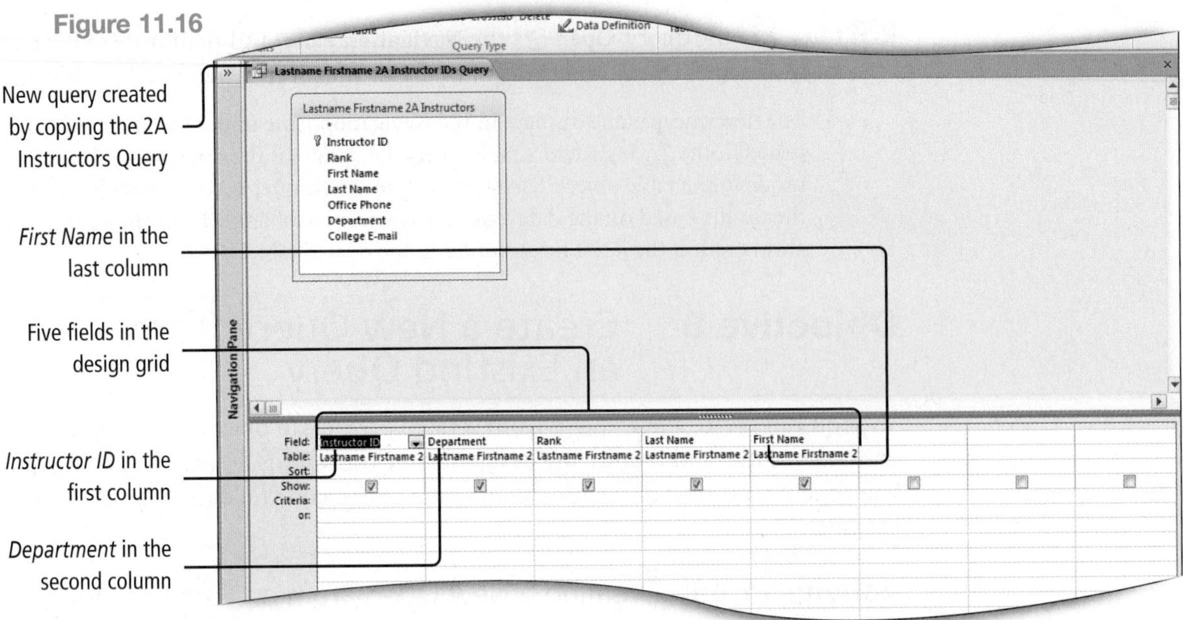

7 On the **Design tab**, in the **Results group**, click the **Run** button.

This query answers the question, *What is the Instructor ID, Department, Rank, Last Name, and First Name for every instructor in the 2A Instructors table?* The results of the query are a subset of the records contained in the 2A Instructors table. The records are sorted by the primary key field—Instructor ID.

8 From **Backstage** view, display the query in **Print Preview**. Create a paper or electronic printout if instructed to do so, and then **Close Print Preview**.

9 **Close** [X] the query, and in the message box, click **Yes** to save the changes to the design—deleting a field, moving two fields, and adding a field. **Open** [»] the **Navigation Pane**.

The query is saved and closed. The new query name displays in the Navigation Pane under the related table. Recall that when you save a query, only the *design* of the query is saved; the records reside in the related table object or objects.

Objective 6 | Sort Query Results

You can sort the results of a query in ascending or descending order in either Datasheet view or Design view. Use Design view if your query results should display in a specified sort order, or if you intend to use the sorted results in a report.

Activity 11.10 | Sorting Query Results

In this activity, you will save an existing query with a new name, and then sort the query results by using the Sort row in Design view.

1 On the **Navigation Pane**, click your **2A Instructor IDs Query**. Display **Backstage** view, and then click **Save Object As**. In the **Save As** dialog box, type **Lastname Firstname 2A Department Sort Query** and then click **OK**. Click the **Home tab**, and then drag the right edge of the **Navigation Pane** to the right to increase its width so that the names of the new query and the relationship report display fully.

Access creates a new query, based on a copy of your 2A Instructors ID Query; that is, the new query includes the same fields in the same order as the query on which it is based.

2 In the **Navigation Pane**, right-click your **2A Department Sort Query**, and then click **Design View. Close** [«] the **Navigation Pane.**

3 In the design grid, in the **Sort** row, click in the **Last Name** field to display the insertion point and an arrow. Click the **Sort arrow**, and then in the list, click **Ascending**. Compare your screen with Figure 11.17.

Figure 11.17

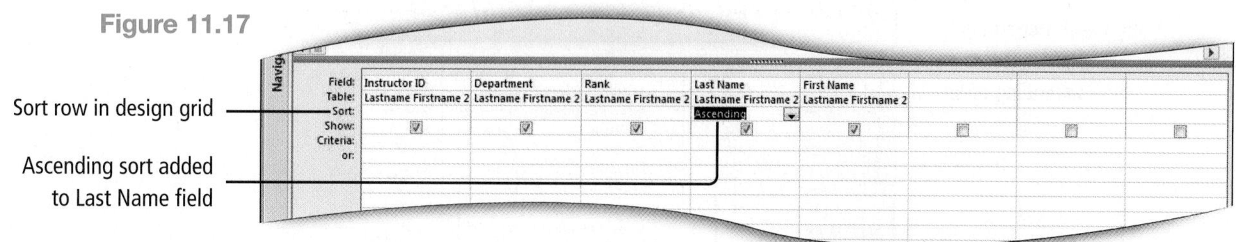

4 On the **Design tab** in the **Results group**, click the **Run** button.

In the query result, the records are sorted in ascending alphabetical order by the Last Name field, and two instructors have the same last name of *Widimer*.

5 On the **Home tab** in the **Views group**, click the **View** button to switch to **Design** view.

6 In the **Sort** row, click in the **First Name** field, click the **Sort arrow**, and then click **Ascending**. **Run** the query.

In the query result, the records are sorted first by the Last Name field. If instructors have the same last name, then Access sorts those records by the First Name field. The two instructors with the last name of *Widimer* are sorted by their first names.

7 Switch to **Design** view. In the **Sort** row, click in the **Department** field, click the **Sort arrow**, and then click **Descending**. **Run** the query; if necessary, scroll down to display the last records, and then compare your screen with Figure 11.18.

In Design view, fields with a Sort designation are sorted from left to right. That is, the sorted field on the left becomes the outermost sort field, and the sorted field on the right becomes the innermost sort field.

Thus, the records are sorted first in descending alphabetical order by the Department field—the leftmost sort field. Then, within each same department name field, the Last Names are sorted in ascending alphabetical order. And, finally, within each same last name field, the First Names are sorted in ascending alphabetical order.

If you run a query and the sorted results are not what you intended, be sure that the fields are displayed from left to right according to the groupings that you desire.

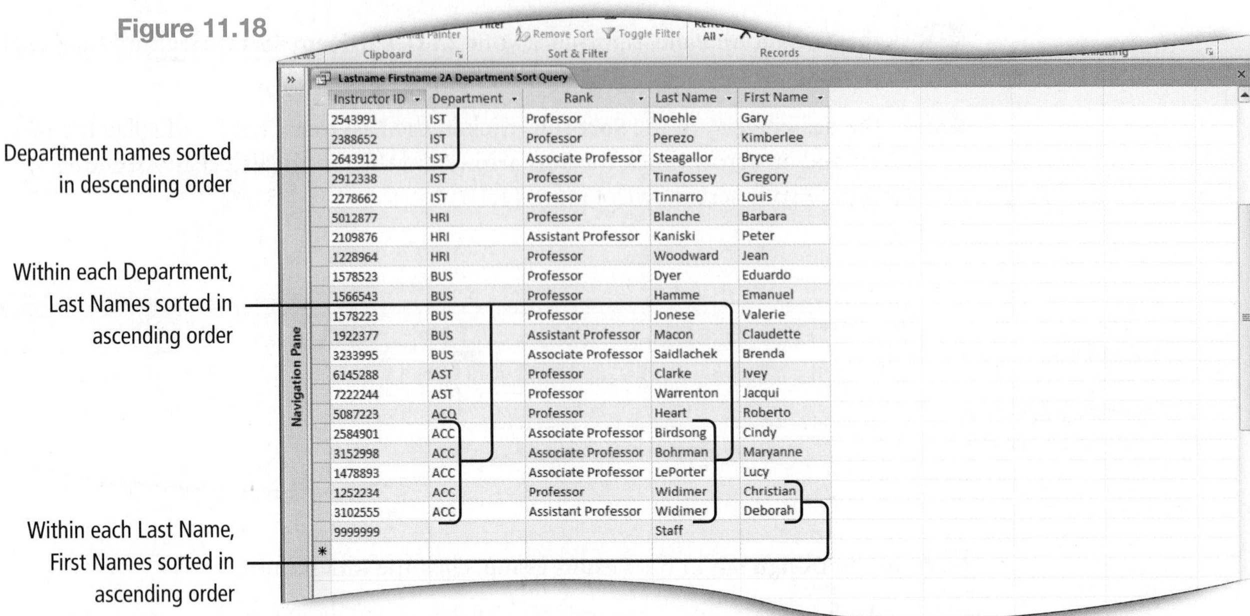

Instructor ID	Department	Rank	Last Name	First Name
2543991	IST	Professor	Noehle	Gary
2388652	IST	Professor	Perezo	Kimberlee
2643912	IST	Associate Professor	Steagallor	Bryce
2912338	IST	Professor	Tinafossey	Gregory
2278662	IST	Professor	Tinnarro	Louis
5012877	HRI	Professor	Blanche	Barbara
2109876	HRI	Assistant Professor	Kaniski	Peter
1228964	HRI	Professor	Woodward	Jean
1578523	BUS	Professor	Dyer	Eduardo
1566543	BUS	Professor	Hamme	Emanuel
1578223	BUS	Professor	Jonese	Valerie
1922377	BUS	Assistant Professor	Macon	Claudette
3233995	BUS	Associate Professor	Saidlachek	Brenda
6145288	AST	Professor	Clarke	Ivey
7222244	AST	Professor	Warrenton	Jacqui
5087223	ACQ	Professor	Heart	Roberto
2584901	ACC	Associate Professor	Birdsong	Cindy
3152998	ACC	Associate Professor	Bohrman	Maryanne
1478893	ACC	Associate Professor	LePorter	Lucy
1252234	ACC	Professor	Widimer	Christian
3102555	ACC	Assistant Professor	Widimer	Deborah
9999999			Staff	

Figure 11.18

8 Display the query in **Print Preview**. Create a paper or electronic printout if instructed to do so, and then **Close Print Preview. Close** ☒ the query. In the message box, click **Yes** to save the changes to the query design.

> **More Knowledge | Sorting**
>
> If you add a sort order to the *design* of a query, it remains as a permanent part of the query design. If you use the sort buttons in the Datasheet view, they will override the sort order of the query design, and can be saved as part of the query. A sort order designated in Datasheet view does not display in the Sort row of the query design grid.

Objective 7 | Specify Criteria in a Query

Queries locate information in a database based on ***criteria*** that you specify as part of the query. Criteria are conditions that identify the specific records for which you are looking.

Criteria enable you to ask a more specific question; therefore, you will get a more specific result. For example, if you want to find out how many instructors are in the IST department, limit the results to that specific department, and then only the records that match the specified department will display.

Activity 11.11 | Specifying Text Criteria in a Query

In this activity, you will assist Dean Judkins by creating a query to answer the question *How many instructors are in the IST Department?*

1 Be sure that all objects are closed and that the **Navigation Pane** is closed. Click the **Create tab**, and then in the **Queries group**, click the **Query Design** button.

2 In the **Show Table** dialog box, **Add** the **2A Instructors** table to the table area, and then **Close** the **Show Table** dialog box.

3 Expand the field list to display all of the fields and the table name. Add the following fields to the design grid in the order given: **Department**, **Instructor ID**, **Rank**, **First Name**, and **Last Name**.

4 In the **Criteria** row of the design grid, click in the **Department** field, type **IST** and then press Enter. Compare your screen with Figure 11.19.

Access places quotation marks around the criteria to indicate that this is a ***text string***—a sequence of characters. Use the Criteria row to specify the criteria that will limit the results of the query to your exact specifications. The criteria is not case sensitive; so you can type *ist* instead of IST.

Figure 11.19

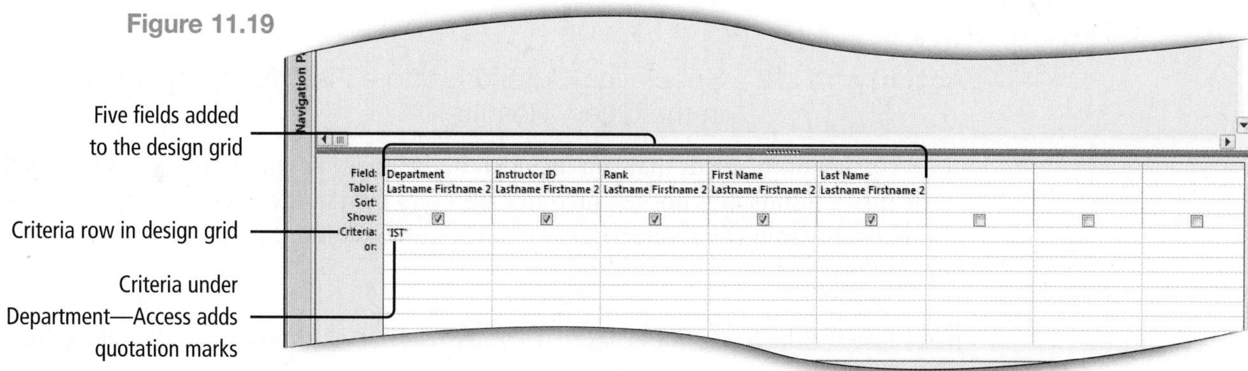

Note | Pressing Enter After Adding Criteria

If you press Enter or click in another column or row in the query design grid after you have added your criteria, you can see how Access alters the criteria so it can interpret what you have typed. Sometimes, there is no change, such as when you add criteria to a number or currency field. Other times, Access may capitalize a letter or add quotation marks or other symbols to clarify the criteria. Whether or not you press Enter after adding criteria has no effect on the query results. It is used here to help you see how the program behaves.

5 **Run** the query, and then compare your screen with Figure 11.20.

Thirteen records display that meet the specified criteria—records that have *IST* in the Department field.

Figure 11.20

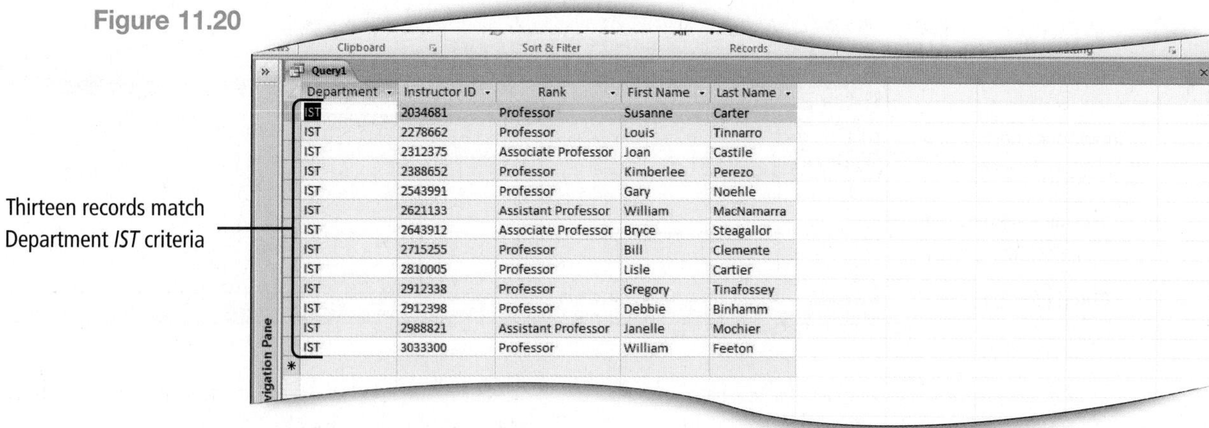

Department	Instructor ID	Rank	First Name	Last Name
IST	2034681	Professor	Susanne	Carter
IST	2278662	Professor	Louis	Tinnarro
IST	2312375	Associate Professor	Joan	Castile
IST	2388652	Professor	Kimberlee	Perezo
IST	2543991	Professor	Gary	Noehle
IST	2621133	Assistant Professor	William	MacNamarra
IST	2643912	Associate Professor	Bryce	Steagallor
IST	2715255	Professor	Bill	Clemente
IST	2810005	Professor	Lisle	Cartier
IST	2912338	Professor	Gregory	Tinafossey
IST	2912398	Professor	Debbie	Binhamm
IST	2988821	Assistant Professor	Janelle	Mochier
IST	3033300	Professor	William	Feeton

Alert! | Do Your Query Results Differ?

If you mistype the criteria, or enter it under the wrong field, or make some other error, the result will display no records. This indicates that there are no records in the table that match the criteria as you entered it. If this occurs, return to Design view and re-examine the query design. Verify that the criteria is typed in the Criteria row, under the correct field, and without typing errors. Then run the query again.

6 **Save** [Save icon] the query as **Lastname Firstname 2A IST Query** and then display the query in **Print Preview**. Create a paper or electronic printout if instructed to do so, and then **Close Print Preview**.

7 **Close** [X] the query, **Open** [»] the **Navigation Pane**, and then notice that the **2A IST Query** object displays under the **2A Instructors** table—its data source.

Recall that queries in the Navigation Pane display an icon of two overlapping tables.

Activity 11.12 | Specifying Criteria Using a Field Not Displayed in the Query Results

So far, all of the fields that you included in the query design have also been included in the query results. It is not required to have every field in the query display in the results. In this activity, you will create a query to answer the question, *Which instructors have a rank of Professor?*

1 **Close** [«] the **Navigation Pane**. Click the **Create tab**, and then in the **Queries group**, click the **Query Design** button.

2 From the **Show Table** dialog box, **Add** the **2A Instructors** table to the table area, and then **Close** the dialog box. Expand the field list.

3 Add the following fields, in the order given, to the design grid: **Instructor ID**, **First Name**, **Last Name**, and **Rank**.

4 In the **Sort** row, in the **Last Name** field, click the **Sort arrow**; click **Ascending**.

5 In the **Criteria** row, click in the **Rank** field, type **professor** and then press Enter. Compare your screen with Figure 11.21.

Recall that criteria is not case sensitive. As you start typing *professor*, a list of functions display, from which you can select if including a function in your criteria. When you press Enter, the insertion point moves to the next criteria box and quotation marks are added around the text string that you entered.

Figure 11.21

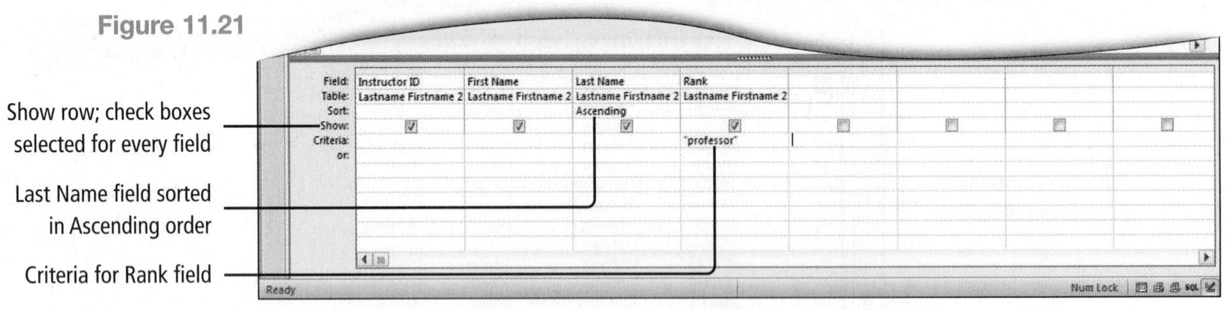

6 In the design grid, in the **Show** row, notice that the check box is selected for every field. **Run** the query to view the query results.

Nineteen records meet the criteria. In the Rank column each record displays *Professor*, and the records are sorted in ascending alphabetical order by the Last Name field.

7 Switch to **Design** view. In the design grid, under **Rank**, in the **Show** row, click to clear the check box.

Because it is repetitive and not particularly useful to have *Professor* display for each record in the query results, clear this check box so that the field does not display. However, you should run the query before clearing the Show check box to be sure that the correct records display.

8 **Run** the query, and then notice that the *Rank* field does not display.

The query results display the same 19 records, but the *Rank* field does not display. Although the Rank field is still included in the query criteria for the purpose of identifying specific records, it is not necessary to display the field in the results. When appropriate, clear the Show check box to avoid cluttering the query results with data that is not useful.

9 **Save** the query as **Lastname Firstname 2A Professor Rank Query** and then display the query in **Print Preview**. Create a paper or electronic printout if instructed to do so, and then **Close Print Preview**. **Close** the query.

Activity 11.13 | Using *Is Null* Criteria to Find Empty Fields

Sometimes you must locate records where data is *missing*. You can locate such records by using ***Is Null***—empty—as the criteria in a field. Additionally, you can display only the records where a value *has* been entered in a field by using ***Is Not Null*** as the criteria, which will exclude records where the specified field is empty. In this activity, you will design a query to find out *Which scheduled courses have no credits listed?*

1 Click the **Create tab**. In the **Queries group**, click the **Query Design** button. Add the **2A Schedule** table to the table area, **Close** the **Show Table** dialog box, and then expand the field list.

2 Add the following fields to the design grid in the order given: **Subject**, **Catalog#**, **Section**, **Course Name**, and **Credits**.

3 In the **Criteria** row, click in the **Credits** field, type **is null** and then press Enter.

Access capitalizes *is null*. The criteria *Is Null* examines the field and looks for records that do *not* have any values entered in the Credits field.

4 In the **Sort** row, click in the **Subject** field, click the **Sort arrow**, and then click **Ascending**. **Sort** the **Catalog#** field in **Ascending** order, and then **Sort** the **Section** field in **Ascending** order. Compare your screen with Figure 11.22.

Figure 11.22

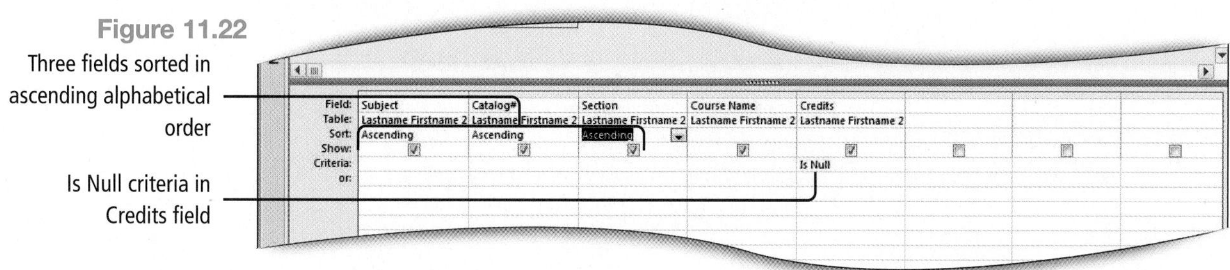

5 **Run** the query, and then compare your screen with Figure 11.23.

Five scheduled courses do not have credits listed—the Credits field is empty. The records are sorted in ascending order first by the Subject field, then by the Catalog # field, and then by the Section. Using the information displayed in the query results, a course scheduler can more easily locate the records in the table to enter the credits.

Figure 11.23

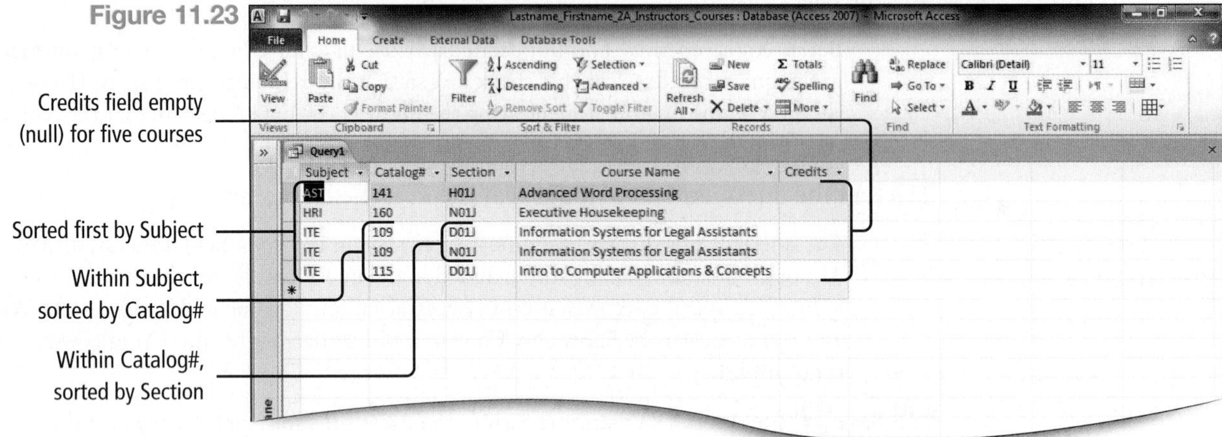

6 **Save** the query as **Lastname Firstname 2A No Credits Query** and then display the query in **Print Preview**. Create a paper or electronic printout if instructed to do so, and then **Close Print Preview**.

7 **Close** the query. **Open** the **Navigation Pane**, and then notice that the **2A No Credits Query** object displays under the **2A Schedule** table object, which is the query's data source.

8 From **Backstage** view, click **Close Database**, and then click **Exit** to close the Access program. As directed by your instructor, submit your database and the eight paper or electronic printouts—relationship report, sorted table, and six queries—that are the results of this project.

End **You have completed Project 11A**

Project 11B Athletic Scholarships Database

Project Activities

In Activities 11.14 through 11.26, you will assist Randy Shavrain, Athletic Director for Capital Cities Community College, in developing and querying his Athletic Scholarships database. Your results will look similar to Figure 11.24.

Project Files

For Project 11B, you will need the following files:

a02B_Athletes_Scholarships
a02B_Athletes (Excel file)

You will save your database as:

Lastname_Firstname_2B_Athletic_Scholarships

Project Results

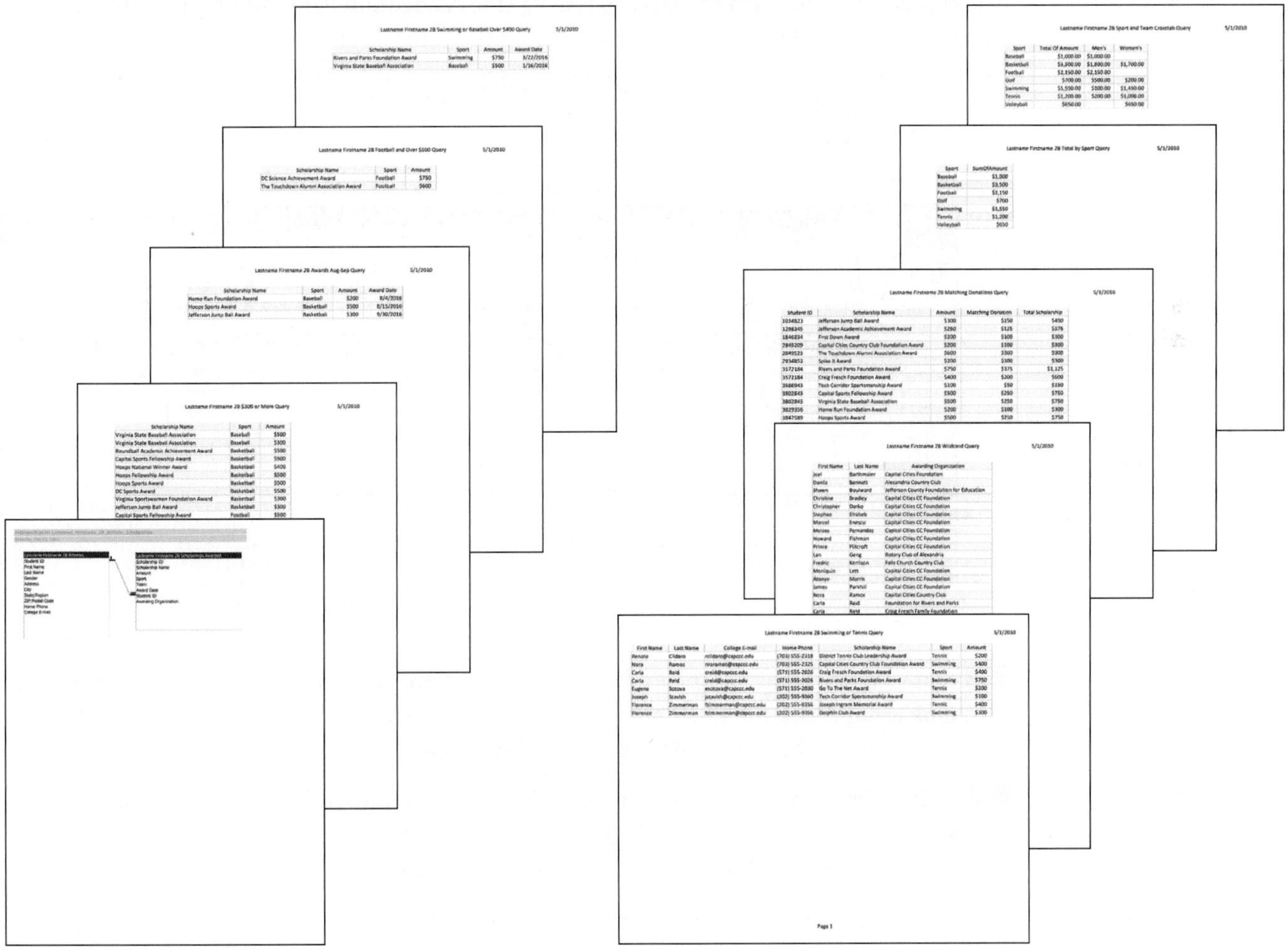

Figure 11.24
Project 11B Athletic Scholarships

Objective 8 | Specify Numeric Criteria in a Query

Criteria can be set for fields containing numeric data. When you design your table, set the appropriate data type for fields that will contain numbers, currency, or dates so that mathematical calculations can be performed.

Activity 11.14 | Opening an Existing Database and Importing a Spreadsheet

In this activity, you will open, rename, and save an existing database, and then import an Excel spreadsheet that Mr. Shavrain wants to bring into Access as a new table.

1. **Start** Access. In **Backstage** view, click **Open**. From your student files, open **a02B_Athletes_Scholarships**.

2. From **Backstage** view, click **Save Database As**. In the **Save As** dialog box, navigate to your **Access Chapter 11** folder, and then in the **File name** box, type **Lastname_Firstname_2B_Athletic_Scholarships** and then press Enter.

3. On the **Message Bar**, click the **Enable Content** button. In the **Navigation Pane**, **Rename** **2B Scholarships Awarded** to **Lastname Firstname 2B Scholarships Awarded**, and then double-click to open the table. **Close** « the **Navigation Pane**, and then examine the data in the table. Compare your screen with Figure 11.25.

   In this table, Mr. Shavrain tracks the names and amounts of scholarships awarded to student athletes. Students are identified only by their Student ID numbers, and the primary key is the Scholarship ID field.

Figure 11.25

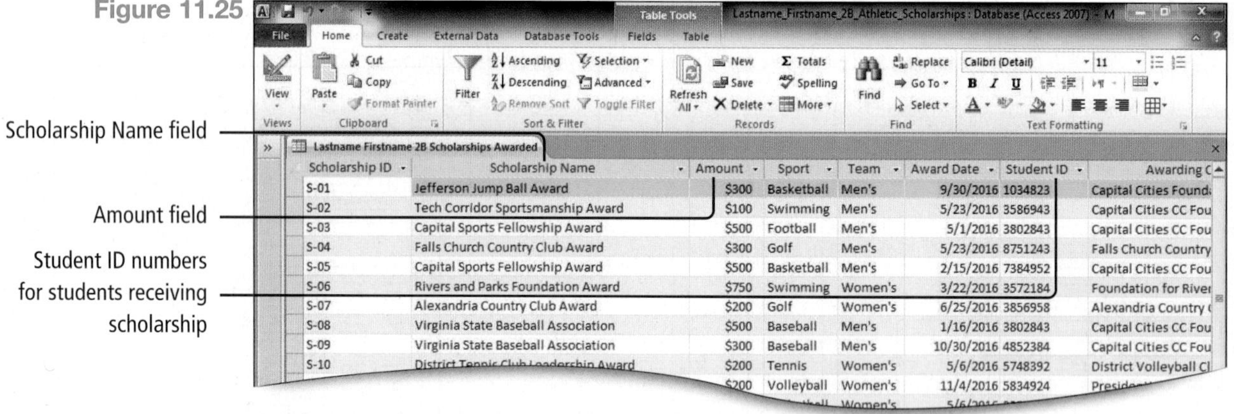

4. **Close** ✕ the table. On the Ribbon, click the **External Data tab**, and then in the **Import & Link group**, click the **Excel** button. In the **Get External Data – Excel Spreadsheet** dialog box, to the right of the **File name** box, click **Browse**.

5. In the **File Open** dialog box, navigate to your student data files, and then double-click **a02B_Athletes**. Be sure that the **Import the source data into a new table in the current database** option button is selected, and then click **OK**.

   The Import Spreadsheet Wizard opens and displays the spreadsheet data.

6. Click **Next**. In the upper left portion of the **Import Spreadsheet Wizard** dialog box, select the **First Row Contains Column Headings** check box. Click **Next**, and then click **Next** again.

7 In the upper portion of the Wizard, click the **Choose my own primary key** option button, and then be sure that **Student ID** displays.

In the new table, Student ID will be the primary key. No two students have the same Student ID.

8 Click **Next**. In the **Import to Table** box, type **Lastname Firstname 2B Athletes** and then click **Finish**. In the **Get External Data – Excel Spreadsheet** Wizard, click **Close**, and then **Open** [»] the **Navigation Pane**. Widen the **Navigation Pane** so that the table names display fully.

9 **Open** the new **2B Athletes** table, and then on the **Home tab**, switch to **Design View**.

10 For the **Student ID** field, click in the **Data Type** box, click the **arrow**, and then click **Text**. For the **ZIP/Postal Code** field, change the **Data Type** to **Text**, and then set the **Field Size** to **5** Click in the **State/Region** field, set the **Field Size** to **2** and then switch back to **Datasheet View**, saving the changes.

Recall that numeric data that will not be used in any calculations, such as the Student ID, should have a Data Type of *Text*.

11 In the message box, click **Yes**—no data will be lost. **Close** [«] the **Navigation Pane**. Take a moment to review the imported data. Using the **Select All** button [ ], apply **Best Fit** to all of the fields. Click in any field to cancel the selection, **Save** [ ] the table, and then **Close** [×] the table.

Activity 11.15 | Creating Table Relationships

In this activity, you will create a one-to-many relationship between the 2B Athletes table and the 2B Scholarships Awarded table by using the common field—*Student ID*.

1 Click the **Database Tools tab**, and then in the **Relationships group**, click the **Relationships** button.

2 In the **Show Table** dialog box, **Add** the **2B Athletes** table, and then **Add** the **2B Scholarships Awarded** table to the table area. **Close** the **Show Table** dialog box.

3 Move and resize the two field lists to display all of the fields and the entire table name, and then position the field lists so that there is approximately one inch of space between the two field lists.

Resizing and repositioning the field lists is not required, but doing so makes it easier for you to view the field lists and the join line when creating relationships.

4 In the **2B Athletes** field list, point to the **Student ID** field. Hold down the left mouse button, drag into the **2B Scholarships Awarded** field list on top of the **Student ID** field, and then release the mouse button to display the **Edit Relationships** dialog box.

5 Point to the title bar of the **Edit Relationships** dialog box, and then drag it below the two field lists. In the **Edit Relationships** dialog box, be sure that **Student ID** is displayed as the common field for both tables.

The two tables relate in a *one-to-many* relationship—*one* athlete can have *many* scholarships. The common field between the two tables is the Student ID field. In the 2B Athletes table, Student ID is the primary key. In the 2B Scholarships Awarded table, Student ID is the foreign key.

6 In the **Edit Relationships** dialog box, select the **Enforce Referential Integrity** check box. Click **Create**, and then compare your screen with Figure 11.26.

The one-to-many relationship is established. The *1* and ∞ indicate that referential integrity is enforced, which ensures that a scholarship cannot be awarded to a student whose Student ID is not in the 2B Athletes table. Similarly, you cannot delete a student athlete from the 2B Athletes table if there is a scholarship listed for that student in the 2B Scholarships Awarded table.

Figure 11.26

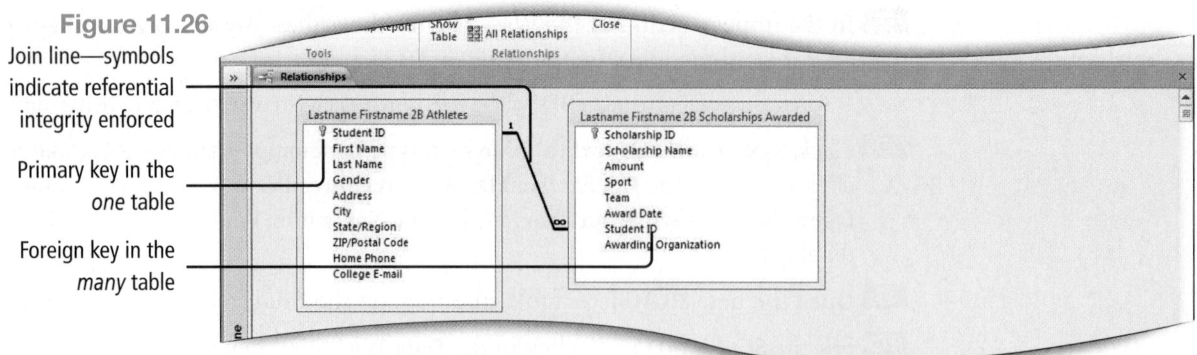

7 On the **Design tab**, in the **Tools group**, click the **Relationship Report** button. Create a paper or electronic printout if instructed to do so.

8 **Save** the report as **Lastname Firstname 2B Relationships** and then click **OK**. **Close** the report, and then **Close** the **Relationships** window.

9 **Open** the **Navigation Pane**, open the **2B Athletes** table, and then **Close** the **Navigation Pane**. On the left side of the table, in the first record, click the **plus sign** (+) to display the subdatasheet for the record.

In the first record, for *Joel Barthmaier*, one related record exists in the 2B Scholarships Awarded table. The related record displays because you created a relationship between the two tables using Student ID as the common field.

10 **Close** the **2B Athletes** table.

Activity 11.16 | Specifying Numeric Criteria in a Query

Mr. Shavrain wants to know *Which scholarships are in the amount of $300, and for which sports?* In this activity, you will specify criteria in the query so that only the records of scholarships in the amount of $300 display.

1 Click the **Create tab**. In the **Queries group**, click the **Query Design** button.

2 In the **Show Table** dialog box, **Add** the **2B Scholarships Awarded** table to the table area, and then **Close** the **Show Table** dialog box. Expand the field list to display all of the fields and the entire table name.

3 Add the following fields to the design grid in the order given: **Scholarship Name**, **Sport**, and **Amount**.

4 In the **Sort** row, click in the **Sport** field. Click the **Sort arrow**, and then click **Ascending**.

5 In the **Criteria** row, click in the **Amount** field, type **300** and then press Enter. Compare your screen with Figure 11.27.

When entering currency values as criteria, do not type the dollar sign. Include a decimal point only if you are looking for a specific amount that includes cents—for example 300.49. Access does not insert quotation marks around the criteria because the field's data type is Number.

Figure 11.27

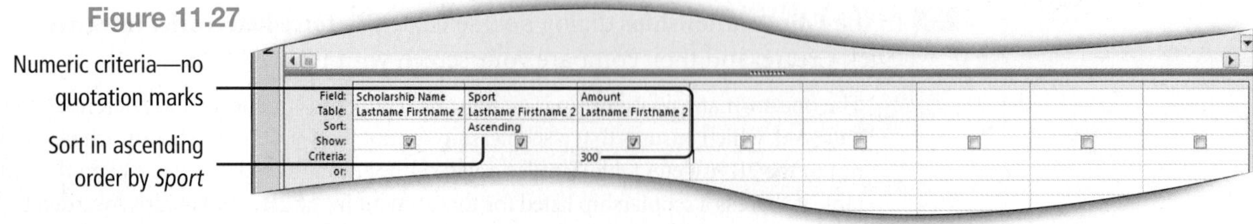

6 On the **Design tab**, in the **Results group**, click the **Run** button to view the results.

Five scholarships were awarded in the exact amount of $300. In the navigation area, *1 of 5* displays to indicate the number of records that match the criteria.

7 On the **Home tab**, in the **Views group**, click the **View** button to switch to **Design** view.

Activity 11.17 | Using Comparison Operators

Comparison operators are symbols that evaluate each field value to determine if it is the same (=), greater than (>), less than (<), or in between a range of values as specified by the criteria.

If no comparison operator is specified, equal (=) is assumed. For example, in the previous activity, you created a query to display only records where the *Amount* is 300. The comparison operator of = was assumed, and Access displayed only records that had values equal to 300.

1 Be sure your query is displayed in **Design** view. In the **Criteria** row, click in the **Amount** field, delete the existing criteria, type **>300** and then press Enter.

2 On the **Design tab**, in the **Results group**, click the **Run** button.

Fourteen records have an Amount that is greater than $300. The results show the records for which the Amount is *greater than* $300, but do not display amounts that are *equal to* $300.

3 Switch to **Design** view. In the **Criteria** row, under **Amount**, delete the existing criteria. Type **<300** and then press Enter. **Run** the query.

Eleven records display and each has an Amount less than $300. The results show the records for which the Amount is *less than* $300, but does not include amounts that are *equal to* $300.

4 Switch to **Design** view. In the **Criteria** row, click in the **Amount** field, delete the existing criteria, type **>=300** and then press Enter.

5 **Run** the query, and then compare your screen with Figure 11.28.

Nineteen records display, including the records for scholarships in the exact amount of $300. The records include scholarships *greater than* or *equal to* $300. In this manner, comparison operators can be combined. This query answers the question, *Which scholarships have been awarded in the amount of $300 or more, and for which sports, with the Sport names in alphabetical order?*

Figure 11.28

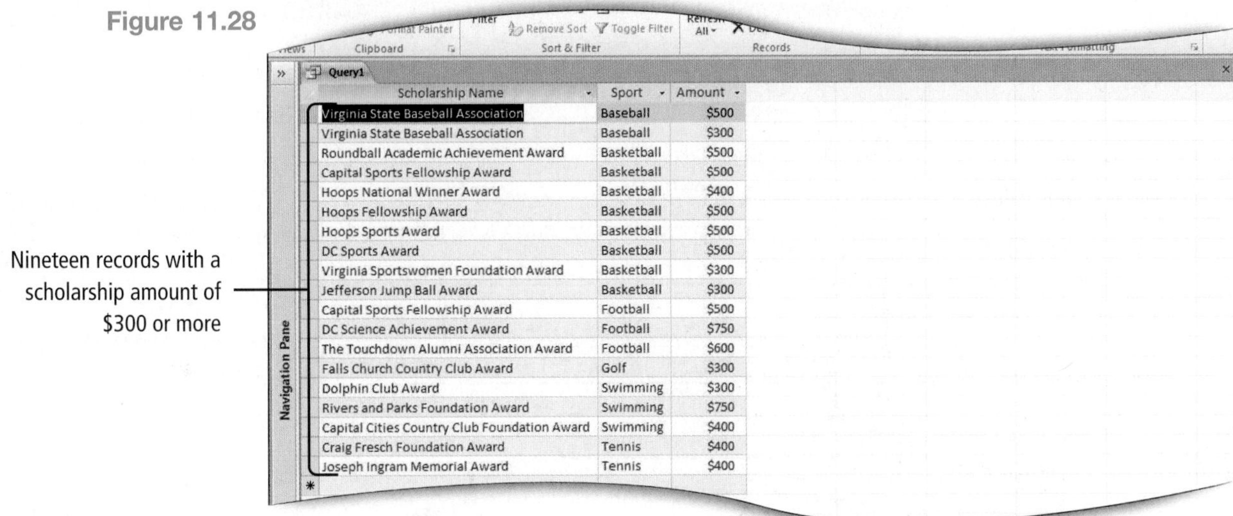

Scholarship Name	Sport	Amount
Virginia State Baseball Association	Baseball	$500
Virginia State Baseball Association	Baseball	$300
Roundball Academic Achievement Award	Basketball	$500
Capital Sports Fellowship Award	Basketball	$500
Hoops National Winner Award	Basketball	$400
Hoops Fellowship Award	Basketball	$500
Hoops Sports Award	Basketball	$500
DC Sports Award	Basketball	$500
Virginia Sportswomen Foundation Award	Basketball	$300
Jefferson Jump Ball Award	Basketball	$300
Capital Sports Fellowship Award	Football	$500
DC Science Achievement Award	Football	$750
The Touchdown Alumni Association Award	Football	$600
Falls Church Country Club Award	Golf	$300
Dolphin Club Award	Swimming	$300
Rivers and Parks Foundation Award	Swimming	$750
Capital Cities Country Club Foundation Award	Swimming	$400
Craig Fresch Foundation Award	Tennis	$400
Joseph Ingram Memorial Award	Tennis	$400

6 **Save** the query as **Lastname Firstname 2B $300 or More Query** and then display the query in **Print Preview**. Create a paper or electronic printout if instructed to do so, and then **Close Print Preview**.

7 **Close** the query. **Open** the **Navigation Pane**, and notice that the new query displays under the table from which it retrieved the records—*2B Scholarships Awarded.*

Activity 11.18 | Using the Between ... And Comparison Operator

The ***Between ... And operator*** is a comparison operator that looks for values within a range. It is useful when you need to locate records that are within a range of dates; for example, scholarships awarded between August 1 and September 30. In this activity, you will create a new query from an existing query, and then add criteria to look for values within a range of dates. The query will answer the question *Which scholarships were awarded between August 1 and September 30?*

1 On the **Navigation Pane**, click the **2B $300 or More Query** object to select it. Display **Backstage** view and click **Save Object As**. In the **Save As** dialog box, type **Lastname Firstname 2B Awards Aug-Sep Query** and then click **OK**.

2 Click the **Home tab**. Open the **2B Awards Aug-Sep Query** object, **Close** the **Navigation Pane**, and then switch to **Design** view. From the **2B Scholarships Awarded** field list, add the **Award Date** as the fourth field in the design grid.

3 In the **Criteria** row, click in the **Amount** field, and then delete the existing criteria so that the query is not restricted by amount. In the **Criteria** row, click in the **Award Date** field, type **between 8/1/16 and 9/30/16** and then press Enter.

4 In the selection bar of the design grid, point to the right edge of the **Award Date** column to display the pointer, and then double-click. Compare your screen with Figure 11.29.

The width of the Award Date column is increased to fit the longest entry, enabling you to see all of the criteria. Access places pound signs (#) around dates and capitalizes *between* and *and*. This criteria instructs Access to look for values in the Award Date field that begin with 8/1/16 and end with 9/30/16. Both the beginning and ending dates will be included in the query results.

Figure 11.29

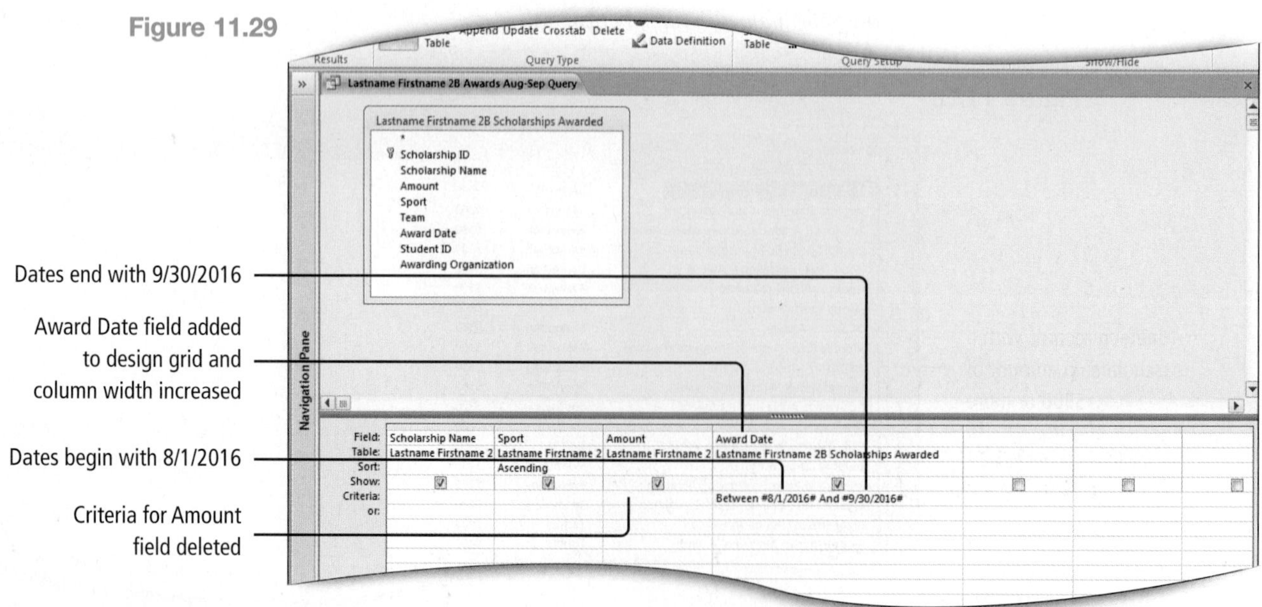

5 **Run** the query, and notice that three scholarships were awarded between 08/1/16 and 9/30/16.

6 Display the query in **Print Preview**, create a paper or electronic printout if instructed to do so, and then **Close Print Preview**.

7 **Close** [×] the query. In the message box, click **Yes** to save the changes to the query design. **Open** [»] the **Navigation Pane**, and notice that the new query displays under the table that is its data source—*2B Scholarships Awarded.*

Objective 9 | Use Compound Criteria

You can specify more than one condition—criteria—in a query; this is called ***compound criteria***. Compound criteria use AND and OR ***logical operators***. Logical operators enable you to enter criteria for the same field or different fields.

Activity 11.19 | Using AND Criteria in a Query

Compound criteria use an ***AND condition*** to display records in the query results that meet all parts of the specified criteria. In this activity, you will help Mr. Shavrain answer the question *Which scholarships over $500 were awarded for Football?*

1 **Close** [«] the **Navigation Pane.** On the Ribbon, click the **Create tab**. In the **Queries group**, click the **Query Design** button. **Add** the **2B Scholarships Awarded** table to the table area. **Close** the **Show Table** dialog box, and then expand the field list.

2 Add the following fields to the design grid in the order given: **Scholarship Name**, **Sport**, and **Amount**.

3 In the **Criteria** row, click in the **Sport** field, type **football** and then press Enter.

4 In the **Criteria** row, in the **Amount** field, type **>500** and then press Enter. Compare your screen with Figure 11.30.

You create the AND condition by placing the criteria for both fields on the same line in the Criteria row. The results will display only records that contain *Football* AND an amount greater than *$500*.

Figure 11.30

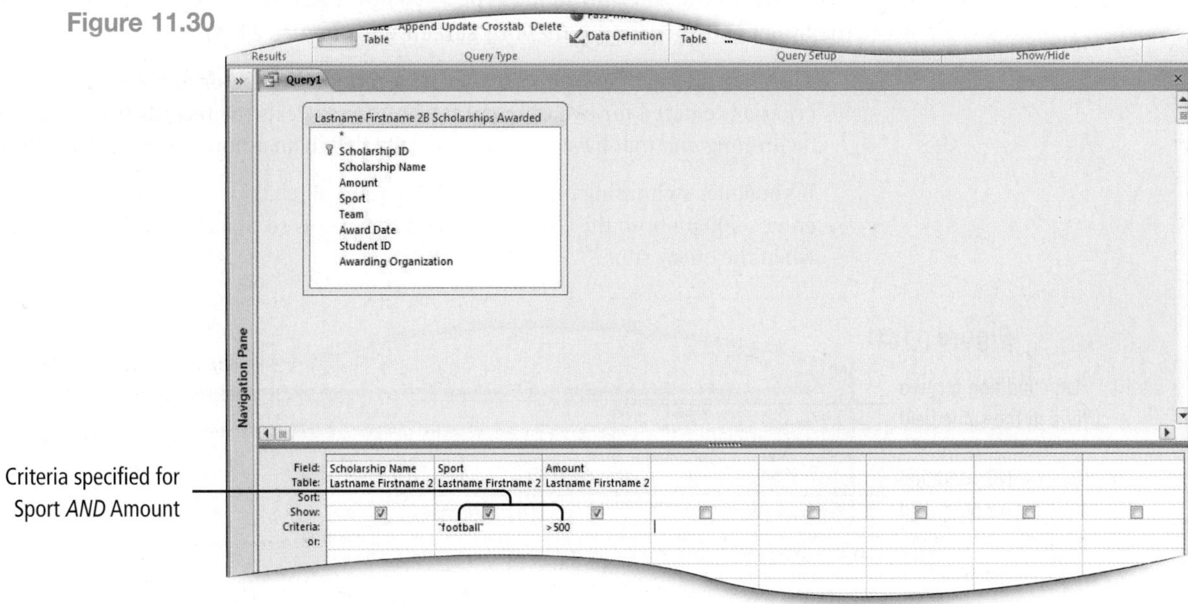

5 On the **Design tab**, in the **Results group**, click the **Run** button.

Two records display that match both conditions—Football in the Sport field *and* greater than $500 in the Amount field.

6 **Save** the query as **Lastname Firstname 2B Football and Over $500 Query** and then click **OK** or press Enter. **Close** the query.

7 **Open** the **Navigation Pane**, and then click one time to select the **2B Football and Over $500 Query** object. Display the query in **Print Preview**, create a paper or electronic printout if instructed to do so, and then **Close Print Preview**.

You can print any selected object from the Navigation Pane—the object does not have to be open to print.

8 **Close** the **Navigation Pane**.

Activity 11.20 | Using OR Criteria in a Query

Use the ***OR condition*** to specify multiple criteria for a single field, or multiple criteria for different fields when you want to display the records that meet any of the conditions. In this activity, you will help Mr. Shavrain answer the question *Which scholarships over $400 were awarded in the sports of Baseball or Swimming, and what is the award date of each?*

1 Click the **Create tab**. In the **Queries group**, click the **Query Design** button.

2 **Add** the **2B Scholarships Awarded** table. **Close** the dialog box, expand the field list, and then add the following four fields to the design grid in the order given: **Scholarship Name**, **Sport**, **Amount**, and **Award Date**.

3 In the **Criteria** row, click in the **Sport** field, and then type **baseball**

4 In the design grid, on the **or** row, click in the **Sport** field, type **swimming** and then press Enter. **Run** the query.

The query results display seven scholarship records where the Sport is either Baseball *or* Swimming. Use the OR condition to specify multiple criteria for a single field.

5 Switch to **Design** view. In the **or** row, under **Sport**, delete *swimming*. In the **Criteria** row, under **Sport**, delete *baseball*. Type **swimming or baseball** and then in the **Criteria** row, click in the **Amount** field. Type **>400** and then press Enter. Increase the width of the **Sport** column. Compare your screen with Figure 11.31.

This is an alternative way to use the OR compound operator in the Sport field. Because criteria is entered for two different fields, Access selects the records that are Baseball *or* Swimming *and* that have a scholarship awarded in an amount greater than $400.

If you enter swimming on the Criteria row and baseball on the or row, then you must enter >400 on both the Criteria row and the or row so that the correct records display when the query runs.

Figure 11.31

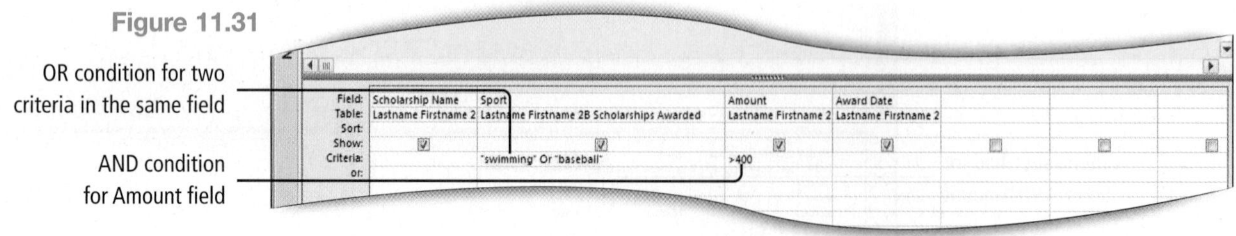

6 **Run** the query to display the two records that match the conditions.

7 **Close** [×] the query. In the message box, click **Yes** to save changes to the query. In the **Save As** dialog box, type **Lastname Firstname 2B Swimming or Baseball Over $400 Query** and then click **OK**.

8 **Open** [»] the **Navigation Pane**, increase the width of the **Navigation Pane** to display the full name of all objects, and then click one time to select the **2B Swimming or Baseball Over $400 Query** object. Display the query in **Print Preview**, create a paper or electronic printout if instructed to do so, and then **Close Print Preview**. **Close** [«] the **Navigation Pane**.

Objective 10 | Create a Query Based on More Than One Table

In a relational database, you can retrieve information from more than one table. Recall that a table in a relational database contains all of the records about a single topic. Tables are joined by relating the primary key field in one table to a foreign key field in another table. This common field creates a relationship, so you can include data from more than one table in a query.

For example, the Athletes table contains all of the information about the student athletes—name, address, and so on. The Scholarships Awarded table includes the scholarship name, amount, and so on. When an athlete receives a scholarship, only the Student ID field is included with the scholarship to identify who received the scholarship. It is not necessary to include any other data about the athletes in the Scholarships Awarded table; doing so would result in redundant data.

Activity 11.21 | Creating a Query Based on More Than One Table

In this activity, you will create a query that selects records from two tables. This is possible because a relationship has been created between the two tables in the database. The query will answer the questions *What is the name, e-mail address, and phone number of athletes who have received swimming or tennis scholarships, and what is the name and amount of the scholarship?*

1 Click the **Create tab**. In the **Queries group**, click the **Query Design** button. **Add** the **2B Athletes** table and the **2B Scholarships Awarded** table to the table area, and then **Close** the **Show Table** dialog box. Expand the two field lists, and then drag the **2B Scholarships Awarded** field list to the right so that there is approximately one inch of space between the field lists.

The join line displays because you previously created a relationship between the tables. It indicates a *one-to-many* relationship—*one* athlete can have *many* scholarships.

2 From the **2B Athletes** field list, add the following fields to the design grid in the order given: **First Name**, **Last Name**, **College E-mail**, and **Home Phone**.

3 In the **Sort** row, click in the **Last Name** field. Click the **Sort arrow**, and then click **Ascending** to sort the records in alphabetical order by last name.

4. From the **2B Scholarships Awarded** field list, add the following fields to the design grid in the order given: **Scholarship Name**, **Sport**, and **Amount**.

5. In the **Criteria** row, click in the **Sport** field. Type **swimming or tennis** and then press Enter.

6. In the design grid, increase the width of the **Home Phone** and **Scholarship Name** columns to display the entire table name on the **Table** row. If necessary, scroll to the right to display the *Home Phone* and *Scholarship Name* fields in the design grid, and then compare your screen with Figure 11.32.

   When extracting data from multiple tables, the information on the Table row is helpful, especially when different tables include the same field names, such as address, but different data, such as a student's address or a coach's address.

Figure 11.32

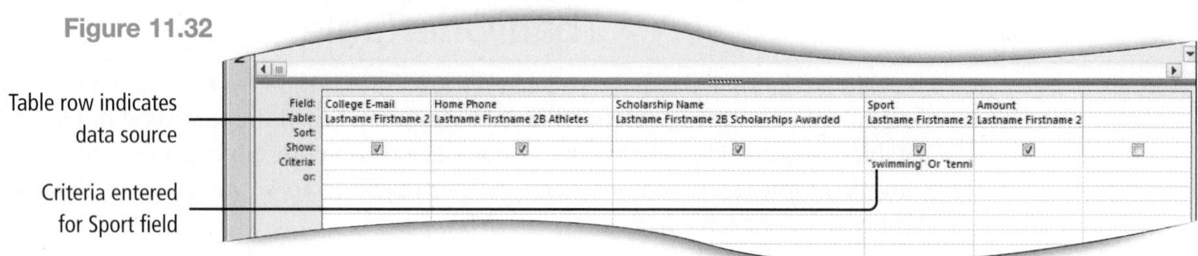

7. **Run** the query, and then compare your screen with Figure 11.33.

   Information for eight student athletes displays. The First Name and Last Name fields are included in the query results even though the common field—*Student ID*—is *not* included in the query design. Because Student ID is included in both tables, and a one-to-many relationship was created between the tables, the Student ID field is used to select the records in both tables by using one query. Two students—*Carla Reid* and *Florence Zimmerman*—received scholarships in both Swimming and Tennis. Recall that *one* student athlete can receive *many* scholarships.

Figure 11.33

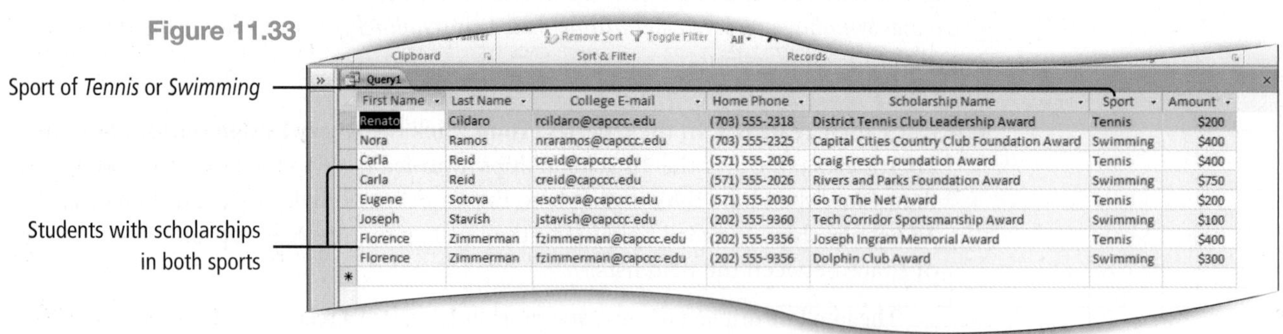

8. Save the query as **Lastname Firstname 2B Swimming or Tennis Query** and then display the query in **Print Preview**. Set the **Margins** to **Normal**, and then change the orientation to **Landscape**. Create a paper or electronic printout if instructed to do so, and then **Close Print Preview**.

9. **Close** the query, **Open** the **Navigation Pane**, and then compare your screen with Figure 11.34.

   Your new query—*2B Swimming or Tennis Query*—displays under both tables from which it retrieved records.

Figure 11.34

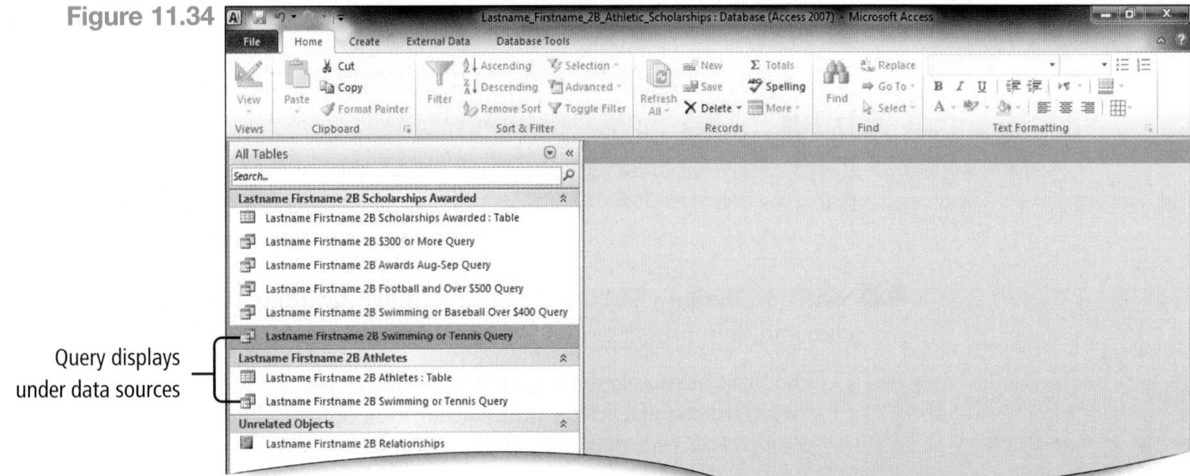

Objective 11 | Use Wildcards in a Query

Wildcard characters serve as a placeholder for one or more unknown characters in the criteria. When you are unsure of the particular character or set of characters to include in criteria, use wildcard characters in place of the characters.

Activity 11.22 | Using a Wildcard in a Query

Use the asterisk (*) to represent one or more characters. For example, if you use the * wildcard in the criteria Fo*, the results will display Foster, Forrester, Forrest, Fossil, or any word beginning with *Fo*. In this activity, you will use the asterisk (*) wildcard in the criteria row to answer the question *Which athletes received scholarships from local Rotary Clubs, country clubs, or foundations?*

1 **Close** « the **Navigation Pane**. On the Ribbon, click the **Create tab**. In the **Queries group**, click the **Query Design** button.

2 **Add** both tables to the table area, **Close** the **Show Table** dialog box, and then expand the field lists.

3 Add the following fields to the design grid in the order given: from the **2B Athletes** table, **First Name** and **Last Name**; from the **2B Scholarships Awarded** table, **Awarding Organization**.

4 In the **Sort** row, click in the **Last Name** field. Click the **arrow**, and then click **Ascending**.

5 In the **Criteria** row, under **Awarding Organization**, type **rotary*** and then press Enter.

The wildcard character * is a placeholder to match one or more characters. After pressing Enter, Access adds *Like* to the beginning of the criteria.

6 **Run** the query, and then compare your screen with Figure 11.35.

Three athletes received scholarships from Rotary Clubs. The results are sorted alphabetically by the Last Name field.

Access | Chapter 11

Figure 11.35

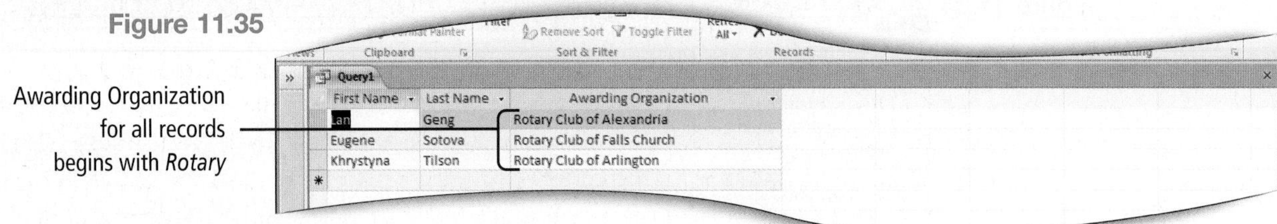

7 Switch to **Design** view. On the **or** row, under **Awarding Organization**, type ***country club** and then press Enter.

The * can be used at the beginning, middle, or end of the criteria. The position of the * wildcard character determines the location of the unknown characters. Here you will search for records that end in *Country Club*.

8 **Run** the query to display six records, and notice that three records begin with *Rotary*, and three records end with *Country Club*—sorted alphabetically by Last Name.

9 Switch to **Design** view. Under **Awarding Organization** and under **Like "*country club"**, type ***foundation*** and then press Enter. Compare your screen with Figure 11.36.

The query will also display records that have the word *Foundation* anywhere—beginning, middle, or end—in the field. Three *OR* criteria have been entered for the Awarding Organization field—the query results will display students who have received scholarships from an organization name that begins with Rotary, *or* that ends in County Club, *or* that has Foundation anywhere in the middle of the name.

Figure 11.36

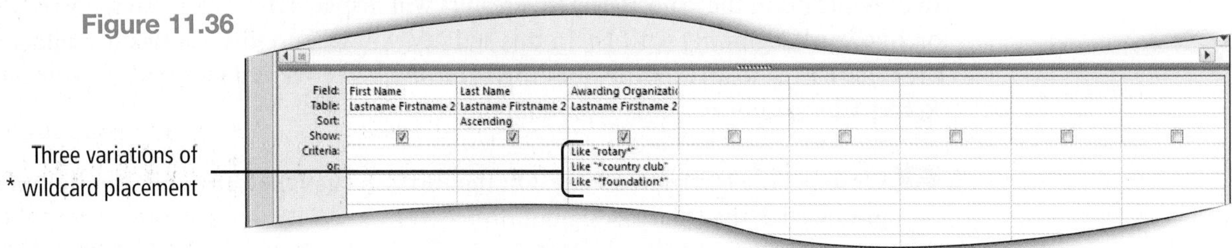

10 **Run** the query to display 28 records.

Twenty-eight scholarships were from a Country Club, *or* a Rotary Club, *or* a Foundation.

11 **Save** the query as **Lastname Firstname 2B Wildcard Query** and then display the results in **Print Preview**. Create a paper or electronic printout if instructed to do so, and then **Close Print Preview**.

12 **Close** the query, and then **Open** the **Navigation Pane**.

Because the 2B Wildcard Query object retrieved data from two tables, it displays below the 2B Scholarships Awarded table *and* the 2B Athletes table—the data sources.

> **More Knowledge | Search for a Single Unknown Character by Using the ? Wildcard**
>
> The question mark (?) is a wildcard that is used to search for unknown single characters. For each question mark included in criteria, any character can be inserted. For example, if you use *b?d* as a criteria, the query might locate bid, bud, bed, or any three-character word beginning with *b* and ending with *d*. If *b??d* is entered as the criteria, the results could include bind, bend, bard, or any four-character word beginning with *b* and ending with *d*.

Objective 12 | Use Calculated Fields in a Query

Queries can create calculated values that are stored in a ***calculated field***. A calculated field stores the value of a mathematical operation. For example, you can multiply two fields together, such as Total Credit Hours and Tuition Per Credit Hour to get a Total Tuition Due amount for each student without having to include a specific field for this amount in the table, which reduces the size of the database and provides more flexibility.

There are two steps to produce a calculated field in a query. First, name the field that will store the calculated values. Second, write the ***expression***—the formula—that performs the calculation. Each field name used in the calculation must be enclosed within its own pair of square brackets, and the new field name must be followed by a colon (:).

Activity 11.23 | Using Calculated Fields in a Query

For each scholarship received by student athletes, the Capital Cities Community College Alumni Association will donate an amount equal to 50 percent of each scholarship. In this activity, you will create a calculated field to determine the additional amount each scholarship is worth. The query will answer the question *What is the value of each scholarship if the Alumni Association makes a matching 50% donation?*

1. **Close** « the **Navigation Pane**, and then click the **Create tab**. In the **Queries group**, click the **Query Design** button.

2. **Add** the **2B Scholarships Awarded** table to the table area, **Close** the **Show Table** dialog box, and then expand the field list. Add the following fields to the design grid in the order given: **Student ID**, **Scholarship Name**, and **Amount**.

3. In the **Sort** row, click in the **Student ID** field; sort **Ascending**.

4. In the **Field** row, right-click in the first empty column to display a shortcut menu, and then click **Zoom**.

   The Zoom dialog box gives you more working space so that you can see the entire calculation as you type it. The calculation can also be typed directly in the empty Field box in the column.

5. In the **Zoom** dialog box, type **Matching Donation:[Amount]*0.5** and then compare your screen with Figure 11.37.

   The first element, *Matching Donation*, is the new field name where the calculated values will display. Following that is a colon (:), which separates the new field name from the expression. *Amount* is enclosed in square brackets because it is an existing field name in the 2B Scholarships Awarded table; it contains the numeric data on which the calculation will be performed. Following the right square bracket is an asterisk (*), which in math calculations signifies multiplication. Finally, the percentage (0.5 or 50%) displays.

Figure 11.37

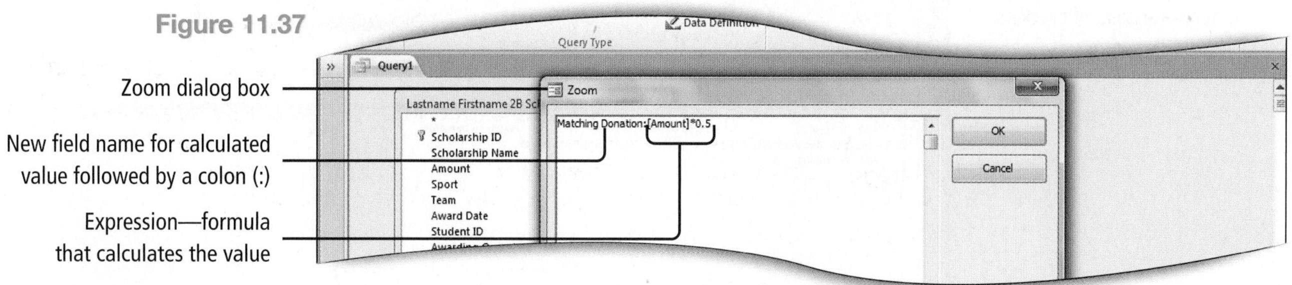

Access | Chapter 11

6 In the **Zoom** dialog box, click **OK**, and then **Run** the query. Compare your screen with Figure 11.38.

The query results display three fields from the 2B Scholarships Awarded table plus a fourth field—*Matching Donation*—in which a calculated value displays. Each calculated value equals the value in the Amount field multiplied by 0.5.

Figure 11.38

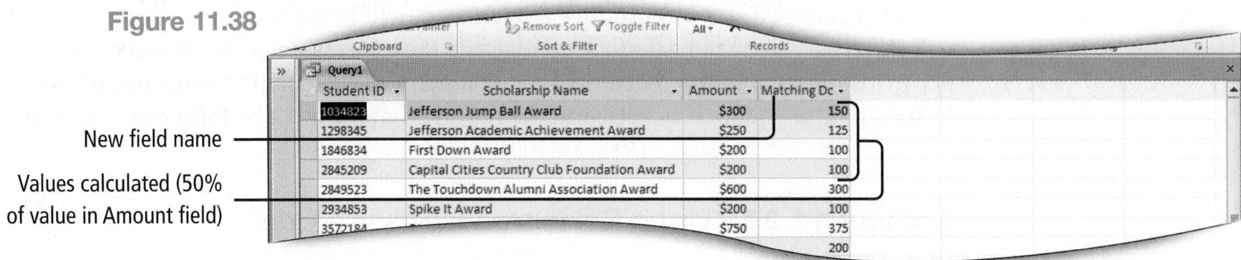

Alert! | Does Your Screen Differ?

If your calculations in a query do not work, switch to Design view and carefully check the expression you typed. Spelling or syntax errors prevent calculated fields from working properly.

7 Notice the formatting of the **Matching Donation** field—there are no dollar signs, commas, or decimal places; you will adjust this formatting later.

When using a number, such as 0.5, in an expression, the values in the calculated field may not be formatted the same as in the existing field.

8 Switch to **Design** view. In the **Field** row, in the first empty column, right-click, and then click **Zoom**. In the **Zoom** dialog box, type **Total Scholarship:[Amount]+[Matching Donation]** and then compare your screen with Figure 11.39.

Each existing field name—*Amount* and *Matching Donation*—must be enclosed in separate pairs of brackets.

Figure 11.39

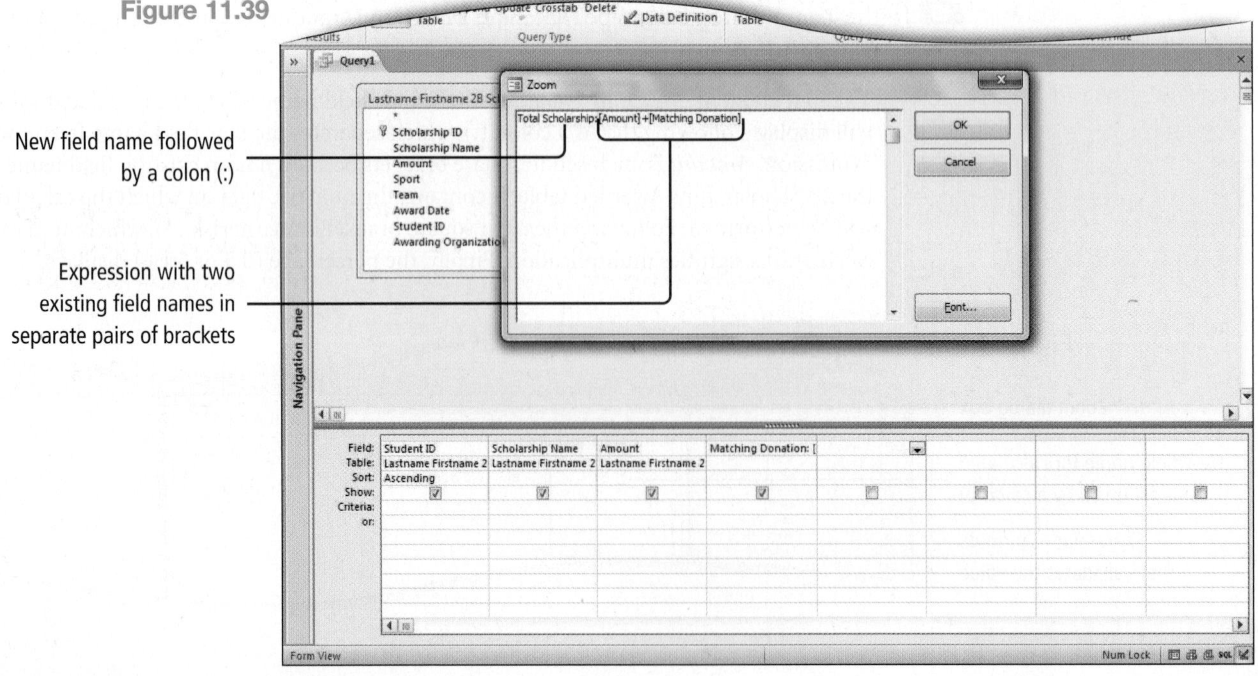

9 In the **Zoom** dialog box, click **OK**, and then **Run** the query to view the results.

Total Scholarship is calculated by adding together the Amount field and the Matching Donation field. The Total Scholarship column includes dollar signs, commas, and decimal points, which carried over from the Currency format in the Amount field.

10 Switch to **Design** view. In the **Field** row, click in the **Matching Donation** field box.

Another Way

Right-click the Matching Donation field name, and then click Properties.

11 On the **Design tab**, in the **Show/Hide group**, click the **Property Sheet** button.

The ***Property Sheet*** displays on the right side of your screen. A Property Sheet is a list of characteristics—properties—for fields in which you can make precise changes to each property associated with the field. The left column displays the Property name, for example, Description. To the right of the Property name is the Property setting box.

12 In the **Property Sheet**, on the **General tab**, click in the **Format** property setting box, and then click the **arrow** that displays. Compare your screen with Figure 11.40.

A list of formats for the Matching Donation field displays.

Figure 11.40

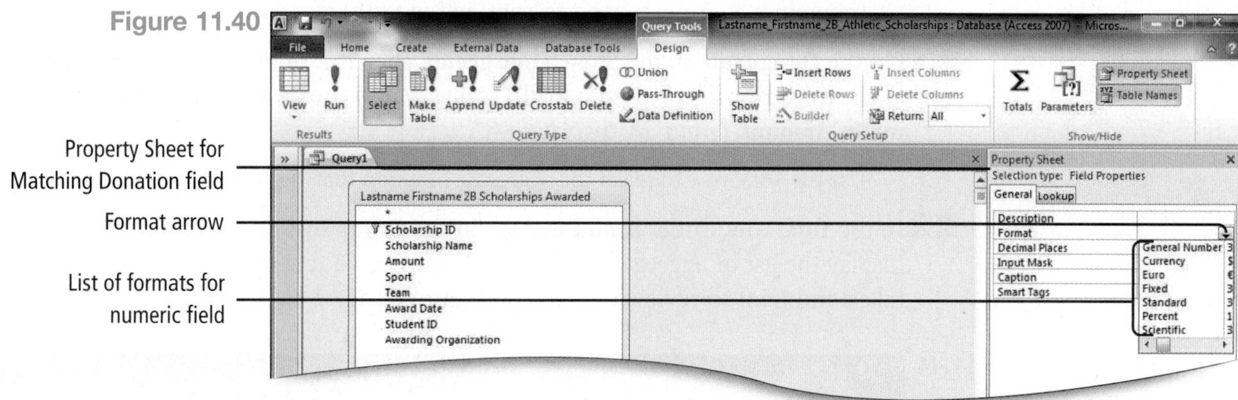

13 In the list, click **Currency**. Click the next property, **Decimal Places**, click the **arrow**, and then click **0**.

14 In the design grid, in the **Field** row, click in the **Total Scholarship** field. On the **Property Sheet**, set the **Format** to **Currency** and the **Decimal Places** to **0**.

15 **Close** the **Property Sheet**, and then **Run** the query. Select all of the columns and apply **Best Fit**.

The Matching Donation and Total Scholarship fields are formatted as Currency with 0 decimal places.

16 **Save** the query as **Lastname Firstname 2B Matching Donations Query** and then display the query results in **Print Preview**. Change the **Orientation** to **Landscape**. Create a paper or electronic printout if instructed to do so, and then **Close Print Preview**. **Close** the query.

Objective 13 | Calculate Statistics and Group Data in a Query

In Access queries, you can perform statistical calculations on a group of records. Calculations that are performed on a group of records are called ***aggregate functions***.

Activity 11.24 | Using the MIN, MAX, AVG, and SUM Functions in a Query

In this activity, you will use the minimum, maximum, average, and sum functions in a query to examine the amounts of scholarships awarded. The last query will answer the question *What is the total dollar amount of all scholarships awarded?*

1 On the **Create tab**, in the **Queries group**, click the **Query Design** button.

2 **Add** the **2B Scholarships Awarded** table to the table area, **Close** the **Show Table** dialog box, and then expand the field list. Add the **Amount** field to the design grid.

Include only the field you want to summarize in the query, so that the aggregate function (minimum, maximum, average, sum, and so forth) is applied to that single field.

3 On the **Design tab**, in the **Show/Hide group**, click the **Totals** button to add a **Total** row as the third row in the design grid. Notice that in the design grid, on the **Total** row, under **Amount**, *Group By* displays.

Use the Total row to select the aggregate function that you want to use for the field.

4 In the **Total** row, under **Amount**, click in the **Group By** box, and then click the **arrow** to display the list of aggregate functions. Compare your screen with Figure 11.41, and take a moment to review the table in Figure 11.42.

Figure 11.41

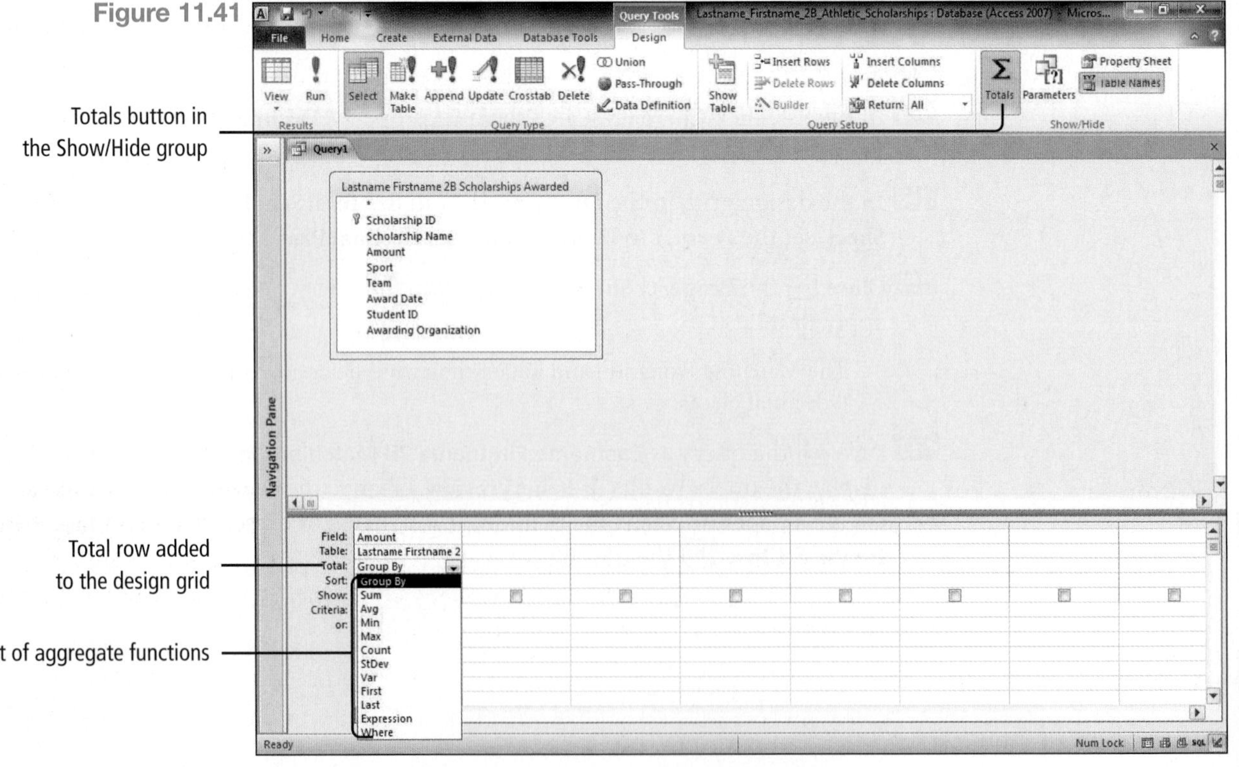

Aggregate Functions	
Function Name	**What It Does**
Sum	Totals the values in a field.
Avg	Averages the values in a field.
Min	Locates the smallest value in a field.
Max	Locates the largest value in a field.
Count	Counts the number of records in a field.
StDev	Calculates the Standard Deviation for the values in a field.
Var	Calculates the Variance for the values in a field.
First	Displays the First value in a field.
Last	Displays the Last value in a field.
Expression	Creates a calculated field that includes an aggregate function.
Where	Limits records to those that match a condition specified in the Criteria row.

Figure 11.42

5 From the list of functions, click **Min**, and then **Run** the query. Double-click the right edge of the column heading to apply Best Fit to the column.

Access calculates the minimum (smallest) scholarship award—*$100.00*. The field name *MinOfAmount* displays for the calculation. This query answers the question, *What is the minimum (smallest) scholarship amount awarded?*

6 Switch to **Design** view. In the **Amount** field, in the **Total** row, select the **Max** function, and then **Run** the query.

The maximum (largest) scholarship amount is *$750.00*.

7 Switch to **Design** view, select the **Avg** function, and then **Run** the query.

The average scholarship amount awarded is *$358.33*.

8 Switch to **Design** view. Select the **Sum** function, and then **Run** the query.

Access sums the Amount field for all records and displays a result of $*10,750.00*. The field name, SumOfAmount, displays. This query answers the question, *What is the total dollar amount of all the scholarships awarded?*

Activity 11.25 | Grouping Data in a Query

Aggregate functions can also be used to calculate totals by groups of data. For example, to group (summarize) the amount of scholarships awarded to each student, you include the Student ID field, in addition to the Amount field, and then group all of the records for each student together to calculate a total awarded to each student. Similarly, you can calculate how much is awarded for each sport.

1 Switch to **Design** view. Drag the **Student ID** field to the first column of the design grid—**Amount** becomes the second column. On the **Total** row, under **Student ID**, notice that *Group By* displays.

This query groups—summarizes—the records by StudentID and calculates a total Amount for each student.

2 **Run** the query, and then compare your screen with Figure 11.43.

The query calculates the total amount of all scholarships for each student.

Figure 11.43

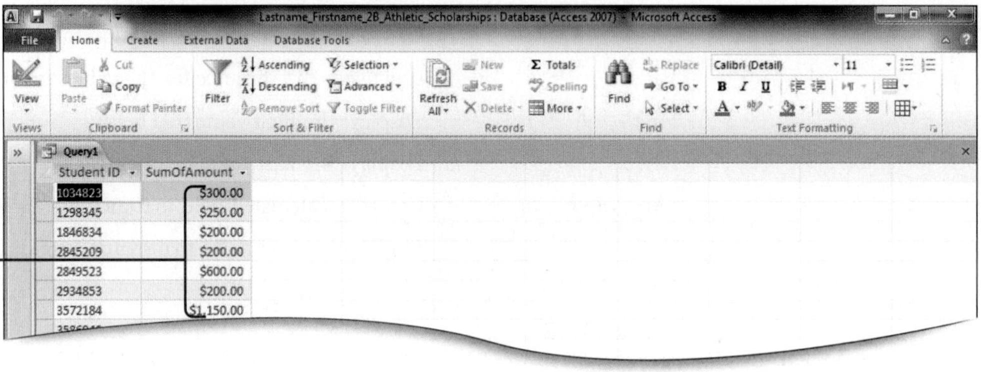

Total scholarship amount awarded to each student

3 Switch to **Design** view. In the design grid, delete the **Student ID** field, and then drag the **Sport** field to the first column—**Amount** becomes the second column.

4 In the design grid, click in the **Amount** field, and then on the **Design tab**, in the **Show/Hide group**, click the **Property Sheet** button.

5 In the **Property Sheet**, set the **Format** to **Currency**, set the **Decimal Places** to **0**, and then **Close** the **Property Sheet**.

6 **Run** the query, and then compare your screen with Figure 11.44.

Access summarizes the data by sport. Basketball scholarships are the largest total Amount—*$3,500*.

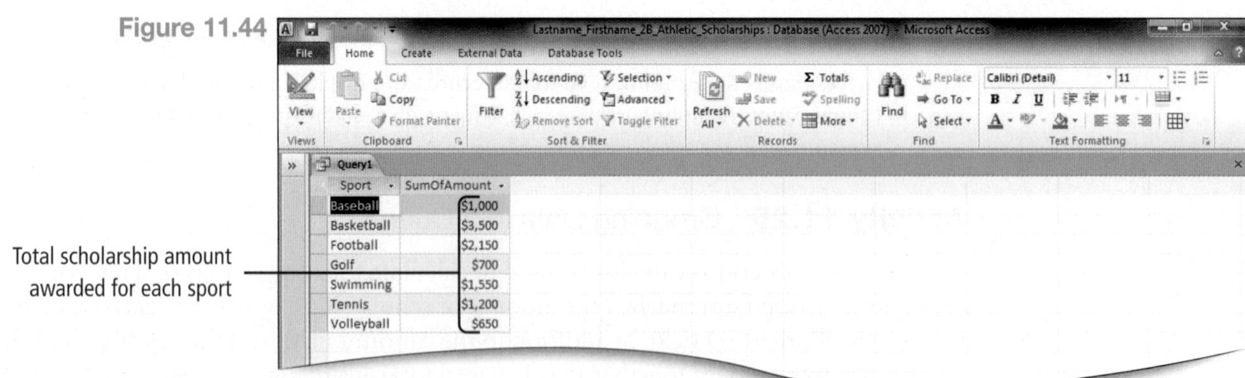

Figure 11.44

7 **Save** the query as **Lastname Firstname 2B Total by Sport Query** and then display the query results in **Print Preview**. Create a paper or electronic printout if instructed to do so, and then **Close Print Preview**. **Close** the query.

Objective 14 | Create a Crosstab Query

A ***crosstab query*** uses an aggregate function for data that can be grouped by two types of information and displays data in a compact, spreadsheet-like format. A crosstab query always has at least one row heading, one column heading, and one summary field. Use a crosstab query to summarize a large amount of data in a small space that is easy to read.

Activity 11.26 | Creating a Crosstab Query Using One Table

In this activity, you will create a crosstab query that displays the total amount of scholarships awarded for each sport and for each team—women's or men's.

1 On the **Create tab**, in the **Queries group**, click the **Query Wizard** button. In the **New Query** dialog box, click **Crosstab Query Wizard**, and then click **OK**.

2 In the **Crosstab Query Wizard**, click **Table: 2B Scholarships Awarded** and then click **Next**.

3 To select the row headings, under **Available Fields**, double-click **Sport** to sort the scholarship amounts by the different sports. Click **Next**, and then compare your screen with Figure 11.45.

The sports are displayed as *row headings*; here you are prompted to select *column* headings.

Figure 11.45

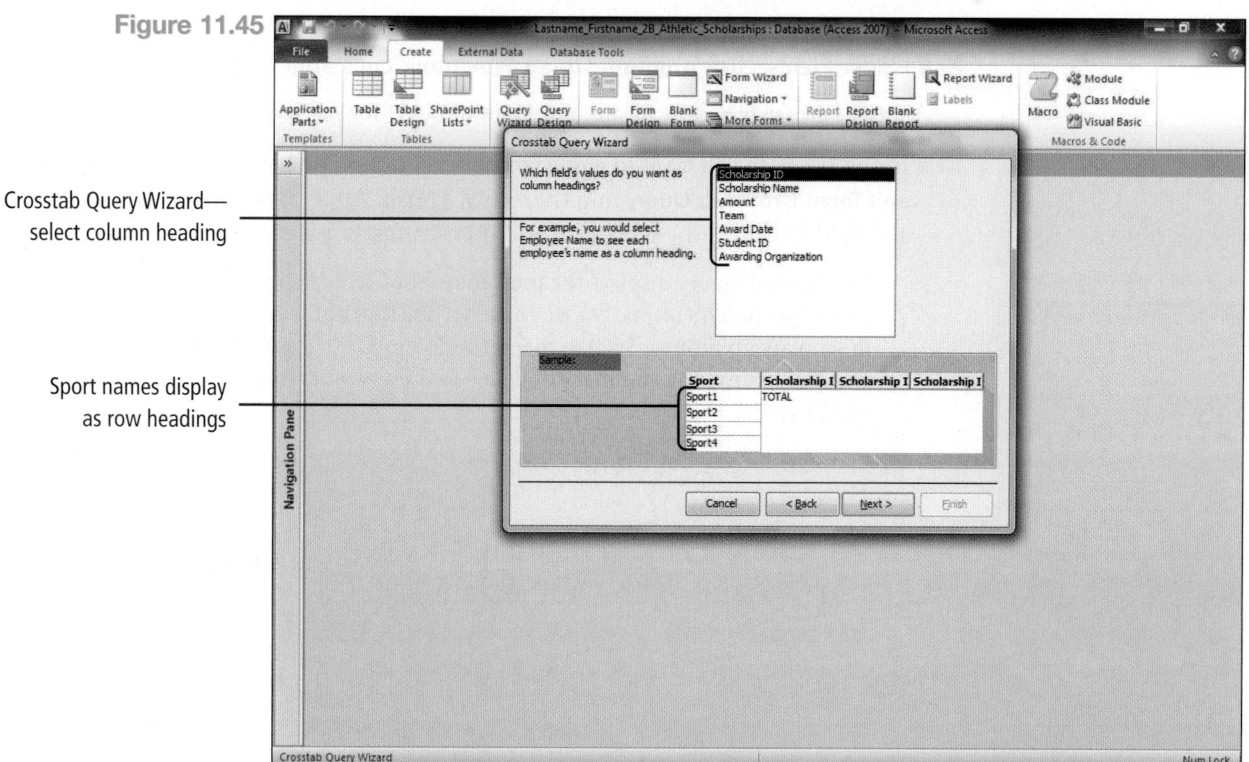

4 To select the column headings, in the field list, click **Team**. Click **Next**, and then compare your screen with Figure 11.46.

The teams will be listed as column headings; here you are prompted to select a field to summarize.

Figure 11.46

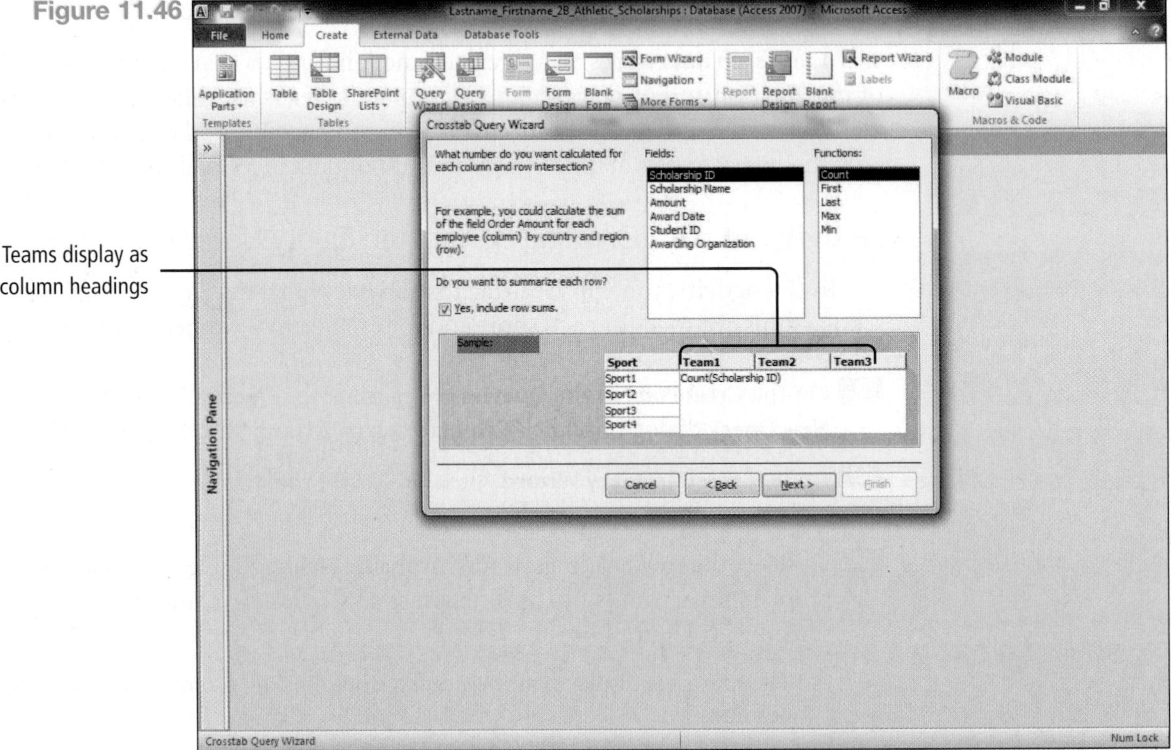

5 Under **Fields**, click **Amount**. Under **Functions**, click **Sum**, and then click **Next**.

The crosstab query will sum the Amount field for each sport and team.

6 In the **What do you want to name your query?** box, type **Lastname Firstname 2B Sport and Team Crosstab Query** and then click **Finish**. Apply **Best Fit** to the columns, click in any field to cancel the selection, and then compare your screen with Figure 11.47.

The crosstab query displays the total amount of scholarships awarded by sport and also by men's or women's teams. For example, for the sport of Golf, a total of $700 was awarded in scholarship money; $500 to men's teams and $200 to women's teams. A crosstab query is useful to display a summary of data based on two different fields—in this case, by sport and by teams.

Figure 11.47

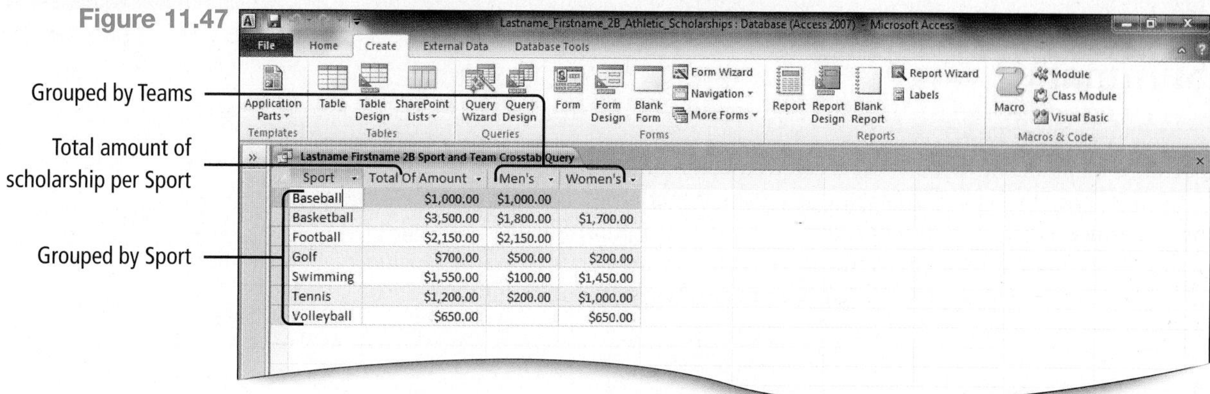

7 Display the query results in **Print Preview**. Create a paper or electronic printout if instructed to do so, and then **Close Print Preview**. **Close** [×] the query, and click **Yes** to save changes to the query layout.

8 **Open** [»] the **Navigation Pane**. In **Backstage** view, click **Close Database**, and then click **Exit**. As directed by your instructor, submit your database and the ten paper or electronic printouts—relationship report and nine queries—that are the results of this project.

> **More Knowledge | Creating a Crosstab Query Using Two Related Tables**
>
> To create a crosstab query using fields from more than one table, you must first create a select query with the fields from both tables that will be included in the crosstab query.

End **You have completed Project 11B**

Content-Based Assessments

Summary

Sorting data in a table reorders the records based on one or more fields. Use queries to ask complex questions about the data in a database in a manner that Access can interpret. Save queries so they can be run as needed against current records. Use queries to limit the fields that display, add criteria to restrict the number of records in the query results, create calculated values, include data from more than one table, and to display data grouped by two types of information.

Key Terms

Aggregate functions 630
AND Condition 621
Ascending order 601
Between ... And operator 620
Calculated field 627
Comparison operators 619
Compound criteria 621
Criteria 610
Crosstab query 633
Data source 604
Descending order 601
Design grid 605
Expression 627
Field list 597
Foreign key 599
Innermost sort field 603
Is Not Null 613
Is Null 613
Join line 599
Logical operators 621
Message Bar 595
One-to-many relationship 596
OR condition 622
Outermost sort field 603
Property Sheet 629
Referential integrity 599
Relationship 596
Run 606
Select query 604
Sorting 601
Subdatasheet 601
Subset 604
Table area 605
Text string 611
Trust Center 595
Wildcard character 625

Matching

Match each term in the second column with its correct definition in the first column by writing the letter of the term on the blank line in front of the correct definition.

G 1. The area below the Ribbon that displays information such as security alerts.
O 2. An area where you can view the security and privacy settings for your Access installation.
K 3. An association that you establish between two tables based on common fields.
H 4. A relationship between two tables where one record in the first table corresponds to many records in the second table.
C 5. A list of field names in a table.
D 6. The field that is included in the related table so the field can be joined with the primary key in another table for the purpose of creating a relationship.
J 7. A set of rules that ensures that the data between related tables is valid.
F 8. The line joining two tables that visually indicates the common fields and the type of relationship.
N 9. A format for displaying related records in a datasheet when you click the plus sign (+) next to a record in a table on the one side of a relationship.
M 10. The process of arranging data in a specific order based on the value in a field.

A Ascending
B Descending
C Field list
D Foreign key
E Innermost
F Join line
G Message Bar
H One-to-many relationship
I Outermost
J Referential integrity
K Relationship
L Select query
M Sorting
N Subdatasheet
O Trust Center

_____ 11. A sorting order that arranges text in alphabetical order (A to Z) or numbers from lowest to highest.

_____ 12. A sorting order that arranges text in reverse alphabetical order (Z to A) or numbers from highest to lowest.

_____ 13. When sorting on multiple fields in Datasheet view, the field that is used for the first level of sorting.

_____ 14. When sorting on multiple fields in Datasheet view, the field that is used for the second level of sorting.

_____ 15. A database object that retrieves (selects) specific data from one or more tables and then displays the results in Datasheet view.

Multiple Choice

Circle the correct answer.

1. The lower area of the Query window that displays the design of the query is the:
   A. design grid **B.** property sheet **C.** table area
2. The process in which Access searches the records in the table, finds the records that match specified criteria, and then displays the records in a datasheet is:
   A. select **B.** run **C.** sort
3. Conditions in a query that identify the specific records for which you are looking are known as:
   A. aggregate functions **B.** criteria **C.** expressions
4. A criteria that searches for fields that are empty is:
   A. Is Empty **B.** Is Not Null **C.** Is Null
5. The symbols of =, >, and < are known as:
   A. aggregate functions **B.** comparison operators **C.** logical operators
6. A comparison operator that looks for values within a range is:
   A. And **B.** Between ... And **C.** Or
7. The logical operator that requires all conditions to be met is:
   A. AND **B.** Is Null **C.** OR
8. A wildcard character that serves as a placeholder for one or more unknown characters is the:
   A. * **B.** ? **C.** /
9. A field that stores the value of a mathematical operation is:
   A. an aggregate field **B.** a calculated field **C.** an expression
10. A query that uses an aggregate function for data that can be grouped by two types of information is:
    A. an aggregate query **B.** a calculated query **C.** a crosstab query

Apply 11A skills from these Objectives:

1. Open an Existing Database
2. Create Table Relationships
3. Sort Records in a Table
4. Create a Query in Design View
5. Create a New Query from an Existing Query
6. Sort Query Results
7. Specify Criteria in a Query

Skills Review | Project 11C Music Department

In the following Skills Review, you will assist Dr. William Jinkens, the Capital Cities Community College Music Director, in using his database to answer various questions about the instruments in the Music Department's inventory. Your results will look similar to Figure 11.48.

Project Files

For Project 11C, you will need the following file:

a02c_Music_Department

You will save your database as:

Lastname_Firstname_2C_Music_Department

Project Results

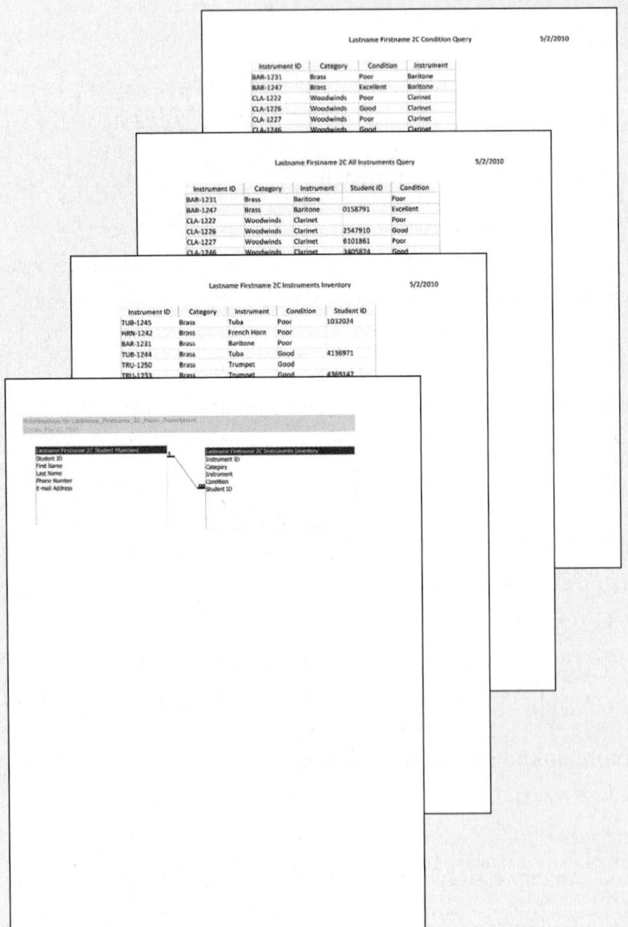

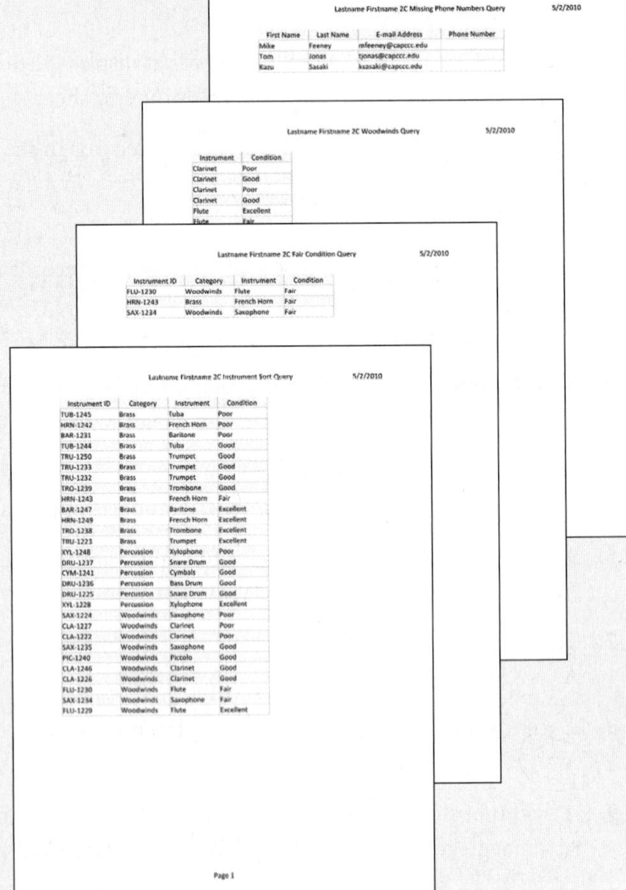

Figure 11.48

(Project 11C Music Department continues on the next page)

Skills Review | Project 11C Music Department (continued)

1 **Start** Access. In **Backstage** view, click **Open**. Navigate to the student files that accompany this textbook, and then open the **a02C_Music_Department** database.

a. Click the **File tab** to return to **Backstage** view, and then click **Save Database As**. In the **Save As** dialog box, navigate to your **Access Chapter 11** folder. In the **File name** box, select the file name, and then type **Lastname_Firstname_2C_Music_Department** and then press Enter. In the **Message Bar**, click **Enable Content**.

b. **Rename** the **2C Student Musicians** table to **Lastname Firstname 2C Student Musicians** and then **Rename** the **2C Instruments Inventory** to **Lastname Firstname 2C Instruments Inventory** Widen the **Navigation Pane** to display fully both table names.

2 **Open** both tables to examine the contents of each, **Close** the tables, and then **Close** the **Navigation Pane**.

a. Click the **Database Tools tab**, and in the **Relationships group** click the **Relationships** button. Drag the **Show Table** dialog box down into the lower right portion of your screen.

b. In the **Show Table** dialog box, click your **2C Student Musicians**, and then click **Add**. Double-click your **2C Instruments Inventory** to add the table to the **Relationships** window. In the **Show Table** dialog box, click **Close**.

c. Drag the **2C Instruments Inventory** field list—the field list on the right—to the right about 3 inches. In the **2C Student Musicians** field list—the field list on the left—position your mouse pointer over the lower right corner of the field list to display the ⤡ pointer, and then drag to the right to increase the width of the field list until the entire name of the table in the title bar displays and all of the field names display. Then use the ⤡ pointer to resize the **2C Instruments Inventory** field list so that all of the field names and the table name display.

d. In the **2C Student Musicians** field list, point to **Student ID**, hold down the left mouse button, and then drag down and to the right to the **2C Instruments Inventory** field list until your mouse pointer is on top of **Student ID**. Then release the mouse button. Drag the **Edit Relationships** dialog box to the lower portion of your screen. The relationship between the two tables is a one-to-many relationship; *one* student can play *many* instruments.

e. In the **Edit Relationships** dialog box, click to select the **Enforce Referential Integrity** check box, and then click the **Create** button. On the **Design tab**, in the **Tools group**, click the **Relationship Report** button. On the **Print Preview tab**, in the **Page Size group**, change the **Margins** to **Normal**, and then create a paper or electronic printout as directed.

f. **Save** the relationship report with the default name. **Close** the report, and then **Close** the **Relationships** window. From the **Navigation Pane**, open the **2C Instruments Inventory** table, and then **Close** the **Navigation Pane**.

3 In the **Condition** field, click any record. On the **Home tab**, in the **Sort & Filter group**, click the **Descending** button to sort the records from *Poor* to *Excellent*. In the field names row, click the **Category arrow**, and then click **Sort A to Z** to sort the records first by *Category* and then by *Condition*.

a. Display **Backstage** view, click **Print**, and then click **Print Preview**. Create a paper or electronic copy as directed. **Close Print Preview**, **Close** the table, and then click **No**; you do not need to save the sort changes.

4 Click the **Create tab**, and then in the **Queries group**, click the **Query Design** button. In the **Show Table** dialog box, double-click your **2C Instruments Inventory** table, and then **Close** the **Show Table** dialog box. Expand the field list.

a. Double-click **Instrument ID** to add the field to the design grid. Point to the **Category** field, hold down the left mouse button, and then drag the field down into the design grid until you are pointing to the **Field** row in the second column. Release the mouse button.

b. In design grid, in the **Field** row, click in the third column, and then click the **arrow** that displays. From the list, click **Instrument** to add the field to the design grid. Using the technique of your choice, add the **Student ID** field to the fourth column and the **Condition** field to the fifth column in the design grid.

c. On the **Design tab**, in the **Results group**, click the **Run** button. This query answers the question, *What is the Instrument ID, Category, Instrument, Student ID, and Condition of all of the instruments in the 2C Instruments Inventory table?*

d. **Save** the query as **Lastname Firstname 2C All Instruments Query** and then click **OK**. Display the query in **Print Preview**, and then create a paper or electronic printout as directed. **Close Print Preview**.

(Project 11C Music Department continues on the next page)

Skills Review | Project 11C Music Department (continued)

5 Display **Backstage** view, click **Save Object As**. In the **Save As** dialog box, type **Lastname Firstname 2C Condition Query** and then click **OK** to create a new query based on an existing query. Click the **Home tab**, and then switch to **Design** view.

a. In the design grid, point to the thin gray selection bar above the **Student ID** field name until the [↓] pointer displays. Click to select the **Student ID** column, and then press Del.

b. In the gray selection bar, select the **Instrument ID** column. Point to the **selection bar** to display the [pointer] pointer, and then drag to the right until a dark vertical line displays on the right side of the **Condition** column. Release the mouse button to position the **Instrument ID** field in the fourth column.

c. **Run** the query. The query results display four fields. This query answers the question, *What is the Category, Instrument, Condition, and Instrument ID for every Instrument in the 2C Instruments Inventory table?*

d. Display the query in **Print Preview**, and then create a paper or electronic printout as directed. **Close Print Preview**, **Close** the query, and in the message box, click **Yes** to save the changes to the design—you moved two fields. **Open** the **Navigation Pane**.

6 **Open** your **2C All Instruments Query**. **Save** the query object as **Lastname Firstname 2C Instrument Sort Query** and then click the **Home tab**. **Close** the **Navigation Pane**. Switch to **Design** view.

a. In the design grid, delete the **Student ID** field. In the **Sort** row, click in the **Category** field. Click the **Sort arrow**, and then in the list, click **Ascending**. In the **Sort** row, click in the **Condition** field, click the **Sort arrow**, and then click **Descending**. **Run** the query. This query answers the question, *For every Instrument ID, within each Category (with Category sorted in ascending order), what Instruments are in the inventory and what is the instrument's Condition (with Condition sorted in descending order)?*

b. Display the query in **Print Preview**. Create a paper or electronic printout if instructed to do so, and then **Close Print Preview**. **Close** the query. In the message box, click **Yes** to save the changes to the query design.

7 Click the **Create tab**, and then in the **Queries group**, click the **Query Design** button. **Add** your **2C Instruments Inventory** table to the table area, and then **Close** the **Show Table** dialog box. Expand the field list. Add the following fields to the design grid in the order given: **Instrument ID**, **Category**, **Instrument**, and **Condition**.

a. In the design grid, on the **Criteria** row, click in the **Condition** field, type **fair** and then press Enter. **Run** the query; three records display that meet the specified criteria—records that have *fair* in the Condition field.

b. **Save** the query as **Lastname Firstname 2C Fair Condition Query** and then create a paper or electronic printout as directed. **Close Print Preview**, and then **Close** the query.

c. **Create** a new query in **Query Design** view. **Add** the **2C Instruments Inventory** table to the table area, and then expand the field list. Add the following fields, in the order given, to the design grid: **Category**, **Instrument**, and **Condition**.

d. In the **Criteria** row, click in the **Category** field, type **woodwinds** and then press Enter. Under **Category**, in the **Show** row, click to clear the check box, and then **Run** the query. Ten instruments are categorized as woodwinds. Recall that if all results use the same criteria, such as *woodwinds*, it is not necessary to display the data in the query results.

e. **Save** the query as **Lastname Firstname 2C Woodwinds Query** and then create a paper or electronic printout as directed. **Close Print Preview**. **Close** the query.

f. **Create** a new query in **Query Design** view. **Add** the **2C Student Musicians** table to the table area, and then expand the field list. Add the following fields, in the order given, to the design grid: **First Name**, **Last Name**, **E-mail Address**, and **Phone Number**.

g. In the **Criteria** row, click in the **Phone Number** field, type **is null** and then press Enter. In the **Sort** row, click in the **Last Name** field, click the **Sort arrow**, and then click **Ascending**. **Run** the query. Three student musicians do not have a phone number stored in the 2C Student Musicians table.

h. **Save** the query as **Lastname Firstname 2C Missing Phone Numbers Query** and then create a paper or electronic printout as directed. **Close Print Preview**, and then **Close** the query. **Open** the **Navigation Pane**.

i. Display **Backstage** view, click **Close Database**, and then click **Exit** to close the Access program. As directed by your instructor, submit your database and the eight paper or electronic printouts—relationship report, sorted table, and six queries—that are the results of this project.

End **You have completed Project 11C**

Content-Based Assessments

Apply 11B skills from these Objectives:

- 8 Specify Numeric Criteria in a Query
- 9 Use Compound Criteria
- 10 Create a Query Based on More Than One Table
- 11 Use Wildcards in a Query
- 12 Use Calculated Fields in a Query
- 13 Calculate Statistics and Group Data in a Query
- 14 Create a Crosstab Query

Skills Review | Project 11D Concerts and Sponsors

In the following Skills Review, you will assist Dr. William Jinkens, the Capital Cities Community College Music Director, in answering questions about concerts, sponsors, box office receipts, dates, and concert locations. Your results will look similar to Figure 11.49.

Project Files

For Project 11D, you will need the following files:

a02D_Concerts_Sponsors
a02D_Sponsors (Excel file)

You will save your database as:

Lastname_Firstname_2D_Concerts_Sponsors

Project Results

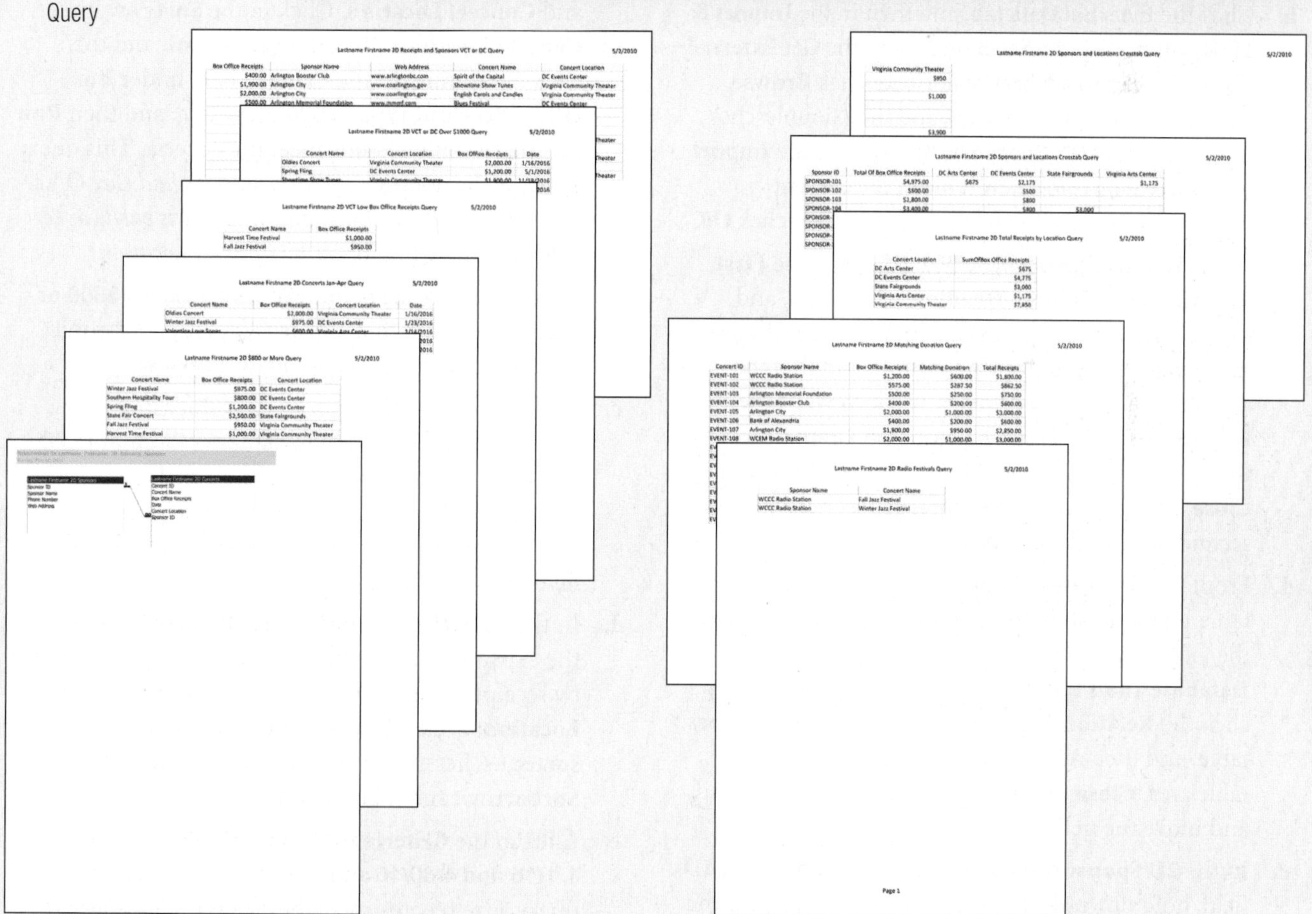

Figure 11.49

(Project 11D Concerts and Sponsors continues on the next page)

Content-Based Assessments

Skills Review | Project 11D Concerts and Sponsors (continued)

1 **Start** Access. In the **Backstage** view, click **Open**. Navigate to the student files that accompany this textbook, and then open the **a02D_Concerts_Sponsors** database.

a. Click the **File tab** to return to **Backstage** view, and then click **Save Database As**. In the **Save As** dialog box, navigate to your **Access Chapter 11** folder. In the **File name** box, select the file name, and then type **Lastname_Firstname_2D_Concerts_Sponsors** and then press Enter. In the **Message Bar**, click **Enable Content**. **Rename** the **2D Concerts** table to **Lastname Firstname 2D Concerts** and then widen the **Navigation Pane** to display the entire table name.

b. Click the **External Data tab**, and then in the **Import & Link group**, click the **Excel** button. In the **Get External Data – Excel Spreadsheet** dialog box, click **Browse**. Navigate to your student files, and then double-click the Excel file **a02D_Sponsors**. Be sure that the **Import the source data into a new table in the current database** option button is selected, and then click **OK**.

c. In the **Import Spreadsheet Wizard**, select the **First Row Contains Column Headings** check box, and then click **Next**. Click **Next** again. Click the **Choose my own primary key** option button, and then be sure that **Sponsor ID** displays. Click **Next**. In the **Import to Table** box, type **Lastname Firstname 2D Sponsors** and then click **Finish**. In the Wizard, click **Close**. The imported Excel spreadsheet becomes the second table in the database.

d. From the **Navigation Pane**, open your **2D Sponsors** table. Apply **Best Fit** to all columns, and then **Close** the table, saving changes to the design. Click the **Database Tools tab**, and in the **Relationships group**, click the **Relationships** button. **Add** the **2D Sponsors** table, and then **Add** the **2D Concerts** table to the table area. **Close** the **Show Table** dialog box. Expand and move the field lists as necessary.

e. In the **2D Sponsors** field list, point to the **Sponsor ID** field, hold down the left mouse button, drag into the **2D Concerts** field list, position the mouse pointer on top of the **Sponsor ID** field, and then release the mouse button. In the **Edit Relationships** dialog box, select the **Enforce Referential Integrity** check box, and then click the **Create** button. A one-to-many relationship is established; *one* sponsor organization can sponsor *many* concerts.

f. On the **Design tab**, in the **Tools group**, click the **Relationship Report** button. Create a paper or electronic printout as directed, and then **Close** the report. In the message box, click **Yes**; and then in the **Save As** dialog box, click **OK** to save the report with the default name. **Close** the **Relationships** window, and then **Close** the **Navigation Pane**.

2 Click the **Create tab**, and then in the **Queries group**, click the **Query Design** button. **Add** the **2D Concerts** table to the table area, **Close** the **Show Table** dialog box, and then expand the field list.

a. Add the following fields to the design grid in the order given: **Concert Name**, **Box Office Receipts**, and **Concert Location**. Click in the **Sort** row under **Concert Location**, click the **Sort arrow**, and then click **Ascending**. In the **Criteria** row, under **Box Office Receipts**, type **>=800** press Enter, and then **Run** the query. Nine records meet the criteria. This query answers the question, *Which concerts had Box Office Receipts of $800 or more, and where was each concert held in alphabetical order by Concert Location?*

b. **Save** the query as **Lastname Firstname 2D $800 or More Query** and then create a paper or electronic printout as directed. **Close Print Preview**.

c. With the query still open, display **Backstage** view, click **Save Object As**, type **Lastname Firstname 2D Concerts Jan-Apr Query** and then click **OK**. Click the **Home tab**, and then switch to **Design** view. From the **2D Concerts** field list, add **Date** as the fourth field in the design grid.

d. In the **Criteria** row, under **Box Office Receipts**, delete the existing criteria so that the query is not restricted by receipts. Click in the **Sort** row under **Concert Location**, click the **Sort arrow**, and then click **(not sorted)**. Click in the **Sort** row under **Date**, click the **Sort arrow**, and then click **Ascending**.

e. Click in the **Criteria** row under **Date**, type **between 1/1/16 and 4/30/16** and then press Enter. **Run** the query. Five records meet the criteria. This query answers the question, *What is the Concert Name, Box Office Receipts, Concert Location, and Date, in chronological order between January 1, 2016, and April 30, 2016, of concerts held?* **Print** or submit electronically as directed. **Close Print Preview**, **Close** the query, and then click **Yes** to save the changes to the query design.

(Project 11D Concerts and Sponsors continues on the next page)

Skills Review | Project 11D Concerts and Sponsors (continued)

3 **Create** a query in **Query Design** view. **Add** the **2D Concerts** table to the table area, **Close** the **Show Table** dialog box, and then expand the field list. Add the following fields to the design grid in the order given: **Concert Name**, **Concert Location**, and **Box Office Receipts**.

a. In the **Criteria** row, under **Concert Location**, type **Virginia Community Theater** and then press Enter. In the **Criteria** row, under **Box Office Receipts**, type **<=1000** and then press Enter. In the **Concert Location** field, clear the **Show** check box. **Run** the query; two records display. This query answers the question, *Which concerts that were held at the Virginia Community Theater had Box Office Receipts of $1,000 or less?*

b. **Save** the query as **Lastname Firstname 2D VCT Low Box Office Receipts Query** and then create a paper or electronic printout as directed. **Close** the query.

c. **Create** a query in **Query Design** view. **Add** the **2D Concerts** table to the table area, **Close** the **Show Table** dialog box, and then expand the field list. Add the following fields to the design grid: **Concert Name**, **Concert Location**, **Box Office Receipts**, and **Date**.

d. In the **Criteria** row, under **Concert Location**, type **Virginia Community Theater or DC Events Center** and press Enter. In the **Criteria** row, under **Box Office Receipts**, type **>1000** and then press Enter. In the **Sort** row, under **Date**, click the **Sort arrow**, and then click **Ascending**.

e. **Run** the query. Four records display. This query answers the question, *Which concerts held at either the Virginia Community Theater or the DC Events Center had Box Office Receipts of more than $1,000 and on what dates, in chronological order, were the concerts held?*

f. **Save** the query as **Lastname Firstname 2D VCT or DC Over $1000 Query** and then create a paper or electronic printout as directed. **Close Print Preview**, and then **Close** the query.

4 **Create** a query in **Query Design** view, **Add** both tables to the table area, and then expand the field lists. Reposition the field lists so that **2D Sponsors** is on the left side. From the **2D Sponsors** field list, add the following fields to the design grid in the order given: **Sponsor Name** and **Web Address**. Click in the **Sort** row under **Sponsor Name**, click the **Sort arrow**, and then click **Ascending**.

a. From the **2D Concerts** field list, add the following fields to the design grid in the order give: **Concert Name**, **Concert Location**, and **Box Office Receipts**.

b. In the **Criteria** row, under **Concert Location**, type **Virginia Community Theater** and then click in the **or** row, under **Concert Location**. Type **DC Events Center** and then press Enter.

c. In the design grid, select the **Box Office Receipts** field, and then drag it to the first field position in the grid. **Run** the query; 12 records display. This query answers the question, *What were the Box Office Receipts, Sponsor Name, sponsor Web Address, Concert Name, and Concert Location of all concerts held at either the Virginia Community Theater or the DC Events Center, sorted alphabetically by Sponsor Name?*

d. **Save** the query as **Lastname Firstname 2D Receipts and Sponsors VCT or DC Query** and then display the query results in **Print Preview**. Change the orientation to **Landscape**, change the **Margins** to **Normal**, and then create a paper or electronic printout as directed. **Close** the query.

5 **Create** a query in **Query Design** view, **Add** both tables to the table area, **Close** the **Show Table** dialog box, and then expand the field lists. Reposition the field lists so that **2D Sponsors** is on the left side.

a. From the **2D Sponsors** field list, add the **Sponsor Name** field to the design grid. From the **2D Concerts** field list, add the **Concert Name** field to the design grid.

b. In the **Criteria** row, under **Sponsor Name**, type ***radio*** and then press Enter. In the **Criteria** row, under **Concert Name**, type ***festival** and then press Enter.

c. **Run** the query; two records have the word *Radio* somewhere in the Sponsor Name and the word *Festival* at the end of the Concert Name. This query answers the question, *Which radio stations are sponsoring Festival-type concerts?* **Save** the query as **Lastname Firstname 2D Radio Festivals Query** and then create a paper or electronic printout as directed. **Close** the query.

6 **Create** a query in **Query Design** view. **Add** both tables to the table area, **Close** the **Show Table** dialog box, and then expand the field lists. If necessary, reposition the

(Project 11D Concerts and Sponsors continues on the next page)

Skills Review | Project 11D Concerts and Sponsors (continued)

field lists so that *2D Sponsors* is on the left side. From the field lists, add the following fields to the design grid in the order given: **Concert ID**, **Sponsor Name**, and **Box Office Receipts**. Click in the **Sort** row under **Concert ID**, click the **Sort arrow**, and then click **Ascending**.

- **a.** Sponsors have indicated that they will donate an additional amount to the Music Department based on 50 percent of the Box Office Receipts. On the **Field** row, right-click in the first empty column to display a shortcut menu, and then click **Zoom**. In the **Zoom** dialog box, type **Matching Donation:[Box Office Receipts]*0.5** and then click **OK**.
- **b. Run** the query to view the new field—*Matching Donation*. Switch to **Design** view. In the **Field** row, in the first empty column, right-click, and then click **Zoom**. In the **Zoom** dialog box, type **Total Receipts: [Box Office Receipts]+[Matching Donation]** and then click **OK**. **Run** the query to view the results.
- **c.** Switch to **Design** view. In the field row, click in the **Matching Donations** field. In the **Show/Hide group**, click the **Property Sheet** button, and then set the **Format** to **Currency** and the **Decimal Places** to **2**. **Close** the **Property Sheet**.
- **d. Run** the query. This query answers the question *In ascending order by Concert ID, assuming each sponsor makes a matching 50 percent donation based on each concert's Box Office Receipts, what is the Sponsor Name, Box Office Receipts, Matching Donation, and Total Receipts for each concert?*
- **e.** Select all of the columns, and then apply **Best Fit**. **Save** the query as **Lastname Firstname 2D Matching Donation Query** and then display the query results in **Print Preview**. Change the orientation to **Landscape**, and then create a paper or electronic printout as directed. **Close** the query.

7 **Create** a query in **Query Design** view. **Add** the **2D Concerts** table to the table area, **Close** the **Show Table** dialog box, and then expand the field list. Add the **Box Office Receipts** field to the design grid.

- **a.** On the **Design tab**, in the **Show/Hide group**, click the **Totals** button, which adds a *Total* row as the third row in the design grid. On the **Total** row, under **Box Office Receipts**, click in the **Group By** box. Click the **arrow**, and then click the **Sum** function.
- **b.** With the field still selected, display the **Property Sheet**, set the **Decimal Places** to **0**, and then **Close** the **Property Sheet**. **Run** the query. The total Box Office Receipts for all the concerts was *$17,475*. Apply **Best Fit** to the **SumOfBox Office Receipts** column.
- **c.** Switch to **Design** view. In the design grid, add the **Concert Location** field as the first field of the design grid. **Run** the query. This query answers the question *For each Concert Location, what are the total Box Office Receipts?*
- **d. Save** the query as **Lastname Firstname 2D Total Receipts by Location Query** and then create a paper or electronic printout as directed. **Close** the query.

8 **Create** a query using the **Query Wizard**. In the **New Query** dialog box, click **Crosstab Query Wizard**, and then click **OK**. Be sure that **2D Concerts** is selected, and then click **Next**.

- **a.** Under **Available Fields**, double-click **Sponsor ID** so that you can display Box Office Receipts by Sponsor ID, and then click **Next**. In the field list, click **Concert Location** to add the locations as column headings, and then click **Next**.
- **b.** Under **Fields**, click **Box Office Receipts**. Under **Functions**, click **Sum**, and then click **Next**.
- **c.** Name the query **Lastname Firstname 2D Sponsors and Locations Crosstab Query** and then click **Finish**. Click the **Home tab**, switch to **Design** view, click in the **Box Office Receipts** column, display the **Property Sheet**, and then set the **Decimal Places** to **0**. **Close** the **Property Sheet**, **Run** the query, and apply **Best Fit** to all of the columns. This query answers the question *By Sponsor ID, what are the total Box Office Receipts for each Concert Location?*
- **d.** Display the query results in **Print Preview**. Change the orientation to **Landscape**, change the **Margins** to **Normal**, and then create a paper or electronic printout as directed—two pages result. **Close** the query, saving changes to the design.
- **e. Open** the **Navigation Pane**. Increase the width of the **Navigation Pane** to display fully all of the object names. Display **Backstage** view, click **Close Database**, and then click **Exit**. As directed by your instructor, submit your database and the ten paper or electronic printouts—relationship report and nine queries—that are the results of this project.

End **You have completed Project 11D**

Apply **11A** skills from these Objectives:

1. Open an Existing Database
2. Create Table Relationships
3. Sort Records in a Table
4. Create a Query in Design View
5. Create a New Query from an Existing Query
6. Sort Query Results
7. Specify Criteria in a Query

Mastering Access | Project 11E Grants and Organizations

In the following Mastering Access project, you will assist Susan Elkington, Director of Grants for the college, in using her database to answer questions about public and private grants awarded to the college departments. Your results will look similar to Figure 11.50.

Project Files

For Project 11E, you will need the following file:

a02E_Grants_Organizations

You will save your database as:

Lastname_Firstname_2E_Grants_Organizations

Project Results

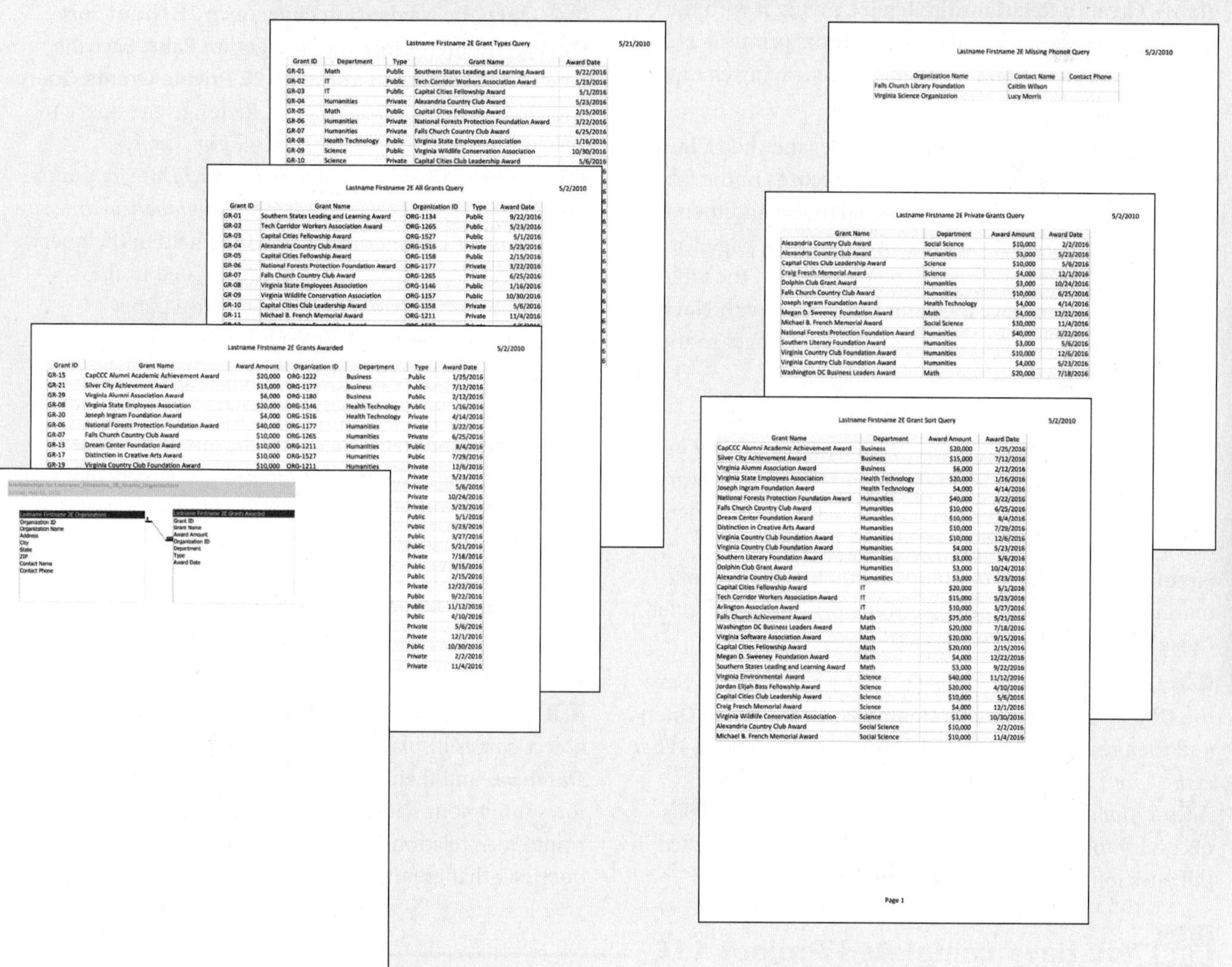

Figure 11.50

(Project 11E Grants and Organizations continues on the next page)

Mastering Access | Project 11E Grants and Organizations (continued)

1 **Start** Access. From your student files, open the **a02E_Grants_Organizations** database. Save the database in your **Access Chapter 11** folder as **Lastname_Firstname_2E_Grants_Organizations** and then enable the content. In the **Navigation Pane**, **Rename** the tables by adding **Lastname Firstname** to the beginning of each table name, and then widen the **Navigation Pane** to display fully both table names. **Open** both tables and examine their contents to become familiar with the data. **Close** both tables, and leave the **Navigation Pane** open.

2 Create a *one-to-many* relationship between the **2E Organizations** table and the **2E Grants Awarded** table based on the **Organization ID** field, and then **Enforce Referential Integrity**. *One* organization can award *many* grants. Create a **Relationship Report**, saving it with the default name. Create a paper or electronic printout as directed, and then **Close** all open objects, saving changes if prompted.

3 **Open** the **2E Grants Awarded** table, and then **Close** the **Navigation Pane**. **Sort** so that the records in the table are in alphabetical order by the **Department** and then in descending order by **Award Amount**. Create a paper or electronic printout as directed, being sure that the table prints on only one page by using **Landscape**, with **Normal** margins. **Close** the table, and do *not* save changes to the table.

4 **Create** a query in **Query Design** view, using the **2E Grants Awarded** table to answer the question, *What is the Grant ID, Grant Name, Award Amount, Type, and Award Date for all of the grants?* Display the fields in the order listed in the question. **Save** the query as **Lastname Firstname 2E All Grants Query** and then, with **Normal** margins, create a paper or electronic printout as directed. **Close Print Preview**, and leave the query open.

5 Use **2E All Grants Query** to create a new query. **Save** the **Object As Lastname Firstname 2E Grant Types Query** and then redesign the query to answer the question, *What is the Grant ID, Department, Type, Grant Name, and Award Amount for all grants?* Display the only the fields necessary to answer the question and in the order listed in the question. With **Normal** margins, create a paper or electronic printout as directed. **Close** the query, saving the design changes.

6 From the **Navigation Pane**, open the **2E All Grants Query**, and then **Close** the **Navigation Pane**. **Save** the **Object As Lastname Firstname 2E Grant Sort Query** and then switch to **Design** view. Redesign the query to answer the question, *What is the Grant Name, Department, Award Amount, and Award Date for grants sorted first in alphabetical order by Department and then in descending order by Amount?* Display only the fields necessary to answer the question and in the order listed in the question. With **Normal** margins, create a paper or electronic printout as directed. **Close** the query, saving changes to the query design.

7 **Open** the **Navigation Pane**, open **2E Grant Sort Query**, and then **Close** the **Navigation Pane**. **Save** the **Object As Lastname Firstname 2E Private Grants Query** and then switch to **Design** view. Redesign the query to answer the question, *What is the Grant Name, Department, Award Amount, and Award Date for grants that have a Type of Private, sorted in alphabetical order by Grant Name?* Do *not* display the **Type** field in the query results; display the fields in the order listed in the question. With **Normal** margins, create a paper or electronic printout as directed. **Close** the query, saving changes to the query design.

8 **Create** a query in **Query Design** view, using the **2E Organizations** table to answer the question, *What is the Organization Name and Contact Name where the Contact Phone number is missing from the table, sorted in alphabetical order by the Organization Name?* Two records meet the criteria. **Save** the query as **Lastname Firstname 2E Missing Phone# Query** and then create a paper or electronic printout as directed. **Close** the query.

9 **Open** the **Navigation Pane** and widen it so that all object names display fully. In **Backstage** view, click **Close Database**, and then click **Exit**. As directed by your instructor, submit your database and the seven paper or electronic printouts—relationship report, sorted table, and five queries—that are the results of this project.

End **You have completed Project 11E**

Apply 11B skills from these Objectives:

- **8** Specify Numeric Criteria in a Query
- **9** Use Compound Criteria
- **10** Create a Query Based on More Than One Table
- **11** Use Wildcards in a Query
- **12** Use Calculated Fields in a Query
- **13** Calculate Statistics and Group Data in a Query
- **14** Create a Crosstab Query

Mastering Access | Project 11F Events and Clients

In the following Mastering Access project, you will assist Hank Schwan, the Capital Cities Community College Facilities Manager, in using his database to answer questions about facilities that the college rents to community and private organizations at times when the facilities are not in use for college activities. Your results will look similar to Figure 11.51.

Project Files

For Project 11F, you will need the following files:

a02F_Events_Clients
a02F_Rental_Clients (Excel file)

You will save your database as:

Lastname_Firstname_2F_Events_Clients

Project Results

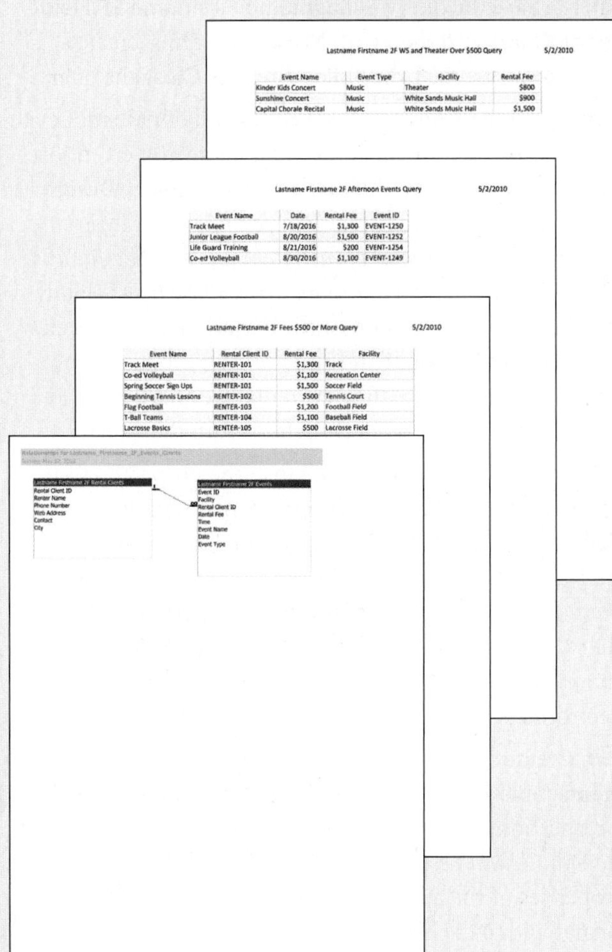

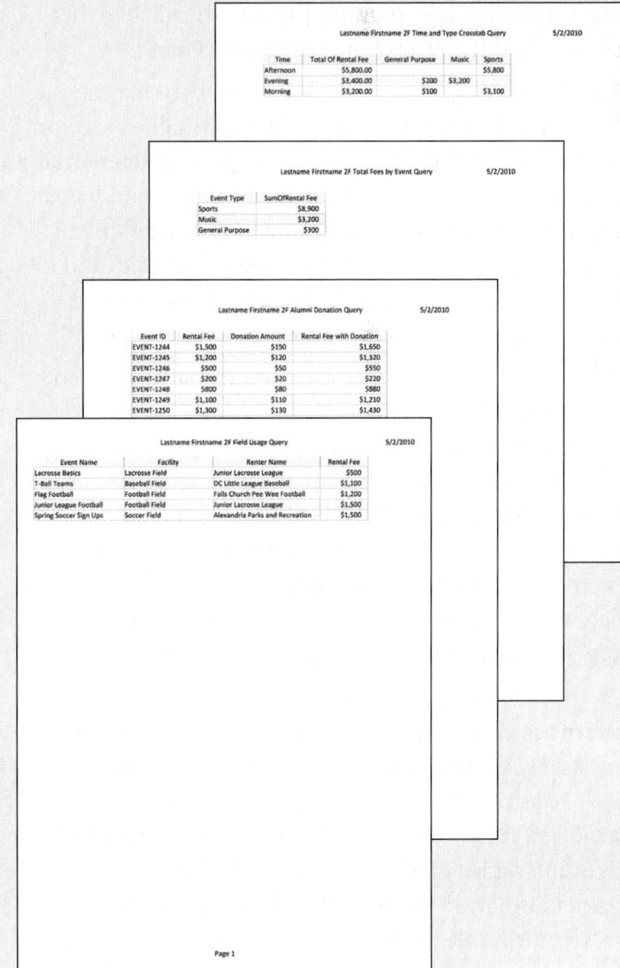

Figure 11.51

(Project 11F Events and Clients continues on the next page)

Mastering Access | Project 11F Events and Clients (continued)

1 **Start** Access. From your student files, open the **a02F_Events_Clients** database. Save the database in your **Access Chapter 11** folder as **Lastname_Firstname_2F_Events_Clients** and then enable the content. In the **Navigation Pane**, **Rename** the table by adding **Lastname Firstname** to the beginning of the table name.

2 **Import** the **a02F_Rental_Clients** Excel spreadsheet from the student data files that accompany this textbook into the current database as a new table. Designate the first row of the spreadsheet as column headings. Select the **Rental Client ID** field as the primary key. Name the table **Lastname Firstname 2F Rental Clients** and then widen the **Navigation Pane** to display fully the two table names. **Open** both tables and examine their contents to become familiar with the data. In the **2F Rental Clients** table, apply **Best Fit** to all of the columns. **Close** both tables, saving changes, and then **Close** the **Navigation Pane**.

3 Create a *one-to-many* relationship between the **2F Rental Clients** table and the **2F Events** table based on the **Rental Client ID** field, and then **Enforce Referential Integrity**. *One* rental client can have *many* events. Create a **Relationship Report**, saving it with the default name. Create a paper or electronic printout as directed, and then **Close** all open objects, saving changes if prompted.

4 **Create** a query in **Query Design** view using the **2F Events** table to answer the question, *What is the Event Name, Rental Client ID, and Rental Fee for events with fees greater than or equal to $500, in ascending order by Rental Client ID, and in which Facility was the event held?* Display the fields in the order listed in the question. Eleven records meet the criteria. **Save** the query as **Lastname Firstname 2F Fees $500 or More Query** Create a paper or electronic printout as directed. Leave the query open.

5 Using the **2F Fees $500 or More Query** object, create a new query, and save it as **Lastname Firstname 2F Afternoon Events Query** Redesign the query to answer the questions, *Which Events were held in the Afternoon between 7/1/16 and 8/31/16, in chronological order by date, what was the Rental Fee, and what was the Event ID?* (Hint: Open the 2F Events table to see how the Time field data is stored.). Do *not* display the **Time** field in the results, and do *not* restrict the results by **Rental Fee**. Four records meet the criteria. Create a paper or electronic printout as directed, **Close** the query, and save changes to the design.

6 **Create** a query in **Query Design** view using the **2F Events** table to answer the question, *Which Events and Event Types were held in either the White Sands Music Hall or the Theater that had Rental Fees greater than $500?* Display the fields in the order listed in the question. Three records meet the criteria. **Save** the query as **Lastname Firstname 2F WS and Theater Over $500 Query** and then create a paper or electronic printout as directed. **Close** the query.

7 **Create** a query in **Query Design** view using both tables to answer the question, *Which Events were held on one of the sports fields, for which Renter Name, and what was the Rental Fee in order of lowest fee to highest fee?* (Hint: Use a wildcard with the word *Field*.) Display the fields in the order listed in the question. Five records meet the criteria. **Save** the query as **Lastname Firstname 2F Field Usage Query** and then with **Normal** margins, create a paper or electronic printout as directed. **Close** the query.

8 The college Alumni Association will donate money to the Building Fund in an amount based on 10 percent of total facility rental fees. **Create** a query in **Query Design** view to answer the question, *In ascending order by Event ID, what will be the total of each Rental Fee if the Alumni Association donates an additional 10% of each fee?* (Hint: First compute the amount of the donation, name the new field **Donation Amount** and run the query to view the results. Then calculate the new rental fee and name the new field **Rental Fee with Donation**) **Run** the query.

Switch back to **Design** view, change the properties of the new fields to display in **Currency** format with **0** decimal places, and then **Run** the query again. For *EVENT-1244*, the *Donation Amount* is *$150* and the *Rental Fee with Donation* is *$1,650*. Apply **Best Fit** to the columns in the query results. **Save** the query as **Lastname Firstname 2F Alumni Donation Query** and then create a paper or electronic printout as directed. **Close** the query.

9 **Create** a query in **Query Design** view using the **2F Events** table and the **Sum** aggregate function to answer the question, *In descending order by Rental Fee, what are the total Rental Fees for each Event Type?* Change the properties of the appropriate field to display **Currency** format with **0** decimal places, and then **Run** the query. For a *Sports* Event Type, Rental Fees total *$8,900*. Apply **Best Fit** to the columns in the query results. **Save** the query as **Lastname Firstname 2F Total Fees by Event Query** and then create a paper or electronic printout as directed. **Close** the query.

(Project 11F Events and Clients continues on the next page)

Mastering Access | Project 11F Events and Clients (continued)

10 By using the **Query Wizard**, create a **Crosstab Query** based on the **2F Events** table. Select **Time** as the **row headings** and **Event Type** as the **column headings**. **Sum** the **Rental Fee** field. Name the query **Lastname Firstname 2F Time and Type Crosstab Query** Change the design to display **Currency** format with **0** decimal places in the appropriate column, and then apply **Best Fit** to all of the columns. This query answers the question *What are the total Rental Fees for each time of the day and for each Event Type?* Create a paper or electronic printout as directed. **Close** the query, saving changes to the design.

11 **Open** the **Navigation Pane** and widen it so that all object names display fully. In **Backstage** view, click **Close Database**, and then click **Exit**. As directed by your instructor, submit your database and the eight paper or electronic printouts—relationship report and seven queries—that are the results of this project.

End **You have completed Project 11F**

Apply 11A and 11B skills from these Objectives:

1 Open an Existing Database
2 Create Table Relationships
3 Sort Records in a Table
4 Create a Query in Design View
5 Create a New Query from an Existing Query
6 Sort Query Results
7 Specify Criteria in a Query
8 Specify Numeric Criteria in a Query
9 Use Compound Criteria
10 Create a Query Based on More Than One Table
11 Use Wildcards in a Query
12 Use Calculated Fields in a Query
13 Calculate Statistics and Group Data in a Query
14 Create a Crosstab Query

Mastering Access | Project 11G Students and Scholarships

In the following Mastering Access project, you will assist Thao Nguyen, Director of Academic Scholarships, in using her database to answer questions about scholarships awarded to students. Your results will look similar to Figure 11.52.

Project Files

For Project 11G, you will need the following file:

a02G_Students_Scholarships

You will save your database as:

Lastname_Firstname_2G_Students_Scholarships

Project Results

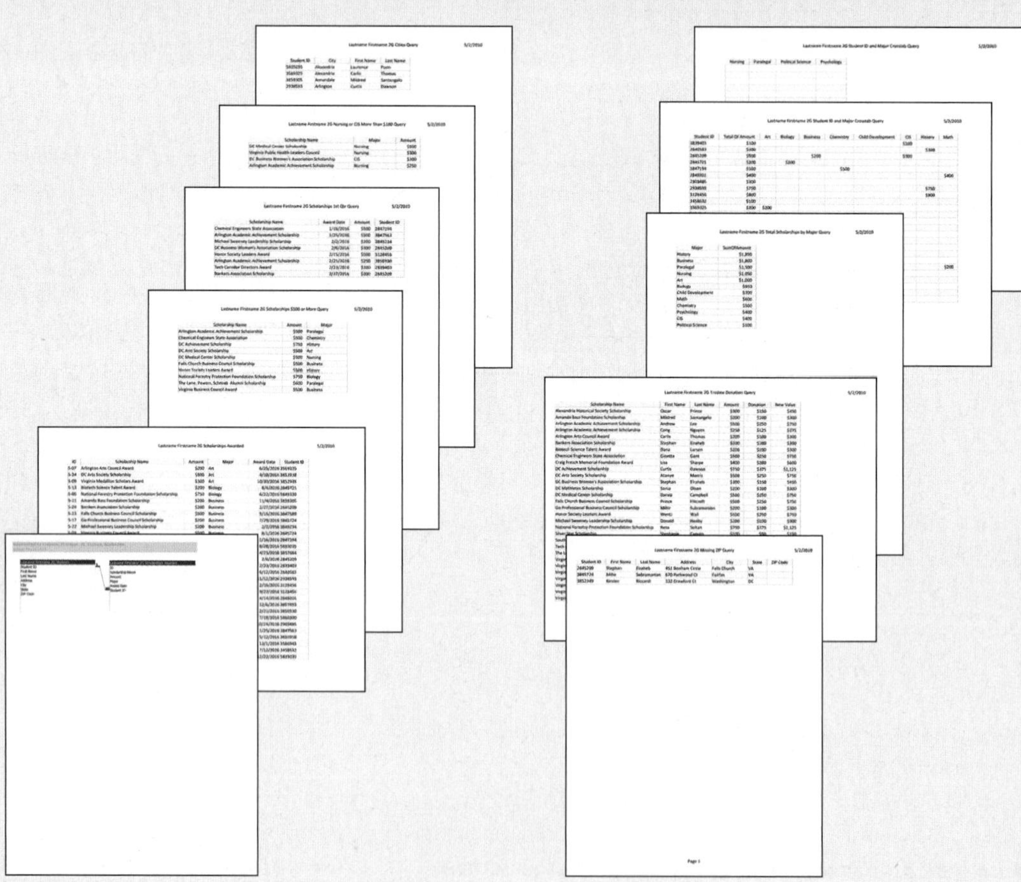

Figure 11.52

(Project 11G Students and Scholarships continues on the next page)

Mastering Access | Project 11G Students and Scholarships (continued)

1 **Start** Access. From your student files, open the **a02G_Students_Scholarships** database. Save the database in your **Access Chapter 11** folder as **Lastname_Firstname_2G_Students_Scholarships** and then enable the content. **Rename** both tables by adding **Lastname Firstname** to the beginning of the table name, and then widen the **Navigation Pane** to display fully the object names.

2 **Open** the two database tables to become familiar with the data. **Close** the tables, and then create a *one-to-many* relationship between the **2G Students** table and the **2G Scholarships Awarded** table based on the **Student ID** field, and then **Enforce Referential Integrity**; *one* student can have *many* scholarships. Create the **Relationship Report**, and create a paper or electronic printout as directed, saving it with the default name. **Close** all open objects.

3 Open the **2G Scholarships Awarded** table, and then **Sort** the appropriate fields in **Ascending** order so that the records are sorted by the **Major** field. Within each Major, the records should be sorted by **Scholarship Name**. Create a paper or electronic printout, being sure to print the results on one page. **Close** the table, and do *not* save changes to the table design. **Close** the **Navigation Pane**.

4 **Create** a query in **Query Design** view using the **2G Scholarships Awarded** table to answer the question, *In alphabetical order by Scholarship Name, what is the Amount and Major for scholarships greater than or equal to $500?* Display the fields in the order listed in the question. Ten records meet the criteria. **Save** the query as **Lastname Firstname 2G Scholarships $500 or More Query** and create a paper or electronic printout as directed. **Close Print Preview**, and leave the query open.

5 Using the **2G Scholarships $500 or More Query**, create a query. **Save** the **Object As Lastname Firstname 2G Scholarships 1st Qtr Query** and then redesign the query to answer the question *Which scholarships were awarded, in chronological order by Award Date, between 1/1/16 and 3/31/16, for what amount, and what was Student ID of the student?* Display the fields in the order listed in the question, display *only* the fields listed in the question, do not restrict the amount, and sort only by date. Eight records meet the criteria. Create a paper or electronic printout as directed. **Close** the query, saving changes.

6 **Create** a query in **Query Design** view using the **2G Scholarships Awarded** table to answer the question, *Which scholarships were awarded for either Nursing or CIS majors for amounts of more than $100, listed in descending order by amount?* Display the fields in the order listed in the question. Four records meet the criteria. (Hint: If five records display, switch to **Design view** and combine the majors on one criteria line using OR.) **Save** the query as **Lastname Firstname 2G Nursing or CIS More Than $100 Query** and then create a paper or electronic printout as directed. **Close** the query.

7 **Create** a query in **Query Design** view. Use the **2G Students** table and a wildcard to answer the question, *In alphabetical order by City and in alphabetical order by Last Name, what are the Student ID, City, First Name, and Last Name of students from cities that begin with the letter A?* Display the fields in the order listed in the question. Four records meet the criteria. **Save** the query as **Lastname Firstname 2G Cities Query** Create a paper or electronic printout as directed. **Close** the query.

8 **Create** a query in **Query Design** view using the **2G Students** table and all of the table's fields to answer the question *For which students is the ZIP Code missing?* Three students are missing ZIP Codes. **Save** the query as **Lastname Firstname 2G Missing ZIP Query** and then with **Normal** margins, create a paper or electronic printout as directed. **Close** the query. Using the information that displays in the query results, an enrollment clerk can use a reference to look up the ZIP codes for the students and then enter the ZIP codes in the student records in the underlying table.

9 For each scholarship, the Board of Trustees of the college will donate an amount equal to 50 percent of each scholarship. **Create** a query in **Query Design** view. Use both tables and calculated fields to answer the question, *In alphabetical order by scholarship name, and including the first and last name of the scholarship recipient, what will the value of each scholarship be if the Board of Trustees makes a matching 50 percent donation?* (Hint: First compute the amount of the donation, naming the new field **Donation** and then calculate the new scholarship value, naming the new field **New Value**).

Run the query, switch back to **Design** view, and as necessary, change the properties of all the numeric fields to display in **Currency** format with **0** decimal places, and then **Run** the query. For the *Alexandria Historical Society Scholarship*, the *Donation* is *$150* and the *New Value* is *$450*. Apply **Best Fit** to the columns in the query results. **Save** the query as **Lastname Firstname 2G Trustee Donation Query** and then create a paper or electronic printout as directed, being sure to print the results on one page. **Close** the query.

(Project 11G Students and Scholarships continues on the next page)

Mastering Access | Project 11G Students and Scholarships (continued)

10 **Create** a new query in **Query Design** view. Use the **2G Scholarships Awarded** table and the **Sum** aggregate function to answer the question *For each major, in descending order by amount, what are the total scholarship amounts?* Display the fields in the order listed in the question. Use the **Property Sheet** to display the sums in the **Currency** format with **0** decimal places. *History* majors received *$1,850* in scholarships. Apply **Best Fit** to the columns in the query results. **Save** the query as **Lastname Firstname 2G Total Scholarships by Major Query** and then create a paper or electronic printout as directed. **Close** the query.

11 **Create** a **Crosstab Query** using the **2G Scholarships Awarded** table. Use the **Student ID** field as row headings and the **Major** field as column headings to answer the question *For each student or major, what is the total scholarship Amount awarded?* Name the query **Lastname Firstname 2G Student ID and Major Crosstab Query** In **Design** view, apply **0** decimal places to the appropriate fields. Apply **Best Fit** to the columns in the query results. **Save** the query, and then as directed, create a paper or electronic printout in **Landscape** orientation—the query results will print on two pages. **Close** the query.

12 **Open** the **Navigation Pane** and widen it to display all of the object names. In **Backstage** view, click **Close Database**, and then click **Exit**. As directed by your instructor, submit your database and the ten paper or electronic printouts—relationship report, sorted table, and eight queries—that are the results of this project.

End **You have completed Project 11G**

Apply a combination of the 11A and 11B skills.

GO! Fix It | Project 11H Social Sciences Division

Project Files

For Project 11H, you will need the following file:

a02H_Social_Sciences

You will save your database as:

Lastname_Firstname_2H_Social_Sciences

In this project, you will correct query design errors in a database used by the Dean of Social Sciences. From the student files that accompany this textbook, open the file a02H_Social_Sciences, and then save the database in your Access Chapter 11 folder as **Lastname_Firstname_2H_Social Sciences**

To complete the project you must find and correct errors in relationships, query design, and column widths. In addition to errors that you find, you should know:

- A relationship should be created between the 2H Social Sciences Faculty table and the 2H Anthropology Dept Course Schedule table. A relationship report should be created and named **Lastname Firstname 2H Relationship Report** One faculty member can teach many courses.
- You should add your last name and first name to each query name; do *not* rename the tables.
- Several queries do not accurately reflect the result implied in the query name. Open each query and examine and correct the design of any queries that do not accurately reflect the query name.
- Be sure that all of the object names in the Navigation Pane display fully.
- Create a paper or electronic printout of the relationship report and the four queries as directed by your instructor.

End **You have completed Project 11H**

Apply a combination of the 11A and 11B skills.

GO! Make It | Project 11I Faculty Awards

Project Files

For Project 11I, you will need the following file:

a02I_Faculty_Awards

You will save your database as:

Lastname_Firstname_2I_Faculty_Awards

Start Access, navigate to your student files, and then open the a02I_Faculty_Awards database file. Save the database in your Access Chapter 11 folder as **Lastname_Firstname_2I_Faculty Awards** Rename the two tables to include your name, create a relationship and relationship report. Then create two queries as shown in Figure 11.53. Create paper or electronic printouts as directed.

Project Results

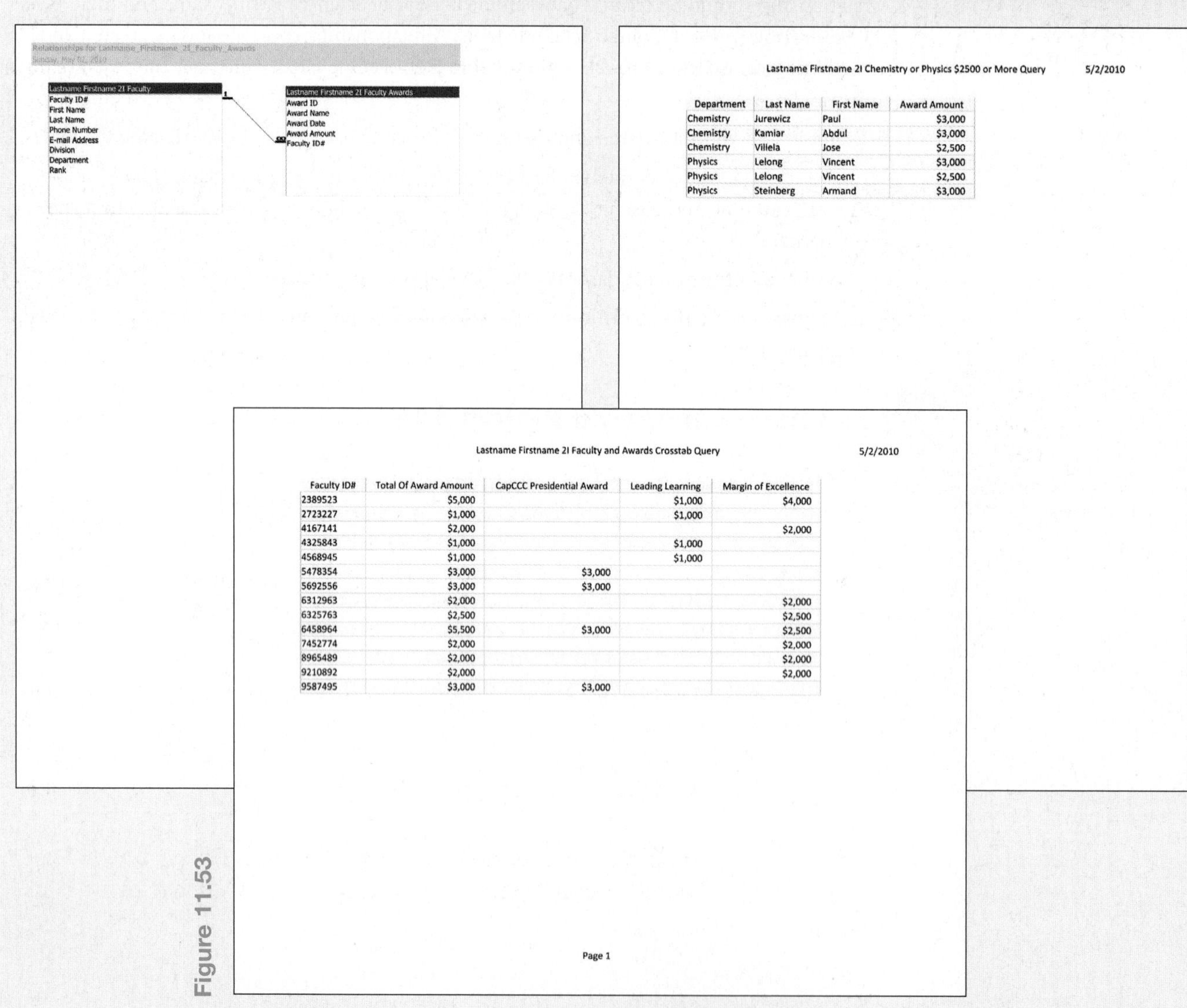

Lastname Firstname 2I Chemistry or Physics $2500 or More Query 5/2/2010

Department	Last Name	First Name	Award Amount
Chemistry	Jurewicz	Paul	$3,000
Chemistry	Kamiar	Abdul	$3,000
Chemistry	Villela	Jose	$2,500
Physics	Lelong	Vincent	$3,000
Physics	Lelong	Vincent	$2,500
Physics	Steinberg	Armand	$3,000

Lastname Firstname 2I Faculty and Awards Crosstab Query 5/2/2010

Faculty ID#	Total Of Award Amount	CapCCC Presidential Award	Leading Learning	Margin of Excellence
2389523	$5,000		$1,000	$4,000
2723227	$1,000		$1,000	
4167141	$2,000			$2,000
4325843	$1,000		$1,000	
4568945	$1,000		$1,000	
5478354	$3,000	$3,000		
5692556	$3,000	$3,000		
6312963	$2,000			$2,000
6325763	$2,500			$2,500
6458964	$5,500	$3,000		$2,500
7452774	$2,000			$2,000
8965489	$2,000			$2,000
9210892	$2,000			$2,000
9587495	$3,000	$3,000		

Page 1

Figure 11.53

End **You have completed Project 11I**

Apply a combination of the 11A and 11B skills.

GO! Solve It | Project 11J Student Refunds

Project Files

For Project 11J, you will need the following file:

a02J_Student_Refunds

You will save your database as:

Lastname_Firstname_2J_Student_Refunds

Start Access, navigate to your student files and open the a02J_Student_Refunds database file. Save the database in your Access Chapter 11 folder as **Lastname_Firstname_2J_Student Refunds** Rename the tables by adding **Lastname Firstname** to the beginning of each table name. Create a relationship between the tables—one student can have many refunds—and then create a relationship report.

Create and save a query to answer the question, *What is the First Name and Last Name of the students who are eligible for a refund and who live in Alexandria or Falls Church sorted alphabetically by Last Name within City?* Create and save a query to answer the question, *What is the total Refund Amount for Full Time and Part Time Students?* Create and save a query to answer the question, *In ascending order by Refund Eligibility Date, what is the Last Name and First Name of students receiving a Refund of more than $50 between the dates of 8/1/16 and 12/31/16?* Apply Best Fit to all the query results, and then create paper or electronic printouts of the report and queries as directed.

Performance Element	Performance Level: Exemplary: You consistently applied the relevant skills	Proficient: You sometimes, but not always, applied the relevant skills	Developing: You rarely or never applied the relevant skills
Create relationship and relationship report	Relationship and relationship report created correctly.	Relationship and relationship report created with one error.	Relationship and relationship report created with two or more errors, or missing entirely.
Create City query	Query created with correct name, fields, sorting, and criteria.	Query created with three elements correct and one incorrect.	Query created with two or more elements incorrect, or missing entirely.
Create Refund query	Query created with correct name, fields, and criteria.	Query created with two elements correct and one incorrect.	Query created with two or more elements incorrect, or missing entirely.
Create Refund Eligibility query	Query created with correct name, fields, sorting, and criteria.	Query created with three elements correct and one incorrect.	Query created with two or more two elements incorrect, or missing entirely.

End **You have completed Project 11J**

Apply a combination of the 11A and 11B skills.

GO! Solve It | Project 11K Leave

Project Files

For Project 11K, you will need the following file:

a02K_Leave

You will save your database as:

Lastname_Firstname_2K_Leave

Start Access, navigate to your student files, and then open the a02K_Leave database file. Save the database in your Access Chapter 11 folder as **Lastname_Firstname_2K_Leave** Rename the tables by adding **Lastname Firstname** to the beginning of each table name. Create a relationship between the tables—one employee can have many leave transactions—and a relationship report.

Create and save a query to answer the question, *Which employees, identified alphabetically by Last Name, have used Personal Leave?* Create and save a query to answer the question, *Which employees, identified alphabetically by Last Name, have no Phone Number?* Create and save a query to answer the question, *How many Leave Transactions were for Vacation leave grouped by the Employee# field?* (Hint: In the Total row of your query, use the Count function.) Create and save a crosstab query to answer the question, *What is the total number of leave transactions for each Employee # (row) by Leave Classification (column)?* Apply Best Fit to all of the query results, and then create paper or electronic printouts of the report and queries as directed by your instructor.

Performance Element	Performance Level		
	Exemplary: You consistently applied the relevant skills	**Proficient:** You sometimes, but not always, applied the relevant skills	**Developing:** You rarely or never applied the relevant skills
Create relationship and relationship report	Relationship and relationship report created correctly.	Relationship and relationship report created with one error.	Relationship and relationship report created with two or more errors, or missing entirely.
Create Personal Leave query	Query created with correct name, fields, sorting, and criteria.	Query created with three elements correct and one incorrect.	Query created with two or more elements incorrect, or missing entirely.
Create Phone Number query	Query created with correct name, fields, and criteria.	Query created with two elements correct and one incorrect.	Query created with two or more elements incorrect, or missing entirely.
Create Vacation Leave query	Query created with correct name, fields, grouping, and aggregate function.	Query created with three elements correct and one incorrect.	Query created with two or more elements incorrect, or missing entirely.
Create Crosstab query	Query created with correct name, row headings, column headings, and aggregate function.	Query created with three elements correct and one incorrect.	Query created with two or more elements incorrect, or missing entirely.

End You have completed Project 11K

Outcomes-Based Assessments

Rubric

The following outcomes-based assessments are *open-ended assessments*. That is, there is no specific correct result; your result will depend on your approach to the information provided. Make *Professional Quality* your goal. Use the following scoring rubric to guide you in *how* to approach the problem and then to evaluate *how well* your approach solves the problem.

The *criteria*—Software Mastery, Content, Format and Layout, and Process—represent the knowledge and skills you have gained that you can apply to solving the problem. The *levels of performance*—Professional Quality, Approaching Professional Quality, or Needs Quality Improvements—help you and your instructor evaluate your result.

	Your completed project is of Professional Quality if you:	**Your completed project is Approaching Professional Quality if you:**	**Your completed project Needs Quality Improvements if you:**
1-Software Mastery	Choose and apply the most appropriate skills, tools, and features and identify efficient methods to solve the problem.	Choose and apply some appropriate skills, tools, and features, but not in the most efficient manner.	Choose inappropriate skills, tools, or features, or are inefficient in solving the problem.
2-Content	Construct a solution that is clear and well organized, contains content that is accurate, appropriate to the audience and purpose, and is complete. Provide a solution that contains no errors in spelling, grammar, or style.	Construct a solution in which some components are unclear, poorly organized, inconsistent, or incomplete. Misjudge the needs of the audience. Have some errors in spelling, grammar, or style, but the errors do not detract from comprehension.	Construct a solution that is unclear, incomplete, or poorly organized; contains some inaccurate or inappropriate content; and contains many errors in spelling, grammar, or style. Do not solve the problem.
3-Format and Layout	Format and arrange all elements to communicate information and ideas, clarify function, illustrate relationships, and indicate relative importance.	Apply appropriate format and layout features to some elements, but not others. Overuse features, causing minor distraction.	Apply format and layout that does not communicate information or ideas clearly. Do not use format and layout features to clarify function, illustrate relationships, or indicate relative importance. Use available features excessively, causing distraction.
4-Process	Use an organized approach that integrates planning, development, self-assessment, revision, and reflection.	Demonstrate an organized approach in some areas, but not others; or, use an insufficient process of organization throughout.	Do not use an organized approach to solve the problem.

Outcomes-Based Assessments

Apply a combination of the **11A** and **11B** skills.

GO! Think | Project **11L** Coaches

Project Files

For Project 11L, you will need the following file:

a02L_Coaches

You will save your database as:

Lastname_Firstname_2L_Coaches

Use the skills you have practiced in this chapter to assist Randy Shavrain, the Athletic Director, in answering questions about the coaches in your database **Lastname_Firstname_2L_Coaches** Create and save the relationship report with the default name, and save the queries you create with your name in the query title. Create paper or electronic printouts of the report and queries as directed by your instructor.

Mr. Shavrain needs to determine: 1) *In alphabetical order by Last Name, what is the Last Name and First Name of every coach involved with Dive activities?* 2) *In alphabetical order by Last Name, what is the Last Name and First Name of every coach involved with Basketball or Football activities?* 3) *In alphabetical order by Last Name, what is the Last Name and First Name of every coach with a Skill Specialty in Volleyball?*

End **You have completed Project 11L**

Apply a combination of the **11A** and **11B** skills.

GO! Think | Project **11M** Club Donations

Project Files

For Project 11M, you will need the following file:

a02M_Club_Donations

You will save your database as:

Lastname_Firstname_2M_Club_Donations

Use the skills you have practiced in this chapter to assist Dr. Kirsten McCarty, Vice President of Student Services, in answering questions about donations collected by students to support student services in your database **Lastname_Firstname_2M_Club_Donations** Create and save the relationship report with the default name, and save the queries you create with your name in the query title. Create paper or electronic printouts of the report and queries as directed.

Dr. McCarty needs to determine: 1) *In ascending order by Last Name, what is the Last Name and First Name of donors who gave donations that are $25 or more?* 2) *What is the total of all donations grouped alphabetically by the Club Affiliation?* 3) *In alphabetical order by the student Last Name, and including the Donation ID#, what will the value of each donation be if the local sports store makes a matching 10 percent donation?* 4) *What are the total donations by Club Affiliation and Student ID?*

End **You have completed Project 11M**

Outcomes-Based Assessments

Apply a combination of the 11A and 11B skills.

You and GO! | Project 11N Personal Inventory

Project Files

For Project 11N, you will need the following file:

New blank Access database

You will save your database as:

Lastname_Firstname_2N_Personal_Inventory

Create a personal database containing a household inventory of your possessions. Name the new database **Lastname_Firstname_2N_Personal_Inventory** Create one or more tables with at least 10 records. Include fields such as item, room location, value, date of purchase. Your table should have items stored in several locations. Sort the table in descending order by the value of the item. Create a paper or electronic printout. Clear all sorts, and then close the table. Create at least three queries to answer specific questions about your inventory. Name the queries to reflect the question asked. Create paper or electronic printouts of your queries.

End You have completed Project 11N

Apply a combination of the 11A and 11B skills.

GO! Collaborate | Project 11O Bell Orchid Hotels Group Running Case

This project relates to the **Bell Orchid Hotels**. Your instructor may assign this group case project to your class. If your instructor assigns this project, he or she will provide you with information and instructions to work as part of a group. The group will apply the skills gained thus far to help the Bell Orchid Hotels achieve their business goals.

End You have completed Project 11O

Forms, Filters, and Reports

OUTCOMES At the end of this chapter you will be able to:	**OBJECTIVES** Mastering these objectives will enable you to:
PROJECT 12A Create forms to enter and display data in a database.	1. Create and Use a Form to Add and Delete Records (p. 663) 2. Create a Form by Using the Form Wizard (p. 669) 3. Modify a Form in Layout View and in Design View (p. 671) 4. Filter Records (p. 679)
PROJECT 12B Create reports to display database information.	5. Create a Report by Using the Report Tool (p. 685) 6. Create Reports by Using the Blank Report Tool and the Report Wizard (p. 688) 7. Modify the Design of a Report (p. 695) 8. Print a Report and Keep Data Together (p. 699)

Andresr/Shutterstock

In This Chapter

In this chapter, you will create forms to enter data and view data in database tables. Forms can display one record at a time, with fields placed in the same order to match a paper source document to make it easier to enter the new information or view existing information. Records in a form or table can be filtered to display only a portion of the total records based on matching specific values.

In this chapter, you will create reports that summarize data stored in a query or table in a professional-looking manner suitable for printing. After your report is created, you can modify the design so that the final report is laid out in a format that is useful to the person reading it.

The projects in this chapter relate to **Capital Cities Community College**, which is located in the Washington D. C. metropolitan area. The college provides high-quality education and professional training to residents in the cities surrounding the nation's capital. Its four campuses serve over 50,000 students and offer more than 140 certificate programs and degrees at the associate's level. CapCCC has a highly acclaimed Distance Education program and an extensive Workforce Development program. The college makes positive contributions to the community through cultural and athletic programs and partnerships with businesses and non-profit organizations.

Project 12A Students and Majors

Project Activities

In Activities 12.01 through 12.11, you will assist Juanita Ramirez, Director of Enrollment Services, in using an Access database to track new students and their major fields of study. Your completed forms will look similar to Figure 12.1.

Project Files

For Project 12A, you will need the following file:

a03A_Students_Majors

You will save your document as:

Lastname_Firstname_3A_Students_Majors

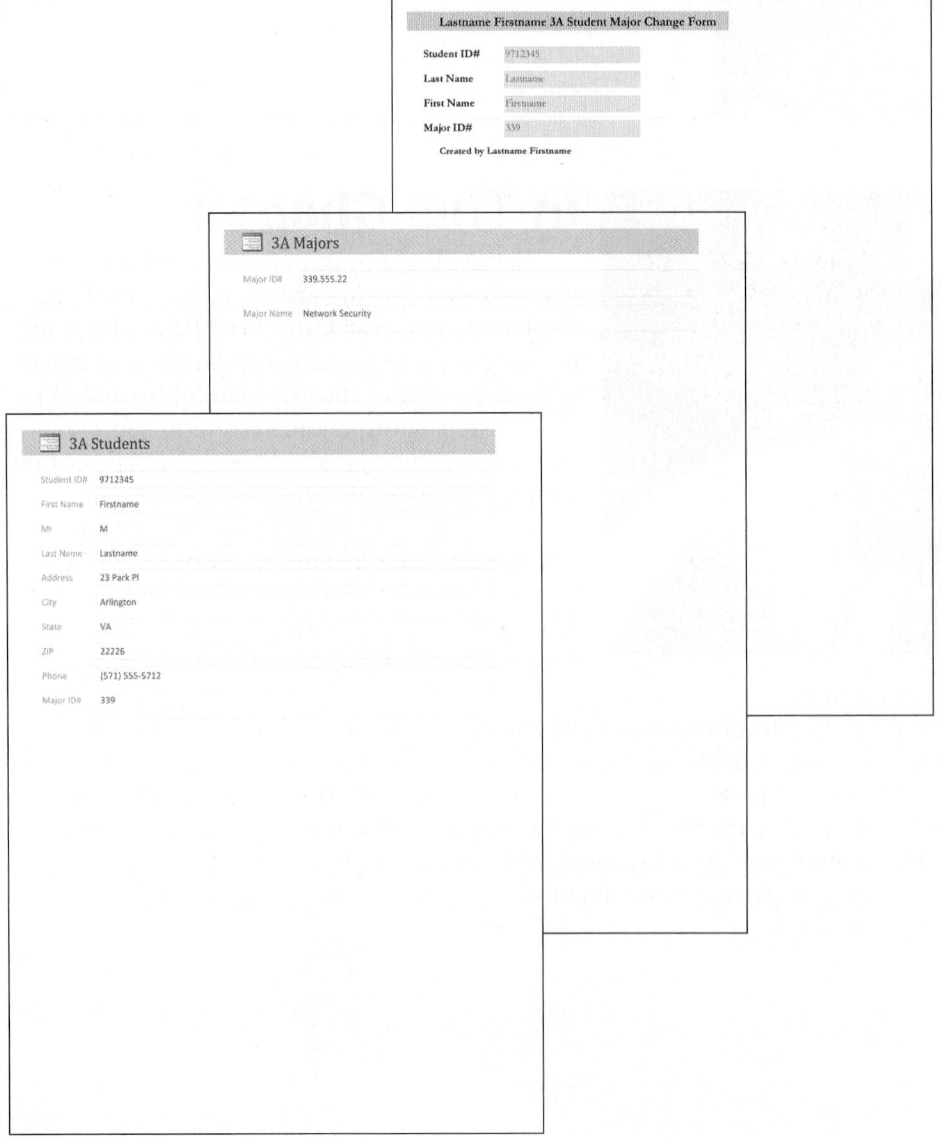

Figure 12.1
Project 12A Students and Majors

Project Results

Objective 1 | Create and Use a Form to Add and Delete Records

A ***form*** is an Access object you can use to enter new records into a table, or to edit, delete, or display existing records in a table. A form is useful to control access to the data. For example, you can design a form for college Registration Assistants who can see and enter the courses scheduled and fees paid by an individual student. However, they cannot see or enter grades in the student's record.

Some Access forms display only one record at a time; other forms display multiple records at the same time. A form that displays only one record at a time is useful not only to the individual who performs the ***data entry***—typing the actual records—but also to anyone who has the job of viewing information in a database. For example, when you visit the Records Office at your college to obtain a transcript, someone displays your record on a screen. For the viewer, it is much easier to look at one record at a time, using a form, than to look at all of the student records in the database.

Activity 12.01 | Creating a Form

There are several ways to create a form in Access, but the fastest and easiest way is to use the ***Form tool***. With a single mouse click, all fields from the underlying data source are placed on the form. You can use the new form immediately, or you can modify it in Layout view or in Design view.

The Form tool incorporates all of the information—both the field names and the individual records—from an existing table or query and then instantly creates the form for you. Records that you edit or create using a form automatically update the underlying table or tables. In this activity, you will create a form and then use it to add new student records to the database.

1. **Start** Access. In **Backstage** view, click **Open**. Navigate to the student data files for this textbook, and then open the **a03A_Students_Majors** database.

2. Display **Backstage** view, click **Save Database As**, and then in the **Save As** dialog box, navigate to the location where you are saving your databases for this chapter. Create a new folder named **Access Chapter 12** and then click **Open**.

3. In the **File name** box, select the file name, and then type **Lastname_Firstname_3A_Students_Majors** and then press Enter. On the **Message Bar**, click the **Enable Content** button. Notice that there are two tables in this database.

4. On the Ribbon, click the **Database Tools tab**. In the **Relationships group**, click the **Relationships** button. Compare your screen with Figure 12.2.

   One major is associated with *many* students. Thus, a one-to-many relationship has been established between the 3A Majors table and the 3A Students table using the Major ID# field as the common field.

Figure 12.2

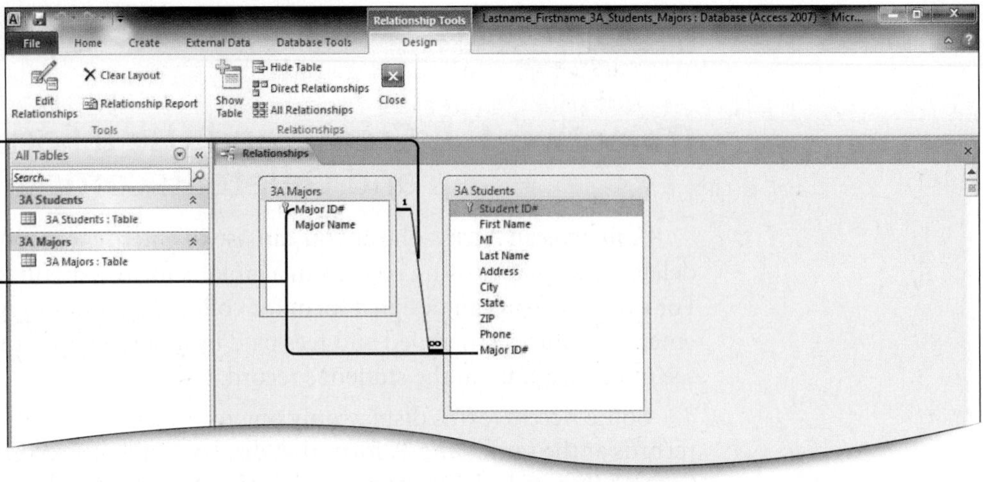

Join line with symbols indicating one-to-many relationship and referential integrity

Major ID# is common field

5 **Close** [X] the **Relationships** window. From the **Navigation Pane**, open the **3A Students** table. Notice the ten fields—*Student ID#, First Name, MI, Last Name, Address, City, State, ZIP, Phone,* and *Major ID#*. **Close** [X] the table.

6 In the **Navigation Pane**, be sure the **3A Students** table is selected. Click the **Create tab**, and then in the **Forms group**, click the **Form** button. **Close** [«] the **Navigation Pane**, and then compare your screen with Figure 12.3.

Access creates the form based on the currently selected object—the 3A Students table—and displays the form in ***Layout view***. In Layout view, you can modify the form while it is displaying data. For example, you can adjust the size of the text boxes to fit the data.

Access creates the form in a simple top-to-bottom layout, with all ten fields in the table lined up in a single column. The data for the first record in the table displays.

Figure 12.3

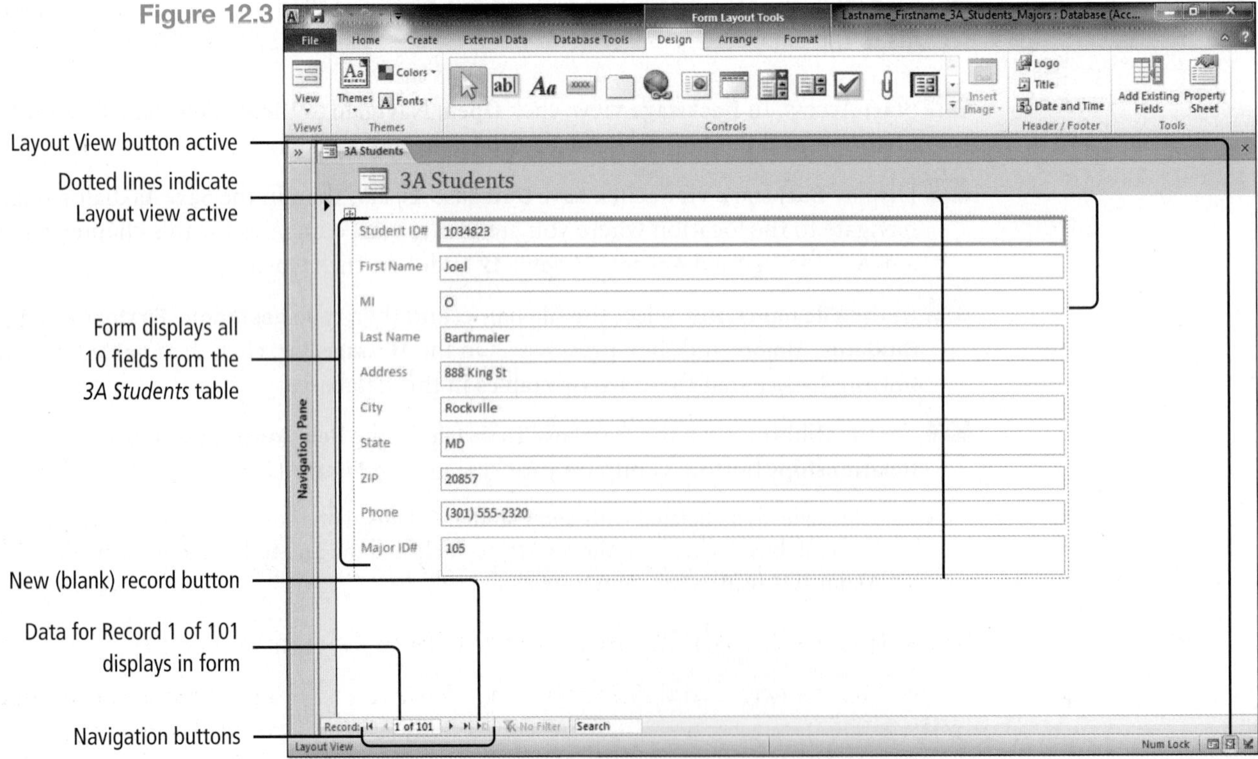

7 In the navigation area, click the **Next record** button ▸ four times. The fifth record—*Student ID 1298345*—displays. In the navigation area, click the **Last record** button ▸| to display the record for *Student ID 9583924*, and then click the **First record** button |◂ to display the record for *Student ID 1034823*.

You can use the navigation buttons to scroll among the records to display any single record.

8 **Save** the form as **Lastname Firstname 3A Student Form** and then **Close** ✕ the form object.

9 **Open** » the **Navigation Pane**, and then, if necessary, increase the width of the **Navigation Pane** to display the entire form name. Notice that your new form displays under the table with which it is related—the **3A Students** table.

10 In the **Navigation Pane**, click to select the **3A Majors** table. Click the **Create tab**, and then in the **Forms group**, click the **Form** button. **Close** « the **Navigation Pane**, and then compare your screen with Figure 12.4. Notice that *Major ID 105*, for *Diagnostic Medical Sonography*, has five students selecting this major.

If a form's record has related records in another table, the related records display in the form because of the established one-to-many relationship between the underlying tables.

Figure 12.4

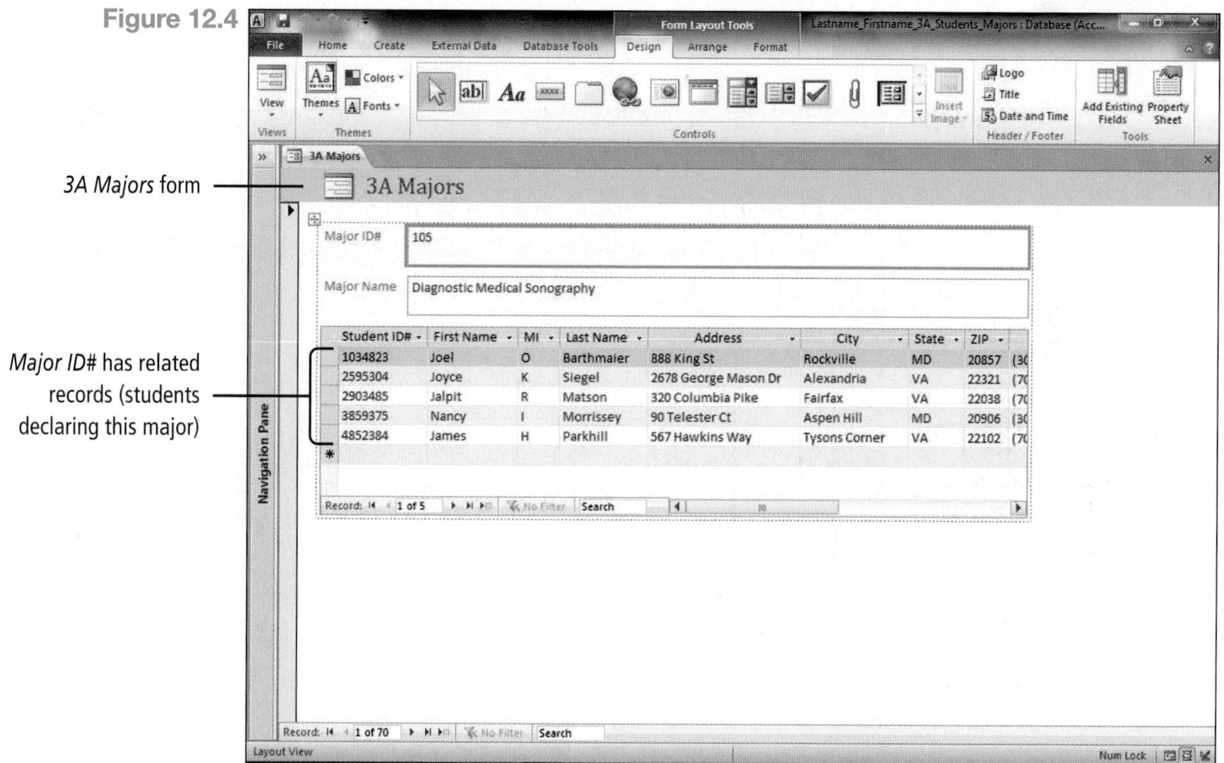

11 **Close** ✕ the **3A Majors** form. In the message box, click **Yes**. In the **Save As** dialog box, name the form **Lastname Firstname 3A Major Form** and then click **OK**.

Activity 12.02 | Adding Records to a Table by Using a Form

By using a single-record form to add and delete records, you can reduce the number of data entry errors, because the individual performing the data entry is looking at only one record at a time. Recall that your database is useful only if the information is accurate—just like your personal address book is useful only if it contains accurate addresses and phone numbers.

Forms are based on—also referred to as ***bound*** to—the table where the records are stored. When a record is entered in a form, the new record is added to the underlying table. The reverse is also true—when a record is added to a table, the new record can be viewed in the related form. In this activity, you will add a new record to the 3A Students table by using the form that you just created.

1. **Open** [»] the **Navigation Pane**, open your **3A Student Form** object, and then **Close** [«] the **Navigation Pane**. In the navigation area, click the **New (blank) record** button [▶*] to display a new blank form.

> **Another Way**
>
> Press the Enter key, provided there are no special buttons on the form, such as a link to create a new form or a link to print the form.

2. In the **Student ID#** field, type **9712345** and then press Tab.

   Use the Tab key to move from field to field in a form. This is known as ***tab order***—the order in which the insertion point moves from one field to the next when you press the Tab key. As you start typing, the pencil icon displays in the ***record selector bar*** at the left—the bar used to select an entire record. This icon displays when a record is created or edited.

3. Using your own first name and last name, continue entering the data as shown in the following table, and then compare your screen with Figure 12.5.

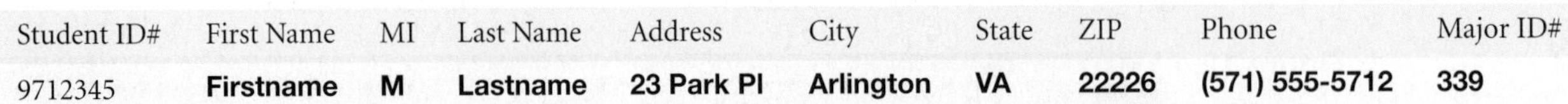

Student ID#	First Name	MI	Last Name	Address	City	State	ZIP	Phone	Major ID#
9712345	**Firstname**	**M**	**Lastname**	**23 Park Pl**	**Arlington**	**VA**	**22226**	**(571) 555-5712**	**339**

Figure 12.5

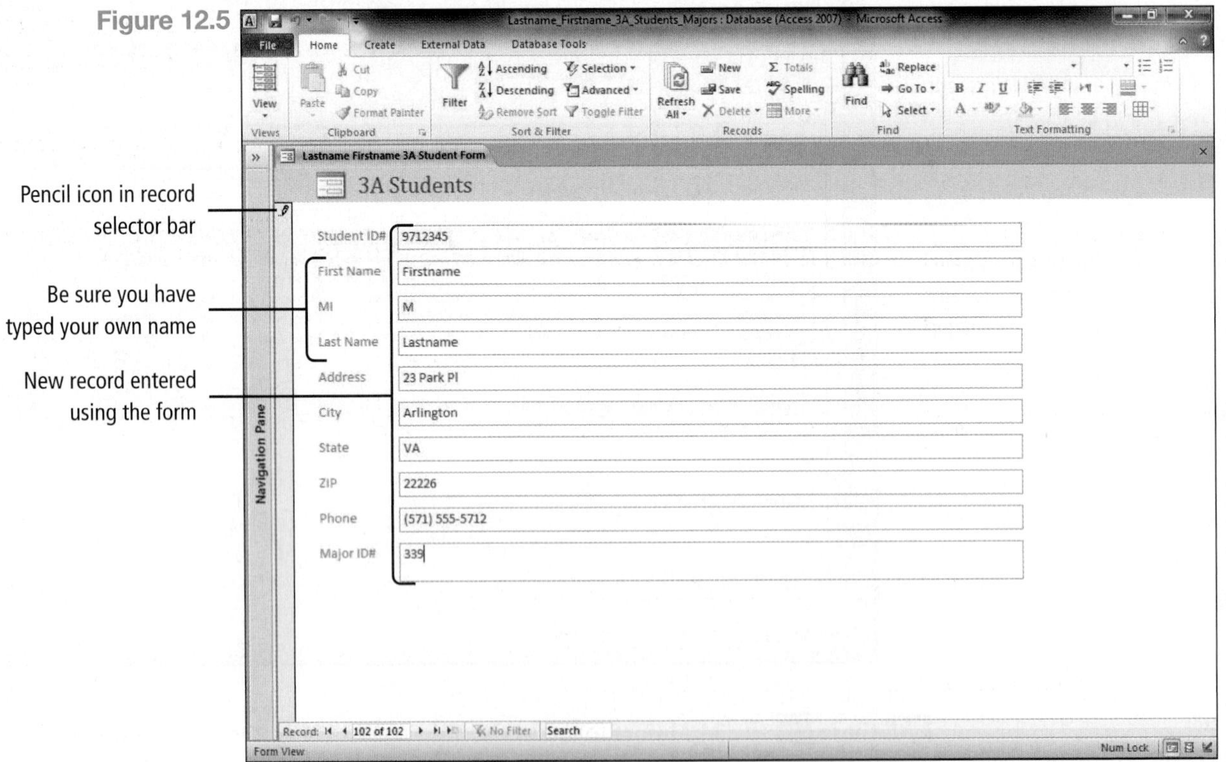

4. With your insertion point in the last field, press Tab to save the record and display a new blank record. **Close** [×] the **3A Student Form** object.

5. **Open** [»] the **Navigation Pane**. Open the **3A Students** table. In the navigation area, click the **Last record** button [▶|] to verify that the record you entered in the form is stored in the underlying table. **Close** [×] the **3A Students** table.

6 From the **Navigation Pane**, open the **3A Major Form** object. At the bottom of your screen, in the navigation area for the form—*not* the navigation area for the subdatasheet—click the **New (blank) record** button ▶. In the blank form, enter the information in the following table:

Major ID#	Major Name
339.555.22	**Network Security**

7 **Close** ☒ your **3A Major Form** object. From the **Navigation Pane**, open the **3A Majors** table, and then scroll down to verify that the new record for Major ID# *339.555.22 Network Security* displays in the table—records are sorted by the *Major ID#* field. **Close** ☒ the table.

Activity 12.03 | Deleting Records from a Table by Using a Form

You can delete records from a database table by using a form. In this activity, you will delete Major ID# 800.03 because the program has been discontinued.

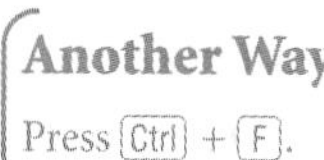

1 From the **Navigation Pane**, open your **3A Major Form** object. On the **Home tab**, in the **Find group**, click the **Find** button to open the **Find and Replace** dialog box.

2 In the **Look In** box, notice that *Current field* displays. In the **Find What** box, type **800.03** and then click **Find Next**. Compare your screen with Figure 12.6, and confirm that the record for **Major ID# 800.03** displays.

Because you clicked in the Major ID# field before opening the dialog box, Access searches for the data in this field.

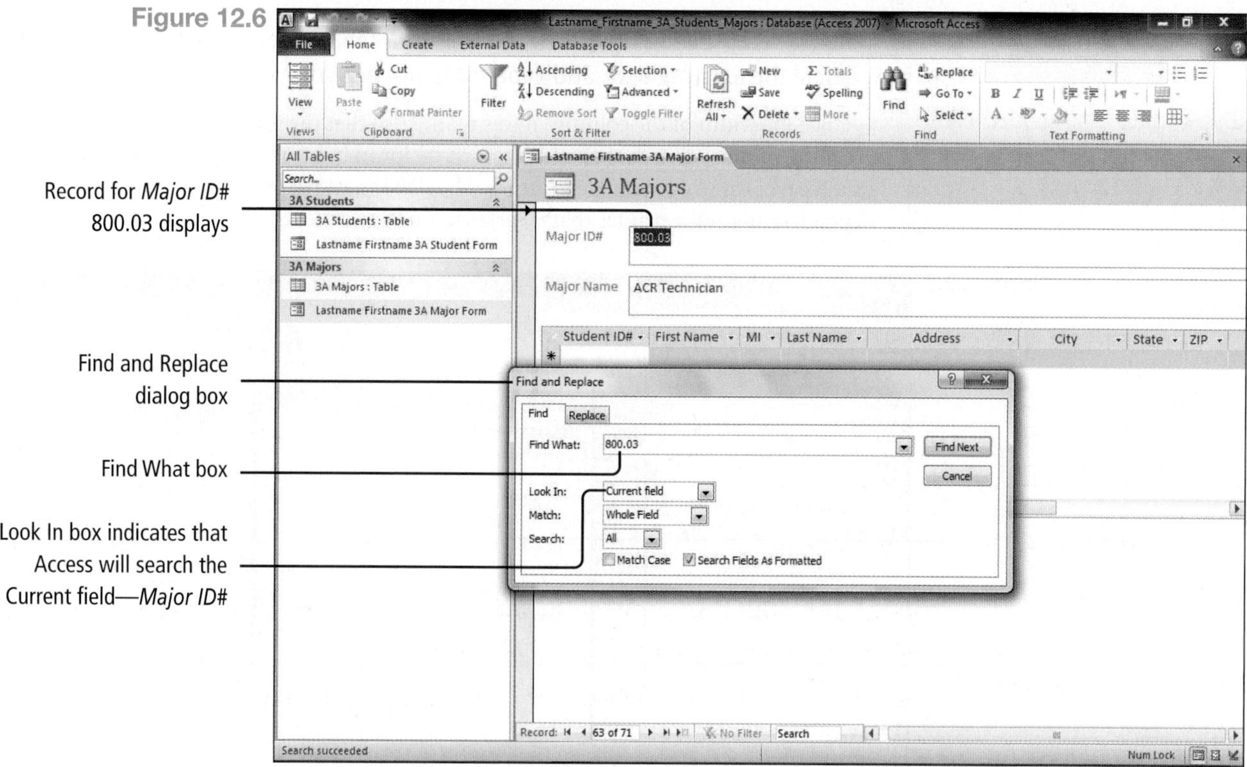

Figure 12.6

3 **Close** the **Find and Replace** dialog box. On the **Home tab**, in the **Records group**, click the **Delete button arrow**, and then click **Delete Record** to delete the record for Major ID# 800.03.

Access removes the record from the screen and displays a message alerting you that you are about to delete *1 record(s)*. If you click Yes to delete the record, you cannot use the Undo button to reverse the action. If you delete a record by mistake, you must re-create the record by reentering the data. Because no students are associated with this major, you can delete it from the table.

4 In the message box, click **Yes** to delete the record. In the navigation area for the form, notice that the number of records in the table is *70*. **Close** the form.

5 From the **Navigation Pane**, open the **3A Majors** table. Examine the table to verify that the *Major ID# 800.03* record no longer exists, and then **Close** the table.

Adding and deleting records in a form updates the records stored in the underlying table.

Activity 12.04 | Printing a Form

Clicking the Print button while a form is displayed causes *all* of the records to print in the form layout. In this activity, you will print only *one* record.

1 From the **Navigation Pane**, open your **3A Student Form** object. Press Ctrl + F to display the **Find and Replace** dialog box. In the **Find What** box, type **9712345** and then click **Find Next** to display the record with your name. **Close** the **Find and Replace** dialog box.

2 Display **Backstage** view. Click the **Print tab**, and then in the **Print group**, click **Print**. In the **Print** dialog box, under **Print Range**, click the **Selected Record(s)** option button. In the lower left corner of the dialog box, click **Setup**.

3 In the **Page Setup** dialog box, click the **Columns tab**. Under **Column Size**, in the **Width** box, delete the existing text, and type **7.5** Compare your screen with Figure 12.7.

Change the width of the column in this manner so that the form prints on one page. Forms are not typically printed, so the width of the column in a form may be greater than the width of the paper on which you are printing. The maximum column width that you can enter is dependent upon the printer that is installed on your system.

Figure 12.7

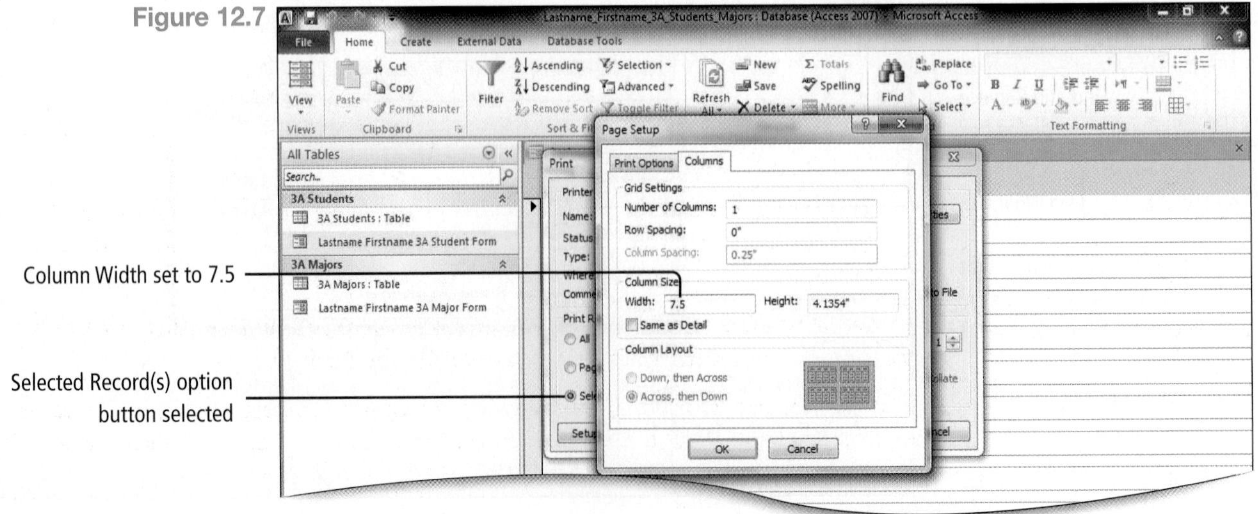

4 Click **OK** to close the **Page Setup** dialog box, and then, to create an electronic printout of this single form, see the instructions in the Note below. To print on paper, click **OK** to close the **Print** dialog box and to print only your record in the form layout.

> **Note | To Print a Single Form in PDF**
>
> To create a PDF electronic printout of a single record in a form, change the column width to 7.5 as described in step 3 above, and then in the Print dialog box, click Cancel. On the left edge of the form, click anywhere in the Record Selector bar so that it is black—selected. On the Ribbon, click the External Data tab. In the Export group, click the PDF or XPS button. In the Publish as PDF or XPS dialog box, navigate to the location where you are storing your files for this project. In the File name box, notice that your form name is automatically entered for you. Then, in the lower left corner of the dialog box, if necessary, select the Open file after publishing check box. In the lower right corner of the dialog box, click the Options button. In the Options dialog box, under Range, click the Selected records option button, click OK, and then click Publish. Close the Adobe Reader or Acrobat window, and then hold this file until you complete the project and submit it as directed by your instructor.

5 **Close** [X] the **3A Student Form** object. Using the techniques you just practiced, open your **3A Major Form** object, display the record for the **Major ID#** of **339.555.22**, and then print only that record, or create an electronic printout of only that record. Then **Close** [X] the **3A Major Form** object.

If there are no related records in the subdatasheet, the empty subdatasheet does not display in the printed form.

Objective 2 | Create a Form by Using the Form Wizard

The ***Form Wizard*** creates a form quickly like the Form tool, but gives you more flexibility in the design, layout, and number of fields. The design of the form should be planned for the individuals who use the form—either for entering new records or viewing records. For example, when your college counselor displays information, it may be easier for the counselor to view the information if the fields are arranged in a layout that differs from the manner in which the Form Tool arranges them.

Activity 12.05 | Creating a Form by Using the Form Wizard

At Capital Cities Community College, when a student changes his or her major, the student fills out a paper form. To make it easier to change the information in the database, you will create an Access form that matches the layout of the paper form. This will make it easier for the individual who changes the data in the database.

1 In the **Navigation Pane**, click to select the **3A Students** table. On the **Create tab**, in the **Forms group**, click the **Form Wizard** button.

The Form Wizard walks you step by step through the process of creating a form by asking questions. In the first Form Wizard dialog box, you select the fields to include on the form. The fields can come from more than one table or query.

2 Under **Tables/Queries**, in the text box, click the **arrow** to display a list of available tables and queries from which you can create the form.

There are two tables in the database from which you can create a new form. Because you selected the 3A Students table on the Navigation Pane, the 3A Students table is the selected table.

3 Click **Table: 3A Students**, and then compare your screen with Figure 12.8.

The field names from the 3A Students table display in the Available Fields list.

Figure 12.8

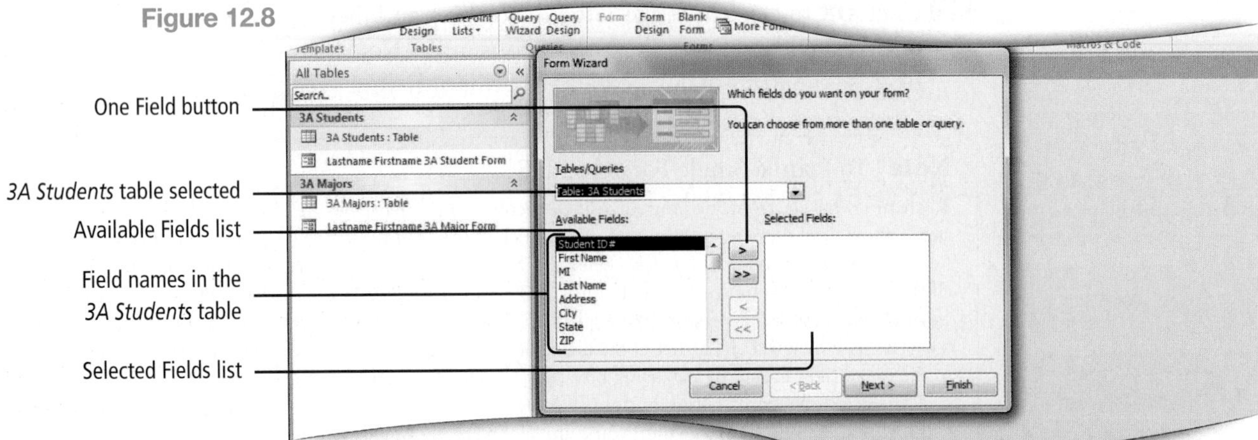

Another Way

Double-click the field name.

4 Use the **One Field** button > to move the following fields to the **Selected Fields** list: **First Name**, **Last Name**, and **Major ID#**. Compare your screen with Figure 12.9.

Three fields from the 3A Students table display in the Selected Fields list.

Figure 12.9

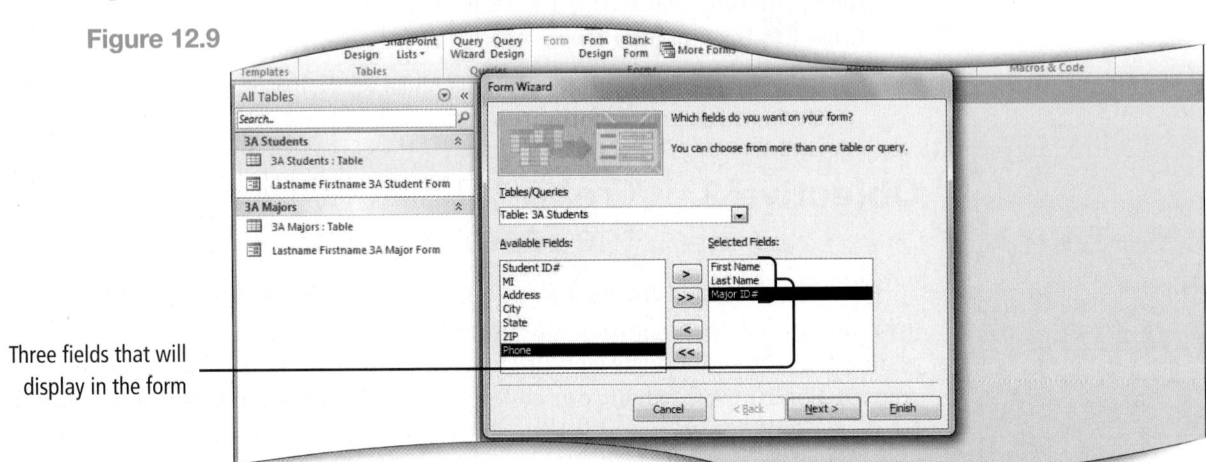

5 Click **Next**. Be sure **Columnar** is selected as the layout, and then click **Next**. Under **What title do you want for your form?**, select the existing text, and then type **Lastname Firstname 3A Student Major Change Form** and then click **Finish** to close the wizard and create the form. If necessary, increase the width of the Navigation Pane to display the entire form name, and then compare your screen with Figure 12.10.

The form is saved and added to the Navigation Pane under its data source. The first record in the underlying table displays in ***Form view***, which is used to view, add, delete, and modify records stored in a table.

Figure 12.10

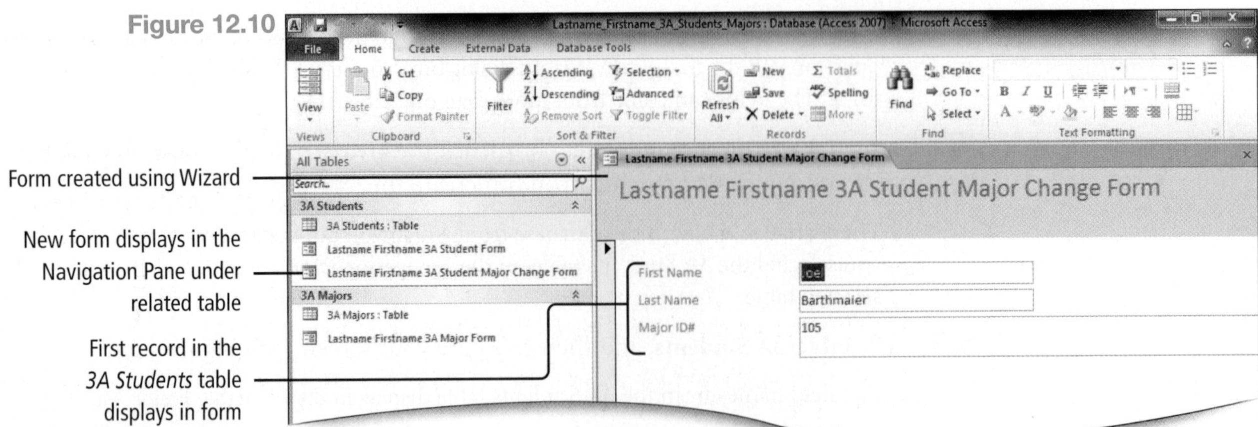

Objective 3 | Modify a Form in Layout View and in Design View

After you create a form, you can make changes to it. For example, you can group the fields, resize the fields, and change the style of the form.

Activity 12.06 | Grouping Controls and Applying a Theme to a Form in Layout View

Layout view enables you to make changes to the design of a form while displaying the data from the underlying table. Most changes to a form can be made in Layout view.

> **Another Way**
>
> On the Home tab, in the Views group, click the View button arrow, and then click Layout View; or, right-click the object tab, and then click Layout View.

1 **Close** « the **Navigation Pane** and be sure your **3A Student Major Change Form** object displays. In the lower right corner of your screen, on the status bar, click the **Layout View** button, and then compare your screen with Figure 12.11.

The field names and data for the first record display in ***controls***—objects on a form that display data, perform actions, and let you view and work with information.

The data in the first record displays in ***text box controls***. The most commonly used control is the text box control, which typically displays data from the underlying table. A text box control is a ***bound control***—its source data comes from a table or query.

The field names—*First Name*, *Last Name*, and *Major ID#*—display in ***label controls***. Access places a label control to the left of a text box control. A label control contains descriptive information that displays on the form, usually the field name. A control that does not have a source of data, for example a label that displays the title of the form, is an ***unbound control***.

Figure 12.11

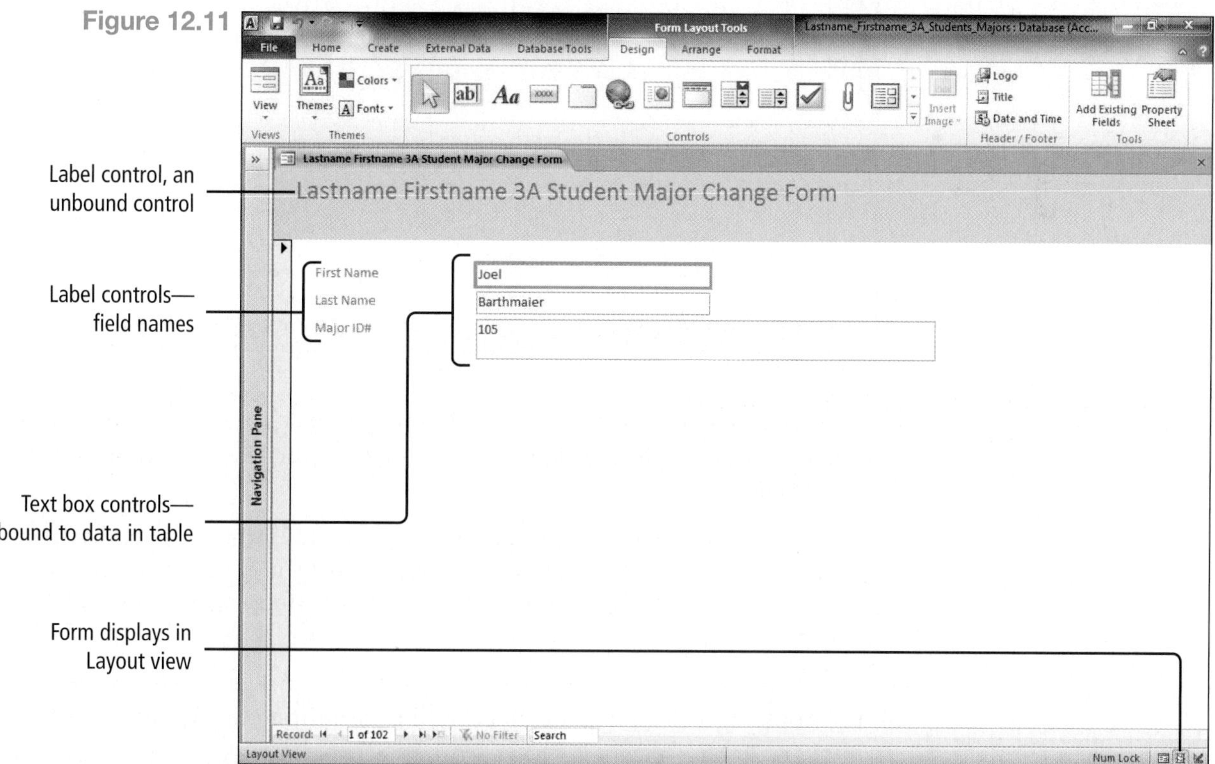

2 Click the **First Name label control**. Hold down Shift, and then click the **Last Name label control**, the **Major ID# label control**, and the **three text box controls** to select all label and text box controls.

> **Alert! | Do Your Controls Change Order When Selecting?**
>
> If, when selecting controls, the controls change order, click Undo and select the controls again. Be careful not to drag the mouse when you are selecting multiple controls.

3 With all six controls selected—surrounded by a colored border—on the Ribbon, click the **Arrange tab**. In the **Table group**, click the **Stacked** button. Click the **First Name Label control** to deselect all of the controls and to surround the **First Name label control** with a colored border. Compare your screen with Figure 12.12.

This action groups the controls together in the ***Stacked layout*** format—a layout similar to a paper form, with labels to the left of each field. Grouping the controls enables you to easily move and edit controls as you redesign your form.

A dotted line forms a border around the field names and data. Above and to the left of the first field name—*First Name*—the ***layout selector*** [⊞] displays, with which you can select and move the entire group of controls.

Figure 12.12

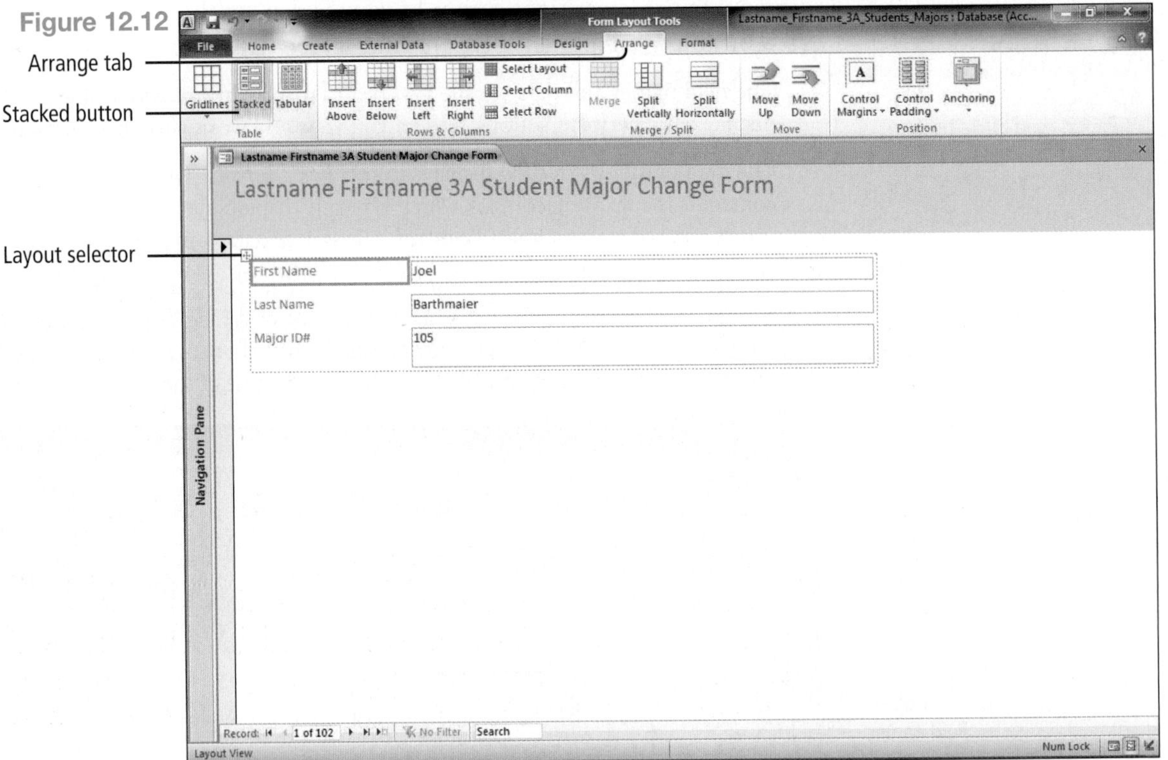

4 Click the **Design tab**, and then in the **Themes group**, click the **Themes** button. In the **Themes** gallery, locate and right-click the **Couture** theme. Click **Apply Theme to This Object Only**.

The ***Themes*** button enables you to apply a predefined format to all of the database objects or to the current object. Right-click a theme so that you can apply the theme to a single object within the database. Apply a theme before performing other formatting to the text in your form.

> **Note** | Applying a Theme to an Object and Determining the Applied Theme
>
> If you click a theme rather than right-clicking it and selecting an option, the theme is applied to all objects in the database. To determine the applied theme, in the Themes group, point to the Themes button. The ScreenTip displays the current theme.

5 Click anywhere in the title *3A Student Major Change Form* to select it. Click the **Format tab**. In the **Font group**, click the **Font Size arrow**, and then click **14**. Click the **Bold** button [**B**] to add bold emphasis to the text. Click the **Font Color button arrow**, and then under **Theme Colors**, in the last column, click the last color—**Brown, Accent 6, Darker 50%**.

Activity 12.07 | Modifying a Form in Design View

Design view presents a detailed view of the structure of your form. Because the form is not actually running when displayed in Design view, you cannot view the underlying data. However, some tasks, such as resizing sections, must be completed in Design view.

> **Another Way**
>
> On the Home tab, in the Views group, click the View button arrow, and then click Design View; or, right-click the object tab, and then click Design View.

1. On the status bar, click the **Design View** button. Compare your screen with Figure 12.13.

   This Design view of a form displays three sections—***Form Header***, ***Detail***, and ***Form Footer***—each designated by a ***section bar*** at the top of each section. The form header contains information, such as a form's title, that displays at the top of the screen in Form view and is printed at the top of the first page when records are printed as forms. The detail section displays the records from the underlying table, and the form footer displays at the bottom of the screen in Form view and is printed after the last detail section on the last page of a printout.

Figure 12.13

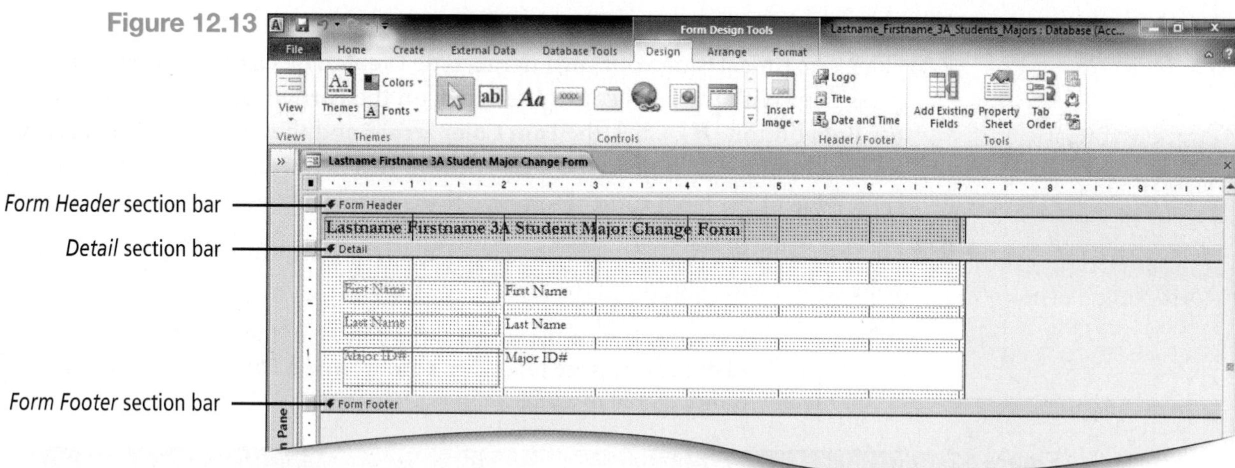

2. At the bottom of the form, point to the *lower* edge of the **Form Footer section bar** to display the pointer, and then drag downward approximately **0.5 inch** to increase the height of the Form Footer section. Compare your screen with Figure 12.14.

Figure 12.14

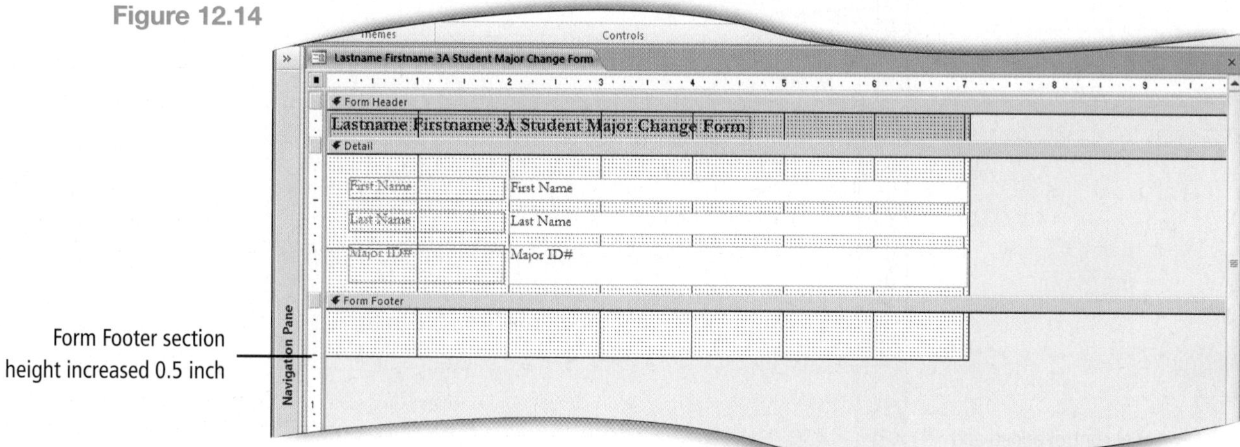

3. On the **Design tab**, in the **Controls group**, click the **Label** button. Move the pointer into the **Form Footer** section, and then position the plus sign of the pointer in the **Form Footer** section at approximately **0.25 inch on the horizontal ruler** and even with the lower edge of the **Form Footer section bar** as shown in Figure 12.15.

Figure 12.15

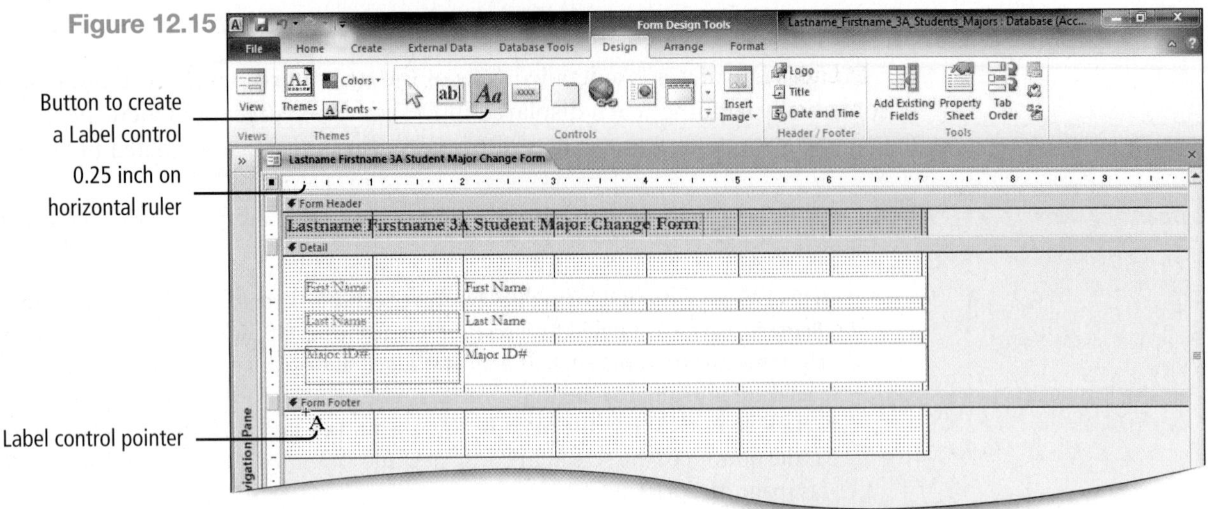

4 Click one time. Using your own name, type **Created by Lastname Firstname** and then press Enter. With the label control selected, on the **Format tab**, in the **Font group**, click the **Bold** button **B**. Click the **Font Color arrow**, and then under **Theme Colors**, in the fourth column, click the first color—**Brown, Text 2**. If necessary, double-click the right edge of the label control to resize the control so that all of the data displays.

> **Another Way**
>
> On the Home tab, in the Views group, click the View button arrow, and then click Form View; or, right-click the object tab, and then click Form View.

5 On the right side of the status bar, click the **Form View** button, and then compare your screen with Figure 12.16.

Form Footer text displays on the screen at the bottom of the form and prints only on the last page if all of the forms are printed as a group. In the ***Form view***, you can add, delete, or modify records stored in a table.

Figure 12.16

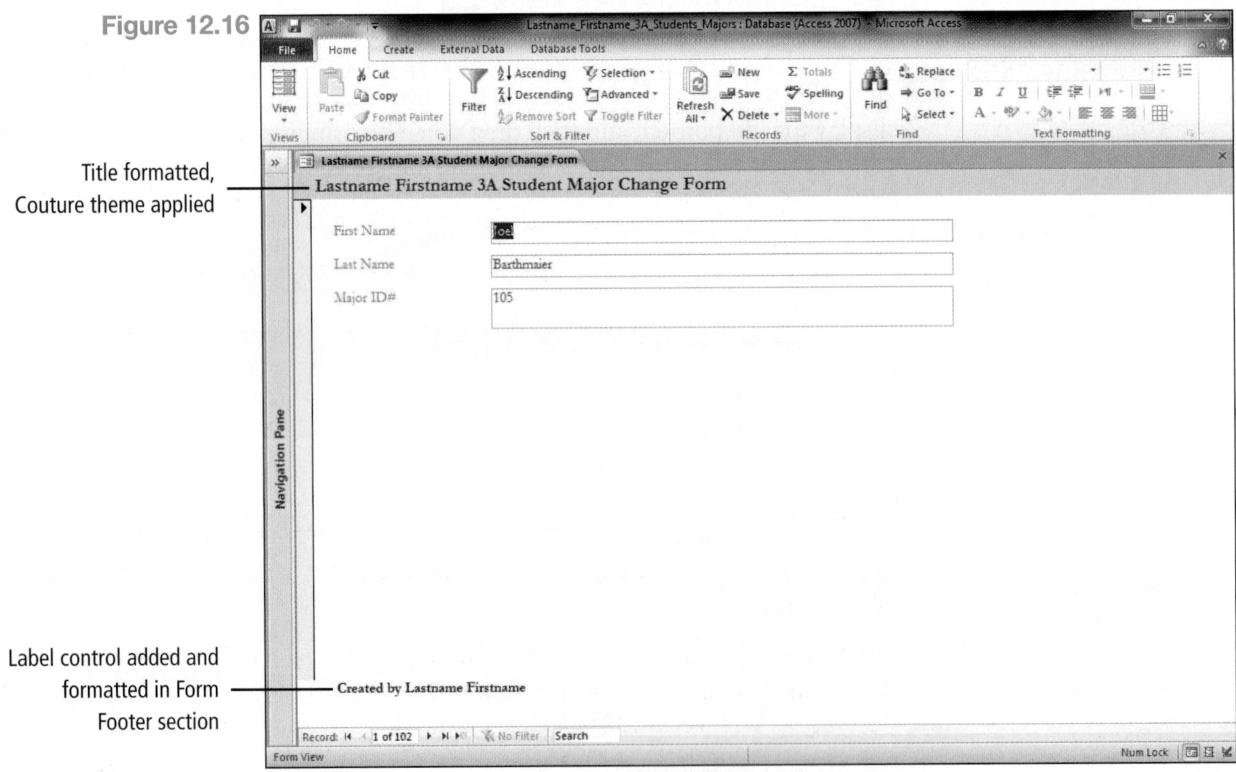

6 **Save** the changes you have made to the design of your form. Leave your **3A Student Major Change Form** open for the next activity.

Activity 12.08 | Adding, Resizing, and Moving Controls in Layout View

In Layout view, you can change the form's ***control layout***—the grouped arrangement of controls.

1 At the right side of the status bar, click the **Layout View** button.

Recall that the layout selector, which displays to the left and above the First Name label control, enables you to select and move the entire group of controls in Layout view.

2 On the **Design tab**, in the **Tools group**, click the **Add Existing Fields** button to display the **Field List** pane, which lists the fields in the underlying table—3A Students. Compare your screen with Figure 12.17.

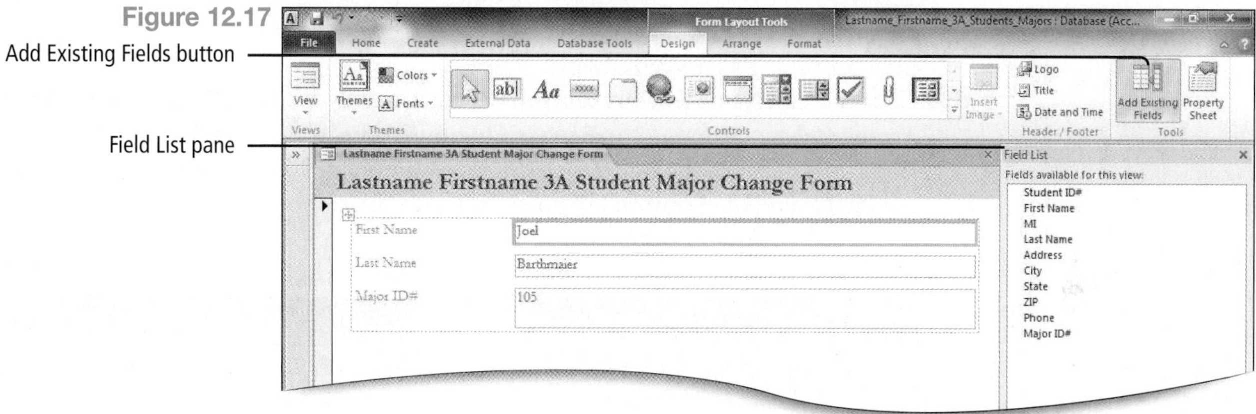

Figure 12.17

3 In the **Field List** pane, click **Student ID#**, and then drag to the left until the pointer displays above the **First Name label control** and a colored line displays above the control. Release the mouse button, and then compare your screen with Figure 12.18. If you are not satisfied with the result, click Undo and begin again.

This action adds the Student ID# label and text box controls to the form above the First Name controls.

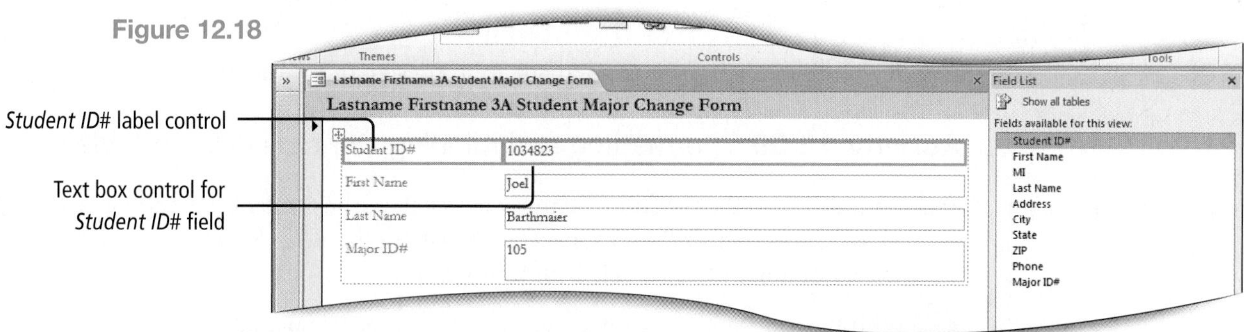

Figure 12.18

4 **Close** the **Field List** pane. Click the **Student ID# text box control**, which currently displays *1034823*, to surround it with a border and to remove the border from the label control.

5 Point to the right edge of the **text box control** until the pointer displays, and then drag to the left until all of the right edges of the text box controls align under the *C* in *Controls* in the Ribbon's **Controls group** above. Compare your screen with Figure 12.19.

All four text box controls are resized simultaneously. By decreasing the width of the text box controls, you have more space in which to rearrange the form controls. In Layout view, because you can see your data, you can determine visually that the space you have allotted is adequate to display all of the data in every field.

Figure 12.19

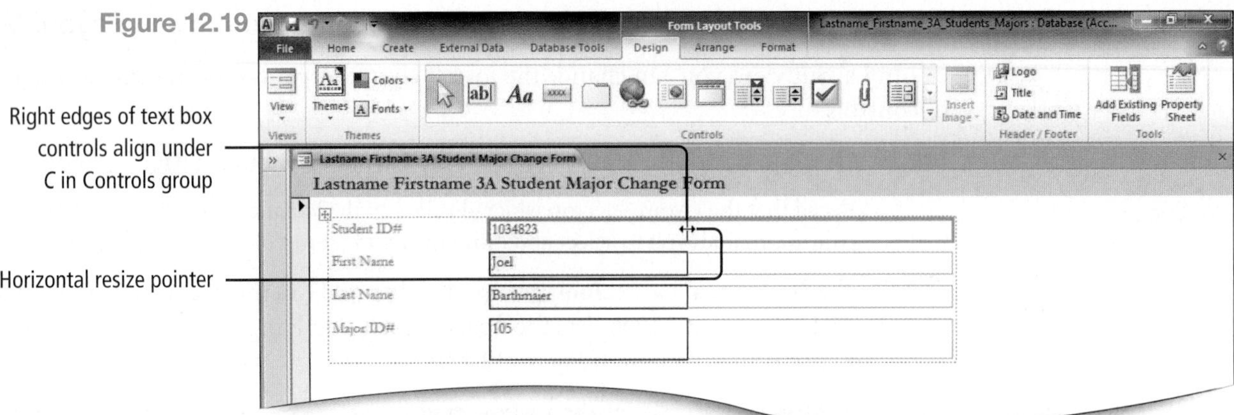

> **Another Way**
> Drag the selected label controls to the desired location and then release the mouse button.

6 Click the **Last Name text box control**, which currently displays *Barthmaier*. Click the **Arrange tab**, and then in the **Rows & Columns group**, click the **Select Row** button. In the **Move group**, click the **Move Up** button one time to move the controls above the **First Name label control** as shown in Figure 12.20.

Figure 12.20

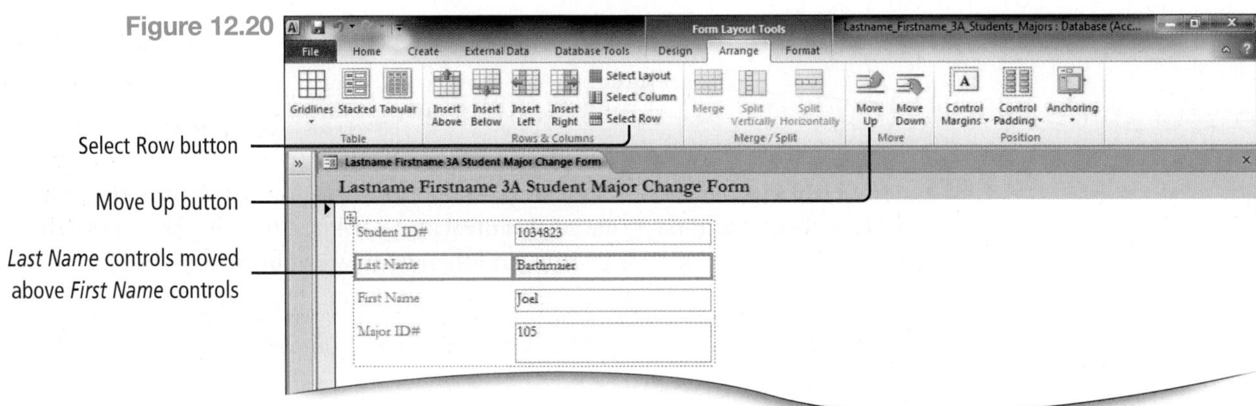

7 **Save** the changes you have made to the design of your form.

Activity 12.09 | Formatting and Aligning Controls in Layout View

> **Another Way**
> Click the first control, hold down Shift, and then click the last control.

1 With the form displayed in Layout view, click in the **Student ID# text box control**, which displays *1034823*. On the **Arrange tab**, in the **Rows & Columns group**, click the **Select Column** button to select all four text box controls.

2 With the four text box controls selected, click the **Format tab**. In the **Font group**, click the **Background Color button arrow**. Under **Theme Colors**, in the fifth column, click the second color—**Brown, Accent 1, Lighter 80%**.

The text box controls display a background color of light brown. This formatting does not affect the label controls on the left.

3 Click the **Student ID# label control**. On the **Arrange tab**, in the **Rows & Columns group**, click the **Select Column** button. Click the **Format tab**, change the **Font Color**—*not* the Background Color—to **Brown, Text 2**—in the fourth column, the first color—and then apply **Bold** B. Click in a blank area of the screen to cancel the selection, and then compare your screen with Figure 12.21.

Figure 12.21

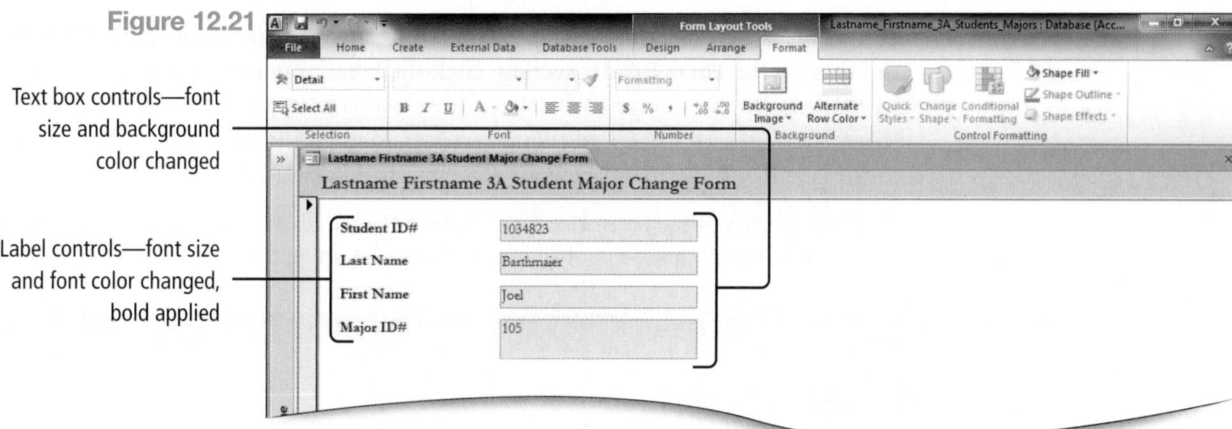

Another Way

Click any control, and then on the Arrange tab, in the Rows & Columns group, click the Select Layout button.

4. Click any **label control** to display the layout selector, and then click the **layout selector** [⊞] to select all of the controls.

   Clicking the layout selector enables you to edit all of the controls at one time.

5. On the **Format tab**, in the **Font group**, click the **Font Size button arrow**, and then click **12** to change the font size of the text in all of the controls.

6. With all of the controls still selected, on the Ribbon, click the **Design tab**. In the **Tools group**, click the **Property Sheet** button. In the **Property Sheet** pane, if necessary, click the **Format tab**, and then compare your screen with Figure 12.22.

   The ***Property Sheet*** for the selected controls displays. Each control has an associated Property Sheet where precise changes to the properties—characteristics—of selected controls can be made. At the top of the Property Sheet, to the right of *Selection type:*, *Multiple selection* displays because you have more than one control selected.

Figure 12.22

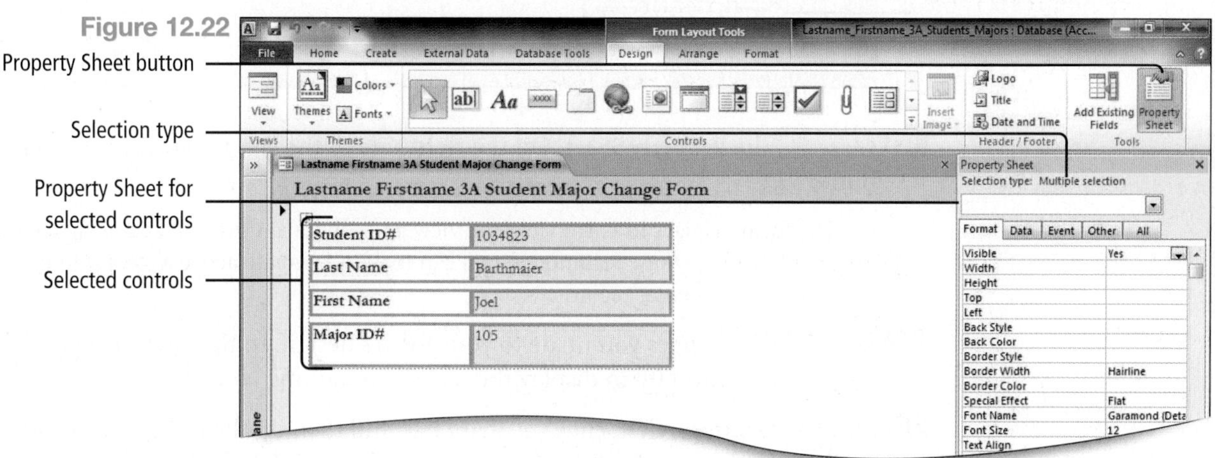

7. In the **Property Sheet**, click the word **Height**, type **0.25** and then press [Enter].

   The height of each control changes to 0.25 inch.

8. Click the **Student ID# label control** to select only that label control. Click the **Arrange tab**, and then in the **Rows & Columns group**, click the **Select Column** button. In the **Property Sheet**, click **Width** to select its value to the right. Type **1.25** and then press [Enter].

   The width of each selected label control changes to 1.25 inches.

9 In the **Form Footer section**, click the **label control** with your name. Hold down Shift, and then in the **Form Header section**, click the **label control** that displays the title *3A Student Major Change Form*. With these two controls selected, in the **Property Sheet**, click **Left**. Type **0.5** and then press Enter to align the left edge of the selected label controls at 0.5 inch. Compare your screen with Figure 12.23.

The left edges of the Form Header and Form Footer label controls align at 0.5 inch. In this manner, you can place a control in a specific location on the form.

Figure 12.23

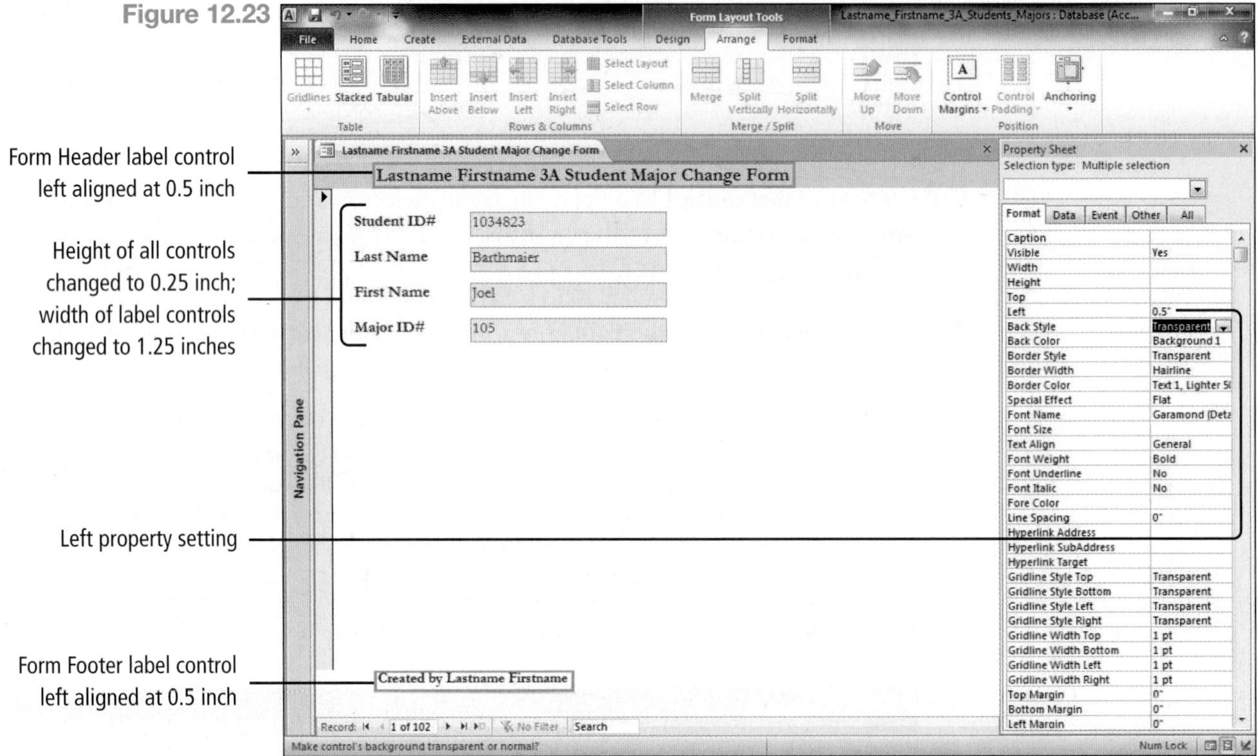

10 **Close** the **Property Sheet**. On the right side of the status bar, click the **Form View** button.

The form displays in Form view, the view an individual uses when entering data in the form. By using these techniques, you can make a form attractive and easy to use for those who view and enter records.

11 **Save** the changes you made to your form's design. In the navigation area, click the **Last record** button to display the record containing your name.

12 Display **Backstage** view, click the **Print tab**, and then on the right, click **Print**. In the **Print** dialog box, under **Print Range**, click the **Selected Record(s)** option button. Create a paper or electronic printout as directed. To create an electronic printout, follow the directions given at the end of Activity 2.04.

Because you decreased the width of the text box controls, you do *not* have to adjust the Column Size width in the Page Setup dialog box as you did with the form you created using the Form tool.

13 With the **3A Student Major Change Form** object displayed in **Form** view, in the navigation area, click the **First record** button to prepare for the next activity.

Objective 4 | Filter Records

Filtering records in a form is the process of displaying only a portion of the total records—a ***subset***—based on matching specific values. Filters are commonly used to provide a quick answer, and the result is not generally saved for future use. For example, by filtering records in a form, you can quickly display a subset of records for students majoring in Information Systems Technology, which is identified by the Major ID# of 339.

One reason that you create a form is to provide a user interface for the database. For example, the Registration Assistants at your college may not, for security reasons, have access to the entire student database. Rather, by using a form, they can access and edit only some information—the information necessary for their jobs. Filtering records within a form provides individuals who do not have access to the entire database a way to ask questions of the database without constructing a query, and also to save a filter that is used frequently.

Activity 12.10 | Filtering Data by Selection of One Field

The counselor would like to see records for students who are majoring in Information Systems Technology. In a form, you can use the ***Filter By Selection*** command—which retrieves only the records that contain the value in the selected field and which temporarily removes the records that do *not* contain the value in the selected field.

1. With your **3A Student Major Change Form** object displayed in **Form** view, in the first record, click in the shaded **Major ID# text box control**. On the **Home tab**, in the **Find group**, click the **Find** button. In the **Find and Replace** dialog box, in the **Find What** box, type **339** If necessary, in the Match box, click the arrow, and then click Whole Field. Click **Find Next**, and then compare your screen with Figure 12.24.

   This action finds and displays a record with 339—the Major ID# for Information Systems Technology—so that you can filter the records using the selected value.

Figure 12.24

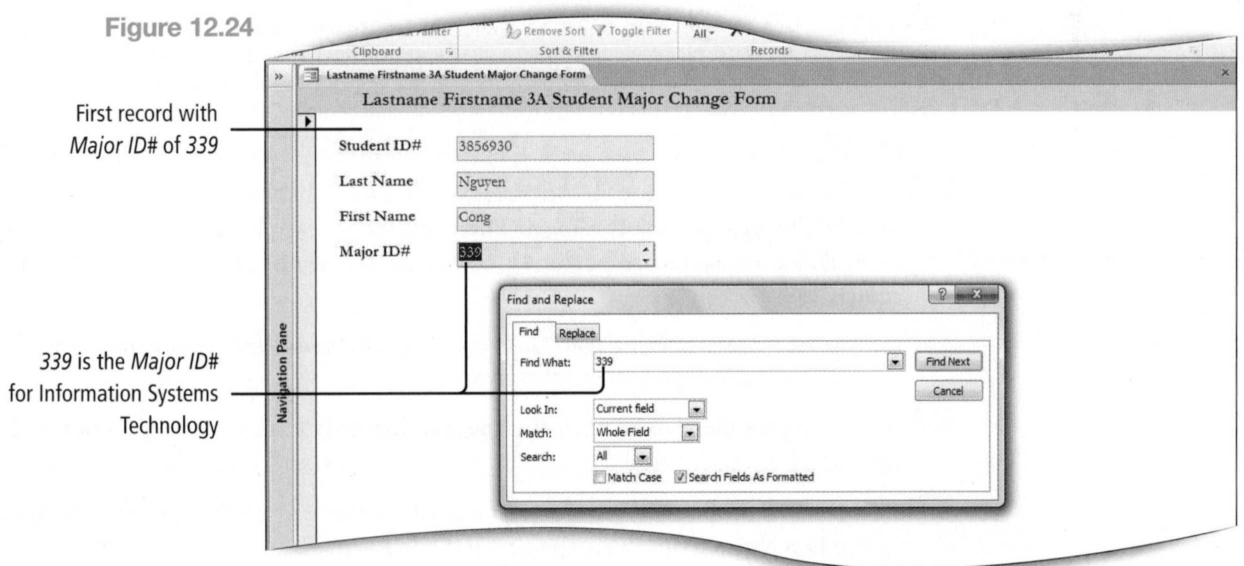

2. **Close** the **Find and Replace** dialog box. In the **Sort & Filter group**, click the **Selection** button, and then click **Equals "339"**. Compare your screen with Figure 12.25.

   Seven records match the contents of the selected Student Major ID# field—*339*—the ID# for the Information Systems Technology major. In the navigation area, a *Filtered* button with a funnel icon displays next to the number of records. *Filtered* also displays on the right side of the status bar to indicate that a filter is applied. On the Home tab, in the Sort & Filter group, the Toggle Filter button is active.

Figure 12.25

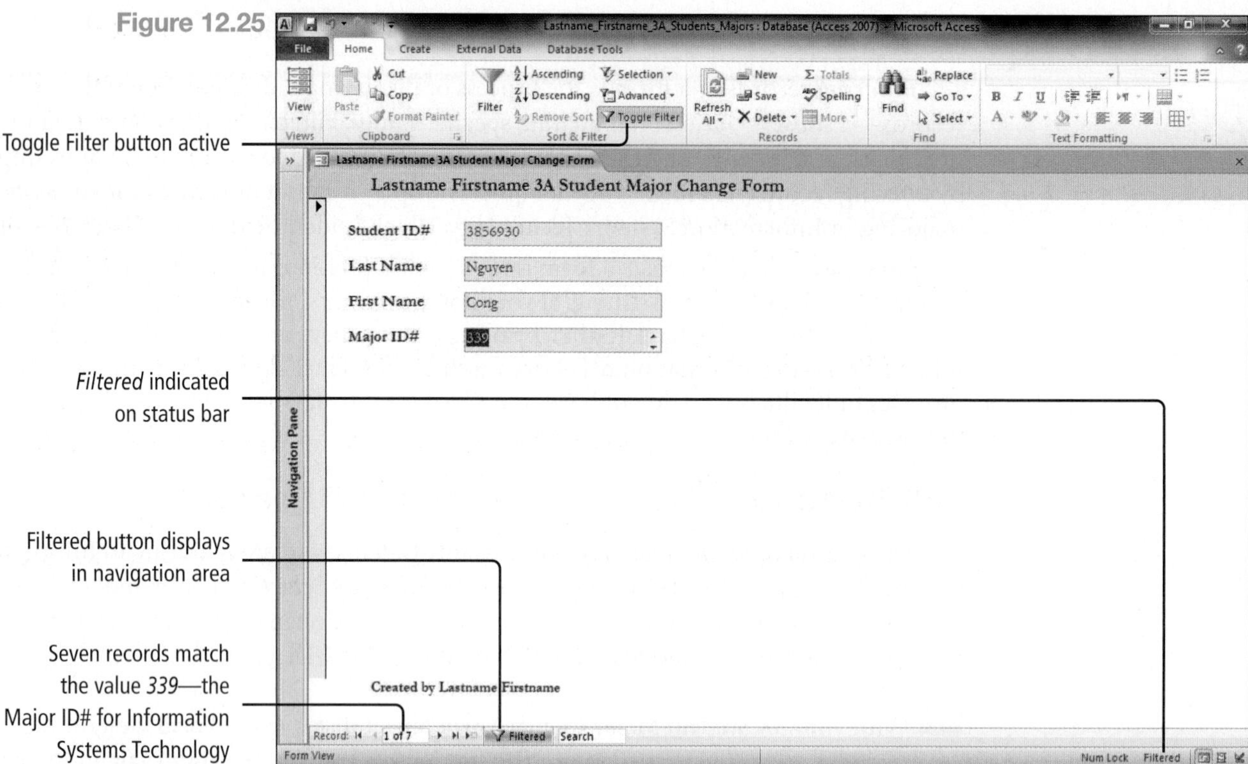

Another Way

Click the Filtered button in the navigation area.

3 On the **Home tab**, in the **Sort & Filter group**, click the **Toggle Filter** button to remove the filter and display all 102 records. Notice the **Unfiltered** button in the navigation area, which indicates that no filter is active.

> **Note** | Toggle Filter Button
>
> On the Home tab, the Toggle Filter button is used to apply or remove a filter. If no filter has been created, the button is not active—it is not highlighted. After a filter is created, this button becomes active. Because it is a toggle button used to apply or remove filters, the ScreenTip that displays for this button alternates between Apply Filter—when a filter is created but is not currently applied—and Remove Filter—when a filter is applied.

4 Be sure that the first record—for *Joel Barthmaier*—displays. On the **Home tab**, in the **Sort & Filter group**, click the **Toggle Filter** button to reapply the filter. In the navigation area, click the **Last record** button to display the last of the seven records that match *339*.

The record for *Student ID# 9712345* displays—the record with your name. In this manner, you can toggle a filter on or off as needed.

5 In the **Sort & Filter group**, click the **Toggle Filter** button to remove the filter and display all of the records.

6 In the navigation area, click the **Next record** button two times to display **Record 3**. In the **Last Name** field, select the first letter—**E**—of *Eckert*. On the **Home tab**, in the **Sort & Filter group**, click the **Selection** button. Click **Begins with "E"**.

A new filter is applied that displays three records in which the *Last Name* begins with the letter *E*.

7 In the navigation area, click the **Filtered** button to remove the filter and display all of the records.

8 **Save** the changes to your form, and then **Close** the form.

The filter is saved with the form even though the filter is not currently applied.

Activity 12.11 | Using Filter By Form and Advanced Filter/Sort

Use the ***Filter By Form*** command to filter the records in a form based on one or more fields, or based on more than one value in the same field. The Filter By Form command offers greater flexibility than the Filter by Selection command and can be used to answer a question that requires matching multiple values.

In this activity, you will use filtering techniques to help Juanita Ramirez determine how many students live in Alexandria or Arlington. Then you will determine how many students live in Arlington who are majoring in Information Systems Technology.

1. **Open** [»] the **Navigation Pane**, open your **3A Student Form** object, and then **Close** [«] the **Navigation Pane**.

2. On the **Home tab**, in the **Sort & Filter group**, click the **Advanced** button, and then click **Filter By Form**. Compare your screen with Figure 12.26.

   The Filter by Form window displays all of the field names, but without any data. In the empty text box for each field, you can type a value or choose from a list of available values. The *Look for* and *Or* tabs display at the bottom.

Figure 12.26

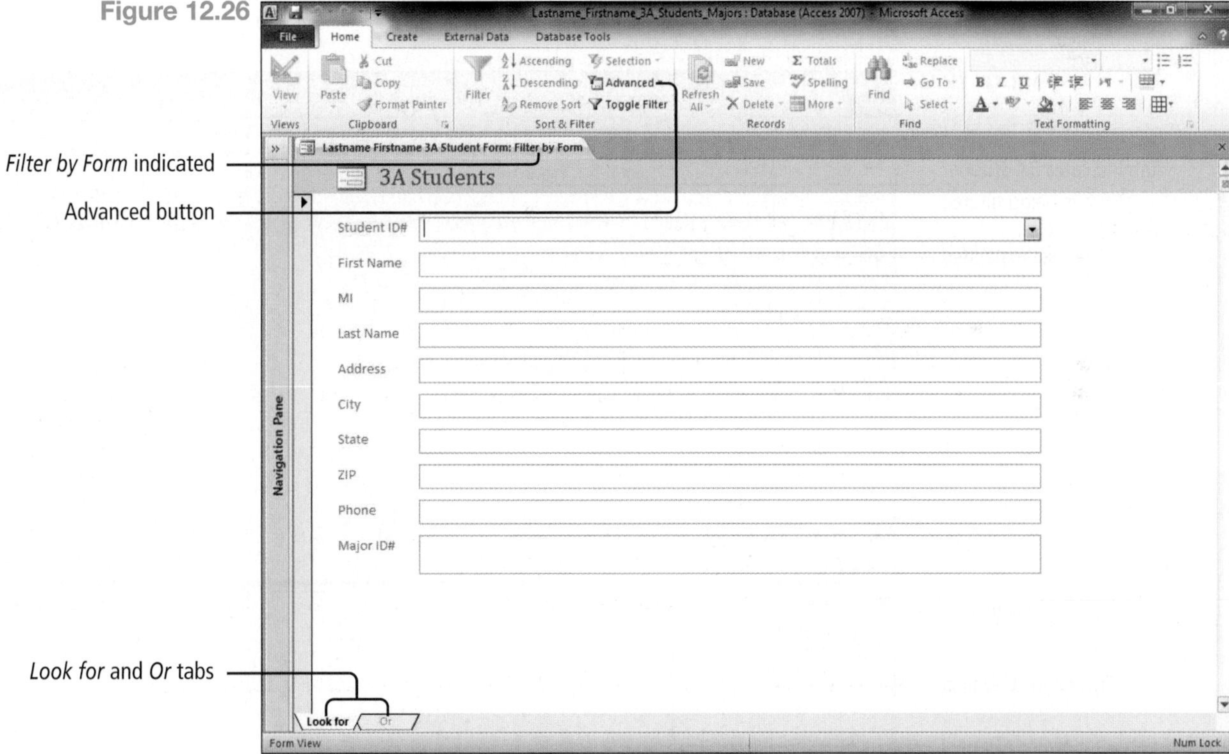

3. Click in the **City text box control**. At the right edge of the text box control, click the **arrow** that displays. In the list, click **Alexandria**. In the **Sort & Filter group**, click the **Toggle Filter** button.

   As displayed in the navigation area, eight student records include *Alexandria* in the City field.

Access | Chapter 12

> **Another Way**
>
> Click in the text box control and type the criteria separated by the word *or*. For example, in the City text box control, type *Alexandria or Arlington*.

4 In the **Sort & Filter group**, click the **Advanced** button, and then click **Filter By Form**. At the bottom left of the window, click the **Or tab**. Click the **City text box control arrow**, and then click **Arlington**. In the **Sort & Filter group**, click the **Toggle Filter** button.

As displayed in the navigation area, eighteen student records include either Alexandria *or* Arlington in the City field. You have created an ***OR condition***; that is, records display where, in this instance, either of two values—Alexandria *or* Arlington—is present in the selected field.

5 In the **Sort & Filter group**, click the **Advanced** button, and then click **Clear All Filters** to display all of the records.

6 Click the **Advanced** button again, and then from the list, click **Advanced Filter/Sort**. Expand the field list.

The Advanced Filter design grid displays. The design grid is similar to the query design grid.

7 From the **3A Students** field list, add the **City** field and then the **Major ID#** field to the design grid. In the **Criteria** row for the **City** field, type **Arlington** and then click in the **Criteria** row for the **Major ID#** field. Type **339** and then press Enter. Compare your screen with Figure 12.27.

Figure 12.27

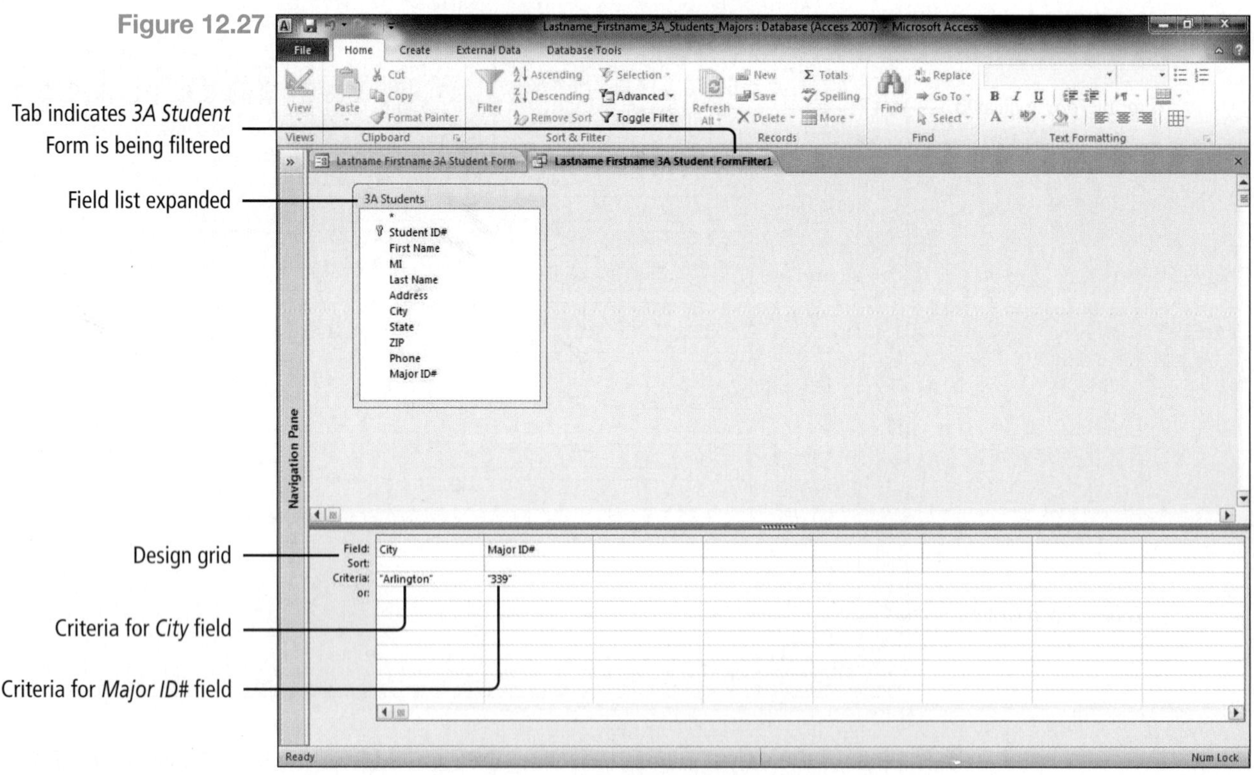

8 In the **Sort & Filter group**, click the **Toggle Filter** button.

Two records match the criteria. You have created an ***AND condition***; that is, only records display where both values—Arlington *and* 339—are present in the selected fields. There are two Information Systems Technology majors who live in Arlington.

9 In the **Sort & Filter group**, click the **Toggle Filter** button to display all of the records.

In the navigation area, *Unfiltered* displays, which indicates that a filter was created for this form. Unless you Clear All Filters, the filter is saved with the form when the form is closed. When you reopen the form, you can click on the Toggle Filter button or the Unfiltered button to reapply the filter.

10 **Close** [×] all open objects, and then **Open** [»] the **Navigation Pane**. Display **Backstage** view, click **Close Database**, and then click **Exit**. As directed by your instructor, submit your database and the three paper or electronic printouts that are the results of this project.

> **More Knowledge | Using the Filter Button**
>
> You can filter a form in a manner similar to the way you filter records in a table. Click in the text box control of the field you wish to use for the filter. On the Home tab, in the Sort & Filter group, click the Filter button to display a shortcut menu. Select the (Select All) check box to clear the option, and then select the data by which you want to filter by clicking the check boxes preceding the data. To remove the filter, redisplay the menu, and then select the (Select All) check box.

End **You have completed Project 12A**

Project 12B Job Openings

Project Activities

In Activities 12.12 through 12.19, you will assist Damon Bass, Career Center Director for Capital Cities Community College, in using an Access database to track the employers and job openings advertised for the annual Career Fair. Your completed reports will look similar to Figure 12.28.

Project Files

For Project 12B, you will need the following file:

a03B_Job_Openings

You will save your database as:

Lastname_Firstname_3B_Job_Openings

Project Results

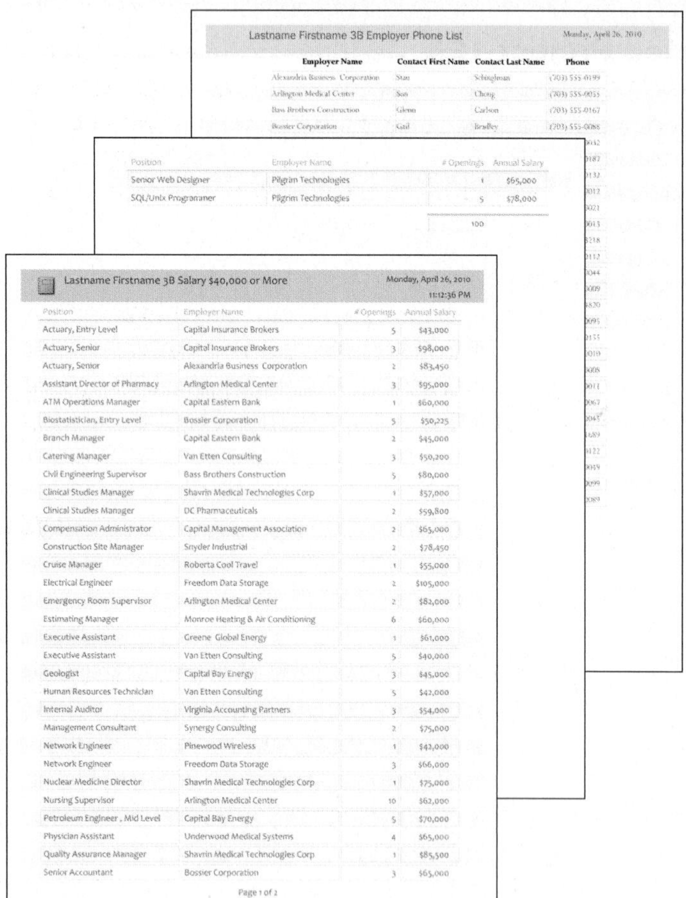

Lastname Firstname 3B Employer Phone List — Monday, April 26, 2010

Employer Name	Contact First Name	Contact Last Name	Phone
Alexandria Business Corporation	Stan	Schinglman	(703) 555-0199
Arlington Medical Center	Sun	Chong	(703) 555-0055
Bass Brothers Construction	Glenn	Carlson	(703) 555-0167
Bossier Corporation	Gail	Bradley	(703) 555-0086

Position	Employer Name	# Openings	Annual Salary
Senior Web Designer	Pilgrim Technologies	1	$65,000
SQL/Unix Programaner	Pilgrim Technologies	5	$78,000
		100	

Lastname Firstname 3B Salary $40,000 or More — Monday, April 26, 2010 11:12:36 PM

Position	Employer Name	# Openings	Annual Salary
Actuary, Entry Level	Capital Insurance Brokers	5	$43,000
Actuary, Senior	Capital Insurance Brokers	3	$98,000
Actuary, Senior	Alexandria Business Corporation	2	$83,450
Assistant Director of Pharmacy	Arlington Medical Center	3	$95,000
ATM Operations Manager	Capital Eastern Bank	1	$60,000
Biostatistician, Entry Level	Bossier Corporation	5	$50,225
Branch Manager	Capital Eastern Bank	2	$45,000
Catering Manager	Van Etten Consulting	3	$50,200
Civil Engineering Supervisor	Bass Brothers Construction	5	$80,000
Clinical Studies Manager	Shavrin Medical Technologies Corp	1	$57,000
Clinical Studies Manager	DC Pharmaceuticals	2	$59,800
Compensation Administrator	Capital Management Association	2	$65,000
Construction Site Manager	Snyder Industrial	2	$78,450
Cruise Manager	Roberta Cool Travel	1	$55,000
Electrical Engineer	Freedom Data Storage	2	$105,000
Emergency Room Supervisor	Arlington Medical Center	2	$82,000
Estimating Manager	Monroe Heating & Air Conditioning	6	$60,000
Executive Assistant	Greene Global Energy	1	$61,000
Executive Assistant	Van Etten Consulting	5	$40,000
Geologist	Capital Bay Energy	3	$45,000
Human Resources Technician	Van Etten Consulting	5	$42,000
Internal Auditor	Virginia Accounting Partners	3	$54,000
Management Consultant	Synergy Consulting	2	$75,000
Network Engineer	Pinewood Wireless	1	$42,000
Network Engineer	Freedom Data Storage	3	$66,000
Nuclear Medicine Director	Shavrin Medical Technologies Corp	1	$75,000
Nursing Supervisor	Arlington Medical Center	10	$62,000
Petroleum Engineer , Mid Level	Capital Bay Energy	5	$70,000
Physician Assistant	Underwood Medical Systems	4	$65,000
Quality Assurance Manager	Shavrin Medical Technologies Corp	1	$85,500
Senior Accountant	Bossier Corporation	3	$65,000

Page 1 of 2

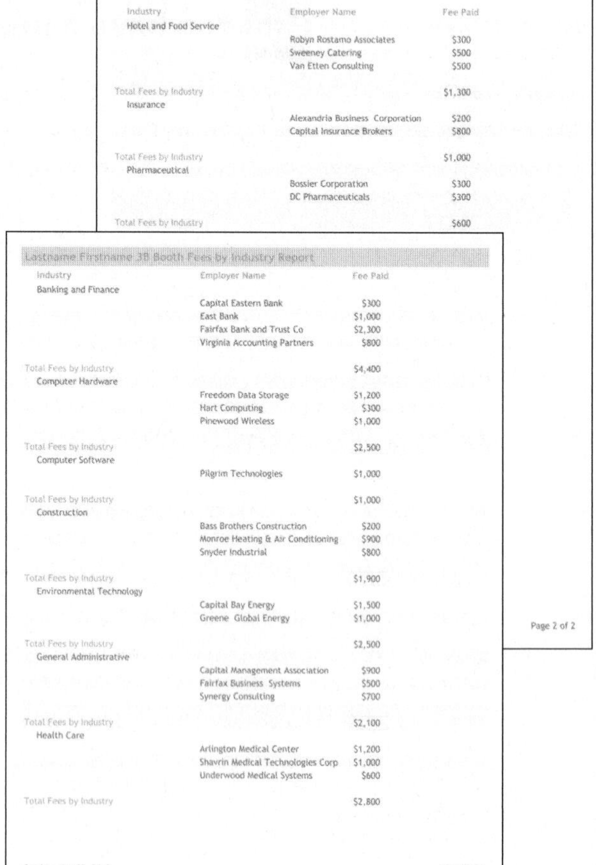

Industry	Employer Name	Fee Paid
Hotel and Food Service		
	Robyn Rostamo Associates	$300
	Sweeney Catering	$500
	Van Etten Consulting	$500
Total Fees by Industry		$1,300
Insurance		
	Alexandria Business Corporation	$200
	Capital Insurance Brokers	$800
Total Fees by Industry		$1,000
Pharmaceutical		
	Bossier Corporation	$300
	DC Pharmaceuticals	$300
Total Fees by Industry		$600

Page 2 of 2

Lastname Firstname 3B Booth Fees by Industry Report

Industry	Employer Name	Fee Paid
Banking and Finance		
	Capital Eastern Bank	$300
	East Bank	$1,000
	Fairfax Bank and Trust Co	$2,300
	Virginia Accounting Partners	$800
Total Fees by Industry		$4,400
Computer Hardware		
	Freedom Data Storage	$1,200
	Hart Computing	$300
	Pinewood Wireless	$1,000
Total Fees by Industry		$2,500
Computer Software		
	Pilgrim Technologies	$1,000
Total Fees by Industry		$1,000
Construction		
	Bass Brothers Construction	$200
	Monroe Heating & Air Conditioning	$900
	Snyder Industrial	$800
Total Fees by Industry		$1,900
Environmental Technology		
	Capital Bay Energy	$1,500
	Greene Global Energy	$1,000
Total Fees by Industry		$2,500
General Administrative		
	Capital Management Association	$900
	Fairfax Business Systems	$500
	Synergy Consulting	$700
Total Fees by Industry		$2,100
Health Care		
	Arlington Medical Center	$1,200
	Shavrin Medical Technologies Corp	$1,000
	Underwood Medical Systems	$600
Total Fees by Industry		$2,800

Sunday, May 23, 2010 — Page 1 of 2

Figure 12.28
Project 12B Job Openings

Objective 5 | Create a Report by Using the Report Tool

A ***report*** is a database object that summarizes the fields and records from a query or from a table, in an easy-to-read format suitable for printing. A report consists of information extracted from queries or tables and also the report's design items, such as labels, headings, and graphics. The queries or tables that provide the underlying data for a report are referred to as the report's ***record source***.

Activity 12.12 | Creating a Report by Using the Report Tool

The ***Report tool*** is the fastest way to create a report. This tool displays all of the fields and records from the record source that you select. You can use the Report tool to look at the underlying data quickly in an easy-to-read format, after which you can save the report and modify it in Layout view or in Design view. In this activity, you will use the Report tool to create a report from a query that lists all of the job openings with an annual salary of at least $40,000.

1 **Start** Access. In **Backstage** view, click **Open**. Navigate to the student data files for this textbook, and then open the **a03B_Job_Openings** database.

2 In **Backstage** view, click **Save Database As**. In the **Save As** dialog box, navigate to your **Access Chapter 12** folder. In the **File name** box, type **Lastname_Firstname_3B_Job_Openings** and then press Enter. On the **Message Bar**, click **Enable Content**. Notice that in this database, there are two tables and one query that uses both tables as its record source.

3 On the Ribbon, click the **Database Tools tab**. In the **Relationships group**, click the **Relationships** button. Compare your screen with Figure 12.29. If your relationships do not display, in the Relationships group, click the All Relationships button.

One employer is associated with *many* job openings. Thus, a one-to-many relationship has been established between the 3B Employers table and the 3B Job Openings table by using the Employer ID# field as the common field.

Figure 12.29

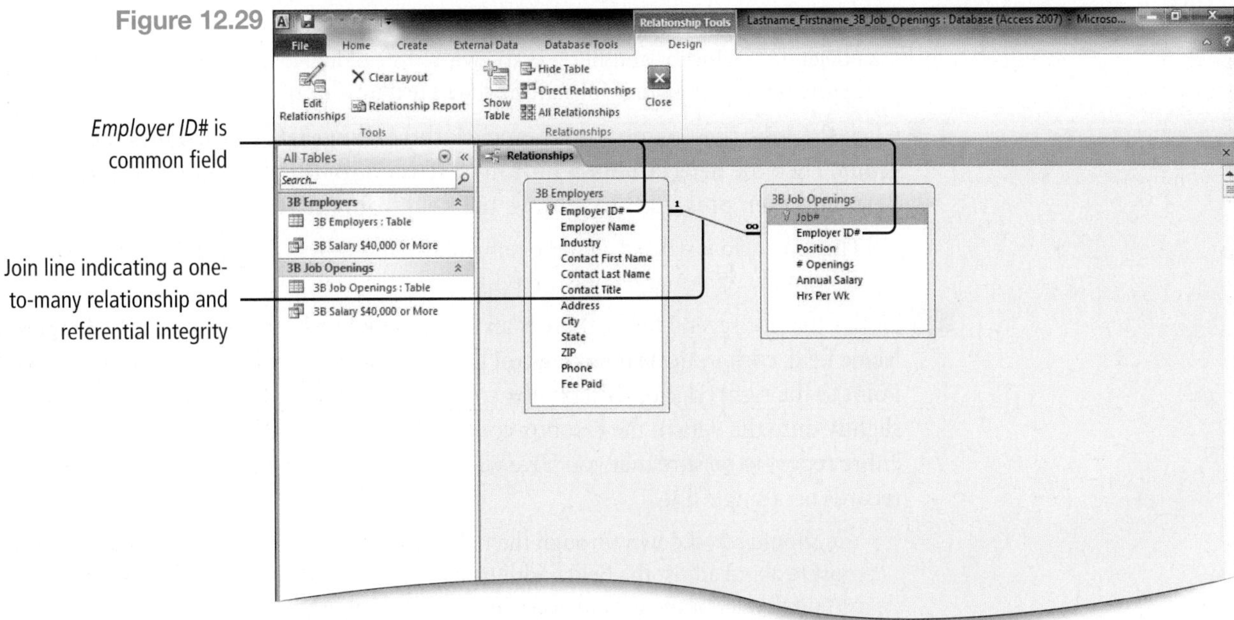

Access | Chapter 12

4 **Close** [X] the **Relationships** window. Open both tables, and look at the fields and data in each table. Open the query to examine the data, and then switch to **Design** view to examine the design grid. When you are finished, **Close** [X] all objects.

The query answers the question *What is the Job#, Position, Employer Name, and # of Openings for jobs that have an Annual Salary of $40,000 or more?*

5 In the **Navigation Pane**, click to select the **3B Salary $40,000 or More** query. Click the **Create tab**, and then in the **Reports group**, click the **Report** button. **Close** [«] the **Navigation Pane**, and then compare your screen with Figure 12.30.

Access creates the 3B Job Openings report and displays it in Layout view. The report includes all of the fields and all of the records in the query. In Layout view, you can see the margins and page breaks in the report.

Figure 12.30

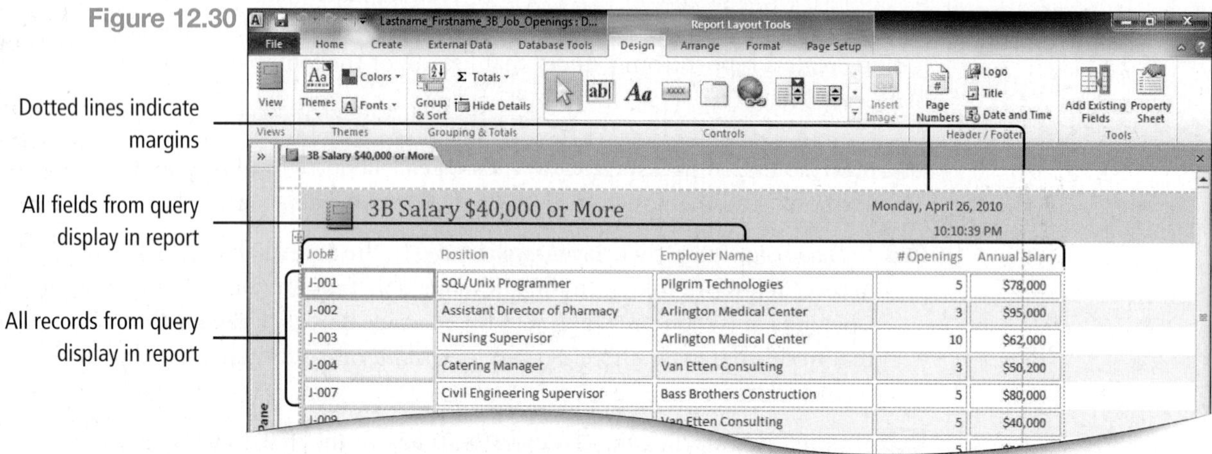

Activity 12.13 | Modifying a Report in Layout View and Printing a Report

1 On the **Design tab**, in the **Themes group**, click the **Themes** button. From the gallery of themes, scroll down, locate, and then right-click the **Waveform** theme. Click **Apply Theme to This Object Only**.

Recall that right-clicking a theme enables you to apply a predefined format to the active object only, which is another way to give a professional look to a report. Apply a theme before performing other formatting to the text in your report.

2 Click the **Job#** field name, and then click the **Arrange tab**. In the **Rows & Columns group**, click the **Select Column** button to select both the field name and the data in the field, and then press [Del] to remove the field from the report.

The Job# field is deleted, and the remaining fields move to the left. No fields extend beyond the right margin of the report.

3 Notice that for several fields, there is an extra blank line in the record. In the **Employer Name** field, click in the **text box control** that displays *Monroe Heating & Air Conditioning*. Point to the right edge of the text box control to display the [↔] pointer. Drag to the right slightly until the data in the text box control displays on one line. Scroll down to view the entire report to be sure that you have widened the column enough to accommodate all records on a single line.

You should scroll down through the report to find the text box control that displays the most text and adjust the field width using that text box control. In this manner, you can be certain that all of the data in every text box control displays on one line.

4 Click the **Position** field name, and then click the **Home tab**. In the **Sort & Filter group**, click the **Ascending** button to sort the records in the report alphabetically by Position.

5 Scroll down to the bottom of the report, and then click the **Annual Salary calculated control**, which displays a total that is truncated at the bottom. Press Del to remove this total.

Access automatically adds a calculated control to sum any field that is formatted as currency. Here, the total is not a useful number and this can be deleted.

6 At the top of the report, click the **# Openings** field name. Click the **Design tab**. In the **Grouping & Totals group**, click the **Totals** button, and then click **Sum**.

7 Scroll down to display the last line of the report. Click in the **# Openings calculated control**, point to the bottom edge of the control to display the ↕ pointer, and then double-click to resize the control. Compare your screen with Figure 12.31.

The total number of job openings for positions with a salary equal to or greater than $40,000 is 100. Use Layout view to make quick changes to a report created with the Report tool. The Report tool is not intended to create a perfectly formatted formal report, but it is a way to summarize the data in a table or query quickly in an easy-to-read format suitable for printing and reading.

Figure 12.31

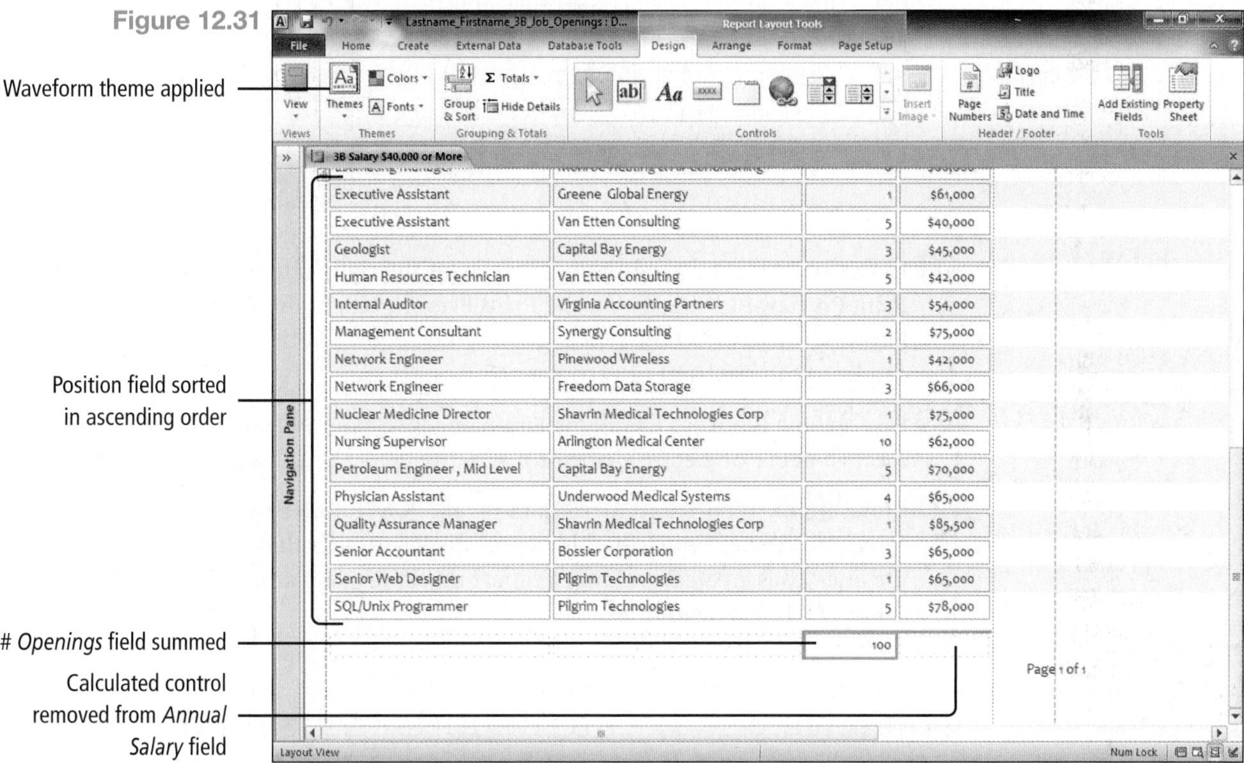

8 At the bottom of the report, notice that the **Page Number control** does not fit entirely within the margins. Click the **Page Number control** that displays *Page 1 of 1*, and then drag the pointer to the left until the page number control is visually centered between the margins of the report.

Always look at the headers and footers to determine if the data will print on one page.

9 Scroll up to display the top of the report. In the **Report Header** section, click the label control that displays *3B Salary $40,000 or More*. Click the **Format tab**, and then in the **Font group**, change the **Font Size** to **14**. Click the **label control** again so that you can edit the title. Using your own name, add **Lastname Firstname** to the beginning of the title, and then press Enter. If necessary, point to the right edge of the label control to display the ↔ pointer, and then double-click to fit the width of the text in the control.

10 Click any field in the report. In the upper left corner of the report, click the **layout selector** [icon], and then drag it slightly downward and to the right until the columns are visually centered between the margins of the report. If your columns rearrange, on the Quick Access Toolbar, click Undo and begin again. Compare your screen with Figure 12.32.

Using the layout selector, you can move the entire layout of the label controls and text box controls to horizontally center the records on the page. It is easier to control this movement if you drag downward slightly while moving the selector to the right.

Figure 12.32

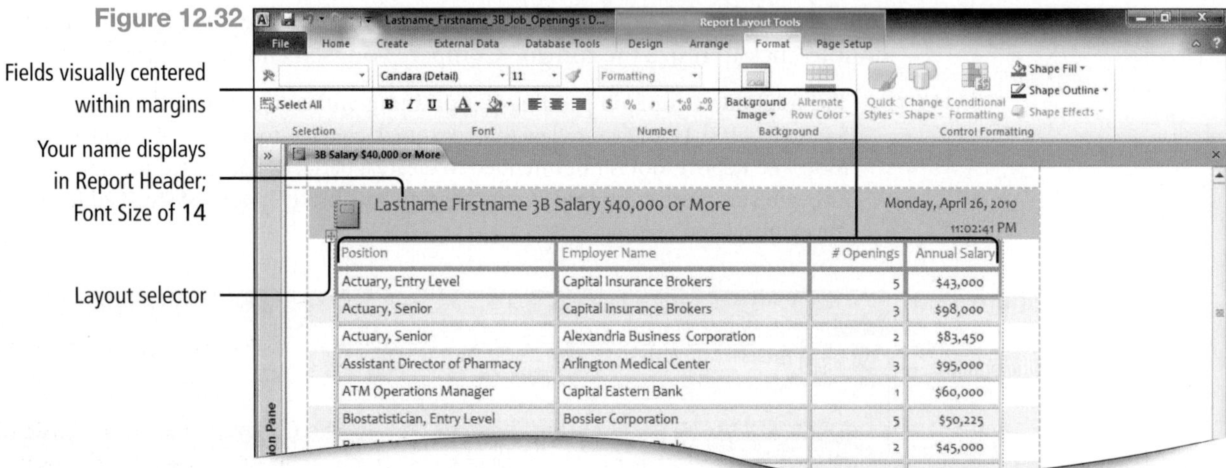

Another Way

In the object window, right-click the object tab, and then click Print Preview.

11 In the lower right corner of your screen, at the right side of the status bar, click the **Print Preview** button [icon]. On the **Print Preview tab**, in the **Zoom group**, click the **Two Pages** button to view the two pages of your report. Notice that the page number displays at the bottom of each page.

12 **Save** [icon] the report as **Lastname Firstname 3B Salary $40,000 or More Report** and then create a paper or electronic printout as directed. Then **Close Print Preview**.

13 **Close** [icon] the report, and then **Open** [icon] the **Navigation Pane**. Expand the width of the **Navigation Pane**. Notice that the report displays under the source tables from which the query was created, and that a report object displays a small green notebook icon. **Close** [icon] the **Navigation Pane**.

Objective 6 | Create Reports by Using the Blank Report Tool and the Report Wizard

Use the ***Blank Report tool*** to create a report without predefined labels and fields. This is an efficient way to create a report, especially if you plan to include only a few fields in your report.

Activity 12.14 | Creating a Report by Using the Blank Report Tool

In this activity, you will build a report that lists only the Employer Name, Contact First Name, Contact Last Name, and Phone fields, which Mr. Bass will use as a quick reference for phoning the employers to verify the details of their Career Fair participation.

1 On the **Create tab**, in the **Reports group**, click the **Blank Report** button.

A blank report displays in Layout view, and the Field List pane displays.

2 In the **Field List** pane, click **Show all tables**, and then click the **plus sign** (+) next to **3B Employers** to display the field names in the table. Compare your screen with Figure 12.33.

Figure 12.33

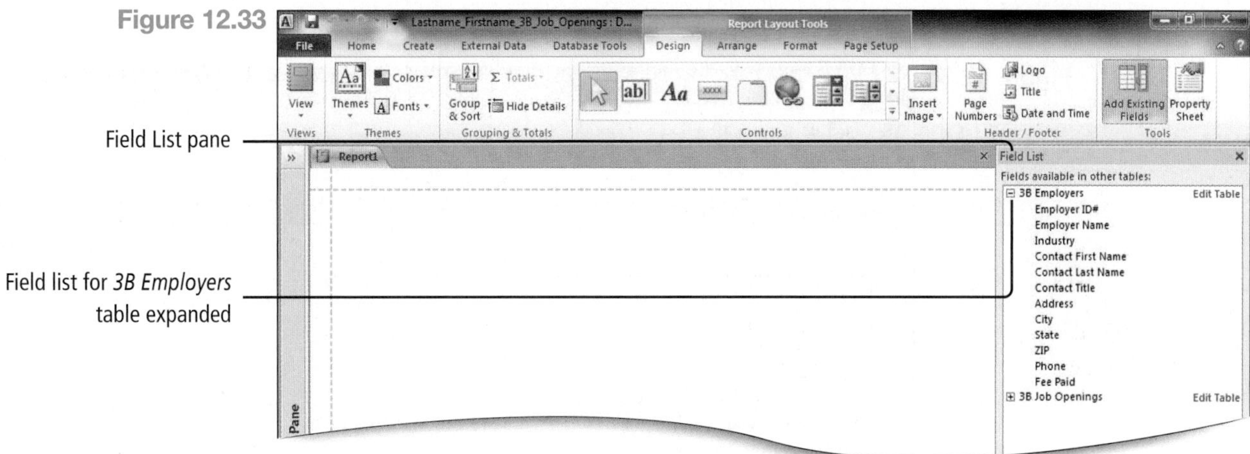

3 In the **Field List** pane, point to the **Employer Name** field, right-click, and then click **Add Field to View**.

The Employer Name field and its data display as the first column of the report. Using the Report tool, you build the report field by field in the order that you want the fields to display.

4 From the **Field List** pane, drag the **Contact First Name** field into the blank report—anywhere to the right of *Employer Name*. Double-click the **Contact Last Name** field to add it as the third field in the report. Use any technique that you just practiced to add the **Phone** field as the fourth field in the report, and then compare your screen with Figure 12.34.

Figure 12.34

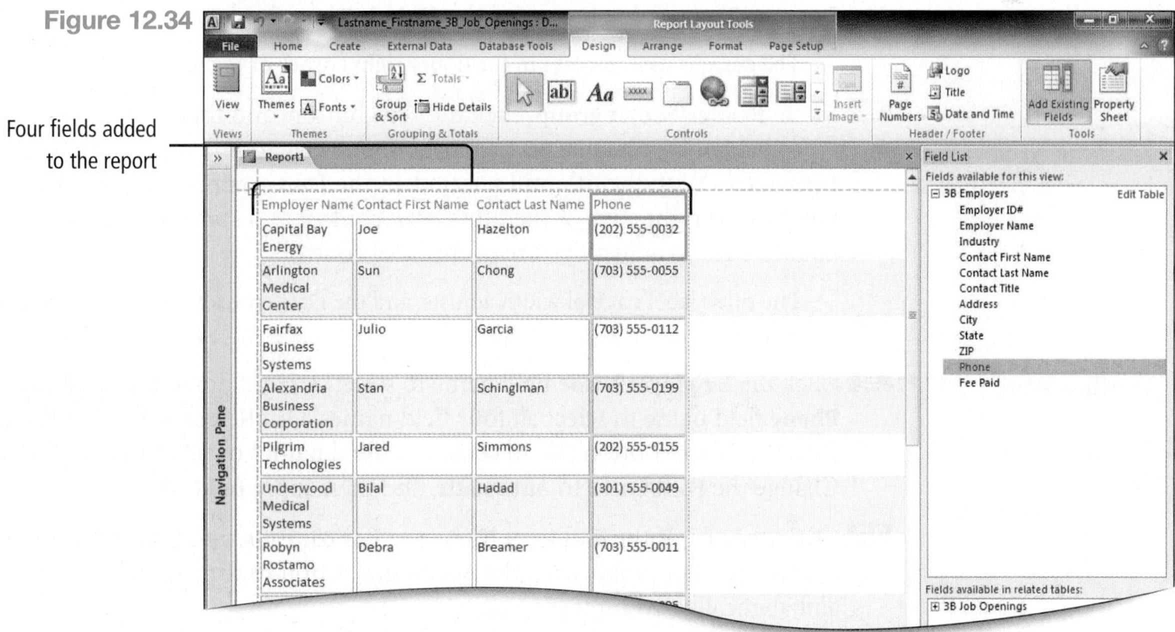

5 **Close** the **Field List** pane. On the **Design tab**, in the **Themes group**, click the **Themes** button. Right-click the **Equity** theme, and then click **Apply Theme to This Object Only**.

Recall that you should select a theme before making other formatting changes.

6 Under **Employer Name**, click in the **text box control** that displays *Monroe Heating & Air Conditioning*. Point to the right edge of the text box control to display the ↔ pointer, and then drag to the right until the data in the text box control displays on one line and there is a small amount of space between the name and the next column. Compare your screen with Figure 12.35.

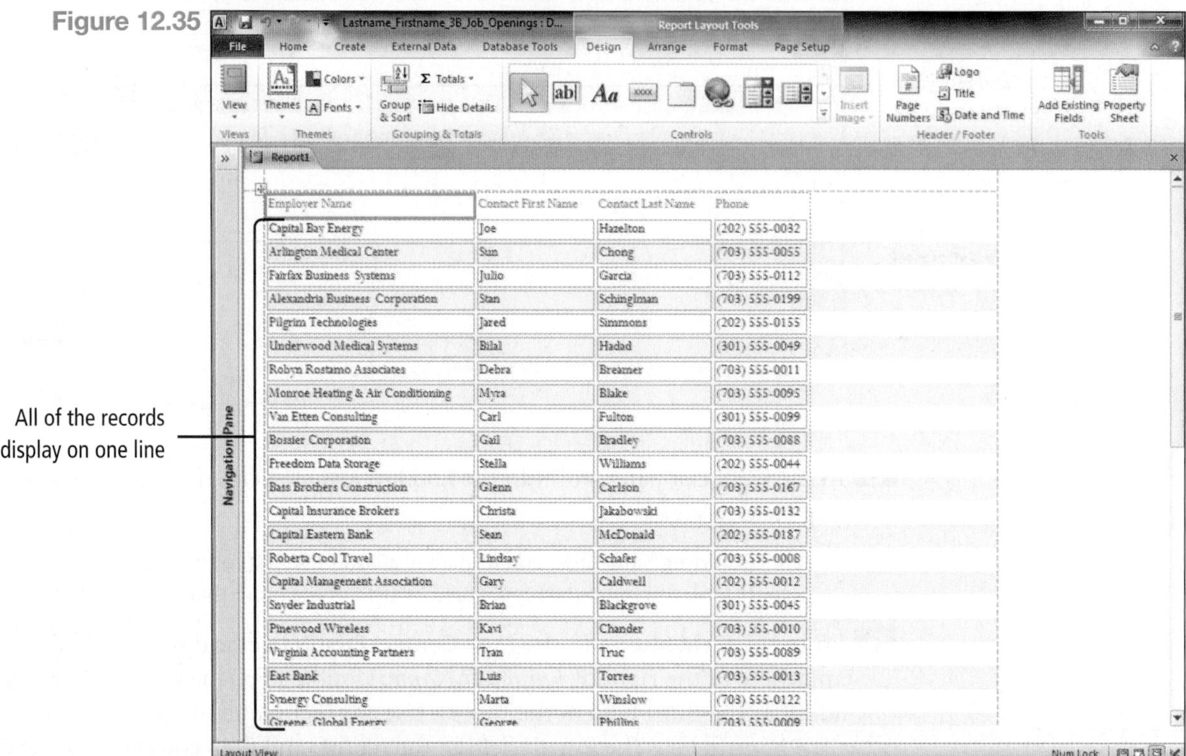

Figure 12.35

7 On the **Design tab**, in the **Header/Footer group**, click the **Date and Time** button. In the **Date and Time** dialog box, clear the **Include Time** check box, and then click **OK**.

The current date displays in the upper right corner of the report.

8 In the **Header/Footer group**, click the **Title** button, and then using your own name, type **Lastname Firstname 3B Employer Phone List** and then press Enter. Click the **Format tab**. With the title still selected, in the **Font group**, change the **Font Size** to **14**. Point to the right edge of the title's label control to display the ↔ pointer, and then double-click to adjust the size of the label control.

The title's label control width adjusts, and the Date control moves to the left within the margin.

> **Another Way**
>
> Click the first field name, and then click the Arrange tab. In the Rows & Columns group, click the Select Row button.

9 Click the **Employer Name** field name to select it. Hold down Shift, and then click the **Phone** field name to select all four field names. On the **Format tab**, in the **Font group**, click the **Center** button to center the field names over the data in the columns. Change the **Font Color** to **Automatic**, and then apply **Bold** **B**.

10 Click any one of the **Employer Name text box controls**, and then click the **Home tab**. In the **Sort & Filter group**, click the **Ascending** button to sort the records in the report alphabetically by Employer Name.

11 In the upper left corner of the report, click the **layout selector**, and then drag it downward slightly and to the right to visually center the fields between the margins. Compare your screen with Figure 12.36.

Recall that it is easier to control this movement if you drag down slightly while moving the layout selector.

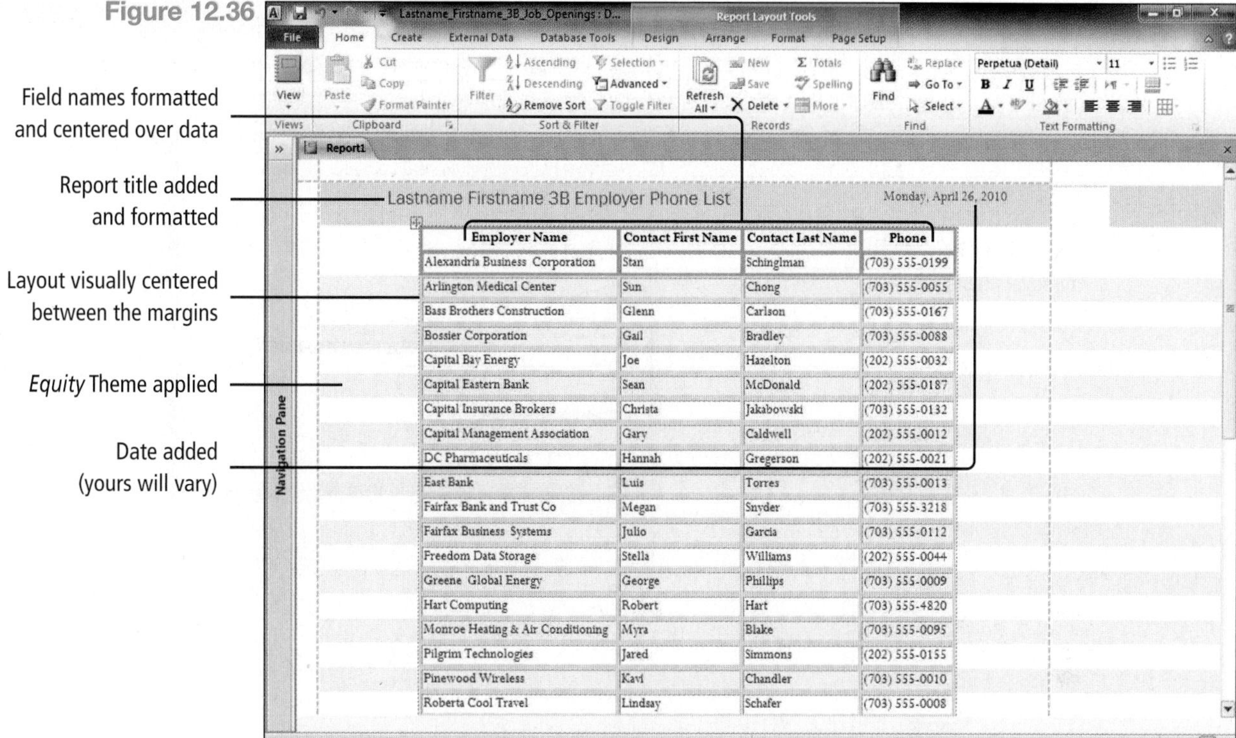

Figure 12.36

12 **Save** the report as **Lastname Firstname 3B Employer Phone List** and then on the status bar, click the **Print Preview** button. Create a paper or electronic printout as directed.

13 **Close Print Preview**, and then **Close** the report. **Open** the **Navigation Pane**, and notice that the report displays below the *3B Employers* table—the underlying data source. **Close** the **Navigation Pane**.

Activity 12.15 | Creating a Report by Using the Report Wizard

Use the ***Report Wizard*** when you need flexibility and want to control the report content and design. The Report Wizard enables you to specify how the data is grouped and sorted. You can use fields from more than one table or query, assuming you have created the appropriate relationships between the tables. The Report Wizard is similar to the Form Wizard; it creates a report by asking you a series of questions and then designs the report based on your answers.

In this activity, you will prepare a report for Mr. Bass that displays the employers, grouped by industry, and the total fees paid by employers for renting a booth at the Career Fair.

1 Click the **Create tab**, and then in the **Reports group**, click the **Report Wizard** button.

Here you select the tables or queries from which you want to extract information, and then select the fields to include in the report. You can also select more than one table or query.

2 Click the **Tables/Queries arrow**, and then click **Table: 3B Employers**. Move the following fields to the **Selected Fields** list in the order given: **Industry**, **Employer Name**, and **Fee Paid** (scroll down as necessary to locate the *Fee Paid* field). Compare your screen with Figure 12.37.

Figure 12.37

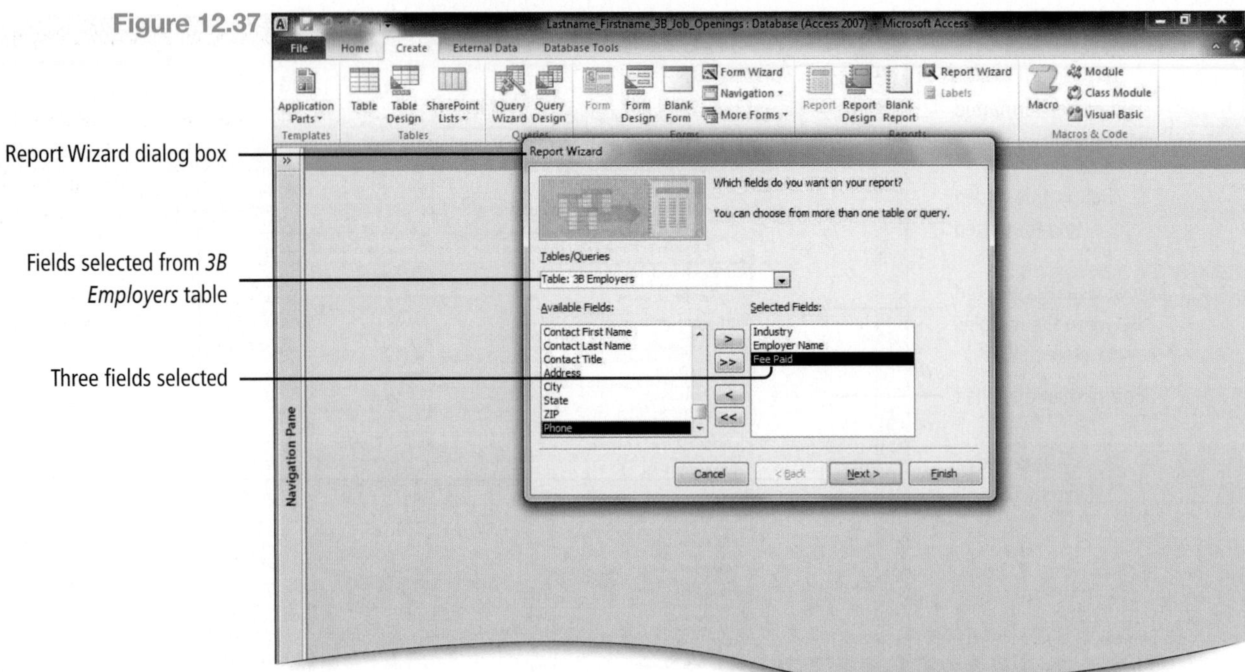

3 Click **Next**, and notice that in this dialog box, you can add grouping levels. A preview of the grouping level displays on the right side of the dialog box.

Grouping data helps to organize and summarize the data in your report.

4 With **Industry** selected, click the **One Field** button [>], and then compare your screen with Figure 12.38.

The preview window displays how the data will be grouped in the report. Grouping data in a report places all of the records that have the same data in a field together as a group—in this instance, each *Industry* will display as a group.

Figure 12.38

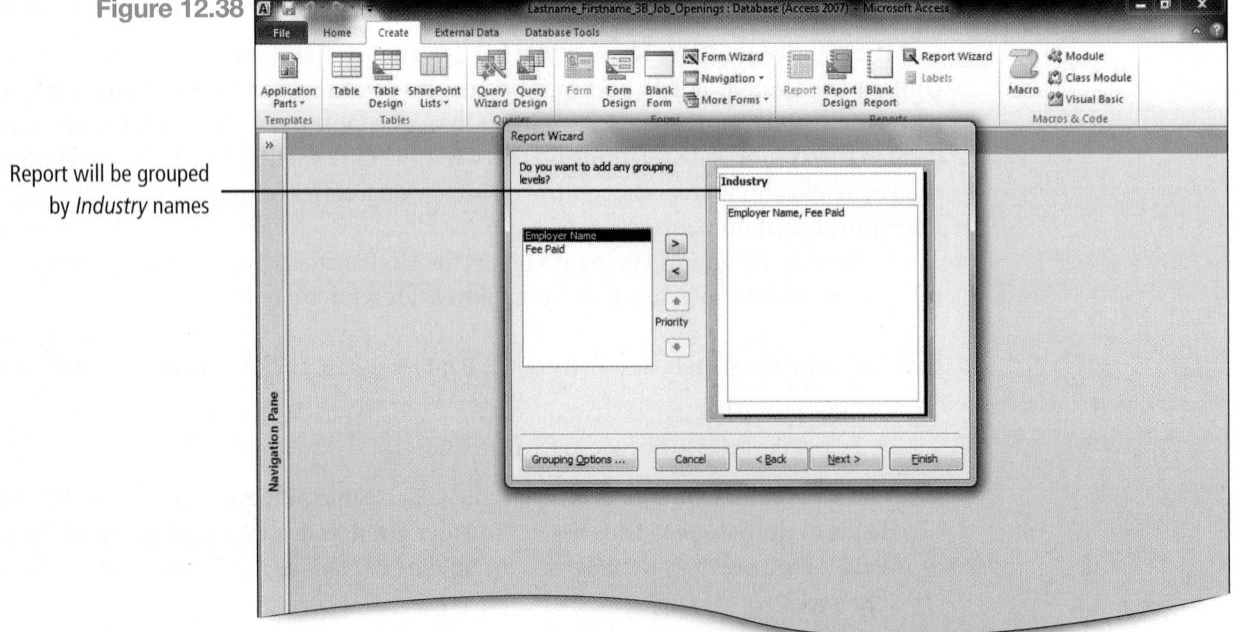

5 Click **Next**, and then click the **1** box **arrow**. Click **Employer Name**, and then compare your screen with Figure 12.39.

Here you indicate how you want to sort and summarize the information. You can sort on up to four fields. The Summary Options button displays because the data is grouped and contains numerical or currency data. The records in the report will sort alphabetically by Employer Name within Industry. Sorting records in a report presents a more organized report.

Figure 12.39

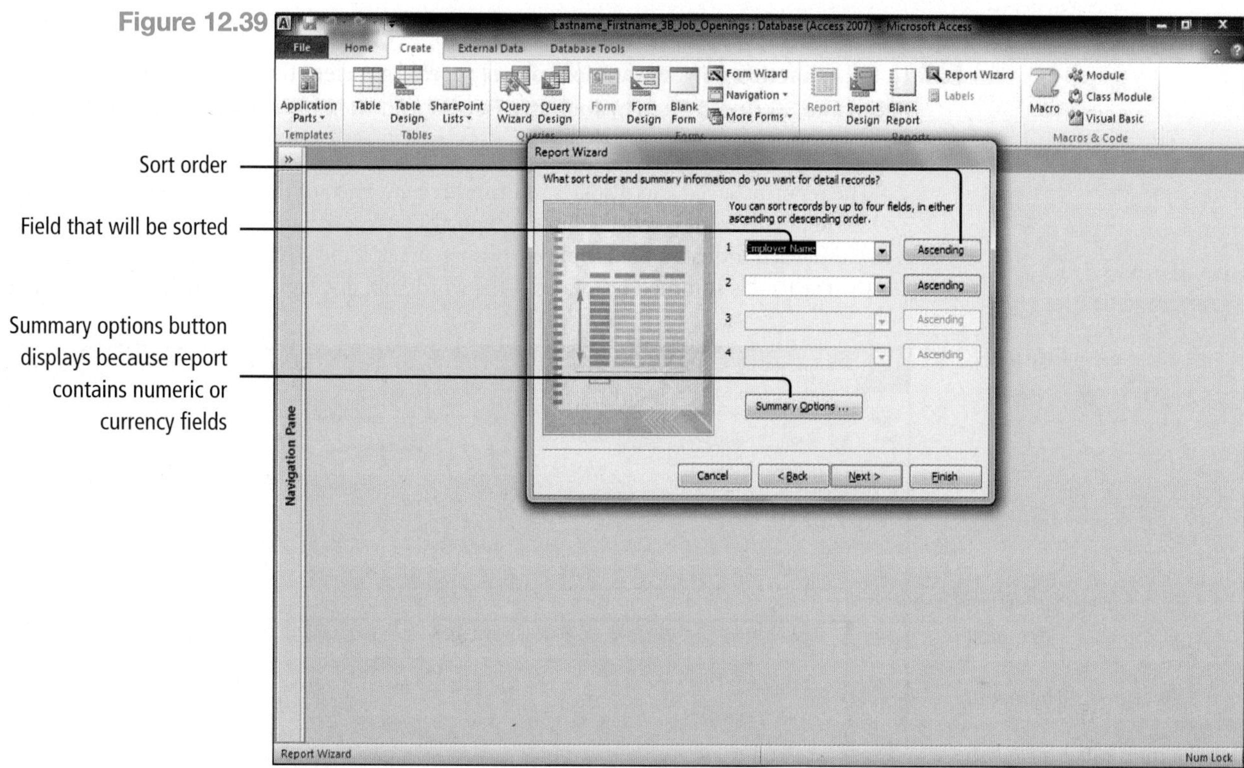

6 In the **Report Wizard** dialog box, click the **Summary Options** button, and then compare your screen with Figure 12.40.

The Summary Options dialog box displays. The Fee Paid field can be summarized by selecting one of four options—Sum, Avg, Min, or Max. You can also choose to display only summary information or to display both details—each record—and the summary information.

Figure 12.40

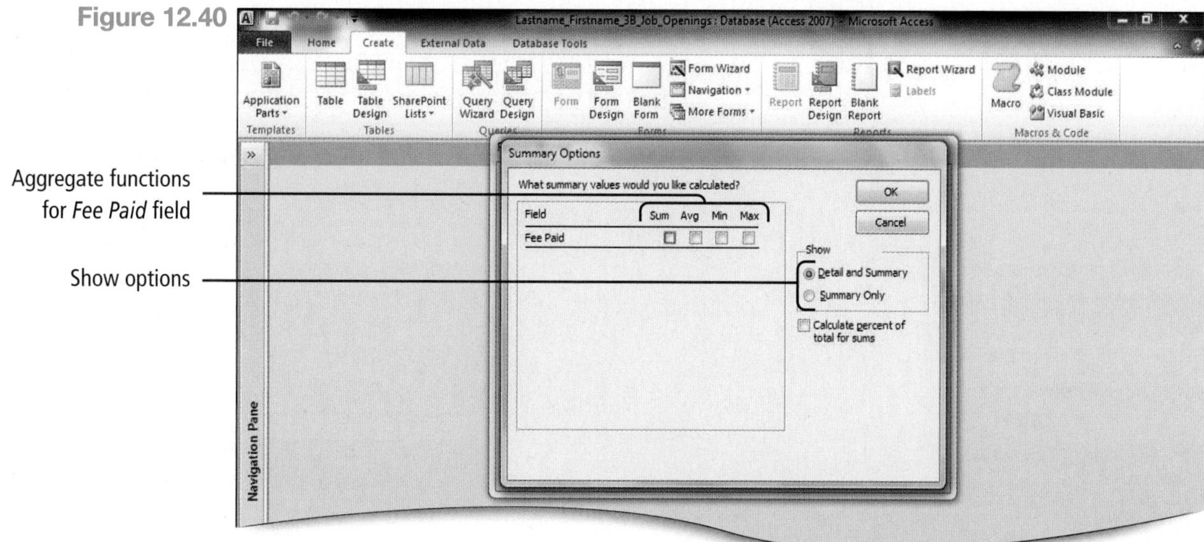

7 To the right of **Fee Paid**, select the **Sum** check box. Under **Show**, be sure that the **Detail and Summary** option button is selected, click **OK**, and then click **Next**.

Here you select the layout and the page orientation. A preview of the layout displays on the left.

8 Click each **Layout** option button, noticing the changes in the preview box, and then click the **Stepped** option button to select it as the layout for your report. Under **Orientation**, be sure that **Portrait** is selected. At the bottom, be sure that the **Adjust the field width so all fields fit on a page** check box is selected, and then click **Next**.

9 In the **What title do you want for your report?** box, select the existing text, type **Lastname Firstname 3B Booth Fees by Industry Report** and then click **Finish**. Compare your screen with Figure 12.41.

The report is saved and displays in Print Preview. Each of the specifications you defined in the Report Wizard is reflected in the report. The records are grouped by Industry, and then within each Industry, the Employer Names are alphabetized. Within each Industry grouping, the Fee Paid is summed or totaled—the word *Sum* displays at the end of each grouping.

Figure 12.41

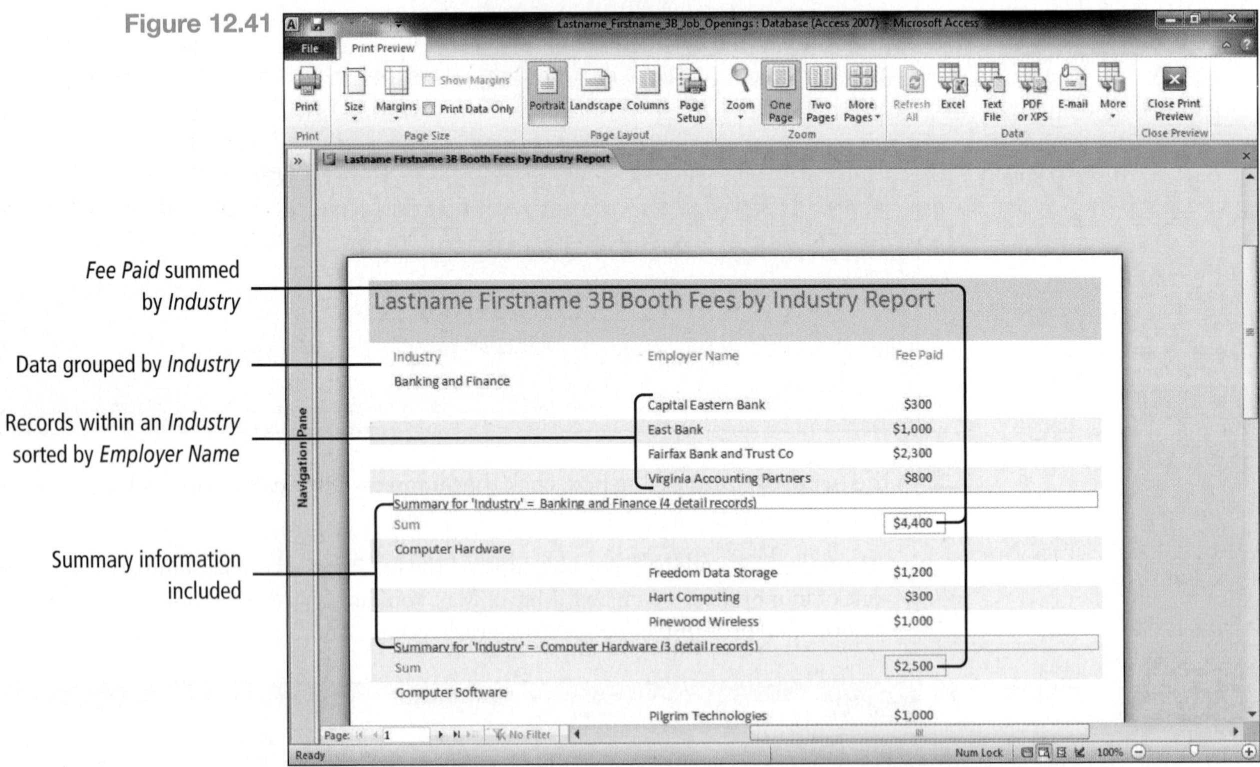

10 **Close Print Preview**. On the status bar, click the **Layout View** button.

Objective 7 | Modify the Design of a Report

After you create your report, you can modify its design by using tools and techniques similar to those you used to modify the design of a form. You can change the format of controls, add controls, remove controls, or change the placement of controls in the report. Most report modifications can be made in Layout view.

Activity 12.16 | Formatting and Deleting Controls in Layout View

1. With your **3B Booth Fees by Industry** report in **Layout** view, on the **Design tab**, in the **Themes group**, click the **Themes** button. In the **Themes gallery**, scroll down, and right-click the **Opulent** theme. Click **Apply Theme to This Object Only**.

2. Click the title—**3B Booth Fees by Industry Report**—to display a border around the label control, and then click the **Format tab**. In the **Font group**, change the **Font Size** to **14**, and then apply **Bold** **B**.

3. Within each *Industry* grouping, notice the **Summary for 'Industry'** information.

   Access includes a summary line that details what is being summarized (in this case, summed) and the number of records that are included in the summary total. Now that Mr. Bass has viewed the report, he has decided this information is not necessary and can be removed.

4. Click any one of the **Summary for 'Industry' controls**.

   The control that you clicked is surrounded by a dark border, and all of the related controls are surrounded by paler borders to indicate that all are selected.

> **Another Way**
>
> Right-click any of the selected controls, and then click Delete.

5. Press Del to remove the controls from the report. Compare your screen to Figure 12.42.

Figure 12.42

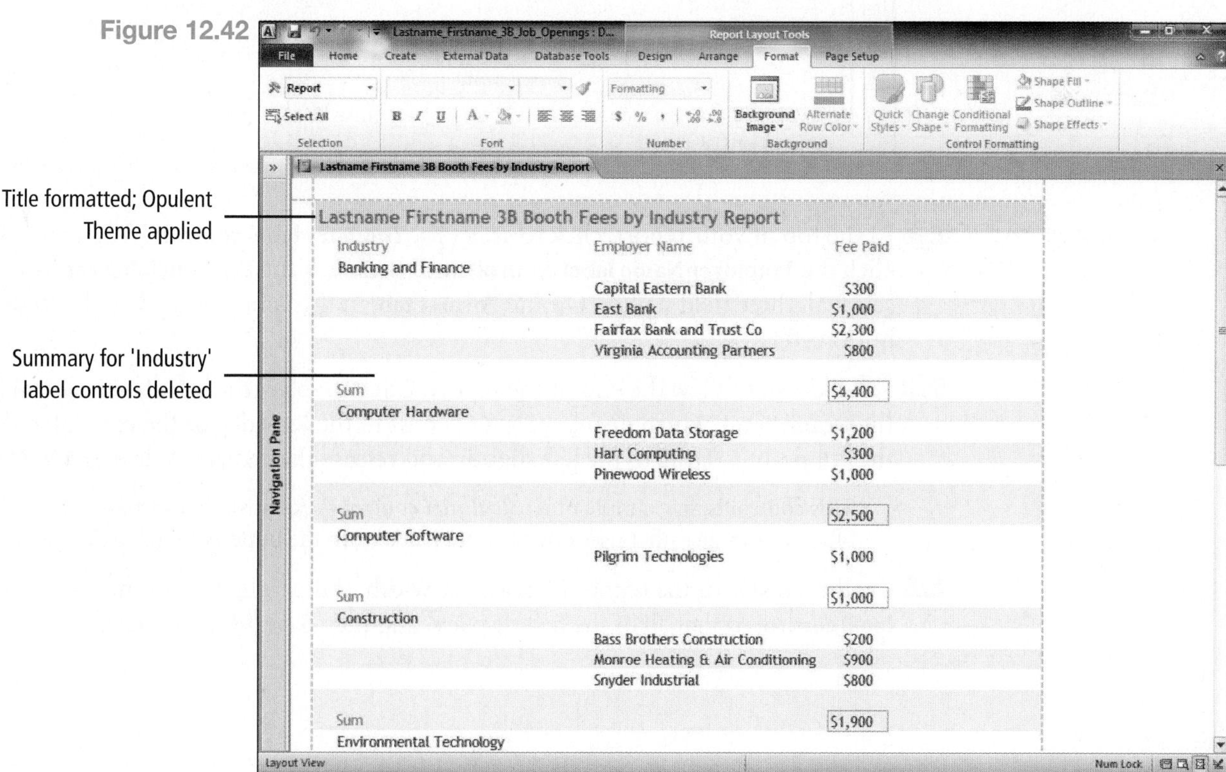

6. **Save** the changes you have made to the report.

Activity 12.17 | Modifying Controls in Layout View

In this activity, you will modify the text in controls, move controls, resize controls, and add a control to the report, all of which is easily accomplished in Layout view.

1 On the left side of the report, click one of the **Sum label controls** to select all of the controls, and then double-click to select the text. Type **Total Fees by Industry** and then press Enter. Compare your screen with Figure 12.43.

The new text more clearly states what is being summed.

Figure 12.43

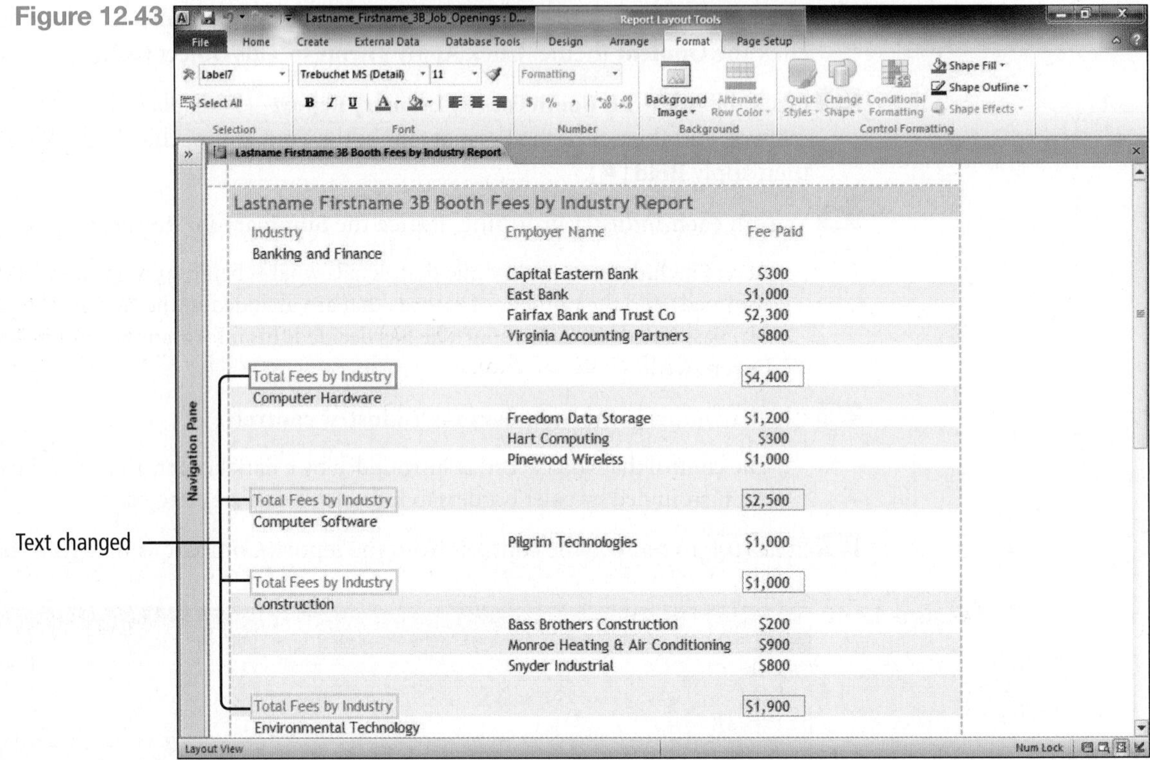

2 At the top of your report, click to select the **Industry label control.** Hold down Shift, click the **Employer Name label control**, and then click the **Fee Paid label control** to select all three field names. On the **Format tab**, in the **Font group**, click the **Bold** button **B**.

3 Scroll down to view the end of the report. Click to select the **calculated control** for the **Grand Total**, which displays *20,400*. Point to the left edge of the control to display the ↔ pointer. Drag to the left slightly and release the mouse to display **$20,400.**

This control is an example of a ***calculated control***—a control that contains an expression, often a formula—that uses one or more fields from the underlying table or query.

4 On the left side of the report, increase the width of the right edge of the **Grand Total label control** so that all of the text displays, and then **Save** the report.

Activity 12.18 | Aligning Controls in Design View

Design view gives you a more detailed view of the structure of your report. You can see the header and footer sections for the report, for the page, and for groups. In Design view, your report is not actually running, so you cannot see the underlying data while you are working. In the same manner as forms, you can add labels to the Page Footer section or increase the height of sections. Some tasks, such as aligning controls, can also be completed in Design view.

1 On the status bar, click the **Design View** button, and then compare your screen with Figure 12.44.

The Design view for a report is similar to the Design view for a form. You can modify the layout of the report in this view, and use the dotted grid pattern to align controls. This report contains a ***Report Header***, a ***Page Header***, a ***Group Header***, which in this instance is the *Industry* grouping, a Detail section that displays the data, a ***Group Footer*** (*Industry*), a ***Page Footer***, and a ***Report Footer***.

The Report Header displays information at the top of the *first page* of a report. The Page Header displays information at the top of *every page* of a report. The Group Header and Group Footer display the field label by which the data has been grouped—*Industry* in this instance. If you do not group data in a report, the Group Header does not display. Similarly, if you do not summarize data, the Group Footer does not display.

Figure 12.44

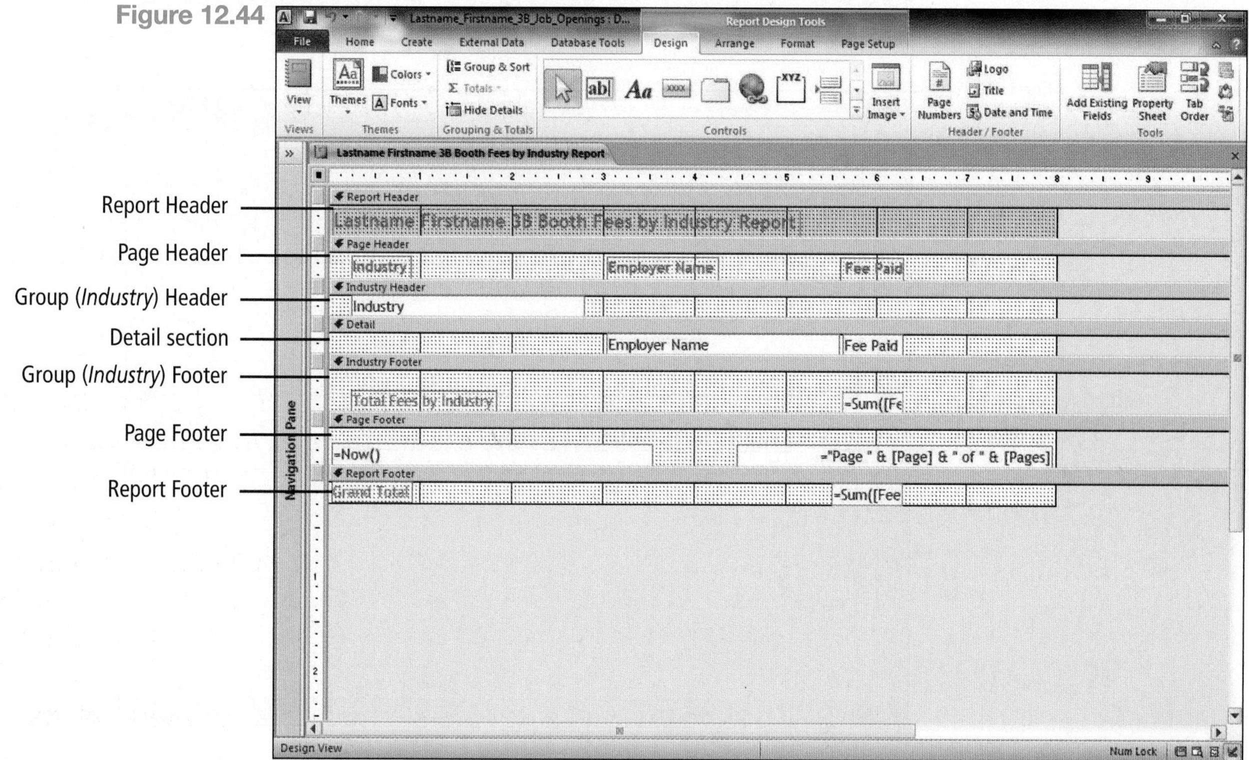

2 In the **Page Footer** section of the report, examine the two controls in this section.

The Page Footer displays information at the bottom of *every page* in the report, including the page number and the current date inserted by those controls.

The ***date control*** on the left side, displayed as *=Now( )*, inserts the current date each time the report is opened. The ***page number control*** on the right side, displayed as *="Page " & [Page] & " of " & [Pages]*, inserts the page number, for example Page 1 of 2, in the report when the report is displayed in Print Preview or when printed. Both of these are examples of functions that are used by Access to create controls in a report.

3 In the **Industry Footer** section, click the **Total Fees by Industry label control**. Hold down Shift. In the **Report Footer** section, click the **Grand Total label control** to select both controls.

4 On the **Arrange tab**, in the **Sizing & Ordering group**, click the **Align** button, and then click **Left**. **Save** the report, and then compare your screen with Figure 12.45.

The left edge of the Grand Total label control is aligned with the left edge of the Total Fees by Industry label control. When using the Align Left feature, Access aligns the left edges of controls with the control that is farthest to the left in the report. Similarly, when using the Align Right feature, Access aligns the right edges of controls with the control that is farthest to the right in the report.

Figure 12.45

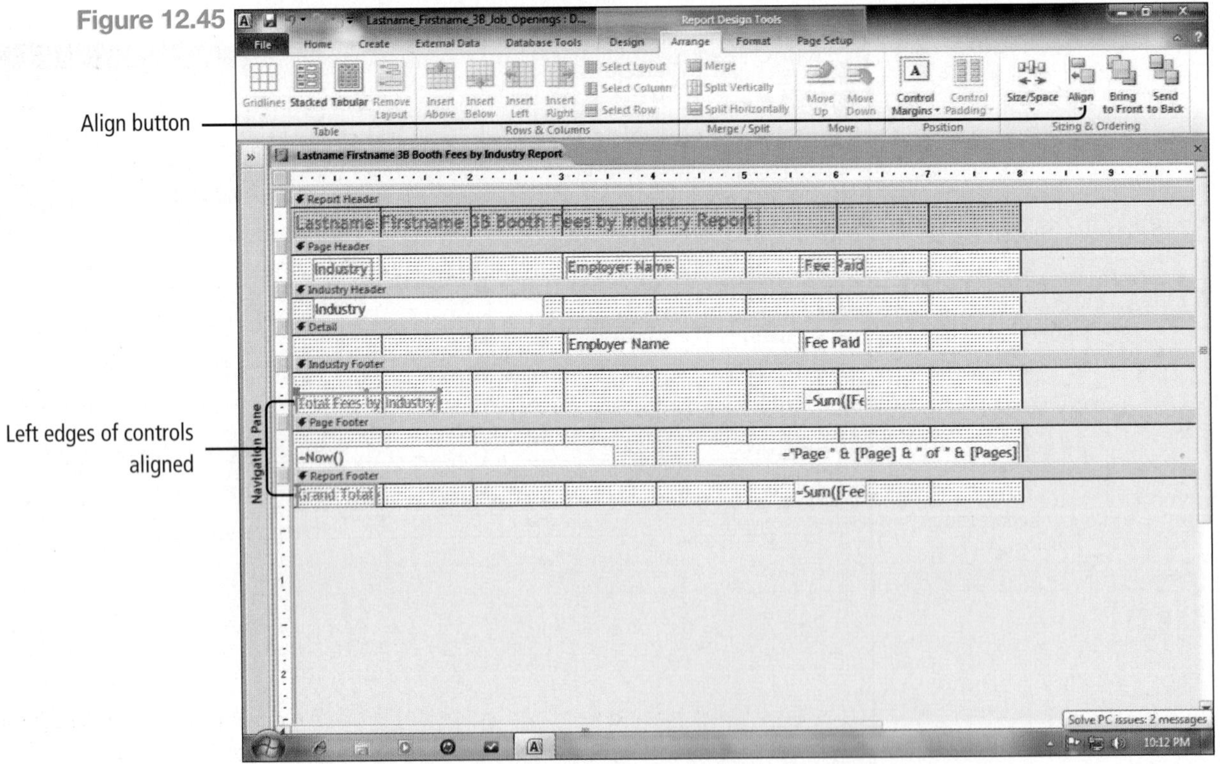

5 Switch to **Layout** view to display the underlying data in the controls. Scroll down, and notice that the **Total Fees by Industry label controls** and the **Grand Total label control** are left aligned.

Objective 8 | Print a Report and Keep Data Together

Before you print a report, examine the preview of the report to ensure that all of the labels and data display fully and to make sure that all of the data is properly grouped. Sometimes a page break occurs in the middle of a group of data, leaving the labels on one page and the data or totals on another page.

Activity 12.19 | Keeping Data Together and Printing a Report

It is possible to keep the data in a group together so it does not break across a page unless, of course, the data itself exceeds the length of a page.

1 On the status bar, click the **Print Preview** button. If necessary, in the **Zoom group**, click the **Two Pages** button, and then compare your screen with Figure 12.46.

This report will print on two pages. One record and the summary data for the *Hotel and Food Service* group display at the top of page 2, which is separated from the rest of the grouping.

Figure 12.46

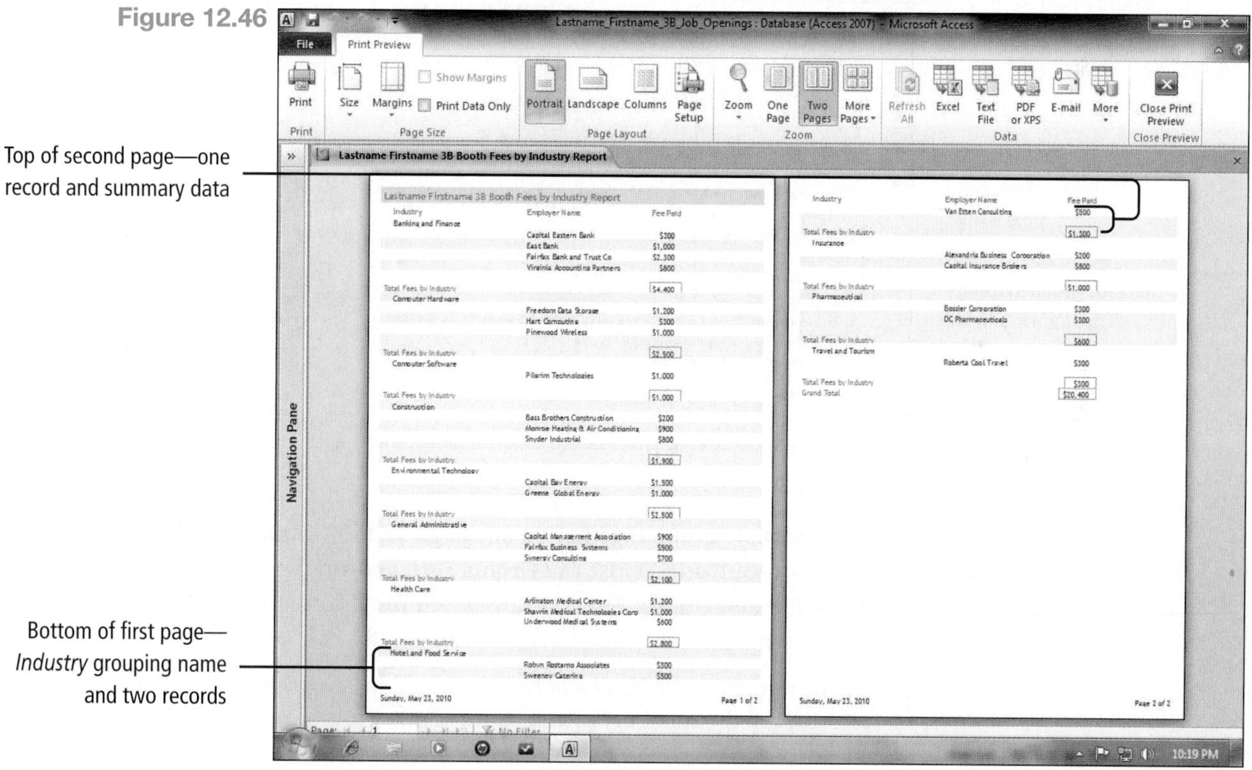

2 Click the **Close Print Preview** button to return to **Layout** view. On the **Design tab**, in the **Grouping & Totals group**, click the **Group & Sort** button.

At the bottom of the screen, the ***Group, Sort, and Total pane*** displays. Here you can control how information is grouped, sorted, or totaled. Layout view is the preferred view in which to accomplish such tasks, because you can see how the changes affect the display of the data.

3 In the **Group, Sort, and Total** pane, on the **Group on Industry bar**, click **More**. To the right of **do not keep group together on one page**, click the **arrow**, and then compare your screen with Figure 12.47.

The *keep whole group together on one page* command keeps each industry group together, from the name in the group header through the summary in the group footer. Next to *Group on Industry, with A on top* indicates that the industry names display in ascending sort order. The default setting is *do not keep group together on one page.*

Figure 12.47

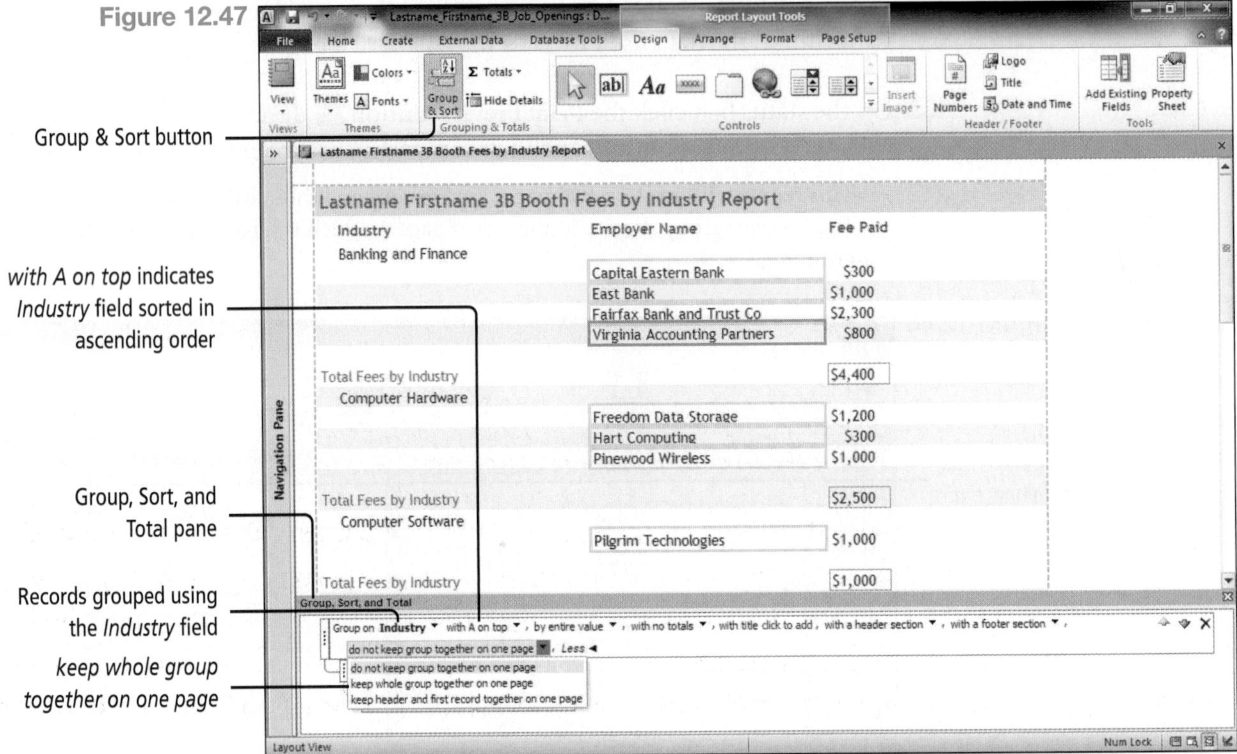

4 Click **keep whole group together on one page**. In the **Grouping & Totals group**, click the **Group & Sort** button to close the **Group, Sort, and Total** pane. On the status bar, click the **Print Preview** button. If necessary, in the Zoom group, click the Two Pages button. Compare your screen with Figure 12.48.

All the records in the *Hotel and Food Service* industry group—the group header, the three records, and the summary information—display together at the top of page 2.

Figure 12.48

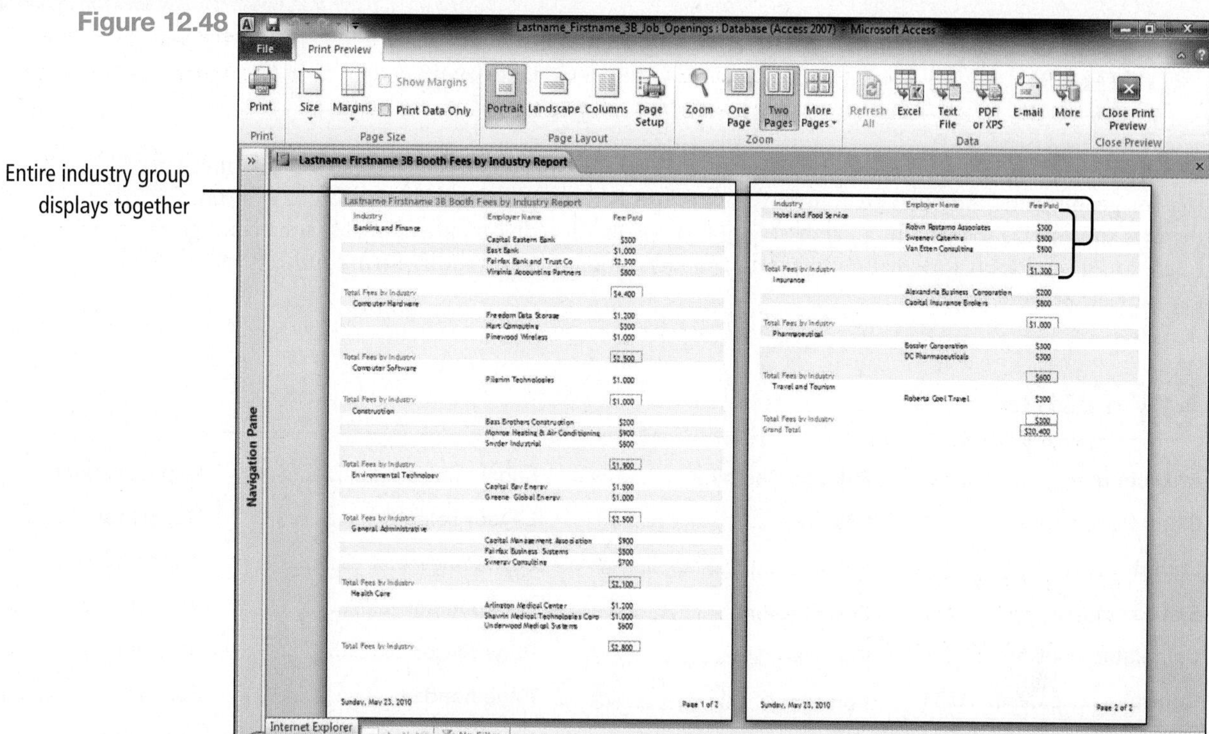

5 **Save** the report. Create a paper or electronic copy of the report as directed.

6 **Close Print Preview**, and then **Close** the report. **Open** the **Navigation Pane**, and, if necessary, increase the width of the pane so that all object names display fully.

7 Display **Backstage** view, click **Close Database**, and then click **Exit**. As directed by your instructor, submit your database and the three paper or electronic printouts that are the results of this project.

End **You have completed Project 12B**

Content-Based Assessments

Summary

A form is an object for either entering or viewing information in a database—it creates a user interface for people using the database. A form is easy to use, because it can display one record at a time. Reports summarize the data in a database in a professional-looking manner suitable for printing. There are several tools for creating forms and reports, and you can modify forms and reports in Layout view or Design view.

Key Terms

- **AND condition**.................682
- **Blank Report tool**..........688
- **Bound**..........................666
- **Bound control**................671
- **Calculated control**........696
- **Control**..........................671
- **Control layout**................675
- **Data entry**......................663
- **Date control**..................698
- **Design view**....................673
- **Detail section**................673
- **Filter by Form**................681
- **Filter by Selection**..........679
- **Filtering**..........................679
- **Form**..............................663
- **Form footer**....................673
- **Form header**..................673
- **Form tool**........................663
- **Form view**......................670
- **Form Wizard**..................669
- **Group footer**..................697
- **Group header**................697
- **Group, Sort, and Total pane**..................699
- **Label control**..................671
- **Layout selector**..............672
- **Layout view**....................664
- **OR condition**..................682
- **Page footer**....................697
- **Page header**..................697
- **Page number control**....698
- **Property Sheet**..............677
- **Record selector bar**......666
- **Record source**..............685
- **Report**..........................685
- **Report footer**................697
- **Report header**................697
- **Report tool**....................685
- **Report Wizard**................691
- **Section bar**....................673
- **Stacked layout**..............672
- **Subset**..........................679
- **Tab order**......................666
- **Text box control**............671
- **Theme**..........................672
- **Unbound control**............671

Matching

Match each term in the second column with its correct definition in the first column by writing the letter of the term on the blank line in front of the correct definition.

____ 1. The Access view in which you can make changes to a form or report while viewing the data.

____ 2. The term used to describe objects and controls that are based on data that is stored in tables.

____ 3. An Access view that displays the detailed structure of a query, form, or report.

____ 4. Information, such as a form's title, that displays at the top of the screen in Form view and is printed at the top of the first page when records are printed as forms.

____ 5. The section of a form or report that displays the records from the underlying table or query.

____ 6. Information at the bottom of the screen in Form view that prints after the last detail section on the last page.

____ 7. A gray bar in a form or report that identifies and separates one section from another.

____ 8. An object on a form or report that displays data, performs actions, and lets you work with information.

____ 9. The graphical object on a form or report that displays the data from the underlying table or query.

A Bound
B Bound control
C Calculated control
D Control
E Control layout
F Date control
G Design view
H Detail section
I Form footer
J Form header
K Label control
L Layout view
M Section bar
N Text box control
O Unbound control

_____ 10. A control that retrieves its data from an underlying table or query.

_____ 11. A control on a form or report that contains descriptive information, typically a field name.

_____ 12. A control that does not have a source of data, such as a title in a form or report.

_____ 13. The grouped arrangement of controls on a form or report.

_____ 14. A control that contains an expression, often a formula, that uses one or more fields from the underlying table or query.

_____ 15. A control on a form or report that inserts the current date each time the form or report is opened.

Multiple Choice

Circle the correct answer.

1. An Access object to enter new records into a table, edit or delete existing records in a table, or display existing records is a:
   A. bound control   **B.** form   **C.** report

2. The order that the insertion point moves from one field to another in a form when you press Tab is the:
   A. data entry order   **B.** control order   **C.** tab order

3. A small symbol that displays in the upper left corner of a selected control layout in a form or report that is displayed in Layout view and that is used to move an entire group of controls is the:
   A. control layout   **B.** label control   **C.** layout selector

4. A list of characteristics for controls on a form or report in which you can make precise changes to each property associated with the control is the:
   A. bound control   **B.** control layout   **C.** Property Sheet

5. The process of displaying only a portion of the total records (a subset) based on matching a specific value is:
   A. filtering   **B.** reporting   **C.** zooming

6. An Access command that filters the records in a form based on one or more fields, or based on more than one value in the field is Filter by:
   A. Form   **B.** Selection   **C.** Subset

7. A condition in which records that match at least one of the specified values are displayed is:
   A. AND   **B.** BOTH   **C.** OR

8. A database object that summarizes the fields and records from a table or query in an easy-to-read format suitable for printing is a:
   A. control   **B.** form   **C.** report

9. Information printed at the end of each group of records and that is used to display summary information for the group is called a:
   A. group footer   **B.** group header   **C.** Group, Sort, and Total pane

10. A predefined format that can be applied to the entire database or to individual objects in the database is called a:
    A. group header   **B.** subset   **C.** theme

Content-Based Assessments

Apply **12A** skills from these Objectives:

1. Create and Use a Form to Add and Delete Records
2. Create a Form by Using the Form Wizard
3. Modify a Form in Layout View and in Design View
4. Filter Records

Skills Review | Project 12C Student Advising

In the following Skills Review, you will assist Gerald Finn, the Dean of Information Technology, in using an Access database to track students and their faculty advisors. Your completed forms will look similar to Figure 12.49.

Project Files

For Project 12C, you will need the following file:

a03C_Student_Advising

You will save your database as:

Lastname_Firstname_3C_Student_Advising

Project Results

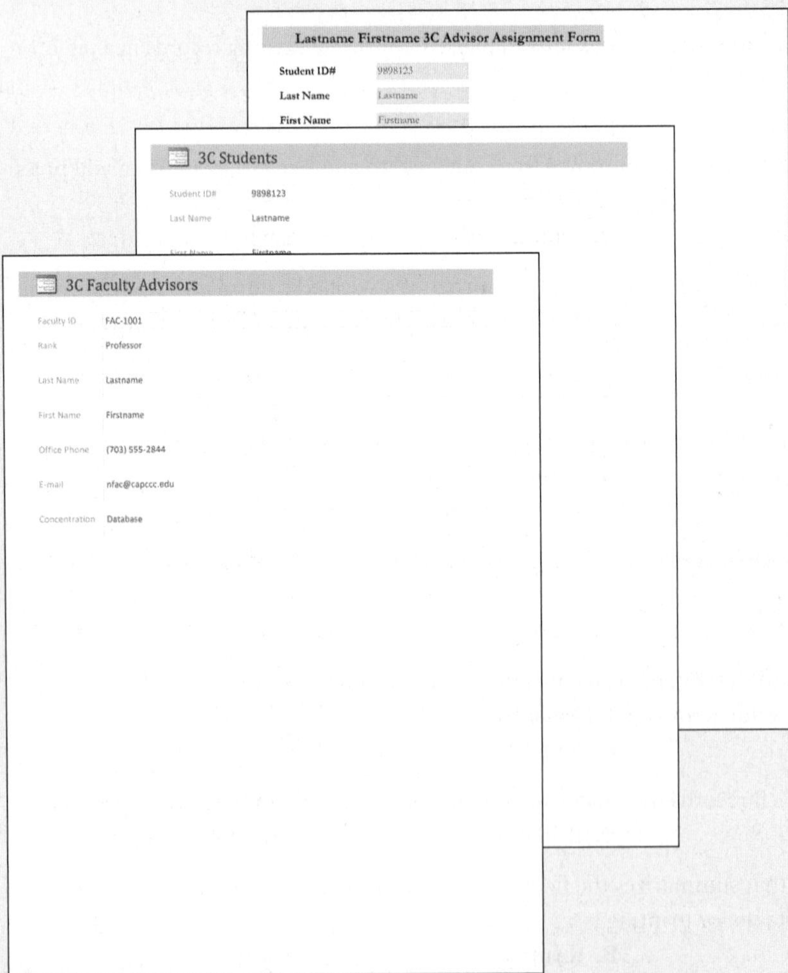

Figure 12.49

(Project 12C Student Advising continues on the next page)

Skills Review | Project 12C Student Advising (continued)

1 **Start** Access. In **Backstage** view, click **Open**, and then from your student files open the **a03C_Student_Advising** database. In **Backstage** view, click **Save Database As.** Save the database in your **Access Chapter 12** folder as **Lastname_Firstname_3C_Student_Advising** On the **Message Bar**, click the **Enable Content** button.

a. On the **Database Tools tab**, in the **Relationships group**, click the **Relationships** button. Notice the one-to-many relationship between the 3C Faculty Advisors table and the 3C Students table using the Faculty ID and Faculty Advisor ID fields as the common fields. *One* faculty member can advise *many* students. Recall that common fields do not need to have the same name; they must have the same data type. **Close** the **Relationships** window.

b. In the **Navigation Pane**, select the **3C Students** table. Click the **Create tab**, and then in the **Forms group**, click the **Form** button. **Save** the form as **Lastname Firstname 3C Student Form** and then **Close** the form object.

c. In the **Navigation Pane**, select the **3C Faculty Advisors** table. Click the **Create tab**, and then in the **Forms group**, click the **Form** button. **Close** the **Navigation Pane**, and then notice that *Faculty ID FAC-2877*, for *Professor Treiman*, has been assigned one student for advising.

d. **Close** the form, saving it as **Lastname Firstname 3C Faculty Advisor Form**

2 **Open** the **Navigation Pane**, and increase the width to display fully the object names. Open your **3C Student Form** object, and then **Close** the **Navigation Pane**. In the navigation area, click the **New (blank) record** button. In the **Student ID#** field, type **9898123** and then press Tab.

a. Using your own name, continue entering the data as shown in **Table 1**.

b. In the last field, press Tab to save the record and display a new blank record. **Close** the **3C Student Form** object, and then **Open** the **Navigation Pane.**

c. **Open** your **3C Faculty Advisor Form** object, and then **Close** the **Navigation Pane**. Notice that in the first record, your record displays in the subdatasheet for Professor Treiman. At the bottom of your screen, in the navigation area for the form—not the navigation area for the related records in the form itself—click the **New (blank) record** button. In the blank form, using your own name, enter the information in **Table 2**, being sure to press Tab after entering the data in the last field.

d. In the navigation area, click the **First record** button. Click in the **Last Name** field, and then on the **Home tab**, in the **Find group**, click the **Find** button to open the **Find and Replace** dialog box. In the **Find What** box, type **Holland** and then click **Find Next**. **Close** the **Find and Replace** dialog box.

e. On the **Home tab**, in the **Records group**, click the **Delete button arrow**, and then click **Delete Record** to delete the record for Professor Holland—because Professor Holland has no student advisees assigned, he can be deleted from the table. In the message box, click **Yes** to delete the record. In the navigation area for the form, notice that the number of records in the table is *18*.

f. Use the **Find** button to display the form for the **Faculty ID** of **FAC-1001** Display **Backstage** view. Click the **Print tab**, and then in the right panel, click **Print**. In the **Print** dialog box, under **Print Range**, click the **Selected Record(s)** option button, and then click **Setup**. In the **Page Setup** dialog box, click the **Columns tab**. Under **Column Size**, in the **Width** box, delete the existing text, type **7.5** and then click **OK** two times to print only your record in the form layout, or create an electronic printout. **Close** the **3C Faculty Advisor Form** object, and then **Open** the **Navigation Pane**.

Table 1

Student ID#	Last Name	First Name	Phone Number	E-mail	Concentration	Faculty Advisor ID
9898123	**Lastname**	**Firstname**	**(703) 555-1257**	**ns0001@capccc.edu**	**Network Security**	**FAC-2877**

(Return to Step 2-b)

Table 2

Faculty ID	Rank	Last Name	First Name	Office Phone	E-mail	Concentration
FAC-1001	**Professor**	**Lastname**	**Firstname**	**(703) 555-2844**	**nfac@capccc.edu**	**Database**

(Return to Step 2-d)

(Project 12C Student Advising continues on the next page)

Skills Review | Project 12C Student Advising (continued)

g. Open your **3C Student Form** object, and then **Close** the **Navigation Pane**. Click in the **Last Name** field. Press Ctrl + F to display the **Find and Replace** dialog box. Enter the information to find the record where the **Last Name** field contains your **Lastname** and then **Print** only the selected record, changing the **Column Size Width** to **7.5** or create an electronic printout. **Close** the **3C Student Form** object, and then **Open** the **Navigation Pane**.

3 In the **Navigation Pane**, click to select the **3C Students** table. On the **Create tab**, in the **Forms group** click the **Form Wizard** button.

a. Under **Tables/Queries**, be sure that **Table: 3C Students** displays. Using the **One Field** button or by double-clicking, move the following fields to the **Selected Fields** list in the order specified: **First Name**, **Last Name**, and **Faculty Advisor ID**.

b. Click **Next**. Be sure **Columnar** is selected as the layout, and then click **Next**. In the box **What title do you want for your form?**, select the existing text, and then type **Lastname Firstname 3C Advisor Assignment Form** and then click **Finish** to close the wizard and create the form.

4 **Close** the **Navigation Pane**. Be sure your **3C Advisor Assignment Form** displays. In the lower right corner of your screen, click the **Layout View** button. Click the **First Name label control**. Hold down Shift, and then click the **Last Name label control**, the **Faculty Advisor ID label control**, and the **three text box controls** to select all of the controls. On the Ribbon, click the **Arrange tab**. In the **Table group**, click the **Stacked** button to group the controls. Click the **First Name label control** to deselect all of the controls and to surround the label control with a colored border.

a. On the **Design tab**, in the **Themes group**, click the **Themes** button. Right-click the **Couture** theme, and then click **Apply Theme to This Object Only**.

b. Click anywhere in the title *3C Advisor Assignment Form* to select it. On the **Format tab**, in the **Font group**, click the **Font Size button arrow**, and then click **16**. Click the **Bold** button. Click the **Font Color button arrow**, and then under **Theme Colors**, in the last column, click the last color—**Brown, Accent 6, Darker 50%**.

c. On the status bar, click the **Design View** button. Point to the *lower* edge of the **Form Footer section bar** to display the ‡ pointer, and then drag downward approximately **0.5 inch**. On the **Design tab**, in the **Controls group**, click the **Label** button. Position the plus sign of the +A pointer in the **Form Footer** section at **0.25 inch on the horizontal ruler** and even with the lower edge of the Form Footer section bar. Click one time.

d. Using your own name, type **Created by Lastname Firstname** and then press Enter. Click the **Format tab**. With the label control selected, in the **Font group**, click the **Bold** button, and then change the **Font Color** to **Brown, Text 2**—in the fourth column, the first color. Point to a sizing handle to display one of the resize pointers, and then double-click to fit the control to the text you typed.

5 **Save** the form, and then switch to **Layout** view. On the **Design tab**, in the **Tools group**, click the **Add Existing Fields** button. In the **Field List** pane, point to **Student ID#**, and then drag to the left until the I pointer is above the *First Name* label control and a thick colored line displays above the control. Release the mouse button to add the Student ID# controls to the form.

a. **Close** the **Field List** pane. Click the **Last Name text box control**, which currently displays *Barthmaier*, to surround it with a border. Point to the right edge of the **text box control** until the ↔ pointer displays, and then drag to the left until there is approximately **1"** of space between *Barthmaier* and the right edge of the text box control.

b. On the **Arrange tab**, in the **Rows & Columns** group, click the **Select Row** button. In the **Move group**, click the **Move Up** button one time to move the **Last Name controls** above the **First Name controls**. **Save** the form.

6 Click the **Student ID# text box control**, which displays *1034823*. In the **Rows & Columns group**, click the **Select Column** button to select all four text box controls. On the **Format tab**, in the **Font group**, click the **Background Color button arrow**. Under **Theme Colors**, in the fifth column, click the second color—**Brown, Accent 1, Lighter 80%**.

a. Click the **Student ID# label control**. On the **Arrange tab**, in the **Rows & Columns group**, click the **Select Column** button to select all four label controls. Click the **Format tab**, change the **Font Color**—*not* the Background Color—to **Brown, Text 2**—in the fourth column, the first color. Then apply **Bold**.

(Project 12C Student Advising continues on the next page)

Skills Review | Project 12C Student Advising (continued)

b. Click the **layout selector** [⊞] to select all of the controls. Change the **Font Size** to **12**. On the Ribbon, click the **Design tab**, and then in the **Tools group**, click the **Property Sheet** button. In the **Property Sheet**, click the word **Height**, type **0.25** and then press Enter to adjust the height of all of the controls.

c. Click the **Student ID# label control** to select only that label. Click the **Arrange tab**, and then in the **Rows & Columns group**, click the **Select Column** button. In the **Property Sheet**, click **Width**, type **1.5** and then press Enter.

d. In the **Form Footer section**, click the label control with your name. Hold down Shift, and then in the **Form Header section**, in the **label control** that displays *3C Advisor Assignment Form*, click to select both controls. In the **Property Sheet**, change the **Left** property to **0.5** and then press Enter. **Save** the form.

e. Close the **Property Sheet**, and then switch to **Form** view. In the navigation area, click the **Last record** button to display the record containing your name. Display **Backstage** view, click the **Print tab**, and then click **Print**. In the **Print** dialog box, under **Print Range**, click the **Selected Record(s)** option button. Create a paper or electronic printout as directed, and then **Close Print Preview**.

7 With the form displayed in **Form** view, click the **First record** button, click the **Faculty Advisor ID label control** to select the text in the text box control. On the **Home tab**, in the **Find group**, click the **Find** button. In the **Find and Replace** dialog box, in the **Find What** box, type **FAC-9119** and then click **Find Next** to find and display the record for *Amanda Bass*. **Close** the **Find and Replace** dialog box. In the **Sort & Filter group**, click the **Selection** button, and then click **Equals "FAC-9119"**. In the navigation area, notice that two students have been assigned to the faculty member with the *FAC-9119* advisor number.

a. In the **Sort & Filter group**, click the **Toggle Filter** button to remove the filter and display all 27 records. **Close** the form, and save changes.

b. Open the **Navigation Pane**, open your **3C Student Form** object, and then **Close** the **Navigation Pane**. On the **Home tab**, in the **Sort & Filter group**, click the **Advanced** button, and then click **Filter By Form**. Click in the **Concentration text box control**. At the right edge of the text box control, click the **arrow** that displays. In the list, click Programming. In the **Sort & Filter group**, click the **Toggle Filter** button, and notice that two students have a *Concentration* of *Programming*.

c. In the **Sort & Filter group**, click the **Advanced** button, and then click **Filter By Form**. At the bottom left side of the window, click the **Or tab**. Click the **Concentration text box control arrow**, and then click **Networking**. In the **Sort & Filter group**, click the **Toggle Filter** button. Seven students have a Concentration of *Programming* or *Networking*. In the **Sort & Filter group**, click the **Toggle Filter** button to display all of the records. **Save** and then **Close** the form.

d. Open the **Navigation Pane**; be sure all object names display fully. Display **Backstage** view, click **Close Database**, and then click **Exit**. As directed by your instructor, submit your database and the three paper or electronic printouts that are the results of this project.

End You have completed Project 12C

Apply 12B skills from these Objectives:

5 Create a Report by Using the Report Tool
6 Create Reports by Using the Blank Report Tool and the Report Wizard
7 Modify the Design of a Report
8 Print a Report and Keep Data Together

Skills Review | Project 12D Workshop Rooms

In the following Skills Review, you will assist Michelina Cortez, the Director of Workforce Development, in using an Access database to track the details about workshops offered by community members for the public and for students at the Washington Campus of Capital Cities Community College. Your completed reports will look similar to Figure 12.50.

Project Files

For Project 12D, you will need the following file:

a03D_Workshop_Rooms

You will save your database as:

Lastname_Firstname_3D_Workshop_Rooms

Project Results

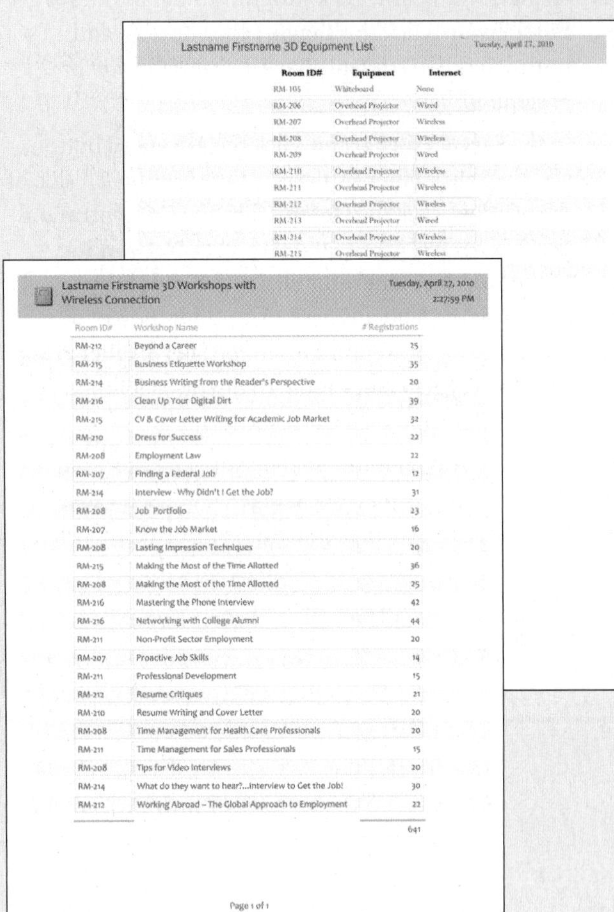

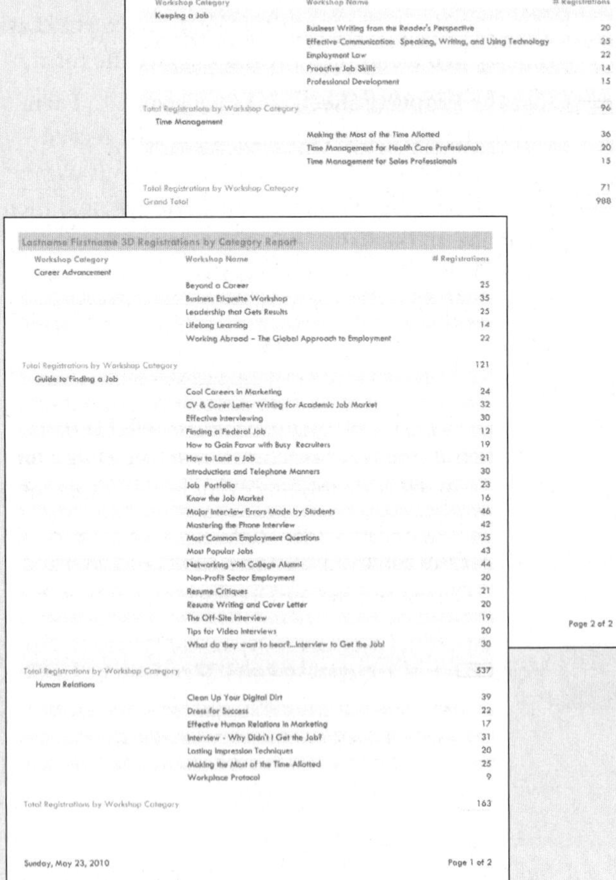

Figure 12.50

(Project 12D Workshop Rooms continues on the next page)

Skills Review | Project 12D Workshop Rooms (continued)

1 **Start** Access. In **Backstage** view, click **Open**. From your student files, open the **a03D_Workshop_Rooms** database. In **Backstage** view, save the database in your **Access Chapter 12** folder as **Lastname_Firstname_3D_Workshop_Rooms** and then in the **Message Bar**, click the **Enable Content** button. On the Ribbon, click the **Database Tools tab**, and then click the **Relationships** button. If your relationships do not display, in the Relationships group, click the All Relationships button. *One* room is associated with *many* workshops. Thus, a one-to-many relationship has been established between the 3D Rooms table and the 3D Workshops table using Room ID# as the common field. **Close** the **Relationships** window.

a. Open the two tables to examine the data, and then open the query in **Design** view to examine the design grid. This query answers the question *What is the Room ID#, Workshop Name, Workshop Category, and # Registrations for workshops that have wireless Internet connections available?* **Close** all open objects. In the **Navigation Pane**, select the **3D Workshops with Wireless Connection** query. Click the **Create tab**, and then in the **Reports group**, click the **Report** button. **Close** the **Navigation Pane**.

b. On the **Design tab**, in the **Themes group**, click the **Themes** button, right-click the **Waveform** theme, and then click **Apply Theme to This Object Only**.

c. Click the **Workshop Category** field name. Click the **Arrange tab**, and then in the **Rows & Columns group**, click the **Select Column** button. Press Del to remove the field from the report.

d. Click the **Room ID#** field name, and then drag the right edge of the control to the left until there is approximately **0.5** inch of space between the room number and the right edge of the field. Scroll down the report, and then in the **Workshop Name** field—second column—click in the **text box control** that displays *What do they want to hear?... Interview to Get the Job!* Drag the right edge of the control to the right until the data in the control displays on one line. With the **Workshop Name** field selected, click the **Home tab**. In the **Sort & Filter group**, click the **Ascending** button.

e. Scroll down to the bottom of the report, and notice that Access counted the number of records in the report—*26* displays under the Room ID# field. Click this **calculated control**, and then press Del. At the top of the report, click the **# Registrations** field name. On the **Design tab**, in the **Grouping & Totals group**, click the **Totals** button, and then click **Sum**. Scroll down to the bottom of the report, and then click the calculated control. Point to the bottom edge of the control to display the ↕ pointer, and then double-click to resize the control. The total number of registrations for the workshops that have a wireless connection is *641*.

f. Click the **Page number control**, and then drag the control to the left until the control is visually centered between the left and right margins of the report. At the top of the report, in the **Report Header** section, click the text *3D Workshops with Wireless Connection*. On the **Format tab**, in the **Font group**, change the **Font Size** to **14**, and then click the **label control** again to position the insertion point in the title. Using your own name, add **Lastname Firstname** to the beginning of the title. Click any field in the report. Above and to the left of the **Room ID#** field name, click the **layout selector** ⊞, and then drag it down slightly and to the right until the fields are visually centered between the margins of the report. **Save** the report as **Lastname Firstname 3D Workshops with Wireless Connection Report**

g. On the status bar, click the **Print Preview** button. On the **Print Preview tab**, in the **Zoom group**, click the **Two Pages** button, and notice that the report will print on one page. Create a paper or electronic printout as directed, and then **Close Print Preview**.

h. **Close** the report, and then **Open** the **Navigation Pane**. If necessary, increase the width of the **Navigation Pane** to display the entire report name, and then **Close** the **Navigation Pane**.

2 Click the **Create tab**, and then in the **Reports group**, click the **Blank Report** button. If the Field List pane does not display, on the Design tab, in the Tools group, click the Add Existing Fields button. In the **Field List** pane, click **Show all tables**, and then click the **plus sign** (+) next to **3D Rooms**. Point to the **Room ID#** field, right-click, and then click **Add Field to View**. From the **Field List** pane, drag the **Equipment** field into the blank report—anywhere to the right of *Room ID#*. Double-click the **Internet** field to add it as the third field in the report, and then **Close** the **Field List** pane.

a. On the **Design tab**, in the **Themes group**, click the **Themes** button, and then right-click the **Equity** theme. Click **Apply Theme to This Object Only**.

(Project 12D Workshop Rooms continues on the next page)

Skills Review | Project 12D Workshop Rooms (continued)

Under the **Equipment** field name, click in any **text box control** that displays *Overhead Projector*. Point to the right edge of the control to display the ↔ pointer, and then drag to the right until the text in the control displays on one line and there is a small amount of space between the text and the next column.

b. On the **Design tab**, in the **Header/Footer group**, click the **Date and Time** button. Clear the **Include Time** check box, and then click **OK**. In the **Header/Footer group**, click the **Title** button. Using your own name, type **Lastname Firstname 3D Equipment List** and then press Enter.

c. With the title still selected, on the **Format tab**, in the **Font group**, change the **Font Size** to **14**. On the right edge of the **label control** for the title, double-click to resize the title's label control.

d. Click the **Room ID#** field name to select it. Hold down Shift, and then click the **Internet** field name to select all three field names. On the **Format tab**, in the **Font group**, click the **Center** button to center the field names over the data in the fields. Change the **Font Color** to **Automatic**, and then apply **Bold**. Click the **layout selector** ⊞, and then drag it down slightly and to the right to visually center the fields between the margins. **Save** the report as **Lastname Firstname 3D Equipment List**

e. On the status bar, click the **Print Preview** button. Create a paper or electronic printout as directed, and then **Close Print Preview**. **Close** the report.

3 Click the **Create tab**, and then in the **Reports group**, click the **Report Wizard** button. Click the **Tables/Queries arrow**, and then click **Table: 3D Workshops**. Double-click the following fields in the order given to move them to the **Selected Fields** list: **Workshop Category**, **Workshop Name**, and **# Registrations**. Click **Next**.

a. With **Workshop Category** selected, click the **One Field** button to group the report by this field, and then click **Next**. Click the **1** box **arrow**, and then click **Workshop Name** to sort the records within each Workshop Category by the Workshop Name. Click the **Summary Options** button. To the right of **# Registrations**, select the **Sum** check box. Under **Show**, be sure that the **Detail and Summary** option button is selected, click **OK**, and then click **Next**.

b. Under **Layout**, be sure that the **Stepped** option button is selected. Under **Orientation**, be sure that **Portrait** is selected, and at the bottom of the **Report Wizard** dialog box, be sure that the **Adjust the field width so all fields fit on a page** check box is selected. Click **Next**, In the **What title do you want for your report?** box, select the existing text, type **Lastname Firstname 3D Registrations by Category Report** and then click **Finish**. **Close Print Preview**, and then on the status bar, click the **Layout View** button.

4 On the **Design tab**, in the **Themes group**, click the **Themes** button, right-click the **Median** theme, and then click **Apply Theme to This Object Only**. Click the title of the report. On the **Format tab**, in the **Font group**, change the **Font Size** to **14**, and then apply **Bold**. Click one of the **Summary for 'Workshop Category' controls**, and then press Del.

a. On the left side of the report, click one of the **Sum label controls**, and then double-click to select the text inside the control. Type **Total Registrations by Workshop Category** and then press Enter.

b. At the top of your report, click the **Workshop Category label control**. Hold down Shift, click the **Workshop Name label control**, and then click the **# Registrations label control** to select all three field names. On the **Format tab**, in the **Font group**, click the **Bold** button.

c. On the status bar, click the **Design View** button. In the **Report Footer section**, click the **Grand Total label control**. Hold down Shift, and in the **Workshop Category Footer section**, click the **Total Registrations by Workshop Category label control** to select both controls. On the **Arrange tab**, in the **Sizing & Ordering group**, click the **Align** button, and then click **Left** to align the left edges of the two controls.

5 On the status bar, click the **Print Preview** button. In the **Zoom group**, click the **Two Pages** button to view how your report is currently laid out. Notice that at the bottom of Page 1 and the top of Page 2, the records in the **Keeping a Job** category are split between the two pages. Click **Close Print Preview**. On the status bar, click the **Layout View** button.

(Project 12D Workshop Rooms continues on the next page)

Skills Review | Project 12D Workshop Rooms (continued)

a. On the **Design tab**, in the **Grouping & Totals group**, click the **Group & Sort** button. In the **Group, Sort, and Total** pane, on the **Group on Workshop Category bar**, click **More**. Click the **do not keep group together on one page arrow**, and then click **keep whole group together on one page**. On the **Design tab**, in the **Grouping & Totals group**, click the **Group & Sort** button to close the **Group, Sort, and Total** pane. **Save** the report.

b. On the status bar, click the **Print Preview** button. Notice that the entire **Workshop Category** grouping of **Keeping a Job** displays together at the top of Page 2. Create a paper or electronic printout as directed, and then **Close Print Preview**. **Save**, and then **Close** the report. **Open** the **Navigation Pane**, and if necessary, increase the width of the Navigation Pane so that all object names display fully. In **Backstage** view, click **Close Database**, and then click **Exit**. As directed by your instructor, submit your database and the three paper or electronic printouts that are the results of this project.

End **You have completed Project 12D**

Apply 12A skills from these Objectives:

1 Create and Use a Form to Add and Delete Records
2 Create a Form by Using the Form Wizard
3 Modify a Form in Layout View and in Design View
4 Filter Records

Mastering Access | Project 12E Raffle Sponsors

In the following Mastering Access project, you will assist Alina Ngo, Dean of Student Services at the Central Campus of Capital Cities Community College, in using her database to track raffle items and sponsors for the New Student Orientation sessions. Your completed forms will look similar to Figure 12.51.

Project Files

For Project 12E, you will need the following file:

a03E_Raffle_Sponsors

You will save your database as:

Lastname_Firstname_3E_Raffle_Sponsors

Project Results

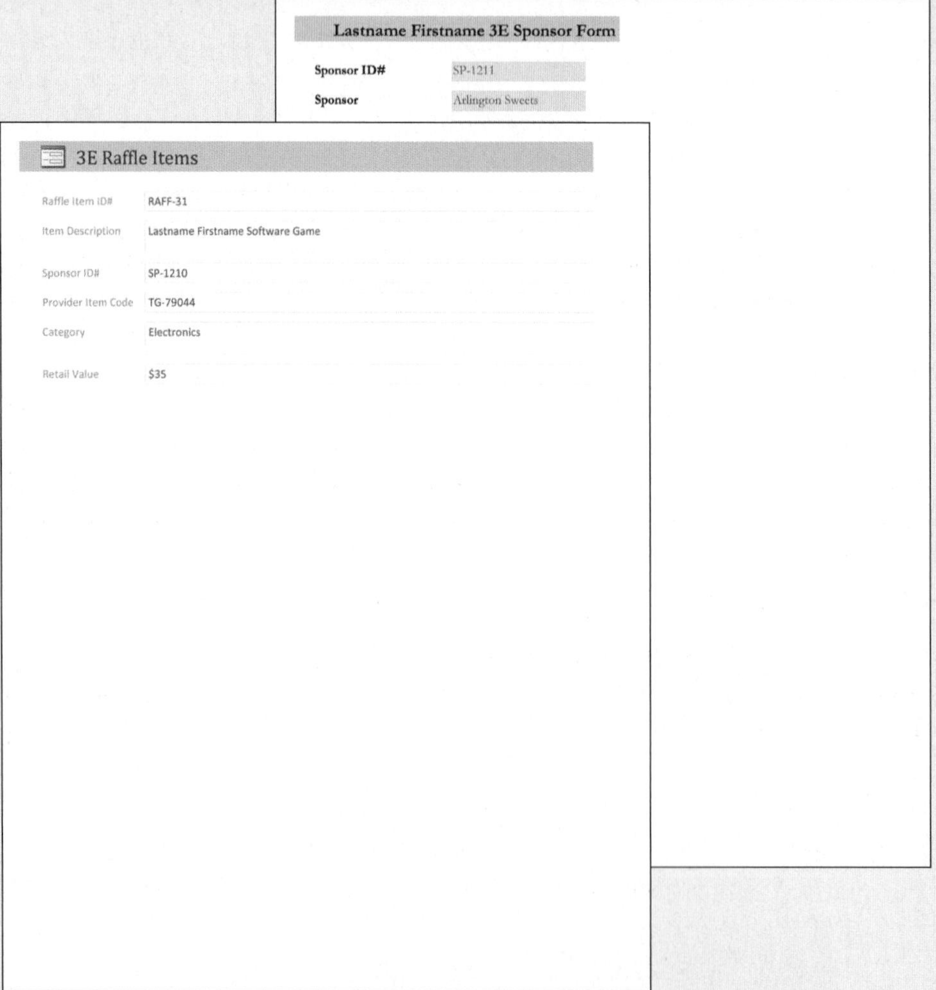

Figure 12.51

(Project 12E Raffle Sponsors continues on the next page)

Content-Based Assessments

Mastering Access | Project 12E Raffle Sponsors (continued)

1 **Start** Access. From your student data files, **Open** the **a03E_Raffle_Sponsors** database. Save the database in your **Access Chapter 12** folder as **Lastname_Firstname_3E_Raffle_Sponsors** and then enable the content. View the relationship between the 3E Sponsors table and the 3E Raffle Items table. *One* sponsor can provide *many* raffle items for the New Student Orientation sessions.

2 Based on the **3E Raffle Items** table, use the **Form** tool to create a form. **Save** the form as **Lastname Firstname 3E Raffle Item Form** and then switch to **Form** view. Add the new record as shown in **Table 1**, using your own name in the **Item Description** field.

3 Display the first record, and, if necessary, click in the Raffle Item ID# field. Use the **Find** button to display the record for the **Raffle Item ID#** of **RAFF-06**, and then **Delete** the record. Display the record you entered for **RAFF-31**, and then **Print** the **Selected Record**, changing the column width to **7.5"** or create an electronic printout. **Close** the form, saving changes if prompted.

4 Based on the **3E Sponsors** table, use the **Form Wizard** tool to create a form. Include the following fields in the order given: **Sponsor**, **Contact Last Name**, **Contact First Name**, and **Phone Number**. Use a **Columnar** layout, and as the title type **Lastname Firstname 3E Sponsor Form**

5 In **Layout** view, apply the **Stacked** layout to all of the controls, and then apply the **Couture** theme to this object only. For the title of the form, change the **Font Size** to **16**, apply **Bold**, and change the **Font Color** to **Brown**, **Accent 6**, **Darker 50%**. In **Design** view, increase the height of the **Form Footer** section to approximately **0.5 inch**. In the **Form Footer** section and using your own name, add a **label control** that displays **Created by Lastname Firstname** For the **label control**, change the **Font Color** to **Brown, Text 2**, apply **Bold**, and then adjust the control to fit the text in the control.

6 **Save** the form, and then switch to **Layout** view. Display the **Field List** pane, and then add the **Sponsor ID#** field to the form above the **Sponsor** field. **Close** the **Field List** pane, and then move the **Contact First Name** controls directly above the **Contact Last Name** controls. Display **Record 5**—this record's Sponsor name is the longest entry of all records. Decrease the width of the **Sponsor text box control** until there is approximately **1 inch** between *Inc* and the right edge of the control. **Save** the form.

7 Select all five **text box controls**, set the **Background Color** to **Brown, Accent 1, Lighter 80%**. Select all of the **label controls**, set the **Font Color** to **Brown, Text 2**, and then apply **Bold**. With the controls selected, display the **Property Sheet**. For the **label controls**, set the **Width** to **1.75** Select all of the **label controls** and **text box controls**, set the **Font Size** to **12**, and the **Height** property to **0.25** In the **Form Header** and **Form Footer** sections, select the **label controls** with the title and your name. Set the **Left** property to **0.5**

8 **Close** the **Property Sheet**, **Save** the form, and then switch to **Form** view. Using your first name and last name, add the record as shown in **Table 2**, being sure to use the Tab key to move among fields and to save the record.

9 Display the record you just added and then **Print** the **Selected Record**, or create an electronic printout as directed. **Close** the form.

10 Open your **3E Raffle Item Form** object. Using the **Advanced Filter/Sort** tool, create a filter that displays eight records with a **Category** of **Clothing** or **Dining** After verifying that eight records display, use the **Toggle Filter** button to display all 30 records. **Save** the form.

11 **Close** all open objects. **Open** the **Navigation Pane**, and, if necessary, increase the width of the **Navigation Pane** to display fully all of the object names. Display **Backstage** view. Click **Close Database**, and then click **Exit**. As directed by your instructor, submit your database and the two paper or electronic printouts that are the results of this project.

Table 1

Raffle Item ID#	Item Description	Sponsor ID#	Provider Item Code	Category	Retail Value
RAFF-31	**Lastname Firstname Software Game**	**SP-1210**	**TG-79044**	**Electronics**	**35**

(Return to Step 3)

Table 2

Sponsor ID#	Sponsor	Contact First Name	Contact Last Name	Phone Number
SP-1211	**Arlington Sweets**	**Firstname**	**Lastname**	**(703) 555-5355**

(Return to Step 9)

End **You have completed Project 12E**

Mastering Access | Project 12F Contractor Services

Apply 12B skills from these Objectives:

5 Create a Report by Using the Report Tool
6 Create Reports by Using the Blank Report Tool and the Report Wizard
7 Modify the Design of a Report
8 Print a Report and Keep Data Together

In the following Mastering Access project, you will assist Roger Lockheart, Director of Facilities at the Jefferson Campus of Capital Cities Community College, in using a database to track facility and contractor services for an open house for prospective college students. Your completed reports will look similar to Figure 12.52.

Project Files

For Project 12F, you will need the following file:

a03F_Contractor_Services

You will save your database as:

Lastname_Firstname_3F_Contractor_Services

Project Results

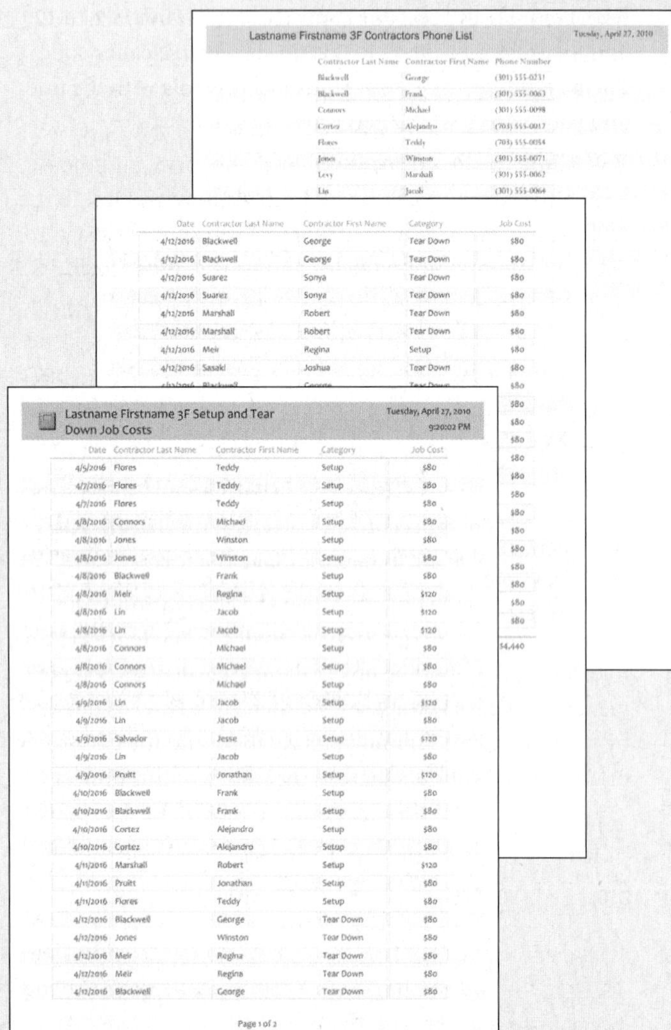

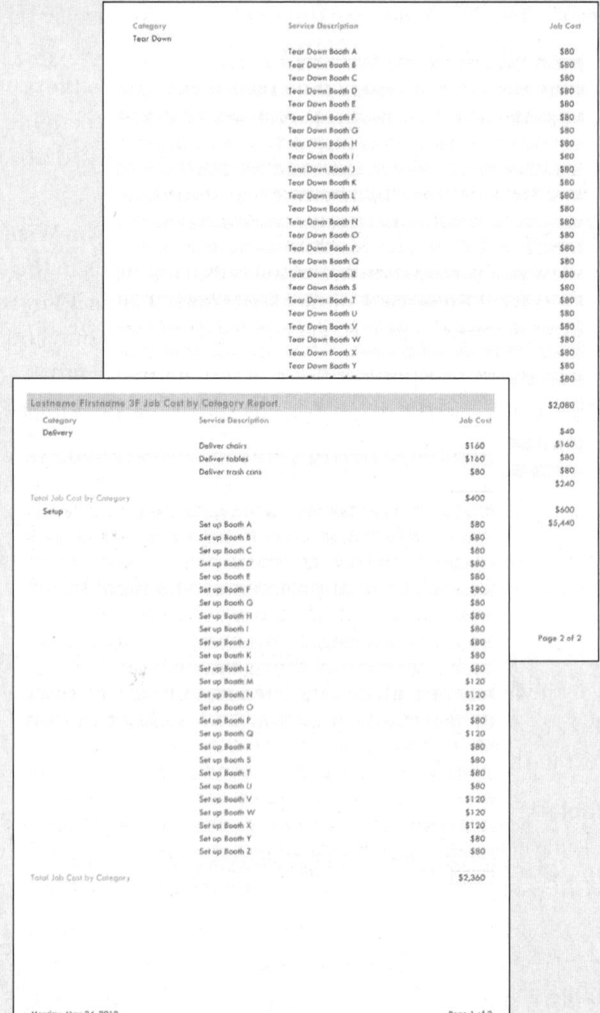

Figure 12.52

(Project 12F Contractor Services continues on the next page)

Content-Based Assessments

Mastering Access | Project 12F Contractor Services (continued)

1 **Start** Access. From your student files, **Open** the **a03F_Contractor_Services** database. Save the database in your **Access Chapter 12** folder as **Lastname_Firstname_3F_Contractor_Services** and then enable the content. View the relationship between the 3F Contractors table and the 3F Facility Services table. *One* contractor can provide *many* facility services. **Close** the **Relationships** window. Based on the **3F Setup and Tear Down Job Costs** query, use the **Report** tool to create a report, and then **Close** the **Navigation Pane**. This query answers the question *What is the Date, Job ID, Contractor ID, Contractor Last Name, Contractor First Name, Category, and Job Cost of setup and tear down jobs?*

2 Apply the **Waveform** theme to this object only. **Delete** the **Job ID** and **Contractor ID** fields from the report. Decrease the widths of the **Contractor Last Name**, **Contractor First Name**, and **Category** fields until there is approximately **0.25 to 0.5 inch** of space between the longest entry in each field—including the field name—and the right edge of each control. Be sure that there is enough space for *Tear Down* to display on one line. **Sort** the **Date** field in ascending order.

Scroll down to the bottom of the report, and increase the height of the **calculated control** that displays *$4,440*. Drag the **page number control** to the left to visually center it between the margins of the report. For the title, change the **Font Size** to **16**, and then using your last name and first name, add **Lastname Firstname** to the beginning of the title. Using the **layout selector** [⊞], visually center the fields between the left and right margins. **Save** the report as **Lastname Firstname 3F Setup and Tear Down Job Costs Report** and then create a paper or electronic printout as directed—two pages will print. **Close** the report. **Open** the **Navigation Pane**, and increase the width of the **Navigation Pane** to display the entire report name. **Close** the **Navigation Pane**.

3 Use the **Blank Report** tool to create a report based on the **3F Contractors** table. Add the fields to the report in the order given: **Contractor Last Name**, **Contractor First Name**, and **Phone Number**. **Close** the **Field List** pane. Apply the **Equity** theme to this object only. Increase the width of the **Contractor Last Name** field so that the field name displays fully. Add the **Date** to the Report Header section—do not include the time. Add a **Title** of **Lastname Firstname 3F Contractors Phone List** to the report, and change the **Font Size** to **14**. Decrease the width of the **title's label control** to fit the text and to move the date control to the left within the right margin. Apply **Bold** to the three field names. **Sort** the **Contractor Last Name** field in **Ascending** order. Using the **layout selector** [⊞], visually center the fields between the report margins. **Save** the report as **Lastname Firstname 3F Contractors Phone List** and then create a paper or electronic printout as directed. **Close Print Preview**, and then **Close** the report.

4 Use the **Report Wizard** to create a report based on the **3F Facility Services** table. Select the following fields in the order given: **Category**, **Service Description**, and **Job Cost**. **Group** the report by **Category**, **Sort** by **Service Description**, and **Sum** the **Job Cost** field. Select the **Stepped** layout and **Portrait** orientation. For the report title, type **Lastname Firstname 3F Job Cost by Category Report** and then switch to **Layout** view.

5 Apply the **Median** theme to this object only. For the title, change the **Font Size** to **14**, and apply **Bold**. **Delete** the **Summary for 'Category' controls**. Scroll down to the bottom of the report, and click the **text box control** that displays *Wireless network for laptop lane*. Decrease the width of the control until there is approximately **0.25 inch** of space between the end of the word *lane* and the right edge of the label control. At the bottom of the report, for the last record *Wireless network for laptop lane*, to the right, click the **text box control** that displays #—the number or pound sign displays because the text box control is not wide enough to display the entire value. Hold down [Shift], and immediately below the selected control, click the **Sum calculated control**, and then under that, click the **Grand Total calculated control**. Drag the left edge of the three selected controls to the left approximately **0.5 inch** to display the amounts fully. **Save** the report.

6 Change the text in the **Sum label control** to **Total Job Cost by Category** and then at the top of the report, select the three **field names**, and apply **Bold**. **Save** the report.

7 Switch to **Design** view. Click the **label control** that displays *Total Job Cost by Category*, and then align the left edge of the control with the left edge of the **label control** that displays *Grand Total*. **Save** the report.

8 Display the report in **Print Preview** in the **Two Pages** arrangement, examine how the groupings break across pages, **Close Print Preview**, and then switch to **Layout** view. Display the **Group, Sort, and Total** pane, and then select **keep whole group together on one page**. Close the

(Project 12F Contractor Services continues on the next page)

Mastering Access | Project 12F Contractor Services (continued)

Group, Sort, and Total pane. Display the report in **Print Preview** in the **Two Pages** arrangement, and then notice that the entire **Tear Down** grouping displays on Page 2. **Save** the report.

 Create a paper or electronic printout as directed, **Close Print Preview**, and then **Close** the report. **Open** the **Navigation Pane**, and then display **Backstage** view. Click **Close Database**, and then click **Exit**. As directed by your instructor, submit your database and the three paper or electronic printouts that are the results of this project.

End You have completed Project 12F

Apply **12A** and **12B** skills from these Objectives:

1. Create and Use a Form to Add and Delete Records
2. Create a Form by Using the Form Wizard
3. Modify a Form in Layout View and in Design View
4. Filter Records
5. Create a Report by Using the Report Tool
6. Create Reports by Using the Blank Report Tool and the Report Wizard
7. Modify the Design of a Report
8. Print a Report and Keep Data Together

Mastering Access | Project 12G Career Books

In the following Mastering Access project, you will assist Teresa Johnson, Head Librarian at the Capital Campus of Capital Cities Community College, in using a database to track publishers and book titles to assist students in finding employment. Your completed forms and reports will look similar to Figure 12.53.

Project Files

For Project 12G, you will need the following file:

a03G_Career_Books

You will save your database as:

Lastname_Firstname_3G_Career_Books

Project Results

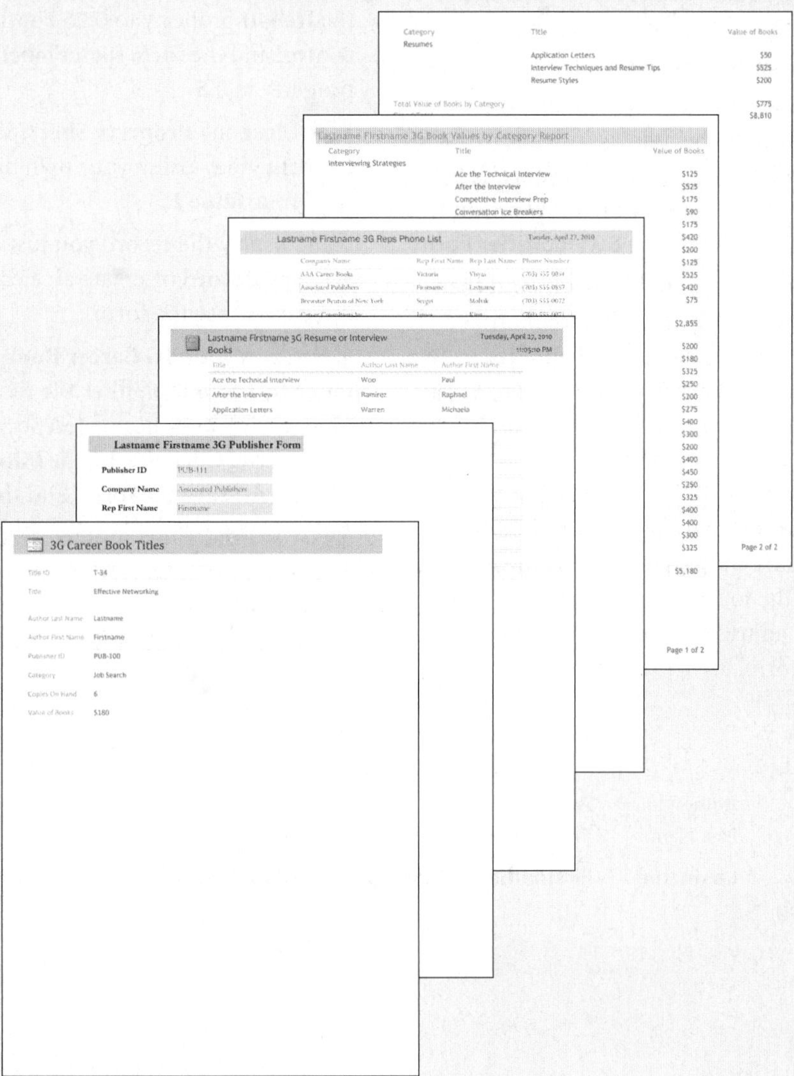

Figure 12.53

(Project 12G Career Books continues on the next page)

Mastering Access | Project 12G Career Books (continued)

1 **Start** Access. From your student files, open the **a03G_Career_Books** database. **Save** the database in your **Access Chapter 3** folder as **Lastname_Firstname_3G_Career_Books** and then enable the content. Review the relationship between the 3G Publishers table and the 3G Career Book Titles table. *One* publisher can publish *many* books.

2 Based on the **3G Career Book Titles** table, use the **Form** tool to create a form. Switch to **Form** view, and then using your own name, add the record as shown in **Table 1**.

3 **Save** the form as **Lastname Firstname 3G Career Book Form** and then display the first record. Use the **Find** button to display the record for the **Title ID** of **T-18**, and then **Delete** the record. Display the record you entered for **T-34**, and then **Print** the **Selected Record**, changing the column width to **7.5"** or create an electronic printout. **Close** the form, saving changes if prompted.

4 Use the **Form Wizard** to create a form based on the **3G Publishers** table. Include the following fields: **Company Name**, **Rep Last Name**, **Rep First Name**, **Job Title**, and **Phone Number**. Use a **Columnar** layout, and as the title, type **Lastname Firstname 3G Publisher Form**

5 In **Layout** view, select all of the controls, and then apply the **Stacked** layout. Apply the **Couture** theme to this object only. For the title, change the **Font Size** to **16**, apply **Bold**, and change the **Font Color** to **Brown, Accent 6, Darker 50%**—in the last column, the last color. In **Design** view, increase the height of the **Form Footer** section approximately **0.5 inch**. In the **Form Footer** section, add a **label control** that displays **Created by Lastname Firstname** and then change the **Font Color** to **Brown, Text 2**—in the fourth column, the first color. Apply **Bold**, and then adjust the control to fit the data in the control. **Save** the form.

6 In **Layout** view, display the **Field List** pane, and then add the **Publisher ID** field to the form above the **Company Name** field. **Close** the **Field List** pane. Move the **Rep First Name** field directly above the **Rep Last Name** field. Click the **Job Title text box control**, and then drag the right edge of the control to the left until there is approximately **1 inch** of space between *Representative* and the right edge of the control. **Save** the form.

7 Select all of the **text box controls**, set the **Background Color** to **Brown, Accent 1, Lighter 80%**—in the fifth column, the second color. Select all of the **label controls**. Set the **Font Color** to **Brown, Text 2**, apply **Bold**, and then set the **Width** property to **1.5** Select all of the **label controls** and **text box controls**, set the **Font Size** to **12**, and then set the **Height** property to **0.25** For the **form header label control** and the **form footer label control**, set the **Left** property to **0.5**

8 **Close** the **Property Sheet**, **Save** the form, and switch to **Form** view. Using your own name, add a new record as shown in **Table 2**.

9 Display the record you just added and then **Print** the **Selected Record** or create an electronic printout as directed. **Close** the form.

10 **Open** your **3G Career Book Form** object. Using the **Filter By Form** tool, filter the records to display the **Category** of **Resumes** or **Job Search**. Twenty books meet the criteria. Click the **Toggle Filter** button to display all 31 records. **Save** the form, and then **Close** the form.

11 Use the **Report** tool to create a report based on the **3G Resume or Interview Books** query. Apply the **Waveform** theme to this object only. **Delete** the **Publisher ID**, **Category**, and **Company Name** fields from the report.

Table 1

Title ID	Title	Author Last Name	Author First Name	Publisher ID	Category	Copies On Hand	Value of Books
T-34	Effective Networking	Lastname	Firstname	PUB-100	Job Search	6	180

(Return to Step 3)

Table 2

Publisher ID	Company Name	Rep First Name	Rep Last Name	Job Title	Phone Number
PUB-111	Associated Publishers	Firstname	Lastname	Sales Associate	(703) 555-0857

(Return to Step 9)

(Project 12G Career Books continues on the next page)

Mastering Access | Project 12G Career Books (continued)

Decrease the widths of the **Author Last Name** and **Author First Name** fields so that there is approximately **0.5 inch** between the word *Name* in the field name and the right edge of the label controls. Increase the width of the **Title** field until each title displays on one line. **Sort** the **Title** field in **Ascending** order.

Click the **Title** field name, and then on the **Design tab**, click the **Totals** button. Add a control that counts the number of records, and then increase the height of the control so that *14* displays fully in the calculated control. Drag the **page number control** to the left to visually center it between the report margins. For the title of the report, change the **Font Size** to **14**, and then using your own name, add **Lastname Firstname** to the beginning of the title. Using the **layout selector** [⊞], visually center the fields between the left and right margins. **Save** the report as **Lastname Firstname 3G Resume or Interview Books Report** and then create a paper or electronic printout as directed. **Close** the report.

12 Use the **Blank Report** tool to create a report based on the **3G Publishers** table. Add the following fields to the report in the order listed: **Company Name**, **Rep First Name**, **Rep Last Name**, and **Phone Number**. **Close** the **Field List** pane, and then apply the **Equity** theme to this object only. Increase the width of the **Company Name** field so that the text in each record displays on one line. Add the **Date** to the report, add a **Title** of **Lastname Firstname 3G Reps Phone List** For the title, change the **Font Size** to **14**, and then adjust the width of the title's label control, being sure that the date displays within the right margin of the report. Apply **Bold** to all of the field names, and then **Center** the field names over the data. **Sort** the **Company Name** field in **Ascending** order. Using the **layout selector**, visually center the fields between the left and right margins. **Save** the report as **Lastname Firstname 3G Reps Phone List** and then create a paper or electronic printout as directed. **Close** the report.

13 Use the **Report Wizard** to create a report based on the **3G Career Book Titles** table, Select the following fields: **Category**, **Title**, and **Value of Books**. **Group** the report by **Category**, **Sort** by **Title**, and **Sum** the **Value of Books** field. Select the **Stepped** layout, and **Portrait** orientation as the report title, type **Lastname Firstname 3G Book Values by Category Report** and then switch to **Layout** view.

14 Apply the **Opulent Theme** to this object only. For the title of the report, change the **Font Size** to **14** and then apply **Bold**. **Delete** the **Summary for 'Category' controls**. Scroll down to the bottom of the report, and in the **Title** field, click the **text box control** that displays *Interview Techniques and Resume Tips*, which is the longest entry in the field. Point to the right edge of the **text box control**, and then drag the pointer to the left until there is approximately **0.25 inch** between *Tips* and the right edge of the text box control. Scroll to the top of the report, and then click in the **Value of Books label control**. Double-click the left edge of the **label control** to increase the width of the label control and to display fully the text in the label control. **Save** the report.

15 Scroll down to the bottom of the report, and then on the right side of the report, increase the width of the **Sum calculated controls** and the **Grand Total calculated control** so that the entire figure, including the dollar sign, displays—the Grand Total is *$8,810*. Change the text in the **Sum label controls** to **Total Value of Books by Category** and then increase the width of the **Grand Total label control** to display fully the text in the control. **Save** the report.

16 At the top of the report, apply **Bold** to the three field names. Select any of the **Title text box controls**. Display the **Property Sheet**, set the **Height to 0.25**. **Close** the **Property Sheet**. In **Design** view, align the left edge of the **label control** that displays *Total Value of Books by Category* with the left edge of the **label control** that displays *Grand Total*. **Save** the report.

17 Display the report in **Print Preview** in the **Two Pages** arrangement, examine how the groupings break across pages, and then **Close Print Preview**. In **Layout** view, display the **Group, Sort, and Total** pane, and then click **keep whole group together on one page**. Close the **Group, Sort, and Total** pane. **Save** the report. Display the report in **Print Preview** in the **Two Pages** arrangement, and then notice that the entire **Resumes** grouping displays on Page 2. Create a paper or electronic printout as directed, and then **Close Print Preview**.

18 **Close** the report, and then **Open** the **Navigation Pane**. If necessary, increase the width of the Navigation Pane to display all of the object names fully. In **Backstage** view, click **Close Database**, and then click **Exit**. As directed by your instructor, submit your database and the five paper or electronic printouts that are the results of this project.

End **You have completed Project 12G**

Apply a combination of the 12A and 12B skills.

GO! Fix It | Project 12H Resume Workshops

Project Files

For Project 12H, you will need the following file:

a03H_Resume_Workshops

You will save your database as:

Lastname_Firstname_3H_Resume_Workshops

In this project, you will make corrections to and update an Access database that stores information about resume workshops that are scheduled for students. Start Access, navigate to the student files that accompany this textbook, and then open the a03H_Resume_Workshops database. Save the database in your Access Chapter 12 folder as **Lastname_Firstname_3H_Resume_Workshops** and enable the content.

To complete the project, you should know that:

- In the Participant Form object, all the field heights should be the same, and your name and 3H should display in the title. Create a filter that finds records where the Workshop Fee is $35—five records meet the criteria. Toggle the filter off, and then save the form. In the first record, enter your first name and last name in the appropriate fields. Then, as directed, create a paper or electronic printout of only this record.
- In the Resume Workshop Form object, in the header, change Lastname Firstname to your own last name and first name. Add a label control to the Form Footer section. Using your own name, type **Created by Lastname Firstname** and then bold the text. Save the form. Find the record for Workshop ID# R-002, and then, as directed, create a paper or electronic printout of only this record.
- In the Participant Input Form object, you should adjust the height and width of the controls so that the text in the controls displays on one line. The font sizes for the label controls and text box controls should match. Add your name and 3H to the title, and be sure that the title displays on one line. For the title, change the font size so that the title does not extend to the right of the text box controls beneath it. In the Form Footer section, create a label typing **Created by Lastname Firstname** and then bold the text in the label. Add a light blue background color to the text box controls, and then save the form. Display the record with your name and then, as directed, create a paper or electronic printout of only this record.
- For the Participant Fees Report, apply the Opulent theme to this object only. Add a title to the report that includes your name and 3H. Adjust the font size and the width of the label control, and be sure that the date control displays within the right margin of the report. Center the data in the Workshop ID text box controls. Center the layout between the margins, and add a total for the Workshop Fee column that sums the fees. Sort the Date Fee Received field in ascending order. Save the report, and then create a paper or electronic printout as directed.
- In the Participants by Workshop Name report, apply the Equity theme to this object only. Add your name and 3H to the title, and reduce the Font Size. Adjust controls so that all of the data displays fully. Delete the Summary for 'Workshop ID#' control. Change the text in the Sum label controls so that they reflect what is being summed. Align the left edges of the Sum and Grand Total label controls. Add the date to the Report Header section. Be sure that the groupings are kept together when printed. Create a paper or electronic printout as directed.

End You have completed Project 12H

Apply a combination of the 12A and 12B skills.

GO! Make It | Project 12I Study Abroad

Project Files

For Project 12I, you will need the following file:

a03I_Study_Abroad

You will save your database as:

Lastname_Firstname_3I_Study_Abroad

From the student files that accompany this textbook, open the a03I_Study_Abroad database, and then save the database in your Access Chapter 12 folder as **Lastname_Firstname_3I_Study_Abroad** Using the Blank Report tool, create the report shown in Figure 12.54. Apply the Slipstream theme, and then create a paper or electronic printout as directed.

Project Results

Lastname Firstname 3I Trip Dates and Cost Report

Destination	Cost of Trip	Departure Date	Return Date
Costa Rica	$3,000	2/15/2016	2/25/2016
Egypt	$4,300	2/16/2016	2/26/2016
Great Britain	$6,000	3/22/2016	4/4/2016
Greece	$6,000	5/5/2016	5/15/2016
Ireland	$5,000	5/23/2016	6/2/2016
Italy	$4,500	5/1/2016	5/8/2016
Mexico	$2,000	2/8/2016	2/18/2016
Panama	$2,900	4/30/2016	5/5/2016
Paris	$7,580	5/6/2016	5/17/2016
Rome	$7,250	5/2/2016	5/12/2016
Singapore	$5,000	4/12/2016	4/20/2016
South Africa	$4,780	3/3/2016	3/10/2016
Switzerland	$5,400	2/25/2016	3/3/2016
Tokyo	$4,950	3/4/2016	3/12/2016
Tuscan Valley	$5,600	2/4/2016	2/14/2016

Figure 12.54

End You have completed Project 12I

Content-Based Assessments

Apply a combination of the 12A and 12B skills.

GO! Solve It | Project 12J Job Offers

Project Files

For Project 12J, you will need the following file:

a03J_Job_Offers

You will save your database as:

Lastname_Firstname_3J_Job_Offers

From the student files that accompany this textbook, open the a03J_Job_Offers database file, save the database in your Access Chapter 12 folder as **Lastname_Firstname_3J_Job_Offers** and then enable the content.

Kevin Bodine, coordinator of the Student Employment Office, would like one form and two reports created from the Job Offers database. Using the skills you have practiced in this chapter, create an attractive form that can be used to update student candidate records. Using your own information, add a new record as Student ID# **9091246** with a College Major of **Business** and a Phone Number of **(703) 555-9876** Leave the Internship Completed field blank. Save the form as **Lastname Firstname 3J Candidate Update Form** and then create a paper or electronic printout of only your record.

Mr. Bodine wants an attractive report listing the Organization Name and the Offer Amount of each job offered to a student, grouped by the Student ID#, sorted in ascending order by the Organization Name. The Offer Amount field should display the maximum amount offered. Create and save the report as **Lastname Firstname 3J Job Offers by Student ID# Report** and then create a paper or electronic printout as directed.

Mr. Bodine also wants an attractive report of the names, college majors, and phone numbers of the student candidates, grouped by college majors and then sorted by the Last Name field. Save the report as **Lastname Firstname 3J Student Candidates by Major Report** and then create a paper or electronic printout as directed.

Performance Criteria	Performance Level		
	Exemplary You consistently applied the relevant skills	**Proficient** You sometimes, but not always, applied the relevant skills	**Developing** You rarely or never applied the relevant skills
Create 3J Candidate Update Form	Form created with correct fields in easy-to-follow format and record entered for student.	Form created with no more than two missing elements.	Form created with more than two missing elements.
Create 3J Job Offers by Student ID# Report	Report created with correct fields, grouped and sorted correctly, and in an attractive format.	Report created with no more than two missing elements.	Report created with more than two missing elements.
Create 3J Student Candidates by Major Report	Report created with correct fields, grouped and sorted correctly, and in an attractive format.	Report created with no more than two missing elements.	Report created with more than two missing elements.

End You have completed Project 12J

Apply a combination of the 12A and 12B skills.

GO! Solve It | Project 12K Financial Aid

Project Files

For Project 12K, you will need the following file:

a03K_Financial_Aid

You will save your database as:

Lastname_Firstname_3K_Financial_Aid

From the student files that accompany this textbook, open the a03K_Financial_Aid database file, and then save the database in your Access Chapter 12 folder as **Lastname_Firstname_3K_Financial_Aid**

Marguerite Simons, the Financial Aid Director, wants an attractive, easy-to-follow form that can be used to update the Financial Aid Students table. Using your first name and last name, add a new record with the following information:

Student ID#	Financial Aid ID	Home Phone#	College E-mail
1472589	**FA-07**	**(703) 555-3874**	**ns589@capccc.edu**

Save the form as **Lastname Firstname 3K FA Student Update Form** and then create a paper or electronic printout of only your record.

Ms. Simons also wants an attractively formatted report listing the Award Name, the Student ID# and the Award Amount for financial aid offered to students, grouped by the Award name and sorted in ascending order by the Student ID# field (Hint: Use data from both tables). The Award Amount should be summed. Save the report as **Lastname Firstname 3K Amount by Award Name Report** and then create a paper or electronic printout of the report.

		Performance Level		
		Exemplary You consistently applied the relevant skills	**Proficient** You sometimes, but not always, applied the relevant skills	**Developing** You rarely or never applied the relevant skills
Performance Criteria	Create 3K FA Student Update Form	Form created with correct fields in easy-to-follow format and record entered for student.	Form created with no more than two missing elements.	Form created with more than two missing elements.
	Create 3K Amount by Award Name Report	Report created with correct fields, grouped and sorted correctly, and in an attractive format.	Report created with no more than two missing elements.	Report created with more than two missing elements.

End You have completed Project 12K

Outcomes-Based Assessments

Rubric

The following outcomes-based assessments are *open-ended assessments*. That is, there is no specific correct result; your result will depend on your approach to the information provided. Make *Professional Quality* your goal. Use the following scoring rubric to guide you in *how* to approach the problem, and then to evaluate *how well* your approach solves the problem.

The *criteria*—Software Mastery, Content, Format and Layout, and Process—represent the knowledge and skills you have gained that you can apply to solving the problem. The *levels of performance*—Professional Quality, Approaching Professional Quality, or Needs Quality Improvements—help you and your instructor evaluate your result.

	Your completed project is of Professional Quality if you:	**Your completed project is Approaching Professional Quality if you:**	**Your completed project Needs Quality Improvements if you:**
1-Software Mastery	Choose and apply the most appropriate skills, tools, and features and identify efficient methods to solve the problem.	Choose and apply some appropriate skills, tools, and features, but not in the most efficient manner.	Choose inappropriate skills, tools, or features, or are inefficient in solving the problem.
2-Content	Construct a solution that is clear and well organized, contains content that is accurate, appropriate to the audience and purpose, and is complete. Provide a solution that contains no errors in spelling, grammar, or style.	Construct a solution in which some components are unclear, poorly organized, inconsistent, or incomplete. Misjudge the needs of the audience. Have some errors in spelling, grammar, or style, but the errors do not detract from comprehension.	Construct a solution that is unclear, incomplete, or poorly organized; contains some inaccurate or inappropriate content; and contains many errors in spelling, grammar, or style. Do not solve the problem.
3-Format and Layout	Format and arrange all elements to communicate information and ideas, clarify function, illustrate relationships, and indicate relative importance.	Apply appropriate format and layout features to some elements, but not others. Overuse features, causing minor distraction.	Apply format and layout that does not communicate information or ideas clearly. Do not use format and layout features to clarify function, illustrate relationships, or indicate relative importance. Use available features excessively, causing distraction.
4-Process	Use an organized approach that integrates planning, development, self-assessment, revision, and reflection.	Demonstrate an organized approach in some areas, but not others; or, use an insufficient process of organization throughout.	Do not use an organized approach to solve the problem.

Outcomes-Based Assessments

Apply a combination of the 12A and 12B skills.

GO! Think | Project 12L Food Services

Project Files

For Project 12L, you will need the following file:

a03L_Food_Services

You will save your database as:

Lastname_Firstname_3L_Food_Services

Use the skills you have practiced in this chapter to assist Luciano Perez, the Hospitality Director, in creating a form and a report to assist him with the staff scheduling of food services for a two-day student orientation workshop. Create an attractive form that he can use to update the 3L Staff table saving the form as **Lastname Firstname 3L Staff Update Form** Using your own name, add a new record with the following information:

Staff ID: **STAFF-1119** Phone Number: **(703) 555-0845** Title: **Server**

Create a paper or electronic printout of only your record. Create an attractive, easy-to-read report for calling staff members when the schedule changes. Name the report **Lastname Firstname 3L Staff Phone List** and then create a paper or electronic printout of the report as directed.

End **You have completed Project 12L**

Apply a combination of the 12A and 12B skills.

GO! Think | Project 12M Donors and Gifts

Project Files

For Project 12M, you will need the following file:

a03M_Donors_Gifts

You will save your database as:

Lastname_Firstname_3M_Donors_Gifts

Use the skills you have practiced in this chapter to assist the Dean of Information Technology in using her database to create attractive forms and reports. The Dean would like an attractive form that would enable her work study student to enter the information in the Donors table. Create and save a form naming it **Lastname Firstname 3M Donor Update Form** Using your own name, add a new record with the following information:

Donor ID: **DNR-1212** Donor: **Lastname Foundation** Phone Number: **(703) 555-6091**

Create a paper or electronic printout of only your record. Create a donor list with the donor, contact names, and phone numbers so that the Dean can call the donors to thank them for donating gifts that will be distributed during the high school recruitment tours. Save the report as **Lastname Firstname 3M Donor Phone List** and then create a paper or electronic printout as directed.

Create a report grouped by Category and sorted by Item Description that includes the Retail Value totals and a Grand Total of the Retail Value of the gift items. Create a page footer control that displays **Created by Lastname Firstname** and then save the report as **Lastname Firstname 3M Gift Amounts by Category Report** and then create a paper or electronic printout as directed.

End **You have completed Project 12M**

Apply a combination of the 12A and 12B skills

You and GO! | Project 12N Personal Inventory

Project Files

For Project 12N, you will need the following file:

Lastname_Firstname_2N_Personal_Inventory (your file from Chapter 3)

You will save your database as:

Lastname_Firstname_3N_Personal_Inventory

If you have your database from Project 3N, save it in your Access Chapter 12 folder as **Lastname_Firstname_3N_Personal_Inventory** If you do not have the database from Project 3N, create a new database, saving it in your Access Chapter 12 folder with the same name given above. In the database, create one table with at least 18 records. Include fields such as item, room location, value, and date of purchase. Your table should have items stored in several locations.

Using the table, create an attractive form, naming it **Lastname Firstname 3N Inventory Update Form** Using the form, enter at least three records and then create a paper or electronic printout of one of the new records. Using the table, create an attractive report including fields for the room location, item name, and value or purchase price of the item—you may add more fields if you desire. Group the report by the room location, and sort by the value or purchase price of the item, summarizing the values. Name the report **Lastname Firstname 3N Room Values Report** and then create a paper or electronic printout as directed.

End You have completed Project 12N

Apply a combination of the 2A and 2B skills.

GO! Collaborate | Project 12O Bell Orchid Hotels Group Running Case

This project relates to the **Bell Orchid Hotels**. Your instructor may assign this group case project to your class. If your instructor assigns this project, he or she will provide you with information and instructions to work as part of a group. The group will apply the skills gained thus far to help the Bell Orchid Hotels achieve their business goals.

End You have completed Project 12O

Business Running Case

Razvan CHIRNOAGA/Shutterstock

This project relates to **Front Range Action Sports**, which is one of the country's largest retailers of sports gear and outdoor recreation merchandise. The company has large retail stores in Colorado, Washington, Oregon, California, and New Mexico, in addition to a growing online business. Major merchandise categories include fishing, camping, rock climbing, winter sports, action sports, water sports, team sports, racquet sports, fitness, golf, apparel, and footwear.

In this project, you will apply skills you practiced from the Objectives in Access Chapters 9 through 12. You will create a database for Frank Osei, Vice President of Finance, that contains inventory and supplier information. In addition, you will create queries that answer specific questions relating to the inventory items and suppliers, forms for entering and updating information, and reports. Your printed results will look similar to Figure 2.1.

Project Files

For Project BRC1, you will need the following files:

New blank Access database
aBRC1_Inventory (Excel workbook)
aBRC1_Suppliers (Excel workbook)

You will save your database as:

Lastname_Firstname_BRC1_Inventory_Suppliers

Project Results

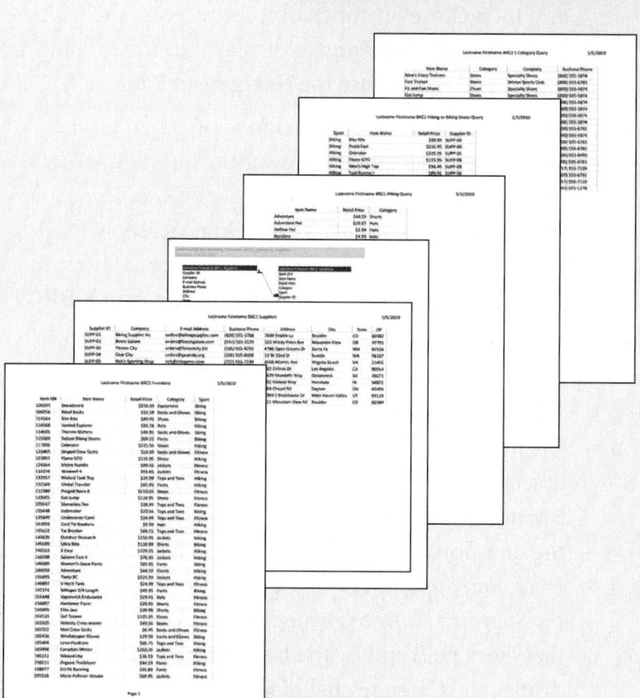

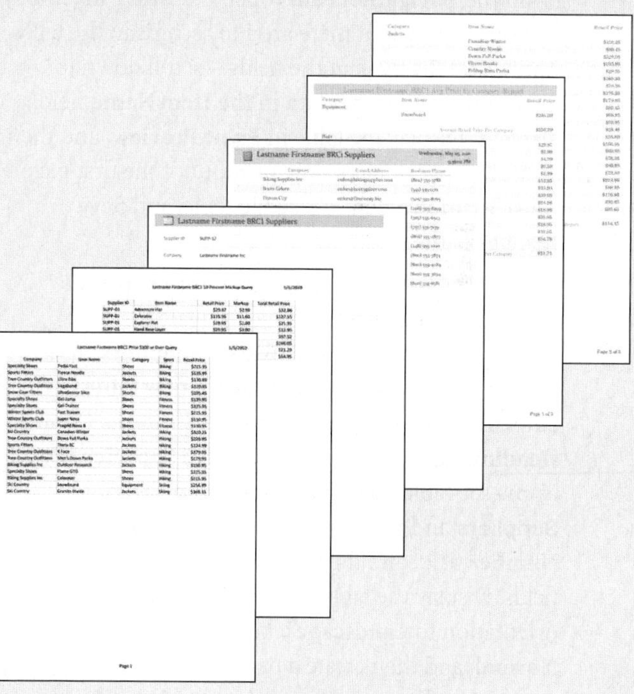

Figure 2.1

Business Running Case

Front Range Action Sports

1 **Start** Access to create a new **Blank database**. In the location where you are storing your projects, create a new folder named **Front Range Action Sports** or navigate to this folder if you have already created it. **Save** the database as **Lastname_Firstname_BRC1_Inventory_Suppliers**

a. Rename the **ID** field to **Item ID#** and change the **Data Type** to **Text**. Then create the fields as shown in **Table 1**.

b. Enter the two records as shown in **Table 2**.

c. **Close** the table, **Save** it as **Lastname Firstname BRC1 Inventory** and then increase the width of the **Navigation Pane** to display the entire table name. On the **External Data tab**, in the **Import & Link group**, click the **Excel** button. Navigate to your student files, double-click **aBRC1_Inventory**, and then **Append a copy of the records** to the **BRC1 Inventory** table. From the **Navigation Pane**, open the **BRC1 Inventory** table and verify that there are 116 records in the table. Apply **Best Fit** to all of the fields—scroll down to be sure that all of the data in the **Item Name** field displays. Display the table in **Print Preview**, and then create a paper or electronic printout of the first page. **Close Print Preview**, **Close** the table, and **Save** changes to the layout of the table.

d. On the **External Data tab**, in the **Import & Link group**, click the **Excel** button. Navigate to your student files, double-click **aBRC1_Suppliers**, and then **Import the source data into a new table in the current database**. Click **First Row Contains Column Headings** and set the primary key to **Supplier ID**. Name the table **Lastname Firstname BRC1 Suppliers** and then **Open** the table. **Delete** the **Fax Number** field, and then apply **Best Fit** to all of the fields. Display the table in **Print Preview**, change the orientation to **Landscape**, change the **Margins** to **Normal**, and then create a paper or electronic printout as directed. **Close Print Preview**, **Close** the table, and save changes to the layout of the table. On the **Navigation Pane**, click the **Navigation Pane arrow**, and then click **Tables and Related Views**.

e. Click the **Database Tools tab**, and then in the **Relationships group**, click the **Relationships** button. In the **Show Table** dialog box, double-click **BRC1 Suppliers**, double-click **BRC1 Inventory**, and then **Close** the dialog box. Expand the field lists, and then in the **BRC1 Suppliers** field list, point to **Supplier ID**. Drag to the right into the **BRC1 Inventory** field list on top of the **Supplier ID** field, release the mouse button, click **Enforce Referential Integrity**, and then click **Create**. *One* supplier can supply *many* inventory items. Create a **Relationship Report**, **Save** the report with the default name, and then create a paper or electronic printout as directed. **Close Print Preview**, and then **Close** any open objects. Increase the width of the **Navigation Pane** to display the entire report name, and then **Close** the **Navigation Pane**.

2 Create a query in **Query Design** view, based on the **BRC1 Inventory** table to answer the question, *What is the Item Name (in alphabetical order), Retail Price, and Category for the Sport of Hiking?* Do not display the **Sport** field in the query results. Forty records meet the criteria. **Save** the query as **Lastname Firstname BRC1 Hiking Query** and then create a paper or electronic printout as directed. **Close Print Preview**, and then **Close** the query.

a. Create a copy of the **BRC1 Hiking Query**, saving the object as **Lastname Firstname BRC1 Hiking or Biking Shoes Query** Redesign the query to answer the question, *What is the Sport, Item Name, Retail Price, and Supplier ID for the Category of Shoes where the Sport is Hiking or Biking?* **Sort** the records by the **Sport** field and by the **Item Name** field. Do not display the **Category** field in the query results. Nine records meet the criteria. Create a paper or electronic

Table 1

Data Type	Text	Text	Currency	Text	Text	Text
Field Name	Item ID#	**Item Name**	**Retail Price**	**Category**	**Sport**	**Supplier ID**

(Return to Step 1-b)

Table 2

Item#	Item Name	Retail Price	Category	Sport	Supplier ID#
106555	**Snowboard**	**256.99**	**Equipment**	**Skiing**	**SUPP-06**
106556	**Wool Socks**	**12.59**	**Socks and Gloves**	**Skiing**	**SUPP-04**

(Return to Step 1-c)

(Business Running Case: Front Range Action Sports continues on the next page)

Front Range Action Sports (continued)

printout as directed. **Close Print Preview**, and **Close** the query.

b. Create a query in **Query Design** view, based on the **BRC1 Suppliers** table and the **BRC1 Inventory** table to answer the question, *What is the Item Name, Category, Company, and Business Phone for Categories that begin with the letter S, and sorted by Category, for the Sport of Fitness?* Do not display the **Sport** category in the query results. Eighteen records meet the criteria. **Save** the query as **Lastname Firstname BRC1 S Category Query** and then create a paper or electronic printout as directed. **Close Print Preview**, and **Close** the query.

c. Create a query in **Query Design** view, based on the **BRC1 Suppliers** table and the **BRC1 Inventory** table to answer the question, *What is the Company, Item Name, Category, Sport, and Retail Price for items that have a retail price of $100 or greater sorted in ascending order by Sport and then in descending order by Retail Price?* Twenty records meet the criteria. **Save** the query as **Lastname Firstname BRC1 Price $100 or Over Query** and then create a paper or electronic printout as directed, changing the margins to **Normal**. **Close Print Preview**, and **Close** the query.

d. Create a query in **Query Design** view, based on the **BRC1 Inventory** table to answer the question, *For Supplier ID of SUPP-01, for each Item Name and Retail Price, what is the markup of each item if marked up 10%, and what is the final price?* All numeric fields should be formatted as **Currency**, **2 Decimal** places. Apply **Best Fit** to all of the fields, **Save** the query as **Lastname Firstname BRC1 10 Percent Markup Query** and then create a paper or electronic printout as directed. **Close Print Preview**, and then **Close** the query.

3 Based on the **BRC1 Suppliers** table, use the **Form** tool to create a form. Switch to **Form** view, and then using your own first name and last name for the **Company** field, add a new record as shown in **Table 3**.

a. Save the form as **Lastname Firstname BRC1 Supplier Form** and then create a paper or electronic printout of only the record you just created in the form, changing the **Column Width** to **7.5"** **Close Print Preview**, and then **Close** the form.

4 Based on the **BRC1 Suppliers** table, use the **Report** tool to create a new report. **Delete** the following fields from the report: **Supplier ID**, **Address**, **City**, **State**, and **ZIP**. Apply the **Paper** theme to this object only. **Sort** the **Company** field in **Ascending** order. Decrease the width of the **Business Phone** field to accommodate the longest entry in the field. **Bold** the field names, and **Center** the **Company** and **E-mail Address** field names over the data. Use the **layout selector** to visually center the layout between the left and right margins, and then visually center the **page number control** between the left and right margins. (Hint: scroll to the right to display the control.) **Save** the report as **Lastname Firstname BRC1 Suppliers Contact List** Display the report in **Print Preview**, and then create a paper or electronic printout as directed. **Close Print Preview**, and then **Close** the report.

5 Using the **Report Wizard**, create a report based on the **BRC1 Inventory** table. Add the following fields to the report: **Category**, **Item Name**, and **Retail Price**. **Group** by **Category**. **Sort** in **Ascending** order by **Item Name**. Find the **Average** of the **Retail Price** field. Select the **Stepped Layout**, and then as the report title, type **Lastname Firstname BRC1 Avg Price by Category Report**

a. In **Print Preview**, display the report by **Two Pages** and notice how the groupings are split between pages, that the **Retail Price** field name displays only *Price*, and that the prices in the text box and calculated controls display ###. **Close Print Preview**, and then switch to **Layout** view. Apply the **Oriel** theme to the report and no other objects.

b. Click the **Item Name** field name, hold down Shift, and then click the **text box control** that displays *Snowboard*. Decrease the width of the field until there is approximately **2** inches between **Item Name** and the right edge of the text box control. Scroll down the

Table 3

Supplier ID	Company	E-mail Address	Business Phone	Address	City	State	ZIP
SUPP-12	Lastname Firstname Inc	info@watersports.biz	(305) 555-6543	14 South Beach Rd	Miami	FL	33125

(Business Running Case: Front Range Action Sports continues on the next page)

(Return to Step 3-a)

Front Range Action Sports (continued)

report to be sure that all Item Names display fully. Scroll to the top of the report, and then click the **Retail Price** field name, which displays only a portion of the word *Price*. Hold down Shift, click the **text box control** below the field name, which displays ###, and then click the **calculated control** that also displays ###. Increase the width of the controls by pointing to the left edge of any one of the selected controls and dragging it to the left until the entire field name—**Retail Price**—displays as the field name.

c. Delete the **Summary for 'Category' label controls**. Change the text in the **Avg label control** from *Avg* to **Average Retail Price Per Category** and then move the **label control** to the right until the right edge of the control is approximately **0.25 inch** from the left edge of its associated calculated control.

d. Click in the **title** of the report, and then change the **Font Size** to **16**. Visually center the title between the left and right margins of the report. Select all of the field names, and then apply **Bold** and **Italic**.

e On the **Design tab**, in the **Grouping & Totals** group, click the **Group & Sort** button. In the **Group, Sort, and Total** pane, click **More**. Click the **do not keep group together on one page arrow**, and then click **keep whole group together on one page**. In the **Grouping & Totals group**, click the **Group & Sort** button to close the **Group, Sort, and Total** pane. **Save** the report.

f. Display the report in **Print Preview** by **Two Pages**, and notice how the groupings are kept together on one page. On the **Print Preview tab**, in the **Print group**, click the **Print** button. In the **Print** dialog box, under **Print Range**, click **Pages**. In the **From** box, type **1** and in the **To** box, type **2** and then click **OK** to create a paper printout—or create an electronic printout as directed. **Close Print Preview**, and then **Close** the report.

6 **Open** the **Navigation Pane**, and if necessary, widen the pane to display fully all object names. Display **Backstage** view, click **Close Database**, and then click **Exit**.

End You have completed Business Running Case 1

Getting Started with Microsoft Office PowerPoint

OUTCOMES

At the end of this chapter you will be able to:

OBJECTIVES

Mastering these objectives will enable you to:

PROJECT 13A

Create a new PowerPoint presentation.

1. Create a New Presentation (p. 733)
2. Edit a Presentation in Normal View (p. 737)
3. Add Pictures to a Presentation (p. 744)
4. Print and View a Presentation (p. 747)

PROJECT 13B

Edit and format a PowerPoint presentation.

5. Edit an Existing Presentation (p. 753)
6. Format a Presentation (p. 757)
7. Use Slide Sorter View (p. 760)
8. Apply Slide Transitions (p. 763)

© Steve Murray / Alamy

In This Chapter

In this chapter you will study presentation skills, which are among the most important skills you will learn. Good presentation skills enhance your communications—written, electronic, and interpersonal. In this technology-enhanced world, communicating ideas clearly and concisely is a critical personal skill. Microsoft PowerPoint 2010 is presentation software with which you create electronic slide presentations. Use PowerPoint to present information to your audience effectively. You can start with a new, blank presentation and add content, pictures, and themes, or you can collaborate with colleagues by inserting slides that have been saved in other presentations.

The projects in this chapter relate to **Lehua Hawaiian Adventures**. Named for the small, crescent-shaped island that is noted for its snorkeling and scuba diving, Lehua Hawaiian Adventures offers exciting but affordable adventure tours. Hiking tours go off the beaten path to amazing remote places on the islands. If you prefer to ride into the heart of Hawaii, try the cycling tours. Lehua Hawaiian Adventures also offers Jeep tours. Whatever you prefer—mountain, sea, volcano—our tour guides are experts in the history, geography, culture, and flora and fauna of Hawaii.

Project 13A Company Overview

Project Activities

In Activities 13.01 through 13.13, you will create the first four slides of a new presentation that Lehua Hawaiian Adventures tour manager Carl Kawaoka is developing to introduce the tour services that the company offers. Your completed presentation will look similar to Figure 13.1.

Project Files

For Project 13A, you will need the following files:

New blank PowerPoint presentation
p01A_Helicopter
p01A_Beach

You will save your presentation as:

Lastname_Firstname_1A_LHA_Overview

Project Results

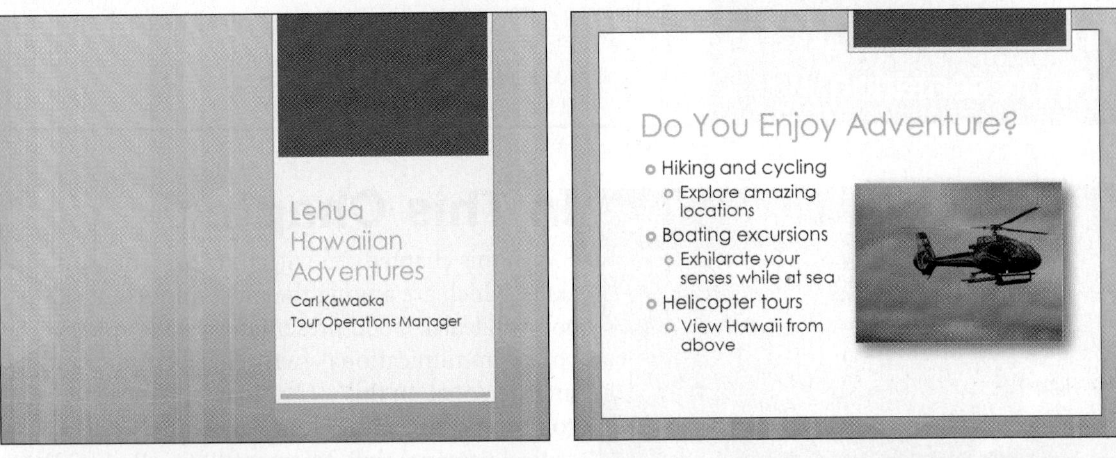

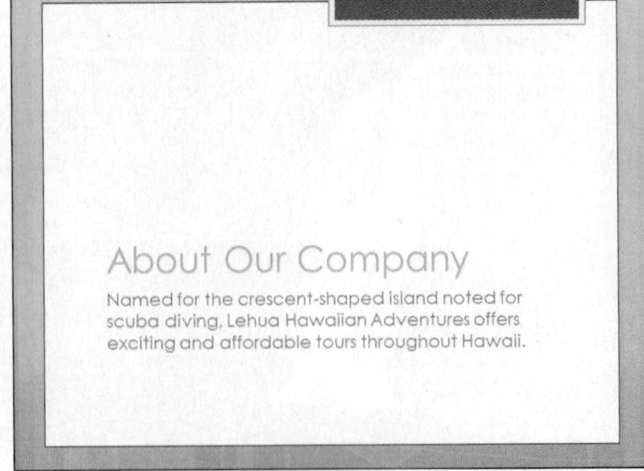

Figure 13.1
Project 13A LHA Overview

Objective 1 | Create a New Presentation

Microsoft PowerPoint 2010 is software with which you can present information to your audience effectively. You can edit and format a blank presentation by adding text, a presentation theme, and pictures.

Activity 13.01 | Identifying Parts of the PowerPoint Window

In this activity, you will start PowerPoint and identify the parts of the PowerPoint window.

1 **Start** PowerPoint to display a new blank presentation in Normal view, and then compare your screen with Figure 13.2.

Normal view is the primary editing view in PowerPoint where you write and design your presentations. Normal view includes the Notes pane, the Slide pane, and the Slides/ Outline pane.

Figure 13.2

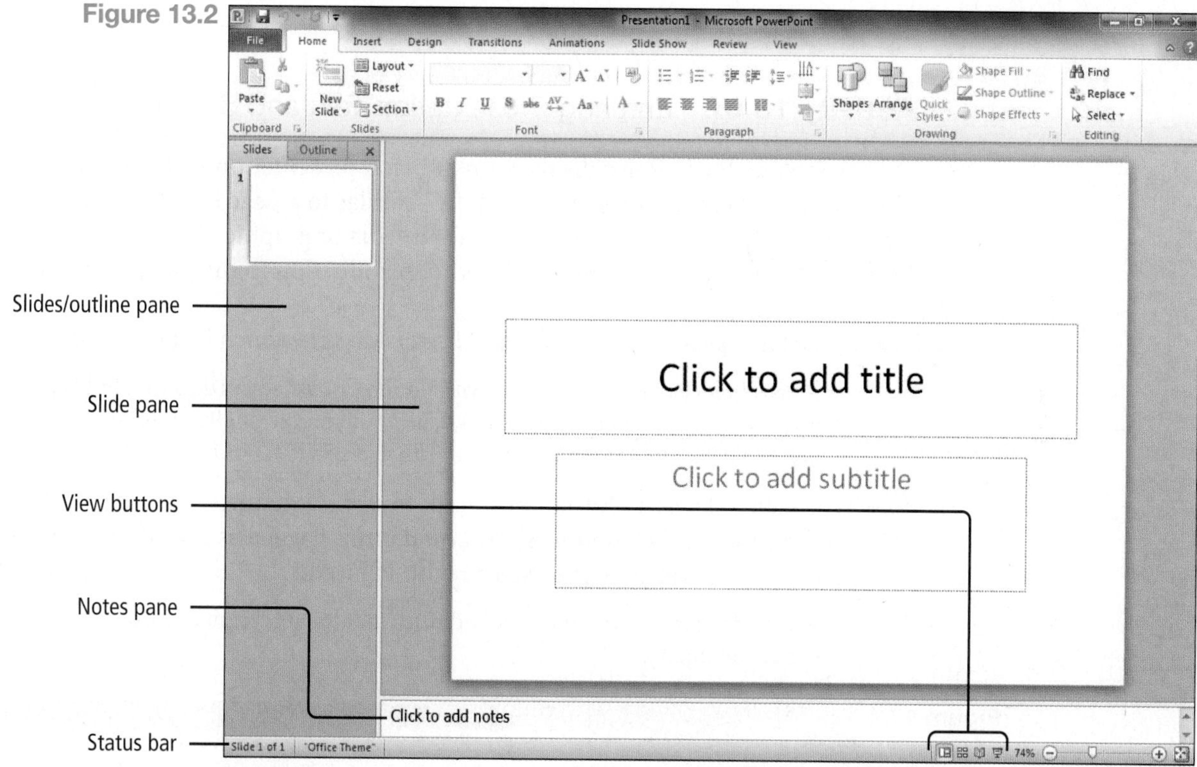

2 Take a moment to study the parts of the PowerPoint window described in the table in Figure 13.3.

Microsoft PowerPoint Screen Elements

Screen Element	Description
Notes pane	Displays below the Slide pane and provides space for you to type notes regarding the active slide.
Slide pane	Displays a large image of the active slide.
Slides/Outline pane	Displays either the presentation in the form of miniature images called ***thumbnails*** (Slides tab) or the presentation outline (Outline tab).
Status bar	Displays, in a horizontal bar at the bottom of the presentation window, the current slide number, number of slides in a presentation, theme, View buttons, Zoom slider, and Fit slide to current window button; you can customize this area to include additional helpful information.
View buttons	Control the look of the presentation window with a set of commands.

Figure 13.3

Activity 13.02 | Entering Presentation Text and Saving a Presentation

On startup, PowerPoint displays a new blank presentation with a single ***slide***—a ***title slide*** in Normal view. A presentation slide—similar to a page in a document—can contain text, pictures, tables, charts, and other multimedia or graphic objects. The title slide is the first slide in a presentation and provides an introduction to the presentation topic.

1 In the **Slide pane**, click in the text *Click to add title*, which is the title ***placeholder***.

A placeholder is a box on a slide with dotted or dashed borders that holds title and body text or other content such as charts, tables, and pictures. This slide contains two placeholders, one for the title and one for the subtitle.

2 Type **Lehua Hawaiian Adventures** point to *Lehua*, and then right-click. On the shortcut menu, click **Ignore All** so *Lehua* is not flagged as a spelling error in this presentation. Compare your screen with Figure 13.4.

Recall that a red wavy underline indicates that the underlined word is not in the Microsoft Office dictionary.

Figure 13.4

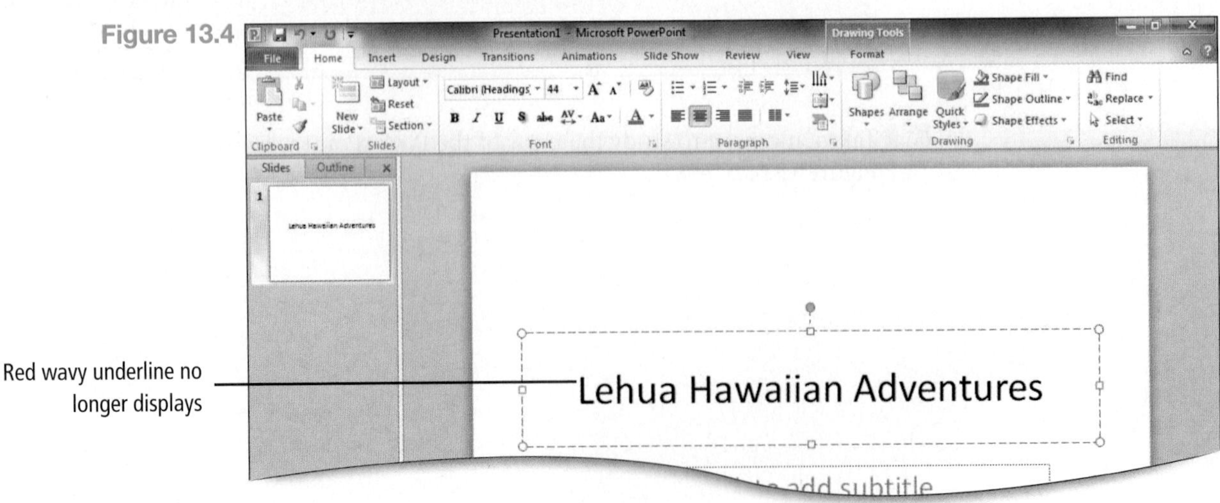

3 Click in the subtitle placeholder, and then type **Carl Kawaoka**

4 Press Enter to create a new line in the subtitle placeholder. Type **Tour Manager**

5 Right-click **Kawaoka**, and then on the shortcut menu, click **Ignore All**. Compare your screen with Figure 13.5.

Figure 13.5

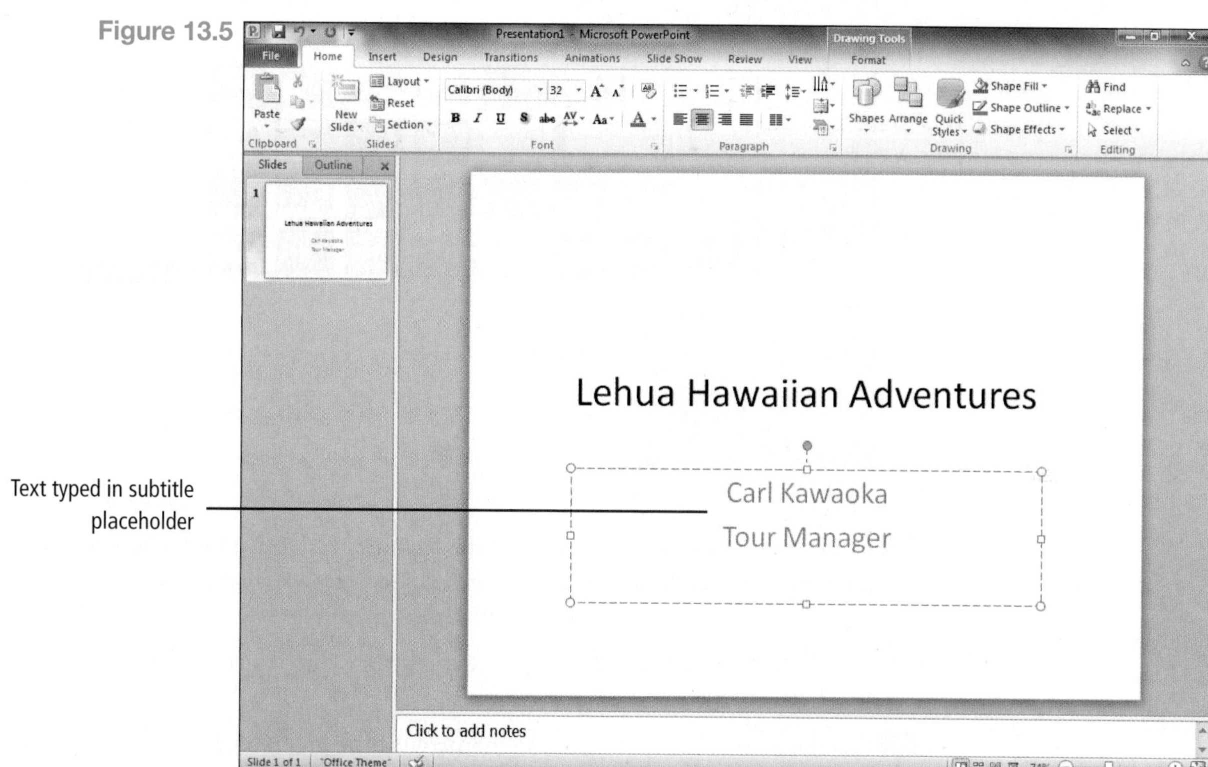

6 In the upper left corner of your screen, click the **File tab** to display **Backstage** view, click **Save As**, and then in the **Save As** dialog box, navigate to the location where you will store your files for this chapter. Create a new folder named **PowerPoint Chapter 13** In the **File name** box, replace the existing text with **Lastname_Firstname_1A_LHA_Overview** and then click **Save**.

Activity 13.03 | Applying a Presentation Theme

A ***theme*** is a set of unified design elements that provides a look for your presentation by applying colors, fonts, and effects.

1 On the Ribbon, click the **Design tab**. In the **Themes group**, click the **More** button to display the **Themes** gallery. Compare your screen with Figure 13.6.

Figure 13.6

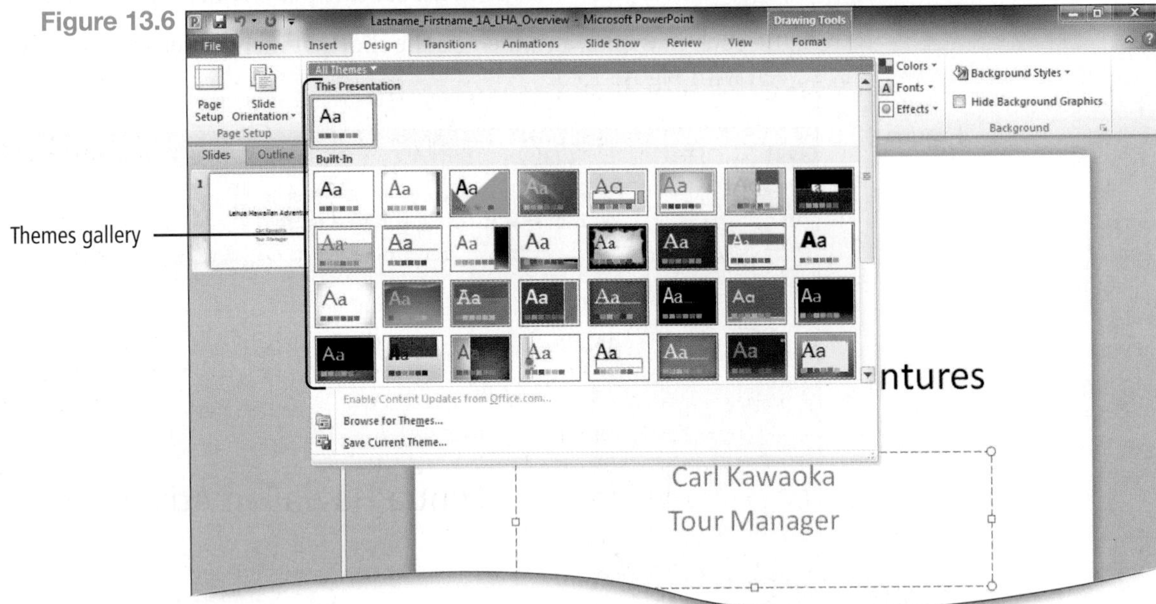

2 Under **Built-In**, point to several of the themes and notice that a ScreenTip displays the name of each theme and the Live Preview feature displays how each theme would look if applied to your presentation.

The first theme that displays is the Office theme. Subsequent themes are arranged alphabetically.

3 Use the ScreenTips to locate the theme with the green background—**Austin**—as shown in Figure 13.7.

Figure 13.7

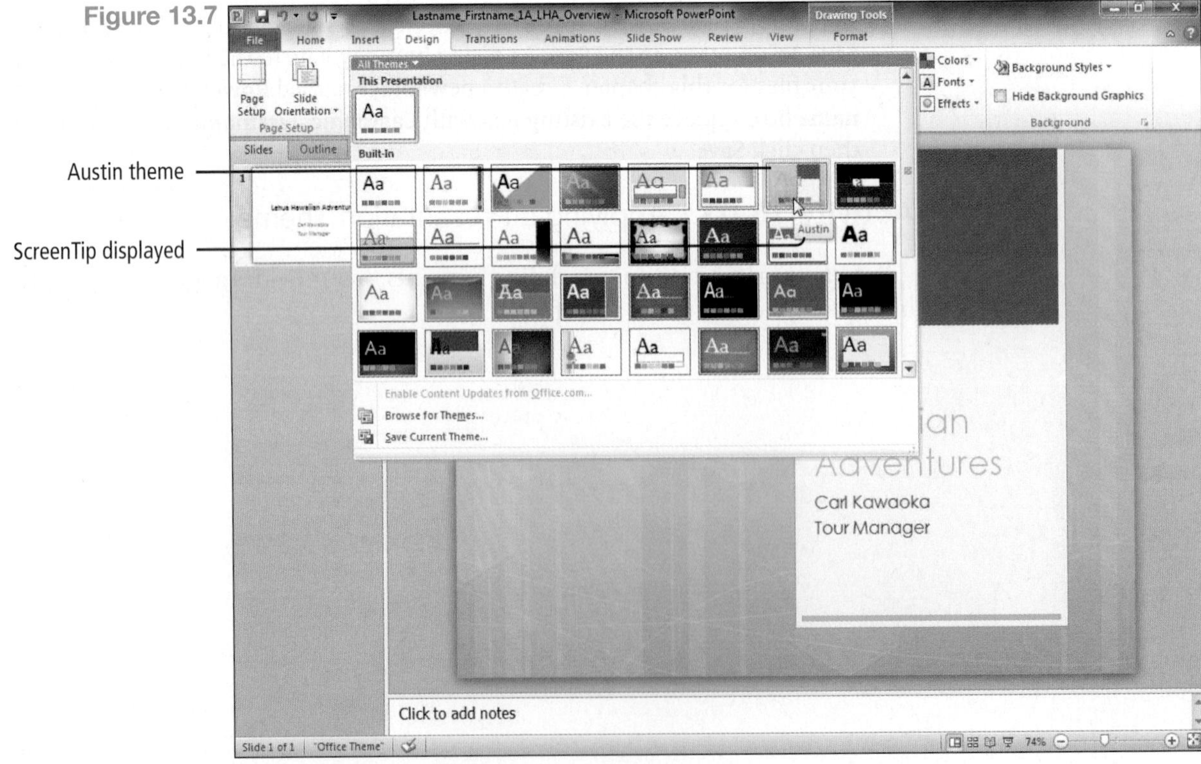

4 Click the **Austin** theme to change the presentation theme and then **Save** your presentation.

Objective 2 | Edit a Presentation in Normal View

Editing is the process of modifying a presentation by adding and deleting slides or by changing the contents of individual slides.

Activity 13.04 | Inserting a New Slide

To insert a new slide in a presentation, display the slide that will precede the slide that you want to insert.

1 On the **Home tab**, in the **Slides group**, point to the **New Slide** button. Compare your screen with Figure 13.8.

The New Slide button is a split button. Recall that clicking the main part of a split button performs a command and clicking the arrow opens a menu, list, or gallery. The upper, main part of the New Slide button, when clicked, inserts a slide without displaying any options. The lower part—the New Slide button arrow—when clicked, displays a gallery of slide ***layouts.*** A layout is the arrangement of elements, such as title and subtitle text, lists, pictures, tables, charts, shapes, and movies, on a slide.

Figure 13.8

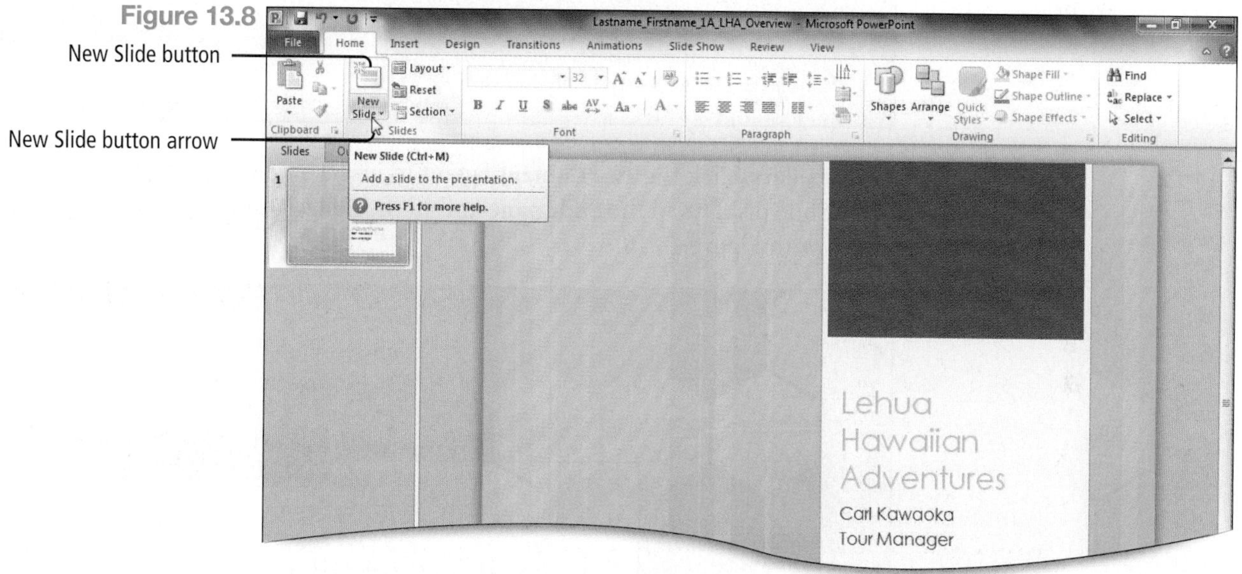

2 In the **Slides group**, click the lower portion of the New Slide button—the **New Slide button arrow**—to display the gallery, and then compare your screen with Figure 13.9.

Figure 13.9

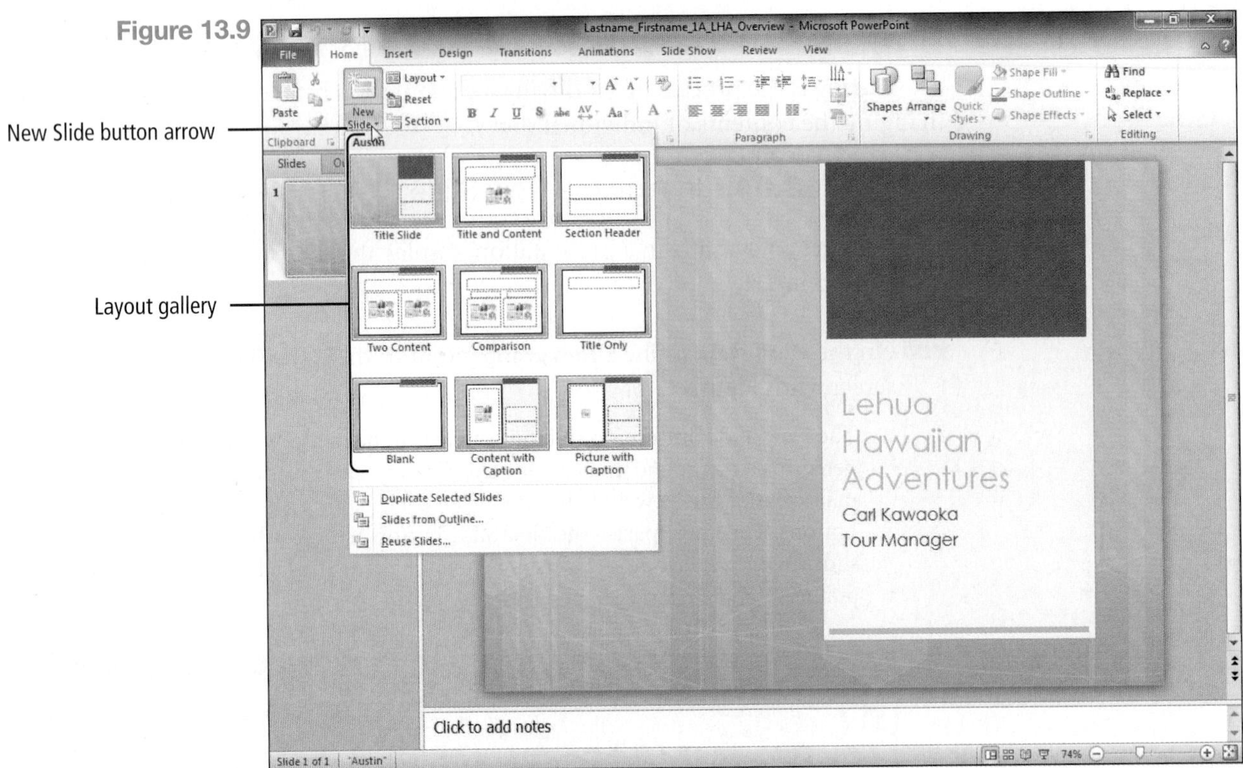

3 In the gallery, click the **Two Content** layout to insert a new slide. Notice that the new blank slide displays in the **Slide pane** and in the **Slides/Outline pane**. Compare your screen with Figure 13.10.

Figure 13.10

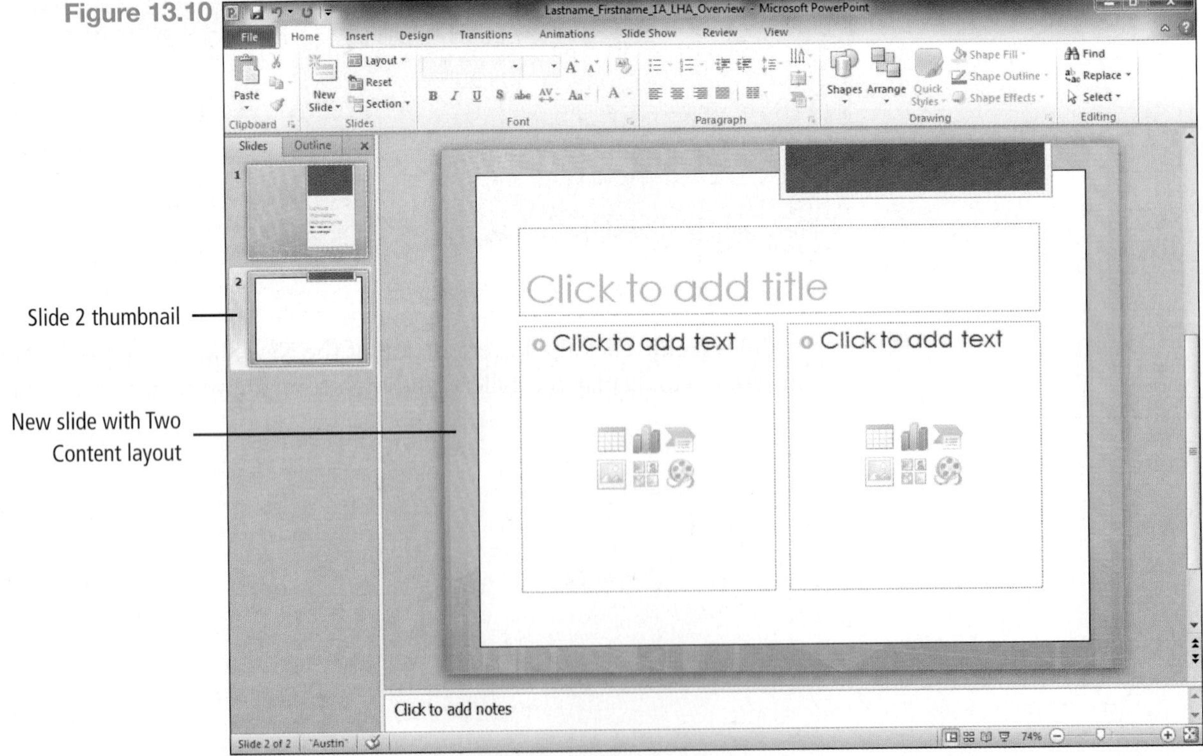

4 In the **Slide pane**, click the text *Click to add title*, and then type **Do You Enjoy Adventure?**

5 On the left side of the slide, click anywhere in the content placeholder. Type **Hiking and cycling** and then press Enter.

6 Type **Explore locations** and then compare your screen with Figure 13.11.

Figure 13.11

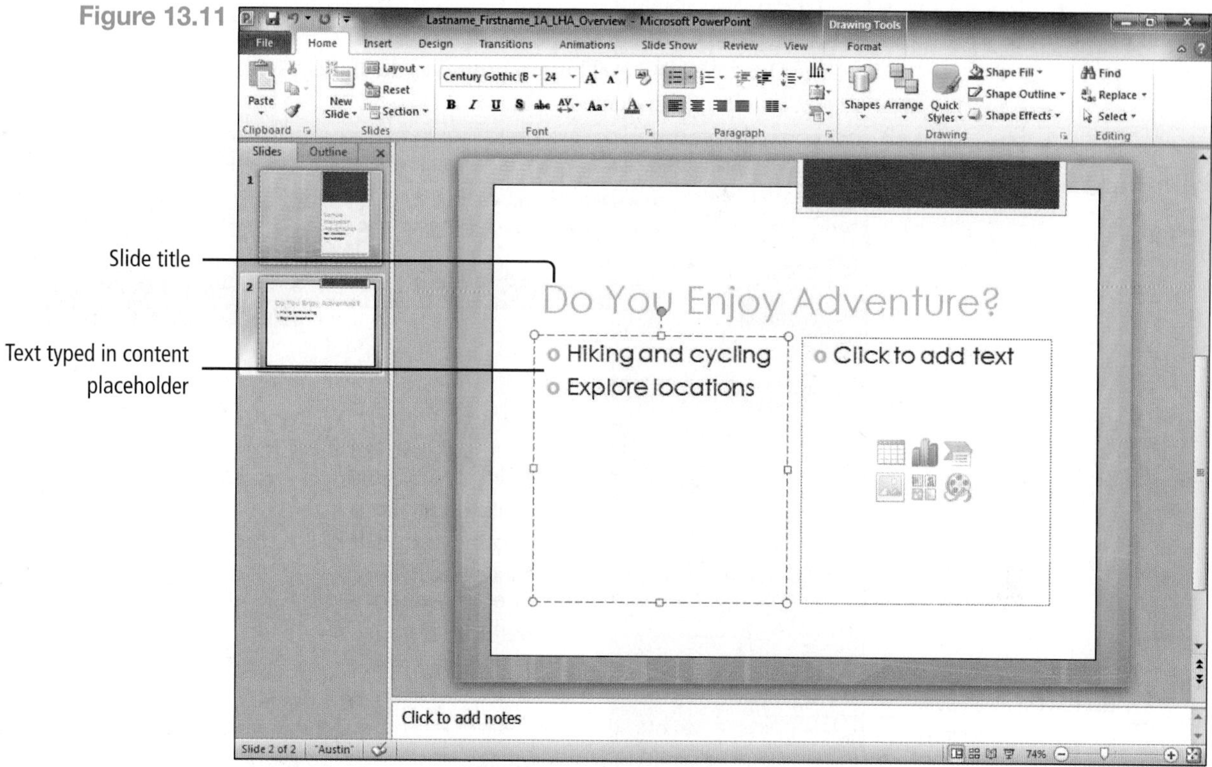

7 **Save** your presentation.

Activity 13.05 | Increasing and Decreasing List Levels

Text in a PowerPoint presentation is organized according to ***list levels***. List levels, each represented by a bullet symbol, are similar to outline levels. On a slide, list levels are identified by the bullet style, indentation, and the size of the text.

The first level on an individual slide is the title. Increasing the list level of a bullet point increases its indent and results in a smaller text size. Decreasing the list level of a bullet point decreases its indent and results in a larger text size.

1 On **Slide 2**, if necessary, click at the end of the last bullet point after the word *locations*, and then press Enter to insert a new bullet point.

2 Type **Boating excursions** and then press Enter.

3 Press Tab, and then notice that the green bullet is indented. Type **Exhilarate your senses while at sea**

By pressing Tab at the beginning of a bullet point, you can increase the list level and indent the bullet point.

4 Press Enter. Notice that a new bullet point displays at the same level as the previous bullet point. Then, on the **Home tab**, in the **Paragraph group**, click the **Decrease List Level** button. Type **Helicopter tours** and then compare your screen with Figure 13.12.

The Decrease List Level button promotes the bullet point. The text size increases and the text is no longer indented.

Figure 13.12

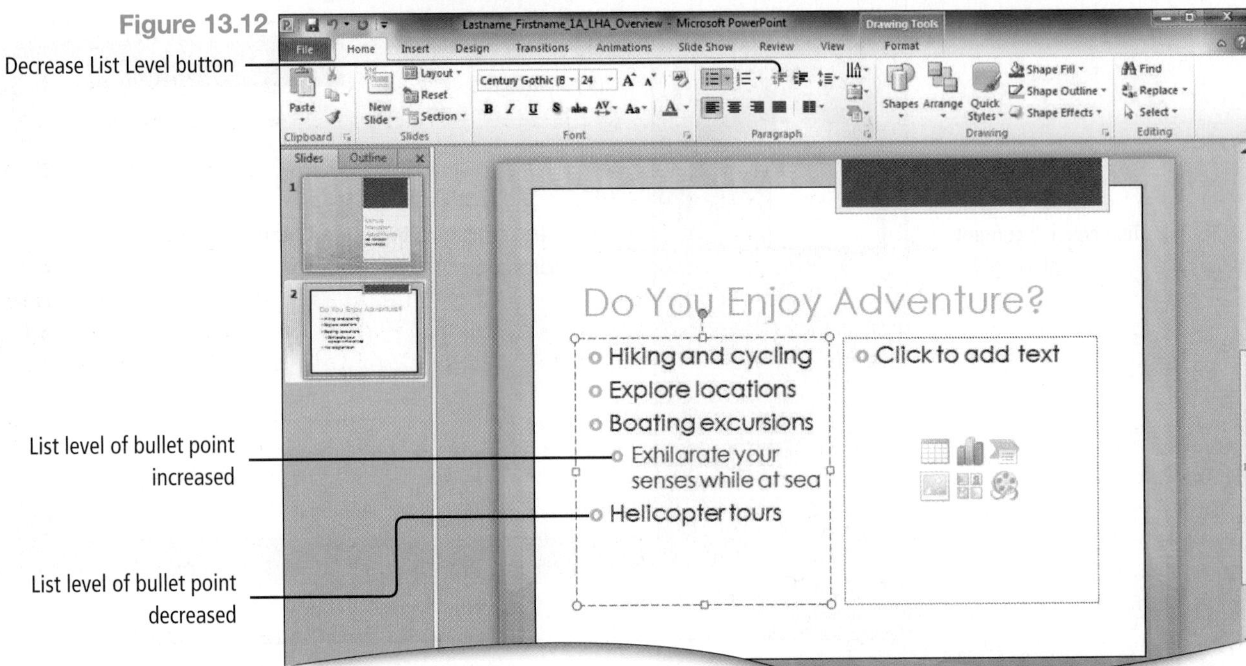

5 Press Enter, and then press Tab to increase the list level. Type **View Hawaii from above**

6 Click anywhere in the second bullet point—*Explore locations.* On the **Home tab**, in the **Paragraph group**, click the **Increase List Level** button. Compare your screen with Figure 13.13.

The bullet point is indented and the size of the text decreases.

Figure 13.13

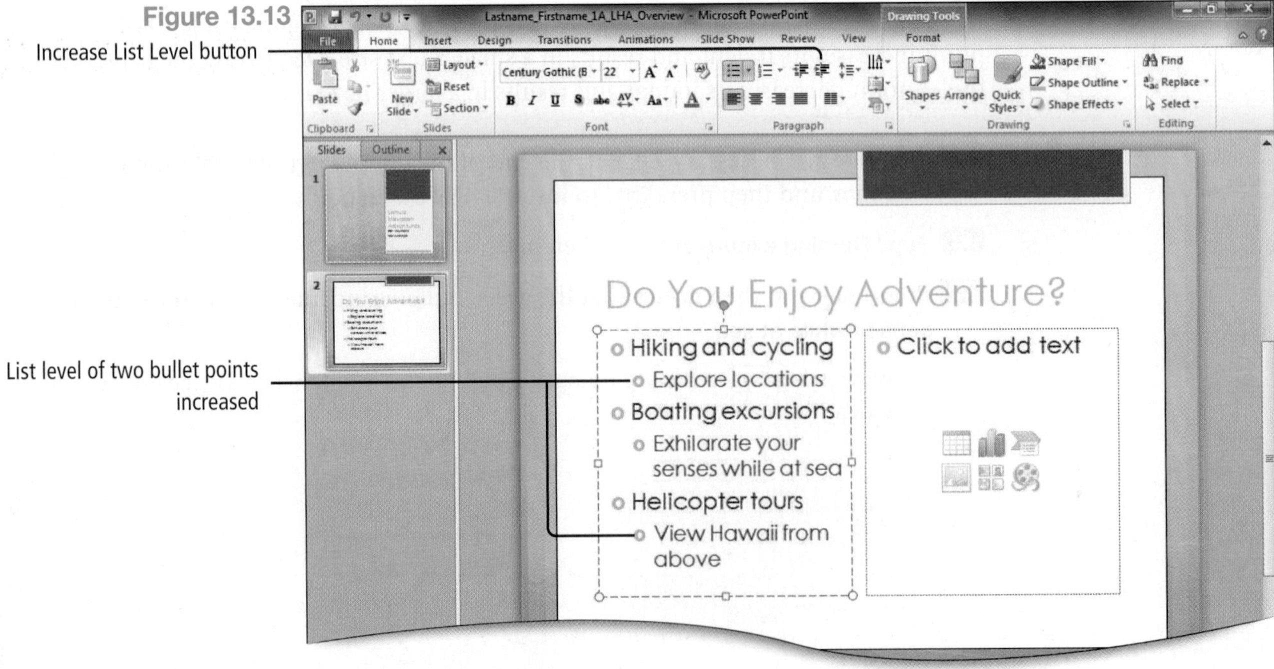

7 **Save** your presentation.

Activity 13.06 | Adding Speaker's Notes to a Presentation

Recall that when a presentation is displayed in Normal view, the Notes pane displays below the Slide pane. Use the Notes pane to type speaker's notes that you can print below a picture of each slide. Then, while making your presentation, you can refer to these printouts while making a presentation, thus reminding you of the important points that you want to discuss during the presentation.

1 With **Slide 2** displayed, on the **Home tab**, in the **Slides group**, click the **New Slide button arrow** to display the **Slide Layout** gallery, and then click **Section Header**.

The section header layout changes the look and flow of a presentation by providing text placeholders that do not contain bullet points.

2 Click in the title placeholder, and then type **About Our Company**

3 Click in the content placeholder below the title, and then type **Named for the crescent-shaped island noted for scuba diving, Lehua Hawaiian Adventures offers exciting and affordable tours throughout Hawaii.** Compare your screen with Figure 13.14.

Figure 13.14

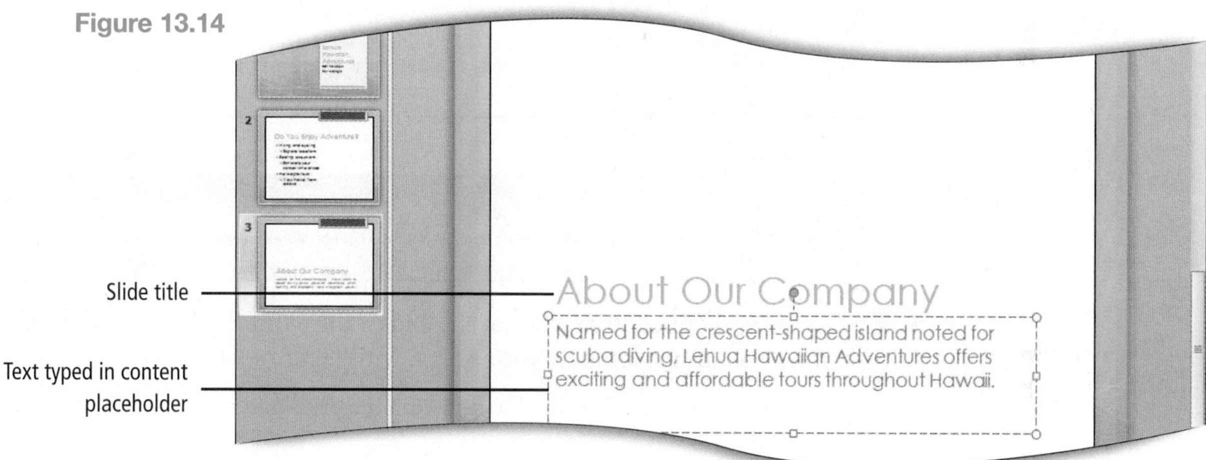

4 Below the slide, click in the **Notes pane**. Type **Lehua Hawaiian Adventures is based in Honolulu but has offices on each of the main Hawaiian islands.** Compare your screen with Figure 13.15, and then **Save** your presentation.

Figure 13.15

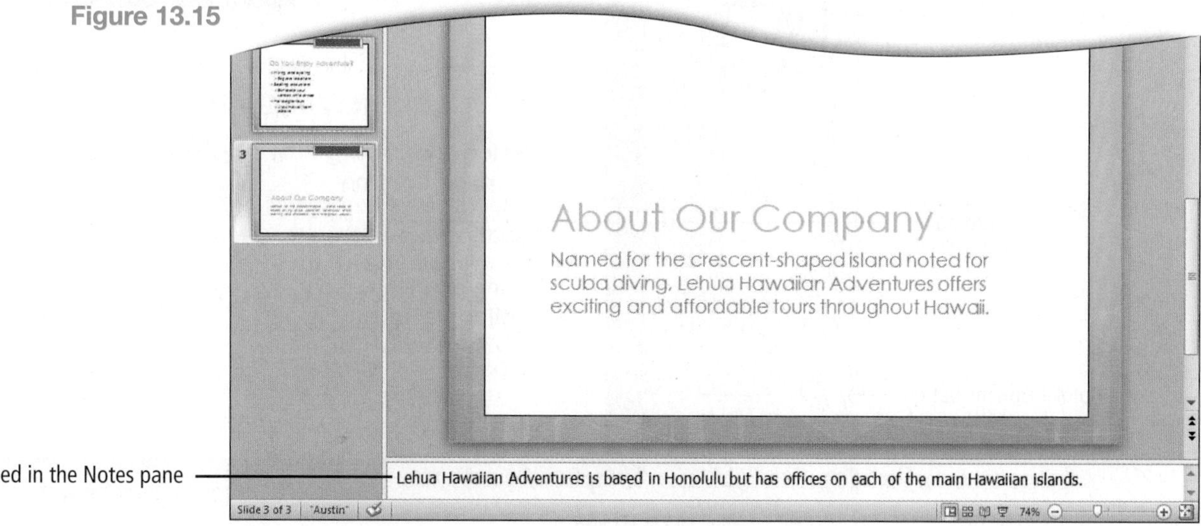

Activity 13.07 | Displaying and Editing Slides in the Slide Pane

To edit a presentation slide, display the slide in the Slide pane.

1 Look at the **Slides/Outline pane**, and then notice that the presentation contains three slides. At the right side of the PowerPoint window, in the vertical scroll bar, point to the scroll box, and then hold down the left mouse button to display a ScreenTip indicating the slide number and title.

2 Drag the scroll box up until the ScreenTip displays *Slide: 2 of 3 Do You Enjoy Adventure?* Compare your slide with Figure 13.16, and then release the mouse button to display **Slide 2**.

Figure 13.16

3 In the second bullet point, click at the end of the word *Explore*. Press Spacebar, and then type **amazing** Compare your screen with Figure 13.17.

The placeholder text is resized to fit within the placeholder. The AutoFit Options button displays.

Figure 13.17

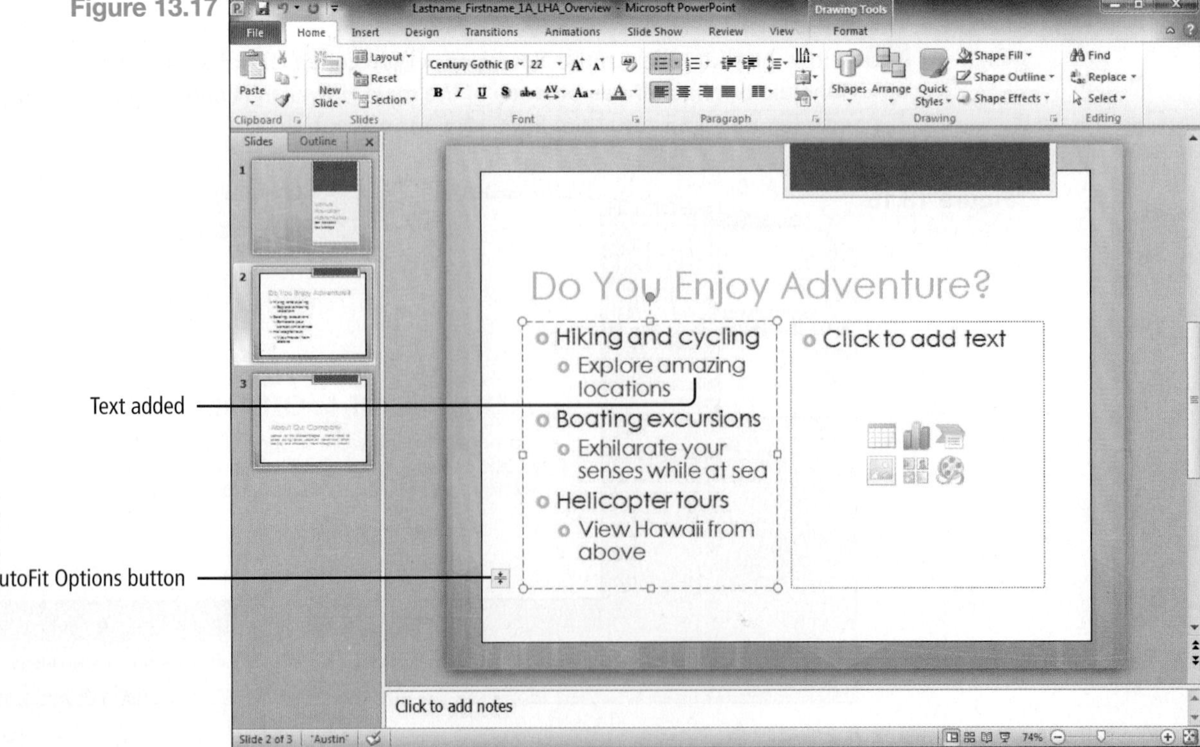

4 Click the **AutoFit Options** button, and then click **AutoFit Text to Placeholder**.

The *AutoFit Text to Placeholder* option keeps the text contained within the placeholder by reducing the size of the text. The *Stop Fitting Text to This Placeholder* option turns off the AutoFit option so that the text can flow beyond the placeholder border; the text size remains unchanged.

5 Below the vertical scroll bar, locate the **Previous Slide** and **Next Slide** buttons as shown in Figure 13.18.

Figure 13.18

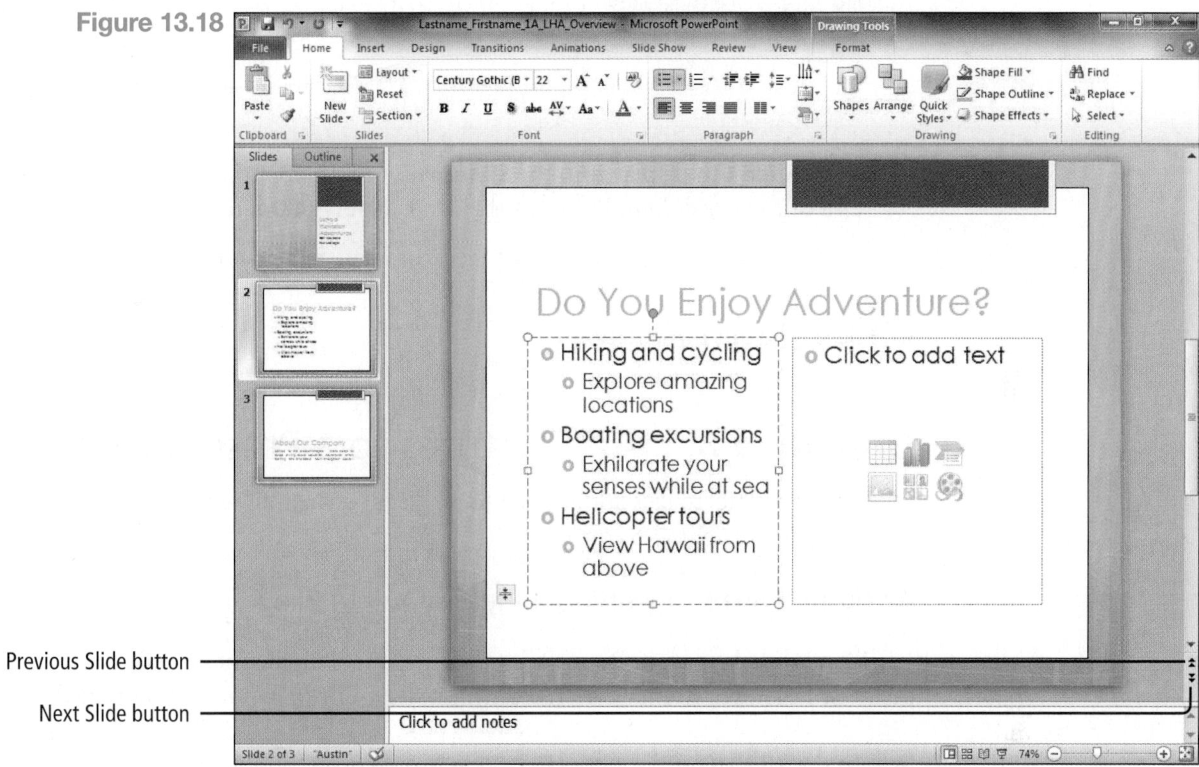

6 In the vertical scroll bar, click the **Previous Slide** button so that **Slide 1** displays. Then click the **Next Slide** button two times until **Slide 3** displays.

By clicking the Next Slide or the Previous Slide buttons, you can scroll through your presentation one slide at a time.

7 On the left side of the PowerPoint window, in the **Slides/Outline pane**, point to **Slide 1**, and then notice that a ScreenTip displays the slide title. Compare your screen with Figure 13.19.

In the Slides/Outline pane, the slide numbers display to the left of the slide thumbnails.

Figure 13.19

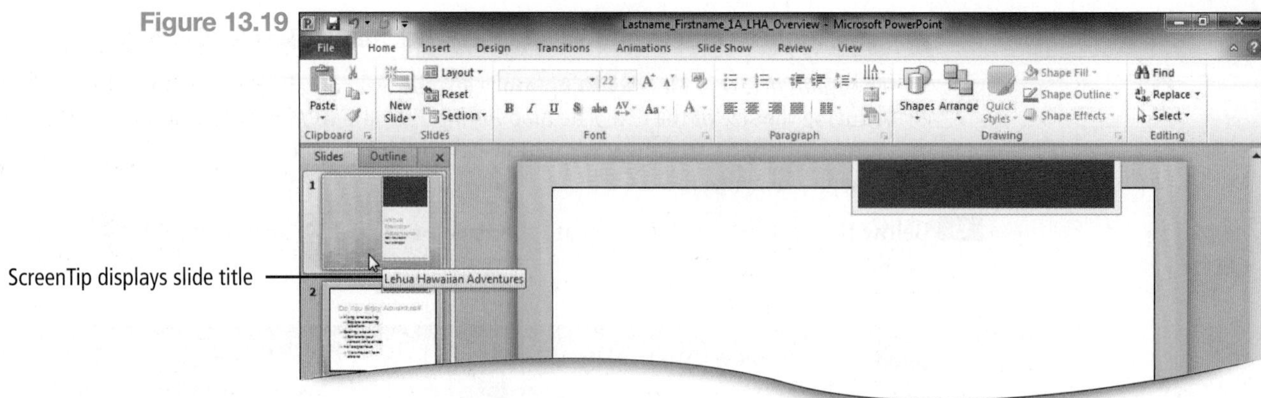

8 Click **Slide 1** to display it in the **Slide pane**, and then in the slide subtitle, click at the end of the word *Tour*. Press Spacebar, and then type **Operations**

Clicking a slide thumbnail is the most common method used to display a slide in the Slide pane.

9 **Save** your presentation.

Objective 3 | Add Pictures to a Presentation

Photographic images add impact to a presentation and help the audience visualize the message you are trying to convey.

Activity 13.08 | Inserting a Picture from a File

Many slide layouts in PowerPoint accommodate digital picture files so that you can easily add pictures you have stored on your system or on a portable storage device.

1 In the **Slides/Outline pane**, click **Slide 2** to display it in the **Slide pane**. On the **Home tab**, in the **Slides group**, click the **New Slide button arrow** to display the **Slide Layout** gallery. Click **Picture with Caption** to insert a new **Slide 3**. Compare your screen with Figure 13.20.

In the center of the large picture placeholder, the *Insert Picture from File* button displays.

Figure 13.20

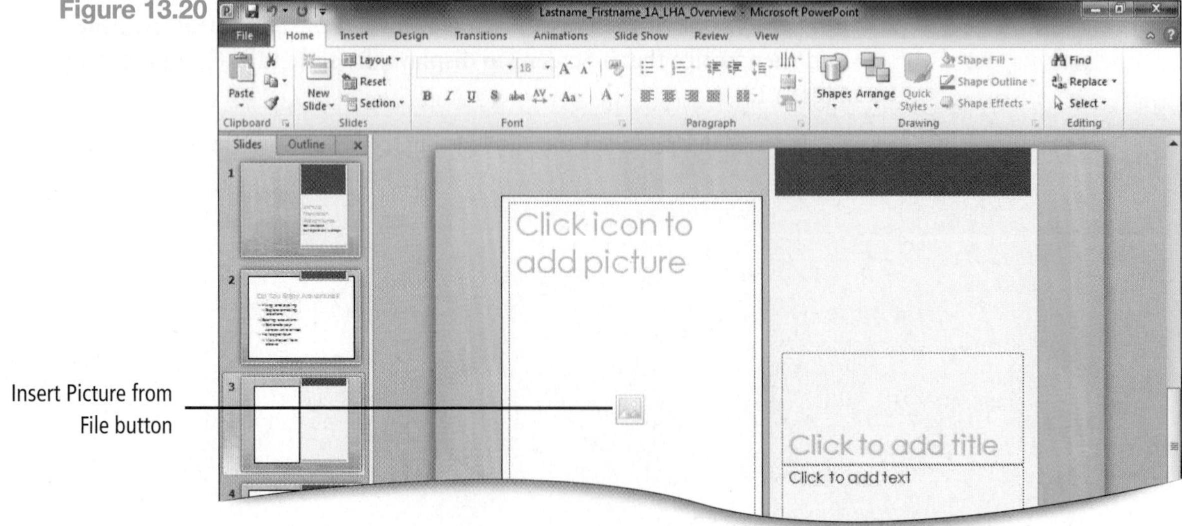

2 In the picture placeholder, click the **Insert Picture from File** button to open the **Insert Picture** dialog box. Navigate to the location in which your student files are stored, click **p01A_Beach**, then click **Insert** to insert the picture in the placeholder.

3 To the right of the picture, click in the title placeholder. Type **Prepare to be Amazed!**

4 Below the title, click in the caption placeholder, and then type **Mountain, sea, volcano. Our tour guides are experts in the history, geography, culture, and flora and fauna of Hawaii.** Compare your screen with Figure 13.21.

Figure 13.21

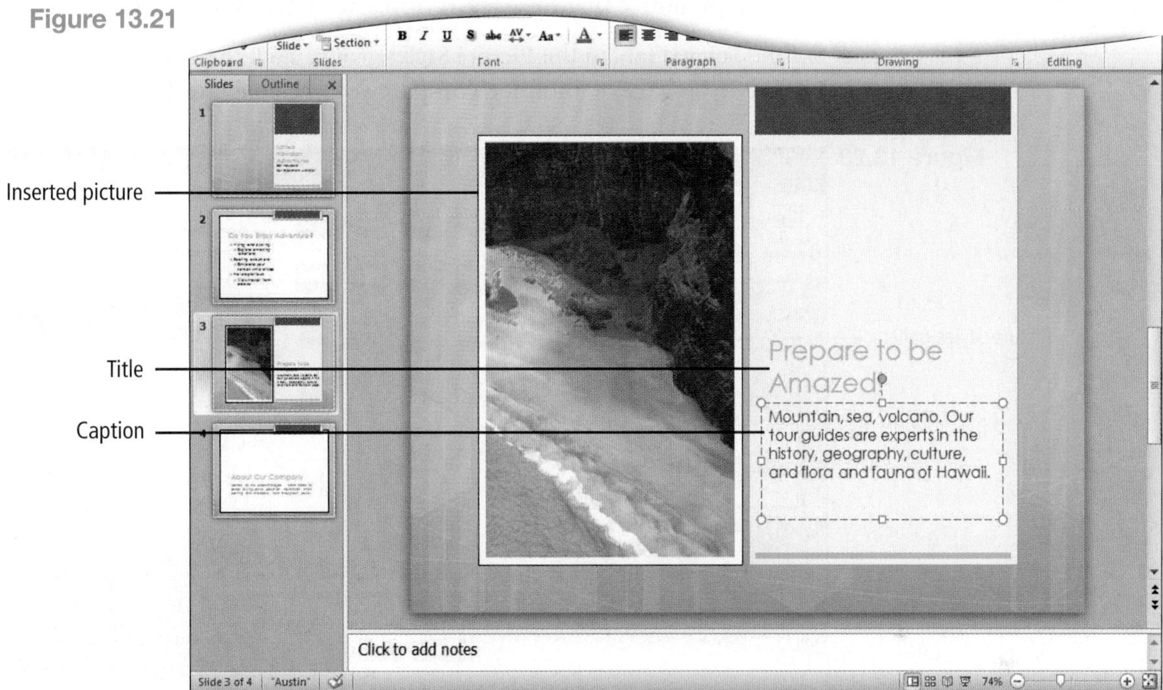

5 Display **Slide 2**. In the placeholder on the right side of the slide, click the **Insert Picture from File** button. Navigate to your student files, and then click **p01A_Helicopter**. Click **Insert**, and then compare your screen with Figure 13.22.

Small circles and squares—***sizing handles***—surround the inserted picture and indicate that the picture is selected and can be modified or formatted. The ***rotation handle***—a green circle above the picture—provides a way to rotate a selected image.

Figure 13.22

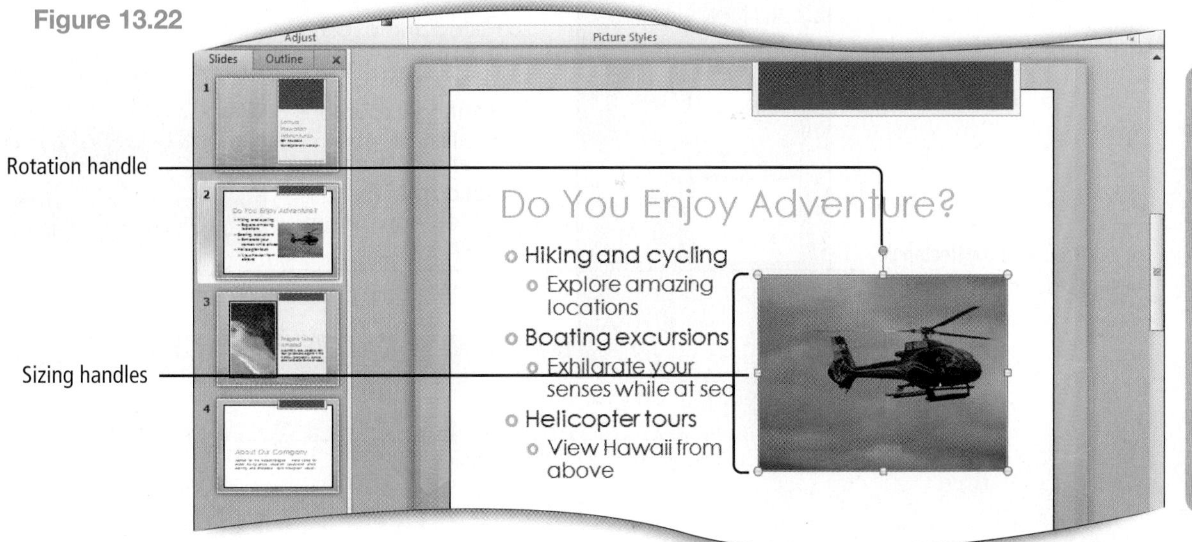

6 **Save** the presentation.

Activity 13.09 | Applying a Style to a Picture

The Picture Tools add the Format tab to the Ribbon, which provides numerous ***styles*** that you can apply to your pictures. A style is a collection of formatting options that you can apply to a picture, text, or an object.

1 With **Slide 2** displayed, if necessary, click the picture of the helicopter to select it. On the Ribbon, notice that the Picture Tools are active and the Format tab displays.

2 On the **Format tab**, in the **Picture Styles group**, click the **More** button to display the **Picture Styles** gallery, and then compare your screen with Figure 13.23.

Figure 13.23

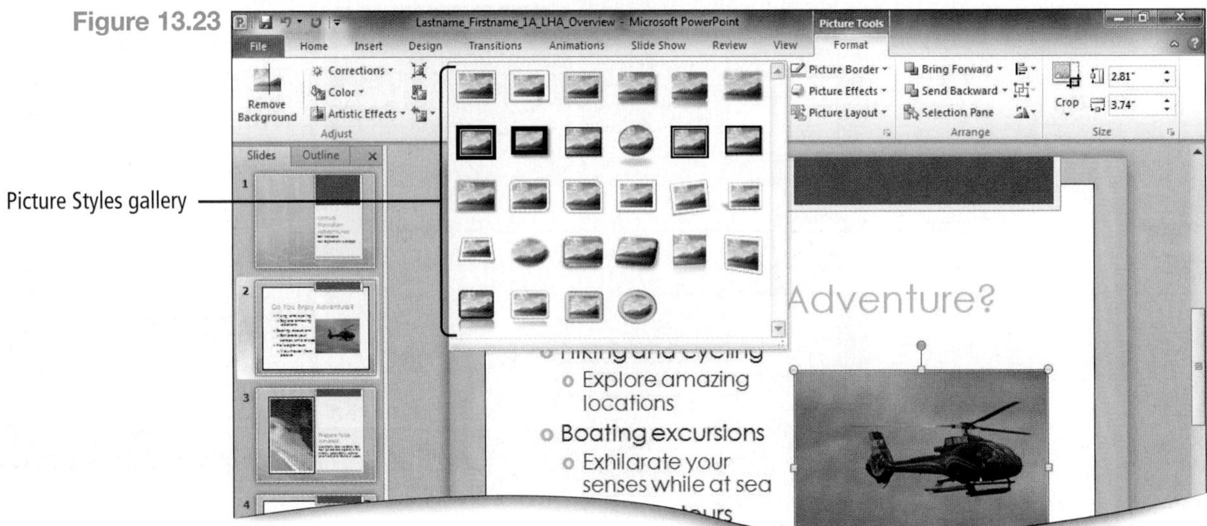

3 In the gallery, point to several of the picture styles to display the ScreenTips and to view the effect on your picture. In the first row, click **Drop Shadow Rectangle**.

4 Click in a blank area of the slide, and then compare your screen with Figure 13.24.

Figure 13.24

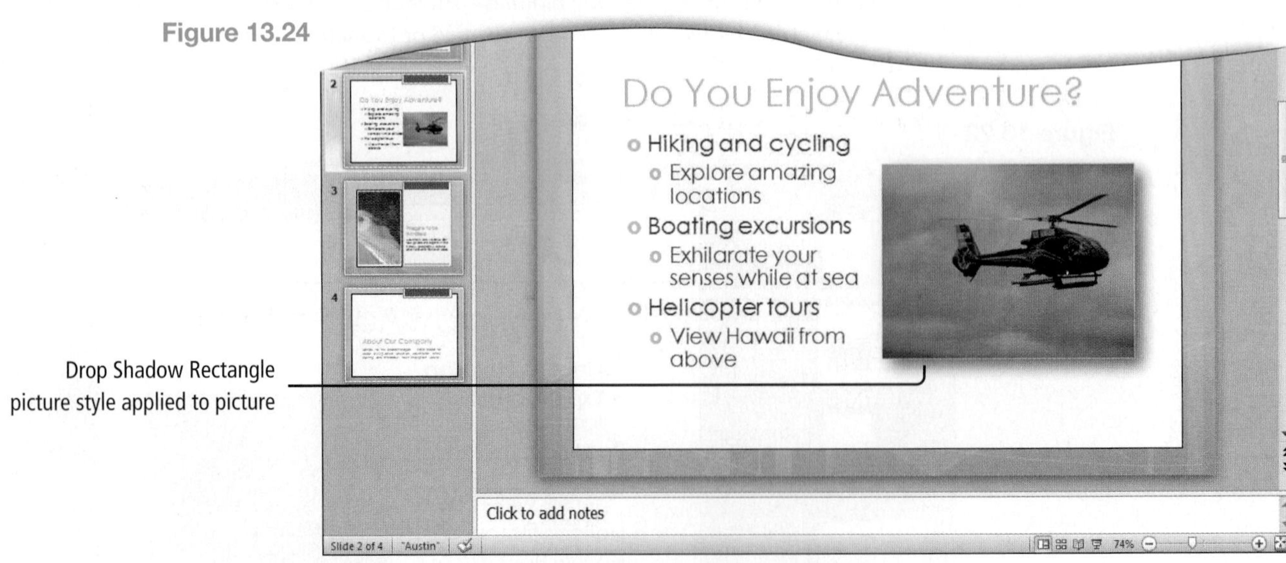

5 **Save** the presentation.

Activity 13.10 | Applying and Removing Picture Artistic Effects

Artistic effects are formats applied to images that make pictures resemble sketches or paintings.

1 With **Slide 2** displayed, select the picture of the helicopter.

2 Click the **Format tab**, and then in the **Adjust group**, click the **Artistic Effects** button to display the **Artistic Effects** gallery. Compare your screen with Figure 13.25.

Figure 13.25

3 In the gallery, point to several of the artistic effects to display the ScreenTips and to have Live Preview display the effect on your picture. Then, in the second row, click the **Paint Strokes** effect.

4 With the picture still selected, on the **Format tab**, in the **Adjust group**, click the **Artistic Effects** button to display the gallery. In the first row, click the first effect—**None**—to remove the effect from the picture and restore the previous formatting.

5 **Save** the presentation.

Objective 4 | Print and View a Presentation

Activity 13.11 | Viewing a Slide Show

When you view a presentation as an electronic slide show, the entire slide fills the computer screen, and an audience can view your presentation if your computer is connected to a projection system.

Another Way

Press F5 to start the slide show from the beginning. Or, display the first slide you want to show and click the Slide Show button on the lower right side of the status bar; or press Shift + F5.

1 On the Ribbon, click the **Slide Show tab**. In the **Start Slide Show group**, click the **From Beginning** button.

The first slide fills the screen, displaying the presentation as the audience would see it if your computer was connected to a projection system.

2 Click the left mouse button or press Spacebar to advance to the second slide.

3 Continue to click or press Spacebar until the last slide displays, and then click or press Spacebar one more time to display a black slide.

After the last slide in a presentation, a ***black slide*** displays, indicating that the presentation is over.

4 With the black slide displayed, click the left mouse button or press Spacebar to exit the slide show and return to the presentation.

Activity 13.12 | Inserting Headers and Footers

A ***header*** is text that prints at the top of each sheet of ***slide handouts*** or ***notes pages***. Slide handouts are printed images of slides on a sheet of paper. Notes pages are printouts that contain the slide image on the top half of the page and notes that you have created on the Notes pane in the lower half of the page.

In addition to headers, you can insert ***footers***—text that displays at the bottom of every slide or that prints at the bottom of a sheet of slide handouts or notes pages.

1 Click the **Insert tab**, and then in the **Text group**, click the **Header & Footer** button to display the **Header and Footer** dialog box.

2 In the **Header and Footer** dialog box, click the **Notes and Handouts tab**. Under **Include on page**, select the **Date and time** check box, and as you do so, watch the Preview box in the lower right corner of the Header and Footer dialog box.

The Preview box indicates the placeholders on the printed Notes and Handouts pages. The two narrow rectangular boxes at the top of the Preview box indicate placeholders for the header text and date. When you select the Date and time check box, the placeholder in the upper right corner is outlined, indicating the location in which the date will display.

3 If necessary, click the Update automatically option button so that the current date prints on the notes and handouts each time the presentation is printed.

4 If necessary, *clear* the Header check box to omit this element. Notice that in the **Preview** box, the corresponding placeholder is not selected.

5 Select the **Page number** and **Footer** check boxes, and then notice that the insertion point displays in the **Footer** box. Using your own name, type **Lastname_Firstname_1A_LHA_Overview** so that the file name displays as a footer, and then compare your dialog box with Figure 13.26.

Figure 13.26

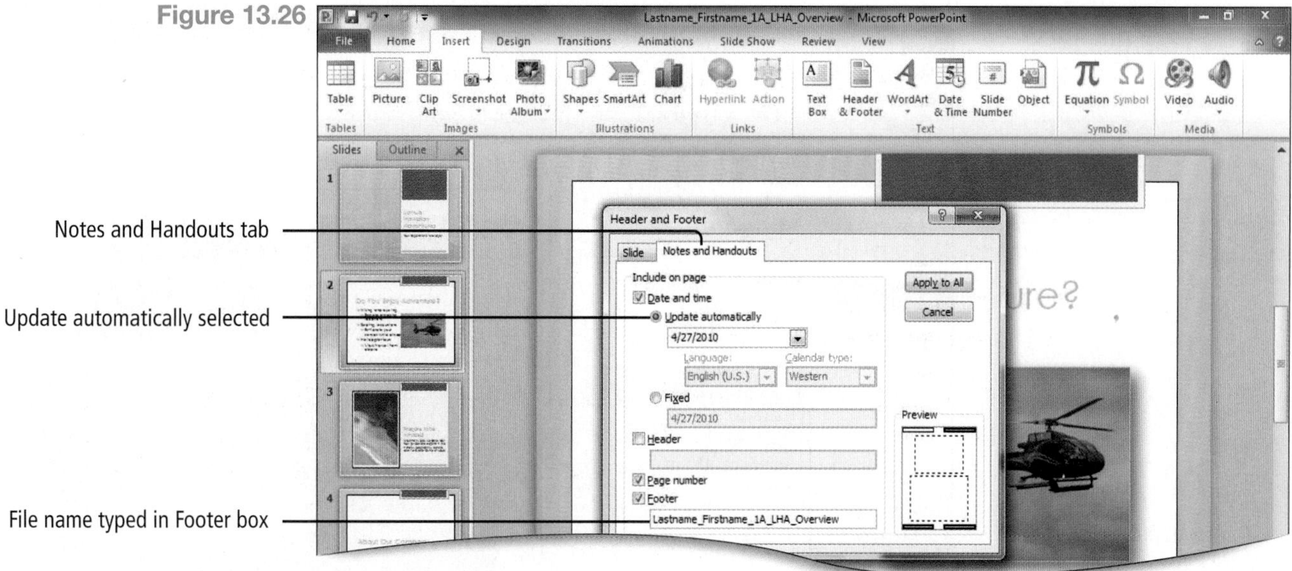

6 In the upper right corner of the dialog box, click **Apply to All**. **Save** your presentation.

> **More Knowledge | Adding Footers to Slides**
>
> You can also add footers to the actual slides, which will display during your presentation, by using the Slide tab in the Header and Footer dialog box. Headers cannot be added to individual slides.

Activity 13.13 | Printing a Presentation

Use Backstage view to preview the arrangement of slides on the handouts and notes pages.

1 Display **Slide 1**. Click the **File tab** to display **Backstage** view, and then click the **Print tab.**

The Print tab in Backstage view displays the tools you need to select your settings and also to view a preview of your presentation. On the right, Print Preview displays your presentation exactly as it will print.

2 In the **Settings group**, click **Full Page Slides**, and then compare your screen with Figure 13.27.

The gallery displays either the default print setting—Full Page Slides—or the most recently selected print setting. Thus, on your system, this button might indicate the presentation Notes Pages, Outline, or one of several arrangements of slide handouts—depending on the most recently used setting.

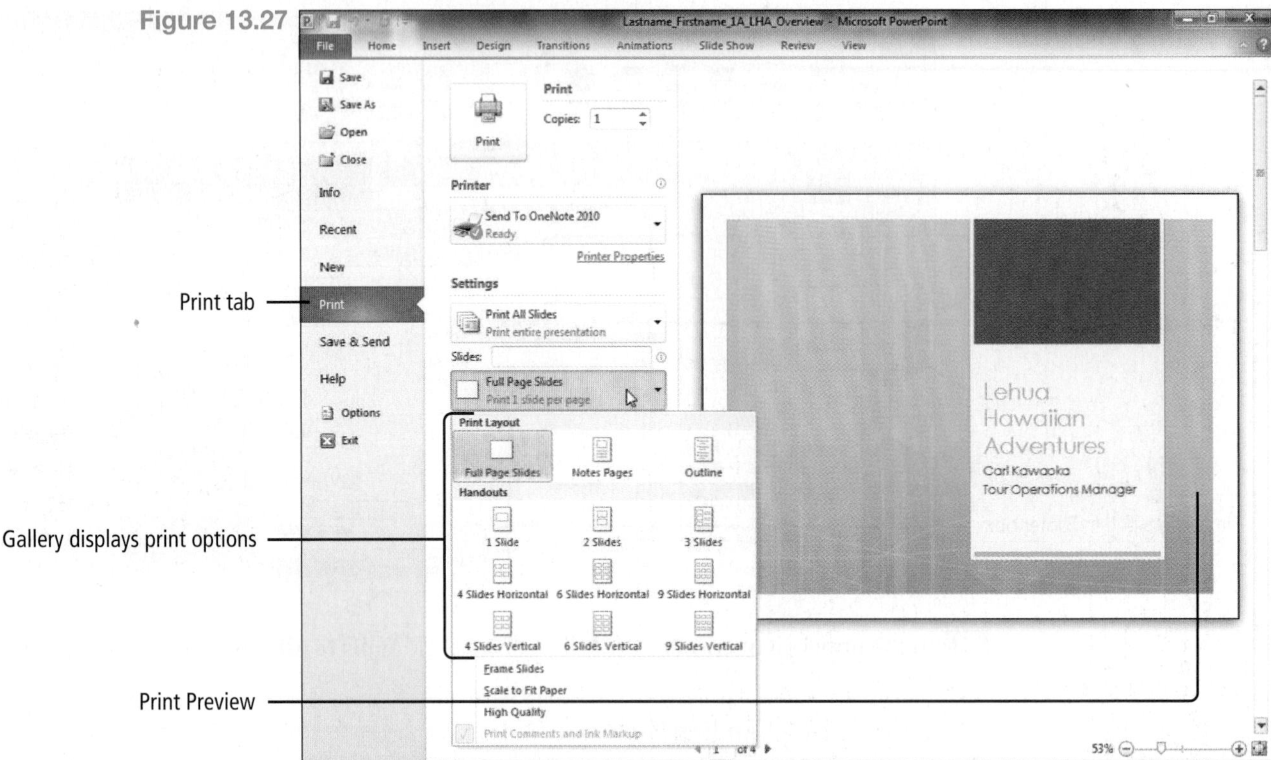

Figure 13.27

3 In the gallery, under **Handouts**, click **4 Slides Horizontal**. Notice that the **Print Preview** on the right displays the slide handout, and that the current date, file name, and page number display in the header and footer.

In the Settings group, the Portrait Orientation option displays so that you can change the print orientation from Portrait to Landscape. The Portrait Orientation option does not display when Full Page Slides is chosen.

4 To print your handout, be sure your system is connected to a printer, and then in the **Print group**, click the **Print** button.

The handout will print on your default printer—on a black and white printer, the colors will print in shades of gray. Backstage view closes and your file redisplays in the PowerPoint window.

5 Click the **File tab** to display **Backstage** view, and then click the **Print tab**. In the **Settings group**, click **4 Slides Horizontal**, and then under **Print Layout**, click **Notes Pages** to view the presentation notes for **Slide 1**; recall that you created notes for **Slide 4**.

Indicated below the Notes page are the current slide number and the number of pages that will print when Notes page is selected. You can use the Next Page and Previous Page arrows to display each Notes page in the presentation.

6 At the bottom of the **Print Preview**, click the **Next Page** button ▶ three times so that **Page 4** displays. Compare your screen with Figure 13.28.

The notes that you created for Slide 4 display below the image of the slide.

Figure 13.28

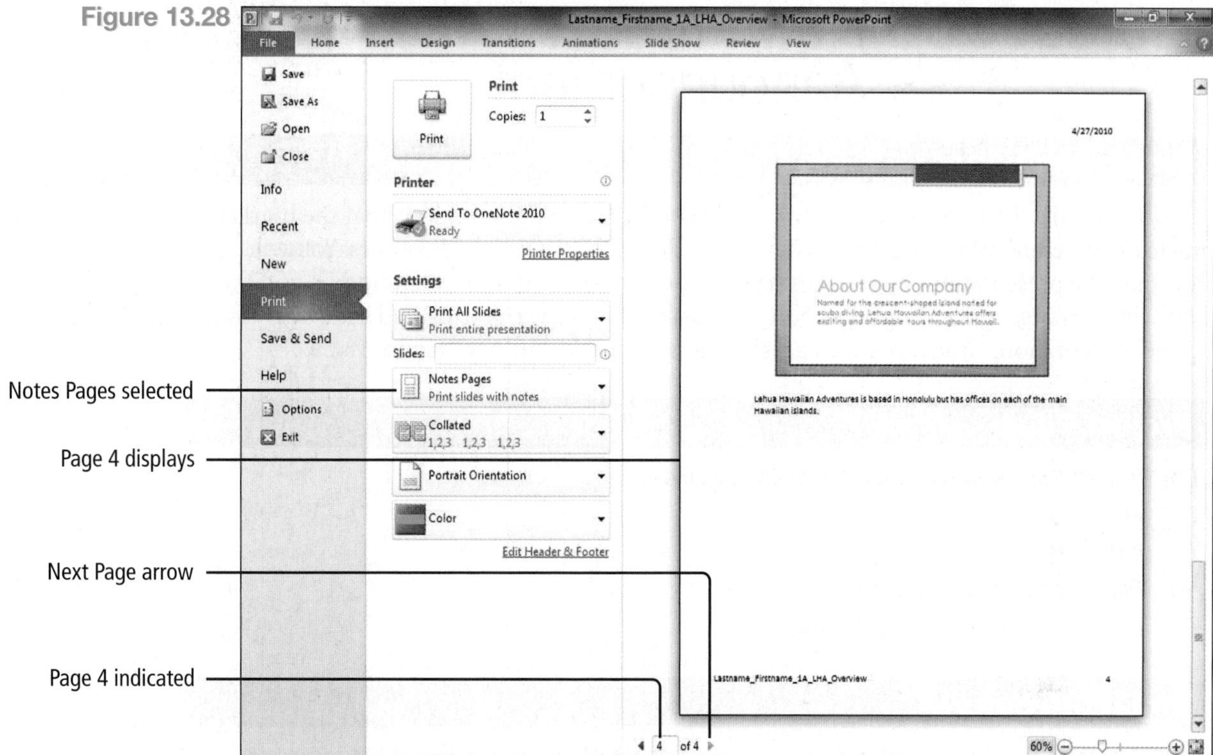

7 In the **Settings group**, click in the **Slides** box, and then type **4** so that only the Notes pages for **Slide 4** will print. In the **Settings group**, click **Notes Pages**, and then below the gallery, select **Frame Slides**. In the **Print group**, click the **Print** button to print the Notes page.

8 Click the **File tab** to redisplay **Backstage** view, be sure the **Info tab** is active, and then in the third panel, click **Properties**. Click **Show Document Panel**, and then in the **Author** box, delete any text and type your firstname and lastname.

9 In the **Subject** box, type your course name and section number. In the **Keywords** box, type **company overview** and then **Close** the Document Information Panel.

10 **Save** your presentation. On the right end of the title bar, click the **Close** button to close the presentation and close PowerPoint.

End **You have completed Project 13A**

Project 13B New Product Announcement

Project Activities

In Activities 13.14 through 13.23, you will combine two presentations that the marketing team at Lehua Adventure Travels developed describing their new Ecotours. You will combine the presentations by inserting slides from one presentation into another, and then you will rearrange and delete slides. You will also apply font formatting and slide transitions to the presentation. Your completed presentation will look similar to Figure 13.29.

Project Files

For Project 13B, you will need the following files:

p01B_Ecotours
p01B_Slides

You will save your presentation as:

Lastname_Firstname_1B_Ecotours

Project Results

Figure 13.29
Project 13B—Ecotours

Objective 5 | Edit an Existing Presentation

Recall that editing refers to the process of adding, deleting, and modifying presentation content. You can edit presentation content in either the Slide pane or the Slides/Outline pane.

Activity 13.14 | Displaying and Editing the Presentation Outline

You can display the presentation outline in the Slides/Outline pane and edit the presentation text. Changes that you make in the outline are immediately displayed in the Slide pane.

1 **Start** PowerPoint. From your student files, open **p01B_Ecotours**. On the **File tab**, click **Save As**, navigate to your **PowerPoint Chapter 13** folder, and then using your own name, save the file as **Lastname_Firstname_1B_Ecotours**

2 In the **Slides/Outline pane**, click the **Outline tab** to display the presentation outline. If necessary, below the Slides/Outline pane, drag the scroll box all the way to the left so that the slide numbers display. Compare your screen with Figure 13.30.

The outline tab is wider than the Slides tab so that you have additional space to type your text. Each slide in the outline displays the slide number, slide icon, and the slide title in bold.

Figure 13.30

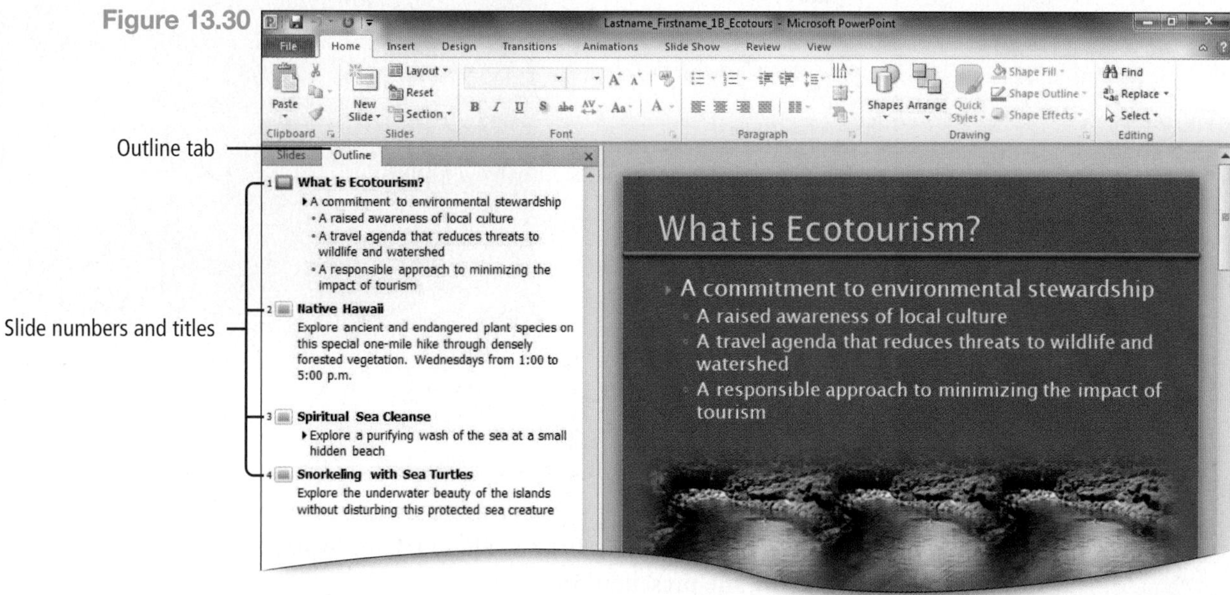

3 In the **Outline tab**, in **Slide 1**, select the last three bullet points, and then compare your screen with Figure 13.31.

Figure 13.31

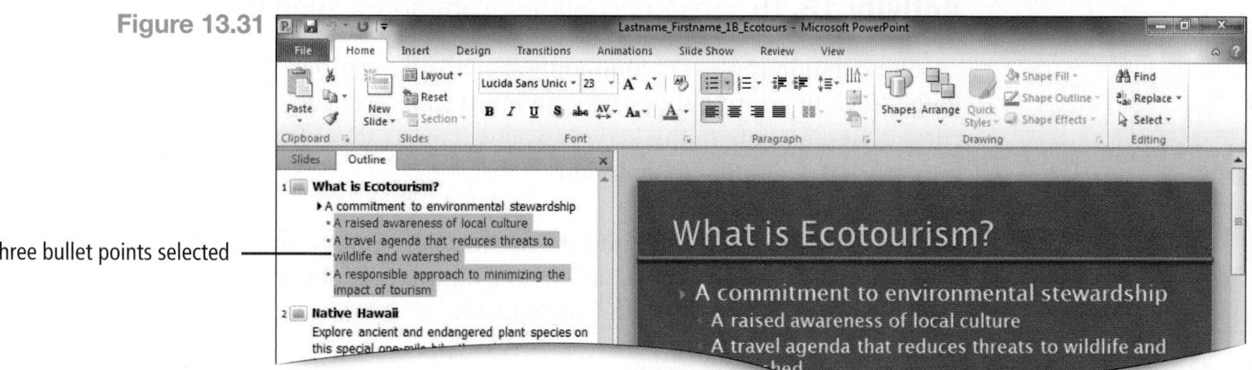

4 On the **Home tab**, in the **Paragraph group**, click the **Decrease List Level** button one time to decrease the list level of the selected bullet points.

When you type in the outline or change the list level, the changes also display in the Slide pane.

5 In the **Outline tab**, click anywhere in **Slide 3**, and then click at the end of the last bullet point after the word *beach*. Press Enter to create a new bullet point at the same list level as the previous bullet point. Type **Offered Tuesdays and Thursdays one hour before sunset, weather permitting**

6 Press Enter to create a new bullet point. Type **Fee: $30** and then compare your screen with Figure 13.32.

Figure 13.32

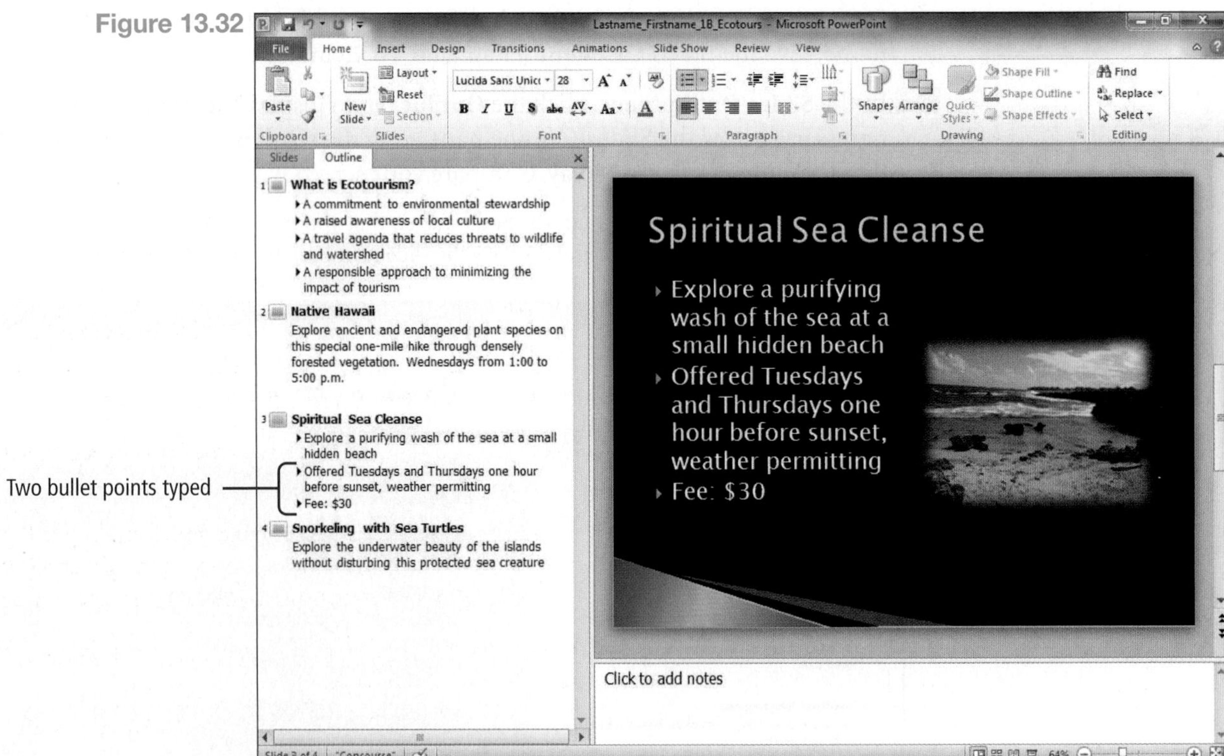

7 In the **Slides/Outline pane**, click the **Slides tab** to display the slide thumbnails, and then **Save** the presentation.

You can type text in the Slide tab or in the Outline tab. Displaying the Outline tab enables you to view the entire flow of the presentation.

Activity 13.15 | Inserting Slides from an Existing Presentation

Presentation content is commonly shared among group members in an organization. Rather than re-creating slides, you can insert slides from an existing presentation into the current presentation. In this activity, you will insert slides from an existing presentation into your 1B_Ecotours presentation.

1 Display **Slide 1**. On the **Home tab**, in the **Slides group**, click the **New Slide button arrow** to display the **Slide Layout** gallery and additional commands for inserting slides. Compare your screen with Figure 13.33.

Figure 13.33

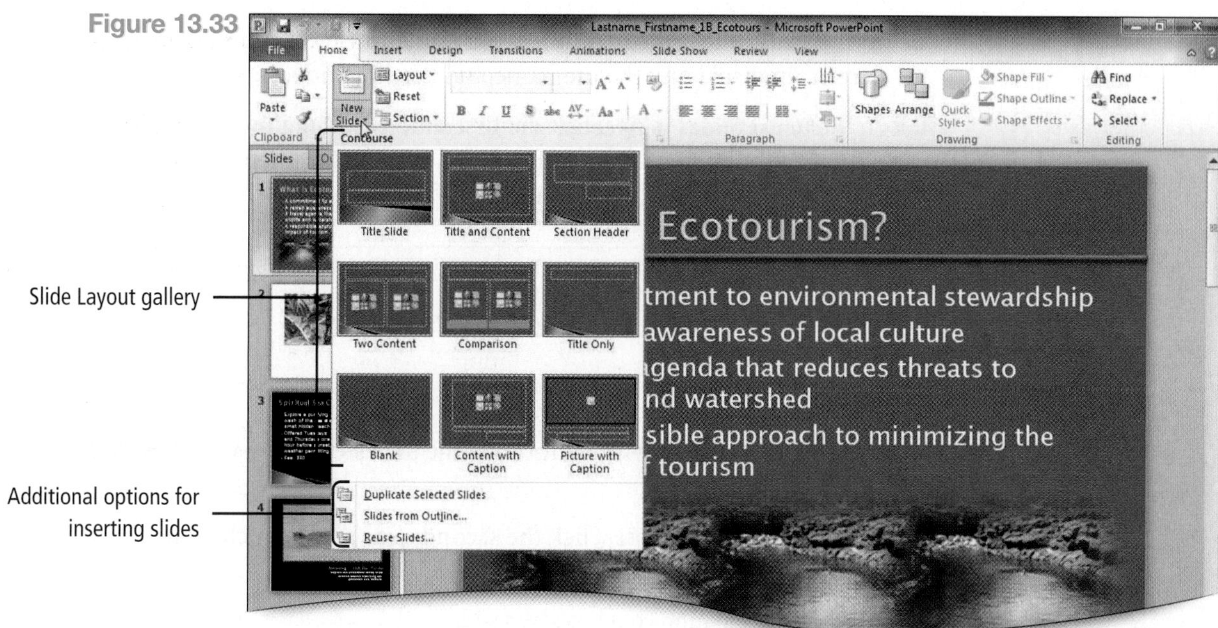

2 Below the gallery, click **Reuse Slides** to open the Reuse Slides pane on the right side of the PowerPoint window.

3 In the **Reuse Slides** pane, click the **Browse** button, and then click **Browse File**. In the **Browse** dialog box, navigate to the location where your student files are stored, and then double-click **p01B_Slides** to display the slides in the Reuse Slides pane.

4 At the bottom of the **Reuse Slides** pane, select the **Keep source formatting** check box, and then compare your screen with Figure 13.34.

By selecting the *Keep source formatting* check box, you retain the formatting applied to the slides when inserted into the existing presentation. When the *Keep source formatting* check box is cleared, the theme formatting of the presentation in which the slides are inserted is applied.

Figure 13.34

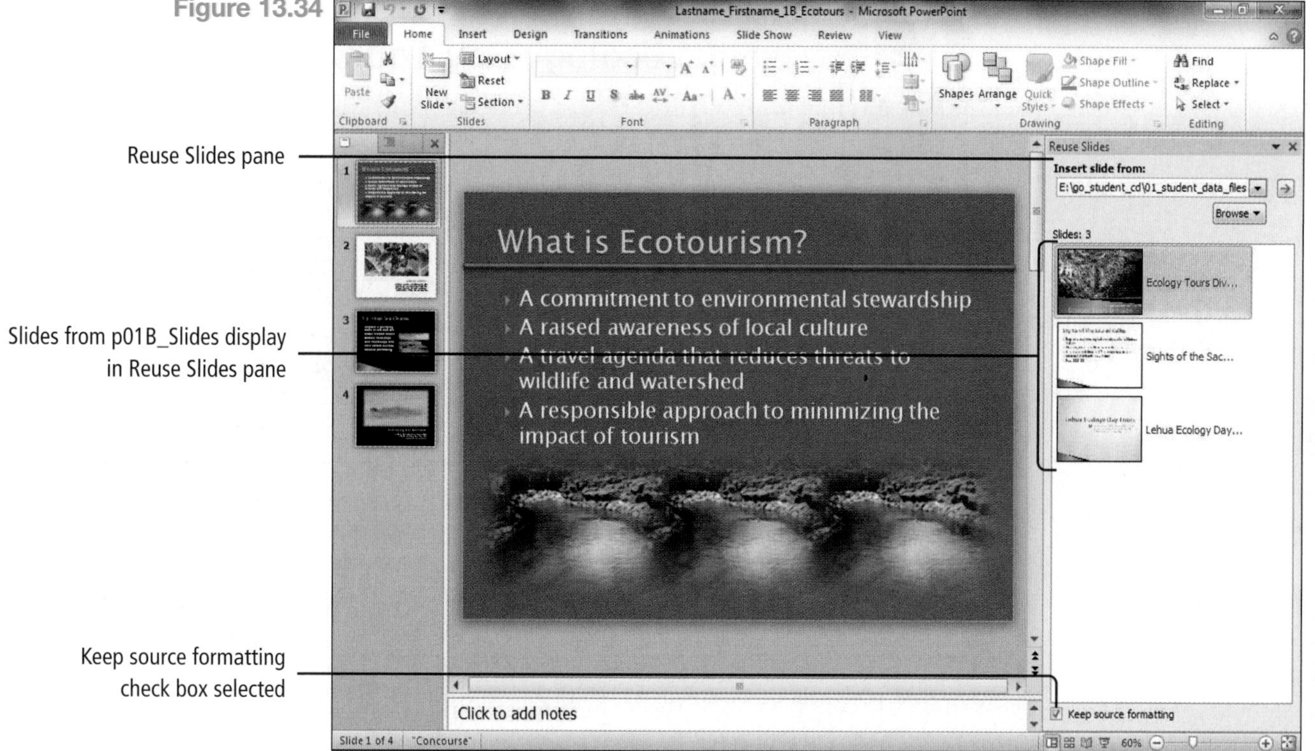

5 In the **Reuse Slides** pane, point to each slide to view a zoomed image of the slide and a ScreenTip displaying the file name and the slide title.

6 In the **Reuse Slides** pane, click the first slide—**Ecology Tours Division**—to insert the slide into the current presentation after Slide 1, and then notice that the original slide background formatting is retained.

> **Note | Inserting Slides**
>
> You can insert slides into your presentation in any order; remember to display the slide that will precede the slide that you want to insert.

7 In your **1B_Ecotours** presentation, in the **Slides/Outline pane**, click **Slide 5** to display it in the **Slide pane**.

8 In the **Reuse Slides** pane, click the second slide and then click the third slide to insert both slides after **Slide 5**.

Your presentation contains seven slides.

9 On **Slide 7**, point to *Lehua*, and then right-click to display the shortcut menu. Click **Ignore all**. Use the same technique to ignore the spelling of the word *Ecotour*. Compare your screen with Figure 13.35.

Figure 13.35

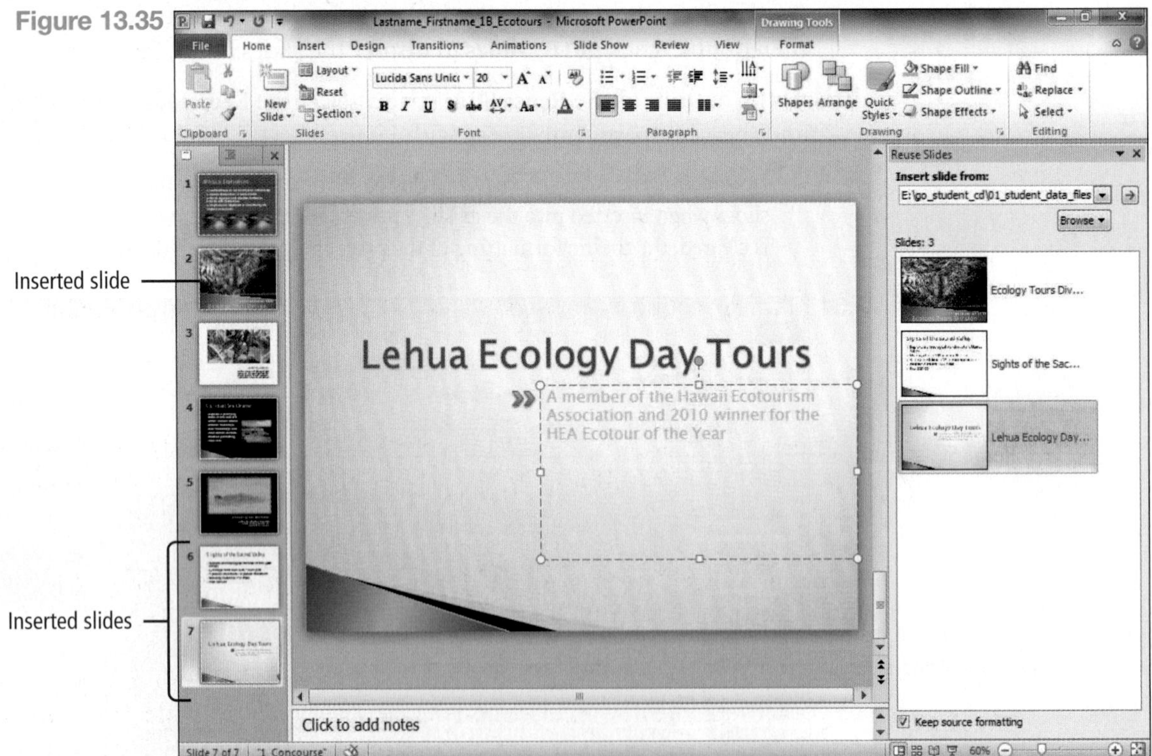

10 **Close** [X] the **Reuse Slides** pane; click **Save**.

> **More Knowledge | Inserting All Slides**
>
> You can insert all of the slides from an existing presentation into the current presentation at one time. In the Reuse Slides pane, right-click one of the slides that you want to insert, and then click Insert All Slides.

Activity 13.16 | Finding and Replacing Text

The Replace command enables you to locate all occurrences of specified text and replace it with alternative text.

1 Display **Slide 1**. On the **Home tab**, in the **Editing group**, click the **Replace** button. In the **Replace** dialog box, in the **Find what** box, type **Ecology** and then in the **Replace with** box, type **Eco** Compare your screen with Figure 13.36.

Figure 13.36

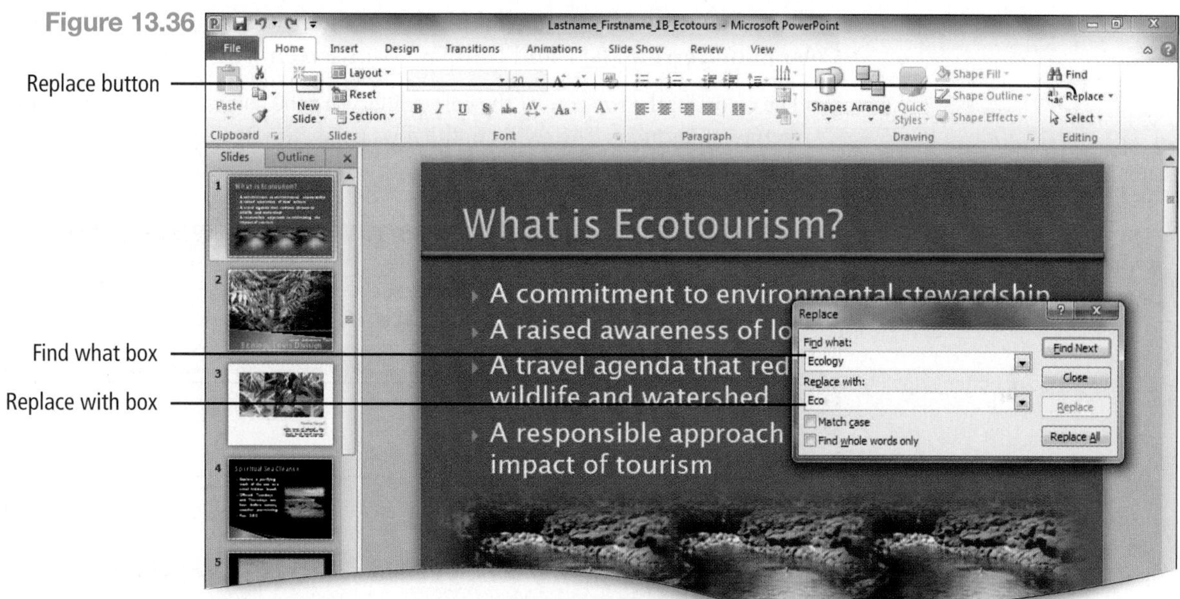

2 In the **Replace** dialog box, click the **Replace All** button.

A message box displays indicating the number of replacements that were made.

3 In the message box, click **OK**, **Close** the **Replace** dialog box, and then click **Save**.

Objective 6 | Format a Presentation

Formatting refers to changing the appearance of the text, layout, and design of a slide. You will find it easiest to do most of your formatting changes in PowerPoint in the Slide pane.

Activity 13.17 | Changing Fonts, Font Sizes, Font Styles, and Font Colors

Recall that a font is a set of characters with the same design and shape and that fonts are measured in points. Font styles include bold, italic, and underline, and you can apply any combination of these styles to presentation text. Font styles and font color are useful to provide emphasis and are a visual cue to draw the reader's eye to important text.

1 On the right side of the **Slides/Outline pane**, drag the scroll box down until **Slide 7** displays, and then click **Slide 7** to display it in the **Slides** pane.

When a presentation contains a large number of slides, a scroll box displays to the right of the slide thumbnails so that you can scroll and then select the thumbnails.

2 Select the title text—*Lehua Eco Day Tours*. Point to the Mini toolbar, and then click the **Font button arrow** to display the available fonts. Click **Arial Black**.

3 Select the light green text in the placeholder below the title, and then on the Mini toolbar, change the **Font** to **Arial Black** and the **Font Size** to **28**. Then, click the **Font Color button arrow** [A ▾], and compare your screen with Figure 13.37.

The colors in the top row of the color gallery are the colors associated with the presentation theme—*Concourse*. The colors in the rows below the first row are light and dark variations of the theme colors.

Figure 13.37

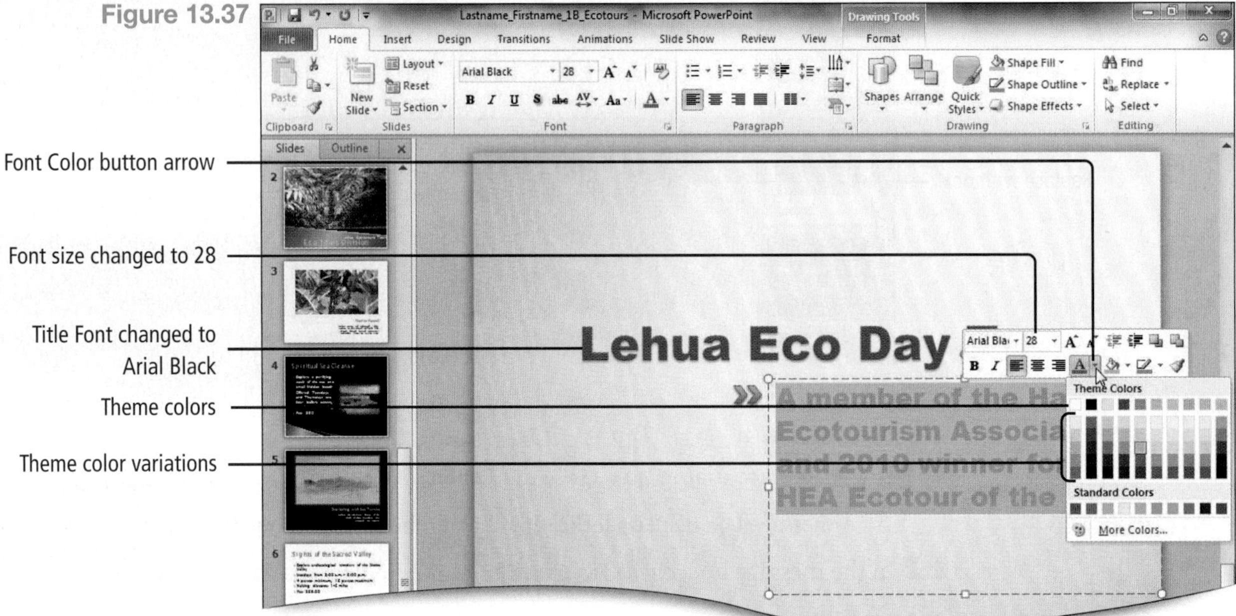

4 Point to several of the colors and notice that a ScreenTip displays the color name and Live Preview displays the selected text in the color to which you are pointing.

5 In the second column of colors, click the first color—**Black, Text 1**—to change the font color. Notice that on the Home tab and Mini toolbar, the lower part of the Font Color button displays the most recently applied font color—Black.

When you click the Font Color button instead of the Font Color button arrow, the color displayed in the lower part of the Font Color button is applied to selected text without displaying the color gallery.

6 Display **Slide 2**, and then select the title *Eco Tours Division*. On the Mini toolbar, click the **Font Color button** [A ▾] to apply the font color **Black, Text 1** to the selection. Select the subtitle—*Lehua Adventure Tours*—and then change the **Font Color** to **Black, Text 1**. Compare your screen with Figure 13.38.

Figure 13.38

7 Display **Slide 3**, and then select the title—*Native Hawaii.* From the Mini toolbar, apply **Bold** [B] and **Italic** [I], and then **Save** your presentation.

Activity 13.18 | Aligning Text and Changing Line Spacing

In PowerPoint, ***text alignment*** refers to the horizontal placement of text within a placeholder. You can align left, centered, right, or justified.

1 Display **Slide 2**. Click anywhere in the title—*Eco Tours Division.*

2 On the **Home tab**, in the **Paragraph group**, click the **Align Text Right** button to right align the text within the placeholder.

3 Display **Slide 7**. Click anywhere in the text below the title. In the **Paragraph group**, click the **Line Spacing** button. In the list, click **1.5** to change from single-spacing between lines to one-and-a-half spacing between lines. **Save** your presentation, and then compare your screen with Figure 13.39.

Figure 13.39

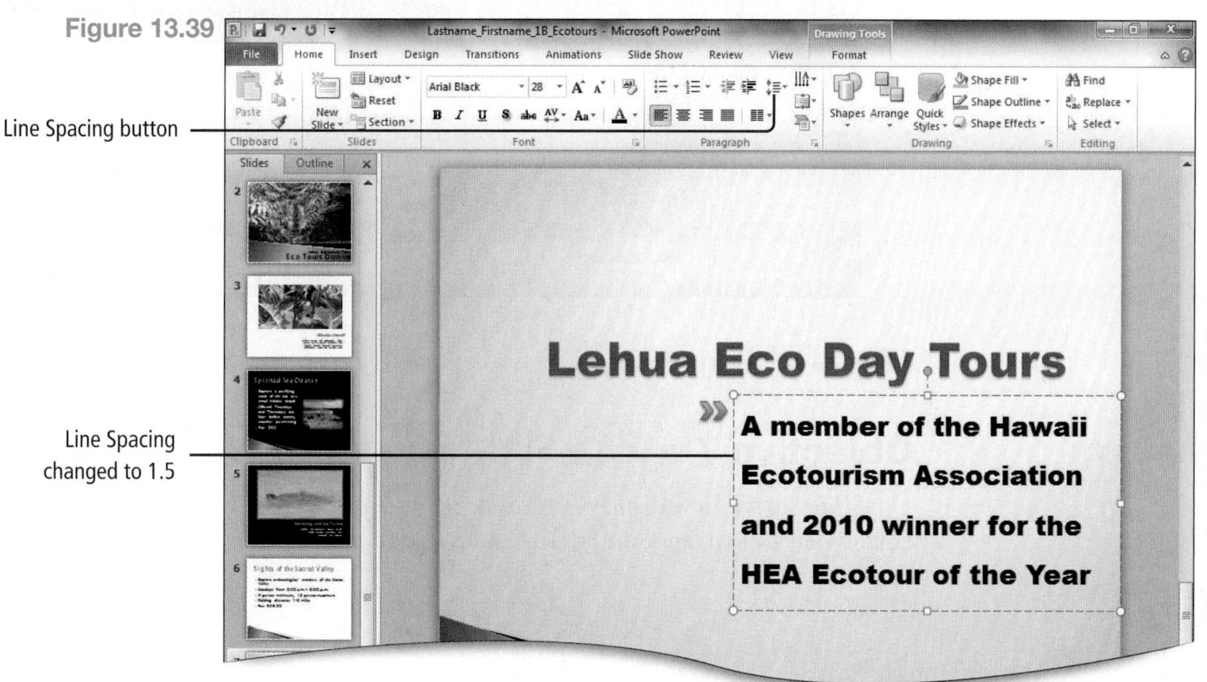

Activity 13.19 | Modifying Slide Layout

Recall that the slide layout defines the placement of the content placeholders on a slide. PowerPoint includes predefined layouts that you can apply to your slide for the purpose of arranging slide elements.

For example, a Title Slide contains two placeholder elements—the title and the subtitle. When you design your slides, consider the content that you want to include, and then choose a layout with the elements that will display the message you want to convey in the best way.

1 Display **Slide 3**. On the **Home tab**, in the **Slides group**, click the **Layout** button to display the **Slide Layout** gallery. Notice that *Content with Caption* is selected.

The selection indicates the layout of the current slide.

2 Click **Picture with Caption** to change the slide layout, and then compare your screen with Figure 13.40.

The Picture with Caption layout emphasizes the picture more effectively than the Content with Caption layout.

Figure 13.40

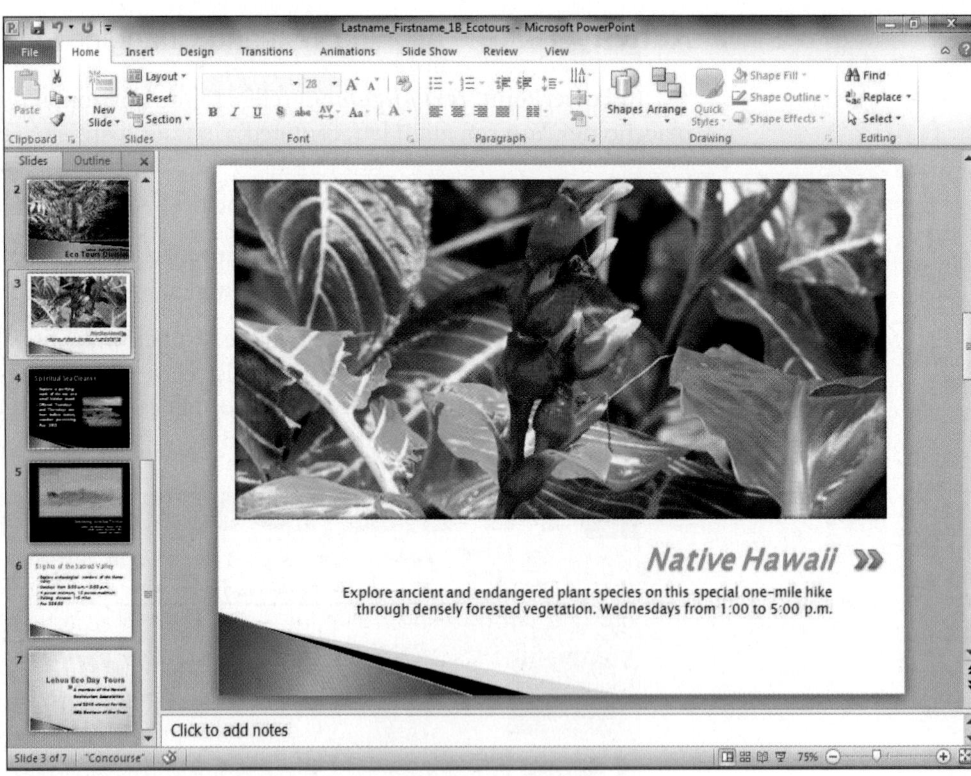

3 **Save** your presentation.

Objective 7 | Use Slide Sorter View

Slide Sorter view displays thumbnails of all of the slides in a presentation. Use Slide Sorter view to rearrange and delete slides and to apply formatting to multiple slides.

Activity 13.20 | Deleting Slides in Slide Sorter View

> **Another Way**
> On the Ribbon, click the View tab, and then in the Presentation Views group, click Slide Sorter.

1 In the lower right corner of the PowerPoint window, click the **Slide Sorter** button to display all of the slide thumbnails.

2 Compare your screen with Figure 13.41.

Your slides may display larger or smaller than those shown in Figure 13.41.

Figure 13.41

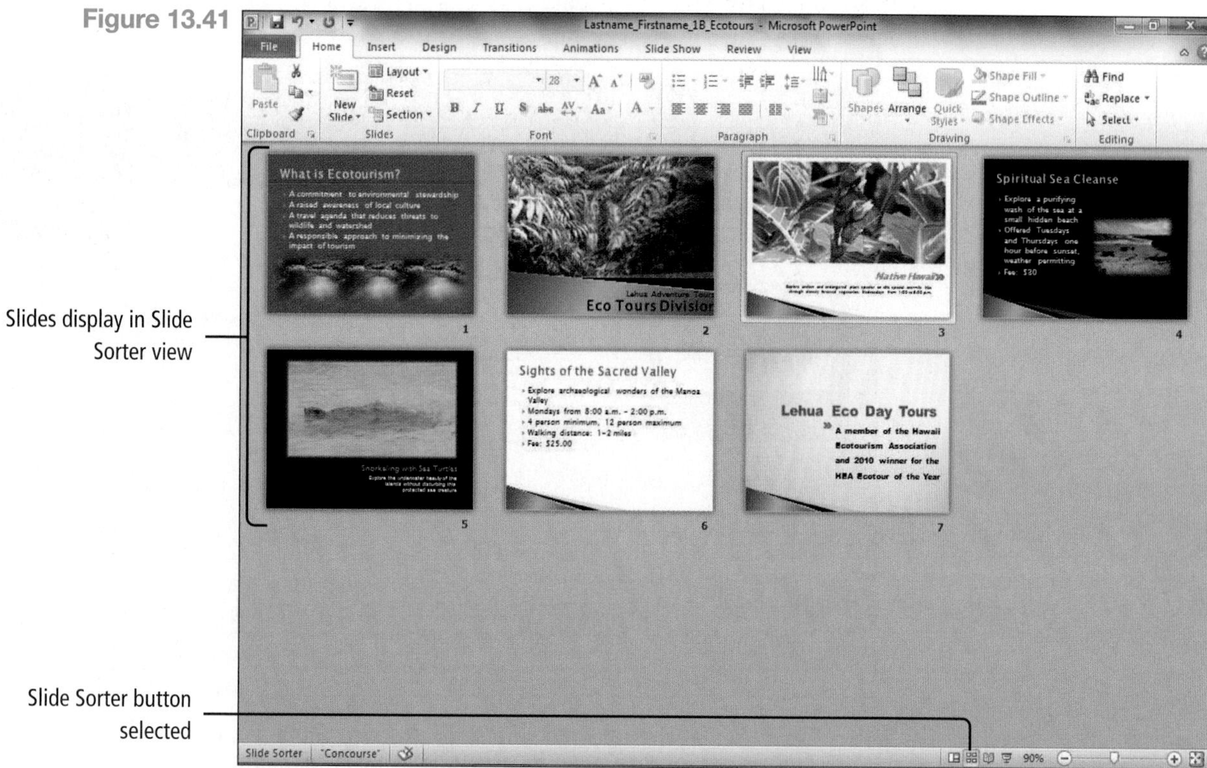

3 Click **Slide 6**, and notice that a thick outline surrounds the slide, indicating that it is selected. On your keyboard, press Del to delete the slide. Click **Save**.

Activity 13.21 | Moving Slides in Slide Sorter View

1 With the presentation displayed in Slide Sorter view, point to **Slide 2**. Hold down the left mouse button, and then drag the slide to the left until the vertical move bar and pointer indicating the position to which the slide will be moved is positioned to the left of **Slide 1**, as shown in Figure 13.42.

Figure 13.42

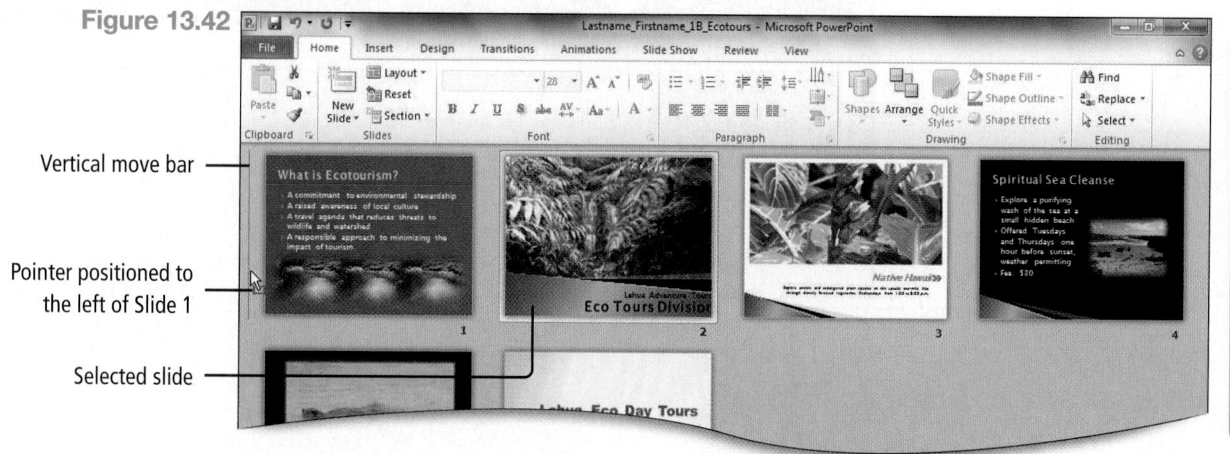

2 Release the mouse button to move the slide to the Slide 1 position in the presentation.

3 Click **Slide 4**, hold down Ctrl, and then click **Slide 5**. Compare your screen with Figure 13.43.

Both slides are outlined, indicating that both are selected. By holding down Ctrl, you can create a group of selected slides.

Figure 13.43

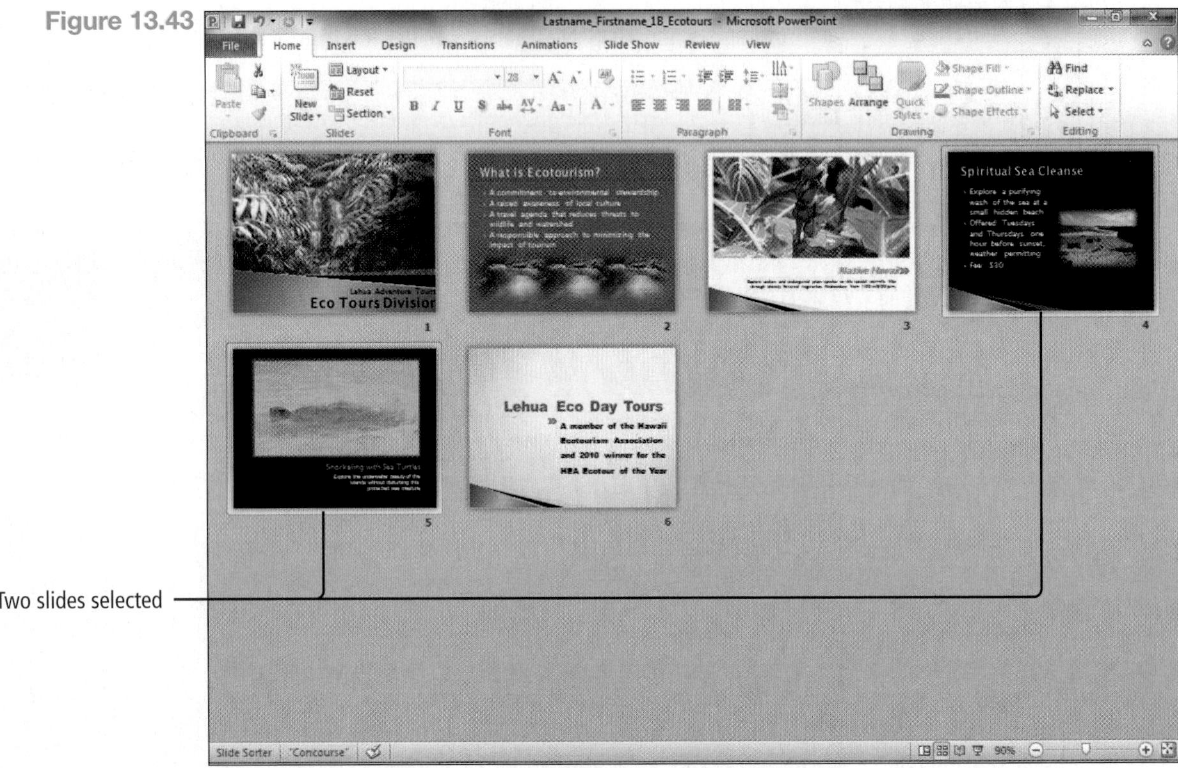

Two slides selected

4 Point to either of the selected slides, hold down the left mouse button, and then drag to position the vertical move bar to the left of **Slide 3**. Release the mouse button to move the two slides, and then compare your screen with Figure 13.44.

Figure 13.44

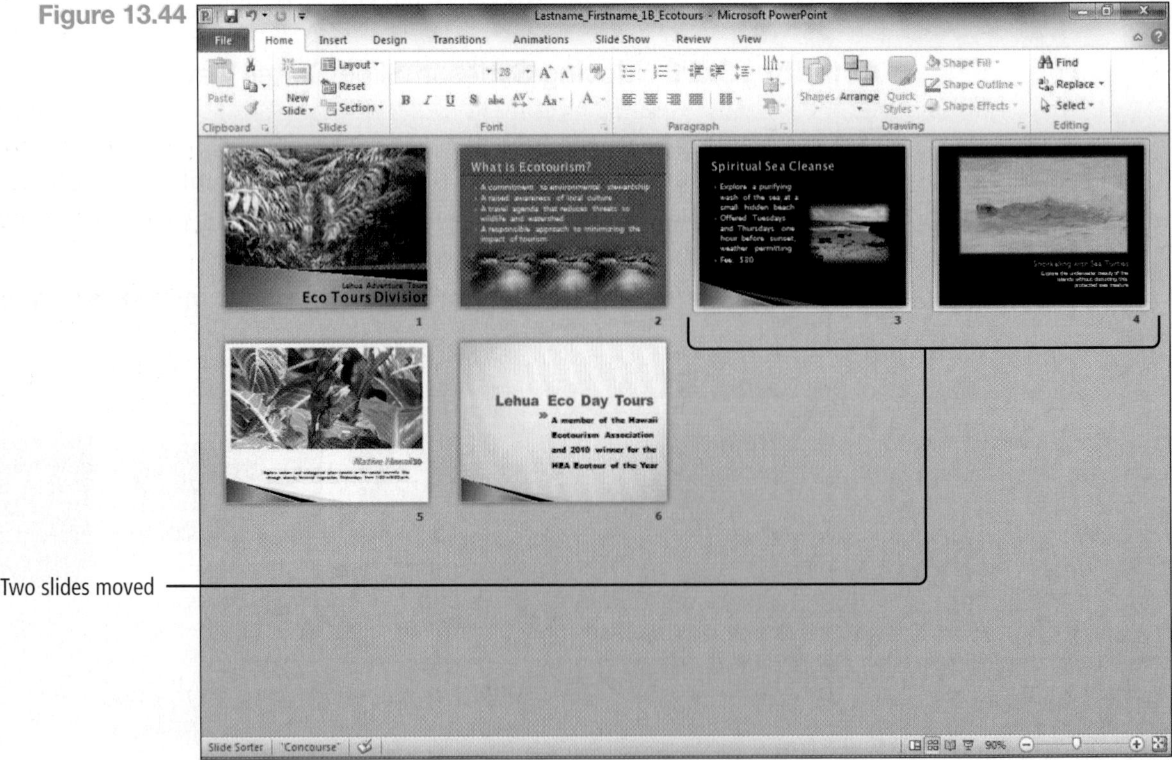

Two slides moved

5 In the status bar, click the **Normal** button to return to Normal view. **Save** your presentation.

Objective 8 | Apply Slide Transitions

Slide transitions are the motion effects that occur in Slide Show view when you move from one slide to the next during a presentation. You can choose from a variety of transitions, and you can control the speed and method with which the slides advance.

Activity 13.22 | Applying Slide Transitions to a Presentation

1 Display **Slide 1**. On the **Transitions tab**, in the **Transition to This Slide group**, click the **More** button to display the **Transitions** gallery. Compare your screen with Figure 13.45.

Figure 13.45

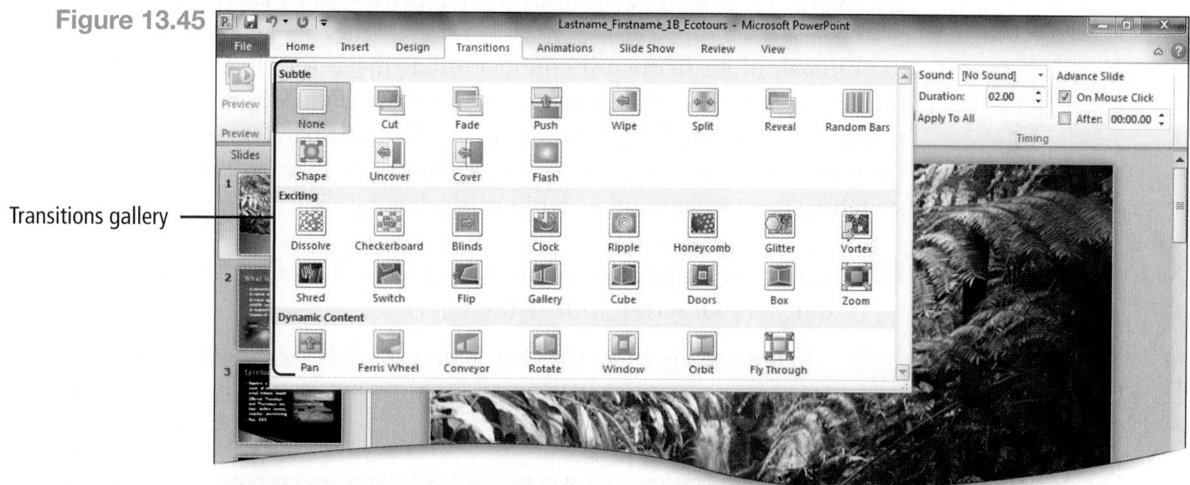

2 Under **Exciting**, click **Doors** to apply and view the transition. In the **Transition to This Slide group**, click the **Effect Options** button to display the directions from which the slide enters the screen. Click **Horizontal**.

The Effect Options vary depending upon the selected transition and include the direction from which the slide enters the screen or the shape in which the slide displays during the transition.

3 In the **Timing group**, notice that the **Duration** box displays *01.40*, indicating that the transition lasts 1.40 seconds. Click the **Duration** box **up spin arrow** two times so that *01.75* displays. Under **Advance Slide**, verify that the **On Mouse Click** check box is selected; select it if necessary. Compare your screen with Figure 13.46.

When the On Mouse Click option is selected, the presenter controls when the current slide advances to the next slide by clicking the mouse button or by pressing Spacebar.

Figure 13.46

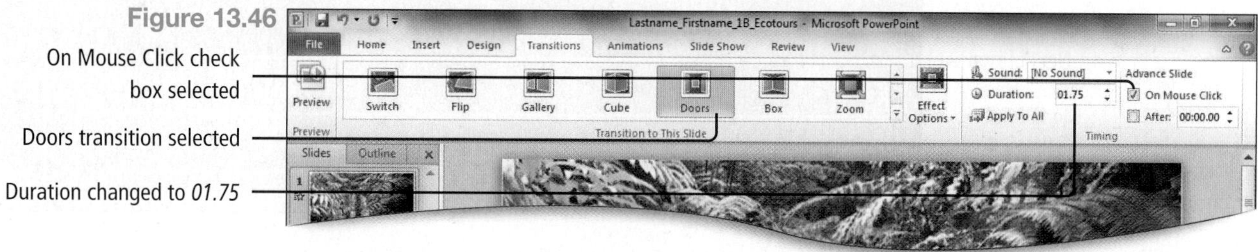

4 In the **Timing group**, click the **Apply To All** button so that the Doors, Horizontal with a Duration of 1.75 seconds transition is applied to all of the slides in the presentation. Notice that in the Slides/Outline pane, a star displays below the slide number providing a visual cue that a transition has been applied to the slide.

5 Click the **Slide Show tab**. In the **Start Slide Show group**, click the **From Beginning** button, and then view your presentation, clicking the mouse button to advance through the slides. When the black slide displays, click the mouse button one more time to display the presentation in Normal view. **Save** your presentation.

More Knowledge | Applying Multiple Slide Transitions

You can apply more than one type of transition in your presentation by displaying the slides one at a time, and then clicking the transition that you want to apply instead of clicking the Apply To All button.

Activity 13.23 | Displaying a Presentation in Reading View

Organizations frequently conduct online meetings when participants are unable to meet in one location. The ***Reading view*** in PowerPoint displays a presentation in a manner similar to a slide show but the taskbar, title bar, and status bar remain available in the presentation window. Thus, a presenter can easily facilitate an online conference by switching to another window without closing the slide show.

Another Way

On the View tab, in the Presentation Views group, click Reading View.

1 In the lower right corner of the PowerPoint window, click the **Reading View** button. Compare your screen with Figure 13.47.

In Reading View, the status bar contains the Next and Previous buttons, which are used to navigate in the presentation, and the Menu button which is used to print, copy, and edit slides.

Figure 13.47

2 In the status bar, click the **Next** button to display **Slide 2**. Press Spacebar to display **Slide 3**. Click the left mouse button to display **Slide 4**. In the status bar, click the **Previous** button to display **Slide 3**.

Another Way

Press Esc to exit Reading view and return to Normal view.

3 In the status bar, click the **Menu** button to display the Reading view menu, and then click **End Show** to return to Normal view.

4 On the **Insert tab**, in the **Text group**, click the **Header & Footer** button, and then click the **Notes and Handouts tab**. Under **Include on page**, select the **Date and time** check box, and if necessary, select **Update automatically**. Clear the **Header** check box, and then select the **Page number** and **Footer** check boxes. In the **Footer** box, using your own name, type **Lastname_Firstname_1B_Ecotours** and then click **Apply to All**.

5 Display **Backstage** view, and then on the right, click **Properties**. Click **Show Document Panel**, and then in the **Author** box, delete any text and type your firstname and lastname. In the **Subject** box, type your course name and section number, and in the **Keywords** box, type **ecotours, ecotourism Close** the Document Information Panel.

6 **Save** your presentation. Submit your presentation electronically or print **Handouts, 6 Slides Horizontal**, as directed by your instructor.

7 **Close** the presentation and **Exit** PowerPoint.

More Knowledge | Broadcasting a Slide Show

You can broadcast a slide show to remote viewers by using the PowerPoint Broadcast Service or another broadcast service. To broadcast a slide show, on the Slide Show tab, in the Start Slide Show group, click Broadcast Slide Show, and then follow the instructions in the Broadcast Slide Show dialog box to start the broadcast.

End **You have completed Project 13B**

Content-Based Assessments

Summary

In this chapter, you created a new PowerPoint presentation and edited an existing presentation by reusing slides from another presentation. You entered, edited, and formatted text in Normal view; worked with slides in Slide Sorter view; and viewed the presentation as a slide show. You also added emphasis to your presentations by inserting pictures, applying font formatting, and modifying layout, alignment, and line spacing.

Key Terms

Artistic effects 747	**Notes page** 748	**Slide Sorter view**............760
Black slide......................748	**Notes pane** 734	**Slide transitions** 763
Editing 737	**Placeholder**....................734	**Slides/Outline pane** 734
Footer 748	**Reading view** 764	**Style**................................746
Formatting......................755	**Rotation handle** 745	**Text alignment** 759
Header............................748	**Sizing handles**................745	**Theme** 735
Layout 737	**Slide**..............................734	**Thumbnails** 734
List level 739	**Slide handouts** 748	**Title slide**........................734
Normal view 733	**Slide pane** 734	

Matching

Match each term in the second column with its correct definition in the first column by writing the letter of the term on the blank line in front of the correct definition.

_____ 1. The PowerPoint view in which the window is divided into three panes—the Slide pane, the Slides/Outline pane, and the Notes pane.

_____ 2. A presentation page that can contain text, pictures, tables, charts, and other multimedia or graphic objects.

_____ 3. The first slide in a presentation, the purpose of which is to provide an introduction to the presentation topic.

_____ 4. A box on a slide with dotted or dashed borders that holds title and body text or other content such as charts, tables, and pictures.

_____ 5. A set of unified design elements that provides a look for your presentation by applying colors, fonts, and effects.

_____ 6. An outline level in a presentation represented by a bullet symbol and identified in a slide by the indentation and the size of the text.

_____ 7. Small circles and squares that indicate that a picture is selected.

_____ 8. A green circle located above a selected picture with which you can rotate the selected image.

_____ 9. A collection of formatting options that can be applied to a picture, text, or object.

_____ 10. A slide that displays at the end of every slide show to indicate that the presentation is over.

_____ 11. Printed images of slides on a sheet of paper.

A Black slide
B Formatting
C List level
D Normal view
E Notes page
F Placeholder
G Rotation handle
H Sizing handles
I Slide
J Slide handouts
K Slide transitions
L Style
M Text alignment
N Theme
O Title slide

E 12. A printout that contains the slide image on the top half of the page and notes that you have created in the Notes pane on the lower half of the page.

B 13. The process of changing the appearance of the text, layout, and design of a slide.

M 14. The term that refers to the horizontal placement of text within a placeholder.

K 15. Motion effects that occur in Slide Show view when you move from one slide to the next during a presentation.

Multiple Choice

Circle the correct answer.

1. In Normal view, the pane that displays a large image of the active slide is the:
   A. Slide pane **B.** Slides/Outline pane **C.** Notes pane

2. In Normal view, the pane that displays below the Slide pane is the:
   A. Slide Sorter pane **B.** Slides/Outline pane **C.** Notes pane

3. The buttons in the lower right corner that control the look of the presentation window are the:
   A. Normal buttons **B.** View buttons **C.** Thumbnails buttons

4. The process of modifying a presentation by adding and deleting slides or by changing the contents of individual slides is referred to as:
   A. Editing **B.** Formatting **C.** Aligning

5. The arrangement of elements, such as title and subtitle text, lists, pictures, tables, charts, shapes, and movies, on a PowerPoint slide is referred to as:
   A. Theme modification **B.** Editing **C.** Layout

6. Text that prints at the top of a sheet of slide handouts or notes pages is a:
   A. Header **B.** Footer **C.** Page number

7. Text that displays at the bottom of every slide or that prints at the bottom of a sheet of slide handouts or notes.
   A. Header **B.** Footer **C.** Page number

8. The command that locates all occurrences of specific text and replace it with alternative text is:
   A. Replace **B.** Find **C.** Edit

9. The view in which all of the slides in your presentation display in miniature is:
   A. Slide Sorter view **B.** Normal view **C.** Reading view

10. A view similar to Slide Show view but that also displays the title bar, status bar, and taskbar is:
    A. Slide Sorter view **B.** Normal view **C.** Reading view

Content-Based Assessments

Apply 13A skills from these Objectives:

1. Create a New Presentation
2. Edit a Presentation in Normal View
3. Add Pictures to a Presentation
4. Print and View a Presentation

Skills Review | Project 13C Tour Hawaii

In the following Skills Review, you will create a new presentation by inserting content and pictures, adding notes and footers, and applying a presentation theme. Your completed presentation will look similar to Figure 13.48.

Project Files

For Project 13C, you will need the following files:

New blank PowerPoint presentation
p01C_Harbor
p01C_View

You will save your presentation as:

Lastname_Firstname_1C_Tour_Hawaii

Project Results

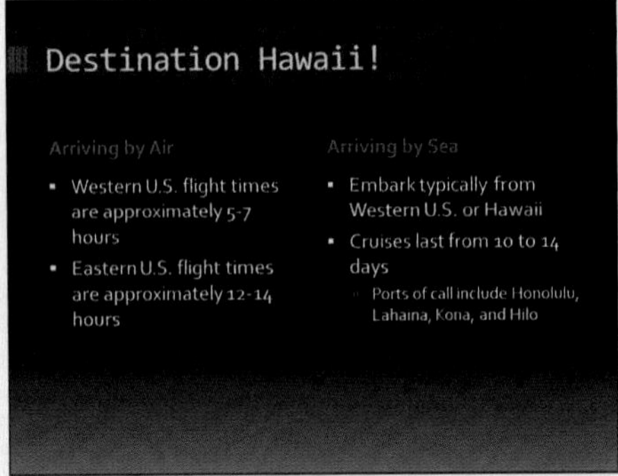

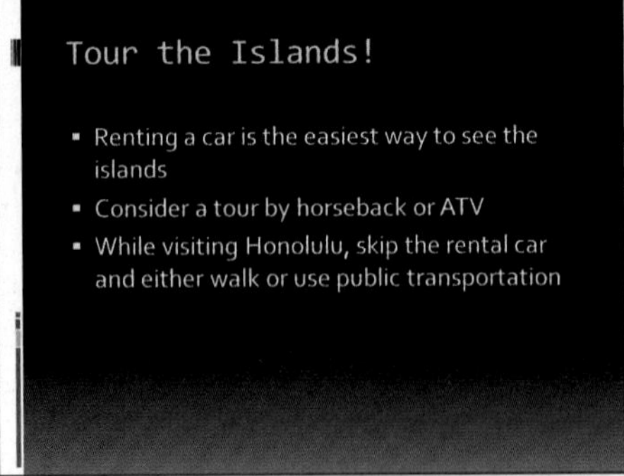

Figure 13.48

(Project 13C Tour Hawaii continues on the next page)

Content-Based Assessments

Skills Review | Project 13C Tour Hawaii (continued)

1 **Start** PowerPoint to display a new blank presentation in Normal view.

a. In the **Slide pane**, click in the title placeholder, which contains the text *Click to add title.* Type **Traveling the Islands**

b. Click in the subtitle placeholder, and then type **Tips from Lehua Hawaiian Adventures**

c. Right-click *Lehua,* and then on the shortcut menu, click **Ignore All**.

d. On the Ribbon, click the **Design tab**. In the **Themes group**, click the **More** button to display the **Themes gallery**. Recall that the themes display alphabetically. Using the ScreenTips, locate and then click **Metro** to apply the Metro theme to the presentation.

e. On the Quick Access Toolbar, click the **Save** button, navigate to your **PowerPoint Chapter 13** folder, and then **Save** the presentation as **Lastname_Firstname_1C_Tour_Hawaii**

2 On the **Home tab**, in the **Slides group**, click the **New Slide button arrow**. In the gallery, click the **Picture with Caption** layout to insert a new slide.

a. In the **Slide pane**, click the text *Click to add title,* and then type **Plan Ahead!**

b. Click in the text placeholder below the title, and then type **A little planning will go a long way toward creating a memorable and trouble-free vacation to the islands.**

c. In the picture placeholder, click the **Insert picture from File** button, and then navigate to your student data files. Click **p01C_View**, and then press Enter to insert the picture.

d. With the picture selected, on the **Format tab**, in the **Picture Styles group**, click the **More** button to display the **Picture Styles** gallery. Use the ScreenTips to locate, and then click the style **Soft Edge Oval**.

e. In the **Adjust group**, click the **Artistic Effects** button, and then in the fourth row, click the second effect—**Texturizer**.

3 On the **Home tab**, in the **Slides group**, click the **New Slide button arrow**. In the gallery, click the **Comparison** layout to insert a new slide. In the title placeholder, type **Destination Hawaii!**

a. Below the title, on the left side of the slide, click in the placeholder containing the pink words *Click to add text.* Type **Arriving by Air**

b. On the right side of the slide, click in the placeholder containing the pink words *Click to add text.* Type **Arriving by Sea**

c. On the left side of the slide, click in the content placeholder. Type **Western U.S. flight times are approximately 5–7 hours** and then press Enter. Type **Eastern U.S. flight times are approximately 12–14 hours**

d. On the right side of the slide, click in the content placeholder. Type **Embark typically from Western U.S. or Hawaii** and then press Enter. Type **Cruises last 10 to 14 days**

e. Press Enter, and then on the **Home tab**, in the **Paragraph group**, click the **Increase List Level** button, and then type **Ports of call include Honolulu, Lahaina, Kona, and Hilo**

f. Right-click *Lahaina,* and then on the shortcut menu, click **Ignore All**. **Save** your presentation.

4 On the **Home tab**, in the **Slides group**, click the **New Slide button arrow**. In the gallery, click **Title and Content** to insert a new slide. In the title placeholder, type **Tour the Islands!**

a. In the content placeholder, type the following three bullet points:

Renting a car is the easiest way to see the islands

Consider a tour by horseback or ATV

While visiting Honolulu, skip the rental car and either walk or use public transportation

b. Below the slide, click in the **Notes pane**, and then type **Rental car company offices are located at each major airport.**

5 Insert a **New Slide** using the **Picture with Caption** layout.

a. In the title placeholder, type **Explore!** In the text placeholder, type **Regardless of the mode of transportation that you choose, explore Hawaii for an unforgettable vacation!**

b. In the center of the large picture placeholder, click the **Insert Picture from File** button. Navigate to your student files, and then insert **p01C_Harbor**.

c. With the picture selected, on the **Format tab**, in the **Picture Styles group**, click the **More** button to display the **Picture Styles** gallery. In the first row, click the sixth style—**Soft Edge Rectangle**.

(Project 13C Tour Hawaii continues on the next page)

Content-Based Assessments

Skills Review | Project 13C Tour Hawaii (continued)

6 On the Ribbon, click the **Slide Show tab**. In the **Start Slide Show group**, click the **From Beginning** button.

a. Click the left mouse button or press Spacebar to advance to the second slide. Continue to click or press Spacebar until the last slide displays, and then click or press Spacebar one more time to display a black slide.

b. With the black slide displayed, click the left mouse button or press Spacebar to exit the slide show and return to the presentation.

7 Click the **Insert tab**, and then in the **Text group**, click the **Header & Footer** button to display the **Header and Footer** dialog box.

a. In the **Header and Footer** dialog box, click the **Notes and Handouts tab**. Under **Include on page**, select the **Date and time** check box. If necessary, click the Update automatically option button so that the current date prints on the notes and handouts.

b. If necessary, clear the Header check box to omit this element. Select the **Page number** and **Footer** check boxes. In the **Footer** box, type **Lastname_Firstname_1C_Tour_Hawaii** and then click **Apply to All**.

c. Click the **File tab** to display **Backstage** view, and then on the right, click **Properties**. Click **Show Document Panel**, and then in the **Author** box, delete any text and type your firstname and lastname. In the **Subject** box, type your course name and section number, and in the **Keywords** box, type **travel tips, tour tips, trip planning Close** the Document Information Panel.

d. **Save** your presentation. Submit your presentation electronically or print **Handouts, 6 Slides Horizontal** as directed by your instructor. **Close** the presentation.

End You have completed Project 13C

Apply **13B** skills from these Objectives:

- **5** Edit an Existing Presentation
- **6** Format a Presentation
- **7** Use Slide Sorter View
- **8** Apply Slide Transitions

Skills Review | Project **13D** Luau Information

In the following Skills Review, you will edit an existing presentation by inserting slides from another presentation, applying font and slide formatting, and applying slide transitions. Your completed presentation will look similar to Figure 13.49.

Project Files

For Project 13D, you will need the following files:

p01D_Luau_Information
p01D_History_of_Luaus

You will save your presentation as:

Lastname_Firstname_1D_Luau_Information

Project Results

History of the Luau

- Luaus are traditional Hawaiian celebrations
  - Originally called 'aha 'aina, these celebrations became known as luaus about 150 years ago
- The term luau originates from the Hawaiian and other Hawaiian languages, and is the name for the taro leaf
  - Taro leaves are combined with others foods, such as chicken or fish, and then baked in coconut milk

The Modern Luau

- King Kamehameha II introduced the modern luau in 1819
- Luaus were celebrated when a child became of age, when a new canoe was launched, or when warriors returned home after long journeys
- Today, luaus celebrate events such as weddings, graduations, and first birthdays

Celebrating a Luau

- Traditional luau feasts were eaten on the ground and without utensils
- Mats were rolled out and held beautiful centerpieces made of leaves, ferns, and flowers
- Foods were cooked in an underground oven

Luau Delicacies

- Roasted pulled pork cooked in an imu
- Poi: Mashed taro root
- Laulau: Taro leaf tips and fish or chicken wrapped in ti leaves
- Lomi salmon: A salted fish marinated in lemon juice, tomatoes, and onions
- Plantain bananas, yams, fresh fruits

Experience Hawaiian Culture
On a Beautiful Hawaiian Beach

Contact Lehua Hawaiian Adventures for additional information about attending an authentic Hawaiian Luau

Figure 13.49

(Project 13D Luau Information continues on the next page)

Content-Based Assessments

Skills Review | Project 13D Luau Information (continued)

1 **Start** PowerPoint. From your student files, open **p01D_Luau_Information**. Click the **File tab** to display **Backstage** view, click **Save As**, navigate to your **PowerPoint Chapter 13** folder, and then using your own name, **Save** the file as **Lastname_Firstname_1D_Luau_Information** Take a moment to examine the content of the presentation.

a. In the **Slides/Outline pane**, click the **Outline tab** to display the presentation outline.

b. In the **Outline tab**, in **Slide 2**, click anywhere in the last bullet point, which begins with the text *Luaus were celebrated.*

c. On the **Home tab**, in the **Paragraph group**, click the **Decrease List Level** button one time.

d. In the **Outline tab**, click at the end of the second bullet after the word *journeys*. Press Enter to create a new bullet point at the same list level as the previous bullet point. Type **Today, luaus celebrate events such as weddings, graduations, and first birthdays**

e. In the **Slides/Outline pane**, click the **Slides tab** to display the slide thumbnails.

2 Display **Slide 1**. On the **Home tab**, in the **Slides group**, click the **New Slide button arrow** to display the **Slide Layout** gallery and additional options for inserting slides.

a. Below the gallery, click **Reuse Slides** to open the **Reuse Slides** pane on the right side of the PowerPoint window.

b. In the **Reuse Slides** pane, click the **Browse** button, and then click **Browse File**. In the **Browse** dialog box, navigate to your student files, and then double-click **p01D_History_of_Luaus**.

c. At the bottom of the **Reuse Slides** pane, select the **Keep source formatting** check box.

d. In the **Reuse Slides** pane, click the first slide—*Luau Information*—to insert the slide into the current presentation after **Slide 1**. In the **Reuse Slides** pane, click the second slide—**Celebrating a Luau** to insert it as the third slide in your presentation.

e. In your **1D_Luau_Information** presentation, in the **Slides/Outline pane**, click **Slide 5** to display it in the **Slide pane**.

f. In the **Reuse Slides** pane, click the third slide—*History of the Luau*—and then click the fourth slide—*Luau Delicacies*—to insert both slides after **Slide 5**. In the **Reuse Slides** pane, click the **Close** button.

3 Display **Slide 1**, and then select the title—*Feasting Polynesian Style.*

a. Point to the Mini toolbar, and then click the **Font arrow** to display the available fonts. Click **Arial**, and then click the **Font Size arrow**. Click **44** to change the font size. Use the Mini toolbar to apply **Bold** and **Italic** to the title.

b. Select the subtitle—*A History of the Luau.* Use the Mini toolbar to change the **Font** to **Arial** and the **Font Size** to **28**.

c. On the **Home tab**, in the **Editing group**, click the **Replace** button. In the **Replace** dialog box, click in the **Find what** box. Type **Polynesian** and then in the **Replace with** box, type **Hawaiian**

d. In the **Replace** dialog box, click the **Replace All** button to replace three occurrences of *Polynesian* with *Hawaiian.* Click **OK** to close the message box, and then in the **Replace** dialog box, click the **Close** button.

e. Display **Slide 6**, and then select the second bullet point, which begins *Originally.* On the Mini toolbar, click the **Font Color button arrow**. Under **Theme Colors**, in the sixth column, click the first color—**Teal, Accent 2**.

f. Select the last bullet point, which begins *Taro leaves.* On the Mini toolbar, click the **Font Color button** to apply **Teal, Accent 2** to the selection.

4 With **Slide 6** displayed, click anywhere in the title.

a. On the **Home tab**, in the **Paragraph group**, click the **Center** button to center the text within the placeholder.

b. Display **Slide 7**, and then **Center** the slide title.

c. Display **Slide 5**, and then click anywhere in the text in the lower portion of the slide. In the **Paragraph group**, click the **Line Spacing** button. In the list, click **1.5** to change from single-spacing between lines to one-and-a-half spacing between lines.

d. Display **Slide 3**. On the **Home tab**, in the **Slides group**, click the **Layout** button to display the **Slide Layout** gallery. Click **Title and Content** to change the slide layout.

5 In the lower right corner of the PowerPoint window, in the **View** buttons, click the **Slide Sorter** button to display the slide thumbnails in Slide Sorter view.

(Project 13D Luau Information continues on the next page)

Skills Review | Project 13D Luau Information (continued)

a. Click **Slide 2**, and then notice that a thick outline surrounds the slide, indicating that it is selected. Press Del to delete the slide.

b. Point to **Slide 5**, hold down the mouse button, and then drag to position the vertical move bar to the left of **Slide 2**. Release the mouse button to move the slide.

c. Point to **Slide 5**, hold down the mouse button, and then drag so that the vertical move bar displays to the right of **Slide 6**. Release the mouse button to move the slide so that it is the last slide in the presentation.

d. Point to **Slide 4**, hold down the mouse button, and then drag so that the vertical move bar displays to the left of **Slide 3**. Release the mouse button to move the slide.

e. In the **View** buttons, click the **Normal** button to return the presentation to Normal view.

6 Display **Slide 1**. On the **Transitions tab**, in the **Transition to This Slide group**, click the **Wipe** button to apply the Wipe transition to the slide.

a. In the **Transition to This Slide group**, click the **Effect Options** button, and then click **From Top**.

b. In the **Timing group**, click the **Duration** box **up spin arrow** twice to change the Duration to *01.50*.

c. In the **Timing group**, under **Advance Slide**, verify that the **On Mouse Click** check box is selected, and select it if necessary.

d. In the **Timing group**, click the **Apply To All** button so that the transition settings are applied to all of the slides in the presentation.

e. Click the **Slide Show tab**. In the **Start Slide Show group**, click the **From Beginning** button, and then view your presentation, clicking the mouse button to advance through the slides. When the black slide displays, click the mouse button one more time to display the presentation in Normal view.

f. On the **Insert tab**, in the **Text group**, click the **Header & Footer** button to display the **Header and Footer** dialog box. Click the **Notes and Handouts tab**. Under **Include on page**, select the **Date and time** check box, and then if necessary, select Update automatically.

g. Clear the **Header** check box if necessary, and then select the **Page number** and **Footer** check boxes. In the **Footer** box, using your own name, type **Lastname_Firstname_1D_Luau_Information** and then click **Apply to All**.

h. Click the **File tab**, and then on the right side of the window, click **Properties**. Click **Show Document Panel**, and then in the **Author** box, delete any text and type your firstname and lastname. In the **Subject** box, type your course name and section number, and in the **Keywords** box, type **luau, Hawaiian history, Hawaiian culture Close** the Document Information Panel.

i. **Save** your presentation. Submit your presentation electronically or print **Handouts, 6 Slides Horizontal** as directed by your instructor. **Close** the presentation.

End **You have completed Project 13D**

Content-Based Assessments

Apply 13A skills from these Objectives:

1. Create a New Presentation
2. Edit a Presentation in Normal View
3. Add Pictures to a Presentation
4. Print and View a Presentation

Mastering PowerPoint | Project 13E Boat Tours

In the following Mastering PowerPoint project, you will create a new presentation describing the types of boat tours offered by Lehua Hawaiian Adventures. Your completed presentation will look similar to Figure 13.50.

Project Files

For Project 13E, you will need the following files:

New blank PowerPoint presentation
p01E_Catamaran
p01E_Raft

You will save your presentation as:

Lastname_Firstname_1E_Boat_Tours

Project Results

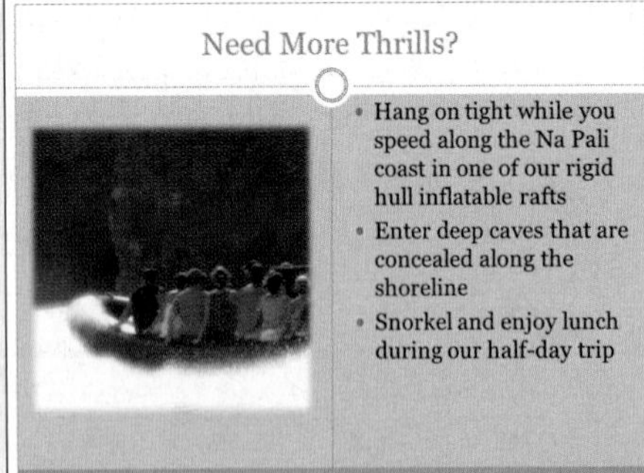

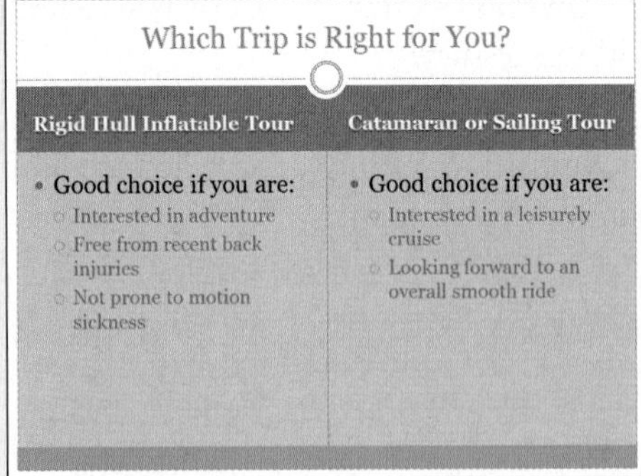

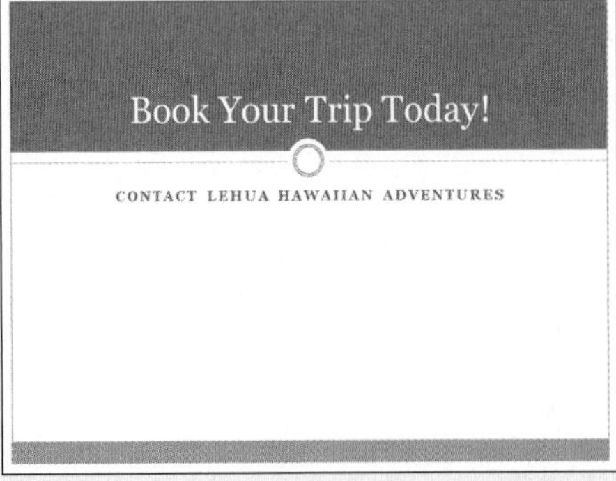

Figure 13.50

(Project 13E Boat Tours continues on the next page)

Mastering PowerPoint | Project 13E Boat Tours (continued)

1 **Start** PowerPoint to display a new blank presentation, and then change the **Design** by applying the **Civic** theme. As the title of this presentation type **Viewing Na Pali by Sea** and as the subtitle type **With Lehua Hawaiian Adventures**

2 Correct spelling errors on this slide by choosing the **Ignore All** option for the words *Pali* and *Lehua*. Save the presentation in your **PowerPoint Chapter 13** folder as **Lastname_Firstname_1E_Boat_Tours**

3 Insert a **New Slide** using the **Content with Caption** layout. In the title placeholder, type **Looking to Relax?** In the large content placeholder on the right side of the slide, from your student files, insert the picture **p01E_Catamaran**. Format the picture with the **Compound Frame, Black** picture style and the **Texturizer** artistic effect.

4 In the text placeholder, type **If an easy day of sailing is your style, consider a morning or sunset cruise on our forty-person catamaran. Our experienced crew will sail our vessel along the Na Pali coast for a view of waterfalls, caves, and beaches. Spinner dolphins often swim alongside and whales can be spotted January through March.**

5 Insert a **New Slide** using the **Two Content** layout. In the title placeholder, type **Need More Thrills?** In the content placeholder on the left side of the slide, from your student files, insert the picture **p01E_Raft**. Format the picture with the **Soft Edge Rectangle** picture style and the **Glow Diffused** artistic effect. In the content placeholder on the right side of the slide, type the following three bullet points:

Hang on tight while you speed along the Na Pali coast in one of our rigid hull inflatable rafts

Enter deep caves that are concealed along the shoreline

Snorkel and enjoy lunch during our half-day trip

6 Insert a **New Slide** using the **Comparison** layout. In the title placeholder, type **Which Trip is Right for You?** In the orange placeholder on the left side of the slide, type **Rigid Hull Inflatable Tour** and in the orange placeholder on the right side of the slide, type **Catamaran or Sailing Tour**

7 In the content placeholder on the left, type each of the following bullet points, increasing the list level for the last three bullet points as indicated:

Good choice if you are:

- **Interested in adventure**
- **Free from recent back injuries**
- **Not prone to motion sickness**

8 In the content placeholder on the right, type each of the following bullet points, increasing the list level for the last two bullet points as indicated:

Good choice if you are:

- **Interested in a leisurely cruise**
- **Looking forward to an overall smooth ride**

9 On **Slide 4**, type the following notes in the **Notes pane: If you need assistance deciding which boat tour is right for you, we'll be happy to help you decide.** Insert a **New Slide** using the **Section Header** layout. In the title placeholder, type **Book Your Trip Today!** In the text placeholder, type **Contact Lehua Hawaiian Adventures**

10 Insert a **Header & Footer** on the **Notes and Handouts**. Include the **Date and time** updated automatically, the **Page number**, and a **Footer**—using your own name—with the text **Lastname_Firstname_1E_Boat_Tours** and apply to all the slides.

11 Display the **Document Information Panel**. Replace the text in the **Author** box with your own firstname and lastname. In the **Subject** box, type your course name and section number, and in the **Keywords** box, type **Na Pali, boat tours, sailing Close** the Document Information Panel.

12 **Save** your presentation, and then view the slide show from the beginning. Submit your presentation electronically or print **Handouts, 6 Slides Horizontal** as directed by your instructor. **Close** the presentation.

End **You have completed Project 13E**

Apply **13B** skills from these Objectives:

- 5 Edit an Existing Presentation
- 6 Format a Presentation
- 7 Use Slide Sorter View
- 8 Apply Slide Transitions

Mastering PowerPoint | Project 13F Helicopter Tour

In the following Mastering PowerPoint project, you will edit a presentation describing the helicopter tours offered by Lehua Hawaiian Adventures. Your completed presentation will look similar to Figure 13.51.

Project Files

For Project 13F, you will need the following files:

p01F_Helicopter_Tour
p01F_Aerial_Views

You will save your presentation as:

Lastname_Firstname_1F_Helicopter_Tour

Project Results

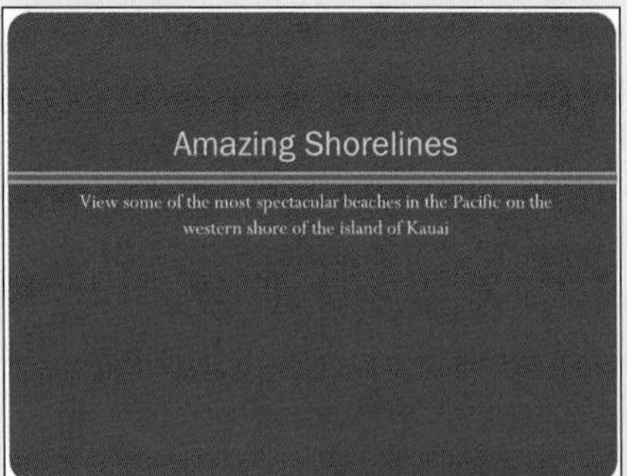

Figure 13.51

(Project 13F Helicopter Tour continues on the next page)

Mastering PowerPoint | Project 13F Helicopter Tour (continued)

1 **Start** PowerPoint, and then from your student data files, open the file **p01F_Helicopter_Tour**. In your **PowerPoint Chapter 13** folder, **Save** the file as **Lastname_Firstname_1F_Helicopter_Tour**

2 Display the presentation **Outline**. In the **Outline tab**, in **Slide 2**, increase the list level of the bullet point that begins *Formed by erosion*. In the **Outline tab**, click at the end of the second bullet point after the word *Kauai*. Press Enter, and then decrease the list level of the new bullet point. Type **Lava flows changed the canyon landscape over the course of centuries**

3 In the **Slides/Outline pane**, click the **Slides tab** to display the slide thumbnails, and then display **Slide 1**. Display the **Reuse Slides** pane, and then click the **Browse** button. Click **Browse File**, and then in the **Browse** dialog box, from your student files, open **p01F_Aerial_Views**. Select the **Keep source formatting** check box, and then from this group of slides, insert the first and second slides—*Aerial View of Kauai* and *Dramatic Overhead*.

4 In the **Slides/Outline pane**, click **Slide 4** to display it in the **Slide pane**, and then from the **Reuse Slides** pane, insert the third, fourth, fifth, and sixth slides—*Na Pali Coast, Honopu Beach, Amazing Shorelines, Tunnels Beach*. **Close** the **Reuse Slides** pane.

5 Display **Slide 1**, and then select the title—*Maui from the Sky*. Change the **Font** to **Arial**, and the **Font Size** to **44**. Change the **Font Color** to **White, Text 1**. Display the **Replace** dialog box. **Replace All** occurrences of the word **Maui** with **Kauai** and then **Close** the **Replace** dialog box.

6 Display **Slide 5**, and then select the paragraph in the content placeholder. Apply **Bold** and **Italic**, and then **Center** the text. Change the **Line Spacing** to **1.5**. Display **Slide 7**, and then change the **Slide Layout** to **Section Header**. **Center** the text in both placeholders.

7 In **Slide Sorter** view, delete **Slide 2**. Then select **Slides 6** and **7** and move both slides so that they are positioned after **Slide 3**. In **Normal** view, display **Slide 1**. Apply the **Split** transition and change the **Effect Options** to **Horizontal Out**. Apply the transition to all of the slides in the presentation. View the slide show from the beginning.

8 **Insert** a **Header & Footer** on the **Notes and Handouts**. Include the **Date and time** updated automatically, the **Page number**, and a **Footer** with the text **Lastname_Firstname_1F_Helicopter_Tour** Apply to all the slides.

9 Check spelling in the presentation. If necessary, select the Ignore All option if proper names are indicated as misspelled.

10 Display the **Document Information Panel**. Replace the text in the **Author** box with your own firstname and lastname. In the **Subject** box, type your course name and section number, and in the **Keywords** box, type **helicopter, Kauai** **Close** the Document Information Panel.

11 **Save** your presentation, and then submit your presentation electronically or print **Handouts, 4 Slides Horizontal** as directed by your instructor. **Close** the presentation.

End **You have completed Project 13F**

Content-Based Assessments

Apply 13A and 13B skills from these Objectives:

1. Create a New Presentation
2. Edit a Presentation in Normal View
3. Add Pictures to a Presentation
4. Print and View a Presentation
5. Edit an Existing Presentation
6. Format a Presentation
7. Use Slide Sorter View
8. Apply Slide Transitions

Mastering PowerPoint | Project 13G Volcano Tour

In the following Mastering PowerPoint project, you will edit an existing presentation that describes the tour of Volcanoes National Park offered by Lehua Hawaiian Adventures. Your completed presentation will look similar to Figure 13.52.

Project Files

For Project 13G, you will need the following files:

p01G_Crater_Information
p01G_Lava
p01G_Volcano_Tour

You will save your presentation as:

Lastname_Firstname_1G_Volcano_Tour

Project Results

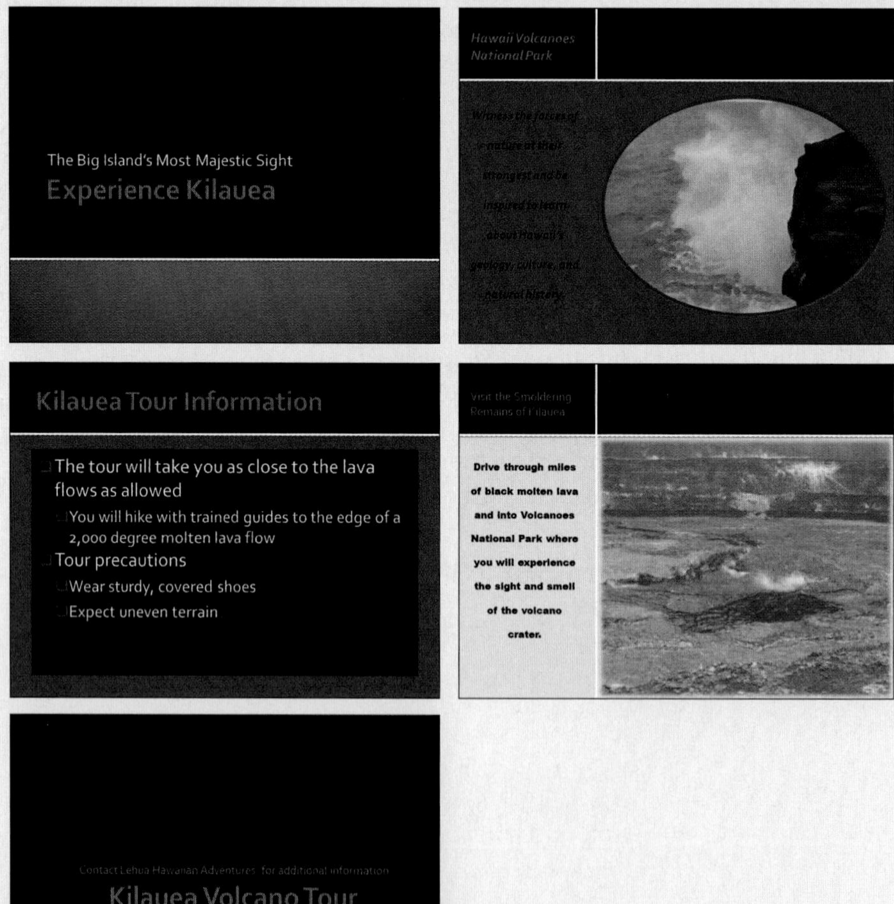

Figure 13.52

(Project 13G Volcano Tour continues on the next page)

Mastering PowerPoint | Project 13G Volcano Tour (continued)

1 **Start** PowerPoint, and then from your student files, open the file **p01G_Volcano_Tour**. In your **PowerPoint Chapter 13** folder, **Save** the file as **Lastname_Firstname_1G_Volcano_Tour**

2 Replace all occurrences of the text **Diamond Head** with **Kilauea** Display **Slide 3**, open the **Reuse Slides** pane, and then from your student files browse for and display the presentation **p01G_Crater_Information**. If necessary, clear the Keep source formatting check box, and then insert both slides from the **p01G_Crater_Information** file. **Close** the **Reuse Slides** pane.

3 Display the presentation outline, and then in **Slide 3**, increase the list level of the bullet point beginning *You will hike*. In either the **Slide pane** or the **Outline**, click at the end of the last bullet point after the word *flow*, and then insert a new bullet point. Decrease its list level. Type **Tour precautions** and then press Enter. Increase the list level, and then type the following two bullet points.

Wear sturdy, covered shoes

Expect uneven terrain

4 Display the slide thumbnails. In **Slide 1**, select the subtitle—*The Big Island's Most Majestic Sight*—and then change the **Font Color** to **White, Text 1** and the **Font Size** to **28**. On **Slide 2**, center the caption text located below the slide title and apply **Bold** and **Italic**. Change the **Line Spacing** to **2.0**. Click in the content placeholder on the right, and then from your student files, insert the picture **p01G_Lava**. Format the picture with the **Beveled Oval, Black** picture style and the **Paint Brush** artistic effect.

5 In **Slide Sorter** view, move **Slide 5** between **Slides 3** and **4**. In **Normal** view, on **Slide 5**, change the slide **Layout** to **Title Slide**, and then type the following notes in the **Notes pane**: **Recent volcanic activity at the national park site may result in changes to the tour itinerary.** Apply the **Uncover** transition and change the **Effect Options** to **From Top**. Change the **Timing** by increasing the **Duration** to **01.50**. Apply the transition effect to all of the slides. View the slide show from the beginning.

6 **Insert** a **Header & Footer** on the **Notes and Handouts**. Include the **Date and time** updated automatically, the **Page number**, and a **Footer**, using your own name, with the text **Lastname_Firstname_1G_Volcano_Tour**

7 Check spelling in the presentation. If necessary, select the Ignore All option if proper names are indicated as misspelled.

8 Display the **Document Information Panel**. Replace the text in the **Author** box with your own firstname and lastname. In the **Subject** box, type your course name and section number, and in the **Keywords** box, type **Kilauea, volcano** **Close** the Document Information Panel.

9 **Save** your presentation. Submit your presentation electronically or print **Handouts, 6 Slides Horizontal** as directed by your instructor. **Close** the presentation.

End **You have completed Project 13G**

Content-Based Assessments

Apply a combination of the 13A and 13B skills.

GO! Fix It | Project 13H Hawaii Guide

Project Files

For Project 13H, you will need the following files:

p01H_Hawaii_Guide
p01H_Islands

You will save your presentation as:

Lastname_Firstname_1H_Hawaii_Guide

In this project, you will edit a presentation prepared by Lehua Hawaiian Adventures that describes some of the activities on each of the Hawaiian Islands. From the student files that accompany this textbook, open the file p01H_Hawaii_Guide, and then save the file in your chapter folder as **Lastname_Firstname_1H_Hawaii_Guide**

To complete the project, you should know:

- All of the slides in the p01H_Islands presentation should be reused in this presentation and inserted after Slide 2. Correct two spelling errors and ignore all instances of proper names that are indicated as misspelled.
- The Opulent theme should be applied.
- Slides 3 through 8 should be arranged alphabetically according to the name of the island
- On the Maui and Molokai slides, the list level of the second bullet points should decreased.
- The Layout for Slide 2 should be Section Header, the slide should be moved to the end of the presentation, and the Flip transition using the Left effect option should be applied to all of the slides in the presentation.
- Document Properties should include your name, course name and section, and the keywords **guide, islands** A Header & Footer should be inserted on the Notes and Handouts that includes the Date and time updated automatically, the Page number, and a Footer with the text **Lastname_Firstname_1H_Hawaii_Guide**

Save your presentation and submit electronically or print Handouts, 4 Slides Horizontal as directed by your instructor. Close the presentation.

End You have completed Project 13H

Apply a combination of the 13A and 13B skills.

GO! Make It | Project 13I Dolphin Encounter

Project Files

For Project 13I, you will need the following files:

p01I_Dolphin_Encounters
p01I_Dolphin

You will save your presentation as:

Lastname_Firstname_1I_Dolphin_Encounters

From your student files, open p01I_Dolphin_Encounters, and then save it in your PowerPoint Chapter 13 folder as **Lastname_Firstname_1I_Dolphin_Encounters**

By using the skills you practiced in this chapter, create the slide shown in Figure 13.53 by inserting a new Slide 2 with the layout and text shown in the figure. The title font size is 36, and the font color is Black, Background 1. The caption text font is Arial, and the font size is 16 with bold and italic applied. To complete the slide, from your student files, insert the picture p01H_Dolphin. Insert the date and time updated automatically, the file name, and a page number in the Notes and Handouts footer. In the Document Information Panel, add your name and course information and the keyword **dolphin** Save your presentation, and then print or submit electronically as directed by your instructor.

Project Results

Figure 13.53

End You have completed Project 13I

Apply a combination of the 13A and 13B skills.

GO! Solve It | Project 13J Planning Tips

Project Files

For Project 13J, you will need the following file:

p01J_Planning_Tips

You will save your presentation as:

Lastname_Firstname_1J_Planning_Tips

Open the file p01J_Planning_Tips and save it as **Lastname_Firstname_1J_Planning_Tips** Complete the presentation by applying a theme and by correcting spelling errors. Format the presentation attractively by applying appropriate font formatting and by changing text alignment and line spacing. Change the layout of at least one slide to a layout that will accommodate a picture. Insert a picture that you have taken yourself, or use one of the pictures in your student data files that you inserted in other projects in this chapter. On the last slide, insert an appropriate picture, and then apply picture styles to both pictures. Apply slide transitions to all of the slides in the presentation, and then insert a header and footer that includes the date and time updated automatically, the file name in the footer, and the page number. Add your name, your course name and section number, and the keywords **planning, weather** to the Properties area. Save and print or submit as directed by your instructor.

Performance Elements	Performance Level		
	Exemplary: You consistently applied the relevant skills	**Proficient:** You sometimes, but not always, applied the relevant skills	**Developing:** You rarely or never applied the relevant skills
Apply a theme	An appropriate theme was applied to the presentation.	A theme was applied but was not appropriate for the presentation.	A theme was not applied.
Apply font and slide formatting	Font and slide formatting is attractive and appropriate.	Adequately formatted but difficult to read or unattractive.	Inadequate or no formatting.
Use appropriate pictures and apply styles attractively	Two appropriate pictures are inserted and styles are applied attractively.	Pictures are inserted but styles are not applied or are inappropriately applied.	Pictures are not inserted.

End You have completed Project 13J

Apply a combination of the 13A and 13B skills.

GO! Solve It | Project 13K Hikes

Project Files

For Project 13K, you will need the following file:

p01K_Hikes

You will save your presentation as:

Lastname_Firstname_1K_Hikes

Open the file p01K_Hikes and save it as **Lastname_Firstname_1K_Hikes** Complete the presentation by applying an appropriate theme. Move Slide 2 to the end of the presentation, and then change the layout to one appropriate for the end of the presentation. Format the presentation attractively by applying font formatting and by changing text alignment and line spacing. Review the information on Slide 3, and then increase list levels appropriately on this slide. Apply picture styles to the two pictures in the presentation and an artistic effect to at least one picture. Apply slide transitions to all of the slides. Insert a header and footer that includes the date and time updated automatically, the file name in the footer, and the page number. Add your name, your course name and section number, and the keywords **hiking Akaka Falls, Waimea Canyon** to the Properties area. Save and print or submit as directed by your instructor.

	Performance Level		
	Exemplary: You consistently applied the relevant skills	**Proficient:** You sometimes, but not always, applied the relevant skills	**Developing:** You rarely or never applied the relevant skills
Performance Elements: Apply a theme	An appropriate theme was applied to the presentation.	A theme was applied but was not appropriate for the presentation.	A theme was not applied.
Apply appropriate formatting	Formatting is attractive and appropriate.	Adequately formatted but difficult to read or unattractive.	Inadequate or no formatting.
Apply appropriate list levels	List levels are applied appropriately.	Some, but not all, list levels are appropriately applied.	Changes to list levels were not made.

End You have completed Project 13K

Outcomes-Based Assessments

Rubric

The following outcomes-based assessments are *open-ended assessments*. That is, there is no specific correct result; your result will depend on your approach to the information provided. Make *Professional Quality* your goal. Use the following scoring rubric to guide you in *how* to approach the problem, and then to evaluate *how well* your approach solves the problem.

The *criteria*—Software Mastery, Content, Format and Layout, and Process—represent the knowledge and skills you have gained that you can apply to solving the problem. The *levels of performance*—Professional Quality, Approaching Professional Quality, or Needs Quality Improvements—help you and your instructor evaluate your result.

	Your completed project is of Professional Quality if you:	**Your completed project is Approaching Professional Quality if you:**	**Your completed project Needs Quality Improvements if you:**
1-Software Mastery	Choose and apply the most appropriate skills, tools, and features and identify efficient methods to solve the problem.	Choose and apply some appropriate skills, tools, and features, but not in the most efficient manner.	Choose inappropriate skills, tools, or features, or are inefficient in solving the problem.
2-Content	Construct a solution that is clear and well organized, contains content that is accurate, appropriate to the audience and purpose, and is complete. Provide a solution that contains no errors in spelling, grammar, or style.	Construct a solution in which some components are unclear, poorly organized, inconsistent, or incomplete. Misjudge the needs of the audience. Have some errors in spelling, grammar, or style, but the errors do not detract from comprehension.	Construct a solution that is unclear, incomplete, or poorly organized; contains some inaccurate or inappropriate content; and contains many errors in spelling, grammar, or style. Do not solve the problem.
3-Format and Layout	Format and arrange all elements to communicate information and ideas, clarify function, illustrate relationships, and indicate relative importance.	Apply appropriate format and layout features to some elements, but not others. Overuse features, causing minor distraction.	Apply format and layout that does not communicate information or ideas clearly. Do not use format and layout features to clarify function, illustrate relationships, or indicate relative importance. Use available features excessively, causing distraction.
4-Process	Use an organized approach that integrates planning, development, self-assessment, revision, and reflection.	Demonstrate an organized approach in some areas, but not others; or, use an insufficient process of organization throughout.	Do not use an organized approach to solve the problem.

Apply a combination of the 13A and 13B skills.

GO! Think | Project 13L Big Island

Project Files

For Project 13L, you will need the following files:

New blank PowerPoint presentation
p01L_Fishing
p01L_Monument

You will save your presentation as:

Lastname_Firstname_1L_Big_Island

Carl Kawaoka, Tour Operations Manager for Lehua Hawaiian Adventures, is developing a presentation describing sea tours on the Big Island of Hawaii to be shown at a travel fair on the mainland. In the presentation, Carl will be showcasing the company's two most popular sea excursions: The Captain Cook Monument Snorkeling Tour and the Kona Deep Sea Fishing Tour.

On the Captain Cook Monument Snorkeling Tour, guests meet at 8:00 a.m. at the Lehua Hawaiian Adventures Kona location and then board a 12-passenger rigid hull inflatable raft. Captained by a U.S. Coast Guard licensed crew, the raft is navigated along the Hawaii coastline, exploring sea caves, lava tubes, and waterfalls. Upon arrival at the Monument, guests snorkel in Hawaii's incredible undersea world of colorful fish, sea turtles, and stingrays. Lehua Hawaiian Adventures provides the lunch, snacks, drinks, and snorkeling equipment and asks that guests bring their own towels, sunscreen, swim suits, and sense of adventure. This tour lasts 5 hours and the fee is $85.

On the Kona Deep Sea Fishing Tour, guests meet at 7:00 a.m. at the Lehua Hawaiian Adventures Kona location and then board a 32-foot Blackfin fishing boat. The boat is captained by a U.S. Coast Guard licensed crew of three. A maximum of six guests are allowed on each trip, which sails, weather permitting, every Wednesday, Friday, and Saturday. For deep sea fishing, there is no better place than the Kona coast. On full-day adventures, it is common for guests to catch marlin, sailfish, ahi, ono, and mahi-mahi. This tour lasts 8 hours and the fee is $385.

Using the preceding information, create a presentation that Carl can show at the travel fair. The presentation should include four to six slides describing the two tours. Apply an appropriate theme and use slide layouts that will effectively present the content. From your student files, insert the pictures p01L_Fishing and p01L_Monument on appropriate slides and apply picture styles or artistic effects to enhance the pictures. Apply font formatting and slide transitions, and modify text alignment and line spacing as necessary. Save the file as **Lastname_Firstname_1L_Big_Island** and then insert a header and footer that include the date and time updated automatically, the file name in the footer, and the page number. Add your name, your course name and section number, and the keywords **sea tours, deep sea fishing, snorkeling tours** to the Properties area. Save and print or submit as directed by your instructor.

End You have completed Project 13L

Apply a combination of the 13A and 13B skills.

GO! Think | Project 13M Beaches

Project Files

For Project 13M, you will need the following files:

New blank PowerPoint presentation
p01M_Black_Sand
p01M_Kite_Surf
p01M_Lithified_Cliffs
p01M_Reef
p01M_Tide_Pools

You will save your presentation as:

Lastname_Firstname_1M_Beaches

Katherine Okubo, President of Lehua Hawaiian Adventures, is making a presentation to groups of tourists at a number of hotels on the Hawaiian Islands. She would like to begin the presentation with an introduction to the beaches of Hawaii before discussing the many ways in which her company can assist tourists with selecting the places they would like to visit. The following paragraphs contain some of the information about the shorelines and beaches that Katherine would like to include in the presentation.

The shorelines of Hawaii vary tremendously, from black sand beaches with pounding surf to beaches of pink and white sand with calm waters perfect for snorkeling. Many of the shorelines provide picturesque hiking, shallow tide pools for exploring, beautiful reef where fish and turtles delight snorkelers, and waves that the most adventurous kite and board surfers enjoy. The terrain and the water make it easy for visitors to find a favorite beach in Hawaii.

The northern shore of Oahu is famous for its surfing beaches, while the southern shores of Kauai provide hikers with amazing views of the lithified cliffs formed by the power of the ocean. Black sand beaches are common on Hawaii, formed by the lava flows that created the islands. The reef that buffers many beaches from the open ocean is home to a wide variety of sea life that can be enjoyed while scuba diving and snorkeling.

Using the preceding information, create the first four to six slides of a presentation that Katherine can show during her discussion. Apply an appropriate theme and use slide layouts that will effectively present the content. Several picture files listed at the beginning of this project have been provided that you can insert in your presentation. Apply font formatting, picture styles, and slide transitions, and modify text alignment and line spacing as necessary. Save the file as **Lastname_Firstname_1M_Beaches** and then insert a header and footer that include the date and time updated automatically, the file name in the footer, and the page number. Add your name, your course name and section number, and the keywords **beaches, Black Sands beach, tide pools, lithified cliffs, scuba, snorkeling** to the Properties area. Save and print or submit as directed by your instructor.

End You have completed Project 13M

Outcomes-Based Assessments

Apply a combination of the 13A and 13B skills.

You and GO! | Project 13N Travel

Project Files

For Project 13N, you will need the following files:

New blank PowerPoint presentation

You will save your presentation as:

Lastname_Firstname_1N_Travel

Choose a place to which you have traveled or would like to travel. Create a presentation with at least six slides that describes the location, the method of travel, the qualities of the location that make it interesting or fun, the places you can visit, and any cultural activities in which you might like to participate. Choose an appropriate theme, slide layouts, and pictures, and then format the presentation attractively. Save your presentation as **Lastname_Firstname_1N_Travel** and submit as directed.

End **You have completed Project 13N**

Apply a combination of the 13A and 13B skills.

GO! CD-ROM

GO! Collaborate | Project 13O Bell Orchid Hotels Group Running Case

This project relates to the **Bell Orchid Hotels**. Your instructor may assign this group case project to your class. If your instructor assigns this project, he or she will provide you with information and instructions to work as part of a group. The group will apply the skills gained thus far to help the Bell Orchid Hotels achieve their business goals.

End **You have completed Project 13O**

Formatting PowerPoint Presentations

OUTCOMES

At the end of this chapter you will be able to:

OBJECTIVES

Mastering these objectives will enable you to:

PROJECT 14A

Format a presentation to add visual interest and clarity.

1. Format Numbered and Bulleted Lists (p. 791)
2. Insert Clip Art (p. 795)
3. Insert Text Boxes and Shapes (p. 800)
4. Format Objects (p. 804)

PROJECT 14B

Enhance a presentation with WordArt and diagrams.

5. Remove Picture Backgrounds and Insert WordArt (p. 813)
6. Create and Format a SmartArt Graphic (p. 818)

Nikolay Okhitin\Shutterstock

In This Chapter

A PowerPoint presentation is a visual aid in which well-designed slides help the audience understand complex information while keeping them focused on the message. Color is an important element that enhances your slides and draws the audience's interest by creating focus. When designing the background and element colors for your presentation, be sure that the colors you use provide contrast so that the text is visible on the background

Fascination Entertainment Group operates 15 regional theme parks across the United States, Mexico, and Canada. Park types include traditional theme parks, water parks, and animal parks. This year the company will launch three of its new "Fascination Parks" where attractions combine fun and the discovery of math and science information, and where teens and adults enjoy the free Friday night concerts.

Project 14A Employee Training Presentation

Project Activities

In Activities 14.01 through 14.14, you will format a presentation for Yuki Hiroko, Director of Operations for Fascination Entertainment Group, that describes important safety guidelines for employees. Your completed presentation will look similar to Figure 14.1.

Project Files

For Project 14A, you will need the following file:

p02A_Safety

You will save your presentation as:

Lastname_Firstname_2A_Safety

Project Results

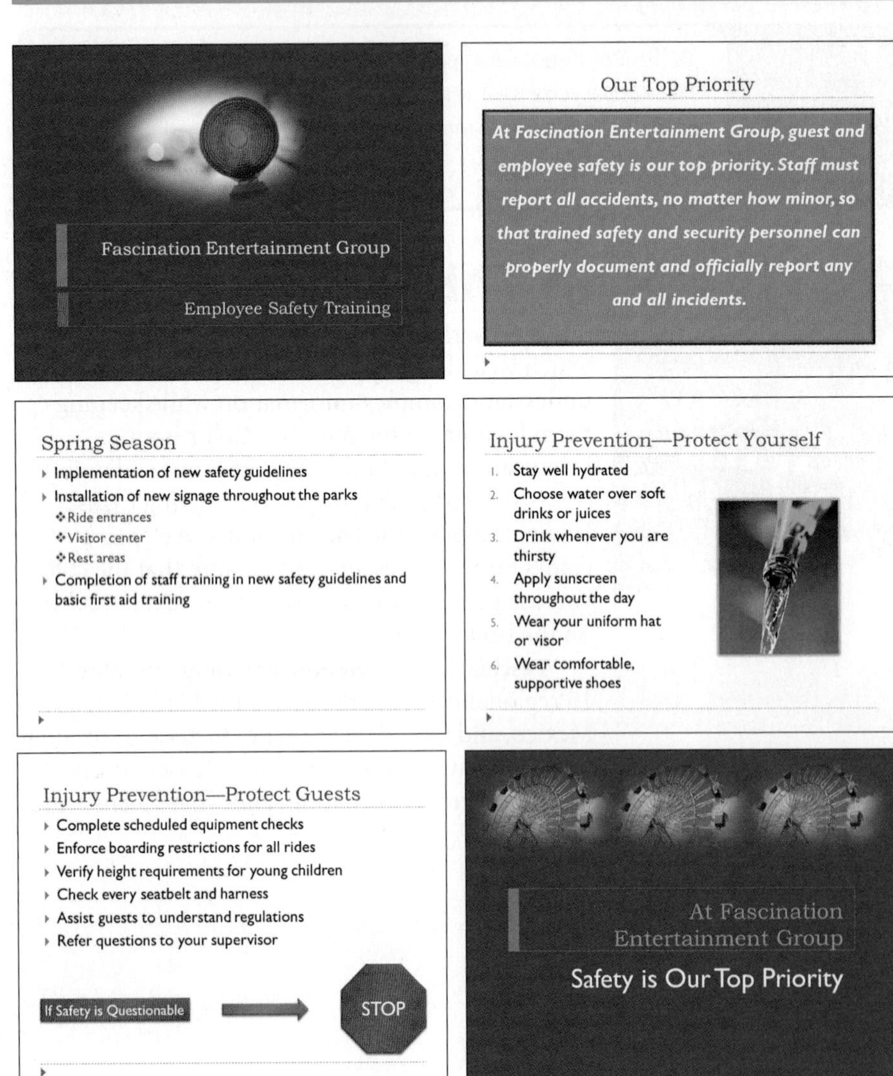

Figure 14.1
Project 14A Safety

Objective 1 | Format Numbered and Bulleted Lists

Recall that formatting is the process of changing the appearance of the text, layout, or design of a slide. You can format slide content by changing the bulleted and numbered list styles and colors.

Activity 14.01 | Selecting Placeholder Text

Recall that a placeholder is a box on a slide with dotted or dashed borders that holds title and body text or other content such as charts, tables, and pictures. You can format placeholder contents by selecting text or by selecting the entire placeholder.

1 **Start** PowerPoint. From the student files that accompany this textbook, locate and open **p02A_Safety**. On the **File tab**, click **Save As**, and then navigate to the location where you are storing your projects for this chapter. Create a new folder named **PowerPoint Chapter 14** and then in the **File name** box and using your own name, type **Lastname_Firstname_2A_Safety** Click **Save** or press Enter. Take a moment to view each slide and become familiar with the contents of this presentation.

2 Display **Slide 2**. Click anywhere in the content placeholder with the single bullet point, and then compare your screen with Figure 14.2.

A dashed border displays, indicating that you can make editing changes to the placeholder text.

Figure 14.2

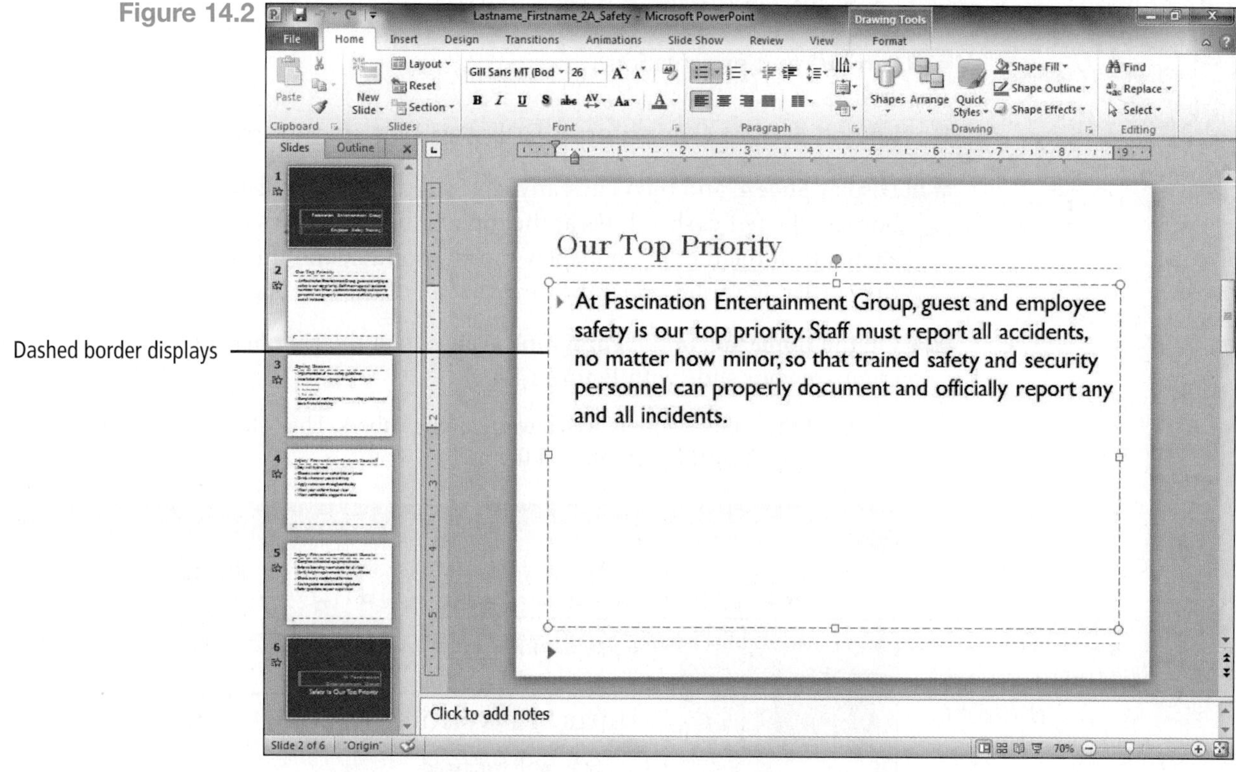

3 Point anywhere on the dashed border to display the pointer, and then click one time to display the border as a solid line. Compare your screen with Figure 14.3.

When a placeholder's border displays as a solid line, all of the text in the placeholder is selected, and any formatting changes that you make will be applied to *all* of the text in the placeholder.

Figure 14.3

Solid border indicates that all placeholder text is selected

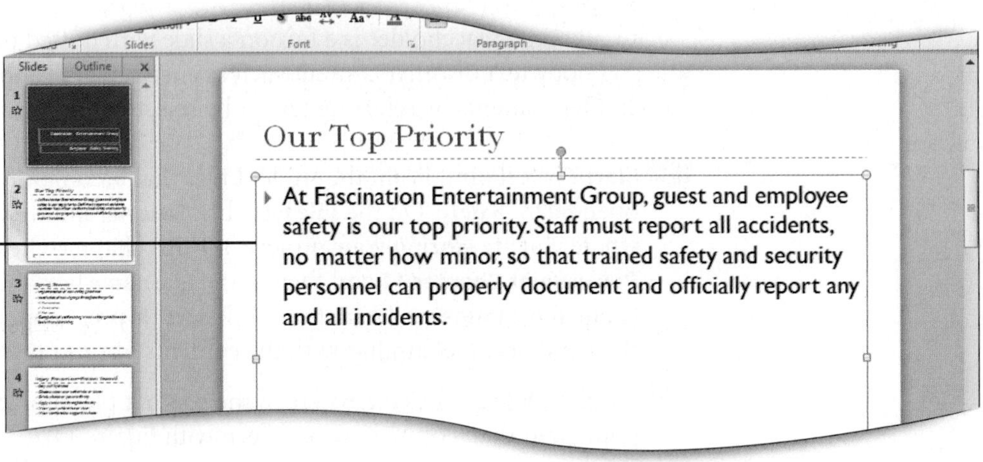

Our Top Priority

At Fascination Entertainment Group, guest and employee safety is our top priority. Staff must report all accidents, no matter how minor, so that trained safety and security personnel can properly document and officially report any and all incidents.

4 With the border of the placeholder displaying as a solid line, click in the **Font Size** box to select the number, and then type **30** and press Enter. Notice that the font size of *all* of the placeholder text increases.

5 **Save** your presentation.

Activity 14.02 | Changing a Bulleted List to a Numbered List

1 Display **Slide 4**, and then click anywhere in the bulleted list. Point to the blue dashed border (the red dashed lines at the top and bottom are part of the decorative elements of the theme) to display the pointer, and then click one time to display the border as a solid line indicating that all of the text is selected.

2 On the **Home tab**, in the **Paragraph group**, click the **Numbering** button, and then compare your slide with Figure 14.4.

All of the bullet symbols are converted to numbers. The color of the numbers is determined by the presentation theme.

Figure 14.4

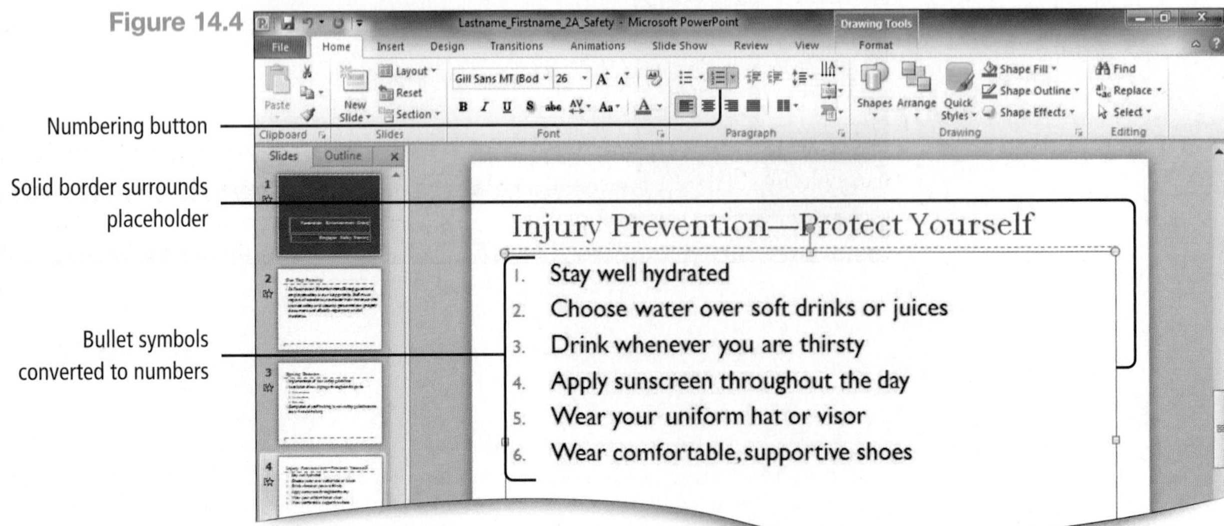

> **Alert! | Did You Display the Numbering Gallery?**
>
> If you clicked the Numbering button arrow instead of the Numbering button, the Numbering gallery displays. Click the Numbering button arrow again to close the gallery, and then click the Numbering button to convert the bullets to numbers.

3 **Save** your presentation.

Activity 14.03 | Modifying a Bulleted List Style

The presentation theme includes default styles for the bullet points in content placeholders. You can customize a bullet by changing its style, color, and size.

1 Display **Slide 3**, and then select the three second-level bullet points—*Ride entrances*, *Visitor center*, and *Rest areas*.

2 On the **Home tab**, in the **Paragraph group**, click the **Bullets button arrow** to display the **Bullets** gallery, and then compare your screen with Figure 14.5.

The Bullets gallery displays several bullet characters that you can apply to the selection.

Figure 14.5

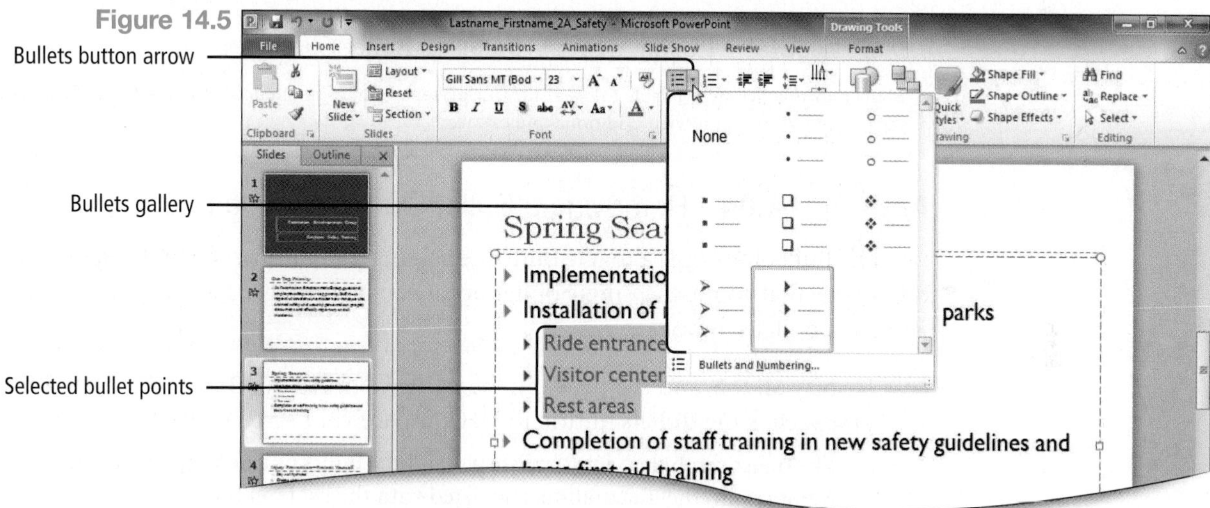

> **Alert! | Were the Bullets Removed?**
>
> If the bullets were removed, then you clicked the Bullets button instead of the Bullets button arrow. Click the Bullets button arrow, and then continue with Step 3.

3 At the bottom of the **Bullets** gallery, click **Bullets and Numbering**. In the **Bullets and Numbering** dialog box, point to each bullet style to display its ScreenTip. Then, in the second row, click **Star Bullets**. If the Star Bullets are not available, in the second row of bullets, click the second bullet style, and then click the Reset button.

4 Below the gallery, click the **Color** button. Under **Theme Colors**, in the sixth column, click the fifth color—**Red, Accent 2, Darker 25%**. In the **Size** box, select the existing number, type **100** and then compare your dialog box with Figure 14.6.

Figure 14.6

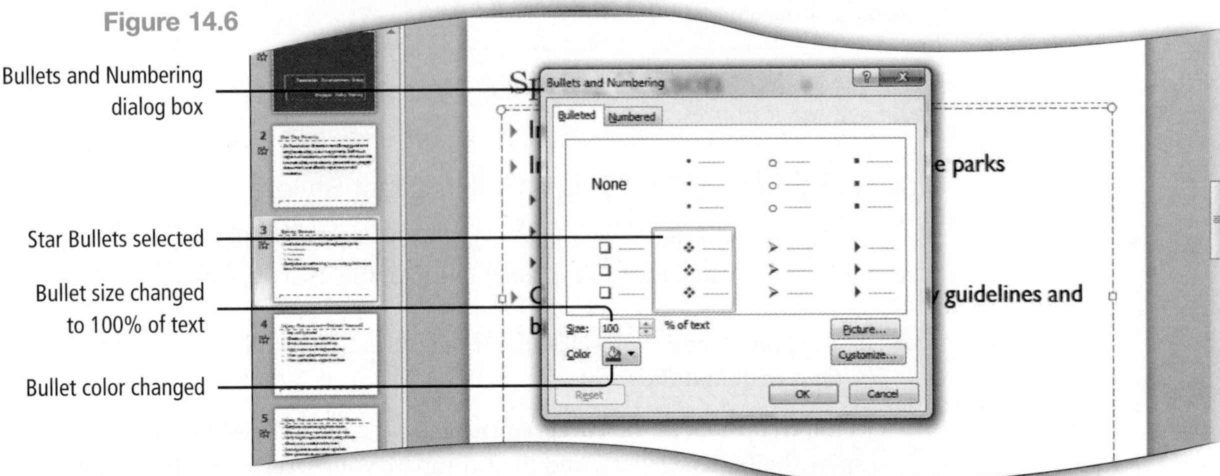

5 Click **OK** to apply the bullet style, and then **Save** your presentation.

> **More Knowledge | Using Other Symbols as Bullet Characters**
>
> Many bullets styles are available to insert in your presentation. In the Bullets and Numbering dialog box, click the Customize button to view additional bullet styles.

Activity 14.04 | Removing a Bullet Symbol from a Bullet Point

The Bullet button is a toggle button, enabling you to turn the bullet symbol on and off. A slide that contains a single bullet point can be formatted as a single paragraph *without* a bullet symbol.

1 Display **Slide 2**, and then click in the paragraph. On the **Home tab**, in the **Paragraph group**, click the **Bullets** button. Compare your screen with Figure 14.7.

The bullet symbol no longer displays, and the bullet button is no longer selected. Additionally, the indentation associated with the list level is removed.

2 **Center** the paragraph. On the **Home tab**, in the **Paragraph group**, click the **Line Spacing** button, and then click **1.5**.

Figure 14.7

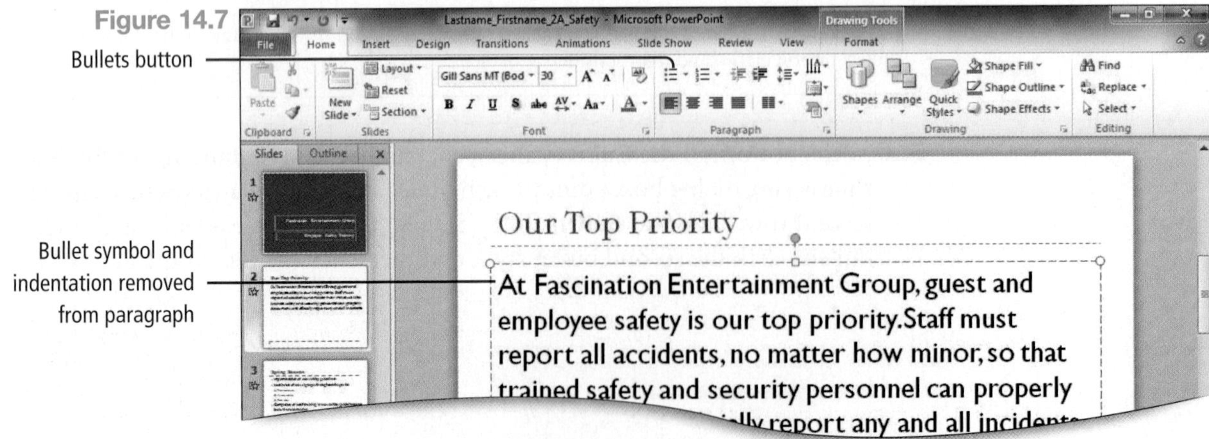

3 Click the dashed border to display the solid border and to select all of the text in the paragraph, and then apply **Bold** and **Italic**. Click in the slide title, and then click the **Center** button. **Save** your presentation.

Objective 2 | Insert Clip Art

There are many sources from which you can insert images into a presentation. One type of image that you can insert is a ***clip***—a single media file such as art, sound, animation, or a movie.

Activity 14.05 | Inserting Clip Art

1 Display **Slide 4**, and then on the **Home tab**, in the **Slides group**, click the **Layout** button. Click **Two Content** to change the slide layout.

2 In the placeholder on the right side of the slide, click the **Clip Art** button to display the **Clip Art** pane, and then compare your screen with Figure 14.8.

Figure 14.8

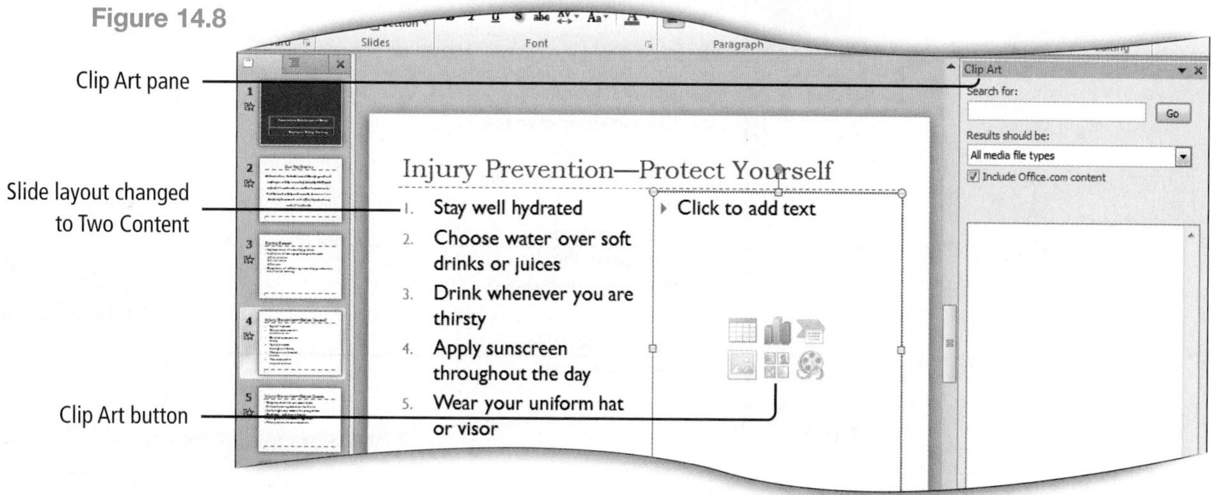

3 In the **Clip Art** pane, click in the **Search for** box, and then replace any existing text with **bottled water** so that PowerPoint can search for images that contain the keyword *bottled water*.

4 Click the **Results should be arrow**, and then click as necessary to *clear* the **Illustrations**, **Videos**, and **Audio** check boxes and to select only the **Photographs** check box. Compare your screen with Figure 14.9.

With the Photographs check box selected, PowerPoint will search for images that were created with a digital camera or a scanner.

Figure 14.9

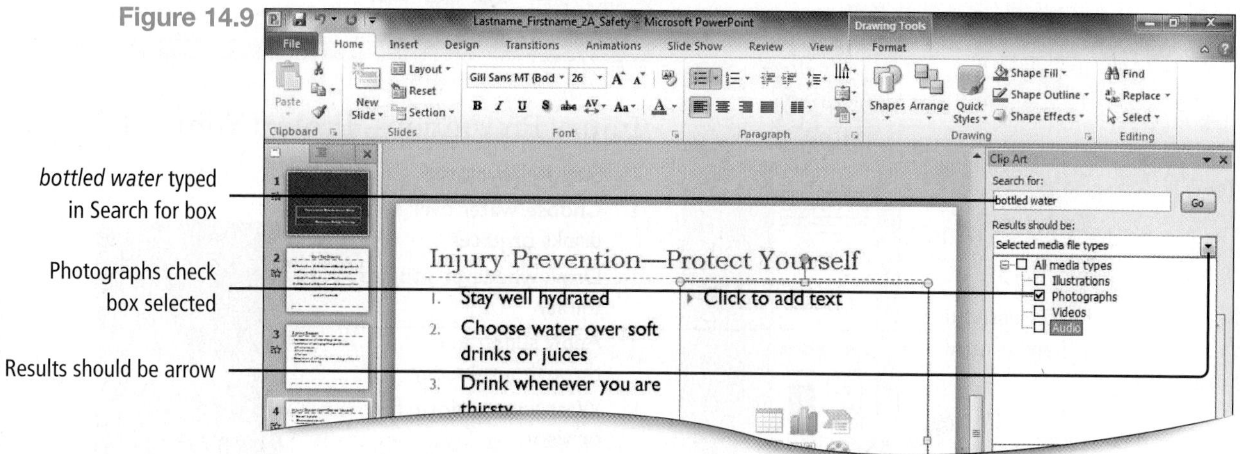

PowerPoint | Chapter 14

5 In the **Clip Art** pane, click the **Results should be arrow** to close the list. Then, if necessary, select the **Include Office.com content** check box so that images available on Office.com are included in the search.

6 In the **Clip Art** pane, click **Go** to display clips in the Clip Art pane. Scroll through the clips, and then locate and point to the image of the water pouring from a glass water bottle on a blue background. Compare your screen with Figure 14.10.

When you point to an image in the Clip Art pane, a ScreenTip displays the keywords and information about the size of the image.

Figure 14.10

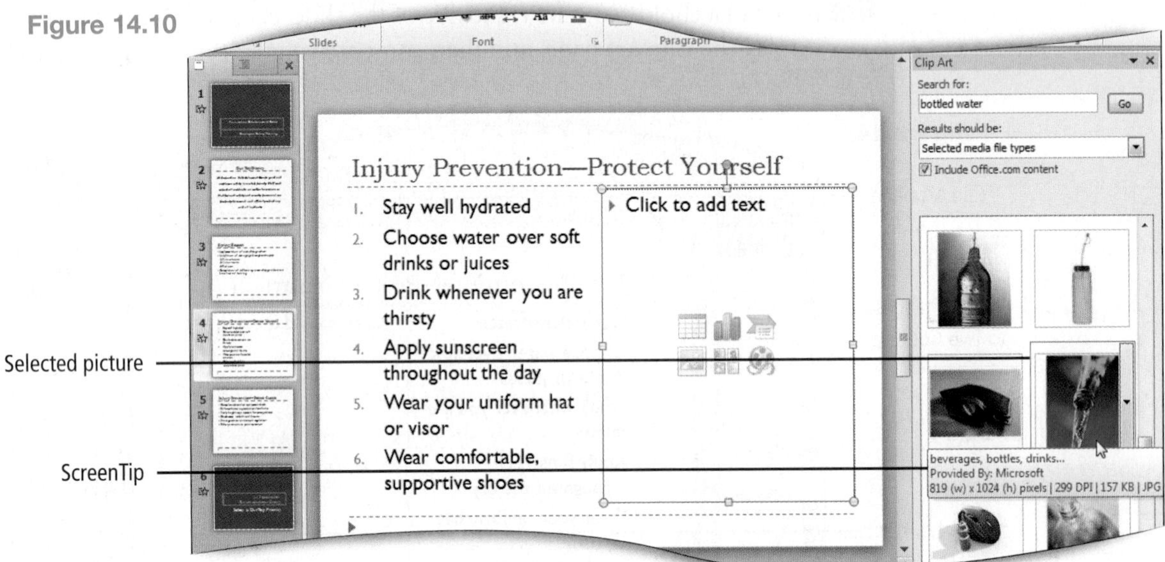

> **Alert!** | **Is the Water Bottle Picture Unavailable?**
>
> If you are unable to locate the suggested picture, choose another similar image.

7 Click the water bottle picture to insert it in the content placeholder on the right side of the slide. **Close** [X] the **Clip Art** pane, and then compare your slide with Figure 14.11.

On the Ribbon, the Picture Tools display, and the water bottle image is surrounded by sizing handles, indicating that it is selected.

Figure 14.11

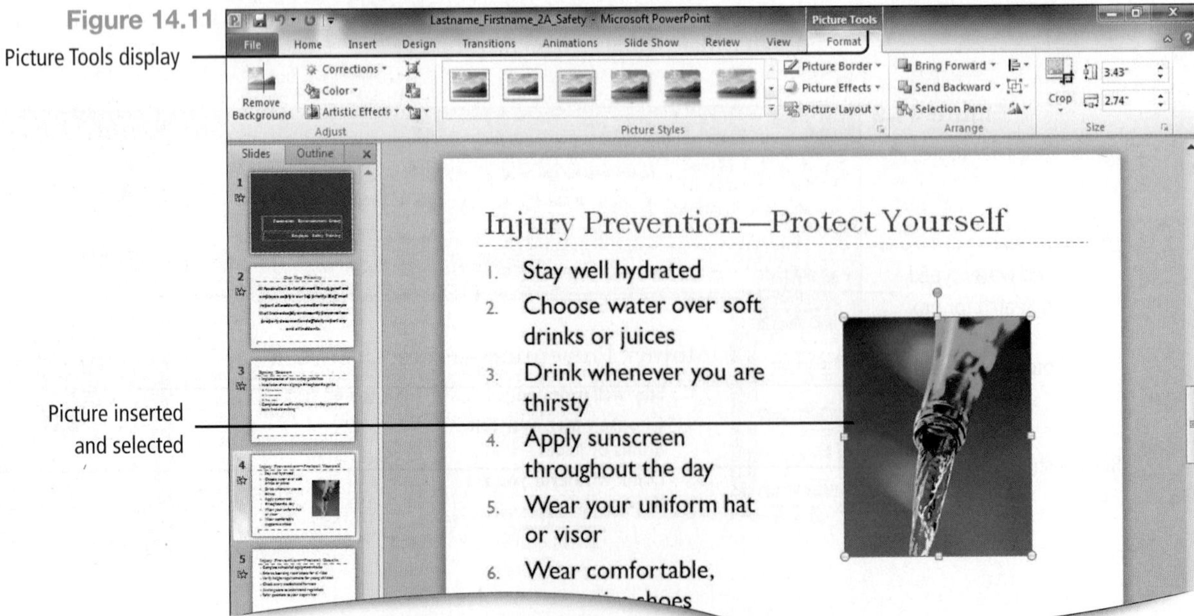

8 Display **Slide 1**. Click the **Insert tab**, and then in the **Images group**, click **Clip Art**.

9 In the **Clip Art** pane, in the **Search for** box, search for **red lights** and then click **Go**. Scroll as necessary to locate the picture of the single red warning light. Point to the picture, and then compare your screen with Figure 14.12.

If you cannot locate the picture, select another appropriate image.

Figure 14.12

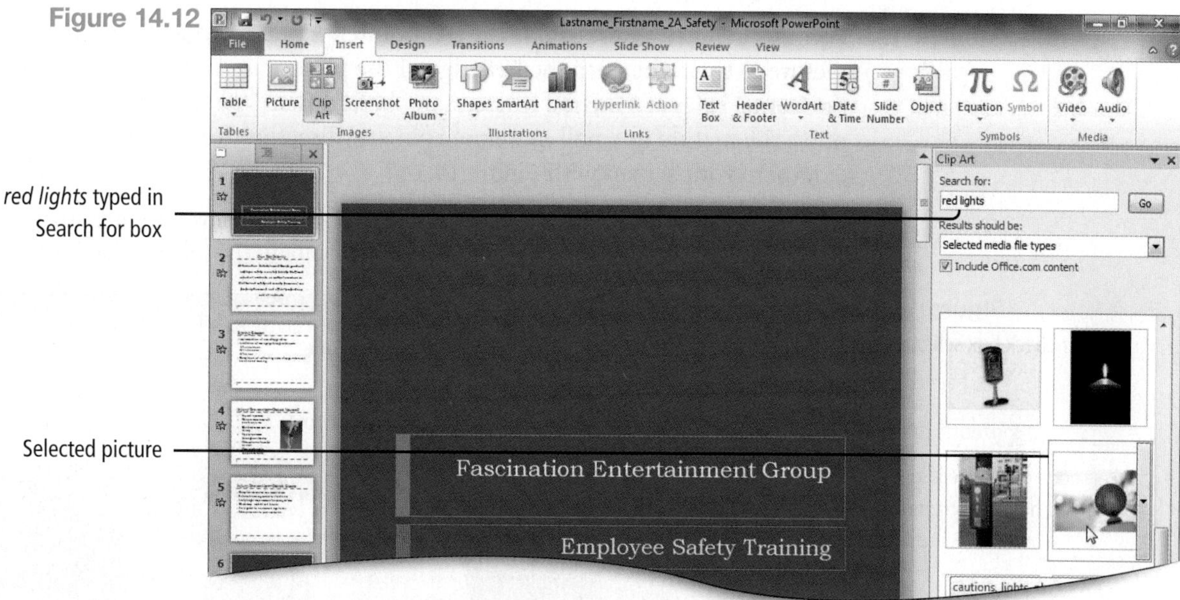

10 Click the **red light** picture to insert it in the center of the slide, and then **Close** the **Clip Art** pane. **Save** your presentation.

When you use the Clip Art command on the Ribbon instead of the Clip Art button in a content placeholder, PowerPoint inserts the image in the center of the slide.

Activity 14.06 | Moving and Sizing Images

Recall that when an image is selected, it is surrounded by sizing handles that you can drag to resize the image. You can also resize an image using the Shape Height and Shape Width boxes on the Format tab. When you point to the image, rather than pointing to a sizing handle, the move pointer—a four-headed arrow—displays, indicating that you can move the image.

> **Another Way**
> Alternatively, drag a corner sizing handle to resize an image proportionately.

1 If necessary, select the picture of the red light. On the **Format tab**, in the **Size group**, click in the **Shape Height** box, and then replace the selected number with **3.5**

2 Press Enter to resize the image. Notice that the picture is resized proportionately, and the **Width** box displays *5.26*. Compare your screen with Figure 14.13.

When a picture is resized in this manner, the width adjusts in proportion to the picture height.

Figure 14.13

3 Display the **View tab**. In the **Show group**, verify that the **Ruler** check box is selected and if necessary, select it. On the horizontal and vertical rulers, notice that *0* displays in the center.

Horizontally, the PowerPoint ruler indicates measurements from the center *out* to the left and to the right. Vertically, the PowerPoint ruler indicates measurements from the center up and down.

4 Point to the picture to display the [pointer icon] pointer. Hold down Shift, and then drag the picture to the right until the left edge of the picture is aligned with the **left half of the horizontal ruler at 3 inches**. If necessary, hold down Ctrl and press an arrow key to move the picture in small increments in any direction for a more precise placement. Compare your screen with Figure 14.14.

Pressing Shift while dragging an object constrains object movement in a straight line either vertically or horizontally. Here, pressing Shift maintains the vertical placement of the picture.

Figure 14.14

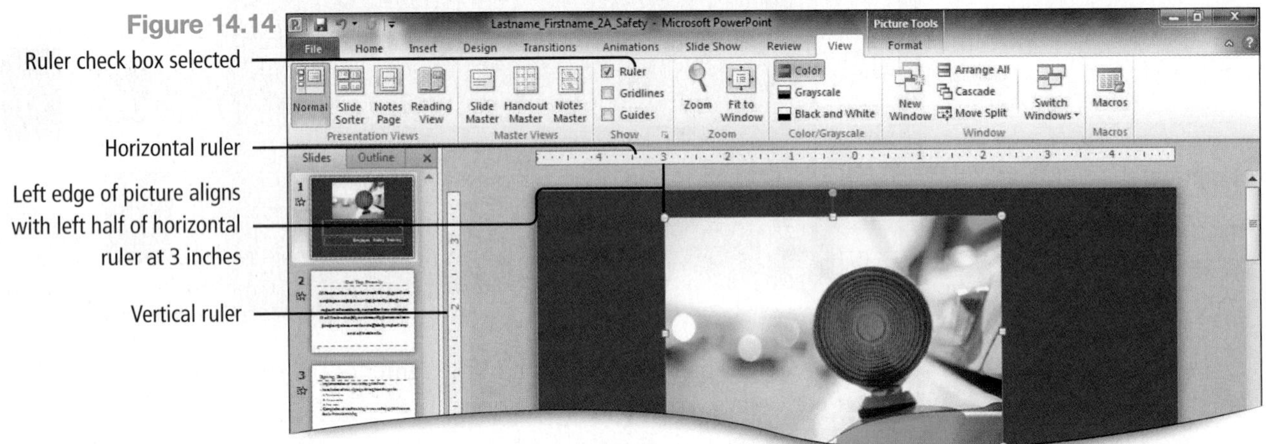

5 Display **Slide 6**. On the **Insert tab**, in the **Images group**, click the **Clip Art** button. In the **Clip Art** pane, search for **amusement park** and then click **Go**. Locate and click the picture of the Ferris wheel with the sky and clouds in the background, and then compare your slide with Figure 14.15.

Figure 14.15

6 **Close** [X] the **Clip Art** pane, and be sure that the picture is still selected. On the **Format tab**, in the **Size group**, click in the **Shape Height** box [icon]. Replace the displayed number with **2.5** and then press Enter to resize the picture. Compare your screen with Figure 14.16.

Figure 14.16

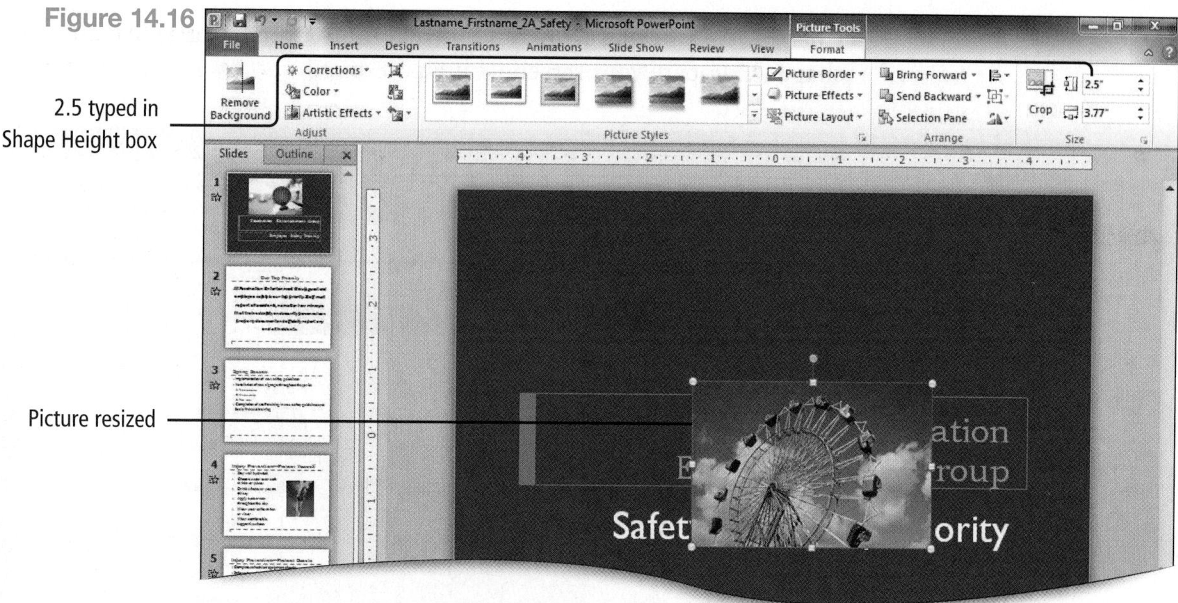

7 **Save** your presentation.

> **More Knowledge | Moving an Object by Using the Arrow Keys**
>
> You can use the directional arrow keys on your keyboard to move a picture, shape, or other object in small increments. Select the object so that its outside border displays as a solid line. Then, on your keyboard, hold down the Ctrl key and press the directional arrow keys to move the selected object in precise increments.

Activity 14.07 | Changing the Shape of a Picture

An inserted picture is rectangular in shape; however, you can modify a picture by changing its shape.

1 Display **Slide 1**, and then select the picture.

2 On the **Format tab**, in the **Size group**, *point* to the **Crop button arrow**, and then compare your screen with Figure 14.17.

The Crop button is a split button. The upper section—the Crop button—enables the ***crop*** feature, which reduces the size of a picture by removing vertical or horizontal edges. The lower section—the Crop arrow—displays cropping options, such as the option to crop a picture to a shape.

Figure 14.17

3 Click the **Crop button arrow**, and then point to **Crop to Shape** to display a gallery of shapes. Compare your screen with Figure 14.18.

Figure 14.18

4 Under **Basic Shapes**, in the first row, click the first shape—**Oval**—to change the picture's shape to an oval. **Save** your presentation.

Objective 3 | Insert Text Boxes and Shapes

You can use objects, including text boxes and shapes, to draw attention to important information or to serve as containers for slide text. Many shapes, including lines, arrows, ovals, and rectangles, are available to insert and position anywhere on your slides.

Activity 14.08 | Inserting a Text Box

A ***text box*** is an object with which you can position text anywhere on a slide.

1 Display **Slide 5** and verify that the rulers display. Click the **Insert tab**, and then in the **Text group**, click the **Text Box** button.

2 Move the pointer to several different places on the slide, and as you do so, in the horizontal and vertical rulers, notice that ***ruler guides***—dotted vertical and horizontal lines that display in the rulers indicating the pointer's position—move also.

Use the ruler guides to help you position objects on a slide.

3 Position the pointer so that the ruler guides are positioned on the **left half of the horizontal ruler at 4.5 inches** and on the **lower half of the vertical ruler at 1.5 inches**, and then compare your screen with Figure 14.19.

Figure 14.19

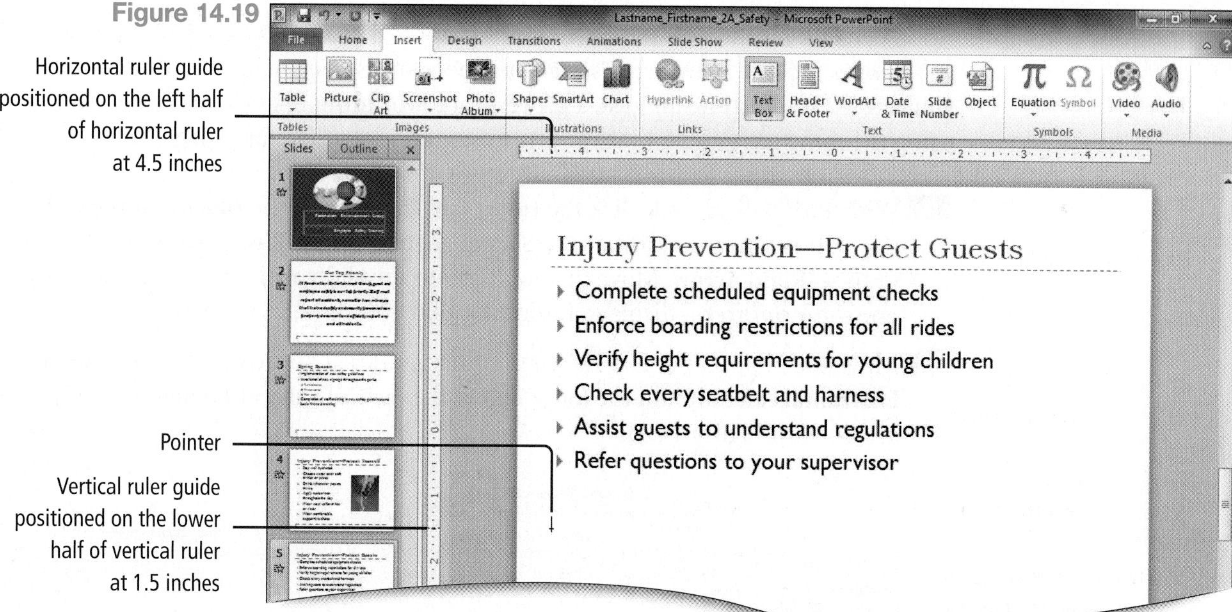

4 Click one time to create a narrow rectangular text box. With the insertion point blinking inside the text box, type **If Safety is Questionable** Notice that as you type, the width of the text box expands to accommodate the text. Compare your screen with Figure 14.20.

Do not be concerned if your text box is not positioned exactly as shown in Figure 14.20.

Figure 14.20

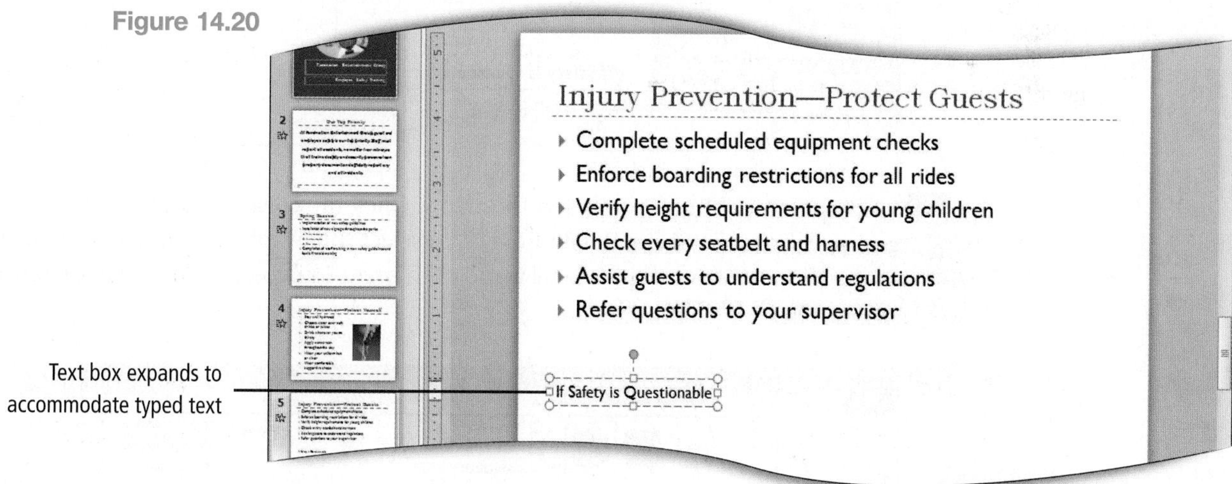

Alert! | Does the Text in the Text Box Display Vertically, One Character at a Time?

If you move the pointer when you click to create the text box, PowerPoint sets the width of the text box and does not widen to accommodate the text. If this happened to you, your text may display vertically instead of horizontally or it may display on two lines. Click Undo, and then repeat the steps again, being sure that you do not move the mouse when you click to insert the text box.

5 Select the text that you typed, change the **Font Size** to **24** and then **Save** your presentation.

You can format the text in a text box by using the same techniques that you use to format text in any other placeholder. For example, you can change the font, font style, font size, and font color.

Activity 14.09 | Inserting, Sizing, and Positioning Shapes

Shapes include lines, arrows, stars, banners, ovals, rectangles, and other basic shapes you can use to illustrate an idea, a process, or a workflow. Shapes can be sized and moved using the same techniques that you use to size and move clip art images.

1 With **Slide 5** displayed, click the **Insert tab**, and then in the **Illustrations group**, click the **Shapes** button to display the **Shapes** gallery. Under **Block Arrows**, click the first shape—**Right Arrow**. Move the pointer into the slide until the ⊞ pointer—called the ***crosshair pointer***—displays, indicating that you can draw a shape.

2 Move the ⊞ pointer to position the ruler guides at approximately **zero on the horizontal ruler** and on the **lower half of the vertical ruler at 1.5 inches**. Compare your screen with Figure 14.21.

Figure 14.21

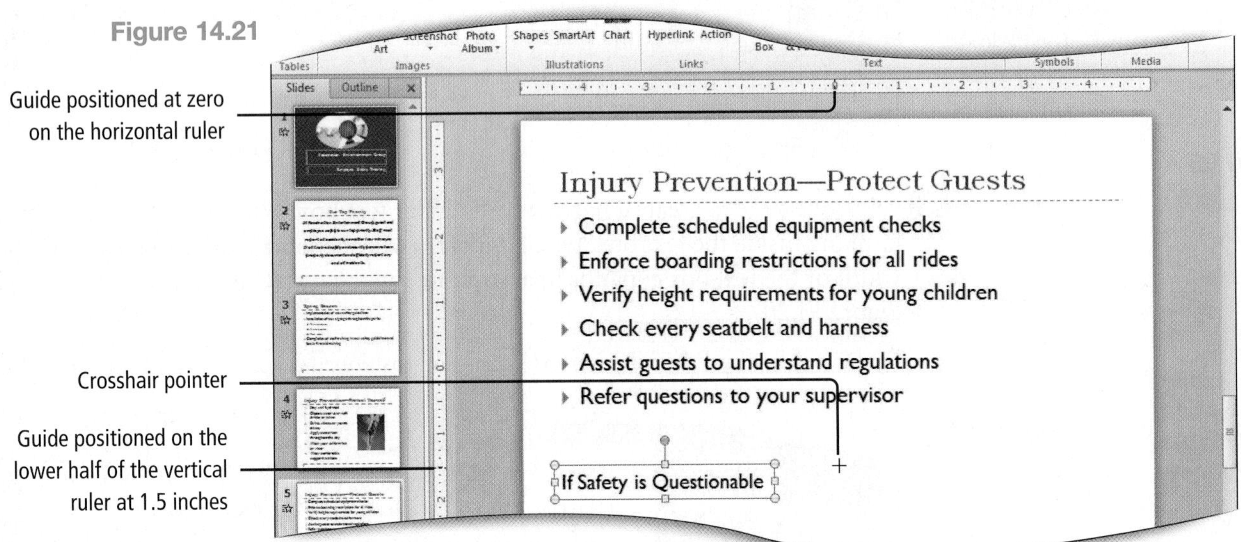

3 Click the mouse button to insert the arrow. Click the **Format tab**, and then in the **Size group**, click in the **Shape Height** box to select the number. Type **.5** and then click in the **Shape Width** box. Type **2** and then press Enter to resize the arrow. Compare your screen with Figure 14.22.

Figure 14.22

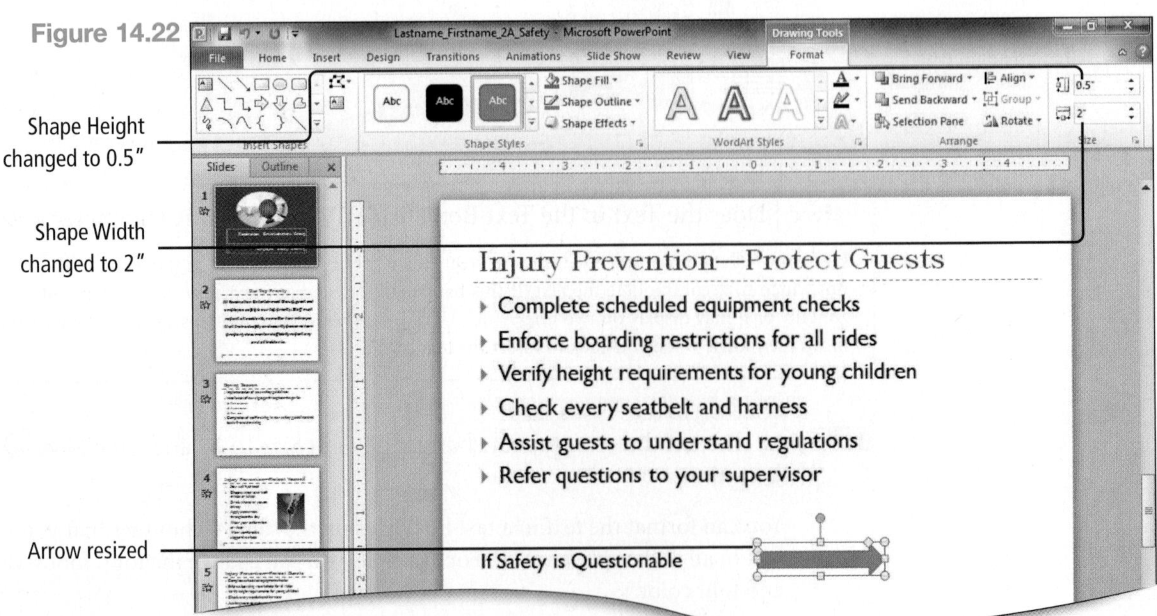

4 On the **Format tab**, in the **Insert Shapes group**, click the **More** button. In the gallery, under **Basic Shapes**, in the first row, click the second to last shape—**Octagon**.

5 Move the pointer to position the ruler guides on the **right half of the horizontal ruler at 2.5 inches** and on the **lower half of the vertical ruler at 1 inch**, and then click one time to insert an octagon.

6 On the **Format tab**, in the **Size group**, click in the **Shape Height** box to select the number. Type **2** and then click in the **Shape Width** box. Type **2** and then press Enter to resize the octagon. Compare your slide with Figure 14.23. Do not be concerned if your shapes are not positioned exactly as shown in the figure.

Figure 14.23

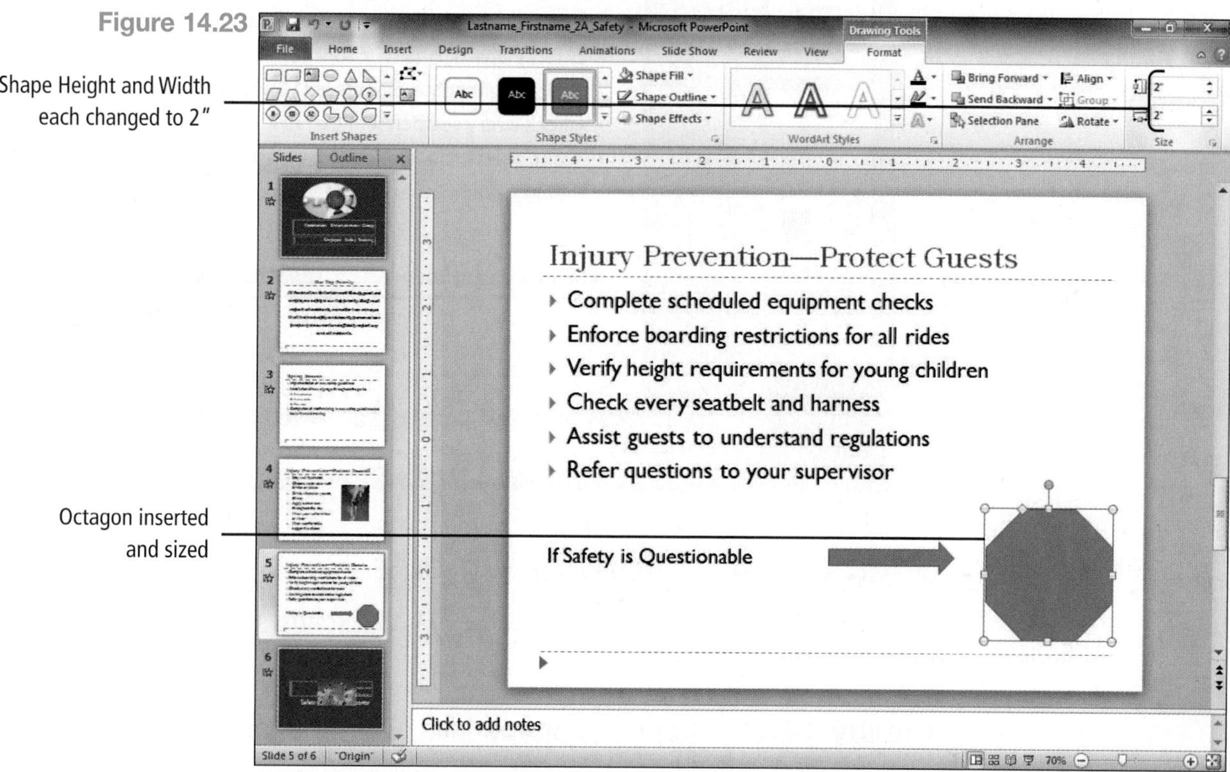

7 **Save** your presentation.

Activity 14.10 | Adding Text to Shapes

Shapes can serve as a container for text. After you add text to a shape, you can change the font and font size, apply font styles, and change text alignment.

1 On **Slide 5**, if necessary, click the octagon so that it is selected. Type **STOP** and notice that the text is centered within the octagon.

PowerPoint | Chapter 14

2 Select the text *STOP*, and then on the Mini toolbar, change the **Font Size** to **32**. Compare your screen with Figure 14.24, and then **Save** your presentation.

Figure 14.24

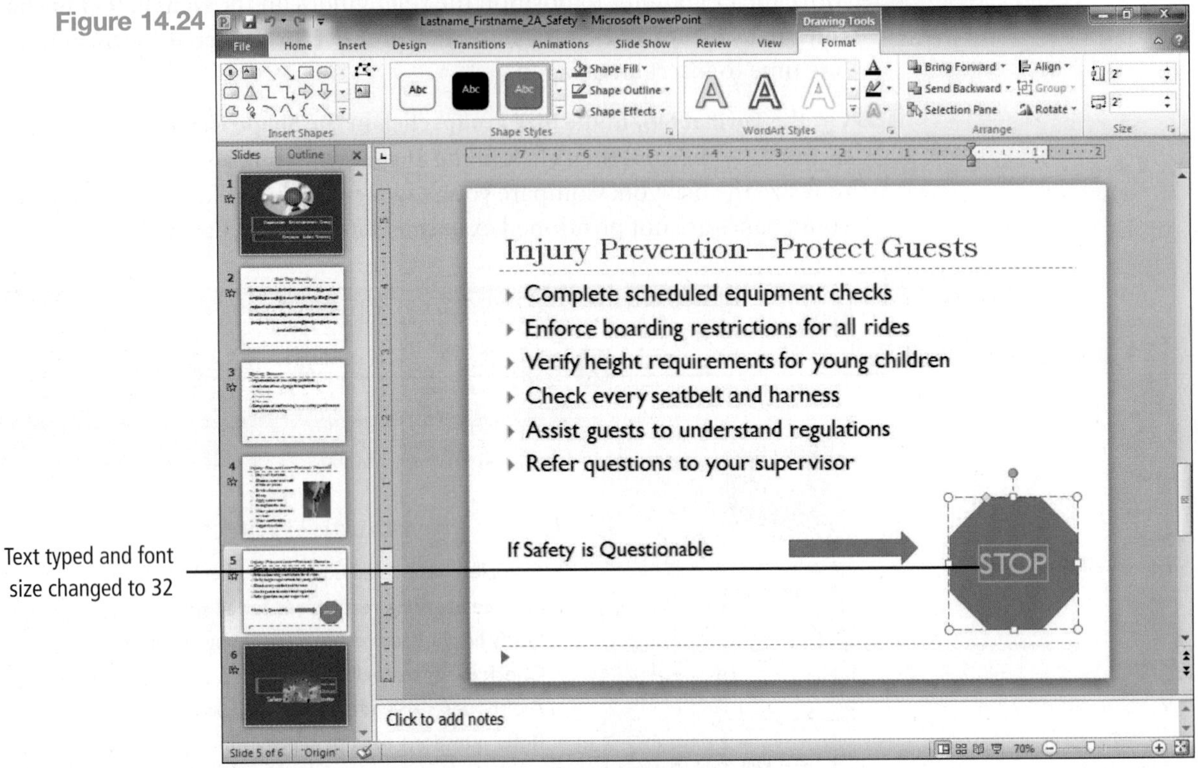

Text typed and font size changed to 32

Objective 4 | Format Objects

Apply styles and effects to clip art, shapes, and text boxes to complement slide backgrounds and colors.

Activity 14.11 | Applying Shape Fills, Outlines, and Styles

Changing the inside ***fill color*** and the outside line color is a distinctive way to format a shape. A fill color is the inside color of text or of an object. Use the Shape Styles gallery to apply predefined combinations of these fill and line colors and also to apply other effects.

1 On **Slide 5**, click anywhere in the text *If Safety is Questionable* to select the text box. On the **Format tab**, in the **Shape Styles group**, click the **More** button to display the **Shape Styles** gallery.

2 In the last row, click the third style—**Intense Effect - Red, Accent 2**. Select the **octagon** shape, and then apply the same style you applied to the text box—**Intense Effect - Red, Accent 2**.

3 Select the **arrow**, and then display the **Shape Styles** gallery. In the last row, click the second style—**Intense Effect - Blue, Accent 1**.

4 Click in a blank part of the slide so that no objects are selected, and then compare your screen with Figure 14.25.

Figure 14.25

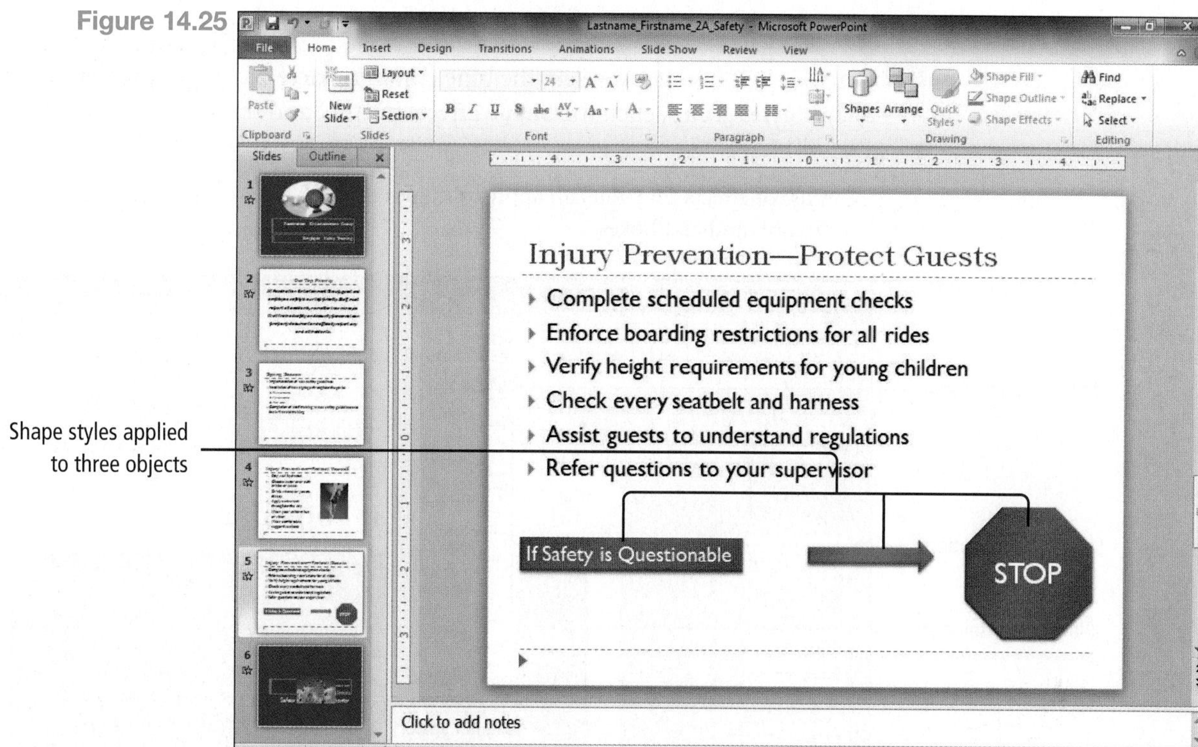

5 Display **Slide 2**, and then click anywhere in the paragraph of text to select the content placeholder.

6 On the **Format tab**, in the **Shape Styles group**, click the **Shape Fill** button, and then point to several of the theme colors and watch as Live Preview changes the inside color of the text box. In the fifth column, click the first color—**Blue, Accent 1**.

7 In the **Shape Styles group**, click the **Shape Outline** button. Point to **Weight**, click **3 pt**, and notice that a thick outline surrounds the text placeholder. Click in a blank area of the slide so that nothing is selected, and then compare your slide with Figure 14.26.

You can use combinations of shape fill, outline colors, and weights to format an object.

Figure 14.26

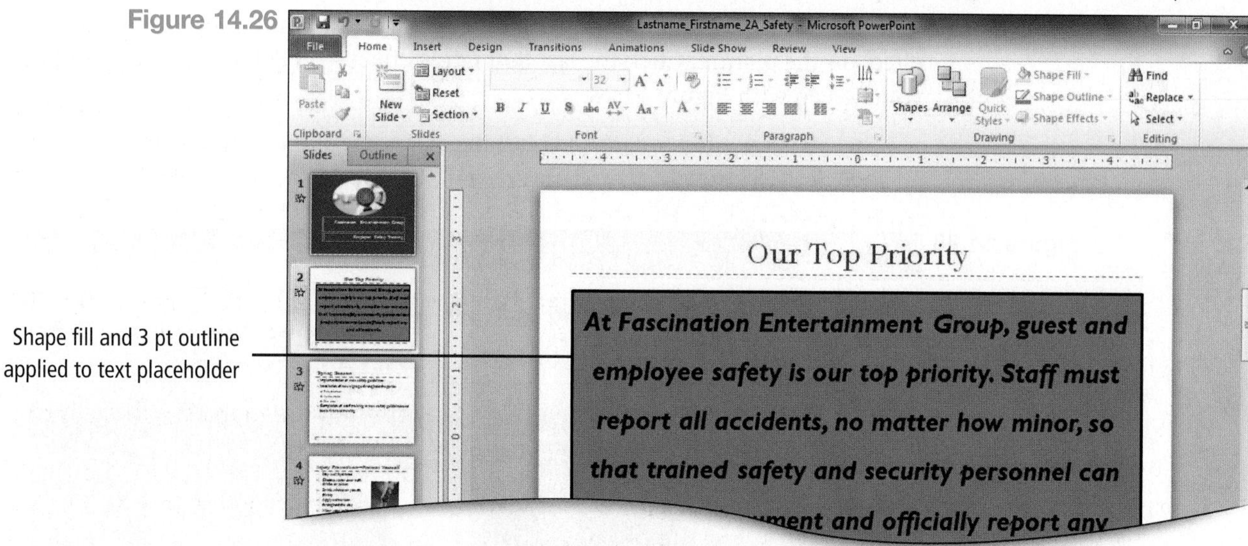

8 Click in the paragraph, and then press Ctrl + A to select all of the paragraph text, right-click in the selection to display the Mini toolbar, and then click the **Font Color button arrow** to display the **Theme Colors** gallery. Click the first color—**White, Background 1**. **Save** your presentation.

Activity 14.12 | Applying Shape and Picture Effects

1 On **Slide 2**, if necessary, select the blue content placeholder. On the **Format tab**, in the **Shape Styles group**, click the **Shape Effects** button, and then compare your screen with Figure 14.27.

A list of effects that you can apply to shapes displays. These effects can also be applied to pictures and text boxes.

Figure 14.27

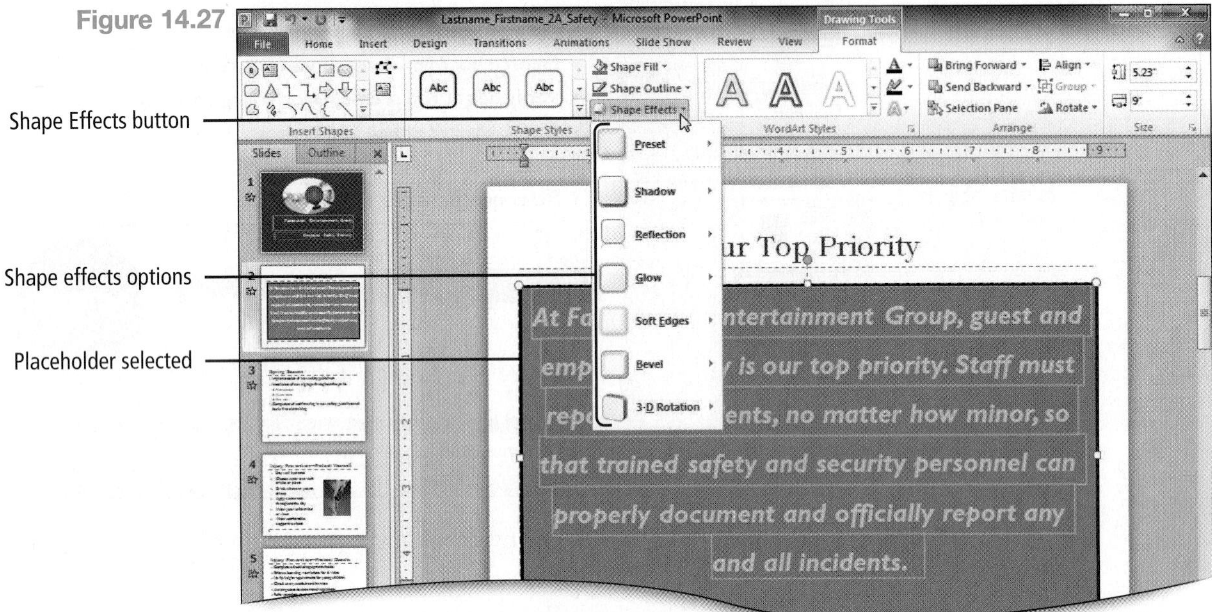

2 Point to **Bevel** to display the **Bevel** gallery. Point to each bevel to view its ScreenTip and to use Live Preview to examine the effect of each bevel on the content placeholder. In the last row, click the last bevel—**Art Deco**.

3 Display **Slide 1**, and then select the picture. On the **Format tab**, in the **Picture Styles group**, click the **Picture Effects** button.

4 Point to **Soft Edges**, and then in the **Soft Edges** gallery, point to each style to view its effect on the picture. Click the last **Soft Edges** effect—**50 Point**, and then compare your screen with Figure 14.28.

The soft edges effect softens and blurs the outer edge of the picture so that it blends into the slide background.

Figure 14.28

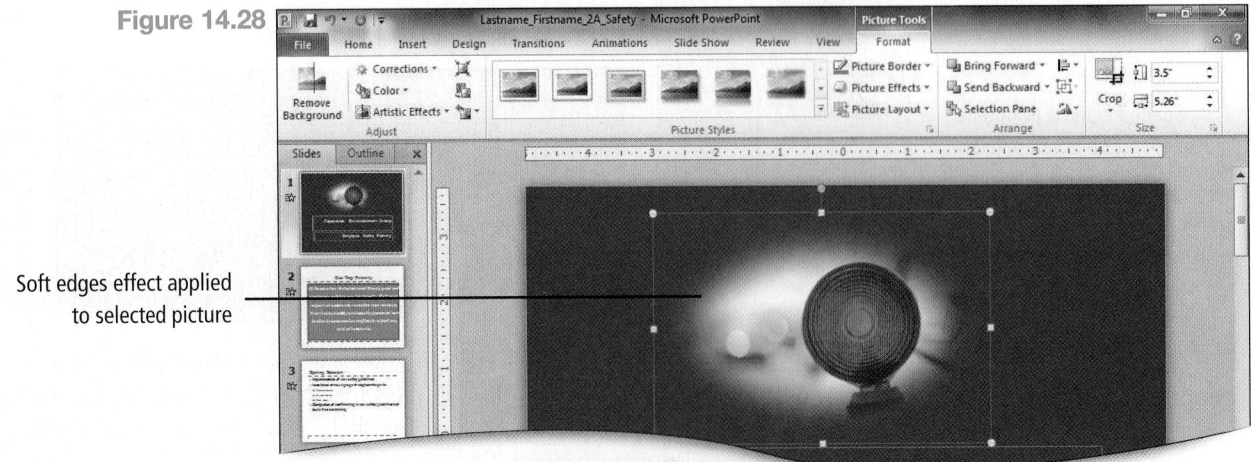

5 Display **Slide 4**, and then select the picture. On the **Format tab**, in the **Picture Styles group**, click the **Picture Effects** button, and then point to **Glow**.

6 Point to several of the effects to view the effect on the picture, and then under **Glow Variations**, in the second row, click the second glow effect—**Red, 8 pt glow, Accent color 2**. Click in a blank area of the slide to deselect the picture. Compare your slide with Figure 14.29, and then **Save** your presentation.

The glow effect applies a colored, softly blurred outline to the selected object.

Figure 14.29

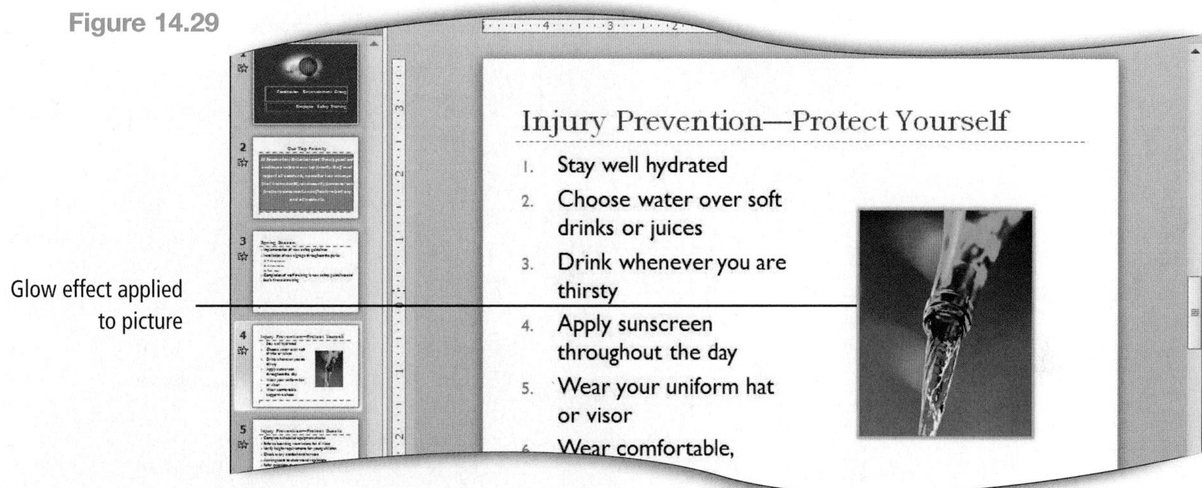

Activity 14.13 | Duplicating Objects

1 Display **Slide 6**, point to the picture to display the pointer, and then drag up and to the left so that the upper left corner of the picture aligns with the upper left corner of the slide.

2 Press and hold down Ctrl, and then press D one time. Release Ctrl.

A duplicate of the picture overlaps the original picture and the duplicated image is selected.

3 Point to the duplicated picture to display the pointer, and then drag down and to the right approximately 1 inch in both directions so that both pictures are visible. Compare your screen with Figure 14.30. Do not be concerned if your pictures are not positioned exactly as shown in the figure.

Figure 14.30

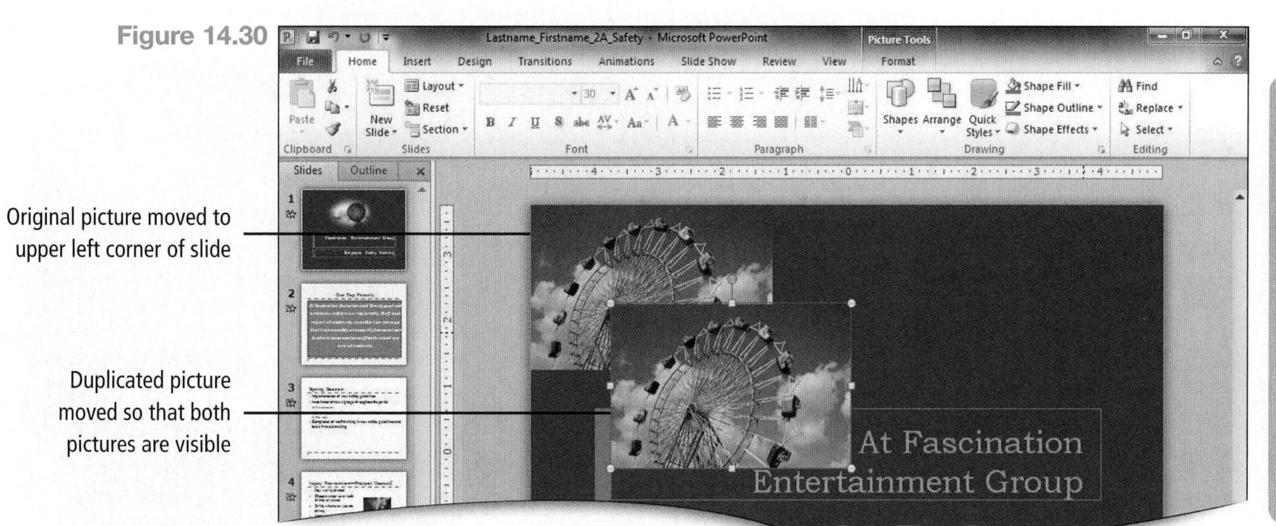

4 With the duplicated image selected, hold down Ctrl, and then press D to insert a third copy of the image.

5 Click anywhere on the slide so that none of the three pictures are selected. **Save** your presentation, and then compare your screen with Figure 14.31. Do not be concerned if your pictures are not positioned exactly as shown.

Figure 14.31

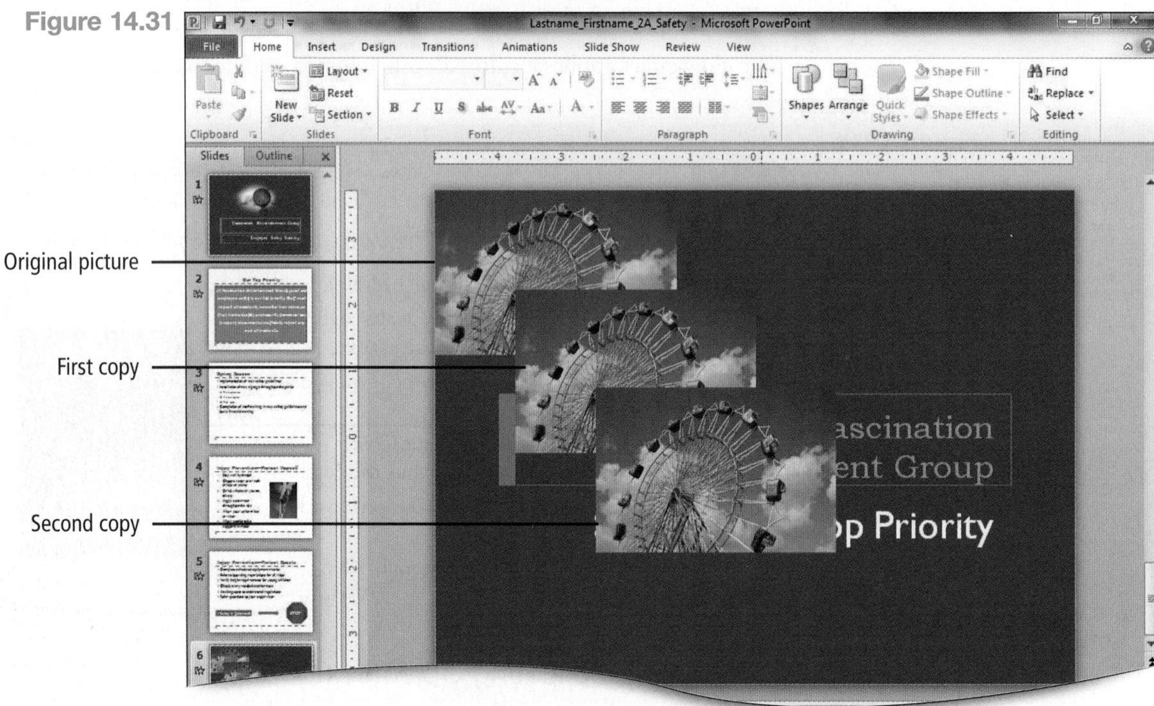

Activity 14.14 | Aligning and Distributing Objects

When you insert multiple objects on a slide, you can use commands on the Ribbon to align and distribute the objects precisely.

Another Way

Hold down Shift and click each object that you want to select.

1 With **Slide 6** displayed, position the pointer in the gray area of the Slide pane just outside the upper left corner of the slide to display the pointer. Drag down and to the right to draw a transparent blue rectangle that encloses the three pictures. Compare your slide with Figure 14.32.

Figure 14.32

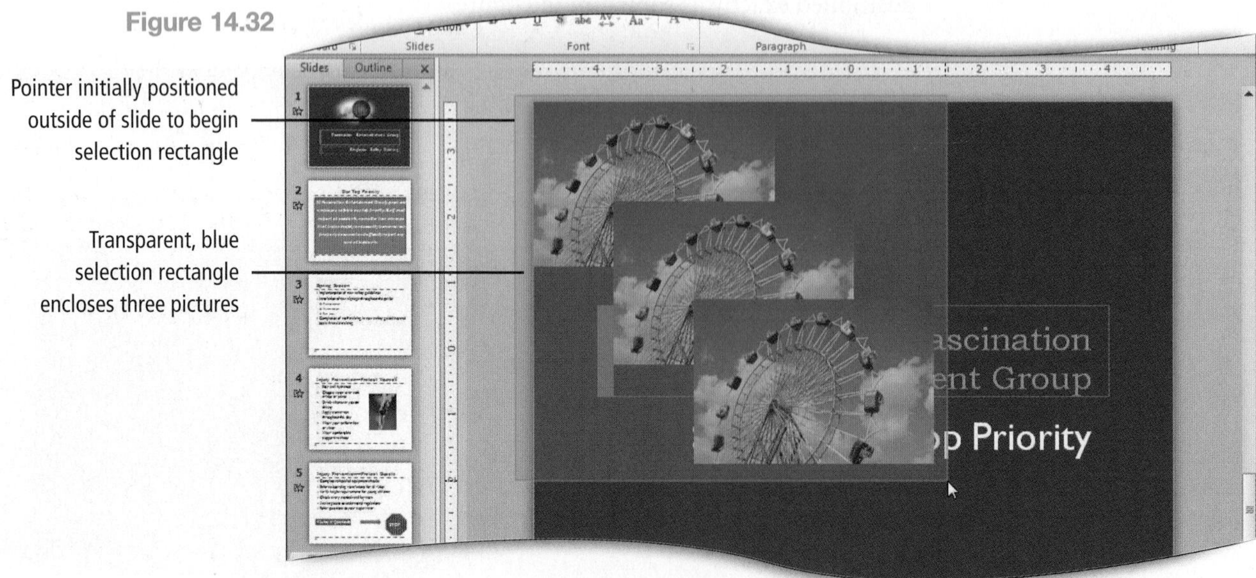

2 Release the mouse button to select the three objects, and then compare your screen with Figure 14.33.

Objects completely enclosed by a selection rectangle are selected when the mouse button is released.

Figure 14.33

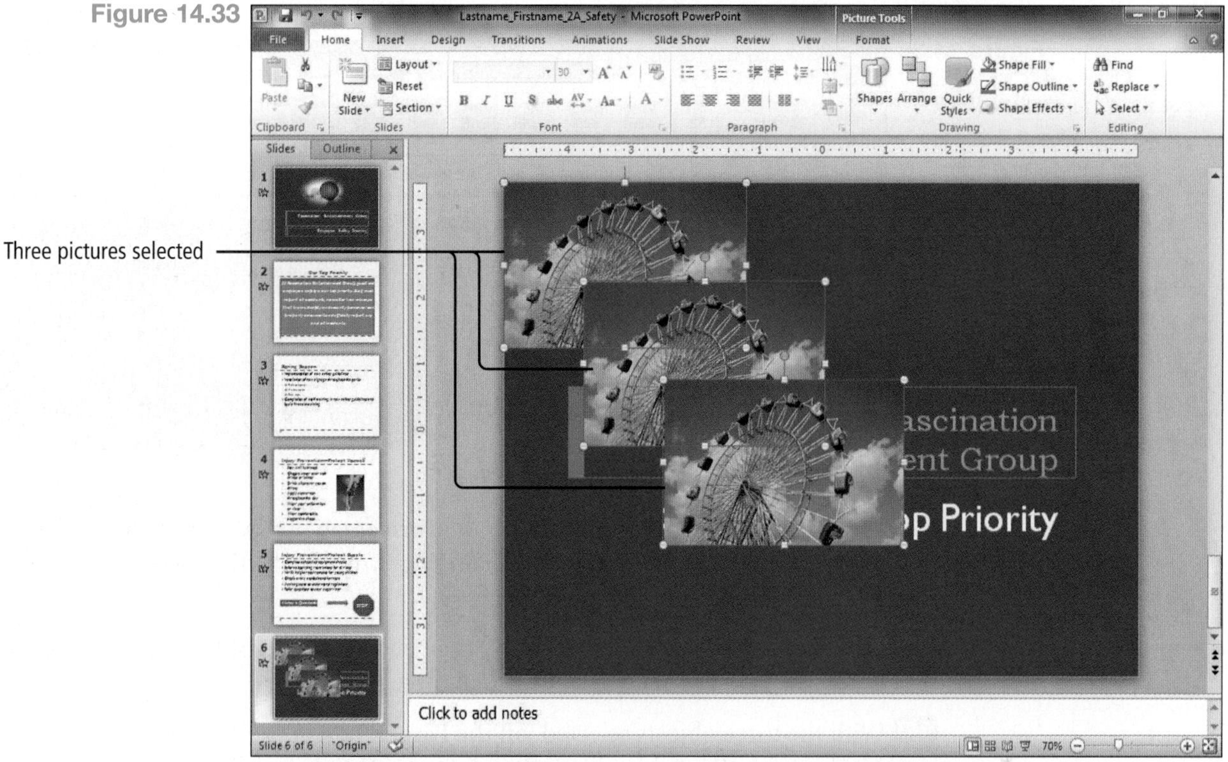

Three pictures selected

3 Click the **Format tab**, and then in the **Arrange group**, click the **Align** button. Toward the bottom of the menu, click **Align to Slide** to activate this setting.

When you select an alignment option, this setting will cause the objects to align with the edges of the slide.

4 On the **Format tab**, in the **Arrange group**, click the **Align** button again, and then click **Align Top**.

The top of each of the three pictures aligns with the top edge of the slide.

5 Click in a blank area of the slide so that nothing is selected. Then, click the third picture. Point to the picture so that the pointer displays, and then drag to the right so that its upper right corner aligns with the upper right corner of the slide.

6 Hold down Shift and click the remaining two pictures so that all three pictures are selected. On the **Format tab**, in the **Arrange group**, click the **Align** button. Click **Align Selected Objects** to activate this setting.

When you select an alignment option, this setting will cause the objects that you select to align relative to each other.

7 With the three pictures still selected, on the **Format tab**, in the **Arrange group**, click the **Align** button again, and then click **Distribute Horizontally**. Compare your screen with Figure 14.34.

The three pictures are spaced and distributed evenly across the top of the slide and aligned with the top edge of the slide.

Figure 14.34

Pictures aligned with top edge of slide and distributed evenly across top edge of slide

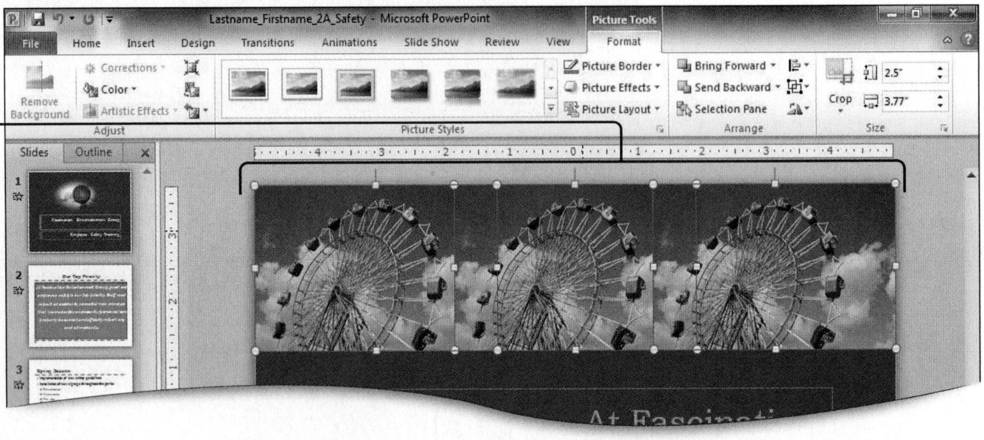

8 With the three pictures selected, on the **Format tab**, in the **Picture Styles group**, click the **Picture Effects** button. Point to **Soft Edges**, and then click **50 Point** to apply the picture effect to all three images.

9 Display **Slide 5**, hold down Shift, and then at the bottom of the slide, click the **text box**, the **arrow**, and the **octagon** to select all three objects.

10 With the three objects selected, on the **Format tab**, in the **Arrange group**, click the **Align** button. Be sure that **Align Selected Objects** is still active—a check mark displays to its left. Then, click **Align Middle**. Click the **Align** button again, and then click **Distribute Horizontally**.

The midpoint of each object aligns and the three objects are distributed evenly.

11 Click anywhere on the slide so that none of the objects are selected, and then compare your screen with Figure 14.35.

Figure 14.35

Text box, arrow, and shape are aligned and distributed

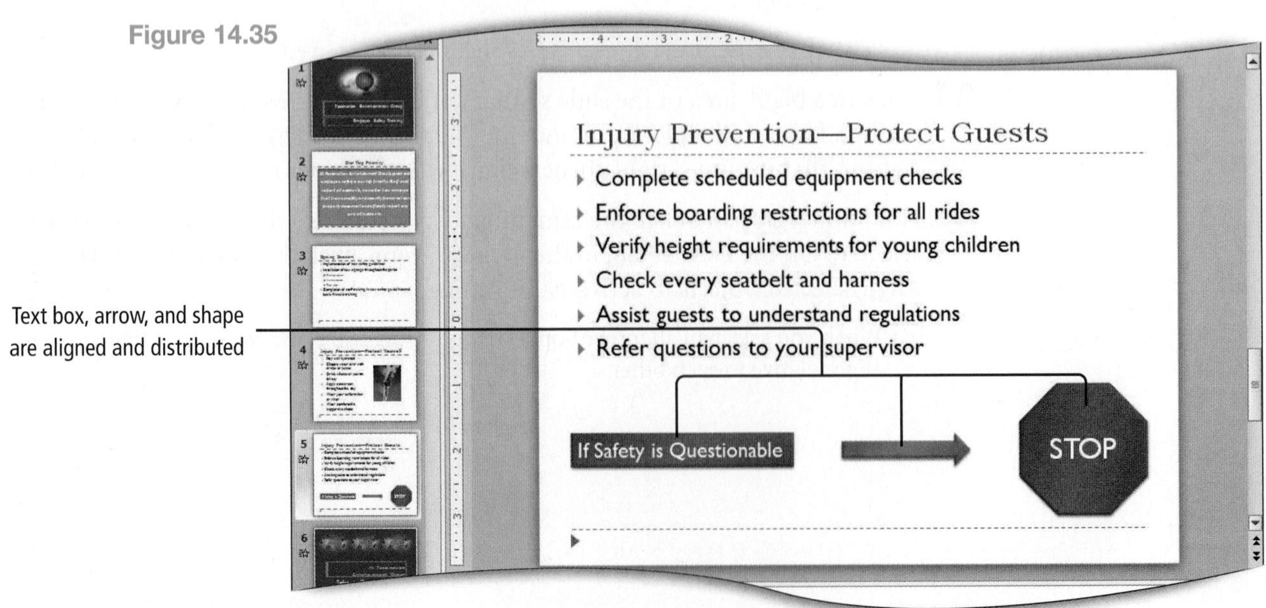

12 On the **Slide Show tab**, in the **Start Slide Show group**, click the **From Beginning** button, and then view the slide show. Press Esc when the black slide displays.

13 On the **Insert tab**, in the **Text group**, click the **Header & Footer** button to display the **Header and Footer** dialog box. Click the **Notes and Handouts tab**. Under **Include on page**, select the **Date and time** check box, and then select **Update automatically**. If necessary, clear the Header check box. Select the **Page number** and **Footer** check boxes. In the **Footer** box, using your own name, type **Lastname_Firstname_2A_Safety** and then click **Apply to All**.

14 Display the **Document Properties**. Replace the text in the **Author** box with your own firstname and lastname, in the **Subject** box, type your course name and section number, and in the **Keywords** box, type **safety, injury prevention Close** the **Document Information Panel**.

15 **Save** your presentation. Print **Handouts 6 Slides Horizontal**, or submit your presentation electronically as directed by your instructor.

16 **Close** the presentation and exit PowerPoint.

End You have completed Project 14A

PowerPoint | Chapter 14

Project 14B Event Announcement

Project Activities

In Activities 14.15 through 14.24, you will format slides in a presentation for the Fascination Entertainment Group Marketing Director that informs employees about upcoming events at the company's amusement parks. You will enhance the presentation using SmartArt and WordArt graphics. Your completed presentation will look similar to Figure 14.36.

Project Files

For Project 14B, you will need the following files:

p02B_Celebrations
p02B_Canada_Contact
p02B_Mexico_Contact
p02B_US_Contact

You will save your presentation as:

Lastname_Firstname_2B_Celebrations

Project Results

Figure 14.36
Project 14B Celebrations

Objective 5 | Remove Picture Backgrounds and Insert WordArt

To avoid the boxy look that results when you insert an image into a presentation, use ***Background Removal*** to flow a picture into the content of the presentation. Background Removal removes unwanted portions of a picture so that the picture does not appear as a self-contained rectangle.

WordArt is a gallery of text styles with which you can create decorative effects, such as shadowed or mirrored text. You can choose from the gallery of WordArt styles to insert a new WordArt object or you can customize existing text by applying WordArt formatting.

Activity 14.15 | Removing the Background from a Picture and Applying Soft Edge Options

1 **Start** PowerPoint. From your student files, open **p02B_Celebrations**. On the **View tab**, in the **Show group**, if necessary, select the Ruler check box. In your **PowerPoint Chapter 14** folder, save the file as **Lastname_Firstname_2B_Celebrations**

2 Display **Slide 6**. Notice how the picture is a self-contained rectangle and that it has a much darker black background than the presentation. Click the picture to select it, and then on the **Format tab**, in the **Adjust group**, click the **Remove Background** button. Compare your screen with Figure 14.37.

PowerPoint determines what portion of the picture is the foreground—the portion to keep—and which portion is the background—the portion to remove. The background is overlaid in magenta, leaving the remaining portion of the picture as it will look when the background removal is complete. A rectangular selection area displays that can be moved and sized to select additional areas of the picture. The Background Removal options display in the Refine group on the Ribbon.

Figure 14.37

3 On the **selection rectangle**, point to the left center sizing handle to display the ⟺ pointer, and then drag to the left so that the left edge of the selection area aligns with the dashed border surrounding the picture. Compare your screen with Figure 14.38.

When you move or size the selection area, the areas outside the selection are treated as background and are removed. Thus, you have control over which portions of the picture that you keep. Here, by resizing the selection area on the left, a larger area of each *flower* in the fireworks is included in the foreground of the picture. On the right side of the fireworks picture, some dark red shadowing is visible as part of the picture.

Figure 14.38

Another Way

In the status bar, use the Zoom Slider options to increase the Zoom to 100%.

4 On the **View tab**, in the **Zoom group**, click the **Zoom** button. In the **Zoom** dialog box, select **100%**, and then click **OK** to increase the size of the slide in the Slide pane. Notice on the right side of the fireworks picture the dark red shadowing in a triangular shape that is visible between some of the outer flowers of the fireworks display. Compare your slide with Figure 14.39.

Figure 14.39

5 On the **Background Removal tab**, in the **Refine group**, click the **Mark Areas to Remove** button, and then position the pencil pointer so that the ruler guides align on the **right half of the horizontal ruler at 1 inch** and on the **lower half of the vertical ruler at 0.5 inch**. Click one time to insert a deletion mark, and then compare your screen with Figure 14.40. If your mark is not positioned as shown in the figure, click Undo and begin again.

You can surround irregular-shaped areas that you want to remove with deletion marks. Here, you can begin to surround the dark red shadow by placing a deletion mark in one corner of the red triangular area.

Figure 14.40

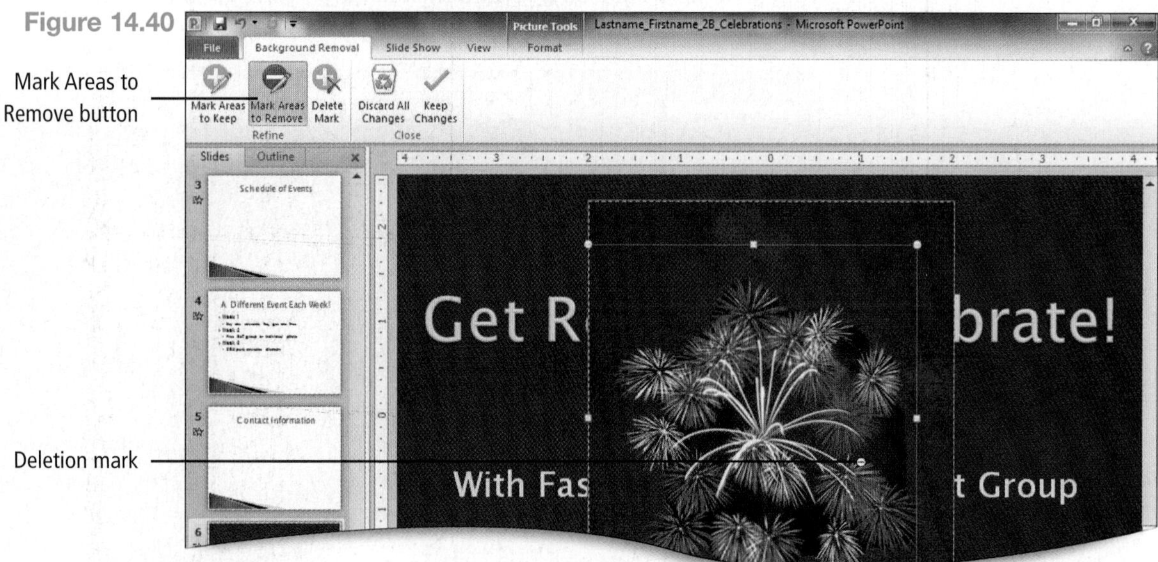

6 With the pencil pointer still active, position the pointer to align the ruler guides on the **right half of the horizontal ruler at approximately 1.5 inches** and on the **lower half of the vertical ruler to 0.75 inch** so that the pointer is aligned on the right edge of the dark red triangle. Click one time to insert another mark. Compare your screen with Figure 14.41.

The two inserted marks provide PowerPoint sufficient information to remove the triangular-shaped red and black shadowed area. If the area is not removed as shown in the figure, insert additional deletion marks as necessary.

Figure 14.41

7 On the **Background Removal tab**, in the **Close group**, click the **Keep Changes** button to remove the background. On the far right edge of the status bar, click the **Fit slide to current window** button.

8 With the picture selected, on the **Format tab**, in the **Picture Styles group**, click the **Picture Effects** button, point to **Soft Edges**, and then click **50 Point**. In the **Adjust group**, click the **Artistic Effects** button, and then in the fourth row, click the third effect—**Crisscross Etching**.

9 In the **Size group**, click in the **Shape Height** box, replace the number with **3.5** and then press Enter. In the **Arrange group**, click the **Align** button, and then click **Align Center**. Click the **Align** button again, and then click **Align Middle**. Compare your slide with Figure 14.42, and then **Save** your presentation.

Figure 14.42

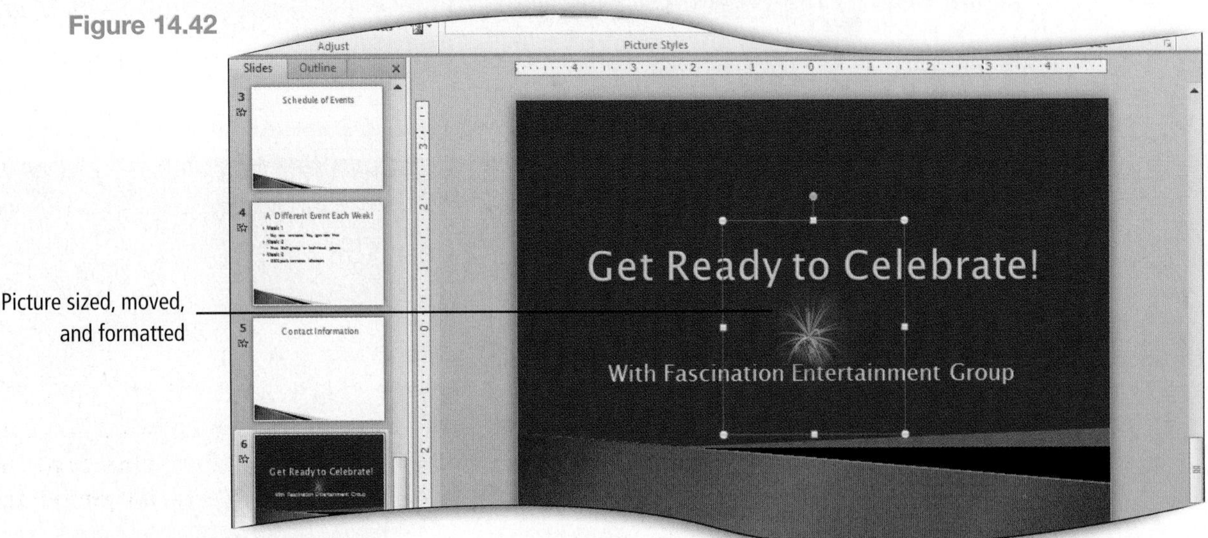

Activity 14.16 | Applying WordArt Styles to Existing Text

1 On **Slide 6**, click anywhere in the word *Get* to activate the title placeholder, and then select the title—*Get Ready to Celebrate*. Click the **Format tab**, and then in the **WordArt Styles group**, click the **More** button.

The WordArt Styles gallery displays in two sections. If you choose a WordArt style in the Applies to Selected Text section, you must first select all of the text to which you want to apply the WordArt. If you choose a WordArt style in the Applies to All Text in the Shape section, the WordArt style is applied to all of the text in the placeholder or shape.

2 Under **Applies to Selected Text**, in the first row, click the fourth style—**Fill – White, Outline – Accent 1**, and then compare your screen with Figure 14.43.

Figure 14.43

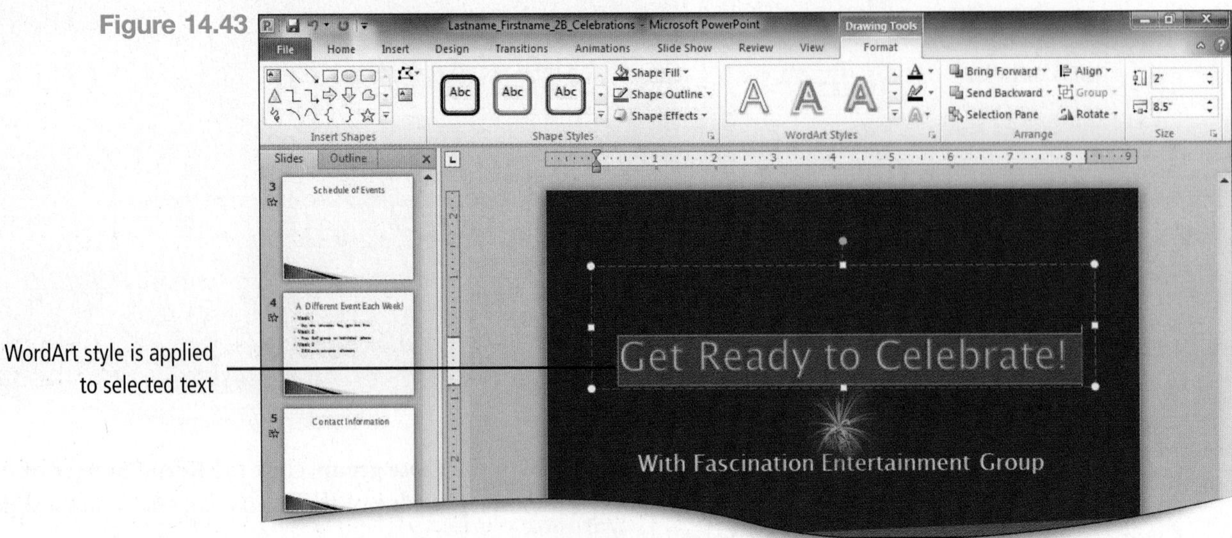

3 With the text still selected, in the **WordArt Styles group**, click the **Text Fill button arrow** [A]. Under **Theme Colors**, in the sixth column, click the fourth color—**Dark Red, Accent 2, Lighter 40%**, and then compare your screen with Figure 14.44.

Figure 14.44

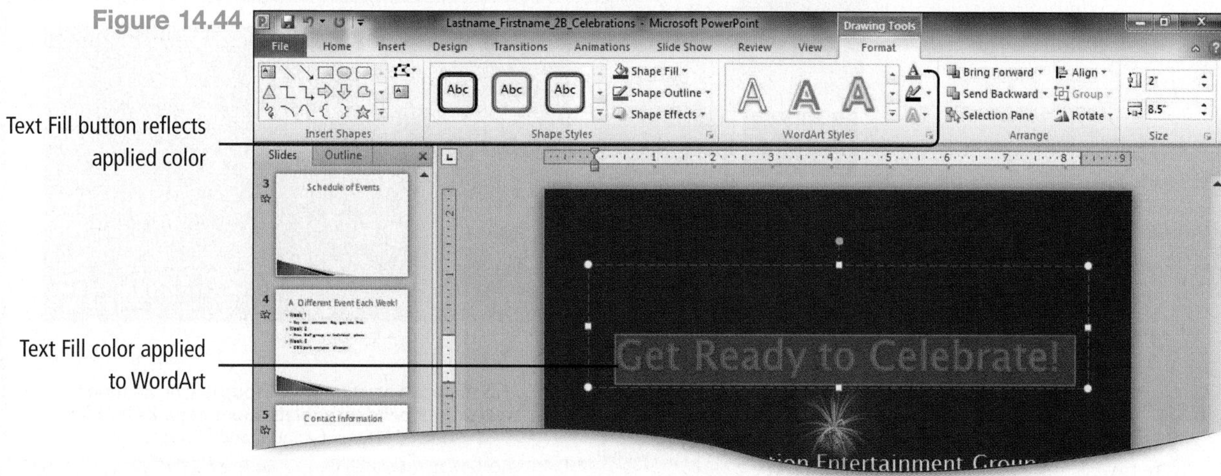

4 Display **Slide 1**, and then click anywhere in the title—*Fascination Entertainment Group*.

5 Click the **Format tab**, and then in the **WordArt Styles group**, click the **More** button [▾] to display the **WordArt Styles** gallery. Under **Applies to All Text in the Shape**, in the first row, click the third style—**Fill – Dark Red, Accent 2, Warm Matte Bevel**, and then compare your screen with Figure 14.45.

Figure 14.45

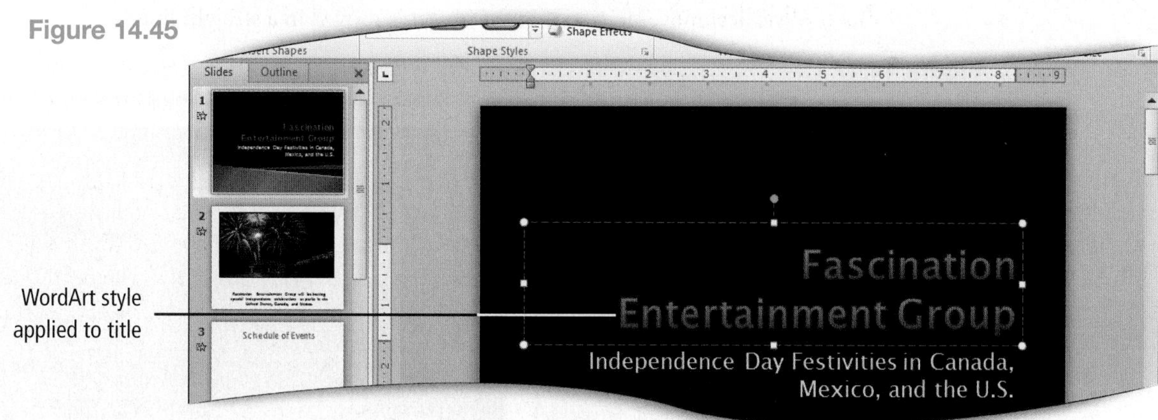

6 **Save** [💾] your presentation.

Activity 14.17 | Inserting a WordArt Object

In addition to formatting existing text using WordArt, you can insert a new WordArt object anywhere on a slide.

1 Display **Slide 2**. Click the **Insert tab**, and then in the **Text group**, click the **WordArt** button. In the gallery, in the last row, click the third WordArt style—**Fill – Dark Red, Accent 2, Matte Bevel**.

In the center of your slide, a WordArt placeholder displays *Your text here*. Text that you type will replace this text and the placeholder will expand to accommodate the text. The WordArt is surrounded by sizing handles with which you can adjust its size.

2 Type **Get Ready for 2014!** to replace the WordArt placeholder text. Compare your screen with Figure 14.46.

Figure 14.46

3 Point to the WordArt border to display the pointer. Hold down Shift, and then drag down to position the WordArt between the picture and the text at the bottom of the slide and centered between the left and right edge of the slide. Use Ctrl + any of the arrow keys to move the WordArt in small increments. Compare your slide with Figure 14.47 and move the WordArt again if necessary.

Recall that holding down Shift when dragging an object constrains the horizontal and vertical movement so that the object is moved in a straight line.

Figure 14.47

4 **Save** your presentation.

Objective 6 | Create and Format a SmartArt Graphic

A ***SmartArt graphic*** is a visual representation of information that you create by choosing from among various layouts to communicate your message or ideas effectively. SmartArt graphics can illustrate processes, hierarchies, cycles, lists, and relationships. You can include text and pictures in a SmartArt graphic, and you can apply colors, effects, and styles that coordinate with the presentation theme.

Activity 14.18 | Creating a SmartArt Graphic from Bulleted Points

You can convert an existing bulleted list into a SmartArt graphic. When you create a SmartArt graphic, consider the message that you are trying to convey, and then choose an appropriate layout. The table in Figure 14.48 describes types of SmartArt layouts and suggested purposes.

Microsoft PowerPoint SmartArt Graphic Types

Graphic Type	Purpose of Graphic
List	Shows non-sequential information
Process	Shows steps in a process or timeline
Cycle	Shows a continual process
Hierarchy	Shows a decision tree or displays an organization chart
Relationship	Illustrates connections
Matrix	Shows how parts relate to a whole
Pyramid	Shows proportional relationships with the largest component on the top or bottom
Picture	Includes pictures in the layout to communicate messages and ideas

Figure 14.48

Another Way

Right-click on a bulleted list to display the shortcut menu, and then click **Convert to SmartArt**.

1 Display **Slide 4**, and then click anywhere in the bulleted list placeholder. On the **Home tab**, in the **Paragraph group**, click the **Convert to SmartArt** button. Below the gallery, click **More SmartArt Graphics**.

Three sections comprise the Choose a SmartArt Graphic dialog box. The left section lists the SmartArt graphic types. The center section displays the SmartArt graphics according to type. The third section displays the selected SmartArt graphic, its name, and a description of its purpose.

2 On the left side of the **Choose a SmartArt Graphic** dialog box, click **List**. Use the ScreenTips to locate and then click **Vertical Bullet List**. Compare your screen with Figure 14.49.

Figure 14.49

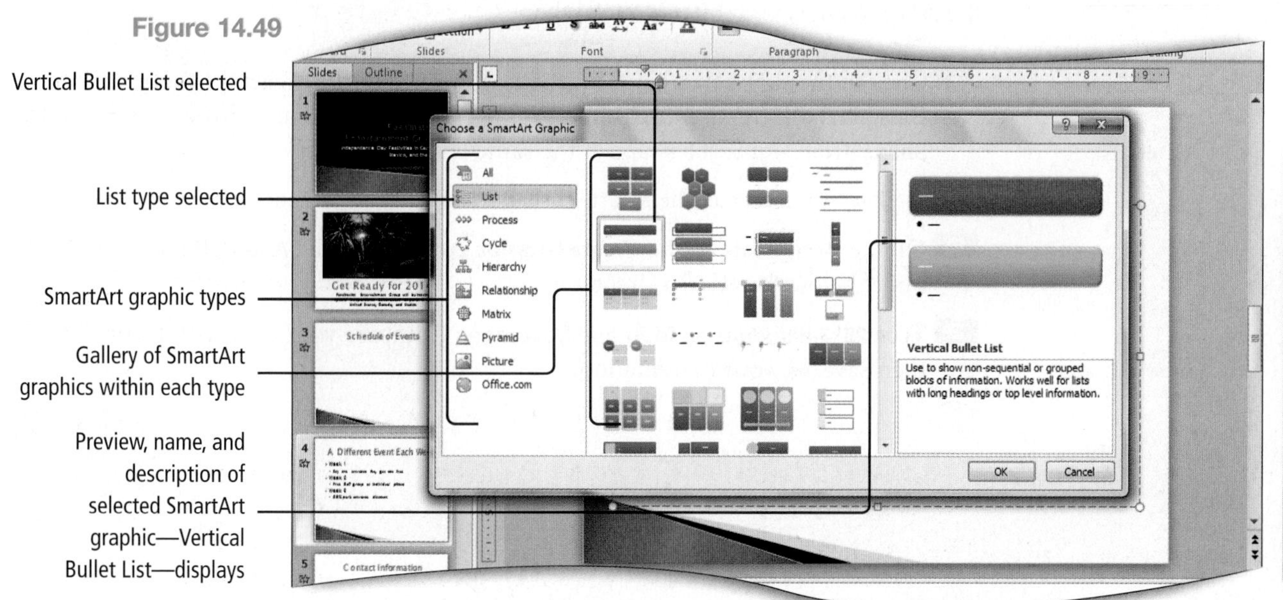

3 In the **Choose a SmartArt Graphic** dialog box, click **OK**. If the Text Pane displays to the right of the SmartArt graphic, click its Close button ☒.Compare your screen with Figure 14.50, and then **Save** your presentation.

It is not necessary to select all of the text in the list. By clicking in the list, PowerPoint converts all of the bullet points to the selected SmartArt graphic. On the Ribbon, the SmartArt contextual tools display two tabs—Design and Format. The thick border surrounding the SmartArt graphic indicates that it is selected and displays the area that the object will cover on the slide.

Figure 14.50

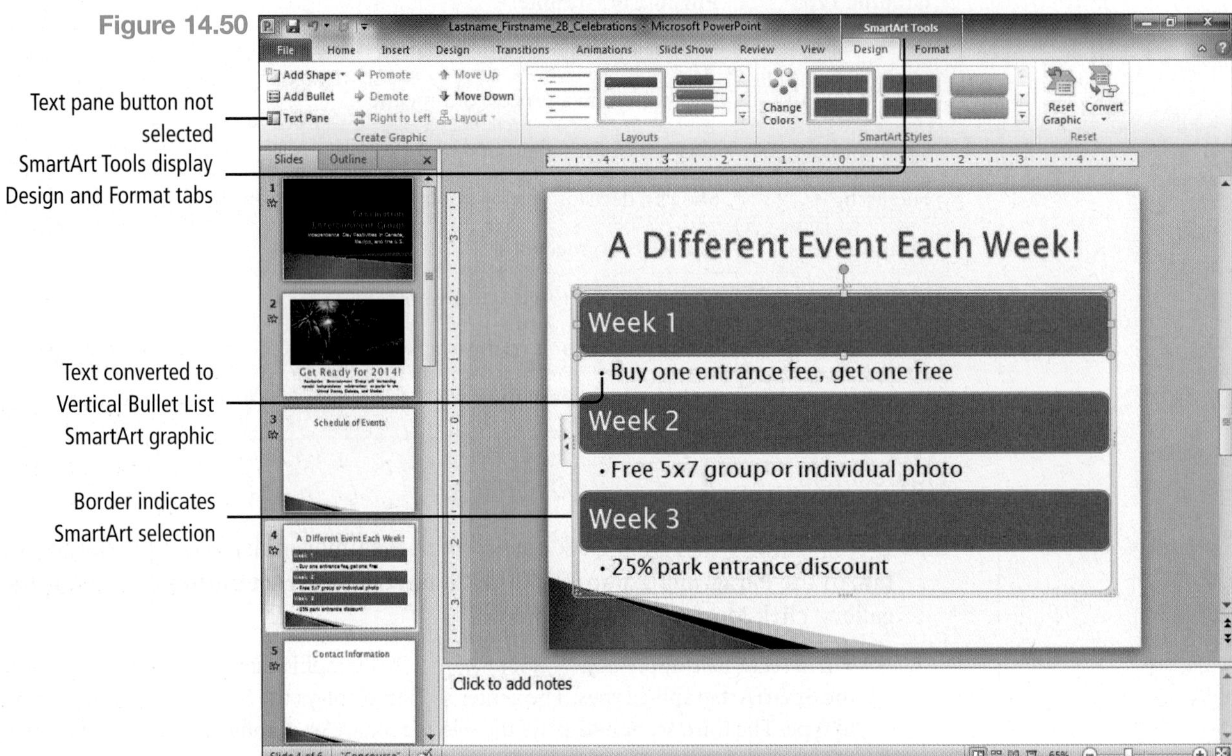

Activity 14.19 | Adding Shapes in a SmartArt Graphic

If a SmartArt graphic does not have enough shapes to illustrate a concept or display the relationships, you can add more shapes.

> **Another Way**
>
> Right-click the shape, point to **Add Shape**, and then click **Add Shape After**.

1 Click in the shape that contains the text *Week 3*. In the **SmartArt Tools**, click the **Design tab**. In the **Create Graphic group**, click the **Add Shape arrow**, and then click **Add Shape After** to insert a shape at the same level. Type **Week 4**

The text in each of the SmartArt shapes resizes to accommodate the added shape.

2 On the **Design tab**, in the **Create Graphic group**, click the **Add Bullet** button to add a bullet below the *Week 4* shape.

3 Type **25% discount on food and beverages** Compare your slide with Figure 14.51, and then **Save** your presentation.

Figure 14.51

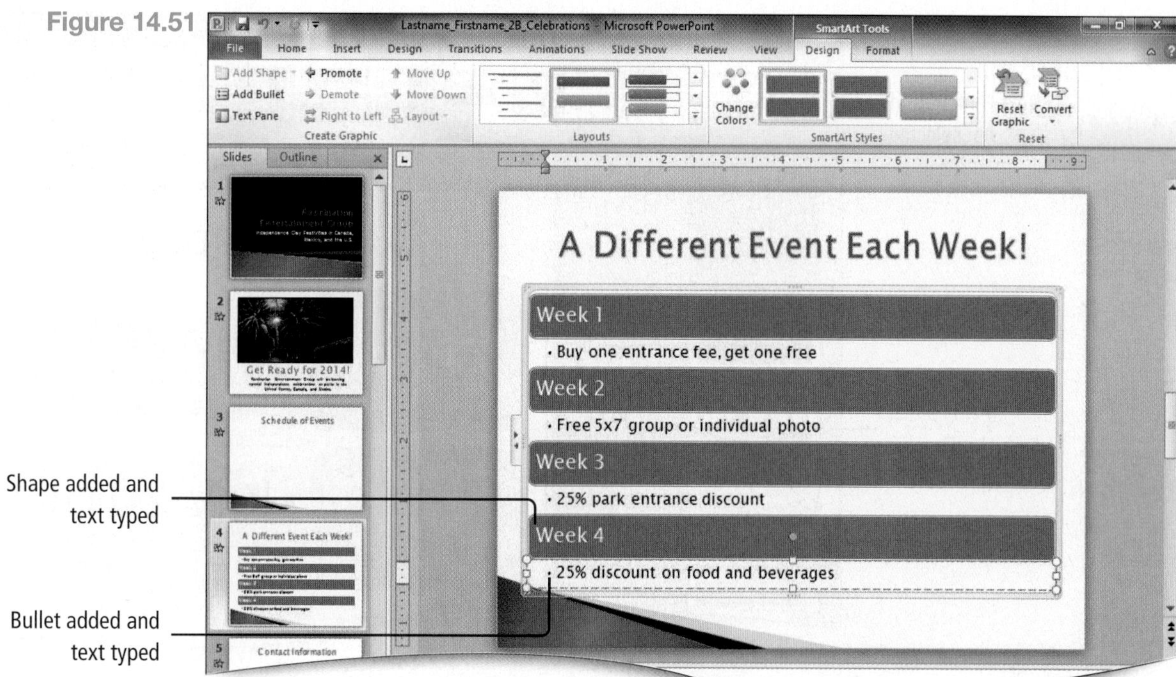

Activity 14.20 | Creating a SmartArt Graphic Using a Content Layout

1 Display **Slide 3**. In the center of the content placeholder, click the **Insert SmartArt Graphic** button to open the **Choose a SmartArt Graphic** dialog box.

2 On the left, click **Process**, and then scroll as necessary and use the ScreenTips to locate **Vertical Arrow List**. Click **Vertical Arrow List**. Compare your screen with Figure 14.52.

Figure 14.52

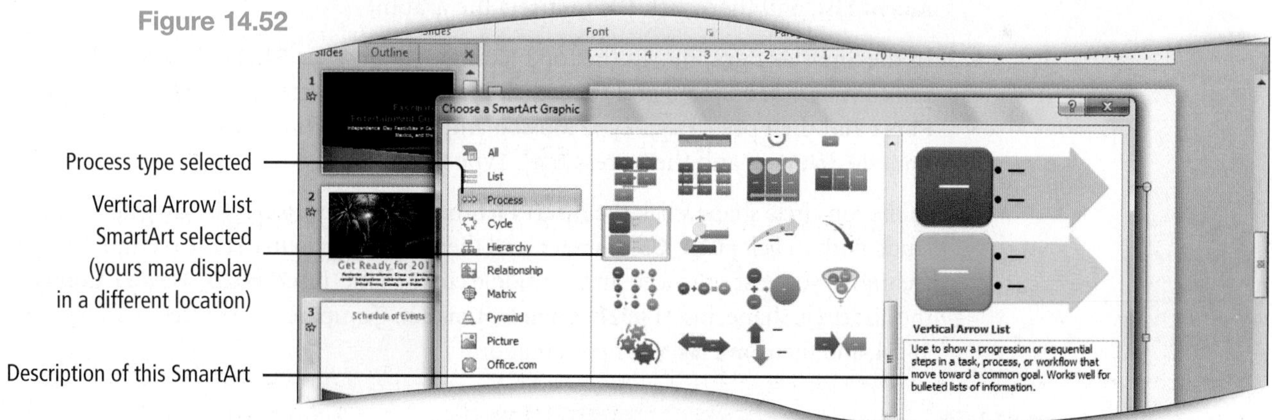

3 Click **OK** to insert the SmartArt graphic.

The SmartArt graphic displays with two rounded rectangle shapes and two arrow shapes. You can type text directly into the shapes or you can type text in the Text Pane, which may display to the left of your SmartArt graphic. You can display the Text Pane by clicking the Text Pane tab on the left side of the SmartArt graphic border, or by clicking the Text Pane button in the Create Graphic group. Depending on your software settings, the Text Pane may display.

4 In the SmartArt graphic, click in the first orange rectangle, and then type **Canada** In the arrow shape to the immediate right, click in the first bullet point. Type **July 2014** and then press Del to remove the second bullet point in the arrow shape.

5 Click in the second orange rectangle, and then type **U.S.** In the arrow shape to the immediate right, click in the first bullet point. Type **July 2014** and then press Del. Compare your slide with Figure 14.53.

Figure 14.53

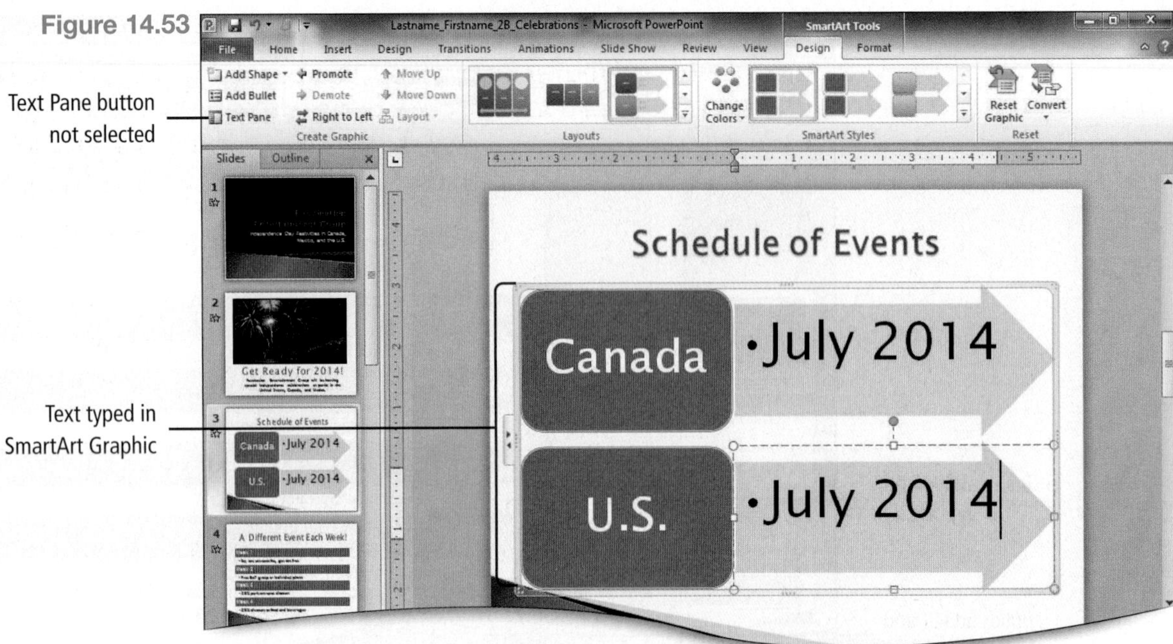

6 Click in the *U.S.* rectangle. On the **Design tab**, in the **Create Graphic group**, click the **Add Shape arrow**. Click **Add Shape After** to insert a new rectangle and arrow. Type **Mexico** and then in the arrow shape to the right, type **September 2014**

7 Display **Slide 5**. In the center of the content placeholder, click the **Insert SmartArt Graphic** button. In the **Choose a SmartArt Graphic** dialog box, click **Picture**, and then scroll as necessary to locate **Vertical Picture Accent List**. Click **Vertical Picture Accent List**, and then click **OK** to insert the graphic.

8 In the SmartArt graphic, in the top rectangle shape, type **Rachel Lewis** and then press Enter. Type **United States** and then click in the middle rectangle shape. Type **Javier Perez** and then press Enter. Type **Mexico** and then click in the last rectangle shape, type **Annette Johnson** and then press Enter. Type **Canada**

9 In the top circle shape, click the **Insert Picture from File** button. Navigate to your student files, click **p02B_US_Contact**, and then press Enter to insert the picture. Using the technique you just practiced, in the middle circle shape, insert **p02B_Mexico_Contact**. In the last circle shape, insert **p02B_Canada_Contact**. Compare your screen with Figure 14.54, and then **Save** your presentation.

Figure 14.54

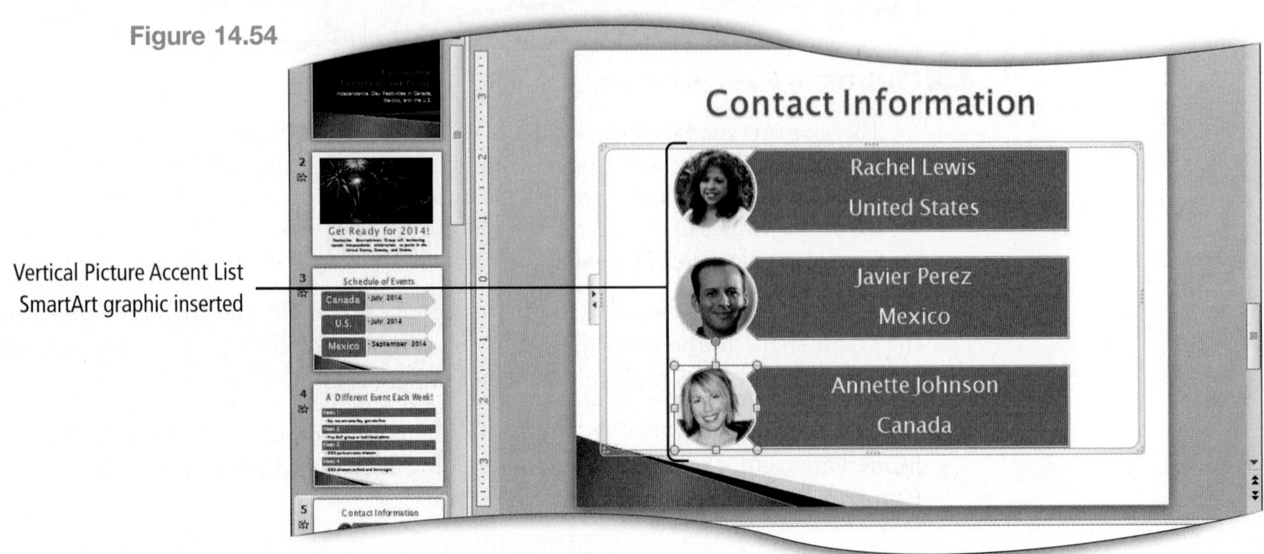

Activity 14.21 | Changing the SmartArt Layout

1 Display **Slide 3**, and then click anywhere in the SmartArt graphic. In the **SmartArt Tools**, click the **Design tab**. In the **Layouts group**, click the **More** button, and then click **More Layouts**. In the **Choose a SmartArt Graphic** dialog box, click **Hierarchy**. Locate and click **Hierarchy List**, and then click **OK**.

2 Compare your slide with Figure 14.55, and then **Save** the presentation.

Figure 14.55

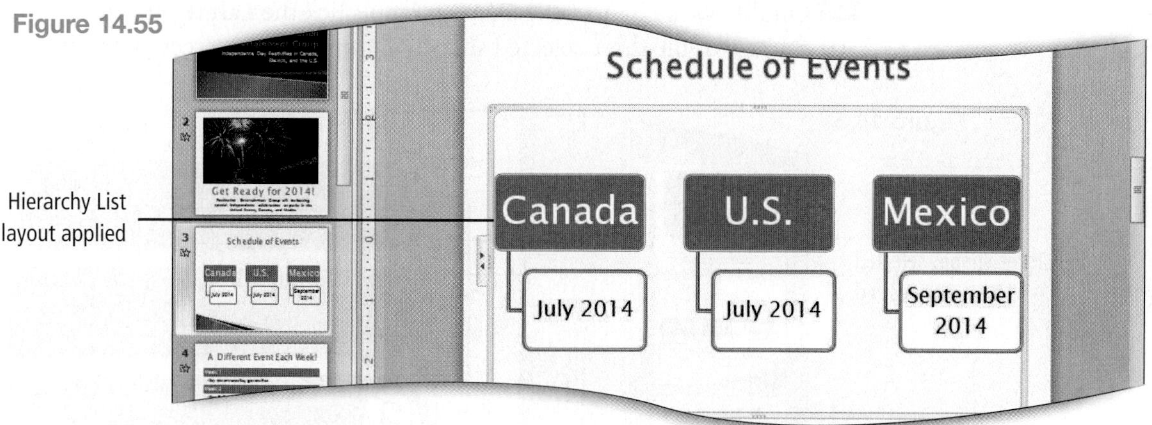

Activity 14.22 | Changing the Color and Style of a SmartArt Graphic

SmartArt Styles are combinations of formatting effects that you can apply to SmartArt graphics.

1 With **Slide 3** displayed and the SmartArt graphic selected, on the **Design tab**, in the **SmartArt Styles group**, click the **Change Colors** button. In the color gallery, under **Colorful**, click the first style—**Colorful - Accent Colors**—to change the color.

2 On the **Design tab**, in the **SmartArt Styles group**, click the **More** button to display the **SmartArt Styles gallery**. Under **3-D**, click the second style, **Inset**. Compare your slide with Figure 14.56.

Figure 14.56

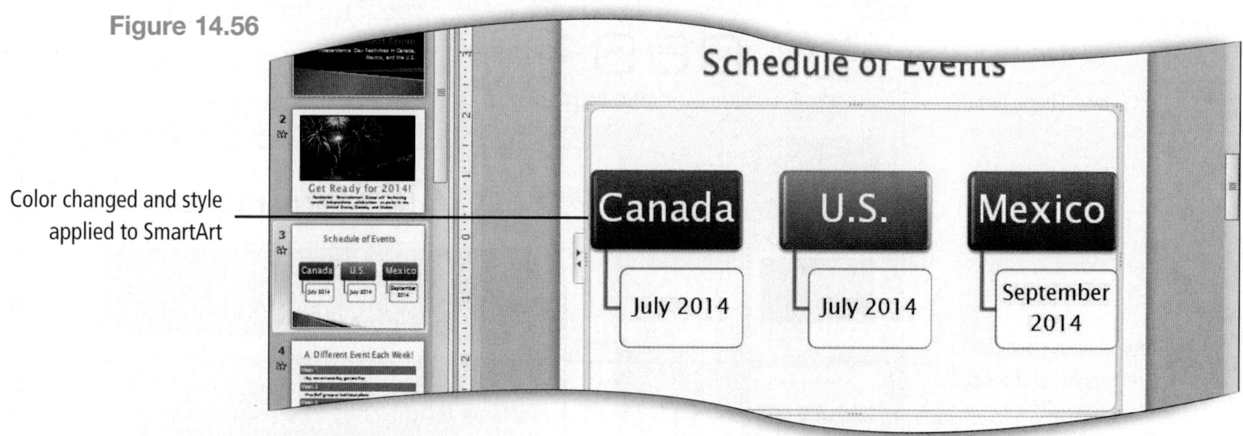

3 Display **Slide 5**, and select the SmartArt. On the **Design tab**, in the **SmartArt Styles group**, click the **Change Colors** button. Under **Accent 2**, click the second style—**Colored Fill - Accent 2**. On the **Design tab**, in the **SmartArt Styles group**, click the **More** button. Under **Best Match for Document**, click the last style, **Intense Effect**. **Save** the presentation.

Activity 14.23 | Customizing the Size and Shape of a SmartArt Graphic

You can select individual or groups of shapes in a SmartArt graphic and make them larger or smaller, and you can change selected shapes to another type of shape.

1 With **Slide 5** displayed, click in the upper red shape that contains the text *Rachel Lewis*. Hold down Shift, and then click in each of the two remaining red shapes containing the text *Javier Perez* and *Annette Johnson* so that all three text shapes are selected.

2 On the **Format tab**, in the **Shapes group**, click the **Larger** button two times to increase the size of the three selected shapes. Compare your screen with Figure 14.57.

Figure 14.57

3 With the three shapes selected, on the **Home tab**, in the **Font group**, increase the **Font Size** to **28**.

4 Select the first circle picture, and then hold down Shift and click the remaining two circles so that all three circles are selected. In the **SmartArt Tools**, on the **Format tab**, in the **Shapes group**, click the **Change Shape** button. Under **Rectangles**, click the first shape—**Rectangle**—to change the circles to rectangles. With the three shapes selected, in the **Shapes group**, click the **Larger** button two times. Compare your screen with Figure 14.58, and then **Save** the presentation.

Figure 14.58

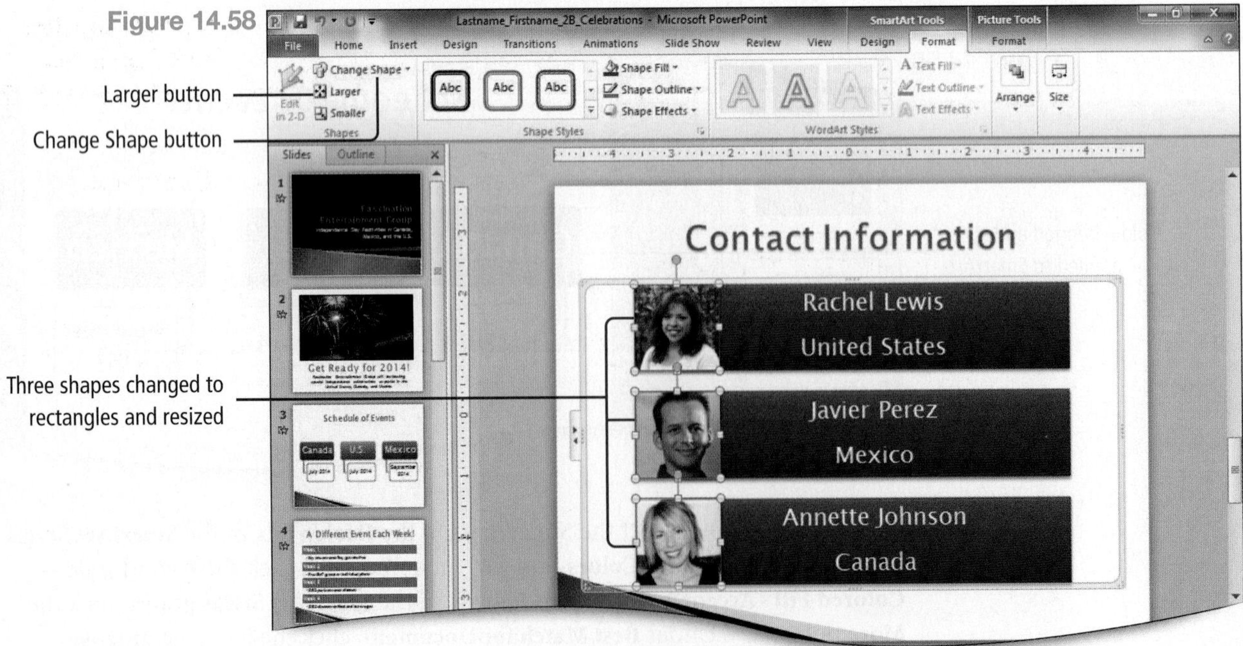

Activity 14.24 | Converting a SmartArt to Text

1 Display **Slide 4**, and then click anywhere in the SmartArt graphic. On the **Design tab**, in the **Reset group**, click the **Convert** button, and then click **Convert to Text** to convert the SmartArt graphic to a bulleted list. Compare your screen with Figure 14.59.

Figure 14.59

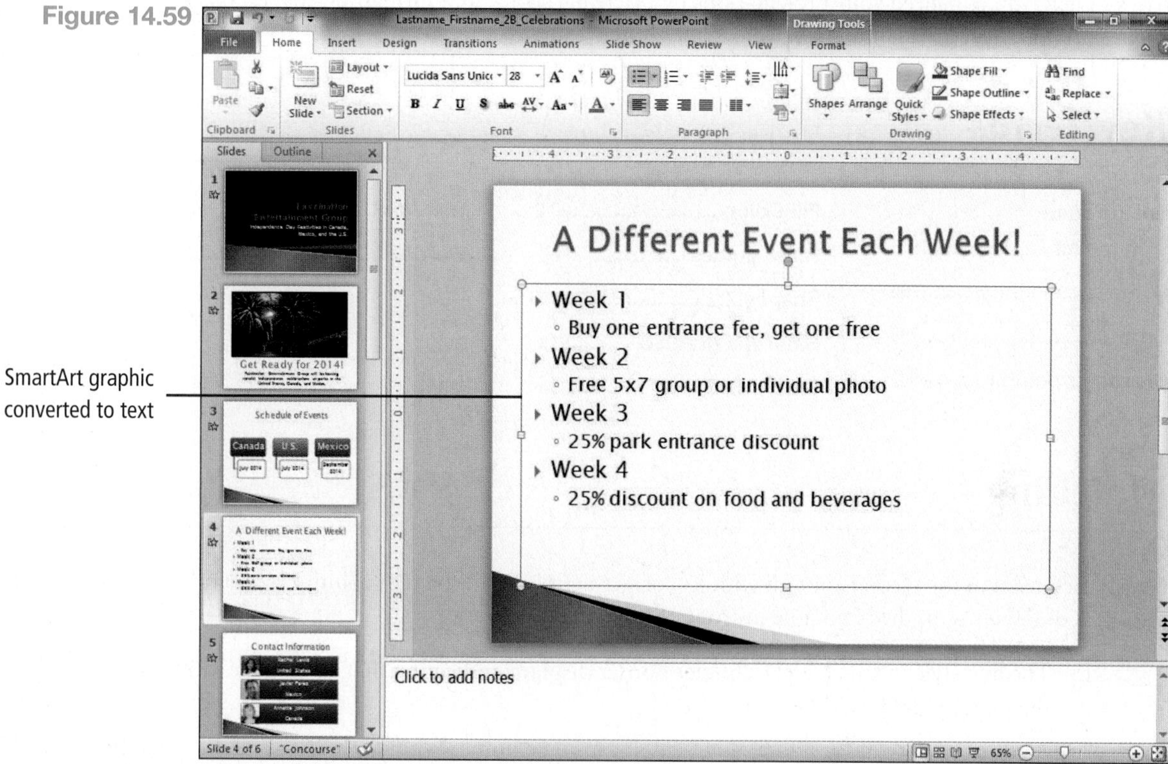

SmartArt graphic converted to text

2 Display the **Document Properties**. Replace the text in the **Author** box with your own firstname and lastname, in the **Subject** box, type your course name and section number, and in the **Keywords** box, type **Independence day, celebrations** **Close** the **Document Information Panel**.

3 Insert a **Header & Footer** on the **Notes and Handouts**. Include the **Date and time updated automatically**, the **Page number**, and a **Footer** with the text **Lastname_Firstname_2B_Celebrations** Apply to all the slides. View the presentation from the beginning, and then make any necessary adjustments.

4 **Save** your presentation. Print **Handouts 6 Slides Horizontal**, or submit your presentation electronically as directed by your instructor.

5 **Close** the presentation.

End You have completed Project 14B

Content-Based Assessments

Summary

In this chapter, you formatted a presentation by changing the bullet style and by applying WordArt styles to text. You enhanced your presentations by inserting, sizing, and formatting shapes, pictures, and SmartArt graphics, resulting in a professional-looking presentation.

Key Terms

Background Removal 813
Clip 795
Crop 799
Crosshair pointer 802
Fill Color 804
Ruler guides 800
Shapes 802
SmartArt graphic 818
SmartArt Styles 823
Text box 800
WordArt 813

Matching

Match each term in the second column with its correct definition in the first column by writing the letter of the term on the blank line in front of the correct definition.

A Align to Slide
B Clip
C Crop
D Crosshair pointer
E Fill color
F Move pointer
G Paragraph
H Ruler guides
I Shapes
J Shape Styles
K SmartArt graphic
L SmartArt Styles
M Solid
N Text box
O WordArt

____ 1. The line style in which a placeholder border displays, indicating that all of the text in the placeholder is selected.

____ 2. A common format for a slide that contains a single point without a bullet symbol.

____ 3. A single media file, for example art, sound, animation, or a movie.

____ 4. A four-headed arrow-shaped pointer that indicates that you can reposition an object or image.

____ 5. An object within which you can position text anywhere on the slide.

____ 6. Vertical and horizontal lines that display in the rulers to provide a visual indication of the pointer position so that you can draw a shape.

____ 7. Lines, arrows, stars, banners, ovals, or rectangles used to illustrate an idea, a process, or a workflow.

____ 8. The pointer that indicates that you can draw a shape.

____ 9. The inside color of text or an object.

____ 10. A style gallery displaying predefined combinations of shape fill and line colors.

____ 11. A setting used to align selected objects.

____ 12. The command that reduces the size of a picture by removing vertical or horizontal edges.

____ 13. A gallery of text styles from which you can create shadowed or mirrored text.

____ 14. A visual representation of information that you create by choosing from among layouts to communicate your message or ideas.

____ 15. Combinations of formatting effects that are applied to SmartArt graphics.

Content-Based Assessments

Multiple Choice

Circle the correct answer.

1. The color of the numbers or bullet symbols in a list is determined by the:
   A. Slide layout **B.** Presentation theme **C.** Gallery
2. When you point to an image in the Clip Art pane, the screen element that displays the keywords and information about the size of the image is the:
   A. ScreenTip **B.** Navigation bar **C.** Menu
3. To horizontally or vertically position selected objects on a slide relative to each other, use the:
   A. Align tools **B.** Distribute tools **C.** Crop tools
4. The command that removes unwanted portions of a picture so that the picture does not appear as a self-contained rectangle is:
   A. Shape height **B.** Picture adjust **C.** Background removal
5. The SmartArt type that shows steps in a process or timeline is:
   A. Radial **B.** Process **C.** List
6. The SmartArt type that shows a continual process is:
   A. Hierarchy **B.** Radial **C.** Cycle
7. The SmartArt type with which you can show a decision tree or create an organization chart is:
   A. Matrix **B.** Pyramid **C.** Hierarchy
8. The SmartArt type that illustrates connections is:
   A. Picture **B.** Radial **C.** Relationship
9. The SmartArt type that shows how parts relate to a whole is:
   A. Matrix **B.** Pyramid **C.** Radial
10. The SmartArt type that shows proportional relationships with the largest component on the top or bottom is:
    A. Matrix **B.** Pyramid **C.** Relationship

Content-Based Assessments

Apply 14A skills from these Objectives:

1. Format Numbered and Bulleted Lists
2. Insert Clip Art
3. Insert Text Boxes and Shapes
4. Format Objects

Skills Review | Project 14C Concerts

In the following Skills Review, you will format a presentation by inserting and formatting Clip Art, text boxes, and shapes, and by modifying bullets and numbering. Your completed presentation will look similar to Figure 14.60.

Project Files

For Project 14C, you will need the following file:

p02C_Concerts

You will save your presentation as:

Lastname_Firstname_2C_Concerts

Project Results

- Located in the main plaza at each park
- Grandstand seating will be available
  - Seating is limited
  - Reserved seating is available through the information booth
- Concerts begin at 7:30 pm

Join Us as We Rock the Night!

1. Eighties Rock
2. Top Forty
3. Country Hits
4. Fifties and Sixties
5. Rhythm & Blues
6. Children's Favorites

A Different Band Each Week!

Figure 14.60

(Project 14C Concerts continues on the next page)

Content-Based Assessments

Skills Review | Project 14C Concerts (continued)

1 **Start** PowerPoint. From the student files that accompany this textbook, locate and open **p02C_Concerts**. **Save** the presentation in your **PowerPoint Chapter 14** folder as **Lastname_Firstname_2C_Concerts**

a. If necessary, display the Rulers. With **Slide 1** displayed, on the **Insert tab**, in the **Illustrations group**, click the **Shapes** button, and then under **Basic Shapes**, in the second row, click the fifth shape—**Frame**.

b. Move the pointer to align the ruler guides with the **left half of the horizontal ruler at 3 inches** and with the **upper half of the vertical ruler at 2.5 inches**, and then click to insert the Frame.

c. On the **Format tab**, in the **Size group**, click in the **Shape Height** box to select the number, and then type **1.7** Click in the **Shape Width** box. Replace the selected number with **5.5** and then press Enter to resize the shape.

d. With the frame selected, type **Fascination Entertainment Group Presents** and then change the **Font Size** to **24**. On the **Format tab**, in the **Shape Styles group**, click the **Shape Fill** button, and then under **Theme Colors**, in the fourth column, click the first color—**Lavender, Text 2**.

2 On the **Insert tab**, in the **Images group**, click the **Clip Art** button to display the **Clip Art** pane.

a. In the **Clip Art** pane, click in the **Search for** box and replace any existing text with **compositions musical notes** Click the **Results should be arrow**, and then click as necessary to so that only the **Photographs** check box is selected. Include Office.com content. Click **Go** to display the musical notes pictures.

b. Click the black and white picture of the two lines of music on a music sheet, and then **Close** the **Clip Art** pane. With the picture selected, on the **Format tab**, in the **Size group**, click in the **Shape Height** box. Replace the selected number with **2.5** and then press Enter to resize the image.

c. Point to the picture and then drag down and to the right so that it is centered just below the title—*Concerts in the Park*—and its top edge aligns with the lower edge of the black rounded rectangle.

d. With the picture selected, on the **Format tab**, in the **Size group**, click the **Crop arrow**, and then point to **Crop to Shape**. Under **Basic Shapes**, click the first shape—**Oval**. In the **Picture Styles group**, click the **Picture Effects** button, point to **Soft Edges**, and then click **25 Point**.

e. On the **Insert tab**, in the **Text group**, click the **Text Box** button. Move the pointer to position the ruler guides on the **horizontal ruler at 0 inches** and on the **lower half of the vertical ruler at 2.5 inches**, and then click to insert the text box.

f. On the **Format tab**, in the **Shape Styles group**, click the **More** button. In the first row, click the second style—**Colored Outline - Pink, Accent 1**. Type **Back by Popular Demand!**

g. With the text box selected, hold down Shift, and then click the frame shape, the title placeholder, and the picture so that all four objects are selected. Under **Drawing Tools**, on the **Format tab**, in the **Arrange group**, click the **Align** button, and then click **Align to Slide**. Click the **Align** button again, and then click **Align Center**. **Save** the presentation.

3 Display **Slide 2**, and then click in the title placeholder containing the text *Every Friday in June and July*.

a. On the **Home tab**, in the **Paragraph group**, click the **Bullets** button to remove the bullet symbol from the title.

b. On the left side of the slide, in the content placeholder, click the **Clip Art** button. In the **Clip Art** pane, in the **Search for** box, search for **cymbals** set the results to **Photographs**, include Office.com content, and then click **Go**. Insert the picture of the drum set on a white background.

c. On the **Format tab**, in the **Picture Styles group**, click the **Picture Effects** button, point to **Soft Edges**, and then click **50 Point**. **Close** the **Clip Art** pane.

4 Display **Slide 3**, and then select the third and fourth bullet points—the two, second-level bullet points.

a. On the **Home tab**, in the **Paragraph group**, click the **Bullets button arrow**, and then click **Bullets and Numbering**. In the first row of bullets, click the last style—**Filled Square Bullets**. Replace the number in the **Size** box with **125** and then click the **Color** button. In the eighth column, click the first color—**Gold, Accent 4**—and then click **OK** to change the bullet style.

b. Display **Slide 4**, and then click the bulleted list placeholder. Click the dashed border so that it displays as a solid line, and then on the **Home tab**, in the **Paragraph group**, click the **Numbering button** to change the bullets to numbers.

(Project 14C Concerts continues on the next page)

Content-Based Assessments

Skills Review | Project 14C Concerts (continued)

5 Display **Slide 5**. On the **Insert tab**, in the **Images group**, click the **Clip Art** button. In the **Clip Art** pane, in the **Search for** box, search for **electric guitar in monochrome** and then click **Go**. Insert the picture of the black electric guitar on the white, blue, and black background.

a. Change the picture **Height** to **4.5** and then drag the picture down and to the left so that its upper left corner aligns with the upper left corner of the black rectangle on the slide background. **Close** the **Clip Art** pane.

b. With the picture selected, on the **Format tab**, in the **Picture Styles group**, click **Picture Effects**, and then point to **Reflection**. Click the first reflection variation—**Tight Reflection, touching**.

c. With the picture selected, hold down Ctrl, and then press D to create a duplicate of the picture. Drag the duplicated picture to the right about 1 inch, and then hold down Ctrl and press D to create another duplicate.

d. Point to the third guitar picture that you inserted, and then drag to the right so that its upper right corner aligns with the upper right corner of the black rectangle on the slide background.

e. Hold down Shift, and then click the first two guitar pictures so that all three pictures are selected. On the **Format tab**, in the **Arrange group**, click the **Align** button, and then click **Align Selected Objects**. Click the **Align** button again, and then click **Align Top**. Click the **Align** button again, and then click **Distribute Horizontally**.

f. **Insert** a **Header & Footer** on the **Notes and Handouts**. Include the **Date and time updated automatically**, the **Page number**, and a **Footer** with the text **Lastname_Firstname_2C_Concerts** Click **Apply to All**.

g. Display the **Document Properties**. Replace the text in the **Author** box with your own firstname and lastname, in the **Subject** box, type your course name and section number, and in the **Keywords** box, type **concerts, summer events** **Close** the **Document Information Panel**.

h. View your slide show from the beginning, and then **Save** your presentation. Submit your presentation electronically or print **Handouts 6 Slides Horizontal** as directed by your instructor. **Close** the presentation and exit PowerPoint.

End **You have completed Project 14C**

Content-Based Assessments

Apply **14B** skills from these Objectives:

5 Remove Picture Backgrounds and Insert WordArt

6 Create and Format a SmartArt Graphic

Skills Review | Project 14D Corporate Events

In the following Skills Review, you will format a presentation by inserting and formatting WordArt and SmartArt graphics. Your completed presentation will look similar to Figure 14.61.

Project Files

For Project 14D, you will need the following file:

p02D_Corporate_Events

You will save your presentation as:

Lastname_Firstname_2D_Corporate_Events

Project Results

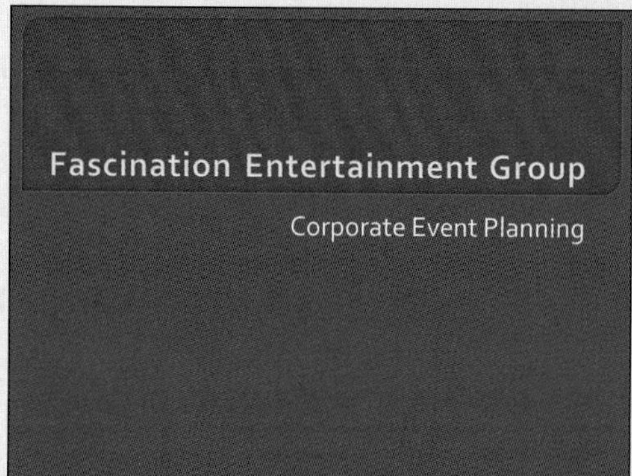

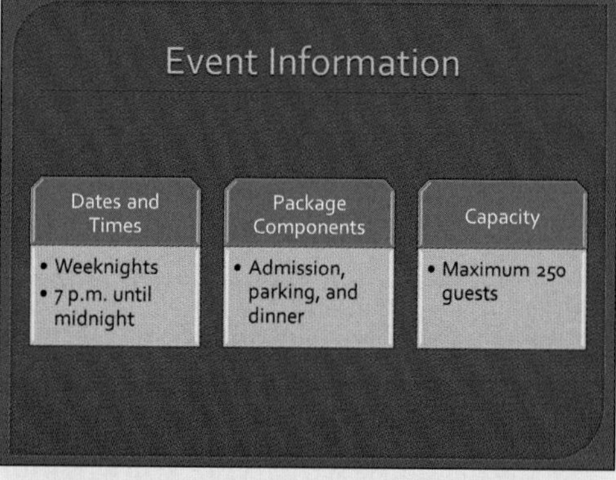

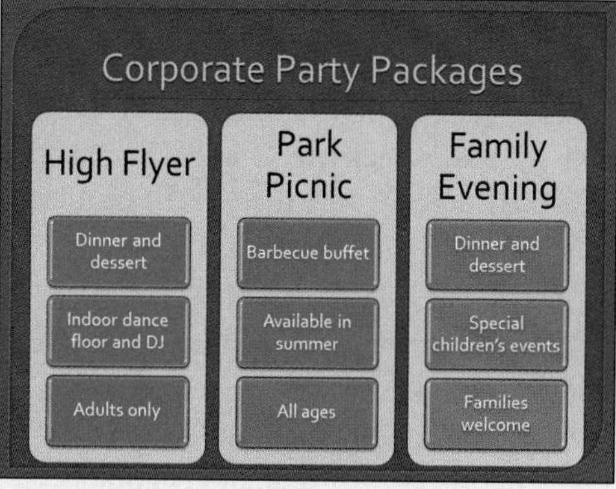

Figure 14.61

(Project 14D Corporate Events continues on the next page)

Skills Review | Project 14D Corporate Events (continued)

1 **Start** PowerPoint. From the student files that accompany this textbook, locate and open **p02D_Corporate_Events**. **Save** the presentation in your **PowerPoint Chapter 14** folder as **Lastname_Firstname_2D_Corporate_Events**

a. With **Slide 1** displayed, select the title—*Fascination Entertainment Group*. On the **Format tab**, in the **WordArt Styles group**, click the **More** button. Under **Applies to All Text in the Shape**, click the first style—**Fill - White, Warm Matte Bevel**. Change the **Font Size** to **40** so that all of the text displays on one line.

b. Display **Slide 2**. On the **Insert tab**, in the **Text group**, click the **WordArt** button. In the **WordArt** gallery, in the second row, click the second style—**Fill - Lime, Accent 6, Outline - Accent 6, Glow - Accent 6**. With the text *Your text here* selected, type **Corporate Events**

c. Point to the dashed, outer edge of the WordArt placeholder, hold down Shift, and drag straight down so that the WordArt is positioned between the picture and the text at the bottom of the slide.

d. With the WordArt selected, on the **Format tab**, in the **Arrange group**, click the **Align** button, and then click **Align Center** so that the WordArt is horizontally centered on the slide. **Save** the presentation.

2 Display **Slide 3**. In the center of the content placeholder, click the **Insert SmartArt Graphic** button to open the **Choose a SmartArt Graphic** dialog box. On the left, click **List**, and then use the ScreenTips to locate and then click **Vertical Bullet List**. Click **OK**.

a. In the SmartArt graphic, click *Text* in the first blue rectangle. Type **Dates and Times** and then click the bullet symbol below the first blue rectangle. Type **Weeknights** and then press Enter to insert a new bullet point. Type **7 p.m. until midnight**

b. Click in the second blue rectangle. Type **Package Components** and then click the bullet symbol below the second blue rectangle. Type **Admission, parking, and dinner**

c. Click in the *Package Components* rectangle, and then on the **SmartArt Tools Design tab**, in the **Create Graphic group**, click the **Add Shape arrow**. Click **Add Shape After** to insert a blue rectangle. Type **Capacity** and then on the **SmartArt Tools Design tab**, in the **Create Graphic group**, click the **Add Bullet** button. Type **Maximum 250 guests**

d. With the SmartArt selected, on the **SmartArt Tools Design tab**, in the **Layouts group**, click the **More** button, and then click **More Layouts**. On the left side of the dialog box, click **List**, and then in the center section of the dialog box, locate and click **Horizontal Bullet List**. Click **OK** to change the SmartArt layout.

e. On the **SmartArt Tools Design tab**, in the **SmartArt Styles group**, click the **More** button. Under **3-D**, in the first row, click the third style—**Cartoon**.

f. Hold down Shift, and then select the **Dates and Times**, **Package Components**, and **Capacity** rectangles. On the **Format tab**, in the **Shapes group**, click the **Change Shape** button, and then under **Rectangles**, click the fourth shape—**Snip Same Side Corner Rectangle**. **Save** the presentation.

3 Display **Slide 4**. In the content placeholder, right-click anywhere in the bulleted list. On the shortcut menu, point to **Convert to SmartArt**, and at the bottom of the gallery, click **More SmartArt Graphics**. On the left side of the **Choose a SmartArt Graphic** dialog box, click **Relationship**. Locate and click **Grouped List**, and then click **OK** to convert the list to a SmartArt graphic.

a. On the **SmartArt Tools Design tab**, in the **SmartArt Styles group**, click the **Change Colors** button. In the **Color** gallery, under **Accent 1**, click the last style—**Transparent Gradient Range - Accent 1**.

b. On the **Design tab**, in the **SmartArt Styles group**, click the **More** button to display the **SmartArt Styles gallery**. Under **3-D**, in the first row, click the third style—**Cartoon**. **Save** the presentation.

4 Display **Slide 5**, and if necessary, display the Rulers. On the **Insert tab**, in the **Text group**, click the **WordArt** button. In the **WordArt** gallery, in the first row, click the fourth style—**Fill - White, Outline - Accent 1**. With the text *Your text here* selected, type **Corporate_events@feg.com**

a. Point to the dashed, outer edge of the WordArt placeholder, and then drag down so that the top edge of the WordArt aligns with the **lower half of the vertical ruler at 1 inch**.

b. With the WordArt selected, on the **Format tab**, in the **Arrange group**, click the **Align** button, and then click **Align Center** so that the WordArt is horizontally centered on the slide.

(Project 14D Corporate Events continues on the next page)

Skills Review | Project 14D Corporate Events (continued)

c. **Insert** a **Header & Footer** on the **Notes and Handouts**. Include the **Date and time updated automatically**, the **Page number**, and a **Footer** with the text **Lastname_Firstname_2D_Corporate_Events** and **Apply to All**.

d. Display the **Document Properties**. Replace the text in the **Author** box with your own firstname and lastname, in the **Subject** box, type your course name and section number, and in the **Keywords** box, type **corporate events, group packages Close** the **Document Information Panel**. View the presentation from the beginning.

e. **Save** your presentation. Submit your presentation electronically or print **Handouts 6 Slides Horizontal** as directed by your instructor. **Close** the presentation and exit PowerPoint.

End You have completed Project 14D

Content-Based Assessments

Apply **14A** skills from these Objectives:

1. Format Numbered and Bulleted Lists
2. Insert Clip Art
3. Insert Text Boxes and Shapes
4. Format Objects

Mastering PowerPoint | Project 14E Roller Coasters

In the following Mastering PowerPoint project, you will format a presentation describing new roller coaster attractions at the Fascination Entertainment Group theme parks. Your completed presentation will look similar to Figure 14.62.

Project Files

For Project 14E, you will need the following file:

p02E_Roller_Coasters

You will save your presentation as:

Lastname_Firstname_2E_Roller_Coasters

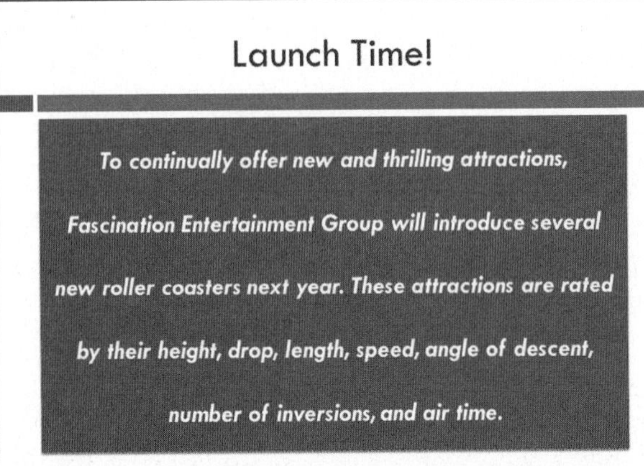

New Coasters for 2016

1. Intensity
   - 2,933 foot steel coaster
   - Scheduled for completion in March
   - Merrillville Park
2. Hang Time
   - 7,438 foot steel coaster
   - Scheduled for completion in May
   - Montreal Park
3. Last Chance
   - 4,564 foot steel coaster
   - Scheduled for completion in July
   - Atlanta Park

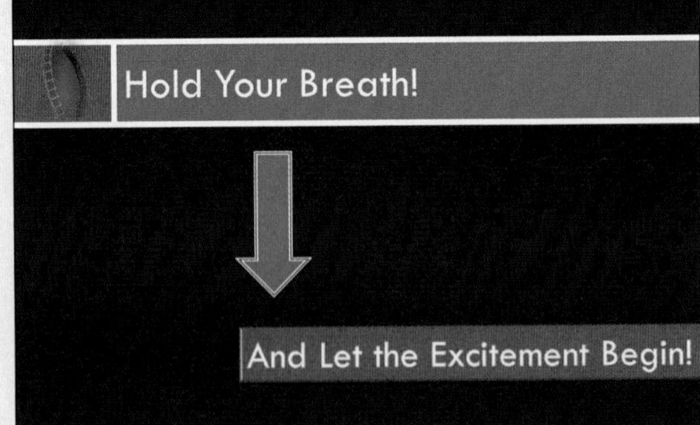

Figure 14.62

(Project 14E Roller Coasters continues on the next page)

Mastering PowerPoint | Project 14E Roller Coasters (continued)

1 **Start** PowerPoint. From the student files that accompany this textbook, locate and open **p02E_Roller_Coasters**. In your **PowerPoint Chapter 14** folder, **Save** the file as **Lastname_Firstname_2E_Roller_Coasters**

2 On **Slide 2**, remove the bullet symbol from the paragraph. **Center** the paragraph, apply **Bold** and **Italic** to the text, and then set the **Line Spacing** to **2.0**. With the content placeholder selected, display the **Shape Styles** gallery, and then in the fifth row, apply the third style—**Moderate Effect - Red, Accent 2**.

3 On **Slide 3**, apply **Numbering** to the first-level bullet points—*Intensity, Hang Time,* and *Last Chance*. Under each of the numbered items, change all of the hollow circle bullet symbols to **Filled Square Bullets**, and then change the bullet color to **Dark Blue, Text 2**—the first color in the fourth column.

4 In the content placeholder on the right side of the slide, insert a **Clip Art** photograph by searching for **roller coaster** Insert the close-up picture of the roller coaster with the red cars on the blue sky background, as shown in Figure 14.62 at the beginning of this project. Crop the picture shape to **Rounded Rectangle**, and then modify the **Picture Effect** by applying the last **Bevel** style—**Art Deco**.

5 On **Slide 4**, insert the picture of the white looped roller coaster on the lighter blue sky background. Change the picture **Height** to **1.5** and then apply a **25 Point Soft Edges** effect. Drag the picture up and to the left to position it in the center of the red rectangle to the left of the slide title. Deselect the picture.

6 From the **Shapes** gallery, under **Block Arrows**, insert a **Down Arrow** aligned with the **left half of the horizontal ruler at 1 inch** and the **upper half of the vertical ruler at 0.5 inches**. On the **Format tab**, from the **Shape Styles** gallery, in the third row, apply the second style—**Light 1 Outline, Colored Fill - Blue, Accent 1**. Change the **Shape Height** to **2** and the **Shape Width** to **1**

7 Insert a **Text Box** aligned with the **left half of the horizontal ruler at 1.5 inches** and with the **lower half of the vertical ruler at 2 inches**. On the **Format tab**, from the **Shape Styles** gallery, in the last row, apply the third style—**Intense Effect - Red, Accent 2**. In the inserted text box, type **And Let the Excitement Begin!** Change the **Font Size** to **40**, and then if necessary, drag the text box so that its right edge aligns with the right edge of the slide. Select the arrow and the text box, and then apply **Align Left** alignment using the **Align Selected Objects** option.

8 Select the title, the arrow, and the text box. Distribute the objects vertically using the **Align Selected Objects** option. Apply the **Box** transition to all of the slides in the presentation, and then view the slide show from the beginning.

9 **Insert** a **Header & Footer** on the **Notes and Handouts**. Include the **Date and time updated automatically**, the **Page number**, and a **Footer** with the text **Lastname_Firstname_2E_Roller_Coasters** Apply to all.

10 Display the **Document Properties**. Replace the text in the **Author** box with your own firstname and lastname, in the **Subject** box, type your course name and section number, and in the **Keywords** box, type **roller coasters, new attractions** Close the **Document Information Panel**.

11 **Save** your presentation. Submit your presentation electronically or print **Handouts 4 Slides Horizontal** as directed by your instructor. **Close** the presentation and exit PowerPoint.

End **You have completed Project 14E**

Content-Based Assessments

Apply **14B** skills from these Objectives:

- **5** Remove Picture Backgrounds and Insert WordArt
- **6** Create and Format a SmartArt Graphic

Mastering PowerPoint | Project **14F** Coaster Club

In the following Mastering PowerPoint project, you will format a presentation describing an event sponsored by Fascination Entertainment Group for roller coaster club members. Your completed presentation will look similar to Figure 14.63.

Project Files

For Project 14F, you will need the following file:

p02F_Coaster_Club

You will save your presentation as:

Lastname_Firstname_2F_Coaster_Club

Project Results

About Coaster Enthusiasts

Coaster enthusiasts travel the world to find the tallest, fastest, and longest coasters. They will expect park employees to understand coaster terminology and be able to answer questions about the coasters at all of our park locations and also those at competing parks.

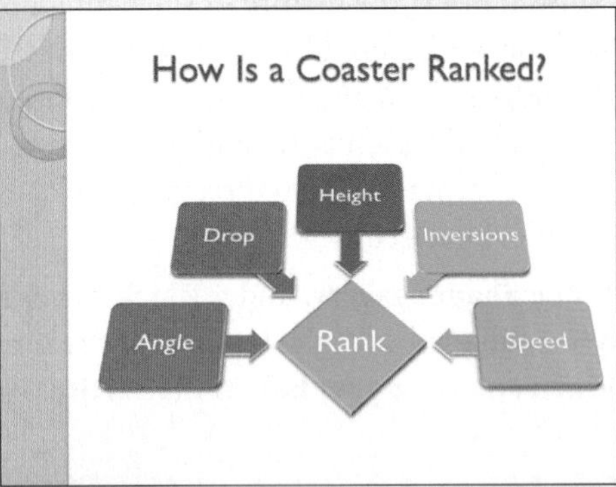

KNOW THE FOLLOWING INFORMATION FOR EACH OF OUR ROLLER COASTERS!

- Angle
  - Degree of steepest angle
- Drop
  - Distance from top of largest drop to bottom
- Height
  - Distance from highest point of track to ground
- Inversions
  - Number of times rider goes upside-down
- Speed
  - Maximum speed achieved by coaster

Figure 14.63

(Project 14F Coaster Club continues on the next page)

Mastering PowerPoint | Project 14F Coaster Club (continued)

1 **Start** PowerPoint. From the student files that accompany this textbook, open **p02F_Coaster_Club**, and then **Save** the file in your **PowerPoint Chapter 14** folder as **Lastname_Firstname_2F_Coaster_Club**

2 On **Slide 1**, select the title and display the **WordArt** gallery. In the last row, apply the third WordArt style—**Fill - Aqua, Accent 2, Matte Bevel**. On **Slide 2**, convert the bulleted list to a **SmartArt** graphic by applying the **Vertical Bracket List** graphic. Change the SmartArt color to **Colorful Range - Accent Colors 3 to 4**, and then apply the **Inset 3-D** style.

3 On **Slide 4**, in the content placeholder, insert a **Relationship** type **SmartArt** graphic—**Converging Radial**. In the circle shape, type **Rank** In the left rectangle, type **Angle** in the middle rectangle, type **Drop** and in the right rectangle type **Height** Add a shape after the *Height* rectangle, and then type **Inversions** Add a shape after the *Inversions* rectangle, and then type **Speed** so that your SmartArt contains five rectangular shapes pointing to the circle shape.

4 Change the SmartArt color to **Colorful Range - Accent Colors 3 to 4**, and then apply the **3-D Flat Scene** style. Change the circle shape to the **Diamond** basic shape. On the **Format tab**, in the **Shapes group**, click the **Larger** button two times to increase the size of the diamond.

5 On **Slide 5**, select the content placeholder, and then from the **Shape Styles** gallery, in the last row, apply the third style—**Intense Effect - Aqua, Accent 2**. Change the **Font Color** of all the text in the content placeholder to **Black, Text 1**.

6 On **Slide 6**, insert a **WordArt**—the third style in the last row—**Fill - Aqua, Accent 2, Matte Bevel**. Replace the WordArt text with **Mark Your Calendars!** Change the **Font Size** to **48**, and align the right edge of the WordArt placeholder with the right edge of the slide.

7 **Insert** a **Header & Footer** on the **Notes and Handouts**. Include the **Date and time updated automatically**, the **Page number**, and a **Footer** with the text **Lastname_Firstname_2F_Coaster_Club** Apply to all.

8 Display the **Document Properties**. Replace the text in the **Author** box with your own firstname and lastname, in the **Subject** box, type your course name and section number, and in the **Keywords** box, type **roller coasters, coaster club, events** Close the **Document Information Panel**.

9 **Save** your presentation, and then view the slide show from the beginning. Submit your presentation electronically or print **Handouts 6 Slides Horizontal** as directed by your instructor. **Close** the presentation and exit PowerPoint.

End **You have completed Project 14F**

Content-Based Assessments

Apply **14A** and **14B** skills from these Objectives:

1 Format Numbered and Bulleted Lists
2 Insert Clip Art
3 Insert Text Boxes and Shapes
4 Format Objects
5 Remove Picture Backgrounds and Insert WordArt
6 Create and Format a SmartArt Graphic

Mastering PowerPoint | Project 14G Orientation

In the following Mastering PowerPoint project, you will edit an existing presentation that is shown to Fascination Entertainment Group employees on their first day of a three-day orientation. Your completed presentation will look similar to Figure 14.64.

Project Files

For Project 14G, you will need the following files:

p02G_Orientation
p02G_Maya_Ruiz
p02G_David_Jensen
p02G_Ken_Lee

You will save your presentation as:

Lastname_Firstname_2G_Orientation

Project Results

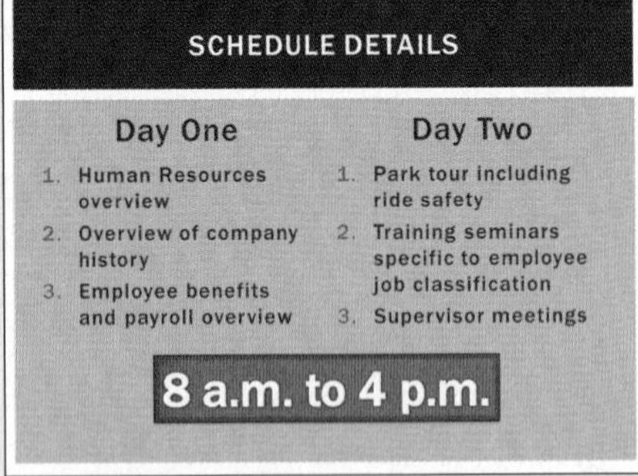

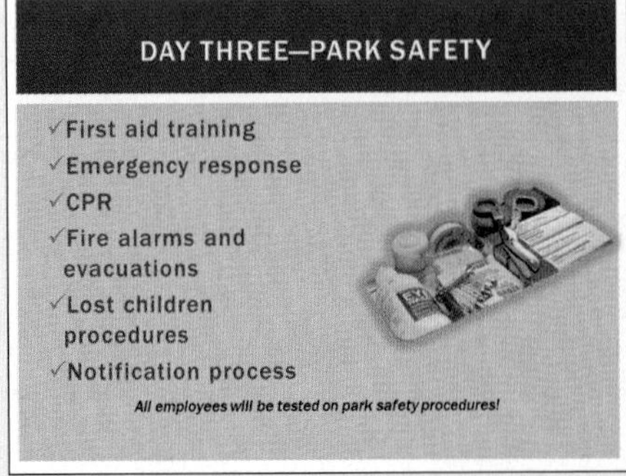

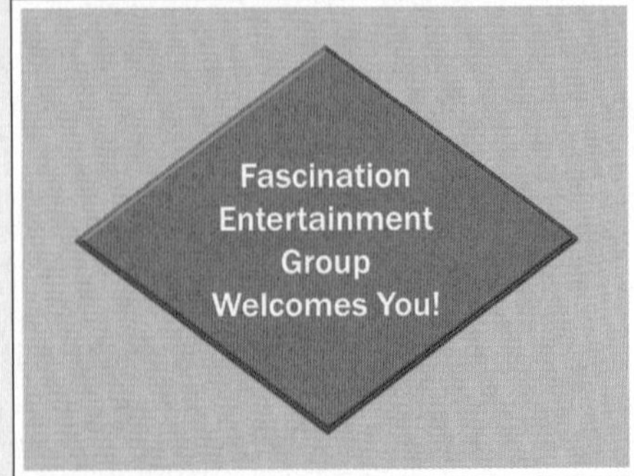

Figure 14.64

(Project 14G Orientation continues on the next page)

Mastering PowerPoint | Project 14G Orientation (continued)

1 **Start** PowerPoint, and then from your student data files, open the file **p02G_Orientation**. In your **PowerPoint Chapter 14** folder, **Save** the file as **Lastname_Firstname_2G_Orientation**

2 On **Slide 1**, format the title as a **WordArt** using the fourth style in the first row—**Fill - White, Outline - Accent 1**. Select the five pictures, and then using the **Align to Slide** option, align the pictures using the **Distribute Vertically** and **Align Right** commands. On **Slide 2**, change the **Shape Style** of the content placeholder to the second style in the last row—**Intense Effect - Tan, Accent 1**.

3 On **Slide 3**, convert the bulleted list to the **Picture** type **SmartArt** graphic—**Title Picture Lineup**. Change the color to **Colorful Range - Accent Colors 5 to 6**, and then apply the **3-D Inset** style. In the three picture placeholders, from your student files insert the following pictures: **p02G_Maya_Ruiz**, **p02G_David_Jensen**, and **p02G_Ken_Lee**.

4 On **Slide 4**, change the two bulleted lists to **Numbering**. Then, insert a **WordArt** using the **Fill - White, Drop Shadow** style with the text **8 a.m. to 4 p.m.** and position the WordArt centered below the two content placeholders. Apply a **Shape Style** to the WordArt using **Intense Effect - Tan, Accent 1**.

5 On **Slide 5**, change the bullet symbols to **Checkmark Bullets**, and then in the placeholder on the right, insert a **Clip Art** photograph by searching for **first aid kit** Insert the picture of the opened first aid box, and then remove the background from the picture so that only the items in the kit display. Mark areas to keep and remove as necessary. Change the **Shape Height** to **3.25** and then apply the **Brown, 18 pt glow, Accent color 4** picture effect.

6 On **Slide 5**, insert a **Text Box** aligned with the **left half of the horizontal ruler at 4 inches** and with the **lower half of the vertical ruler at 2.5 inches**. In the text box, type **All employees will be tested on park safety procedures!** Apply **Italic**, and then **Align Center** the text box using the **Align to Slide** option.

7 Insert a **New Slide** with the **Blank** layout. From the **Shapes** gallery, under **Basic Shapes**, insert a **Diamond** of any size anywhere on the slide. Then, resize the diamond so that its **Shape Height** is **6** and its **Shape Width** is **8** Using the **Align to Slide** option, apply the **Align Center**, and **Align Middle** alignment commands. Apply the **Moderate Effect - Tan, Accent 1** shape style to the diamond, and then in the diamond, type **Fascination Entertainment Group Welcomes You!** Change the **Font Size** to **40**, and then apply the **Art Deco Bevel** effect to the diamond shape.

8 **Insert** a **Header & Footer** on the **Notes and Handouts**. Include the **Date and time updated automatically**, the **Page number**, and a **Footer** with the text **Lastname_Firstname_2G_Orientation** Apply to all.

9 Display the **Document Properties**. Replace the text in the **Author** box with your own firstname and lastname, in the **Subject** box, type your course name and section number, and in the **Keywords** box, type **orientation, employee training** **Close** the **Document Information Panel**.

10 **Save** your presentation, and then view the slide show from the beginning. Submit your presentation electronically or print **Handouts 6 Slides Horizontal** as directed by your instructor. **Close** the presentation and exit PowerPoint.

End **You have completed Project 14G**

Apply a combination of the 14A and 14B skills.

GO! Fix It | Project 14H Summer Jobs

Project Files

For Project 14H, you will need the following file:

p02H_Summer_Jobs

You will save your presentation as:

Lastname_Firstname_2H_Summer_Jobs

In this project, you will edit several slides from a presentation prepared by the Human Resources Department at Fascination Entertainment Group regarding summer employment opportunities. From the student files that accompany this textbook, open the file p02H_Summer_Jobs, and then save the file in your chapter folder as **Lastname_Firstname_2H_Summer_Jobs**

To complete the project you should know:

- The Theme should be changed to Module and two spelling errors should be corrected.
- On Slide 1, the pictures should be aligned with the top of the slide and distributed horizontally.
- On Slide 2, the bulleted list should be converted to a Vertical Box List SmartArt and an attractive style should be applied. The colors should be changed to Colorful Range - Accent Colors 5 to 6.
- On Slide 3, the bulleted list should be formatted as a numbered list.
- On Slide 4, insert a Fill - White, Drop Shadow WordArt with the text **Apply Today!** and position the WordArt centered approximately 1 inch below the title placeholder.
- Document Properties should include your name, course name and section, and the keywords **summer jobs, recruitment** A Header & Footer should be inserted on the Notes and Handouts that includes the Date and time updated automatically, the Page number, and a Footer with the text **Lastname_Firstname_2H_Summer_Jobs**

Save and submit your presentation electronically or print Handouts 4 Slides Horizontal as directed by your instructor. Close the presentation.

End You have completed Project 14H

Apply a combination of the 14A and 14B skills.

GO! Make It | Project 14I Renovation Plans

Project Files

For Project 14I, you will need the following file:

New blank PowerPoint presentation

You will save your presentation as:

Lastname_Firstname_2I_Renovation_Plans

By using the skills you practiced in this chapter, create the first two slides of the presentation shown in Figure 14.65. Start PowerPoint to begin a new blank presentation, and apply the Urban theme and the Aspect color theme. Type the title and subtitle shown in Figure 14.65, and then change the background style to Style 12 and the title font size to 40. Apply the Fill - Black, Background 1, Metal Bevel WordArt style to the title. Save the file in your PowerPoint Chapter 14 folder as **Lastname_Firstname_2I_Renovation_Plans**

To locate the picture on Slide 1, search for a clip art photograph with the keyword **carnival rides** Resize the picture Height to **2** and then apply soft edges, duplicate, align, and distribute the images as shown in the figure.

Insert a new Slide 2 using the Content with Caption layout. Insert the Basic Matrix SmartArt layout shown in Figure 14.65 and change the color and style as shown. Type the title and caption text, changing the title Font Size to 28 and the caption text Font Size to 18. Modify line spacing and apply formatting to the caption text as shown in Figure 14.65. Insert the date, file name, and page number in the Notes and Handouts footer. In the Document Information Panel, add your name and course information and the Keywords **renovation, goals** Save, and then print or submit electronically as directed by your instructor.

Project Results

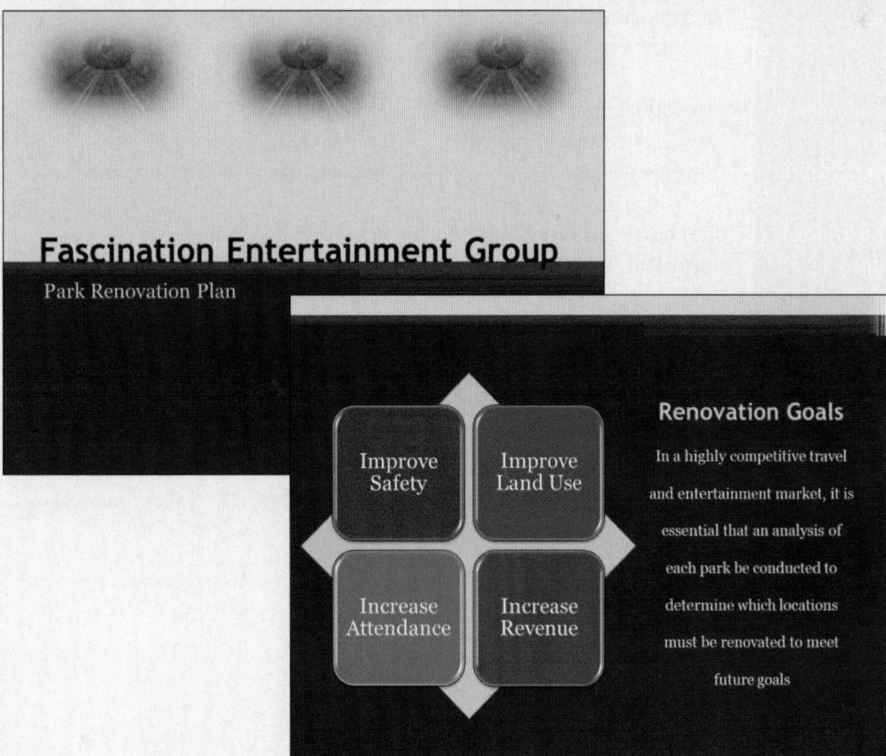

Figure 14.65

End You have completed Project 14I

Content-Based Assessments

Apply a combination of the 14A and 14B skills.

GO! Solve It | Project 14J Business Summary

Project Files

For Project 14J, you will need the following file:

p02J_Business_Summary

You will save your presentation as:

Lastname_Firstname_2J_Business_Summary

Open the file p02J_Business_Summary and save it in your chapter folder as **Lastname_Firstname_2J_Business_Summary** Format the presentation attractively by applying appropriate font formatting and by changing text alignment and line spacing. Insert at least one clip art image and change the picture shape and effect. On Slide 2, align and format the text box and shape attractively and insert a clip art image that can be duplicated, aligned, and distributed across the bottom edge of the slide. On Slide 3, insert an appropriate photo on the right. On Slide 4, convert the bulleted list to an appropriate SmartArt graphic and format the graphic appropriately. Apply slide transitions to all of the slides in the presentation and insert a header and footer that includes the date and time updated automatically, the file name in the footer, and the page number. Add your name, your course name and section number, and the keywords **business summary, revenue** to the Properties area. Save, and then print or submit electronically as directed by your instructor.

Performance Elements	Performance Level: Exemplary: You consistently applied the relevant skills	Proficient: You sometimes, but not always, applied the relevant skills	Developing: You rarely or never applied the relevant skills
Insert and format appropriate clip art	Appropriate clip art was inserted and formatted in the presentation.	Clip art was inserted but was not appropriate for the presentation or was not formatted.	Clip art was not inserted.
Insert and format appropriate SmartArt graphic	Appropriate SmartArt graphic was inserted and formatted in the presentation.	SmartArt graphic was inserted but was not appropriate for the presentation or was not formatted.	SmartArt graphic was not inserted.
Format text boxes and shapes attractively	Text boxes and shapes were formatted attractively.	Text boxes and shapes were formatted but the formatting was inappropriately applied.	Inadequate or no formatting.
Insert transitions	Appropriate transitions were applied to all slides.	Transitions were applied to some, but not all slides.	Transitions were not applied.

End **You have completed Project 14J**

Apply a combination of the **14A** and **14B** skills.

GO! Solve It | Project 14K Hotel

Project Files

For Project 14K, you will need the following file:

p02K_Hotel

You will save your presentation as:

Lastname_Firstname_2K_Hotel

Open the file p02K_Hotel and save it as **Lastname_Firstname_2K_Hotel** Complete the presentation by inserting a clip art image on the first slide and applying appropriate picture effects. On Slide 2, format the bullet point as a single paragraph, and then on Slide 3, convert the bulleted list to an appropriate SmartArt graphic. Change the SmartArt color and apply a style. On Slide 4, insert and attractively position a WordArt with the text **Save the Date!** Apply slide transitions to all of the slides. Insert a header and footer that includes the date and time updated automatically, the file name in the footer, and the page number. Add your name, your course name and section number, and the keywords **hotel, accommodations** to the Properties area. Save your presentation. Print or submit as directed by your instructor.

Performance Elements	Performance Level: Exemplary: You consistently applied the relevant skills	Proficient: You sometimes, but not always, applied the relevant skills	Developing: You rarely or never applied the relevant skills
Insert and format appropriate clip art	Appropriate clip art was inserted and formatted in the presentation.	Clip art was inserted but was not appropriate for the presentation or was not formatted.	Clip art was not inserted.
Insert and format appropriate SmartArt graphic	Appropriate SmartArt graphic was inserted and formatted in the presentation.	SmartArt graphic was inserted but was not appropriate for the presentation or was not formatted.	SmartArt graphic was not inserted.
Insert and format appropriate WordArt	Appropriate WordArt was inserted and formatted in the presentation.	WordArt was inserted but was not appropriate for the presentation or was not formatted.	WordArt was not inserted.
Insert transitions	Appropriate transitions were applied to all slides.	Transitions were applied to some, but not all slides.	Transitions were not applied.

End **You have completed Project 14K**

Outcomes-Based Assessments

Rubric

The following outcomes-based assessments are *open-ended assessments*. That is, there is no specific correct result; your result will depend on your approach to the information provided. Make *Professional Quality* your goal. Use the following scoring rubric to guide you in *how* to approach the problem, and then to evaluate *how well* your approach solves the problem.

The *criteria*—Software Mastery, Content, Format and Layout, and Process—represent the knowledge and skills you have gained that you can apply to solving the problem. The *levels of performance*—Professional Quality, Approaching Professional Quality, or Needs Quality Improvements—help you and your instructor evaluate your result.

	Your completed project is of Professional Quality if you:	**Your completed project is Approaching Professional Quality if you:**	**Your completed project Needs Quality Improvements if you:**
1-Software Mastery	Choose and apply the most appropriate skills, tools, and features and identify efficient methods to solve the problem.	Choose and apply some appropriate skills, tools, and features, but not in the most efficient manner.	Choose inappropriate skills, tools, or features, or are inefficient in solving the problem.
2-Content	Construct a solution that is clear and well organized, contains content that is accurate, appropriate to the audience and purpose, and is complete. Provide a solution that contains no errors in spelling, grammar, or style.	Construct a solution in which some components are unclear, poorly organized, inconsistent, or incomplete. Misjudge the needs of the audience. Have some errors in spelling, grammar, or style, but the errors do not detract from comprehension.	Construct a solution that is unclear, incomplete, or poorly organized; contains some inaccurate or inappropriate content; and contains many errors in spelling, grammar, or style. Do not solve the problem.
3-Format and Layout	Format and arrange all elements to communicate information and ideas, clarify function, illustrate relationships, and indicate relative importance.	Apply appropriate format and layout features to some elements, but not others. Overuse features, causing minor distraction.	Apply format and layout that does not communicate information or ideas clearly. Do not use format and layout features to clarify function, illustrate relationships, or indicate relative importance. Use available features excessively, causing distraction.
4-Process	Use an organized approach that integrates planning, development, self-assessment, revision, and reflection.	Demonstrate an organized approach in some areas, but not others; or, use an insufficient process of organization throughout.	Do not use an organized approach to solve the problem.

Apply a combination of the 14A and 14B skills.

GO! Think | Project 14L Interactive Ride

Project Files

For Project 14L, you will need the following file:

New blank PowerPoint presentation

You will save your presentation as:

Lastname_Firstname_2L_Interactive_Ride

As part of its mission to combine fun with the discovery of math and science, Fascination Entertainment Group is opening a new, interactive roller coaster at its South Lake Tahoe location. FEG's newest coaster is designed for maximum thrill and minimum risk. In a special interactive exhibit located next to the coaster, riders can learn about the physics behind this powerful coaster and even try their hand at building a coaster.

Guests will begin by setting the height of the first hill, which determines the coaster's maximum potential energy to complete its journey. Next they will set the exit path, and build additional hills, loops, and corkscrews. When completed, riders can submit their coaster for a safety inspection to find out whether the ride passes or fails.

In either case, riders can also take a virtual tour of the ride they created to see the maximum speed achieved, the amount of negative G-forces applied, the length of the track, and the overall thrill factor. They can also see how their coaster compares with other coasters in the FEG family, and they can e-mail the coaster simulation to their friends.

Using the preceding information, create a presentation that Marketing Director, Annette Chosek, will present at a travel fair describing the new attraction. The presentation should include four to six slides with at least one SmartArt graphic and one clip art image. Apply an appropriate theme and use slide layouts that will effectively present the content, and use text boxes, shapes, and WordArt if appropriate. Apply font formatting and slide transitions, and modify text alignment and line spacing as necessary. Save the file as **Lastname_Firstname_2L_Interactive_Ride** and then insert a header and footer that includes the date and time updated automatically, the file name in the footer, and the page number. Add your name, your course name and section number, and the keywords **roller coaster, new rides** to the Properties area. Print or submit as directed by your instructor.

End **You have completed Project 14L**

Outcomes-Based Assessments

Apply a combination of the **14A** and **14B** skills.

GO! Think | Project **14M** Research

Project Files

For Project 14M, you will need the following file:

New blank PowerPoint presentation

You will save your presentation as:

Lastname_Firstname_2M_Research

As the number of theme park vacations continues to rise, Fascination Entertainment Group is developing plans to ensure that its top theme parks are a true vacation destination. Fascination Entertainment Group research has verified that visitors use several factors in determining their theme park destinations: top attractions, overall value, and nearby accommodations.

Visitors, regardless of age, look for thrills and entertainment at a good value. Fascination Entertainment Group owns four of North America's top 15 coasters and two of its top 10 water parks, thus making the parks prime attraction destinations. Typical costs for visitors include park entrance fees, food and beverages, souvenirs, transportation, and lodging. Beginning this year, FEG will offer vacation packages. Package pricing will vary depending on number of adults, number of children, length of stay, and number of parks attended (i.e., theme park, water park, and zoo). Each park will continue to offer annual passes at a discount.

Research shows that visitors who travel more than 100 miles one way will consider the need for nearby accommodations. For its top 10 theme parks, Fascination Entertainment Group will open hotels at any parks that do not currently have them within the next two years. Until then, the company will partner with area hotels to provide discounts to theme park visitors.

Using the preceding information, create the first four slides of a presentation that the Fascination Entertainment Group marketing director can show at an upcoming board of directors meeting. Apply an appropriate theme and use slide layouts that will effectively present the content. Include clip art and at least one SmartArt graphic. Apply font and WordArt formatting, picture styles, and slide transitions, and modify text alignment and line spacing as necessary. If appropriate, insert and format a text box or a shape. Save the file as **Lastname_Firstname_2M_Research** and then insert a header and footer that includes the date and time updated automatically, the file name in the footer, and the page number. Add your name, your course name and section number, and the keywords **visitor preferences, research findings** to the Properties area. Print or submit as directed by your instructor.

End **You have completed Project 14M**

Outcomes-Based Assessments

Apply a combination of the 14A and 14B skills.

You and GO! | Project 14N Theme Park

Project Files

For Project 14N, you will need the following file:

New blank PowerPoint presentation

You will save your presentation as:

Lastname_Firstname_2N_Theme_Park

Research your favorite theme park and create a presentation with at least six slides that describes the park, its top attractions, nearby accommodations, and the reasons why you enjoy the park. Choose an appropriate theme, slide layouts, and pictures, and format the presentation attractively, including at least one SmartArt graphic and one WordArt object or shape. Save your presentation as Lastname_Firstname_2N_Theme_Park and submit as directed.

End You have completed Project 14N

Apply a combination of the 14A and 14B skills.

GO! Collaborate | Project 14O Bell Orchid Hotels Group Running Case

This project relates to the **Bell Orchid Hotels**. Your instructor may assign this group case project to your class. If your instructor assigns this project, he or she will provide you with information and instructions to work as part of a group. The group will apply the skills gained thus far to help the Bell Orchid Hotels achieve their business goals.

End You have completed Project 14O

Enhancing a Presentation with Animation, Video, Tables, and Charts

OUTCOMES

At the end of this chapter you will be able to:

OBJECTIVES

Mastering these objectives will enable you to:

PROJECT 15A
Customize a presentation with animation and video.

1. Customize Slide Backgrounds and Themes (p. 851)
2. Animate a Slide Show (p. 858)
3. Insert a Video (p. 865)

PROJECT 15B
Create a presentation that includes data in tables and charts.

4. Create and Modify Tables (p. 875)
5. Create and Modify Charts (p. 880)

Travis Houston/Shutterstock

In This Chapter

Recall that a presentation theme applies a consistent look to a presentation. You can customize a presentation by modifying the theme and by applying animation to slide elements, and you can enhance your presentations by creating tables and charts that help your audience understand numeric data and trends just as pictures and diagrams help illustrate a concept. The data that you present should determine whether a table or a chart would most appropriately display your information. Styles applied to your tables and charts unify these slide elements by complementing your presentation theme.

The projects in this chapter relate to **Golden Grove**, a growing city located between Los Angeles and San Diego. Just 10 years ago the population was under 100,000; today it has grown to almost 300,000. Community leaders have always focused on quality and economic development in decisions on housing, open space, education, and infrastructure, making the city a model for other communities its size around the United States. The city provides many recreational and cultural opportunities with a large park system, thriving arts, and a friendly business atmosphere.

Project 15A Informational Presentation

Project Activities

In Activities 15.01 through 15.11, you will edit and format a presentation that Mindy Walker, Director of Golden Grove Parks and Recreation, has created to inform residents about the benefits of using the city's parks and trails. Your completed presentation will look similar to Figure 15.1.

Project Files

For Project 15A, you will need the following files:

p03A_Park
p03A_Pets
p03A_Trails
p03A_Walking_Trails
p03A_Trails_Video

You will save your presentation as:

Lastname_Firstname_3A_Walking_Trails

Project Results

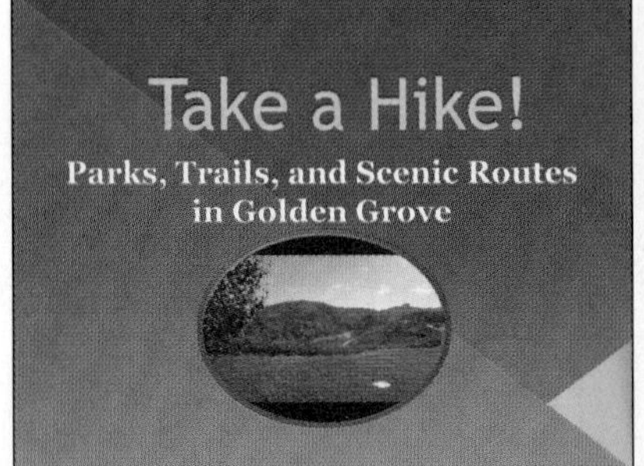

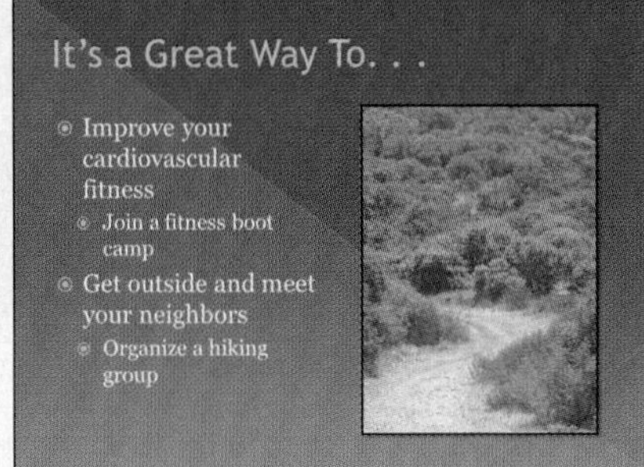

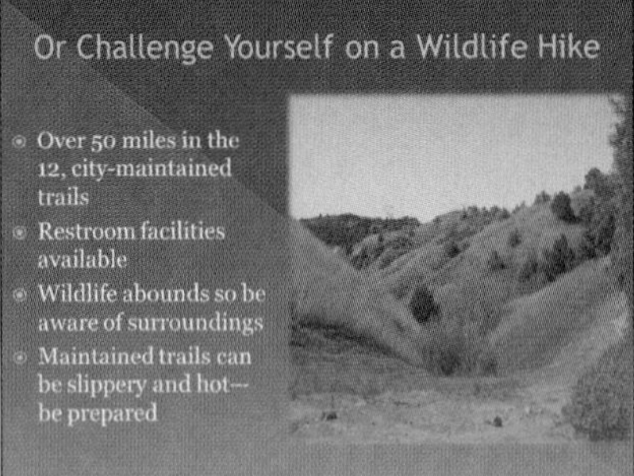

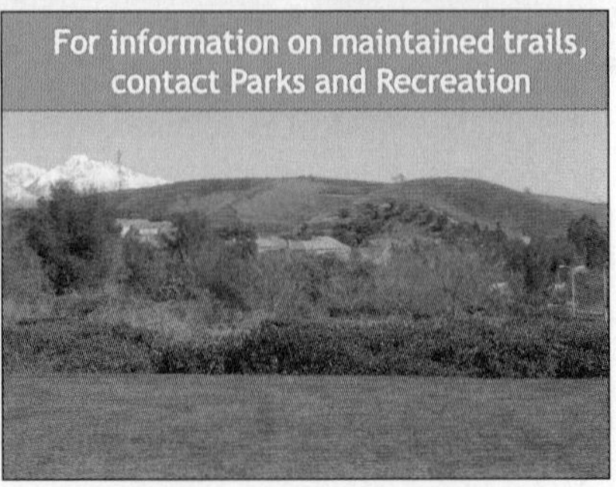

Figure 15.1
Project 15A Walking Trails

Objective 1 | Customize Slide Backgrounds and Themes

You have practiced customizing presentations by applying themes with unified design elements, backgrounds, and colors that provide a consistent look in your presentation. Additional ways to customize a slide include changing theme fonts and colors, applying a background style, modifying the background color, or inserting a picture on the slide background.

Activity 15.01 | Changing the Theme Colors and Theme Fonts

Recall that the presentation theme is a coordinated, predefined set of colors, fonts, lines, and fill effects. In this activity, you will open a presentation in which the Verve theme is applied, and then you will change the ***theme colors***—a set of coordinating colors that are applied to the backgrounds, objects, and text in a presentation.

In addition to theme colors, every presentation theme includes ***theme fonts*** that determine the font to apply to two types of slide text—headings and body. The ***Headings font*** is applied to slide titles and the ***Body font*** is applied to all other text. When you apply a new theme font to the presentation, the text on every slide is updated with the new heading and body fonts.

1 From the student files that accompany this textbook, locate and open **p03A_Walking_Trails**. Display **Backstage** view, click **Save As**, and then navigate to the location where you are storing your projects for this chapter. Create a new folder named **PowerPoint Chapter 15** and then in the **File name** box and using your own name, type **Lastname_Firstname_3A_Walking_Trails** Click **Save** or press Enter.

2 Click the **Design tab**, and then in the **Themes group**, click the **Colors** button to display the list of theme colors. Point to several themes and notice the color changes on **Slide 1**. Scroll the **Theme Colors** list, and then click **Metro** to change the theme colors.

Changing the theme colors does not change the overall design of the presentation. In this presentation, the *Verve* presentation theme is still applied to the presentation. By modifying the theme colors, you retain the design of the *Verve* theme. The colors of the *Metro* theme, which coordinate with the pictures in the presentation, are available as text, accent, and background colors.

3 With **Slide 1** displayed, click anywhere in the title placeholder. Click the **Home tab**, and then in the **Font group**, click the **Font button arrow**. Notice that at the top of the **Font** list, under **Theme Fonts**, Century Gothic (Headings) and Century Gothic (Body) display. Compare your screen with Figure 15.2.

Figure 15.2

4. Click anywhere on the slide to close the Font list. Click the **Design tab**, and then in the **Themes group**, click the **Fonts** button.

   This list displays the name of each theme and the pair of fonts in the theme. The first and larger font in each pair is the Headings font and the second and smaller font in each pair is the Body font.

5. Point to several of the themes and watch as Live Preview changes the title and subtitle text. Then, scroll to the bottom of the **Theme Fonts** list and click **Urban**. Compare your screen with Figure 15.3, and then **Save** your presentation.

Figure 15.3

Activity 15.02 | Applying a Background Style

1. With **Slide 1** displayed, on the **Design tab**, in the **Background group**, click the **Background Styles** button. Compare your screen with Figure 15.4.

   A ***background style*** is a slide background fill variation that combines theme colors in different intensities or patterns.

Figure 15.4

2 Point to each of the background styles to view the style on **Slide 1**. Then, in the first row, *right-click* **Style 2** to display the shortcut menu. Click **Apply to Selected Slides** and then compare your screen with Figure 15.5.

The background style is applied only to Slide 1.

3 **Save** your presentation.

Figure 15.5

More Knowledge | **Applying Background Styles to All Slides in a Presentation**

To change the background style for all of the slides in the presentation, click the background style that you want to apply and the style will be applied to every slide.

Activity 15.03 | Hiding Background Graphics

Many of the PowerPoint 2010 themes contain graphic elements that display on the slide background. In the Verve theme applied to this presentation, the background includes a triangle and lines that intersect near the lower right corner of the slide. Sometimes the background graphics interfere with the slide content. When this happens, you can hide the background graphics.

1 Display **Slide 6**, and notice that on this slide, you can clearly see the triangle and lines on the slide background.

You cannot delete these objects because they are a part of the slide background; however, you can hide them.

2 Display **Slide 5**, and notice that the background graphics distract from the connecting lines on the diagram. On the **Design tab**, in the **Background group**, select the **Hide Background Graphics** check box, and then compare your slide with Figure 15.6.

The background objects no longer display behind the SmartArt diagram.

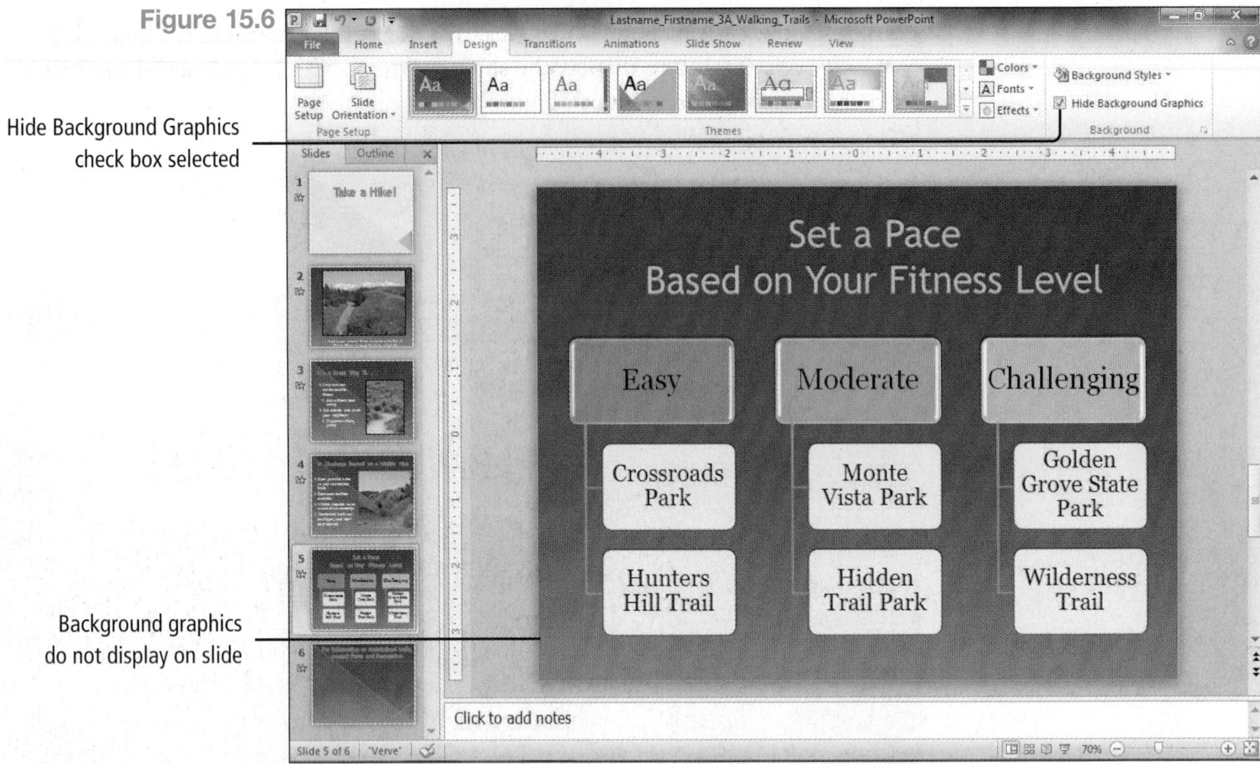

Figure 15.6

3. **Save** the presentation.

Activity 15.04 | Formatting a Slide Background with a Picture

You can insert a picture on a slide background so the image fills the entire slide.

1. Display **Slide 3**, and then click the **Home tab**. In the **Slides group**, click the **New Slide arrow**, and then click the **Title Only** layout to insert a new slide with the Title Only layout.
2. With the new **Slide 4** displayed, click the **Design tab**. In the **Background group**, select the **Hide Background Graphics** check box, and then click the **Background Styles** button. Below the displayed gallery, click **Format Background**.

   In the Format Background dialog box, you can customize a slide background by changing the formatting options.
3. If necessary, on the left side of the dialog box, click Fill. On the right side of the dialog box, under **Fill**, click the **Picture or texture fill** option button, and then notice that on the slide background, a textured fill displays. Compare your screen with Figure 15.7.

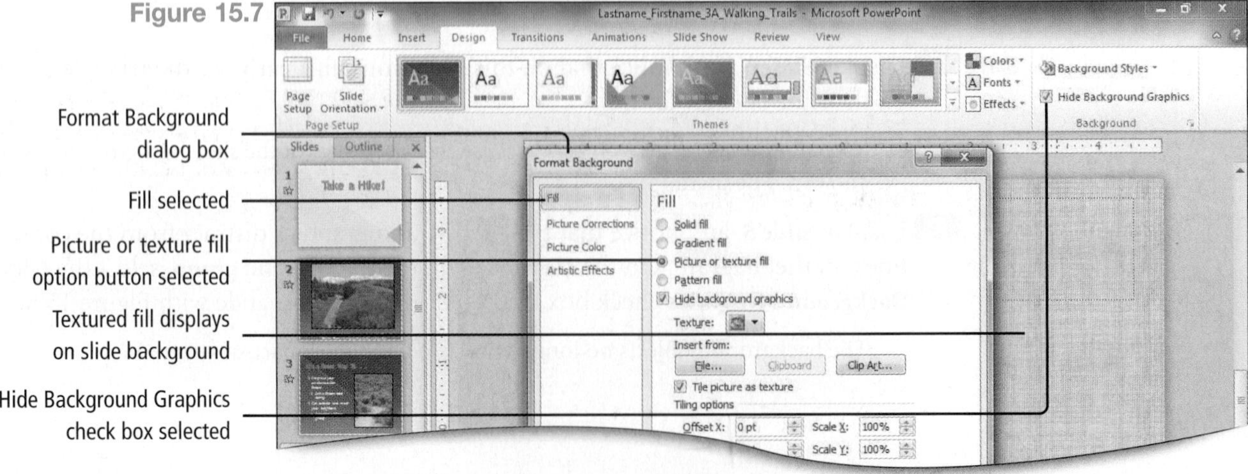

Figure 15.7

4 Under **Insert from**, click the **File** button to display the **Insert Picture** dialog box. Navigate to your student files, and then click **p03A_Pets**. Click **Insert**, and then at the bottom of the **Format Background** dialog box, click **Close**. Compare your slide with Figure 15.8 and notice that the picture displays as the background of Slide 4.

When a picture is applied to a slide background using the Format Background option, the picture is not treated as an object. The picture fills the background and you cannot move it or size it.

Figure 15.8

5 Click in the title placeholder, type **Find a Pet Friendly Trail** and then notice that the background picture does not provide sufficient contrast with the text to display the title effectively.

6 With your insertion point still in the title placeholder, click the **Format tab**. In the **Shape Styles group**, click the **Shape Fill button arrow**. In the fifth column, click the last color—**Green, Accent 1, Darker 50%**. Select the title text, and then on the **Format tab**, in the **WordArt Styles group**, in the first row, click the third style—**Fill - White, Drop Shadow**. **Center** the text.

The green fill color and the white WordArt style provide good contrast against the slide background so that the text is readable.

7 Point to the outer edge of the title placeholder to display the pointer, and then drag the placeholder up and to the left so that its upper left corner aligns with the upper left corner of the slide. Point to the center right sizing handle and drag to the right so that the placeholder extends to the right edge of the slide. Click outside of the placeholder, and then compare your slide with Figure 15.9.

Figure 15.9

8 Display **Slide 5**, and then insert a **New Slide** with the **Title Only** layout. On the **Design tab**, in the **Background group**, select the **Hide Background Graphics** check box, and then click the **Background Styles** button. Click **Format Background**.

9 Under **Fill**, click the **Picture or texture fill** option button. Under **Insert from**, click **File**. Navigate to your student files, click **p03A_Trails**, click **Insert**, and then **Close** the dialog box. In the title placeholder, type **Get Outside! Get Fit! Get Walking!** and then **Center** the text.

10 Select the text, and then change the **Font Size** to **36**. Then, apply the same **Shape Fill** color and **WordArt** style to the title placeholder that you applied to the title on **Slide 4**. Size the placeholder so that it extends from the left edge of the slide to the right edge of the slide, and then drag the placeholder up so that its upper edge aligns with the upper edge of the slide. Click outside of the title so that it is not selected. Compare your slide with Figure 15.10.

The green fill color and white text provide good contrast with the slide background and complement the green color of the grass on the slide.

Figure 15.10

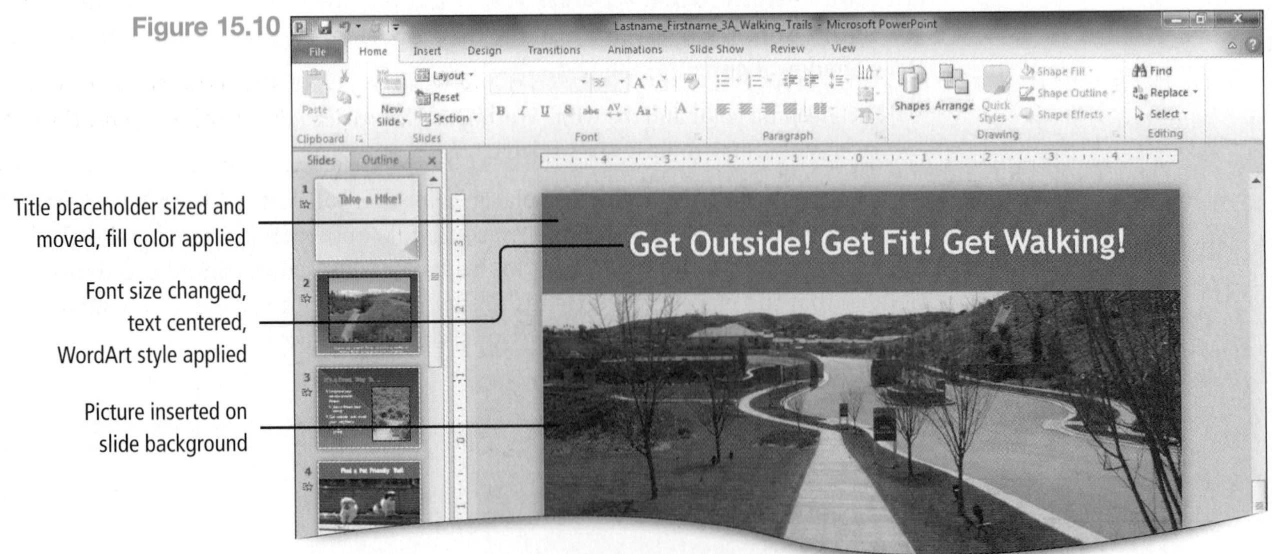

11 Display **Slide 8**, and then format the slide background with a picture from your student files—**p03A_Park**. On the **Design tab**, in the **Background group**, select the **Hide Background Graphics** check box.

12 Select the title placeholder. On the **Format tab**. In the **Shape Styles group**, click the **More** button. In the **Shape Styles** gallery, in the second row, click the sixth style—**Colored Fill – Periwinkle, Accent 5**.

13 Select the text, and then on the **Format tab**, in the **WordArt Styles group**, click the third style—**Fill - White, Drop Shadow**. Click outside of the placeholder, and then compare your slide with Figure 15.11. **Save** the presentation.

Figure 15.11

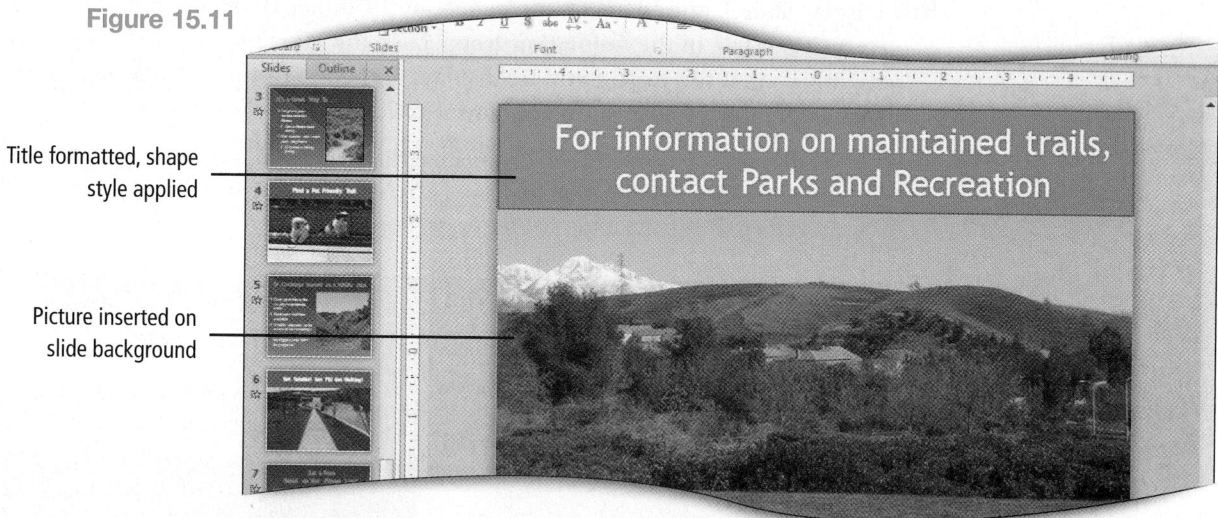

Activity 15.05 | Applying a Background Fill Color and Resetting a Slide Background

1 Display **Slide 1**, and then click the **Design tab**. In the **Background group**, click the **Background Styles** button, and then click **Format Background**.

2 In the **Format Background** dialog box, if necessary, click the Solid fill option button. Under **Fill Color**, click the **Color** button. Under **Theme Colors**, in the first column, click the last color—**White, Background 1, Darker 50%**. Click **Close**.

The solid fill color is applied to the slide background.

3 On the **Design tab**, in the **Background group**, click the **Background Styles** button. Below the gallery, click **Reset Slide Background**, and then **Save** the presentation.

After making many changes to a slide background, you may decide that the original theme formatting is the best choice for displaying the text and graphics on a slide. The Reset Slide Background feature restores the original theme and color theme formatting to a slide.

Objective 2 | Animate a Slide Show

Animation is a visual or sound effect added to an object or text on a slide. Animation can focus the audience's attention, providing the speaker with an opportunity to emphasize important points using the slide element as an effective visual aid.

Activity 15.06 | Applying Animation Entrance Effects and Effect Options

Entrance effects are animations that bring a slide element onto the screen. You can modify an entrance effect by using the animation Effect Options command.

1 Display **Slide 3**, and then click anywhere in the bulleted list placeholder. On the **Animations tab**, in the **Animation group**, click the **More** button. If necessary, scroll slightly so that the word *Entrance* displays at the top of the Animation gallery, and then compare your screen with Figure 15.12.

Recall that an entrance effect is animation that brings an object or text onto the screen. An ***emphasis effect*** is animation that emphasizes an object or text that is already displayed. An ***exit effect*** is animation that moves an object or text off the screen.

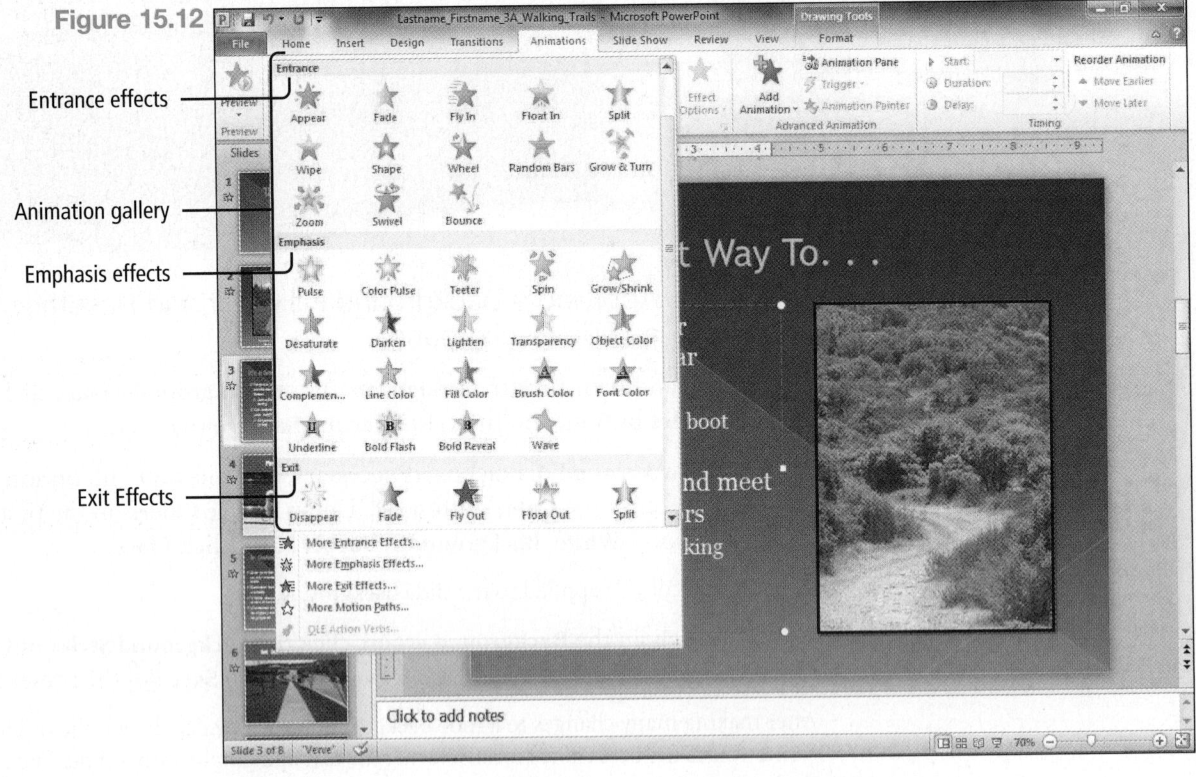

Figure 15.12

2 Under **Entrance**, click **Split**, and then notice the animation applied to the list. Compare your screen with Figure 15.13.

The numbers *1* and *2* display to the left of the bulleted list placeholder, indicating the order in which the bullet points will be animated during the slide show. For example, the first bullet point and its subordinate bullet are both numbered *1*. Thus, both will display at the same time.

Figure 15.13

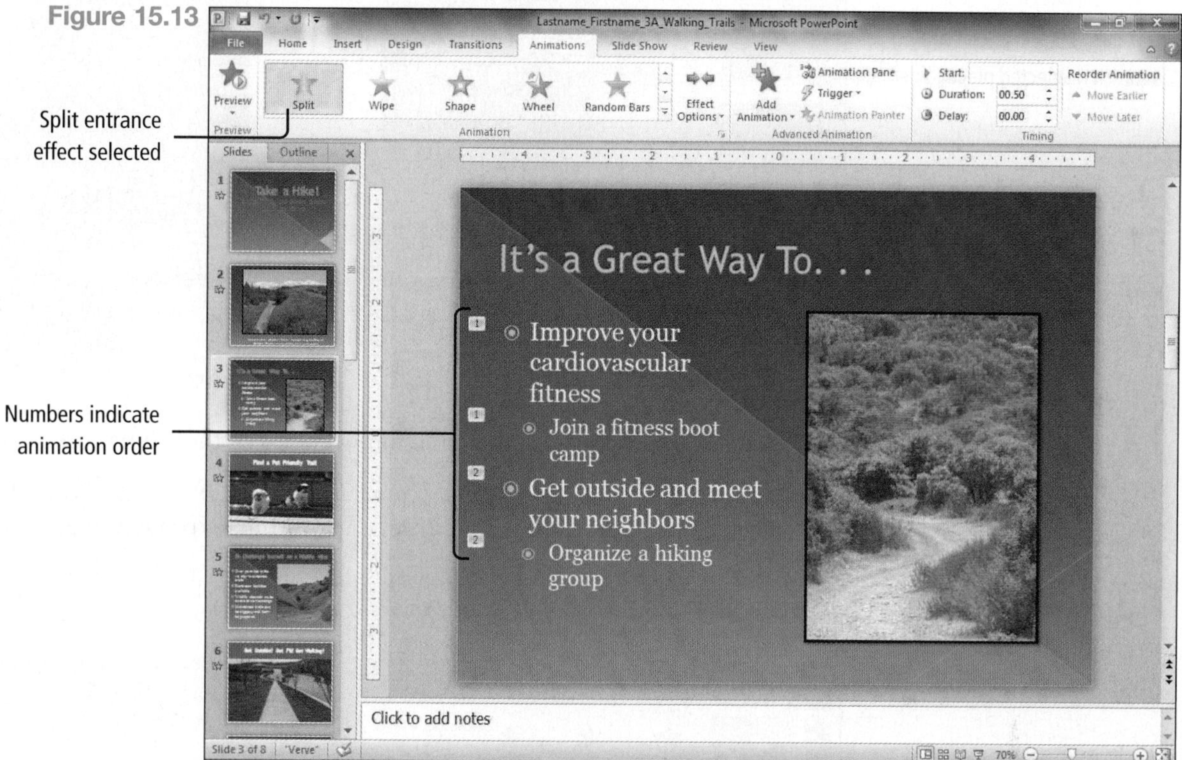

3 Select the bulleted text placeholder. In the **Animation group**, click the **Effect Options** button, and then compare your screen with Figure 15.14.

The Effect Options control the direction and sequence in which the animation displays. Additional options may be available with other entrance effects.

PowerPoint | Chapter 15

Figure 15.14

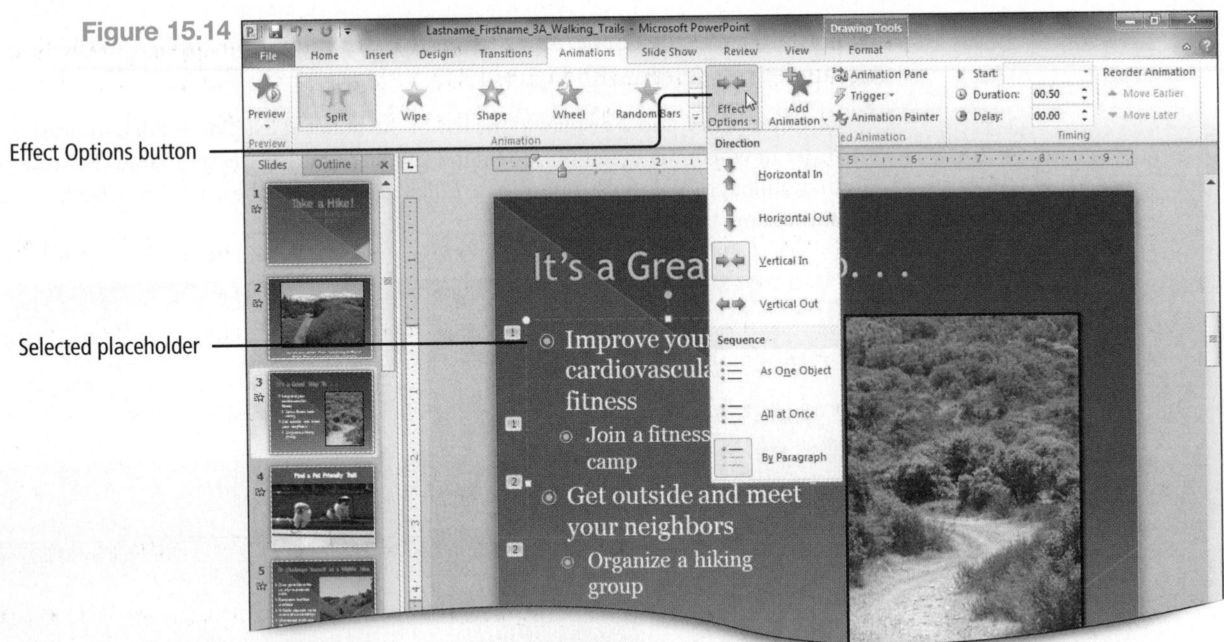

4 Click **Vertical Out** and notice the direction from which the animation is applied.

5 Select the picture. In the **Animation group**, click the **More** button, and then below the gallery, click **More Entrance Effects**. Compare your screen with Figure 15.15.

The Change Entrance Effect dialog box displays additional entrance effects grouped in four categories: Basic, Subtle, Moderate, and Exciting.

Figure 15.15

6 In the lower right corner of the **Change Entrance Effect** dialog box, verify that the **Preview Effect** check box is selected. Under **Basic**, click **Dissolve In**, and then watch as Live Preview displays the selected entrance effect. Click **OK**.

The number *3* displays next to the picture, indicating that it is third in the slide animation sequence.

7 Select the title. On the **Animations tab**, in the **Animation group**, click the **More** button, and then under **Entrance**, click **Split** to apply the animation to the title.

The number *4* displays next to the title, indicating that it is fourth in the slide animation sequence.

8 **Save** the presentation.

Activity 15.07 | Setting Animation Timing Options

Timing options control when animated items display in the animation sequence.

1 With **Slide 3** displayed, on the **Animations tab**, in the **Preview group**, click the **Preview** button.

The list displays first, followed by the picture, and then the title. The order in which animation is applied is the order in which objects display during the slide show.

2 Select the title. On the **Animations tab**, in the **Timing group**, under **Reorder Animation**, click the **Move Earlier** button two times, and then compare your screen with Figure 15.16.

To the left of the title placeholder, the number *1* displays. You can use the Reorder Animation buttons to change the order in which text and objects are animated during the slide show.

Figure 15.16

3 With the title selected, on the **Animations tab**, in the **Timing group**, click the **Start button arrow** to display three options—*On Click*, *With Previous*, and *After Previous*. Compare your screen with Figure 15.17.

The ***On Click*** option begins the animation sequence for the selected slide element when the mouse button is clicked or the Spacebar is pressed. The ***With Previous*** option begins the animation sequence at the same time as the previous animation or slide transition. The ***After Previous*** option begins the animation sequence for the selected slide element immediately after the completion of the previous animation or slide transition.

Figure 15.17

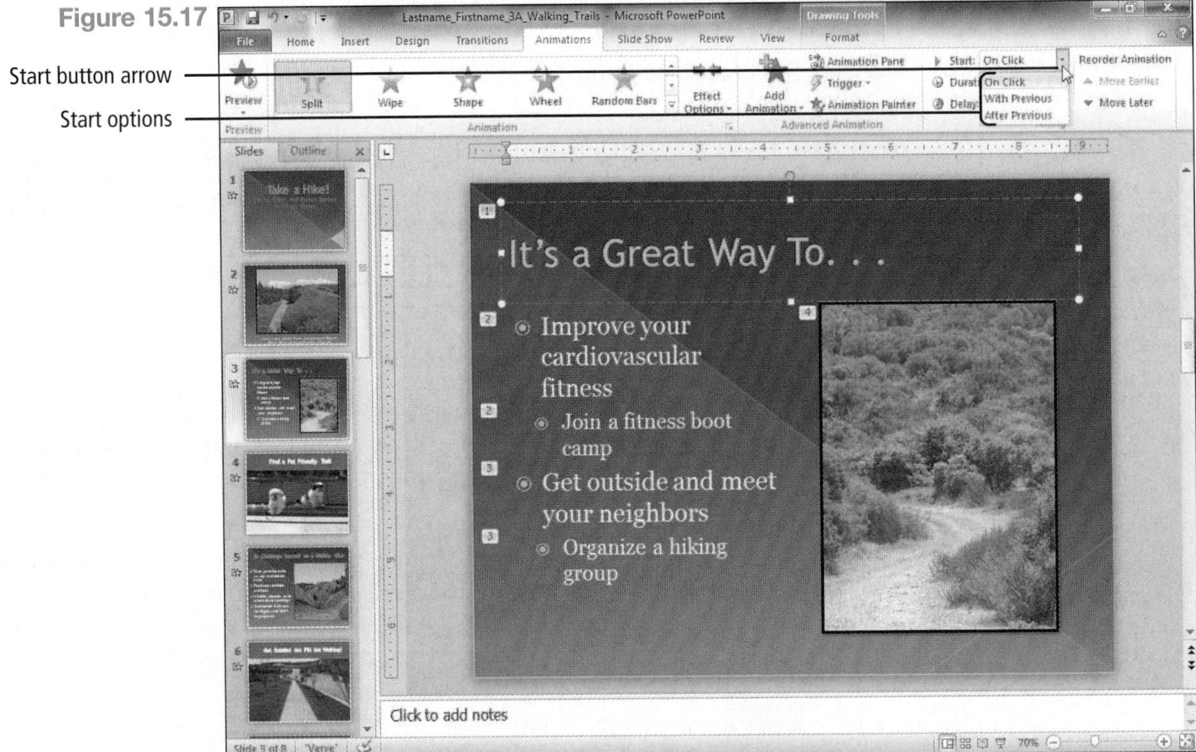

4 Click **After Previous**, and then notice that the number *1* is changed to *0*, indicating that the animation will begin immediately after the slide transition; the presenter does not need to click the mouse button or press Spacebar to display the title.

5 Select the picture, and then in the **Timing group**, click the **Start arrow**. Click **With Previous** and notice that the number is changed to *2*, indicating that the animation will begin at the same time as the second set of bullet points in the bulleted list.

6 On the **Animations tab**, in the **Preview group**, click the **Preview** button and notice that the title displays first, and that the picture displays at the same time as the second set of bullet points.

7 Display **Slide 1**, and then click in the title placeholder. On the **Animations tab**, in the **Animation group**, click the **Entrance** effect **Fly In**, and then click the **Effect Options** button. Click **From Top**. In the **Timing group**, click the **Start arrow**, and then click **After Previous.**

The number *0* displays to the left of the title indicating that the animation will begin immediately after the slide transition.

8 With the title selected, in the **Timing group**, click the **Duration** down arrow so that *00.25* displays in the **Duration** box. Compare your screen with Figure 15.18.

Duration controls the speed of the animation. You can set the duration of an animation by typing a value in the Duration box, or you can use the spin box arrows to increase and decrease the duration in 0.25-second increments. When you decrease the duration, the animation speed increases. When you increase the duration, the animation is slowed.

Figure 15.18

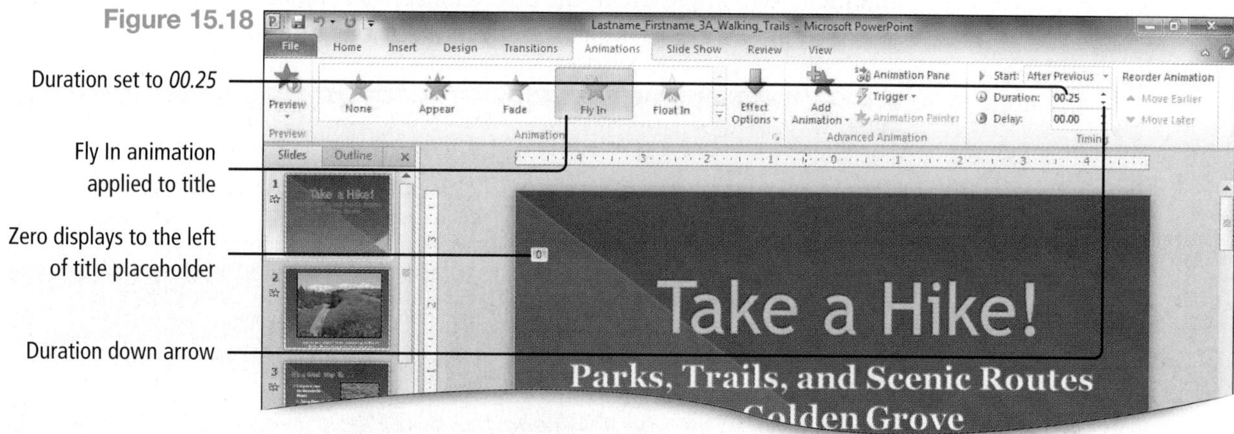

9 Select the subtitle, and then in the **Animation group**, apply the **Fly In** entrance effect. In the **Timing group**, click the **Start arrow**, and then click **After Previous**. In the **Timing group**, select the value in the **Delay** box, type **00.50** and then press Enter. Compare your screen with Figure 15.19.

You can use Delay to begin a selected animation after a specified amount of time has elapsed. Here, the animation is delayed by one-half of a second after the completion of the previous animation—the title animation. You can type a value in the Delay or Duration boxes, or you can use the up and down arrows to change the timing.

Figure 15.19

10 View the slide show from the beginning and notice the animation on Slides 1 and 3. When the black slide displays, press Esc to return to Normal view, and then **Save** the presentation.

Activity 15.08 | Using Animation Painter and Removing Animation

Animation Painter is a feature that copies animation settings from one object to another.

1. Display **Slide 3**, and then click anywhere in the bulleted list. On the **Animations tab**, in the **Advanced Animation group**, click the **Animation Painter** button. Display **Slide 5**, and then point anywhere in the bulleted list placeholder to display the Animation Painter pointer. Compare your screen with Figure 15.20.

Figure 15.20

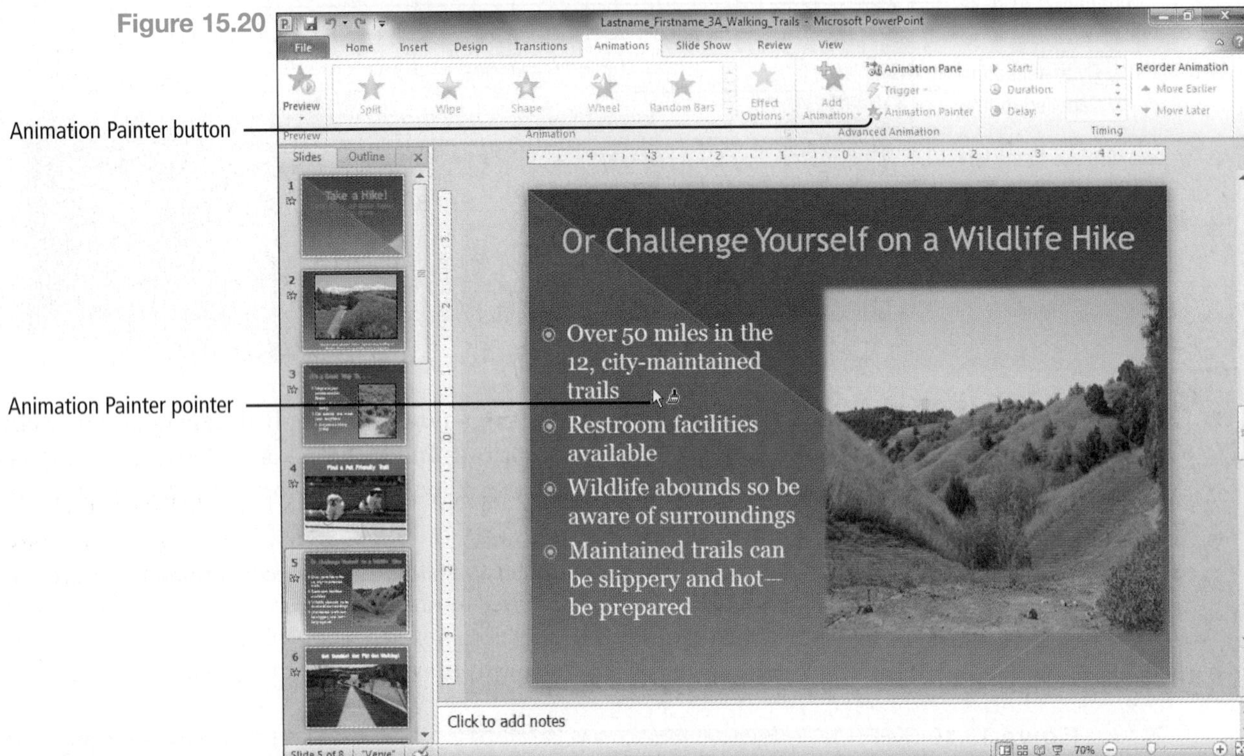

2. Click the bulleted list to copy the animation settings from the list on **Slide 3** to the list on **Slide 5**.

3. Display **Slide 3**, and then select the picture. Using the technique that you just practiced, use **Animation Painter** to copy the animation from the picture on **Slide 3** to the picture on **Slide 5**. With **Slide 5** displayed, compare your screen with Figure 15.21.

   The numbers displayed to the left of the bulleted list and the picture indicate that animation is applied to the objects.

Figure 15.21

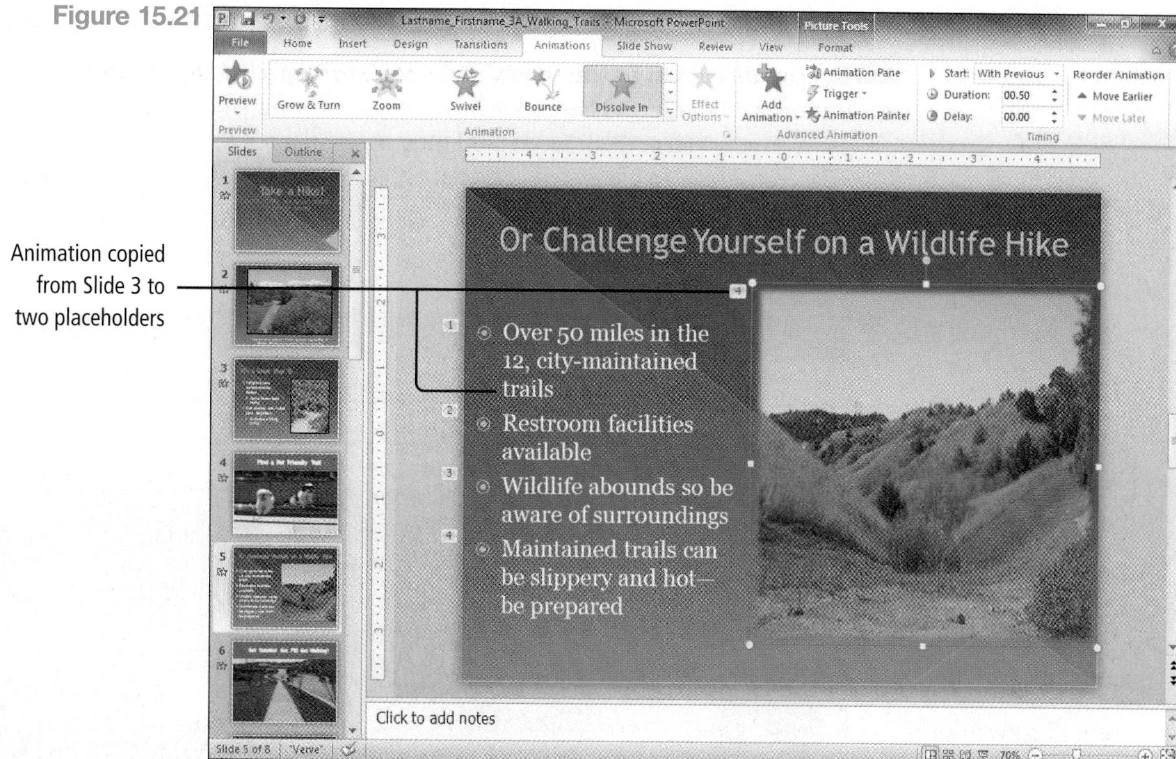

4 Display **Slide 3**, and then click in the title placeholder. On the **Animations tab**, in the **Animation group**, click the **More** button. At the top of the gallery, click **None** to remove the animation from the title placeholder. Compare your screen with Figure 15.22, and then **Save** the presentation.

Figure 15.22

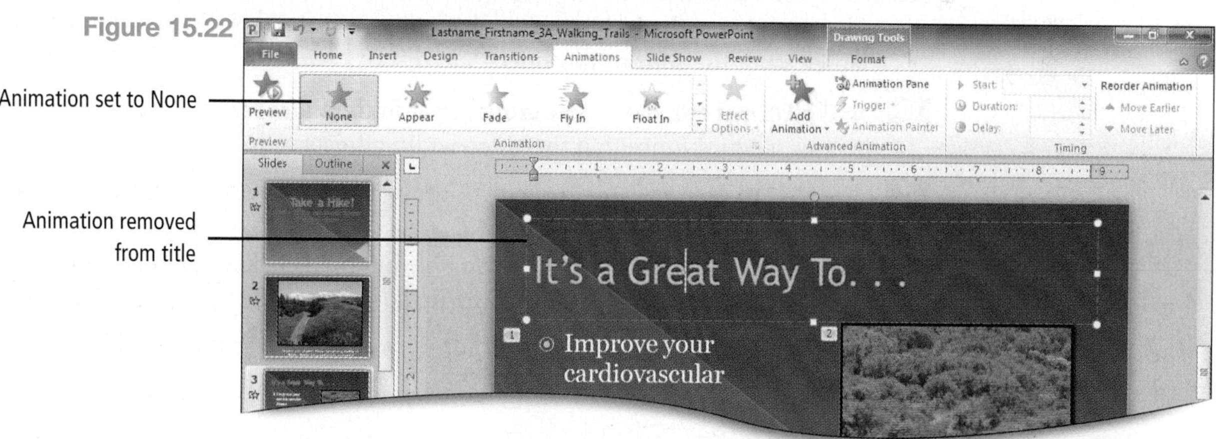

Objective 3 | Insert a Video

You can insert, size, and move videos in a PowerPoint presentation, and you can format videos by applying styles and effects. Video editing features in PowerPoint 2010 enable you to trim parts of a video and to fade the video in and out during a presentation.

Activity 15.09 | Inserting a Video

1 Display **Slide 1**. On the **Insert tab**, in the **Media group**, click the upper part of the **Video** button. In the **Insert Video** dialog box, navigate to your student files, and then click **p03A_Trails_Video**. Click **Insert**, and then compare your screen with Figure 15.23.

The video displays in the center of the slide, and playback and volume controls display in the control panel below the video. Video formatting and editing tools display on the Ribbon.

Figure 15.23

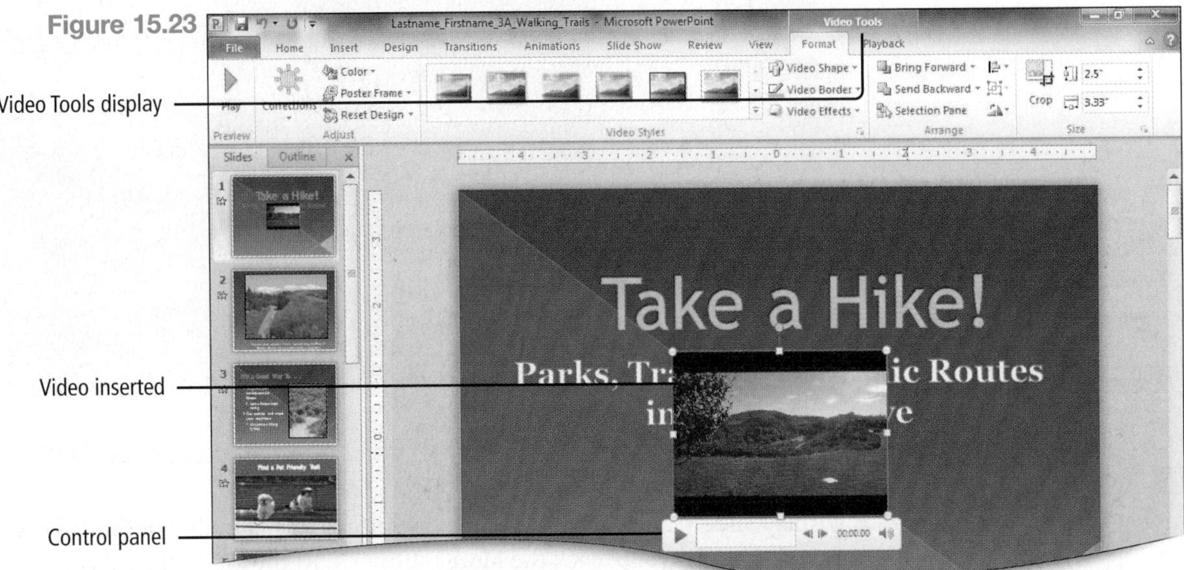

2 Below the video, on the control panel, click the **Play/Pause** button ▶ to view the video and notice that as the video plays, the control panel displays the time that has elapsed since the start of the video.

3 On the **Format tab**, in the **Size group**, click in the **Video Height** box. Type **3** and then press Enter. Notice that the video width adjusts proportionately.

4 Point to the video to display the pointer, and then drag the video down so that the top of the video is aligned at **zero on the vertical ruler**. On the **Format tab**, in the **Arrange group**, click the **Align** button, and then click **Align Center** to center the video horizontally on the slide. Compare your screen with Figure 15.24.

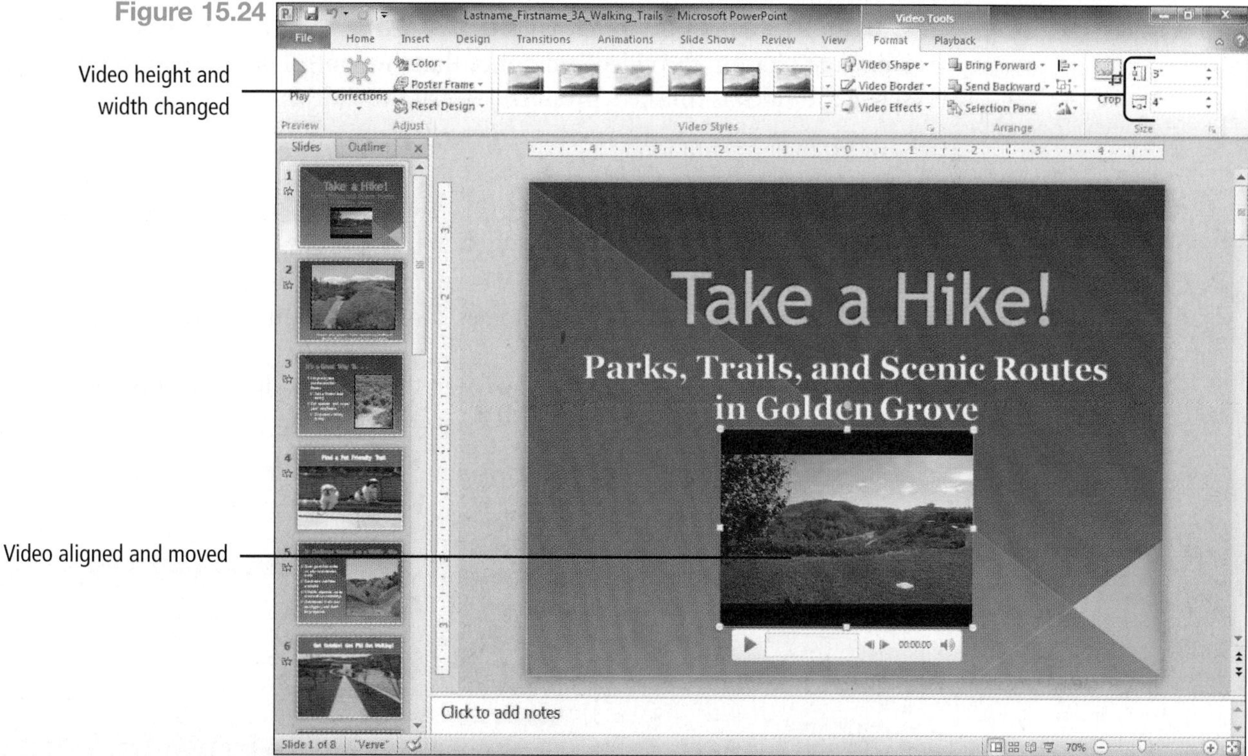

Figure 15.24

5 In the lower right corner of the PowerPoint window, in the **View** buttons, click the **Slide Show** button to display **Slide 1** in the slide show.

6 Point to the video to display the pointer, and then compare your screen with Figure 15.25.

When you point to the video during the slide show, the control panel displays.

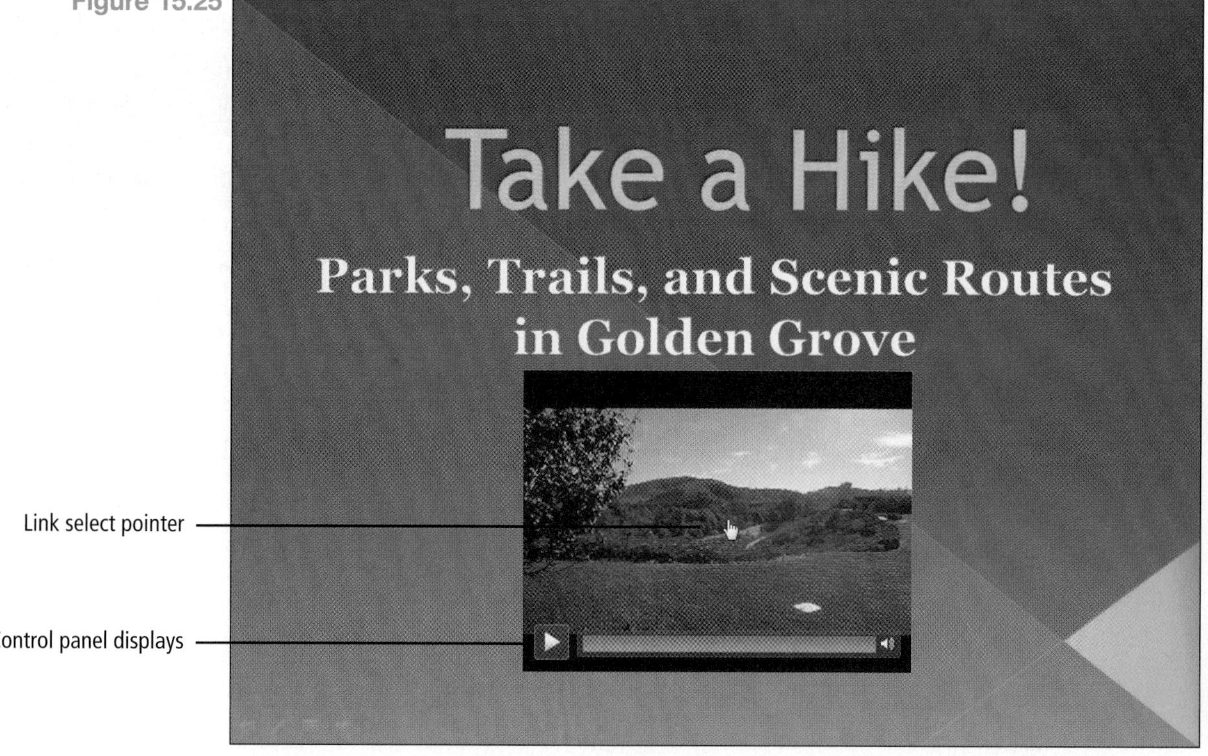

Figure 15.25

7 With the pointer displayed, click the mouse button to view the video. Move the pointer away from the video and notice that the control panel no longer displays. When the video is finished, press Esc to exit the slide show.

8 **Save** the presentation.

Activity 15.10 | Formatting a Video

You can apply styles and effects to a video and change the video shape and border. You can also recolor a video so that it coordinates with the presentation theme.

1 With **Slide 1** displayed, select the video. On the **Format tab**, in the **Video Styles group**, click the **More** button to display the **Video Styles** gallery.

2 Using the ScreenTips to view the style name, under **Moderate**, click the first style—**Compound Frame, Black**. Compare your screen with Figure 15.26.

Figure 15.26

3 In the **Video Styles group**, click the **Video Shape** button, and then under **Basic Shapes**, click the first shape—**Oval**. In the **Video Styles group**, click the **Video Border** button, and then in the third column, click the fifth color—**Blue-Gray, Background 2, Darker 25%**. In the **Video Styles group**, click the **Video Effects** button, point to **Bevel**, and then click the last bevel—**Art Deco**. Compare your screen with Figure 15.27.

You can format a video with any combination of styles and effects.

Figure 15.27

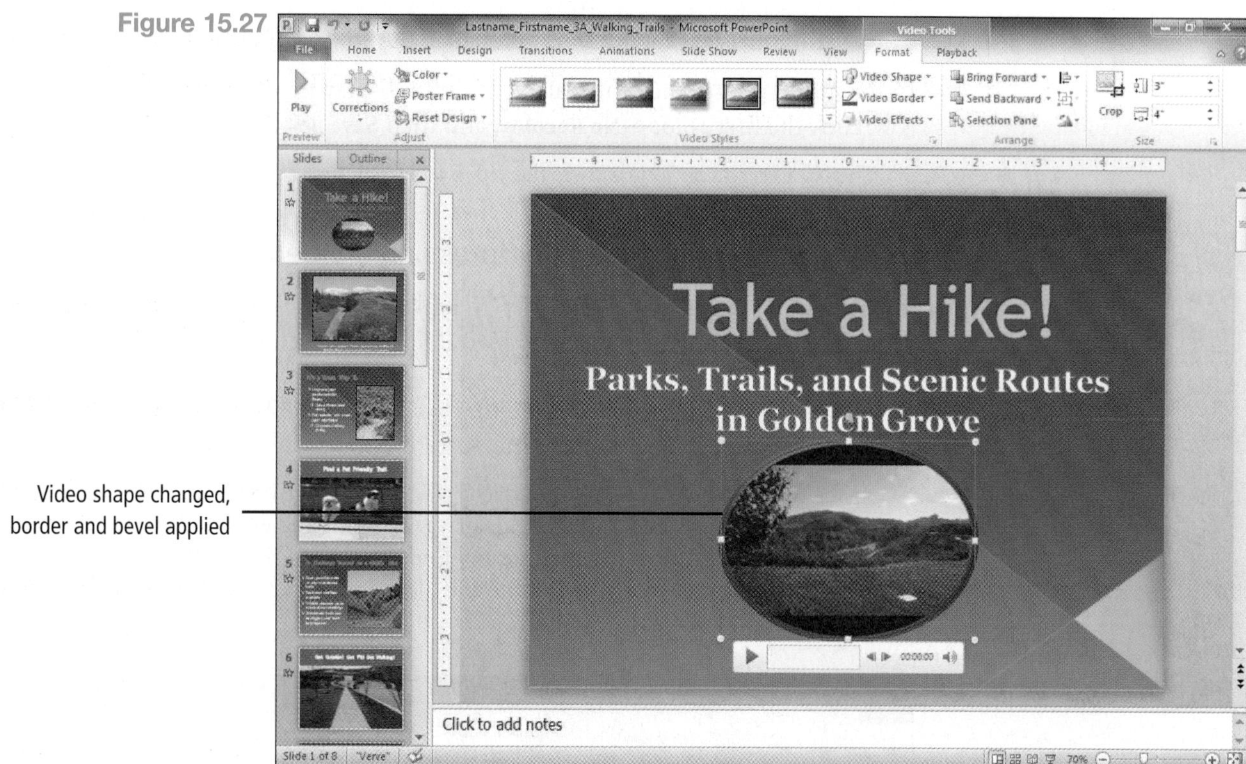

4 If necessary, select the video. On the **Format tab**, in the **Adjust group**, click the **Color** button to display the **Recolor** gallery.

The first row of the Recolor gallery displays options to recolor the video in grayscale, sepia, washout, or black and white variations. The remaining rows in the gallery display options to recolor the video in the theme colors.

5 In the **Recolor** gallery, in the second row, point to the first style—**Light Blue, Text color 2 Dark** and notice that Live Preview displays the video in the selected color. Compare your screen with Figure 15.28.

Figure 15.28

6 Click **Light Blue, Text color 2 Dark** to change the color of the video.

7 In the **Adjust group**, click the **Color** button to display the Recolor gallery. In the first row, click the first color—**No Recolor**, and then **Save** the presentation.

The No Recolor option restores the video to its original color.

Activity 15.11 | Editing and Compressing a Video

You can ***trim***—delete parts of a video to make it shorter—and you can compress a video file to reduce the file size of your PowerPoint presentation.

1 If necessary, select the video. On the **Playback tab**, in the **Editing group**, click the **Trim Video** button, and then compare your screen with Figure 15.29.

At the top of the displayed Trim Video dialog box, the file name and the video duration display. Below the video, a timeline displays with start and end markers indicating the video start and end time. Start Time and End Time boxes display the current start and end of the video. The Previous Frame and Next Frame buttons move the video forward and backward one frame at a time.

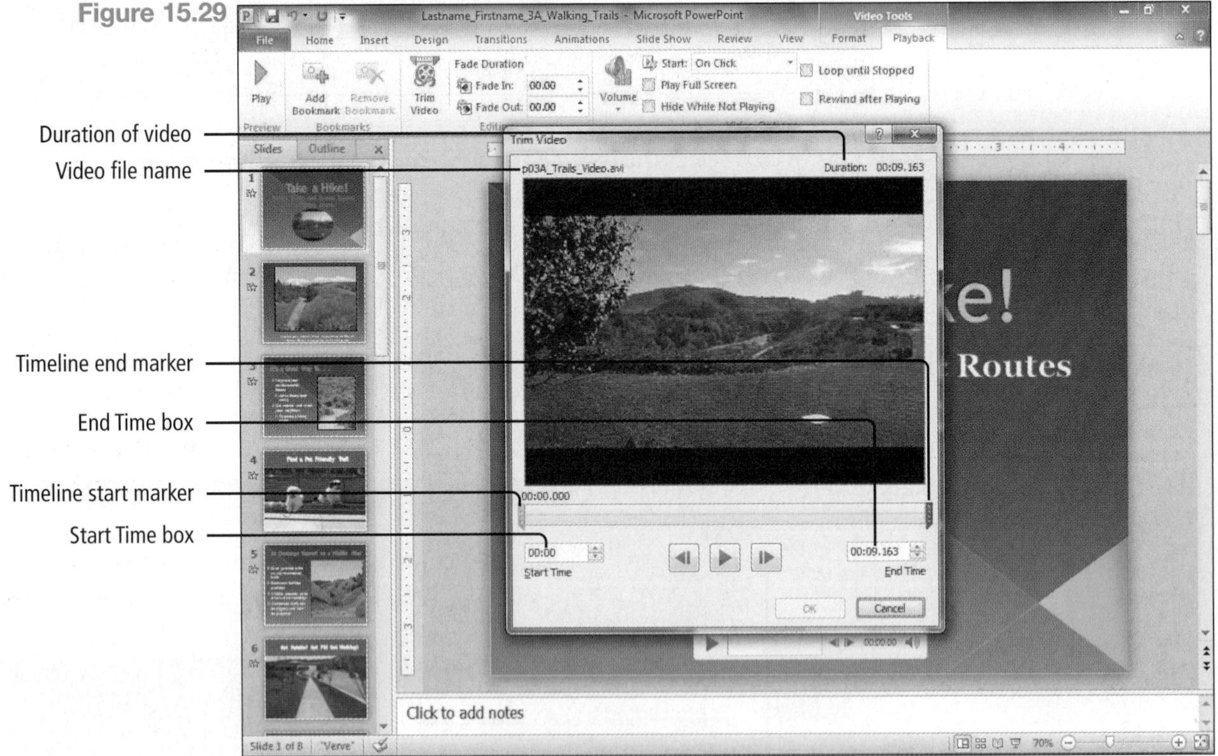

Figure 15.29

Another Way

Drag the red ending marking until its ScreenTip displays the ending time that you want; or type in the box.

2 Click in the **End Time** box, and then use the spin box arrows to set the End Time to **0:07.040**. Compare your screen with Figure 15.30.

The blue section of the timeline indicates the portion of the video that will play during the slide show. The gray section indicates the portion of the video that is trimmed.

Figure 15.30

3 Click **OK** to apply the trim settings.

4 Display **Backstage** view, and then on the **Info tab**, click the **Compress Media** button. Read the description of each video quality option, and then click **Low Quality.** Compare your screen with Figure 15.31.

The Compress Media dialog box displays the slide number on which the selected video is inserted, the video file name, the original size of the video file, and when compression is complete, the amount that the file size was reduced.

Figure 15.31

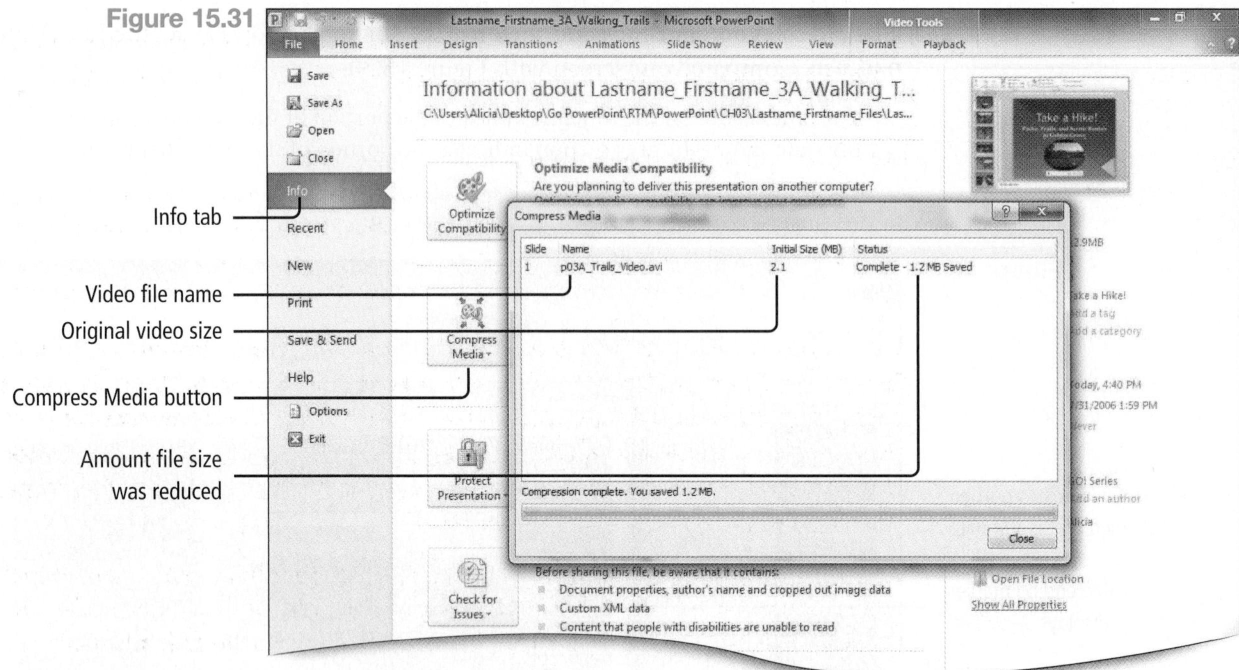

5 In the **Compress Media** dialog box, click **Close**, and then click the **Home tab** to return to **Slide 1**.

6 If necessary, select the video. On the **Playback tab**, in the **Video Options group**, click the **Start arrow**, and then click **Automatically** so that during the slide show, the video will begin automatically. Compare your screen with Figure 15.32.

Figure 15.32

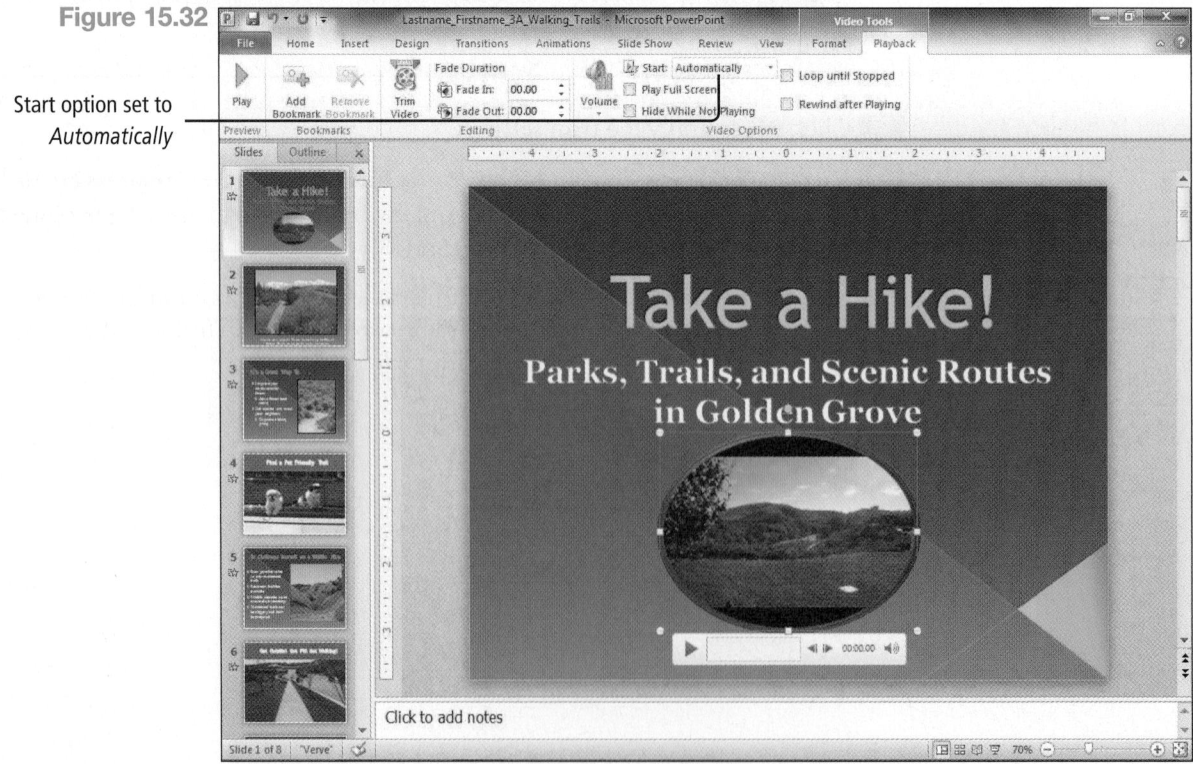

7 Click the **Slide Show tab**, in the **Start Slide Show group**, click the **From Beginning** button, and then view the slide show. Press Esc when the black slide displays.

Note | Your Video May Look Blurry

On playback, a compressed video may look slightly blurry. If you are certain that your presentation file will not be transmitted over the Internet, for example, in an e-mail message or in your learning management system, it is not necessary to compress the video.

8 On the **Insert tab**, in the **Text group**, click the **Header & Footer** button to display the **Header and Footer** dialog box. Click the **Notes and Handouts tab**. Under **Include on page**, select the **Date and time** check box, and then select **Update automatically**. If necessary, clear the **Header** check box, and then select the **Page number** and **Footer** check boxes. In the **Footer** box, using your own name, type **Lastname_Firstname_3A_Walking_Trails** and then click **Apply to All**.

9 Show the **Document Panel**. Replace the text in the **Author** box with your own firstname and lastname. In the **Subject** box, type your course name and section number, and in the **Keywords** box, type **trails, hiking Close** the **Document Information Panel.**

10 **Save** your presentation. Print **Handouts 4 Slides Horizontal**, or submit your presentation electronically as directed by your instructor.

11 **Close** the presentation and exit PowerPoint.

End You have completed Project 15A

Project 15B Summary and Analysis Presentation

Project Activities

In Activities 15.12 through 15.17, you will add a table and two charts to a presentation that Mindy Walker, Director of Parks and Recreation, is creating to inform the City Council about enrollment trends in Golden Grove recreation programs. Your completed presentation will look similar to Figure 15.33.

Project Files

For Project 1B, you will need the following file:

p03B_Recreation_Enrollment

You will save your presentation as:

Lastname_Firstname_3B_Recreation_Enrollment

Project Results

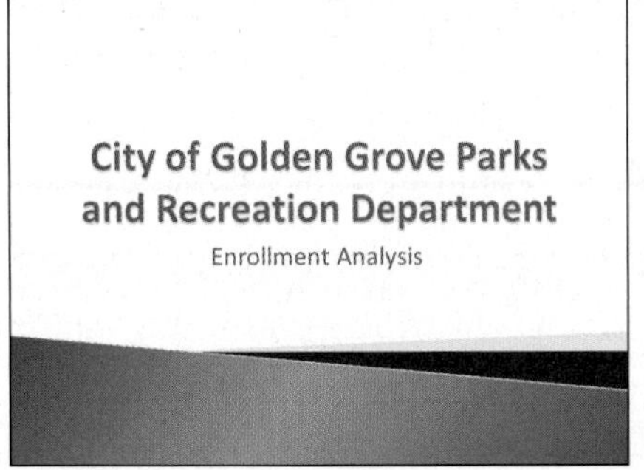

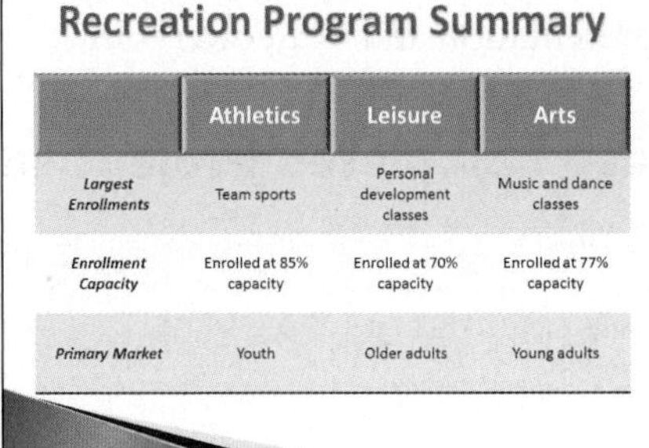

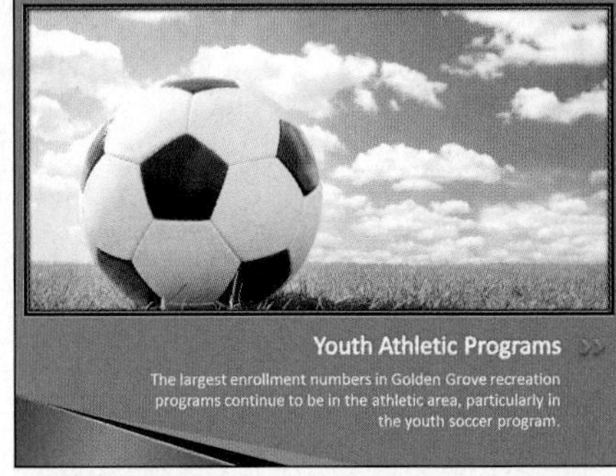

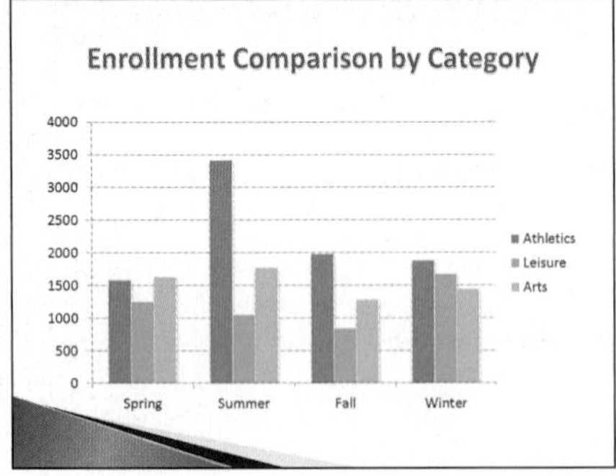

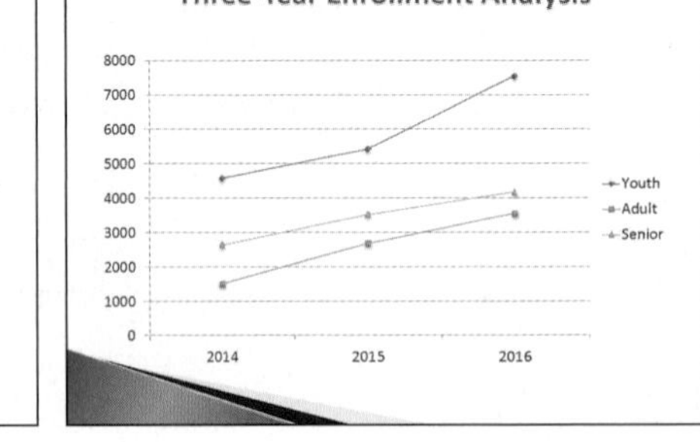

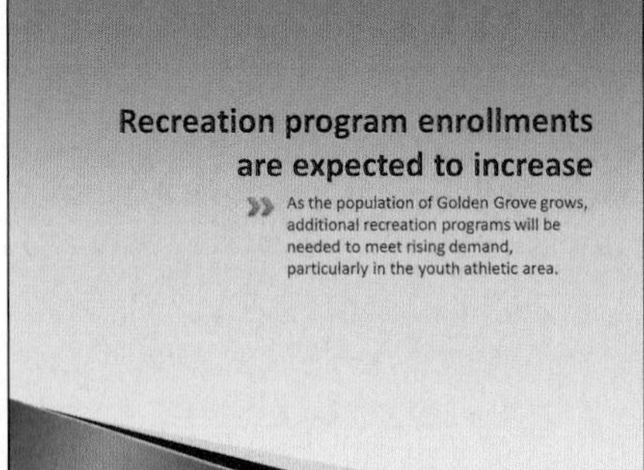

Figure 15.33
Project 15B Recreation Enrollment

Objective 4 | Create and Modify Tables

A ***table*** is a format for information that organizes and presents text and data in columns and rows. The intersection of a column and row is referred to as a ***cell*** and is the location in which you type text in a table.

Activity 15.12 | Creating a Table

There are several ways to insert a table in a PowerPoint slide. For example, you can use the Draw Table pointer, which is useful when the rows and columns contain cells of different sizes. Another way is to insert a slide with a Content Layout and then click the Insert Table button. Or, click the Insert tab and then click Table. In this activity, you will use a Content Layout to create a table.

1 **Start** PowerPoint. From your student files, open **p03B_Recreation_Enrollment**, and then **Save** the presentation in your **PowerPoint Chapter 15** folder as **Lastname_Firstname_3B_Recreation_Enrollment**

2 With **Slide 1** displayed, on the **Home tab**, in the **Slides group**, click the **New Slide** button to insert a slide with the **Title and Content** layout. In the title placeholder, type **Recreation Program Summary** and then **Center** the title.

3 In the content placeholder, click the **Insert Table** button to display the **Insert Table** dialog box. In the **Number of columns** box, type **3** and then press Tab. In the **Number of rows** box, type **2** and then compare your screen with Figure 15.34.

Here you enter the number of columns and rows that you want the table to contain.

Figure 15.34

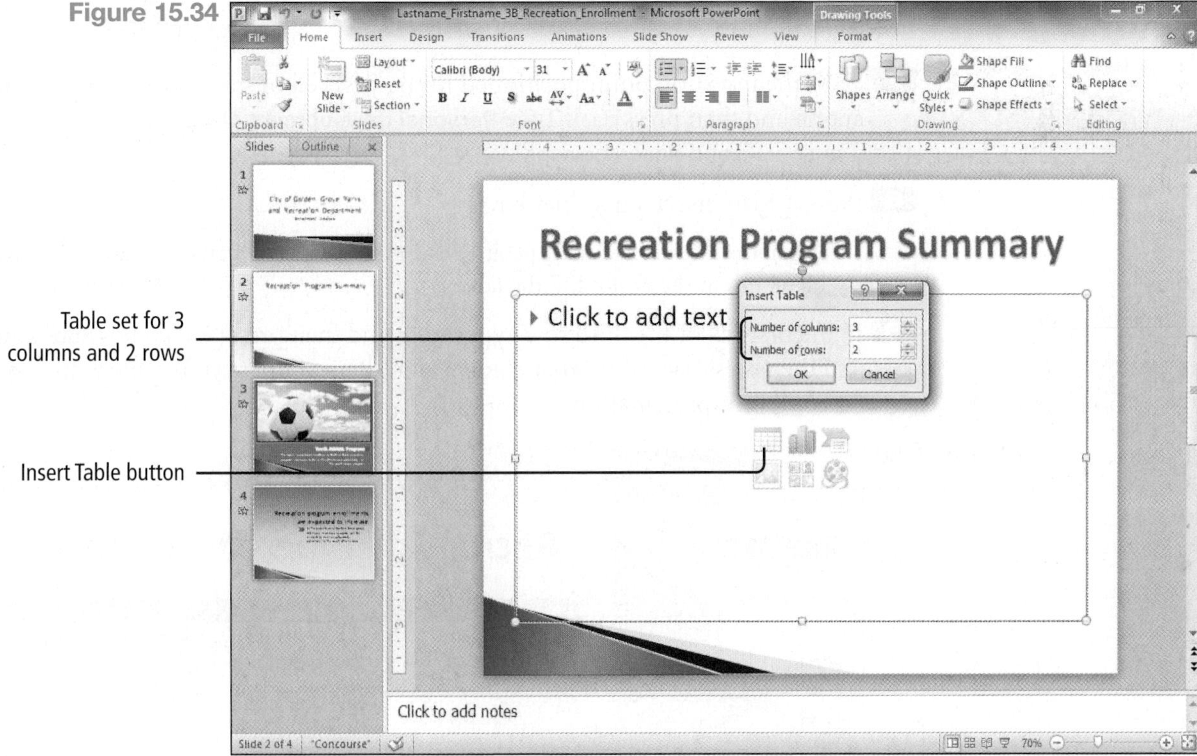

4 Click **OK** to create a table with three columns and two rows. Notice that the insertion point is blinking in the upper left cell of the table.

The table extends from the left side of the content placeholder to the right side, and the three columns are equal in width. By default, a style is applied to the table.

5 With the insertion point positioned in the first cell of the table, type **Athletics** and then press Tab.

Pressing Tab moves the insertion point to the next cell in the same row. If the insertion point is positioned in the last cell of a row, pressing Tab moves the insertion point to the first cell of the next row.

> **Alert! | Did You Press Enter Instead of Tab?**
>
> In a table, pressing Enter creates another line in the same cell. If you press Enter by mistake, you can remove the extra line by pressing Backspace.

6 With the insertion point positioned in the second cell of the first row, type **Leisure** and then press Tab. Type **Arts** and then press Tab to move the insertion point to the first cell in the second row. Compare your table with Figure 15.35.

Figure 15.35

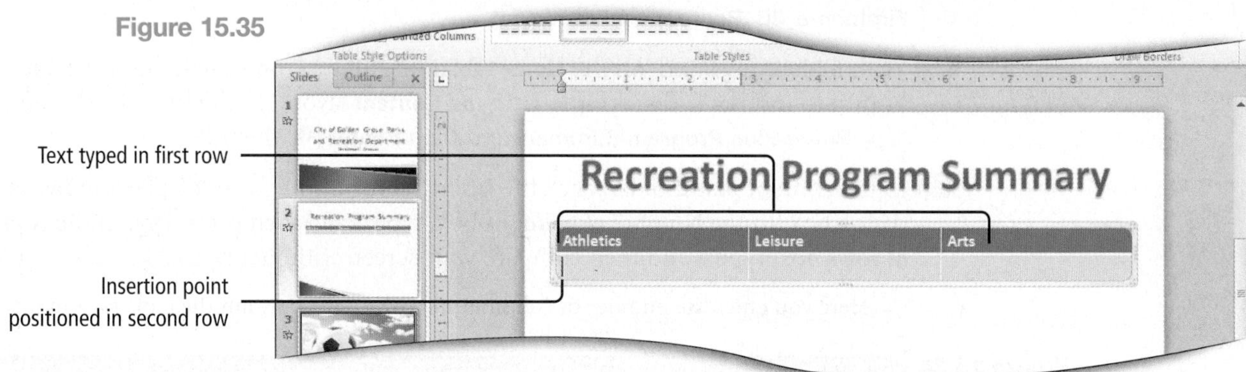

7 With the insertion point positioned in the first cell of the second row, type **Team sports** and then press Tab. Type **Personal development classes** and then press Tab. Type **Music and dance classes**

8 Press Tab to insert a new blank row.

When the insertion point is positioned in the last cell of a table, pressing Tab inserts a new blank row at the bottom of the table.

9 In the first cell of the third row, type **Youth** and then press Tab. Type **Older adults** and then press Tab. Type **Young adults** and then compare your table with Figure 15.36. **Save** your presentation.

Figure 15.36

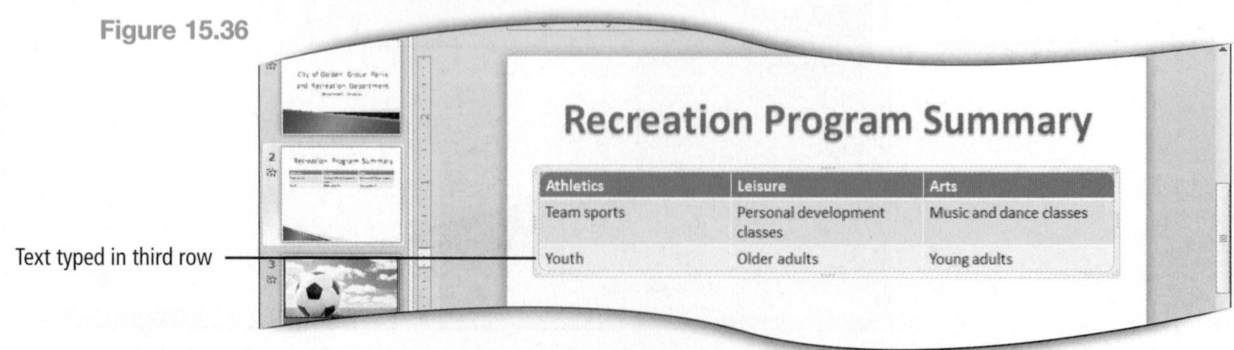

> **Alert! | Did You Add an Extra Row to the Table?**
>
> Recall that when the insertion point is positioned in the last cell of the table, pressing Tab inserts a new blank row. If you inadvertently inserted a blank row in the table, on the Quick Access Toolbar, click Undo.

Activity 15.13 | Modifying the Layout of a Table

You can modify the layout of a table by inserting or deleting rows and columns, changing the alignment of the text in a cell, adjusting the height and width of the entire table or selected rows and columns, and by merging multiple cells into one cell.

1 Click in any cell in the first column, and then click the **Layout tab**. In the **Rows & Columns group**, click the **Insert Left** button.

A new first column is inserted and the width of the columns is adjusted so that all four columns are the same width.

2 In the *second* row, click in the first cell, and then type **Largest Enrollments**

3 In the third row, click in the first cell, and then type **Primary Market** Compare your table with Figure 15.37.

Figure 15.37

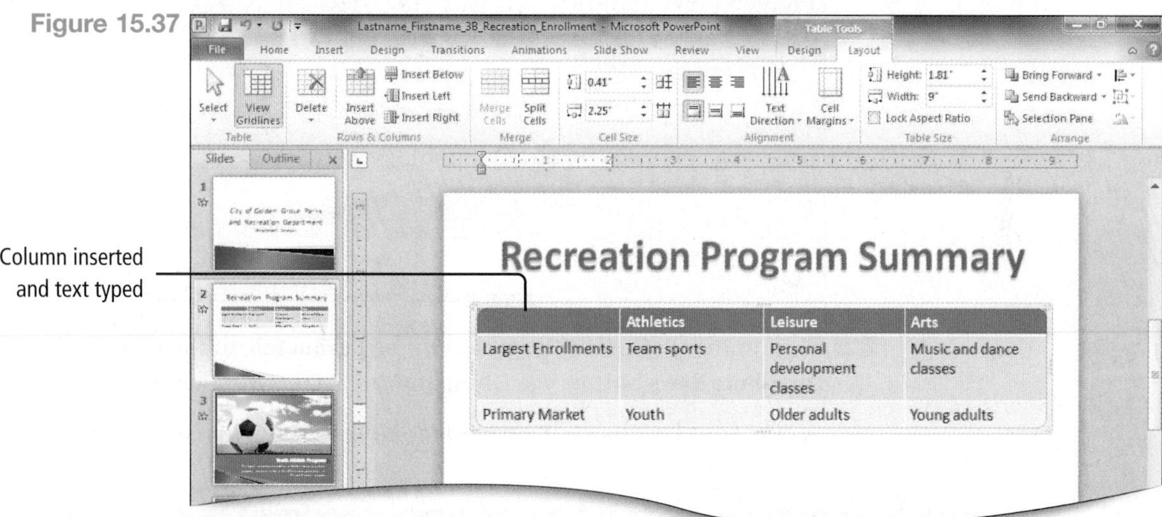

4 With the insertion point positioned in the third row, on the **Layout tab**, in the **Rows & Columns group**, click the **Insert Above** button to insert a new third row. In the first cell, type **Enrollment Capacity** and then press Tab. Type the remaining three entries, pressing Tab to move from cell to cell: **Enrolled at 85% capacity** and **Enrolled at 70% capacity** and **Enrolled at 77% capacity**

5 At the center of the lower border surrounding the table, point to the cluster of four dots—the sizing handle—to display the ↕ pointer. Compare your screen with Figure 15.38.

Figure 15.38

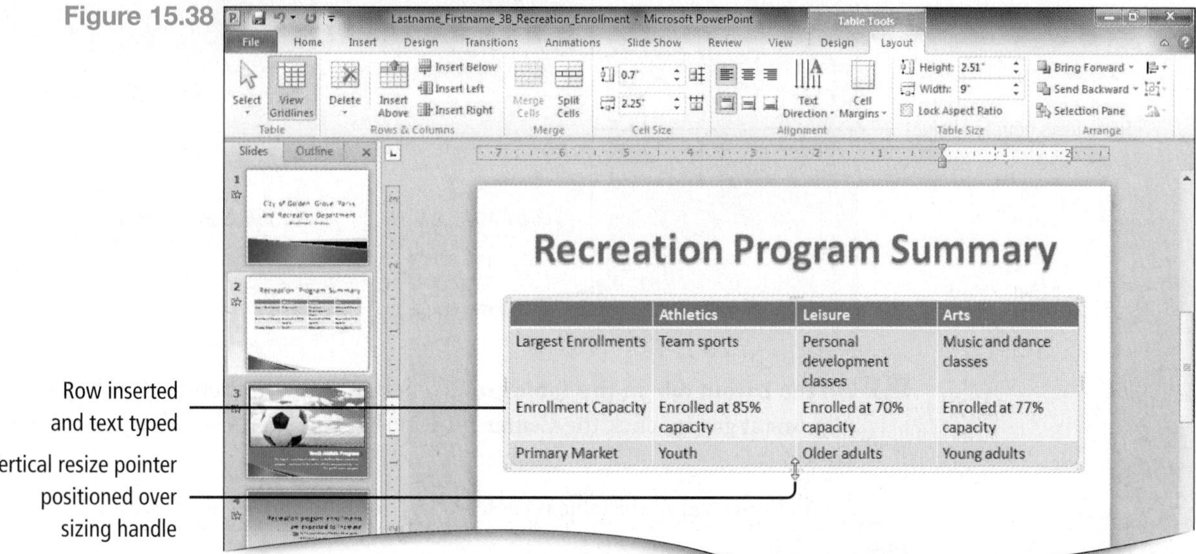

6 Drag down to resize the table until the lower left corner of the table outline is just above the graphic in the lower left corner of the slide. Compare your screen with Figure 15.39.

Figure 15.39

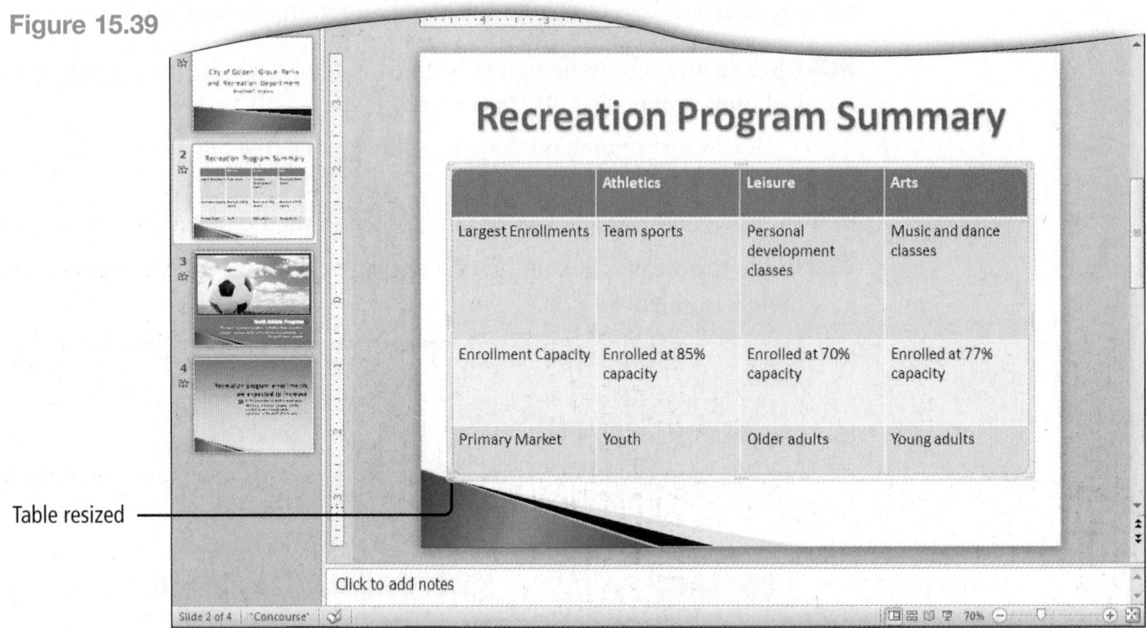

7 Click in the first cell of the table. On the **Layout tab**, in the **Cell Size group**, click the **Distribute Rows** button. Compare your table with Figure 15.40.

The Distribute Rows command adjusts the height of the rows in the table so that they are equal.

Figure 15.40

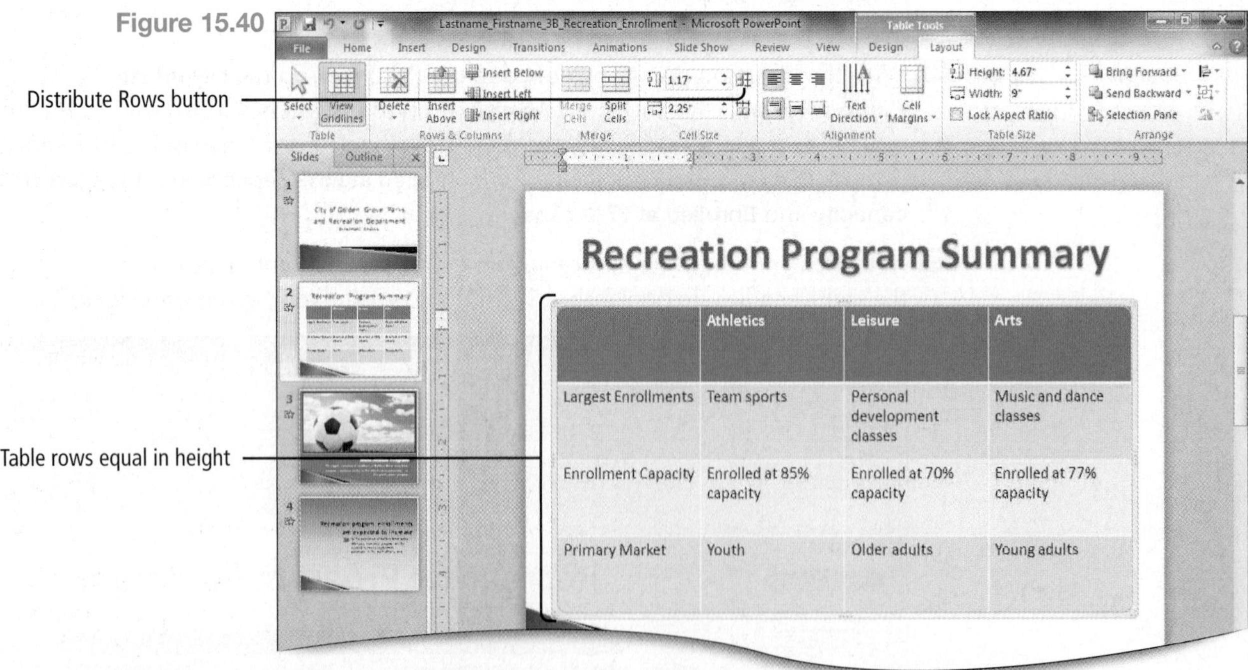

8 On the **Layout tab**, in the **Table group**, click **Select**, and then click **Select Table**. In the **Alignment group**, click the **Center** button, and then click the **Center Vertically** button.

All of the text in the table is centered horizontally and vertically within the cells.

9 **Save** your presentation.

> **More Knowledge | Deleting Rows and Columns**
>
> To delete a row or column from a table, click in the row or column that you want to delete. Click the Layout tab, and then in the Rows & Columns group, click Delete. In the displayed list, click Delete Columns or Delete Rows.

Activity 15.14 | Modifying a Table Design

You can modify the design of a table by applying a ***table style***. A table style formats the entire table so that it is consistent with the presentation theme. There are color categories within the table styles—Best Match for Document, Light, Medium, and Dark.

1. Click in any cell in the table. In the **Table Tools**, click the **Design tab**, and then in the **Table Styles group**, click the **More** button. In the displayed **Table Styles** gallery, point to several of the styles to view the Live Preview of the style.
2. Under **Medium**, scroll as necessary, and then in the third row, click the third button—**Medium Style 3 – Accent 2**—to apply the style to the table.
3. On the **Design tab**, in the **Table Style Options group**, clear the **Banded Rows** check box. Notice that each row except the header row displays in the same color.

   The check boxes in the Table Style Options group control where Table Style formatting is applied.
4. Select the **Banded Rows** check box.
5. Move the pointer outside of the table so that it is positioned to the left of the first row in the table to display the pointer, as shown in Figure 15.41.

Figure 15.41

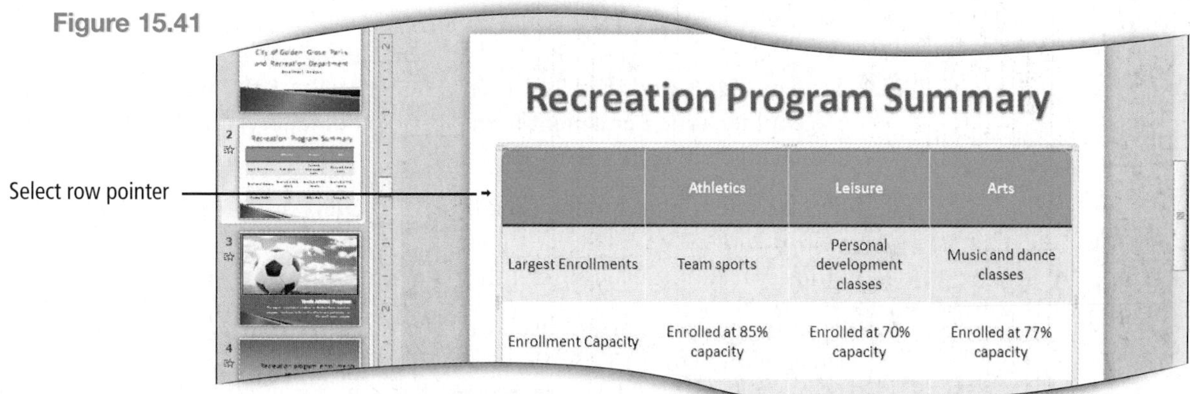

6. With the pointer pointing to the first row in the table, click the mouse button to select the entire row so that you can apply formatting to the selection. Move the pointer into the selected row, and then right-click to display the Mini toolbar and shortcut menu. On the Mini toolbar, change the **Font Size** to **28**.
7. With the first row still selected, in the **Table Tools**, on the **Design tab**, in the **Table Styles group**, click the **Effects** button. Point to **Cell Bevel**, and then under **Bevel**, click the first bevel—**Circle**.
8. Position the pointer above the first column to display the pointer, and then right-click to select the first column and display the shortcut menu. Click **Bold** and **Italic**.
9. Click in a blank area of the slide, and then compare your slide with Figure 15.42. **Save** the presentation.

Figure 15.42

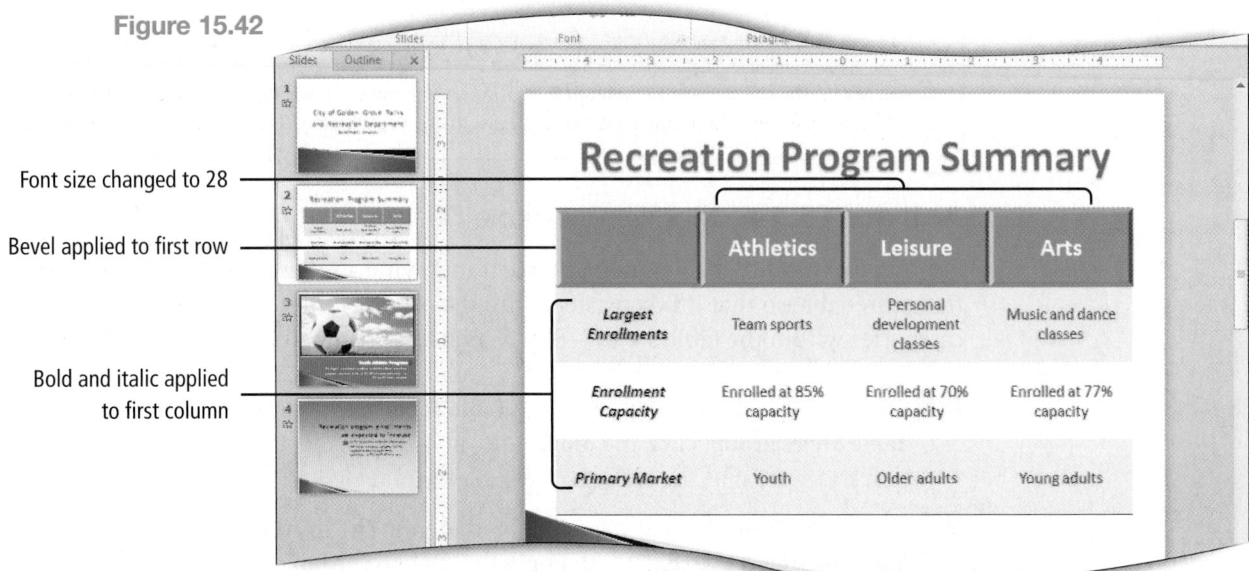

Objective 5 | Create and Modify Charts

A ***chart*** is a graphic representation of numeric data. Commonly used chart types include bar and column charts, pie charts, and line charts. A chart that you create in PowerPoint is stored in an Excel worksheet that is incorporated into the PowerPoint file.

Activity 15.15 | Creating a Column Chart and Applying a Chart Style

A ***column chart*** is useful for illustrating comparisons among related numbers. In this activity, you will create a column chart that compares enrollment in each category of recreation activities by season.

1. Display **Slide 3**, and then add a **New Slide** with the **Title and Content** layout. In the title placeholder, type **Enrollment Comparison by Category** and then **Center** the title and change the **Font Size** to **36**.
2. In the content placeholder, click the **Insert Chart** button to display the **Insert Chart** dialog box. Notice the types of charts that you can insert in your presentation. If necessary, on the left side of the dialog box, click Column.
3. Point to the first chart to display the ScreenTip *Clustered Column*. Compare your screen with Figure 15.43.

Figure 15.43

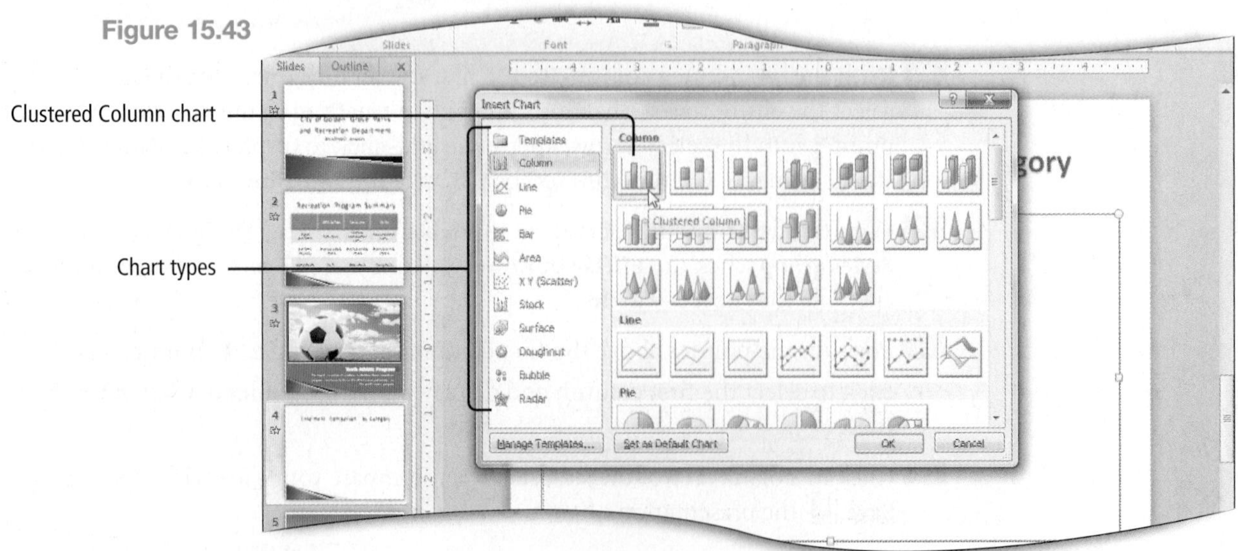

4 Click **Clustered Column**. Click **OK**, and then compare your screen with Figure 15.44.

The PowerPoint window displays a column chart on one side of your screen. On the other side of your screen, an Excel worksheet displays columns and rows. A cell is identified by the intersecting column letter and row number, forming the ***cell reference***.

The worksheet contains sample data in a data range outlined in blue, from which the chart in the PowerPoint window is generated. The column headings—*Series 1*, *Series 2*, and *Series 3* display in the chart ***legend*** and the row headings—*Category 1*, *Category 2*, *Category 3*, and *Category 4*—display as ***category labels***. The legend identifies the patterns or colors that are assigned to the data series in the chart. The category labels display along the bottom of the chart to identify the categories of data.

Figure 15.44

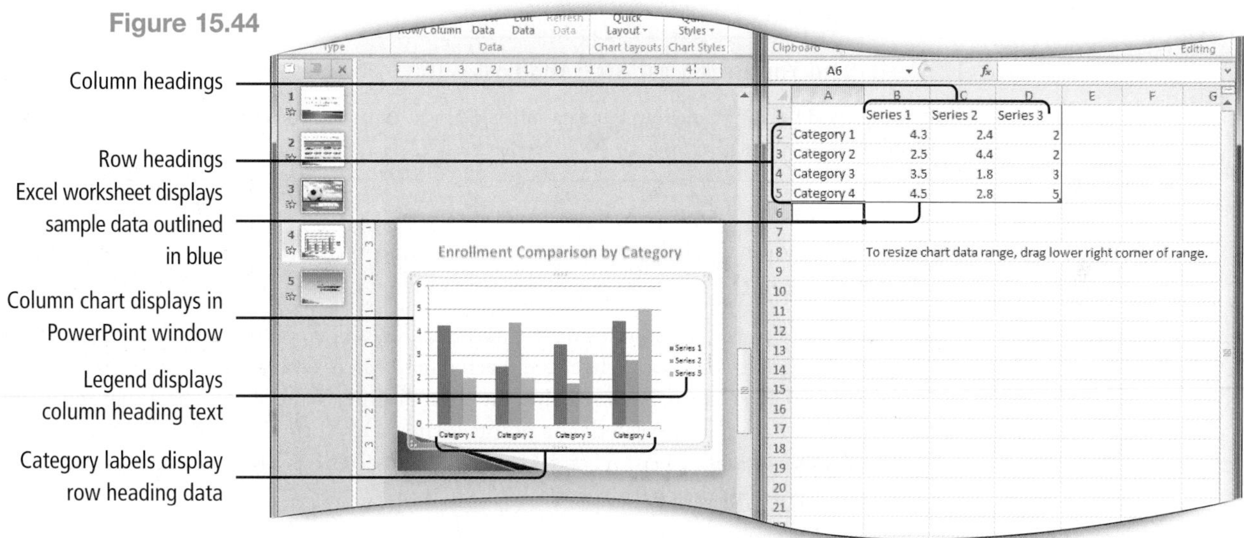

5 In the Excel window, click in cell **B1**, which contains the text *Series 1*. Type **Athletics** and then press Tab to move to cell **C1**.

The chart legend is updated to reflect the change in the Excel worksheet.

6 In cell **C1**, which contains the text *Series 2*, type **Leisure** and then press Tab to move to cell **D1**. Type **Arts** and then press Tab. Notice that cell **A2**, which contains the text *Category 1*, is selected. Compare your screen with Figure 15.45.

The blue box outlining the range of cells defines the area in which you are entering data. When you press Tab in the rightmost cell, the first cell in the next row becomes active.

Figure 15.45

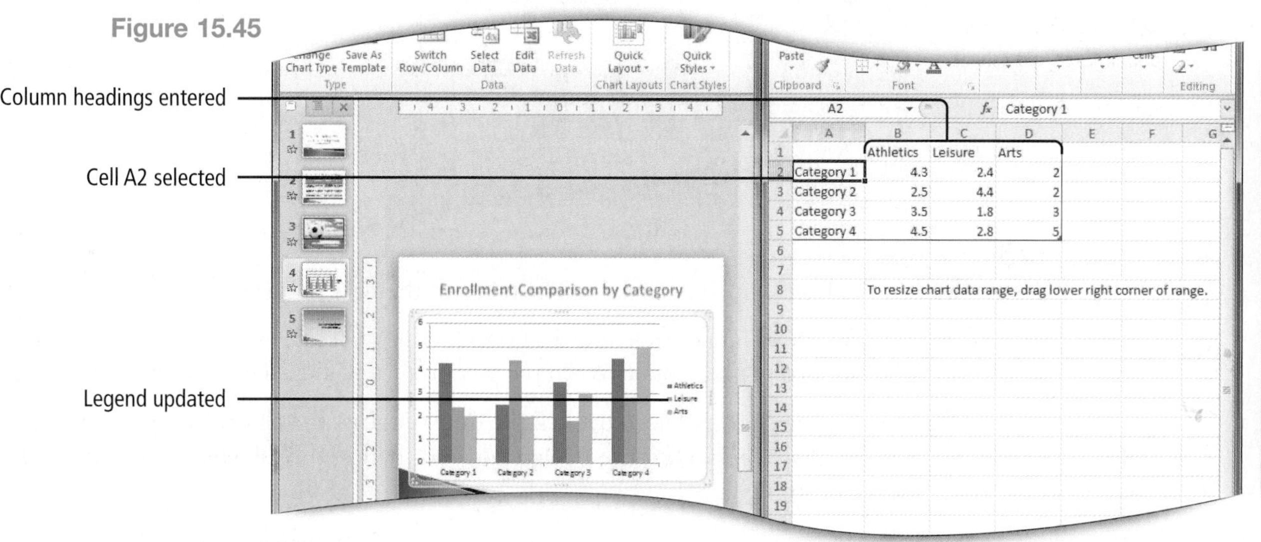

7 Beginning in cell **A2**, type the following data, pressing Tab to move from cell to cell.

	Athletics	Leisure	Arts
Spring	**1588**	**1263**	**1639**
Summer	**3422**	**1058**	**1782**
Fall	**1987**	**852**	**1293**
Winter	**1889**	**1674**	

8 In cell **D5**, which contains the value 5, type **1453** and then press Enter.

Pressing Enter in the last cell of the blue outlined area maintains the existing data range.

> **Alert! | Did You Press Tab After the Last Entry?**
>
> If you pressed Tab after entering the data in cell D5, you expanded the chart range. In the Excel window, click Undo.

9 Compare your worksheet and your chart with Figure 15.46. Correct any typing errors by clicking in the cell that you want to change, and then retype the data.

Each of the 12 cells containing the numeric data that you entered is a ***data point***—a value that originates in a worksheet cell. Each data point is represented in the chart by a ***data marker***—a column, bar, area, dot, pie slice, or other symbol in a chart that represents a single data point. Related data points form a ***data series***; for example, there is a data series for *Athletics*, *Leisure*, and *Arts*. Each data series has a unique color or pattern represented in the chart legend.

Figure 15.46

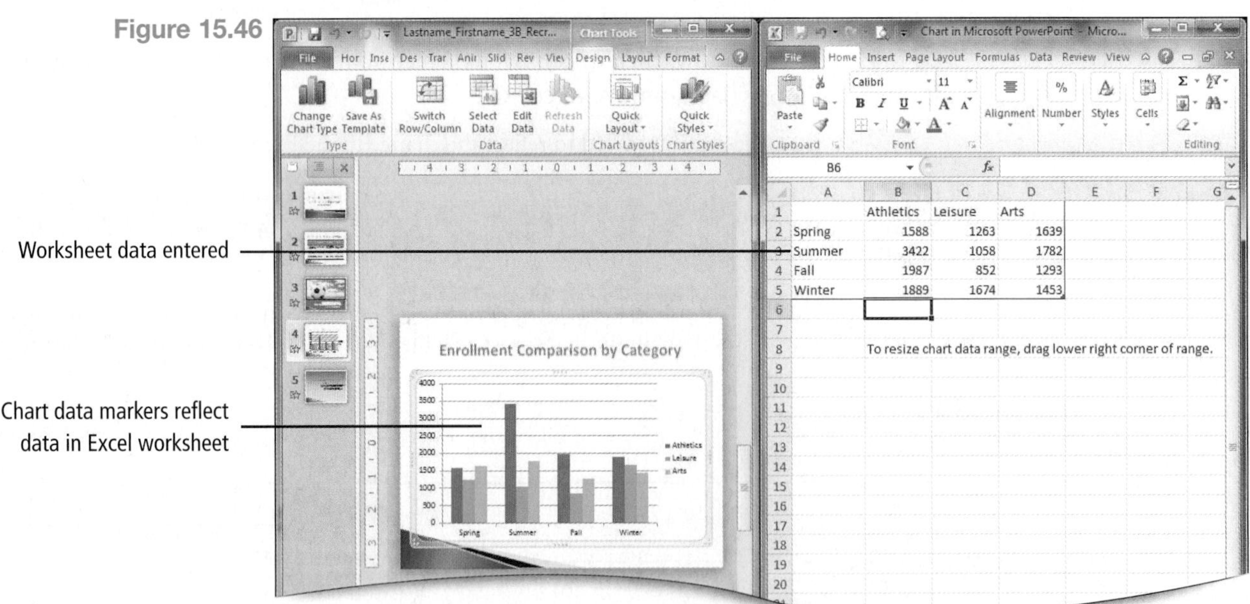

10 In the Excel window, click the **File tab**, and then click **Close**.

You are not prompted to save the Excel worksheet because the worksheet data is a part of the PowerPoint presentation. When you save the presentation, the Excel data is saved with it.

11 Be sure the chart is selected; click the outer edge of the chart if necessary to select it. In the **Chart Tools**, click the **Design tab**, and then in the **Chart Styles group**, click the **More** button.

12 In the **Chart Styles** gallery, the chart styles are numbered sequentially. Use ScreenTips to display the style numbers. Click **Style 10** to apply the style to the chart.

13 **Save** your presentation.

> **More Knowledge | Editing the Chart Data After Closing Excel**
>
> You can redisplay the Excel worksheet and make changes to the data after you have closed Excel. To do so, in PowerPoint, click the chart to select it, and then on the Design tab in the Data group, click Edit Data.

Activity 15.16 | Creating a Line Chart and Deleting Chart Data

To analyze and compare annual data over a three-year period, the presentation requires an additional chart. Recall that there are a number of different types of charts that you can insert in a PowerPoint presentation. In this activity, you will create a ***line chart***, which is commonly used to illustrate trends over time.

1 With **Slide 4** displayed, add a **New Slide** with the **Title and Content** layout. In the title placeholder, type **Three-Year Enrollment Analysis** and then **Center** the title and change the **Font Size** to **36**.

2 In the content placeholder, click the **Insert Chart** button. On the left side of the displayed **Insert Chart** dialog box, click **Line**, and then on the right, under **Line**, click the fourth chart—**Line with Markers**. Click **OK**.

3 In the Excel worksheet, click in cell **B1**, which contains the text *Series 1*. Type **Youth** and then press Tab. Type **Adult** and then press Tab. Type **Senior** and then press Tab.

4 Beginning in cell **A2**, type the following data, pressing Tab to move from cell to cell. If you make any typing errors, click in the cell that you want to change, and then retype the data.

	Youth	Adult	Senior
2014	**4586**	**1534**	**2661**
2015	**5422**	**2699**	**3542**
2016	**7565**	**3572**	**4183**

5 In the Excel window, position the pointer over **row heading 5** so that the pointer displays. Compare your screen with Figure 15.47.

Figure 15.47

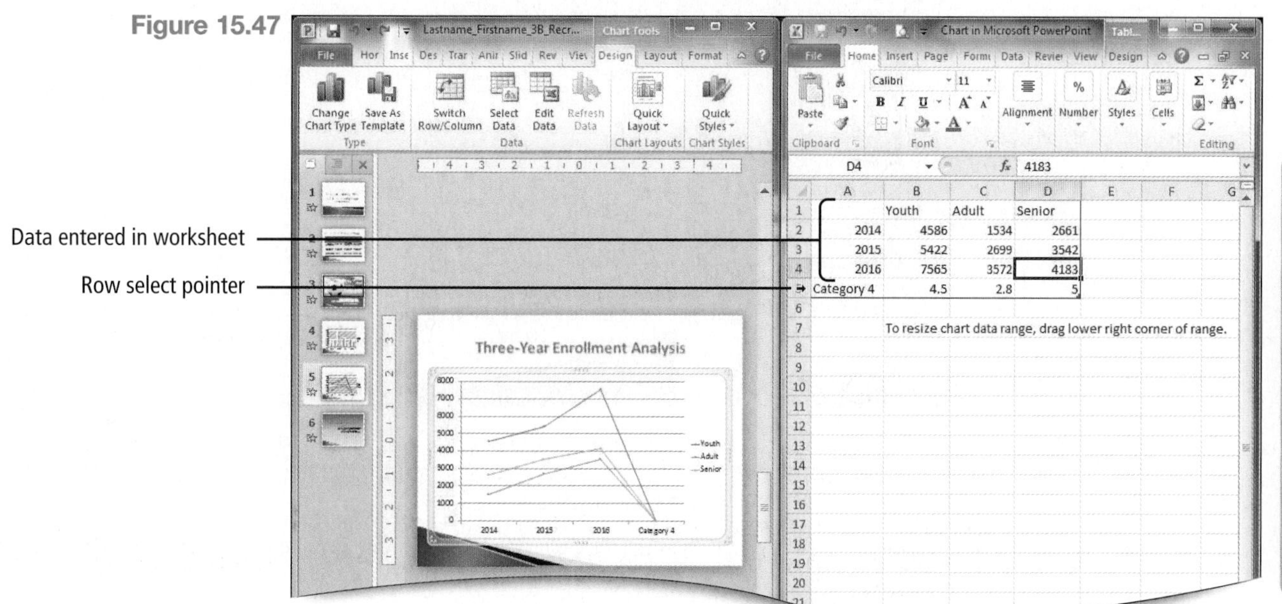

6 With the [pointer icon] pointer displayed, *right-click* to select the row and display the shortcut menu. On the shortcut menu, click **Delete** to delete the extra row from the worksheet, and then compare your screen with Figure 15.48.

The data in the worksheet contains four columns and four rows, and the blue outline defining the chart data range is resized. You must delete columns and rows that you do not want to include in the chart. You can add additional rows and columns by typing column and row headings and then entering additional data. When data is typed in cells adjacent to the chart range, the range is resized to include the new data.

Figure 15.48

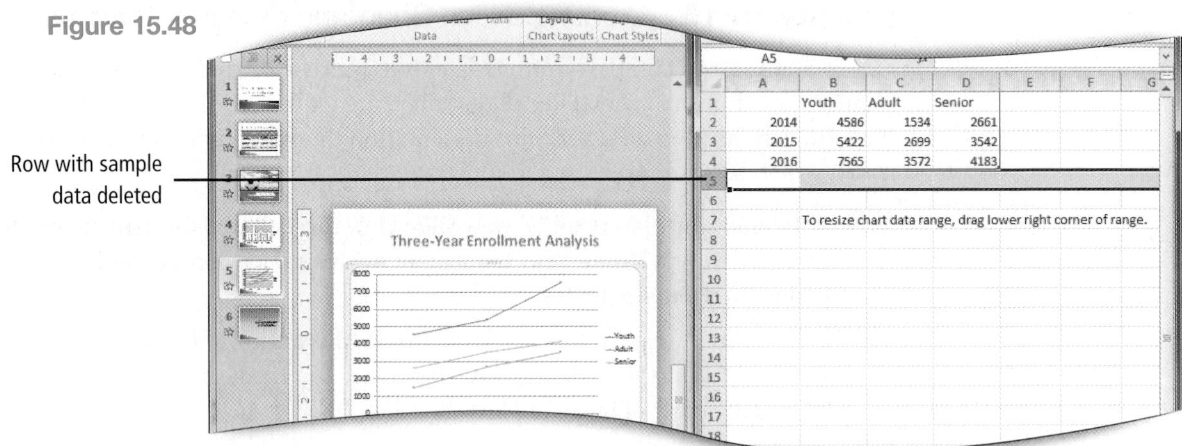

7 **Close** [Close button] the Excel window. In the **Chart Styles group**, click the **More** button [More button]. In the **Chart Styles** gallery, click **Style 26**, and then compare your slide with Figure 15.49. **Save** [Save button] your presentation.

Figure 15.49

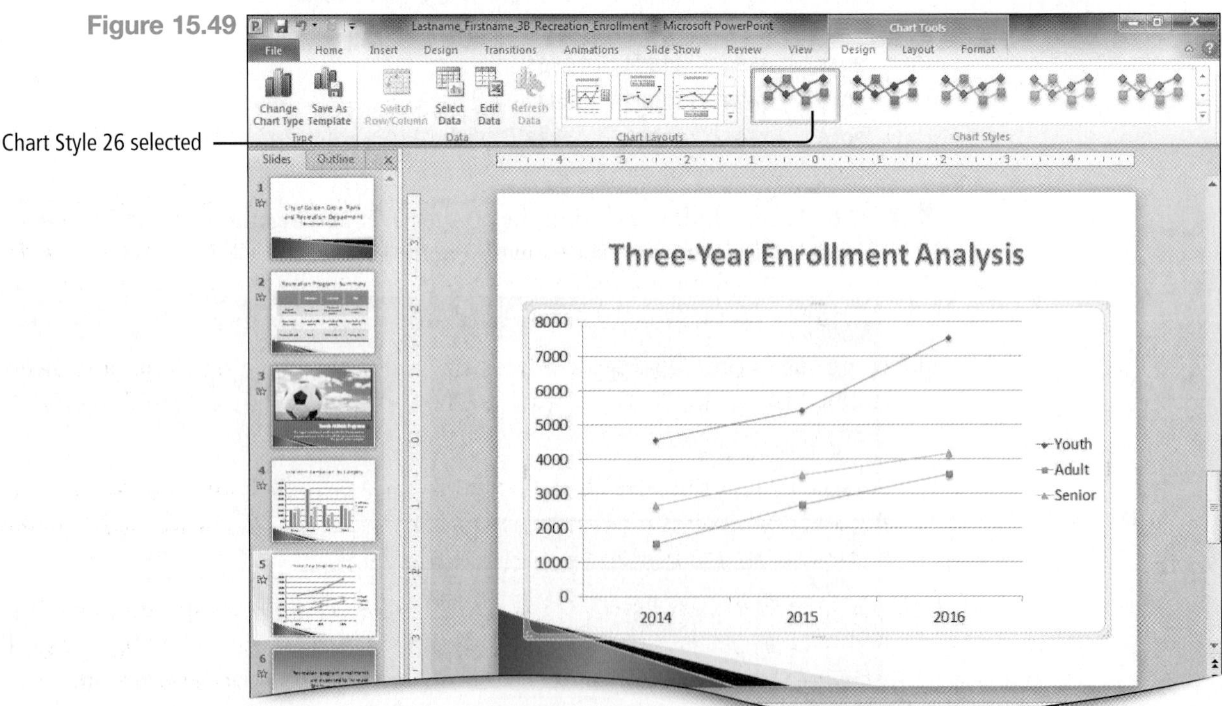

> **More Knowledge | Deleting Columns**
>
> To delete a worksheet column, position the pointer over the column letter that you want to select so that the [pointer icon] pointer displays. Right-click to select the column and display the shortcut menu. Click Delete.

Activity 15.17 | Animating a Chart

1 Display **Slide 4**, and then click the column chart to select it. On the **Animations tab**, in the **Animation group**, click the **More** button, and then under **Entrance**, click **Split**.

2 In the **Animation group**, click the **Effect Options** button, and then under **Sequence**, click **By Series**. Compare your screen with Figure 15.50.

The By Series option displays the chart one data series at a time, and the numbers 1, 2, 3, and 4 to the left of the chart indicate the four parts of the chart animation sequence. The chart animation sequence includes the background, followed by the Athletics data series for each season, and then the Leisure series, and then the Arts series.

Figure 15.50

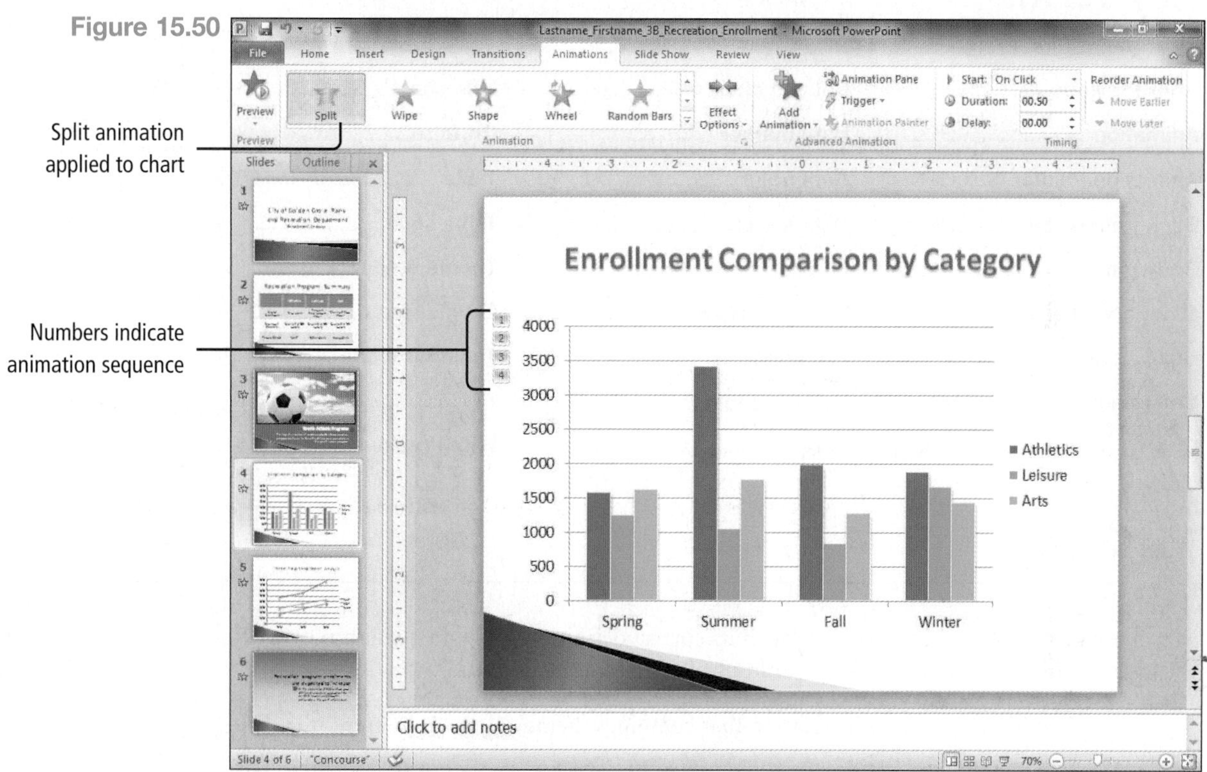

3 Click the **Slide Show tab**. In the **Start Slide Show group**, click **From Current Slide** to view the animation on **Slide 4**. Press Spacebar to display the legend and labels. Press Spacebar again to display the *Athletics* data.

4 Continue to press Spacebar to advance through the remaining animation effects. After the animations for Slide 4 are complete, press Esc to end the slide show and return to the presentation.

5 Insert a **Header & Footer** for the **Notes and Handouts**. Include the **Date and time updated automatically**, the **Page number**, and a **Footer** with the file name **Lastname_Firstname_3B_Recreation_Enrollment**

6 Show the **Document Panel**. Replace the text in the **Author** box with your own firstname and lastname. In the **Subject** box, type your course name and section number, and in the **Keywords** box, type **enrollment, recreation Close** the **Document Information Panel**.

7 **Save** your presentation. Print **Handouts 6 Slides Horizontal**, or submit your presentation electronically as directed by your instructor. **Close** the presentation and exit PowerPoint.

End **You have completed Project 15B**

Content-Based Assessments

Summary

In this chapter, you formatted a presentation by applying background styles, inserting pictures on slide backgrounds, and changing the theme fonts. You enhanced your presentation by inserting video, applying animation effects, and by changing effect and timing options. You practiced creating tables to present information in an organized manner, and you used charts to visually represent data.

Key Terms

After Previous 862	**Column chart** 880	**Line chart** 883
Animation 858	**Data marker** 882	**On Click**..........................862
Animation Painter..........864	**Data point** 882	**Table** 875
Background style 852	**Data series** 882	**Table style** 879
Body font.........................851	**Emphasis effect** 858	**Theme colors** 851
Category label 881	**Entrance effect**..............858	**Theme font** 851
Cell..................................875	**Exit effect** 858	**Timing options** 861
Cell reference 881	**Headings font** 851	**Trim** 870
Chart 880	**Legend**...........................881	**With Previous** 862

Matching

Match each term in the second column with its correct definition in the first column by writing the letter of the term on the blank line in front of the correct definition.

____ 1. A slide background fill variation that combines theme colors in different intensities.
____ 2. A theme that determines the font applied to two types of slide text—headings and body.
____ 3. Of the two types of fonts in the theme font, the type that is applied to slide titles.
____ 4. Of the two types of fonts in the theme font, the type that is applied to all slide text except titles.
____ 5. A visual or sound effect added to an object or text on a slide.
____ 6. Animations that bring a slide element onto the screen.
____ 7. Animation that emphasizes an object or text that is already displayed.
____ 8. Animation that moves an object or text off the screen.
____ 9. A format for information that organizes and presents text and data in columns and rows.
____ 10. The intersection of a column and row.
____ 11. Formatting applied to an entire table so that it is consistent with the presentation theme.
____ 12. A graphic representation of numeric data.
____ 13. A type of chart used to compare data.
____ 14. A combination of the column letter and row number identifying a cell.
____ 15. A chart element that identifies the patterns or colors that are assigned to the each data series in the chart.

A Animation
B Background style
C Body font
D Cell
E Cell reference
F Chart
G Column chart
H Emphasis effect
I Entrance effect
J Exit effect
K Headings font
L Legend
M Table
N Table style
O Theme font

Content-Based Assessments

Multiple Choice

Circle the correct answer.

1. The set of coordinating colors applied to the backgrounds, objects, and text in a presentation is called:
   A. theme colors **B.** colors set **C.** coordinating colors
2. The command that is used to prevent background graphics from displaying on a slide is:
   A. Hide Background Styles **B.** Cover Background Graphics **C.** Hide Background Graphics
3. Animation options that control when animated items display in the animation sequence are called:
   A. timing options **B.** effect options **C.** sequence options
4. A feature that copies animation settings from one object to another is:
   A. copy **B.** format painter **C.** animation painter
5. The action of deleting parts of a video to make it shorter is referred to as:
   A. edit **B.** trim **C.** crop
6. A chart element that identifies categories of data is a:
   A. data marker **B.** category label **C.** category marker
7. A column, bar, area, dot, pie slice, or other symbol in a chart that represents a single data point is a:
   A. data marker **B.** data point **C.** data series
8. A chart value that originates in a worksheet cell is a:
   A. data marker **B.** data point **C.** data series
9. A group of related data points is called a:
   A. data marker **B.** data point **C.** data series
10. A type of chart that shows trends over time is a:
    A. pie chart **B.** column chart **C.** line chart

Content-Based Assessments

Apply **15A** skills from these Objectives:

1. Customize Slide Backgrounds and Themes
2. Animate a Slide Show
3. Insert a Video

Skills Review | Project 15C Lake

In the following Skills Review, you will format a presentation by applying slide background styles, colors, pictures, and animation. Your completed presentation will look similar to Figure 15.51.

Project Files

For Project 15C, you will need the following files:

p03C_Lake
p03C_Scenery
p03C_Lake_Video

You will save your presentation as:

Lastname_Firstname_3C_Lake

Project Results

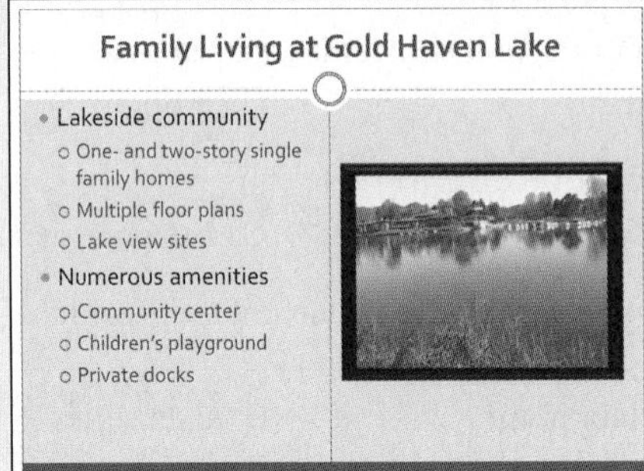

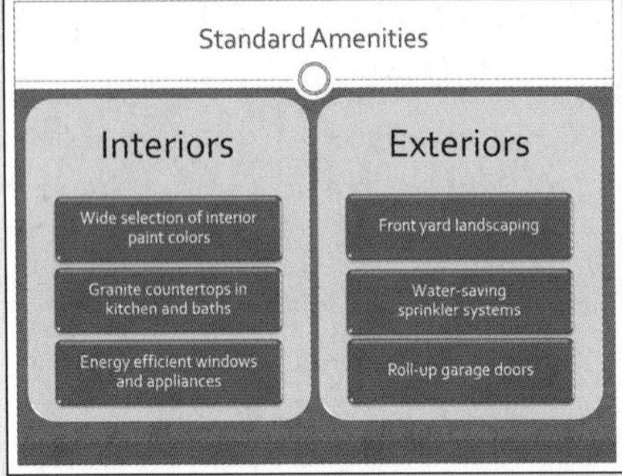

Figure 15.51

(Project 15C Lake continues on the next page)

Skills Review | Project 15C Lake (continued)

1 **Start** PowerPoint, from your student files open **p03C_Lake**, and then **Save** the presentation in your **PowerPoint Chapter 15** folder as **Lastname_Firstname_3C_Lake**

a. On the **Design tab**, in the **Themes group**, click the **Colors** button, and then click **Aspect** to change the theme colors. On the **Design tab**, in the **Themes group**, click the **Fonts** button, and then click **Module** to change the theme fonts.

b. Display **Slide 2**, and then on the **Home tab**, in the **Slides group**, click the **New Slide arrow**. Click **Title Only** to insert a new slide with the Title Only layout. On the **Design tab**, in the **Background group**, select the **Hide Background Graphics** check box. Click in the title placeholder, and then type **Enjoy the Lakeside Scenery**

c. On the **Design tab**, in the **Background group**, click the **Background Styles** button. Below the gallery, click **Format Background**, and then in the **Format Background** dialog box, verify that on the left side, **Fill** is selected. On the right side of the dialog box, under **Fill**, click the **Picture or texture fill** option button. Under **Insert from**, click the **File** button, and then navigate to your student data files. Click **p03C_Scenery**, and then click **Insert**. In the **Format Background** dialog box, click **Close** to format the slide background with the picture.

d. Click in the title placeholder. On the **Format tab**, in the **Shape Styles group**, click the **More** button, and then in the second row, click the fourth style—**Colored Fill - Dark Blue, Accent 3**.

e. Point to the outer edge of the title placeholder to display the [move] pointer, and then drag the placeholder up and to the left so that its top left corner aligns with the top left corner of the slide. Point to the center right sizing handle and drag to the right so that placeholder extends to the right edge of the slide.

2 Display **Slide 4**. On the **Design tab**, in the **Background group**, click the **Background Styles** button. In the second row, point to the third button—**Style 7**. *Right-click* to display the shortcut menu, and then click **Apply to Selected Slides** to apply the dark gray, patterned background to Slide 4.

a. Display **Slide 5**. On the **Design tab**, in the **Background group**, click the **Background Styles** button. Below the gallery, click **Format Background**.

b. In the **Format Background** dialog box, verify that on the left side, **Fill** is selected. On the right side, under **Fill**, click the **Solid Fill** option button, and then under **Fill Color**, click the **Color** button. In the seventh column, click the first color—**Dark Blue, Accent 3**, and then click **Close** to apply the background fill color to the slide.

3 Display **Slide 2**, and then on the **Insert tab**, in the **Media group**, click the **Video** button. Navigate to your student files, and then click **p03_Lake_Video**. Click **Insert** to insert the video.

a. With the video selected, on the **Format tab**, in the **Size group**, replace the value in the **Video Height** box with **3.25** and then press Enter.

b. Point to the video, and then hold down Shift and drag to the right so that its right edge aligns at **4.5 inches on the right side of the horizontal ruler**.

c. With the video selected, on the **Format tab**, in the **Video Styles group**, click the **Video Border** button, and then in the seventh column, click the first color—**Dark Blue, Accent 3**. Click the **Video Effects** button, point to **Bevel**, and then click the last style—**Art Deco**.

d. With the video selected, on the **Playback tab**, in the **Video Options group**, click the **Start arrow**, and then click **Automatically**. In the **Editing group**, click the **Trim Video** button. In the **Trim Video** dialog box, in the **End Time** box, use the spin box arrows to set the end time to **00:6.520** Click **OK**.

e. Display **Backstage** view. On the **Info page**, in the center panel, click the **Compress Media** button, and then click **Low Quality**. Recall that compressing in this manner facilitates sending your file over the Internet in an e-mail or in a learning management system, although it may make the video less clear when played. When the compression is complete, **Close** the **Compress Media** dialog box, and then click the **Home tab** to return to the presentation.

4 On **Slide 2**, click anywhere in the bulleted list placeholder. On the **Animations tab**, in the **Animation group**, click the **More** button, and then under **Entrance**, click **Split**.

a. In the **Animation group**, click the **Effect Options** button, and then click **Vertical Out**.

(Project 15C Lake continues on the next page)

Content-Based Assessments

Skills Review | Project 15C Lake (continued)

- **b.** In the **Timing group**, click the **Start arrow**, and then click **With Previous** so that the list displays at the same time as the video begins to play.
- **c.** In the **Timing group**, click the **Duration up arrow** two times so that *01.00* displays in the **Duration** box. Click the **Delay up arrow** one time so that *00.25* displays in the **Delay** box.

5 Display **Slide 5**, and then click in the title placeholder. On the **Animations tab**, in the **Animation group**, click the **More** button, and then under **Entrance**, click **Wipe**. In the **Timing group**, click the **Start arrow**, and then click **After Previous**.

- **a.** Select the title, and then in the **Advanced Animation group**, click the **Animation Painter** button. Click the subtitle to apply the title animation effects to the subtitle.
- **b.** Display **Slide 1**, and then select the title. On the **Animations tab**, in the **Animation group**, click the **More** button, and then click **None** to remove the animation from the title.
- **c.** On the **Slide Show tab**, in the **Start Slide Show group**, click **From Beginning**, and then view your presentation, clicking the mouse button to advance through the slides.
- **d.** Insert a **Header & Footer** for the **Notes and Handouts**. Include the **Date and time updated automatically**, the **Page number**, and a **Footer** with the file name **Lastname_Firstname_3C_Lake** Click **Apply to All**.
- **e.** Show the **Document Panel**. Replace the text in the **Author** box with your own firstname and lastname. In the **Subject** box, type your course name and section number, and in the **Keywords** box, type **Gold Haven, lake Close** the **Document Information Panel**.
- **f.** **Save** your presentation. Print **Handouts 6 Slides Horizontal**, or submit your presentation electronically as directed by your instructor. **Close** the presentation.

End You have completed Project 15C

Apply **15B** skills from these Objectives:

- **4** Create and Modify Tables
- **5** Create and Modify Charts

Skills Review | Project 15D School Enrollment

In the following Skills Review, you will format a presentation by inserting and formatting a table, column chart, and line chart. Your completed presentation will look similar to Figure 15.52.

Project Files

For Project 15D, you will need the following file:

p03D_School_Enrollment

You will save your presentation as:

Lastname_Firstname_3D_School_Enrollment

Project Results

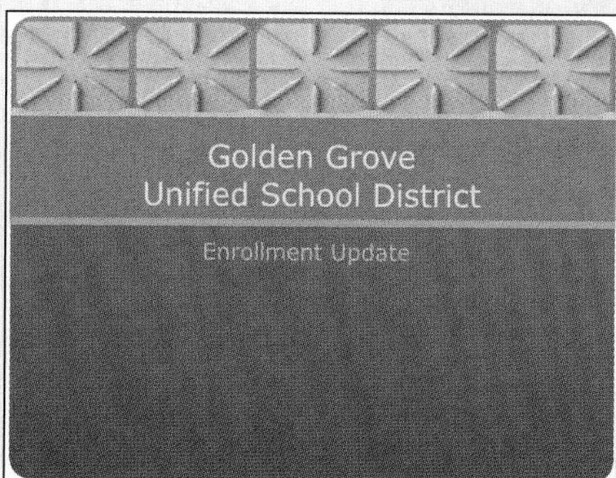

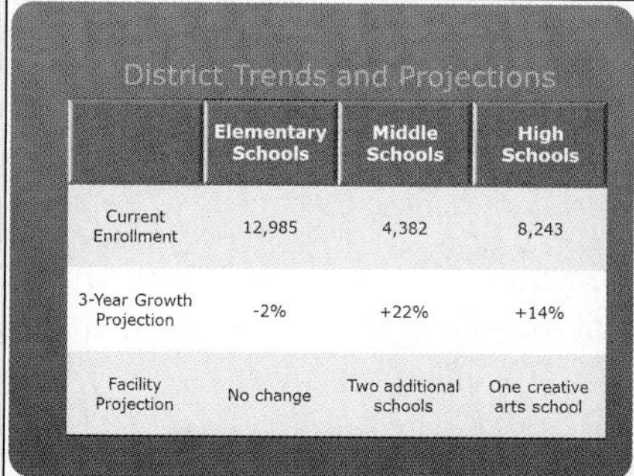

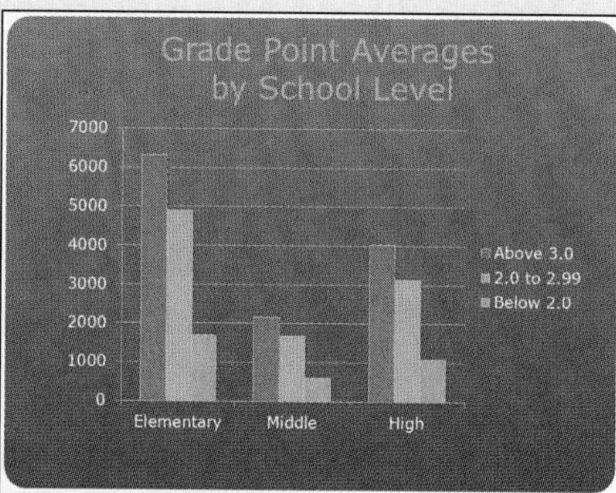

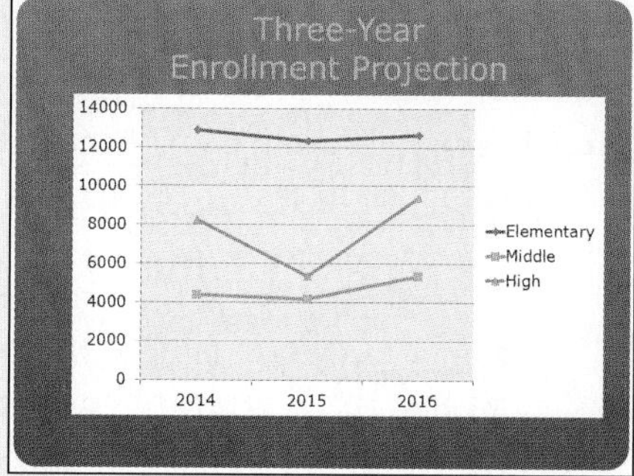

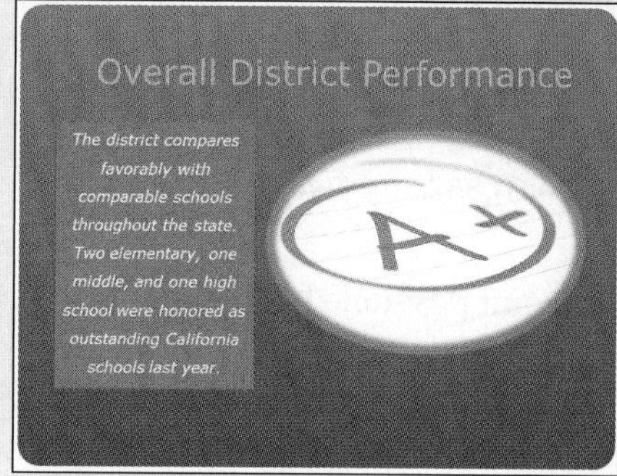

Figure 15.52

(Project 15D School Enrollment continues on the next page)

Content-Based Assessments

Skills Review | Project 15D School Enrollment (continued)

1 **Start** PowerPoint, from your student files open **p03D_School_Enrollment**, and then **Save** the presentation in your **PowerPoint Chapter 15** folder as **Lastname_Firstname_3D_School_Enrollment**

a. Display **Slide 2**. In the content placeholder, click the **Insert Table** button to display the **Insert Table** dialog box. In the **Number of columns** box, type **3** and then press Tab. In the **Number of rows** box, type **2** and then click **OK** to create the table.

b. In the first row of the table, click in the *second* cell. Type **Elementary Schools** and then press Tab. Type **High Schools** and then press Tab to move the insertion point to the first cell in the second row.

c. With the insertion point positioned in the first cell of the second row, type **Current Enrollment** and then press Tab. Type **12,985** and then press Tab. Type **8,243** and then press Tab to insert a new blank row. In the first cell of the third row, type **Facility Projection** and then press Tab. Type **No change** and then press Tab. Type **One creative arts school**

d. With the insertion point positioned in the last column, on the **Layout tab**, in the **Rows & Columns group**, click the **Insert Left** button. Click in the top cell of the inserted column, and then type **Middle Schools** In the second and third rows of the inserted column, type **4,382** and **Two additional schools**

e. With the insertion point positioned in the third row, on the **Layout tab**, in the **Rows & Columns group**, click the **Insert Above** button. Click in the first cell of the row you inserted, type **3-Year Growth Projection** and then press Tab. Type the remaining three entries in the row as follows: **-2%** and **+22%** and **+14%**

2 At the center of the lower border surrounding the table, point to the cluster of four dots—the sizing handle—and make the table larger by dragging down until the lower edge of the table aligns at **3 inches on the lower half of the vertical ruler.**

a. Click in the first cell of the table. On the **Layout tab**, in the **Cell Size group**, click the **Distribute Rows** button.

b. On the **Layout tab**, in the **Table group**, click **Select**, and then click **Select Table**. In the **Alignment group**, click the **Center** button, and then click the **Center Vertically** button.

c. Click in any cell in the table. In the **Table Tools**, click the **Design tab**, and then in the **Table Styles group**, click the **More** button. Under **Medium**, in the third row, click the second style—**Medium Style 3 – Accent 1**—to apply the style to the table.

d. Move the pointer outside of the table so that is positioned to the left of the first row in the table to display the ➡ pointer, click one time to select the entire row. Click the **Design tab**, and then in the **Table Styles group**, click the **Effects** button. Point to **Cell Bevel**, and then under **Bevel**, click the first bevel—**Circle**. Change the **Font Size** of the text in the first row to **20**.

3 Display **Slide 3**. In the content placeholder, click the **Insert Chart** button to display the **Insert Chart** dialog box. Click the first chart—*Clustered Column*—and then click **OK**.

a. In the Excel window, click in cell **B1**, which contains the text *Series 1*. Type **Above 3.0** and then press Tab to move to cell **C1**.

b. In cell **C1**, which contains the text *Series 2*, type **2.0 to 2.99** and then press Tab to move to cell **D1**, which contains the text *Series 3*. Type **Below 2.0** and then press Tab.

c. Beginning in cell **A2**, type the following data, pressing Tab to move from cell to cell.

	Above 3.0	2.0 to 2.99	Below 2.0
Elementary	**6318**	**4900**	**1676**
Middle	**2147**	**1665**	**596**
High	**4039**	**3132**	**1070**

d. In the Excel window, position the pointer over **row heading 5** so that the ➡ pointer displays. Then, *right-click* to select the row and display the shortcut menu. On the shortcut menu, click **Delete. Close** the Excel window.

e. If necessary, click the edge of the chart so that it is selected. In the **Chart Tools**, click the **Design tab**, and then in the **Chart Styles group**, click the **More** button. In the **Chart Styles** gallery, click **Style 10** to apply the style to the chart.

f. With the chart selected, click the **Animations tab**, and then in the **Animation group**, click the **More** button. Under **Entrance**, click **Split**. In the

(Project 15D School Enrollment continues on the next page)

Content-Based Assessments

Skills Review | Project 15D School Enrollment (continued)

Animation group, click the **Effect Options** button, and then under **Sequence**, click **By Series**.

4 Display **Slide 4**. In the content placeholder, click the **Insert Chart** button. On the left side of the displayed **Insert Chart** dialog box, click **Line**, and then under **Line**, click the fourth chart—**Line with Markers**. Click **OK**.

a. In the Excel worksheet, click in cell **B1**, which contains the text *Series 1*. Type **Elementary** and then press Tab. Type **Middle** and then press Tab. Type **High** and then press Tab.

b. Beginning in cell **A2**, type the following data, pressing Tab to move from cell to cell.

	Elementary	Middle	High
2014	12895	4382	8243
2015	12322	4156	5346
2016	12637	5346	9397

c. In the Excel window, position the pointer over **row heading 5** so that the ➡ pointer displays. Then, right-click to select the row and display the shortcut menu. On the shortcut menu, click **Delete**. **Close** the Excel window.

d. On the **Chart Tools Design tab**, in the **Chart Styles group**, click the **More** button. In the **Chart Styles** gallery, click **Style 34**.

e. Insert a **Header & Footer** for the **Notes and Handouts**. Include the **Date and time updated automatically**, the **Page number**, and a **Footer** with the file name **Lastname_Firstname_3D_School_Enrollment** Click **Apply to All**.

f. Show the **Document Panel**. Replace the text in the **Author** box with your own firstname and lastname. In the **Subject** box, type your course name and section number, and in the **Keywords** box, type **enrollment, schools** **Close** the **Document Information Panel**.

g. View the slide show from the beginning, and then **Save** your presentation. Print **Handouts 6 Slides Horizontal**, or submit your presentation electronically as directed by your instructor. **Close** the presentation and exit PowerPoint.

End **You have completed Project 15D**

Content-Based Assessments

Apply 15A skills from these Objectives:

1. Customize Slide Backgrounds and Themes
2. Animate a Slide Show
3. Insert a Video

Mastering PowerPoint | Project 15E Spotlight Neighborhood

In the following Mastering PowerPoint project, you will format a presentation created by the Golden Grove Public Relations department that announces the winner of the Spotlight Neighborhood award. Your completed presentation will look similar to Figure 15.53.

Project Files

For Project 1E, you will need the following files:

p03E_Spotlight_Neighborhood
p03E_Neighborhood
p03E_Neighborhood_Video

You will save your presentation as:

Lastname_Firstname_3E_Spotlight_Neighborhood

Project Results

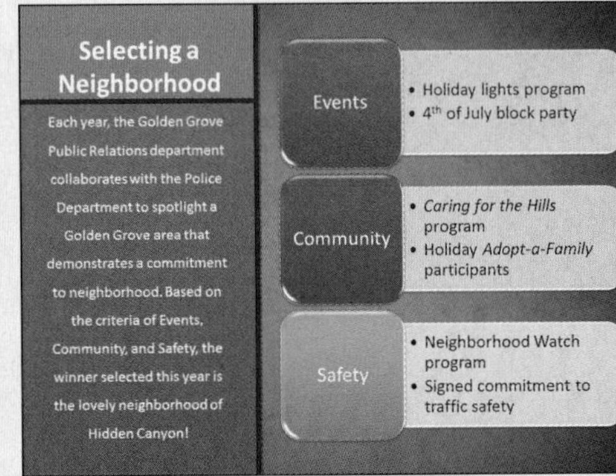

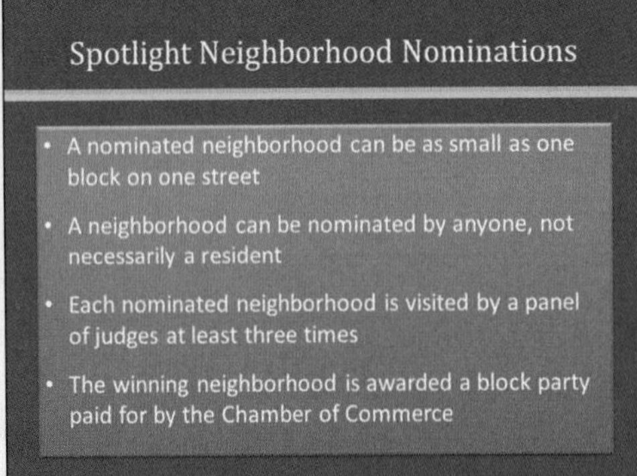

Figure 15.53

(Project 15E Spotlight Neighborhood continues on the next page)

Mastering PowerPoint | Project 15E Spotlight Neighborhood (contin-

1 **Start** PowerPoint. From the student files that accompany this textbook, locate and open **p03E_Spotlight_Neighborhood**. Change the **Theme Colors** for the presentation to **Office**, and the **Theme Fonts** to **Adjacency**. **Save** the presentation in your **PowerPoint Chapter 15** folder as **Lastname_Firstname_3E_Spotlight_Neighborhood**

2 On **Slide 1**, hide the background graphics, and then format the slide background by inserting a picture from your student files—**p03E_Neighborhood**. To the title, apply the first **WordArt** style—**Fill - Tan Text 2, Outline - Background 2**.

3 On **Slide 2**, display the **Background Styles** gallery, right-click **Background Style 12**, and then apply the style to this slide only. Select the paragraph on the left side of the slide, and then change the **Font Color** to **White, Text 1**. With the paragraph selected, apply the **Split** entrance effect, and then change the **Effect Options** to **Horizontal Out**. Change the **Start** setting to **After Previous**, and then change the **Duration** to **01.00**. Animate the **SmartArt** graphic by applying the **Fade** entrance effect and so that it starts **With Previous**.

4 On **Slide 3**, format the **Background Style** by applying a **Solid fill—Dark Blue, Text 2**. Change the **Font Color** of the title text to **White, Background 1**. Remove the entrance effect from the title.

5 On **Slide 4**, hide the background graphics, and then apply background **Style 12**. From your student files, insert the video **p03E_Neighborhood_Video**. Change the **Video Height** to **4** and **Align Center** the video. Format the video by applying, from the **Video Styles** gallery, an **Intense** style—**Monitor, Gray**. Change the **Start** setting to **Automatically**.

6 Display **Slide 2**, and then use **Animation Painter** to apply the animation from the paragraph on the left side of the slide to the bulleted list on **Slide 3**.

7 **Insert** a **Header & Footer** on the **Notes and Handouts**. Include the **Date and time updated automatically**, the **Page** number, and a **Footer** with the text **Lastname_Firstname_3E_Spotlight_Neighborhood**

8 Update the **Document Properties** with your name, course name and section number, and the **Keywords** **spotlight neighborhood** **Close** the **Document Information Panel**.

9 **Save** your presentation, and then view the slide show from the beginning. Submit your presentation electronically, or print **Handouts 4 Slides Horizontal** as directed by your instructor. **Close** the presentation.

End **You have completed Project 15E**

Content-Based Assessments

Apply **15B** skills from these Objectives:

4 Create and Modify Tables

5 Create and Modify Charts

Mastering PowerPoint | Project 15F Water Conservation

In the following Mastering PowerPoint project, you will format a presentation that the Golden Grove Chief Water Engineer will present at a community forum. Your completed presentation will look similar to Figure 15.54.

Project Files

For Project 1F, you will need the following file:

p03F_Water_Conservation

You will save your presentation as:

Lastname_Firstname_3F_Water_Conservation

Project Results

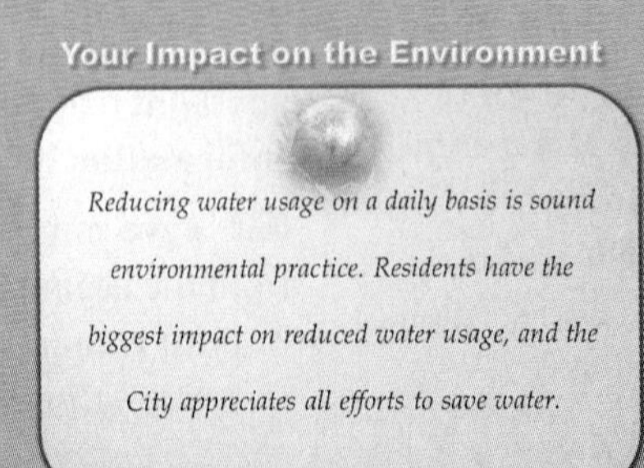

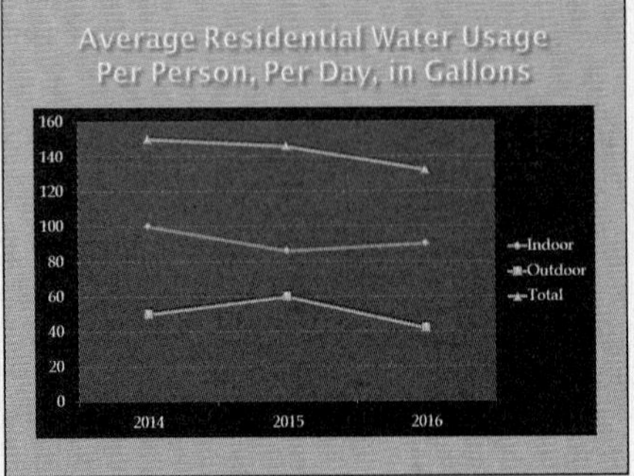

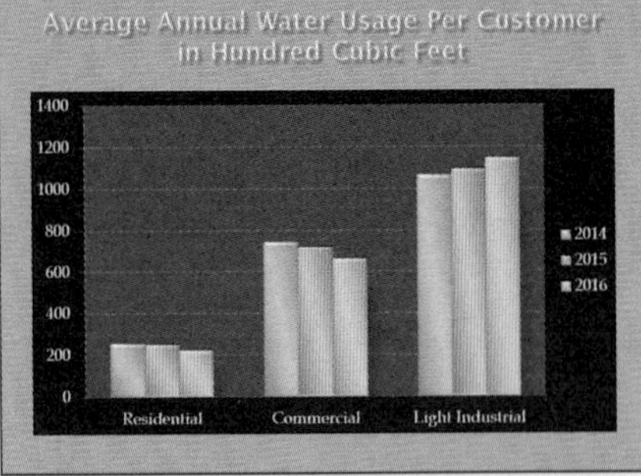

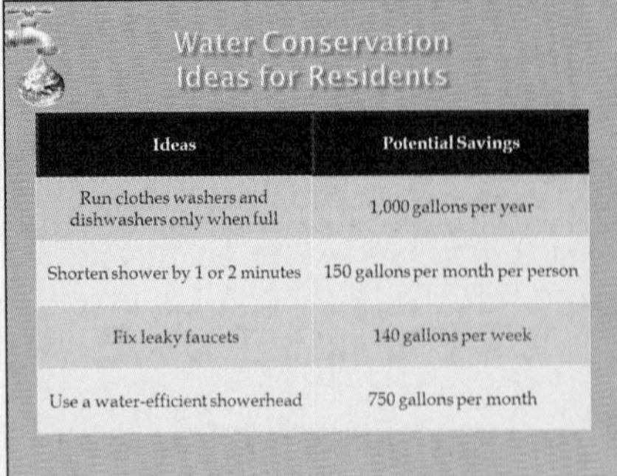

Figure 15.54

(Project 15F Water Conservation continues on the next page)

Mastering PowerPoint | Project 15F Water Conservation (continued)

1 **Start** PowerPoint. From your student files open **p03F_Water_Conservation**, and then **Save** the presentation in your **PowerPoint Chapter 15** folder as **Lastname_Firstname_3F_Water_Conservation**

2 On **Slide 3**, in the content placeholder, insert a **Line with Markers** chart. In the Excel worksheet, in cell **B1**, type **Indoor** and then enter the following data:

	Indoor	Outdoor	Total
2014	100	50	150
2015	86	60	146
2016	90	42	132

3 In the Excel window, delete **row 5**, and then **Close** the Excel window. Apply **Chart Style 42** to the chart, and then apply the **Wipe** entrance effect to the chart.

4 On **Slide 5**, in the content placeholder, insert a **Clustered Column** chart. In the Excel worksheet, in cell **B1**, type **2014** and then enter the following data:

	2014	2015	2016
Residential	256	249	225
Commercial	746	718	660
Light Industrial	1065	1092	1146

5 In the Excel window, delete **row 5**, and then **Close** the Excel window. Apply **Chart Style 42** to the chart, and then apply the **Wipe** entrance effect to the chart. Change the **Effect Options** so that the animation is applied **By Series**. Change the **Timing** so that the animation starts **After Previous**.

6 On **Slide 6**, in the content placeholder, insert a **Table** with **2 columns** and **5 rows**, and then type the text in **Table 1** at the bottom of the page.

7 Resize the table so that its lower edge extends to **3 inches on the lower half of the vertical ruler**, and then distribute the table rows. Align the table text so that it is centered horizontally and vertically within the cells. Apply table style **Medium Style 2**, and then apply a **Circle Bevel** to the first row. Change the table text **Font Size** to **20**.

8 Insert a **Header & Footer** for the **Notes and Handouts**. Include the **Date and time updated automatically**, the **Page number**, and a **Footer** with the file name **Lastname_Firstname_3F_Water_Conservation** Update the **Document Properties** with your name, course name and section number, and the **Keywords water conservation** **Close** the **Document Information Panel**.

9 View the slide show from the beginning, and then **Save** your presentation. Print **Handouts 4 Slides Horizontal**, or submit your presentation electronically as directed by your instructor. **Close** the presentation.

Table 1

Ideas	Potential Savings
Run clothes washers and dishwashers only when full	1,000 gallons per year
Shorten shower by 1 or 2 minutes	150 gallons per month per person
Fix leaky faucets	140 gallons per week
Use a water-efficient showerhead	750 gallons per month

(Return to Step 7)

End You have completed Project 15F

Content-Based Assessments

Apply 15A and 15B skills from these Objectives:

1. Customize Slide Backgrounds and Themes
2. Animate a Slide Show
3. Insert a Video
4. Create and Modify Tables
5. Create and Modify Charts

Mastering PowerPoint | Project 15G Restaurants

In the following Mastering PowerPoint project, you will format a presentation that the Golden Grove Public Relations Director will show at a meeting of the National Restaurant Owners Association to encourage new restaurant and catering business in the city. Your completed presentation will look similar to Figure 15.55.

Project Files

For Project 15G, you will need the following files:

p03G_Restaurants
p03G_Town_Center
p03G_Catering

You will save your presentation as:

Lastname_Firstname_3G_Restaurants

Project Results

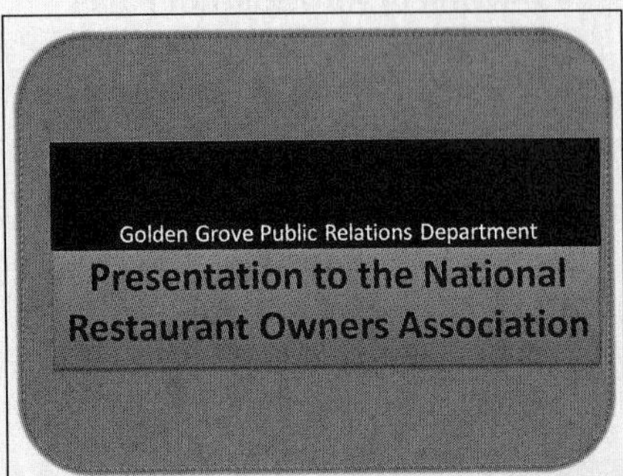

Golden Grove City Profile

Population	218,381	Expected 5-year increase: 12%
Households	62,394	Expected 5-year increase: 3%
Average years in residence	6.8	62% families with children
Owner occupied	75%	Expected to increase with new construction

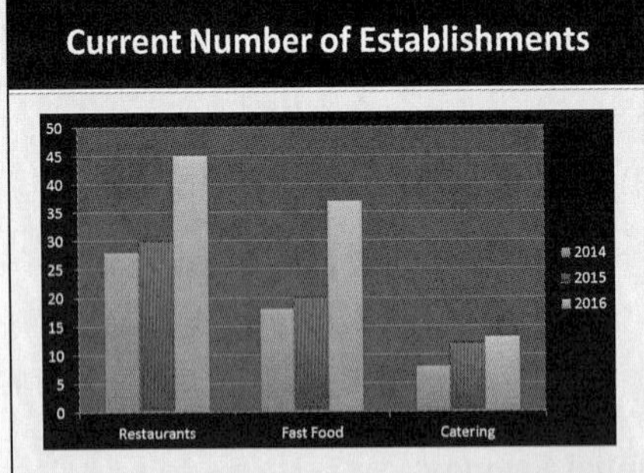

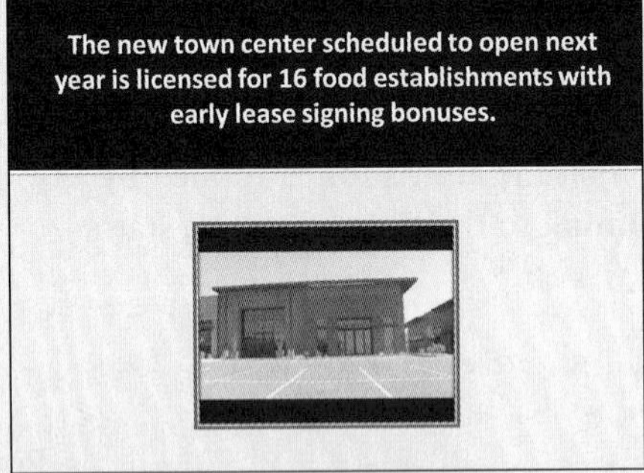

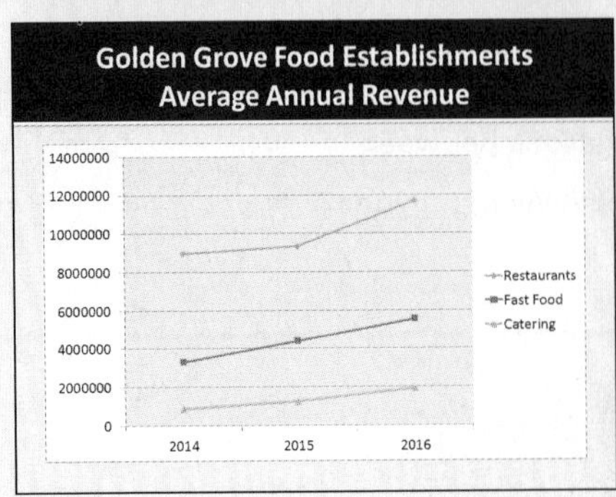

Figure 15.55

(Project 15G Restaurants continues on the next page)

Mastering PowerPoint | Project 15G Restaurants (continued)

1 **Start** PowerPoint. From the student files that accompany this textbook, locate and open **p03G_Restaurants**. Change the **Theme Colors** for the presentation to **Apothecary**, and the **Theme Fonts** to **Composite**. **Save** the presentation in your **PowerPoint Chapter 15** folder as **Lastname_Firstname_3G_Restaurants**

2 On **Slide 2**, insert a **Table** with **3 columns** and **4 rows**. Apply table style **Medium Style 3 - Accent 2**, and then type the information in **Table 1**, shown at the bottom of this page, into the inserted table.

3 On the **Design tab**, in the **Table Style Options group**, select *only* the **First Column** and **Banded Rows** check boxes. Resize the table so that its lower edge extends to **3 inches on the lower half of the vertical ruler**, and then distribute the table rows. Align the table text so that it is centered horizontally and vertically within the cells, and then change the **Font Size** of all of the table text to **24**.

4 On **Slide 3**, display the **Background Styles** gallery, right-click **Background Style 3**, and then apply the style to this slide only. Animate the **SmartArt** graphic using the **Wipe** entrance effect starting **After Previous**. Apply the **Split** entrance effect to the bulleted list placeholder, and then change the **Effect Options** to **Vertical Out**.

5 On **Slide 4**, insert a **Clustered Column** chart. In the Excel worksheet, in cell **B1** type **2014** and then enter the following data:

	2014	2015	2016
Restaurants	28	30	45
Fast Food	18	20	37
Catering	8	12	13

6 In the Excel window, delete **row 5**, and then **Close** the Excel window. Apply **Chart Style 42** to the chart, and then apply the **Wipe** entrance effect to the chart.

7 On **Slide 5**, from your student files, insert the video **p03G_Town_Center**. Change the **Video Height** to **3** and then drag the video down so that its top edge aligns at **zero on the vertical ruler**. Apply the **Align Center** alignment option, display the **Video Styles** gallery, and then apply the first **Moderate** style—**Compound Frame, Black**. Change the **Video Border** to **Gray-50%, Accent 1, Darker 50%**—in the fifth column, the last color.

8 On the **Playback tab**, change the **Video Options** to **Start** the video **Automatically**. **Trim** the video so that the **End Time** is **00:05.560**

9 On **Slide 6**, in the content placeholder, insert a **Line with Markers** chart. In the Excel worksheet, in cell **B1**, type **Restaurants** and then enter the following data:

	Restaurants	Fast Food	Catering
2014	8956231	3284680	856700
2015	9326852	4369571	1235640
2016	11689730	5526895	1894325

10 In the Excel window, delete **row 5**, and then **Close** the Excel window. Apply **Chart Style 34** to the chart, and then use **Animation Painter** to copy the animation from the column chart on **Slide 4** to the line chart on **Slide 6**.

11 On **Slide 7**, hide the background graphics. Format the slide background by inserting a picture from your student files—**p03G_Catering**. Change the title placeholder **Shape Fill** color to **Black, Text 1**, and then change the **Font Color** to **Red, Accent 2**. Size the placeholder so that it extends from the left edge of the slide to the right edge of the slide, and then position it so that its lower edge aligns with the lower edge of the slide. **Center** the text.

12 Insert a **Header & Footer** for the **Notes and Handouts**. Include the **Date and time updated automatically**, the **Page number**, and a **Footer** with the file name **Lastname_Firstname_3G_Restaurants** Update the **Properties** with your name, course name and section number, and the **Keywords catering, restaurants** **Close** the **Document Information Panel**.

13 View the slide show from the beginning, and then **Save** your presentation. Print **Handouts 4 Slides Horizontal**, or submit your presentation electronically as directed by your instructor. **Close** the presentation.

Table 1

Population	218,381	Expected 5-year increase: 12%
Households	62,394	Expected 5-year increase: 3%
Average years in residence	6.8	62% families with children
Owner occupied	75%	Expected to increase with new construction

(Return to Step 3)

End **You have completed Project 15G**

Content-Based Assessments

Apply a combination of the **15A** and **15B** skills.

GO! Fix It | Project 15H Housing Developments

Project Files

For Project 15H, you will need the following file:

p03H_Housing_Developments

You will save your presentation as:

Lastname_Firstname_3H_Housing_Developments

In this project, you will edit several slides from a presentation prepared by the Golden Grove Planning Department regarding real estate developments in the city. From the student files that accompany this textbook, open the file p03H_Housing_Developments, and then save the file in your chapter folder as **Lastname_Firstname_3H_Housing_Developments**

To complete the project, you should know:

- The Theme Colors should be changed to Module and the Theme Fonts should be changed to Apex.
- The titles on Slides 2 and 3 should be centered.
- On Slide 2, the table style Light Style 2 - Accent 2 should be applied and a column should be added to right of the last column in the table. In the inserted column, the following text should be entered in the three cells: **Bering** and **37%** and **August 2016**
- On Slides 3 and 4, the charts should be animated with the Wipe entrance effect.
- Document Properties should include your name, course name and section, and the keywords **property tax, housing** A Header & Footer should be inserted on the Notes and Handouts that includes the Date and time updated automatically, the Page number and a Footer with the text **Lastname_Firstname_3H_Housing_Developments**

Save and submit your presentation electronically or print Handouts 4 Slides Horizontal as directed by your instructor. Close the presentation.

End **You have completed Project 15H**

Content-Based Assessments

Apply a combination of the 15A and 15B skills.

GO! Make It | Project 15I Arboretum

Project Files

For Project 15I, you will need the following files:

New blank PowerPoint presentation
p03I_Flowers

You will save your presentation as:

Lastname_Firstname_3I_Arboretum

Start PowerPoint to begin a new blank presentation, and apply the Opulent theme. Save the file in your PowerPoint Chapter 15 folder as **Lastname_Firstname_3I_Arboretum**

By using the skills you practiced in this chapter, create the first two slides of the presentation shown in Figure 15.56. The layout for Slide 1 is Title Only, and the background is formatted with the picture from your student data file— p03I_Flowers. The title Shape Fill color is Purple, Accent 2, Darker 50%. On Slide 2, insert and format the table as shown. Change the Font Size of the text in the first row to 32. Insert the file name, date, and page number in the Notes and Handouts footer. In the Document Information Panel, add your name and course information and the Keywords **arboretum, events** Save, and then print or submit electronically as directed by your instructor.

Project Results

UPCOMING EVENTS

Event	Description	Dates
Festival of Flowers	A presentation of annual spring blooms	May 1-7
Landscaping 101	A four-day course on selecting appropriate flora for your yard	Every Saturday in June and July
Summer Nature Adventure	A botanical discovery camp for children ages 8 to 12	August 1 - 14

Figure 15.56

End **You have completed Project 15I**

Apply a combination of the 15A and 15B skills.

GO! Solve It | Project 15J Aquatic Center

Project Files

For Project 15J, you will need the following file:

p03J_Aquatic_Center

You will save your presentation as:

Lastname_Firstname_3J_Aquatic_Center

Open the file p03J_Aquatic_Center and save it as **Lastname_Firstname_3J_Aquatic_Center** Complete the presentation by changing the Theme Fonts and then formatting the slide background of at least one of the slides using a Background Style or Solid Fill color. On Slide 4, insert and format a table with the following information regarding the fee schedule for swim passes.

Membership	Monthly	Seasonal
Youth	$10	$25
Adult	$25	$50
Senior	$15	$30

Apply appropriate animation and slide transitions to the slides. Insert a header and footer that includes the date and time updated automatically, the file name in the footer, and the page number. Add your name, your course name and section number, and the keywords **aquatic center, swim program** to the Properties area. Save and then print, or submit it as directed by your instructor.

		Performance Level		
		Exemplary: You consistently applied the relevant skills	**Proficient:** You sometimes, but not always, applied the relevant skills	**Developing:** You rarely or never applied the relevant skills
Performance Elements	Format slide with a background style	Slide background style was applied to at least one slide and text displayed with good contrast against the background.	Slide background was formatted but text did not display well against the chosen background.	Slide background was not formatted with a background style.
	Insert and format appropriate table	Appropriate table was inserted and formatted.	A table was inserted but was not appropriately formatted.	Table was not inserted.
	Apply appropriate animation	Appropriate animation was applied to the presentation.	Animation was applied but was not appropriate for the presentation.	Animation was not applied.

End **You have completed Project 15J**

Apply a combination of the 15A and 15B skills.

GO! Solve It | Project 15K Power

Project Files

For Project 15K, you will need the following files:

p03K_Power
p03K_Tower

You will save your presentation as:

Lastname_Firstname_3K_Power

Open the file p03K_Power and save it as **Lastname_Firstname_3K_Power** Complete the presentation by applying a theme and then formatting the slide background of one of the slides with the picture found in your student files—p03K_Tower. Adjust the size, position, fill color, and font color of the slide titles as necessary so that the title text displays attractively against the background picture. Format the background of at least one other slide using a Background Style or Solid Fill color. Insert a new Slide 3 that includes an appropriate title and a table with the following information regarding the power sources that the City uses.

Power Sources	Percent Used by City
Natural gas	32%
Hydroelectric	17%
Renewables	18%
Coal	23%
Nuclear	10%

On Slide 4, insert and format an appropriate chart to demonstrate the revenue collected from residential power sales over the past three years. Revenue in 2014 was 35.5 million dollars, in 2015 revenue was 42.6 million dollars, and in 2016 revenue was 48.2 million dollars. Apply appropriate animation and slide transitions to the slides. Insert a header and footer that includes the date and time updated automatically, the file name in the footer, and the page number. Add your name, your course name and section number, and the keywords **power sources, revenue** to the Properties area. Save and then print or submit the presentation as directed by your instructor.

Performance Elements	Performance Level: Exemplary: You consistently applied the relevant skills	Proficient: You sometimes, but not always, applied the relevant skills	Developing: You rarely or never applied the relevant skills
Format two slide backgrounds with pictures and styles	Two slide backgrounds were formatted attractively and text displayed with good contrast against backgrounds.	Slide backgrounds were formatted but text did not display well against the chosen background, or only one slide background was formatted.	Slide backgrounds were not formatted with pictures or styles.
Insert and format appropriate table and chart	Appropriate table and chart were inserted and formatted and the entered data was accurate.	A table and a chart were inserted but were not appropriate for the presentation or either a table or a chart was omitted.	Table and chart were not inserted.
Apply appropriate animation	Appropriate animation was applied to the presentation.	Animation was applied but was not appropriate for the presentation.	Animation was not applied.

End **You have completed Project 15K**

Outcomes-Based Assessments

Rubric

The following outcomes-based assessments are *open-ended assessments*. That is, there is no specific correct result; your result will depend on your approach to the information provided. Make *Professional Quality* your goal. Use the following scoring rubric to guide you in *how* to approach the problem, and then to evaluate *how well* your approach solves the problem.

The *criteria*—Software Mastery, Content, Format and Layout, and Process—represent the knowledge and skills you have gained that you can apply to solving the problem. The *levels of performance*—Professional Quality, Approaching Professional Quality, or Needs Quality Improvements—help you and your instructor evaluate your result.

	Your completed project is of Professional Quality if you:	**Your completed project is Approaching Professional Quality if you:**	**Your completed project Needs Quality Improvements if you:**
1-Software Mastery	Choose and apply the most appropriate skills, tools, and features and identify efficient methods to solve the problem.	Choose and apply some appropriate skills, tools, and features, but not in the most efficient manner.	Choose inappropriate skills, tools, or features, or are inefficient in solving the problem.
2-Content	Construct a solution that is clear and well organized, contains content that is accurate, appropriate to the audience and purpose, and is complete. Provide a solution that contains no errors in spelling, grammar, or style.	Construct a solution in which some components are unclear, poorly organized, inconsistent, or incomplete. Misjudge the needs of the audience. Have some errors in spelling, grammar, or style, but the errors do not detract from comprehension.	Construct a solution that is unclear, incomplete, or poorly organized; contains some inaccurate or inappropriate content; and contains many errors in spelling, grammar, or style. Do not solve the problem.
3-Format and Layout	Format and arrange all elements to communicate information and ideas, clarify function, illustrate relationships, and indicate relative importance.	Apply appropriate format and layout features to some elements, but not others. Overuse features, causing minor distraction.	Apply format and layout that does not communicate information or ideas clearly. Do not use format and layout features to clarify function, illustrate relationships, or indicate relative importance. Use available features excessively, causing distraction.
4-Process	Use an organized approach that integrates planning, development, self-assessment, revision, and reflection.	Demonstrate an organized approach in some areas, but not others; or, use an insufficient process of organization throughout.	Do not use an organized approach to solve the problem.

Apply a combination of the 15A and 15B skills.

GO! Think | Project 15L Animal Sanctuary

Project Files

For Project 15L, you will need the following file:

New blank PowerPoint presentation

You will save your presentation as:

Lastname_Firstname_3L_Animal Sanctuary

The Golden Grove Animal Sanctuary, a non-profit organization, provides shelter and care for animals in need, including dogs, cats, hamsters, and guinea pigs. The Sanctuary, which celebrates its tenth anniversary in July, has cared for more than 12,000 animals since it opened and is a state-of-the-art facility. Funding for the Sanctuary comes in the form of business sponsorships, individual donations, and pet adoption fees. The following table indicates revenue generated by the Sanctuary during the past three years.

	Fees	Donations	Sponsorships
2014	125,085	215,380	175,684
2015	110,680	256,785	156,842
2016	132,455	314,682	212,648

In addition to shelter services, the Sanctuary offers community service and training programs, veterinarian services, and vaccine clinics. Examples of these services include Canine Obedience classes, microchipping ($25 fee), and the Healthy Pet Hotline (free). Canine Obedience classes are for puppies and adult dogs to improve obedience, socialization, and behavior. Classes last two, three, or four months and cost $150 to $250.

Using the preceding information, create the first five slides of a presentation that the director of the Golden Grove Animal Sanctuary will show at an upcoming pet fair. Apply an appropriate theme and use slide layouts that will effectively present the content. Include a line chart with the revenue data, a table with the community service programs information, and at least one slide formatted with a dog or cat on the slide background. Apply styles to the table and chart, and apply animation and slide transitions to the slides. Use the techniques that you practiced in this chapter so that your presentation is professional and attractive. Save the file as **Lastname_Firstname_3L_Animal_Sanctuary** and then insert a header and footer that includes the date and time updated automatically, the file name in the footer, and the page number. Add your name, your course name and section number, and the keywords **animals, pets** to the Properties area. Save and then print or submit the presentation as directed by your instructor.

End **You have completed Project 15L**

Outcomes-Based Assessments

Apply a combination of the **15A** and **15B** skills.

GO! Think | Project **15M** Water Sources

Project Files

For Project 15M, you will need the following file:

New blank PowerPoint presentation

You will save your presentation as:

Lastname_Firstname_3M_Water_Sources

The Golden Grove Department of Water and Power operations are financed solely through sales of water and electric services. A portion of capital expenditures are funded through the sale of municipal bonds. The city's water supply is generated from a number of sources, with 35% from the Sierra Nevada aqueduct system, 42% from water districts, 18% from groundwater, and 5% from recycled sources. This supply provides water for the City's residents and commercial and industrial customers.

In the past three years, the Department has renovated several reservoirs and pump stations, resulting in better reserves and emergency preparedness capacity. The following table details the in-city reservoir capacities over the past three years. Water capacity is measured in acre feet, in which one acre foot is equal to approximately 325,000 gallons. Years in which zero or low capacity is specified indicates years in which the reservoir was undergoing renovation.

	2014	2015	2016
Elkhart Reservoir	350	1250	2243
Gold Lake Reservoir	3685	865	2865
Diamond Canyon Reservoir	2650	3850	4635

Using the preceding information, create a title slide and four additional slides of a presentation that the Golden Grove Chief Water Engineer can show at an upcoming City Council meeting. Apply an appropriate theme and use slide layouts that will effectively present the content. Include a table that details the water supply sources, and a column chart with the reservoir information. Apply animation and slide transitions and use the techniques that you practiced in this chapter so that your presentation is professional and attractive. Save the file as **Lastname_Firstname_3M_Water_Sources** and then insert a header and footer that includes the date and time updated automatically, the file name in the footer, and the page number. Add your name, your course name and section number, and the keywords **reservoirs, water capacity** to the Properties area. Save, and then print or submit the presentation as directed by your instructor.

End **You have completed Project 15M**

Outcomes-Based Assessments

Apply a combination of the 15A and 15B skills.

You and GO! | Project 15N Recreation Programs

Project Files

For Project 1N, you will need the following file:

New blank PowerPoint presentation

You will save your presentation as:

Lastname_Firstname_3N_Recreation_Programs

Research the recreation programs available in the city in which you live, and then create a presentation about the program. Include a table that describes some of the activities, the location in which they are held, and the fees. Choose an appropriate theme, slide layouts, and pictures, and format the presentation attractively, including at least one slide with a picture on the slide background. Save your presentation as **Lastname_Firstname_3N_Recreation_Programs** and submit as directed.

You have completed Project 15N

Apply a combination of the 15A and 15B skills.

GO! Collaborate | Project 15O Bell Orchid Hotels Group Running Case

This project relates to the **Bell Orchid Hotels**. Your instructor may assign this group case project to your class. If your instructor assigns this project, he or she will provide you with information and instructions to work as part of a group. The group will apply the skills gained thus far to help the Bell Orchid Hotels achieve their business goals.

End **You have completed Project 15O**

Business Running Case

This project relates to **Front Range Action Sports**, which is one of the country's largest retailers of sports gear and outdoor recreation merchandise. The company has large retail stores in Colorado, Washington, Oregon, California, and New Mexico, in addition to a growing online business. Major merchandise categories include fishing, camping, rock climbing, winter sports, action sports, water sports, team sports, racquet sports, fitness, golf, apparel, and footwear.

In this project, you will apply skills you practiced from the Objectives in PowerPoint Chapters 13 through 15. You will develop a presentation that Irene Shviktar, Vice President of Marketing, will show at a corporate marketing retreat that summarizes the company's plans to expand the winter sports product line. Your completed presentation will look similar to Figure 2.1.

Project Files

For Project BRC1, you will need the following files:

pBRC1_Company_Overview
pBRC1_Heights
pBRC1_Lake
pBRC1_Mountain
pBRC1_Skiing
pBRC1_Winter_Products

You will save your presentation as:

Lastname_Firstname_BRC1_Winter_Products

Project Results

Figure 2.1

Business Running Case

Front Range Action Sports (continued)

1 **Start** PowerPoint. From the student files that accompany this textbook, locate and open **pBRC1_Winter_Products**. In the location where you are storing your projects, create a new folder named **Front Range Action Sports** or navigate to this folder if you have already created it. **Save** the presentation as **Lastname_Firstname_BRC1_Winter_Products**

- **a.** Display **Slide 1**. Change the presentation theme to **Concourse**, and then change the **Theme Colors** to **Office**. Change the **Theme Fonts** to **Elemental**. On **Slide 1**, format the background with a picture from your student files—**pBRC1_Skiing**.
- **b.** Display the **Reuse Slides** pane. Browse your student files, and display in the **Reuse Slides** pane **pBRC1_Company_Overview**. Insert the second slide—**Mission**—as **Slide 2**, and then **Close** the **Reuse Slides** pane. Remove the bullet symbol from the paragraph, **Center** the text, and then apply **Bold** and **Italic**.
- **c.** With **Slide 2** displayed, change the **Line Spacing** of the content placeholder text to **2.0**. Change the **Shape Fill** to the first color in the fourth column—**Dark Blue, Text 2**, and then change the **Font Color** to **White, Background 1**. Format the placeholder with the first **Bevel** shape effect—**Circle**—and then hide the background graphics on the slide.
- **d.** Display **Slide 3**, and then in the picture placeholder, from your student files insert **pBRC1_Heights**. Apply the first **Glow** picture effect—**Blue, 5 pt glow, Accent color 1**. Format the slide background by applying **Style 12**, being sure to apply the background only to **Slide 3**.

2 Display **Slide 4**, and then in the content placeholder, insert the **Process** SmartArt graphic **Alternating Flow**. Change the color to **Colorful - Accent Colors**, and then apply **3-D Cartoon** style.

- **a.** In the **red shape**, type **Washington and California Resorts** and then click in the first bullet point in the rounded rectangle above the red shape. Type **Mammoth Mountain and Lake Tahoe in California** Click in the second bullet point, and then type **Mission Ridge and Crystal Mountain in Washington**
- **b.** In the **green shape**, type **Our Market Position** and then click in the first bullet point in the rounded rectangle below the green shape. Type **Trusted brand name in the sporting world** In the second bullet point, type **Winter sports product line not fully marketed in the Western United States**
- **c.** In the **purple shape**, type **Poised for Growth** and then click in the first bullet point in the rounded rectangle above the purple shape. Type **New warehouses in Washington** In the second bullet point, type **Proposed retail division in Northern California**
- **d.** Animate the SmartArt by applying the **Wipe** entrance effect. Change the **Start** option so that the SmartArt animation begins **After Previous**.

3 Display **Slide 5**, and then apply background **Style 3** to the slide. In both content placeholders, change the bullet symbol to **Star Bullets**, and then change the bullet **Color** to **Olive Green, Accent 3**. In the **blue shapes** at the bottom of the slide, change the **Font Color** to **White, Text 1**.

- **a.** Insert a **Down Arrow** shape by clicking on the slide with the guides aligned with the **left half of the horizontal ruler at 3 inches** and with the **lower half of the vertical ruler at 1 inch**.
- **b.** Change the arrow **Shape Height** to **1** and the **Shape Width** to **0.5** and then apply the fourth **Shape Style** in the first row—**Colored Outline - Olive Green, Accent 3**. Select the arrow, the content placeholder on the left, and the *Skiing* shape, and then on the **Format tab**, in the **Arrange group**, click the **Align** button. Click **Align Selected Objects**. Click the **Align** button again, and then click **Align Center**.
- **c.** Duplicate the arrow shape, and then drag the duplicated arrow so that its left edge aligns with the **right half of the horizontal ruler at 2 inches** and its top edge aligns with the **lower half of the vertical ruler at 1 inch**. Select the arrow, the content placeholder on the right, and the *Snowboarding* shape, and then using the **Align Selected Objects** option apply **Align Center**. Select the two arrows, and then using the **Align Selected Objects** option, apply **Align Top** to the two arrow shapes.

(Business Running Case: Front Range Action Sports continues on the next page)

Front Range Action Sports (continued)

4 With **Slide 5** displayed, insert a **New Slide** with the **Two Content** layout and then apply background **Style 3** to the inserted slide. Type the slide title **Our Most Popular Winter Products** Change the **Font Size** to **32** and then **Center** the title.

a. In the content placeholder on the left, type the following six bullet points:

Snowboards
Boots
Goggles
Bindings
Skis
Jackets

b. Change the bulleted list to **Numbering**, and then change the number **Color** to **White, Text 1**.

c. In the placeholder on the right, insert a **Clip Art** by searching for a **Photograph** with the keyword **snowboard** Insert the black and white silhouette picture of the person holding a snowboard behind his back. If you cannot locate the picture, choose another image, and then **Close** the Clip Art pane.

d. Change the **Height** of the picture to **5** and then move the picture so that its upper left corner aligns with **zero on the horizontal ruler** and with the **upper half of the vertical ruler at 2.5 inches**. Apply a **Soft Edges** picture effect of **25 Point**.

	Oregon	Colorado	British Columbia
2012	12.2	17.5	6.5
2013	14.5	19.2	8.7
2014	11.9	18.6	10.6
2015	17.6	22.4	11.3

e. Display **Slide 7**, and then in the content placeholder, insert a **Clustered Column** chart. In the **Excel** worksheet, enter the following data.

f. **Close** the Excel worksheet. Apply **Chart Style 26**, and then animate the chart by applying the **Wipe** entrance effect.

5 Display **Slide 8**, and then hide the background graphics on the slide. Format the background with a picture from your student files—**pBRC1_Lake**.

Targeted Retail Expansion	2013 Goal	2016 Goal
Northern California	Three new franchises with rental services	Four new franchises
Central and Eastern Washington	Four new franchises with rental services and lessons	Eight new franchises with rental services

a. Select the title placeholder, and then using the **Align to Slide** option, align the title using the **Align Top** and **Align Center** options.

b. Display **Slide 9**, and then in the content placeholder, insert a **Table** with **3** columns and **3** rows. Type the following text in the table.

c. Apply the **Light Style 2 - Accent 1** table style, and then resize the table so that its lower left corner touches the graphic in the lower left corner of the slide. Distribute the table rows.

d. To the first row, apply the first **Cell Bevel** effect—**Circle**, and then change the **Font Size** to **24**. Center all of the text in the table horizontally and vertically, and then apply the **Wipe** entrance effect to the table.

6 Display **Slide 10**. Apply background **Style 3** to the slide, and then hide the background graphics. To the title, apply the fourth **WordArt** style in the first row **Fill - White, Outline -Accent 1**.

a. With **Slide 10** displayed, from your student files, insert the picture **pBRC1_Mountain**. Change the picture **Height** to **2.5** and then apply a **Soft Edges** picture effect of **25 Point**. Use the **Crop to Shape** option to change the picture shape to the tenth **Basic Shape** in the third row—**Cloud**. **Align Center** and **Align Middle** the picture using the **Align to Slide** option.

b. On **Slide 10**, insert a **WordArt** using the fourth **WordArt** style in the first row **Fill - White, Outline - Accent 1**. Type **Moving to the Top of the Winter Sports Action** and then change the **Font Size** to **28**. Drag the WordArt down so that its top edge aligns with the **lower half of the vertical ruler at 1 inch**. Select the title placeholder, picture, and WordArt, and then using the **Align to Slide** option, apply **Align Center**.

(Business Running Case: Front Range Action Sports continues on the next page)

Business Running Case

Front Range Action Sports (continued)

c. To all of the slides in the presentation, apply the **Box** transition, and then change the **Effect Options** to **From Top**. Display **Slide 6**, and then apply the **Split** entrance effect to the numbered list.

d. Display **Slide 3**. In the **Notes pane**, type **The key elements necessary to achieve our 2016 goals are the expansion of the winter sports product line, an aggressive marketing campaign, and new retail locations in California and Washington.**

e. Insert a **Header & Footer** for the **Notes and Handouts**. Include the **Date and time** updated automatically, the **Page number**, and a **Footer** with the file name

End **You have completed Business Running Case 1**

Glossary

3-D The shortened term for *three-dimensional*, which refers to an image that appears to have all three spatial dimensions—length, width, and depth.

Absolute cell reference A cell reference that refers to cells by their fixed position in a worksheet; an absolute cell reference remains the same when the formula is copied.

Accounting Number Format The Excel number format that applies a thousand comma separator where appropriate, inserts a fixed U.S. Dollar sign aligned at the left edge of the cell, applies two decimal places, and leaves a small amount of space at the right edge of the cell to accommodate a parenthesis for negative numbers.

Active cell The cell, surrounded by a black border, ready to receive data or be affected by the next Excel command.

Address bar The bar at the top of a folder window with which you can navigate to a different folder or library, or go back to a previous one.

After Previous An animation command that begins the animation sequence for the selected PowerPoint slide element immediately after the completion of the previous animation or slide transition.

Aggregate functions Calculations such as MIN, MAX, AVG, and SUM that are performed on a group of records.

Alignment The placement of paragraph text relative to the left and right margins.

All Programs An area of the Start menu that displays all the available programs on your computer system.

American Psychological Association (APA) One of two commonly used style guides for formatting research papers.

Anchor The symbol that indicates to which paragraph an object is attached.

AND condition A condition in which only records where all of the values are present in the selected fields.

Animation A visual or sound effect added to an object or text on a slide.

Animation Painter A feature that copies animation settings from one object to another.

Append To add on to the end of an object; for example, to add records to the end of an existing table.

Application Another term for a program.

Arguments The values that an Excel function uses to perform calculations or operations.

Arithmetic operators The symbols +, –, *, /, %, and ^ used to denote addition, subtraction (or negation), multiplication, division, percentage, and exponentiation in an Excel formula.

Artistic effects Formats applied to images that make pictures resemble sketches or paintings.

Ascending order A sorting order that arranges text in alphabetical order (A to Z) or numbers from the lowest to highest number.

Auto Fill An Excel feature that generates and extends values into adjacent cells based on the values of selected cells.

AutoComplete (Excel) A feature that speeds your typing and lessens the likelihood of errors; if the first few characters you type in a cell match an existing entry in the column, Excel fills in the remaining characters for you.

AutoCorrect A feature that corrects common spelling errors as you type, for example, changing *teh* to *the*.

AutoFit An Excel feature that adjusts the width of a column to fit the cell content of the widest cell in the column.

AutoNumber data type A data type that describes a unique sequential or random number assigned by Access as each record is entered and that is useful for data that has no distinct field that can be considered unique.

AutoPlay A Windows feature that displays when you insert a CD, a DVD, or other removable device, and which lets you choose which program to use to start different kinds of media, such as music CDs, or CDs and DVDs containing photos.

AutoSum Another name for the *SUM* function.

AVERAGE function An Excel function that adds a group of values, and then divides the result by the number of values in the group.

Axis A line that serves as a frame of reference for measurement and which borders the chart plot area.

Back and Forward buttons Buttons at the top of a folder window that work in conjunction with the address bar to change folders by going backward or forward one folder at a time.

Background Removal A command that removes unwanted portions of a picture so that the picture does not appear as a self-contained rectangle.

Background style A slide background fill variation that combines theme colors in different intensities or patterns.

Backstage tabs The area along the left side of Backstage view with tabs to display various pages of commands.

Backstage view A centralized space for file management tasks; for example, opening, saving, printing, publishing, or sharing a file. A navigation pane displays along the left side with tabs that group file-related tasks together.

Bar tab stop A vertical bar that displays at a tab stop.

Base The starting point; used in calculating the rate of increase, which is the amount of increase divided by the base.

Best Fit An Access command that adjusts the width of a column to accommodate the column's longest entry.

Between . . . And operator A comparison operator that looks for values within a range.

Bevel A shape effect that uses shading and shadows to make the edges of a shape appear to be curved or angled.

Bibliography A list of cited works in a report or research paper also referred to as *Works Cited*, *Sources*, or *References*, depending upon the report style.

Black slide A slide that displays at the end of an electronic slide show indicating that the presentation is over.

Blank database A database that has no data and has no database tools—you must create the data and the tools as you need them.

Blank Report tool An Access tool with which you can create a report from scratch by adding the fields you want in the order in which you want them to display.

Body font A font that is applied to all slide text except titles.

Body The text of a letter.

Bound control A control that retrieves its data from an underlying table or query; a text box control is an example of a bound control.

Bound The term used to describe objects and controls that are based on data that is stored in tables.

Bullets Text symbols such as small circles or check marks that precede each item in a bulleted list.

Bulleted list A list of items with each item introduced by a symbol such as a small circle or check mark, and which is useful when the items in the list can be displayed in any order.

Calculated control A control that contains an expression, often a formula, that uses one or more fields from the underlying table or query.

Calculated field A field that stores the value of a mathematical operation.

Caption A property setting that displays a name for a field in a table, query, form, or report other than that listed as the field name.

Category axis The area along the bottom of a chart that identifies the categories of data; also referred to as the *x-axis*.

Category label A chart element that identifies a category of data.

Category labels The labels that display along the bottom of a chart to identify the categories of data; Excel uses the row titles as the category names.

Cell The intersection of a column and a row.

Cell (Word) The box at the intersection of a row and column in a Word table.

Cell address Another name for a *cell reference.*

Cell content Anything typed into a cell.

Cell reference The identification of a specific cell by its intersecting column letter and row number.

Cell style A defined set of formatting characteristics, such as font, font size, font color, cell borders, and cell shading.

Center alignment An arrangement of text in which the text is centered between the left and right margins.

Center alignment The alignment of text or objects that is centered horizontally between the left and right margin.

Center tab stop A tab stop in which the text centers around the tab stop location.

Chart A graphic representation of numeric data.

Chart (Excel) The graphic representation of data in a worksheet; data presented as a chart is usually easier to understand than a table of numbers.

Chart area The entire chart and all of its elements.

Chart Elements box The box in the Chart Tools tabs from which you can select a chart element so that you can format it.

Chart layout The combination of chart elements that can be displayed in a chart such as a title, legend, labels for the columns, and the table of charted cells.

Chart Layouts gallery A group of predesigned chart layouts that you can apply to an Excel chart.

Chart sheet A workbook sheet that contains only a chart.

Chart style The overall visual look of a chart in terms of its graphic effects, colors, and backgrounds; for example, you can have flat or beveled columns, colors that solid or transparent, and backgrounds that are dark or light.

Chart Styles gallery A group of predesigned chart styles that you can apply to an Excel chart.

Chart types Various chart formats used in a way that is meaningful to the reader; common examples are column charts, pie charts, and line charts.

Citation A note inserted into the text of a research paper that refers the reader to a source in the bibliography.

Click The action of pressing the left button on your mouse pointing device one time.

Clip art Predefined graphics included with Microsoft Office or downloaded from the Web.

Clip A single media file, for example art, sound, animation, or a movie.

Column A vertical group of cells in a worksheet.

Column break indicator A single dotted line with the text *Column Break* that indicates where a manual column break was inserted.

Column chart A chart in which the data is arranged in columns and which is useful for showing data changes over a period of time or for illustrating comparisons among items.

Column chart A type of chart used to compare data.

Column heading The letter that displays at the top of a vertical group of cells in a worksheet; beginning with the first letter of the alphabet, a unique letter or combination of letters identifies each column.

Comma Style The Excel number format that inserts thousand comma separators where appropriate and applies two decimal places; Comma Style also leaves space at the right to accommodate a parenthesis when negative numbers are present.

Command An instruction to a computer program that causes an action to be carried out.

Common dialog boxes The set of dialog boxes that includes Open, Save, and Save As, which are provided by the Windows programming interface, and which display and operate in all of the Office programs in the same manner.

Common field A field in one or more tables that stores the same data.

Comparison operator Symbols that evaluate each value to determine if it is the same (=), greater than (>), less than (<), or in between a range of values as specified by the criteria.

Complimentary closing A parting farewell in a business letter.

Compound criteria Multiple conditions in a query or filter.

Compressed file A file that has been reduced in size and thus takes up less storage space and can be transferred to other computers quickly.

Conditional format A format that changes the appearance of a cell—for example, by adding cell shading or font color—based on a condition; if the condition is true, the cell is formatted based on that condition, and if the condition is false, the cell is *not* formatted.

Constant value Numbers, text, dates, or times of day that you type into a cell.

Content control In a template, an area indicated by placeholder text that can be used to add text, pictures, dates, or lists.

Context sensitive A command associated with activities in which you are engaged; often activated by right-clicking a screen item.

Context sensitive command A command associated with activities in which you are engaged.

Contextual tabs Tabs that are added to the Ribbon automatically when a specific object, such as a picture, is selected, and that contain commands relevant to the selected object.

Control An object on a form or report that displays data, performs actions, and lets you view and work with information.

Control layout The grouped arrangement of controls on a form or report.

Copy A command that duplicates a selection and places it on the Clipboard.

COUNTIF function A statistical function that counts the number of cells within a range that meet the given condition and that has two arguments—the range of cells to check and the criteria.

Criteria (Access) Conditions in a query that identify the specific records for which you are looking.

Criteria (Excel) Conditions that you specify in a logical function.

Crop A command that reduces the size of a picture by removing vertical or horizontal edges.

Crosshair pointer A pointer that indicates that you can draw a shape.

Crosstab query A query that uses an aggregate function for data that can be grouped by two types of information and displays the data in a compact, spreadsheet-like format.

Currency data type An Access data type that describes monetary values and numeric data that can be used in mathematical calculations involving data with one to four decimal places.

Cut A command that removes a selection and places it on the Clipboard.

Data Facts about people, events, things, or ideas.

Data (Excel) Text or numbers in a cell.

Data bar A cell format consisting of a shaded bar that provides a visual cue to the reader about the value of a cell relative to other cells; the length of the bar represents the value in the cell—a longer bar represents a higher value and a shorter bar represents s lower value.

Data entry The action of typing the record data into a database form or table.

Data marker A column, bar, area, dot, pie slice, or other symbol in a chart that represents a single data point; related data points form a data series.

Data point A value that originates in a worksheet cell and that is represented in a chart by a data marker.

Data series Related data points represented by data markers; each data series has a unique color or pattern represented in the chart legend.

Data source (Access) The table or tables from which a form, query, or report retrieves its data.

Data source (Word) A list of variable information, such as names and addresses, that is merged with a main document to create customized form letters or labels.

Data type The characteristic that defines the kind of data that can be entered into a field, such as numbers, text, or dates.

Database management system Database software that controls how related collections of data are stored, organized, retrieved, and secured; also known as a *DBMS*.

Database template A preformatted database designed for a specific purpose.

Database An organized collection of facts about people, events, things, or ideas related to a specific topic or purpose.

Datasheet view The Access view that displays data organized in columns and rows similar to an Excel worksheet.

Date control A control on a form or report that inserts the current date each time the form or report is opened.

Date line The first line in a business letter that contains the current date and that is positioned just below the letterhead if a letterhead is used.

DBMS An acronym for *database management system*.

Decimal tab stop A tab stop in which the text aligns with the decimal point at the tab stop location.

Default The term that refers to the current selection or setting that is automatically used by a computer program unless you specify otherwise.

Descending order A sorting order that arranges text in reverse alphabetical order (Z to A) or numbers from the highest to lowest number.

Deselect The action of canceling the selection of an object or block of text by clicking outside of the selection.

Design grid The lower area of the Query window that displays the design of the query.

Design view An Access view that displays the detailed structure of a query, form, or report; for forms and reports, may be the view in which some tasks must be performed, and only the controls, and not the data, display in this view.

Desktop In Windows, the opening screen that simulates your work area.

Destination table (Access) The table to which you import or append data.

Detail section The section of a form or report that displays the records from the underlying table or query.

Detail sheets The worksheets that contain the details of the information summarized on a summary sheet.

Details pane The area at the bottom of a folder window that displays the most common file properties.

Dialog Box Launcher A small icon that displays to the right of some group names on the Ribbon, and which opens a related dialog box or task pane providing additional options and commands related to that group.

Dialog box A small window that contains options for completing a task.

Displayed value The data that displays in a cell.

Document properties Details about a file that describe or identify it, including the title, author name, subject, and keywords that identify the document's topic or contents; also known as *metadata*.

Dot leader A series of dots preceding a tab that guides the eye across the line.

Double-click The action of clicking the left mouse button two times in rapid succession.

Drag The action of holding down the left mouse button while moving your mouse.

Drag and drop The action of moving a selection by dragging it to a new location.

Drawing objects Graphic objects, such as shapes, diagrams, lines, or circles.

Edit The actions of making changes to text or graphics in an Office file.

Editing The process of modifying a presentation by adding and deleting slides or by changing the contents of individual slides.

Ellipsis A set of three dots indicating incompleteness; when following a command name, indicates that a dialog box will display.

Emphasis effect Animation that emphasizes an object or text that is already displayed.

Enclosures Additional documents included with a business letter.

Endnote In a research paper, a note placed at the end of a document or chapter.

Enhanced ScreenTip A ScreenTip that displays more descriptive text than a normal ScreenTip.

Entrance effect Animation that brings a slide element onto the screen.

Excel table A series of rows and columns that contains related data that is managed independently from the data in other rows and columns in the worksheet.

Exit effect Animation that moves an object or text off the screen.

Expand Formula Bar button An Excel window element with which you can increase the height of the Formula Bar to display lengthy cell content.

Expand horizontal scroll bar button An Excel window element with which you can increase the width of the horizontal scroll bar.

Explode The action of pulling out one or more pie slices from a pie chart for emphasis.

Expression A formula.

Extract To decompress, or pull out, files from a compressed form.

Field A single piece of information that is stored in every record and formatted as a column in a database table.

Field (Word) A placeholder that displays preset content, such as the current date, the file name, a page number, or other stored information.

Field list A list of the field names in a table.

Field properties Characteristics of a field that control how the field displays and how data can be entered in the field.

Fields In a mail merge, the column headings in the data source.

File A collection of information stored on a computer under a single name, for example a Word document or a PowerPoint presentation.

File list In a folder window, the area on the right that displays the contents of the current folder or library.

Fill The inside color of an object.

Fill color The inside color of text or of an object.

Fill handle The small black square in the lower right corner of a selected cell.

Filter The process of displaying only a portion of the data based on matching a specific value to show only the data that meets the criteria that you specify.

Filter by Form An Access command that filters the records in a form based on one or more fields, or based on more than one value in the field.

Filter by Selection An Access command that retrieves only the records that contain the value in the selected field.

Filtering The process of displaying only a portion of the total records (a subset) based on matching a specific value.

Find and replace (Excel) A command that searches the cells in a worksheet—or in a selected range—for matches and then replaces each match with a replacement value of your choice.

First principle of good database design A principle of good database design stating that data is organized in tables so that there is no redundant data.

Flat database A simple database file that is not related or linked to any other collection of data.

Floating object A graphic that can be moved independently of the surrounding text characters.

Folder window In Windows, a window that displays the contents of the current folder, library, or device, and contains helpful parts so that you can navigate.

Folder A container in which you store files.

Font A set of characters with the same design and shape.

Font styles Formatting emphasis such as bold, italic, and underline.

Footer (PowerPoint) Text that displays at the bottom of every slide or that prints at the bottom of a sheet of slide handouts or notes pages.

Footer A reserved area for text or graphics that displays at the bottom of each page in a document.

Footnote In a research paper, a note placed at the bottom of the page.

Foreign key The field that is included in the related table so the field can be joined with the primary key in another table for the purpose of creating a relationship.

Form A database object used to enter data, edit data, or display data from a table or query.

Form (Access) An Access object you can use to enter new records into a table, edit or delete existing records in a table, or display existing records.

Form footer Information at the bottom of the screen in Form view that is printed after the last detail section on the last page.

Form header Information, such as a form's title, that displays at the top of the screen in Form view and is printed at the top of the first page when records are printed as forms.

Form tool The Access tool that creates a form with a single mouse click, which includes all of the fields from the underlying data source (table or query).

Form view The Access view in which you can view the records, but you cannot change the layout or design of the form.

Form Wizard The Access tool that creates a form by asking a series of questions.

Format (Excel) Changing the appearance of cells and worksheet elements to make a worksheet attractive and easy to read.

Format as you type The Excel feature by which a cell takes on the formatting of the number typed into the cell.

Format Painter An Office feature that copies formatting from one selection of text to another.

Formatting The process of establishing the overall appearance of text, graphics, and pages in an Office file—for example, in a Word document.

Formatting (PowerPoint) The process of changing the appearance of the text, layout, and design of a slide.

Formatting marks Characters that display on the screen, but do not print, indicating where the Enter key, the Spacebar, and the Tab key were pressed; also called *nonprinting characters.*

Formula AutoComplete An Excel feature which, after typing an = (equal sign) and the beginning letter or letters of a function name, displays a list of function names that match the typed letter(s).

Formula An equation that performs mathematical calculations on values in a worksheet.

Formula Bar An element in the Excel window that displays the value or formula contained in the active cell; here you can also enter or edit values or formulas.

Freeze Panes A command that enables you to select one or more rows or columns and freeze (lock) them into place; the locked rows and columns become separate panes.

Function A predefined formula—a formula that Excel has already built for you—that performs calculations by using specific values in a particular order or structure.

Fund A sum of money set aside for a specific purpose.

Gallery An Office feature that displays a list of potential results instead of just the command name.

General format The default format that Excel applies to numbers; this format has no specific characteristics—whatever you type in the cell will display, with the exception that trailing zeros to the right of a decimal point will not display.

General fund The term used to describe money set aside for the normal operating activities of a government entity such as a city.

Goal Seek A what-if analysis tool that finds the input needed in one cell to arrive at the desired result in another cell.

Graphics Pictures, clip art images, charts, or drawing objects.

Group footer Information printed at the end of each group of records; used to display summary information for the group.

Group header Information printed at the beginning of each new group of records, for example, the group name.

Group, Sort, and Total pane A pane that displays at the bottom of the screen in which you can control how information is sorted and grouped in a report; provides the most flexibility for adding or modifying groups, sort orders, or totals options on a report.

Groups On the Office Ribbon, the sets of related commands that you might need for a specific type of task.

Hanging indent An indent style in which the first line of a paragraph extends to the left of the remaining lines, and that is commonly used for bibliographic entries.

Header (PowerPoint) Text that prints at the top of each sheet of slide handouts or notes pages.

Header A reserved area for text or graphics that displays at the top of each page in a document.

Headings font The font that is applied to slide titles.

Horizontal window split box (Excel) An Excel window element with which you can split the worksheet into two horizontal views of the same worksheet.

HTML See Hypertext Markup Language (HTML).

Hypertext Markup Language (HTML) The language used to format documents that can be opened using any Web browser.

Icons Pictures that represent a program, a file, a folder, or some other object.

IF function A function that uses a logical test to check whether a condition is met, and then returns one value if true, and another value if false.

Import The process of copying data from another file, such as a Word table or an Excel workbook, into a separate file, such as an Access database.

Info tab The tab in Backstage view that displays information about the current file.

Information Data that is organized in a useful manner.

Inline object An object or graphic inserted in a document that acts like a character in a sentence.

Innermost sort field When sorting on multiple fields in Datasheet view, the field that will be used for the second level of sorting.

Insert Worksheet button Located on the row of sheet tabs, a sheet tab that, when clicked, inserts an additional worksheet into the workbook.

Insertion point A blinking vertical line that indicates where text or graphics will be inserted.

Inside address The name and address of the person receiving the letter; positioned below the date line.

Is Not Null A criteria that searches for fields that are not empty.

Is Null A criteria that searches for fields that are empty.

Join line In the Relationships window, the line joining two tables that visually indicates the related field and the type of relationship.

Justified alignment An arrangement of text in which the text aligns evenly on both the left and right margins.

Keyboard shortcut A combination of two or more keyboard keys, used to perform a task that would otherwise require a mouse.

KeyTips The letter that displays on a command in the Ribbon and that indicates the key you can press to activate the command when keyboard control of the Ribbon is activated.

Label control A control on a form or report that contains descriptive information, typically a field name.

Labels Another name for a text value, and which usually provides information about number values.

Landscape orientation A page orientation in which the paper is wider than it is tall.

Layout The arrangement of elements, such as title and subtitle text, lists, pictures, tables, charts, shapes, and movies, on a PowerPoint slide.

Layout selector A small symbol that displays in the upper left corner of a selected control layout in a form or report that is displayed in Layout view or Design view; used to move an entire group of controls.

Layout view The Access view in which you can make changes to a form or report while the object is running—the data from the underlying data source displays.

Leader characters Characters that form a solid, dotted, or dashed line that fills the space preceding a tab stop.

Left alignment An arrangement of text in which the text aligns at the left margin, leaving the right margin uneven.

Left alignment (Excel) The cell format in which characters align at the left edge of the cell; this is the default for text entries and is an example of formatting information stored in a cell.

Left tab stop A tab stop in which the text is left aligned at the tab stop and extends to the right.

Legend A chart element that identifies the patterns or colors that are assigned to the categories in the chart.

Lettered column headings The area along the top edge of a worksheet that identifies each column with a unique letter or combination of letters.

Letterhead The personal or company information that displays at the top of a letter.

Library In Windows, a collection of items, such as files and folders, assembled from various locations that might be on your computer, an external hard drive, removable media, or someone else's computer.

Line break indicator A small nonprinting bent arrow that displays where a manual line break was inserted.

Line chart A chart type that is useful to display trends over time; time displays along the bottom axis and the data point values are connected with a line.

Line spacing The distance between lines of text in a paragraph.

Link A connection to data in another file.

List level An outline level in a presentation represented by a bullet symbol and identified in a slide by the indentation and the size of the text.

Live Preview A technology that shows the result of applying an editing or formatting change as you point to possible results—*before* you actually apply it.

Location Any disk drive, folder, or other place in which you can store files and folders.

Logical functions A group of functions that test for specific conditions and that typically use conditional tests to determine whether specified conditions are true or false.

Logical operators Operators that combine criteria using AND and OR. With two criteria, AND requires that both conditions be met and OR requires that either condition be met.

Logical test Any value or expression that can be evaluated as being true or false.

Mail merge A Microsoft Word feature that joins a main document and a data source to create customized letters or labels.

Main document In a mail merge, the document that contains the text or formatting that remains constant.

Major unit The value in a chart's value axis that determines the spacing between tick marks and between the gridlines in the plot area.

Manual column break An artificial end to a column to balance columns or to provide space for the insertion of other objects.

Manual line break The action of ending a line, before the normal end of the line, without creating a new paragraph.

Manual page break The action of forcing a page to end and placing subsequent text at the top of the next page.

Margins The space between the text and the top, bottom, left, and right edges of the paper.

MAX function An Excel function that determines the largest value in a selected range of values.

MEDIAN function An Excel function that finds the middle value that has as many values above it in the group as are below it; it differs from AVERAGE in that the result is not affected as much by a single value that is greatly different from the others.

Merge & Center A command that joins selected cells in an Excel worksheet into one larger cell and centers the contents in the new cell.

Message Bar The area directly below the Ribbon that displays information such as security alerts when there is potentially unsafe, active content in an Office 2010 document that you open.

Metadata Details about a file that describe or identify it, including the title, author name, subject, and keywords that identify the document's topic or contents; also known as *document properties*.

Microsoft Access A database program, with which you can collect, track, and report data.

Microsoft Excel A spreadsheet program, with which you calculate and analyze numbers and create charts.

Microsoft InfoPath An Office program that enables you to create forms and gather data.

Microsoft Office 2010 A Microsoft suite of products that includes programs, servers, and services for individuals, small organizations, and large enterprises to perform specific tasks.

Microsoft OneNote An Office program with which you can manage notes that you make at meetings or in classes.

Microsoft Outlook An Office program with which you can manage e-mail and organizational activities.

Microsoft PowerPoint A presentation program, with which you can communicate information with high-impact graphics.

Microsoft Publisher An Office program with which you can create desktop publishing documents such as brochures.

Microsoft SharePoint Workspace An Office program that enables you to share information with others in a team environment.

Microsoft Word A word processing program, also referred to as an authoring program, with which you create and share documents by using its writing tools.

MIN function An Excel function that determines the smallest value in a selected range of values.

Mini toolbar A small toolbar containing frequently used formatting commands that displays as a result of selecting text or objects.

Modern Language Association (MLA) One of two commonly used style guides for formatting research papers.

Multiple Items form A form that enables you to display or enter multiple records in a table.

Name Box An element of the Excel window that displays the name of the selected cell, table, chart, or object.

Nameplate The banner on the front page of a newsletter that identifies the publication; also referred to as a *banner*, *flag*, or *masthead*.

Navigate The process of exploring within the organizing structure of Windows.

Navigate (Excel) The process of moving within a worksheet or workbook.

Navigation area An area at the bottom of the Access window that indicates the number of records in the table and contains controls (arrows) with which you can navigate among the records.

Navigation Pane (Access) An area of the Access window that displays and organizes the names of the objects in a database; from here, you open objects for use.

Navigation pane (Windows) In a folder window, the area on the left in which you can navigate to, open, and display favorites, libraries, folders, saved searches, and an expandable list of drives.

New from existing The Word command that opens an existing document as a new unnamed document, so that you can use it as a starting point for a new document.

No Spacing style The Word style that inserts *no* extra space following a paragraph and uses single spacing.

Nonprinting characters Characters that display on the screen, but do not print, indicating where the Enter key, the Spacebar, and the Tab key were pressed; also called *formatting marks*.

Normal template The template that serves as a basis for all new Word documents.

Normal view (Excel) A screen view that maximizes the number of cells visible on your screen and keeps the column letters and row numbers close to the columns and rows.

Normal view (PowerPoint) The primary editing view in PowerPoint in which you write and design your presentations; consists of the Notes pane, Slide pane, and the Slides/Outline pane.

Normalization The process of applying design rules and principles to ensure that your database performs as expected.

Note In a research paper, information that expands on the topic, but that does not fit well in the document text.

Notes page A printout that contains the slide image on the top half of the page and notes that you have created on the Notes pane in the lower half of the page.

Notes pane The PowerPoint screen element that displays below the Slide pane with space to type notes regarding the active slide.

NOW function An Excel function that retrieves the date and time from your computer's calendar and clock and inserts the information into the selected cell.

Nudge The action of moving an object on the page in small precise increments.

Number format A specific way in which Excel displays numbers in a cell.

Number values Constant values consisting of only numbers.

Numbered list A list of items in which each item is introduced by a consecutive number to indicate definite steps, a sequence of actions, or chronological order.

Numbered row headings The area along the left edge of a worksheet that identifies each row with a unique number.

Object window An area of the Access window that displays open objects, such as tables, forms, queries, or reports; by default, each object displays on its own tab.

Objects The basic parts of a database that you create to store your data and to work with your data; for example, tables, forms, queries, and reports.

Office Clipboard A temporary storage area that holds text or graphics that you select and then cut or copy.

On Click An animation command that begins the animation sequence for the selected PowerPoint slide element when the mouse button is clicked or the spacebar is pressed.

One-to-many relationship A relationship between two tables where one record in the first table corresponds to many records in the second table—the most common type of relationship in Access.

Open dialog box A dialog box from which you can navigate to, and then open on your screen, an existing file that was created in that same program.

Operators The symbols with which you can specify the type of calculation you want to perform in an Excel formula.

Option button A round button that allows you to make one choice among two or more options.

Options dialog box A dialog box within each Office application where you can select program settings and other options and preferences.

OR condition A condition in which records that match at least one of the specified values are displayed.

Order of operations The mathematical rules for performing multiple calculations within a formula.

Outermost sort field When sorting on multiple fields in Datasheet view, the field that will be used for the first level of sorting.

Page break indicator A dotted line with the text *Page Break* that indicates where a manual page break was inserted.

Page footer Information printed at the end of every page in a report; used to print page numbers or other information that you want to display at the bottom of every report page.

Page header (Access) Information printed at the top of every page of a report.

Page Layout view A screen view in which you can use the rulers to measure the width and height of data, set margins for printing, hide or display the numbered row headings and the lettered column headings, and change the page orientation; this view is useful for preparing your worksheet for printing.

Page number control A control on a form or report that inserts the page numbers when displayed in Print Preview or when printed.

Pane (Excel) A portion of a worksheet window bounded by and separated from other portions by vertical and horizontal bars.

Paragraph symbol The symbol ¶ that represents a paragraph.

Parenthetical citation In the MLA style, a citation that refers to items on the *Works Cited* page, and which is placed in parentheses; the citation includes the last name of the author or authors, and the page number in the referenced source.

Paste The action of placing text or objects that have been copied or moved from one location to another location.

Paste area The target destination for data that has been cut or copied using the Office Clipboard.

Paste Options Icons that provide a Live Preview of the various options for changing the format of a pasted item with a single click.

Paste Options gallery (Excel) A gallery of buttons that provides a Live Preview of all the Paste options available in the current context.

PDF (Portable Document Format) file A file format that creates an image that preserves the look of your file, but that cannot be easily changed; a popular format for sending documents electronically, because the document will display on most computers.

Percent for new value = base percent + percent of increase The formula for calculating a percentage by which a value increases by adding the base percentage—usually 100%—to the percent increase.

Percentage rate of increase The percent by which one number increases over another number.

Picture element A point of light measured in dots per square inch on a screen; 64 pixels equals 8.43 characters, which is the average number of digits that will fit in a cell in an Excel worksheet using the default font.

Picture styles Frames, shapes, shadows, borders, and other special effects that can be added to an image to create an overall visual style for the image.

Pie chart A chart that shows the relationship of each part to a whole.

Pixel The abbreviated name for a *picture element.*

Placeholder text Text in a content control that indicates the type of information to be entered in a specific location.

Placeholder A box on a slide with dotted or dashed borders that holds title and body text or other content such as charts, tables, and pictures.

Plot area The area bounded by the axes of a chart, including all the data series.

Point The action of moving your mouse pointer over something on your screen.

Point and click method The technique of constructing a formula by pointing to and then clicking cells; this method is convenient when the referenced cells are not adjacent to one another.

Pointer Any symbol that displays on your screen in response to moving your mouse.

Points A measurement of the size of a font; there are 72 points in an inch, with 10-12 points being the most commonly used font size.

Populate The action of filling a database table with records.

Portrait orientation A page orientation in which the paper is taller than it is wide.

Preview pane button In a folder window, the button on the toolbar with which you can display a preview of the contents of a file without opening it in a program.

Primary key The field that uniquely identifies a record in a table; for example, a Student ID number at a college.

Print Preview A view of a document as it will appear when you print it.

Print Titles An Excel command that enables you to specify rows and columns to repeat on each printed page.

Program A set of instructions that a computer uses to perform a specific task, such as word processing, accounting, or data management; also called an *application*.

Program-level control buttons In an Office program, the buttons on the right edge of the title bar that minimize, restore, or close the program.

Property Sheet A list of characteristics—properties—for fields or controls on a form or report in which you can make precise changes to each property associated with the field or control.

Protected view A security feature in Office 2010 that protects your computer from malicious files by opening them in a restricted environment until you enable them; you might encounter this feature if you open a file from an e-mail or download files from the Internet.

Pt. The abbreviation for *point*; for example when referring to a font size.

Query A database object that retrieves specific data from one or more database objects—either tables or other queries—and then, in a single datasheet, displays only the data you specify.

Quick Access Toolbar In an Office program, the small row of buttons in the upper left corner of the screen from which you can perform frequently used commands.

Quick Commands The commands Save, Save As, Open, and Close that display at the top of the navigation pane in Backstage view.

Range Two or more selected cells on a worksheet that are adjacent or nonadjacent; because the range is treated as a single unit, you can make the same changes or combination of changes to more than one cell at a time.

Range finder An Excel feature that outlines cells in color to indicate which cells are used in a formula; useful for verifying which cells are referenced in a formula.

Range finder An Excel feature that outlines cells in color to indicate which cells are used in a formula; useful for verifying which cells are referenced in a formula.

Rate = amount of increase/base The mathematical formula to calculate a rate of increase.

Read-Only A property assigned to a file that prevents the file from being modified or deleted; it indicates that you cannot save any changes to the displayed document unless you first save it with a new name.

Reading view A view in PowerPoint that displays a presentation in a manner similar to a slide show but in which the taskbar, title bar, and status bar remain available in the presentation window.

Record selector bar The bar at the left edge of a record when it is displayed in a form, and which is used to select an entire record.

Record All of the categories of data pertaining to one person, place, thing, event, or idea, and which is formatted as a row in a database table.

Record In a mail merge, a row of information that contains data for one person.

Record selector box The small box at the left of a record in Datasheet view that, when clicked, selects the entire record.

Record source The tables or queries that provide the underlying data for a form or report.

Redundant In a database, information that is repeated in a manner that indicates poor database design.

Referential integrity A set of rules that Access uses to ensure that the data between related tables is valid.

Relational database A sophisticated type of database that has multiple collections of data within the file that are related to one another.

Relationship An association that you establish between two tables based on common fields.

Relative cell reference In a formula, the address of a cell based on the relative position of the cell that contains the formula and the cell referred to.

Report A database object that summarizes the fields and records from a table or query in an easy-to-read format suitable for printing.

Report footer Information printed once at the end of a report; used to print report totals or other summary information for the entire report.

Report header Information printed once at the beginning of a report; used for logos, titles, and dates.

Report tool The Access tool that creates a report with one mouse click, which displays all of the fields and records from the record source that you select—a quick way to look at the underlying data.

Report Wizard An Access feature with which you can create a report by answering a series of questions; Access designs the report based on your answers.

Ribbon The user interface in Office 2010 that groups the commands for performing related tasks on tabs across the upper portion of the program window.

Ribbon tabs The tabs on the Office Ribbon that display the names of the task-oriented groups of commands.

Right alignment An arrangement of text in which the text aligns at the right margin, leaving the left margin uneven.

Right tab stop A tab stop in which the text is right aligned at the tab stop and extends to the left.

Right-click The action of clicking the right mouse button one time.

Rotation handle A green circle that provides a way to rotate a selected image.

Rounding A procedure in which you determine which digit at the right of the number will be the last digit displayed and then increase it by one if the next digit to its right is 5, 6, 7, 8, or 9.

Row A horizontal group of cells in a worksheet.

Row heading The numbers along the left side of an Excel worksheet that designate the row numbers.

Ruler guides Dotted vertical and horizontal lines that display in the rulers indicating the pointer's position.

Run The process in which Access searches the records in the table(s) included in the query design, finds the records that match the specified criteria, and then displays the records in a datasheet; only the fields that have been included in the query design display.

Salutation The greeting line of a business letter.

Sans serif A font design with no lines or extensions on the ends of characters.

Scale to Fit Excel commands that enable you to stretch or shrink the width, height, or both, of printed output to fit a maximum number of pages.

Scaling (Excel) The process of shrinking the width and/or height of printed output to fit a maximum number of pages.

Screenshot An image of an active window on your computer that you can paste into a document.

ScreenTip A small box that that displays useful information when you perform various mouse actions such as pointing to screen elements or dragging.

Scroll bar A vertical or horizontal bar in a window or a pane to assist in bringing an area into view, and which contains a scroll box and scroll arrows.

Scroll box The box in the vertical and horizontal scroll bars that can be dragged to reposition the contents of a window or pane on the screen.

Search box In a folder window, the box in which you can type a word or a phrase to look for an item in the current folder or library.

Second principle of good database design A principle stating that appropriate database techniques are used to ensure the accuracy of data entered into a table.

Section A portion of a document that can be formatted differently from the rest of the document.

Section bar A gray bar in a form or report that identifies and separates one section from another; used to select the section and to change the size of the adjacent section.

Section break A double dotted line that indicates the end of one section and the beginning of another section.

Select To highlight, by dragging with your mouse, areas of text or data or graphics, so that the selection can be edited, formatted, copied, or moved.

Select All box A box in the upper left corner of the worksheet grid that, when clicked, selects all the cells in a worksheet.

Select query A type of Access query that retrieves (selects) data from one or more tables or queries, displaying the selected data in a datasheet; also known as a *simple select query*.

Series A group of things that come one after another in succession; for example, January, February, March, and so on.

Serif font A font design that includes small line extensions on the ends of the letters to guide the eye in reading from left to right.

Shapes Lines, arrows, stars, banners, ovals, rectangles, and other basic shapes with which you can illustrate an idea, a process, or a workflow.

Sheet tab scrolling buttons Buttons to the left of the sheet tabs used to display Excel sheet tabs that are not in view; used when there are more sheet tabs than will display in the space provided.

Sheet tabs The labels along the lower border of the Excel window that identify each worksheet.

Shortcut menu A menu that displays commands and options relevant to the selected text or object.

Simple select query Another name for a select query.

Single File Web Page A document saved using HTML and that opens using a Web browser.

Single-record form A form that enables you to display or enter one record at a time in a table.

Sizing handles Small circles and squares that indicate that a picture is selected.

Slide A presentation page that can contain text, pictures, tables, charts, and other multimedia or graphic objects.

Slide handouts Printed images of slides on a sheet of paper.

Slide pane A PowerPoint screen element that displays a large image of the active slide.

Slide Sorter view A presentation view that displays thumbnails of all of the slides in a presentation.

Slide transitions The motion effects that occur in Slide Show view when you move from one slide to the next during a presentation.

Slides/Outline pane A PowerPoint screen element that displays the presentation either in the form of thumbnails (Slides tab) or in outline format (Outline tab).

Small caps A font effect, usually used in titles, that changes lowercase text into capital (uppercase) letters using a reduced font size.

SmartArt graphic A visual representation of information that you can create by choosing from among many different layouts to communicate your message or ideas effectively.

SmartArt Styles Combinations of formatting effects that you can apply to SmartArt graphics.

SmartArt A designer-quality visual representation of your information that you can create by choosing from among many different layouts to effectively communicate your message or ideas.

Sort The process of arranging data in a specific order based on the value in each field.

Source file When importing a file, refers to the file being imported.

Sparkline A tiny chart in the background of a cell that gives a visual trend summary alongside your data; makes a pattern more obvious.

Spin box A small box with an upward- and downward-pointing arrow that lets you move rapidly through a set of values by clicking.

Split button A button divided into two parts and in which clicking the main part of the button performs a command and clicking the arrow opens a menu with choices.

Spreadsheet Another name for a *worksheet.*

Stacked layout A control layout format that is similar to a paper form, with label controls placed to the left of each textbox control. The controls are grouped together for easy editing.

Start button The button on the Windows taskbar that displays the Start menu.

Start menu The Windows menu that provides a list of choices and is the main gateway to your computer's programs, folders, and settings.

Statistical functions Excel functions, including the AVERAGE, MEDIAN, MIN, and MAX functions, which are useful to analyze a group of measurements.

Status bar (Excel) The area along the lower edge of the Excel window that displays, on the left side, the current cell mode, page number, and worksheet information; on the right side, when numerical data is selected, common calculations such as Sum and Average display.

Status bar The area along the lower edge of an Office program window that displays file information on the left and buttons to control how the window looks on the right.

Structure In Access, the underlying design of a table, including field names, data types, descriptions, and field properties.

Style A group of formatting commands, such as font, font size, font color, paragraph alignment, and line spacing that can be applied to a paragraph with one command.

Style (PowerPoint) A collection of formatting options that can be applied to a picture, text, or an object.

Style guide A manual that contains standards for the design and writing of documents.

Subdatasheet A format for displaying related records when you click the plus sign (+) next to a record in a table on the *one* side of a relationship.

Subfolder A folder within a folder.

Subject line The optional line following the inside address in a business letter that states the purpose of the letter.

Subpoints Secondary-level information in a SmartArt graphic.

Subset A portion of the total records available.

SUM function A predefined formula that adds all the numbers in a selected range of cells.

Summary sheet A worksheet where totals from other worksheets are displayed and summarized.

Synonyms Words with the same or similar meaning.

Tab order The order in which the insertion point moves from one field to another in a form when you press the Tab key.

Tab stop Specific locations on a line of text, marked on the Word ruler, to which you can move the insertion point by pressing the Tab key, and which is used to align and indent text.

Table A format for information that organizes and presents text and data in columns and rows.

Table (Access) The database object that stores data organized in an arrangement of columns and rows, and which is the foundation of an Access database.

Table (Word) An arrangement of information organized into rows and columns.

Table area The upper area of the Query window that displays field lists for the tables that are used in the query.

Table style Formatting applied to an entire table so that it is consistent with the presentation theme.

Tables and Related Views An arrangement in the Navigation Pane that groups objects by the table to which they are related.

Tabs On the Office Ribbon, the name of each activity area in the Office Ribbon.

Tags Custom file properties that you create to help find and organize your own files.

Task pane A window within a Microsoft Office application in which you can enter options for completing a command.

Template An existing document that you use as a starting point for a new document; it opens a copy of itself, unnamed, and then you use the structure—and possibly some content, such as headings—as the starting point for the new document.

Text alignment (PowerPoint) The horizontal placement of text within a placeholder.

Text box A movable resizable container for text or graphics.

Text box (PowerPoint) An object within which you can position text anywhere on a slide.

Text box control The graphical object on a form or report that displays the data from the underlying table or query; a text box control is known as a bound control.

Text control A content control that accepts only a text entry.

Text data type An Access data type that describes text, a combination of text and numbers, or numbers that are not used in calculations, such as a number that is an identifier like a Student ID.

Text effects Decorative formats, such as shadowed or mirrored text, text glow, 3-D effects, and colors that make text stand out.

Text string A sequence of characters.

Text values Constant values consisting of only text, and which usually provides information about number values; also referred to as *labels*.

Text wrapping The manner in which text displays around an object.

Theme A predefined format that can be applied to the entire database or to individual objects in the database.

Theme A predesigned set of colors, fonts, lines, and fill effects that look good together and that can be applied to your entire document or to specific items.

Theme (PowerPoint) A set of unified design elements that provides a look for your presentation by applying colors, fonts, and effects.

Theme colors A set of coordinating colors that are applied to the backgrounds, objects, and text in a presentation.

Theme font A theme that determines the font applied to two types of slide text—headings and body.

Thesaurus A research tool that provides a list of synonyms.

Thumbnails (PowerPoint) Miniature images of presentation slides.

Tick marks The short lines that display on an axis at regular intervals.

Timing options Animation options that control when animated items display in the animation sequence.

Title bar The bar at the top edge of the program window that indicates the name of the current file and the program name.

Title slide The first slide in a presentation the purpose of which is to provide an introduction to the presentation topic.

Toggle button A button that can be turned on by clicking it once, and then turned off by clicking it again.

Toolbar In a folder window, a row of buttons with which you can perform common tasks, such as changing the view of your files and folders or burning files to a CD.

Top-level points The main text points in a SmartArt graphic.

Trim The action of deleting parts of a video to make it shorter.

Triple-click The action of clicking the left mouse button three times in rapid succession.

Truncated Refers to data that is cut off or shortened.

Trust Center An area of the Access program where you can view the security and privacy settings for your Access installation.

Trusted Documents A security feature in Office 2010 that remembers which files you have already enabled; you might encounter this feature if you open a file from an e-mail or download files from the Internet.

Unbound control A control that does not have a source of data, such as a title in a form or report.

Underlying formula The formula entered in a cell and visible only on the Formula Bar.

Underlying value The data that displays in the Formula Bar.

USB flash drive A small data storage device that plugs into a computer USB port.

Value Another name for a *constant value*.

Value after increase = base x percent for new value The formula for calculating the value after an increase by multiplying the original value—the base—by the percent for new value (see the *Percent for new value* formula).

Value axis A numerical scale on the left side of a chart that shows the range of numbers for the data points; also referred to as the *y-axis*.

Vertical window split box (Excel) A small box on the vertical scroll bar with which you can split the window into two vertical views of the same worksheet.

Views button In a folder window, a toolbar button with which you can choose how to view the contents of the current location.

Volatile A term used to describe an Excel function that is subject to change each time the workbook is reopened; for example the NOW function updates itself to the current date and time each time the workbook is opened.

What-if analysis The process of changing the values in cells to see how those changes affect the outcome of formulas in a worksheet.

Wildcard character In a query, a character that serves as a placeholder for one or more unknown characters in your criteria; an asterisk (*) represents one or more unknown characters, and a question mark (?) represents a single unknown character.

Window A rectangular area on a computer screen in which programs and content appear, and which can be moved, resized, minimized, or closed.

Windows Explorer The program that displays the files and folders on your computer, and which is at work anytime you are viewing the contents of files and folders in a window.

Windows taskbar The area along the lower edge of the Windows desktop that contains the Start button and an area to display buttons for open programs.

With Previous An animation command that begins the animation sequence on a PowerPoint slide at the same time as the previous animation or slide transition.

Wizard A feature in Microsoft Office that walks you step by step through a process.

WordArt A gallery of text styles with which you can create decorative effects, such as shadowed or mirrored text.

Wordwrap The feature that moves text from the right edge of a paragraph to the beginning of the next line as necessary to fit within the margins.

Workbook An Excel file that contains one or more worksheets.

Workbook-level buttons Buttons at the far right of the Ribbon tabs that minimize or restore a displayed workbook.

Workbook-level buttons Buttons at the far right of the Ribbon tabs that minimize or restore a displayed workbook.

Works Cited In the MLA style, a list of cited works placed at the end of a research paper or report.

Worksheet The primary document that you use in Excel to work with and store data, and which is formatted as a pattern of uniformly spaced horizontal and vertical lines.

Writer's identification The name and title of the author of a letter, placed near the bottom of the letter under the complimentary closing—also referred to as the *writer's signature block.*

Writer's signature block The name and title of the author of a letter, placed near the bottom of the letter, under the complimentary closing—also referred to as the *writer's identification.*

x-axis Another name for the *category axis.*

x-axis Another name for the horizontal *(category) axis.*

y-axis Another name for the *value axis.*

y-axis Another name for the vertical *(value) axis.*

Zoom The action of increasing or decreasing the viewing area on the screen.

Index

Symbols and Numbers

*** (asterisk), definition, 625**
= (equal to operator), 411
>= (greater than or equal to operator), 411
< (less than operator), 411
<= (less than or equal to operator), 411
3-D (three-dimensional), formatting pie charts, 469–470

A

absolute cell references
- copying formulas, 368–370
- definition, 368, 465
- dollar signs, 369

Access, 37
Access 2010
- Business Running Cases, 727–730
- content-based assessments, 570–589, 636–656, 702–723
- outcomes-based assessments, 590–592, 657–659, 724–726

accessing Web sites from Address bar, 121–124
Accessories programs, 75–80. ***See also*** **Calculator; Paint; Snipping Tool**
Accounting Number Format, 351
active window, 76
active worksheets, 340
Ad-Aware, 54
Add a Favorite dialog box, 119
Add button, 119
Administrative Tools, 34
Adobe Photoshop/Illustrator, 39
address bar, 65–66, 118–119, 121–124
Address Bar down arrow, 123
addresses. ***See*** **Web addresses**
- cells (worksheets), 340
- labels, 301, 305
- mail merges, 300

Advanced Filter/Sort, filtering records, 681–683
Advanced Micro Devices (AMD), 14
adware, 52
Aero interface, 68, 81–83
After Previous option (animation timing option), 862
aggregate functions, queries, 631
Alerts!
- file type difference, 98
- gadgets, 71
- hidden taskbar, 74
- icon differences, 64
- screen differences, 63
- window variances (Windows Explorer window), 65, 68

alignment
- controls, Design view, 697–698
- form controls, 676–678
- number values, worksheets, 345
- objects, presentations, 808–811
- pictures, documents, 166–167
- tab alignment options, 188
- text
  - documents, 178–179
  - slides, 759
  - worksheets, 341, 343–344
- video (presentations), 867

All Programs **command, 74–75**
alphanumeric keys, 11
Alt key and Tab key, 83
ALU (arithmetic logic unit), 14
AMD (Advanced Micro Devices), 14
anchors, 166
AND condition, 621, 682
animation
- definition, 858
- slide shows, 858–865
  - Animation Painter, 864–865
  - charts, 885
  - Effect Options, 858–861
  - entrance effects, 858–861
  - removing animation, 864–865
  - timing options, 861–863

Animation Painter, 864–865
antispyware software, 53–54
antivirus software, 53–54
Appearance (Control Panel), 34
appending, definition, 539
Apple Macintosh computers (Macs), 6
application software, 35–40
Apply to box, 298
Architecture backgrounds, 70
arguments, 404
arithmetic logic unit (ALU), 14
arithmetic operator symbols, 366–368
arrow keys, 12
arrow keys, moving objects, 799
artistic effects (pictures), 167, 747
Artistic Effects gallery, 747
ascending order
- definition, 601
- sorting records, 601–602

assessments
- content-based assessments
  - Access 2010, 570–589, 636–656, 702–723
  - Excel 2010, 378–395, 442–459, 500–517
  - PowerPoint 2010, 766–783, 826–843, 886–903
  - Word 2010, 194–211, 250–269, 306–325
- outcomes-based assessments
  - Access 2010, 590–592, 657–659, 724–726
  - Excel 2010, 396–399, 460–462, 518–521
  - PowerPoint 2010, 784–787, 844–847, 904–907
  - Word 2010, 212–214, 270–272, 326–328

associated Web site name, 130
asterisk (*), definition, 625
audio ports, 26
Auto Fill, inserting data into worksheets, 342–343
Auto Fill Options button, 342
AutoComplete, inserting data into worksheets, 340–341
AutoCorrect, recording entries, 233–234
AutoCorrect Options button, 185

AutoFit, adjusting column widths, 361
AutoFit Options button, 742–743
AutoFit Text to Placeholder option, 743
auto-hide feature (for taskbar), 74
automated maintenance tasks, 45–46
automatic numbered lists, activating, 185
AutoNumber data type, definition, 536
Auto Play dialog box, 90
AutoSum button, 348
AVERAGE function, 403–405
averaging values (functions), 404
Avery 5160 address label, 301
AVG Anti-Virus, 53
AVG function, queries, 630–631
axes (line charts) formatting, 493–494

B

Back button, 120
***Back* command, 75**
backgrounds, desktop, 70
Background Removal commands, 813
Background Styles button, 852
Background Styles gallery, 852
backgrounds
  removing from pictures, presentations, 813–816
  slides
    adding pictures, 854–857
    fill colors, 857
    hiding graphics, 853–854
    resetting, 857
    styles, 852–853
Backstage view
  Print tab, 174
backup tape drives, 23
Bar tab alignment option, 188
Best Fit, definition, 548
Between...And operator, definition, 620
bevels, 469
bibliographies
  definition, 282
  page breaks, 285–286
Bing, 133
Blank Report tool
  creating reports, 688–691
  definition, 688
block style cover letters, 234–236
www.bls.gov, 122, 129, 137
Bluetooth (wireless technology), 26
BMP files, 98
body (cover letters), 233
Body font, 851
boot process, 30
borders
  adding to paragraphs, documents, 298–299
  cells, 344
  documents, adding, 167–168
  placeholders (slides), 792
  text, documents, 298
  Word tables, 226–228
  worksheets, financial information, 352
Borders and Shading dialog box, 298
botnets, 52
bound, definition, 666
bound controls, definition, 671
broadcasting slide shows, 765
browsers, 117
browsers, Web, 40
Budget file, 98
bulleted lists
  converting to numbered lists, 792–793
  creating, 183–184
  customizing bullets, 187
  definition, 183
  formatting, presentations, 791–794
  spacing between bulleted points, 184
  styles, presentations, 793–794
  tables (Word), creating, 220–221
bullets
  creating SmartArt graphics (presentations), 819–820
  customizing
    documents, 187
    presentations, 793–794
  definition, 183
  list levels (presentations), 739–740
  removing bullet symbols from, presentations, 794
  SmartArt, 193
  subpoints, 191
burn (record), 21
burner, CD, 22
bus topology, 43
Business Communication texts, creating cover letters, 234–236
business letters
  creating letterheads, 230–231
  recording AutoCorrect entries, 233–234
Business Running Cases
  Access 2010, 727–730
  Excel 2010, 523–526
  PowerPoint 2010, 909–912
  Word 2010, 329–333
buttons. *See* individual names of buttons
By Series option (chart animation sequence), 885
bytes, 16

C

.ca, 122
calculated fields
  definition, 627
  queries, 627–629
calculations
  AutoSum button, 348
  AVERAGE function, 403–405
  formulas
    absolute cell references, 368–370
    range finder, 368
  increasing values, 486–487
  MAX function, 406
  MEDIAN function, 405–406
  MIN function, 406
  NOW function, 414–415
  percentage, 486
  percentage rate of increase, 481–484
  percentages, 370
  status bar, 368
  SUM function, 346–348, 403–405
Calculator, 75
Caps Lock key, 12

card readers, 4
carpal tunnel syndrome, 11
cartridges, laser/ink-jet, 18
category axis, 353, 493
category labels (charts), 353, 881
caution, on Internet, 53
CD burner, 22
CD (Compact Disc), 91
CD drives, 22
CD-R, 21
CD-ROMs, 21
CD-RW, 21
CD-RW drive, 22
CDs (compact discs), 21
cell content, definition, 340
cell references, presentation charts, 881
cells (Word tables), merging, 223–224
cells (worksheets), 340–341
addresses, 340
borders, 344
clearing contents, 427–428
copying formulas with fill handles, 348–349
data points, 354
displayed values, 345
error messages, resolving, 407–408
Find and Replace feature, 413–414
Format Painter, 484–486
formatting
clearing formats, 427–428
financial numbers, 351–352
Merge & Center command, 350–351
with Percent Style, 372
styles, 350–351
moving contents, 407–408
pasting groups, 488–490
ranges, 344
conditional formatting, 412
inserting data by, 365–366
selecting, 350
references, 340, 349
series, Auto Fill, 342
styles, 350–351
center alignment, 178–179
Center tab alignment option, 188
central processing units. *See* CPUs
Change Entrance Effect dialog box, 860
chart area, formatting, 472–473
Chart Layouts gallery, 355
Chart Tools, 353
charts
chart sheets
creating, 465–467
printing workbooks, 477–479
formatting, 495–497
presentations
animation, 885
category labels, 881
cell references, 881
column charts, 880–883
column headings, 881
creating, 880–883
data markers, 882
data points, 882
data series, 882
deleting columns, 884
deleting data from, 883–884
editing data, 883
legends, 881
line charts, 883–884
styles, 880–883
printing, 479
worksheets
category axis, 353
category labels, 353
chart types, 353
column charts, 352–356
data markers, 354
data series, 354
definition, 352
formatting, 472–473
layouts, 355
legends, 353
line
creating, 491–492
formatting axes, 493–494
pie
applying percentages to labels, 468–469
coloring pie slices, 471–472
creating, 465–467
data markers, 467
data points, 467
data series, 467
definition, 465
exploding pie slices, 471–472
formatting with 3-D, 469–470
legends, 467
rotating, 470–471
rows, inserting into line charts, 491–492
sparklines, 352, 356–357
inserting, 439
summary sheets, 436–437
styles, 355
text boxes, inserting, 473–474
types, 353
updating, 474
value axis, 353
x-axis, 353
y-axis, 353
citations
adding to research papers, 282–285
corporate authors, 283
definition, 282
Web sites, 284
clearing cell contents (worksheets), 427–428
click (right-click, double-click), 66
clicks (mouse clicks), 12–13
clients, 43
client/server networks, 42–43
clip art
inserting into presentations, 795–797
newsletters, 294–295
Clip Art button, 797
Clip Art commands, 797
Clip Art pane, 795–796
clip art. *See also* graphics; images; pictures
Clock, Language, Region (Control Panel), 34
Close button, 119
for gadgets, 72
for windows, 65–66

closing
- databases, 558
- queries, 606

closing windows, 87
coaxial cables, 40
colors
- fills, slide backgrounds, 857
- fonts, presentations, 757–759
- pie slices, 471–472
- shapes, presentations, 804–805
- sheet tabs, 424–425
- SmartArt graphics, 823
- themes, presentations, 851–852

column break indicators, 294
column breaks
- inserting into newsletters, 293–294
- manual column breaks, 291

column charts
- presentations, 880–883
- worksheets, 352–356

column headings (charts), presentations, 881
column sparklines, 439
columns
- charts (presentations), deleting, 884
- newsletters
  - changing text to two columns, 291–292
  - inserting breaks, 293–294
  - justifying text, 293
  - multiple columns, 292–293
- tables (databases), changing width, 547–549
- tables (documents), changing width, 221–222
- worksheets, 339
  - default width, 343
  - deleting, 372–374
  - freezing panes, 415–416
  - headings, 339
  - inserting, 372–374
  - sizing, 343–344
  - unfreezing panes, 415–416
  - width, 374–376

columns, in file list, 93
.com, 122, 135
Comma Style, 351
Command bar, 64, 119
Commands, 120–121
- Background Removal, 813
- Clip Art, 797
- Distribute Rows, 878
- Filter By Form, definition, 681
- Filter By Selection, definition, 679
- Freeze Panes, 415–416
- Merge & Center, 350–351
- New from existing, 231–232
- Paste Special, 488–490
- Print Titles, 419
- Scale to Fit, 419
- Spelling and Grammar, 241

commas, typing numbers in cells (worksheets), 485
common fields, definition, 530
communication/organizational software, 39
Compact Disc (CD), 21, 91
comparison operators, 411, 619
complimentary closings (cover letters), 233
compound criteria, specifying in database queries, 621–623
Compress Media dialog box, 871
compressed video, 870–873
compressing files, 100–102
computer fluency, 1–2, 44, 55
computer hardware. *See* hardware
Computer icon, 66
computers
- defined, 2
- evaluation of, 26–29
- fluency on, 1–2, 44, 55
- functions of, 2–4
- hardware, 9–29
- maintenance, 44–51
- safe computing practices, 44–54
- systems, components of, 4
- types of, 5–9
- viruses and, 51–55
- zombies, 54

conditional formatting
- COUNTIF function, 409–410
- data bars, 412–413
- Highlight Cells Rules, 412–413
- IF function, 410–412
- logical tests, 410–412
- ranges, 412

configuration, 5, 26, 42–43
connectivity ports, 25
consecutive operators, order of operations, 483
constant values, definition, 340
Content layout, creating SmartArt graphics, 821–822
content placeholders (slides)
- definition, 734
- Preview box, 748
- selecting, 791–792
- slide text, 741, 743
- title placeholder, formatting, 855–857

Content with Caption layout (presentations), 760
content-based assessments
- Access 2010, 570–589, 636–656, 702–723
- Excel 2010, 378–395, 442–459, 500–517
- PowerPoint 2010, 766–783, 826–843, 886–903
- Word 2010, 194–211, 250–269, 306–325

context-sensitive commands, 66
context sensitive Fill Series option, 342
contextual tabs, 356
control keys, 11
Control Panel, 34, 69, 103
control unit, 14
controls
- bound, 671
- date, 698
- definition, 671
- forms
  - alignment, 676–678
  - formatting, 676–678
  - layout, 675–676
- grouping in forms, 671–673
- label, 671
- page number, 698
- reports
  - aligning in Design view, 697–698
  - formatting and deleting, 695
  - modifying, 696
- text box, 671
- unbound, 671

cookies, 52

copying
charts (worksheets)
formulas
absolute cell references, 368–370
worksheets, 348–349
worksheet data (Paste Options gallery), 429–430
copying files, 95–97
copyright laws, 136, 141
corner sizing handles, 164
corporate authors, citations, 283
COUNTIF function, 409–410
cover letters
creating, 234–236
creating letterheads, 230–231
finding/replacing text, 236–238
recording AutoCorrect entries, 233–234
CPUs (central processing units), 10, 14–16
criteria (databases), 610
Crop button, 799
cropping pictures in presentations, 799
crosstab queries, 633–635
custom formats, conditional formatting, 412
customizing. *See also* formatting
bullets
documents, 187
presentations, 793–794
desktop, 68–70
presentations
Animation Painter, 864–865
background fill colors, 857
background pictures, 854–857
fonts, 851–852
hiding background graphics, 853–854
removing animation, 864–865
slide backgrounds, 852–853
theme colors, 851–852
SmartArt graphics, 824
taskbar, 82–84
Cycle SmartArt graphic, 819

D

Data, 2
definition, 340, 529
grouping in queries, 631–633
importing Excel data into Access tables, 539–541
data bars
conditional formatting, 412–413
definition, 413
data entry
definition, 663
inserting data by ranges, 365–366
worksheets, 340–341
Auto Fill, 340–341
AutoComplete, 340–341
keyboard shortcuts, 340–341
numbers, 344–345
data management systems, definition, 529
data markers (charts)
presentations, 882
worksheets, 354
data mining, 37
data points, 354
charts (presentations), 882
pie charts (worksheets), 467
data series, 354
charts (presentations), 882
pie charts (worksheets), 467
data sources, definition, 299, 606
data types
assigning, 533–536
changing, 536
definition, 534
databases
closing, 558
creating, 560–564
definition, 529
design, 529–530
flat, definition, 529
forms
adding records to tables, 665–667
creating with Form tool, 663–665
deleting records from tables, 667–668
filtering records, 679–683
modifying, 671–678
printing, 554–556
opening, 595–596
organizing objects in Navigation Pane, 564–565
relational, definition, 529
renaming, 595
reports
creating with Blank Report tool, 688–691
creating with Report tool, 685–688
creating with Report Wizard, 691–694
design modifications, 695–698
printing, 568–569, 699–701
saving, 558
security alerts, 595–596
tables
adding descriptions, 543–544
adding records, 537–539, 665–667
adding second tables, 542–552
assigning data type and naming fields, 533–536
calculated fields in queries, 627–629
changing data types, 536
changing structure, 542–552
closing queries, 606
column widths, 547–549
creating, 566–568
creating queries, 604–609, 623–625
crosstab queries, 633–635
deleting fields, 542–543
importing data from Excel workbooks, 539–541
importing Excel worksheets, 545–547
modifying field sizes, 543–544
Multiple Items form, 561–564
new blank databases, 531–533
printing, 549–552, 568–569
printing queries, 606
relationships, 596–601
renaming, 538, 595–596
renaming fields, 536
reports, 556–558
running queries, 606
saving queries, 606
sorting queries, 608–610

databases *(Continued)*
sorting records, 601–604
specifying criteria in queries, 610–623
statistical calculations, 630–633
viewing primary keys in Design view, 544–545
templates, definition, 530, 560
themes, 671–673
database software, 37
Datasheet view, definition, 534
date controls, definition, 698
date lines
definition, 233
position, 234
dates
NOW function, 414–415
worksheets
formatting, 425–427
inserting, 425–427
Decimal tab alignment option, 188
Decrease List Level button, 740
decreasing list levels (presentations), 739–740
dedicated servers, 43
default home page, 120
default search engine, 133–134
defaults, 161
Delay box (animation timing), 863
deleting. *See also* removing
chart data in presentations, 883–884
columns
in charts (presentations), 884
in worksheets, 372–374
controls in Layout view, 695
files, 97–100
records in tables, 667–668
Recycle Bin, 64, 99, 103
rows in worksheets, 372–374
slides in Slide Sorter view, 761
table fields in Design view, 542–543
video (trimming), 870
worksheets, 359
deleting Web addresses from Favorites list, 132–133
deletion marks, surrounding shapes with, 815
denial-of-service (DoS) attacks, 54
Department of Defense, 115
Department of Education Web site, 123, 135
Department of Labor, Bureau of Labor Statistics Web site, 122
descending order
definition, 601
sorting records, 601–602
descriptions, adding to table fields, 543–544
Descriptions for files, 103–105
Design tab, Table Tools, 217
Design view
aligning controls, 697–698
creating queries, 604–606
definition, 534, 673
deleting table fields, 542–543
modifying forms, 673–674
viewing primary keys, 544–545
desktop, 63–70
exploring, 63–68
personalizing/customizing, 68–70
shortcuts added to, 77–78
desktop backgrounds, 70
desktop computers, 5–6
Desktop Icon Settings dialog box, 71
destination tables, definition, 540
Detail section (Design view), definition, 673
Details pane, 65–68, 89–90, 93, 97, 100, 103–104
details sheets, changing values to update summary sheets, 438–439
device, 20
diagonal resize pointer, 85
dialog boxes, 30, 69
See also specific dialog boxes
Borders and Shading, 298
Change Entrance Effect, 860
Compress Media, 871
Find and Replace, 237
Font, 297
Format Axis, 497
Format Background, 854
Format Cells, 412
Format Chart Area, 495–496
Function Arguments, 405, 414–415
Goal Seek, 476
Object, displaying, 162
Page Setup, 478
Source Manager, 285
Spelling and Grammar, 241
Style, 280
Trim Video, 870
digital cameras, 13, 19
digital subscriber line. *See* DSL
Digital Video (or Versatile) Disc (DVD), 91
digital video discs (DVDs), 21
Digital Video Interface (DVI) ports, 26
digital video recorders, 13
disc-labeling technology, LightScribe, 21
Disk Cleanup, 48–49
Disk Defragmenter, 44
Disk Operating System (DOS), 30
displayed values, definition, 345
displaying
formulas in worksheets, 360–361
function names in Formula Bar, 404–405
functions (Formula AutoComplete), 482
Object dialog box, 162
presentations
in Reading view, 764–765
in Slides/Outline pane, 753–754
slides, 742–744
subdatasheet records, 600–601
displaying windows, 80–81
Distribute Rows command, 878
distributing objects in presentations, 808–811
division, order of operations, 483
docking stations, 6
documents
borders, 167–168
bulleted lists
creating, 183–184
customizing bullets, 187
definition, 183
spacing between bulleted points, 184
citations, 282–285
corporate authors, 283
Web sites, 284
clip art, 294–295

columns
  changing text to two columns, 291–292
  inserting breaks, 293–294
  justifying text, 293
cover letters
  creating, 234–236
  finding/replacing text, 236–238
  letterheads, 230–231
  recording AutoCorrect entries, 233–234
creating, 161–163
  from existing documents, 231–233
  from templates, 244–249
default settings, 161
fonts, 161, 296–297
footers
  adding file names to, 172–174
  fields, 172
  file names, 277
footnotes, 277–279, 280–282
formatting, multiple columns, 292–293
hanging indents, 287
headings, 276
letterheads, creating, 230–231
line spacing, 180–181
lines, 161
mail merges, 299–304
  previewing, 304–305
  printing, 304–305
main, definition, 299
margins, 161, 177–178
nameplates, 292
numbered lists
  creating, 184–186
  definition, 183
page breaks, 285–286
page numbers
  formatting, 275–277
  suppressing, 277
paragraphs
  adding shading, 298–299
  adding spacing after, 181–183
  alignment, 178–179
  anchors, 166
  borders, 298–299
  line break indicators, 297
  No Spacing style, 230
  spacing, 161, 279
pictures
  artistic effects, 167
  inserting, 164–165
  moving, 166–167
  sizing, 164–165
  sizing handles, 164
  styles, 167
  wrapping text around, 165–166
previewing, 172–175
printing, 172–175
proofreading, 240–244
  grammar errors, 241–243
  spelling errors, 241–243
  Thesaurus, 243–244
  management, 287–289
reference pages, creating, 286–287
screenshots, 296
section breaks, 292
sections, 292
sentence spacing, 161
shapes
  formatting, 170–172
  inserting, 168–169
  moving, 170–172
  sizing, 170–172
SmartArt
  bullets, 193
  definition, 190
  inserting, 190–191
  modifying, 191–193
statistics, 288
tab stops
  dot leaders, 190
  leader characters, 190
  modifying, 189–190
  setting, 188–189
tables
  adding rows, 222–223
  adding text, 218–220
  borders, 226–228
  changing column widths, 221–222
  creating, 217
  creating bulleted lists, 220–221
  fields, 301
  formatting text, 224–226
  inserting, 240
  merging cells, 223–224
  records, 301
text
  alignment, 178–179
  borders, 298
  finding, 236–238
  formatting, 163–164, 275–277
  indenting, 181–183, 277
  inserting, 161–163
  line spacing, 180–181
  moving, 238–239
  replacing, 236–238
  replacing placeholder text, 245–247
  selecting, 238–239
  wordwrap, 161
text boxes
  formatting, 170–172
  inserting, 168–169
  moving, 170–172
  sizing, 170–172
Documents (library), 89
Documents of Firstname Lastname folder, 92, 98
docx extension, 233
dollar signs, absolute cell references, 369
domain name, 122
DOS (Disk Operating System), 30
DoS (denial-of-service) attacks, 54
dot leaders, 190
dot matrix printers, 18
dot pitch, 17
dots per inch (dpi), 19
dotx extension, 233
double spacing, 180–181
double-click, 66
double-click (mouse click), 13
Download.com, 54
downloading, 117, 135–138

dpi (dots per inch), 19
drag, 85
drag and dropping
moving cell data, 407–408
moving text, 238–239
selecting text, 238–239
Drag gadget (gadget control), 72
drag (mouse function), 13
Draw Table pointer, 875
drawing objects, 163
drive letters, 67, 91
drives, 67. *See also* hard drives
Drop Shadow Rectangle picture, 746
DSL (digital subscriber line), 25
dual core processors, 14
duplicating objects in presentations, 807–808
DVD (Digital Video (or Versatile) Disc), 91
DVD drives, 22
DVD-Roms, 21
DVD-R/RW, 21
DVDs (digital video discs), 21
DVI (Digital Video Interface) ports, 26
Dvorak keyboard, 11

E

Ease of Access (Control Panel), 34
editing. *See also* modifying
definition, 737
presentations
charts, 883
in Normal view, 737–744
in Slides/Outline pane, 753–754
slides, 742–744
table column widths (databases), 547–549
video, 870–873
workbooks, 474
worksheets
grouping worksheets for edits, 430–431
values, 371
.edu, 122
Effect Options, 763, 858–861
effects
artistic effects, 167, 747
documents, text effects, 163–164
emphasis, definition, 858
exit, definition, 858
presentations
pictures, 806–807
shapes, 806–807
shape effects, bevels, 469
video, 868–870
electronic printouts of PDFs (Access), 551
embedded computers, 9
emphasis effect, definition, 858
enabling
endnotes, definition, 277
Enter key, pasting in worksheets, 430
entering data. *See also* data entry; inserting, definition, 663
entrance effects (slide shows), 858–861
Equal to operator (=), 411
ergonomic keyboards, 11
error messages, resolving, 407–408
Esc key, 11
Ethernet ports, 25
eTrust Pest Patrol, 54
Excel, 36, 80, 97, 107
Excel 2010
Business Running Cases, 523–526
content-based assessments, 378–395, 442–459, 500–517
outcomes-based assessments, 396–399, 460–462, 518–521
starting, 337–338
Excel pointer, 339
exit effect, definition, 858
Expand Formula Bar button, 339
Expand horizontal scroll bar button, 338
expansion cards, 10
expansion slots, 10
exploding pie slices, 471–472
Explorer. *See* Internet Explorer icon; Windows Explorer
exponentiation, order of operations, 483
exporting
expressions
definition, 627
order of operations, 483
external hard drive, 89
Extract all files button, 101

F

FAFSA (Free Application for Federal Student Aid), 128
www.fafsa.ed.gov, 128
Fair Use Guidelines, 141
Family Safety (Control Panel), 34
Fast Ethernet, 26
Favorites, 65–66
Favorites bar, 118, 124, 129–132
Favorites button, 118–119, 129–132
Favorites Center, 119, 124, 129
Favorites list
address added to, 130–131
Web site display with, 131–132
fiber optic, 40
field list, definition, 597
fields
database tables
definition, 529
deleting, 542–543
modifying, 543–544
naming, 533–536
properties, 543
renaming, 536
footers, 172
Is Null/Is Not Null criteria, 613–614
sorting records, 603–604
tables, documents, 301
file extensions, 98
file list, 65–67, 93–95
File Transfer Protocol. *See* FTP
file types, 98
files. *See also specific files*
compressing, 100–102
copying, 95–97
descriptions for, 103–105
finding, 105–107
folders/files management (project 1B), 88–107
moving/renaming/deleting, 97–100
names
adding to footers, 277
adding to footers (documents), 172–174

as templates, 233
source, definition, 539
tags on, 103–105
file-sharing services, 53
fill handles
copying formulas, 348–349
Fill Series option, context sensitive, 342
fills
colors, slide backgrounds, 857
shapes, presentations, 804–805
Filter By Form command, definition, 681
Filter By Selection command, definition, 679
filtering
definition, 679
records, 679–683
Filter By Form command, 681–683
Filter By Selection command, 679–680
tables in worksheets, 417–419
financial numbers, formatting in worksheets, 351–352
Find and Replace dialog box, 237
Find and Replace feature, worksheets, 413–414
finding
templates, 244–245
text
documents, 236–238
slides, 757
finding folders/files, 105–107
Firewall and Advanced Security, 34
firewalls, 34, 54
FireWire ports, 25
First Line Indent tab alignment option, 188
first principle of good database design, definition, 530
flash drives (USB/thumb drives), 22, 89–99, 102
flash memory, 22
flat databases, definition, 529
floating objects, 165
floppy disk drives, 22
fluency with computers, 1–2, 44, 55
folders. *See also specific folders*
creating, 91–92
finding, 105–107
folders/files management (Project 2B), 88–107
moving, 93–95
renaming, 93–95
search, 105–107
Font Color button, 758
Font dialog box, 297
font size setting, 161
fonts
Body, 851
documents, 161, 296–297
Headings, 851
presentations, 757–759
themes (presentations), 851–852
footers
documents
adding file names to, 172–174
fields, 172
file names, 277
objects (Access), 551
presentations
adding, 748–749
definition, 748
slides, 749
worksheets, creating, 357–359
footnotes
definition, 277
research papers, 277–282
Form Footer (Design view), definition, 673
Form Header (Design view), definition, 673
Form tool, definition, 663
Form view, definition, 556
Form Wizard
creating forms, 669–670
definition, 669
format as you type, 485
Format Axis dialog box, 497
Format Background dialog box, 854
Format Cells dialog box, 412
Format Chart Area dialog box, 495–496
Format Painter, 484–486
formats, typing telephone numbers, 537
formatting. *See also* customizing
axes, line charts, 493–494
bulleted lists, presentations, 791–794
cells (worksheets)
clearing formats, 427–428
financial numbers, 351–352
Merge & Center command, 350–351
styles, 350–351
with Percent Style, 372
chart area, 472–473
charts, 495–497
chart area, 472–473
controls, Layout view, 695
dates, worksheets, 425–427
documents, multiple columns, 292–293
form controls, 676–678
Format Painter, 484–486
numbered lists, presentations, 791–794
page numbers (research papers), 275–277
pie charts with 3-D, 469–470
plot areas, 495–497
presentations, 757–760
background pictures, 854–857
bulleted lists, 791–794
fonts, 757–759
layouts, 760
line spacing, 759
numbered lists, 791–794
text alignment, 759
resumes, 248–249
shapes, documents, 170–172
slides, Keep source formatting check box, 755
sparklines, 356–357
text
documents, 163–164
research papers, 275–277
in tables, documents, 224–226
text boxes, documents, 170–172
title placeholders (slides), 855–857
video (presentations), 868–870
worksheets, 440–441
grouped worksheets, 432–435
large worksheets, 419–422
formatting marks
definition, 161
forms
creating
Form tool, 663–665

forms *(Continued)*
Form Wizard, 669–670
definition, 552
modifying, 671–678
control alignment, 676–678
control layout, 675–676
Design view, 673–674
Layout view, 671–673
printing, 554–556, 668–669
records
adding to tables, 665–667
deleting from tables, 667–668
filtering, 679–683
Formula AutoComplete, 482
Formula Bar, 338
copied formulas, 489
displaying function names, 404–405
underlying values, 345
formulas (worksheets)
absolute cell references, 368–370, 465
arithmetic operators, 366–368
AutoSum button, 348
calculating percentage rate of increase, 481–484
calculating values after increases, 486–487
copying, 348–349
creating in grouped worksheets, 432–435
definition, 340
displaying, 360–361
hiding, 360–361
moving cell data, 407–408
Paste Special command, 488–490
point and click method, 347
printing, 360–361
range finder, 368
relative cell references, 349, 465, 487
status bar calculations, 368
worksheets, 346–348
Formulas Bar, underlying formulas, 347
Forward button, 120–121, 123
.fr, 122
frames, 137–138
Free Application for Federal Student Aid (FAFSA), 128
Freeze Panes command, 415–416
freezing panes, 415–416
FTP (File Transfer Protocol), 122
Full-screen Snip, 78, 84, 95, 102, 107
Function Arguments dialog box, 405, 414–415
function keys, 12
functions
arguments, 404
AVERAGE, 403–405
definition, 346, 403
displaying, Formula AutoComplete, 482
logical
COUNTIF, 409–410
IF, 410–412
NOW, 414–415
statistical
definition, 403
MAX, 406
MEDIAN, 405–406
MIN, 406
ranges, averaging values, 404
ScreenTips, 404
SUM, 403–405
worksheets, SUM, 346–348
funds, definition, 465

G

gadget controls, 72–73
gadgets, 64, 71–73
Gadgets dialog box, 71, 73
galleries
Artistic Effects, 747
Background Styles, 852
Chart Layouts, 355
Numbering, 793
Paste Options, 429–430
Recolor, 869
Shape Styles, 804
Themes, 736
WordArt, 475
WordArt Styles, 816–817
gaming computers, 5
GB (gigabytes), 16, 23
General format, 345, 366
general funds, definition, 465
General tab, 29
GHz (gigahertz), 15, 23
Gigabit Ethernet, 25–26
gigabytes (GB), 16, 23
gigahertz (GHz), 15, 23
GO! Web site, 131–133
Goal Seek dialog box, 476
Goal Seek what-if analysis, 475–477
Google, 53, 133–134
.gov, 122, 128, 135
grammar errors, proofreading documents, 240–244
graphical user interface (GUI), 63. *See also* Aero interface
graphics, 163. *See also* clip art; images; pictures
downloading, 137–138
printing, 140–141, 143
size, spin boxes, 165
slides, hiding background graphics, 853–854
SmartArt
adding shapes to, 820–821
bullets, 193
colors, 823
converting to text, 825
creating from bullet points, 819–820
creating with Content layout, 821–822
customizing shape, 824
definition, 190, 818
inserting into documents, 190–191
layouts, 821–822, 823
modifying, 191–193
size, 824
styles, 823
text, 821–822
types, 819
spin boxes, 165
Greater than or equal to operator (>=), 411
grid area, Worksheet grid area, 338
gridlines, tick marks, 494
Group, Sort, and Total pane, definition, 699
groups
cells, pasting, 488–490
data, queries, 631–633

worksheets
editing, 430–431
formatting grouped worksheets, 432–435
GUI. *See* **graphical user interface**

H

hackers, 51
handheld computers, 6
Hanging Indent tab alignment option, 188
hanging indents, 287
hard disk drives, 22
hard drives. ***See also*** **flash drives**
defined, 67
external, 89
letter notation for, 67, 91
local, 89, 91, 95
removable, 67, 89–90, 92, 95, 107
hardware, 4–29, 63
Hardware and Sound (Control Panel), 34
headers
objects (Access), 551
presentations
adding, 748–749
definition, 748
headings
column headings (worksheets), 339
research papers, 276
Headings font, 851
headset/headphones, 4
healthy computers. ***See*** **maintenance**
height
sizing images in presentations, 797–799
video (presentations), 867
hiding
background graphics, slides, 853–854
formulas, worksheets, 360–361
taskbar, 74
windows, 80–81
Hierarchy SmartArt graphic, 819
Highlight Cells Rules, conditional formatting, 412–413
History list, 120–121, 124, 129–130
history of Internet, 115
Home button, 120–121
home page, 118, 120
horizontal rulers (PowerPoint 2010), 798
horizontal scroll bar, 82, 86
Horizontal window split box, 339
HTML (Hypertext Markup Language), 249
HTML documents, 126
HTTP (Hypertext Transfer Protocol), 122–123, 137
hyperlinks, 35, 119, 126–129, 138
Hypertext Markup Language (HTML), 249
Hypertext Transfer Protocol. ***See*** **HTTP**

I

icons, 30, 64. ***See also*** **shortcuts**
computer, 66
defined, 64
on desktop, 77–78
differences in, 64
IF function, 410–412
Illustrator, 39
IM (instant messaging), 39
images (presentations). ***See also*** **clip art; graphics; pictures**
moving, 797–799
sizing, 797–799
importing
definition, 539
workbook data into Access tables, 539–541
worksheets, 545–547
specifying numeric criteria in a query, 616–617
Increase List Level button, 740
increasing list levels (presentations), 739–740
increasing values, calculating values after increases, 486–487
indentation
hanging indents, 287
page breaks, 286
text in documents, 181–183, 277
information, 2
information, definition, 529
information processing cycle, 3–4
ink-jet printer cartridge, 18
ink-jet printers, 18
inline objects, 164
innermost sort field, definition, 603
input (information processing cycle), 3–4
input devices, 11–13
Insert Picture from File button, 744
Insert Worksheet button, 338
inserting
clip art into newsletters, 294–295
column breaks into newsletters, 293–294
columns into worksheets, 372–374
controls into forms, 675–676
data by ranges into worksheets, 365–366
data into worksheets, Auto Fill, 342–343
dates into worksheets, 425–427
descriptions into table fields, 543–544
file names into footers, documents, 172–174
footers into presentations, 748–749
footnotes into research papers, 277–279
headers into presentations, 748–749
numbers into worksheets, 344–345
page breaks into documents, 285–286
pictures
into documents, 164–165
into presentations from files, 744–746
records into database tables, 537–539, 665–667
rows
into charts, 491–492
into tables (presentations), 876
into tables (documents), 222–223
into worksheets, 372–374
screenshots into newsletters, 296
shapes
into documents, 168–169
into presentations, 802–803
slides into presentations, 737–739, 754–756
SmartArt graphics, 190–191
sparklines, 439
speaker notes into presentations, 741
tables
into databases, 542–552
into documents, 240
into documents, 161–163
into tables (documents), 218–220
into worksheets, 340–341

inserting *(Continued)*
text boxes
into documents, 168–169
into presentations, 800–801
text into presentations, 734–735
video into presentations, 865–868
WordArt into worksheets, 475
WordArt objects into slides, 817–818
insertion point, 12
inside addresses
definition, 233
spacing, 234
instant messaging (IM), 39
Instant Search box, 133, 134
Intel CPUs, 14
Internet, 12, 42, 49–50, 53. *See also* Web sites
history of, 115
navigating, 120–130
searching, 133–135
World Wide Web and, 117–118, 122
Internet Explorer 122
History list, 120–121, 124, 129–130
screen elements, 117–120
starting, 117–120
as Web browser, 117
Internet Explorer icon, 64
Internet Explorer's Tools menu, 53
Internet Service Providers (ISP), 117, 120
intranets, 42
Invitation file, 97
IrDA port, 26
Is Not Null criteria (fields), 613–614
Is Null criteria (fields), 613–614
iTunes, 53

J

join line, definition, 599
joysticks, 13
JPEG/JPG files, 79, 84, 98, 100, 104–106
jump list, 83
justification (text alignment), 178, 293

K

Kazaa, 53
Keep source formatting check box, 755
keyboard keys
nudging, 167
keyboard shortcuts
inserting data into worksheets, 340–341
navigating worksheets, 343
key loggers, 52
key terms, 55–57, 109
keyboards, 11–12
kilobits, 24
kilobytes, 16

L

labels
category labels, 353
charts, presentations, 881
controls, definition, 671
mail merge, 301, 305
pie charts, applying percentages, 468–469
worksheets, 340
landscape orientation, 750
LANs (local area networks), 41
large worksheets
formatting, 419–422
printing, 419–422
Larger size (gadget control), 72
laser mouse, 11
laser printer cartridge, 18
laser printers, 18
Layout tab, Table Tools, 217
Layout view
aligning controls, 676–678
control layout (forms), 675–676
definition, 555
deleting, 696
formatting controls, 676–678, 695
modifying controls, 696
modifying forms, 671–673
modifying reports, 686–688
layouts
charts, worksheets, 355
databases
form controls, 675–676
Stacked layout format, definition, 672
presentations, 737–738, 741
slides, 760
SmartArt graphics
changing, 823
Content layout, 821–822
tables, presentations, 877–878
LCD (liquid crystal display) monitors, 16–17
leader characters, 190
left alignment, 178, 341
Left Indent tab alignment option, 188
Left tab alignment option, 188
legends, 353
pie charts, 467
presentation charts, 881
Less than operator (<), 411
Less than or equal to operator (<=), 411
Lettered column headings, 339
letterheads, creating, 230–231
letters. *See* business letters; cover letters; documents
libraries, 89
Library pane, 65–66
Life Saving Service Drawings folder, 94–95, 104
LightScribe disc-labeling technology, 21
line break indicators, 297
line charts
axes, formatting, 493–494
creating, 491–492
presentations, creating, 883–884
line spacing, 161
documents, 180–181
No Spacing style, 230
slides, 759
Link Select pointer, 119, 126
links, definition, 539
links, sponsored, 135. *See also* hyperlinks
Linux, 32–33
liquid crystal display. *See* LCD monitors

list levels (presentations)
decreasing, 739–740
increasing, 739–740
List SmartArt graphic, 819
lists. *See* bulleted lists; numbered lists
Live Preview
copying in worksheets, 429
video, 869
Live Search, 133
local area networks. *See* LANs
local disk, 89, 91, 95
logical functions
COUNTIF, 409–410
IF, 410–412
logical tests, 410–412
Lotus, 35–39
***LSS Boat* tag, 106–107**
LSS Drawings, 95, 102–103
LSS-Charlotte NY Station, 104
LSS-Dragging Surfboat to Beach, 103
LSS-Surf Boat in High Surf, 104

M

Mac OS, 32
Macs (Apple Macintosh computers), 6
magnetic storage, 20
Mail Merge Wizard, 302–304
opening, 299–302
mail merges (documents), 299–302
labels, 301, 305
main document, definition, 299
mainframe computers, 8
maintenance (computer maintenance), 44–51
Major unit value, 494
managing files/folders (Project 2B), 88–107
manual column breaks, 291
manual line breaks, 297
manual page breaks, 285–286
definition, 286
indentation, 286
margins
documents, 161, 177–178
Match case check box, 238
Matrix SmartArt graphic, 819
MAX function, 406
queries, 630–631
Maximize button, 79, 89, 118
maximizing windows, 79–80
MB (megabytes), 16, 23
McAfee VirusScan, 53
media, 20–23, 40
MEDIAN function, 405–406
megabits, 25
megabytes (MB), 16, 23
megahertz (MHz), 15, 23
memory, 89, 15–16, 20, 22. *See* RAM
Menu bar, 65–66
menus, 30, 66
Merge & Center command, 350–351
merging, table cells, documents, 223–224
Message Bar, definition, 595
metadata, 103. *See also* tags
MFDs (multifunction devices), 18–19
MHTML, 136–138
MHz (megahertz), 15, 23
microcomputers, 5–6
microphones, 4, 11, 13
microprocessor chip, 10
Microsoft Access, 37
Microsoft Access Database window, 533
Microsoft Access Opening window, 531
www.microsoft.com, 118, 121, 124, 137
Microsoft Excel, 36
Microsoft Office, 31, 39, 80, 97–98, 100, 104
Microsoft Office Access 2010
Business Running Cases, 727–730
content-based assessments, 570–589, 636–656, 702–723
outcomes-based assessments, 590–592, 657–659, 724–726
Microsoft Office Clipboard
copying/pasting in worksheets, 429
Microsoft Office Excel 2010
Business Running Cases, 523–526
content-based assessments, 378–395, 442–459, 500–517
outcomes-based assessments, 396–399, 460–462, 518–521
starting, 337–338
Microsoft Office PowerPoint 2010
Business Running Cases, 909–912
content-based assessments, 766–783, 826–843, 886–903
outcomes-based assessments, 784–787, 844–847, 904–907
starting, 733–734
Microsoft Office Word 2010
Business Running Cases, 329–333
content-based assessments, 194–211, 250–269, 306–325
outcomes-based assessments, 212–214, 270–272, 326–328
Microsoft PowerPoint, 38
Microsoft Windows, 31
Microsoft Word, 35
.mil, 122
MIDI ports, 26
MIN function, 406, 630–631
Minimize button, 118–119
minimizing windows, 79–80
mining, data, 37
misspelled words, recording AutoCorrect entries, 233–234
MLA style
citations, 282–285
footnotes, 279–282
formatting page numbers, 275–277
formatting text, 275–277
indenting text, 277
parenthetical references, 284
reference pages, 286–287
mobile devices, 6
modem ports, 25
modems, 4
modifying. *See also* editing
controls, Layout view, 696
fields, 543–544
forms, 671–678
control alignment, 676–678
control layout, 675–676
Design view, 673–674
Layout view, 671–673
reports, 556–558, 686–688, 695–698
monitors, 4, 16–17
Morpheus, 53
motherboards, 10

mouse, 12–13
double-click, 66
pointer, 64
right-click, 66
mouse pointer, 12, 119
moving. *See also* removing
cell data, 407–408
files, 97–100
folders, 93–95
form controls, 675–676
images in presentations, 797–799
objects, arrow keys, 799
pictures in documents, 166–167
shapes, 170–172, 799
slides in Slide Sorter view, 761–763
text, documents, 238–239
text boxes, 170–172
windows, 84–87
worksheets, 440–441
Music (library), 89
multifunction devices (MFDs), 18–19
multimedia control keys, 12
multimedia keyboards, 11
multimedia projectors, 19
multiple processors, 112 multiple 61.65 spacing, 180–181
multiple columns, newsletters, 291–293
Multiple Items form
building tables, 561–564
definition, 561
multiple open windows, 80, 82
multiple open Web pages, 125
multiple slide transitions, 764
multiplication, order of operations, 483
multitasking, 8

N

Name Box, 338
nameplates, newsletters, 292
names
database table fields, 533–536
database tables, 538, 595–596
databases, 595
workbooks, 337–338
worksheets, 424–425
names, window, 75
Napster, 53
navigating Windows Explorer, 89–91
navigation
slides, 743
workbooks, 339–340
worksheets, 339–340, 424–425
keyboard shortcuts, 343
navigation area, definition, 541
navigation of Internet, 120–130
Navigation pane, 65–66, 90
definition, 534
organizing objects, 564–565
Tables and Related Views category, 564
Network and Internet (Control Panel), 34
network topology, 43–44
networks, 7, 40–44
New from existing command, 231–232
New Slide button, 737
New Slide button arrow, 737
newsletters
clip art, 294–295
columns
changing text to two columns, 291–292
inserting breaks, 293–294
justifying text, 293
columns, inserting breaks, 293–294
formatting multiple columns, 292–293
nameplates, 292
paragraphs
adding shading, 298–299
borders, 298–299
screenshots, 296
section breaks, 292
sections, 292
small caps, 296–297
Next Slide button, 743
No Spacing style, 230
nodes, 40, 43
nonimpact printers, 18
nonprinting characters, definition, 161
nonvolatile memory, 15
Normal template, 230
Normal view, 359
editing presentations, 737–744
PowerPoint, 733
normalization, definition, 530
Norton AntiVirus, 53
Not equal to operator, 411
notebook computers, 6
notes
definition, 277
symbols, 279
notes pages, 748
footers, 748–749
headers, 748–749
Notes pane, 733–734, 741
notification area, 64
NOW function, 414–415
nudging, 167
number formats
definition, 345
General format, 345, 366
number values, definition, 340
numbered lists
automatic, activating, 185
converting bulleted lists to, 792–793
creating, 184–186
definition, 183
formatting, presentations, 791–794
Numbered row headings, 339
Numbering button, 792–793
Numbering gallery, 793
numbers
financial, formatting in worksheets, 351–352
Format Painter, 484–486
inserting into worksheets, 344–345
rounding, 348
numeric criteria, specifying in queries, 616–621
numeric keypad, 12

O

Object button arrow, 162
Object dialog box, displaying, 162

object window, definition, 534
objects
databases
headers and footers, 551
organizing in Navigation pane, 564–565
PDF electronic printouts, 551
definition, 531
drawing, 163
floating, 165
inline, 164
moving with arrow keys, 799
presentations
aligning, 808–811
distributing, 808–811
duplicating, 807–808
selecting, 809
WordArt, inserting WordArt into slides, 817–818
Office (Microsoft), 31, 39
Office Clipboard
copying/pasting in worksheets, 429
On Click option (animation timing option), 862
On Mouse Click option, 763
opening
databases, 595–596
Mail Merge Wizard, 299–302
templates, 244–245
open-source software, 32–33
open windows, multiple, 80, 82
operating systems, 63, 109. *See also* Windows 7
operating systems (OS), 30–34
operators
arithmetic, 366–368
comparison, 411
definition, 366
order of operations, 483
optical storage, 20–21
Options (gadget control), 72
OR condition, 622–623
definition, 682
order of operations, 483
.org, 122
organizational/communication software, 39
OS. *See* operating systems
outcomes-based assessments
Access 2010, 590–592, 657–659, 724–726
Excel 2010, 396–399, 460–462, 518–521
PowerPoint 2010, 784–787, 904–907
Word 2010, 212–214, 250–269, 326–328
outermost sort field, definition, 603
Outline tab, viewing presentations, 754
outlines
presentations, editing, 753–754
shapes, 804–805
output (information processing cycle), 3–4
output devices, 16–19

P

P100P (peer-to-peer) networks, 42–43
page breaks, 285–286
indentation, 286
indicators, definition, 286
Page Layout view, 357
page number control, definition, 698
page numbers
documents
formatting, 275–277
suppressing, 277
formatting, 275–277
notes, page numbers, 279
Page Setup dialog box, 478
pages. *See* Web pages
pages per minute (ppm), 19
Paint (program), 81–82
painting (artistic effects), 747
panes
freezing, 415–416
unfreezing, 415–416
paragraphs
alignment, 178–179
documents
adding shading, 298–299
adding spacing after paragraphs, 181–183
alignment, 178–179
anchors, 166
borders, 298–299
indenting text, 277
line break indicators, 297
line spacing, 180–181
No Spacing style, 230
spacing, 161, 279
parallel ports, 24–25
parentheses (formulas), calculating percentage rate of increase, 481–484
parenthetical references, 282, 284
paste area (Office Clipboard), 429
Paste Options gallery, 429–430
Paste Special command, 488–490
pasting
charts (worksheets)
Enter key, 430
Paste Special command, 488–490
worksheets data, Paste Options gallery, 429–430
patches, 53
path, 126–127
PCs (personal computers), 6
PDAs (personal digital assistants), 6
PDF electronic printouts, objects (Access), 551
peer-to-peer (P100P) networks, 42–43
Penn State Web site, 124–125
percent for new value = base percent + percent of increase, 486
Percent Style, formatting cells (worksheets), 372
percentage rate of increase, calculating, 481–484
percentages
applying to labels in pie charts, 468–469
calculations, 370, 486–487
peripherals, 9
permanent memory, 15, 20
personal computers (PCs), 6
personal digital assistants. *See* PDAs
Personal Identification Number. *See* PIN
Personalization (Control Panel), 34
Personalization window, 68–70
Pest Patrol, 54
petabyte, 16
Photoshop, 39
picture elements. *See* pixels
Picture SmartArt graphic, 819

Picture Tools, 796
Picture with Caption layout (presentations), 760
pictures. *See also* clip art; graphics; images
documents
artistic effects, 167
inserting, 164–165
moving, 166–167
sizing, 164–165
sizing handles, 164
styles, 167
wrapping text around, 165–166
presentations
adding background pictures to slides, 854–857
artistic effects, 747
changing shape, 799–800
cropping, 799
effects, 806–807
inserting from files, 744–746
removing backgrounds, 813–816
rotation handles, 745
sizing handles, 745
soft edge options, 813–816
styles, 746–747
Pictures (library), 89
pie charts
coloring pie slices, 471–472
creating, 465–467
data markers, 467
data points, 467
data series, 467
definition, 465
exploding pie slices, 471–472
formatting with 3-D, 469–470
labels, applying percentages, 468–469
legends, 467
rotating, 470–471
Personal Identification Number. *See* PIN
PIN (Personal Identification Number), 128
pinned program area, 74
pinning shortcuts, to Start menu, 76–77
pixels, 17
pixels, definition, 343
PKZIP, 100
placeholder text (documents)
definition, 246
templates, replacing, 245–247
placeholders (slides)
definition, 734
Preview box, 748
selecting, 791–792
slide text, AutoFit options, 743
title placeholder, formatting, 855–857
plot areas
formatting, 495–497
line charts, 493
tick marks, 494
Pocket PCs, 6
point and click method, creating formulas, 347
pointer (mouse pointer), 12
populations, calculating increasing values, 486–487
Pop-up Blocker, 49–50
portals, 120
portrait orientation, 750
ports, 10, 24–26
positioning shapes, presentations, 802–803
power lines, 40
PowerPoint 2010, 38
Business Running Cases, 909–912
content-based assessments, 766–783, 826–843, 886–903
outcomes-based assessments, 784–787, 844–847, 904–907
starting, 733–734
PowerPoint window, 733–734
ppm (pages per minute), 19
presentation software, 38
presentations
charts
animation, 885
category labels, 881
cell references, 881
column, 880–883
column headings, 881
creating, 880–883
data markers, 882
data points, 882
data series, 882
deleting columns, 884
deleting data from, 883–884
editing data, 883
legends, 881
line charts, 883–884
styles, 880–883
clip art, inserting, 795–797
customizing
Animation Painter, 864–865
background fill colors, 857
background pictures, 854–857
fonts, 851–852
hiding background graphics, 853–854
removing animation, 864–865
slide backgrounds, 852–853
theme colors, 851–852
displaying
Reading view, 764–765
Slides/Outline pane, 753–754
editing
in Normal view, 737–744
in Slides/Outline pane, 753–754
footers
adding, 748–749
definition, 748
formatting, 757–760
background pictures, 854–857
bulleted lists, 791–794
fonts, 757–759
layouts, 760
line spacing, 759
numbered lists, 791–794
text alignment, 759
headers
adding, 748–749
definition, 748
images
moving, 797–799
sizing, 797–799
layouts, 737–738, 741
objects
aligning, 808–811
distributing, 808–811
duplicating, 807–808
selecting, 809

pictures
  artistic effects, 747
  changing shape, 799–800
  cropping, 799
  effects, 806–807
  inserting from files, 744–746
  removing backgrounds, 813–816
  rotation handles, 745
  sizing handles, 745
  soft edge options, 813–816
  styles, 746–747
printing, 749–751
saving, 734–735
shapes
  adding text, 803–804
  changing shapes of pictures, 799–800
  definition, 802
  effects, 806–807
  fill colors, 804–805
  fills, 804–805
  inserting, 802–803
  outlines, 804–805
  positioning, 802–803
  sizing, 802–803
  styles, 804–805
  surrounding with deletion marks, 815
slide shows, 747–748
  animation, 858–865
  broadcasting, 765
slides
  deleting in Slide Sorter view, 761
  displaying, 742–744
  editing, 742–744
  footers, 749
  hiding background graphics, 853–854
  inserting, 737–739
  inserting into presentations from existing presentations, 754–756
  layouts, 737–738, 760
  line spacing, 759
  moving in Slide Sorter view, 761–763
  navigation, 743
  text alignment, 759
  thumbnails, 744
  transitions, 763–764
  transitions (slide timing options), 861–863
SmartArt graphics
  creating from bullet points, 819–820
  types, 819
status bars, 733–734
tables
  creating, 875–876
  inserting rows, 876
  layouts, 877–878
  rows, 876
  styles, 875, 879–880
text
  applying WordArt styles, 816–817
  content placeholders. *See* placeholders
  inserting, 734–735
  list levels, 739–740
text boxes, inserting, 800–801
themes, 735–736
  changing colors, 851–852
  fonts, 851–852
  Reset Slide Background feature, 857
video, 865–868
  compressing, 870–873
  editing, 870–873
  formatting, 868–870
  trimming, 870
Preview box, 748
Preview button, 69
previewing
  documents, 172–175
  mail merge documents, 304–305
  worksheets, Print Preview, 357–359
Previous Slide button, 743
primary keys, viewing in Design view, 544–545
Print dialog box, 87
Print Preview
  previewing documents, 172–175
  previewing worksheets, 357–359
  Print tab (Backstage view), 749
Print tab (Backstage view), 174, 749
Print Titles command, 419
printer speed, 19
printers, 4, 18–19
printing
  charts, 479
  database tables, 549–552
  documents, 172–175
  forms, 554–556, 668–669
  formulas, 360–361
  graphics (from Web pages), 140–141, 143
  mail merge documents, 304–305
  presentations, 749–751
  queries, 606
  relationship reports, 600–601
  reports, 556–558, 568–569, 686–688, 699–701
  single forms, 669
  tables, 568–569
  text (from Web pages), 141–143
  titles, in worksheets, 419–422
  Web pages, 138–139, 143
  workbooks, with chart sheets, 477–479
  worksheets, 360, 498–499
    all worksheets, 441
    large worksheets, 419–422
privacy threats. *See* viruses
private networks, 42
process (information processing cycle), 3–4
Process SmartArt graphic, 819
processors. *See* CPUs
programmable, 2
programs, 29, 34
projectors, multimedia, 19
protection, from viruses, 53–54
proofreading
  documents, 240–244
    grammar errors, 241–243
    spelling errors, 241–243
    Thesaurus, 243–244
  worksheets, checking spelling, 363–365
properties
  fields, 543
Properties dialog box, 74, 84, 104–105
property management, documents, 287–289
protocols, 122. *See also* FTP; HTTP
www.psu.edu, 124
pubic networks, 42

public domain, 141
punctuation, documents, 240–244
Pyramid SmartArt graphic, 819

Q

quad processors, 14
queries, 552–554
  aggregate functions, 631
  AND condition, 621–622
  calculated fields, 627–629
  closing, 606
  creating
    Design view, 604–606
    from existing queries, 607–608
    multiple tables, 623–625
  crosstab, 633–635
  definition, 552
  grouping data, 631–633
  OR condition, 622–623
  printing, 606
  running, 606
  saving, 606
  select, 606
  simple select, 552
  sorting, 608–610
  specifying criteria, 610–614
    compound criteria, 621–623
    numeric criteria, 616–621
  statistical calculations, 630–633
  wildcards, 625–626
  QWERTY keyboard, 11

R

RAM (random access memory), 10, 15–16
random access memory. ***See*** **RAM**
range finder (formulas), 368
ranges (worksheets), 344
  conditional formatting, 412
  converting tables to data ranges, 419
  functions, averaging values, 404
  inserting data by, 365–366
  selecting, 350
rate = amount of increase/base, 482
Reading view, displaying presentations, 764–765
read-only memory (ROM), 15
Recent Pages button down arrow, 123
recently used programs, 74
Recolor gallery, 869
record (burn), 21
record selector box, definition, 537
record source, definition, 685
recording AutoCorrect entries, 233–234
records
  adding to tables, forms, 665–667
  database tables
    adding, 537–539
    definition, 529
  deleting from tables, forms, 667–668
  filtering, forms, 679-683
  sorting, 601–604
  tables, documents, 301
Recycle Bin, 64, 99, 103
red wavy underlines, 734
redundant data, definition, 530
reference pages, creating, 286–287
referential integrity, 596–601
Refresh button, 120
refresh rate, 17
relational databases, definition, 529
Relationship SmartArt graphic, 819
relationships, database tables, 596–601, 617–618
relative cell addresses, calculating increasing values, 487
relative cell references, 349, 465
removable drives/storage devices, 67, 89–90, 92, 95, 107. ***See also*** **flash drives**
removing. ***See also*** **deleting**
  animation from slides, 864–865
  auto-hide feature, 74
  backgrounds from pictures, presentations, 813–816
  bullet symbols from bullet points, 794
  gadgets, 71–72
  pinned programs, 74
  template controls, 248–249
renaming
  files, 97–100
  folders, 93–95
Reorder Animation buttons, 861
replacing text
  documents, 236–238
  slides, 757
Report tool
  creating reports, 685–688
  definition, 685
Report Wizard
  creating reports, 691–694
  definition, 691
reports
  controls
    aligning in Design view, 697–698
    formatting and deleting, 695
  creating, 556–558
    Blank Report tool, 688–691
    Report tool, 685–688
    Report Wizard, 691–694
  definition, 552, 685
  design modifications, 695–698
  footnotes, 277–279
  modifying, 556–558, 686–688
  printing, 556–558, 568–569, 686–688, 699–701
  viewing, 568
research papers
  citations, 282–285
    corporate authors, 283
    Web sites, 284
  creating
    formatting page numbers, 275–277
    formatting text, 275–277
  footnotes, 277–279
    modifying, 279–282
  headings, 276
  page breaks, 285–286
  reference pages, creating, 286–287
Reset Slide Background feature, 857
resize pointer, diagonal, 85
resizing windows, 84–87
resolution, 17
resolving, database security alerts, 595–596

responsible computer users. ***See*** **safe computing practices**
Restore Down button, 76, 79–80, 82, 118–119
restore points, 47–48
resumes
adding text to tables, 218–220
changing column widths, 221–222
creating
removing template controls, 248–249
replacing placeholder text, 245–247
templates, 244–245
creating bulleted lists in tables, 220–221
creating tables, 217
formatting, 248–249
formatting text in table cells, 224–226
merging table cells, 223–224
saving as Web pages, 249
table borders, 226–228
restoring windows, 79–80
Ribbon(screen saver), 69
groups. *See* groups
right alignment, 178
Right tab alignment option, 188
right-click(mouse click), 13, 66
right-drag, 13
ring topology, 44
ROM (read-only memory), 15
rotate handles, 164
rotating
pie charts, 470–471
text, worksheets, 408
rotation handles, definition, 745
rounding, 348
rows
charts, inserting into line charts, 491–492
tables (presentations), 876
tables (documents), adding, 222–223
worksheets, 340
Comma Style, 351
deleting, 372–374
freezing panes, 416
unfreezing panes, 416
ruler guides, inserting text boxes into presentations, 800–801
running queries, 554, 606

S

safe computing practices, 44–54
salutations (cover letters), definition, 233, 235
Save As dialog box, 78–79, 84, 87, 95, 107
saving
databases, 558
as templates, 233
presentations, 734–735
queries, 606
resumes as Web pages, 249
workbooks, 337–338
Scale to Fit command, 419
scaling worksheets, 361, 419–422
scanners, 4, 13
Scholarships & grants page, 126–127
screen
differences in, 63
elements, 64
scroll box, 86
screen elements (Internet Explorer62), 117–120
Screen Saver Settings dialog box, 69
screen savers, 68–69
screenshots, newsletters, 296
screen shots (snips), 78. ***See also*** **Snipping Tool**
ScreenTips, 65–66, 94, 120, 125
clip art (presentations), 796
functions, 404
scroll, 13
scroll bars, 118–119, 338
horizontal, 82, 86
vertical, 82, 84–86, 97, 98
scroll wheel, 13
scrolling windows, 84–87
Search and Destroy, 54
Search box, 65–66, 86, 237
search engines, 133–135
search folder, 105–107
Search History option, 129
Search programs and files box, 76
second principle of good database design, definition, 530
section bar (Design view), definition, 673
section breaks, 292
section header layout (presentations), 741
sections, newsletters, 292
security
alerts, databases, 595–596
Security Configuration Manager, 34
security settings, 50–51
Select All box, 339
select queries, definition, 552, 606
selecting
cell ranges, 350
objects, presentations, 809
placeholders, 791–792
text, documents, 238–239
Send to **command, 77–78**
sentences (documents), spacing, 161
sequence of slides (timing options), 861–863, 885
serial ports, 24
series
Auto Fill, 342
pie charts, 467
presentation charts, 882
servers, 7, 42–43
shading, adding to paragraphs (documents), 298–299
Shape Height box, 797
Shape Styles gallery, 804
shapes
definition, 168
documents
formatting, 170–172
inserting, 168–169
moving, 170–172
sizing, 170–172
effects, bevels, 469
moving, arrow keys, 799
presentations
adding text, 803–804
changing shapes of pictures, 799–800
definition, 802
effects, 806–807
fill colors, 804–805
fills, 804–805
inserting, 802–803
outlines, 804–805

shapes *(Continued)*
positioning, 802–803
sizing, 802–803
styles, 804–805
surrounding with deletion marks, 815
SmartArt graphics
adding, 820–821
customizing, 824
Sheet tab scrolling buttons, 338
sheet tabs, 338, 359, 424–425
shortcut menus, 13, 66
shortcuts (keyboard)
desktop, 77–78
inserting data into worksheets, 340–341
navigating worksheets, 343
Start menu, 76–77
taskbar, 78–79
Show desktop button, 81, 84–85
***Show more details* command, 97**
***Show on Desktop*, 66**
Simple Query Wizard, creating queries, 552–554
simple select queries, definition, 552
Single File Web Page, 249
single forms, printing, 669
single spacing, 180–181
single-record form, definition, 562
sites. *See* Web sites
sizing
columns (worksheets), 343–344
fonts (presentations), 757–759
form controls, 675–676
graphics, spin boxes, 165
images, presentations, 797–799
pictures, 164–165
shapes
documents, 170–172
presentations, 802–803
SmartArt graphics, 824
text boxes, documents, 170–172
sizing handles, 164, 745
slices (pie)
coloring, 471–472
exploding, 471–472
slide handouts, 748
footers, 748–749
headers, 748–749
Slide pane, 733–734, 744
Slide Show gadget, 73
Slide Show view, slide transitions, 763–764
slide shows
animation, 858–865
Animation Painter, 864–865
charts, 885
Effect Options, 858–861
entrance effects, 858–861
removing animation, 864–865
timing options, 861–863
broadcasting, 765
viewing, 747–748
Slide Sorter view, 760
deleting slides, 761
moving slides in, 761–763
slide transitions. *See* transitions
slides
backgrounds
adding pictures, 854–857
fill colors, 857
hiding graphics, 853–854
resetting, 857
styles, 852–853
definition, 734
deleting in Slide Sorter view, 761
displaying, 742–744
editing, 742–744
footers, 749
formatting, Keep source formatting check box, 755
graphics, hiding background graphics, 853–854
inserting, 737–739
inserting into presentations, from existing presentations, 754–756
layouts, 737–738, 741, 760
line spacing, 759
moving in Slide Sorter view, 761–763
navigation, 743
placeholders
AutoFit options, 743
definition, 734
Preview box, 748
text
alignment, 759
finding, 757
replacing, 757
thumbnails, 744
title, definition, 734
titles, 741
transitions, 763–764
transitions (slide timing options), 861–863
WordArt, inserting WordArt objects, 817–818
Slides pane
displaying slides, 742–744
editing slides, 742–744
Slides/Outline pane, 733–734
displaying presentations, 753–754
editing presentations, 753–754
slide numbers, 743
small caps
definition, 296
newsletters, 296–297
Smaller size (gadget control), 72
SmartArt graphics
bullets, 193
colors, 823
converting into text, 825
creating
Content layout, 821–822
from bullet points, 819–820
customizing shape, 824
definition, 190, 817–818
inserting into documents, 190–191
layouts
changing, 823
Content, 821–822
modifying, 191–193
shapes, adding, 820–821
size, 824
styles, 823
text, 821–822
converting SmartArt into text, 825
types, 819
Snipping Tool, 78–79, 84, 95, 102, 107

snips (screen shots), 78
soft copy, 16
soft edge options (pictures), 813–816
software, 29–40, 53–54
software suites, 39
sorting
  queries, 608–610
  records, 601–604
  tables, worksheets, 417–419
source files, definition, 539
Source Manager dialog box, 285
spacing
  adding after paragraphs, 181–183
  bulleted points, 184
  date line, 234
  inside addresses, 234
  lines, 161, 180–181
    slides, 759
  No Spacing style, 230
  paragraphs, 161, 279
  salutations, 235
  sentences (documents), 161
spam, 52, 54
sparklines, 352
  creating, 356–357
  formatting, 356–357
  inserting, 439
  summary sheets, 436–437
speaker notes (presentations), adding, 741
speakers, 4, 19
special purpose ports, 26
speech-recognition technology, 6
spelling
  checking
    documents, 241–243
    worksheets, 363–365
  recording AutoCorrect entries, 233–234
  red wavy underlines, 734
Spelling and Grammar command, 241
Spelling and Grammar dialog box, 241
spin boxes, graphics, 165
splash screen, 28
split animation, charts (presentations), 885
sponsored links, 135
spreadsheet software, 36
spreadsheets. *See* worksheets
Spybot Search and Destroy, 54
spyware, 52–53
square text wrapping, 166
Stacked layout format, definition, 672
star topology, 44
Start button, 64
State financial aid page, 127–128
Start menu, 72–79
starting
  Excel 2010, 337–338
  PowerPoint 2010, 733–734
statistical calculations, queries, 630–633
statistical functions
  definition, 403
  MAX, 406
  MEDIAN, 405–406
  MIN, 406
statistics (document), 288
status area. *See* notification area
status bars, 118–119
  calculations, 368
  Excel 2010, 338
  presentations, 733–734
Stop button, 120
Stop Fitting Text to This Placeholder option, 743
storage. *See also* flash drives; hard drives
  devices, 91
  drives, 67
  memory, 89
  removable devices, 67, 89–90, 92, 95, 107
  temporary, 89
storage (information processing cycle), 3–4
storage devices, 20–23
storage media, 20–23
structure (table fields), definition, 534
structure (tables), 542–552
www.students.gov, 126–127
Style dialog box, 280
styles
  backgrounds, slides, 852–853
  bulleted lists, presentations, 793–794
  charts
    presentations, 880–883
    worksheets, 355
  fonts, presentations, 757–759
  formatting cells (worksheets), 350–351
  pictures
    documents, 167
    presentations, 746–747
  shapes, presentations, 804–805
  SmartArt graphics, 823
  tables, presentations, 875, 879–880
  video, 868–870
  WordArt, applying to text in presentations, 816–817
stylus, 6
subdatasheet records, displaying, 600–601
submenus, 74
subpoints, 191
subsets, definition, 679
suites, software, 39
SUM function, 346–348, 403–405, 630–631
summary sheets
  changing values in detail sheets to update, 438–439
  creating with sparklines, 436–437
supercomputers, 8
suppressing page numbers, 277
Survey Letter, 98
S-video ports, 26
symbols
  arithmetic operators, 367
  bullet points
    customizing, 794
    list levels (presentations), 739–740
    removing, 794
  bullets
    customizing, 187
    definition, 183
  dollar signs, absolute cell references, 369
  notes, 279
synonyms, Thesaurus, 243–244
System and Security (Control Panel), 34
system boards. *See* motherboards

system software, 29–30
system tray. *See* notification area
system unit, 4, 9–10

T

Tab key, Alt key and, 83
tab stops
dot leaders, 190
leader characters, 190
modifying, 189–190
setting, 188–189
Table Tools, 217
tables
databases
adding descriptions, 543–544
adding records, 537–539, 665–667
adding tables, 542–552
assigning data types, 533–536
calculated fields in queries, 627–629
changing structure, 542–552
closing queries, 606
column widths, changing, 547–549
creating, 566–568
creating queries, 604–608, 623–625
crosstab queries, 633–635
definition, 529
deleting fields, 542–543
forms, 554-556, 663-683
importing data from Excel workbooks, 539–541
importing Excel worksheets, 545–547
modifying field size, 543–544
Multiple Items form, 561–564
naming fields, 533–536
new blank databases, 531–533
printing, 549–552, 568–569
printing queries, 606
queries, 552–554
relationships, 596–601
renaming, 538, 595–596
renaming fields and changing data types, 536
reports, 556–558
saving queries, 606
sorting queries, 608–610
sorting records, 601–604
specifying criteria in a query, 610–623
statistical calculations and queries, 630–633
viewing primary keys in Design view, 544–545
definition, 875
destination, definition, 540
documents
adding rows, 222–223
adding text, 218–220
borders, 226–228
changing column widths, 221–222
creating, 217
creating bulleted lists, 220–221
fields, 301
formatting, 221–228, 240
formatting text, 224–226
merging cells, 223–224
inserting, 240
presentations
creating, 875–876
inserting rows, 876
layouts, 877–878
rows, 876
styles, 875, 879–880
records, documents, 301
worksheets
converting into ranges of data, 419
creating, 416–417
filtering, 417–419
sorting, 417–419
Tables and Related Views category (Navigation pane), 564
tablet computers, 6
Tabs, 118–120, 125
Contextual, 356
Design, 217
Layout, 217
Outline, viewing presentations, 754
Print (Backstage view), Print Preview, 749
Sheet, 359
Sheet tabs, 338
sheet tabs, colors, 424–425
tags, 103–107
tape backup drives, 23
Task Scheduler, 45–46
taskbar, 64
auto-hide feature for, 74
customizing, 82–84
defined, 64
telephone numbers, formatting for typing, 537
telephone wires, 40
templates
creating documents, 230–233, 244–249
databases
creating databases, 560–564
definition, 530
finding, 244–245
Normal template, 230
opening, 244–245
placeholder text, replacing, 245–247
removing controls, 248–249
saving files as, 233
temporary memory, 15. *See also* RAM
temporary storage, 89
terabytes (TR), 16
terms (key terms), 55–57, 109
text
documents
adding to tables, 218–220
alignment, 178–179
borders, 298
finding, 236–238
formatting, 163–164, 275–277
indenting, 181–183, 277
inserting, 161–163
line spacing, 180–181
moving, 238–239
replacing, 236–238
replacing placeholder text, 245–247
selecting, 238–239
wordwrap, 161
wrapping around pictures, 165–166
newsletters, justifying text in columns, 293
presentations
adding to shapes, 803–804
alignment on slides, 759
applying WordArt styles, 816–817

content placeholders. *See* placeholders
converting SmartArt into text, 825
finding, 757
inserting, 734–735
list levels, 739–740
replacing, 757
SmartArt graphics, 821–822
worksheets
alignment, 343–344
inserting, 340–341
left alignment, 341
rotating, 408
wrapping, 374–376
text box controls, definition, 671
text boxes
charts, inserting, 473–474
definition, 168, 473
documents
formatting, 170–172
inserting, 168–169
moving, 170–172
sizing, 170–172
presentations, inserting, 800–801
Text data type, definition, 535
text effects, formatting documents, 163–164
Text Pane, creating SmartArt graphics, 821–822
text values, definition, 340
Textbook Sites folder, 131–132
themes
database forms, 671–673
presentations, 735–736
changing colors, 851–852
definition, 735
fonts, 851–852
Reset Slide Background feature, 857
Themes gallery, presentations, 736
Thesaurus, 243–244
three-dimensional (3-D), formatting pie charts, 469–470
thumb drives. *See* flash drives
thumbnails, 82
thumbnails, slides, 744
tick marks, 494
times, NOW function, 414–415
timing options, slide shows, 861–863
title bar, 65–66, 119
title placeholders (slides), formatting, 855–857
titles
slides, 734, 741
tables, merging cells, 223–224
worksheets, printing, 419–422
TLD. *See* top-level domain
toggle keys, 12
token-ring topology, 44
toolbar, 65–66
toolbar commands, 120–121
Tools menu (Internet Explorer), 53
top-level domain (TLD), 122, 124, 128, 135
top-level points, definition, 191
touch screen, 6
touch screen monitors, 16–17
transitions, 763–764, 861–863
Trim Video dialog box, 870
trimming, video, 870
trojan horses, 52
Trust Center, definition, 595
Tucows, 54
twisted pairs cables, 40
typing
correcting errors, 537
format as you type, 485
telephone numbers, 537

U

unbound controls, definition, 671
underlying formulas, 347
underlying values
definition, 345
error messages, 407–408
unfreezing panes, 415–416
unhiding taskbar, 74
universal serial bus. *See* USB
unshielded twisted pair (UTP) cables, 40
updates, software, 53
updating
charts (worksheets), 474
URL (Uniform Resource Locator), 122, 125–127, 129–130, 137, 139
defined, 118
path, 126–127
USB (universal serial bus) flash drives, 22, 91
USB (universal serial bus) ports, 25
U.S. Department of Defense, 115
U.S. Department of Education Web site, 123, 135
U.S. Department of Labor, Bureau of Labor Statistics Web site, 122
www.usa.gov, 121–123, 130
User Accounts (Control Panel), 34
user friendly, 30
user interface, 30
utility programs, 34
UTP (unshielded twisted pair) cables, 40

V

value after increase = base X percent for new value, 486
value axis
definition, 353
line charts, 493
vertical rulers (PowerPoint 2010), 798
vertical scroll bar, 82, 84–86, 97–98
Vertical window split box, 338
video
compressing, 870–873
editing, 870–873
formatting, 868–870
inserting into presentations, 865–868
Live Preview, 869
trimming, 870
video conference, 41
video recorders, digital, 13
Videos (library), 89
View buttons, 733–734
View setting, 161
viewing
primary keys in Design view, 544–545
reports, 568
slide shows, 747–748
views
Backstage, 174

views *(Continued)*
Design
aligning controls, 697–698
creating queries, 604–606
modifying forms, 673–674
Layout
control layout (forms), 675–676
formatting and aligning controls, 676–678
formatting and deleting controls, 695
modifying controls, 696
modifying forms, 671–673
modifying reports, 686–688
Normal, 359, 733
Page Layout, 357
Reading, displaying presentations, 764–765
Slide Show, slide transitions, 763–764
Slide Sorter, 760
deleting slides, 761
moving slides in, 761–763
worksheets, 357–359
views, for History list, 129
Virtual PC for Mac (Microsoft), 32
virtual servers, 7
virus protection, 135, 137
viruses, 51–55
Vista. *See* Windows Vista
VoIP (Voice over Internet Protocol), 41
volatile memory, 15. *See also* RAM
Volunteers file, 97

W

WANs (wide area networks), 42
Weather gadget, 71–73
Web addresses
adding to Favorites list, 130–131
deleting from Favorites list, 132–133
parts of, 122
Web browsers, 40, 117
webcams, 4
Web graphics. *See* graphics
Web pages, 118
associated, 130
downloading/saving, 136–137
graphics, downloading, 137–138
hyperlinks, 119, 126–129, 138
multiple, 125
printing, 138–139, 143
saving resumes as, 249
Scholarships & grants, 126–127
State financial aid, 127–128
tabs, 118–120, 125
text, printing, 141–142, 143
Web sites
accessing from Address bar, 121–124
Address bar, 121–124
www.bls.gov, 122, 129, 137
citations, 284
defined, 118
Department of Education, 123, 135
Department of Labor, Bureau of Labor Statistics, 122
displaying with Favorites list, 131–132
www.fafsa.ed.gov, 128
GO!, 131–133
www.microsoft.com, 118, 121, 124, 137
Penn State, 124–125
www.psu.edu, 124
www.students.gov, 126–127
www.usa.gov, 121–123, 130
what-if analysis
answering what-if questions, 488–490
calculating percentage rate of increase, 481–484
calculating values after increases, 486–487
Format Painter, 484–486
formatting while typing, 484–486
Goal Seek, 475–477
Paste Special command, 488–490
what-if questions, 488–490
wide area networks. *See* WANs
width
columns (worksheets), 343, 374–376
images (presentations), 797–799
table columns (databases), 547–549
table columns (documents), 221–222
video (presentations), 867
wildcards
definition, 625
queries, 625–626
windows, 30, 63, 109
active, 76
Aero interface, 68, 81–83
closing, 87
displaying, 80–81
familiarization (Project 2A), 62–87
hiding, 80–81
maximizing, 79–80
Microsoft Access Database, 533
Microsoft Access Opening, 531
minimizing, 79–80
moving, 84–87
multiple open windows, 80, 82
name, 75
parts of, 65–66
Personalization, 68–70
PowerPoint, 733–734
resizing, 84–87
restoring, 79–80
scrolling, 84–87
thumbnails of, 82
Windows105, 27–28, 34, 45–51
Windows Explorer, 28–29, 34, 65–66, 89–91
defined, 65, 89
navigating, 89–91
opening, 89
window, variances in, 65, 68
Windows key, 11
Windows Live toolbar, 118
Windows Task Manager, 34
Windows Vista, 27–28, 31, 45, 47–50, 53–54
Windows XP, 16, 27–28, 54
WinZip, 100
wireless keyboards, 11
wireless laser mouse, 11
wireless networks, 40
wireless technology, 26
With Previous option (animation timing option), 862
wizards
Form Wizard, creating forms, 669–670
Mail Merge Wizard, 299–304
Report Wizard

creating reports, 691–694
definition, 691
Simple Query Wizard, creating queries, 552–554
Word (Microsoft Word), 35
Word 2010
Business Running Cases, 329–333
content-based assessments, 194–211, 250–269, 306–325
outcomes-based assessments, 212–214, 270–272, 326–328
Word document files, 98
word processing software, 35
WordArt
inserting WordArt objects into slides, 817–818
styles, applying to text in presentations, 816–817
worksheets, inserting, 475
WordArt Styles gallery, 816–817
WordPad, 76
wordwrap, definition, 161
workbook-level buttons, 338
workbooks
chart sheets, creating, 465–467
definition, 337
editing, 474
names, 337–338
navigation, 339–340
NOW function, 414–415
printing, with chart sheets, 477–479
saving, 337–338
worksheets. *See also* worksheets
deleting, 359
formatting, 440–441
moving, 440–441
printing, 441
Works Cited
creating, 286–287
definition, 282
Worksheet grid area, 338
worksheets
active, 340
borders, financial information, 352
calculations, increasing values, 486–487
cells, 340–341
addresses, 340
borders, 344
clearing contents, 427–428
copying formulas with fill handles, 348–349
data points, 354
displayed values, 345
Find and Replace feature, 413–414
Format Painter, 484–486
formatting with Percent Style, 372
Merge & Center command, 350–351
moving contents, 407–408
pasting groups, 488–490
ranges, 344
references, 340
charts. *See* charts (worksheets)
columns, 339
default width, 343
deleting, 372–374
freezing panes, 415–416
headings, 339
inserting, 372–374
sizing, 343–344
unfreezing panes, 415–416
width, 374–376
conditional formatting
COUNTIF function, 409–410
data bars, 412–413
Highlight Cells Rules, 412–413
IF function, 410–412
logical tests, 410–412
ranges, 412
copying data, Paste Options gallery, 429–430
data entry, 340–341
Auto Fill, 340–341
AutoComplete, 340–341
keyboard shortcuts, 340–341
numbers, 344–345
dates
formatting, 425–427
inserting, 425–427
definition, 337
deleting, 359
details sheets, changing values to update summary sheets, 438–439
editing values, 371
error messages, resolving, 407–408
footers, creating, 357–359
formatting, 440–441
grouped worksheets, 432–435
large worksheets, 419–422
formulas, 346–348
absolute cell references, 368–370, 465
arithmetic operators, 366–368
AutoSum button, 348
calculating percentage rate of increase, 481–484
calculating values after increases, 486–487
copying, 348–349
creating in grouped worksheets, 432–435
definition, 340
displaying, 360–361
hiding, 360–361
Paste Special command, 488–490
point and click method, 347
printing, 360–361
range finder, 368
relative cell references, 465
freezing panes, 415–416
functions
AVERAGE, 403–405
averaging values, 404
COUNTIF, 409–410
definition, 403
IF, 410–412
MAX, 406
MEDIAN, 405–406
MIN, 406
NOW, 414–415
ScreenTips, 404
statistical, 403
SUM, 346–348, 403–405
grouping, 430–431
importing, 545–547, 616–617
importing data into Access tables, 539–541
labels, 340
moving, 440–441
names, 424–425

worksheets *(Continued)*
navigation, 339–340, 343, 424–425
number values, 340
pasting data, Paste Options gallery, 429–430
previewing, 357–359
printing, 360, 498–499
all worksheets, 441
large worksheets, 419–422
ranges
inserting data by, 365–366
selecting, 350
rows, 340
Comma Style, 351
deleting, 372–374
freezing panes, 416
unfreezing panes, 416
scaling, 361
sheet tabs, colors, 424–425
spelling, checking, 363–365
summary sheets
changing values in detail sheets to update, 438–439
creating with sparklines, 436–437
tables
converting to ranges of data, 419
creating, 416–417
filtering, 417–419
sorting, 417–419
text
alignment, 343–344
inserting, 340–341
left alignment, 341
rotating, 408
values, 340
wrapping, 374–376
titles, printing, 419–422
unfreezing panes, 415–416
views, 357–359
what-if analysis
answering what-if questions, 488–490
calculating percentage rate of increase, 481–484
calculating values after increases, 486–487
Format Painter, 484–486
formatting while typing, 484–486
Goal Seek, 475–477
WordArt, inserting, 475
World Wide Web (www), 117–118, 122. *See also* Internet
worms, 51–52
wrapping text
around pictures, documents, 165–166
in worksheets, 374–376
writer's identification (cover letters), definition, 233
writer's signature block (cover letters), definition, 233

X–Z

x-axis, 353, 493
XML Files folder, 94, 100
y-axis, 353, 493
Yahoo!, 53
Zombies, 54
zipped files, 100–102